Criminal Law and Procedure

Cases and Materials

ELEVENTH EDITION

Kent Roach
Faculty of Law
University of Toronto

Benjamin L. Berger
Osgoode Hall Law School
York University

Emma Cunliffe
Peter A. Allard School of Law
University of British Columbia

The Hon. James Stribopoulos
Ontario Court of Justice
Adjunct Professor
Osgoode Hall Law School
York University

Toronto, Canada
2015

Emond Montgomery Publications Limited
60 Shaftesbury Avenue
Toronto ON M4T 1A3
http://www.emond.ca/lawschool

Printed in Canada.
Reprinted May 2018.

We acknowledge the financial support of the Government of Canada.
Nous reconnaissons l'appui financier du gouvernement du Canada.

Canada

Vice president, publishing: Anthony Rezek
Managing editor, development: Kelly Dickson
Director, editorial and production: Jim Lyons
Copy editor: Rodney Rawlings
Production editors: Laura Bast, Nancy Ennis, Cindy Fujimoto
Proofreader: David Handelsman
Permissions editor: Lisa Brant

Library and Archives Canada Cataloguing in Publication

Roach, Kent, 1961-, author
    Criminal law and procedure : cases and materials / Kent Roach, Faculty of Law, University of Toronto, Benjamin L. Berger, Osgoode Hall Law School, York University, Emma Cunliffe, Peter A. Allard School of Law, University of British Columbia, Justice James Stribopoulos, Ontario Court of Justice, Osgoode Hall Law School, York University (Adjunct). — Eleventh edition.

Revision of: Criminal law and procedure. 10th ed. Toronto : Emond Montgomery Publications, 2010.
ISBN 978-1-55239-548-6 (bound)

    1. Criminal law—Canada—Cases.   2. Criminal procedure—Canada—Cases.
I. Berger, Benjamin L., 1977-, author   II. Cunliffe, Emma, author   III. Stribopoulos, James, author   IV. Title.

KE8809.R63 2015   345.71   C2015-903437-X
KF9220.ZA2R63 2015

Preface to the Eleventh Edition

This book has its origins in ML Friedland's innovative teaching materials *Cases and Materials on Criminal Law and Procedure*, first published in 1967.

This edition retains the basic structure of previous editions. Following the pattern started with the tenth edition, we continue to include fuller extracts of leading cases than appeared in previous editions, while maintaining a manageable size for the volume as a whole. We have also included more secondary and contextual readings, giving students access to scholarly literature on the criminal law while enriching the text's attention to issues of Aboriginal justice, racial and ethnic bias, gender in the criminal law, and other matters of deep social importance to the criminal justice system.

The years have, in our view, confirmed the wisdom of Professor Friedland's original decision to teach criminal law in its broader procedural, theoretical, social, and institutional context. For this reason, Part One of the book continues to contain, in addition to introductory chapters on the sources of and limits on the criminal law, chapters on police powers and the trial process. This last includes a sustained examination of the wrongful conviction of Donald Marshall Jr.—a study of what Professor Friedland called, in *The Trials of Israel Lipski*, "the inherent fallibility of the criminal trial process and the constant danger of error." Indeed, the wisdom of Professor Friedland's approach, which in earlier editions involved a case study of the Steven Truscott case, has only been affirmed by history. Nearly 50 years after his original murder conviction, Mr. Truscott's conviction was overturned by the Ontario Court of Appeal: see *Truscott (Re)*, 2007 ONCA 575, 225 CCC (3d) 321.

We are well aware that the chapters on police powers and the trial process are no substitute for a full course on criminal procedure and recognize that instructors who wish to focus on Part One might wish to omit Chapters 3 and 4. Nevertheless, we hope those chapters will be used by some, including those who study criminal justice outside the law schools, as a means of setting the substantive criminal law in its institutional context. In this edition, drawing on a series of wrongful convictions related to faulty expert evidence, we have added new discussions to Chapter 4 that examine professional responsibility issues—for prosecutors, defence lawyers, expert witnesses, and judges—raised by wrongful convictions and guilty pleas. We have also expanded this chapter's discussion of the important issue of prosecutorial discretion.

In Part Two, we examine the fundamental principles of criminal liability. Chapter 5, addressing *actus reus*, is substantially reorganized. The chapter foregrounds the concept of voluntariness, offers an updated section on causation that reflects the Supreme Court's important decision in *Maybin*, and concludes by using the principle of contemporaneity to introduce questions of the relationship between *actus reus* and *mens rea*. Chapters 6 to 8 then consider various dimensions of fault, integrating recent developments in the area, including the affirmation of presumptions of subjective fault in *ADH*.

Part Three on extensions of criminal liability remains an important feature of the book, which recognizes the importance of accomplice, organizational, and inchoate liability. Again, we appreciate that some instructors might wish to leave these topics to the end of the course.

We continue to find it useful to study the complex and dynamic laws of sexual assault and homicide on their own and these make up Part Four, which we call "the special part," on sexual assault and homicide. We have thoroughly revised and restructured this part, beginning with a discussion of the gendered dynamics of sexual assault and the problem of attrition in this field. Recent cases, such as *JA* and *Mabior*, have been incorporated.

Part Five deals with defences. The chapters in that part have been significantly updated and revised in light of recent jurisprudential and legislative developments. Our combined chapter on mental disorder and automatism includes 2014 amendments affecting the disposition of those not criminally responsible on account of mental disorder. We have moved up the chapter on self-defence, in part because of the increased importance and breadth of that defence under the 2012 reforms. This also allows our discussion of the general part to conclude with the related defences of necessity and duress, including a full extract of the landmark *Ryan* decision.

Part Six consists of a newly revised chapter on sentencing, one that pays particular attention to constitutional limits on sentencing, including the Supreme Court's recent decision in *Nur*. Again, this chapter is no substitute for a full course on the critically important subject of sentencing; but its inclusion is an important part of our vision for this casebook.

We are indebted to Marty Friedland's pioneering work in criminal law and procedure and to the faith that he had put in us to continue these materials.

We are grateful for the significant contributions Justice Patrick Healy made to the tenth edition, many of which continue to benefit this one. We understand his decision to focus on his judicial duties and wish him the very best.

We owe a debt of thanks to a number of instructors who have used the book and offered many helpful and generous suggestions, and in this regard would especially like to thank Professors Gerry Ferguson and Allan Manson.

We are grateful to all at Emond Publishing for their hard work and commitment to this project, and in particular we thank Jim Lyons for coordinating and directing the project; Kelly Dickson for her support and guidance as managing editor; Laura Bast for her excellent work as production editor; and Nancy Ennis, Rodney Rawlings, and David Handelsman for their work typesetting, copy-editing, and proofreading this edition. We have also been ably assisted by an outstanding set of students at Osgoode Hall Law School who have worked closely with us in reviewing and editing this book; thank you to Amy Brubacher, Rachel Devon, Kiran Kang, Dana Phillips, Anthony Sangiuliano, and Andrea Sobko for their excellent work.

Finally, in recognition of his integral and lasting conceptualization of this book as one that would explore the criminal process in all its facets, with deep admiration for his immense contributions to Canadian criminal justice over the past 55 years, we respectfully and affectionately dedicate the eleventh edition of this book to "Marty," aka ML Friedland, CC, QC.

KR
BLB
EC
JS
May 2015

Acknowledgments

A book of this nature borrows heavily from other published material. We have attempted to request permission from, and to acknowledge in the text, all sources of such material. We wish to make specific references here to the authors, publishers, journals, and institutions that have generously given permission to reproduce in this text works already in print. If we have inadvertently overlooked an acknowledgment or failed to secure a permission, we offer our sincere apologies and undertake to rectify the omission in the next edition.

Aboriginal Affairs and Northern Development Canada   ME Turpel, "On the Question of Adapting the Canadian Criminal Justice System for Aboriginal Peoples: Don't Fence Me In" in *Aboriginal Peoples and the Justice System: Report of the National Round Table on Aboriginal Justice Issues* (Ottawa: Minister of Supply and Services Canada, 1993). Reprinted with permission of Aboriginal Affairs and Northern Development Canada.

British Academy   P Devlin, "The Enforcement of Morals" (Maccabaean Lecture in Jurisprudence of the British Academy, 18 March 1959), Proceedings of the British Academy volume XLV © The British Academy 1960. Reprinted with permission.

Canadian Bar Association   Chapters 9(9), (10), and (11) of the Canadian Bar Association *Code of Professional Conduct* (2009). Reprinted with permission of the Canadian Bar Association.

Canadian Bar Review   AW Mewett, "The Criminal Law, 1867-1967" (1967) 45 Can Bar Rev 726 at 726-30. Reprinted with the permission of the Canadian Bar Review.

Canada Law Book   T Archibald, K Jull & K Roach, "The Changed Face of Corporate Criminal Liability" (2004) 48 Crim LQ 367. Reproduced by permission of Canada Law Book, a division of Thomson Reuters Canada Limited.

Canada Law Book   C Boyle & M MacCrimmon, "The Constitutionality of Bill C-49: Analyzing Sexual Assault as if Equality Really Mattered" (1999) 41 Crim LQ 198 at 214-17. Reproduced by permission of Canada Law Book, a division of Thomson Reuters Canada Limited.

Carswell   ML Friedland, "Criminal Justice and the Division of Power in Canada" in *A Century of Criminal Justice* (Toronto: Carswell, 1984). Reprinted by permission of Carswell, a division of Thomson Reuters Canada Ltd.

Carswell   M Shaffer, "Coerced into Crime: Battered Women and the Defence of Duress" (1999) 4 Can Crim L Rev 272 at 307-8, 329-30. Reproduced by permission of Carswell, a division of Thomson Reuters Canada Limited.

Department of Justice   *Recodifying Criminal Law Report 31*, Law Reform Commission of Canada 1987. Reproduced with the permission of the Department of Justice Canada, 2015.

Department of Justice   *Special Committee on Pornography and Prostitution* (the Fraser Committee). Law Reform Commission of Canada, 1985. Reproduced with the permission of the Department of Justice Canada, 2015.

Hart Publishing   BL Berger, "Mental Disorder and the Instability of Blame in Criminal Law" in F Tanguay-Renaud & J Stribopoulos, eds, *Rethinking Criminal Law Theory: New Canadian Perspectives on the Philosophy of Domestic, Transnational, and International Criminal Law* (Portland, Or: Hart, 2012) 117 at 117, 121, 131. Reprinted with the permission of Hart Publishing, an imprint of Bloomsbury Publishing Plc.

House of Commons   *The Challenge of Change: A Study of Canada's Criminal Prostitution Laws*. Report of the Standing Committee on Justice and Human Rights. House of Commons (December 2006). Reprinted with permission.

Immediate Media Company   HLA Hart, "Immorality and Treason," *The Listener* (30 July 1959). Reprinted by permission of Immediate Media Company.

Irwin Law   D Layton & M Proulx, *Ethics and Criminal Law*, 2nd ed (Toronto: Irwin Law, 2015). Reprinted with permission.

Journal of Criminal Law and Criminology   SH Kadish, "The Criminal Law and the Luck of the Draw" (1994) 84 J Crim L & Criminology 679 at 679, 681-82. Reprinted by special permission of Northwestern University School of Law.

Law Society of Upper Canada   "Defending a Criminal Case" (1969). Copyright 1969, The Law Society of Upper Canada. Reproduced with permission of the Law Society of Upper Canada.

McGill Law Journal   BL Berger, "Emotions and the Veil of Voluntarism: The Loss of Judgment in Canadian Criminal Defences" (2006) 51 McGill LJ 99 at 111-12, 114-17, 126. Reprinted with the permission of Benjamin L. Berger.

Michigan Law Review   WJ Stuntz, "The Pathological Politics of Criminal Law" (2001) 100 Mich L Rev 505 at 506. Reprinted with the permission of the estate of William Stuntz.

Oxford University Press   Jeremy Horder, *Provocation and Responsibility* (Oxford: Clarendon Press, 1992). Reprinted by permission of Oxford University Press.

Province of Manitoba   *Report of the Aboriginal Justice Inquiry of Manitoba* (1991). Reprinted with the permission of the Province of Manitoba.

Province of Nova Scotia   *Royal Commission on the Donald Marshall Jr Prosecution* (1989). Reprinted with the permission of the Province of Nova Scotia.

Senate of Canada   *Honourable Rob Nicholson, Minister of Justice and Attorney General of Canada addressing amendments to the Criminal Code before the Standing Senate Committee on Legal and Constitutional Affairs on May 12, 2012.* Reprinted with the permission of the Senate of Canada.

Simon & Schuster   G Fletcher, *A Crime of Self-Defense* (New York: Free Press, 1988). Reprinted with the permission of Free Press, a division of Simon & Schuster, Inc. from *A Crime of Self-Defense: Bernhard Goetz and the Law on Trial* by George P. Fletcher. Copyright © 1988 by George P. Fletcher. All rights reserved.

Supreme Court Law Review   G Ferguson, "The Intoxication Defence: Constitutionally Impaired and in Need of Rehabilitation" (2012) 57 SCLR (2nd) 111 at 135-37. Reprinted with the permission of Gerry Ferguson.

UBC Law Review   I Grant, "The Syndromization of Women's Experience" (1991) 25 UBC L Rev 51 at 51-53. Reprinted with permission of the UBC Law Review Society.

UBC Press   EA Sheehy, *Defending Battered Women on Trial: Lessons from the Transcripts* (Vancouver: University of British Columbia Press, 2014). Reprinted with permission of the Publisher. © University of British Columbia Press 2014. All rights reserved with the Publisher.

University of Toronto Press   M Randall, "Sexual Assault Law, Credibility and 'Ideal Victims': Consent, Resistance and Victim Blaming" (2010) 22 CJWL 398 at 398-99. Reprinted by permission of the publisher.

University of Toronto Press   K Roach, *Due Process and Victims' Rights: The New Law and Politics of Criminal Justice* (Toronto: University of Toronto Press, 1999). Reprinted with permission of the publisher.

University of Toronto Press   K Roach, "Mind the Gap: Canada's Different Criminal and Constitutional Standards of Fault" (2011) 61 UTLJ 545. Reprinted by permission of the publisher.

Summary Table of Contents

PART TWO   PRINCIPLES OF CRIMINAL LIABILITY

PART THREE   EXTENSIONS OF CRIMINAL LIABILITY

PART SIX   DISPOSITION

Detailed Table of Contents

PART TWO   PRINCIPLES OF CRIMINAL LIABILITY

PART SIX   DISPOSITION

Table of Cases

A page number in boldface type indicates that the text of the case or a portion thereof is reproduced. A page number in lightface type indicates that the case is quoted briefly or discussed by the authors. Cases mentioned within excerpts are not listed.

PART ONE

Introduction to Criminal Law and Procedure

Sources of Criminal Law

This chapter provides an introduction to the sources of Canadian criminal law in (1) the Constitution as the supreme law; (2) statute law and in particular the *Criminal Code* of Canada; and (3) common law or judge-made decisions of courts including decisions interpreting the Constitution and the *Criminal Code*. The first part of the chapter provides an overview of the book. The second part examines the criminal law in the context of the constitutional division of powers between the federal and provincial governments and the constitutional rights provided in the *Canadian Charter of Rights and Freedoms* and mechanisms for justifying limits on those rights. The remaining part of this chapter examines the codification of the criminal law in the *Criminal Code*, the objectives of codification, constitutional prohibitions on vagueness and overbreadth in the criminal law, and the various approaches to the interpretation of the *Criminal Code*.

I. OVERVIEW OF THE BOOK

The criminal law is the result of a complex process that starts with the decision of a legislature to define something as prohibited. Criminal law in Canada is enacted by the federal Parliament, which under s 91(27) of the *Constitution Act, 1867* has exclusive jurisdiction over criminal law and procedure. The *Criminal Code* of Canada contains many offences, ranging from traditional crimes, such as murder, assault, robbery, and theft, to newer crimes, such as operating or having care and control over a vehicle with a blood alcohol level "over 80," and participating in the activities of a criminal organization or a terrorist group. Some offences, such as assault or sexual assault, protect bodily integrity, while others, such as theft, protect property. Crimes relating to firearms and drunk driving offences attempt to prevent conduct that presents a significant risk of harm to others. Crimes against the possession and sale of illegal drugs or obscene material may also prevent harm, but they also proclaim standards of socially acceptable behaviour.

The *Canadian Charter of Rights and Freedoms* (Part I of the *Constitution Act, 1982*, being Schedule B to the *Canada Act 1982* (UK), 1982, c 11), usually referred to simply as the Charter, places limits on the criminal law (Chapter 2). For example, criminal offences that prohibit various forms of expression must be justified by the state as demonstrably justified and reasonable limits under s 1 of the Charter.

Criminal laws are designed primarily to denounce and punish inherently wrongful behaviour and to deter people from committing crimes or engaging in behaviour that presents a serious risk of harm. Courts consider these purposes when sentencing offenders, but they are also concerned with the incapacitation and rehabilitation of the particular offenders and providing reparation to the victim and the community for the crime committed.

The *Criminal Code* contains many offences but they constitute only a small number of all the offences in Canada. Most offences are regulatory. Regulatory offences can be enacted by the federal Parliament, provinces, or municipalities. They include traffic offences, such as speeding, polluting, engaging in a regulated activity without a licence or without keeping proper records, and offences relating to harmful commercial practices, such as using misleading advertising or not complying with health and safety regulations. The punishment for regulatory offences is usually a fine, but may include imprisonment. In any event, the accused is frequently a corporation that cannot be imprisoned but that can be fined or placed on probation. The primary purpose of regulatory offences is to deter risky behaviour and prevent harm rather than punish intrinsically wrongful and harmful behaviour. Generally, fewer restrictions are placed on the state in the investigation and prosecution of regulatory crimes.

The Criminal Process

The criminal law assumes concrete meaning when it is administered through the criminal justice system. The bulk of this spending (61 percent) is on the police; 22 percent on corrections, including federal and provincial prisons; 9 percent on courts; 5 percent on legal aid, to fund the defence of those accused of crime; and 3 percent on prosecutors. See A Taylor-Butts, "Justice Spending in Canada, 2000/01" (2002) 22:11 Juristat 1.

The criminal process has traditionally started with the investigation of crime by the police (Chapter 3) and the criminal trial process, which includes pre-trial proceedings, such as the decision whether to grant bail and the selection of the jury (Chapter 4). These phases of the criminal process must be procedurally fair or the accused will be able to seek a remedy for the violation of his or her rights under the *Canadian Charter of Rights and Freedoms*.

Principles of Criminal Liability

At the criminal trial, the morally innocent should not be found guilty and punished. As required by the presumption of innocence, the Crown must generally prove beyond a reasonable doubt to the judge or jury that the accused committed the prohibited act or *actus reus* (Chapter 5) with the required fault element or *mens rea* (Chapter 7). The *actus reus* is usually defined as an overt act, such as the taking of another person's property. The legislature can, however, define the prohibited conduct as an omission or a failure to take action. For example, a parent can be guilty of the criminal offence of failing to provide the necessities of life to his or her child.

A great variety of fault elements are used in criminal and regulatory offences. Sometimes the fault element is specified in the wording of an offence by phrases such as "intentionally," "knowingly," "recklessly," or "negligently." Frequently, however, the courts will have to infer what type of fault element is required. Often a distinction between "subjective" and "objective" fault elements is drawn. A subjective fault or mental element depends on what was in the particular accused's mind at the time that the criminal act was committed. In determining this, the judge or jury must consider all the evidence presented, even if it reveals factors that are peculiar to the accused, such as the accused's diminished intelligence. On the other hand, an objective fault element does not depend on the accused's own state of mind but rather on what a reasonable person in the circumstances would have known or done. Ignorance of the law is generally not an excuse (Chapter 8), but the accused's ignorance of, or mistakes about, certain facts may prevent the prosecutor from establishing the necessary fault (Chapter 7).

There are special rules for determining liability for non-criminal regulatory offences (Chapter 6). Most regulatory offences, known in Canada as strict liability offences, require the accused to establish a defence of due diligence or lack of negligence after the state has proven the prohibited act beyond a reasonable doubt. Other regulatory offences, known as absolute liability offences, only require proof of the prohibited act and do not allow any defence of due diligence or require proof of any fault. When such offences are combined with imprisonment, they can be constitutionally problematic because they can punish individuals and corporations even though they could not have reasonably been expected to have prevented the prohibited act.

Although the simplest form of criminal liability is an individual committing a complete crime with the necessary fault or *mens rea*, there are important extensions of criminal liability examined in Part Three of this book.

Often a crime is committed by more than one person. A person who assists in the commission of an offence can be convicted of the same offence as the person who actually commits the offence (Chapter 9). The parties' provisions in s 21 of the *Criminal Code* mean that people who have different levels of involvement in a crime may be found guilty of the same offence. The extent of an offender's participation in a crime will be considered by the judge when determining the appropriate sentence.

A person may be guilty of the separate offence of attempting a codified crime even if he or she does not succeed in carrying out the prohibited act, such as an unlawful killing (Chapter 9). Section 24 of the *Criminal Code* states that anyone having an intent to commit an offence, who does or omits to do anything beyond mere preparation to commit a criminal offence, is guilty of attempting to commit the offence, regardless of whether it was possible to commit an offence. A person punished for an attempted crime is punished more for his or her intent to commit the crime than the harm caused.

There is a separate regime in the *Criminal Code* for determining the liability of corporations and other organizations, which requires not only that employees or other representatives of the corporation engage in activity that is criminal, but also that some fault be attributed to a "senior officer" in the corporation (Chapter 11).

Many of the most important principles of criminal law have been developed in the context of a few particular crimes, some of which are examined in Part Four. The law of sexual assault has been particularly dynamic over the last three decades and is examined in Chapter 12. The law of homicide, involving the important distinction between murder and manslaughter, as well as the classification of murder as first- or second-degree murder, is examined in Chapter 13. There is one defence that applies only in homicide cases and reduces what would otherwise be an intentional murder to the less serious offence of manslaughter. It is the defence of provocation, which is examined in Chapter 14.

Principles of Exculpation

Even if he or she has committed the prohibited act with the required fault, the accused may still be acquitted if a defence applies. Chapter 15 examines the related defences of mental disorder and automatism as they relate to the accused's capacity to be at fault and to be held responsible for criminal acts. The mental disorder defence leads to a special disposition in which the accused, although not convicted, may be subject to further detention or treatment. Chapter 16 examines the complex defences of intoxication as they apply to various crimes. Intoxication most often acts as a defence that raises a reasonable doubt about whether the accused had the required fault or intent for a serious crime such as murder. At the same time, intoxication often does not negate fault for a less serious crime such as manslaughter. As will be seen, it is more controversial when intoxication is used as a defence to a less serious crime.

Chapter 17 examines self-defence, a defence that has long been codified in the Code but was recently amended in an attempt to make it simpler. Chapters 18 and 19 examine the related defences of necessity and duress, which excuse crimes committed by people in agonizing circumstances where they have no reasonable choice but to commit the crime. In this chapter and others, we will see that some restrictions on defences may be unconstitutional and violate s 7 of the Charter because they deprive people of liberty in a manner that is not in accordance with the principles of fundamental justice.

Disposition

No examination of criminal justice would be complete without some examination of the sentencing principles that govern the disposition of an accused who has been found guilty (Chapter 20). The judge at sentencing has wide discretion to tailor punishment to the offender's degree of responsibility and also to consider what punishment will best deter, rehabilitate, or incapacitate the particular offender; deter others from committing the same crime; and provide reparation to the community and victims for the crime. On sentencing, see A Manson et al, *Sentencing and Penal Policy in Canada*, 2nd ed (Toronto: Emond Montgomery, 2008).

II. THE CRIMINAL LAW AND THE CONSTITUTION

The supreme source of criminal law in Canada is the Constitution, as represented by both the division of powers between federal and provincial governments in ss 91 and 92 of the *Constitution Act, 1867* and the rights and freedoms in the 1982 *Canadian Charter of Rights and Freedoms*.

The Canadian Charter of Rights and Freedoms

The Charter pervades the whole of criminal law from the initial decision to criminalize conduct, through the investigation of crime by police, the prosecution of offences, the determination of criminal liability, and even the sentencing of offenders. Almost every chapter in this book will examine some aspect of the Charter. We recognize, however, that the Charter may be unfamiliar to some students and for this reason what follows is a brief introduction to the Charter.

The Charter, as part of the supreme law of Canada, applies to the activities of Canadian legislatures and governmental officials such as the police. It differs from the *Canadian Bill of Rights* enacted in 1960 both because it is part of the Constitution and because it applies to all governments and not just the federal government.

The Charter guarantees a number of rights including freedom of expression and equality rights. The legal rights set out in ss 7 to 14 of the Charter are designed to protect those subject to criminal investigation, those charged and tried for criminal offences, and those punished for crime. The broadest legal right is contained in s 7 and it can potentially apply at any of the above stages of the criminal process. It provides as follows:

> Everyone has the right to life, liberty and security of the person and the right not to be deprived thereof except in accordance with the principles of fundamental justice.

Sections 8 to 10 of the Charter protect those subject to investigation by the state. Section 8 provides the right to be secure against unreasonable searches or seizures, while s 9 provides the right not to be arbitrarily detained or imprisoned. Upon arrest or detention, individuals have a number of rights under s 10, including the right to retain and instruct counsel without delay and to be informed of that right.

Sections 11 to 14 of the Charter protect those who are charged and tried for offences. For example, before trial, a person who is charged has a right not to be denied reasonable bail without just cause (s 11(e)) and to be tried within a reasonable time (s 11(b)). At trial, the accused has, among other rights, the right to be presumed innocent until proven guilty in a court of law in a fair and public hearing by an independent and impartial tribunal (s 11(d)) and the right to a jury trial in certain circumstances (s 11(f)). When finally acquitted or found guilty and punished for the offence, the accused has the right not to be tried or punished for it again (s 11(h)).

Everyone has the right not to be subjected to any cruel and unusual treatment or punishment (s 12) and this is the right that is most relevant to sentencing issues.

Another right that has increased relevance to criminal justice is s 15(1) of the Charter, which provides:

> Every individual is equal before and under the law and has the right to the equal protection and
> equal benefit of the law without discrimination and, in particular, without discrimination based
> on race, national or ethnic origin, colour, religion, sex, age or mental or physical disability.

Laws and practices can be found to infringe s 15(1) of the Charter. At the same time, a concern about equality can be considered as a rationale for some laws such as those prohibiting hate speech or obscenity.

If a law or practice is found to infringe a Charter right, it is open for the state to prove under s 1 of the Charter that it is a reasonable limit prescribed by law and demonstrably justified in a free and democratic society. If the law or practice is not so justified, then under s 52 of the *Constitution Act, 1982* any law that is inconsistent with the Charter is to the extent of the inconsistency of no force or effect.

In addition to the remedy of striking laws down, the courts have broad powers to order remedies for Charter violations, including unconstitutional police practices. Section 24(1) of the Charter provides that those whose Charter rights have been infringed may apply to a court of competent jurisdiction to obtain such remedy as the court considers appropriate and just. Section 24(2) governs the remedy of exclusion of evidence obtained in a manner that violates Charter rights by providing that evidence shall be excluded from a criminal trial if it is established that, having regard to all the circumstances, its admission would bring the administration of justice into disrepute.

Finally, it should be noted that in the context of the legal rights discussed above, not only can the state try to justify laws that violate rights as reasonable limits under s 1, but it can also provide that an Act or a provision thereof shall operate notwithstanding s 2 or ss 7 to 15 of the Charter (s 33). This power has rarely been used by governments and never used with respect to the criminal law.

For some further readings on the Charter, see P Hogg, *Constitutional Law of Canada*, 5th ed (Toronto: Carswell, 2007); D Stuart, *Charter Justice in Canadian Criminal Law*, 6th ed (Toronto: Carswell, 2014); and R Sharpe & K Roach, *The Charter of Rights and Freedoms*, 5th ed (Toronto: Irwin Law, 2013).

The Criminal Law and the Division of Powers

Section 91(27) of the *Constitution Act, 1867* vests in the federal Parliament exclusive jurisdiction to legislate in relation to "the Criminal Law, except the Constitution of Courts of Criminal Jurisdiction, but including the Procedure in Criminal Matters." The federal Parliament also has jurisdiction under s 91(28) to establish, maintain, and manage penitentiaries, which have been considered to be the place of detention for persons serving terms of imprisonment for two years or more.

The provinces have jurisdiction under s 92(15) to impose punishment by way of fine, penalty, or imprisonment in order to enforce valid provincial laws. The provinces also have jurisdiction over the administration of justice under s 92(14), the establishment of "Reformatory Prisons" (s 92(6)) (the place of detention for persons serving terms of imprisonment for less than two years), and "Asylums" (s 92(7)), as well as property and civil rights (s 92(13)).

The federal government appoints the judges of the higher superior trial courts under s 96 of the *Constitution Act, 1867* while the provinces appoint judges to provincial courts, where most criminal trials are held. The federal government also appoints appeal court judges including those on the Supreme Court of Canada.

The following excerpt outlines the historical and contemporary importance of federal jurisdiction over criminal law and procedure.

ML Friedland, "Criminal Justice and the Division of Power in Canada"
in ML Friedland, ed, *A Century of Criminal Justice*
(Toronto: Carswell, 1984) ch 2 (footnotes omitted)

Confederation

The discussion and legislative debates leading to Confederation show that there was no controversy over whether legislative power over criminal law and procedure should be given to the federal government. Centralizing the criminal law power was in deliberate contrast to the American Constitution which left control over the criminal law power to the individual states.

Why was the criminal law power given to the federal government? Sir John A. Macdonald, then the Attorney-General, expressed what must have been the consensus at the time when, in the parliamentary debates in 1865, he stated:

> The criminal law too—the determination of what is a crime and what is not and how crime shall be punished—is left to the General Government. This is a matter almost of necessity. It is of great importance that we should have the same criminal law throughout these provinces—that what is a crime in one part of British America, should be a crime in every part—that there should be the same protection of life and property in one as in another.

He then commented on the American division of authority:

> It is one of the defects in the United States system, that each separate state has or may have a criminal code of its own,—that what may be a capital offence in one state, may be a venial offence, punishable slightly, in another. But under our Constitution we shall have one body of criminal law, based on the criminal law of England, and operating equally throughout British America, so that a British American, belonging to what province he may, or going to any other part of the Confederation, knows what his rights are in that respect, and what his punishment will be if an offender against the criminal laws of the land. I think this is one of the most marked instances in which we take advantage of the experience derived from our observations of the defects in the Constitution of the neighboring Republic.

There is no doubt that the Civil War in the United States was a major factor in the desire of many to place some of the more important powers and symbols of nationhood within the legislative authority of the federal government. The criminal law plays an important role in society in stating fundamental values. This can be seen today in the discussions taking place on such criminal law issues as the law of abortion, the law relating to homosexual conduct, the question of the reintroduction of capital punishment, and the activities of the police and the security service. ...

Scope of the Criminal Law Power

A hundred years ago, the courts gave the criminal law power a very wide meaning. In 1882, in *Russell v. The Queen*, the Privy Council seemed to uphold the validity of the Canada Temperance Act of 1878 under the criminal law power. The Court stated:

> Laws ... designed for the promotion of public order, safety, or morals, and which subject those who contravene them to criminal procedure and punishment, belong to the subject of public wrongs rather than to that of civil rights. They are of a nature which fall within the general authority of Parliament to make laws for the order and good government of Canada, and have direct relation to criminal law, which is one of the enumerated classes of subjects assigned exclusively to the Parliament of Canada.

But doubt was thrown on *Russell* by Lord Watson in 1896 in the *Local Prohibition* case. He explained *Russell* as based on the "peace, order and good government" clause, and went so far as to say, in one example, that "an Act restricting the right to carry weapons of offence, or their sale to young persons, within the province would be within the authority of the provincial legislature" and not of the federal parliament. Lord Watson's enhancement of provincial power over "property and civil rights" at the expense of federal powers such as the criminal law power was also found in Lord Haldane's judgments in the 20th century.

In 1922, in the *Board of Commerce* case, Lord Haldane severely restricted the criminal law power to cases "where the subject matter is one which by its very nature belongs to the domain of criminal jurisprudence." But later decisions have broadened that definition. Lord Atkin in the *P.A.T.A.* case in 1931 gave the following definition: "The criminal quality of an act cannot be discerned by intuition; nor can it be discovered by reference to any standard but one: Is the act prohibited with penal consequences?" But just as Haldane's definition was too narrow, Lord Atkin's has proven to be too wide. The federal government cannot take jurisdiction simply by imposing a criminal penalty. The *Margarine Reference* case in 1951 demonstrated this limitation on the criminal law power. The Supreme Court held that to forbid manufacture and sale of margarine for economic purposes is "to deal directly with the civil rights of individuals in relation to particular trade within the Provinces." A similar approach was taken by the Supreme Court in 1979 with respect to the marketing of apples under the Canada Agricultural Products Standards Act in *Dominion Stores Ltd. v. The Queen* and with respect to the marketing of "light beer" under the federal Food and Drugs Acts in the *Labatt Breweries* case. In both cases the majority of the Supreme Court held that the criminal law power could not justify the legislation and so declared parts of the federal legislation *ultra vires*.

... The recently enacted gun control provisions have been challenged—unsuccessfully—in a number of cases. The Supreme Court of Canada has not yet dealt with the issue. When it does, no doubt it will disregard Lord Watson's statement, quoted earlier, and uphold the federal legislation. Controlling firearms is directly related to the criminal law. One of the reasons why the United States has a gun problem is because of the absence of strong federal legislation which would effectively prevent guns being sent from lax gun control states to other states. ...

[The Supreme Court did indeed hold that gun control laws, including those providing that it was a criminal offence to have an unlicensed or unregistered gun, were within the federal jurisdiction. It concluded that "the regulation of guns as dangerous products is a valid purpose within the criminal law power." See *Reference re Firearms Act (Can)*, 2000 SCC 31 at para 33, [2000] 1 SCR 783. See also *Quebec (AG) v Canada (AG)*, 2015 SCC 14 confirming the federal government could not only repeal the long gun registry but destroy records so that Quebec could not use them to create its own registry. The recent trend seems to be back to an expansive approach to Parliament's criminal law power to include matters such as offences that restrict the advertising of tobacco or the introduction of substances that are toxic to the environment. See *RJR-MacDonald Inc v Canada (Attorney General)*, [1995] 3 SCR 199; *R v Hydro-Québec*, [1997] 3 SCR 213. See generally The Constitutional Law Group, *Canadian Constitutional Law*, 4th ed (Toronto: Emond Montgomery, 2010) ch 11.]

Provincial Legislation

Provincial laws can be struck down either for lack of constitutional power under section 92 or for conflict with federal legislation. Under both heads the Supreme Court of Canada has tended to uphold provincial law. A trio of cases in 1960 showed the reluctance of the Supreme Court of Canada to declare provincial legislation inoperative because of existing federal legislation. Of course it will do so if it conflicts with federal legislation. But what is meant by conflicts? In *O'Grady v. Sparling* the Supreme Court upheld provincial careless driving legislation, although the federal Criminal Code makes it an offence to operate a motor vehicle in a criminally negligent manner. In *Stephens v. The Queen* the Supreme Court upheld provincial competence to require a driver involved in an accident to stop, provide particulars, and offer assistance, in spite of a provision in the Criminal Code making the same conduct an offence, though with the added element of "intent to escape civil or criminal liability." Finally, in *Smith v. The Queen* the Supreme Court upheld a section of the Ontario Securities Act making it an offence to furnish false information in any document required to be filed or furnished under the Act, although the Criminal Code makes it an offence for a person to publish a prospectus which he knows is false in a material particular with intent to induce persons to become shareholders in a company. In none of these cases was there held to be a conflict. ...

... The tendency to uphold provincial legislation can also be seen in a number of recent Supreme Court of Canada cases in which provincial legislation was challenged as not falling within section 92. In 1978 in *Dupond* the majority of the Supreme Court of Canada upheld a Montreal by-law designed to prevent assemblies and passed to cope with occurrences such as the F.L.Q. rallies. The same year the Supreme Court in the *McNeil* case upheld Nova Scotia legislation which permitted the banning of the movie, "Last Tango in Paris," even though there was also federal obscenity legislation in the Criminal Code. In 1982, in the *Schneider* case, the Supreme Court upheld provincial legislation providing for the compulsory treatment of heroin addicts. In the most recent Supreme Court case, *Westendorp v. The Queen*, however, the Court struck down a Calgary by-law which had attempted to deal with prostitution by prohibiting a person from remaining on the street for the purpose of prostitution or approaching another person on the street for the purpose of prostitution. Laskin C.J., for a unanimous Supreme Court, held that the by-law was "a colourable attempt to deal, not with a public nuisance but with the evil of prostitution. ...

If a province or municipality may translate a direct attack on prostitution into street control through reliance on public nuisance, it may do the same with respect to trafficking in drugs, and, may it not, on the same view, seek to punish assaults that take place on city streets as an aspect of street control!" Thus, just as there are limits on federal legislation, there are limits on the creation of provincial offences.

[A provincial attempt to prohibit the performance of an abortion other than in a hospital has been held to be an invalid provincial attempt to enact criminal laws. See *R v Morgentaler*, [1993] 3 SCR 463. Note that five years earlier, the court had struck down federal *Criminal Code* provisions that restricted abortions to those performed in a hospital and approved by a hospital committee on the grounds that they violated s 7 of the Charter by depriving women of security of the person in a manner that did not accord with the principles of fundamental justice: *R v Morgentaler*, [1988] 1 SCR 30. Provincial forfeiture procedures were upheld in *Chatterjee v Ontario*, 2009 SCC 19, [2009] 1 SCR 624, even though they overlapped with *Criminal Code* provisions.]

[Sections 26 to 32 of Quebec's Bill 52, *An Act Respecting End-of-Life Care*, SQ 2014, c 2 provide for medical assistance in dying if certain conditions are satisfied: being of full age and capacity, being at the end of life and having a serious and incurable illness, and having a second, independent medical doctor determine the fulfillment of these conditions. Does this statute conflict with the assisted suicide offence in s 241 of the *Criminal Code*? Note that the Supreme Court in *Carter v Canada*, 2015 SCC 5 struck this criminal offence down as violating s 7 of the Charter but gave Parliament a year to consider enacting new legislation. If Parliament enacts a new regime, will/should it prevail if it conflicts with the Quebec regime? How should courts reconcile competing federal and provincial jurisdiction over health care issues such as assisted dying?]

Administering the Criminal Law

Section 92(14) of the B.N.A. Act gives the provinces authority over "the administration of justice in the province, including the constitution, maintenance, and organization of provincial courts, both of civil and of criminal jurisdiction, and including procedure in civil matters in those courts." Does this give the provinces or the federal government the primary power to prosecute federal offences enacted under the criminal law power? In 1979 in the *Hauser* case the Supreme Court was called on to decide whether the federal government could control prosecutions under the Narcotic Control Act [SC 1996, c 19]. The Court held that the federal government had this power, although, to the surprise of many, not on the basis that the Narcotic Control Act was criminal law, but rather because it was enacted under the "peace, order and good government" clause. The Court, therefore, left open the question of what would happen when the issue related directly to enforcing the criminal law.

Two important cases decided by the Supreme Court in 1983 dealt with that question. In *A.G. Canada v. Canadian National Transportation Ltd. et al.* the issue was whether the federal government has the power to control prosecutions under the Combines Investigation Act. Section 2 of the Criminal Code gives the power to prosecute federal offences not under the Criminal Code to the Attorney-General of Canada. Chief Justice Laskin gave the judgment for the majority of the seven-member court, holding that the Combines Act is valid under section 91(27), the criminal law power, and that the federal government has exclusive authority to control prosecutions. The majority judgment did not deal with the validity of the legislation under any other head of federal power. Dickson J. upheld federal prosecutorial authority for violations of the *Combines Investigation Act* under the federal "trade and commerce" power. With respect to the criminal law power, Dickson J. maintained the position he had taken in his dissent in *Hauser* that only the provincial Attorney-General can validly prosecute criminal enactments. ...

In *The Queen v. Wetmore and Kripp*, released the same day as the Canadian National Transportation case, the issue was the power to prosecute under the federal Food and Drugs Act. Again, Laskin C.J. held that because the Act fell under the criminal law power the federal government could control who had the power to prosecute. Dickson J., dissenting and characterizing the view of the majority as "blind centralism," held that the legislation was only valid under the criminal law power and thus it was the provincial, not the federal Attorney General who had the power to prosecute. ...

The result of the cases, then, appears to be that the federal government has exclusive power to prosecute federal offences. This power can, however, be delegated to the provincial Attorney General as is done directly in section 2 of the Criminal Code for Criminal Code offences. ...

Thus far the courts have not dealt directly with the question of whether the federal government could, if it wished, control prosecutions under the Criminal Code itself. The issue is not likely to arise because section 2 of the Code now gives this power to the provincial Attorneys General. ...

[Section 2 still generally defines the attorney general in charge of prosecuting *Criminal Code* offences as the provincial attorney general but also now grants the federal attorney general concurrent jurisdiction to prosecute terrorism offences or offences that were committed outside of Canada but can be prosecuted in Canada.]

Do you agree with those, such as Chief Justice Laskin, who support a strong and exclusive federal jurisdiction in matters concerning criminal justice? What would be the advantages and disadvantages of giving the provinces more power in these matters?

Dickson J, as he then was, stated in his dissent in *R v Hauser*, [1979] 1 SCR 984 at 1032 that part of the Confederation bargain was that while the criminal law was to be enacted by the federal Parliament, its administration was to be left in the hands of local and provincial authorities "where it could be more flexibly administered":

> The position of decentralized control, which had obtained in England from time immemorial, and in Canada prior to Confederation, with local administration of justice, local police forces, local juries, and local prosecutors, was perpetuated and carried forward into the Constitution through s. 92(14). The administration of criminal justice was to be kept in local hands and out of the control of central government.

Before the enactment of the Charter, exclusive federal jurisdiction over criminal law and procedure was one of the few means to strike down provincial legislation that threatened civil liberties.

Switzman v Elbling and AG of Quebec
Supreme Court of Canada
[1957] SCR 285

KERWIN CJ: Section 1 provides

> 1. This Act may be cited as *Act Respecting Communistic Propaganda.*

Sections 3 and 12 read:

> 3. It shall be illegal for any person, who possesses or occupies a house within the Province, to use it or allow any person to make use of it to propagate communism or bolshevism by any means whatsoever.
> 12. It shall be unlawful to print, to publish in any manner whatsoever or to distribute in the Province any newspaper, periodical, pamphlet, circular, document or writing whatsoever propagating or tending to propagate communism or bolshevism.

Sections 4 to 11 provide that the Attorney-General, upon satisfactory proof that an infringement of s. 3 has been committed, may order the closing of the house; authorize any peace officer to execute such order, and provide a procedure by which the owner may apply by petition to a judge of the Superior Court to have the order revised. Section 13 provides for imprisonment of anyone infringing or participating in the infringement of s. 12. ...

The validity of the statute was attacked upon a number of grounds, but, in cases where constitutional issues are involved, it is important that nothing be said that is unnecessary. In my view it is sufficient to declare that the Act is legislation in relation to the criminal law over which, by virtue of head 27 of s. 91 of the *British North America Act,* the Parliament of Canada has exclusive legislative authority. The decision of this Court in *Bédard v. Dawson et al.* (1923), 40 C.C.C. 404 is clearly distinguishable. As Mr. Justice Barclay points out, the real object of the Act here under consideration is to prevent propagation of communism within the Province and to punish anyone who does so—with provisions authorizing steps for the closing of premises used for such object. The *Bédard* case was concerned with the control and enjoyment of property. ... It is not necessary to refer to other authorities, because, once the conclusion is reached that the pith and substance of the impugned Act is in relation to criminal law, the conclusion is inevitable that the Act is unconstitutional.

[Seven other judges concurred with Kerwin CJ in the result. Taschereau J dissented and relied on *Bédard v Dawson* (1923), 40 CCC 404 (SCC), which had upheld a Quebec law aimed at closing "disorderly houses" after there had been *Criminal Code* convictions for gambling or prostitution offences. Taschereau J stated that the provinces had the power to legislate to prevent crime such as treason and sedition.]

Even after the enactment of the Charter, the inability of the provinces to enact laws classified as criminal laws was still applied by the courts.

R v Morgentaler
Supreme Court of Canada
[1993] 3 SCR 463

SOPINKA J: The question in this appeal is whether the *Nova Scotia Medical Services Act*, RSNS 1989, c. 281, and the regulation made under the Act, N.S. Reg. 152/89, are *ultra vires* the province of Nova Scotia on the ground that they are in pith and substance criminal law. The Act and regulation make it an offence to perform an abortion outside a hospital. ...

In January 1988, this Court ruled that the *Criminal Code* provisions relating to abortion were unconstitutional because they violated women's Charter guarantee of security of the person: *R. v. Morgentaler*, [1988] 1 S.C.R. 30 (*Morgentaler* (1988)). At the same time the Court reaffirmed its earlier decision that the provisions were a valid exercise of the federal criminal law power: *Morgentaler v. The Queen*, [1976] 1 S.C.R. 616 (*Morgentaler* (1975)). The 1988 decision meant that abortion was no longer regulated by the criminal law. It was no longer an offence to obtain or perform an abortion in a clinic such as those run by the respondent. ... This legislation deals, by its terms, with a subject historically considered to be part of the criminal law—the prohibition of the performance of abortions with penal consequences. It is thus suspect on its face. Its legal effect partially reproduces that of the now defunct s. 251 of the *Criminal Code*, in so far as both precluded the establishment and operation of free-standing abortion clinics. ... The primary objective of this legislation was to prohibit abortions outside hospitals as socially undesirable conduct and any concern with the safety and security of pregnant women or with health care policy, hospitals or the regulation of the medical profession was merely ancillary. This legislation involves the regulation of the place where an abortion may be obtained, not from the viewpoint of health care policy, but from the viewpoint of public wrongs or crimes. ...

[Lamer CJ and La Forest, L'Heureux-Dubé, Gonthier, Cory, McLachlin, Iacobucci, and Major JJ concurred with Sopinka J in declaring the impugned law to be an unconstitutional provincial invasion of the federal criminal law power.]

Reference re Firearms Act (Can)
Supreme Court of Canada
2000 SCC 31, [2000] 1 SCR 783

THE COURT: In 1995, Parliament amended the *Criminal Code*, R.S.C., 1985, c C-46, by enacting the *Firearms Act*, S.C. 1995, c. 39, commonly referred to as the gun control law, to require the holders of all firearms to obtain licences and register their guns. In 1996, the Province of Alberta challenged Parliament's power to pass the gun control law by a reference to the Alberta Court of Appeal. The Court of Appeal by a 3:2 majority upheld Parliament's power to pass the law. The Province of Alberta now appeals that decision to this Court. ...

The answer to this question lies in the Canadian Constitution. The Constitution assigns some matters to Parliament and others to the provincial legislatures: *Constitution Act, 1867*. The federal government asserts that the gun control law falls under its criminal law power, s. 91(27), and under its general power to legislate for the "Peace, Order and good Government" of Canada. Alberta, on the other hand, says the law falls under its power over property and civil rights, s. 92(13). All agree that to resolve this dispute, the Court must first determine what the gun control law is really about—its "pith and substance"—and then ask which head or heads of power it most naturally falls within.

We conclude that the gun control law comes within Parliament's jurisdiction over criminal law. The law in "pith and substance" is directed to enhancing public safety by controlling access to firearms through prohibitions and penalties. This brings it under the federal criminal law power. While the law has regulatory aspects, they are secondary to its primary criminal law purpose. The intrusion of the law into the provincial jurisdiction over property and civil rights is not so excessive as to upset the balance of federalism. ...

Yet another argument is that the ownership of guns is not criminal law because it is not immoral to own an ordinary firearm. There are two difficulties with this argument. The first is that while the ownership of ordinary firearms is not in itself regarded by most Canadians as immoral, the problems associated with the misuse of firearms are firmly grounded in morality. Firearms may be misused to take human life and to assist in other immoral acts, like theft and terrorism. Preventing such misuse can be seen as an attempt to curb immoral acts. Viewed thus, gun control is directed at a moral evil.

The second difficulty with the argument is that the criminal law is not confined to prohibiting immoral acts: see *Proprietary Articles Trade Association v. Attorney-General for Canada*, [1931] A.C. 310 (P.C.). While most criminal conduct is also regarded as immoral, Parliament can use the criminal law to prohibit activities which have little relation to public morality. For instance, the criminal law has been used to prohibit certain restrictions on market competition. ... Therefore, even if gun control did not involve morality, it could still fall under the federal criminal law power.

We recognize the concerns of northern, rural and aboriginal Canadians who fear that this law does not address their particular needs. They argue that it discriminates against them and violates treaty rights, and express concerns about their ability to access the scheme, which may be administered from a great distance. These apprehensions are genuine, but they do not go to the question before us—Parliament's jurisdiction to enact this law. Whether a law could have been designed better or whether the federal government should have engaged in more consultation before enacting the law has no bearing on the division of powers analysis applied by this Court. If the law violates a treaty or a provision of the Charter, those affected can bring their claims to Parliament or the courts in a separate case. The reference questions, and hence this judgment, are restricted to the issue of the division of powers.

We also appreciate the concern of those who oppose this Act on the basis that it may not be effective or it may be too expensive. Criminals will not register their guns, Alberta argued. The only real effect of the law, it is suggested, is to burden law-abiding farmers and hunters with red tape. These concerns were properly directed to and considered by

Parliament; they cannot affect the Court's decision. The efficacy of a law, or lack thereof, is not relevant to Parliament's ability to enact it under the division of powers analysis. … The cost of the program, another criticism of the law, is equally irrelevant to our constitutional analysis.

On federalism and the criminal law, see P Hogg, *Constitutional Law of Canada*, 5th ed (Toronto: Carswell, 2007) ch 18; E Colvin & S Anand, *Principles of Criminal Law*, 3rd ed (Toronto: Carswell, 2007) ch 1; and P Monahan & B Shaw, *Constitutional Law*, 4th ed (Toronto: Irwin Law, 2013) ch 11.

III. CODIFICATION: THE CRIMINAL LAW AS A STATUTE

History of the Criminal Code

The history of the Canadian *Criminal Code* is briefly stated in the following extract.

AW Mewett, "The Criminal Law, 1867-1967"
(1967) 45 Can Bar Rev 726 at 726-30 (footnotes omitted)

For a large part of the nineteenth century, the idea of codification of the criminal law had been mooted in England and elsewhere in the English-speaking world. In 1838 in England the first Criminal Law Commissioners were appointed to report on and draft such a code and in 1878, largely as a result of the work of Sir James Stephen, the English Draft Code, dealing with indictable offences, was formulated. Although this formed the basis of two Bills presented to the English Parliament, both attempts to introduce a comprehensive criminal code were abortive.

In Canada, the Bill Respecting Criminal Law of 1892 was expressed by Sir John Thompson to be founded on the Draft Code prepared by the Royal Commission in Great Britain in 1880, on Stephen's *Digest of the Criminal Law*, the edition of 1887, Burbidge's *Digest of the Canadian Criminal Law* of 1889 and the Canadian statutory law. He quoted from the *Commission Report* to define the codification as follows:

> It is a reduction of the existing law to an orderly written system, freed from needless technicalities, obscurities and other defects which the experience of its administration has disclosed. It aims at the reduction to a system of that kind of substantive law relating to crimes and the law of procedure, both as to indictable offences and as to summary convictions.

A series of amendments resulted in the consolidations of 1906 and 1927, but neither of these could be called revisions. In 1947, a Royal Commission to Revise the Criminal Code was appointed, reported in 1952 and in 1953 the Revised Code was enacted. This revision did not greatly alter the structure or substance of the original Code, no attempt being made to consider or redefine fundamental criminal law concepts. The system of punishments was rationalized, certain procedural reforms were introduced and a relatively small number of specific offences were either redefined or introduced.

One significant change was that enacted by section 8 [now s 9] stating:

Notwithstanding anything in this Act or any other Act, no person shall be convicted or discharged under section 736
  (a) of an offence at common law,
  (b) of an offence under an Act of the Parliament of England, or of Great Britain, or of the United Kingdom of Great Britain and Ireland, or
  (c) of an offence under an Act or ordinance in force in any province, territory or place before that province, territory or place became a province of Canada,
but nothing in this section affects the power, jurisdiction or authority that a court, judge, justice or provincial court judge had, immediately before April 1, 1955, to impose punishment for contempt of court.

Prior to the enactment of section 8 of the 1953 revision, prosecutions were successful for such common law offences as abuse of office in taking fees wrongfully, public mischief, champerty and maintenance and perhaps barratry.

It was thus not until 1953 that all common law offences were abolished throughout Canada. It is interesting to note that, in contrast, the first English Draft Code proposed the abolition of all common law offences not specifically enacted in the Code. It could not, however, be maintained that prosecution for common law offences was a very frequent occurrence in Canada after 1892, and the Revision Commissioners decided that there was no point in preserving them after 1953. Instead, all those thought applicable to Canada were specifically enacted. ...

On the other hand, faced with the difficulty, if not impossibility of attempting to codify the common law defences, the Commissioners merely recommended, and Parliament enacted, section 7(2) [now s 8(3)] providing:

Every rule and principle of the common law that renders any circumstance a justification or excuse for an act or a defence to a charge continues in force and applies in respect of proceedings for an offence under this Act or any other Act of the Parliament of Canada, except insofar as they are altered by or are inconsistent with this Act or any other Act of the Parliament of Canada.

For the history of the *Criminal Code* enacted in Canada, see G Parker, "The Origins of the Canadian Criminal Code" in DH Flaherty, *Essays in the History of Canadian Law* (Toronto: Osgoode Society, 1981) ch 7; D Brown, *The Genesis of the Canadian Criminal Code of 1892* (Toronto: University of Toronto Press, 1989); and AW Mewett, "The Canadian Criminal Code, 1892-1992" (1993) 72 Can Bar Rev 1. For an alternative code that was not adopted in Canada, see ML Friedland, "R.S. Wright's Model Criminal Code: A Forgotten Chapter in the History of the Criminal Law" in ML Friedland, ed, *A Century of Criminal Justice* (Toronto: Carswell, 1984) ch 1.

Common Law Defences

Why should offences at common law (i.e., judge-made law as opposed to legislation) be prohibited under s 9(a) of the *Criminal Code* but not defences, excuses, or justifications?

Amato v The Queen
Supreme Court of Canada
[1982] 2 SCR 418

[In this case, Estey J interpreted s 7(3) (now s 8(3)) of the *Criminal Code* to allow the judicial development of a defence of entrapment. The subsequent development of entrapment will be examined in Chapter 3.]

ESTEY J: If there be a defence of entrapment available to the accused in the circumstances of this appeal it cannot be of statutory origin for it is not to be found in the *Criminal Code.* If a defence arises in the common law it can only find its way into the courts through s. 7(3) of the Code:

> 7(3) Every rule and principle of the common law that renders any circumstance a justification or excuse for an act or a defence to a charge continues in force and applies in respect of proceedings for an offence under this Act or any other Act of the Parliament of Canada, except in so far as they are altered by or are inconsistent with this Act or any other Act of the Parliament of Canada.

This provision in turn only supports the application of such a defence if s-s. (3) has a continuing prospective character when properly construed. The Chief Justice assumes this to be the case in *R. v. Kirzner* (1977), 38 C.C.C. (2d) 131 at p. 138, 81 D.L.R. (3d) 229 at p. 236, [1978] 2 S.C.R. 487 at p. 496:

> I do not think that s. 7(3) should be regarded as having frozen the power of the Courts to enlarge the content of the common law by way of recognizing new defences, as they may think proper according to circumstances that they consider may call for further control of prosecutorial behaviour or of judicial proceedings.

… [T]he common law would be allowed to develop defences not inconsistent with the provisions of the Code if the construction adopted was prospective. For this conclusion I find support in the Report of the Imperial Commissioners on the Draft Code of 1879, s. 19 of which is the forerunner of our present s. 7(3). The commissioners explained the inclusion of s. 19 (now s. 7(3)) as follows, at volume I, p. 10, of their report:

> But whilst we exclude from the category of indictable offences any culpable act or omission not provided for by this or some other Act of Parliament, there is another branch of the unwritten law which introduces different considerations; namely, the principles which declare what circumstances amount to a justification or excuse for doing that which would be otherwise a crime, or at least would alter the quality of the crime.
>
> … At present we desire to state that in our opinion it is, if not absolutely impossible, at least not practicable, to foresee all the various combinations of circumstances which may happen, but which are of so unfrequent occurrence that they have not hitherto been the subject of judicial consideration, although they might constitute a justification or excuse, and to use language at once so precise and clear and comprehensive as to include all cases that ought to be included, and not to include any case that ought to be excluded.
>
> We have already expressed our opinion that it is on the whole expedient that no crimes not specified in the Draft Code should be punished, though in consequence some guilty

persons may thus escape punishment. But we do not think it desirable that, if a particular combination of circumstances arises of so unusual a character that the law has never been decided with reference to it, there should be any risk of a Code being so framed as to deprive an accused person of a defence to which the common law entitles him, and that it might become the duty of the judge to direct the jury that they must find him guilty, although the facts proved did show that he had a defence on the merits, and would have an undoubted claim to be pardoned by the Crown. While, therefore, digesting and declaring the law as applicable to the ordinary cases, we think that the common law so far as it affords a defence should be preserved in all cases not expressly provided for. This we have endeavoured to do by Section 19 of the Draft Code.

It might also be noted that in recent years this court has adverted to common law defences of duress (*R. v. Paquette* (1976), 30 C.C.C. (2d) 417, 70 D.L.R. (3d) 129, [1977] 2 S.C.R. 189), necessity (*Morgentaler v. The Queen* (1975), 20 C.C.C. (2d) 449, 53 D.L.R. (3d) 161, [1976] 1 S.C.R. 616), and due diligence (*R. v. City of Sault Ste. Marie* (1978), 40 C.C.C. (2d) 353, 85 D.L.R. (3d) 161, [1978] 2 S.C.R. 1299), without exclusive concern for the state of the law prior to the 1892 introduction of the *Criminal Code*.

Applying the ordinary rule of construction where statutes and common law meet I conclude that s. 7(3) is the authority for the courts of criminal jurisdiction to adopt, if appropriate in the view of the court, defences including the defence of entrapment. The components of such a defence and the criteria for its application raise other issues.

Justice Estey dissented in this case, but the full court eventually endorsed a defence of entrapment in *R v Mack*, [1988] 2 SCR 903 as contained in Chapter 3.

The Law Reform Commission of Canada has proposed that all defences be set out in a new *Criminal Code* "in the interest of comprehensiveness." The commission notes that it would still be "open to the courts to develop other defences insofar as is required by the reference to 'principles of fundamental justice' in section 7 of the *Charter*": *Recodifying Criminal Law, Report 31* (Ottawa: Law Reform Commission of Canada, 1987) at 28. Is this a wise departure from s 8(3) of the present Code as interpreted in *Amato, supra*? Note that the subcommittee of the Standing Committee on Justice and the Solicitor-General examining the General Part of the *Criminal Code* recommended in its report of February 1993 that the Code should codify existing defences but continue to allow for the recognition of new defences.

Common Law Offences

Even before the abolition of common law offences by the 1953 *Criminal Code*, the Supreme Court of Canada in *Frey v Fedoruk*, [1950] SCR 517 (a civil action for false imprisonment and malicious prosecution) had decided not to increase the number of common law offences and thus refused to declare it to be an offence to be a "peeping tom."

Frey v Fedoruk
Supreme Court of Canada
[1950] SCR 517

[Frey was caught and detained by Fedoruk after Frey was observed at 11:00 p.m. looking into a window of a woman's room in Fedoruk's house. Frey was charged that he "unlawfully did act in a manner likely to cause a breach of the peace by peeping." He was convicted at trial but the conviction was overturned on the basis that there was no such offence. Frey then brought a civil suit as a plaintiff against Fedoruk and others for false imprisonment. Fedoruk argued as a defendant that he was justified in restraining Frey because Frey was committing a criminal offence.]

CARTWRIGHT J (speaking for 6 out of 7 members of the Supreme Court sitting on the case stated in part): ... This appeal raises questions as to whether the conduct of the Plaintiff, which is popularly described as that of a "peeping tom," constitutes a criminal offence and if so, whether the Defendants Fedoruk and Stone were justified in arresting the Plaintiff without a warrant.

The majority of the Court of Appeal (O'Halloran, J.A. speaking for the majority) were of opinion that the Plaintiff was guilty of a criminal offence at Common Law, and that the Defendants were justified in the circumstances in arresting him without a warrant.

The only charge laid against the Plaintiff was that he:

> ... unlawfully did act in a manner likely to cause a breach of the peace by peeping at night through the window of the house of S. Fedoruk, there situated, against the peace of our Lord the King, his Crown and dignity; Contrary to the form of Statute in such case made and provided.

On this charge the Plaintiff was convicted by a police magistrate sitting for the summary trial of an indictable offence. The formal conviction concludes with the words:

> and I adjudge the said Bernard Frey for his said offence to keep the Peace and be of good behaviour for the term of one year.

If it should be admitted as a principle that conduct may be treated as criminal because, although not otherwise criminal, it has a natural tendency to provoke violence by way of retribution, it seems to me that great uncertainty would result. I do not think it safe by the application of such a supposed principle to declare an act or acts criminal which have not, up to the present, been held to be criminal in any reported case.

O'Halloran, J.A. does not refer to any reported case in which the conduct of a "peeping tom" has been held to be a criminal offence. As mentioned above, we were referred to no such case by counsel, and I have not been able to find one.

I do not understand O'Halloran, J.A. to suggest in his elaborate reasons that there is precedent for the view that the Plaintiff's conduct in this case was criminal. Rather he appears to support the finding of the trial Judge to that effect on the grounds stated in the following paragraph:

> Criminal responsibility at Common law is primarily not a matter of precedent, but of application of generic principle to the differing facts of each case. It is for the jury to apply to

the facts of the case as they find them, the generic principle the Judge gives them. Thus by their general verdict the jury in practical effect decide both the law and the facts in the particular case, and have consistently done so over the centuries, and cf. Coke on Littleton (1832 Ed.) vol. 1, note 5, para. 155(b). The fact finding Judge in this case, as the record shows, had not the slightest doubt on the evidence before him that what the appellant had been accused of was a criminal offence at Common Law.

I am of the opinion that the proposition implicit in the paragraph quoted above ought not to be accepted. I think that if adopted, it would introduce great uncertainty into the administration of the Criminal Law, leaving it to the judicial officer trying any particular charge to decide that the acts proved constituted a crime or otherwise, not by reference to any defined standard to be found in the code or in reported decisions, but according to his individual view as to whether such acts were a disturbance of the tranquility of people tending to provoke physical reprisal.

John Willis saw the Supreme Court's decision in *Frey v Fedoruk* not to expand the range of common law crimes to cover "peeping toms" as a decision to place "the protection of the individual from the risk of oppression" above "the protection of the state from the risk of disorder." He stated that the decision

> enunciates in ringing tones the grand old slogan that Canadians are not at the mercy of the whims of officials, even those officials who are independent of the government in power and called judges. So long as the principle is vindicated, it matters not that the police cannot any longer afford to the householder the protection he has been led to expect.

Willis observed that in England the common law crime of public mischief has been useful in addressing problems such as group libel and "hoaxing the police": "Case Comment" (1950) 28 Can Bar Rev 1023.

When in 1953 Parliament enacted the present s 9 of the *Criminal Code* abolishing all but the common law offence of contempt of court, it also introduced an offence of trespassing at night: SC 1953-54, c 51, s 162 (now s 177). The offence provides:

> Every one who, without lawful excuse, the proof of which lies on him, loiters or prowls at night on the property of another person near a dwelling-house situated on that property is guilty of an offence punishable on summary conviction.

The conspiracy section of the Canadian *Criminal Code* (s 465) had a provision that was repealed in 1985 (RSC 1985, c 27, s 61(3)), which stated:

> Every one who conspires with any one
>   (a) to effect an unlawful purpose, or
>   (b) to effect a lawful purpose by unlawful means,
> is guilty of an indictable offence and is liable to imprisonment for two years.

In *Shaw v DPP*, [1962] AC 220, the House of Lords in England held that the publishers of a directory of prostitutes were guilty of the common law offence of conspiracy to corrupt public morals. There was subsequently considerable controversy as to whether that decision was applicable in Canada to the offence listed above. In *Gralewicz et al v The Queen*, [1980] 2

SCR 493 the Supreme Court of Canada clarified the issue by stating that in the conspiracy section "unlawful purpose means contrary to law, that is prohibited by federal or provincial legislation." See now s 465 of the Code. Paragraph (1)(d) provides:

> (d) every one who conspires with any one to commit an offence punishable on summary conviction is guilty of an offence punishable on summary conviction.

Section 9 of the *Criminal Code* abolishes common law or judge-made offences with the exception of contempt of court. The next case tried to challenge the use of the common law contempt offence under s 7 of the Charter by arguing that codification of crimes was a principle of fundamental justice. In *United Nurses of Alberta v AG Alberta*, [1992] 1 SCR 901, the accused union was fined $400,000 for contempt of court by disobeying court directives not to go on strike. McLachlin J stated for the Supreme Court of Canada:

> It is argued that the offence of criminal contempt violates s. 7 of the *Canadian Charter of Rights and Freedoms* because it is not codified and is vague and arbitrary. …
>
> The union's first position is that all uncodified common law crimes are unconstitutional. It is a fundamental principle of justice, it submits, that all crimes must be codified. Criminal contempt, although mentioned in s. 9 of the *Code*, is not codified, both its *actus reus* and *mens rea* being defined at common law.
>
> We were referred to no authority in support of the proposition that fundamental justice requires codification of all crimes. The union cites the principle that there must be no crime or punishment except in accordance with fixed, predetermined law. But the absence of codification does not mean that a law violates this principle. For many centuries, most of our crimes were uncodified and were not viewed as violating this fundamental rule. Nor, conversely, is codification a guarantee that all is made manifest in the *Code*. Definition of elements of codified crimes not infrequently requires recourse to common law concepts: see *R. v. Jobidon* (1991), 66 C.C.C. (3d) 454, where the majority of this court, per Gonthier J., noted the important role the common law continues to *play* in the criminal law. The union also relies on the fact that this court has said it is for Parliament, not the courts, to create new offences: *Frey v. Fedoruk* (1950), 97 C.C.C. 1, [1950] 3 D.L.R. 513, [1950] S.C.R. 517; s. 9 of the *Criminal Code*. But this does not mean that the courts should refuse to recognize the common law crime of contempt of court which pre-dated codification and which is expressly preserved by s. 9 of the *Criminal Code*. I conclude that lack of codification in itself does not render the common law crime of criminal contempt of court unconstitutional.
>
> The next argument is that the crime of criminal contempt is so vague and difficult to apply that it violates the fundamental principle of justice that the law should be fixed, predetermined and accessible and understandable by the public. …
>
> In this case there was ample evidence to support the conclusion that the union chose to defy court orders openly and continuously, with full knowledge that its defiance would be widely publicized and, even putting the union's case at its best, it did not care whether this would bring the court into disrepute.
>
> Criminal contempt, thus defined, does not violate the Charter. It is neither vague nor arbitrary. A person can predict in advance whether his or her conduct will constitute a crime. The trial judges below had no trouble applying the right test, suggesting that the concept is capable of application without difficulty. Thus the case that the crime of contempt violates the principles of fundamental justice has not been made out.

The union's appeal was dismissed and the conviction affirmed.

With the exception of the common law offence of contempt, courts cannot create new common law crimes. The next case, however, demonstrates how courts can interpret an existing provision in a manner that effectively extends the offence and applies the extended provision retroactively to the case at hand.

R v Jobidon
Supreme Court of Canada
[1991] 2 SCR 714

[The accused was charged with manslaughter by the unlawful act of assault. He fought the victim first in a barroom in Sudbury and later in the parking lot of the bar. The victim, who was drunk but larger than the accused and had boxing experience, had got the better of the fight in the bar. In the parking lot, however, Jobidon rendered the victim unconscious with the first blow to the face and then followed that up with several more blows causing the victim to go into a coma and eventually die. The accused was acquitted of manslaughter at trial on the basis that the victim had consented to the fight. Section 265(1)(a) defines assault as the intentional application of force to another person "without the consent of [the other] person." The Crown successfully appealed to the Court of Appeal, which concluded that for reasons of public policy there could be no consent to such an assault and entered a conviction of manslaughter. The accused appealed to the Supreme Court.]

GONTHIER J (L'Heureux-Dubé, La Forest, Cory, and Iacobucci JJ concurring): At issue in the present appeal is the role of consent in the criminal offence of assault. More particularly, the issue is whether the absence of consent is an essential element of this offence when it relates to a fist fight where bodily harm is intentionally caused.

· · ·

The appellant argued that the Ontario Court of Appeal erred in its interpretation of s. 265 of the *Criminal Code*. Rather than apply the common law understanding of the role of consent—which sometimes limits its effectiveness as a bar to assault—the court should have accorded full effect to Haggart's consent, as apparently required by s. 265(1)(a) of the *Code*.

Section 265(1)(a) states that an assault occurs when, "without the consent of another person, he applies force intentionally to that other person, directly or indirectly." Section 265(2) provides that "This section applies to all forms of assault, including sexual assault, sexual assault with a weapon, threats to a third party or causing bodily harm and aggravated sexual assault." In the appellant's opinion, the trial judge's finding of consent meant that all the elements of the offence of assault had not been proved. The appellant should therefore have been acquitted on that basis, since the legislature intended that consent should serve as a bar to conviction.

According to the appellant, the legislature could have specified that in certain situations, or in respect of certain forms of conduct, absence of consent would not be an operative element of the offence. It has done so with other offences. Parliament has provided that no person is entitled to consent to have death inflicted on him (s. 14). It restricted the concept in ss. 150.1 and 159 of the *Code* by denying defences to sexual offences based on a child's consent. It also did this in s. 286 by negating the validity of a young person's consent to abduction. But with the assault provisions in s. 265, it chose not to insert policy-based limitations on the role of consent. Moreover, in s. 265(3), Parliament expressly specified the circumstances in which consent would be vitiated on grounds of involuntariness, but the circumstances described in that subsection do not include the policy limitation applied to fist fights by the English Court of Appeal in the *Attorney General's Reference, ... infra.*

The appellant further observed that, in England, the crime of assault is not defined in a criminal code but in the common law, to which common law limitations and exceptions more naturally apply. In Canada, we have a code of general principles by which, it is presumed, ambiguity is to be construed in favour of the liberty of the subject.

The basic offence of assault originally came to post-Confederation Canada as a crime of common law.

· · ·

Canada did not adopt its first criminal code until 1893. So, the English law was the primary foundation of Canadian criminal law. As Canadian courts gradually added to the English jurisprudence, our criminal common law increasingly became a blend of English and Canadian authorities. For decades, though, the definition of assault in Canadian criminal law remained virtually identical to the English common law version. That essential identity was not disturbed when Canada proclaimed its *Criminal Code* on July 1, 1893 since Canada's codification was very moderate, merely "expressing the common law in neat statutory language to be interpreted by common law judges." (G. Parker, "The Origins of the Canadian *Criminal Code*," in D.H. Flaherty, ed., *Essays in the History of Canadian Law* (1981), vol. I, at p. 263. See also Law Reform Commission of Canada, *Towards a Codification of Canadian Criminal Law* (1976).) ...

It can be seen from this brief overview that the absence of consent to intentionally applied force was a material component of the offence of assault throughout its existence in Canada. But it is also evident that consent would not be legally effective in all circumstances. For instance, it would be vitiated by fraud. Various limitations on the validity of consent have a long lineage in the history of the offence. To observe those limitations one must advert to the common law.

· · ·

The controversy in this appeal stems from the apparent contradiction between the holding of the Ontario Court of Appeal in the instant appeal and the wording of s. 265(1)(a). By that wording, once the trial judge found that the deceased had consented to a fight with Jobidon, it appears as if he could not have committed the unlawful act of assault since s. 265(2) states a general rule that s. 265 applies to all forms of assault, including assault causing bodily harm. Consequently, given the reference to absence of consent in s. 265(1), proof of consent to a fist fight in which force is intentionally applied and which results in bodily harm would seem to serve as a defence for Jobidon.

· · ·

Parliament could have specified whether the term "consent" is aimed simply at the kind of *activity* being purportedly consented to (here a fist fight), or whether it refers to consent to a *trivial injury* which does not amount to bodily harm (such as might be sustained in sporting activities), or whether for the defence to apply the consent must be as to the *precise extent of harm actually caused* by the application of force. At any point in the history of the provision Parliament could have taken the opportunity to specify whether the common law, which already had had much to say about assault and the requirement of consent, was being emptied of relevance. But it did not do these things. Nor did it have to.

Just as the common law has built up a rich jurisprudence around the concepts of agreement in contract law, and *volenti non fit injuria* in the law of negligence, it has also generated a body of law to illuminate the meaning of consent and to place certain limitations on its legal effectiveness in the criminal law. It has done this in respect of assault. In the same way that the common law established principles of public policy negating the legal effectiveness of certain types of contracts—contracts in restraint of trade for example—it has also set limits on the types of harmful actions to which one can validly consent, and shelter an assailant from the sanctions of our criminal law.

All criminal offences in Canada are now defined in the *Code* (s. 9). But that does not mean the common law no longer illuminates these definitions nor gives content to the various principles of criminal responsibility those definitions draw from. As the Law Reform Commission of Canada has noted in its 31st report on recodification, the basic premises of our criminal law—the necessary conditions for criminal liability—are at present left to the common law. (*Recodifying Criminal Law*, at pp. 17, 28 and 34.). ... The *Code* itself, in s. 8, explicitly acknowledges the ongoing common law influence: ...

> 8. ...
>
> (2) The criminal law of England that was in force in a province immediately before April 1, 1955 continues in force in the province except as altered, varied, modified or affected by this Act or any other Act of the Parliament of Canada.
>
> (3) Every rule and principle of the common law that renders any circumstance a justification or excuse for an act or a defence to a charge continues in force and applies in respect of proceedings for an offence under this Act or any other Act of Parliament except in so far as they are altered by or are inconsistent with this Act or any other Act of Parliament.

Section 8 expressly indicates that the common law rules and principles continue to apply, but only to the extent that they are not inconsistent with the *Code* or other Act of Parliament and have not been altered by them.

· · ·

In light of this communicated understanding of the antecedents and purpose of s. 8(3), it can hardly be said that the common law's developed approach to the role and scope of consent as a defence to assault has no place in our criminal law. If s. 8(3) and its interaction with the common law can be used to develop entirely new defences not inconsistent with the *Code*, it surely authorizes the courts to look to pre-existing common law rules and principles to give meaning to, and explain the outlines and boundaries of an existing defence or justification, indicating where they will not be recognized as legally effective— provided of course that there is no clear language in the *Code* which indicates that the *Code* has displaced the common law. That sort of language cannot be found in the *Code*. As such, the common law legitimately serves in this appeal as an archive in which one may locate situations or forms of conduct to which the law will not allow a person to consent.

· · ·

In *Matthew v. Ollerton* (1693), Comb. 218, 90 E.R. 438, it was held that a man may not license another to beat him as that act amounted to a breach of the peace. This principle was repeated in *Boulter v. Clarke* (1747), Bull. N.P. 16, where it was determined that it is no defence to a charge of assault that the two persons fought by mutual consent. Coleridge J. reaffirmed the doctrine in *R. v. Lewis* (1844), 1 Car. & K. 419, 174 E.R. 874, a case involving a fight between two men outside a dance hall, which had resulted in the death of a man from blows sustained to his head. Coleridge J. stated, at p. 875: "it ought to be known, that, whenever two persons go out to strike each other, and do so, each is guilty of an assault."

It will be seen that this nullification of the defence of consent in fist fight cases in England has continued forward uninterruptedly to the present day. In Canada the same principle was applied for many decades before the appropriateness of such invalidation was ever brought into question. Indeed it was for reasons of public policy that the Court of Appeal nullified Haggart's [the victim in this case] consent.

. . .

It would have been quite impractical, if not impossible, for Parliament to establish an adequate list of exceptions to apply to all situations, old and new. Policy-based limits are almost always the product of a balancing of individual autonomy (the freedom to choose to have force intentionally applied to oneself) and some larger societal interest. That balancing may be better performed in the light of actual situations, rather than in the abstract, as Parliament would be compelled to do.

With the offence of assault, that kind of balancing is a function the courts are well-suited to perform. ... The common law is the register of the balancing function of the courts—a register Parliament has authorized the courts to administer in respect of policy-based limits on the role and scope of consent in s. 265 of the *Code*.

. . .

Foremost among the policy considerations supporting the Crown is the social uselessness of fist fights. As the English Court of Appeal noted in the *Attorney General's Reference*, it is not in the public interest that adults should willingly cause harm to one another without a good reason. There is precious little utility in fist fights or street brawls. These events are motivated by unchecked passion. They so often result in serious injury to the participants. Here it resulted in a tragic death to a young man on his wedding day.

There was a time when pugilism was sheltered by the notion of "chivalry." Duelling was an activity not only condoned, but required by honour. Those days are fortunately long past. Our social norms no longer correlate strength of character with prowess at fisticuffs. Indeed when we pride ourselves for making positive ethical and social strides, it tends to be on the basis of our developing reason. This is particularly true of the law, where reason is cast in a privileged light. Erasing longstanding limits on consent to assault would be a regressive step, one which would retard the advance of civilised norms of conduct.

Quite apart from the valueless nature of fist fights from the combatants' perspective, it should also be recognized that consensual fights may sometimes lead to larger brawls and to serious breaches of the public peace. In the instant case, this tendency was openly observable. At the prospect of a fight between Jobidon and the deceased, in a truly macabre fashion many patrons of the hotel deliberately moved to the parking lot to witness the gruesome event. That scene easily could have erupted in more widespread aggression between allies of the respective combatants. Indeed it happened that the brothers of Jobidon and Haggart also took to each other with their fists.

Given the spontaneous, often drunken nature of many fist fights, I would not wish to push a deterrence rationale too far. Nonetheless, it seems reasonable to think that, in some cases, common law limitations on consent might serve some degree of deterrence to these sorts of activities.

Related to a deterrence rationale is the possibility that, by permitting a person to consent to force inflicted by the hand of another, in rare cases the latter may find he derives some form of pleasure from the activity, especially if he is doing so on a regular basis. It is perhaps not inconceivable that this kind of perversion could arise in a domestic or marital setting where one or more of the family members are of frail or unstable mental health. As one criminal law theorist has written:

> [T]he self-destructive individual who induces another person to kill or to mutilate him implicates the latter in the violation of a significant social taboo. The person carrying out the killing or the mutilation crosses the threshold into a realm of conduct that, the second time, might be more easily carried out. And the second time, it might not be particularly significant whether the victim consents or not. Similarly, if someone is encouraged to inflict a sadomasochistic beating on a consenting victim, the experience of inflicting the beating might loosen the actor's inhibitions against sadism in general.

(G. Fletcher, *Rethinking Criminal Law* (1978), at pp. 770-71.)

Of course this appeal does not concern sadism or intentional killing. But it comes close to mutilation. In any event, the weight of the argument could hold true for fights. If aggressive individuals are legally permitted to get into consensual fist fights, and they take advantage of that license from time to time, it may come to pass that they eventually lose all understanding that that activity *is* the subject of a powerful social taboo. They may too readily find their fists raised against a person whose consent they forgot to ascertain with full certitude. It is preferable that these sorts of omissions be strongly discouraged.

Wholly apart from deterrence, it is most unseemly from a moral point of view that the law would countenance, much less provide a backhanded sanction to the sort of interaction displayed by the facts of this appeal. The sanctity of the human body should militate against the validity of consent to bodily harm inflicted in a fight.

· · ·

The policy preference that people not be able to consent to intentionally inflicted harms is heard not only in the register of our common law. The *Criminal Code* also contains many examples of this propensity. As noted above, s. 14 of the *Code* viewed the legal effectiveness of a person's consent to have death inflicted on him under any circumstances. The same policy appears to underlie ss. 150.1, 159 and 286 in respect of younger people, in the contexts of sexual offences, anal intercourse, and abduction, respectively. All this is to say that the notion of policy-based limits on the effectiveness of consent to some level of inflicted harms is not foreign. Parliament as well as the courts have been mindful of the need for such limits. Autonomy is not the only value which our law seeks to protect.

Some may see limiting the freedom of an adult to consent to applications of force in a fist fight as unduly paternalistic; a violation of individual self-rule. Yet while that view may commend itself to some, those persons cannot reasonably claim that the law does not know such limitations. All criminal law is "paternalistic" to some degree—top-down guidance is inherent in any prohibitive rule. That the common law has developed a strong resistance to recognizing the validity of consent to intentional applications of force in fist fights and brawls is merely one instance of the criminal law's concern that Canadian citizens treat each other humanely and with respect.

· · ·

Conclusion

How, and to what extent is consent limited?

The law's willingness to vitiate consent on policy grounds is significantly limited. Common law cases restrict the extent to which consent may be nullified; as do the relevant policy considerations. The unique situation under examination in this case, a weaponless fist fight between two adults, provides another important boundary.

The limitation demanded by s. 265 as it applies to the circumstances of this appeal is one which vitiates consent between adults intentionally to apply force causing serious hurt or non-trivial bodily harm to each other in the course of a fist fight or brawl. (This test entails that a minor's apparent consent to an adult's intentional application of force in a fight would also be negated.) This is the extent of the limit which the common law requires in the factual circumstances of this appeal. It may be that further limitations will be found to apply in other circumstances. But such limits, if any, are better developed on a case by case basis, so that the unique features of the situation may exert a rational influence on the extent of the limit and on the justification for it.

Stated in this way, the policy of the common law will not affect the validity or effectiveness of freely given consent to participate in rough sporting activities, so long as the intentional applications of force to which one consents are within the customary norms and rules of the game. Unlike fist fights, sporting activities and games usually have a significant social value; they are worthwhile.

· · ·

Finally, the preceding formulation avoids nullification of consent to intentional applications of force which cause only minor hurt or trivial bodily harm. The bodily harm contemplated by the test is essentially equivalent to that contemplated by the definition found in s. 267(2) of the *Code*, dealing with the offence of assault causing bodily harm. The section defines bodily harm as "any hurt or injury to the complainant that interferes with the health or comfort of the complainant and that is more than merely transient or trifling in nature."

On this definition, combined with the fact that the test is restricted to cases involving adults, the phenomenon of the "ordinary" schoolyard scuffle, where boys or girls immaturely seek to resolve differences with their hands, will not come within the scope of the limitation. That has never been the policy of the law and I do not intend to disrupt the status quo.

· · ·

I would uphold the decision of the Court of Appeal. The appeal is dismissed.

[Sopinka J, with Stevenson J concurring (in dissent), also agreed on the facts that there was an assault and this provided a basis for the manslaughter conviction:]

SOPINKA J: I have had the advantage of reading the reasons of Gonthier J. and while I agree with his disposition of the matter I am unable to agree with his reasons. This appeal involves the role that consent plays in the offence of criminal assault. Unlike my colleague I am of the view that consent cannot be read out of the offence. I come to this conclusion for two reasons: (1) consent is a fundamental element of many criminal offences, including assault, and (2) the statutory provision creating the offence of assault explicitly provides for the element of consent.

• • •

I see no evidence in the clear and simple language of s. 265 that it intended to outlaw consensual fighting in the interests of avoiding breaches of the peace or to allow it if a judge thought that it occurred in circumstances that were socially useful. Rather, the policy reflected in s. 265 is to make the absence of consent a requirement in the definition of the offence but to restrict consent to those intentional applications of force in respect of which there is a clear and effective consent by a victim who is free of coercion or misrepresentation. Instead of reading the words "without the consent of another person" out of s. 265 I am of the opinion that the intention of Parliament is respected by close scrutiny of the scope of consent to an assault. Instead of attempting to evaluate the utility of the activity the trial judge will scrutinize the consent to determine whether it applied to the very activity which is the subject of the charge. The more serious the assault the more difficult it should be to establish consent.

• • •

Section 265 states that "[a] person commits an assault when *without the consent of another person*, he applies force intentionally to that other person ..." (emphasis added). My colleague Gonthier J. concludes that on the basis of cases which applied the common law, that section should be interpreted as excluding the absence of consent as an element of the *actus reus* in respect of an assault with intent to commit intentional bodily harm. In coming to his conclusion my colleague relies on a number of English authorities. The issue was not finally resolved in England until the decision of the English Court of Appeal on a reference to it by the Attorney General in 1980. See *Attorney General's Reference (No. 6 of 1980)*, [1981] 2 All E.R. 1057. Unconstrained by the expression of legislative policy, the court moulded the common law to accord with the court's view of what was in the public interest. On this basis the court discarded the absence of consent as an element in assaults in which actual bodily harm was either caused or intended. Exceptions were created for assaults that have some positive social value such as sporting events. In Canada, the criminal law has been codified and the judiciary is constrained by the wording of sections defining criminal offences. The courts' application of public policy is governed by the expression of public policy in the *Criminal Code*. If Parliament intended to adopt the public policy which the English Court of Appeal developed it used singularly inappropriate language. It made the absence of consent a specific requirement and provided that this applied to *all* assaults without exception. ...

In my opinion the above observations as to the appropriate use of public policy are sufficient to conclude that the absence of consent cannot be swept away by a robust application of judge-made policy. This proposition is strengthened and confirmed by the specific dictates of the *Code* with reference to the essential elements of a criminal offence. Section 9(a) of the *Code* provides that "[n]otwithstanding anything in this Act or any other Act, no person shall be convicted ... (a) of an offence at common law." The effect of my colleague's approach is to create an offence where one does not exist under the terms of the *Code* by application of the common law. The offence created is the intentional application of force with the consent of the victim. I appreciate that my colleague's approach is to interpret the section in light of the common law but, in my view, use of the common law to eliminate an element of the offence that is required by statute is more than interpretation and is contrary to not only the spirit but also the letter of s. 9(a). One of the basic reasons for s. 9(a) is the importance of certainty in determining what conduct constitutes a criminal offence. That is the reason we have codified the offences in the *Criminal Code*. An accused should not have to search the books to discover the common law in order to determine if the offence charged is indeed an offence at law. ...

Application to This Appeal

Given the danger inherent in the violent activity in this case, the scope of the consent required careful scrutiny. The trial judge found that the consent given by Haggart did not extend to a continuation of the fight once he had lost consciousness. By striking Haggart once he was unconscious, the accused acted beyond the scope of the consent of Haggart and thus committed the *actus reus* of assault.

. . .

Having found that the accused committed an assault, and given that Mr. Haggart died as a result of that unlawful act, the accused is therefore guilty of manslaughter via *Criminal Code* ss. 222(5)(a) and 234. I would therefore dispose of the appeal as proposed by Gonthier J.

NOTE AND QUESTIONS

Should common law policy constraints on assault such as are contemplated by the majority in *Jobidon* be applied to sado-masochistic sexual activities between consenting adults? The House of Lords in a 3:2 decision in *R v Brown* (1993), 97 Cr App R 44 said yes, as did the Ontario Court of Appeal in *R v Welch* (1995), 101 CCC (3d) 216 (Ont CA).

The Supreme Court revisited *Jobidon* in *R v Paice*, 2005 SCC 22, [2005] 1 SCR 339 at para 18 and concluded: "*Jobidon* requires serious harm both intended and caused for consent to be vitiated." Charron J explained:

> Indeed, if the test were otherwise and a conviction possible if bodily harm were *either* intended or caused, the result would be to criminalize numerous activities that were never intended by Parliament to come within the ambit of the assault provisions and would go beyond the policy considerations identified in *Jobidon*. For example, if causation alone sufficed, a person who agreed to engage in a playful wrestling match with another could end up being criminally responsible if, even by accident, he caused serious bodily harm to the other during the course of play. This Court in *Jobidon* was very mindful not to overextend the application of the principle to like situations. [Emphasis added.]

In the sexual assault causing bodily harm context, courts have now indicated that consent will only be vitiated if, in an assault of a sexual nature, the accused both caused bodily harm and subjectively intended to inflict it. *R v Quashie* (2005), 198 CCC (3d) 337 at para 58 (Ont CA); *R v Zhao*, 2013 ONCA 293 at para 107. Do these refinements help justify the policy of vitiating consent on common law public policy grounds?

Codification and Certainty in the Criminal Law

Codification is thought to advance some of the most fundamental values of the criminal law. Many of these values are captured in the maxim *nullum crimen sine lege, nulla poena sine lege*: "there must be no crime or punishment except in accordance with fixed, predetermined law."

One aspect of this principle is that crimes not be created or punished on a retroactive basis. This has been protected in ss 11(g) and (i) of the Charter, which provide that any person charged with an offence has the right:

> (g) not to be found guilty on account of any act or omission unless, at the time of the act or omission, it constituted an offence under Canadian or international law or was criminal according to the general principles of law recognized by the community of nations; ...
>
> (i) if found guilty of the offence and if the punishment for the offence has been varied between the time of commission and the time of sentencing, to the benefit of the lesser punishment.

The legislative enactment and retroactive imposition of a crime would in most cases violate not only s 11(g) of the Charter but also the principles of fundamental justice in s 7 of the Charter. But what about a novel judicial interpretation of the law (such as in *R v Jobidon*, *supra*) that has the effect of extending the ambit of a criminal offence?

Another value of codification is that the criminal law should be certain.

In *R v Nova Scotia Pharmaceutical Society*, [1992] 2 SCR 606, the Supreme Court affirmed the existence of a void for vagueness doctrine under the Charter. Gonthier J stated:

> Vagueness can be raised under s. 7 of the Charter, since it is a principle of fundamental justice that laws may not be too vague. It can also be raised under s. 1 of the Charter *in limine*, on the basis that an enactment is so vague as not to satisfy the requirement that a limitation on Charter rights be "prescribed by law." ...
>
> The "doctrine of vagueness" is founded on the rule of law, particularly on the principles of fair notice to citizens and limitation of enforcement discretion. ...
>
> *(a) Fair notice to the citizen*
>
> Fair notice to the citizen, as a guide to conduct and a contributing element to a full answer and defence, comprises two aspects.
>
> First of all, there is the more formal aspect of notice, that is acquaintance with the actual text of a statute. In the criminal context, this concern has more or less been set aside by the common law maxim, "Ignorance of the law is no excuse," embodied in s. 19 of the *Criminal Code*. ... Some authors have expressed the opinion that this maxim contradicts the rule of law, and should be revised in the light of the growing quantity and complexity of penal legislation: see E. Colvin, "Criminal Law and The Rule of Law," in P. Fitzgerald, ed., *Crime, Justice & Codification: Essays in commemoration of Jacques Fortin* (Toronto: Carswell, 1986), p. 125, at p. 151, and J.C. Jeffries, Jr., "Legality, Vagueness, and the Construction of Penal Statutes" (1985), 71 *Va. L. Rev.* 189 at p. 209. Since this argument was not raised in this case, I will refrain from ruling on this issue. In any event, given that, as this court has already recognized, case law applying and interpreting a particular section is relevant in determining whether the section is vague, formal notice is not a central concern in a vagueness analysis. ...
>
> Fair notice may not have been given when enactments are in somewhat general terms, in a way that does not readily permit citizens to be aware of their substance, when they do not relate to any element of the substratum of values held by society. It is no coincidence that these enactments

are often found vague. For instance, the vagrancy ordinance invalidated by the United States Supreme Court in *Papachristou v. City of Jacksonville*, 405 U.S. 156 (1972), or the compulsory identification statute struck down in *Kolender v. Lawson*, 461 U.S. 352 (1983), fall in this group.

(b) Limitation of law enforcement discretion

Lamer J. in the *Prostitution Reference* (1990), 56 C.C.C. (3d) 65, used the phrase "standardless sweep," first coined by the United States Supreme Court in *Smith v. Goguen*, 415 U.S. 566 (1974) at p. 575, to describe the limitation of enforcement discretion rationale for the doctrine of vagueness. It has become the prime concern in American constitutional law: *Kolender*, at pp. 357-8. Indeed, today it has become paramount, given the considerable expansion in the discretionary powers of enforcement agencies that has followed the creation of the modern welfare state.

A law must not be so devoid of precision in its content that a conviction will automatically flow from the decision to prosecute. Such is the crux of the concern for limitation of enforcement discretion. When the power to decide whether a charge will lead to conviction or acquittal, normally the preserve of the judiciary, becomes fused with the power to prosecute because of the wording of the law, then a law will be unconstitutionally vague.

For instance, the wording of the vagrancy ordinance invalidated by the United States Supreme Court in *Papachristou*, and quoted at length in the *Prostitution Reference* at p. 86, was so general and so lacked precision in its content that a conviction would ensue every time the law enforcer decided to charge someone with the offence of vagrancy. The words of the ordinance had no substance to them, and they indicated no particular legislative purpose. They left the accused completely in the dark, with no possible way of defending himself before the court.

In this case the Supreme Court of Canada unanimously held that s 32(1)(c) of the then *Combines Investigation Act*, RSC 1970, c C-23, which made it an offence to "lessen, unduly, competition," was not impermissibly vague. In most cases, challenges under s 7 of the Charter to offences on the basis of vagueness have failed, with the courts often stressing that courts can still place a limiting interpretation on expansively worded statutes. See K Roach, *Criminal Law*, 6th ed (Toronto: Irwin Law, 2015) ch 2 and 3, and D Stuart, *Charter Justice in Canadian Criminal Law*, 6th ed (Toronto: Carswell, 2014) at 125-33.

The next case was one of the first striking down a criminal offence on the basis of overbreadth under s 7. As will be examined in the next chapter in the extract *Canada (Attorney General) v Bedford,* 2013 SCC 72, [2013] 3 SCR 1101, the principles of fundamental justice have continued to evolve so that laws can potentially be struck down not only if they are excessively vague or overbroad but also if they are arbitrary or grossly disproportionate to their legislative aims. The court in *Bedford* observed that arbitrariness, overbreadth, and gross disproportionality "compare the rights infringement caused by the law with the objective of the law, not with the law's effectiveness" (at para 123). That is, they do not look to how well the law achieves its object, or to how much of the population the law benefits. They do not consider ancillary benefits to the general population. Furthermore, none of the principles measure the percentage of the population that is negatively impacted. The analysis is qualitative, not quantitative. The question under s. 7 is whether *anyone's* life, liberty or security of the person has been denied by a law that is inherently bad; a grossly disproportionate, overbroad, or arbitrary effect on one person is sufficient to establish a breach of s. 7." *Ibid* at para 123.

Other principles of fundamental justice that impact criminal and regulatory offences and defences will be examined in other parts of the book, most notably in Chapters 6, 7, 13, 16, and 18.

R v Heywood
Supreme Court of Canada
[1994] 3 SCR 761

[The case involved s 179(1)(b) of the *Criminal Code*, which provided that it was an offence for a person with a past sexual violence conviction to be "found loitering in or near a school ground, playground, public park or bathing area." The British Columbia Court of Appeal quashed the conviction of a man with two prior convictions of sexual assault of young girls after he was "found loitering in or near … a playground." He had been found photographing young children at play after a store had alerted the Victoria police that he had brought photos of the crotch area of young girls to be developed. The Crown appealed to the Supreme Court.]

CORY J (Lamer CJ, Sopinka, Iacobucci, and Major JJ concurring): … Overbreadth and vagueness are different concepts, but are sometimes related in particular cases. As the Ontario Court of Appeal observed in *R. v. Zundel* (1987), 58 O.R. (2d) 129, at pp. 157-58, cited with approval by Gonthier J. in *R. v. Nova Scotia Pharmaceutical Society*, [[1992] 2 SCR 606], the meaning of a law may be unambiguous and thus the law will not be vague; however, it may still be overly broad. Where a law is vague, it may also be overly broad, to the extent that the ambit of its application is difficult to define. Overbreadth and vagueness are related in that both are the result of a lack of sufficient precision by a legislature in the means used to accomplish an objective. In the case of vagueness, the means are not clearly defined. In the case of overbreadth the means are too sweeping in relation to the objective.

Overbreadth analysis looks at the means chosen by the state in relation to its purpose. In considering whether a legislative provision is overbroad, a court must ask the question: are those means necessary to achieve the State objective? If the State, in pursuing a legitimate objective, uses means which are broader than is necessary to accomplish that objective, the principles of fundamental justice will be violated because the individual's rights will have been limited for no reason. The effect of overbreadth is that in some applications the law is arbitrary or disproportionate. …

In summary, s. 179(1)(b) is overly broad to an extent that it violates the right to liberty proclaimed by s. 7 of the Charter for a number of reasons. First, it is overly broad in its geographical scope embracing as it does all public parks and beaches no matter how remote and devoid of children they may be. Secondly, it is overly broad in its temporal aspect with the prohibition applying for life without any process for review. Thirdly, it is too broad in the number of persons it encompasses. Fourthly, the prohibitions are put in place and may be enforced without any notice to the accused.

I am strengthened in this conclusion by a consideration of the new s. 161 of the *Criminal Code*, S.C. 1993, c. 45, s. 1, which was enacted shortly after the decision of the British Columbia Court of Appeal in this case. …

It can be seen that this section is limited to clearly defined geographical areas where children are or can reasonably be expected to be present. Further, the prohibition may be for life or a shorter period and a system of review is provided. Additionally, the order of prohibition is made part of the sentencing procedure so that the accused is aware of and notified of the prohibitions. It is thus apparent that overly broad provisions are not essential or necessary in order to achieve the aim of s. 179(1)(b).

GONTHIER J (La Forest, L'Heureux-Dubé, and McLachlin JJ concurring (in dissent)): The interpretation I advocate eliminates Cory J.'s concern that the prohibition is overbroad. A lifetime prohibition of activities with a malevolent or ulterior purpose related to reoffending is in no way objectionable or overbroad. Such a prohibition would impose a restriction on the liberty of the affected individuals to which ordinary citizens are not subject, but that restriction is directly related to preventing reoffending. The affected persons' history of offending, the uncertainties prevalent in treating offenders and a desire to disrupt the cycle of reoffending justify what is, in effect, a minor intrusion which does not breach the principles of fundamental justice. ...

In addition to overbreadth, the absence of any notice of the prohibition contained in s. 179(1)(b) was relied upon by Cory J. in concluding that s. 7 of the Charter was violated. The basis for this conclusion was that notice is provided for in the case of certain other prohibitions contained in the Code and that the lack of notice in the case of s. 179(1)(b) "is unfair and unnecessarily so." In so concluding, Cory J. would make notice, albeit in limited circumstances, a principle of fundamental justice. With all due respect, I cannot agree. It is a basic tenet of our legal system that ignorance of the law is not an excuse for breaking the law. This fundamental principle has been given legislative expression in s. 19 of the *Criminal Code*: "Ignorance of the law by a person who commits an offence is not an excuse for committing that offence." Though formal notice of the content of s. 179(1)(b) might be preferable, I can see no basis for transforming the legislator's decision to provide notice in respect of certain Code prohibitions into a principle of fundamental justice.

Section 161(1) provides that in the case of a person convicted of a sexual offence with respect to a person under 16 years of age, the court may, in addition to other punishments, prohibit the offender from:

(a) attending a public park or public swimming area where persons under the age of 16 years are present or can reasonably be expected to be present, or a daycare centre, schoolground, playground or community centre;

(a.1) being within two kilometres, or any other distance specified in the order, of any dwelling-house where the victim identified in the order ordinarily resides or of any other place specified in the order;

(b) seeking, obtaining or continuing any employment, whether or not the employment is remunerated, or becoming or being a volunteer in a capacity, that involves being in a position of trust or authority towards persons under the age of 16 years;

(c) having any contact—including communicating by any means—with a person who is under the age of 16 years, unless the offender does so under the supervision of a person whom the court considers appropriate; or

(d) using the Internet or other digital network, unless the offender does so in accordance with conditions set by the court.

In *R v Budreo* (2000), 32 CR (5th) 127, the Ontario Court of Appeal held that the reference to a "community centre" in a similar peace bond provision in s 810.1 of the Code was overbroad to the objective of protecting children from sexual violence because children might not be present in such centres. The court declared the reference to "community centres" to be unconstitutional. The next case, however, suggests that the Supreme Court is now more willing to save potentially overbroad unconstitutional legislation by interpreting the legislation (sometimes called "reading the legislation down") to constitutional limits as Justice Gonthier attempted to do in his dissent in *Heywood*.

Canadian Foundation for Children, Youth and the Law v Canada (Attorney General)
Supreme Court of Canada
2004 SCC 4, [2004] 1 SCR 76

[In this case, the Supreme Court considered whether s 43 of the *Criminal Code* authorizing the use of force "by way of correction toward a pupil or child … if the force does not exceed what is reasonable under the circumstances" was void because of vagueness or overbreadth. The majority of the court also rejected arguments that it violated ss 2 and 15 of the Charter.]

McLACHLIN CJ (Gonthier, Iacobucci, Major, Bastarache, Binnie, and LeBel JJ concurring): …

[15] A law is unconstitutionally vague if it "does not provide an adequate basis for legal debate" and "analysis"; "does not sufficiently delineate any area of risk"; or "is not intelligible." The law must offer a "grasp to the judiciary": *R. v. Nova Scotia Pharmaceutical Society*, [1992] 2 S.C.R. 606, at pp. 639-40.

Certainty is not required. As Gonthier J. pointed out in *Nova Scotia Pharmaceutical, supra*, at pp. 638-39,

> … conduct is guided by approximation. The process of approximation sometimes results in quite a narrow set of options, sometimes in a broader one. *Legal dispositions therefore delineate a risk zone*, and cannot hope to do more, unless they are directed at individual instances. [Emphasis added.]

[16] A law must set an intelligible standard both for the citizens it governs and the officials who must enforce it. The two are interconnected. A vague law prevents the citizen from realizing when he or she is entering an area of risk for criminal sanction. It similarly makes it difficult for law enforcement officers and judges to determine whether a crime has been committed. This invokes the further concern of putting too much discretion in the hands of law enforcement officials, and violates the precept that individuals should be governed by the rule of law, not the rule of persons. The doctrine of vagueness is directed generally at the evil of leaving "basic policy matters to policemen, judges, and juries for resolution on an ad hoc and subjective basis, with the attendant dangers of arbitrary and discriminatory application": *Grayned v. City of Rockford*, 408 U.S. 104 (1972), at p. 109. …

[19] The purpose of s. 43 is to delineate a sphere of non-criminal conduct within the larger realm of common assault. It must, as we have seen, do this in a way that permits people to know when they are entering a zone of risk of criminal sanction and that avoids

ad hoc discretionary decision-making by law enforcement officials. People must be able to assess when conduct approaches the boundaries of the sphere that s. 43 provides.

[20] To ascertain whether s. 43 meets these requirements, we must consider its words and court decisions interpreting those words. The words of the statute must be considered in context, in their grammatical and ordinary sense, and with a view to the legislative scheme's purpose and the intention of Parliament: *Rizzo & Rizzo Shoes Ltd. (Re)*, [1998] 1 S.C.R. 27, at para. 21; *Bell ExpressVu Limited Partnership v. Rex*, [2002] 2 S.C.R. 559, 2002 SCC 42, at para. 26. Since s. 43 withdraws the protection of the criminal law in certain circumstances, it should be strictly construed: see *Ogg-Moss v. The Queen*, [1984] 2 S.C.R. 173, at p. 183.

[21] Section 43 delineates who may access its sphere with considerable precision. The terms "schoolteacher" and "parent" are clear. The phrase "person standing in the place of a parent" has been held by the courts to indicate an individual who has assumed "all the obligations of parenthood": *Ogg-Moss, supra*, at p. 190. These terms present no difficulty.

[22] Section 43 identifies less precisely what conduct falls within its sphere. It defines this conduct in two ways. The first is by the requirement that the force be "by way of correction." The second is by the requirement that the force be "reasonable under the circumstances." The question is whether, taken together and construed in accordance with governing principles, these phrases provide sufficient precision to delineate the zone of risk and avoid discretionary law enforcement. ...

[27] [T]he law has long used reasonableness to delineate areas of risk, without incurring the dangers of vagueness. The law of negligence, which has blossomed in recent decades to govern private actions in nearly all spheres of human activity, is founded upon the presumption that individuals are capable of governing their conduct in accordance with the standard of what is "reasonable." But reasonableness as a guide to conduct is not confined to the law of negligence. The criminal law also relies on it. The *Criminal Code* expects that police officers will know what constitutes "reasonable grounds" for believing that an offence has been committed, such that an arrest can be made (s. 495); that an individual will know what constitutes "reasonable steps" to obtain consent to sexual contact (s. 273.2(b)); and that surgeons, in order to be exempted from criminal liability, will judge whether performing an operation is "reasonable" in "all the circumstances of the case" (s. 45). These are merely a few examples; the criminal law is thick with the notion of "reasonableness." ...

[30] The first limitation arises from the behaviour for which s. 43 provides an exemption, simple non-consensual application of force. Section 43 does not exempt from criminal sanction conduct that causes harm or raises a reasonable prospect of harm. It can be invoked only in cases of non-consensual application of force that results neither in harm nor in the prospect of bodily harm. This limits its operation to the mildest forms of assault. People must know that if their conduct raises an apprehension of bodily harm they cannot rely on s. 43. Similarly, police officers and judges must know that the defence cannot be raised in such circumstances.

[31] Within this limited area of application, further precision on what is reasonable under the circumstances may be derived from international treaty obligations. Statutes should be construed to comply with Canada's international obligations: *Ordon Estate v. Grail*, [1998] 3 S.C.R. 437, at para. 137. Canada's international commitments confirm that physical correction that either harms or degrades a child is unreasonable. ...

[36] Determining what is "reasonable under the circumstances" in the case of child discipline is also assisted by social consensus and expert evidence on what constitutes reasonable corrective discipline. The criminal law often uses the concept of reasonableness to accommodate evolving mores and avoid successive "fine-tuning" amendments. It is implicit in this technique that current social consensus on what is reasonable may be considered. It is wrong for caregivers or judges to apply their own subjective notions of what is reasonable; s. 43 demands an objective appraisal based on current learning and consensus. Substantial consensus, particularly when supported by expert evidence, can provide guidance and reduce the danger of arbitrary, subjective decision making.

[37] Based on the evidence currently before the Court, there are significant areas of agreement among the experts on both sides of the issue (trial decision, para. 17). Corporal punishment of children under two years is harmful to them, and has no corrective value given the cognitive limitations of children under two years of age. Corporal punishment of teenagers is harmful, because it can induce aggressive or antisocial behaviour. Corporal punishment using objects, such as rulers or belts, is physically and emotionally harmful. Corporal punishment which involves slaps or blows to the head is harmful. These types of punishment, we may conclude, will not be reasonable.

[38] Contemporary social consensus is that, while teachers may sometimes use corrective force to remove children from classrooms or secure compliance with instructions, the use of corporal punishment by teachers is not acceptable. Many school boards forbid the use of corporal punishment, and some provinces and territories have legislatively prohibited its use by teachers: see, e.g., *Schools Act, 1997*, S.N.L. 1997, c S-12.2, s. 42; *School Act*, R.S.B.C. 1996, c. 412, s. 76(3); *Education Act*, S.N.B. 1997, c. E-1.12, s. 23; *School Act*, R.S.P.E.I. 1988, c. S-2.1, s. 73; *Education Act*, S.N.W.T. 1995, c. 28, s. 34(3); *Education Act*, S.Y. 1989-90, c. 25, s. 36. ... Section 43 will protect a teacher who uses reasonable, corrective force to restrain or remove a child in appropriate circumstances. Substantial societal consensus, supported by expert evidence and Canada's treaty obligations, indicates that corporal punishment by teachers is unreasonable.

[39] Finally, judicial interpretation may assist in defining "reasonable under the circumstances" under s. 43. It must be conceded at the outset that judicial decisions on s. 43 in the past have sometimes been unclear and inconsistent, sending a muddled message as to what is and is not permitted. In many cases discussed by Arbour J., judges failed to acknowledge the evolutive nature of the standard of reasonableness, and gave undue authority to outdated conceptions of reasonable correction. On occasion, judges erroneously applied their own subjective views on what constitutes reasonable discipline—views as varied as different judges' backgrounds. In addition, charges of assaultive discipline were seldom viewed as sufficiently serious to merit in-depth research and expert evidence or the appeals which might have permitted a unified national standard to emerge. However, "[t]he fact that a particular legislative term is open to varying interpretations by the courts is not fatal": *Reference re ss. 193 and 195.1(1)(c) of the Criminal Code (Man.)*, [1990] 1 S.C.R. 1123, at p. 1157. This case, and those that build on it, may permit a more uniform approach to "reasonable under the circumstances" than has prevailed in the past. Again, the issue is not whether s. 43 has provided enough guidance in the past, but whether it expresses a standard that can be given a core meaning in tune with contemporary consensus.

[40] When these considerations are taken together, a solid core of meaning emerges for "reasonable under the circumstances," sufficient to establish a zone in which discipline

risks criminal sanction. Generally, s. 43 exempts from criminal sanction only minor corrective force of a transitory and trifling nature. On the basis of current expert consensus, it does not apply to corporal punishment of children under two or teenagers. Degrading, inhuman or harmful conduct is not protected. Discipline by the use of objects or blows or slaps to the head is unreasonable. Teachers may reasonably apply force to remove a child from a classroom or secure compliance with instructions, but not merely as corporal punishment. Coupled with the requirement that the conduct be corrective, which rules out conduct stemming from the caregiver's frustration, loss of temper or abusive personality, a consistent picture emerges of the area covered by s. 43. It is wrong for law enforcement officers or judges to apply their own subjective views of what is "reasonable under the circumstances"; the test is objective. The question must be considered in context and in light of all the circumstances of the case. The gravity of the precipitating event is not relevant.

[41] The fact that borderline cases may be anticipated is not fatal. As Gonthier J. stated in *Nova Scotia Pharmaceutical*, at p. 639, "… it is inherent to our legal system that some conduct will fall along the boundaries of the area of risk; no definite prediction can then be made. Guidance, not direction, of conduct is a more realistic objective."

[42] Section 43 achieves this objective. It sets real boundaries and delineates a risk zone for criminal sanction. The prudent parent or teacher will refrain from conduct that approaches those boundaries, while law enforcement officers and judges will proceed with them in mind. It does not violate the principle of fundamental justice that laws must not be vague or arbitrary.

[43] My colleague, Arbour J., by contrast, takes the view that s. 43 is unconstitutionally vague, a point of view also expressed by Deschamps J. Arbour J. argues first that the foregoing analysis amounts to an impermissible reading down of s. 43. This contention is answered by the evidence in this case, which established a solid core of meaning for s. 43; to construe terms like "reasonable under the circumstances" by reference to evidence and argument is a common and accepted function of courts interpreting the criminal law. To interpret "reasonable" in light of the evidence is not judicial amendment, but judicial interpretation. It is a common practice, given the number of criminal offences conditioned by the term "reasonable." If "it is the function of the appellate courts to rein in overly elastic interpretations" (Binnie J., at para. 122), it is equally their function to define the scope of criminal defences.

[44] Arbour J. also argues that unconstitutional vagueness is established by the fact that courts in the past have applied s. 43 inconsistently. Again, the inference does not follow. Vagueness is not argued on the basis of whether a provision has been interpreted consistently in the past, but whether it is capable of providing guidance for the future. Inconsistent and erroneous applications are not uncommon in criminal law, where many provisions admit of difficulty; we do not say that this makes them unconstitutional. Rather, we rely on appellate courts to clarify the meaning so that future application may be more consistent. I agree with Arbour J. that Canadians would find the decisions in many of the past cases on s. 43 to be seriously objectionable. However, the discomfort of Canadians in the face of such unwarranted acts of violence toward children merely demonstrates that it is possible to define what corrective force is reasonable in the circumstances. Finally, Arbour J. argues that parents who face criminal charges as a result of corrective force will be able to rely on the defences of necessity and "de minimis." The defence of necessity, I agree, is available, but only in situations where corrective force is not in issue, like saving

a child from imminent danger. As for the defence of de minimis, it is equally or more vague and difficult in application than the reasonableness defence offered by s. 43.

Overbreadth

[45] Section 43 of the *Criminal Code* refers to corrective force against children generally. The Foundation argues that this is overbroad because children under the age of two are not capable of correction and children over the age of 12 will only be harmed by corrective force. These classes of children, it is argued, should have been excluded.

[46] This concern is addressed by Parliament's decision to confine the exemption to reasonable correction, discussed above. Experts consistently indicate that force applied to a child too young to be capable of learning from physical correction is not corrective force. Similarly, current expert consensus indicates that corporal punishment of teenagers creates a serious risk of psychological harm: employing it would thus be unreasonable. There may however be instances in which a parent or school teacher reasonably uses corrective force to restrain or remove an adolescent from a particular situation, falling short of corporal punishment. Section 43 does not permit force that cannot correct or is unreasonable. It follows that it is not overbroad. ...

ARBOUR J (Deschamps J concurring (in dissent)):

[131] This appeal raises the constitutional validity of s. 43 of the *Criminal Code*, R.S.C. 1985, c. C-46, which justifies the reasonable use of force by way of correction by parents and teachers against children in their care. Although I come to a conclusion which may not be very different from that reached by the Chief Justice, I do so for very different reasons. The Chief Justice significantly curtails the scope of the defence of s. 43 of the *Code*, partly on the basis that s. 43 should be strictly construed since it withdraws the protection of the criminal law in certain circumstances. According to her analysis, s. 43 can only be raised as a defence to a charge of simple (common) assault; it applies only to corrective force, used against children older than two but not against teenagers; it cannot involve the use of objects, and should not consist of blows to the head; and it should not relate to the "gravity" of the conduct attracting correction.

[132] With respect, in my opinion, such a restrictive interpretation of a statutory defence is inconsistent with the role of courts *vis-à-vis* criminal defences, both statutory and common law defences. Furthermore, this restrictive interpretation can only be arrived at if dictated by constitutional imperatives. Canadian courts have not thus far understood the concept of reasonable force to mean the "minor corrective force" advocated by the Chief Justice. In my view, the defence contained in s. 43 of the *Code*, interpreted and applied inconsistently by the courts in Canada, violates the constitutional rights of children to safety and security and must be struck down. Absent action by Parliament, other existing common law defences, such as the defence of necessity and the "de minimis" defence, will suffice to ensure that parents and teachers are not branded as criminals for their trivial use of force to restrain children when appropriate.

[133] Section 43 of the *Code* justifies the use of force by parents and teachers by way of correction. The force that is justified is force that is "reasonable under the circumstances." The section does not say that forcible correction is a defence only to common assault. Nor has it been understood to be so restrictive: see *R. v. Pickard*, [1995] B.C.J.

No. 2861 (QL) (Prov. Ct.); *R. v. G.C.C.* (2001), 206 Nfld. & P.E.I.R. 231 (Nfld. S.C.T.D.); *R. v. Fritz* (1987), 55 Sask. R. 302 (Q.B.); *R. v. Bell*, [2001] O.J. No. 1820 (QL) (S.C.J.); and *R. v. N.S.*, [1999] O.J. No. 320 (QL) (Ct. J. (Gen. Div.)), where s. 43 was successfully raised as a defence against charges of assault with a weapon and/or assault causing bodily harm.

[134] In the *Code*, the justifiable use of force may be advanced as a defence against a wide range of offences that have at their origin the application of force. These offences range from common assault, to assault causing bodily harm and eventually to manslaughter. ...

[135] In the case at bar, the critical inquiry turns on the meaning of the phrases "force by way of correction" and "reasonable under the circumstances" (s. 43 of the *Code*). To say, as the Chief Justice does, that this defence cannot be used to justify any criminal charge beyond simple assault, that the section cannot justify the use of corrective force against a child under 2 or against a teenager, and that force is never reasonable if an object is used, is a laudable effort to take the law where it ought to be. However, s. 43 can only be so interpreted if the law, as it stands, offends the Constitution and must therefore be curtailed. Absent such constitutional constraints, it is neither the historic nor the proper role of courts to enlarge criminal responsibility by limiting defences enacted by Parliament. In fact, the role of the courts is precisely the opposite.

[136] Setting aside any constitutional considerations for the moment, courts are expressly prohibited by s. 9 of the *Code* from creating new common law offences. All criminal offences must be enacted by statute. On the other hand, the courts have been and continue to be the guardians of common law defences. This reflects the role of courts as enforcers of fundamental principles of criminal responsibility including, in particular, the fundamental concept of fault which can only be reduced or displaced by statute. ...

[138] In this case, we have been asked to either curtail or abolish altogether a defence created by Parliament. If we are to do this, as I believe we must, it should be for higher constitutional imperatives. Absent a finding of a constitutional violation by Parliament, the reading down of a statutory defence as is done by the Chief Justice amounts to, in my respectful opinion, an abandonment by the courts of their proper role in the criminal process.

[139] Courts, including this Court, have until now properly focussed on what constitutes force that is "reasonable under the circumstances." No pre-emptive barriers have been erected. Nothing in the words of the statute, properly construed, suggests that Parliament intended that some conduct be excluded at the outset from the scope of s. 43's protection. This is the law as we must take it in order to assess its constitutionality. To essentially rewrite it before validating its constitutionality is to hide the constitutional imperative.

[140] The role of the courts when applying defences must be contrasted with the role of courts when they are called upon to examine the constitutional validity of criminal offences. In such cases, it is entirely appropriate for the courts to interpret the provisions that proscribe conduct in a manner that least restricts "the liberty of the subject," consistent with the wording of the statute and the intent of Parliament. This is what was done in *R. v. Sharpe*, [2001] 1 S.C.R. 45, 2001 SCC 2, for example. But such a technique cannot be employed to restrict the scope of statutory defences without the courts compromising the core of their interplay with Parliament in the orderly development and application of the criminal law.

[141] In the end, I will conclude, not unlike the Chief Justice, that the use of corrective force by parents and teachers against children under their care is only permitted when

the force is minimal and insignificant. I so conclude not because this is what the *Code* currently provides but because it is what the Constitution requires. ...

[183] "Reasonableness" with respect to s. 43 is linked to public policy issues and one's own sense of parental authority. "Reasonableness" will always entail an element of subjectivity. As McCombs J. recognized in the case at bar, "[b]ecause the notion of reasonableness varies with the beholder, it is perhaps not surprising that some of the judicial decisions applying s. 43 to excuse otherwise criminal assault appear to some to be inconsistent and unreasonable" ((2000), 49 O.R. (3d) 662, at para. 4). It is clear, however, that the concept of reasonableness, so widely used in the law generally, and in the criminal law in particular, is not in and of itself unconstitutionally vague. "Reasonableness" functions as an intelligible standard in many other criminal law contexts. ...

[189] I doubt that it can be said, on the basis of the existing record, that the justification of corporal punishment of children when the force used is "reasonable under the circumstances" gives adequate notice to parents and teachers as to what is and is not permissible in a criminal context. Furthermore, it neither adequately guides the decision-making power of law enforcers nor delineates, in an acceptable fashion, the boundaries of legal debate. The Chief Justice rearticulates the s. 43 defence as the delineation of a "risk zone for criminal sanction" (para. 18). I do not disagree with such a formulation of the vagueness doctrine in this context. Still, on this record, the "risk zone" for victims and offenders alike has been a moving target.

[190] In the Chief Justice's reasons, it is useful to note how much work must go into making the provision constitutionally sound and sufficiently precise: (1) the word "child" must be construed as including children only over age 2 and younger than teenage years; (2) parts of the body must be excluded; (3) implements must be prohibited; (4) the nature of the offence calling for correction is deemed not a relevant contextual consideration; (5) teachers are prohibited from utilizing corporal punishment; and (6) the use of force that causes injury that is neither transient nor trifling (assault causing bodily harm) is prohibited (it seems even if the force is used by way of restraint). At some point, in an effort to give sufficient precision to provide notice and constrain discretion in enforcement, mere interpretation ends and an entirely new provision is drafted. As this Court concluded in *R. v. Heywood*, [1994] 3 S.C.R. 761, at p. 803:

> The changes which would be required to make s. 179(1)(b) [here, s. 43] constitutional would not constitute reading down or reading in; rather, *they would amount to judicial rewriting of the legislation*. [Emphasis added.]

The restrictions put forth by the Chief Justice with respect to the scope of the defence have not emerged from the existing case law. These restrictions are far from self-evident and would not have been anticipated by many parents, teachers or enforcement officials.

[191] In my view, we cannot cure vagueness from the top down by declaring that a proper legal debate has taken place and that anything outside its boundaries is simply wrong and must be discarded. Too many people have been engaged in attempting to define the boundaries of that very debate for years in Canadian courtrooms to simply dismiss their conclusions because they do not conform with a norm that was never apparent to anyone until now. As demonstrated earlier, s. 43 has been subject to considerable disparity in application, some courts justifying conduct that other courts have found wholly unreasonable, despite valiant efforts by the lower courts to give intelligible content to the

provision. Attempts at judicial interpretation which would structure the discretion in s. 43 have, in my opinion, failed to provide coherent or cogent guidelines that would meet the standard of notice and specificity generally required in the criminal law. Thus, despite the efforts of judges, some of whom have openly expressed their frustration with what has been described as "no clear test" and a "legal lottery" in the criminal law (McGillivray, "'He'll learn it on his body': Disciplining childhood in Canadian law" [(1997) 5 Intl J Child Rts 193], at p. 228; James, ... per Weagant Prov. J., at paras. 11-12), the ambit of the justification remains about as unclear as when it was first codified in 1892. As Lamer C.J. stated in *R. v. Morales*, [1992] 3 S.C.R. 711, at p. 729:

> A standardless sweep does not become acceptable simply because it results from the whims of judges and justices of the peace rather than the whims of law enforcement officials. Cloaking whims in judicial robes is not sufficient to satisfy the principles of fundamental justice.

This would not only raise the already high bar set in *Nova Scotia Pharmaceutical, supra*; it would essentially make it unreachable.

[192] As a result, I find that the phrase "reasonable under the circumstances" in s. 43 of the *Code* violates children's security of the person interest and that the deprivation is not in accordance with the relevant principle of fundamental justice, in that it is unconstitutionally vague.

Construction or Interpretation of the Criminal Code

The *Criminal Code* has historically been interpreted in a "strict" manner designed to give the accused the benefit of a doubt concerning any textual ambiguity. Is this a wise policy for the courts to pursue? In recent years, there has been a trend to making resort to the doctrine of strict construction only if there is an ambiguity in a statute after it has been given a purposive interpretation designed to achieve its objectives. What is left of the doctrine of strict construction of the criminal law?

R v Paré
Supreme Court of Canada
[1987] 2 SCR 618

WILSON J (for the Court): Section 214(5)(b) [see now s 231(5)] of the *Criminal Code*, RSC 1970, c. C-34, as amended by 1974-75-76, c. 105, s. 4, which was in force at the time of the commission of the offence provided that murder is first degree murder when the death is caused by a person while the person is committing indecent assault. The respondent, Marc-André Paré, indecently assaulted and murdered a seven-year-old boy, Steeve Duranleau. The central issue in this appeal is whether the respondent murdered the child "while committing" the indecent assault. ...

The Facts

On July 13, 1982, at about 1:30 in the afternoon the respondent Marc-André Paré, then 17 years old, met Steeve Duranleau, a seven-year-old boy. At Paré's suggestion the two went swimming. After about 15 minutes in the pool Paré offered to take Duranleau to look at some used cars. The offer was only a pretense. Paré's real motive was to get Duranleau alone in order to have sexual relations with him.

After changing, Paré and Duranleau went to a parking-lot where they looked at some used cars. Near the parking-lot was a bridge that crossed the St. Charles River. Paré lured Duranleau under the bridge. Duranleau wanted to leave but Paré told him not to and held him by the arm. Paré sat there for the next 10 minutes holding Duranleau by the arm. Then Paré told Duranleau to lie on his back and keep quiet. Paré pulled Duranleau's shorts down and lowered his own pants and underwear. He then lay on top of Duranleau and indecently assaulted him. After ejaculating beside Duranleau's penis, Paré sat up and got dressed.

At this point Duranleau told Paré that he intended to tell his mother about the incident. Paré told him that he did not want him to tell his mother and that, if he did, he would kill him. After this exchange of words Paré was certain that the boy would tell his mother as soon as he could. Paré made Duranleau lie on his back. He waited for two minutes with his hand on Duranleau's chest. He then killed Duranleau by strangling him with his hands, hitting him on the head several times with an oil filter, and strangling him with a shoe-lace.

The accused was charged as follows (translation):

> That in Quebec City, Quebec, on or around 13 July 1982, he illegally and intentionally killed S.D., thereby committing murder in the first degree contrary to ss. 212-214(5)-218 of the *Criminal Code*.

At trial the accused admitted all the facts outlined above. On December 7, 1982, the accused was found guilty of first degree murder. The accused's appeal to the Quebec Court of Appeal was dismissed on April 2, 1985 (per L'Heureux-Dubé, Beauregard and LeBel JJ.A.), the court substituting a verdict of second degree murder for the jury's verdict of first degree murder.

The Courts Below

The Court of Appeal for Quebec

Beauregard and LeBel JJ.A. gave separate reasons; Madame Justice L'Heureux-Dubé agreed with both. Beauregard J.A. examined the case-law and decided that s. 214(5) of the *Criminal Code* should be restrictively interpreted. He concluded that "while committing" must be contrasted with "after having finished committing." A murder committed after the accused had committed the indecent assault was not a first degree murder. Accordingly, when the trial judge said to the jury that a murder committed "on the occasion of" an indecent assault was a first degree murder, he did not invite the jury to consider the really critical question, namely, whether the murder was committed during the commission of the indecent assault or after the indecent assault was over.

Beauregard J.A. was of the opinion that a properly directed jury would not have been convinced beyond a reasonable doubt that the accused murdered his victim while committing the indecent assault. Consequently, he dismissed the appeal and substituted a verdict of second degree murder for the verdict of first degree murder.

LeBel J.A. did not agree with Beauregard J.A.'s conclusion that s. 214(5) required the murder and the indecent assault to be absolutely simultaneous. Even if the section were to be construed restrictively, he stated, it must not be deprived of all effect. By reading

s. 214(5) in conjunction with s. 213 LeBel J.A. concluded that the words "while committing" demanded a close temporal connection between the indecent assault and the murder. Moreover, he concluded that the murder must be an immediate consequence of the first offence for s. 214(5) to apply. LeBel J.A. found it difficult to conclude that a jury more completely informed of the nuances of the sections in question would have necessarily returned the same verdict. The charge given to the jury, he stated, effectively prevented the jury from directing its attention to the proper meaning of s. 214(5). Therefore, despite his reservations about Beauregard J.A.'s conclusions of law, LeBel J.A. agreed with his disposition of the case.

Section 214(5): "While Committing"

The Literal Meaning

Did the respondent murder Duranleau while committing an indecent assault? Counsel for the respondent submit that he did not. The argument here is simple. The murder occurred, it is submitted, after the indecent assault was complete. Thus, by a literal reading of s. 214(5) Paré did not murder Duranleau "while committing" an indecent assault.

This argument is a forceful one but by no means decisive. The literal meaning of words could equally be termed their acontextual meaning. As Professor Dworkin points out, the literal or acontextual meaning of words is "the meaning we would assign them if we had no special information about the context of their use or the intentions of their author": see R. Dworkin, Law's Empire (1986), p. 17, Cambridge, Harvard University Press. Thus, the words "while committing" could have one meaning when disembodied from the *Criminal Code* and another entirely when read in the context of the scheme and purpose of the legislation. It is the latter meaning that we must ascertain. ...

The Case-Law

Further support for the narrow interpretation is found in two subsequent cases: *R. v. Kjeldsen* (1980), 53 C.C.C. (2d) 55, [1980] 3 W.W.R. 411, 20 A.R. 267 (Alta. C.A.) and *R. v. Sargent* (1983), 5 C.C.C. (3d) 429, 22 Sask. R. 230 (Sask. C.A.). In the latter case, the victim was killed after she had been raped by either the appellant or his companion or both. Hall J.A., speaking for the court concluded at p. 436:

> It is manifest that the jury, in returning a verdict of guilty of first degree murder accepted those portions of the evidence which were most unfavourable to the appellant. However, in that event, there is no basis upon which the jury could return the verdict which they did. If the jury found, on the evidence before them, that a rape had occurred, it is clear that the death of the deceased did not occur while that offence was being committed. That is, there was no evidence to support the finding that the actions which resulted in the death of Lenny Lou Cosgrove were perpetrated by the appellant (either alone or with Massong) while committing the offence of rape. On the only evidence before the jury, the murder was committed after the actual rape. Therefore the provisions of s. 214(5) do not apply to establish the offence of first degree murder: see *R. v. Kjeldsen.*

Kjeldsen took the same approach. In that case the appellant raped his victim and then tied her up. A short time later she freed herself and the appellant then killed her. At trial the appellant was convicted of first degree murder. The Court of Appeal substituted a conviction of second degree murder. The court did not analyze the meaning of the words "while committing" in s. 214(5) but appeared to assume that these words required the underlying offence and the murder to occur simultaneously (p. 85).

The courts, however, have not been unanimous in adopting the narrow interpretation. In *R. v. Stevens* (1984), 11 C.C.C. (3d) 518, another case of rape and murder, Martin J.A. held that there was sufficient evidence on which a jury could conclude that the murder took place during the commission of an indecent assault. He went on, however, to make some interesting comments on the interpretation of the words "while committing" in s. 214(5). At p. 541 he states:

> Thus, it appears clear that where death is caused after the underlying offence is complete and the act causing death is committed for the purpose of facilitating the flight of the offender, the murder is not under ss. 213 and 214(5)(b) first degree murder.
>
> I do not wish, however, to be taken as holding that where the act causing death and the acts constituting the rape, attempted rape, indecent assault or an attempt to commit indecent assault, as the case may be, all form part of one continuous sequence of events forming a single transaction, that death would not be caused during the commission of the offence, even though the underlying offence in s. 213 in a sense could be said to be then complete.

The suggestion here is that the words "while committing" in s. 214(5) do not require an exact coincidence of the murder with the underlying offence. Rather, they require a close temporal and causative link between the two. Which of the competing interpretations should be adopted?

Strict Construction

Counsel for the respondent argue that the doctrine of strict construction of criminal statutes requires that this court adopt the interpretation most favourable to the accused. According to this argument the words "while committing" must be narrowly construed so as to elevate murder to first degree only when the death and the underlying offence occur simultaneously. In order to assess the validity of this position we must examine the doctrine of strict construction.

The doctrine is one of ancient lineage. It reached its pinnacle of importance in a former age when the death penalty attached to a vast array of offences. As Stephen Kloepfer points out in his article "The Status of Strict Construction in Canadian Criminal Law" (1983), 15 Ottawa L. Rev. 553 at pp. 556-60, the doctrine was one of many tools employed by the judiciary to soften the impact of the Draconian penal provisions of the time. Over the past two centuries criminal law penalties have become far less severe. Criminal law remains, however, the most dramatic and important incursion that the state makes into individual liberty. Thus, while the original justification for the doctrine has been substantially eroded, the seriousness of imposing criminal penalties of any sort demands that reasonable doubts be resolved in favour of the accused.

This point was underlined by Dickson J. in *Marcotte v. Deputy Attorney-General of Canada* (1974), 19 C.C.C. (2d) 257 at p. 262, 51 D.L.R. (3d) 259 at p. 264, [1976] 1 S.C.R. 108 at p. 115:

It is unnecessary to emphasize the importance of clarity and certainty when freedom is at stake. No authority is needed for the proposition that if real ambiguities are found, or doubts of substance arise, in the construction and application of a statute affecting the liberty of a subject, then that statute should be applied in such a manner as to favour the person against whom it is sought to be enforced. If one is to be incarcerated, one should at least know that some Act of Parliament requires it in express terms, and not, at most, by implication. ...

Applying the Doctrine

As we have noted above, it is clearly grammatically possible to construe the words "while committing" in s. 214(5) as requiring murder to be classified as first degree only if it is exactly coincidental with the underlying offence. This, however, does not end the question. We still have to determine whether the narrow interpretation of "while committing" is a reasonable one, given the scheme and purpose of the legislation.

In my view, the construction that counsel for the respondent would have us place on these words is not one that could reasonably be attributed to Parliament. The first problem with the exactly simultaneous approach flows from the difficulty in defining the beginning and end of an indecent assault. In this case, for example, after ejaculation the respondent sat up and put his pants back on. But for the next two minutes he kept his hands on his victim's chest. Was this continued contact part of the assault? It does not seem to me that important issues of criminal law should be allowed to hinge upon this kind of distinction. An approach that depends on this kind of distinction should be avoided if possible.

A second difficulty with the exactly simultaneous approach is that it leads to distinctions that are arbitrary and irrational. In the present case, had the respondent strangled his victim two minutes earlier than he did, his guilt of first degree murder would be beyond dispute. The exactly simultaneous approach would have us conclude that the two minutes he spent contemplating his next move had the effect of reducing his offence to one of second degree murder. This would be a strange result. The crime is no less serious in the latter case than in the former; indeed, if anything, the latter crime is more serious since it involves some element of deliberation. An interpretation of s. 214(5) that runs contrary to common sense is not to be adopted if a reasonable alternative is available.

In my view, such an interpretation has been provided by Martin J.A. in *Stevens, supra*. As noted above, Martin J.A. suggested that "where the act causing death and the acts constituting the rape, attempted rape, indecent assault or an attempt to commit indecent assault, as the case may be, all form part of one continuous sequence of events forming a single transaction" the death was caused "while committing" an offence for the purposes of s. 214(5). This interpretation eliminates the need to draw artificial lines to separate the commission and the aftermath of an indecent assault. Further, it eliminates the arbitrariness inherent in the exactly simultaneous approach. I would, therefore, respectfully adopt Martin J.A.'s single transaction analysis as the proper construction of s. 214(5).

This approach, it seems to me, best expresses the policy considerations that underlie the provision. Section 214, as we have seen, classifies murder as either first or second degree. All murders are serious crimes. Some murders, however, are so threatening to the public that Parliament has chosen to impose exceptional penalties on the perpetrators. One such class of murders is that found in s. 214(5), murders done while committing a hijacking, a kidnapping and forcible confinement, a rape, or an indecent assault. An understanding of why this class of murder is elevated to murder in the first degree is a helpful guide to the interpretation of the language.

The Law Reform Commission of Canada addressed this issue in its paper on *Homicide* (Working Paper 33, 1984). At p. 79 the paper states:

> … there is a lack of rationale in the law. Subsection 214(5) provides that, whether planned and deliberate or not, murder is first degree murder when committed in the course of certain listed offences. It is curious that the list there given is considerably shorter than that given in section 213 which makes killing murder if done in the commission of certain specified offences. Inspection and comparison of the two lists, however, reveal no organizing principle in either of them and no rationale for the difference between them.

With respect, I disagree. The offences listed in s. 214(5) are all offences involving the unlawful domination of people by other people. Thus an organizing principle for s. 214(5) can be found. This principle is that where a murder is committed by someone already abusing his power by illegally dominating another, the murder should be treated as an exceptionally serious crime. Parliament has chosen to treat these as murders in the first degree.

Refining then on the concept of the "single transaction" referred to by Martin J.A. in *Stevens, supra*, it is the continuing illegal domination of the victim which gives continuity to the sequence of events culminating in the murder. The murder represents an exploitation of the position of power created by the underlying crime and makes the entire course of conduct a "single transaction." This approach, in my view, best gives effect to the philosophy underlying s. 214(5).

Conclusion

The respondent murdered Steeve Duranleau two minutes after indecently assaulting him. The killing was motivated by fear that the boy would tell his mother about the indecent assault. The jury found the respondent guilty of first degree murder. They were entitled to do so. The murder was temporally and causally connected to the underlying offence. It formed part of one continuous sequence of events. It was part of the same transaction.

I would allow the appeal and restore the conviction of first degree murder.

The Supreme Court has affirmed in a number of subsequent cases that courts should only resort to strict construction of the criminal law if there is an ambiguity after the law has been interpreted in a purposive manner. For example, in *Bell ExpressVu Limited Partnership v Rex*, 2002 SCC 42, [2002] 2 SCR 559, the Court endorsed Elmer Driedger's definitive formulation, found in his *Construction of Statutes*, 2nd ed (Toronto: Butterworths, 1983) at 87:

> Today there is only one principle or approach, namely, the words of an Act are to be read in their entire context and in their grammatical and ordinary sense harmoniously with the scheme of the Act, the object of the Act, and the intention of Parliament.

The Court added:

> Driedger's modern approach has been repeatedly cited by this Court as the preferred approach
> to statutory interpretation across a wide range of interpretive settings ... . I note as well that, in
> the federal legislative context, this Court's preferred approach is buttressed by s. 12 of the *Inter-*
> *pretation Act*, R.S.C. 1985, c I-21, which provides that every enactment "is deemed remedial, and
> shall be given such fair, large and liberal construction and interpretation as best ensures the at-
> tainment of its objects." ... Other principles of interpretation—such as the strict construction of
> penal statutes and the "Charter values" presumption—only receive application where there is
> ambiguity as to the meaning of a provision.

Because the *Criminal Code* as a federal statute is equally authoritative in both English and
French, both versions of the law should be consulted. The Court has stated that

> when one of the two versions of a provision of a bilingual statute has a broader meaning than
> the other, the common meaning of the two versions is normally the one that is derived from the
> version with a more restricted meaning. This rule is especially relevant in a criminal context, as
> the accused may, depending on which version he or she reads, form a different conception of the
> elements of the offence in question. ... [I]t is important to ensure that all accused persons, re-
> gardless of the official language in which they read s. 462.31, have the same understanding of
> the elements of the offence of laundering proceeds of crime. The two versions must therefore
> publicize exactly the same description of the offence. It would not be fair to propose an interpret-
> ation whereby in one language the elements of the *actus reus* would be met, but not in the other.
> If we adopted the English version, which is broader than the French one, this Court would be
> making an undue judicial amendment of the statute. For these reasons, the Court must favour
> the French version.

R v Daoust, 2004 SCC 6 at paras 35, 37, [2004] 1 SCR 217.

On the interpretation of the criminal law, see K Roach, *Criminal Law*, 6th ed (Toronto: Irwin
Law, 2015) ch 3 and D Stuart, *Canadian Criminal Law*, 7th ed (Toronto: Carswell, 2014) at
38-42.

Limits on Criminal Law

The criminal law is the most intrusive and violent tool at the disposal of the state. Although we look to the criminal law to respond when we find serious instances of social breakdown, the immense power of the criminal law—its ability to deprive an individual of his or her basic liberty—raises the difficult question of whether there are limits on the kinds of ends for which it can be used. This chapter addresses this hotly debated and rich issue of the permissible scope of the criminal law. In so doing, it also continues to explore the limitations that the Constitution, and in particular the Charter, places on criminal laws.

The first section of this chapter introduces the philosophical debate regarding the limits of the criminal law, focusing on the key question of whether the criminal law should respond only to harm or whether it also has a role in proclaiming and enforcing the values or moral views of the community. After introducing the so-called harm principle, this issue is explored by looking at the famous "Hart–Devlin" debate, turning then to recent decisions of the Supreme Court of Canada that address whether the concept of harm is an appropriate guide to the limits of the criminal law.

The second and third sections of this chapter offer case studies of particular social issues that have sharply raised the question of the limits of the criminal law. Section II presents the controversial issue of whether prostitution/sex work is an issue properly dealt with by the criminal law. The final section of this chapter raises the very difficult question of the criminalization of hate speech.

I. THE LIMITS OF THE CRIMINAL LAW:
DEBATING THE HARM PRINCIPLE

In the search for limits on the proper use of the criminal law, the thought of 19th-century liberal political theorist John Stuart Mill is an important touchstone. Mill articulated a position that you will see referred to by the thinkers and in the decisions that follow. In his essay *On Liberty*, he argued that government power ought to be used as sparingly as possible, leaving as much space as possible for each individual to exercise his or her liberty of thought, expression, and action. Although there is a great deal more to his argument, Mill's position has been equated with one particularly influential passage in which he described the central thesis of his essay:

> The object of this Essay is to assert one very simple principle, as entitled to govern absolutely the dealings of society with the individual in the way of compulsion and control, whether the means used be physical force in the form of legal penalties, or the moral coercion of public opinion. That principle is, that the sole end for which mankind are warranted, individually or collectively, in interfering with the liberty of action of any of their number, is self-protection. That the only purpose for which power can be rightfully exercised over any member of a civilized community, against his will, is to prevent harm to others. His own good, either physical or moral, is not a sufficient warrant. He cannot rightfully be compelled to do or forbear because it will be better for him to do so, because it will make him happier, because, in the opinions of others, to do so would be wise, or even right. These are good reasons for remonstrating with him, or reasoning with him, or persuading him, or entreating him, but not for compelling him, or visiting him with any evil in case he do otherwise. To justify that, the conduct from which it is desired to deter him, must be calculated to produce evil to some one else. The only part of the conduct of any one, for which he is amenable to society, is that which concerns others. In the part which merely concerns himself, his independence is, of right, absolute. Over himself, over his own body and mind, the individual is sovereign.

This principle enunciated by Mill is referred to as the "harm principle" and, as you can see, it distinguishes between the use of government power to achieve moral ends, which Mill views as illegitimate, and the use of such coercive power to prevent harm to others—the only permissible use of such force.

Mill's thought has thus formed the basis for the central debate regarding the limits of the criminal law—namely, whether it is legitimate to use the most extreme and violent tool at the disposal of the state, the criminal law, to enforce morality or whether criminal laws must always be based on preventing harm to others. What are the proper limits of the criminal law? This issue has been the matter of much contemporary academic debate. See e.g. J Feinberg, *The Moral Limits of the Criminal Law*, vols 1-4 (New York: Oxford University Press, 1984-1988); BE Harcourt, "The Collapse of the Harm Principle" (1999) 90 J Crim L & Criminology 109; and SD Smith, "Is the Harm Principle Illiberal?" (2006) 51 Am J Juris 1. However, as Mill's essay shows, the question of the limits of the criminal law has a long pedigree, raising themes that have been vigorously debated over the history of the development of modern criminal law.

In 1957, the Committee on Homosexual Offences and Prostitution, created to consider whether prostitution and homosexual acts should be prohibited by the criminal law in the United Kingdom, issued its final report, often referred to as the "Wolfenden Report," after the committee's chairperson, Lord Wolfenden. The committee concluded that "homosexual behaviour between consenting adults in private should no longer be a criminal offence." This conclusion and the reasoning set out in the Wolfenden Report set off one of the most important debates in 20th-century jurisprudence, a debate centrally concerned with defining the proper limits of the criminal law.

The so-called Hart–Devlin debate was inaugurated by a lecture delivered by Sir Patrick Devlin, then a high court judge in England who later became a member of the House of Lords. The following excerpt is from this famous lecture.

P Devlin, "The Enforcement of Morals"
Maccabaean Lecture in Jurisprudence of the British Academy
(London: Oxford University Press, 1959)

The Report of the Committee on Homosexual Offences and Prostitution, generally known as the Wolfenden Report, is recognized to be an excellent study of two very difficult legal and social problems. But it has also a particular claim to the respect of those interested in jurisprudence; it does what law reformers so rarely do; it sets out clearly and carefully what in relation to its subjects it considers the function of law to be. Statutory additions to the criminal law are too often made on the simple principle that "there ought to be a law against it." The greater part of the law relating to sexual offences is the creation of statute and it is difficult to ascertain any logical relationship between it and the moral ideas which most of us uphold. Adultery, fornication, and prostitution are not, as the Report points out, criminal offences: homosexuality between males is a criminal offence but between females is not. Incest was not an offence until it was declared so by statute only fifty years ago. Does the legislature select these offences haphazardly or are there some principles which can be used to determine what part of the moral law should be embodied in the criminal? … This sort of question is of practical importance, for a law that appears to be arbitrary and illogical, in the end and after the wave of moral indignation that has put it on the statute books subsides, forfeits respect. As a practical question it arises more frequently in the field of sexual morals than in any other, but there is no special answer to be found in that field. The inquiry must be general and fundamental. What is the connexion between crime and sin and to what extent, if at all, should the criminal law of England concern itself with the enforcement of morals and punish sin or immorality as such?

The statements of principle in the Wolfenden Report provide an admirable and modern starting-point for such an inquiry. In the course of my examination of them I shall find matter for criticism … .

Early in the Report, the Committee puts forward:

> Our own formulation of the function of the criminal law so far as it concerns the subject of this enquiry. In this field, its function, as we see it, is to preserve public order and decency, to protect the citizen from what is offensive or injurious, and to provide sufficient safeguards against exploitation and corruption of others, particularly those who are specially vulnerable because they are young, weak in body or mind, inexperienced, or in a state of special physical, official or economic dependence.
>
> It is not, in our view, the function of the criminal law to intervene in the private lives of citizens, or to seek to enforce any particular pattern of behaviour, further than is necessary to carry out the purposes we have outlined.

· · ·

I must disclose at the outset that I have as a judge an interest in the result of the inquiry which I am seeking to make as a jurisprudent. As a judge who administers the criminal law and who has often to pass sentence in a criminal court, I should feel handicapped in my task if I thought that I was addressing an audience which had no sense of sin or which thought of crime as something quite different … . I must admit that I begin with a feeling that a complete separation of crime from sin (I use the term throughout this lecture in the wider meaning) would not be good for the moral law and might be disastrous for the criminal. But can this sort of feeling be justified as a matter of jurisprudence? And if it be a right feeling, how should the relationship between the criminal and the moral law be stated? Is there a good theoretical basis for it, or is it just a practical working alliance, or is it a bit of both? ...

... The smooth functioning of society and the preservation of order require that a number of activities should be regulated. The rules that are made for that purpose and are enforced by the criminal law are often designed simply to achieve uniformity and convenience and rarely involve any choice between good and evil. Rules that impose a speed limit or prevent obstruction on the highway have nothing to do with morals. Since so much of the criminal law is composed of rules of this sort, why bring morals into it at all? Why not define the function of the criminal law in simple terms as the preservation of order and decency and the protection of the lives and property of citizens and elaborate those terms in relation to any particular subject in the way in which it is done in the Wolfenden Report? The criminal law in carrying out these objects will undoubtedly overlap the moral law. Crimes of violence are morally wrong and they are also offences against good order; therefore they offend against both laws. But this is simply because the two laws in pursuit of different objectives happen to cover the same area. Such is the argument.

· · ·

It is true that for many centuries the criminal law was much concerned with keeping the peace and little, if at all, with sexual morals. But it would be wrong to infer from that that it had no moral content or that it would ever have tolerated the idea of a man being left to judge for himself in matters of morals. The criminal law of England has from the very first concerned itself with moral principles. A simple way of testing this point is to consider the attitude which the criminal law adopts towards consent.

Subject to certain exceptions inherent in the nature of particular crimes, the criminal law has never permitted consent of the victim to be used as a defence. In rape, for example, consent negatives an essential element. But consent of the victim is no defence to a charge of murder. It is not a defence to any form of assault that the victim thought his punishment well deserved and submitted to it; to make a good defence the accused must prove that the law gave him the right to chastise and that he exercised it reasonably. Likewise, the victim may not forgive the aggressor and require the prosecution to desist; the right to enter a *nolle prosequi* [stay of proceedings] belongs to the Attorney-General alone.

Now if the law existed for the protection of the individual, there would be no reason why he should avail himself of it if he did not want it. The reason why a man may not consent to the commission of an offence against himself beforehand or forgive it afterwards is because it is an offence against society. It is not that society is physically injured; that would be impossible. Nor need any individual be shocked, corrupted, or exploited; everything may be done in private. Nor can it be explained on the practical ground that a violent man is a potential danger to others in the community who have therefore a direct interest in his apprehension and punishment as being necessary to their own protection. That would be true of a man whom the victim is prepared to forgive but not of one who gets his consent first; a murderer who acts only upon the consent, and maybe the request, of his victim is no menace to others, but he does threaten one of the great moral principles upon which society is based, that is, the sanctity of human life. There is only one explanation of what has hitherto been accepted as the basis of the criminal law and that is that there are certain standards of behaviour or moral principles which society requires to be observed; and the breach of them is an offence not merely against the person who is injured but against society as a whole.

Thus, if the criminal law were to be reformed so as to eliminate from it everything that was not designed to preserve order and decency or to protect citizens (including the protection of youth from corruption), it would overturn a fundamental principle. It would also end a number of specific crimes. Euthanasia or the killing of another at his own request, suicide, attempted suicide and suicide pacts, duelling, abortion, incest between brother and sister, are all acts which can be done in private and without offence to others and need not involve the corruption or exploitation of others. Many people think that the law on some of these subjects is in need of reform, but no one hitherto has gone so far as to suggest that they should all be left outside the criminal law as matters of private morality. They can be brought within it only as a matter of moral principle. …

I think it clear that the criminal law as we know it is based upon moral principle. In a number of crimes its function is simply to enforce a moral principle and nothing else. The law, both criminal and civil, claims to be able to speak about morality and immorality generally. Where does it get its authority to do this and how does it settle the moral principles which it enforces? Undoubtedly, as a matter of history, it derived both from Christian teaching. But I think that the strict logician is right when he says that the law can no longer rely on doctrines in which citizens are entitled to disbelieve. It is necessary therefore to look for some other source. …

… What makes a society of any sort is community of ideas, not only political ideas but also ideas about the way its members should behave and govern their lives; these latter ideas are its morals. Every society has a moral structure as well as a political one: or rather, since that might suggest two independent systems, I should say that the structure of every society is made up both of politics and morals. Take, for example, the institution of marriage. Whether a man should be allowed to take more than one wife is something about which every society has to make up its mind one way or the other. In England we believe in the Christian idea of marriage and therefore adopt monogamy as a moral principle. Consequently the Christian institution of marriage has become the basis of family life and so part of the structure of our society. It is there not because it is Christian. It has got there because it is Christian, but it remains there because it is built into the house in which we live and could not be removed without bringing it down. The great majority of those who live in this country accept it because it is the Christian idea of marriage and for them the only true one. But a non-Christian is bound by it, not because it is part of Christianity but because, rightly or wrongly, it has been adopted by the society in which he lives. It would be useless for him to stage a debate designed to prove that polygamy was theologically more correct and socially preferable; if he wants to live in the house, he must accept it as built in the way in which it is.

We see this more clearly if we think of ideas or institutions that are purely political. Society cannot tolerate rebellion; it will not allow argument about the rightness of the cause. Historians a century later may say that the rebels were right and the Government was wrong and a percipient and conscientious subject of the State may think so at the time. But it is not a matter which can be left to individual judgment. …

I return to the statement that I have already made, that society means a community of ideas; without shared ideas on politics, morals, and ethics no society can exist. Each one of us has ideas about what is good and what is evil; they cannot be kept private from the society in which we live. If men and women try to create a society in which there is no fundamental agreement about good and evil they will fail; if having based it on common agreement, the agreement goes, the society will disintegrate. For society is not something that is kept together physically; it is held by the invisible bonds of common thought. If the bonds were too far relaxed the members would drift apart. A common morality is part of the bondage. The bondage is part of the price of society; and mankind, which needs society, must pay its price. ...

I think, therefore, that it is not possible to set theoretical limits to the power of the State to legislate against immorality. It is not possible to settle in advance exceptions to the general rule or to define inflexibly areas of morality into which the law is in no circumstances to be allowed to enter. Society is entitled by means of its laws to protect itself from dangers, whether from within or without. Here again I think that the political parallel is legitimate. The law of treason is directed against aiding the king's enemies and against sedition within. The justification for this is that established government is necessary for the existence of society and therefore its safety against violent overthrow must be secured. But an established morality is as necessary as good government to the welfare of society. Societies disintegrate from within more frequently than they are broken up by external pressures. There is disintegration when no common morality is observed and history shows that the loosening of moral bonds is often the first stage of disintegration, so that society is justified in taking the same steps to preserve its moral code as it does to preserve its government and other essential institutions. The suppression of vice is as much the law's business as the suppression of subversive activities; it is no more possible to define a sphere of private morality than it is to define one of private subversive activity. ... You may argue that if a man's sins affect only himself it cannot be the concern of society. If he chooses to get drunk every night in the privacy of his own home, is any one except himself the worse for it? But suppose a quarter or a half of the population got drunk every night, what sort of society would it be? You cannot set a theoretical limit to the number of people who can get drunk before society is entitled to legislate against drunkenness. The same may be said of gambling. ...

... How are the moral judgements of society to be ascertained? By leaving it until now, I can ask it in the more limited form that is now sufficient for my purpose. How is the law-maker to ascertain the moral judgements of society? It is surely not enough that they should be reached by the opinion of the majority; it would be too much to require the individual assent of every citizen. English law has evolved and regularly uses a standard which does not depend on the counting of the heads. It is that of the reasonable man. He is not to be confused with the rational man. He is not expected to reason about anything and his judgement may be largely a matter of feeling. It is the viewpoint of the man in the street—to use an archaism familiar to all lawyers—the man in the Clapham omnibus. He might also be called the right-minded man. For my purpose I should like to call him the man in the jury box, for the moral judgement of society must be something about which any twelve men or women drawn at random might after discussion be expected to be unanimous. This was the standard the judges applied in the days before Parliament was as active as it is now and when they laid down rules of public policy. They did not think of themselves as making law but simply as stating principles which every right-minded person would accept as valid. ...

Nothing should be punished by the law that does not lie beyond the limits of tolerance. It is not nearly enough to say that a majority dislike a practice; there must be a real feeling of reprobation. Those who are dissatisfied with the present law on homosexuality often say that the opponents of reform are swayed simply by disgust. If that were so it would be wrong, but I do not think one can ignore disgust if it is deeply felt and not manufactured. Its presence is a good indication that the bounds of toleration are being reached. Not everything is to be tolerated. No society can do without intolerance, indignation, and disgust; they are the forces behind the moral law, and indeed it can be argued that if they or something like them are not present the feelings of society cannot be weighty enough to deprive the individual of freedom of choice. ...

The limits of tolerance shift. This is supplementary to what I have been saying but of sufficient importance in itself to deserve statement as a separate principle which lawmakers have to bear in mind. I suppose that moral standards do not shift; so far as they come from divine revelation they do not, and I am willing to assume that the moral judgements made by a society always remain good for that society. But the extent to which society will tolerate—I mean tolerate, not approve—departures from moral standards varies from generation to generation. It may be that over all tolerance is always increasing. The pressure of the human mind, always seeking greater freedom of thought, is outwards against the bonds of society forcing their gradual relaxation. It may be that history is a tale of contraction and expansion and that all developed societies are on their way to dissolution. I must not speak of things I do not know ... . I return therefore to the simple and observable fact that in matters of morals the limits of tolerance shift. Laws, especially those which are based on morals, are less easily moved. It follows as another good working principle that in any new matter of morals the law should be slow to act. By the next generation the swell of indignation may have abated and the law be left without the strong backing which it needs. But it is then difficult to alter the law without giving the impression that moral judgement is being weakened. This is now one of the factors that is strongly militating against any alteration to the law on homosexuality. ...

The last and biggest thing to be remembered is that the law is concerned with the minimum and not with the maximum; there is much in the Sermon on the Mount that would be out of place in the Ten Commandments. We all recognize the gap between the moral law and the law of the land. No man is worth much who regulates his conduct with the sole object of escaping punishment, and every worthy society sets for its members standards which are above those of the law ... .

Society cannot live without morals. Its morals are those standards of conduct which the reasonable man approves. A rational man, who is also a good man, may have other standards. If he has no standards at all he is not a good man and need not be further considered. If he has standards, they may be very different; he may, for example, not disapprove of homosexuality or abortion. In that case he will not share in the common morality; but that should not make him deny that it is a social necessity ... .

A man who concedes that morality is necessary to society must support the use of those instruments without which morality cannot be maintained. The two instruments are those of teaching, which is doctrine, and of enforcement, which is the law.

Devlin developed his ideas more fully in a volume published in 1965, which bore the same title as this lecture, *The Enforcement of Morals*.

Shortly after Devlin's speech, HLA Hart, a professor of jurisprudence at Oxford and one of the most prominent modern theorists of law, responded in a short piece published in *The Listener*.

HLA Hart, "Immorality and Treason"
The Listener (30 July 1959) 162 at 162-63

The most remarkable feature of Sir Patrick's lecture is his view of the nature of morality—the morality which the criminal law may enforce. Most previous thinkers who have repudiated the liberal point of view have done so because they thought that morality consisted either of divine commands or of rational principles of human conduct discoverable by human reason. Since morality for them had this elevated divine or rational status as the law of God or reason, it seemed obvious that the state should enforce it, and that the function of human law should not be merely to provide men with the opportunity for leading a good life, but actually to see that they lead it. Sir Patrick does not rest his repudiation of the liberal point of view on these religious or rationalist conceptions. Indeed much that he writes reads like an abjuration of the notion that reasoning or thinking has much to do with morality. English popular morality has no doubt its historical connexion with the Christian religion: "That," says Sir Patrick, "is how it got there." But it does not owe its present status or social significance to religion any more than to reason.

What, then, is it? According to Sir Patrick it is primarily a matter of feeling. "Every moral judgment," he says, "is a feeling that no right-minded man could act in any other way without admitting that he was doing wrong." Who then must feel this way if we are to have what Sir Patrick calls a public morality? He tells us that is "the man in the street," "the man in the jury box," or (to use the phrase so familiar to English lawyers) "the man on the Clapham omnibus." For the moral judgments of society so far as the law is concerned are to be ascertained by the standards of the reasonable man, and he is not to be confused with the rational man. Indeed, Sir Patrick says "he is not expected to reason about anything and his judgment may be largely a matter of feeling."

Intolerance, Indignation, and Disgust

But what precisely are the relevant feelings, the feelings which may justify use of the criminal law? Here the argument becomes a little complex. Widespread dislike of a practice is not enough. There must, says Sir Patrick, be "a real feeling of reprobation." Disgust is not enough either. What is crucial is a combination of intolerance, indignation, and disgust. These three are the forces behind the moral law, without which it is not "weighty enough to deprive the individual of freedom of choice." Hence there is, in Sir Patrick's outlook, a crucial difference between the mere adverse moral judgment of society and one which is inspired by feeling raised to the concert pitch of intolerance, indignation, and disgust.

This distinction is novel and also very important. For on it depends the weight to be given to the fact that when morality is enforced individual liberty is necessarily cut down .... .

A Shared Morality

If this is what morality is—a compound of indignation, intolerance, and disgust—we may well ask what justification there is for taking it, and turning it as such, into criminal law with all the misery which criminal punishment entails. Here Sir Patrick's answer is very clear and simple. A collection of individuals is not a society; what makes them into a society is among other things a shared or public morality. This is as necessary to its existence as an organized government. So society may use the law to preserve its morality like anything else essential to it. "The suppression of vice is as much the law's business as the suppression of subversive activities." The liberal point of view which denies this is guilty of "an error in jurisprudence": for it is no more possible to define an area of private morality than an area of private subversive activity. There can be no "theoretical limits" to legislation against immorality just as there are no such limits to the power of the state to legislate against treason and sedition.

Surely all this, ingenious as it is, is misleading. Mill's formulation of the liberal point of view may well be too simple. The grounds for interfering with human liberty are more various than the single criterion of "harm to others" suggests: cruelty to animals or organizing prostitution for gain do not, as Mill himself saw, fall easily under the description of harm to others. Conversely, even where there is harm to others in the most literal sense, there may well be other principles limiting the extent to which harmful activities should be repressed by law. So there are multiple criteria, not a single criterion, determining when human liberty may be restricted. Perhaps this is what Sir Patrick means by a curious distinction which he often stresses between theoretical and practical limits. But with all its simplicities the liberal point of view is a better guide than Sir Patrick to clear thought on the proper relation of morality to the criminal law: for it stresses what he obscures—namely, the points at which thought is needed before we turn popular morality into criminal law.

Society and Moral Opinion

No doubt we would all agree that a consensus of moral opinion on certain matters is essential if society is to be worth living in. Laws against murder, theft, and much else would be of little use if they were not supported by a widely diffused conviction that what these laws forbid is also immoral. So much is obvious. But it does not follow that everything to which the moral vetoes of accepted morality attach is of equal importance to society; nor is there the slightest reason for thinking of morality as a seamless web: one which will fall to pieces carrying society with it, unless all its emphatic vetoes are enforced by law. Surely even in the face of the moral feeling that is up to concert pitch—the trio of intolerance, indignation, and disgust—we must pause to think. We must ask a question at two different levels which Sir Patrick never clearly enough identifies or separates. First, we must ask whether a practice which offends moral feeling is harmful, independently of its repercussion on the general moral code. Secondly, what about repercussion on the moral code? Is it really true that failure to translate this item of general morality into criminal law will jeopardize the whole fabric of morality and so of society?

We cannot escape thinking about these two different questions merely by repeating to ourselves the vague nostrum: "This is part of public morality and public morality must be preserved if society is to exist." Sometimes Sir Patrick seems to admit this, for he says in words which both Mill and the Wolfenden Report might have used, that there must be the maximum respect for individual liberty consistent with the integrity of society. Yet this, as his contrasting examples of fornication and homosexuality show, turns out to mean only that the immorality which the law may punish must be generally felt to be intolerable. This plainly is no adequate substitute for a reasoned estimate of the damage to the fabric of society likely to ensue if it is not suppressed.

Nothing perhaps shows more clearly the inadequacy of Sir Patrick's approach to this problem than his comparison between the suppression of sexual immorality and the suppression of treason or subversive activity. Private subversive activity is, of course, a contradiction in terms because "subversion" means overthrowing government, which is a public thing. But it is grotesque, even where moral feeling against homosexuality is up to concert pitch, to think of the homosexual behaviour of two adults in private as in any way like treason or sedition either in intention or effect. We can make it *seem* like treason only if we assume that deviation from a general moral code is bound to affect that code, and to lead not merely to its modification but to its destruction. The analogy could begin to be plausible only if it was clear that offending against this item of morality was likely to jeopardize the whole structure. But we have ample evidence for believing that people will not abandon morality, will not think any better of murder, cruelty, and dishonesty, merely because some private sexual practice which they abominate is not punished by the law.

Because this is so the analogy with treason is absurd. Of course "No man is an island": what one man does in private, if it is known, may affect others in many different ways. Indeed it may be that deviation from general sexual morality by those whose lives, like the lives of many homosexuals, are noble ones and in all other ways exemplary will lead to what Sir Patrick calls the shifting of the limits of tolerance. But if this has any analogy in the sphere of government it is not the overthrow of ordered government, but a peaceful change in its form. So we may listen to the promptings of common sense and of logic, and say that though there could not logically be a sphere of private treason there is a sphere of private morality and immorality.

Sir Patrick's doctrine is also open to a wider, perhaps a deeper, criticism. In his reaction against a rationalist morality and his stress on feeling, he has I think thrown out the baby and kept the bath water; and the bath water may turn out to be very dirty indeed. When Sir Patrick's lecture was first delivered *The Times* greeted it with these words: "There is a moving and welcome humility in the conception that society should not be asked to give its reason for refusing to tolerate what in its heart it feels intolerable." This drew from a correspondent in Cambridge the retort: "I am afraid that we are less humble than we used to be. We once burnt old women because, without giving our reasons, we felt in our hearts that witchcraft was intolerable."

This retort is a bitter one, yet its bitterness is salutary. We are not, I suppose, likely, in England, to take again to the burning of old women for witchcraft or to punishing people for associating with those of a different race or colour, or to punishing people again for adultery. Yet if these things were viewed with intolerance, indignation, and disgust, as the second of them still is in some countries, it seems that on Sir Patrick's principles no rational criticism could be opposed to the claim that they should be punished by law. We could only pray, in his words, that the limits of tolerance might shift.

Curious Logic

It is impossible to see what curious logic has led Sir Patrick to this result. For him a practice is immoral if the thought of it makes the man on the Clapham omnibus sick. So be it. Still, why should we not summon all the resources of our reason, sympathetic understanding, as well as critical intelligence, and insist that before general moral feeling is turned into criminal law it is submitted to scrutiny of a different kind from Sir Patrick's? Surely, the legislator should ask whether the general morality is based on ignorance, superstition, or misunderstanding; whether there is false conception that those who practise what it condemns are in other ways dangerous or hostile to society; and whether the misery to many parties, the blackmail and the other evil consequences of criminal punishment, especially for sexual offences, are well understood. It is surely extraordinary that among the things which Sir Patrick says are to be considered before we legislate against immorality these appear nowhere; not even as "practical considerations," let alone "theoretical limits." To any theory which, like this one, asserts that the criminal law may be used on the vague ground that the preservation of morality is essential to society and yet omits to stress the need for critical scrutiny, our reply should be: "Morality, what crimes may be committed in thy name!"

As Mill saw, and de Tocqueville showed in detail long ago in his critical but sympathetic study of democracy, it is fatally easy to confuse the democratic principle that power should be in the hands of the majority with the utterly different claim that the majority, with power in their hands, need respect no limits. Certainly there is a special risk in a democracy that the majority may dictate how all should live. This is the risk we run, and should gladly run; for it is the price of all that is so good in democratic rule. But loyalty to democratic principles does not require us to maximize this risk: yet this is what we shall do if we mount the man in the street on the top of the Clapham omnibus and tell him that if only he feels sick enough about what other people do in private to demand its suppression by law no theoretical criticism can be made of his demand.

In the years following, Hart published a number of pieces that elaborated on the views expressed in this short article. See *Law, Liberty and Morality* (London: Oxford University Press, 1963); *The Morality of the Criminal Law* (Jerusalem: Magnes Press, 1964); and "Social Solidarity and the Enforcement of Morality" (1967) 35 U Chicago L Rev 1. Another important legal theorist, Ronald Dworkin, also criticized Devlin's views at the time in "Lord Devlin and the Enforcement of Morals" (1966) 75 Yale LJ 986.

The Hart–Devlin debate has been the subject of considerable subsequent commentary and academic reflection. Much remains critical of Devlin's views, but there are significant threads in contemporary discussions suggesting that aspects of his general argument are valuable and remain relevant. See e.g. S Wexler, "The Intersection of Law and Morals" (1976) 54 Can Bar Rev 351; R George, "Social Cohesion and the Legal Enforcement of Morals: A Reconsideration of the Hart-Devlin Debate" (1990) Am J Juris 15; and JP McCutcheon, "Morality and the Criminal Law: Reflections on Hart-Devlin" (2003) 47 Crim LQ 15.

The following letter, signed by Lord Devlin and others, was published in *The Times* (London) on May 11, 1965:

Sir,—In 1957 the Wolfenden Committee recommended, after three years study of the evidence, that homosexual behaviour between consenting adults in private should no longer be a criminal offence. ...

Seven years ago a distinguished list of signatories wrote in your columns that the existing law clearly no longer represented either Christian or liberal opinion in this country, and that its continued enforcement would do more harm than good to the community as a whole.

We hope that in response to [a motion in the House of Lords] Her Majesty's Government will now recognize the necessity for this reform and will introduce legislation.

Yours faithfully,
[other signatories]
Devlin: House of Lords

The law was changed in England and Wales in 1967 so that homosexual conduct between two consenting adults in private would no longer be an offence: *Sexual Offences Act 1967*, c 60.

In 1969 the Canadian Parliament passed a proviso that the crimes of buggery and gross indecency did not apply to any act committed in private between a husband and wife or any two consenting persons over 21 years of age: SC 1968-69, c 38, s 7. Then Justice Minister Pierre Trudeau explained the reform on the basis that the state had no place in the bedrooms of the nation. In 1988, the offences were replaced with an offence of anal intercourse that did not apply to private acts between a husband and wife or any two persons over the age of 18. (See s 159 of the *Criminal Code*.) The Ontario and Quebec Courts of Appeal subsequently declared this provision unconstitutional on the basis that it unjustifiably discriminated against gay men under the age of 18: *R v M(C)* (1995), 98 CCC (3d) 481 (Ont CA); *R v Roy* (1998), 125 CCC (3d) 442 (Que CA).

Recall that Devlin used the example of the "Christian idea" of monogamous, heterosexual marriage as an instance of an idea about which there is such moral consensus that it "is built into the house in which we live and could not be removed without bringing it down." As you may know, the Supreme Court of Canada affirmed the constitutionality of Parliament's bill establishing the legality of same-sex marriage in *Reference re Same-Sex Marriage*, 2004 SCC 79, [2004] 3 SCR 698. Section 293 of the *Criminal Code* prohibits polygamy, imposing a maximum punishment of five years' imprisonment for committing this offence. In January 2009, Winston Blackmore and James Oler, both leaders of fundamentalist Mormon communities in Bountiful, British Columbia, were charged with engaging in polygamy. These charges brought the criminal law in direct competition with the s 2(a) guarantee of freedom of religion and sharply engaged the question of the limits of the criminal law. Is the criminal prohibition on polygamy a harm-based offence or is it a piece of morals legislation? For discussion of this issue, see BL Berger, "Moral Judgment, Criminal Law and the Constitutional Protection of Religion" in J Cameron & J Stribopoulos, eds, *The Charter and Criminal Justice: Twenty-Five Years Later* (Toronto: LexisNexis, 2008) 513; SG Drummond, "Polygamy's Inscrutable Criminal Mischief" (2009) 47 Osgoode Hall LJ 317; and A Campbell, "Bountiful Voices" (2009) 47 Osgoode Hall LJ 183.

Many aspects of criminal law raise questions as to the limits and propriety of "morals legislation." *R v Jobidon*, [1991] 2 SCR 714, extracted in Chapter 1, is an example having to do with the complex issue of consent. In *Jobidon*, Justice Gonthier held that an individual could not consent to a serious assault. Among the reasons that he offered, Justice Gonthier explained that "it is most unseemly from a moral point of view that the law would countenance, much less provide a backhanded sanction to the sort of interaction displayed by the facts of this appeal. The sanctity of the human body should militate against the validity of consent to bodily harm inflicted in a fight." Anticipating the charge that limiting the ability of an individual to consent to bodily harm would be "unduly paternalistic," Justice Gonthier answered that "[a]ll criminal law is 'paternalistic' to some degree." The issue of whether the law will permit consent to sado-masochistic sexual practices has been considered by the House of Lords in *R v Brown* (1993), 97 Cr App R 44, and by the Ontario Court of Appeal in *R v Welch* (1995), 101 CCC (3d) 216 (Ont CA). Both courts held that consent could not be a defence to a charge of sexual assault causing bodily harm. Lord Templeman for the majority in the House of Lords in *Brown* stated that "society is entitled and bound to protect itself against a cult of violence. Pleasure derived from the infliction of pain is an evil thing. Cruelty is uncivilized." Lord Slynn in his dissent argued that it was not for the courts "in the interest of 'paternalism' … or in order to protect people from themselves" to imply limits on consent. The Ontario Court of Appeal relied on *Jobidon* and held that "the consent of the complainant, assuming it was given, cannot detract from the inherently degrading and dehumanizing nature of the conduct. Although the law must recognize individual freedom and autonomy, when the activity in question involves pursuing sexual gratification by deliberately inflicting pain upon another that gives rise to bodily harm, then the personal interest of the individuals must yield to the more compelling societal interests which are challenged by such behaviour."

The appropriate limits of the criminal law, and the role of the harm principle in setting these limits, have been the subject of recent consideration by the Supreme Court of Canada in cases involving the simple possession of marijuana and criminal indecency.

R v Malmo-Levine; R v Caine
Supreme Court of Canada
2003 SCC 74, [2003] 3 SCR 571

GONTHIER and BINNIE JJ (McLachlin CJ and Iacobucci, Major, and Bastarache JJ concurring): [1] In these appeals, the Court is required to consider whether Parliament has the legislative authority to criminalize simple possession of marihuana and, if so, whether that power has been exercised in a manner that is contrary to the *Canadian Charter of Rights and Freedoms*. The appellant Caine argues in particular that it is a violation of the principles of fundamental justice for Parliament to provide for a term of imprisonment as a sentence for conduct which he says results in little or no harm to other people. The appellant Malmo-Levine puts in issue the constitutional validity of the prohibition against possession for the purpose of trafficking in marihuana.

[2] The British Columbia Court of Appeal rejected the appellants' challenges to the relevant provisions of the *Narcotic Control Act*, R.S.C. 1985, c. N-1 ("NCA"), and, in our view, it was right to do so. Upholding as we do the constitutional validity of the simple possession offence, it follows, for the same reasons, that Malmo-Levine's challenge to the prohibition against possession for the purpose of trafficking must also be rejected.

[3] All sides agree that marihuana is a psychoactive drug which "causes alteration of mental function." That, indeed, is the purpose for which the appellants use it. Certain groups in society share a particular vulnerability to its effects. While members of these groups, whose identity cannot in general be distinguished from other users in advance,

are relatively small as a percentage of all marihuana users, their numbers are significant in absolute terms. The trial judge estimated "chronic users" to number about 50,000. A recent Senate Special Committee report estimated users under 16 (which may overlap to some extent with the chronic user group) also at 50,000 individuals (*Cannabis: Our Position for a Canadian Public Policy* (2002) (the "Senate Committee Report"), vol. I, at pp. 165-66). Pregnant women and schizophrenics are also said to be at particular risk. Advancing the protection of these vulnerable individuals, in our opinion, is a policy choice that falls within the broad legislative scope conferred on Parliament.

[4]   A conviction for the possession of marihuana for personal use carries no mandatory minimum sentence. In practice, most first offenders are given a conditional discharge. Imprisonment is generally reserved for situations that also involve trafficking or hard drugs. Except in very exceptional circumstances, imprisonment for simple possession of marihuana would constitute a demonstrably unfit sentence and, if imposed, would rightly be set aside on appeal. Availability of imprisonment in a statute that deals with a wide variety of drugs from opium and heroin to crack and cocaine is not unconstitutional, and its rare imposition for marihuana offences (as a scheduled drug) can and should be dealt with under ordinary sentencing principles. A fit sentence, by definition, complies with s. 7 of the *Charter*. The mere fact of the *availability* of imprisonment in a statute dealing with a variety of prohibited drugs does not, in our view, make the criminalization of possession of a psychoactive drug like marihuana contrary to the principles of fundamental justice.

[5]   The appellants have assembled much evidence and argument attacking the wisdom of the criminalization of simple possession of marihuana. They say that the line between criminal and non-criminal conduct has been drawn inappropriately and that the evil effects of the law against marihuana outweigh the benefits, if any, associated with its prohibition. These are matters of legitimate controversy, but the outcome of that debate is not for the courts to determine. The Constitution provides no more than a framework. Challenges to the wisdom of a legislative measure within that framework should be addressed to Parliament. Our concern is solely with the issue of constitutionality. We conclude that it is within Parliament's legislative jurisdiction to criminalize the possession of marihuana should it choose to do so. Equally, it is open to Parliament to decriminalize or otherwise modify any aspect of the marihuana laws that it no longer considers to be good public policy.

[6]   The appeals are therefore dismissed.

[Justices Gonthier and Binnie reviewed the facts and decisions below before turning to the analysis of the two key issues in the case: (1) whether the prohibition on possession of marijuana was a valid use of the federal criminal law power and, if so, (2) whether s 7 of the Charter nevertheless prohibits Parliament from criminalizing this conduct.]

V. Analysis

[21]   The controversy over the criminalization of the use of marihuana has raged in Canada for at least 30 years. In 1972, the Commission of Inquiry into the Non-Medical Use of Drugs (the "Le Dain Commission"), in its preliminary report entitled *Cannabis*, recommended that the prohibition against its use be removed from the *criminal* law. In 1974, the federal government introduced Bill S-19, which would have removed penal

sanctions for possession of marihuana for a first offence and substituted a monetary fine in its place. The Bill, however, died on the Order Paper. ...

[22] The trial judge in *Caine* estimated that over 600,000 Canadians now have criminal records for cannabis-related offences, and that widespread use despite the criminal prohibition encourages disrespect for the law. At the time of the hearing of the appeal in this Court, the government announced its intention of introducing a bill to eliminate the availability of imprisonment for simple possession. Bill C-38, as introduced, states that possession of amounts less than 15 grams of marihuana will render an individual "guilty of an offence punishable on summary conviction and liable to a fine" (s. 4(5.1)). Furthermore, the offence would be designated as a contravention, pursuant to the *Contraventions Act*, S.C. 1992, c. 47, with the effect that an individual convicted for such possession would not receive a criminal record.

[23] These reports and legislative initiatives were directed to crafting what was thought to be the best legislative response to the marihuana controversy. Whether the Bill should proceed, and if so in what form, is a matter of legislative policy for Parliament to decide. The question before us is purely a matter of law. Is the prohibition, including the availability of imprisonment for simple possession, beyond the powers of Parliament, either because it does not properly fall within Parliament's legislative competence, or because the prohibition, and in particular the availability of imprisonment, violate the *Charter*'s guarantees of rights and freedoms? ...

[Justices Gonthier and Binnie then reviewed the evidence regarding the possible harms associated with marijuana use. They drew from the admissions of the parties, the findings of the Le Dain Commission, above at para 21, certain parliamentary reports, and the trial judge's finding of fact in *Caine*.]

[46] [The trial judge in *Caine*] reviewed the extensive evidence before her court to put in perspective the potential harms associated with the use of marihuana, as presently understood, as follows (at para. 40):

1. the occasional to moderate use of marihuana by a healthy adult is not ordinarily harmful to health, even if used over a long period of time;

2. there is no conclusive evidence demonstrating any irreversible organic or mental damage to the user, except in relation to the lungs and then only to those of a chronic, heavy user such as a person who smokes at least 1 and probably 3-5 marihuana joints per day;

3. there is no evidence demonstrating irreversible, organic or mental damage from the use of marihuana by an ordinary healthy adult who uses occasionally or moderately;

4. marihuana use does cause alteration of mental function and as such should not be used in conjunction with driving, flying or operating complex machinery;

5. there is no evidence that marihuana use induces psychosis in ordinary healthy adults who use [marihuana] occasionally or moderately and, in relation to the

heavy user, the evidence of marihuana psychosis appears to arise only in those having a predisposition towards such a mental illness;

6. marihuana is not addictive;

7. there is a concern over potential dependence in heavy users, but marihuana is not a highly reinforcing type of drug, like heroin or cocaine and consequently physical dependence is not a major problem; psychological dependence may be a problem for the chronic user;

8. there is no causal relationship between marihuana use and criminality;

9. there is no evidence that marihuana is a gateway drug and the vast majority of marihuana users do not go on to try hard drugs … .

10. marihuana does not make people aggressive or violent, but on the contrary it tends to make them passive and quiet;

11. there have been no deaths from the use of marihuana;

12. there is no evidence of an amotivational syndrome, although chronic use of marihuana could decrease motivation, especially if such a user smokes so often as to be in a state of chronic intoxication;

13. assuming current rates of consumption remain stable, the health related costs of marihuana use are very, very small in comparison with those costs associated with tobacco and alcohol consumption.

[47] Having concluded that the use of marihuana is not as harmful as is sometimes claimed, the trial judge went on to state in *Caine* that marihuana is *not* "a completely harmless drug for all individual users" (para. 42). …

[48] Key to [the trial judge's] findings was the identification of perhaps 50,000 chronic users, who cannot be identified in advance, but who pose both a risk to themselves and a potential cost to society … .

· · ·

[61] We have been shown no reason to interfere with these findings of fact. It seems clear that the use of marihuana has less serious and permanent effects than was once claimed, but its psychoactive and health effects can be harmful, and in the case of members of vulnerable groups the harm may be serious and substantial.

[62] We turn, now, to the legal arguments raised by the parties.

D. Division of Powers

[63] The appellant Caine contends that Parliament has no power to criminalize the possession of marihuana for personal use under either the residuary power of peace, order and good government ("POGG") or the criminal law power.

[Justices Gonthier and Binnie briefly discussed the possibility that the prohibition was a valid exercise of the federal government's POGG power, leaving that matter for another day given the court's conclusion that the impugned provisions of the NCA were valid exercises of the criminal law power.]

(b) The Criminal Law Power

. . .

[74] For a law to be classified as a criminal law, it must possess three prerequisites: a valid criminal law purpose backed by a prohibition and a penalty (*Reference re Firearms Act (Can.)*, [2000] 1 S.C.R. 783, 2000 SCC 31, at para. 27). The criminal power extends to those laws that are designed to promote public peace, safety, order, health or other legitimate public purpose. In *RJR-MacDonald Inc. v. Canada (Attorney General)*, [1995] 3 S.C.R. 199, it was held that some legitimate public purpose must underlie the prohibition. In *Labatt Breweries, supra*, in holding that a health hazard may ground a criminal prohibition, Estey J. stated the potential purposes of the criminal law rather broadly as including "public peace, order, security, health and morality" (p. 933). Of course Parliament cannot use its authority improperly, e.g. colourably, to invade areas of provincial competence: *Scowby v. Glendinning*, [1986] 2 S.C.R. 226, at p. 237. ...

[In light of the harms identified by the trial judge and in the other sources canvassed by them, Gonthier and Binnie JJ concluded that these provisions sought to protect vulnerable groups, chronic users, adolescents, and those in the broader society from the potential harms associated with the use of marijuana.]

. . .

[78] The use of marihuana is therefore a proper subject matter for the exercise of the criminal law power. *Butler* held, at p. 504, that if there is a reasoned apprehension of harm Parliament is entitled to act, and in our view Parliament is also entitled to act on reasoned apprehension of harm even if on some points "the jury is still out." In light of the concurrent findings of "harm" in the courts below, we therefore confirm that the NCA in general, and the scheduling of marihuana in particular, properly fall within Parliament's legislative competence under s. 91(27) of the *Constitution Act, 1867*.

[79] Prior to the enactment of the *Charter* in 1982, that finding, which validates the exercise of the criminal law power, would have ended the appellants' challenge. Now, of course, Parliament must not only find legislative authority within the *Constitution Act, 1867*, but it must exercise that authority subject to the individual rights and freedoms guaranteed by the *Charter*.

[80] We therefore turn to the appellants' *Charter* arguments.

E. Section 7 of the Charter

. . .

2. Principles of Fundamental Justice

[Having found that Parliament had the authority to pass legislation prohibiting simple possession of marijuana under its criminal law power, Justices Gonthier and Binnie turned to the question whether s 7 might nevertheless prohibit the government from criminalizing this conduct. They found that the liberty interests of the accused were engaged by the risk of imprisonment and moved on to assess whether this deprivation of liberty offended any principles of fundamental justice. Justices Gonthier and Binnie addressed a number of collateral points before turning to the key question in the case—is the harm principle a principle of fundamental justice?]

· · ·

(d) The "Harm Principle"

[102] The appellants contend that unless the state can establish that the use of marihuana is harmful *to others*, the prohibition against simple possession cannot comply with s. 7. Our colleague Arbour J. accepts this proposition as correct to the extent that "the state resorts to imprisonment" (para. 244). Accordingly, a closer look at the alleged "harm principle" is called for.

· · ·

(I) HISTORY AND DEFINITION OF THE HARM PRINCIPLE

[Justices Gonthier and Binnie quoted JS Mill's harm principle, set out earlier in this chapter, and continued.]

· · ·

[107] … Mill's principle has two essential features. First, it rejects paternalism—that is, the prohibition of conduct that harms only the actor. Second, it excludes what could be called "moral harm." Mill was of the view that such moral claims are insufficient to justify use of the criminal law. Rather, he required clear and tangible harm to the rights and interests of others.

[108] At the same time, Mill acknowledged an exception to his requirement of harm "to others" for vulnerable groups. He wrote that "this doctrine is meant to apply to human beings in the maturity of their faculties. … Those who are still in a state to require being taken care of by others, must be protected against their own actions as well as against external injury" (p. 9).

[109] Mill's statement has the virtues of insight and clarity but he was advocating certain general philosophic principles, not interpreting a constitutional document. Moreover, even his philosophical supporters have tended to agree that justification for state intervention cannot be reduced to a single factor—harm—but is a much more complex matter. …

(II) IS THE HARM PRINCIPLE A PRINCIPLE OF FUNDAMENTAL JUSTICE?

· · ·

[113] … [F]or a rule or principle to constitute a principle of fundamental justice for the purposes of s. 7, it must be a legal principle about which there is significant societal consensus that it is fundamental to the way in which the legal system ought fairly to operate, and it must be identified with sufficient precision to yield a manageable standard against which to measure deprivations of life, liberty or security of the person.

A. *IS THE HARM PRINCIPLE A LEGAL PRINCIPLE?*

[114] In our view, the "harm principle" is better characterized as a description of an important state interest rather than a normative "legal" principle. Be that as it may, even if the harm principle could be characterized as a legal principle, we do not think that it meets the other requirements, as explained below.

B. *THERE IS NO SUFFICIENT CONSENSUS THAT THE HARM PRINCIPLE IS VITAL OR FUNDAMENTAL TO OUR SOCIETAL NOTION OF CRIMINAL JUSTICE*

[115] Contrary to the appellants' assertion, we do not think there is a consensus that the harm principle is the sole justification for criminal prohibition. There is no doubt that our case law and academic commentary are full of statements about the criminal law being aimed at conduct that "affects the public," or that constitutes "a wrong against the public welfare," or is "injurious to the public," or that "affects the community." No doubt, as stated, the *presence* of harm to others may justify legislative action under the criminal law power. However, we do not think that the *absence* of proven harm creates the unqualified barrier to legislative action that the appellants suggest. On the contrary, the state may sometimes be justified in criminalizing conduct that is either not harmful (in the sense contemplated by the harm principle), or that causes harm only to the accused. ...

[117] Several instances of crimes that do not cause harm to others are found in the *Criminal Code*, R.S.C. 1985, c. C-46. Cannibalism is an offence (s. 182) that does not harm another sentient being, but that is nevertheless prohibited on the basis of fundamental social and ethical considerations. Bestiality (s. 160) and cruelty to animals (s. 446) are examples of crimes that rest on their offensiveness to deeply held social values rather than on Mill's "harm principle." ...

• • •

C. *NOR IS THERE ANY CONSENSUS THAT THE DISTINCTION BETWEEN HARM TO OTHERS AND HARM TO SELF IS OF CONTROLLING IMPORTANCE*

• • •

[124] Putting aside, for the moment, the proper approach to the appropriateness of imprisonment (which, as stated, we think should be addressed under s. 12 rather than s. 7), we do not accept the proposition that there is a general prohibition against the criminalization of harm to self. Canada continues to have paternalistic laws. Requirements that people wear seatbelts and motorcycle helmets are designed to "save people from themselves." There is no consensus that this sort of legislation offends our societal notions of justice. Whether a jail sentence is an appropriate penalty for such an offence is another question. However, the objection in that aspect goes to the validity of an assigned punishment—it does not go to the validity of prohibiting the underlying conduct.

[125] A recent discussion policy paper from the Law Commission of Canada entitled *What is a Crime? Challenges and Alternatives* (2003) highlights the difficulties in distinguishing between harm to others and harm to self. It notes that "in a society that recognizes the interdependency of its citizens, such as universally contributing to healthcare or educational needs, harm to oneself is often borne collectively" (p. 17).

[126] In short, there is no consensus that tangible harm to others is a necessary precondition to the creation of a criminal law offence.

D. *THE HARM PRINCIPLE IS NOT A MANAGEABLE STANDARD AGAINST WHICH TO MEASURE DEPRIVATION OF LIFE, LIBERTY OR SECURITY OF THE PERSON*

[127] Even those who agree with the "harm principle" as a regulator of the criminal law frequently disagree about what it means and what offences will meet or offend the harm principle. In the absence of any agreed definition of "harm" for this purpose, allegations

and counter-allegations of non-trivial harm can be marshalled on every side of virtually every criminal law issue, as one author explains:

> The harm principle is effectively collapsing under the weight of its own success. Claims of harm have become so pervasive that the harm principle has become meaningless: the harm principle no longer serves the function of a *critical principle* because non-trivial harm arguments permeate the debate. Today, the issue is no longer *whether* a moral offense causes harm, but rather what type and what amount of harms the challenged conduct causes, and how the harms compare. On those issues, the harm principle is silent. [Emphasis in original.]

> (B.E. Harcourt, "The Collapse of the Harm Principle" (1999), 90 *J. Crim. L. & Criminology* 109, at p. 113)

Professor Harcourt goes on to point out that it is the "hidden normative dimensions ... [that] do the work in the harm principle, not the abstract, simple notion of harm" (p. 185). In other words, the existence of harm (however defined) does no more than open a gateway to the debate; it does not give any precise guidance about its resolution.

[128] Harm, as interpreted in the jurisprudence, can take a multitude of forms, including economic, physical and social (e.g., injury and/or offence to fundamental societal values). In the present appeal, for example, the respondents put forward a list of "harms" which they attribute to marihuana use. The appellants put forward a list of "harms" which they attribute to marihuana prohibition. Neither side gives much credence to the "harms" listed by the other. Each claims the "net" result to be in its favour.

[129] In the result, we do not believe that the content of the "harm" principle as described by Mill and advocated by the appellants provides a manageable standard under which to review criminal or other laws under s. 7 of the *Charter*. Parliament, we think, is entitled to act under the criminal law power in the protection of legitimate state interests other than the avoidance of harm to others, subject to *Charter* limits such as the rules against arbitrariness, irrationality and gross disproportionality, discussed below. ...

[The appellants further argued that criminalizing the use of marijuana, while failing to criminalize the use of other substances like alcohol and tobacco, showed that the law was arbitrary. Justices Gonthier and Binnie rejected this argument, stating that "Parliament may, as a matter of constitutional law, determine what is *not* criminal as well as what is. The choice to use the criminal law in a particular context does not require its use in any other" (at para 140). Justices Gonthier and Binnie also addressed the appellant's argument that exposure to the risk of imprisonment was disproportionate to the nature of the conduct in question, answering that the appropriate standard would be one of "gross disproportionality" and that "the lack of any mandatory minimum sentence together with the existence of well-established sentencing principles mean that the mere availability of imprisonment on a marihuana charge cannot, without more, violate the principle against gross disproportionality" (at para 158).]

· · ·

VI. *Conclusion*

[186] For these reasons, it is our view that the *Charter* challenges must fail and that the appeals should be dismissed.

. . .

ARBOUR J (dissenting in *Caine*):

. . .

[190] We are asked to address, directly for the first time, whether the *Charter* requires that harm to others or to society be an essential element of an offence punishable by imprisonment. In a landmark 1985 case, Lamer J. (as he then was) said: "A law that has the potential to convict a person who has not really done anything wrong offends the principles of fundamental justice and, if imprisonment is available as a penalty, such a law then violates a person's right to liberty under s. 7 of the *Charter*" (*Re B.C. Motor Vehicle Act*, [1985] 2 S.C.R. 486, at p. 492 ("*Motor Vehicle Reference*")). In my view, a "person who has not really done anything wrong" is a person whose conduct caused little or no reasoned risk of harm or whose harmful conduct was not his or her fault. Therefore, for the reasons that follow, I am of the view that s. 7 of the *Charter* requires not only that some minimal mental element be an essential element of any offence punishable by imprisonment, but also that the prohibited act be harmful or pose a risk of harm to others. A law that has the potential to convict a person whose conduct causes little or no reasoned risk of harm to others offends the principles of fundamental justice and, if imprisonment is available as a penalty, such a law then violates a person's right to liberty under s. 7 of the *Charter*. Imprisonment can only be used to punish blameworthy conduct that is harmful to others.

[Justice Arbour reviewed the facts and then dispensed with the division of powers issue largely as the majority had. She found that the interest protected by s 7 had been engaged and, on the central issue of the harm principle as a principle of fundamental justice, continued.]

. . .

[236] The fundamental question raised in these appeals is whether harm is a constitutionally required component of the *actus reus* of any offence punishable by imprisonment. We have seen above that harm may not be the only basis upon which Parliament may decide to prohibit or regulate a given type of conduct. We must now determine whether the *Charter* requires that harm be the sole basis upon which the state may employ the threat of imprisonment as a sanction against a prohibited conduct.

[237] The debate over the harm principle takes place around the traditional confrontation between harm and morality as a basis for restricting an individual's liberty. The liberal view was initially espoused by Victorian philosopher and economist John Stuart Mill in his essay, *On Liberty* ... . Mill's principle was exclusive: "[T]he *only* purpose for which power can be rightfully exercised over any member of a civilized community, against his will, is to prevent harm to others" (p. 8 (emphasis added)).

[238] Mill's assertion was challenged by Sir James Fitzjames Stephen in *Liberty, Equality, Fraternity* (1967), initially published in 1874, who strongly opposed any limitation on the power of the state to enforce morality. Stephen's argument was best captured in a now-famous passage: "[T]here are acts of wickedness so gross and outrageous that, self-protection apart, they must be prevented as far as possible at any cost to the offender, and

punished, if they occur, with exemplary severity" (p. 162). This debate between Mill and Stephen was reignited in England by the recommendation in 1957 of the Committee on Homosexual Offences and Prostitution to decriminalize homosexuality on the basis that it is not the duty of the law to concern itself with immorality as such (*The Wolfenden Report* (1963), at paras. 61-62). The reactions to the *Wolfenden Report* have been vehement. Lord Patrick Devlin, in his Maccabaean Lecture delivered at the British Academy in 1959 (later published: P. Devlin, *The Enforcement of Morals* (1965)), argued that purportedly immoral activities, like homosexuality and prostitution, should remain criminal offences and he became associated with the principle of legal moralism—the principle that moral offences should be regulated because they are immoral (see on this: B.E. Harcourt, "The Collapse of the Harm Principle" (1999), 90 *J. Crim. L. & Criminology* 109, at pp. 111-12; B. Lauzon, *Les champs légitimes du droit criminel et leur application aux manipulations génétiques transmissibles aux générations futures* (2002), at p. 26).

[239] This position is opposed to the liberal view of Professors Hart and Feinberg who reiterated Mill's harm principle. According to J. Feinberg, who adopts a less exclusive view of the harm principle in *The Moral Limits of the Criminal Law* (1984), in the first volume, entitled *Harm to Others*, at p. 26, "[i]t is always a good reason in support of penal legislation that it would probably be effective in preventing ... harm to persons other than the actor." The debate between legal moralism and the harm principle has stimulated academic discussions and much has been written on this topic (see, *inter alia*, in addition to other sources cited throughout these reasons: "Symposium: The Moral Limits of the Criminal Law" (2001), 5 *Buff. Crim. L. Rev.* 1-319; *Mill's On Liberty: Critical Essays* (1997), edited by Gerald Dworkin). Braidwood J.A. referred, at paras. 107-12, to various authors who either adopted the harm principle or incorporated it in their writings. One of the most prominent, H.L. Packer, in his influential *The Limits of the Criminal Sanction* (1968) said, at p. 267, that "harm to others" must be a "limiting criteri[on] for invocation of the criminal sanction." This debate, which has remained focused, as I said earlier, on what should be *criminalized*, also permeated the work of the Law Reform Commissions in Canada on possible reforms of the *Criminal Code*. I need not expand on their recommendations for my purposes. Suffice it to say that Braidwood J.A. referred to various reports, all of which basically advocated that the criminal law should only be used, save in exceptional circumstances, where conduct causes or risks causing significant or grave harm to others or society (see paras. 113-16).

[240] This philosophical and theoretical debate is of great interest and is a useful policy tool for law makers. It may also serve as a guide in the characterization of the harm principle as a principle of fundamental justice. However, as guardians of the *constitutional* principles of fundamental justice, courts are not expected to merely choose from among the competing theories of harm advanced by criminal law theorists. ...

· · ·

[244] I am of the view that the principles of fundamental justice require that whenever the state resorts to imprisonment, a minimum of harm to others must be an essential part of the offence. The state cannot resort to imprisonment as a punishment for conduct that causes little or no reasoned risk of harm to others. Prohibited conduct punishable by imprisonment cannot be harmless conduct or conduct that only causes harm to the perpetrator. As Braidwood J.A. said in *Caine*, "it is common sense that you don't go to jail unless there is a potential that your activities will cause harm to others" (para. 134).

· · ·

[246] As I said before, however, the focus must remain on the choice by the state to resort to imprisonment to sanction conduct that it has decided to prohibit through its criminal law power or otherwise. The power of Parliament to use criminal law is broad and any concern as to what should be criminalized remains in the hands of the elected representatives. However, in my view, be it as a criminal sanction or as a sanction to any other prohibition, imprisonment must, as a constitutional minimum standard, be reserved for those whose conduct causes a reasoned risk of harm to others. "Doing nothing wrong" in that sense means acting in a manner which causes little or no reasoned risk of harm to others or to society. The *Charter* requires that the highest form of restriction of liberty be reserved for those who, at a minimum, infringe on the rights or freedoms of other individuals or otherwise harm society. ...

[247] Where legislation which may deprive individuals of their liberty is aimed at protecting other individuals or society from the risk of harm caused by the prohibited conduct, courts must scrutinize carefully the harm alleged. In victimizing conduct, the attribution of fault is relatively straightforward because of the close links between the actor's culpable conduct and the resulting harm to the victim ... .

[248] Where harm to society as a whole is alleged, how must such harm be assessed? Harm caused to collective interests, as opposed to harm caused to identifiable individuals, is not easy to quantify and even less easy to impute to a distinguishable activity or actor. In order to determine whether specific conduct, which perhaps only causes direct harm to the actor, or which seems rather benign, causes more than little or no risk of harm to others, courts must assess the interest of society in prohibiting and sanctioning the conduct. ...

[249] Societal interests in prohibiting conduct are evaluated by balancing the harmful effects on society if the conduct in question is not prohibited by law against the effects of prohibiting the conduct in question. It would indeed be misleading to engage in an assessment of the state's interest in prohibiting conduct by evaluating solely the collective harm that the state wishes to prevent without also evaluating the collective costs incurred by preventing such harm (see Packer, *supra*, at p. 267: "One cannot meaningfully deal with the question of 'harm to others' without weighing benefits against detriments"). The harm or risk of harm to society caused by the prohibited conduct must outweigh any harm that may result from enforcement. ...

· · ·

[254] It is useful at this stage to briefly revisit the harm caused by marihuana use as found by the trial judges. Although there is no need at this stage to reproduce the findings of the trial judges as to what harms are *not* associated with marihuana use, remember that these findings displaced many commonly held but entirely erroneous assumptions regarding the effects of marihuana use (see para. 192, above). As to the harmful effects of marihuana use, recall that McCart J. held in *Clay* that the consumption of marihuana is "not completely harmless" but "unlikely to create serious harm for most individual users or society" (para. 26).

[255] Howard Prov. Ct. J. in *Caine* summarized her overall findings on harm as follows, at paras. 121-26:

> The evidence before me demonstrates that there is a reasonable basis for believing that the following health risks exist with [marihuana use].

There is a general risk of harm to the users of marihuana from the acute effects of the drug, but these adverse effects are rare and transient. Persons experiencing the acute effects of the drug will be less adept at driving, flying and other activities involving complex machinery. In this regard they represent a risk of harm to others in society. At current rates of use, accidents caused by users under the influence of marihuana cannot be said to be significant.

There is also a risk that any individual who chooses to become a casual user, may end up being a chronic user of marihuana, or a member of one of the vulnerable persons identified in the materials. It is not possible to identify these persons in advance.

As to the chronic users of marihuana, there are health risks for such persons. The health problems are serious ones but they arise primarily from the act of smoking rather than from the active ingredients in marihuana. Approximately 5% of all marihuana users are chron[i]c users. At current rates of use, this comes to approximately 50,000 persons. There is a risk that, upon legalization, rates of use will increase, and with that the absolute number of chronic users will increase.

In addition, there are health risks for those vulnerable persons identified in the materials. There is no information before me to suggest how many people might fall into this group. Given that it includes young adolescents who may be more prone to becoming chronic users, I would not estimate this group to be min[u]scule.

All of the risks noted above carry with them a cost to society, both to the health care and welfare systems. At current rates of use, these costs are negligible compared to the costs associated with alcohol and drugs [sic]. There is a risk that, with legalization, user rates will increase and so will these costs.

[256] The inevitable conclusion is that apart from the risks of impairment while driving, flying or operating complex machinery and the impact of marihuana use on the health care and welfare systems, to which I will return, the harms associated with marihuana use are exclusively health risks for the individual user, ranging from almost non-existent for low/occasional/moderate users of marihuana to relatively significant for chronic users. In my view, as I stated above, harm to self does not satisfy the constitutional requirement that whenever the state resorts to imprisonment, there must be a minimum harm to others as an essential part of the offence. The prohibition of conduct that only causes harm to self, regardless of the gravity of the harm, is not in accordance with the principles of fundamental justice and, if imprisonment is available as a means to enforce the prohibition, a breach of s. 7 of the *Charter* will have been established.

[257] It is important at this stage to address a specific issue raised by my colleagues. Although they find that the purpose of the impugned legislation is the protection of health and public safety in general (see majority reasons at para. 65), my colleagues put great emphasis on the fact that it also aims at protecting vulnerable groups from self-inflicted harm … . Specifically, they recall the state's interest in acting to protect vulnerable groups, citing *New Brunswick (Minister of Health and Community Services) v. G.(J.)*, [1999] 3 S.C.R. 46, at para. 70; and *B.(R.)* [*v Children's Aid Society of Metropolitan Toronto*, [1995] 1 SCR 315], at para. 88. They also claim that the protection of vulnerable groups is a valid exercise of the criminal law power, citing *Rodriguez* [*v British Columbia (Attorney General)*, [1993] 3 SCR 519], at p. 595; *R. v. Morgentaler*, [1988] 1 S.C.R. 30, at pp. 74-75; *R. v. Keegstra*, [1995] 2 S.C.R. 381; [*R v Sharpe*, 2001 SCC 2, [2001] 1 SCR 45]; and [*R v Butler*, [1992] 1 SCR 452]. While the cases referred to by my colleagues clearly illustrate the state's

interest in the protection of vulnerable groups from others who might harm them, they are far from suggesting that it is the vulnerable ones who should be sent to jail for their self-protection. Implicit in my colleagues' argument is that the state would be justified in threatening with imprisonment adolescents with a history of poor school performance, women of childbearing age and persons with pre-existing diseases such as cardiovascular diseases, respiratory diseases, schizophrenia and other drug dependencies, who are at particular risk of harming themselves by using marihuana. I do not think that an exception to the harm principle is justified to allow the state to threaten with imprisonment vulnerable people in order to prevent them from harming themselves. ...

· · ·

[265] In the cases before us, the societal interests in prohibiting marihuana possession must take into account, on the one hand, the burden that marihuana use imposes on the health care and welfare systems, and, on the other, the costs incurred by society because of the prohibition. Howard Prov. Ct. J. noted that at current rates of use, the costs imposed upon the health care and welfare systems by marihuana are negligible compared to the costs associated with alcohol and drugs. As I mentioned earlier, society's tolerance for the harmful effects that the conduct may entail must be assessed, where possible, by reference to its tolerance for comparable conduct. I will thus simply take note of the trial judges' findings that the burden that marihuana use imposes on society is "negligible" or "very, very small" compared to the costs imposed by comparable conduct that society tolerates (i.e., alcohol and tobacco use).

[266] If there remained any doubt as to whether the harms associated with marihuana use justified the state in using imprisonment as a sanction against its possession, this doubt disappears when the harms caused by the prohibition are put in the balance. The record shows and the trial judges found that the prohibition of simple possession of marihuana attempts to prevent a low quantum of harm to society at a very high cost. A "negligible" burden on the health care and welfare systems, coupled with the many significant negative effects of the prohibition, cannot be said to amount to more than little or no reasoned risk of harm to society. I thus conclude that s. 3(1) and (2) of the *Narcotic Control Act*, as it prohibits the possession of marihuana for personal use under threat of imprisonment, violates the right of the appellants to liberty in a manner that is not in accordance with the harm principle, a principle of fundamental justice, contrary to s. 7 of the *Charter*.

· · ·

[Justices LeBel and Deschamps wrote separate dissenting reasons. Justice LeBel would not have declared the harm principle to be a principle of fundamental justice, but reasoned that the criminalization of simple possession of marijuana constituted "the adoption and implementation of a legislative response which is disproportionate to the societal problems at issue" and, as such, was "arbitrary and in breach of s. 7 of the *Charter*" (at para 280). Justice Deschamps, who was also unwilling to raise the harm principle to the status of a principle of fundamental justice for the purposes of s 7 of the Charter, reasoned similarly, concluding instead that the use of the criminal law was arbitrary given the limited harm caused by marijuana use, the availability of less severe legislative tools to address the issue, and the lack of proportionality between the harmful effects of marijuana use and the harm caused by its prohibition.]

As you have read, in *Malmo-Levine*, the Supreme Court of Canada ruled that the harm principle does not qualify as a principle of fundamental justice within the meaning of that term in s 7 of the Charter. Accordingly, it is constitutionally open to Parliament to legislate on the basis of morality alone. Yet an important theme in this chapter, indeed a theme that is worth bearing in mind throughout your study of the criminal law, is that the question of the proper *limits* of the criminal law—whether philosophical or constitutional—is a different question than what constitutes *good* criminal law policy or common law doctrine. The Constitution merely sets boundaries for the criminal law; within these outer boundaries there remain many important choices to be made about the best approach to the criminal law and criminal justice. See e.g. K Roach, "The Dangers of a Charter-Proof and Crime-Based Response to Terrorism" in RJ Daniels, P Macklem & K Roach, *The Security of Freedom* (Toronto: University of Toronto Press, 2001) 131. The Supreme Court's decision in *Malmo-Levine*, while deciding that the harm principle was not a constitutionally imposed limit on criminal law, left open the question of what role "harm" should play when a court is faced with the common law task of interpreting a criminal law. This issue was addressed in the following case.

R v Labaye
Supreme Court of Canada
2005 SCC 80, [2005] 3 SCR 728

McLACHLIN CJ (Major, Binnie, Deschamps, Fish, Abella, and Charron JJ concurring):

1. Introduction

[1] The appellant appeals from a conviction of keeping a "common bawdy-house" for the "practice of acts of indecency" under s. 210(1) of the *Criminal Code*, R.S.C. 1985, c. C-46. The issue is whether the acts committed in his establishment were acts of indecency within the meaning of our criminal law.

[2] Defining indecency under the *Criminal Code* is a notoriously difficult enterprise. The *Criminal Code* offers no assistance, leaving the task to judges. The test developed by the cases has evolved from one based largely on subjective considerations, to one emphasizing the need for objective criteria, based on harm. This heightened emphasis on objective criteria rests on the principle that crimes should be defined in a way that affords citizens, police and the courts a clear idea of what acts are prohibited. (See *Reference re ss. 193 and 195.1(1)(c) of the Criminal Code (Man.)*, [1990] 1 S.C.R. 1123, *per* Lamer J.) We generally convict and imprison people only where it is established beyond a reasonable doubt that they have violated objectively defined norms. Crimes relating to public indecency are no exception.

[3] This appeal requires us to apply the norms developed in recent cases to the operation of clubs established to facilitate group sex, a practice colloquially referred to as "swinging." This in turn invites further refinement of the objective criteria for indecency under the *Criminal Code*.

[4] I conclude that the appellant's conviction should be quashed.

2. Facts

[5] The appellant operated a club in Montréal, called L'Orage. The purpose of the club was to permit couples and single people to meet each other for group sex. Only members and their guests were admitted to the club. Prospective members were interviewed to ensure that they were aware of the nature of the activities of the club and to exclude applicants who did not share the same views on group sex. Members paid an annual membership fee.

[6] At the time of the events giving rise to the charge against the appellant, the club L'Orage had three floors. The first floor was occupied by a bar, the second a salon, and the third the "apartment" of the appellant. A doorman manned the main door of the club, to ensure that only members and their guests entered. Two doors separated access to the third floor apartment from the rest of the club. One was marked *"Privé"* (Private) and the other locked with a numeric key pad.

[7] Members of the club were supplied with the appropriate code and permitted to access the third floor apartment. This was the only place where group sex took place. A number of mattresses were scattered about the floor of the apartment. There people engaged in acts of cunnilingus, masturbation, fellatio and penetration. On several occasions observed by the police, a single woman engaged in sex with several men, while other men watched and masturbated.

[8] Entry to the club and participation in the activities were voluntary. No one was forced to do anything or watch anything. No one was paid for sex. While men considerably outnumbered women on the occasions when the police visited, there is no suggestion that any of the women were there involuntarily or that they did not willingly engage in the acts of group sex.

· · ·

4. Analysis

4.1 The Legal Test for Criminal Indecency

4.1.1 The History of Criminal Indecency

[13] Section 210(1) of the *Criminal Code* makes it an offence, punishable by two years in prison, to keep a common bawdy-house. A bawdy-house is defined in s. 197(1) of the *Code* as a place kept, occupied, or resorted to "by one or more persons for the purpose of prostitution or the practice of acts of indecency." The only question in this case is whether what went on at L'Orage constituted "acts of indecency."

[14] Indecency has two meanings, one moral and one legal. Our concern is not with the moral aspect of indecency, but with the legal. The moral and legal aspects of the concept are, of course, related. Historically, the legal concepts of indecency and obscenity, as applied to conduct and publications, respectively, have been inspired and informed by the moral views of the community. But over time, courts increasingly came to recognize that morals and taste were subjective, arbitrary and unworkable in the criminal context, and that a diverse society could function only with a generous measure of tolerance for minority mores and practices. This led to a legal norm of objectively ascertainable harm instead of subjective disapproval.

[15] Canadian law on indecent acts, from its origins in the English common law, has been firmly anchored in societal rather than purely private moral concerns. For example, in the early case of *R. v. Hicklin* (1868), L.R. 3 Q.B. 360, Cockburn C.J. stated that the test for obscenity was whether the material would tend to deprave and corrupt other members of society.

[16] However, depravity and corruption vary with the eye of the beholder, and the *Hicklin* test proved difficult to apply in an objective fashion. Convictions often depended more on the idiosyncrasies and the subjective moral views of the judge or jurors than objective criteria of what might deprave or corrupt. Nevertheless, the *Hicklin* test remained in place for almost a century.

[17] In 1959, the Canadian Parliament introduced a new "undue exploitation of sex" test for obscene materials: s. 150(8) of the *Criminal Code*, S.C. 1953-54, c. 51 (added by S.C. 1959, c. 41, s. 11) (now s. 163(8)). In considering this test, the Supreme Court emphasized the failings of the previous test and the need for new criteria "which have some certainty of meaning and are capable of objective application and which do not so much depend as before upon the idiosyncrasies and sensitivities of the tribunal of fact, whether judge or jury": *Brodie v. The Queen*, [1962] S.C.R. 681, at p. 702, *per* Judson J.

[18] Borrowing on decisions from Australia and New Zealand emphasizing the foundation of criminal legislation on obscenity and indecency in societal norms, the Court adopted a test based on the community standard of tolerance. On its face, the test was objective, requiring the trier of fact to determine what the community would tolerate. Yet once again, in practice it proved difficult to apply in an objective fashion. How does one determine what the "community" would tolerate were it aware of the conduct or material? In a diverse, pluralistic society whose members hold divergent views, who is the "community"? And how can one objectively determine what the community, if one could define it, would tolerate, in the absence of evidence that community knew of and considered the conduct at issue? In practice, once again, the test tended to function as a proxy for the personal views of expert witnesses, judges and jurors. In the end, the question often came down to what they, as individual members of the community, would tolerate. Judges and jurors were unlikely, human nature being what it is, to see themselves and their beliefs as intolerant. It was far more likely that they would see themselves as reasonable, representative members of the community. The chances of a judge or juror saying, "I view this conduct as indecent but I set that view aside because it is intolerant," were remote indeed. The result was that despite its superficial objectivity, the community standard of tolerance test remained highly subjective in application.

• • •

[20] In 1985, the Supreme Court pursued the search for objectivity by introducing a two-part definition of community standards of tolerance in *Towne Cinema Theatres Ltd. v. The Queen*, [1985] 1 S.C.R. 494. The first way to establish obscenity (undue exploitation of sex) was to show that the material violated the norm of tolerance of what Canadians would permit others, whose views they did not share, to do or see (p. 508). The second was to show that the material would have a harmful effect on others in society (p. 505). Although this notion of harm had been implicit in Cockburn C.J.'s definition of obscenity in *Hicklin*, *Towne Cinema* marked the first clear articulation of the relationship between obscenity and harm in Canadian jurisprudence, and represented the beginning of a shift from a community standards test to a harm-based test.

[21] The shift to a harm-based rationale was completed by this Court's decisions in *R. v. Butler*, [1992] 1 S.C.R. 452, and *Little Sisters Book and Art Emporium v. Canada (Minister of Justice)*, [2000] 2 S.C.R. 1120, 2000 SCC 69. In *Butler*, the two-part test for obscenity of *Towne Cinema* was resolved into a single test, in which the community standard of tolerance was determined by reference to the risk of harm entailed by the conduct:

> The courts must determine as best they can what the community would tolerate others being exposed to *on the basis of the degree of harm that may flow from such exposure.* Harm in this context means that it *predisposes persons to act in an anti-social manner* as, for example, the physical or mental mistreatment of women by men, or, what is perhaps debatable, the reverse. Anti-social conduct for this purpose is *conduct which society formally recognizes as incompatible with its proper functioning.* The stronger the inference of a risk of harm the lesser the likelihood of tolerance. [Emphasis added; p 485, *per* Sopinka J]
>
> . . .

[24] Grounding criminal indecency in harm represents an important advance in this difficult area of the law. Harm or significant risk of harm is easier to prove than a community standard. Moreover, the requirement of a risk of harm incompatible with the proper functioning of society brings this area of the law into step with the vast majority of criminal offences, which are based on the need to protect society from harm.

[25] However, it is not always clear precisely how the harm test for indecency applies in particular circumstances. New cases have raised questions as to the nature and degree of harm sufficient to establish indecency. Further definition is required in order to resolve cases like this, and to permit individuals to conduct themselves within the law and the police and courts to enforce the criminal sanction in an objective, fair way.

4.1.2 Toward a Theory of Harm

[26] Developing a workable theory of harm is not a task for a single case. In the tradition of the common law, its full articulation will come only as judges consider diverse situations and render decisions on them. Moreover, the difficulty of the task should not be underestimated. We must proceed incrementally, step by cautious step.

[27] The facts of this case require the further exploration of what types of harm, viewed objectively, suffice to found a conviction for keeping a bawdy-house for the purposes of acts of indecency. This exploration must be based on the purposes that the offence serves. More precisely, what harms are sought to be curtailed by targeting indecent conduct?

. . .

[30] … [T]he analysis to be performed in a particular case involves two steps. The first step is concerned with the *nature* of the harm. It asks whether the Crown has established a harm or significant risk of harm to others that is grounded in norms which our society has formally recognized in its Constitution or similar fundamental laws. The second step is concerned with the *degree* of the harm. It asks whether the harm in its degree is incompatible with the proper functioning of society. Both elements must be proved beyond a reasonable doubt before acts can be considered indecent under the *Criminal Code*.

[31] I now turn to a more detailed consideration of each of the two requirements for establishing indecent acts for the purposes of s. 210 of the *Criminal Code*.

4.1.3 The Nature of the Harm: Harm to Individuals or Society Contrary to Society's Norms

[32] To ground criminal responsibility, the harm must be one which society *formally recognizes* as incompatible with its proper functioning: *Butler*, at p. 485.

[33] The requirement of formal societal recognition makes the test objective. The inquiry is not based on individual notions of harm, nor on the teachings of a particular ideology, but on what society, through its fundamental laws, has recognized as essential. Views about the harm that the sexual conduct at issue may produce, however widely held, do not suffice to ground a conviction. This is not to say that social values no longer have a role to play. On the contrary, to ground a finding that acts are indecent, the harm must be shown to be related to a fundamental value reflected in our society's Constitution or similar fundamental laws, like bills of rights, which constitutes society's formal recognition that harm of the sort envisaged may be incompatible with its proper functioning. Unlike the community standard of tolerance test, the requirement of formal recognition inspires confidence that the values upheld by judges and jurors are truly those of Canadian society. Autonomy, liberty, equality and human dignity are among these values.

. . .

[35] The requirement of formal endorsement ensures that people will not be convicted and imprisoned for transgressing the rules and beliefs of particular individuals or groups. To incur the ultimate criminal sanction, they must have violated values which Canadian society as a whole has formally endorsed.

[36] Three types of harm have thus far emerged from the jurisprudence as being capable of supporting a finding of indecency: (1) harm to those whose autonomy and liberty may be restricted by being confronted with inappropriate conduct; (2) harm to society by predisposing others to anti-social conduct; and (3) harm to individuals participating in the conduct. Each of these types of harm is grounded in values recognized by our Constitution and similar fundamental laws. The list is not closed; other types of harm may be shown in the future to meet the standards for criminality established by *Butler*. But thus far, these are the types of harm recognized by the cases.

[37] Reference to the fundamental values of our Constitution and similar fundamental laws also eliminates types of conduct that do *not* constitute a harm in the required sense. Bad taste does not suffice: *Towne Cinema*, at p. 507. Moral views, even if strongly held, do not suffice. Similarly, the fact that most members of the community might disapprove of the conduct does not suffice: *Butler*, at p. 492. In each case, more is required to establish the necessary harm for criminal indecency.

[Chief Justice McLachlin then elaborated on each of these three *types* of harm that could ground a conviction for criminal indecency before addressing the second step in the majority's proposed approach—namely, assessing the *degree* of harm.]

4.1.4 The Degree of the Harm: Harm Incompatible with the Proper Functioning of Canadian Society

[52] At this stage, the task is to examine the degree of the harm to determine whether it is incompatible with the proper functioning of society. The threshold is high. It proclaims that as members of a diverse society, we must be prepared to tolerate conduct of

which we disapprove, short of conduct that can be objectively shown beyond a reasonable doubt to interfere with the proper functioning of society.

[53] The objective test for criminal indecency that this Court has long insisted must be our goal requires careful and express analysis of whether the alleged harm is on the evidence in the particular case truly incompatible with the proper functioning of Canadian society. This involves value judgements. What is the "proper" functioning of society? At what point do we say an activity is "incompatible" with it?

[54] Value judgements in this domain of the law, like many others, cannot be avoided. But this does not mean that the decision-making process is subjective and arbitrary. First, judges should approach the task of making value judgments with an awareness of the danger of deciding the case on the basis of unarticulated and unacknowledged values or prejudices. Second, they should make value judgments on the basis of evidence and a full appreciation of the relevant factual and legal context, to ensure that it is informed not by the judge's subjective views, but by relevant, objectively tested criteria. Third, they should carefully weigh and articulate the factors that produce the value judgements. By practices such as these, objectivity can be attained.

. . .

[56] Incompatibility with the proper functioning of society is more than a test of tolerance. The question is not what individuals or the community think about the conduct, but whether permitting it engages a harm that threatens the basic functioning of our society. This ensures in part that the harm be related to a formally recognized value, at step one. But beyond this it must be clear beyond a reasonable doubt that the conduct, not only by its nature but also in degree, rises to the level of threatening the proper functioning of our society.

[57] Whether it does so must be determined by reference to the values engaged by the particular kind of harm at stake. If the harm is based on the threat to autonomy and liberty arising from unwanted confrontation by a particular kind of sexual conduct, for example, the Crown must establish a real risk that the way people live will be significantly and adversely affected by the conduct. The number of people unwillingly exposed to the conduct and the circumstances in which they are exposed to it are critical under this head of harm. If the only people involved in or observing the conduct were willing participants, indecency on the basis of this harm will not be made out.

[58] If the harm is based on predisposing others to anti-social behaviour, a real risk that the conduct will have this effect must be proved. Vague generalizations that the sexual conduct at issue will lead to attitudinal changes and hence anti-social behaviour will not suffice. The causal link between images of sexuality and anti-social behaviour cannot be assumed. Attitudes in themselves are not crimes, however deviant they may be or disgusting they may appear. What is required is proof of links, first between the sexual conduct at issue and the formation of negative attitudes, and second between those attitudes and real risk of anti-social behaviour.

[59] Similarly, if the harm is based on physical or psychological injury to participants, it must again be shown that the harm has occurred or that there is a real risk that this will occur. Witnesses may testify as to actual harm. Expert witnesses may give evidence on the risks of potential harm. In considering psychological harm, care must be taken to avoid substituting disgust for the conduct involved, for proof of harm to the participants.

In the case of vulnerable participants, it may be easier to infer psychological harm than in cases where participants operate on an equal and autonomous basis.

[60] These are matters that can and should be established by evidence, as a general rule. When the test was the community standard of tolerance, it could be argued that judges or jurors were in a position to gauge what the community would tolerate from their own experience in the community. But a test of harm or significant risk of harm incompatible with the proper functioning of society demands more. The judge and jurors are generally unlikely to be able to gauge the risk and impact of the harm, without assistance from expert witnesses. To be sure, there may be obvious cases where no one could argue that the conduct proved in evidence is compatible with the proper functioning of society, obviating the need for an expert witness. To kill in the course of sexual conduct, to take an obvious example, would on its face be repugnant to our law and the proper functioning of our society. But in most cases, expert evidence will be required to establish that the nature and degree of the harm makes it incompatible with the proper functioning of society. In every case, a conviction must be based on evidence establishing beyond a reasonable doubt actual harm or a significant risk of actual harm. ...

[61] Where actual harm is not established and the Crown is relying on risk, the test of incompatibility with the proper functioning of society requires the Crown to establish a significant risk. Risk is a relative concept. The more extreme the nature of the harm, the lower the degree of risk that may be required to permit use of the ultimate sanction of criminal law. Sometimes, a small risk can be said to be incompatible with the proper functioning of society. For example, the risk of a terrorist attack, although small, might be so devastating in potential impact that using the criminal law to counter the risk might be appropriate. However, in most cases, the nature of the harm engendered by sexual conduct will require at least a probability that the risk will develop to justify convicting and imprisoning those engaged in or facilitating the conduct.

4.1.5 Summary of the Test

[62] Indecent criminal conduct will be established where the Crown proves beyond a reasonable doubt the following two requirements:

1. That, by its *nature*, the conduct at issue causes harm or presents a significant risk of harm to individuals or society in a way that undermines or threatens to undermine a value reflected in and thus formally endorsed through the Constitution or similar fundamental laws by, for example:

   (a) confronting members of the public with conduct that significantly interferes with their autonomy and liberty; or

   (b) predisposing others to anti-social behaviour; or

   (c) physically or psychologically harming persons involved in the conduct, and

2. That the harm or risk of harm is of a *degree* that is incompatible with the proper functioning of society.

· · ·

[63] This test, applied objectively and on the basis of evidence in successive cases as they arise, is directed to articulating legal standards that enhance the ability of persons engaged in or facilitating sexual activities to ascertain the boundary between non-criminal conduct and criminal conduct. In this way, the basic requirements of the criminal law of fair notice to potential offenders and clear enforcement standards to police will, it is hoped, be satisfied.

4.2 Application of the Test

[64] The first question is whether the conduct at issue harmed, or presented a significant risk of harm to individuals or society.

[65] The sexual acts at issue were conducted on the third floor of a private club, behind doors marked "*Privé*" and accessed only by persons in possession of the proper numerical code. The evidence establishes that a number of steps were taken to ensure that members of the public who might find the conduct inappropriate did not see the activities. Pre-membership interviews were conducted to advise of the nature of the activities and screen out persons not sharing the same interests. Only members and guests were admitted to the premises. A doorman controlled access to the principal door.

[66] On these facts, none of the kinds of harm discussed above was established. The autonomy and liberty of members of the public was not affected by unwanted confrontation with the sexual conduct in question. On the evidence, only those already disposed to this sort of sexual activity were allowed to participate and watch.

[67] Nor was there evidence of the second type of harm, the harm of predisposing people to anti-social acts or attitudes. Unlike the material at issue in *Butler*, which perpetuated abusive and humiliating stereotypes of women as objects of sexual gratification, there is no evidence of anti-social attitudes toward women, or for that matter men. No one was pressured to have sex, paid for sex, or treated as a mere sexual object for the gratification of others. The fact that L'Orage is a commercial establishment does not in itself render the sexual activities taking place there commercial in nature. Members do not pay a fee and check consent at the door; the membership fee buys access to a club where members can meet and engage in consensual activities with other individuals who have similar sexual interests. The case proceeded on the uncontested premise that all participation was on a voluntary and equal basis.

[68] Finally, there is no evidence of the third type of harm—physical or psychological harm to persons participating. The only possible danger to participants on the evidence was the risk of catching a sexually transmitted disease. However, this must be discounted as a factor because, as discussed above, it is conceptually and causally unrelated to indecency.

[69] As stated above, the categories of harm are not closed; in a future case other different harms may be alleged as a basis for criminal indecency. However, no other harms are raised by the evidence in this case. All that is raised, in the final analysis, is the assessment that the conduct amounted to "an orgy" and that Canadian society does not tolerate orgies (Rochon J.A., at para. 133). This reasoning erroneously harks back to the community standard of tolerance test, which has been replaced, as discussed, by the harm-based test developed in *Butler*.

[70] I conclude that the evidence provides no basis for concluding that the sexual conduct at issue harmed individuals or society. *Butler* is clear that criminal indecency or

obscenity must rest on actual harm or a significant risk of harm to individuals or society. The Crown failed to establish this essential element of the offence. The Crown's case must therefore fail. The majority of the Court of Appeal erred, with respect, in applying an essentially subjective community standard of tolerance test and failing to apply the harm-based test of *Butler*.

[71] It is unnecessary to proceed to the second branch of the test. However, if one did, there appears to be no evidence that the degree of alleged harm rose to the level of incompatibility with the proper functioning of society. Consensual conduct behind code-locked doors can hardly be supposed to jeopardize a society as vigorous and tolerant as Canadian society.

[72] I would allow the appeal and set aside the conviction.

BASTARACHE and LeBEL JJ (dissenting):

1. *Introduction*

. . .

[75] The majority is ... departing from the case law of this Court and proposing a new approach to indecency that is, in our view, neither desirable nor workable. It constitutes an unwarranted break with the most important principles of our past decisions regarding indecency. Our colleagues' approach replaces the community standard of tolerance with a test that treats harm as the basis of indecency rather than as a criterion for determining the community's level of tolerance. Whether or not serious social harm is sustained has never been the determinative test for indecency, and it cannot take the place of a contextual analysis of the Canadian community standard of tolerance without completely transforming the concept of indecency and rendering it meaningless.

[76] In contrast to our colleagues, we propose to continue applying the original test for indecency, which focusses on a contextual analysis of the impugned acts and incorporates the concept of harm as a significant, but not determinative, factor to consider in establishing the applicable level of tolerance. Whether or not harm is sustained is merely one of several indicators or contextual factors that make it possible to gauge the degree of tolerance of the Canadian community. In our view, all the contextual factors must be considered in every case. The application of this test to the facts of the case at bar leads to the conclusion that the impugned acts were indecent and that the appellant's establishment was a common bawdy-house within the meaning of s. 210(1) *Cr. C.*

. . .

3.2 *The Concept of Harm and Its Role in the Analysis*

. . .

[95] There can be no doubt that, since *Butler*, social harm has been a very important test for establishing indecency. For example, in *Mara*, at para. 33, this Court stated that the standard of tolerance test for a performance was "if the social harm engendered by the performance, having reference to the circumstances in which it took place, is such that the community would not tolerate it taking place." See also *Little Sisters Book and Art Emporium v. Canada (Minister of Justice)*, [2000] 2 S.C.R. 1120, 2000 SCC 69, at para. 52.

[96] However, despite the importance of the social harm test, it cannot be said to be the only standard by which the tolerance of the Canadian community for sexual practices is to be measured. The very definition of social harm warrants closer examination before this test can be applied to determine the level of tolerance of the Canadian community. ...

[97] ... [S]erious harm is not the sole criterion for determining what the Canadian community will tolerate. Harm is but one indicator of the community standard of tolerance. ...

[98] In principle, we consider the change to the legal order proposed by the majority to be inappropriate, particularly because no valid justification is given for departing from the existing test. We are convinced that this new approach strips of all relevance the social values that the Canadian community as a whole believes should be protected.

. . .

[103] In our opinion, the test adopted by the majority introduces a concept of tolerance that does not seem to be justifiable according to any principle whatsoever. This concept cannot be accepted on the pretext that harm is easier to prove or that it is desirable for this type of offence to have the same rationale as the vast majority of other criminal offences, namely the need to protect the community from harm. Social morality, which is inherent in indecency offences and is expressed through the application of the standard of tolerance, must still be allowed to play a role in all situations where it is relevant. Otherwise, the social values that the Canadian community as a whole considers worth protecting would be stripped of any relevance.

[104] Furthermore, the existence of harm is not a prerequisite for exercising the state's power to criminalize certain conduct. The existence of fundamental social and ethical considerations is sufficient: see *R. v. Malmo-Levine*, [2003] 3 S.C.R. 571, 2003 SCC 74, at p. 635. There is no principle that supports the harmonization of offences.

[105] The philosophical underpinnings of the majority's harm-based approach are found in the liberal theories of J.S. Mill. This philosopher argued that the only purpose for which state power can be rightfully exercised over a member of the community is to prevent harm to others: see J.S. Mill, *On Liberty and Considerations on Representative Government* (1946), at p. 8. This court had occasion to address the principle of harm in *Malmo-Levine*. Although that case concerned the constitutional limits on the state's power to legislate in criminal matters, the majority's reasons stressed that the justification for state intervention cannot be reduced to a single factor. There are multiple criteria for justifying state intervention in criminal matters, even if it restricts human liberty: see *Malmo-Levine*, at para. 109. Offences under the *Criminal Code* are thus based on principles and values other than harm. In the case at bar, the offence relates to social morality. To place excessive emphasis on the criterion of harm will therefore make it impossible to give effect to the moral principles in respect of which there is a consensus in the community.

[106] Our colleagues' position also raises problems relating to the determination of the level of harm required for a finding of indecency. The proposed threshold is, in our view, too demanding and too abstract. There is no justification for adopting a threshold that would require neither more nor less than proof that the sexual practices in issue will lead to social disorder. The Court has not gone that far in its past decisions; rather, it has merely concluded that encouraging anti-social conduct would be incompatible with the proper functioning of society. Why should such a notion be adopted when tolerance is clearly linked to public morality and community values? What is meant by conduct that

is incompatible with the proper functioning of society? How can proof that an act will lead to anti-social conduct be required, assuming that it is defined objectively, and why should it be required when the proceeding may concern acts that in fact fit that definition?

· · ·

[109] According to contemporary Canadian social morality, acts such as child pornography, incest, polygamy and bestiality are unacceptable regardless of whether or not they cause social harm. The community considers these acts to be harmful in themselves. Parliament enforces this social morality by enacting statutory norms in legislation such as the *Criminal Code*. The community does not tolerate degrading acts or sexual exploitation either: *Butler*, at p. 485. Nor is the purchase of sexual favours in public places accepted, as evidenced by the various provisions of the *Criminal Code* that prohibit common bawdy-houses and prostitution. In this second type of situation, morality is conveyed by means of provisions that demand that each individual case be assessed in light of its specific context and circumstances in order to gauge the Canadian community's tolerance for the acts in question. Certain acts are thus prohibited because of their harmful nature. Others are prohibited because of the context and places in which they arise, as in the case at bar. Harm is thus ultimately linked to a concept of social morality. There is also harm where what is acceptable to the community in terms of public morals is compromised.

[110] Thus, the need to prove societal dysfunction to a degree approaching social disorder would appear to unduly restrict the situations in which a court could reach a finding of indecency. The importance of this requirement profoundly alters the traditional concept of tolerance by suggesting that the public will tolerate anything that is contrary to public morals unless it can be established that an act will cause significant social disorder.

· · ·

[116] These reasons are sufficient for rejecting a test for the standard of tolerance that is based solely on harm. Our colleagues' approach has too many shortcomings, both practical and theoretical. It introduces a concept of tolerance that appears to be supported by no principle whatsoever. It is also hard to find support for this position in the case law. We will now set out what we feel to be a more appropriate approach.

[Justices Bastarache and LeBel then set out an approach whereby the Canadian community's tolerance should be determined based on an assessment of two factors: the nature of the acts and their context. Regarding the context in which the acts take place, Bastarache and LeBel JJ explained that the following factors should be considered: (1) the private or public nature of the place; (2) the type of participants and the composition of the audience; (3) the nature of the warning given regarding the acts; (4) the measures taken to limit access to the place; (5) the commercial nature of the place and the acts; (6) the purpose of the acts; (7) the conduct of the participants; and (8) harm suffered by the participants.]

· · ·

4.3 Conclusion Regarding Indecency

[153] In the case at bar, the impugned sexual acts were very explicit acts, and they took place in a commercial establishment that was easily accessible to the general public. This situation caused a certain form of social harm resulting from the failure to meet the minimum standards of public morality. In light of these contextual factors, we are of the

opinion that the sexual acts performed in the appellant's establishment clearly offended the Canadian community standard of tolerance and were therefore indecent. Our analysis does not permit us to conclude that the Canadian community would tolerate the performance, in a commercial establishment to which the public has easy access, of group sexual activities on the scale of those that took place in this case. The appellant's establishment is therefore a common bawdy-house within the meaning of s. 210(1) *Cr. C.*

5. Disposition

[154] We would have dismissed the appeal and upheld the appellant's conviction.

———————————

Canadian Foundation for Children, Youth and the Law v Canada (Attorney General), 2004 SCC 4, [2004] 1 SCR 76, extracted in Chapter 1, is another case that, at core, was concerned with the appropriate uses of the criminal law. Recall that this case addressed the constitutionality of s 43 of the *Criminal Code* authorizing the use of force "by way of correction toward a pupil or child ... if the force does not exceed what is reasonable under the circumstances." Even if one takes the position that corporal punishment of children is an evil that society has an interest in eradicating, is the criminal law the best tool for achieving this goal?

Sir Patrick Devlin represents what one might call a "conservative" position on the use of the criminal law, whereas HLA Hart (like John Stuart Mill) reflects a conventionally "liberal" view. However, the landscape of theoretical perspectives on the appropriate uses and limits of the criminal law is much richer than just these two broad canopies of thought. Feminist theory, for example, has made crucial contributions to modern analysis of the criminal law. It is important to bear in mind that the field of feminist approaches to the criminal law is itself broad and there is no single "feminist" perspective. Nevertheless, feminist legal theories share certain common concerns and certain general orientations to the analysis of the criminal justice system. (See e.g. DG Réaume, "What's Distinctive About Feminist Analysis of Law? A Conceptual Analysis of Women's Exclusion from Law" (1996) 2 Leg Theory 265.) The next section of this chapter addresses prostitution as a case study on the limits of the criminal law. In its 1985 report, the Special Committee on Pornography and Prostitution (the Fraser Committee) canvassed a series of positions on the just scope of the criminal law and offered the following general observations:

> It is the feminist position on the rights question which provides a significant challenge to orthodox liberal theorists. According to feminists, the liberal tends to characterize the rights issue in terms of the infringement by the state on the rights of an individual. Little or no attention is paid to the fact that rights issues often develop out of what is, at base, a conflict in the exercise of rights by two individuals. True, the immediate agent of one side may be the state, but that does not alter the fact that a clash of rights between individuals is involved.
>
> If this is correct, then the legal system is not only called upon to protect rights, but also to choose which right is entitled to greater protection. This is unlikely to give the liberal any trouble when it is clear that the exercise of a right by one has caused harm to the other in the exercise of those rights. Much less clear is the liberal reaction when the opposing right has not, in fact, been abridged in the concrete sense but only in the abstract, for example, when a woman claims a pornographic publication infringes her right to equality in that it treats women as degraded or

subhuman. Here, the liberal would argue that in the absence of a tangible interference with the "victim's" right, there is no warrant for curtailing the offending activity.

The feminist response to this line of argument is that it demonstrates the bankruptcy of the narrow characterization of the harm principle, and points to the need to redefine the notion of rights in liberal theory. As long as rights in the liberal glossary mean liberty in the sense of being free to act without restraint, they have little value in a society in which fundamental inequalities exist. Thus for women, the fact that on the formal level they enjoy the liberty to do certain things is of little consequence if the social environment prevents the exercise of those rights, and there is no correlative duty on the part of others to see that the rights are exercisable. ...

Feminist writers also join issue with the liberals on the interpretation of the "harm" requirement. As the discussion of the liberal view has demonstrated, the philosophical liberal has a limited perception of harm as a basis for invoking legal proscription of restraint. Either measurable harm, for example, economic, physical or mental to an individual, or statistically verifiable general harm must be established.

Feminists react in two ways to this approach. The first is to challenge the assertion that the "harm" principle is necessarily so limited. Given their perception that sexism in our society is endemic, and their belief that eradication of it requires recognition of the special claims of women, they construct a broader notion of harm which includes a social harm, and in particular, the adverse and potentially divisive effects of a significant segment of the male community developing or reinforcing a thoroughly misogynistic attitude.

Secondly, they will argue that, even if a narrower view of harm is adopted, there is enough data to demonstrate that women are victimized by the sexism inherent in pornography and prostitution. They point to an increasing body of research by social psychologists which, it is claimed, suggests a link between pornography and violence against both women and children. The existence of this link is, they argue, supported by a growing number of reported cases in which battered women report that pornography influenced the conduct of their partners. Finally, they claim, common sense would suggest that frequent exposure to this type of material is likely to have an adverse and brutalizing effect on male perceptions of women as well as male sexuality.

In the same way that feminist writers have difficulty with liberal theory, so they reject acceptance of conservative ideas. On the surface, feminist and conservative theory seem to coincide in that they see "harm" as embracing harm to the community or to society in general. Moreover, insofar as feminist theory views the sexual exploitation of women as subversive of society, it has some similarities to the disintegration theory of Devlin. However, feminist writers are quick to point out that similarities are superficial. They see conservative theory as oppressive and unsatisfactory, because its fundamental assumption is that the ideal society is one in which women have a subordinate and submissive role, and in which sexual expression of all but the most orthodox type is frowned upon.

As you look back over the cases that you have read and think about the issues that follow, consider how attention to these themes and principles raised in various feminist analyses might affect one's view of the proper limits and scope of the criminal law.

II. PROSTITUTION/SEX WORK AND THE CRIMINAL LAW

A highly contentious contemporary issue regarding the limits of the criminal law concerns the propriety of using the criminal law to address social concerns arising from prostitution or, as some of those engaged in these activities and their advocates prefer to label it, sex work. The *Criminal Code* does not directly prohibit prostitution, but it prohibits a host of activities related to it. For many years, s 213(1)(c) prohibited communicating for the purposes of engaging in prostitution or obtaining the services of a prostitute; s 212(1)(j) made it a criminal offence to live off the avails of prostitution; and s 210(1) prohibited keeping a "common bawdy-house." These and other provisions have been the subject of sustained public, legislative, and academic scrutiny and debate. As you will see, these debates have focused on the appropriate use and scope of the criminal law, and have been centrally concerned with claims about harm—both the harms thought to be caused by prostitution and the harms created by the criminal law itself.

Consider, for example, the 1985 report of the Special Committee on Pornography and Prostitution in Canada (the Fraser Committee), which offered the following conclusions on the use of the criminal law to regulate prostitution.

The Role of the Criminal Law

… A wide range of views were put to us during the hearings as to the appropriate role of criminal law in dealing with both pornography and prostitution. These ranged from the extreme conservative position that there should be a complete identification of the criminal law of the state with the "moral law," to the extreme libertarian view that the criminal law should intrude only when physical harm had been caused by one person to another.

It is our view that the role of the criminal law lies mid-way between these extremes. The view that criminal law is somehow the solvent of all social ills is, we believe, naive. History has shown that the enactment of draconian laws has typically had a marginal impact on behaviour patterns. …

We appreciate fully that law, especially criminal law, has an important and often invisible impact in moulding and influencing peoples' behaviour, and it is clear that some criminal law provisions affect behaviour beneficially without the instrumentation of enforcement. …

We also disagree with the view that the criminal law should be confined to the tangible harm caused by one individual to another. Although we think that there should be less rather than more intrusion of the criminal law into the lives of citizens, we also think that it has a wider, legitimate ambit than is often claimed for it. Criminal law is, in part, a reflection of the values of society.

Conclusion

We believe that the development of theory which views pornography as an assault on human rights, will have to be integrated into the conceptual framework of the criminal law on pornography. Our recommendations thus include a complete reworking of the *Criminal Code* prohibitions in this area, to create offences based not on concepts of sexual immorality but rather on the offences to equality, dignity and physical integrity which we believe are involved in pornography. The concern for the vulnerability of young persons has prompted us to devise a number of prohibitions against the use of young persons in sexually explicit material, against the sale, distribution or possession of such material, and the accessibility of such material to young people. …

With respect to prostitution, our recommendations feature withdrawal of sanctions against simple soliciting: only when the conduct causes actual adverse effect on neighbours and environment is it criminalized. The adult prostitute is accorded by our proposed regime, some leeway to conduct his or her business in privacy and dignity. We would permit one or two prostitutes to receive customers in their own home, hoping thereby to provide people with a safe alternative to the street and parked cars. In addition, we are recommending that the possibility of allowing small prostitution establishments in non-residential areas be discussed by the federal government and the provinces and territories.

The idea that adults who engage in prostitution can and should be counted upon to take responsibility for themselves has led us to recommend cutting back the criminal prohibitions against procuring and living on the avails of prostitution. Only procuring which is effected by coercion or threats will be criminalized in the case of an adult. So, too, we stipulate that receiving financial support from an adult prostitute should be criminal only when that support is exacted by means of coercion or threats.

Where young persons are concerned, the emphasis of our recommendations is to provide strong protection against exploitation. Procuring children to engage in sexual activity for reward is made criminal even where no threats are used. So, too, is receiving support from the paid sexual activities of young persons. We have recommended adding to the *Criminal Code* a specific prohibition against engaging, or offering or attempting to engage, in sexual activity with a young person. However, we do not recommend criminalizing the behaviour of young persons, except to the extent that they come within the general prohibitions because of their own exploitation of other young persons.

The Supreme Court of Canada had an opportunity to consider the constitutionality of the provisions dealing with prostitution in *Reference re ss 193 and 195.1(1)(c) of the Criminal Code*, [1990] 1 SCR 1123 [*Prostitution Reference*]. The argument put before the Court was that the common bawdy-house and communication offences in the *Criminal Code* were inconsistent with s 7 of the Charter (on grounds of vagueness and unfairness) and that the communication offence offended the s 2(b) protection of freedom of expression. The majority of the Court held that neither prohibition contravened the principles of fundamental justice then recognized in s 7, and that, although the communication law offended s 2(b), the limitation on freedom of expression was justified under s 1 because the legislation was "aimed at the social nuisance of street solicitation and at its eventual elimination" (at 1140). Justice Wilson (L'Heureux-Dubé J concurring) dissented, finding breaches of both s 7 and s 2(b). She concluded that the breach of s 2(b) could not be justified because "to imprison people for exercising their constitutionally protected freedom of expression, even if they are exercising it for purposes of prostitution (which is not itself prohibited), is not a proportionate way of dealing with the public or social nuisance at which the legislation is aimed" (at 1223).

Despite the majority's conclusion that these provisions were constitutionally compliant, serious debate about the criminalization of prostitution/sex work continued after the Court's decision in the *Prostitution Reference*.

In 2006, the Standing Committee on Justice and Human Rights issued a report arising from its study of the nature and effect of criminal laws relating to prostitution in Canada. The report extensively outlined the scope and incidence of prostitution in Canada, the harmful effects of prostitution on women and communities, and the historical legal response to prostitution through the use of the criminal law. The following extract from the committee's report outlines its conclusions regarding the negative and positive effects of criminalizing prostitution-related activities.

The Challenge of Change: A Study of Canada's Criminal Prostitution Laws
Report of the Standing Committee on Justice and Human Rights
House of Commons (December 2006) at 61-70 (footnotes omitted)

A. Negative Effects of Criminalizing Prostitution-Related Activities

Like many of the witnesses heard during the Subcommittee's study, the literature concerning the impact of prostitution laws on the health, safety and wellbeing of prostitutes indicates that criminalization intended to control prostitution related activities in Canada jeopardizes the safety of prostitutes, as well as their access to health and social services.

In the following paragraphs, we examine the concerns raised by witnesses who maintained that the current provisions pertaining to prostitution are harmful to prostitutes' health and safety, as they create an illegal market that is conducive to abuse and exploitation and encourage secrecy and the isolation of those selling sexual services.

1. Section 213 of the Criminal Code: Prohibition of Communication in Public Places for the Purpose of Prostitution

Section 213 is the most frequently enforced of all criminal law provisions relating to prostitution. Since it was introduced in 1985, this provision has accounted for 90% of prostitution-related offences reported by the police. Yet numerous studies have shown that section 213 has not had the deterrent effect desired. It has not adequately reduced the incidence of street prostitution or even the social nuisance associated with its practice. These studies indicate that enforcement of section 213 has instead served to move prostitution activities from one place to another, and in so doing, has made those selling sexual services more vulnerable.

(a) Secrecy and Isolation

During our study, we heard that street level prostitutes face the following paradox in order to ensure their safety and at the same time avoid arrest under section 213 of the *Criminal Code*:

> Working in an isolated area discouraged attention from police and residents but increased risks from bad dates and other aggressors; working in a well-lit, populated area discouraged bad dates but often led to unwanted attention from police and residents.

In many of the cities we visited, a number of witnesses indicated that the enforcement of section 213 forced street prostitution activities into isolated areas, where they asserted that the risk of abuse and violence is very high. These witnesses told us that by forcing people to work in secrecy, far from protection services, and by allowing clients complete anonymity, section 213 endangers those who are already very vulnerable selling sexual service on the street. This is what the director of Pivot Legal Society, Katrina Pacey, told us:

> In these areas, sex workers are more vulnerable to predation, robbery, harassment, and murder. In these areas, they're unable to access help if they're in trouble.

According to Professor Lowman, the isolation resulting from the application of section 213 has made street prostitutes especially vulnerable to violence and abuse. His research suggests that predators who are looking to abuse women are generally drawn to street prostitution because it allows them to remain out of sight and anonymous. Lowman maintains that violent men are not inclined to hire prostitutes who work for an agency or prostitution establishment for fear of being identified. According to him, it should therefore not be surprising that 80% of the women murdered in British Columbia between 1975 and 1994 were street prostitutes and did not work for prostitution establishments or agencies.

The murder and disappearance of a large number of women prostitutes in the last 20 years are cited as the most compelling evidence of the extreme violence to which street prostitutes are subjected. Lowman maintains that these murders and disappearances are also indicative of the deteriorating conditions in prostitution since the introduction of section 213 in 1985:

> I argue that the communicating law [section 213] played a pivotal role in creating a social and legal milieu that facilitated these homicides, and that Canadian prostitution law puts lower-echelon sex workers at risk.

During our hearings, a number of witnesses maintained that the introduction of the communicating law (section 213) also led to the scattering of prostitutes, making them more vulnerable to violence and exploitation. Whereas in the past street prostitutes frequently worked in teams in an effort to reduce the risk of violence (for example by helping take down information such as clients' licence plate numbers and descriptions), they now tend to work in isolation from one another. While this practice has the advantage of attracting less attention from police, it also minimizes information-sharing, making prostitutes more vulnerable to meeting violent clients since they are not as well informed and are often less aware of the resources available to assist them. Similarly, witnesses also indicated that prostitutes in these areas are often unable to obtain assistance and exchange information about health and safety, since access to health and social services, as well as basic services such as public transportation, restaurants and public telephones is generally limited in isolated areas.

Finally, various social service workers reported that they have experienced, greater difficulty reaching street prostitutes to offer health services, information or to provide condoms or lists of bad clients due to the enforcement of section 213.

(b) Frequent Changes of Location Due to Policing and Court Orders

The vulnerability of persons engaging in street prostitution is also related to the fact that they frequently change locations. As a result of an arrest, fear of arrest, or a court order, such people are often forced to move to another area, effectively separating them from friends, co-workers, regular customers and familiar places. A number of witnesses indicated that this instability jeopardizes prostitutes' health, safety and well-being.

(c) Screening Clients

According to a number of witnesses, section 213 also places street prostitutes in danger by forcing them to conclude their negotiations with clients more quickly, often leading them to get into the client's car too quickly. ...

Working out the details of the transaction before getting into a vehicle or going to a private location was considered important by all the prostitutes who testified. They told us that public bargaining would give them an opportunity to assess the likelihood of a potential client having violent tendencies. Summarizing the statements of 91 street prostitutes from Vancouver, Katrina Pacey said:

> Sex workers describe their fear of being caught by police while negotiating the terms of a transaction with a potential client. As a result, they feel rushed in these negotiations and are not able to take the time required to adequately assess a client and to follow their own instincts, or to maybe note if that client has appeared on a bad date list.

Witnesses also suggested that section 213 places prostitutes in a weak bargaining position. Many current and former prostitutes stated that it is more difficult to negotiate prices and services once they are in the vehicle. They are also at a disadvantage because, to avoid being arrested in sting operations, they usually let the client determine the prices and services. Gwen Smith, a member of PEERS Victoria and the Canadian National Coalition of Experiential Women, said in her testimony, "Due to the worry of being trapped by undercover police, women generally let the john name an act for a price first, giving him the advantage in negotiations."

2. Section 210 of the Criminal Code: Prohibition of Bawdy-Houses

Although section 210, which prohibits bawdy houses, is seldom enforced, witnesses indicated that many people are at risk every day of being charged with being found in a common bawdy-house. Throughout our study, witnesses also maintained that this section leaves prostitutes with few options if they wish to sell their sexual services under safer conditions. One prostitute made the following points in a brief submitted to the Subcommittee:

> Preventing those with the objective of engaging in prostitution from creating a safe place to do so only serves to create unsafe places to do business. As the law is now, the only possible way to carry out sex work is by going to home of a client. The unknown factors involved in a home visit (under current code) for the sex worker create a dangerous situation. One does not know if the client has any cemented connections to the address provided and therefore cannot be provided with security even if measures are taken to inform a friend or colleague where they are and who they are with. In fact, article 212 actually prevents a sex worker from taking such precautionary measures.

In addition to prohibiting prostitutes from creating a stable environment, whether by using their residence or some other fixed location, witnesses argued that section 210 makes their lives more insecure by encouraging landlords to rescind the lease of anyone suspected of committing acts of prostitution. ...

[The committee then briefly addressed s 211 of the *Criminal Code*, which prohibits transporting someone to a bawdy house.]

4. Section 212 of the Criminal Code: Procuring a Person to Engage in Prostitution or Living Wholly or in Part on the Avails of Prostitution of Another

According to the testimony of a number of former prostitutes, section 212 increases the isolation of those who engage in prostitution by criminalizing cohabitation and the establishment of an employer-employee relationship. Witnesses indicated that this prohibition is often disadvantageous for prostitutes who in some cases regard such options as having economic and safety benefits. Prostitutes told us that cohabitation is a good way to save money and can also reduce the risk of abuse and violence by reducing prostitutes' isolation. Some witnesses indicated that the relationship with a manager or employer can also be beneficial. Some people reported feeling more comfortable and safer when a third party is responsible for finding and screening clients for them and providing them with a place to carry on their prostitution activities.

5. Other Effects of the Criminalization of Prostitutes

Throughout our study, a number of prostitutes told us that they lived every day with the fear of losing custody of their children, losing their lawful employment, being stigmatized and having to live with the devastating effects of the stigma of being a prostitute for their entire lives.

> [TRANSLATION] The stigma associated with prostitution activity is a powerful social label that discredits and taints anyone to whom it is attached. It radically changes the way that person perceives himself/herself and is perceived as a person. Stigmatization exposes such people to various forms of violence, abuse and contempt. The stigma that sex workers feel or the fear of discrimination has a huge effect on their lives. As a result, they seldom trust government-run systems because they feel judged and categorized by those systems.

To avoid this stigma and facing criminal charges, the Subcommittee heard that the vast majority of prostitutes do not report violence committed against them. ...

Witnesses said that prostitutes are thus deprived of police protection, since the police are seen as an adversary rather than an ally due to criminalization. This leaves prostitutes more vulnerable to predators.

A number of witnesses indicated that criminalization also contributes to the violence against prostitutes by making violence easier to justify. Kara Gillies told us that:

> The criminal laws increase the risk of violence by prohibiting a series of safety-enhancing measures. The law also reinforces the characterization of sex workers as aberrant and therefore, in some way, acceptable targets of derision and abuse.

[The subcommittee also noted the adverse effects of criminal records and the economic insecurity that these provisions can visit on prostitutes.]

B. The Positive Effects of Criminalization

1. An Important Message in the Campaign Against Prostitution in All Its Forms

Other witnesses noted how important the criminalization of clients of prostitution and pimps was in the broader campaign that they feel Canada should conduct to eradicate prostitution in all its forms, whether between consenting adults or not. The witnesses who made this argument regard persons who engage in prostitution as victims of an inherently violent, alienating activity that makes up part of the oppression of women by men.

This viewpoint is reflected in the testimony of Lyne Kurtzman of the Alliance de recherche IREF-Relais femmes of the Université du Québec à Montréal:

> We believe it is time to take a stand on prostitution and to define our position as a society. … prostitution practice [is based on] an unequal relationship between the sexes and specific exploitation of a small percentage of women. We must avoid introducing provisions that remove barriers to the trade in women's bodies and legitimize the fact that men have unlimited access to the bodies of a certain number of women, thus creating two classes of female citizens: so-called respectable citizens and those dedicated to the sexual comfort of men.

Most of the people who define prostitution in these terms feel that it is Parliament's responsibility to censure the act of prostitution by criminalizing men who buy sexual services, as well as those who live on the avails of prostitution of another person, and in so doing, support all women who are engaged in prostitution and who are, consequently, victims of sexual exploitation and inequality between the sexes. The aim of the message is to discourage prostitution. For the proponents of this view, the primary purpose of criminalization is deterrence by sending the message of disapproval of prostitution.

2. An Instrument of Prevention and Intervention for Prostitutes and for Their Clients

Like the vast majority of the witnesses who testified before us, police officers generally recognize that enforcement activity based on section 213 of the *Criminal Code* does not lead to a reduction in the incidence of street prostitution. They agree that such activity merely moves the problem to another area or disperses it. Nevertheless, many police officers view section 213 as a useful and necessary instrument of prevention and intervention.

According to a number of police officers who testified before the Subcommittee, enforcement of section 213 offers them the opportunity to protect female prostitutes from a drug habit, from their pimp or from the inherent dangers of prostitution.

A police officer who testified in a private hearing argued that simply taking prostitutes off the street, even for a short period, is itself a significant benefit of criminalization. This view is also evident in the testimony of Doug Le Pard, Deputy Chief of the Vancouver Police Department:

> When we charge a sex trade worker, it is often in an attempt to create a gap or wedge between the sex trade worker and her pimp. With conditions placed on her, she becomes less of a marketable commodity and less of an asset. With less peer and pimp pressure on her, she may have the chance to work towards getting her life together and exiting the sex trade. Criminal charges can be and are stayed to assist sex trade workers who are seeking to exit the sex trade.
>
> … the criminal law [has been used] as a tool to compel young women to seek or take advantage of resources that may help them exit the sex trade. For example, it might be a condition of probation that requires they meet with a counsellor who can help them develop exit strategies.

During the Subcommittee's hearings, police officers also stated that section 213 was useful in deterring clients. They said that many clients buy sexual services because they do not understand the harm that they are doing to society by engaging in such activities and very often are unaware of the desperate situation of most women who engage in prostitution. Having these factors explained to them in "john school" often discourages them from taking part in this kind of activity. Sergeant Matt Kelly of the Vancouver Police Department's vice squad stated that:

> ... with the johns, section 213 allows us to educate and reduce some of the myths you've heard that exist around the sex trade industry, such as that the women actually enjoy it and they've chosen to go into it. These, of course, are myths.

In the same vein, Staff Sergeant Terry Welsh of the Ottawa Police Service made the following statements:

> Over the past seven years I've been dealing with using section 213 to assist with the education of both the customers and the sex trade workers. In dealing with section 213, it gives me the authority to arrest individuals, give them the option of attending an educational program—john school—and give them the education, show them the risks, the threats, the issues that are on the street to allow them to make a conscious decision about what is really happening in our community.

In this respect, criminalization or arrest is seen as a form of social intervention.

In conclusion, although the witnesses differed in their opinions on the effects of these laws on prostitution and on the appropriate legislative response to prostitution, they all agreed that, at present, the most marginalized individuals are the ones most likely to experience the consequences of criminalization.

The report goes on to assess a number of models for reform. Ultimately, the committee was unable to reach consensus on the proper role of the criminal law in matters of prostitution. The report states that the majority of the committee (composed of Liberal, New Democratic, and Bloc Québécois members) "strongly believe that prostitution is above all a public health issue, and not only a criminal law issue. What they propose is therefore a pragmatic approach that recognizes the importance of prevention, education, treatment and harm reduction measures for all persons involved in the many forms of prostitution, from sexual slavery and survival sex, to the exchange of sexual services between consenting adults" (at 85). The report goes on to explain that "[t]he Conservative members agree that the status quo with respect to the enforcement of laws is unacceptable, but disagree that decriminalization is the solution. ... The Conservatives therefore call for legal and social reforms which would reduce all prostitution through criminal sanctions that clearly target abusers (johns and pimps), and improve the ability of those engaged in prostitution—the victims—to quit. They propose a new approach to criminal justice in which the perpetrators of crime would fund, through heavy fines, the rehabilitation and support of the victims they create" (at 91).

Parliament did not take any legislative steps to reform the laws governing prostitution following this report. Soon, the debate about whether and how the criminal law should deal with issues of sex work and prostitution found its way back into the courts. In British Columbia, a grassroots organization called the Downtown Eastside Sex Workers United Against Violence

(SWUAV) initiated a challenge to the laws criminalizing adult prostitution. That litigation produced an important constitutional law decision on public interest standing (*Canada (Attorney General) v Downtown Eastside Sex Workers United Against Violence Society*, 2012 SCC 45, [2012] 2 SCR 524), a holding that made it easier for those not themselves charged with an offence to nevertheless challenge the constitutionality of a law. However, it was a challenge to the laws initiated in Ontario that brought the issues of the constitutionality of the prostitution laws back to the Supreme Court of Canada in *Canada (Attorney General) v Bedford*, 2013 SCC 72, [2013] 3 SCR 1101. In the intervening years between the *Prostitution Reference* and *Bedford* the social and policy debate carried on, but the jurisprudence governing s 7 of the Charter had also grown and developed. The Court's decision shows both the evolution of the debate surrounding this aspect of Canadian criminal law, as well as the central role that s 7 of the Charter, with its "principles of fundamental justice," has assumed in regulating the scope and limits of the criminal law.

Canada (Attorney General) v Bedford
Supreme Court of Canada
2013 SCC 72, [2013] 3 SCR 1101

THE CHIEF JUSTICE:

[1] It is not a crime in Canada to sell sex for money. However, it is a crime to keep a bawdy-house, to live on the avails of prostitution or to communicate in public with respect to a proposed act of prostitution. It is argued that these restrictions on prostitution put the safety and lives of prostitutes at risk, and are therefore unconstitutional.

[2] These appeals and the cross-appeal are not about whether prostitution should be legal or not. They are about whether the laws Parliament has enacted on how prostitution may be carried out pass constitutional muster. I conclude that they do not. I would therefore make a suspended declaration of invalidity, returning the question of how to deal with prostitution to Parliament.

I. The Case

[3] Three applicants, all current or former prostitutes, brought an application seeking declarations that three provisions of the *Criminal Code*, R.S.C. 1985, c. C-46, are unconstitutional.

[4] The three impugned provisions criminalize various activities related to prostitution. They are primarily concerned with preventing public nuisance, as well as the exploitation of prostitutes. Section 210 makes it an offence to be an inmate of a bawdy-house, to be found in a bawdy-house without lawful excuse, or to be an owner, landlord, lessor, tenant, or occupier of a place who knowingly permits it to be used as a bawdy-house. Section 212(1)(j) makes it an offence to live on the avails of another's prostitution. Section 213(1)(c) makes it an offence to either stop or attempt to stop, or communicate or attempt to communicate with, someone in a public place for the purpose of engaging in prostitution or hiring a prostitute.

[5] However, prostitution itself is not illegal. It is not against the law to exchange sex for money. Under the existing regime, Parliament has confined lawful prostitution to two

categories: street prostitution and "out-calls"—where the prostitute goes out and meets the client at a designated location, such as the client's home. This reflects a policy choice on Parliament's part. Parliament is not precluded from imposing limits on where and how prostitution may be conducted, as long as it does so in a way that does not infringe the constitutional rights of prostitutes.

[6] The applicants allege that all three provisions infringe s. 7 of the *Canadian Charter of Rights and Freedoms* by preventing prostitutes from implementing certain safety measures—such as hiring security guards or "screening" potential clients—that could protect them from violent clients. The applicants also allege that s. 213(1)(c) infringes s. 2(b) of the *Charter*, and that none of the provisions are saved under s. 1.

[7] The backgrounds of the three applicants as revealed in their evidence were reviewed in the application judge's decision (2010 ONSC 4264, 102 O.R. (3d) 321).

[8] Terri Jean Bedford was born in Collingwood, Ontario, in 1959, and as of 2010 had 14 years of experience working as a prostitute in various Canadian cities. She worked as a street prostitute, a massage parlour attendant, an escort, an owner and manager of an escort agency, and a dominatrix. Ms. Bedford had a difficult childhood and adolescence during which she was subjected to various types of abuse. She also encountered brutal violence throughout her career—largely, she stated, while working on the street. In her experience, indoor prostitution is safer than prostitution on the street, although she conceded that safety of an indoor location can vary. Ms. Bedford has been convicted of both keeping and being an inmate of a common bawdy-house, for which she has paid a number of fines and served 15 months in jail.

[9] When she ran an escort service in the 1980s, Ms. Bedford instituted various safety measures, including: ensuring someone else was on location during in-calls, except during appointments with well-known clients; ensuring that women were taken to and from out-call appointments by a boyfriend, husband, or professional driver; if an appointment was at a hotel, calling the hotel to verify the client's name and hotel room number; if an appointment was at a client's home, calling the client's phone to ensure it was the correct number; turning down appointments from clients who sounded intoxicated; and verifying that credit card numbers matched the names of clients. She claimed she was not aware of any incidents of violence by the clientele towards her employees during that time. At some point in the 1990s, Ms. Bedford ran the Bondage Bungalow, where she offered dominatrix services. She also instituted various safety measures at this establishment, and claimed she only experienced one incident of "real violence" (application decision, at para. 30).

[10] Ms. Bedford is not currently working in prostitution but asserted that she would like to return to working as a dominatrix in a secure, indoor location; however, she is concerned that in doing so, she would be exposed to criminal liability. Furthermore, she does not want the people assisting her to be subject to criminal liability due to the living on the avails of prostitution provision.

[11] Amy Lebovitch was born in Montréal in 1979. She comes from a stable background and attended both CEGEP and university. She currently works as a prostitute and has done so since approximately 1997 in various cities in Canada. She worked first as a street prostitute, then as an escort, and later in a fetish house. Ms. Lebovitch considers herself lucky that she was never subjected to violence during her years working on the streets. She moved off the streets to work at the escort agency after seeing other women's injuries and hearing stories of the violence suffered by other street prostitutes. Ms. Lebovitch

maintains that she felt safer in an indoor location; she attributed remaining safety issues mainly to poor management. Ms. Lebovitch experienced one notable instance of violence, which she did not report to the police out of fear of police scrutiny and the possibility of criminal charges.

[12] Presently, Ms. Lebovitch primarily works independently out of her home, where she takes various safety precautions, including: making sure client telephone calls are from unblocked numbers; not taking calls from clients who sound drunk, high, or in another manner undesirable; asking for expectations upfront; taking clients' full names and verifying them using directory assistance; getting referrals from regular clients; and calling a third party—her "safe call"—when the client arrives and before he leaves. Ms. Lebovitch fears being charged and convicted under the bawdy-house provisions and the consequent possibility of forfeiture of her home. She says that the fear of criminal charges has caused her to work on the street on occasion. She is also concerned that her partner will be charged with living on the avails of prostitution. She has never been charged with a criminal offence of any kind. Ms. Lebovitch volunteers as the spokesperson for Sex Professionals of Canada ("SPOC"), and she also records information from women calling to report "bad dates"—incidents that ended in violence or theft. Ms. Lebovitch stated that she enjoys her job and does not plan to leave it in the foreseeable future.

[13] Valerie Scott was born in Moncton, New Brunswick, in 1958. She is currently the executive director of SPOC, and she no longer works as a prostitute. In the past, she worked indoors, from her home or in hotel rooms; she also worked as a prostitute on the street, in massage parlours, and she ran a small escort business. She has never been charged with a criminal offence of any kind. When Ms. Scott worked from home, she would screen new clients by meeting them in public locations. She never experienced significant harm working from home. Around 1984, as awareness about HIV/AIDS increased, Ms. Scott was compelled to work as a street prostitute, since indoor clients felt entitled not to wear condoms. On the street, she was subjected to threats of violence, as well as verbal and physical abuse. Ms. Scott described some precautions street prostitutes took prior to the enactment of the communicating law, including working in pairs or threes and having another prostitute visibly write down the client's licence plate number, so he would know he was traceable if something was to go wrong.

[14] Ms. Scott worked as an activist and, among other things, advocated against Bill C-49 (which included the current communicating provision). Ms. Scott stated that following the enactment of the communicating law, the Canadian Organization for the Rights of Prostitutes ("CORP") began receiving calls from women working in prostitution about the increased enforcement of the laws and the prevalence of bad dates. In response, Ms. Scott was involved in setting up a drop-in and phone centre for prostitutes in Toronto; within the first year, Ms. Scott spoke to approximately 250 prostitutes whose main concerns were client violence and legal matters arising from arrest. In 2000, Ms. Scott formed SPOC to revitalize and continue the work previously done by CORP. As the executive director of this organization, she testified before a Parliamentary Subcommittee on Solicitation Laws in 2005. Over the years, Ms. Scott estimates that she has spoken with approximately 1,500 women working in prostitution. If this challenge is successful, Ms. Scott would like to operate an indoor prostitution business. While she recognizes that clients may be dangerous in both outdoor and indoor locations, she would institute

safety precautions such as checking identification of clients, making sure other people are close by during appointments to intervene if needed, and hiring a bodyguard.

[15] The three applicants applied pursuant to rule 14.05(3)(g.1) of the *Rules of Civil Procedure*, R.R.O. 1990, Reg. 194, for an order that the provisions restricting prostitution are unconstitutional. The evidentiary record consists of over 25,000 pages of evidence in 88 volumes. The affidavit evidence was accompanied by a large volume of studies, reports, newspaper articles, legislation, Hansard and many other documents. Some of the affiants were cross-examined.

IV. *Discussion*

. . .

A. *Preliminary Issues*

(1) *Revisiting the Prostitution Reference*

[38] Certainty in the law requires that courts follow and apply authoritative precedents. Indeed, this is the foundational principle upon which the common law relies.

[39] The issue of when, if ever, such precedents may be departed from takes two forms. The first "vertical" question is when, if ever, a lower court may depart from a precedent established by a higher court. The second "horizontal" question is when a court such as the Supreme Court of Canada may depart from its own precedents.

[40] In this case, the precedent in question is the Supreme Court of Canada's 1990 advisory opinion in the *Prostitution Reference*, which upheld the constitutionality of the prohibitions on bawdy-houses and communicating—two of the three provisions challenged in this case. The questions in that case were whether the laws infringed s. 7 or s. 2(b) of the *Charter*, and, if so, whether the limit was justified under s. 1. The Court concluded that neither of the impugned laws were inconsistent with s. 7, and that although the communicating law infringed s. 2(b), it was a justifiable limit under s. 1 of the *Charter*. ...

[The application judge (the judge of "first instance") in this case held that she was not bound by the *Prostitution Reference* because some of the legal issues were different; the governing law had evolved since 1990, the record before her was richer; and the social, political, and economic context had changed over those 24 years. The chief justice held that a trial judge is not bound to follow a prior higher court decision "when a new legal issue is raised, or if there is a significant change in the circumstances or evidence." Although Chief Justice McLachlin indicated that "the threshold for revisiting a matter is not an easy one to reach," she found that, in this case, with respect to the s 7 argument, there were both new issues raised and substantial legal change in the intervening years. The application judge was therefore entitled to reconsider whether these provisions offended s 7. As to the question of whether the Supreme Court of Canada should depart from its previous decision (the question of "horizontal precedent") McLachlin CJ explained that this turns on a balancing exercise "in which the Court must weigh correctness against certainty."]

. . .

B. *Section 7 Analysis*

[57] In the discussion that follows, I first consider whether the applicants have established that the impugned laws impose limits on security of the person, thus engaging s. 7. I then examine the argument of the appellant Attorneys General that the laws do not cause the alleged harms. I go on to consider whether any limits on security of the person are in accordance with the principles of fundamental justice.

(1) Is Security of the Person Engaged?

[58] Section 7 provides that the state cannot deny a person's right to life, liberty or security of the person, except in accordance with the principles of fundamental justice. At this stage, the question is whether the impugned laws negatively impact or limit the applicants' security of the person, thus bringing them within the ambit of, or engaging, s. 7 of the *Charter.*

[59] Here, the applicants argue that the prohibitions on bawdy-houses, living on the avails of prostitution, and communicating in public for the purposes of prostitution, heighten the risks they face in prostitution—itself a legal activity. The application judge found that the evidence supported this proposition and the Court of Appeal agreed.

[60] For reasons set out below, I am of the same view. The prohibitions at issue do not merely impose conditions on how prostitutes operate. They go a critical step further, by imposing *dangerous* conditions on prostitution; they prevent people engaged in a risky—but legal—activity from taking steps to protect themselves from the risks.

(a) Sections 197 and 210: Keeping a Common Bawdy-House

[61] It is not an offence to sell sex for money. The bawdy-house provisions, however, make it an offence to do so in any "place" that is "kept or occupied" or "resorted to" for the purpose of prostitution (ss. 197 and 210(1) of the *Code*). The reach of these provisions is broad. "Place" includes any defined space, even if unenclosed and used only temporarily (s. 197(1) of the *Code*; *R. v. Pierce* (1982), 37 O.R. (2d) 721 (C.A.)). And by definition, it applies even if resorted to by only one person (s. 197(1); *R. v. Worthington* (1972), 10 C.C.C. (2d) 311 (Ont. C.A.)).

[62] The practical effect of s. 210 is to confine lawful prostitution to two categories: street prostitution and out-calls (application decision, at para. 385). In-calls, where the john comes to the prostitute's residence, are prohibited. Out-calls, where the prostitute goes out and meets the client at a designated location, such as the client's home, are allowed. Working on the street is also permitted, though the practice of street prostitution is significantly limited by the prohibition on communicating in public (s. 213(1)(c)).

[63] The application judge found, on a balance of probabilities, that the safest form of prostitution is working independently from a fixed location (para. 300). She concluded that indoor work is far less dangerous than street prostitution—a finding that the evidence amply supports. She also concluded that out-call work is not as safe as in-call work, particularly under the current regime where prostitutes are precluded by virtue of the living on the avails provision from hiring a driver or security guard. Since the bawdy-house provision makes the safety-enhancing method of in-call prostitution illegal, the application

judge concluded that the bawdy-house prohibition materially increased the risk prostitutes face under the present regime. I agree.

[64] First, the prohibition prevents prostitutes from working in a fixed indoor location, which would be safer than working on the streets or meeting clients at different locations, especially given the current prohibition on hiring drivers or security guards. This, in turn, prevents prostitutes from having a regular clientele and from setting up indoor safeguards like receptionists, assistants, bodyguards and audio room monitoring, which would reduce risks (application decision, at para. 421). Second, it interferes with provision of health checks and preventive health measures. Finally—a point developed in argument before us—the bawdy-house prohibition prevents resort to safe houses, to which prostitutes working on the street can take clients. In Vancouver, for example, "Grandma's House" was established to support street workers in the Downtown Eastside, at about the same time as fears were growing that a serial killer was prowling the streets—fears which materialized in the notorious Robert Pickton. Street prostitutes—who the application judge found are largely the most vulnerable class of prostitutes, and who face an alarming amount of violence (para. 361)—were able to bring clients to Grandma's House. However, charges were laid under s. 210, and although the charges were eventually stayed—four years after they were laid—Grandma's House was shut down. ... For some prostitutes, particularly those who are destitute, safe houses such as Grandma's House may be critical. For these people, the ability to work in brothels or hire security, even if those activities were lawful, may be illusory.

[65] I conclude, therefore, that the bawdy-house provision negatively impacts the security of the person of prostitutes and engages s. 7 of the *Charter*.

(b) Section 212(1)(j): Living on the Avails of Prostitution

[66] Section 212(1)(j) criminalizes living on the avails of prostitution of another person, wholly or in part. While targeting parasitic relationships (*R. v. Downey*, [1992] 2 S.C.R. 10), it has a broad reach. As interpreted by the courts, it makes it a crime for anyone to supply a service to a prostitute, because she is a prostitute (*R. v. Grilo* (1991), 2 O.R. (3d) 514 (C.A.); *R. v. Barrow* (2001), 54 O.R. (3d) 417 (C.A.)). In effect, it prevents a prostitute from hiring bodyguards, drivers and receptionists. The application judge found that by denying prostitutes access to these security-enhancing safeguards, the law prevented them from taking steps to reduce the risks they face and negatively impacted their security of the person (para. 361). As such, she found that the law engages s. 7 of the *Charter*.

[67] The evidence amply supports the judge's conclusion. Hiring drivers, receptionists, and bodyguards, could increase prostitutes' safety (application decision, at para. 421), but the law prevents them from doing so. Accordingly, I conclude that s. 212(1)(j) negatively impacts security of the person and engages s. 7.

(c) Section 213(1)(c): Communicating in a Public Place

[68] Section 213(1)(c) prohibits communicating or attempting to communicate for the purpose of engaging in prostitution or obtaining the sexual services of a prostitute, in a public place or a place open to public view. The provision extends to conduct short

of verbal communication by prohibiting stopping or attempting to stop any person for those purposes (*R. v. Head* (1987), 59 C.R. (3d) 80 (B.C.C.A.)).

[69] The application judge found that face-to-face communication is an "essential tool" in enhancing street prostitutes' safety (para. 432). Such communication, which the law prohibits, allows prostitutes to screen prospective clients for intoxication or propensity to violence, which can reduce the risks they face (paras. 301 and 421). This conclusion, based on the evidence before her, sufficed to engage security of the person under s. 7.

[70] The application judge also found that the communicating law has had the effect of displacing prostitutes from familiar areas, where they may be supported by friends and regular customers, to more isolated areas, thereby making them more vulnerable (paras. 331 and 502).

[71] On the evidence accepted by the application judge, the law prohibits communication that would allow street prostitutes to increase their safety. By prohibiting communicating in public for the purpose of prostitution, the law prevents prostitutes from screening clients and setting terms for the use of condoms or safe houses. In these ways, it significantly increases the risks they face.

[72] I conclude that the evidence supports the application judge's conclusion that s. 213(1)(c) impacts security of the person and engages s. 7.

• • •

(3) Principles of Fundamental Justice

(a) The Applicable Norms

[93] I have concluded that the impugned laws deprive prostitutes of security of the person, engaging s. 7. The remaining step in the s. 7 analysis is to determine whether this deprivation is in accordance with the principles of fundamental justice. If so, s. 7 is not breached.

[94] The principles of fundamental justice set out the minimum requirements that a law that negatively impacts on a person's life, liberty, or security of the person must meet. As Lamer J. put it, "[t]he term 'principles of fundamental justice' is not a right, but a qualifier of the right not to be deprived of life, liberty and security of the person; its function is to set the parameters of that right" (*Re B.C. Motor Vehicle Act*, [1985] 2 S.C.R. 486 ("*Motor Vehicle Reference*"), at p. 512).

[95] The principles of fundamental justice have significantly evolved since the birth of the *Charter*. Initially, the principles of fundamental justice were thought to refer narrowly to principles of natural justice that define procedural fairness. ...

[96] The *Motor Vehicle Reference* recognized that the principles of fundamental justice are about the basic values underpinning our constitutional order. The s. 7 analysis is concerned with capturing inherently bad laws: that is, laws that take away life, liberty, or security of the person in a way that runs afoul of our basic values. The principles of fundamental justice are an attempt to capture those values. Over the years, the jurisprudence has given shape to the content of these basic values. In this case, we are concerned with the basic values against arbitrariness, overbreadth, and gross disproportionality.

[97] The concepts of arbitrariness, overbreadth, and gross disproportionality evolved organically as courts were faced with novel *Charter* claims.

[98] Arbitrariness was used to describe the situation where there is no connection between the effect and the object of the law. In *Morgentaler* [*R v Morgentaler*, [1988] 1 SCR 30], the accused challenged provisions of the *Criminal Code* that required abortions to be approved by a therapeutic abortion committee of an accredited or approved hospital. The purpose of the law was to protect women's health. The majority found that the requirement that all therapeutic abortions take place in accredited hospitals did not contribute to the objective of protecting women's health and, in fact, caused delays that were detrimental to women's health. Thus, the law violated basic values because the effect of the law actually contravened the objective of the law. Beetz J. called this "manifest unfairness" (*Morgentaler*, at p. 120), but later cases interpreted this as an "arbitrariness" analysis (see *Chaoulli v. Quebec (Attorney General)*, 2005 SCC 35, [2005] 1 S.C.R. 791, at para. 133, *per* McLachlin C.J. and Major J.).

[99] In *Chaoulli*, the applicant challenged a Quebec law that prohibited private health insurance for services that were available in the public sector. The purpose of the provision was to protect the public health care system and prevent the diversion of resources from the public system. The majority found, on the basis of international evidence, that private health insurance and a public health system could co-exist. Three of the four-judge majority found that the prohibition was "arbitrary" because there was no real connection on the facts between the effect and the objective of the law.

[100] Most recently, in *PHS* [*Canada (Attorney General) v PHS Community Services Society*, 2011 SCC 44, [2011] 3 SCR 134], this Court found that the Minister's decision not to extend a safe injection site's exemption from drug possession laws was arbitrary. The purpose of drug possession laws was the protection of health and public safety, and the services provided by the safe injection site actually contributed to these objectives. Thus, the effect of not extending the exemption—that is, prohibiting the safe injection site from operating—was contrary to the objectives of the drug possession laws.

[101] Another way in which laws may violate our basic values is through what the cases have called "overbreadth": the law goes too far and interferes with some conduct that bears no connection to its objective. In *R. v. Heywood*, [1994] 3 S.C.R. 761, the accused challenged a vagrancy law that prohibited offenders convicted of listed offences from "loitering" in public parks. The majority of the Court found that the law, which aimed to protect children from sexual predators, was overbroad; insofar as the law applied to offenders who did not constitute a danger to children, and insofar as it applied to parks where children were unlikely to be present, it was unrelated to its objective.

[102] In *R. v. Demers*, 2004 SCC 46, [2004] 2 S.C.R. 489, the challenged provisions of the *Criminal Code* prevented an accused who was found unfit to stand trial from receiving an absolute discharge, and subjected the accused to indefinite appearances before a review board. The purpose of the provisions was "to allow for the ongoing treatment or assessment of the accused in order for him or her to become fit for an eventual trial" (para. 41). The Court found that insofar as the law applied to permanently unfit accused, who would never become fit to stand trial, the objective did "not apply" and therefore the law was overbroad (paras. 42-43).

[103] Laws are also in violation of our basic values when the effect of the law is grossly disproportionate to the state's objective. In *Malmo-Levine*, the accused challenged the prohibition on the possession of marijuana on the basis that its effects were grossly disproportionate to its objective. Although the Court agreed that a law with grossly disproportionate

effects would violate our basic norms, the Court found that this was not such a case: "... the effects on accused persons of the present law, including the potential of imprisonment, fall within the broad latitude within which the Constitution permits legislative action" (para. 175).

[104] In *PHS*, this Court found that the Minister's refusal to exempt the safe injection site from drug possession laws was not in accordance with the principles of fundamental justice because the effect of denying health services and increasing the risk of death and disease of injection drug users was grossly disproportionate to the objectives of the drug possession laws, namely public health and safety.

[105] The overarching lesson that emerges from the case law is that laws run afoul of our basic values when the means by which the state seeks to attain its objective is fundamentally flawed, in the sense of being arbitrary, overbroad, or having effects that are grossly disproportionate to the legislative goal. To deprive citizens of life, liberty, or security of the person by laws that violate these norms is not in accordance with the principles of fundamental justice.

[106] As these principles have developed in the jurisprudence, they have not always been applied consistently. The Court of Appeal below pointed to the confusion that has been caused by the "commingling" of arbitrariness, overbreadth, and gross disproportionality (paras. 143-51). This Court itself recently noted the conflation of the principles of overbreadth and gross disproportionality (*R. v. Khawaja*, 2012 SCC 69, [2012] 3 S.C.R. 555, at paras. 38-40; see also *R. v. S.S.C.*, 2008 BCCA 262, 257 B.C.A.C. 57, at para. 72). In short, courts have explored different ways in which laws run afoul of our basic values, using the same words—arbitrariness, overbreadth, and gross disproportionality—in slightly different ways.

[107] Although there is significant overlap between these three principles, and one law may properly be characterized by more than one of them, arbitrariness, overbreadth, and gross disproportionality remain three distinct principles that stem from what Hamish Stewart calls "failures of instrumental rationality"—the situation where the law is "inadequately connected to its objective or in some sense goes too far in seeking to attain it" (*Fundamental Justice: Section 7 of the Canadian Charter of Rights and Freedoms* (2012), at p. 151). ...

[108] The case law on arbitrariness, overbreadth and gross disproportionality is directed against two different evils. The first evil is the absence of a connection between the infringement of rights and what the law seeks to achieve—the situation where the law's deprivation of an individual's life, liberty, or security of the person is not connected to the purpose of the law. The first evil is addressed by the norms against arbitrariness and overbreadth, which target the absence of connection between the law's purpose and the s. 7 deprivation.

[109] The second evil lies in depriving a person of life, liberty or security of the person in a manner that is grossly disproportionate to the law's objective. The law's impact on the s. 7 interest is connected to the purpose, but the impact is so severe that it violates our fundamental norms.

[110] Against this background, it may be useful to elaborate on arbitrariness, overbreadth and gross disproportionality.

[111] Arbitrariness asks whether there is a direct connection between the purpose of the law and the impugned effect on the individual, in the sense that the effect on the

individual bears some relation to the law's purpose. There must be a rational connection between the object of the measure that causes the s. 7 deprivation, and the limits it imposes on life, liberty, or security of the person (Stewart, at p. 136). A law that imposes limits on these interests in a way that bears *no connection* to its objective arbitrarily impinges on those interests. Thus, in *Chaoulli*, the law was arbitrary because the prohibition of private health insurance was held to be unrelated to the objective of protecting the public health system.

[112] Overbreadth deals with a law that is so broad in scope that it includes *some* conduct that bears no relation to its purpose. In this sense, the law is arbitrary *in part*. At its core, overbreadth addresses the situation where there is no rational connection between the purposes of the law and *some*, but not all, of its impacts. For instance, the law at issue in *Demers* required unfit accused to attend repeated review board hearings. The law was only disconnected from its purpose insofar as it applied to permanently unfit accused; for temporarily unfit accused, the effects were related to the purpose.

[113] Overbreadth allows courts to recognize that the law is rational in some cases, but that it overreaches in its effect in others. Despite this recognition of the scope of the law as a whole, the focus remains on the individual and whether the effect on the individual is rationally connected to the law's purpose. For example, where a law is drawn broadly and targets some conduct that bears no relation to its purpose in order to make enforcement more practical, there is still no connection between the purpose of the law and its effect on the *specific individual*. Enforcement practicality may be a justification for an overbroad law, to be analyzed under s. 1 of the *Charter*.

· · ·

[117] … [I]t may be helpful to think of overbreadth as a distinct principle of fundamental justice related to arbitrariness, in that the question for both is whether there is *no connection* between the effects of a law and its objective. Overbreadth simply allows the court to recognize that the lack of connection arises in a law that goes too far by sweeping conduct into its ambit that bears no relation to its objective.

[118] An ancillary question, which applies to both arbitrariness and overbreadth, concerns how significant the lack of correspondence between the objective of the infringing provision and its effects must be. Questions have arisen as to whether a law is arbitrary or overbroad when its effects are *inconsistent* with its objective, or whether, more broadly, a law is arbitrary or overbroad whenever its effects are *unnecessary* for its objective (see, e.g., *Chaoulli*, at paras. 233-34).

[119] As noted above, the root question is whether the law is inherently bad because there is *no connection*, in whole or in part, between its effects and its purpose. This standard is not easily met. The evidence may, as in *Morgentaler*, show that the effect actually undermines the objective and is therefore "inconsistent" with the objective. Or the evidence may, as in *Chaoulli*, show that there is simply no connection on the facts between the effect and the objective, and the effect is therefore "unnecessary." Regardless of how the judge describes this lack of connection, the ultimate question remains whether the evidence establishes that the law violates basic norms because there is *no connection* between its effect and its purpose. This is a matter to be determined on a case-by-case basis, in light of the evidence.

[120] Gross disproportionality asks a different question from arbitrariness and overbreadth. It targets the second fundamental evil: the law's effects on life, liberty or security

of the person are so grossly disproportionate to its purposes that they cannot rationally be supported. The rule against gross disproportionality only applies in extreme cases where the seriousness of the deprivation is totally out of sync with the objective of the measure. This idea is captured by the hypothetical of a law with the purpose of keeping the streets clean that imposes a sentence of life imprisonment for spitting on the sidewalk. The connection between the draconian impact of the law and its object must be entirely outside the norms accepted in our free and democratic society.

[121] Gross disproportionality under s. 7 of the *Charter* does *not* consider the beneficial effects of the law for society. It balances the negative effect on the individual against the purpose of the law, *not* against societal benefit that might flow from the law. ...

[122] Thus, gross disproportionality is not concerned with the number of people who experience grossly disproportionate effects; a grossly disproportionate effect on one person is sufficient to violate the norm.

[123] All three principles—arbitrariness, overbreadth, and gross disproportionality—compare the rights infringement caused by the law with the objective of the law, not with the law's effectiveness. That is, they do not look to how well the law achieves its object, or to how much of the population the law benefits. They do not consider ancillary benefits to the general population. Furthermore, none of the principles measure the percentage of the population that is negatively impacted. The analysis is qualitative, not quantitative. The question under s. 7 is whether *anyone's* life, liberty or security of the person has been denied by a law that is inherently bad; a grossly disproportionate, overbroad, or arbitrary effect on one person is sufficient to establish a breach of s. 7.

· · ·

(4) Do the Impugned Laws Respect the Principles of Fundamental Justice?

(a) Section 210: The Bawdy-House Prohibition

(I) THE OBJECT OF THE PROVISION

[130] The bawdy-house provision has remained essentially unchanged since it was moved to Part V of the *Criminal Code*, "Disorderly Houses, Gaming and Betting," in the 1953-54 *Code* revision (c. 51, s. 182). In *Rockert v. The Queen*, [1978] 2 S.C.R. 704, Estey J. found "little, if any, doubt" in the authorities that the disorderly house provisions were not directed at the mischief of betting, gaming and prostitution *per se*, but rather at the harm to the community in which such activities were carried on in a notorious and habitual manner (p. 712). This objective can be traced back to the common law origins of the bawdy-house provisions (see, e.g., E. Coke, *The Third Part of the Institutes of the Laws of England: Concerning High Treason, and Other Pleas of the Crown and Criminal Causes* (1817, first published 1644), at pp. 205-6).

[131] The appellant Attorneys General argue that the object of this provision, considered alone and in conjunction with the other prohibitions, is to deter prostitution. The record does not support this contention; on the contrary, it is clear from the legislative record that the purpose of the prohibition is to prevent community harms in the nature of nuisance.

[132] There is no evidence to support a reappraisal of this purpose by Parliament. The doctrine against shifting objectives does not permit a new object to be introduced at this

point (*R. v. Zundel*, [1992] 2 S.C.R. 731). On its face, the provision is only directed at in-call prostitution, and so cannot be said to aim at deterring prostitution generally. To find that it operates with the other *Criminal Code* provisions to deter prostitution generally is also unwarranted, given their piecemeal evolution and patchwork construction, which leaves out-calls and prostitution itself untouched. I therefore agree with the lower courts that the objectives of the bawdy-house provision are to combat neighbourhood disruption or disorder and to safeguard public health and safety.

(ii) COMPLIANCE WITH THE PRINCIPLES OF FUNDAMENTAL JUSTICE

[133] The courts below considered whether the bawdy-house prohibition is overbroad, or grossly disproportionate.

[134] I agree with them that the negative impact of the bawdy-house prohibition on the applicants' security of the person is grossly disproportionate to its objective. I therefore find it unnecessary to decide whether the prohibition is overbroad insofar as it applies to a single prostitute operating out of her own home (C.A., at para. 204). The application judge found on the evidence that moving to a bawdy-house would improve prostitutes' safety by providing the "safety benefits of proximity to others, familiarity with surroundings, security staff, closed-circuit television and other such monitoring that a permanent indoor location can facilitate" (para. 427). Balancing this against the evidence demonstrating that "complaints about nuisance arising from indoor prostitution establishments are rare" (*ibid.*), she found that the harmful impact of the provision was grossly disproportionate to its purpose.

[135] The Court of Appeal acknowledged that empirical evidence on the subject is difficult to gather, since almost all the studies focus on street prostitution. However, it concluded that the evidence supported the application judge's findings on gross disproportionality—in particular, the evidence of the high homicide rate among prostitutes, with the overwhelming number of victims being street prostitutes. The Court of Appeal agreed that moving indoors amounts to a "basic safety precaution" for prostitutes, one which the bawdy-house provision makes illegal (paras. 206-7).

[136] In my view, this conclusion was not in error. The harms identified by the courts below are grossly disproportionate to the deterrence of community disruption that is the object of the law. Parliament has the power to regulate against nuisances, but not at the cost of the health, safety and lives of prostitutes. A law that prevents street prostitutes from resorting to a safe haven such as Grandma's House while a suspected serial killer prowls the streets, is a law that has lost sight of its purpose.

(b) Section 212(1)(j): Living on the Avails of Prostitution

(i) THE OBJECT OF THE PROVISION

[137] This Court has held, *per* Cory J. for the majority in *Downey*, that the purpose of this provision is to target pimps and the parasitic, exploitative conduct in which they engage:

> It can be seen that the majority of offences outlined in s. 195 are aimed at the procurer who entices, encourages or importunes a person to engage in prostitution. Section 195(1)(j) [now s 212(1)(j)] is specifically aimed at those who have an economic stake in the earnings of a

prostitute. It has been held correctly I believe that the target of s. 195(1)(j) is the person who lives parasitically off a prostitute's earnings. That person is commonly and aptly termed a pimp. [p. 32]

[138] The Attorneys General of Canada and Ontario argue that the true objective of s. 212(1)(j) is to target the commercialization of prostitution, and to promote the values of dignity and equality. This characterization of the objective does not accord with *Downey*, and is not supported by the legislative record. It must be rejected.

(II) COMPLIANCE WITH THE PRINCIPLES OF FUNDAMENTAL JUSTICE

[139] The courts below concluded that the living on the avails provision is overbroad insofar as it captures a number of non-exploitative relationships which are not connected to the law's purpose. The courts below also concluded that the provision's negative effect on the security and safety of prostitutes is grossly disproportionate to its objective of protecting prostitutes from harm.

[140] I agree with the courts below that the living on the avails provision is overbroad.

[141] The provision has been judicially restricted to those who provide a service or good to a prostitute because she is a prostitute, thus excluding grocers and doctors, for instance (*Shaw v. Director of Public Prosecutions*, [1962] A.C. 220 (H.L.)). It also has been held to require that exploitation be proven in the case of a person who lives with the prostitute, in order to exclude people in legitimate domestic relationships with a prostitute (*Grilo*). These refinements render the prohibition narrower than its words might suggest.

[142] The question here is whether the law nevertheless goes too far and thus deprives the applicants of their security of the person in a manner unconnected to the law's objective. The law punishes everyone who lives on the avails of prostitution without distinguishing between those who exploit prostitutes (for example, controlling and abusive pimps) and those who could increase the safety and security of prostitutes (for example, legitimate drivers, managers, or bodyguards). It also includes anyone involved in business with a prostitute, such as accountants or receptionists. In these ways, the law includes some conduct that bears no relation to its purpose of preventing the exploitation of prostitutes. The living on the avails provision is therefore overbroad.

[143] The appellant Attorneys General argue that the line between an exploitative pimp and a prostitute's legitimate driver, manager or bodyguard, blurs in the real world. A relationship that begins on a non-exploitative footing may become exploitative over time. If the provision were tailored more narrowly—for example, by reading in "in circumstances of exploitation" as the Court of Appeal did—evidentiary difficulties may lead to exploiters escaping liability. Relationships of exploitation often involve intimidation and manipulation of the kind that make it very difficult for a prostitute to testify. For these reasons, the Attorneys General argue, the provision must be drawn broadly in order to effectively capture those it targets.

[144] This argument is more appropriately addressed under the s. 1 analysis. As stated above, if a law captures conduct that bears no relation to its purpose, the law is overbroad under s. 7; enforcement practicality is one way the government may justify an overbroad law under s. 1 of the *Charter*.

[145] Having found that the prohibition on living on the avails of prostitution is overbroad, I find it unnecessary to consider whether it is also grossly disproportionate to its object of protecting prostitutes from exploitative relationships.

(c) Section 213(1)(c): Communicating in Public for the Purposes of Prostitution

(i) THE OBJECT OF THE PROVISION

[146] The object of the communicating provision was explained by Dickson C.J. in the *Prostitution Reference*:

> Like Wilson J., I would characterize the legislative objective of s. 195.1(1)(c) [now s. 213(1)(c)] in the following manner: the provision is meant to address solicitation in public places and, to that end, seeks to eradicate the various forms of social nuisance arising from the public display of the sale of sex. My colleague Lamer J. finds that s. 195.1(1)(c) is truly directed towards curbing the exposure of prostitution and related violence, drugs and crime to potentially vulnerable young people, and towards eliminating the victimization and economic disadvantage that prostitution, and especially street soliciting, represents for women. I do not share the view that the legislative objective can be characterized so broadly. In prohibiting sales of sexual services in public, the legislation does not attempt, at least in any direct manner, to address the exploitation, degradation and subordination of women that are part of the contemporary reality of prostitution. Rather, in my view, the legislation is aimed at taking solicitation for the purposes of prostitution off the streets and out of public view. ...

[147] It is clear from these reasons that the purpose of the communicating provision is not to eliminate street prostitution for its own sake, but to take prostitution "off the streets and out of public view" in order to prevent the nuisances that street prostitution can cause. The *Prostitution Reference* belies the argument of the Attorneys General that Parliament's overall objective in these provisions is to deter prostitution.

(ii) COMPLIANCE WITH THE PRINCIPLES OF FUNDAMENTAL JUSTICE

[148] The application judge concluded that the harm imposed by the prohibition on communicating in public was grossly disproportionate to the provision's object of removing the nuisance of prostitution from the streets. This was based on evidence that she found established that the ability to screen clients was an "essential tool" to avoiding violent or drunken clients (application decision, at para. 432).

[149] The majority of the Court of Appeal found that the application judge erred in her analysis of gross disproportionality by attaching too little importance to the objective of s. 213(1)(c), and by incorrectly finding on the evidence that face-to-face communication with a prospective customer is essential to enhancing prostitutes' safety (paras. 306 and 310).

[150] In my view, the Court of Appeal majority's reasoning on this question is problematic, largely for the reasons set out by MacPherson J.A., dissenting in part. Four aspects of the majority's analysis are particularly troubling.

[151] First, in concluding that the application judge accorded too little weight to the legislative objective of s. 213(1)(c), the majority of the Court of Appeal criticized her characterization of the object of the provision as targeting "noise, street congestion, and

the possibility that the practice of prostitution will interfere with those nearby" (C.A., at para. 306). But the application judge's conclusion was in concert with the object of s. 213(1)(c) established by Dickson C.J. in the *Prostitution Reference*, which the majority of the Court of Appeal endorsed earlier in their reasons (para. 286).

[152] Compounding this error, the majority of the Court of Appeal inflated the objective of the prohibition on public communication by referring to "drug possession, drug trafficking, public intoxication, and organized crime" (para. 307), even though Dickson C.J. explicitly *excluded* the exposure of "related violence, drugs and crime" to vulnerable young people from the objectives of s. 213(1)(c). At most, the provision's effect on these other issues is an ancillary benefit—and, as such, it should not play into the gross disproportionality analysis, which weighs the actual objective of the provision against its negative impact on the individual's life, liberty and security of the person.

[153] The three remaining concerns with the majority's reasoning relate to the other side of the balance: the assessment of the impact of the provision.

[154] First, the majority of the Court of Appeal erroneously substituted its assessment of the evidence for that of the application judge. It found that the application judge's conclusion that face-to-face communication is essential to enhancing prostitutes' safety was based only on "anecdotal evidence … informed by her own common sense" (para. 311). This was linked to its error, discussed above, in according too little deference to the application judge on findings of social and legislative facts. MacPherson J.A. for the minority, correctly countered that the evidence on this point came from both prostitutes' own accounts and from expert assessments, and provided a firm basis for the application judge's conclusion (paras. 348-50).

[155] Second, the majority ignored the law's effect of displacing prostitutes to more secluded, less secure locations. The application judge highlighted this displacement (at para. 331), citing the evidence found in the report of the House of Commons Standing Committee on Justice and Human Rights Subcommittee on Solicitation Laws (*The Challenge of Change: A Study of Canada's Criminal Prostitution Laws* (2006)) on the effects of s. 213(1)(c). The majority's conclusion that the application judge did not have a proper basis to conclude that face-to-face communication enhances safety may be explained in part by their failure to consider the impact of the provision on displacement.

[156] Related to this is the uncontested fact that the communication ban prevents street workers from bargaining for conditions that would materially reduce their risk, such as condom use and the use of safe houses.

[157] Finally, the majority of the Court of Appeal majority, in rejecting the application judge's conclusions, relied on its own speculative assessment of the impact of s. 213(1)(c):

> While it is fair to say that a street prostitute might be able to avoid a "bad date" by negotiating details such as payment, services to be performed and condom use up front, it is equally likely that the customer could pass muster at an early stage, only to turn violent once the transaction is underway. It is also possible that the prostitute may proceed even in the face of perceived danger, either because her judgment is impaired by drugs or alcohol, or because she is so desperate for money that she feels compelled to take the risk. [para. 312]

[158] It is certainly conceivable, as this passage suggests, that some street prostitutes would not refuse a client even if communication revealed potential danger. It is also conceivable that the danger may not be perfectly predicted in advance. However, that

does not negate the application judge's finding that communication is an essential tool that can decrease risk. The assessment is qualitative, not quantitative. If screening could have prevented one woman from jumping into Robert Pickton's car, the severity of the harmful effects is established.

[159] In sum, the Court of Appeal wrongly attributed errors in reasoning to the application judge and made a number of errors in considering gross disproportionality. I would restore the application judge's conclusion that s. 213(1)(c) is grossly disproportionate. The provision's negative impact on the safety and lives of street prostitutes is a grossly disproportionate response to the possibility of nuisance caused by street prostitution.

C. Do the Prohibitions Against Communicating in Public Violate Section 2(b) of the Charter?

[160] Having concluded that the impugned laws violate s. 7, it is unnecessary to consider this question.

D. Are the Infringements Justified Under Section 1 of the Charter?

[161] The appellant Attorneys General have not seriously argued that the laws, if found to infringe s. 7, can be justified under s. 1 of the *Charter*. Only the Attorney General of Canada addressed this in his factum, and then, only briefly. I therefore find it unnecessary to engage in a full s. 1 analysis for each of the impugned provisions. However, some of their arguments under s. 7 of the *Charter* are properly addressed at this stage of the analysis.

[162] In particular, the Attorneys General attempt to justify the living on the avails provision on the basis that it must be drafted broadly in order to capture all exploitative relationships, which can be difficult to identify. However, the law not only catches drivers and bodyguards, who may actually be pimps, but it also catches clearly non-exploitative relationships, such as receptionists or accountants who work with prostitutes. The law is therefore not minimally impairing. Nor, at the final stage of the s. 1 inquiry, is the law's effect of preventing prostitutes from taking measures that would increase their safety, and possibly save their lives, outweighed by the law's positive effect of protecting prostitutes from exploitative relationships.

[163] The Attorneys General have not raised any other arguments distinct from those considered under s. 7. I therefore find that the impugned laws are not saved by s. 1 of the *Charter*.

V. Result and Remedy

[164] I would dismiss the appeals and allow the cross-appeal. Section 210, as it relates to prostitution, and ss. 212(1)(j) and 213(1)(c) are declared to be inconsistent with the *Canadian Charter of Rights and Freedoms* and hence are void. The word "prostitution" is struck from the definition of "common bawdy-house" in s. 197(1) of the *Criminal Code* as it applies to s. 210 only.

[165] I have concluded that each of the challenged provisions, considered independently, suffers from constitutional infirmities that violate the *Charter*. That does not mean that Parliament is precluded from imposing limits on where and how prostitution may

be conducted. Prohibitions on keeping a bawdy-house, living on the avails of prostitution and communication related to prostitution are intertwined. They impact on each other. Greater latitude in one measure—for example, permitting prostitutes to obtain the assistance of security personnel—might impact on the constitutionality of another measure—for example, forbidding the nuisances associated with keeping a bawdy-house. The regulation of prostitution is a complex and delicate matter. It will be for Parliament, should it choose to do so, to devise a new approach, reflecting different elements of the existing regime.

[The Court suspended the declaration of invalidity for one year to allow Parliament to respond.]

Appeals dismissed and cross-appeal allowed.

Following the Supreme Court of Canada's decision in *Bedford*, attention turned to how Parliament would and should respond. Some argued that this was the moment to move sex work out of the remit of the criminal law, pursuing issues of prevention, health, and regulation instead. Others suggested that the government should adopt the so-called Nordic Model whereby the criminal law would not be used against sex workers themselves, targeting instead consumers and exploiters.

Parliament's response was Bill C-36, the *Protection of Communities and Exploited Persons Act*, which received royal assent on November 6, 2014. The preamble to the Bill reads as follows:

> Whereas the Parliament of Canada has grave concerns about the exploitation that is inherent in prostitution and the risks of violence posed to those who engage in it;
>
> Whereas the Parliament of Canada recognizes the social harm caused by the objectification of the human body and the commodification of sexual activity;
>
> Whereas it is important to protect human dignity and the equality of all Canadians by discouraging prostitution, which has a disproportionate impact on women and children;
>
> Whereas it is important to denounce and prohibit the purchase of sexual services because it creates a demand for prostitution;
>
> Whereas it is important to continue to denounce and prohibit the procurement of persons for the purpose of prostitution and the development of economic interests in the exploitation of the prostitution of others as well as the commercialization and institutionalization of prostitution;
>
> Whereas the Parliament of Canada wishes to encourage those who engage in prostitution to report incidents of violence and to leave prostitution;
>
> And whereas the Parliament of Canada is committed to protecting communities from the harms associated with prostitution. …

The Bill made a host of changes to the *Criminal Code* and related statutes. The heart of Parliament's response can be found in ss 213(1.1) and 286.1 to 286.5, which you should examine. The new legislation is relatively intricate, containing a number of conditions and caveats, and poses some significant interpretive challenges. Indeed, certain key terms and concepts (such as "sexual services" and "commercial enterprise") are not defined, making the ultimate scope and effect of the provisions uncertain. However, the key features of these amendments are the following:

- Prostitution is now excluded from the scope of the common bawdy-house provision.

- The new legislation targets those purchasing sexual services. It is now an offence *to obtain* sexual services for consideration. It is also an offence to communicate with anyone *for the purpose of obtaining* the sexual services of a person for consideration, irrespective of the location of that communication (s 286.1).

- Constraints on communication for those offering sexual services are more limited. Communication for the purpose of *providing or offering* sexual services for consideration is only an offence if that communication takes place in a "public place, or in any place open to public view, that is or is next to a school ground, playground or daycare centre" (s 213.1).

- The crime of living on the avails of prostitution (s 212) is repealed in favour of new provisions that:

  a. make it an offence to receive financial or other material benefit, "knowing that it is obtained by or derived directly or indirectly from" sexual services obtained for consideration (s 286.2(1)), *unless* the benefit arises under certain specified circumstances, such as "a legitimate living arrangement" or the provision of a good or service offered to the general public (s 286.2(4)). Those exemptions from the "material benefit" offence do not apply, however, if the benefit is derived in abusive circumstances (ss 286.2(5)(a)-(c)), if the accused was engaged in procurement (s 286.1(5)(d)), or if the benefit was received "in the context of a commercial enterprise that offers sexual services for consideration" (s 286.2(5)(e)).

  b. establish that everyone commits an offence "who procures a person to offer or provide sexual services for consideration or, for the purpose of facilitating an offence under subsection 286.1(1), recruits, holds, conceals or harbours a person who offers or provides sexual services for consideration, or exercises control, direction or influence over the movements of that person" (s 286.3(1)).

- There is a new offence capturing anyone who "knowingly advertises an offer to provide sexual services for consideration" (s 286.4).

- The "material benefit" (s 286.2(1)) and "advertising" (s 286.4) offences do not apply to those who benefit from or advertise *their own* sexual services (s 286.5(1)).

- The law also states that "[n]o person shall be prosecuted for aiding, abetting, conspiring or attempting to commit an offence under any of sections 286.1 to 286.4 or being an accessory after the fact or counselling a person to be a party to such an offence, if the offence relates to the offering or provision of their own sexual services" (s 286.5(2)).

As you can see, the thrust of the new legislation is to decriminalize many of the activities of sex workers themselves, and to target the criminal law at those who purchase sexual services or exploit sex workers. Recall, however, that the Supreme Court of Canada in *Bedford* was focused on the practical effects of the criminal law on the lives of sex workers, as measured against Parliament's legislative purpose. What do you think these provisions will mean for the lives of sex workers? Do you think that these new provisions will withstand Charter scrutiny?

III. HATE SPEECH

A classic issue that provokes debates about the proper limits of the criminal law is the question of whether hate speech ought to be criminalized. On the one hand, using the criminal law to punish individuals for expressing their beliefs seems highly illiberal and a potentially dangerous path for the criminal law to venture down. On the other hand, many argue that marginalized and vulnerable communities are seriously harmed by the public incitement of hate or the spreading of discriminatory views. As you read the following cases, consider for yourself whether the criminal law ought to be used to regulate hate speech.

R v Keegstra
Supreme Court of Canada
[1990] 3 SCR 697

[The accused, a high school teacher, was accused of promoting hatred against Jews by teaching students at Eckville High School about "an international Jewish conspiracy" and that Jews were "sadistic," "money-loving," "power hungry," and "child killers." The accused was convicted at trial but the conviction was overturned by the Alberta Court of Appeal on the grounds that ss 281.2(2) and 281.2(3)(a) (now ss 319(2) and 319(3)(a)) of the *Criminal Code* violated ss 2(b) and 11(d) of the Charter and were not justified under s 1. The Crown appealed. The Supreme Court upheld ss 281.2(2) and 281.2(3)(a) of the Code in a 4:3 decision.]

DICKSON CJ [Wilson, L'Heureux-Dubé, and Gonthier JJ held for the Court that s 319(2) infringed freedom of expression under s 2(b) of the Charter because it prohibits "communications which convey meaning, namely, those communications which are intended to promote hatred against identifiable groups" but was a justified limit under s 1. He stated]: It is undeniable that media attention has been extensive on those occasions when s. 319(2) has been used. Yet from my perspective, s. 319(2) serves to illustrate to the public the severe reprobation with which society holds messages of hate directed towards racial and religious groups. The existence of a particular criminal law, and the process of holding a trial when that law is used, is thus itself a form of expression, and the message sent out is that hate propaganda is harmful to target group members and threatening to a harmonious society (see Rauf, "Freedom of Expression, the Presumption of Innocence and Reasonable Limits" (1988), 65 C.R. (3d) 356, at p. 359). As I stated in my reasons in *R. v. Morgentaler*, [1988] 1 S.C.R. 30, at p. 70:

> The criminal law is a very special form of governmental regulation, for it seeks to express our society's collective disapprobation of certain acts and omissions.

The many, many Canadians who belong to identifiable groups surely gain a great deal of comfort from the knowledge that the hate-monger is criminally prosecuted and his or her ideas rejected. Equally, the community as a whole is reminded of the importance of diversity and multiculturalism in Canada, the value of equality and the worth and dignity of each human person being particularly emphasized. ... Is s. 319(2) nevertheless overbroad because it captures all public expression intended to promote hatred? ...

[An] important element of s. 319(2) is its requirement that the promotion of hatred be "wilful." The nature of this mental element was explored by Martin J.A. in *R. v. Buzzanga and Durocher* (1979), 49 C.C.C. (2d) 369 (Ont. C.A.) [see Chapter 7]. ... Martin J.A. went on to elaborate on the meaning of "wilfully," concluding that this mental element is satisfied only where an accused subjectively desires the promotion of hatred or foresees such a consequence as certain or substantially certain to result from an act done in order to achieve some other purpose (pp. 384-85). On the facts in *Buzzanga*, the trial judge had informed the jury that "wilfully" could be equated with the intention to create "controversy, furor and an uproar" (p. 386). This interpretation was clearly incompatible with Martin J.A.'s requirement that the promotion of hatred be intended or foreseen as substantially certain, and a new trial was therefore ordered.

The interpretation of "wilfully" in *Buzzanga* has great bearing upon the extent to which s. 319(2) limits the freedom of expression. This mental element, requiring more than merely negligence or recklessness as to result, significantly restricts the reach of the provision, and thereby reduces the scope of the targeted expression. Such a reduced scope is recognized and applauded in the Law Reform Commission of Canada's Working Paper on Hate Propaganda, op. cit., it being said that (at p. 36):

> The principle of restraint requires lawmakers to concern themselves not just with whom they want to catch, but also with whom they do not want to catch. For example, removing an intent or purpose requirement could well result in successful prosecutions of cases similar to *Buzzanga*, where members of a minority group publish hate propaganda against their own group in order to create controversy or to agitate for reform. This crime should not be used to prosecute such individuals.

I agree with the interpretation of "wilfully" in *Buzzanga*, and wholeheartedly endorse the view of the Law Reform Commission. ...

While mindful of the dangers identified by Kerans J.A., I do not find them sufficiently grave to compel striking down s. 319(2). First, to predicate the limitation of free expression upon proof of actual hatred gives insufficient attention to the severe psychological trauma suffered by members of those identifiable groups targeted by hate propaganda. Second, it is clearly difficult to prove a causative link between a specific statement and hatred of an identifiable group. In fact, to require direct proof of hatred in listeners would severely debilitate the effectiveness of s. 319(2) in achieving Parliament's aim. It is well-accepted that Parliament can use the criminal law to prevent the risk of serious harms, a leading example being the drinking and driving provisions in the *Criminal Code*. The conclusions of the Cohen Committee and subsequent study groups show that the risk of hatred caused by hate propaganda is very real, and in view of the grievous harm to be avoided in the context of this appeal, I conclude that proof of actual hatred is not required in order to justify a limit under s. 1.

[Dickson CJ concluded that s 319(3)(a) infringed the presumption of innocence under s 11(d) of the Charter. Note that the presumption of innocence is examined in Chapter 4.]

The judgments of the appeal courts in this case and in the accompanying appeal of *Andrews* [*R v Andrews*, [1990] 3 SCR 870] reveal a divergence of opinion as to whether

s. 11(d) of the Charter is infringed by the truth defence. In the Alberta Court of Appeal, Kerans J.A. viewed as crucial the possibility that an accused can be convicted of wilfully promoting hatred though there exists a reasonable doubt that the statements communicated are true. As the defence places an onus on the accused to prove truth on the balance of probabilities, he thus found it to infringe s. 11(d). In contrast to this conclusion, the Ontario Court of Appeal in *R. v. Andrews, supra,* found that s. 319(3)(a) does not place a true reverse onus upon the accused. Relying upon the majority judgment in *R. v. Holmes,* [1988] 1 S.C.R. 914, Grange J.A. felt that s. 319(3)(a) provides a defence which becomes applicable only after all elements of the offence have been proven beyond a reasonable doubt, a circumstance which was said to avoid infringing the presumption of innocence (p. 225). Grange J.A. distinguished this Court's decision in *R. v. Whyte,* [1988] 2 S.C.R. 3, on the grounds that the statutory presumption challenged in that case related to the proof of an essential element of the offence.

It is not overly difficult to settle the disagreement between the Alberta and Ontario Appeal Courts. Though some confusion may have existed after the decision of this Court in *Holmes,* since in *Whyte* it is clear that the presumption of innocence is infringed whenever the accused is liable to be convicted despite the existence of a reasonable doubt as to guilt in the mind of the trier of fact.

[He then held that the violation of s 11(d) by the reverse onus on the truth defence was justified under s 1.]

The reverse onus in the truth defence operates so as to make it more difficult to avoid conviction where the wilful promotion of hatred has been proven beyond a reasonable doubt. As the wilful promotion of hatred is hostile to Parliament's aims, placing such a burden upon the accused is rationally connected to a valid s. 1 objective. ...

To include falsity as a component of s. 319(2) for example, or even to require only that the accused raise a reasonable doubt as to the truthfulness of the statements, would excessively compromise the effectiveness of the offence in achieving its purpose. The former option would especially hinder Parliament's objective, for many statements are not susceptible to a true/false categorization. In either instance, however, where a reasonable doubt existed as to the falsity of an accused's statements an acquittal would be entered. To accept such a result it would have to be agreed that this relatively small possibility of truthfulness outweighs the harm caused through the wilful promotion of hatred. Yet to my mind the crucial objective of Parliament in this appeal justifies requiring a more convincing demonstration that a hate-monger's statements may be true, as a successful defence provides an excuse despite the presence of the harm sought to be eradicated (see Rauf, op. cit., at pp. 368-69). Having the accused prove truthfulness on the balance of probabilities is an understandable and valued precaution against too easily justifying such harm, and I hence conclude that the reverse onus provision in s. 319(3)(a) represents a minimal impairment of the presumption of innocence. ...

[McLACHLIN J (Sopinka and La Forest JJ concurring) dissented, finding that s 319(2) infringed s 2(b) and was not justified under s 1. She stated:]

Section 319(2) may well have a chilling effect on defensible expression by law-abiding citizens. At the same time, it is far from clear that it provides an effective way of curbing hatemongers. Indeed, many have suggested it may promote their cause. Prosecutions under the *Criminal Code* for racist expression have attracted extensive media coverage. Zundel, prosecuted not under s. 319(2) but for the crime of spreading false news (s. 181), claimed that his court battle had given him "a million dollars worth of publicity": Globe and Mail, March 1, 1985, p. 1. There is an unmistakable hint of the joy of martyrdom in some of the literature for which Andrews, in the companion appeal, was prosecuted:

> The Holocaust Hoax has been so ingrained in the minds of the hated "goyim" by now that in some countries ... challenging its validity can land you in jail. *R. v. Andrews* (1988), 65 O.R. (2d) 161, at p. 165 (C.A.). ...

Not only is the category of speech caught by s. 319(2) defined broadly. The application of the definition of offending speech, i.e. the circumstances in which the offending statements are prohibited, is virtually unlimited. Only private conversations are exempt from state scrutiny. Section 319(2) is calculated to prevent absolutely expression of the offending ideas in any and all public forums through any and all mediums. Speeches are caught. The corner soap-box is no longer open. Books, films and works of art—all these fall under the censor's scrutiny because of s. 319(2) of the *Criminal Code*. ...

In summary, s. 319(2) of the *Criminal Code* catches a broad range of speech and prohibits it in a broad manner, allowing only private conversations to escape scrutiny. Moreover, the process by which the prohibition is effected—the criminal law—is the severest our society can impose and is arguably unnecessary given the availability of alternate remedies. I conclude that the criminalization of hate statements does not impair free speech to the minimum extent permitted by its objectives.

Is the limit on free expression effected by s. 319(2) of the *Criminal Code* reasonable and demonstrably justifiable in a free and democratic society? On all three criteria for proportionality laid down in *Oakes*—rational connection between the legislation with its objectives, infringement to the minimum extent possible, and the balance between the importance of the infringement or the right of free speech and the benefit conferred by the legislation—s. 319(2) of the *Criminal Code* emerges wanting. Accepting that the objectives of the legislation are valid and important and potentially capable of overriding the guarantee of freedom of expression, I cannot conclude that the means chosen to achieve them—the criminalization of the potential or foreseeable promotion of hatred—are proportionate to those ends.

[McLACHLIN J (Sopinka J concurring) found that s 319(3)(a) infringed s 11(d) but was not justified under s 1. She stated:]

A rational connection between the aims of s. 319(3)(a) and its requirement that the accused prove the truth of his statements is difficult to discern. It is argued that without the reverse onus, it would be difficult if not impossible to obtain convictions for much speech promoting hate. If the objection is that it is merely difficult to prove the statements true or false, the answer is that the burden should be on the state because it has superior resources. If the objection is that it is impossible to know if the statements are true or false (i.e. true opinion), then the answer is that it cannot be ruled out that the statements may be more valuable than harmful, if we accept the ultimate value of the exchange of truthful ideas. The same considerations suggest that s. 319(3)(a)'s infringement of the presumption of innocence is neither minimal nor, given the importance of the infringement in the context of prosecutions under s. 319(2), sufficient to outweigh the dubious benefit of such a provision.

Similar considerations arise on the question of whether s. 319(3)(a) of the *Criminal Code* impairs the presumption of innocence under s. 11(d) as little as possible. It is said that hate promotion against identifiable groups is highly unlikely to be true. But that would be small comfort to a particular accused in the case where such a defence lay but he or she, because of restricted means or for whatever other reason, was unable to prove it. The presumption of innocence should not depend on the percentage of cases in which the defence in question may arise. ...

The final test of proportionality between the effects of the infringement and the objectives it promotes encounters other difficulties. We must start from the proposition that Parliament intended the truth to be a defence and that falsehood is an important element of the offence created by s. 319(2) of the *Criminal Code*. That fact, coupled with the centrality of the presumption of innocence in our criminal law, suggests that only a countervailing state interest of the most compelling kind could justify the infringement. But, as discussed in connection with the infringement of the guarantee of freedom of expression, it is difficult to see what benefits s. 319(2) in fact produces in terms of stemming hate propaganda and promoting social harmony and individual dignity. ... I conclude that s. 319(3)(a) is not saved by s. 1 of the Charter.

[The Crown's appeal in *Keegstra* was allowed. The Alberta Court of Appeal subsequently ordered a new trial because the trial judge had denied the accused an opportunity to challenge the impartiality of jurors: *R v Keegstra*, 1991 ABCA 97, 63 CCC (3d) 110. In July 1992, Keegstra was convicted and fined $3,000: 1994 ABCA 293, 92 CCC (3d) 505. Keegstra successfully appealed this conviction to the Alberta Court of Appeal, but a Crown appeal was unanimously allowed and the conviction restored by the Supreme Court in *R v Keegstra*, [1996] 1 SCR 458.]

In *RAV v City of St Paul*, 112 S Ct 2538 (1992), the accused was charged with violating a city ordinance that made it a misdemeanour to display a symbol one knows or has reason to know "arouses anger, alarm or resentment in others on the basis of race, colour, creed, religion or gender." He had burned a cross on the front lawn of a black family. The United States Supreme Court struck down the ordinance as violating the First Amendment.

Justice Scalia in the opinion of the court held the ordinance was invalid because it regulated the content of speech. He stated that under the law:

> ... One could hold up a sign saying, for example, that all "anti-Catholic bigots" are misbegotten; but not that all "papists" are, for that would insult and provoke violence "on the basis of religion." St. Paul has no such authority to license one side of a debate to fight freestyle, while requiring the other to follow Marquis of Queensbury Rules.
>
> ... An ordinance not limited to the favored topics, for example, would have precisely the same beneficial effect. In fact the only interest distinctively served by the content limitation is that of

displaying the city council's special hostility towards the particular biases thus singled out. That is precisely what the First Amendment forbids. The politicians of St. Paul are entitled to express that hostility—but not through the means of imposing unique limitations upon speakers who (however benightedly) disagree.

... Let there be no mistake about our belief that burning a cross in someone's front yard is reprehensible. But St. Paul has sufficient means at its disposal to prevent such behavior without adding the First Amendment to the fire.

Four other judges disagreed with this basis for striking the law down, but said that the law was invalid because it was overbroad. Justice White stated that the law prohibited speech "that causes only hurt feelings, offense, or resentment, and is protected by the First Amendment," unlike "fighting words" that would incite "imminent lawless action."

In *Wisconsin v Mitchell*, 508 US 476 (1993), the United States Supreme Court upheld a state law that increased the maximum penalty if a crime was motivated by hate.

In Canada, s 718.2(a)(i) of the *Criminal Code* provides that "evidence that the offence was motivated by bias, prejudice, or hate based on race, national or ethnic origin, language, colour, religion, sex, age, mental or physical disability, sexual orientation, or any other similar factor" is an aggravating factor at sentencing.

In 2004, the definition of "identifiable group" in s 318(4) for the purpose of hate speech prosecutions was amended to add "sexual orientation" to the existing references to colour, race, religion, and national or ethnic origin. Are there valid arguments, however, that the section still remains underinclusive? Should the definition of identifiable group be expanded to include hate speech on the basis of language, sex, age, or mental or physical disability? Would such groups have a valid claim that they are being denied the equal protection and benefit of the law under s 15 of the Charter?

R v Zundel
Supreme Court of Canada
[1992] 2 SCR 731

[The accused was charged under s 181 of the *Criminal Code* for publishing material denying the Holocaust. He was convicted, but the Ontario Court of Appeal allowed his appeal, (1987), 31 CCC (3d) 97, in part because of concerns about jury selection. Zundel was convicted at his second trial and appealed to the Supreme Court.]

McLACHLIN J (La Forest, L'Heureux-Dubé, and Sopinka JJ concurring): Neither the admittedly offensive beliefs of the appellant, Mr. Zundel, nor the specific publication with regard to which he was charged under s. 181 are directly engaged by these constitutional questions. This appeal is not about the dissemination of hate, which was the focus of this court's decision in *R. v. Keegstra* (1990), 61 C.C.C. (3d) 1, and the reasons of my colleagues Cory and Iacobucci JJ. here. In *Keegstra*, this court ruled that the provisions of the *Criminal Code* which prohibit the dissemination of hate violated the guarantee of freedom of expression but were saved under s. 1 of the *Charter*. This case presents the court with the question of whether a much broader and vaguer class of speech—false statements deemed likely to injure or cause mischief to any public interest—can be saved under s. 1 of the

Charter. In my view, the answer to this question must be in the negative. To permit the imprisonment of people, or even the threat of imprisonment, on the ground that they have made a statement which 12 of their co-citizens deem to be false and mischievous to some undefined public interest, is to stifle a whole range of speech, some of which has long been regarded as legitimate and even beneficial to our society. I do not assert that Parliament cannot criminalize the dissemination of racial slurs and hate propaganda. I do assert, however, that such provisions must be drafted with sufficient particularity to offer assurance that they cannot be abused so as to stifle a broad range of legitimate and valuable speech.

Before we put a person beyond the pale of the Constitution, before we deny a person the protection which the most fundamental law of this land, on its face, accords to the person, we should, in my belief, be entirely certain that there can be no justification for offering protection. The criterion of falsity falls short of this certainty, given that false statements can sometimes have value and given the difficulty of conclusively determining total falsity. Applying the broad, purposive interpretation of the freedom of expression guaranteed by s. 2(b) hitherto adhered to by this court, I cannot accede to the argument that those who deliberately publish falsehoods are for that reason alone precluded from claiming the benefit of the constitutional guarantees of free speech. I would rather hold that such speech is protected by s. 2(b), leaving arguments relating to its value in relation to its prejudicial effect to be dealt with under s. 1.

I turn first to the state's interest in prohibiting the expression here at issue—the question of whether the Crown has established an overriding public objective, to use the language of *R. v. Oakes* (1986), 24 C.C.C. (3d) 321.

In determining the objective of a legislative measure for the purposes of s. 1, the court must look at the intention of Parliament when the section was enacted or amended. It cannot assign objectives, nor invent new ones according to the perceived current utility of the impugned provision: see *R. v. Big M Drug Mart Ltd.* (1985), 18 C.C.C. (3d) 385, at p. 344 [SCR], in which this court rejected the United States doctrine of shifting purposes. Although the application and interpretation of objectives may vary over time (see, e.g., *Butler*, [[1992] 1 SCR 452], per Sopinka J., at pp. 494-496 [SCR]), new and altogether different purposes should not be invented. The case is quite different from the anti-obscenity legislation in *Butler* where the goal historically and to the present day is the same—combatting the "detrimental impact" of obscene materials on individuals and society—even though our understanding or conception of that detrimental impact (a "permissible shift in emphasis") may have evolved, as Sopinka J. noted. My colleagues say that it is a permissible shift in emphasis that the false news provision was originally focused on the "prevention of deliberate slanderous statements against the great nobles of the realm" and is now said to be concerned with "attacks on religious, racial or ethnic minorities." But this is no shift in emphasis with regard to the purpose of the legislation—this is an outright redefinition not only of the purpose of the prohibition but also of the nature of the activity prohibited. To convert s. 181 into a provision directed at encouraging racial harmony is to go beyond any permissible shift in emphasis and effectively rewrite the section.

It is argued that this interpretation represents a mere shift in emphasis because the thrust of s. 181 and its predecessors, like the obscenity provisions in *Butler*, disclosed a single goal: "[t]he protection of the public interest from harm" or from that which would "threaten the integrity of the social fabric." Yet, all *Criminal Code* provisions—as well as much statutory regulation in the public and private law spheres—have as their basic purpose the protection of the public from harm and the maintenance of the integrity of the social fabric. Indeed, one might argue that such was the goal of the obscenity provisions under review in *Butler*, yet the court did not adopt that as the legislation's objective. Instead, it relied upon a specific objective concerning the effect of pornographic materials on individuals and the resultant impact on society. If the simple identification of the (content-free) goal of protecting the public from harm constitutes a "pressing and substantial" objective, virtually any law will meet the first part of the onus imposed upon the Crown under s. 1. I cannot believe that the framers of the *Charter* intended s. 1 to be applied in such a manner. Justification under s. 1 requires more than the general goal of protection from harm common to all criminal legislation; it requires a specific purpose so pressing and substantial as to be capable of overriding the *Charter*'s guarantees. To apply the language used by Sopinka J. in *Butler* (at p. 496 [SCR]); s. 181 cannot be said to be directed to avoidance of publications which "seriously offend the values fundamental to our society," nor is it directed to a "substantial concern which justifies restricting the otherwise full exercise of the freedom of expression."

All this stands in sharp contrast to the hate propaganda provision of the *Criminal Code* at issue in *Keegstra*—s. 319(2). Both the text of that provision and its long and detailed Parliamentary history, involving Canada's international human rights obligations, the Cohen Committee Report (*Report of the Special Committee on Hate Propaganda in Canada* (Ottawa: Queen's Printer, 1966)) and the Report of the Special Committee on the Participation of Visible Minorities in Canadian Society (*Equality Now!* (Ottawa: Supplies & Services, 1984)), permitted ready identification of the objective Parliament had in mind. Section 319(2), under challenge in *Keegstra*, was part of the amendments to the *Criminal Code* "essentially along the lines suggested by the [Cohen] Committee ..." (per Dickson C.J.C. in *Keegstra*, supra, at p. 725 [SCR]). The evil addressed was hate-mongering, particularly in the racial context. The provision at issue on this appeal is quite different. Parliament had identified no social problem, much less one of pressing concern, justifying s. 181 of the *Criminal Code*. To suggest that the objective of s. 181 is to combat hate propaganda or racism is to go beyond its history and its wording and to adopt the "shifting purpose" analysis this court has rejected. Such an objective, moreover, hardly seems capable of being described as a "nuisance," the rubric under which Parliament has placed s. 181, nor as the offence's target of mere "mischief" to a public interest.

Can it be said in these circumstances that the Crown has discharged the burden upon it of establishing that the objective of the legislation is pressing and substantial, in short, of sufficient importance to justify overriding the constitutional guarantee of freedom of expression? I think not. It may be that s. 181 is capable of serving legitimate purposes. But no objective of pressing and substantial concern has been identified in support of its retention in our *Criminal Code*. Other provisions, such as s. 319(2) of the *Criminal Code*, deal with hate propaganda more fairly and more effectively. Still other provisions seem to deal adequately with matters of sedition and state security. ...

Section 181 can be used to inhibit statements which society considers should be inhibited, like those which denigrate vulnerable groups. Its danger, however, lies in the fact that by its broad reach it criminalizes a vast penumbra of other statements merely because they might be thought to constitute a mischief to some public interest, however successive prosecutors and courts may wish to define these terms. The danger is magnified because the prohibition affects not only those caught and prosecuted, but those who may refrain from saying what they would like to because of the fear that they will be caught. Thus worthy minority groups or individuals may be inhibited from saying what they desire to say for fear that they might be prosecuted. Should an activist be prevented from saying "the rainforest of British Columbia is being destroyed" because she fears criminal prosecution for spreading "false news" in the event that scientists conclude and a jury accepts that the statement is false and that it is likely to cause mischief to the British Columbia forest industry? ...

... All it takes is one judge and 12 jurors who believe that certain "falsehoods" compromise a particular "public" interest, and that such falsehoods "must have been" known to the accused, in order to convict. A jury in Port Alberni, British Columbia, may have a very different view of the overall beneficial impact of false statements of fact impugning the lumber industry than a jury in Toronto. ...

In summary, the broad range of expression caught by s. 181—extending to virtually all controversial statements of apparent fact which might be argued to be false and likely to do some mischief to some public interest—combined with the serious consequences of criminality and imprisonment, makes it impossible to say that s. 181 is appropriately measured and restrained having regard to the evil addressed—that it effects a "minimal impairment" to use the language of *Oakes*, supra. Section 181 is materially different, in this regard, from s. 319(2)—the provision upheld under s. 1 by the majority of this court in *Keegstra*.

To summarize, the restriction on expression effected by s. 181 of the *Criminal Code*, unlike that imposed by the hate propaganda provision at issue in *Keegstra*, cannot be justified under s. 1 of the *Charter* as a "reasonable limit prescribed by law as can be demonstrably justified in a free and democratic society." At virtually every step of the *Oakes* test, one is struck with the substantial difference between s. 181 and the provision at issue in *Keegstra*, s. 319(2) of the Code. In contrast to the hate propaganda provision (*Keegstra*), the false news provision cannot be associated with any existing social problem or legislative objective, much less one of pressing concern. It is, as the Law Reform Commission concluded, "anachronistic." But even if the court were to attribute to s. 181 the objective of promoting racial and social tolerance and conclude that such objective was so pressing and substantial as to be capable of overriding a fundamental freedom, s. 181 would still fail to meet the criteria of proportionality which prevailed in *Keegstra*. In *Keegstra*, the majority of this court found the objective of the legislation to be compelling and its effect to be appropriately circumscribed. The opposite is the case with s. 181 of the *Criminal Code*. Section 181 catches not only deliberate falsehoods which promote hatred, but sanctions all false assertions which the prosecutor believes "likely to cause injury or mischief to a public interest," regardless of whether they promote the values underlying s. 2(b). At the same time, s. 181's objective, in so far as an objective can be ascribed to the section, ranks much lower in importance than the legislative goal at stake in *Keegstra*. When the objective of s. 181 is balanced against its invasive reach, there can, in my opinion, be only one conclusion: the limitation of freedom of expression is disproportionate to the objective envisaged.

In their laudable effort to send a message condemning the "hate-mongering" of persons such as the appellant by upholding s. 181 as a reasonable limit, it is my respectful opinion that my colleagues Cory and Iacobucci JJ. make three fundamental errors. First, they effectively rewrite s. 181 to supply its text with a particularity which finds no support in the provision's history or in its rare application in the Canadian context. Second, they underrate the expansive breadth of s. 181 and its potential not only for improper prosecution and conviction but for "chilling" the speech of persons who may otherwise have exercised their freedom of expression. Finally, they go far beyond accepted principles of statutory and *Charter* interpretation in their application of s. 1 of the *Charter*. While I share the concerns of my colleagues, I fear that such techniques, taken to their ultimate extreme, might render nugatory the free speech guarantee of the *Charter*. ...

[CORY and IACOBUCCI JJ (Gonthier J concurring) in dissent agreed that s 181 violated s 2(b) but held that it was justified under s 1 of the Charter.]

This appeal concerns the wilful publication of deliberate, injurious lies and the legislation which seeks to combat the serious harm to society as a whole caused by these calculated and deceitful falsehoods. Our colleague, McLachlin J., has stated that s. 181 violates s. 2(b) of the *Charter* and is not saved under s. 1. We agree with her conclusion, though not with her reasoning, that s. 181 violates s. 2(b) of the *Charter*. However, with respect, we do not agree that the section cannot be justified under s. 1.

The appellant contends that the term "public interest" is so vague that the section is invalid. It is submitted that the term could be used by an unscrupulous government to render criminal any conduct or opinion opposed by the government of the day.

The fact that the term is undefined by the legislation is of little significance. There are many phrases and words contained in the *Criminal Code* which have been interpreted by the courts. It is impossible for legislators to foresee and provide for every eventuality or to define every term that is used. Enactments must have some flexibility. Courts have in the past played a significant role in the definition of words and phrases used in the Code and other enactments. They should continue to do so in the future.

A survey of federal statutes alone reveals that the term "public interest" is mentioned 224 times in 84 federal statutes. The term appears in comparable numbers in provincial statutes. The term does not and cannot have a uniform meaning in each statute. It must be interpreted in light of the legislative history of the particular provision in which it appears and the legislative and social context in which it is used.

A "public interest" likely to be harmed as a result of contravention of s. 181 is the public interest in a free and democratic society that is subject to the rule of law. A free society is one built upon reasoned debate in which all its members are entitled to participate. Section 181, including its reference to "public interest," should, as this court has emphasized, be interpreted in light of *Charter* values.

As a fundamental document setting out essential features of our vision of democracy, the *Charter* provides us with indications as to which values go to the very core of our political structure. A democratic society capable of giving effect to the *Charter*'s guarantees is one which strives toward creating a community committed to equality, liberty and human dignity. The public interest is, therefore, in preserving and promoting these goals.

The term, as it appears in s. 181, should be confined to those rights recognized in the *Charter* as being fundamental to Canadian democracy. It need not be extended beyond that. As an example, the rights enacted in ss. 7, 15 and 27 of the *Charter* should be considered in defining a public interest.

It has been argued that s. 181 is anachronistic and that to attribute to it the purpose of protecting racial and social tolerance is to trigger the invalid shifting purpose doctrine. Those concerns should now be addressed.

It is true the false news provision dates back to 1275. It was submitted that there is really no need at this stage in our history to protect the "great persons of the realm," which was the basis for the section when it was first enacted in the 13th century, and that the provision serves no other purpose. That position cannot be accepted. This section was specifically retained by Parliament in 1955. It has today a very real and pertinent role to play in Canada's multicultural and democratic society.

The tragedy of the Holocaust and the enactment of the *Charter* have served to emphasize the laudable s. 181 aim of preventing the harmful effects of false speech and thereby promoting racial and social tolerance. In fact, it was in part the publication of the evil and invidious statements that were known to be false by those that made them regarding the Jewish people that led the way to the inferno of the Holocaust. The realities of Canada's multicultural society emphasize the vital need to protect minorities and preserve Canada's mosaic of cultures.

Support for the proposition that a shift in emphasis is permissible also stems from the decision in *Butler*, supra. Centuries ago, obscenity laws were enacted to prevent the corruption of the morals of the King's subjects, and therefore to protect the peace of the King and government. ... In *Butler*, however, Sopinka J. found that the objective of the obscenity law is no longer moral disapprobation but rather the avoidance of harm to society.

Sopinka J. concluded by adding that a "permissible shift in emphasis was built into the legislation when, as interpreted by the courts, it adopted the community standards test." ... Similarly, in the present case, the wording of s. 181 includes a permissible shift in emphasis with its test which is based on injury to the public interest.

Just as the community standards test, as applied to the obscenity law, "must necessarily respond to changing mores," ... so too should the test to define "injury to a public interest" take into account the changing values of Canadian society. Those values encompass multiculturalism and equality, precepts specifically included in the provisions of the *Charter*.

At the end of this detailed analysis it is worthwhile to step back and consider what it is that is being placed on the balance.

On one side is s. 181. It infringes to a minimal extent the s. 2(b) right of freedom of expression. In reality, it cannot be said that the prohibition of the wilful publication of false statements that are known to be false is an infringement of the core values of s. 2(b). Rather the infringement is on the extreme periphery of those values. In addition, the section can play an important role in fostering multiculturalism and racial and religious tolerance by demonstrating Canadian society's abhorrence of spreading what are known to be lies that injure and denigrate vulnerable minority groups and individuals.

On the other side, s. 181 provides maximum protection of the accused. It requires the Crown to establish beyond a reasonable doubt that the accused wilfully published false statements of fact presented as truth and that their publication caused or was likely to cause injury to the public interest. Any uncertainty as to the nature of the speech must inure to the benefit of the accused. If ever s. 1 balancing is to be used to demonstrate that a section of the *Criminal Code* is justifiable in a free and democratic society, this is such a case.

Legislation such as this, which is aimed at the protection of society from deceit and aggression, yet provides the widest protection for the accused, should be fostered. Applying the *Charter* to strike s. 181 would be in direct contradiction to the principles established by this court. The section is justifiable in our free and democratic Canadian society.

Appeal allowed; acquittal entered.

The Ontario attorney general subsequently declined to allow a charge against Zundel under s 319(2) of the *Criminal Code*.

The Law Reform Commission of Canada in its Working Paper 50 *Hate Propaganda* (1986) summarized previous reform proposals as follows:

> The Special Parliamentary Committee Report on Participation of Visible Minorities in Canadian Society, *Equality Now*, recommended: (1) the removal of the "wilfully" requirement from subsection 281.2(2), so that it would no longer be necessary to prove that the accused intended to promote hatred; (2) the removal of the requirement of the consent of the Attorney General to a prosecution under subsection 281.2(2); and (3) clarifying that the burden of proof is on the accused to raise the defences provided for by that subsection. The Special Committee on Racial and Religious Hatred of the Canadian Bar Association differed from the conclusions in *Equality Now* in two respects. First, it believed that requiring the consent of the provincial Attorney General could prevent frivolous prosecutions. Second, it believed that two of the existing defences to a charge under subsection 281.2(2) should be abolished. These were: (1) a good faith opinion on a religious subject; and (2) a reasonable belief in the truth of the statements if they were relevant to the public interest and were discussed for the public benefit. The Fraser Committee also recommended the removal of the "wilfully" requirement and the consent of the Attorney General. But, unlike the other reports, it advocated enlarging the definition of "identifiable group" to include the categories of sex, age, and mental or physical disability, at least insofar as the definition applies to section 281.2 of the *Code*.
>
> While these laws and these proposals are useful to us in some degree, those who have either passed laws or have proposed reforms in this area have not adequately considered the fundamental principle of restraint which must shape our criminal law.

The commission examined the offence created under s 319(2) of the *Criminal Code*:

> The crucial issue involving *mens rea* is whether the crime should retain the word "wilfully" or an equivalent phrase which makes the crime effectively one of specific intent, or whether "wilfully" should be dropped altogether to create a crime of recklessness. The preferred view of many persons, as reflected in *Equality Now* and the Fraser Committee report, is that the "wilfully" requirement must be dropped.
>
> With respect, we do not share this view. The principle of restraint requires lawmakers to concern themselves not just with whom they want to catch, but also with whom they do not want to catch. For example, removing an intent or purpose requirement could well result in successful prosecutions of cases similar to *Buzzanga*, where members of a minority group publish hate

propaganda against their own group in order to create controversy or to agitate for reform. This crime should not be used to prosecute such individuals.

In effect, this crime should be used only to catch the most extreme cases of fomenting hatred, when the accused is motivated by enmity. Accordingly, we recommend that this crime should continue to be one of intent or purpose. This is best achieved by removing the "wilfully" requirement and substituting in its place an "intentionally" or "purposely" requirement. This change in wording would not result in any change to the *mens rea* requirement for this crime as set out in *Buzzanga and Durocher*, but it would avoid the problems inherent in the word "wilfully," which has been defined inconsistently in criminal law.

The commission proposed that the definition of identifiable group should be expanded to protect groups identifiable on the basis of race, national or ethnic origin, colour, religion, sex, age, or mental or physical disability.

The commission concluded that the prohibition against the spreading of false news in s 181 of the *Criminal Code* should be abolished:

It is too wide, because it is too vague. It is too vague because it catches any statement which the publisher knows is false, if likely to cause "mischief to a public interest." But what is "mischief to a public interest"? While this phrase may appear to catch only harmful conduct, the appearance is deceptive. Unfortunately, the reported prosecutions under this offence, save for the *Zundel* case, seem unwarranted: for example, a conviction of an angry store owner for saying that Americans were not wanted in Canada; a trial conviction (later overturned on appeal) of an underground newspaper printing a false story that the mayor of Montréal was killed by a dope-crazed hippie.

On the other hand, does section 177 [now s 181] serve a useful purpose when used to prosecute persons like Zundel? Surely not. Using section 177 for this purpose is inappropriate for two reasons. First, denials of the Holocaust should be dealt with for what they are—a form of hate propaganda. Second, on principle, if Parliament intends that promoting hatred be dealt with in a certain way and creates safeguards such as the requirement of the Attorney General's consent to avoid an abusive application of the criminal law, a private prosecutor should not be able to avoid these safeguards by offence shopping elsewhere.

Police Powers

This chapter provides an introduction and basic overview of key common law, statutory, and constitutional constraints on the investigation of crime. The focus will be on the values at stake when the state investigates crime and the challenge of striking an appropriate balance between these important but competing goals. Thought should also be given to how decisions about the limits of the criminal law discussed in Chapter 2 affect the role of the police, for example, with respect to crimes involving drugs or prostitution.

Section I introduces various models of the criminal process, with an emphasis on competing values such as crime control and due process and the role of the Charter in striking a balance between them. Section II considers the common law and constitutional requirements for the taking of statements from suspects, questioning whether or not Canada has moved toward the due process model under the Charter and adopted its own *Miranda* rule. Section III examines the defence of entrapment. Section IV explores the constitutional constraints that have developed under s 8 of the Charter with respect to police powers of search and seizure. Section V examines the constitutional constraints that have developed under s 9 of the Charter with respect to police detention and arrest powers, with an emphasis on the interaction between Charter requirements, the common law, and statutory powers. Finally,

Section VI addresses the source of police powers, introducing the contemporary debate surrounding the judicial creation of police powers in Canada under the "ancillary powers doctrine."

I. MODELS OF THE CRIMINAL PROCESS

K Roach, *Due Process and Victims' Rights:*
The New Law and Politics of Criminal Justice
(Toronto: University of Toronto Press, 1999) (references omitted)

Packer's Two Concepts of Justice

The most successful attempt to construct models of the criminal process was achieved by the American legal scholar Herbert Packer. ... The essence of each of Packer's two models is captured by an evocative metaphor. The criminal process in the crime-control model resembles a high-speed "assembly-line conveyor belt" operated by the police and prosecutors. The end product of the assembly-line is a guilty plea. In contrast, the due-process model is an "obstacle course" in which defence lawyers argue before judges that the prosecution should be rejected because the accused's rights have been violated. The assembly line of the crime-control model is primarily concerned with efficiency, while the due-process model is concerned with fairness to the accused and "quality control" ... .

Prior to the enactment of the Charter and the "due-process revolution" of the 1980s, the formal law of the Canadian criminal justice system embraced crime-control values. The few due-process initiatives that occurred were undertaken by Parliament, not the Supreme Court. This runs contrary to Packer's predictions that courts, not legislatures, would be the champions of due process. It also illustrates the dynamic nature of legal and political culture. In the 1980s, the Supreme Court and Parliament switched roles, with the former taking a proactive due-process lead and Parliament being concerned with crime control and victims' rights, frequently in reaction to due-process court decisions.

Before the Charter, Canadian courts had limited grounds to intervene in the criminal process. ... Canadian courts traditionally placed discovering the truth about the factually guilty before the fair treatment of the accused. Justice Ivan Rand rejected the notion that suspects' statements would be inadmissible because the police failed to read the proper warnings. "It would be a serious error to place the ordinary modes of investigation of crime in a strait-jacket of artificial rules. ... Rigid formulas can be both meaningless to the weakling and absurd to the sophisticated or hardened criminal; and to introduce a new rite as an inflexible preliminary condition would serve no genuine interest of the accused and but add an unreal formalism to that vital branch of the administration of justice." Thus, *Miranda*-type warnings were dismissed by even the most liberal of Canadian judges before the Charter. Consistent with crime-control concerns about truth and reliability, Canadian courts were concerned only about the propriety of police conduct when doubt was "cast on the truth of the statement." Truth, not fairness, mattered.

Commitment to crime control meant a reluctance to exclude relevant evidence even if unfairly obtained. In *Wray* (1970), the Supreme Court admitted into evidence a gun and an involuntary confession taken from a suspect subjected to a coercive ten-hour interrogation during which the police deliberately kept his lawyer at bay. The gun was admissible as reliable evidence, and the confession was admissible to the extent that its reliability was confirmed when the suspect led the police to the murder weapon. The admission of this relevant and truthful evidence was "unfortunate" for the accused, but not "unfair." There was no "judicial authority in this country or in England which supports the proposition that a trial judge has a discretion to exclude admissible evidence because, in his opinion, its admission would be calculated to bring the administration of justice into disrepute." As will be seen, *Wray* would be decided very differently under section 24(2) of the Charter.

Consistent with their general lack of concern about what happened beyond the court-room door, the Supreme Court limited the right against self-incrimination to not being compelled to testify in one's own trial. A refusal by an accused to participate in an iden-tification line-up could be used as incriminating evidence. The accused's blood and other "incriminating conditions of the body" could be admitted into evidence even though involuntarily and illegally obtained. Under the Charter, the Court would extend the right against self-incrimination from the courthouse to the police station and exclude reliable evidence, including incriminating bodily material, because it was unfairly conscripted from the accused.

The crime-control model did not necessarily condone police misconduct, but insisted that it be addressed outside of the accused's trial through civil suits, disciplinary hearings, and criminal prosecutions against the police. During the 1950s, the Supreme Court upheld damage awards stemming from police abuses in Quebec, and the right to seek damages was celebrated as the accused's most viable remedy. The damage remedy, however, was illusory, except for the most persistent and ultimately consistent with crime-control values because it required the accused's rights to be vindicated outside of the criminal process. Americans discontent with the Warren Court's reliance on the exclusionary rule looked longingly north of the border. One critic of the Warren Court invoked the Canadian ex-ample of crime control by quoting a commissioner of the Royal Canadian Mounted Police (RCMP) who argued that "when the policeman exceeds his authority, bring him up short, but when he is doing, as most of them are doing, a tough, thankless and frequently dan-gerous job for you and for all you hold dear, for God's sake get off his back."

Canadian acceptance of broad police powers is best symbolized by writs of assistance which gave members of the RCMP open-ended powers to conduct drug or Customs searches. Consistent with crime-control values, the writs relied on the expertise of police officers to decide when a search was warranted. As late as 1976, there were 935 writs held by RCMP officers which were used to authorize more than 4,000 searches. As one Amer-ican commentator noted with some disgust, the writs empowered a police officer "without prior authorization or subsequent judicial review, to dismantle a house [in a search for narcotics] on their own decision." The use of the writs by English Customs officials had been one of the leading grievances in the American Revolution, and such general warrants were specifically prohibited in the American Bill of Rights. In Canada, however, even the reformist 1969 Ouimet Commission refused to recommend their abolition, and the writs were upheld under the Canadian Bill of Rights because that statutory bill of rights did not grant Canadians rights against unreasonable searches and seizures, and the writs did not interfere with the accused's right to a fair trial in the courtroom. Again, judicial concerns about fairness did not extend beyond the courtroom door. ...

Under the 1960 Canadian Bill of Rights, Canadian courts defined the accused's right in a minimal fashion and refused to grant effective remedies. The right to consult counsel did not include the right to talk to a lawyer in private. A drunk-driving suspect required upon pain of criminal conviction to provide a breath sample at the side of the road was not detained and entitled to consult counsel. Although a denial of the right to counsel could qualify as a reasonable excuse for not providing a breathalyser, the Court would not exclude a breath sample given by a less assertive accused who was also denied counsel. As Laskin J. accurately noted in his dissent, the Court's choice was "to favour the social interest in the repression of crime despite the unlawful invasion of individual interests ... by public officers." ... In short, both the law and the practice of criminal justice before the Charter closely resembled Packer's crime-control model. As will be seen in the next section, the values of crime control almost survived the enactment of the Charter.

The Development of Due Process

Although they are the most frequently litigated part of the Charter, the legal rights and remedies of the accused were never at the heart of Pierre Trudeau's patriation project. Support for due process was at the mercy of the intergovernmental bargaining that defined constitutional politics until the late 1980s. The precarious place of due process in the drafting of the Charter, like other messy facts of history, embarrasses claims that due process was an inevitable development necessary to legitimate and distract a criminal justice system that was losing credibility. ...

[T]he federal government ... diluted the legal rights and remedies in an attempt to obtain provincial support. By October 1980, the right against unreasonable search and seizure had been watered down to the right "not to be subjected to search or seizure except on grounds, and in accordance with procedures, established by law." The writs of assistance, however Draconian, were still established by law. Similarly, detainees had rights against detention, imprisonment, and the denial of bail only if the deprivations of liberty were not "in accordance with procedures established by law." Those subject to detention or arrest had the right to counsel, but not the right to be informed of that right. As under the CBR, only the most knowledgeable and aggressive of accused would benefit from their rights.

The October draft did contain more robust rights such as the presumption of innocence and the right to be tried in a reasonable time, but these rights only ensured fairness in the courtroom. Like all other Charter rights, they were subject to "reasonable limits as are generally accepted in a free and democratic society with a parliamentary system of government." The reference to a parliamentary system of government would encourage courts to defer to the ability of Parliament to enact criminal laws and procedures and was criticized as a "Mack Truck" exception to the guaranteed rights. The October draft also inhibited the development of remedies by providing that all Charter rights (except the traditional right against being called as a witness in one's own trial) did not affect existing laws allowing unfairly obtained but relevant evidence to be admitted in criminal trials or the ability of legislatures to provide their own standards of admissibility.

The October draft preserved, behind a thin façade of rights and due process, the unfettered discretion of police, prosecutors, and legislatures fundamental to the crime-control model. It affirmed due process in the abstract while enabling substantial crime-control limitations on these rights. ...

After the collapse of intergovernmental bargaining, the federal government referred the Charter to a special Joint Committee of the House of Commons and Senate. … Legal rights and remedies were fundamentally strengthened in the Joint Committee process. The Canadian Civil Liberties Association (CCLA), which claimed a membership of only 5,000 individuals was probably the most influential group in beefing up the rights that would be the foundation of Canada's due-process revolution. … Alan Borovoy of the CCLA argued that the October prohibition could have upheld an infamous drug raid in Fort Erie where more than 100 patrons of a bar were searched under the expansive legal powers of the Narcotics Control Act and a writ of assistance possessed by one of the officers. The section was a "verbal illusion in the sense that it may pretend to give us something, but in fact, gives us nothing more than we already have." The B.C. Civil Liberties Association claimed that the provision was worse than nothing and would justify some of the warrantless searches uncovered by the McDonald Commission into RCMP wrongdoing. Despite their small membership, the civil-liberties groups effectively invoked well-publicized police abuses. The Canadian Bar Association (CBA) stressed the danger of a standard that could "be altered by the arbitrary action of a legislature, as well as by the arbitrary action of a public official." The lawyers wanted judges, not Parliament, to have the last word. …

The October draft provided the accused with the right to retain and instruct counsel without delay, but did not require the police to inform detainees of this right. Borovoy successfully proposed that the right be amended so that "nervous, frightened, bewildered" detainees not be interrogated until informed of the right to counsel. … This gave the Supreme Court of Canada a textual basis to require the police to provide *Miranda*-style warnings to those they detained or arrested. Civil-liberties groups and the New Democratic Party failed, however, to entrench the right to legal aid, and this omission was later used by the Court as a reason not to require all provinces to provide 1-800 numbers to ensure that detainees could speak to lawyers.

Section 26 of the October draft of the Charter would have preserved legislative supremacy for laws governing the admissibility of evidence. It was strongly criticized by civil-liberties groups and defence lawyers, but vigorously defended by police and prosecutors. The CBA argued that it preserved parliamentary supremacy when the Charter would give courts "an entrenched right to construe every other specified legal right." In contrast, an association of prosecutors defended section 26 for leaving "the law of evidence to the type of evolution that we have been used to in this country, that is a combination of parliament and the courts." The CBA favoured the judicial supremacy that was fundamental to the due-process model, while the prosecutors wished to conserve legislative supremacy and the crime-control values of the common law. …

The government agreed to delete section 26 in early January 1981 and add a "general remedies" section allowing courts to order whatever remedy they considered to be appropriate and just in the circumstances. [Later, s 24(2) was finalized.] … The only note of caution came from Coline Campbell of the Liberals, who inquired whether the amendment introduced the American "tainted fruit doctrine" and wondered why section 24(2) did not specify the factors to be considered when deciding whether the admission of evidence would bring the administration of justice into disrepute. E.G. Ewaschuk of the Department of Justice reassured her that a judge would consider "the seriousness of the case, the seriousness of the breach by the police, the manner in which the evidence was obtained" before deciding whether to exclude the evidence. Moreover, he argued that the remedy would be triggered only by "very blameworthy, repugnant and very reprehensive" conduct; in short, when "the admission of this evidence would make me vomit, it was obtained in such a reprehensible manner" ... the vomit test did not win judicial favour. In its desire to protect an expanded right against self-incrimination, the Supreme Court developed a quasi-absolutist exclusionary rule which precluded judges from considering the seriousness of the offence charged or the seriousness of the violation.

The provinces eventually obtained the ability to enact legislation, notwithstanding the legal rights. This power has never been used in the criminal justice field despite the political appeal of crime control and victims' rights. It has proven unnecessary because Parliament has used ordinary legislation to respond to, and even overturn, unpopular due-process Charter decisions. This contrasts with the American experience of courts ignoring legislative attempts to overrule *Miranda*, but it is facilitated by the structure of the Charter, which allows government to justify legislation that violates Charter rights as "reasonable limits prescribed by law as can be demonstrably justified in a free and democratic society" (Charter, s. 1).

Are the values of due process and crime control exhaustive of the relevant values in the investigation of crime? What about the question of community standards examined in the last chapter? What about the interests or rights of victims or groups that may be disproportionately subject to some crimes?

II. QUESTIONING SUSPECTS

The Common Law Governing Confessions

Long before the 1982 enactment of the Charter, judges used their law-making authority at common law to develop a body of jurisprudence that requires the exclusion from evidence of confessions not proven to be voluntary.

Consider, as you read this material, whether the purpose of the confessions rule is to deal with the danger that the statement may be untrue or obtained in a manner offensive to community standards, or to control improper police practices, or to protect the accused against self-incrimination, or some combination of all four concerns.

In *Boudreau v The King*, [1949] SCR 262, the Supreme Court of Canada held that the fundamental question relating to the admissibility of a confession made to a person in authority (for example, a police officer) is whether it is *voluntary*. The court in *Boudreau* affirmed the conviction (Estey J dissenting) holding that a warning that the accused is not obliged to say anything but that anything that he or she says may be recorded and given in evidence is not absolutely necessary. Only part of the judgments of Kellock and Rand JJ are reproduced here. Kellock J stated:

> The governing principle is stated by Lord Sumner in *Ibrahim v. The King*, [1914] A.C. 599 at pp. 609-10, as follows: "It has long been established as a positive rule of English criminal law, that no statement by an accused is admissible in evidence against him unless it is shewn by the prosecution to have been a voluntary statement, in the sense that it has not been obtained from him

either by fear of prejudice or hope of advantage exercised or held out by a person in authority. The principle is as old as Lord Hale. The burden of proof in the matter has been decided by high authority in recent times in *Reg. v. Thompson*, [1893] 2 Q.B. 12."

Rand J stated:

> The cases of *Ibrahim v. The King*, [1914] A.C. 599, *R. v. Voisin*, [1918] 1 K.B. 531, and *Prosko v. The King*, 66 D.L.R. 340, 37 Can. C.C. 199, 63 S.C.R. 226, lay it down that the fundamental question is whether the statement is voluntary. No doubt arrest and the presence of officers tend to arouse apprehension which a warning may or may not suffice to remove, and the rule is directed against the danger of improperly instigated or induced or coerced admissions. It is the doubt cast on the truth of the statement arising from the circumstances in which it is made that gives rise to the rule. What the statement should be is that of a man free in volition from the compulsions or inducements of authority and what is sought is assurance that that is the case. The underlying and controlling question then remains: Is the statement freely and voluntarily made? Here the trial Judge found that it was. It would be a serious error to place the ordinary modes of investigation of crime in a strait-jacket of artificial rules; and the true protection against improper interrogation or any kind of pressure or inducement is to leave the broad question to the Court. Rigid formulas can be both meaningless to the weakling and absurd to the sophisticated or hardened criminal; and to introduce a new rite as an inflexible preliminary condition would serve no genuine interest of the accused and but add an unreal formalism to that vital branch of the administration of justice.

In the decades following *Boudreau*, a body of case law developed in Canada regarding the voluntariness requirement. In time, beyond actual violence, threats, or promises, the Supreme Court also came to recognize that voluntariness could be undermined by considerations that had little to do with the reliability of a confession and everything to do with treating suspects fairly. So, for example, voluntariness could be undermined due to shock (*Ward v The Queen*, [1979] 2 SCR 30), hypnosis (*Horvath v The Queen*, [1979] 2 SCR 376 per Beetz J), or "complete emotional disintegration" (*Horvath, supra*, at 400, per Spence J). Similarly, in *Hobbins v The Queen*, [1982] 1 SCR 553 at 556-57, Laskin CJ noted that in determining the voluntariness of a confession, courts should be alert to the coercive effect of an "atmosphere of oppression," even though there was "no inducement held out of hope of advantage or fear of prejudice, and absent any threats of violence or actual violence." As the Supreme Court recognized in *R v Oickle*, 2000 SCC 38, [2000] 2 SCR 3, although the confessions rule is concerned with reliability, it now "also extends to protect a broader conception of voluntariness 'that focuses on the protection of the accused's rights and fairness in the criminal process'" (at para 69).

In *Oickle*, the Supreme Court reiterated that confessions can be rendered involuntary: (1) because of threats or promises that induce the confession; (2) due to an atmosphere of oppression that compels a suspect to speak in order to bring their ordeal to an end; (3) in circumstances where a suspect lacked an "operating mind" when speaking—for example, where a suspect is so intoxicated or mentally disturbed that the suspect lacks knowledge of what he or she is saying and that he or she is saying it to a police officer who can use it to the suspect's detriment; or (4) where the police have engaged in trickery that is so appalling as to shock the community. With this last concern, the Court in *Oickle* recognized that "[w]hile it is still related to voluntariness, its more specific objective is maintaining the integrity of the criminal justice system" (at para 65).

In the end, however, the Court in *Oickle* eschewed the use of hard-and-fast rules when deciding on the admissibility of confessions. Instead, it emphasized the need for a contextual approach. Each case ultimately turns on its facts. The totality of the circumstances must be considered in deciding whether the Crown has established beyond a reasonable doubt that the suspect made a free and voluntary choice to speak to the police—in other words, that the statement was voluntary.

We move next to developments under the Charter. In these next few parts our focus will be on the Charter's legal rights guarantees that operate to constrain the investigative powers of police (ss 7, 8, 9, and 10). For now, the remedial consequence of a Charter violation—that is, the potential exclusion of unconstitutionally obtained evidence under s 24(2)—will be placed on the backburner. The Supreme Court of Canada's most recent direction on the approach to be taken in deciding whether or not to admit or exclude unconstitutionally obtained evidence under s 24(2) of the Charter is contained in *R v Grant*, 2009 SCC 32, [2009] 2 SCR 353. *Grant* is reproduced in Section V below.

Confessions and the Right to Counsel

The next case is one of the Supreme Court's first and seminal decisions interpreting s 10(b) of the Charter, which provides as follows:

> 10. Everyone has the right on arrest or detention …
>   (b) to retain and instruct counsel without delay and to be informed of that right … .

R v Manninen
Supreme Court of Canada
[1987] 1 SCR 1233

LAMER J: On October 26, 1982, there was a robbery at a Mac's Milk store in Toronto …

On October 28th, two days after the robbery, police officers MacIver and Train, acting on information received, attended at E & R Simonizing on Caledonia Rd. in Toronto at around 1:30 p.m. Both officers were in plain clothes. At approximately 2:33 p.m., the respondent drove up to the premises in a car which answered the description of the stolen car used in the armed robbery.

The respondent left the car and proceeded to the office premises where Train was waiting. MacIver, who had been waiting in the parking-lot, investigated the car. He saw a gun butt protruding from under the driver's seat. He put the gun into his hip pocket, and he then followed the respondent into the office. When the respondent entered the office, Train greeted him with "Hi Ron." The respondent asked "Do I know you?" At that stage both officers identified themselves as police officers and showed the respondent their badges. They searched and handcuffed the respondent.

At 2:40 p.m. Train arrested the respondent for theft and possession of the stolen car and for the armed robbery of the Mac's Milk store. He read him his rights from a card which was issued to all police officers when the Charter was proclaimed. The card from which the constable read stated as follows:

Charter of Rights

1. Notice Upon Arrest

   I am arresting you for _____ (briefly describe reasons for arrest).

2. Right to Counsel

   It is my duty to inform you that you have the right to retain and instruct counsel without delay.

   Do you understand?

   Caution to Charged Person

   You (are charged, will be charged) with _____. Do you wish to say anything in answer to the charge? You are not obliged to say anything unless you wish to do so, but whatever you say may be given in evidence.

   Secondary Caution to Charged Person

   If you have spoken to any police officer or to anyone with authority or if any such person has spoken to you in connection with this case, I want it clearly understood that I do not want it to influence you in making any statement.

The respondent made a flippant remark at the reading of the caution and the right to counsel to the effect that "it sounds like an American T.V. programme." Train reread the whole card to the respondent and, at that time, the respondent said: "Prove it. I ain't saying anything until I see my lawyer. I want to see my lawyer."

MacIver then questioned the respondent as follows:

Q. What is your full name?

A. Ronald Charles Manninen.

Q. Where is your address?

A. Ain't got one.

Q. Where is the knife that you had along with this (showing the respondent the CO_2 gun found in the car) when you ripped [off] the Mac's Milk on Wilson Avenue?

A. He's lying. When I was in the store I only had the gun. The knife was in the tool box in the car.

This last answer was relied on by the trial judge in convicting the respondent on the charge of armed robbery. ...

There was an operating telephone in the small office where the respondent was arrested and the police officers used it in the course of the afternoon. The respondent did not make a direct request to use the telephone and the police officers did not volunteer the use of the telephone to the respondent. The trial judge made the following finding: "I find the police had no desire to have him call a lawyer, and intended to call a lawyer back at the station when the arrest was completed. The respondent did not speak to his lawyer until the lawyer called him at the police station at 8:35 p.m. ..."

Violation of the Right to Counsel

Section 10(b) of the Charter provides:

> 10. Everyone has the right on arrest or detention
> (b) to retain and instruct counsel without delay and to be informed of that right ...

It is not disputed that the respondent was informed of his right to retain and instruct counsel without delay. Further, the sufficiency of the communication is not challenged. ...

In my view, s. 10(b) imposes at least two duties on the police in addition to the duty to inform the detainee of his rights. First, the police must provide the detainee with a reasonable opportunity to exercise the right to retain and instruct counsel without delay. The detainee is in the control of the police and he cannot exercise his right to counsel unless the police provide him with a reasonable opportunity to do so. ...

In my view, this aspect of the right to counsel was clearly infringed in this case. The respondent clearly asserted his right to remain silent and his desire to consult his lawyer. There was a telephone immediately at hand in the office, which the officers used for their own purposes. It was not necessary for the respondent to make an express request to use the telephone. The duty to facilitate contact with counsel included the duty to offer the respondent the use of the telephone. Of course, there may be circumstances in which it is particularly urgent that the police continue with an investigation before it is possible to facilitate a detainee's communication with counsel. There was no urgency in the circumstances surrounding the offences in this case.

Further, s. 10(b) imposes on the police the duty to cease questioning or otherwise attempting to elicit evidence from the detainee until he has had a reasonable opportunity to retain and instruct counsel. The purpose of the right to counsel is to allow the detainee not only to be informed of his rights and obligations under the law but, equally if not more important, to obtain advice as to how to exercise those rights. In this case, the police officers correctly informed the respondent of his right to remain silent and the main function of counsel would be to confirm the existence of that right and then to advise him as to how to exercise it. For the right to counsel to be effective, the detainee must have access to this advice before he is questioned or otherwise required to provide evidence.

This aspect of the respondent's right to counsel was clearly infringed in the circumstances of this case. Immediately after the respondent's clear assertion of his right to remain silent and his desire to consult his lawyer, the police officer commenced his questioning as if the respondent had expressed no such desire. Again, there may be circumstances in which it is particularly urgent that the police proceed with their questioning of the detainee before providing him with a reasonable opportunity to retain and instruct counsel, but there was no such urgency in this case.

The Crown contends that there was no infringement of the right to counsel because the respondent had waived his right by answering the police officer's questions. While a person may implicitly waive his rights under s. 10(b), the standard will be very high (*Clarkson* [*v The Queen*, [1986] 1 SCR 383], at pp. 394-95). In my view, the respondent's conduct did not constitute an implied waiver of his right to counsel. It seems that he did not intend to waive his right, as he clearly asserted it at the beginning and at the end of the questioning. Rather, the form of the questioning was such as to elicit involuntary answers. The police officer asked two innocuous questions followed by a baiting question which led the respondent to incriminate himself. In addition, where a detainee has positively asserted his desire to exercise his right to counsel and the police have ignored his request and have proceeded to question him, he is likely to feel that his right has no effect and that he must answer. Finally, the respondent had the right not to be asked questions, and he must not be held to have implicitly waived that right simply because he answered the questions. Otherwise, the right not to be asked questions would only exist where the detainee refused to answer and thus where there is no need for any remedy or exclusionary rule.

For these reasons, I would conclude that the respondent's rights under s. 10(b) were infringed.

Bringing the Administration of Justice into Disrepute

The first point that must be made is that the violation of the respondent's rights to counsel was very serious. The respondent clearly asserted his right to remain silent and to consult his lawyer. There was a telephone at hand. There was no urgency which would justify the immediate questioning or the denial of the opportunity to contact his lawyer. In effect, the police officers simply ignored the rights they had read to him and his assertion of the right to silence and the right to counsel. The Ontario Court of Appeal characterized this violation as "wilful and deliberate" and as an "open and flagrant disregard of the [respondent's] rights," and I fully agree.

Further, the evidence obtained was self-incriminatory. As I stated in [*R v Collins*, [1987] 1 SCR 265], the use of self-incriminatory evidence obtained following a denial of the right to counsel will generally go to the very fairness of the trial and thus, will generally bring the administration of justice into disrepute.

It is true that the offence was a serious one and that the respondent's guilt is clearly established by the statement sought to be excluded, but that cannot justify the admission of the evidence in light of the seriousness of the violation and the effect of the evidence on the fairness of the trial.

[The statement had been admitted at trial and the accused was convicted. The Supreme Court affirmed the Ontario Court of Appeal's decision to quash the conviction, exclude the statement, and order a new trial. Dickson CJ and Beetz, McIntyre, Wilson, Le Dain, and La Forest JJ concurred with Lamer J.]

Despite the holding in *Manninen*, over the intervening years it would appear that at least some police forces developed a practice of delaying contact with counsel until the person arrested is transported back to the police station. A recent decision by the Supreme Court of Canada makes clear that police cannot simply assume that it would be impractical to facilitate contact with counsel elsewhere.

In *R v Taylor*, 2014 SCC 50, [2014] 2 SCR 495, shortly after arriving at the scene of a serious single vehicle accident, police identified the accused as the driver. The accused was ultimately arrested at the scene for impaired driving causing bodily harm. When informed of his s 10(b) Charter rights, he asked to speak to a specific lawyer. Following his arrest, Mr. Taylor was not transported to a police detachment but, as a precaution, was instead taken to hospital. At the hospital no effort was made by police to provide Mr. Taylor an opportunity to speak with his lawyer or determine whether such an opportunity was even logistically or medically feasible. At his trial, Mr. Taylor claimed his s 10(b) Charter right was violated and he sought to exclude from evidence the results of the analysis on some blood samples that were taken from him while in hospital before he had an opportunity to speak with his lawyer.

The Supreme Court was unanimous in finding that the police violated Mr. Taylor's right to counsel. Emphasizing that the right to counsel arises immediately upon arrest or detention, the Court noted that absent an urgent or dangerous situation, "the duty to facilitate access to a lawyer, in turn, arises immediately upon the detainee's request to speak to counsel." This, the Court explained, imposes on an arresting police officer "a constitutional obligation to facilitate the requested access to a lawyer at the first reasonably available opportunity," which requires that a detained individual "have access to a phone to exercise his right to counsel at the *first* reasonable opportunity."

Absent specific evidence to support a conclusion that it would have been impractical to facilitate Mr. Taylor's contact with counsel at the hospital, such as a medical emergency, the absence of a phone, or even problems providing sufficient privacy, the Court concluded that the police had violated Mr. Taylor's right to counsel. According to the Court, a person under arrest "who enters a hospital to receive medical treatment is not in a Charter-free zone." Given that "most hospitals have phones, it is not a question simply of whether the individual is in the emergency room, it is whether the Crown has demonstrated that the circumstances are such that a private phone conversation is not reasonably feasible."

In *Manninen* the Court rejected an argument that there had been an implied waiver of the right to counsel. In doing so, it noted that the standard for an implied waiver of a Charter right is very high and cited its earlier decision in *Clarkson v The Queen*, [1986] 1 SCR 383. In *Clarkson* a majority of the Court held that in order to be valid and effective a purported waiver of the right to counsel must be clear, unequivocal, and informed. "Informed" means that the waiver must be premised on a true appreciation of the consequences of giving up the right. The accused in that case was very drunk when she was arrested for her husband's murder, given the customary police warning, and informed of her right to counsel. In response she said there was "no point" in having counsel and underwent police questioning while still rather drunk and very emotional. In these circumstances, the majority concluded that the purported waiver could not pass the "awareness of the consequences test." Absent a situation of urgency, the police should have delayed their interrogation until the accused was in a condition to properly exercise her s 10(b) right or appreciate the consequences of waiving it. By proceeding with the interrogation, the police violated s 10(b) of the Charter.

The next case builds upon *Clarkson*, elaborating upon the sort of information that a person detained or arrested requires before any purported waiver of the right to counsel will be valid.

R v Brydges
Supreme Court of Canada
[1990] 1 SCR 190

[The accused, a resident of Edmonton, was arrested in Strathclair, Manitoba on a charge of second-degree murder and advised of his right to retain and instruct counsel without delay. When taken to Brandon for interrogation he asked a detective if "they have any free legal aid or anything like that up here" and stated, "Won't be able to afford anyone, hey? That's the main thing." The detective asked if there was a reason for wanting to talk to a lawyer and the accused replied, "Not right now, no." The accused proceeded to answer questions and gave prejudicial statements until he eventually asked to see a lawyer and was provided with one.

The trial judge found that the accused was requesting counsel when he inquired about legal aid and excluded subsequent statements made to the police under s 24(2) of the Charter. As a result the accused was acquitted. The Alberta Court of Appeal reversed and held that the accused had "elected to go it alone."]

LAMER J: A detainee may, either explicitly or implicitly, waive his right to retain and instruct counsel, although the standard will be very high where the alleged waiver is implicit. A majority of this Court in *Clarkson* [*v The Queen*, [1986] 1 SCR 383] concluded as follows in respect of a waiver of the right to counsel at pp. 394-95, a passage that has been cited with approval in subsequent cases dealing with s. 10(b):

> ... it is evident that any alleged waiver of this right by an accused must be carefully considered and that the accused's awareness of the consequences of what he or she is saying is crucial. Indeed, this Court stated with respect to the waiver of statutory procedural guarantees in *Korponay v. Attorney General of Canada*, [1982] 1 S.C.R. 41, at p. 49, that any waiver: "... is dependent upon it being *clear and unequivocal that the person is waiving the procedural safeguard and is doing so with full knowledge of the rights the procedure was enacted to protect and of the effect the waiver will have on those rights in the process*." [Emphasis in original.]

... the appellant specifically stated that "the main thing" was that he was unable to afford counsel. The trial judge found that this amounted to a request for counsel. The appellant, however, was left with the mistaken impression that his inability to afford a lawyer prevented him from exercising his right to counsel. I agree with Harradence J.A. in dissent that in this context the appellant did not understand the full meaning of his right to counsel. In this respect, it can hardly be said that the appellant was in a position to carefully consider the consequences of waiving that which he did not understand. I am therefore of the view that the appellant, given the standard for waiver set out by this Court in *Clarkson* and in subsequent cases, did not waive his right to retain and instruct counsel. ...

The failure of the police to inform the appellant of the existence of Legal Aid or duty counsel at the time that he first indicated a concern about his ability to pay a lawyer, was a restriction on the appellant's right to counsel, insofar as the appellant was left with an erroneous impression of the nature and extent of his s. 10(b) rights. As a result, I would conclude, along with the trial judge and Harradence J.A. in dissent at the Court of Appeal, that the appellant's s. 10(b) rights were violated. ...

[Lamer J concluded that the evidence should be excluded under s 24(2). In doing so, he emphasized that the evidence was of a self-incriminatory nature and that the police made a "serious error."]

... [T]he view that the right to retain and instruct counsel, in modern Canadian society, has come to mean more than the right to retain a lawyer privately. It now also means the right to have access to counsel free of charge where the accused meets certain financial criteria set up by the provincial Legal Aid plan, and the right to have access to immediate, although temporary, advice from duty counsel irrespective of financial status. These considerations, therefore, lead me to the conclusion that as part of the information component of s. 10(b) of the *Charter*, a detainee should be informed of the existence and availability of the applicable systems of duty counsel and Legal Aid in the jurisdiction, in order to give the detainee a full understanding of the right to retain and instruct counsel.

[Lamer J concluded that a transition period of 30 days from the delivery of the judgment was "sufficient time for the police forces to react, and to prepare new cautions." Lamer J allowed the appeal and restored the acquittal. Wilson, Gonthier, and Cory JJ concurred with Lamer J; La Forest J (L'Heureux-Dubé and McLachlin JJ concurring) agreed with Lamer J on the facts of the case, allowing the appeal and restoring the acquittal. They, however, found it "unnecessary to consider the broader issues raised by [Lamer J] in the latter part of his reasons."]

After the Supreme Court's decision in *Brydges*, Ontario set up a toll-free 1-800 number so that detained and arrested people throughout the province could at all hours contact a duty counsel paid by legal aid. Nova Scotia did not.

In *R v Prosper*, [1994] 3 SCR 236, a case originating in Nova Scotia, the Supreme Court rejected that s 10(b) of the Charter, either alone or in conjunction with other provisions, imposes a positive obligation on governments to fund duty counsel programs for those detained outside regular business hours. In coming to this conclusion, the Court emphasized both the text of s 10(b) and its drafting history. The framers, for example, specifically voted against including wording in s 10 that would have created even a relatively limited substantive right to legal assistance (that is, for those "without sufficient means" and "if the interests of justice so require").

The majority in *Prosper* did, however, emphasize that the duty to hold off from trying to elicit incriminating evidence would go some distance toward protecting detainees in those jurisdictions where duty counsel programs are not in place. The majority concluded that in circumstances where a detainee asserts his or her right to counsel and is duly diligent in exercising that right but is prevented from doing so because of the absence of a duty counsel program, s 10(b) requires that the police hold off from trying to elicit incriminating evidence from the detainee until he or she has had a reasonable opportunity to reach counsel. Depending on the circumstances, this could mean waiting until the local legal aid office opens, until a private lawyer willing to provide free summary advice can be reached, or until the detainee is able to speak to duty counsel when brought to court for a bail hearing.

The dissenting judges in *Prosper* (L'Heureux-Dubé, La Forest, and Gonthier JJ) worried that taking the duty to hold off as far as the majority proposed would ring "the death knell of the breathalyzer as a device to help take drunk drivers off the roads in provinces that do not have 24-hour duty counsel service programs or their equivalent."

In the companion Ontario case of *R v Bartle*, [1994] 3 SCR 173, the accused was arrested for drunk driving and informed of his right to counsel and the availability of legal aid, but not the toll-free 1-800 number that Ontario had established shortly after the Court's decision in *Brydges*. The Supreme Court held that Bartle's s 10(b) rights had been violated and excluded the breathalyzer sample under s 24(2) of the Charter.

As the decisions above demonstrate, since the Charter's enactment the Supreme Court of Canada has imbued the simple language found in s 10(b) with much meaning in order to help realize the guarantee's protective purposes. In the next case, it was a disagreement regarding the purpose of the guarantee that ultimately divided the Court with respect to its limits.

R v Sinclair
Supreme Court of Canada
2010 SCC 35, [2010] 2 SCR 310

[Sinclair was charged with second-degree murder. Following his arrest he was apprised of his s 10(b) rights. Back at the police station he spoke to a lawyer on two separate occasions before his formal interrogation commenced. At no time did he express dissatisfaction with the length or quality of these consultations. After about five hours of interrogation, Sinclair expressed discomfort about being interviewed without his lawyer. He was told, however, that his right to counsel had been satisfied by the earlier telephone calls. Altogether, four or five times Sinclair alternately expressed his desire to speak with his lawyer and his intention to remain silent on matters touching on his involvement in the killing. Each time, the interrogating officer emphasized that it was Sinclair's choice to make. The interrogation continued with Sinclair being denied any further opportunity to speak with counsel. Eventually, Sinclair made a number of incriminating statements to the interrogating officer. These were followed by admissions to a police officer posing as another prisoner once Sinclair was lodged in police cells. Finally, he attended with police at the scene and participated in a re-enactment. The Crown proffered all of this evidence as part of its case at trial. The statements were ruled voluntary and found not to have been obtained in violation of his s 10(b) Charter rights. Sinclair was convicted of manslaughter. The British Columbia Court of Appeal affirmed the conviction.]

McLACHLIN CJ and CHARRON J (Deschamps, Rothstein, and Cromwell JJ concurring):

I. Overview

[1] This appeal and its companion cases are about the nature and limits of the right to counsel under s. 10(b) of the *Canadian Charter of Rights and Freedoms*. The issue is whether a detainee who has been properly accorded his or her s. 10(b) rights at the outset of the detention has the constitutional right to further consultations with counsel during the course of the interrogation.

. . .

B. *The Purpose of Section 10(b) of the Charter*

[24] The purpose of s. 10(b) is to provide a detainee with an opportunity to obtain legal advice relevant to his legal situation. In the context of a custodial interrogation, chief among the rights that must be understood by the detainee is the right under s. 7 of the *Charter* to choose whether to cooperate with the police or not.

[25] The purpose of s. 10(b) of the *Charter* and its relationship with the right to silence under s. 7 were stated by McLachlin J. (as she then was) in *R. v. Hebert*, [1990] 2 S.C.R. 151, at pp. 176-77. These rights combine to ensure that a suspect is able to make a choice to speak to the police investigators that is both free and informed.

· · ·

[26] The purpose of the right to counsel is "to allow the detainee not only to be informed of his rights and obligations under the law but, equally if not more important, to obtain advice as to how to exercise those rights": *R. v. Manninen*, [1987] 1 S.C.R. 1233, at pp. 1242-43. The emphasis, therefore, is on assuring that the detainee's decision to cooperate with the investigation or decline to do so is free and informed. Section 10(b) does not guarantee that the detainee's decision is wise; nor does it guard against subjective factors that may influence the decision. Its purpose is simply to give detainees the opportunity to access legal advice relevant to that choice.

· · ·

[32] We conclude that in the context of a custodial interrogation, the purpose of s. 10(b) is to support the detainee's right to choose whether to cooperate with the police investigation or not, by giving him access to legal advice on the situation he is facing. This is achieved by requiring that he be informed of the right to consult counsel and, if he so requests, be given an opportunity to consult counsel.

C. *The Right to Have Counsel Present Throughout the Interview*

· · ·

[36] This returns us to the purpose of s. 10(b). As discussed above, it is to inform the detainee of his or her rights and provide the detainee with an opportunity to get legal advice on how to exercise them. These purposes can be achieved by the right to re-consult counsel where developments make this necessary, as discussed below. They do not demand the continued presence of counsel throughout the interview process.

[37] Mr. Sinclair argues that other countries recognize a right to have counsel present throughout a police interview (see *Miranda v. Arizona*, 384 U.S. 436 (1966), and *Escobedo v. Illinois*, 378 U.S. 478 (1964)), and that Canada should do the same. He relies on academic commentary. See L. Stuesser "The Accused's Right to Silence: No Doesn't Mean No" (2002), 29 *Man. L.J.* 149, at p. 150.

[38] We are not persuaded that the *Miranda* rule should be transplanted in Canadian soil. The scope of s. 10(b) of the *Charter* must be defined by reference to its language; the right to silence; the common law confessions rule; and the public interest in effective law enforcement in the Canadian context. Adopting procedural protections from other jurisdictions in a piecemeal fashion risks upsetting the balance that has been struck by Canadian courts and legislatures.

· · ·

[42] We conclude that s. 10(b) should not be interpreted as conferring a constitutional right to have a lawyer present throughout a police interview. There is of course nothing to prevent counsel from being present at an interrogation where all sides consent, as already occurs. The police remain free to facilitate such an arrangement if they so choose, and the detainee may wish to make counsel's presence a precondition of giving a statement.

D. The Right to Reconsult Counsel

. . .

[47] Section 10(b) should be interpreted in a way that fully respects its purpose of supporting the detainee's s. 7 right to choose whether or not to cooperate with the police investigation. Normally, this purpose is achieved by a single consultation at the time of detention or shortly thereafter. This gives the detainee the information he needs to make a meaningful choice as to whether to cooperate with the investigation or decline to do so. However, as the cases illustrate, sometimes developments occur which require a second consultation, in order to allow the accused to get the advice he needs to exercise his right to choose in the new situation.

[Although the majority emphasized that there is no closed list of changes that will re-engage the right, it noted that the existing cases recognized that a change in circumstances may result from: new procedures involving the detainee; a change in the jeopardy facing the detainee; or reason to believe that the detainee may not have understood the initial advice of the right to counsel.]

[55] The change of circumstances, the cases suggest, must be objectively observable in order to trigger additional implementational duties for the police. It is not enough for the accused to assert, after the fact, that he was confused or needed help, absent objective indicators that renewed legal consultation was required to permit him to make a meaningful choice as to whether to cooperate with the police investigation or refuse to do so.

. . .

[65] We conclude that the principles and case-law do not support the view that a request, without more, is sufficient to retrigger the s. 10(b) right to counsel and to be advised thereof. What is required is a change in circumstances that suggests that the choice faced by the accused has been significantly altered, requiring further advice on the new situation, in order to fulfill the purpose of s. 10(b) of providing the accused with legal advice relevant to the choice of whether to cooperate with the police investigation or not. ...

[Applying these principles to the facts, the majority agreed with the courts below that Sinclair's s 10(b) Charter rights were not violated and therefore dismissed the appeal.

Binnie J dissented, but favoured a somewhat different approach than the other dissenting judges. He did not think police should be required to stop interrogating whenever a suspect asks to speak to a lawyer again, but he also concluded that the majority too narrowly defined the circumstances in which further consultation would be necessary. He concluded that Sinclair's s 10(b) rights were violated because police should have given him a further chance to speak with a lawyer when after several hours of questioning they confronted him with what they claimed was "absolutely overwhelming" evidence. Binnie J would also have excluded the evidence under s 24(2), allowed the appeal, and ordered a new trial.]

. . .

LeBEL and FISH JJ (dissenting, Abella J concurring):

. . .

A. *The Text of Section 10(b)*

. . .

[147] In our view, the plain meaning of s. 10(b) favours an ongoing right to the assistance of counsel. The words "retain" and "instruct" signify a continuing relationship between client and counsel. On this basis alone, it is difficult to see how the s. 10(b) right could be "spent" upon its initial exercise.

[148] Nor does the phrase "on arrest or detention" limit s. 10(b) to a one-time consultation. Section 10(b) is of course triggered "on arrest or detention," which ensures that the detainee is afforded an opportunity to consult counsel as soon as possible, and certainly before any interrogation. Indeed, as Lamer J. (later C.J.) put it in *R. v. Manninen*, [1987] 1 S.C.R. 1233, at p. 1243: "For the right to counsel to be effective, the detainee must have access to this advice before he is questioned or otherwise required to provide evidence."

. . .

[151] The French version of s. 10(b) bolsters our interpretation, despite differing from the English version in two minor, yet significant ways. First, instead of the right to "retain and instruct counsel," the French provision guarantees detainees the right to "*l'assistance d'un avocat*." Second, the French version states that the right is triggered "*en cas d'arrestation*," and not "*on* arrest."

. . .

[154] Accordingly, the plain meaning of s. 10(b), in both French and English, supports a broad application of the right to counsel, which includes an ongoing right to consult with counsel.

B. *The Purpose and Scope of the Section 10(b) Right to Counsel*

. . .

[159] The right to silence, the right against self-incrimination, and the presumption of innocence are interrelated principles and the core values that animate the administration of criminal justice in Canada. They work together to ensure that suspects are never obligated to participate in building the case against them. As this Court has noted time and again, the ability of an accused to exercise these fundamental rights is dependent upon the assistance of counsel.

. . .

[165] When a person is detained but not yet charged, the events that follow will determine whether that person can properly be charged and prosecuted. If that person is in fact charged, what occurred at the pre-charge stage will likely influence the nature of the proceedings that follow. The detainee, under total police control and isolated from family and friends, is particularly vulnerable.

[166] Upon arrest, the suspect will be subject to skilled and persistent interrogation, as occurred in this case. Confronted by bits and pieces of incriminating "evidence," conjectural or real, the detainee may be wrongly persuaded that maintaining his or her right of silence is a futile endeavour: that the advice to remain silent originally provided by counsel is now unsound. Through ignorance of the consequences, the detainee may feel bound to make an incriminatory statement to which the police are not by law entitled. In what may seem counterintuitive to the detainee without legal training, it is often better to remain silent in the face of the "evidence" proffered, leaving it to the court to determine its cogency and admissibility, and forego the inevitable temptation to end the interrogation by providing the inculpatory statement sought by the interrogators.

[167] Access to counsel is therefore of critical importance at this stage to ensure, insofar as possible, that the detainee's constitutional rights are respected and provide the sense of security that legal representation is intended to afford. However, it is also in society's interest that constitutional rights be respected at the pre-trial stage, as doing so ensures the integrity of the criminal process from start to finish. In these circumstances, counsel's advice is not simply a matter of reiterating the detainee's right to silence, but also to explain *why* and *how* that right should be, and can be, effectively exercised. In other words, the lawyer not only tells the detainee not to speak but, perhaps more importantly, *why* he ought not to.

. . .

[177] … Under our Constitution the right to counsel enshrined in s. 10(b) is not "spent" upon its initial exercise following arrest or detention. Nor is its further exercise subject to the permission of the police officers who deliberately ignore the detainee's repeated requests to consult counsel. By persisting instead with their relentless custodial interrogation, despite the detainee's clearly expressed choice not to speak with them, the police flout another constitutional right—the detainee's right to silence. Often if not invariably, they thereby succeed in persuading the detainee that further attempts to exercise either constitutional right will merely postpone the inevitable and prove to be in vain.

. . .

[179] In short, we do not accept that fresh access to counsel is limited to situations where *the police interrogator* is satisfied either that there has been a material change in circumstances, or that the request is not made in an effort to delay or distract. As we have shown, this approach is consistent neither with the text of s. 10(b) itself, nor with its broader purpose. We also reject this approach on the basis that it focusses on the objective observations and conclusions of the police, who have the detainee in their total control, and not on the subjective needs of the accused.

. . .

[201] In concluding that the police conduct in this case violated the appellant's s. 10(b) right to counsel, we take care to make perfectly clear that we are not advocating the adoption of the American rules under *Miranda*. Our purpose here is simply to emphasize that our colleagues' fear that the administration of criminal justice would grind to a halt should custodial detainees be given greater access to counsel is not supported by the experience in jurisdictions where that very right is in place. …

[202] In our respectful view, the right against self-incrimination and the right to silence cannot be eroded by an approach to criminal investigations, and in particular to custodial interrogation, that would favour perceived police efficiency at the expense of

constitutionally protected rights. It is certain that police interrogation is not of itself a breach of the *Charter*, but the needs of police efficacy do not rank higher than the requirements of the *Charter*.

. . .

[213] Accordingly, the police's failure to suspend the interrogation and allow Mr. Sinclair to consult with counsel, in the face of his numerous requests, constituted a breach of his right to counsel, guaranteed by s. 10(b) of the *Charter*.

[After applying the principles governing the exclusion of evidence under s 24(2) identified in *R v Grant*, 2009 SCC 32, [2009] 2 SCR 353, LeBel and Fish JJ concluded that the evidence should be excluded. They would have set aside the conviction and ordered a new trial.]

Appeal dismissed.

Confessions and the Right to Silence

The Charter contains no explicit guarantee of a right to silence. Nevertheless, relying on s 7 of the Charter, the Supreme Court of Canada has recognized such a right, albeit subject to some significant limitations.

R v Hebert
Supreme Court of Canada
[1990] 2 SCR 151

[The accused was arrested for robbery and apprised of his right to counsel. After speaking with counsel, he advised police that he did not wish to make a statement. The accused was then placed in a holding cell with an undercover police officer posing as another prisoner. The undercover officer engaged the accused in conversation, during which the accused made various incriminating statements, which implicated him in the robbery for which he had been arrested.]

McLACHLIN J: This case raises the issue of whether a statement made by a detained person to an undercover police officer violates the rights of the accused under the Canadian Charter of Rights and Freedoms. ...

The appellant's liberty is at stake. Under section 7 of the *Charter*, he can only be deprived of that liberty in accordance with the principles of fundamental justice. The question is whether the manner in which the police obtained a statement from him violates that right. The answer to this question lies in an exploration of the underlying legal principles of our system of justice relevant to a detained person's right to silence. As Lamer J. stated in *Re B.C. Motor Vehicle Act*, [1985] 2 S.C.R. 486, at p. 503:

... the principles of fundamental justice are to be found in the basic tenets of our legal system.

How do we discover the "basic tenets of our legal system" in a case such as this? Initially, it must be by reference to the legal rules relating to the right which our legal system has adopted. As D. J. Galligan points out in "The Right to Silence Reconsidered" (1988), 41 *C.L.P.* 69, at pp. 76-77: "The right ... is general and abstract, concealing a bundle of more specific legal relationships. It is only by an analysis of the surrounding legal rules that those more precise elements of the right can be identified." Thus rules such as the common law confessions rule, the privilege against self-incrimination and the right to counsel may assist in determining the scope of a detained person's right to silence under s. 7.

At the same time, existing common law rules may not be conclusive. It would be wrong to assume that the fundamental rights guaranteed by the *Charter* are cast forever in the straight-jacket of the law as it stood in 1982. ...

[McLachlin J then proceeded to review the common law confessions rule, the privilege against self-incrimination, the right to counsel, as well as the overarching purpose underlying the legal rights guarantees found in the Charter (that is, "it is to the control of the superior power of the state *vis-à-vis* the individual who has been detained by the state, and thus placed in its power, that s. 7 and the related provisions that follow are primarily directed"). The purpose of that review was to discern what the principles of fundamental justice require with respect to the right to silence.]

The common law rules related to the right to silence suggest that the scope of the right in the pre-trial detention period must be based on the fundamental concept of the suspect's right to choose whether to speak to the authorities or remain silent. Any doubt on the question is resolved by consideration of related rights protected by the *Charter*, by the *Charter*'s approach to the question of improperly obtained evidence, and by the fundamental purpose of the right to silence and related procedural guarantees. In keeping with the approach inaugurated by the *Charter*, our courts must adopt an approach to pre-trial interrogation which emphasizes the right of the detained person to make a meaningful choice and permits the rejection of statements which have been obtained unfairly in circumstances that violate that right of choice.

The right to choose whether or not to speak to the authorities is defined objectively rather than subjectively. The basic requirement that the suspect possess an operating mind has a subjective element. But this established, the focus under the *Charter* shifts to the conduct of the authorities *vis-à-vis* the suspect. Was the suspect accorded the right to consult counsel? Was there other police conduct which effectively and unfairly deprived the suspect of the right to choose whether to speak to the authorities or not? ...

This approach may be distinguished from an approach which assumes an absolute right to silence in the accused, capable of being discharged only by waiver. On that approach, all statements made by a suspect to the authorities after detention would be excluded unless the accused waived his right to silence. Waiver, as defined in *Clarkson v. The Queen*, [1986] 1 S.C.R. 383, is a subjective concept dependent, among other things, on the accused's knowing that he is speaking to the authorities. On this approach, *all* statements made by a person in detention which were not knowingly made to a police officer would be excluded because, absent knowledge that the suspect is speaking to a police officer, the Crown cannot establish waiver. This would include statements made to undercover agents (regardless of whether the officer is merely passive or has elicited the statement) as well as conversations with fellow prisoners overheard by the police and statements overheard through mechanical listening devices on the wall. There is nothing in the rules underpinning the s. 7 right to silence or other provisions of the *Charter* that suggests that the scope of the right to silence should be extended this far. By contrast, the approach I advocate retains the objective approach to confessions which has always prevailed in our law and would permit the rule to be subject to the following limits.

First, there is nothing in the rule to prohibit the police from questioning the accused in the absence of counsel after the accused has retained counsel. Presumably, counsel will inform the accused of the right to remain silent. If the police are not posing as undercover officers and the accused chooses to volunteer information, there will be no violation of the *Charter*. Police persuasion, short of denying the suspect the right to choose or depriving him of an operating mind, does not breach the right to silence.

Second, it applies only after detention. Undercover operations prior to detention do not raise the same considerations. The jurisprudence relating to the right to silence has never extended protection against police tricks to the pre-detention period. Nor does the *Charter* extend the right to counsel to pre-detention investigations. The two circumstances are quite different. In an undercover operation prior to detention, the individual from whom information is sought is not in the control of the state. There is no need to protect him from the greater power of the state. After detention, the situation is quite different; the state takes control and assumes the responsibility of ensuring that the detainee's rights are respected.

Third, the right to silence predicated on the suspect's right to choose freely whether to speak to the police or to remain silent does not affect voluntary statements made to fellow cell mates. The violation of the suspect's rights occurs only when the Crown acts to subvert the suspect's constitutional right to choose not to make a statement to the authorities. This would be the case regardless of whether the agent used to subvert the accused's right was a cell mate, acting at the time as a police informant, or an undercover police officer.

Fourth, a distinction must be made between the use of undercover agents to observe the suspect, and the use of undercover agents to actively elicit information in violation of the suspect's choice to remain silent. When the police use subterfuge to interrogate an accused after he has advised them that he does not wish to speak to them, they are improperly eliciting information that they were unable to obtain by respecting the suspect's constitutional right to silence: the suspect's rights are breached because he has been deprived of his choice. However, in the absence of eliciting behaviour on the part of the police, there is no violation of the accused's right to choose whether or not to speak to the police. If the suspect speaks, it is by his or her own choice, and he or she must be taken to have accepted the risk that the recipient may inform the police.

It may be noted that a similar distinction has been made in the United States under the Sixth Amendment, which provides that "In all criminal prosecutions the accused shall … have the assistance of counsel for his defence." American courts have consistently held that the use of undercover police to question an accused in prison violates this amendment as the accused has the right to have his lawyer present when being questioned. The leading case is *Kuhlmann v. Wilson*, 477 U.S. 436 (1986). There, the police paid an informer to listen to and report the accused's incriminating evidence but gave the informer explicit instructions not to elicit any information. The Supreme Court of the United States held that the evidence was admissible, concluding that "the defendant must demonstrate that the police and their informant took some action, beyond merely listening, that was designed deliberately to elicit incriminating remarks" (p. 459). Thus, even under the arguably more stringent American constitutional protection, the law permits the use of a police informant after detention, provided he or she does not take active and intentional steps to elicit a confession. …

Application of the Right to Silence in This Case

The essence of the right to silence is that the suspect be given a choice; the right is quite simply the freedom to choose—the freedom to speak to the authorities on the one hand, and the freedom to refuse to make a statement to them on the other. This right of choice comprehends the notion that the suspect has been accorded the right to consult counsel and thus to be informed of the alternatives and their consequences, and that the actions of the authorities have not unfairly frustrated his or her decision on the question of whether to make a statement to the authorities.

In this case, the accused exercised his choice not to speak to the police when he advised them that he did not wish to make a statement. When he later spoke to the undercover policeman, he was not reversing that decision and choosing to speak to the police. He was choosing to speak to a fellow prisoner, which is quite a different matter. The Crown, in using a trick to negate his decision not to speak, violated his rights.

[McLachlin J emphasized the nature of the evidence obtained, involving the "conscription" of the accused, as well as the serious nature of the Charter violation, involving as it did a wilful and deliberate effort by police to undermine the accused's express assertion of his right to silence, in concluding that the evidence should be excluded under s 24(2) of the Charter.]

[Dickson CJ and Lamer, La Forest, L'Heureux-Dubé, Gonthier, and Cory JJ concurred in the opinion of McLachlin J.]

[In separate concurring reasons, both Wilson and Sopinka JJ were prepared to go even further, concluding that, just like any other Charter right, the standard for waiver identified in *Clarkson* should apply equally to the right to silence.]

In *R v Liew*, [1999] 3 SCR 227, the majority (Lamer CJ dissenting) found that the right to silence was not violated in a case where an undercover police officer posed as a cellmate of the accused but did not initiate the conversation that resulted in incriminating utterances. Rather, the undercover officer had simply responded in keeping with his role. The majority explained:

Hebert does not rule out the use of undercover police officers. Its concern is not with subterfuge *per se*, but with subterfuge that, in actively eliciting information, violates the accused's right to silence by depriving her of her choice whether to speak to the police. Precisely because the detainee retains her freedom in that respect, not all of her speech can be immediately deemed involuntary merely by virtue of her being detained. *Hebert* expressly allows for situations where, though speaking to an undercover officer, the detainee's speech is voluntary, in the sense that she must be taken to have freely accepted the risk of her own actions. No other view is consistent with the enshrinement of her right to choose whether to speak or to remain silent. ...

... [W]e find nothing in the facts of this appeal to support the proposition that the exchange between the appellant and the undercover officer was the functional equivalent of an interrogation. It is of no consequence that the police officer was engaged in a subterfuge, permitted himself to be misidentified, or lied, so long as the responses by the appellant were not actively elicited or the result of interrogation. In a more perfect world, police officers may not have to resort to subterfuge, but equally, in that more perfect world, there would be no crime. For the moment, in this space and time, the police can, within the limits imposed by law, engage in limited acts of subterfuge. In our opinion, that is the case in this appeal.

R v Singh
Supreme Court of Canada
2007 SCC 48, [2007] 3 SCR 405

CHARRON J:

Overview

This appeal concerns the scope of a detainee's pre-trial right to silence under s. 7 of the *Canadian Charter of Rights and Freedoms* and, in particular, the intersection between this *Charter* right as defined in *R. v. Hebert*, [1990] 2 S.C.R. 151, and the common law voluntary confessions rule as restated in *R. v. Oickle*, [2000] 2 S.C.R. 3. As in those cases, the discussion in this appeal focuses on the tension between the rights of the accused and society's interest in the effective investigation and resolution of crimes. ...

The Facts and Proceedings Below

Richard Lof was killed by a stray bullet in April 2002 while standing just inside the doorway of a pub. An argument had erupted in the pub between three Indo-Canadian men and the employees of the club. Lof had nothing to do with the argument. The group took the argument outside into the parking lot. One of the Indo-Canadian men pulled out a gun and fired several shots, one of which struck Lof.

The weapon was never found and no forensic evidence linked Mr. Singh to the shooting. Identification was the central issue at trial. A doorman, who had been four feet from the shooter, identified Mr. Singh as the shooter in a photo line-up. A witness viewed videotape footage of the three Indo-Canadian men inside the pub and identified a man with a baseball cap on backwards as the person who had the gun. The day after the fatal shooting, a police officer photographed Mr. Singh in another pub. That officer reviewed a photo taken from the videotape of the three Indo-Canadian men inside the pub and she identified Mr. Singh as the man wearing his cap backwards.

During the course of the first of two police interviews at the police station after his arrest, Mr. Singh admitted that he had been in the pub on the night of the shooting but he stated that he left before the shooting occurred. He admitted to being in the second pub on the day after the shooting, where he was photographed, and he identified himself in that photograph. He then identified himself as the man with the cap on backwards in the photo from the videotape taken inside the pub on the night of the shooting. These admissions, when taken together with other evidence, later became probative of the issue of identification at trial. Their admissibility is what is at issue on this appeal.

Before the interviews, Mr. Singh was given proper *Charter* and official police warnings and spoke to counsel by phone and in person. During the interviews, Mr. Singh spoke with the interviewing officer about his family, his background, his religious beliefs and his employment. He also discussed injuries he sustained when he was shot at a party. Whenever the discussion turned to the incident in question, however, Mr. Singh was less forthcoming. Although he provided some information regarding his presence at the pub on the night of the shooting, he repeatedly denied his involvement and asserted his right to silence. He indicated that he did not want to talk to the police, that he had nothing to say, that he knew nothing about the shooting, or that he wanted to return to his cell. Before Mr. Singh was shown the photographs in question and made the impugned admissions, he asserted his right to silence 18 times. Each time, the interviewing officer would either affirm that Mr. Singh did not have to say anything, or would explain to Mr. Singh that he had a duty or desire to place the evidence before him and he continued the interview.

[At trial, on a *voir dire* to determine the admissibility of his statements, Singh did not testify. The trial judge concluded that the Crown had proven beyond a reasonable doubt that the statements were voluntarily made. In addition, the trial judge also concluded that Singh had not established on a balance of probabilities that the statements were taken in a manner that violated his right to silence under s 7 of the Charter. Singh was convicted. The British Columbia Court of Appeal dismissed his appeal against conviction.]

Analysis

Mr. Singh concedes that his statements were obtained in conformity with the common law confessions rule—in other words, that they were voluntary. His application to exclude his statements from the evidence is grounded, rather, in the residual protection afforded to the right to silence under ss. 7 and 24 of the *Charter*. …

Since voluntariness is conceded, the scope of the common law confessions rule and its application to the facts of this case are not strictly in issue on this appeal. However, a question is raised concerning the interplay between the confessions rule and the *Charter* right to silence. …

As we shall see, there is considerable overlap between the inquiry into voluntariness and the review under s. 7 of the *Charter* in respect of an alleged breach of the right to silence. This should come as no surprise. First, the right to silence is not a concept that was newly born with the advent of the *Charter*. The right long pre-dated the *Charter* and was embraced in the common law confessions rule. Second, in *Hebert*, this Court's recognition of the residual protection afforded to the pre-trial right to silence under s. 7 of the *Charter* was largely informed by the confessions rule and the scope of the protection it provides to an individual's right to choose whether or not to speak to the authorities. Third, this Court's expansive restatement of the confessions rule in *Oickle*, in turn, was largely informed by a consideration of *Charter* principles, including the right to silence as defined in *Hebert*.

I therefore read the Court of Appeal's comment on the interplay between the confessions rule and the s. 7 right to silence as a recognition of this considerable overlap. Indeed, as I will explain, in the context of a police interrogation of a person in detention, where the detainee knows he or she is speaking to a person in authority, the two tests for determining whether the suspect's right to silence was respected are functionally equivalent. (The symmetry between the confessions rule and related *Charter* rights in so far as the requisite mental capacity is concerned was previously recognized in *R. v. Whittle*, [1994] 2 S.C.R. 914, where the Court held that the operating mind test at common law fully answers the mental capacity requirement for an effective waiver of the right to counsel and the mental capacity necessary to make an active choice with respect to the right to silence.) Therefore, in the context of an interrogation of a detainee by an obvious person in authority, the Court of Appeal was correct to question the utility of a "double-barrelled test of admissibility." In addition, because the Crown bears the burden of establishing voluntariness beyond a reasonable doubt and exclusion is automatic if the test is not met, the common law affords greater protection to the accused and there is no point in conducting a distinct s. 7 inquiry. However, as I will explain, the residual protection afforded to the right to silence under s. 7 of the *Charter* will be of added value to the accused in other contexts.

On the question of voluntariness, as under any distinct s. 7 review based on an alleged breach of the right to silence, the focus is on the conduct of the police and its effect on the suspect's ability to exercise his or her free will. The test is an objective one. However, the individual characteristics of the accused are obviously relevant considerations in applying this objective test.

Therefore, voluntariness, as it is understood today, requires that the court scrutinize whether the accused was denied his or her right to silence. The right to silence is defined in accordance with constitutional principles. A finding of voluntariness will therefore be determinative of the s. 7 issue. In other words, if the Crown proves voluntariness beyond a reasonable doubt, there can be no finding of a *Charter* violation of the right to silence in respect of the same statement. The converse holds true as well. If the circumstances are such that an accused is able to show on a balance of probabilities a breach of his or her right to silence, the Crown will not be in a position to meet the voluntariness test. It is important to understand, however, the proper scope of the constitutionalized right to silence, a question that I will address in a moment. As I will explain, Mr. Singh's real bone of contention lies in the scope of the right to silence now constitutionally entrenched under s. 7 of the *Charter*. However, before I do so, more needs to be said on the interrelation between the confessions rule and the residual protection afforded under s. 7 of the *Charter*.

Much concern was expressed on this appeal about this overlap between the confessions rule and s. 7 of the *Charter*. However, Mr. Singh's argument that his *Charter* right to silence is somehow rendered meaningless by an approach that recognizes the full breadth of the contemporary confessions rule is misguided. First, there is nothing unusual in the fact that common law rules develop along *Charter* lines. The common law confessions rule is no exception. Second, the expanded approach adopted in *Oickle* does not negate, but rather *enhances*, the protection of Mr. Singh's right to silence. As stated already, under the common law rule, the onus is on the Crown to prove voluntariness beyond a reasonable doubt. The mere presence of a doubt as to the exercise of the detainee's free will in making the statement will suffice to ground a remedy. And, by contrast to remedies under the *Charter*, which are subject to the court's discretion under s. 24(2), a violation of the confessions rule always warrants exclusion. In *Oickle*, Iacobucci J. noted the wider protection afforded under the confessions rule in explaining why he rejected the suggestion that the *Charter* should be regarded as subsuming the common law rules. ...

Hebert therefore set out the parameters of the s. 7 *Charter* right to silence to achieve this balance. Some of the limits set out by the Court were responsive to the particular facts in *Hebert* and, consequently, are only relevant to the situation where a detainee is interrogated by an undercover officer. They need not be repeated here. Of relevance in this case are the first two limits. I reproduce the relevant excerpts here:

> First, there is nothing in the rule to prohibit the police from questioning the accused in the absence of counsel after the accused has retained counsel. Presumably, counsel will inform the accused of the right to remain silent. If the police are not posing as undercover officers and the accused chooses to volunteer information, there will be no violation of the *Charter*. *Police persuasion, short of denying the suspect the right to choose or depriving him of an operating mind, does not breach the right to silence.*
>
> Second, it applies only after detention. Undercover operations prior to detention do not raise the same considerations. The jurisprudence relating to the right to silence has never extended protection against police tricks to the pre-detention period. Nor does the Charter extend the right to counsel to pre-detention investigations. The two circumstances are quite different. In an undercover operation prior to detention, the individual from whom information is sought is not in the control of the state. There is no need to protect him from the greater power of the state. After detention, the situation is quite different; the state takes control and assumes the responsibility of ensuring that the detainee's rights are respected. [Emphasis added.]

Mr. Singh takes particular issue with the leeway afforded to the police in questioning the detainee, even after he has retained counsel and has asserted his choice to remain silent. He submits that courts have erroneously interpreted the [italicized] passage above as permitting the police to *ignore* a detainee's expressed wish to remain silent and to use "legitimate means of persuasion." I say two things in response to this argument. First, the use of legitimate means of persuasion is indeed permitted under the present rule—it was expressly endorsed by this Court in *Hebert*. This approach is part of the critical balance that must be maintained between individual and societal interests. Second, the law as it stands does not permit the police to *ignore* the detainee's freedom to choose whether to speak or not, as contended. Under both common law and *Charter* rules, police persistence in continuing the interview, despite repeated assertions by the detainee that he wishes to remain silent, may well raise a strong argument that any subsequently obtained statement was not the product of a free will to speak to the authorities. As we shall see, the trial judge in this case was very much alive to the risk that the statement may be involuntary when a police officer engages in such conduct. ...

It is clear that Mr. Singh's argument on his s. 7 application is based on an expanded notion of the right to silence that does not form part of Canadian law. With respect, my colleague Justice Fish effectively endorses this expanded notion of the right to silence when he poses the question on this appeal as being "whether 'no' means 'yes' where a police interrogator refuses to take 'no' for an answer from a detainee under his total control."

As stated earlier, Mr. Singh only takes issue with the trial judge's inquiry on whether the police respected his constitutional right to remain silent. Although he makes his argument within the confines of his s. 7 *Charter* application, it matters not because, as I have explained, the functional test under the confessions rule is the same. The fallacy in Mr. Singh's argument is that it is entirely based upon an expanded and erroneous notion of the scope of the right to silence protected by the *Charter* which, for reasons I have already given, finds no support in Canadian law. The courts below did not err in their interpretation of *Hebert* as contended.

Mr. Singh alleges no other error in principle and, in my view, understandably so. The trial judge correctly instructed himself in accordance with the law in *Oickle* and *Hebert* and conducted a thorough review of all relevant circumstances. Indeed, his analysis of the applicable jurisprudence and review of the relevant facts are impeccable, particularly with respect to the right to silence. The trial judge reviewed all relevant statements of principle pertaining to the right to silence in *Oickle* and *Hebert* and he considered a number of similar cases where the police had continued their questioning of a suspect despite repeated assertions that the suspect wished to remain silent or end the interview, including Proulx J.A.'s judgment in *R. v. Otis* (2000), 151 C.C.C. (3d) 416 (Que. C.A.), which is particularly instructive on this question. In applying the law to the facts, the trial judge paid particular attention to the inherent danger in the stratagem used by Sgt. Attew which troubles my colleague, stating as follows:

> I must say that this aspect of the matter has caused me some concern. Sergeant Attew was refreshingly frank in saying that he intended to put parts of the police case against Mr. Singh before him in an effort to get him to confess, no matter what. That approach can lead to an undermining of an accused person's right to choose between silence and talking to the police authorities.

After citing the instructive passage in *Hebert* quoted above on where the line should be drawn, the trial judge continued as follows:

> It appears to me that in the case where an interviewer approaches his or her task with a view to the effect that "I will use the stratagem of insisting on presenting the police case to the suspect to encourage the suspect to talk, no matter what the suspect says," that interviewer runs the risk of having his or her conduct construed by the reviewing court as depriving the suspect of the right to make a meaningful choice whether to speak to the authorities or not. But, as Mr. McMurray says quite correctly, it is all a matter of degree. Was Mr. Singh's right to choose to talk or to remain silent undermined or overborne by Sergeant Attew's admitted dedication to his agenda?

The trial judge concluded that "it was not." Justice Fish comes to the opposite conclusion. With respect, the applicable standard of review bears repeating. As reiterated in *Oickle*:

> If a trial court properly considers all the relevant circumstances, then a finding regarding voluntariness is essentially a factual one, and should only be overturned for "some *palpable and overriding* error which affected [the trial judge's] assessment of the facts": *Schwartz v. Canada*, [1996] 1 S.C.R. 254, at p. 279 (quoting *Stein v. The Ship "Kathy K"*, [1976] 2 S.C.R. 802, at p. 808) (emphasis in *Schwartz*).

Mr. Singh has not pointed to any such error. Nor, in my view, is any such error apparent from a review of the videotape of the interviews and the transcript of the *voir dire*. Despite Sgt. Attew's admitted intention to put parts of the police case against Mr. Singh before him in an effort to get him to confess, "no matter what," his conduct of the interview as evidenced on the videotape shows that in so describing his method his bark is much worse than his bite. In my respectful view, the trial judge's ultimate judgment call on this issue is supported by the record and is entitled to deference. Therefore, I see no reason to interfere with his ruling on admissibility.

It must again be emphasized that such situations are highly fact-specific and trial judges must take into account all the relevant factors in determining whether or not the Crown has established that the accused's confession is voluntary. In some circumstances, the evidence will support a finding that continued questioning by the police in the face of the accused's repeated assertions of the right to silence denied the accused a meaningful choice whether to speak or to remain silent: see *Otis*. The number of times the accused asserts his or her right to silence is part of the assessment of all of the circumstances, but is not in itself determinative. The ultimate question is whether the accused exercised free will by choosing to make a statement: *Otis*, at paras. 50 and 54. ...

For these reasons, I would dismiss the appeal.

[McLachlin CJ and Bastarache, Deschamps, and Rothstein JJ concurred.]

FISH J (dissenting):

The question on this appeal is whether "no" means "yes" where a police interrogator refuses to take "no" for an answer from a detainee under his total control. As a matter of constitutional principle, I would answer that question in the negative, allow the appeal and order a new trial. ...

The appellant, Jagrup Singh, asserted his right to silence unequivocally—not once, but *18 times*. Throughout his interrogation, Mr. Singh was imprisoned in a police lock-up. In the trial judge's words, he was "totally under the control of the police authorities," "[did] not have freedom of unescorted movement" and "relie[d] totally on his jailers for the necessities of life" ... . Powerless to end his interrogation, Mr. Singh asked, repeatedly, to be returned to his cell. Yet he was not permitted to do so until he capitulated and made the incriminating statements impugned on this appeal.

Mr. Singh's interrogator understood very well that Mr. Singh had chosen not to speak with the police. The interrogator nonetheless disregarded Mr. Singh's repeated assertions of his right to silence. It is undisputed that he did so "in an effort to get [Mr. Singh] to confess, *no matter what*" (Ruling on the *voir dire*, (emphasis added)).

In his relentless pursuit of this objective, the interrogator urged Mr. Singh, subtly but unmistakably, to forsake his counsel's advice. I find this aspect of the interrogation particularly disturbing.

To the officer's knowledge, Mr. Singh had been advised by his lawyer to exercise his right to silence. The officer, with irony if not cynicism, discounted this "absolutely great advice" (his words) as something he too would say if he were Mr. Singh's lawyer. And he then pressed Mr. Singh to instead answer his questions—"to confess, no matter what." ...

In the trial judge's view, Mr. Singh's repeated assertions of his right to silence signify that "Mr. Singh successfully invoked his right to silence." ...

The judge's reasoning in this regard is superficially attractive but blind to reality. Mr. Singh's repeated assertions of his right to silence demonstrate as convincingly as one can that he had chosen *not to talk to the police* about the incident which led to his arrest. His interrogator systematically disregarded Mr. Singh's wish to remain silent. The more he did so, the stronger the interrogator's message to Mr. Singh that continued resistance was futile: any further assertion by Mr. Singh of his right to silence would likewise be frustrated, merely prolonging the agony of his interrogation. And the trial judge found, as I mentioned earlier, that Mr. Singh was throughout this time "totally under the control of the police authorities" and entirely dependent on them "for the necessities of life."

Where continued resistance has been made to appear futile to one person under the dominance or control of another, as it was in this case, ultimate submission proves neither true consent nor valid waiver. It proves the *failure*, not the *success*, of the disregarded assertions of the right of the powerless and the vulnerable to say "no." ...

Nothing in *Hebert*, or in any other decision of this Court, permits the police to press detainees to waive the *Charter* rights they have firmly and unequivocally asserted, or to deliberately frustrate their effective exercise. This is true of the right to counsel and true as well of the right to silence. ...

I am satisfied that Mr. Singh's admission should have been excluded in accordance with s. 24(2) of the *Charter*. His right to silence under s. 7 was violated and he was conscripted to provide evidence against himself. The use of this evidence rendered the trial unfair, "for it did not exist prior to the violation and it strikes at one of the fundamental tenets of a fair trial, the right against self-incrimination": *R. v. Collins*, [1987] 1 S.C.R. 265, at p. 284. There is no claim that this admission could have been obtained through alternative, non-conscriptive means: see *R. v. Stillman*, [1997] 1 S.C.R. 607, at para. 119. Moreover, it is apparent from my reasons that I consider the breach in this case to be serious. Were it necessary to do so, I would reiterate here my earlier comments in that regard.

For all of these reasons, as stated at the outset, I would exclude Mr. Singh's statements, allow the appeal, and order a new trial.

[Binnie, LeBel, and Abella JJ concurred in the dissenting judgment of Fish J.]

Based on the cases in the last two sections, how far a divide is there between the constitutional standards developed in Canada and those developed by the United States Supreme Court in *Miranda v Arizona*, 384 US 436 (1966)? In *Miranda*, Chief Justice Warren stated:

Our holding will be spelled out with some specificity in the pages which follow but briefly stated it is this: the prosecution many not use statements, whether exculpatory or inculpatory, stemming from custodial interrogation of the defendant unless it demonstrates the use of procedural safeguards effective to secure the privilege against self-incrimination. By custodial interrogation, we mean questioning initiated by law enforcement officers after a person has been taken into custody or otherwise deprived of his freedom of action in any significant way. As for the procedural safeguards to be employed, unless other fully effective means are devised to inform accused persons of their right of silence and to assure a continuous opportunity to exercise it, the following measures are required. Prior to any questioning, the person must be warned that he has a right to remain silent, that any statement he does make may be used as evidence against him, and that he has a right to the presence of an attorney, either retained or appointed. The defendant may waive effectuation of these rights, provided the waiver is made voluntarily, knowingly and intelligently. If, however, he indicates in any manner and at any stage of the process that he wishes to consult with an attorney before speaking there can be no questioning. Likewise, if the individual is alone and indicates in any manner that he does not wish to be interrogated, the police may not question him. The mere fact that he may have answered some questions or volunteered some statements on his own does not deprive him of the right to refrain from answering any further inquiries until he has consulted with an attorney and thereafter consents to be questioned.

The constitutional issue we decide in each of these cases is the admissibility of statements obtained from a defendant questioned while in custody or otherwise deprived of his freedom of action in any significant way. In each, the defendant was questioned by police officers, detectives, or a prosecuting attorney in a room in which he was cut off from the outside world. In none of these cases was the defendant given a full and effective warning of his rights at the outset of the interrogation process. In all the cases, the questioning elicited oral admissions, and in three of them, signed statements as well were admitted at their trials. They all thus share salient features—incommunicado interrogation of individuals in a police-dominated atmosphere, resulting in self-incriminating statements without full warnings of constitutional rights.

In these cases, we might not find the defendants' statements to have been involuntary in traditional terms. Our concern for adequate safeguards to protect precious Fifth Amendment rights is, of course, not lessened in the slightest. In each of the cases, the defendant was thrust into an unfamiliar atmosphere and run through menacing police interrogation procedures. The potentiality for compulsion is forcefully apparent, for example, in *Miranda*, where the indigent Mexican defendant was a seriously disturbed individual with pronounced sexual fantasies, and in *Stewart*, in which the defendant was an indigent Los Angeles Negro who had dropped out of school in the sixth grade. To be sure, the records do not evince overt physical coercion or patent psychological ploys. The fact remains that in none of these cases did the officers undertake to afford appropriate safeguards at the outset of the interrogation to insure that the statements were truly the product of free choice.

It is obvious that such an interrogation environment is created for no purpose other than to subjugate the individual to the will of his examiner. This atmosphere carries its own badge of intimidation. To be sure, this is not physical intimidation, but it is equally destructive of human dignity. The current practice of incommunicado interrogation is at odds with one of our Nation's most cherished principles—that the individual may not be compelled to incriminate himself. Unless adequate protective devices are employed to dispel the compulsion inherent in custodial surroundings, no statement obtained from the defendant can truly be the product of his free choice.

Confessions and "Mr. Big" Investigative Operations

There is one last area surrounding the law of confessions in Canada that is noteworthy and deserving of some brief mention. In the period since *Hebert* was decided, Canadian police developed a unique investigative technique that seemed to take advantage of some of the gaps in the legal protections surrounding confessions: the "Mr. Big" sting. Given the cost of such operations, their use has been reserved for serious unsolved cases.

The Mr. Big sting typically begins with undercover police officers luring the suspect into a fictitious criminal organization created by police. Over an extended period, lasting weeks and even months, the suspect is befriended by the undercover police officers. Through these interactions the suspect learns that involvement with the organization carries with it the potential for significant financial rewards and camaraderie with members of the organization. The final requirement for joining the organization, however, is a meeting with and approval from the boss, known colloquially as "Mr. Big."

The investigation culminates in an interview-like meeting between the suspect and Mr. Big. During the interview, Mr. Big broaches the topic of the crime the police are investigating and questions the suspect about it. The rationale for this discussion can vary. For example, the suspect might be told that Mr. Big requires some incriminating information against the suspect as a form of insurance. Alternatively, the suspect may be told that the organization cannot afford to be vulnerable and can arrange for someone dying of cancer in prison to confess to the crime if the suspect shares all the details. In short, the need for a full confession is made clear to the suspect. During the interview Mr. Big dismisses a suspect's denials of guilt as counterproductive. The interaction invariably makes clear to the suspect that the entry into the organization and a share in its spoils requires a confession. Following such a confession, the suspect is invariably arrested and charged.

Over the past 20 years, confessions secured through Mr. Big operations have proven instrumental in securing convictions in hundreds of very serious criminal cases across Canada. Until recently, efforts by accused persons to exclude such confessions have proven unsuccessful. First, because the suspect does now know he or she is speaking to a person in authority, the confessions rule has no application. Second, because the suspect is not "detained" during such operations, the s 10 Charter rights are not operable. For the same reason, the s 7 right to silence is also not engaged.

The Supreme Court of Canada finally redressed this gap in existing protections in *R v Hart*, 2014 SCC 52, [2014] 2 SCR 544. In acting, the Court cited a concern that Mr. Big confessions could result in wrongful convictions. In that regard, the Court noted that these confessions often follow powerful inducements and even veiled threats, giving rise to a concern that some suspects might confess falsely. Further, this evidence is inherently prejudicial as it portrays the suspect in a very negative light, showing him or her to be someone interested in joining a criminal organization. Given these concerns, the Court decided to employ its authority to develop the common law of evidence to create a new set of rules to govern the admissibility of Mr. Big confessions. After *Hart*, Mr. Big confessions are now presumptively inadmissible. To secure their admission, the Crown will need to convince the presiding judge, on a balance of probabilities, that the probative value of the confession outweighs its prejudicial effect.

In terms of assessing probative value, a judge must begin by evaluating the reliability of the confession in light of the circumstances in which it was made. This can include considerations such as the length of the operation, the number of interactions between the police and the accused, the nature of the relationship between the undercover officers and the accused, the nature and extent of the inducements offered, the presence of any threats, the conduct of the interrogation itself, and the personality of the accused, including his or her age, sophistication, and mental health. In light of all this, a trial judge must assess whether and to what extent the reliability of the confession has been called into doubt by the circumstances in which it was made.

After considering those circumstances, the judge must then look to the confession itself for markers of reliability. Trial judges are to consider the level of detail contained in the confession, whether it leads to the discovery of additional evidence, whether it identifies any elements of the crime that have not been made public, or whether it accurately describes mundane details of the crime the accused would likely not know had he or she not committed it. Confirmatory evidence is not a hard-and-fast requirement, but where it exists it can provide a powerful guarantee of reliability. The greater the concerns raised by the circumstances in which the confession was made, the more important it will be to find markers of reliability in the confession itself or the surrounding evidence.

Potential "prejudice" is not concerned with evidence that establishes an accused's guilt; rather, the concern is with the potential for evidence to distort the fact-finding process by causing the jury to assess the case against the accused on the basis of improper considerations. There is a real risk of so-called *moral prejudice* and *reasoning prejudice* with Mr. Big evidence.

With respect to *moral* prejudice, the jury learns that the accused wanted to join a criminal organization and committed a host of "simulated crimes" that he or she believed were real. Moral prejudice may increase with operations that involve the accused in simulated crimes of violence, or that demonstrate the accused has a history of violence.

With respect to *reasoning* prejudice—the risk that the jury's focus will be distracted from the charges before the court—it too can pose a problem depending on the length of the operation, the amount of time that must be spent detailing it, and any controversy as to whether a particular event or conversation occurred. The court was of the view that the risk of prejudice could be mitigated by the trial judge excluding certain pieces of particularly prejudicial evidence that are unessential to the narrative, or by providing limiting instructions to the jury.

In the end, a trial judge has to weigh the probative value and the prejudicial effect of the confession at issue and decide whether the Crown has met its burden. According to the Supreme Court, because trial judges are best positioned to assess the probative value and prejudicial effect of evidence, their decisions to admit or exclude Mr. Big confessions will be afforded deference on appeal.

Further, the Supreme Court of Canada in *Hart* recognized that even where an assessment of probative value versus prejudicial effect suggests that a confession is admissible, a trial judge retains the discretion to exclude the confession, and perhaps to stay proceedings, if he or she concludes that the conduct of the police in securing it was so abusive that its admission would undermine the fairness of the accused's trial and call into question the integrity of the administration of justice. In other words, exclusion of the confession is warranted if the judge concludes that the conduct of police in securing it amounted to an abuse of process. As will be seen in the next section, concerns about abuse of process are also engaged with respect to the defence of entrapment, and in such cases the court's remedy is a stay that permanently stops the criminal proceedings against the accused, as opposed to the less drastic remedy of exclusion of evidence contemplated in *Hart*.

As for what sort of police conduct would serve to cross the abuse-of-process threshold, the Supreme Court mentions situations in which a confession is actually coerced by either inducements, threats, or actual violence. Unacceptable coercion might also include police preying on suspects' particular vulnerabilities—for example, mental health problems, substance addictions, or youth.

See L Dufraimont, "R v Hart: Standing Up to Mr Big" (2014) 12 CR (7th) 294; V MacDonnell, "R v Sinclair: A New Trend in Balancing Individual Rights Against Societal Interests Outside of Section One of the Charter" (2012) 38 Queen's LJ 137; L Dufraimont, "The Interrogation Trilogy and the Protections for Interrogated Suspects in Canadian Law" (2011) 54 SCLR (2nd) 309; L Dufraimont, "The Common Law Confessions Rule in the Charter Era: Current Law and Future Directions" (2008) 40 SCLR (2nd) 249; J Klukach & D Lumba, "The Right to Pre-Trial Silence: Where Does It Stand and What's Next After Singh?" (2008) 42 SCLR (2nd) 479; M Plaxton, "Faith and Interrogations" (2008) 53 Crim LQ 360; K Roach & ML Friedland, "Borderline Justice: Policing in the Two Niagaras" (1996) 23 Am J Crim L 241; R Harvie & H Foster, "Whittled Away: The Increasing Convergence of Canadian and United States Law Respecting Police Interrogations" (1996) 39 Crim LQ 112; D Paciocco, "The Development of Miranda-Like Doctrines Under the Charter" (1987) 19 Ottawa L Rev 49; D Paciocco, "More on Recent Miranda Developments Under Subsection 10(b) of the Charter" (1987) 19 Ottawa L Rev 573; R Harvie & H Foster, "Different Drummers, Different Drums: The Supreme Court of Canada, American Jurisprudence and the Continuing Revision of Criminal Law Under the Charter" (1992) 24 Ottawa L Rev 39; H Foster & R Harvie, "Ties That Bind? The Supreme Court of Canada, American Jurisprudence and the Revision of Canadian Criminal Law Under the Charter" (1990) 28 Osgoode Hall LJ 729; R Ericson & P Baranek, *The Ordering of Justice* (Toronto: University of Toronto Press, 1982) ch 2; E Ratushny, *Self-Incrimination in the Canadian Criminal Process* (Toronto: Carswell, 1979); and K Moore, "Police Implementation of Charter Decisions: An Empirical Study" (1992) 30 Osgoode Hall LJ 547.

III. ENTRAPMENT

Entrapment issues generally arise in the investigation of so-called consensual crimes. These are crimes that often escape detection because the participants do not complain to police. As Chief Justice Laskin explained in *Kirzner v The Queen*, [1978] 2 SCR 487:

> Methods of detection of offences and of suspected offences and offenders necessarily differ according to the class of crime. Where, for example, violence or breaking, entering and theft are concerned, there will generally be external evidence of an offence upon which the police can act in tracking down the offenders; the victim or his family or the property owner, as the case may be, may be expected to call in the police and provide some clues for the police to pursue. When "consensual" crimes are committed, involving willing persons, as is the case in prostitution, illegal gambling and drug offences, ordinary methods of detection will not generally do. The participants, be they deemed victims or not, do not usually complain or seek police aid; that is what they wish to avoid. The police, if they are to respond to the public disapprobation of such offences as reflected in existing law, must take some initiatives.
>
> They may, for example, use a spy, either a policeman or another person, to obtain information about a consensual offence by infiltration; they may make arrangements with informers who may be parties to offences on which they report to the police to enable the other parties to be apprehended; or the police may use decoys or themselves act under cover to provide others with the opportunity to commit a consensual offence or to encourage its commission. Going one step farther, the police may use members of their force or other persons to instigate the commission of an offence, planning and designing it *ab initio* to ensnare others.

In *R v Mack*, [1988] 2 SCR 903, Justice Lamer adopted the explanation above and added:

I would note that in addition to so-called "victimless" or "consensual" crimes, active law enforcement techniques may be used to combat crimes where there are victims, but those victims are reluctant to go to the police because of intimidation or blackmail, as may be the case with the offence of extortion. Further, some criminal conduct may go unobserved for a long time if the victims are not immediately aware of the fact that they have been the subject of criminal activity, in the case, for example, of commercial fraud and also bribery of public officials. In general it may be said that many crimes are committed in secret and it is difficult to obtain evidence of their commission after the fact.

As discussed in Chapter 1, a defence to a crime such as entrapment can be enacted by the legislature or it can be created by a court. Before the Supreme Court of Canada finally recognized the defence of entrapment in *Mack*, there was no shortage of proposals for legislative reform. As you examine the following proposals, identify the different elements of the proposed entrapment defence and think about how they differ from the entrapment defence eventually recognized by the Supreme Court.

To what extent might an entrapment defence enacted by the legislature reflect "crime control" values as identified by Herbert Packer and discussed in the opening extract to this chapter? Would such values suggest that the entrapment might not be available with respect to serious crimes? Would such values suggest that attention should be paid to whether the accused had a pre-existing intention to commit the crime? To what extent might a judicially created entrapment defence reflect "due process" values? Would such values suggest a focus on objective values associated with protecting the reputation of the justice system? Would such values suggest that judges as opposed to juries should decide whether the entrapment defence exists in a particular case? Note, however, that not everyone accepts Packer's idea that courts will gravitate to due process values and legislatures will gravitate to crime control values. For an argument that courts alone will not be able to sustain due process values that protect the accused without support from the legislature, see J Stribopoulos, "Packer's Blind Spot: Low Visibility Encounters and the Limits of Due Process Versus Crime Control" in F Tanguay-Renaud & J Stribopoulos, eds, *Rethinking Criminal Law Theory: New Canadian Perspectives in the Philosophy of Domestic, Transnational and International Criminal Law* (Oxford: Hart, 2011).

The proposed American Law Institute test (*Model Penal Code and Commentaries*, as adopted at the 1962 annual meeting of the American Law Institute at Washington, DC, May 24, 1962 (Philadelphia: American Law Institute, 1980)) is as follows:

Section 2.13. Entrapment.

(1) A public law enforcement official or a person acting in cooperation with such an official perpetrates an entrapment if for the purpose of obtaining evidence of the commission of an offense, he induces or encourages another person to engage in conduct constituting such offense by either:

(a) making knowingly false representations designed to induce the belief that such conduct is not prohibited; or

(b) employing methods of persuasion or inducement which create a substantial risk that such an offense will be committed by persons other than those who are ready to commit it.

(2) Except as provided in Subsection (3) of this Section, a person prosecuted for an offense shall be acquitted if he proves by a preponderance of evidence that his conduct occurred in response to an entrapment. The issue of entrapment shall be tried by the Court in the absence of the jury.

(3) The defense afforded by this Section is unavailable when causing or threatening bodily injury is an element of the offense charged and the prosecution is based on conduct causing or threatening such injury to a person other than the person perpetrating the entrapment.

Compare the Ouimet Report (*Report of the Canadian Committee on Corrections* (Ottawa, 1969)) at 79-80:

For the reasons previously stated, the Committee recommends the enactment of legislation to provide:

1. That a person is not guilty of an offence if his conduct is instigated by a law enforcement officer or agent of a law enforcement officer, for the purpose of obtaining evidence for the prosecution of such person, if such person did not have a pre-existing intention to commit the offence.

2. Conduct amounting to an offence shall be deemed not to have been instigated where the defendant had a pre-existing intention to commit the offence when the opportunity arose and the conduct which is alleged to have induced the defendant to commit the offence did not go beyond affording him an opportunity to commit it.

3. The defence that the offence has been instigated by a law enforcement officer or his agent should not apply to the commission of those offences which involve the infliction of bodily harm or which endanger life.

Compare Commission of Inquiry Concerning Certain Activities of the Royal Canadian Mounted Police, *Freedom and Security Under the Law* (Ottawa: Minister of Supply and Services Canada, 1981) at 1053:

WE RECOMMEND THAT the Criminal Code be amended to include a defence of entrapment embodying the following principle:

The accused should be acquitted if it is established that the conduct of a member or agent of a police force in instigating the crime has gone substantially beyond what is justifiable having regard to all the circumstances, including the nature of the crime, whether the accused had a pre-existing intent, and the nature and extent of the involvement of the police.

Unfortunately, there was much confusion regarding the availability and contours of an entrapment defence in Canada well into the 1980s. In *Amato v The Queen*, [1982] 2 SCR 418, the Supreme Court was sharply divided on entrapment. In that case, Estey J wrote a dissenting judgment (joined by Laskin CJ and McIntyre and Lamer JJ) that endorsed the defence in terms that would ultimately win the support of a majority of justices at the Supreme Court in *R v Mack*. An extract of Justice Estey's judgment in *Amato*, demonstrating the ability of courts to recognize new common law or judge-made defences under s 8(3) of the *Criminal Code*, was included in Chapter 1.

R v Mack
Supreme Court of Canada
[1988] 2 SCR 903

[The accused was a former drug user with several drug convictions. Over a six-month period he was repeatedly asked by a police informer to supply drugs. The accused repeatedly said no, stating at one point he was interested only in real estate deals. On one occasion the informer took the accused into the woods to shoot a handgun and told the accused: "a person could get lost" in the woods. The accused interpreted this as a threat. On another occasion the informer took the accused to see a purchaser for the drugs (an undercover police officer), who showed the accused $50,000 in cash. The accused was arrested and charged with unlawful possession of narcotics for the purpose of trafficking when he delivered 12 ounces of cocaine (bought on credit for $27,000) to the informer.

He was convicted at trial with the trial judge refusing to enter a stay of proceedings because "it is far more probable that the accused became involved in this transaction for profit, rather than through persistent inducement or fear." The trial judge added that in fairness to the accused if the issue was that the Crown had to negate entrapment beyond a reasonable doubt the trial judge would have such a doubt. The British Columbia Court of Appeal confirmed the accused's conviction and he appealed to the Supreme Court of Canada.]

LAMER J: There is a crucial distinction, one which is not easy to draw, however, between the police or their agents—acting on reasonable suspicion or in the course of a bona fide inquiry—providing an opportunity to a person to commit a crime, and the state actually creating a crime for the purpose of prosecution. The former is completely acceptable as is police conduct that is directed only at obtaining evidence of an offence when committed: see *Amato* [*v The Queen*, [1982] 2 SCR 418], per Estey J., at p. 446. The concern is rather with law enforcement techniques that involve conduct that the citizenry cannot tolerate. In many cases the particular facts may constitute a classic example of what may be referred to as "entrapment" which has been described by an American judge as "the conception and planning of an offense by an officer, and his procurement of its commission by one who would not have perpetrated it except for the trickery, persuasion, or fraud of the officer": *Sorrells v. United States*, 287 U.S. 435 at p. 454 (1932), per Roberts J. ...

The Rationale

The Regulation of the Administration of Justice

It is critical in an analysis of the doctrine of entrapment to be very clear on the rationale for its recognition in Canadian criminal law. Much of what is contained in the opinion of Justice Estey in *Amato*, *supra*, provides this rationale. As was explained by Estey J., central to our judicial system is the belief that the integrity of the court must be maintained. This is a basic principle upon which many other principles and rules depend. If the court is unable to preserve its own dignity by upholding values that our society views as essential, we will not long have a legal system which can pride itself on its commitment to justice and truth and which commands the respect of the community it serves. It is a deeply ingrained value in our democratic system that the ends do not justify the means.

In particular, evidence or convictions may, at times, be obtained at too high a price. This proposition explains why as a society we insist on respect for individual rights and procedural guarantees in the criminal justice system. All of these values are reflected in specific provisions of the Charter such as the right to counsel, the right to remain silent, the presumption of innocence and in the global concept of fundamental justice. Obviously, many of the rights in ss. 7 and 14 of the Charter relate to norms for the proper conduct of criminal investigations and trials, and the courts are called on to ensure that these standards are observed. ...

It is the belief that the administration of justice must be kept free from disrepute that compels recognition of the doctrine of entrapment. In the context of the Charter, this court has stated that disrepute may arise from "judicial condonation of unacceptable conduct by the investigatory and prosecutional agencies": *R. v. Collins v. The Queen*, [1987] 1 S.C.R. 265, at p. 281. ...

It must be stressed, however, that the central issue is not the power of a court to *discipline* police or prosecutorial conduct but, as stated by Estey J. in *Amato, supra* (at p. 461): "the avoidance of the improper invocation by the State of the judicial process and its powers." In the entrapment context, the court's sense of justice is offended by the spectacle of an accused being convicted of an offence which is the work of the state (*Amato, supra*, at p. 447). The court is, in effect, saying it cannot condone or be seen to lend a stamp of approval to behaviour which transcends what our society perceives to be acceptable on the part of the state. The stay of the prosecution of the accused is the manifestation of the court's disapproval of the state's conduct. The issuance of the stay obviously benefits the accused but the court is primarily concerned with a larger issue: the maintenance of the public confidence in the legal and judicial process. In this way, the benefit to the accused is really a derivative one. We should affirm the decision of Estey J., in *Amato, supra*, that *the basis upon which entrapment is recognized lies in the need to preserve the purity of administration of justice*.

The Guilt of the Accused

It is not fruitful, in my view, to deal with impermissible police conduct through the vehicle of substantive criminal law doctrine. There are three problems with the appellant's proposition. First, the conduct of the police or their agents in most cases will not have the effect of negating *mens rea* or, for that matter, *actus reus*. (There may be exceptional cases, however; see, for example, the decision of this Court in *Lemieux v. The Queen*, [1967] S.C.R. 492.)

[In *Lemieux*, a police informant solicited the accused to participate in a burglary. The police arranged with the owner of the house to let them have the key to the house. The Supreme Court quashed the burglary conviction on the grounds that no burglary had in fact been committed since the owner had consented to the break-in for the purpose of entrapping the accused.]

The physical act of the accused is a voluntary one and the accused will have an aware state of mind. The prohibited act will have been committed intentionally and with knowledge of the facts which constitute the offence and the consequences which flow from them. ...

... Secondly, the circumstances in which an accused is placed in an entrapment situation are not agonizing in the sense acknowledged by the defences of duress or necessity.

Where the police conduct does amount to duress, that defence can be pleaded in conjunction with an abuse of process allegation. I would note, however, that any "threats" by the police, even if insufficient to support the defence of duress, will be highly relevant in the assessment of police conduct for the purpose of an abuse of process claim. The third reason why I am unwilling to view entrapment as relating to culpability is that if it did, there would not be a valid basis on which to limit the defence to entrapment by the state. The lack of support for an extension of the defence to provide against entrapment by private citizens demonstrates that the real problem is with the propriety of the *state* employing such law enforcement techniques for the purpose of obtaining convictions. If this is accepted, then it follows that the focus must be on the police conduct. ...

In conclusion, and to summarize, the proper approach to the doctrine of entrapment is that which was articulated by Estey J. in *Amato, supra*, and elaborated upon in these reasons. As mentioned and explained earlier there is entrapment when,

(a) the authorities provide a person with an opportunity to commit an offence without acting on a reasonable suspicion that this person is already engaged in criminal activity or pursuant to a *bona fide* inquiry;

(b) although having such a reasonable suspicion or acting in the course of a *bona fide* inquiry, they go beyond providing an opportunity and induce the commission of an offence.

It is neither useful nor wise to state in the abstract what elements are necessary to prove an entrapment allegation. It is, however, essential that the factors relied on by a court relate to the underlying reasons for the recognition of the doctrine in the first place.

Since I am of the view that the doctrine of entrapment is not dependent upon culpability, the focus should not be on the effect of the police conduct on the accused's state of mind. Instead, it is my opinion that as far as possible an objective assessment of the conduct of the police and their agents is required. The predisposition, or the past, present or suspected criminal activity of the accused, is relevant only as a part of the determination of whether the provision of an opportunity by the authorities to the accused to commit the offence was justifiable. Further, there must be sufficient connection between the past conduct of the accused and the provision of an opportunity, since otherwise the police suspicion will not be reasonable. While predisposition of the accused is, though not conclusive, of some relevance in assessing the initial approach by the police of a person with the offer of an opportunity to commit an offence, *it is never relevant* as regards whether they went beyond an offer, since that is to be assessed with regard to what the average non-predisposed person would have done.

The absence of a reasonable suspicion or a *bona fide* inquiry is significant in assessing the police conduct because of the risk that the police will attract people who would not otherwise have any involvement in a crime and because it is not a proper use of the police power to simply go out and test the virtue of people on a random basis. The presence of reasonable suspicion or the mere existence of a *bona fide* inquiry will, however, never justify entrapment techniques: the police may not go beyond providing an opportunity regardless of their perception of the accused's character and regardless of the existence of an honest inquiry. To determine whether the police have employed means which go further than providing an opportunity, it is useful to consider any or all of the following factors:

- the type of crime being investigated and the availability of other techniques for the police detection of its commission;
- whether an average person, with both strengths and weaknesses, in the position of the accused would be induced into the commission of a crime;
- the persistence and number of attempts made by the police before the accused agreed to committing the offence;
- the type of inducement used by the police including: deceit, fraud, trickery or reward;
- the timing of the police conduct, in particular whether the police have instigated the offence or became involved in ongoing criminal activity;
- whether the police conduct involves an exploitation of human characteristics such as the emotions of compassion, sympathy and friendship;
- whether the police appear to have exploited a particular vulnerability of a person such as a mental handicap or a substance addiction;
- the proportionality between the police involvement, as compared to the accused, including an assessment of the degree of harm caused or risked by the police, as compared to the accused, and the commission of any illegal acts by the police themselves;
- the existence of any threats, implied or express, made to the accused by the police or their agents;
- whether the police conduct is directed at undermining other constitutional values.

This list is not exhaustive, but I hope it contributes to the elaboration of a structure for the application of the entrapment doctrine. ...

Procedural Issues

Who Decides: Judge or Jury?

Both the appellant and respondent agree that objective entrapment, involving police misconduct and not the accused's state of mind, is a question to be decided by the trial judge, and that the proper remedy is a stay of proceedings. I too am of this view. ...

This court has held that the determination of whether the admission of evidence obtained in violation of a Charter right would bring the administration of justice into disrepute is one which should be made by a trial judge (*R. v. Therens*, [1985] 1 S.C.R. 613, *per* Le Dain J., at p. 653). In articulating how a trial judge should engage him or herself in that analysis, I stated in *Collins*, *supra*, that a judge should consider the question from the perspective of a reasonable person, "dispassionate and fully apprised of [all] the circumstances," and I commented that "The reasonable person is usually the average person in the community but only when that community's current mood is reasonable" (*supra*, at p. 282). The issue there, as here, is maintaining respect for the values which, over the long term, hold the community together. One of those very fundamental values is the preservation of the purity of the administration of justice. In my opinion, a judge is particularly well suited to make this determination. ...

Finally, I am of the view that before a judge considers whether a stay of proceedings lies because of entrapment, it must be absolutely clear that the Crown had discharged its burden of proving beyond a reasonable doubt that the accused had committed all the essential elements of the offence. If this is not clear and there is a jury, the guilt or inno-cence of the accused must be determined apart from evidence which is relevant only to the issue of entrapment. This protects the right of an accused to an acquittal where the circumstances so warrant. If the jury decides the accused has committed all of the ele-ments of the crime, it is then open to the judge to stay the proceedings because of entrap-ment by refusing to register a conviction. ...

Who Bears the Burden of Proof and on What Standard?

I have come to the conclusion that it is not inconsistent with the requirement that the Crown prove the guilt of the accused beyond a reasonable doubt to place the onus on the accused to prove on a balance of probabilities that the conduct of the state is an abuse of process because of entrapment. I repeat: the guilt or innocence of the accused is not in issue. The accused has done nothing that entitles him or her to an acquittal; the Crown has engaged in conduct, however, that disentitles it to a conviction. ...

Disposition

From the facts it appears that the police had reasonable suspicion that the appellant was involved in criminal conduct. The issue is whether the police went too far in their efforts to attract the appellant into the commission of the offence.

Returning to the list of factors I outlined earlier, this crime is obviously one for which the state must be given substantial leeway. The drug trafficking business is not one which lends itself to the traditional devices of police investigation. It is absolutely essential, therefore, for police or their agents to get involved and gain the trust and confidence of the people who do the trafficking or who supply the drugs. It is also a crime of enormous social consequence which causes a great deal of harm in society generally. This factor alone is very critical and makes this case somewhat difficult.

The police do not appear, however, to have been interrupting an ongoing criminal enterprise, and the offence was clearly brought about by their conduct and would not have occurred absent their involvement. The police do not appear to have exploited a narcotics addiction of the appellant since he testified that he had already given up his use of narcotics. Therefore, he was not, at the time, trying to recover from an addiction. Nonetheless, he also testified that he was no longer involved in drugs and, if this is true, it suggests that the police were indeed trying to make the appellant take up his former life-style. The persistence of the police requests, as a result of the equally persistent refusals by the appellant, supports the appellant's version of events on this point. The length of time, approximately six months, and the repetition of requests it took before the appellant agreed to commit the offence also demonstrate that the police had to go further than merely providing the appellant with the opportunity once it became evident that he was unwilling to join the alleged drug syndicate.

Perhaps the most important and determinative factor, in my opinion, is the appellant's testimony that the informer acted in a threatening manner when they went for a walk in the woods, and the further testimony that he was told to get his act together after he did not provide the supply of drugs he was asked for. I believe this conduct was unacceptable. If the police must go this far, they have gone beyond providing the appellant with an op-portunity. I do not, therefore, place much significance on the fact that the appellant eventually committed the offence when shown the money. Obviously, the appellant knew much earlier that he could make a profit by getting involved in the drug enterprise and he still refused. I have come to the conclusion that the average person in the position of the appellant might also have committed the offence, if only to finally satisfy this threatening informer and end all further contact. As a result I would, on the evidence, have to find that the police conduct in this case was unacceptable. Thus, the doctrine of entrapment applies to preclude the prosecution of the appellant. In my opinion, the appellant has met the burden of proof and the trial judge should have entered a stay of proceedings for abuse of process.

I would, accordingly, allow the appeal, set aside the conviction of the appellant, order a new trial and enter a stay of proceedings.

[Dickson CJ and Beetz, McIntyre, Wilson, La Forest, and L'Heureux-Dubé JJ concurred with Lamer J.]

In *R v Showman*, [1988] 2 SCR 893, the Supreme Court, applying *Mack*, held that there was no entrapment when a police informer (a former friend of the accused) made several telephone calls to arrange for the accused to sell drugs to an undercover police officer. Lamer J stated: "the police acted on reasonable suspicion and they were fully entitled to provide [the accused] with an opportunity to commit the offence." The police had not gone beyond providing this opportunity in part because "the average narcotic supplier is not going to respond at the very first call" and the appeal to friendship "was not unduly exploitive." Lamer J concluded: "I have no doubt that the average person would not be induced into the commission of an offence as a result of this contact."

In *R v Barnes*, [1991] 1 SCR 449, the Court elaborated on what qualifies as a *"bona fide"* inquiry under *Mack*. The case involved an undercover police "buy and bust" operation in the Granville Mall area of Vancouver, "which is known as an area of considerable drug activity." The undercover officer approached the accused and his friend based on nothing more than a "hunch" that they might be involved in drug trafficking. She asked the accused if he had any "weed." Although the accused initially said he didn't, when the officer persisted the accused agreed to sell her a small amount of cannabis resin for $15. The accused was arrested shortly thereafter. The Supreme Court rejected the availability of entrapment on these facts. According to Lamer CJ, writing for the majority:

> The basic rule articulated in *Mack* is that the police may only present the opportunity to commit a particular crime to an individual who arouses a suspicion that he or she is already engaged in the particular criminal activity. An exception to this rule arises when the police undertake a *bona fide* investigation directed at an area where it is reasonably suspected that criminal activity is occurring. When such a location is defined with sufficient precision, the police may present any person associated with the area with the opportunity to commit the particular offence. Such randomness is permissible within the scope of a *bona fide* inquiry.

Lamer CJ then held that although the police officer in this case did not have a reasonable suspicion that the accused was engaged in criminal activity, the police presented the accused with the opportunity to sell drugs *in the course of a bona fide inquiry.* In my opinion, the police officer involved in this case was engaged in such a *bona fide* investigation. First, there is no question that the officer's conduct was motivated by the genuine purpose of investigating and repressing criminal activity. The police department had reasonable grounds for believing that drug-related crimes were occurring throughout the Granville Mall area. The accused was not, therefore, approached for any questionable motives unrelated to the investigation and repression of crime.

Secondly, the police department directed its investigation at a suitable area within the City of Vancouver. ...

Random virtue-testing, conversely, only arises when a police officer presents a person with the opportunity to commit an offence without a reasonable suspicion that:

(a) the person is already engaged in the particular criminal activity, or
(b) the physical location with which the person is associated is a place where the particular criminal activity is likely occurring.

In this case, the accused was approached by the officer when he was walking near the Granville Mall. The notion of being "associated" with a particular area for these purposes does not require more than being present in the area. As a result, the accused was associated with a location where it was reasonably believed that drug-related crimes were occurring. The officer's conduct was therefore justified under the first branch of the test for entrapment set out in *Mack*.

In a dissenting judgment, McLachlin J expressed concern that the majority's approach would allow police to cast their investigative net far too broadly. She worried that the test endorsed "would permit the police to extend their Granville Mall operation to all of Vancouver if statistics could be found to suggest that drug offences were occurring throughout Vancouver generally." In her view, deciding whether or not police were operating in the course of a bona fide inquiry requires a consideration and balancing of other factors, not only the motive of the police and whether there is crime in the general area, but also the likelihood of crime at the particular location targeted, the seriousness of the crime in question, the number of legitimate activities and persons who might be affected, and the availability of other less intrusive investigative techniques. For McLachlin J, the ultimate question should be whether the interception at the particular location where it took place was reasonable, having regard to the conflicting interests of private citizens in being left alone from state interference and of the state in suppressing crime. If the answer to this question is yes, then the inquiry is bona fide. She concluded that in this case "the individual interest in being left alone and free to pursue one's daily business without being confronted by undercover police operatives vastly outweighs the state's interest in the repression of crime. It follows that the police officer in this case cannot be said to have been acting pursuant to a *bona fide* inquiry. Any other conclusion would be, in my respectful opinion, unfitting in a society which heralds the constitutional protection of individual liberties and places a premium on 'being left alone.'"

The June 1993 *Federal Proposals to Amend the General Principles of the Criminal Code* proposed to codify *Mack*, subject to the following:

Entrapment is not a basis for a stay of proceedings in respect of an offence the commission of which requires the intentional or reckless causing of death or serious bodily harm.

As suggested above, the categorical exclusion of serious offences from the entrapment defence might be an expression of crime control values. The 1993 proposals were never enacted. If they had been, might they have been challenged under s 7 of the Charter? Such a challenge would raise the question of whether the entrapment defence is more than a common law defence that courts can create under s 8(3) "except in so far as they are altered by or are inconsistent" with federal legislation and whether the defence is also based in constitutionally protected principles of fundamental justice. Note that s 7 has played a role with respect to other defences—most notably duress, discussed in Chapter 18.

The accused in several post-9/11 terrorism cases in both the United States and Canada have argued, so far without success, that they were entrapped by extensive stings involving state informers. One report in the United States raised concerns that informers and state agents have sometimes appealed to factors such as suspects' religious and political views, their poverty, and in some cases their mental disabilities. See Human Rights Watch, *Illusion of Justice: Human Rights Abuses in US Terrorism Prosecutions* (New York: Human Rights Institute, Columbia Law School, 2014), online: <http://www.hrw.org/reports/2014/07/21/illusion -justice-0>. What if any of these concerns invoke the abuse of process concerns as discussed above both in *Mack* and in the last section in *Hart*? For arguments that courts should be cautious in applying the non-individualized bona fide inquiry element of the entrapment defence discussed in *Barnes*, *supra*, because of the danger of targeting people for extensive stings simply because of their political or religious beliefs and associations, see K Roach, "Entrapment and Equality in Terrorism Prosecutions" (2011) 80 Miss LJ 1455.

Another factor in terrorism and other serious cases is a reluctance to stay proceedings that prevent a trial on the merits. In *R v Babos*, 2014 SCC 16, [2014] 1 SCR 309, the Supreme Court emphasized that a stay of proceedings should only be entered in the clearest of cases where a trial would aggravate prejudice to either the accused's fair trial or the integrity of the justice system, and where no less-drastic remedy would prevent such a result. The Court stressed that in cases under the "residual category" of concerns about judicial integrity, courts must also balance the social interest served by allowing a trial on the merits (including the seriousness of the offence charged) and their need to dissociate themselves from disreputable conduct. The social interests in allowing allegations of terrorist crimes to be adjudicated on the merits are obviously quite high, and Canadian courts have so far rejected claims of entrapment cases in a number of cases in which they have been raised. See K Roach, "Be Careful What You Wish For: Canadian Terrorism Prosecutions" (2015) 40 Queen's LJ 99. How do such conclusions relate to debates about whether courts can be relied upon to protect the due process rights of the accused?

On entrapment generally see S France, "Problems in the Defence of Entrapment" (1988) 22 UBC L Rev 1; R Park, "The Entrapment Controversy" (1976) 60 Minn LR 163; ML Friedland, "Controlling the Administrators of Criminal Justice" (1988-89) 31 Crim LQ 280; M Stober, "The Limits of Police Provocation in Canada" (1992) 34 Crim LQ 290; B Fisse, "Entrapment as a Defence" (1988) 12 Crim LJ 367; D Camp, "Out of the Quagmire After Jacobson v United States: Towards a More Balanced Entrapment Standard" (1993) 83 J Crim L & Criminology 1055; and E Colvin & S Anand, *Principles of Criminal Law*, 3rd ed (Toronto: Thomson, 2007) at 407-13.

IV. SEARCH AND SEIZURE

Section 8 of the Charter provides as follows:

Everyone has the right to be secure against unreasonable search or seizure.

In the following case the Court considered s 10(1) of the *Combines Investigation Act*, RSC 1970, c C-23, which allowed the director of investigations to enter premises and examine or take away materials on the basis of the director's belief that the evidence was relevant to an investigation. Section 10(3) of that Act provided that, before exercising the power under s 10(1), the director should obtain a certificate of authorization from a member of the Restrictive Trade Practices Commission.

Hunter v Southam Inc
Supreme Court of Canada
[1984] 2 SCR 145

DICKSON J: At the outset it is important to note that the issue in this appeal concerns the constitutional validity of a statute authorizing a search and seizure. It does not concern the reasonableness or otherwise of the manner in which the appellants carried out their statutory authority. It is not the conduct of the appellants, but rather the legislation under which they acted, to which attention must be directed. ...

I begin with the obvious. The *Canadian Charter of Rights and Freedoms* is a purposive document. Its purpose is to guarantee and to protect, within the limits of reason, the enjoyment of the rights and freedoms it enshrines. It is intended to constrain governmental action inconsistent with those rights and freedoms; it is not in itself an authorization for governmental action. In the present case this means, as Prowse J.A. pointed out, that in guaranteeing the right to be secure from unreasonable searches and seizures, s. 8 acts as a limitation on whatever powers of search and seizure the federal or provincial governments already and otherwise possess. It does not in itself confer any powers, even of "reasonable" search and seizure, on these governments. This leads, in my view, to the further conclusion that an assessment of the constitutionality of a search and seizure, or of a statute authorizing a search or seizure, must focus on its "reasonable" or "unreasonable" impact on the subject of the search or the seizure, and not simply on its rationality in furthering some valid government objective.

Since the proper approach to the interpretation of the *Canadian Charter of Rights and Freedoms* is a purposive one, before it is possible to assess the reasonableness or unreasonableness of the impact of a search or of a statute authorizing a search, it is first necessary to specify the purpose underlying s. 8: in other words, to delineate the nature of the interests it is meant to protect.

Historically, the common law protections with regard to governmental searches and seizures were based on the right to enjoy property and were linked to the law of trespass. It was on this basis that in the great case of *Entick v. Carrington* (1765), 19 State Tr. 1029, the court refused to countenance a search purportedly authorized by the Executive, to discover evidence that might link the plaintiff to certain seditious libels. Lord Camden prefaced his discussion of the rights in question by saying, at p. 1066:

The great end, for which men entered into society, was to preserve their property. That right is preserved sacred and incommunicable in all instances where it has not been taken away or abridged by some public law for the good of the whole.

The defendants argued that their oaths as King's messengers required them to conduct the search in question and ought to prevail over the plaintiff's property rights. Lord Camden rejected this contention, at p. 1067:

Our law holds the property of every man so sacred, that no man can set his foot upon his neighbour's close without his leave: if he does he is a trespasser though he does no damage at all; if he will tread upon his neighbour's ground, he must justify it by law.

Lord Camden could find no exception from this principle for the benefit of King's messengers. He held that neither the intrusions nor the purported authorizations were supportable on the basis of the existing law. That law would only have countenanced such an entry if the search were for stolen goods and if authorized by a justice on the basis of evidence upon oath that there was "strong cause" to believe the goods were concealed in the place sought to be searched. In view of the lack of proper legal authorization for the governmental intrusion, the plaintiff was protected from the intended search and seizure by the ordinary law of trespass.

In my view, the interests protected by s. 8 are of a wider ambit than those enunciated in *Entick v. Carrington*. Section 8 is an entrenched constitutional provision. It is not therefore vulnerable to encroachment by legislative enactments in the same way as common law protections. There is, further, nothing in the language of the section to restrict it to the protection of property or to associate it with the law of trespass. It guarantees a broad and general right to be secure from unreasonable search and seizure.

The Fourth Amendment, of the United States Constitution, also guarantees a broad right. It provides:

Amendment IV
The right of the people to be secure in their persons, houses, papers, and effects, against unreasonable searches and seizures, shall not be violated, and no warrants shall issue but upon probable cause, supported by oath or affirmation, and particularly describing the place to be searched, and the persons or things to be seized.

Construing this provision in *Katz v. United States* (1967), 389 U.S. 347, Stewart J., delivering the majority opinion of the United States Supreme Court, declared at p. 351 that "the Fourth Amendment protects people, not places." Justice Stewart rejected any necessary connection between that Amendment and the notion of trespass. With respect, I believe this approach is equally appropriate in construing the protections in s. 8 of the *Canadian Charter of Rights and Freedoms*.

In *Katz*, Stewart J. discussed the notion of a right to privacy, which he described at p. 350 as "the right to be let alone by other people." Although Stewart J. was careful not to identify the Fourth Amendment exclusively with the protection of this right, nor to see the Amendment as the only provision in the *Bill of Rights* relevant to its interpretation, it is clear that this notion played a prominent role in his construction of the nature and the limits of the American constitutional protection against unreasonable search and seizure. In the Alberta Court of Appeal, Prowse J.A. took a similar approach to s. 8, which he described as dealing "with one aspect of what has been referred to as a right of privacy which is the right to be secure against encroachment upon the citizens' reasonable expectation of privacy in a free and democratic society."

Like the Supreme Court of the United States, I would be wary of foreclosing the possibility that the right to be secure against unreasonable search and seizure might protect interests beyond the right of privacy, but for the purposes of the present appeal I am satisfied that its protections go at least that far. The guarantee of security from *unreasonable* search and seizure only protects a *reasonable* expectation. This limitation on the right guaranteed by s. 8, whether it is expressed negatively as freedom from "unreasonable" search and seizure, or positively as an entitlement to a "reasonable" expectation of privacy, indicates that an assessment must be made as to whether in a particular situation the public's interest in being left alone by government must give way to the government's interest in intruding on the individual's privacy in order to advance its goals, notably those of law enforcement.

(A) When Is the Balance of Interests to Be Assessed?

If the issue to be resolved in assessing the constitutionality of searches under s. 10 were whether *in fact* the governmental interest in carrying out a given search outweighed that of the individual in resisting the governmental intrusion upon his privacy, then it would be appropriate to determine the balance of the competing interests *after* the search had been conducted. Such a *post facto* analysis would, however, be seriously at odds with the purpose of s. 8. That purpose is, as I have said, to protect individuals from unjustified State intrusions upon their privacy. That purpose requires a means of *preventing* unjustified searches before they happen, not simply of determining, after the fact, whether they ought to have occurred in the first place. This, in my view, can only be accomplished by a system of *prior authorization*, not one of subsequent validation.

A requirement of prior authorization, usually in the form of a valid warrant, has been a consistent prerequisite for a valid search and seizure both at common law and under most statutes. Such a requirement puts the onus on the State to demonstrate the superiority of its interests to that of the individual. As such it accords with the apparent intention of the Charter to prefer, where feasible, the right of the individual to be free from State interference to the interests of the State in advancing its purposes through such interference.

I recognize that it may not be reasonable in every instance to insist on prior authorization in order to validate governmental intrusions upon individuals' expectations of privacy. Nevertheless, where it is feasible to obtain prior authorization, I would hold that such authorization is a pre-condition for a valid search and seizure. ...

(B) Who Must Grant the Authorization?

The purpose of a requirement of prior authorization is to provide an opportunity, before the event, for the conflicting interests of the State and the individual to be assessed, so that the individual's right to privacy will be breached only where the appropriate standard has been met, and the interests of the State are thus demonstrably superior. For such an authorization procedure to be meaningful it is necessary for the person authorizing the search to be able to assess the evidence as to whether that standard has been met, in an entirely neutral and impartial manner. ...

[Dickson J then examined the functions of the Restrictive Trade Practices Commission and concluded:]

In my view, investing the commission or its members with significant investigatory functions has the result of vitiating the ability of a member of the commission to act in a judicial capacity when authorizing a search or seizure under s. 10(3). ...

(C) On What Basis Must the Balance of Interests Be Assessed?

... The purpose of an objective criterion for granting prior authorization to conduct a search or seizure is to provide a consistent standard for identifying the point at which the interests of the State in such intrusions come to prevail over the interests of the individual in resisting them. To associate it with an applicant's reasonable belief that relevant evidence *may* be uncovered by the search, would be to define the proper standard as the *possibility* of finding evidence. This is a very low standard which would validate intrusion on the basis of suspicion, and authorize fishing expeditions of considerable latitude. It would tip the balance strongly in favour of the State and limit the right of the individual to resist to only the most egregious intrusions. I do not believe that this is a proper standard for securing the right to be free from unreasonable search and seizure.

Anglo-Canadian legal and political traditions point to a higher standard. The common law required evidence on oath which gave "strong reason to believe" that stolen goods were concealed in the place to be searched before a warrant would issue. Section 443 of the *Criminal Code* [now s 487] authorizes a warrant only where there has been information upon oath that there is "reasonable ground to believe" that there is evidence of an offence in the place to be searched. The American *Bill of Rights* provides that "no warrants shall issue but upon probable cause, supported by oath or affirmation. ..." The phrasing is slightly different but the standard in each of these formulations is identical. The State's interest in detecting and preventing crime begins to prevail over the individual's interest in being left alone at the point where credibly-based probability replaces suspicion. History has confirmed the appropriateness of this requirement as the threshold for subordinating the expectation of privacy to the needs of law enforcement. Where the State's interest is not simply law enforcement as, for instance, where State security is involved, or where the individual's interest is not simply his expectation of privacy as, for instance, when the search threatens his bodily integrity, the relevant standard might well be a different one. That is not the situation in the present case. In cases like the present, reasonable and probable grounds, established upon oath, to believe that an offence has been committed and that there is evidence to be found at the place of the search, constitutes the minimum standard, consistent with s. 8 of the Charter, for authorizing search and seizure. In so far as s. 10(1) and (3) of the *Combines Investigation Act* do not embody such a requirement, I would hold them to be further inconsistent with s. 8.

(D) Reading In and Reading Down

The appellants submit that even if subss. 10(1) and 10(3) do not specify a standard consistent with s. 8 for authorizing entry, search and seizure, they should not be struck down as inconsistent with the *Charter*, but rather that the appropriate standard should be read into these provisions. ... In the present case, the overt inconsistency with s. 8 manifested by the lack of a neutral and detached arbiter renders the appellants' submissions on reading in appropriate standards for issuing a warrant purely academic. Even if this were not the case, however, I would be disinclined to give effect to these submissions. While the courts are guardians of the Constitution and of individuals' rights under it, it is the legislature's responsibility to enact legislation that embodies appropriate safeguards to comply with the Constitution's requirements. It should not fall to the courts to fill in the details that will render legislative lacunae constitutional. Without appropriate safeguards legislation authorizing search and seizure is inconsistent with s. 8 of the *Charter*. As I have said, any law inconsistent with the provisions of the Constitution is, to the extent of the inconsistency, of no force or effect. I would hold subss. 10(1) and 10(3) of the *Combines Investigation Act* to be inconsistent with the *Charter* and of no force and effect, as much for their failure to specify an appropriate standard for the issuance of warrants as for their designation of an improper arbiter to issue them.

[Ritchie, Beetz, Estey, McIntyre, Chouinard, Lamer, and Wilson JJ concurred in the judgment of Dickson J.]

Reasonable Expectation of Privacy

Compliance with the minimum constitutional standards demanded by s 8 of the Charter is only necessary if the actions of state officials amount to a search or seizure. As *Hunter v Southam* contemplated, the key to this determination is whether a reasonable expectation of privacy is encroached on. The Supreme Court of Canada has struggled to provide clear and consistent guidance for assessing whether such an intrusion has taken place.

R v Wong
Supreme Court of Canada
[1990] 3 SCR 36

[The accused was charged with keeping a common gaming house and the Crown sought to introduce a videotape of gambling conducted in a Toronto hotel room. The trial judge held that the videotape was obtained in violation of s 8 and should be excluded under s 24(2) of the Charter. The Ontario Court of Appeal reversed that decision on the ground that the accused had no reasonable expectation of privacy in the circumstances, given that he had invited members of the public into the hotel room for the purpose of gambling. The accused appealed to the Supreme Court.]

LA FOREST J (Dickson CJ and L'Heureux-Dubé and Sopinka JJ concurring): ...

Reasonable Expectations of Privacy

... [T]he Court of Appeal, while not taking issue with the proposition that video surveillance could, in appropriate circumstances, constitute a search within the meaning of s. 8 of the *Charter*, held that that result would only follow where the person who was the object of the intrusion had a reasonable expectation of privacy. On the facts of this case, the court concluded that there was no such expectation. It is on this question as to what constitutes a reasonable expectation of privacy that I part company with the Court of Appeal for I am unable to reconcile its conclusion on this point with the approach since taken by this Court in *R. v. Duarte*, [[1990] 1 SCR 30].

[At issue in *R v Duarte* was the constitutionality under s 8 of the Charter of undercover police officers or their agents surreptitiously recording the conversations they have with suspects. The Court held that the making of such recordings *does* encroach upon a reasonable expectation of privacy and requires a warrant. See now ss 184.1 to 184.6 of the *Criminal Code*, enacted in part in response to the holding in *Duarte*.]

In *Duarte*, this Court overturned the conclusion of the Court of Appeal that the risk that our interlocutor will electronically record our words is but a variant of the risk of having that person disclose our words to another. This Court accordingly rejected the notion that "risk analysis" provides an appropriate means of assessing whether a person who was the object of an electronic search had a reasonable expectation of privacy in the circumstances. As explained at p. 48 of that decision, this rejection rested on the conclusion that privacy would be inadequately protected if an assessment of the reasonableness of a given expectation of privacy were made to rest on a consideration whether the person concerned had courted the risk of electronic surveillance. In view of the advanced state of surveillance technology, this would be to adopt a meaningless standard, for, in the final analysis, the technical resources which agents of the state have at their disposal ensure that we now run the risk of having our words recorded virtually every time we speak to another human being. Professor Amsterdam, in his seminal comment on the Fourth Amendment to the American Constitution, drives the point home with a striking image when he suggests that in view of the sophistication of modern eavesdropping technology we can only be sure of being free from surveillance today if we retire to our basements, cloak our windows, turn out the lights and remain absolutely quiet; see "Perspectives On The Fourth Amendment" (1974), 58 *Minn. L. Rev.* 349, at p. 402.

In the place of "risk analysis," *R. v. Duarte* approached the problem of determining whether a person had a reasonable expectation of privacy in given circumstances by attempting to assess whether, by the standards of privacy that persons can expect to enjoy in a free and democratic society, the agents of the state were bound to conform to the requirements of the *Charter* when effecting the intrusion in question. This involves asking whether the persons whose privacy was intruded upon could legitimately claim that in the circumstances it should not have been open to the agents of the state to act as they did without prior judicial authorization. To borrow from Professor Amsterdam's reflections, *supra*, at p. 403, the adoption of this standard invites the courts to assess whether giving their sanction to the particular form of unauthorized surveillance in question would see the amount of privacy and freedom remaining to citizens diminished to a compass inconsistent with the aims of a free and open society.

When the intrusion takes the form of unauthorized and surreptitious electronic audio surveillance, *R. v. Duarte* makes it clear that to sanction such an intrusion would see our privacy diminished in just such an unacceptable manner. While there are societies in which persons have learned, to their cost, to expect that a microphone may be hidden in every wall, it is the hallmark of a society such as ours that its members hold to the belief that they are free to go about their daily business without running the risk that their words will be recorded at the sole discretion of agents of the state. ...

I am firmly of the view that if a free and open society cannot brook the prospect that the agents of the state should, in the absence of judicial authorization, enjoy the right to record the words of whomever they choose, it is equally inconceivable that the state should have unrestricted discretion to target whomever it wishes for surreptitious video surveillance. George Orwell in his classic dystopian novel *1984* paints a grim picture of a society whose citizens had every reason to expect that their every movement was subject to electronic video surveillance. The contrast with the expectations of privacy in a free society such as our own could not be more striking. The notion that the agencies of the state should be at liberty to train hidden cameras on members of society wherever and whenever they wish is fundamentally irreconcilable with what we perceive to be acceptable behaviour on the part of government. As in the case of audio surveillance, to permit unrestricted video surveillance by agents of the state would seriously diminish the degree of privacy we can reasonably expect to enjoy in a free society. There are, as *R. v. Dyment*, [1988] 2 S.C.R. 417, at pp. 428-29, tells us, situations and places which invite special sensitivity to the need for human privacy. Moreover, as *Duarte* indicates, we must always be alert to the fact that modern methods of electronic surveillance have the potential, if uncontrolled, to annihilate privacy.

R. v. Duarte was predicated on the notion that there exists a crucial distinction between exposing ourselves to the risk that others will overhear our words, and the much more pernicious risk that a permanent electronic recording will be made of our words at the sole discretion of the state. Transposing to the technology in question here, it must follow that there is an important difference between the risk that our activities may be observed by other persons, and the risk that agents of the state, in the absence of prior authorization, will permanently record those activities on videotape, a distinction that may in certain circumstances have constitutional implications. To fail to recognize this distinction is to blind oneself to the fact that the threat to privacy inherent in subjecting ourselves to the ordinary observations of others pales by comparison with the threat to privacy posed by allowing the state to make permanent electronic records of our words or activities. It is thus an important factor in considering whether there has been a breach of a reasonable expectation of privacy in given circumstances.

The Applicability of Section 8 of the Charter on the Facts of This Case

I turn from these general observations to the question whether, on the facts of this case, the appellant could be said to have had a reasonable expectation of privacy. The Court of Appeal, after stating, by way of an initial premise, that a person attending a function to which the general public has received an open invitation can have no interest in "being left alone," went on to draw the following conclusions from the facts of this case, at p. 373:

> None of the respondents testified that they had a subjective expectation of privacy and it is difficult to believe that they could give such evidence. It may well be that they were in the same room with strangers. The occupants' only common interest was to gamble illegally for high stakes. All but Santiago Wong were no more than casual visitors to the rooms with no basis for challenging the legality of the search. Neither is it possible that Santiago Wong had any reasonable expectation of privacy. He was booking the room regularly and it was clear

from police observation that the room had been used for gambling on other occasions. Wong had invited and accepted so many people into the room that there could not have been any reasonable expectation of privacy by anyone in the room, least of all Santiago Wong who benefited by the presence of the others.

Video surveillance of persons in a hotel room could in certain circumstances constitute a search of the most intrusive kind. However, in this case, as there was no reasonable expectation of privacy, s. 8 of the Charter cannot have any application.

The Court of Appeal has, in effect, applied a variant of the risk analysis rejected by this court, for it has chosen to rest its conclusion on the notion that the appellant, by courting observation by the other persons in the room, has effectively relinquished any right to maintain a reasonable expectation of freedom from the much more intrusive invasion of privacy constituted by surreptitious video surveillance on the part of the state.

Moreover, it is clear from the excerpt cited above that the Court of Appeal, in assessing the constitutionality of the search, has allowed itself to be influenced by the fact that the appellant was carrying on illegal activities. … If reliance were to be placed on such *ex post facto* reasoning, and the courts to conclude that persons who were the subject of an electronic search could not have had a reasonable expectation of privacy because the search revealed that they were in fact performing a criminal act, the result would inevitably be to adopt a system of subsequent validation for searches. Yet it was precisely to guard against this possibility that this Court in *Hunter v. Southam Inc.*, [[1984] 2 SCR 145], at p. 160, stressed that prior authorization, wherever feasible, was a necessary pre-condition for a valid search and seizure.

Accordingly, it follows logically from what was held in *R. v. Duarte* that it would be an error to suppose that the question that must be asked in these circumstances is whether persons who engage in illegal activity behind the locked door of a hotel room have a reasonable expectation of privacy. Rather, the question must be framed in broad and neutral terms so as to become whether in a society such as ours persons who retire to a hotel room and close the door behind them have a reasonable expectation of privacy.

[La Forest J concluded that the accused's s 8 rights had been violated because the police had not obtained a warrant for the videotaping. He held, however, that the admission of the videotape would not bring the administration of justice into disrepute under s 24(2) because the police acted in good faith and there was no *Criminal Code* provision at the time that would have allowed them to obtain a warrant. Wilson J, dissenting, agreed with La Forest J that the accused's s 8 rights had been violated but would have excluded the videotape under s 24(2).]

LAMER J (McLachlin J concurring): I agree with La Forest J. that a person who retires to a hotel room and closes the door behind him or her will normally have a reasonable expectation of privacy. The nature of the place in which the surveillance occurs will always be an important factor to consider in determining whether the target has a reasonable expectation of privacy in the circumstances. It is not, however, determinative. A person who is situated in what would normally be characterized as a public place (a restaurant, for example) may well have a reasonable expectation of privacy. For example, he or she would not reasonably expect that the police will surreptitiously monitor and record the private conversation taking place at his or her table. By the same token, that which would normally be characterized as a private place (a personal residence, for example) may well, by the manner in which it is utilized, become a place in which one does not have a reasonable expectation of privacy.

The expectation of privacy which normally exists with respect to a hotel room will not be circumscribed by the fact that illegal activity may be taking place in the room, nor will it necessarily be waived by the mere fact that others have been invited to the room. However, in some cases, additional facts may be present which will indicate that the target does not have a reasonable expectation of privacy.

In the case at bar, the appellant was situated in a hotel room. In most cases, a hotel room is a location in which one has a reasonable expectation of privacy. However, in this case the appellant had, indiscriminately, extended invitations to the gaming session which was to take place in the hotel room. He had passed out numerous notices in public restaurants and bars, thereby inviting the public into the hotel room. It is impossible to conclude that a reasonable person, in the position of the appellant, would expect privacy in these circumstances. A reasonable person would know that when such an invitation is extended to the public at large, one can no longer expect that strangers, including the police, will not be present in the room. In this case, the police effected their presence in the room via the video camera which was installed in the drapery valence.

I do not wish to be taken as adopting the "risk analysis" which this court rejected in *Duarte, supra*. I am not equating the risk that strangers will be in the hotel room with the risk that the police will be electronically recording the activity in the hotel room. The issue is not so much concerned with risk as it is with reasonable expectations. Here it was not reasonable for the appellant to expect that strangers, including the police, would not be present in the room.

The appellant may well have had a reasonable expectation of privacy in the hotel room had he extended a few invitations to particular individuals. However, that was not the case here. In my view, and with respect for other views, the appellant had no reasonable expectation of privacy in these circumstances; as a result, no search took place within the meaning of s. 8.

Appeal dismissed.

At the time of *Wong*, the *Criminal Code* did not authorize the use of video cameras. See now s 487.01, which allows for the issuance of general warrants to authorize the use of any investigative technique that might constitute an unreasonable search or seizure.

The normative approach used in *Duarte* and *Wong* for assessing whether a particular investigative technique employed by the state encroaches upon a reasonable expectation of privacy has since been supplemented by a variety of other approaches developed by the Supreme Court of Canada for use in different contexts.

For example, in *R v Plant*, [1993] 3 SCR 281, the Court identified a methodology for assessing informational privacy claims under s 8 of the Charter. *Plant* involved police accessing hydro-consumption records for a residence without a warrant. The Court recognized that s 8 protects a "biographical core of personal information which individuals in a free and democratic society would wish to maintain and control from dissemination to the state. This would include information which tends to reveal intimate details of the lifestyle and personal choices of the individual." It went on to identify a number of factors for assessing whether s 8 is engaged with respect to the accessing of information by police. The factors identified include:

- the nature of the information;
- the nature of the relationship between the party releasing the information and the party asserting confidentiality;
- the place where the information was obtained;
- the manner in which the information was obtained; and
- the seriousness of the crime being investigated.

In *Plant*, which originated in Calgary (where hydro-consumption records were publicly accessible at the time), the Court applied these factors and concluded that there was no reasonable expectation of privacy in the records at issue. As a result, the police could access the records without first obtaining a warrant.

Does a man have a reasonable expectation of privacy in his girlfriend's apartment? In *R v Edwards*, [1996] 1 SCR 128, the Supreme Court emphasized that whether or not a reasonable expectation of privacy attaches will depend on the "totality of the circumstances." It explained that the totality of the circumstances may include, but are not restricted to, the following:

(i)   presence at the time of the search;
(ii)   possession or control of the property or place searched;
(iii) ownership of the property or place;
(iv)   historical use of the property or item;
(v)   the ability to regulate access, including the right to admit or exclude others from the place;
(vi)   the existence of a subjective expectation of privacy; and
(vii) the objective reasonableness of the expectation.

Applying these factors in *Edwards*, the Court concluded that the accused lacked a reasonable expectation of privacy in his girlfriend's apartment. The fact that he had a key and sometimes stayed overnight was outweighed by his lack of authority to regulate access to the premises. According to the majority, this was an especially important factor because it meant that he "could not be free from intrusion or interference" at the apartment. At best, he was no more than a "privileged guest." Consequently, he could not raise a s 8 Charter claim to challenge the illegal manner by which police retrieved evidence against him from the apartment.

Do passengers have a reasonable expectation of privacy in the search of a car in which they are travelling? In *R v Belnavis*, [1997] 3 SCR 341, the Supreme Court applied the factors from *Edwards* in holding that a passenger had no reasonable expectation of privacy with respect to the search of bags and the trunk of a car in which she was travelling.

How can we reconcile the various approaches the Supreme Court of Canada has employed to deciding whether a reasonable expectation of privacy exists in a given context? One way to think of it is to note that each approach supplies a somewhat different means of applying the "totality of the circumstances" test in different contexts where privacy is implicated. For example, the normative approach identified in *Duarte* and *Wong* appears to be applicable in situations involving the state's use of surveillance technologies. With respect to informational privacy claims, the factors identified in *Plant* appear to be controlling. Finally, with respect to territorial or spatial privacy claims, the various considerations identified in *Edwards* seemed decisive. As you read the next case, consider which of these various approaches appears to dominate.

R v Spencer
Supreme Court of Canada
2014 SCC 43, [2014] 2 SCR 212

CROMWELL J:

I. Introduction

[1] The Internet raises a host of new and challenging questions about privacy. This appeal relates to one of them.

[2] The police identified the Internet Protocol (IP) address of a computer that someone had been using to access and store child pornography through an Internet file-sharing program. They then obtained from the Internet Service Provider (ISP), without prior judicial authorization, the subscriber information associated with that IP address. This led them to the appellant, Mr. Spencer. He had downloaded child pornography into a folder that was accessible to other Internet users using the same file-sharing program. He was charged and convicted at trial of possession of child pornography and acquitted on a charge of making it available.

· · ·

II. Analysis

A. Did the police obtaining the subscriber information matching the IP address from the ISP constitute a search?

· · ·

[15] Under s. 8 of the *Charter*, "[e]veryone has the right to be secure against unreasonable search or seizure." This Court has long emphasized the need for a purposive approach to s. 8 that emphasizes the protection of privacy as a prerequisite to individual security, self-fulfilment and autonomy as well as to the maintenance of a thriving democratic society: *Hunter v. Southam Inc.*, [1984] 2 S.C.R. 145, at pp. 156-57; *R. v. Dyment*, [1988] 2 S.C.R. 417, at pp. 427-28; *R. v. Plant*, [1993] 3 S.C.R. 281, at pp. 292-93; *R. v. Tessling*, 2004 SCC 67, [2004] 3 S.C.R. 432, at paras. 12-16; *Alberta (Information and Privacy Commissioner) v. United Food and Commercial Workers, Local 401*, 2013 SCC 62, [2013] 3 S.C.R. 733, at para. 22.

[16] The first issue is whether this protection against unreasonable searches and seizures was engaged here. That depends on whether what the police did to obtain the subscriber information matching the IP address was a search or seizure within the meaning of s. 8 of the *Charter*. The answer to this question turns on whether, in the totality of the circumstances, Mr. Spencer had a reasonable expectation of privacy in the information provided to the police by Shaw. If he did, then obtaining that information was a search.

[17]   We assess whether there is a reasonable expectation of privacy in the totality of the circumstances by considering and weighing a large number of interrelated factors. These include both factors related to the nature of the privacy interests implicated by the state action and factors more directly concerned with the expectation of privacy, both subjectively and objectively viewed, in relation to those interests: see, e.g., *Tessling*, at para. 38; *Ward*, at para. 65. The fact that these considerations must be looked at in the "totality of the circumstances" underlines the point that they are often interrelated, that they must be adapted to the circumstances of the particular case and that they must be looked at as a whole.

[18]   The wide variety and number of factors that may be considered in assessing the reasonable expectation of privacy can be grouped under four main headings for analytical convenience: (1) the subject matter of the alleged search; (2) the claimant's interest in the subject matter; (3) the claimant's subjective expectation of privacy in the subject matter; and (4) whether this subjective expectation of privacy was objectively reasonable, having regard to the totality of the circumstances: *Tessling*, at para. 32; *R. v. Patrick*, 2009 SCC 17, [2009] 1 S.C.R. 579, at para. 27; *R. v. Cole*, 2012 SCC 53, [2012] 3 S.C.R. 34, at para. 40. However, this is not a purely factual inquiry. The reasonable expectation of privacy standard is normative rather than simply descriptive: *Tessling*, at para. 42. Thus, while the analysis is sensitive to the factual context, it is inevitably "laden with value judgments which are made from the independent perspective of the reasonable and informed person who is concerned about the long-term consequences of government action for the protection of privacy": *Patrick*, at para. 14; see also *R. v. Gomboc*, 2010 SCC 55, [2010] 3 S.C.R. 211, at para. 34, and *Ward*, at paras. 81-85.

. . .

(a)   The Subject Matter of the Search

[24]   Mr. Spencer contends that the subject matter of the alleged search was core biographical data, revealing intimate and private information about the people living at the address provided by Shaw which matched the IP address. The Crown, on the other hand, maintains that the subject matter of the alleged search was simply a name, address and telephone number matching a publicly available IP address.

. . .

[31]   Thus, it is clear that the tendency of information sought to support inferences in relation to other personal information must be taken into account in characterizing the subject matter of the search. The correct approach was neatly summarized by Doherty J.A. in *Ward*, at para. 65. When identifying the subject matter of an alleged search, the court must not do so "narrowly in terms of the physical acts involved or the physical space invaded, but rather by reference to the nature of the privacy interests potentially compromised by the state action": *ibid.*

[32]   Applying this approach to the case at hand, I substantially agree with the conclusion reached by Cameron J.A. in *Trapp* and adopted by Caldwell J.A. in this case. The subject matter of the search was not simply a name and address of someone in a contractual relationship with Shaw. Rather, it was the identity of an Internet subscriber which corresponded to particular Internet usage. As Cameron J.A. put it, at para. 35 of *Trapp*:

To label information of this kind as mere "subscriber information" or "customer information," or nothing but "name, address, and telephone number information," tends to obscure its true nature. I say this because these characterizations gloss over the significance of an IP address and what such an address, once identified with a particular individual, is capable of revealing about that individual, including the individual's online activity in the home.

[33] Here, the subject matter of the search is the identity of a subscriber whose Internet connection is linked to particular, monitored Internet activity.

(b) Nature of the Privacy Interest Potentially Compromised by the State Action

[34] The nature of the privacy interest engaged by the state conduct is another facet of the totality of the circumstances and an important factor in assessing the reasonableness of an expectation of privacy. The Court has previously emphasized an understanding of informational privacy as confidentiality and control of the use of intimate information about oneself. In my view, a somewhat broader understanding of the privacy interest at stake in this case is required to account for the role that anonymity plays in protecting privacy interests online.

. . .

[38] To return to informational privacy, it seems to me that privacy in relation to information includes at least three conceptually distinct although overlapping understandings of what privacy is. These are privacy as secrecy, privacy as control and privacy as anonymity.

. . .

[41] There is also a third conception of informational privacy that is particularly important in the context of Internet usage. This is the understanding of privacy as anonymity. In my view, the concept of privacy potentially protected by s. 8 must include this understanding of privacy.

[42] The notion of privacy as anonymity is not novel. It appears in a wide array of contexts ranging from anonymous surveys to the protection of police informant identities. A person responding to a survey readily agrees to provide what may well be highly personal information. A police informant provides information about the commission of a crime. The information itself is not private—it is communicated precisely so that it will be communicated to others. But the information is communicated on the basis that it will not be identified with the person providing it. Consider situations in which the police want to obtain the list of names that correspond to the identification numbers on individual survey results or the defence in a criminal case wants to obtain the identity of the informant who has provided information that has been disclosed to the defence. The privacy interest at stake in these examples is not simply the individual's name, but the link between the identified individual and the personal information provided anonymously. As the intervener the Canadian Civil Liberties Association urged in its submissions, "maintaining anonymity can be integral to ensuring privacy": factum, at para. 7.

. . .

[45] Recognizing that anonymity is one conception of informational privacy seems to me to be particularly important in the context of Internet usage. One form of anonymity, as Westin explained, is what is claimed by an individual who wants to present ideas publicly but does not want to be identified as their author: p. 32. Here, Westin, publishing

in 1970, anticipates precisely one of the defining characteristics of some types of Internet communication. The communication may be accessible to millions of people but it is not identified with its author.

[46] Moreover, the Internet has exponentially increased both the quality and quantity of information that is stored about Internet users. Browsing logs, for example, may provide detailed information about users' interests. Search engines may gather records of users' search terms. Advertisers may track their users across networks of websites, gathering an overview of their interests and concerns. "Cookies" may be used to track consumer habits and may provide information about the options selected within a website, which web pages were visited before and after the visit to the host website and any other personal information provided: see N. Gleicher, "Neither a Customer Nor a Subscriber Be: Regulating the Release of User Information on the World Wide Web" (2009), 118 *Yale L.J.* 1945, at pp. 1948-49; R.W. Hubbard, P. DeFreitas and S. Magotiaux, "The Internet—Expectations of Privacy in a New Context" (2002), 45 *Crim. L.Q.* 170, at pp. 189-91. The user cannot fully control or even necessarily be aware of who may observe a pattern of online activity, but by remaining anonymous—by guarding the link between the information and the identity of the person to whom it relates—the user can in large measure be assured that the activity remains private: see Slane and Austin, at pp. 500-3.

[47] In my view, the identity of a person linked to their use of the Internet must be recognized as giving rise to a privacy interest beyond that inherent in the person's name, address and telephone number found in the subscriber information. A sniffer dog provides information about the contents of the bag and therefore engages the privacy interests relating to its contents. DRA readings provide information about what is going on inside a home and therefore may engage the privacy interests relating to those activities. Similarly, subscriber information, by tending to link particular kinds of information to identifiable individuals, may implicate privacy interests relating not simply to the person's name or address but to his or her identity as the source, possessor or user of that information.

[48] Doherty J.A. made this point with his usual insight and clarity in *Ward*. "Personal privacy" he wrote "protects an individual's ability to function on a day-to-day basis within society while enjoying a degree of anonymity that is essential to the individual's personal growth and the flourishing of an open and democratic society": para. 71. He concluded that some degree of anonymity is a feature of much Internet activity and that, "depending on the totality of the circumstances, ... anonymity may enjoy constitutional protection under s. 8": para. 75. I agree. Thus, anonymity may, depending on the totality of the circumstances, be the foundation of a privacy interest that engages constitutional protection against unreasonable search and seizure.

[49] The intervener the Director of Public Prosecutions raised the concern that recognizing a right to online anonymity would carve out a crime-friendly Internet landscape by impeding the effective investigation and prosecution of online crime. In light of the grave nature of the criminal wrongs that can be committed online, this concern cannot be taken lightly. However, in my view, recognizing that there *may* be a privacy interest in anonymity depending on the circumstances falls short of recognizing any "right" to anonymity and does not threaten the effectiveness of law enforcement in relation to offences committed on the Internet. In this case, for example, it seems clear that the police had ample information to obtain a production order requiring Shaw to release the subscriber information corresponding to the IP address they had obtained.

[50] Applying this framework to the facts of the present case is straightforward. In the circumstances of this case, the police request to link a given IP address to subscriber information was in effect a request to link a specific person (or a limited number of persons in the case of shared Internet services) to specific online activities. This sort of request engages the anonymity aspect of the informational privacy interest by attempting to link the suspect with anonymously undertaken online activities, activities which have been recognized by the Court in other circumstances as engaging significant privacy interests: *R. v. Morelli*, 2010 SCC 8, [2010] 1 S.C.R. 253, at para. 3; *Cole*, at para. 47; *R. v. Vu*, 2013 SCC 60, [2013] 3 S.C.R. 657, at paras. 40-45.

[51] I conclude therefore that the police request to Shaw for subscriber information corresponding to specifically observed, anonymous Internet activity engages a high level of informational privacy. I agree with Caldwell J.A.'s conclusion on this point:

> [A] reasonable and informed person concerned about the protection of privacy would expect one's activities on one's own computer used in one's own home would be private. … In my judgment, it matters not that the personal attributes of the Disclosed Information pertained to Mr. Spencer's sister because Mr. Spencer was personally and directly exposed to the consequences of the police conduct in this case. As such, the police conduct *prima facie* engaged a personal privacy right of Mr. Spencer and, in this respect, his interest in the privacy of the Disclosed Information was direct and personal. [para. 27]

(c) Reasonable Expectation of Privacy

[52] The next question is whether Mr. Spencer's expectation of privacy was reasonable. The trial judge found that there could be no reasonable expectation of privacy in the face of the relevant contractual and statutory provisions (para. 19), a conclusion with which Caldwell J.A. agreed on appeal: para. 42. Cameron J.A., however, was doubtful that the contractual and statutory terms had this effect in the context of this case: para. 98.

· · ·

[53] In this Court, Mr. Spencer maintains that the contractual and statutory terms did not undermine a reasonable expectation of privacy with respect to the subscriber information. He submits that the contractual provisions do nothing more than suggest that the information will not be provided to police unless required by law and that *PIPEDA* [*Personal Information Protection and Electronic Documents Act*], whose purpose is to protect privacy rights, supports rather than negates the reasonableness of an expectation of privacy in this case. The Crown disagrees and supports the position taken on this point by Caldwell J.A. in the Court of Appeal.

[54] There is no doubt that the contractual and statutory framework may be relevant to, but not necessarily determinative of whether there is a reasonable expectation of privacy. So, for example in *Gomboc*, Deschamps J. writing for four members of the Court, found that the terms governing the relationship between the electricity provider and its customer were "highly significant" to Mr Gomboc's reasonable expectation of privacy, but treated it as "one factor amongst many others which must be weighed in assessing the totality of the circumstances": paras. 31-32. She also emphasized that when dealing with contracts of adhesion in the context of a consumer relationship, it was necessary to "procee[d] with caution" when determining the impact that such provision would have on the reasonableness of an expectation of privacy: para. 33. The need for caution in this

context was pointedly underlined in the dissenting reasons of the Chief Justice and Fish J. in that case: paras. 138-42.

[The Court then reviewed the relevant contractual and regulatory framework applicable in this case, which included the terms of the contract between Mr. Spencer's sister and Shaw Communications, and the relevant sections of the federal *Personal Information Protection and Electronic Documents Act.*]

. . .

[65] The overall impression created by these terms is that disclosure at the request of the police would be made only where required or permitted by law. Such disclosure is only permitted by *PIPEDA* in accordance with the exception in s. 7, which in this case would require the requesting police to have "lawful authority" to request the disclosure. For reasons that I will set out in the next section, this request had no lawful authority in the sense that while the police could ask, they had no authority to compel compliance with that request. I conclude that, if anything, the contractual provisions in this case support the existence of a reasonable expectation of privacy, since the Privacy Policy narrowly circumscribes Shaw's right to disclose the personal information of subscribers.

[66] In my view, in the totality of the circumstances of this case, there is a reasonable expectation of privacy in the subscriber information. The disclosure of this information will often amount to the identification of a user with intimate or sensitive activities being carried out online, usually on the understanding that these activities would be anonymous. A request by a police officer that an ISP voluntarily disclose such information amounts to a search.

[67] The intervener the Attorney General of Alberta raised a concern that if the police were not permitted to request disclosure of subscriber information, then other routine inquiries that might reveal sensitive information about a suspect would also be prohibited, and this would unduly impede the investigation of crimes. For example, when the police interview the victim of a crime, core biographical details of a suspect's lifestyle might be revealed. I do not agree that this result follows from the principles set out in these reasons. Where a police officer requests disclosure of information relating to a suspect from a third party, whether there is a search depends on whether, in light of the totality of the circumstances, the suspect has a reasonable expectation of privacy in that information: *Plant*, at p. 293; *Gomboc*, at paras. 27-30, *per* Deschamps J. In *Duarte*, the Court distinguished between a person repeating a conversation with a suspect to the police and the police procuring an audio recording of the same conversation. The Court held that the danger is "not the risk that someone will repeat our words but the much more insidious danger inherent in allowing the state, in its unfettered discretion, to record and transmit our words": at pp. 43-44. Similarly in this case, the police request that the ISP disclose the subscriber information was in effect a request to link Mr. Spencer with precise online activity that had been the subject of monitoring by the police and thus engaged a more significant privacy interest than a simple question posed by the police in the course of an investigation.

[The Court went on to consider whether the search was lawful, concluding that it was not. Therefore, a s 8 violation was found. However, the Court refrained from excluding the evidence under s 24(2), emphasizing that it had been unclear whether such requests constituted a "search" and therefore emphasizing the fact that the police had been acting in good faith. The Court also dealt with the fault element for the offence of "making available" child pornography. Concluding that the trial judge had erred in construing the *mens rea* for that offence, the court affirmed the conviction on the charge of possession of child pornography and upheld the Court of Appeal's order for a new trial on the making available count.]

[McLachlin CJ and LeBel, Abella, Rothstein, Moldaver, Karakatsanis, and Wagner JJ concurred in the judgment of Cromwell J.]

In *R v Kang-Brown*, 2008 SCC 18, [2008] 1 SCR 456 and *R v AM*, 2008 SCC 19, [2008] 1 SCR 569, the Supreme Court concluded that the police intrude on a reasonable expectation of privacy when they use a drug-sniffing dog to detect the odour of narcotics emanating from an individual's person or luggage. The Court drew a distinction between the sort of "meaningless" information gleaned through the use of forward-looking infrared technology (FLIR) to detect heat emanating from a home and the extraordinarily meaningful information gleaned through the use of a drug-sniffing dog—that a narcotic is likely being secreted on an individual's person or among his or her belongings.

On reasonable expectations of privacy and s 8 of the Charter, see S Penney, "The Digitization of Section 8 of the Charter: Reform or Revolution?" (2014) 67 SCLR (2nd) 505; H Stewart, "Normative Foundations for Reasonable Expectations of Privacy" (2011) 54 SCLR (2nd) 335; JS McInnes, "Sniffing Out a Theory of Privacy After Kang-Brown and M(A)" (2009) 47 SCLR (2nd) 53; C Michaelson, "The Limits of Privacy: Some Reflections on Section 8 of the Charter" (2008) 40 SCLR (2nd) 87; S Penney, "Conceptions of Privacy: A Comment on R v Kang-Brown, and R v AM" (2008) 46 Alta L Rev 203; S Penney, "Reasonable Expectations of Privacy and Novel Search Technologies: An Economic Approach" (2007) 97 J Crim L & Criminology 477; AJ Cockfield, "Protecting the Social Value of Privacy in the Context of State Investigations Using New Technologies" (2007) 40 UBC L Rev 41; W MacKinnon, "Tessling, Brown and AM: Towards a Principled Approach to Section 8" (2007) 45 Alta L Rev 79; R Pomerance, "Redefining Privacy in the Face of New Technologies" (2005) 9 Can Crim L Rev 273; LM Austin, "Privacy and the Question of Technology" (2003) 22 Law & Phil 119; and E Paton-Simpson, "Privacy and the Reasonable Paranoid: The Protection of Privacy in Public Places" (2000) 50 UTLJ 305.

Permissible Departures from Hunter v Southam

In *R v Collins*, [1987] 1 SCR 265 the Supreme Court held that in order to be reasonable under s 8 of the Charter, a search or seizure must satisfy three essential preconditions: (1) it must be authorized by law; (2) the law itself must be reasonable; and (3) it must be carried out in a reasonable manner.

Students often have difficulty fitting *Hunter v Southam* together with *Collins*. Unfortunately, the Supreme Court did not explain the relationship between the two cases. *Collins* serves to sketch out a broader framework for assessing reasonableness under s 8 of the Charter. The three requirements it sets down apply to all searches or seizures regardless of context. Later cases made clear that the requirements specified in *Hunter v Southam* only apply in a criminal or quasi-criminal context. In other words, the case prescribes the ingredients for a law to be considered "reasonable" (the second requirement prescribed by *Collins*) when criminal investigative powers are involved. Fewer due process protections—including the absence of a warrant and/or the need for reasonable and probable grounds—are necessary for laws authorizing searches or seizures in other contexts to be considered "reasonable." For example, searches of travellers at the border (see *R v Simmons*, [1988] 2 SCR 495; *R v Jacques*, [1996] 3 SCR 312; and *R v Monney*, [1999] 1 SCR 652), businesses operating in highly regulated fields (see *Comité paritaire de l'industrie de la chemise v Potash*, [1994] 2 SCR 406; *Thomson Newspapers Ltd v Canada*, [1990] 1 SCR 425; and *R v McKinlay Transport Ltd*, [1990] 1 SCR 627), and students by school officials for disciplinary purposes (*R v M(MR)*, [1998] 3 SCR 393) are all subject to less onerous constitutional standards than those specified in *Hunter v Southam*.

Even in the context of criminal investigations, the Supreme Court has occasionally countenanced deviations from the *Hunter v Southam* standards. For example, drug-sniffing dogs can be deployed to search suspects and their belongings on the basis of "reasonable suspicion" rather than "reasonable and probable grounds" that illegal drugs will be located, and without the need for prior judicial authorization. (See *R v Kang-Brown*, *supra*, and *R v AM*, *supra*.) Such a departure from the *Hunter v Southam* standards makes sense, given the comparatively less intrusive nature of such searches and the inherent impracticality of requiring warrants in situations where the police must take action in response to on-the-spot observations. This latter concern was similarly instrumental in the Supreme Court's concluding that searches incidental to arrest (which are prefaced on reasonable and probable grounds) can be undertaken without any need for prior judicial approval (*R v Golden*, 2001 SCC 83, [2001] 3 SCR 679).

What is the difference between "reasonable and probable grounds" and "reasonable suspicion"? The Supreme Court has explained that reasonable suspicion means "something more than a mere suspicion and something less than a belief based upon reasonable and probable grounds" (*Kang-Brown* at para 75). The Court has also said that "reasonable grounds to suspect and reasonable and probable grounds to believe are similar in that they both must be grounded in objective facts" but "reasonable suspicion is a lower standard, as it engages the reasonable possibility, rather than probability, of crime" (*R v Chehil*, 2013 SCC 49, [2013] 3 SCR 220 at para 27). According to the Court, the standard "derives its rigour from the requirement that it be based on objectively discernible facts, which can then be subjected to independent judicial scrutiny" (*Chehil* at para 26). In assessing whether this threshold is met, a reviewing court must have regard to the "totality of the circumstances" (*Chehil* at paras 26, 29). The assessment "must be fact-based, flexible, and grounded in common sense and practical, everyday experience" (*Chehil* at para 29).

The Need for Legal Authority

According to *Collins*, an essential precondition for a search or seizure to be "reasonable" under s 8 of the Charter is that it be authorized by law. As a result, identifying the legal authority pursuant to which the police carried out a particular search or seizure is a critical analytical step when assessing whether their actions complied with s 8. An unlawful search or seizure is necessarily unreasonable. The criminal search powers described above, dog sniff searches, and searches incidental to arrest are common law powers. In other words, they were created by judges using their authority to develop the common law. Other search powers are derived from statute. For example, there are a number of offence-specific search and/or seizure powers contained in the *Criminal Code*: ss 117.02 (weapons in place other than dwelling-house); 117.04 (preventive weapons searches); 199(1) to (2) (gaming and bawdy-house searches); 254(2) to (4) (breath or blood demands with respect to alcohol-related driving offences); 339(3) (stolen timber); 447(2) (seizure of cocks found in a cockpit); and 462 (seizure of counterfeit money).

Many of the legislated search powers just listed pre-date the Charter. While some have been amended in an attempt to comply with the minimum requirements of s 8 of the Charter for criminal investigative searches set down in *Hunter v Southam*, others are constitutionally suspect because they authorize the police to search without any need to first obtain a warrant. Rather than declare such powers invalid, however, in the past the Supreme Court has preferred to read them down so that their availability is limited to situations where exigent circumstances make it impracticable to obtain a warrant: see *R v Grant*, [1993] 3 SCR 223. In *Grant*, the Supreme Court indicated that such circumstances "will generally be held to exist if there is an imminent danger of the loss, removal, destruction or disappearance of the evidence ... if the search or seizure is delayed in order to obtain a warrant" (at 241-42). A mere possibility that evidence may be lost is not sufficient: see *R v Feeney*, [1997] 2 SCR 13 at para 52. And, quite obviously, exigent circumstances will not arise if the police have deliberately structured their actions in a manner that is calculated to create the very urgency that is then claimed as the justification for dispensing with the warrant requirement: see *R v Silveira*, [1995] 2 SCR 297.

Arguably, one of the most important search powers found in the *Criminal Code* is the authority to search pursuant to a warrant.

Prior Judicial Authorization: The Warrant Requirement

Under the *Criminal Code* warrants to search buildings, receptacles, or places are issued by a justice of the peace under s 487. There is an analogous provision available for the investigation of drug offences found in s 11 of the *Controlled Drugs and Substances Act*, SC 1996, c 19 (CDSA). That provision confers slightly more expansive authority because it also authorizes police to search a person found in the location being searched if there are reasonable and probable grounds to believe that the person is in possession of a controlled substance (s 11(5)).

Ordinarily, a warrant to search a place includes authorization to search receptacles within that place—for example, filing cabinets and cupboards. However, the Supreme Court recently made clear that computers are different, given they are vast (and almost permanent) repositories of inherently private information. Therefore, if police plan to search computers found in the location to be searched, they must first satisfy the authorizing justice that they have reasonable grounds to believe some computers they discover will contain things they are looking for. Otherwise, if police come across a computer when executing a warrant that does not authorize a computer search, they should seize it (if they have a basis to believe it may contain evidence) and then seek a separate warrant that specifically authorizes such a search. See *R v Vu*, 2013 SCC 60, [2013] 3 SCR 657.

It is also important to note that, at least with respect to the powers found in s 487 of the Code or s 11(5) of the CDSA, the police can dispense with the need to obtain a warrant where "the conditions for obtaining a warrant exist but by reason of exigent circumstances it would be impracticable to obtain a warrant" (see *Criminal Code*, s 487.11 and CDSA, s 11(7)). In other words, Parliament has codified an exigency exception to the warrant requirement.

Parliament has also legislated a number of warrant provisions applicable to particular types of searches and seizures. So, for example, there are specific warrant provisions for intercepting private communications (s 184.2, that is, wiretapping), seizing DNA samples (s 487.05), taking body impressions (s 487.092, that is, handprints, fingerprints, footprints, foot impression, teeth impression, etc.), using electronic tracking devices (s 492.1, that is, GPS), or employing dial number recorders (s 492.2). There is also a residual general warrant provision that the police can resort to in order to "use any device or investigative technique or procedure or do anything described in the warrant" that would encroach upon a reasonable expectation of privacy but where no other provision authorizes it (s 487.01).

Warrants are issued by a judicial officer. Depending on the relevant provision, that can be either a justice of the peace, a provincial court judge, or a superior court judge. The judicial official reviews a sworn document (the "information") prepared by the police that sets out the supporting grounds. With most of the warrant provisions (not all) the controlling standard is reasonable and probable grounds to believe that the proposed search or seizure will produce evidence of a crime. Some of the search warrant provisions employ the reasonable suspicion standard—for example, warrants to use electronic tracking devices under s 492.1 or dial number recorder warrants under s 492.2. Given that these techniques are less intrusive than a conventional search, the use of the reasonable suspicion standard is very likely constitutional under s 8 of the Charter: see *R v Wise*, [1992] 1 SCR 527.

Despite these safeguards, a number of studies of randomly drawn search warrants have revealed that about 40 percent of warrants were invalidly issued with most legal errors being insufficient establishment of reasonable and probable grounds, including a lack of sourcing, belief based on uncorroborated informants of unknown reliability, and a lack of nexus between the offence and the items to be searched and seized. See C Hill, "The Role of Fault in Section 24(2) of the Charter" in J Cameron, ed, *The Charter's Impact on the Criminal Justice System* (Toronto: Carswell, 1996) at 57ff. A more recent study demonstrated an even higher error rate. See C Hill, S Hutchinson & L Pringle, "Search Warrants: Protection or Illusion?" (2000) 28 CR (5th) 89.

The United States Supreme Court held in *US v Leon*, 468 US 897 (1984) that evidence seized unreasonably but in reasonable reliance on a judicial warrant should not be excluded. Justice White stated for the court:

> Because a search warrant provides the detached scrutiny of a neutral magistrate, which is a more reliable safeguard against improper searches than the hurried judgment of a law enforcement officer engaged in the often competitive enterprise of ferreting out crime ... we have expressed a strong preference for warrants.

He concluded that the exclusionary rule need not be applied to those judicial officers who issue search warrants. He elaborated:

> The exclusionary rule is designed to deter police misconduct rather than to punish the errors of judges and magistrates. Second, there exists no evidence suggesting that judges and magistrates are inclined to ignore or subvert the Fourth Amendment or that lawlessness among these actors requires application of the extreme sanction of exclusion. Third, and most important, we discern no basis and are offered none, for believing that exclusion of evidence seized pursuant to a warrant will have a significant deterrent effect on the issuing judge or magistrate.

Justice Brennan, in dissent, argued that the long-run effect of the majority's ruling "will be to undermine the integrity of the warrant process." He stated that creation of the exception implicitly tells magistrates that they need not take much care in reviewing warrant applications because their mistakes will have virtually no consequence and that the ruling will encourage police to provide the bare minimum of information to obtain a warrant and in doing so insulate themselves from the exclusionary sanction.

What effect should reliance on a search warrant have in deciding whether evidence should be excluded under s 24(2) of the Charter? See *R v Harris et al* (1987), 35 CCC (3d) 1 (Ont CA). In that case, the Court of Appeal admitted evidence under s 24(2) on the basis that the police had acted in good faith in obtaining a warrant even though the warrant was defective and demonstrated, in the trial judge's findings, police negligence. In *R v Hosie* (1996), 107 CCC (3d) 385 (Ont CA), however, the same Court of Appeal excluded drugs seized under a warrant because the information supplied by the police to obtain the warrant was "careless." Rosenberg JA stated: "The Courts should not be seen as condoning the use of language in search warrants which masks the true state of affairs and deprives a judicial officer of the opportunity to fairly assess whether the state's interest in detecting crime outweighs the individual's privacy interest in his or her own home."

V. DETENTION AND ARREST

The Deaths of Helen Betty Osborne and John Joseph Harper
Report of the Aboriginal Justice Inquiry of Manitoba (1991)

At approximately 2:37 a.m., Cross left his patrol car and one minute later, while he was still in the back lane, he heard that the suspect had been arrested. Heading toward the place where the suspect had been arrested, he walked from the lane and then across Logan Avenue. He encountered J.J. Harper on Logan, adjacent to Stanley Knowles Park.

Upon seeing Harper, he approached him and asked for identification. According to Cross, Harper replied that he did not have to tell Cross anything. Cross said Harper then started to walk past him. Cross reached out, placed his hand on Harper's arm and turned him around. At that point, Cross said, Harper pushed him, causing him to fall backward onto the sidewalk. As he fell, he grabbed Harper, pulling him down on top of him. Cross testified that while he was on his back, he struggled with Harper and felt a tugging at his holster. He said that he thought Harper was trying to pull his gun from its holster and, therefore, he reached down to grab his revolver. He said the gun came out of the holster with his and Harper's hands on it. He testified that he and Harper both were tugging at the gun when it went off. The blast hit Harper in the middle of the chest. ...

It is clear from all the evidence that he did not confront Harper until *after* Pruden (the suspect) had been arrested. Cross' evidence was that within a minute of hearing of Pruden's arrest he confronted Harper.

It was obvious that Harper didn't fit major elements of the description of the suspect. Cross and Hodgins described the man whom they had seen fleeing from the stolen car as a "native male, 22 years of age, wearing dark clothing." Harper was a native male wearing dark clothing, but he was 37 years of age, considerably heavier than Pruden and of much stockier build. Pruden had outrun the police, while Harper was walking and apparently not breathing heavily. ...

In an encounter between an officer and a citizen, the officer legitimately may exercise his or her right to ask questions and request identification, and generally the citizen will comply, but also legitimately may exercise his or her right to refuse to do so. Up to this point, both are within their respective legal rights and powers. But, if an officer does not place the citizen under arrest, or if the officer is not making a lawful detention and has no intention of doing so, the officer exceeds his or her authority by grabbing and detaining the citizen forcibly. While the use of force to detain individuals falls within the general scope of a police officer's rights, an officer's actions may amount to an unjustifiable use of police power if he or she uses force without making a lawful arrest or detention. Beyond those parameters the officer's use of force is not authorized or justified. ...

Cross, we believe, got caught up in the excitement of the chase. We believe that he decided to stop and question Harper simply because Harper was a male Aboriginal person in his path. We are unable to find any other reasonable explanation for his being stopped. We do not accept Cross' explanation. It was clearly a retroactive attempt to justify stopping Harper. We believe that Cross had no basis to connect him to any crime in the area and that his refusal or unwillingness to permit Harper to pass freely was, for reasons which we discuss later, racially motivated.

As disclosed by the facts, Cross had neither reasonable nor probable grounds to believe that Harper was the suspect the police were after. He had been informed that the person chased from the very lane he had been watching had been apprehended, and he had no reason to believe that his fellow officers were mistaken. If Cross had doubts or suspicions about the suspect in custody, he erred in not seeking further information by radio from those who had arrested Pruden. Harper was walking, not running, and it is highly unlikely that he would have gone far had Cross decided to radio quickly for further information. Also, according to Cross' own account of the incident, Harper was not behaving or walking in a suspicious manner. It would appear, then, that Harper simply had the misfortune of being an Aboriginal man in dark clothing, in that area late at night. In our opinion, Cross exercised poor judgment in pursuing the matter forcibly as he did after Harper legitimately had refused to identify himself.

The *Report of the Commission on Systemic Racism in the Ontario Criminal Justice System* (1996), after surveying members of different racial groups, reported that black respondents are stopped more frequently by police than Caucasian and Asian respondents. Black respondents also reported higher levels of dissatisfaction with police during such investigative encounters. The commission recommended the development of provincial guidelines for the exercise of police discretion to stop and question members of the public. (There have been similar findings with respect to native Canadians: see *Justice on Trial: Report of the Task Force on the Criminal Justice System and Its Impact on the Indian and Métis People of Alberta* (Edmonton: The Task Force, 1991) at 2-48 to 2-49.) Responding to this evidence, in *R v Brown* (2003), 64 OR (3d) 161 (CA), the Court of Appeal for Ontario acknowledged that racial profiling is a reality in Canada. The court provided the following definition:

Racial profiling is criminal profiling based on race. Racial or colour profiling refers to that phenomenon whereby certain criminal activity is attributed to an identified group in society on the basis of race or colour resulting in the targeting of individual members of that group. In this context, race is illegitimately used as a proxy for the criminality or general criminal propensity of an entire racial group. ... The attitude underlying racial profiling is one that may be consciously or unconsciously held. That is, the police officer need not be an overt racist. His or her conduct may be based on subconscious racial stereotyping.

The Manitoba Court of Appeal has also recognized the phenomenon. See *R v H(CR)*, 2003 MBCA 38 at para 49, 173 Man R (2d) 113. On the topic of racial profiling in Canada more generally, see DM Tanovich, *The Colour of Justice: Policing Race in Canada* (Toronto: Irwin Law, 2006) and S Choudhry & K Roach, "Racial and Ethnic Profiling: Statutory Discretion, Constitutional Remedies and Democratic Accountability" (2003) 41 Osgoode Hall LJ 1.

Constitutional Protection

Section 9 of the Charter provides that "[e]veryone has the right not to be arbitrarily detained or imprisoned." It supplies the constitutional framework for regulating the circumstances in which the state may interfere with the individual's freedom of movement. The purpose of s 9 was explained by the Supreme Court in *R v Grant*, 2009 SCC 32, [2009] 2 SCR 353:

The purpose of s. 9, broadly put, is to protect individual liberty from unjustified state interference. ... "liberty," for *Charter* purposes, is not "restricted to mere freedom from physical restraint," but encompasses a broader entitlement "to make decisions of fundamental importance free from state interference" ... . Thus, s. 9 guards not only against unjustified state intrusions upon physical liberty, but also against incursions on mental liberty by prohibiting the coercive pressures of detention and imprisonment from being applied to people without adequate justification. The detainee's interest in being able to make an informed choice whether to walk away or speak to the police is unaffected by the manner in which the detention is brought about.

Section 9 of the Charter serves the goal of protecting individuals from unjustified state interference with their liberty in two ways.

First, s 9 provides a constitutional mechanism for scrutinizing the decision to detain or arrest in individual cases. For example, in *Grant* the Supreme Court made clear that any unlawful interference with individual liberty is necessarily arbitrary and violates s 9 of the Charter. Consequently, if the police detain or arrest an individual in the absence of the requisite grounds for doing so, s 9 of the Charter is violated.

Beyond illegality, the Supreme Court of Canada also recognized in *R v Storrey*, [1990] 1 SCR 241 at 251-52, that s 9 of the Charter is violated if an arrest is undertaken "because a police officer was biased towards a person of a different race, nationality or colour, or that there was a personal enmity between a police officer directed towards the person arrested." This observation has equal force with respect to all detentions, not just those culminating in arrest. It is difficult to imagine anything more unjustifiable or arbitrary than a detention or arrest undertaken because of a discriminatory motivation. In other words, racial profiling is contrary to s 9 of the Charter. (It undoubtedly also violates the equality guarantee found in s 15(1) of the Charter.)

Beyond individual cases, s 9 also provides a means for scrutinizing legislation that authorizes detention or imprisonment. It prescribes minimum constitutional standards that must be met by any law authorizing state officials to interfere with individual liberty. In this regard, it has usually been the presence of too little or too much discretion in the statutory authority conferred that has proven determinative. Legislation that mandates a loss of liberty without the need to consider any rational criteria or standards has been held to operate "arbitrarily." (See *R v Swain*, [1991] 1 SCR 933.) The Supreme Court has rightly recognized that "it is the absence of discretion which would, in many cases, render arbitrary the law's application" (*R v Lyons*, [1987] 2 SCR 309 at 348). At the same time the Court has found legislation at odds with s 9 of the Charter when it confers unfettered discretion on state agents to detain individuals. In such circumstances, "[a] discretion is arbitrary ... [because] there are no criteria, express or implied, which govern its exercise" (*R v Hufsky*, [1988] 1 SCR 621 at 633).

The protection afforded by s 9 of the Charter is, however, contingent on detention or imprisonment. It is rather obvious whether someone has been imprisoned. Far more controversial is whether or not there has been a detention.

R v Grant
Supreme Court of Canada
2009 SCC 32, [2009] 2 SCR 353

[Grant, a young black man, was walking down a Toronto street at midday when, according to two plainclothes police officers, his manner and clothing attracted their attention. The plainclothes officers requested that a nearby uniformed officer "have a chat" with Grant. The uniformed officer approached Grant, while standing on the sidewalk directly in his intended path. The officer asked Grant "what was going on," and requested his name and address. In response, Grant provided a provincial health card. At one point, Grant, behaving nervously, adjusted his jacket, prompting the officer to tell him to "keep his hands in front of him." By this point, the two plainclothes officers had also approached and flashed their badges before taking up positions behind the uniformed officer. Pointed questions followed, with Grant being asked if he was carrying anything that he shouldn't have, an exchange that culminated in Grant admitting that he was in possession of marijuana and a firearm. Thereafter he was arrested immediately. A key issue on appeal was at what point Grant was detained.]

McLACHLIN CJ and CHARRON J: ... In summary, we conclude as follows:

1. Detention under ss. 9 and 10 of the *Charter* refers to a suspension of the individual's liberty interest by a significant physical or psychological restraint. Psychological detention is established either where the individual has a legal obligation to comply with the restrictive request or demand [that is, traffic stops], or a reasonable person would conclude by reason of the state conduct that he or she had no choice but to comply.

2. In cases where there is no physical restraint or legal obligation, it may not be clear whether a person has been detained. To determine whether the reasonable person in the individual's circumstances would conclude that he or she had been

deprived by the state of the liberty of choice, the court may consider, *inter alia*, the following factors:

a) The circumstances giving rise to the encounter as they would reasonably be perceived by the individual: whether the police were providing general assistance; maintaining general order; making general inquiries regarding a particular occurrence; or, singling out the individual for focused investigation.

b) The nature of the police conduct, including the language used; the use of physical contact; the place where the interaction occurred; the presence of others; and the duration of the encounter.

c) The particular characteristics or circumstances of the individual where relevant, including age; physical stature; minority status; level of sophistication.

[McLachlin CJ and Charron J reasoned that the preliminary approach and general questioning of Grant were not enough to trigger a detention because, at that stage, "a reasonable person would not have concluded he or she was being deprived of the right to choose how to act." Things changed, however, with the direction to "keep his hands in front of him" (although on its own this might not be enough, as it could simply be viewed as a "precautionary directive"). On the whole, McLachlin CJ and Charron J viewed the encounter as "inherently intimidating." In so concluding, they emphasized the arrival of two additional police officers who flashed their badges before taking up "tactical positions," the fact that Grant was being singled out, the posing of interrogation-like questions probing whether he "had anything that he should not," and his relative youth and inexperience. Given this backdrop, McLachlin CJ and Charron J concluded that Grant was detained when the uniformed officer told him to keep his hands in front of him.

Given that the officers had no legal grounds to detain Grant, the detention necessarily violated his s 9 Charter rights. McLachlin CJ and Charron J next turned to consider whether the handgun obtained by police should be excluded from evidence under s 24(2). In the process, they revisited the approach to be taken under s 24(2).]

When must evidence obtained in violation of a person's *Charter* rights be excluded? Section 24(2) of the *Charter* provides the following answer:

> Where, in proceedings under subsection (1), a court concludes that evidence was obtained in a manner that infringed or denied any rights or freedoms guaranteed by this Charter, the evidence shall be excluded if it is established that, *having regard to all the circumstances, the admission of it in the proceedings would bring the administration of justice into disrepute.*

The test set out in s. 24(2)—what would bring the administration of justice into disrepute having regard to all the circumstances—is broad and imprecise. The question is what considerations enter into making this determination. In *Collins* and in *R. v. Stillman*, [1997] 1 S.C.R. 607, this Court endeavoured to answer this question. The *Collins/Stillman* framework, as interpreted and applied in subsequent decisions, has brought a measure of certainty to the s. 24(2) inquiry. Yet the analytical method it imposes and the results it sometimes produces have been criticized as inconsistent with the language and objectives of s. 24(2). In order to understand these criticisms, it is necessary to briefly review the holdings in *Collins* and *Stillman*.

In *Collins*, the Court (*per* Lamer J., as he then was) proceeded by grouping the factors to be considered under s. 24(2) into three categories: (1) whether the evidence will undermine the fairness of the trial by effectively conscripting the accused against himself or herself; (2) the seriousness of the *Charter* breach; and (3) the effect of excluding the evidence on the long-term repute of the administration of justice. While Lamer J. acknowledged that these categories were merely a "matter of personal preference" (p. 284), they quickly became formalized as the governing test for s. 24(2).

Collins shed important light on the factors relevant to determining admissibility of *Charter*-violative evidence under s. 24(2). However, the concepts of trial fairness and conscription under the first branch of *Collins* introduced new problems of their own. Moreover, questions arose about what work (if any) remained to be done under the second and third categories, once conscription leading to trial unfairness had been found. Finally, issues arose as to how to measure the seriousness of the breach under the second branch and what weight, if any, should be put on the seriousness of the offence charged in deciding whether to admit evidence.

The admission of physical or "real" evidence obtained from the body of the accused in breach of his or her *Charter* rights proved particularly problematic. Ten years after *Collins*, the Court revisited this question in *Stillman*. The majority held that evidence obtained in breach of the *Charter* should, at the outset of the s. 24(2) inquiry, be classified as either "conscriptive" or "non-conscriptive." Evidence would be classified as conscriptive where "an accused, in violation of his *Charter* rights, is compelled to incriminate himself at the behest of the state by means of a statement, the use of the body or the production of bodily samples": *Stillman*, at para. 80, *per* Cory J. The category of conscriptive evidence was also held to include real evidence discovered as a result of an unlawfully conscripted statement. This is known as derivative evidence.

Stillman held that conscriptive evidence is generally inadmissible—because of its presumed impact on trial fairness—unless if it would have been independently discovered. Despite reminders that "all the circumstances" must always be considered under s. 24(2) (see *R. v. Burlingham*, [1995] 2 S.C.R. 206, *per* Sopinka J., *R. v. Orbanski*, 2005 SCC 37, [2005] 2 S.C.R. 3, *per* LeBel J.), *Stillman* has generally been read as creating an all-but-automatic exclusionary rule for non-discoverable conscriptive evidence, broadening the category of conscriptive evidence and increasing its importance to the ultimate decision on admissibility.

This general rule of inadmissibility of all non-discoverable conscriptive evidence, whether intended by *Stillman* or not, seems to go against the requirement of s. 24(2) that the court determining admissibility must consider "all the circumstances." The underlying assumption that the use of conscriptive evidence always, or almost always, renders the trial unfair is also open to challenge … . It is difficult to reconcile trial fairness as a multifaceted and contextual concept with a near-automatic presumption that admission of a broad class of evidence will render a trial unfair, regardless of the circumstances in which it was obtained. In our view, trial fairness is better conceived as an overarching systemic goal than as a distinct stage of the s. 24(2) analysis.

This brief review of the impact of *Collins* and *Stillman* brings us to the heart of our inquiry on this appeal: clarification of the criteria relevant to determining when, in "all the circumstances," admission of evidence obtained by a *Charter* breach "would bring the administration of justice into disrepute."

The words of s. 24(2) capture its purpose: to maintain the good repute of the administration of justice. The term "administration of justice" is often used to indicate the processes by which those who break the law are investigated, charged and tried. More broadly, however, the term embraces maintaining the rule of law and upholding *Charter* rights in the justice system as a whole.

The phrase "bring the administration of justice into disrepute" must be understood in the long-term sense of maintaining the integrity of, and public confidence in, the justice system. Exclusion of evidence resulting in an acquittal may provoke immediate criticism. But s. 24(2) does not focus on immediate reaction to the individual case. Rather, it looks to whether the overall repute of the justice system, viewed in the long term, will be adversely affected by admission of the evidence. The inquiry is objective. It asks whether a reasonable person, informed of all relevant circumstances and the values underlying the *Charter*, would conclude that the admission of the evidence would bring the administration of justice into disrepute.

Section 24(2)'s focus is not only long-term, but prospective. The fact of the *Charter* breach means damage has already been done to the administration of justice. Section 24(2) starts from that proposition and seeks to ensure that evidence obtained through that breach does not do further damage to the repute of the justice system.

Finally, s. 24(2)'s focus is societal. Section 24(2) is not aimed at punishing the police or providing compensation to the accused, but rather at systemic concerns. The s. 24(2) focus is on the broad impact of admission of the evidence on the long-term repute of the justice system.

A review of the authorities suggests that whether the admission of evidence obtained in breach of the *Charter* would bring the administration of justice into disrepute engages three avenues of inquiry, each rooted in the public interests engaged by s. 24(2), viewed in a long-term, forward-looking and societal perspective. When faced with an application for exclusion under s. 24(2), a court must assess and balance the effect of admitting the evidence on society's confidence in the justice system having regard to: (1) the seriousness of the *Charter*-infringing state conduct (admission may send the message the justice system condones serious state misconduct), (2) the impact of the breach on the *Charter*-protected interests of the accused (admission may send the message that individual rights count for little), and (3) society's interest in the adjudication of the case on its merits. The court's role on a s. 24(2) application is to balance the assessments under each of these lines of inquiry to determine whether, considering all the circumstances, admission of the evidence would bring the administration of justice into disrepute. ...

(a) Seriousness of the Charter-Infringing State Conduct

• • •

The first line of inquiry relevant to the s. 24(2) analysis requires a court to assess whether the admission of the evidence would bring the administration of justice into disrepute by sending a message to the public that the courts, as institutions responsible for the administration of justice, effectively condone state deviation from the rule of law by failing to dissociate themselves from the fruits of that unlawful conduct. The more severe or deliberate the state conduct that led to the *Charter* violation, the greater the need for the courts to dissociate themselves from that conduct, by excluding evidence linked to that conduct, in order to preserve public confidence in and ensure state adherence to the rule of law.

This inquiry therefore necessitates an evaluation of the seriousness of the state conduct that led to the breach. The concern of this inquiry is not to punish the police or to deter *Charter* breaches, although deterrence of *Charter* breaches may be a happy consequence. The main concern is to preserve public confidence in the rule of law and its processes. In order to determine the effect of admission of the evidence on public confidence in the justice system, the court on a s. 24(2) application must consider the seriousness of the violation, viewed in terms of the gravity of the offending conduct by state authorities whom the rule of law requires to uphold the rights guaranteed by the *Charter*.

State conduct resulting in *Charter* violations varies in seriousness. At one end of the spectrum, admission of evidence obtained through inadvertent or minor violations of the *Charter* may minimally undermine public confidence in the rule of law. At the other end of the spectrum, admitting evidence obtained through a wilful or reckless disregard of *Charter* rights will inevitably have a negative effect on the public confidence in the rule of law, and risk bringing the administration of justice into disrepute.

Extenuating circumstances, such as the need to prevent the disappearance of evidence, may attenuate the seriousness of police conduct that results in a *Charter* breach: *R. v. Silveira*, [1995] 2 S.C.R. 297, *per* Cory J. "Good faith" on the part of the police will also reduce the need for the court to disassociate itself from the police conduct. However, ignorance of *Charter* standards must not be rewarded or encouraged and negligence or wilful blindness cannot be equated with good faith: *R. v. Genest*, [1989] 1 S.C.R. 59, at p. 87, *per* Dickson C.J.; *R. v. Kokesch*, [1990] 3 S.C.R. 3, at pp. 32-33, *per* Sopinka J.; *R. v. Buhay*, 2003 SCC 30, [2003] 1 S.C.R. 631, at para. 59. Wilful or flagrant disregard of the *Charter* by those very persons who are charged with upholding the right in question may require that the court dissociate itself from such conduct. It follows that deliberate police conduct in violation of established *Charter* standards tends to support exclusion of the evidence. It should also be kept in mind that for every *Charter* breach that comes before the courts, many others may go unidentified and unredressed because they did not turn up relevant evidence leading to a criminal charge. In recognition of the need for courts to distance themselves from this behaviour, therefore, evidence that the *Charter*-infringing conduct was part of a pattern of abuse tends to support exclusion.

(b) Impact on the Charter-Protected Interests of the Accused

This inquiry focuses on the seriousness of the impact of the *Charter* breach on the *Charter*-protected interests of the accused. It calls for an evaluation of the extent to which the breach actually undermined the interests protected by the right infringed. The impact of a *Charter* breach may range from fleeting and technical to profoundly intrusive. The more serious the impact on the accused's protected interests, the greater the risk that admission of the evidence may signal to the public that *Charter* rights, however high-sounding, are of little actual avail to the citizen, breeding public cynicism and bringing the administration of justice into disrepute.

To determine the seriousness of the infringement from this perspective, we look to the interests engaged by the infringed right and examine the degree to which the violation impacted on those interests. For example, the interests engaged in the case of a statement to the authorities obtained in breach of the *Charter* include the s. 7 right to silence, or to choose whether or not to speak to authorities (*Hebert*)—all stemming from the principle against self-incrimination: *R. v. White*, [1999] 2 S.C.R. 417, at para. 44. The more serious the incursion on these interests, the greater the risk that admission of the evidence would bring the administration of justice into disrepute.

Similarly, an unreasonable search contrary to s. 8 of the *Charter* may impact on the protected interests of privacy, and more broadly, human dignity. An unreasonable search that intrudes on an area in which the individual reasonably enjoys a high expectation of privacy, or that demeans his or her dignity, is more serious than one that does not.

(c) Society's Interest in an Adjudication on the Merits

Society generally expects that a criminal allegation will be adjudicated on its merits. Accordingly, the third line of inquiry relevant to the s. 24(2) analysis asks whether the truth-seeking function of the criminal trial process would be better served by admission of the evidence, or by its exclusion. This inquiry reflects society's "collective interest in ensuring that those who transgress the law are brought to trial and dealt with according to the law": *R. v. Askov*, [1990] 2 S.C.R. 1199, at pp. 1219-20. Thus the Court suggested in *Collins* that a judge on a s. 24(2) application should consider not only the negative impact of admission of the evidence on the repute of the administration of justice, but the impact of *failing to admit* the evidence.

The concern for truth-seeking is only one of the considerations under a s. 24(2) application. The view that reliable evidence is admissible regardless of how it was obtained (see *R. v. Wray*, [1971] S.C.R. 272) is inconsistent with the *Charter*'s affirmation of rights. More specifically, it is inconsistent with the wording of s. 24(2), which mandates a broad inquiry into all the circumstances, not just the reliability of the evidence.

This said, public interest in truth-finding remains a relevant consideration under the s. 24(2) analysis. The reliability of the evidence is an important factor in this line of inquiry. If a breach (such as one that effectively compels the suspect to talk) undermines the reliability of the evidence, this points in the direction of exclusion of the evidence. The admission of unreliable evidence serves neither the accused's interest in a fair trial nor the public interest in uncovering the truth. Conversely, exclusion of relevant and reliable evidence may undermine the truth-seeking function of the justice system and render the trial unfair from the public perspective, thus bringing the administration of justice into disrepute.

The fact that the evidence obtained in breach of the *Charter* may facilitate the discovery of the truth and the adjudication of a case on its merits must therefore be weighed against factors pointing to exclusion, in order to "balance the interests of truth with the integrity of the justice system": *Mann*, at para. 57, *per* Iacobucci J. The court must ask "whether the vindication of the specific Charter violation through the exclusion of evidence extracts too great a toll on the truth-seeking goal of the criminal trial": *R. v. Kitaitchik* (2002), 166 C.C.C. (3d) 14 (Ont. C.A.), at para. 47, *per* Doherty J.A.

The importance of the evidence to the prosecution's case is another factor that may be considered in this line of inquiry. Like Deschamps J., we view this factor as corollary to the inquiry into reliability, in the following limited sense. The admission of evidence of questionable reliability is more likely to bring the administration of justice into disrepute where it forms the entirety of the case against the accused. Conversely, the exclusion of highly reliable evidence may impact more negatively on the repute of the administration of justice where the remedy effectively guts the prosecution.

It has been suggested that the judge should also, under this line of inquiry, consider the seriousness of the offence at issue. Indeed, Deschamps J. views this factor as very important, arguing that the more serious the offence, the greater society's interest in its prosecution (para. 226). In our view, while the seriousness of the alleged offence may be a valid consideration, it has the potential to cut both ways. Failure to effectively prosecute a serious charge due to excluded evidence may have an immediate impact on how people view the justice system. Yet, as discussed, it is the long-term repute of the justice system that is s. 24(2)'s focus. As pointed out in *Burlingham*, the goals furthered by s. 24(2) "operate independently of the type of crime for which the individual stands accused" (para. 51). And as Lamer J. observed in *Collins*, "[t]he *Charter* is designed to protect the accused from the majority, so the enforcement of the *Charter* must not be left to that majority" (p. 282). The short-term public clamour for a conviction in a particular case must not deafen the s. 24(2) judge to the longer-term repute of the administration of justice. Moreover, while the public has a heightened interest in seeing a determination on the merits where the offence charged is serious, it also has a vital interest in having a justice system that is above reproach, particularly where the penal stakes for the accused are high. ...

In all cases, it is the task of the trial judge to weigh the various indications. No overarching rule governs how the balance is to be struck. Mathematical precision is obviously not possible. However, the preceding analysis creates a decision tree, albeit more flexible than the *Stillman* self-incrimination test. We believe this to be required by the words of s. 24(2). We also take comfort in the fact that patterns emerge with respect to particular types of evidence. These patterns serve as guides to judges faced with s. 24(2) applications in future cases. In this way, a measure of certainty is achieved. Where the trial judge has considered the proper factors, appellate courts should accord considerable deference to his or her ultimate determination.

[McLachlin CJ and Charron J then proceeded to apply these factors to the circumstances of Grant's case. They concluded that the violation was not deliberate or egregious and noted that there was no suggestion that the accused was the target of racial profiling. Although the officers went too far in detaining the accused, McLachlin CJ and Charron J noted that the demarcating line for detention is not always clear and that the officers' mistake was an understandable one. While noting that the impact of breach on the accused's protected interests was significant, they concluded that it was not at the most serious end of the scale. Finally, the gun was highly reliable evidence and was essential to a determination on the merits. The significant impact of the breach on the accused's Charter-protected rights was said to weigh strongly in favour of excluding the gun, while the public interest in the adjudication of the case on its merits was said to weigh strongly in favour of its admission. Ultimately, McLachlin CJ and Charron J concluded that because the police officers were operating in circumstances of considerable legal uncertainty, this tipped the balance in favour of admission.

LeBel, Fish, and Abella JJ concurred in the reasons of McLachlin CJ and Charron J. Both Binnie J and Deschamps J wrote separate but concurring reasons.]

Detention Powers

As noted above, to be constitutional, a detention or arrest must be premised on legal authority. Prior to 1993, Canadian law was clear, police had no power to detain short of carrying out a formal arrest. (See e.g. *R v Esposito* (1985), 24 CCC (3d) 88 at 94 (Ont CA), leave to appeal to SCC refused, [1986] 1 SCR viii.)

All this changed with the Ontario Court of Appeal's decision in *R v Simpson* (1993), 79 CCC (3d) 482 (Ont CA). After applying what has come to be known as the "ancillary powers doctrine" (explained in *Mann* below), the court in *Simpson* recognized a police power at "common law" to briefly detain an individual where police have "articulable cause" that the person is involved in criminal activity. In the decade after *Simpson*, virtually every provincial appellate court in the country endorsed the common law power it recognized. By the time the issue came before the Supreme Court of Canada, the momentum in favour of this new police power was somewhat unstoppable.

R v Mann
Supreme Court of Canada
2004 SCC 52, [2004] 3 SCR 59

IACOBUCCI J: ... This appeal presents fundamental issues on the right of individuals to walk the streets free from state interference, but in recognition of the necessary role of the police in criminal investigation. As such, this case offers another opportunity to consider the delicate balance that must be struck in adequately protecting individual liberties and properly recognizing legitimate police functions. ...

Facts

On December 23, 2000, shortly before midnight, two police officers received a radio dispatch message detailing a break and enter in progress in a neighbouring district of downtown Winnipeg. The suspect was described as a 21-year-old aboriginal male, approximately five feet eight inches tall, weighing about 165 pounds, clad in a black jacket with white sleeves, and thought to be one "Zachary Parisienne."

As the officers approached the scene of the reported crime, they observed an individual walking casually along the sidewalk. They testified that this individual matched the description of the suspect "to the tee." The officers stopped the appellant, Philip Mann, and asked him to identify himself. The appellant stated his name and provided his date of birth to the officers. He also complied with a pat-down search of his person for concealed weapons. The appellant was wearing a pullover sweater with a kangaroo pouch pocket in the front. During the pat-down search, one officer felt a soft object in this pocket. The officer reached into the appellant's pocket and found a small plastic bag containing 27.55 grams of marijuana. In another pocket, the officer found a number of small plastic baggies, two Valium pills and a treaty status card confirming the appellant's identity.

The appellant was subsequently arrested and cautioned for the offence of possession for the purpose of trafficking marijuana contrary to s. 5(2) of the *Controlled Drugs and Substances Act*, S.C. 1996, c. 19. ...

Analysis

Introduction

As stated earlier, the issues in this case require the Court to balance individual liberty rights and privacy interests with a societal interest in effective policing. Absent a law to the contrary, individuals are free to do as they please. By contrast, the police (and more broadly, the state) may act only to the extent that they are empowered to do so by law. The vibrancy of a democracy is apparent by how wisely it navigates through those critical junctures where state action intersects with, and threatens to impinge upon, individual liberties.

Nowhere do these interests collide more frequently than in the area of criminal investigation. *Charter* rights do not exist in a vacuum; they are animated at virtually every stage of police action. Given their mandate to investigate crime and keep the peace, police officers must be empowered to respond quickly, effectively, and flexibly to the diversity of encounters experienced daily on the front lines of policing. Despite there being no formal consensus about the existence of a police power to detain for investigative purposes, several commentators note its long-standing use in Canadian policing practice: see A. Young, "All Along the Watchtower: Arbitrary Detention and the Police Function" (1991), 29 *Osgoode Hall L.J.* 329, at p. 330; and J. Stribopoulos, "A Failed Experiment? Investigative Detention: Ten Years Later" (2003), 41 *Alta. L. Rev.* 335, at p. 339.

At the same time, this Court must tread softly where complex legal developments are best left to the experience and expertise of legislators. As McLachlin J. (as she then was) noted in *Watkins v. Olafson*, [1989] 2 S.C.R. 750, at p. 760, major changes requiring the development of subsidiary rules and procedures relevant to their implementation are better accomplished through legislative deliberation than by judicial decree. It is for that very reason that I do not believe it appropriate for this Court to recognize a general power of detention for investigative purposes. The Court cannot, however, shy away from the task where common law rules are required to be incrementally adapted to reflect societal change. Courts, as its custodians, share responsibility for ensuring that the common law reflects current and emerging societal needs and values: *R. v. Salituro*, [1991] 3 S.C.R. 654, at p. 670. Here, our duty is to lay down the common law governing police powers of investigative detention in the particular context of this case.

Where, as in this case, the relevant common law rule has evolved gradually through jurisprudential treatment, the judiciary is the proper forum for the recognition and ordering of further legal developments, absent legislative intervention. Over time, the common law has moved cautiously to carve out a limited sphere for state intrusions on individual liberties in the context of policing. The recognition of a limited police power of investigative detention marks another step in that measured development. It is, of course, open to Parliament to enact legislation in line with what it deems the best approach to the matter, subject to overarching requirements of constitutional compliance.

As well, Parliament may seek to legislate appropriate practice and procedural techniques to ensure that respect for individual liberty is adequately balanced against the interest of officer safety. In the meantime, however, the unregulated use of investigative detentions in policing, their uncertain legal status, and the potential for abuse inherent in such low-visibility exercises of discretionary power are all pressing reasons why the Court must exercise its custodial role. ...

Section 10(a) of the *Charter* provides that "[e]veryone has the right on arrest or detention to be informed promptly of the reasons therefor." At a minimum, individuals who are detained for investigative purposes must therefore be advised, in clear and simple language, of the reasons for the detention.

Section 10(b) of the *Charter* raises more difficult issues. It enshrines the right of detainees "to retain and instruct counsel without delay and to be informed of that right." Like every other provision of the *Charter*, s. 10(b) must be purposively interpreted. Mandatory compliance with its requirements cannot be transformed into an excuse for prolonging, unduly and artificially, a detention that, as I later mention, must be of brief duration. Other aspects of s. 10(b), as they arise in the context of investigative detentions, will in my view be left to another day. They should not be considered and settled without the benefit of full consideration in the lower courts, which we do not have in this case.

The Common Law Development of Investigative Detention

A number of cases occurring over the years have culminated in the recognition of a limited power of officers to detain for investigative purposes.

The test for whether a police officer has acted within his or her common law powers was first expressed by the English Court of Criminal Appeals in *Waterfield*, [[1963] 3 All ER 659], at pp. 660-661. From the decision emerged a two-pronged analysis where the officer's conduct is *prima facie* an unlawful interference with an individual's liberty or property. In those situations, courts must first consider whether the police conduct giving rise to the interference falls within the general scope of any duty imposed on the officer by statute or at common law. If this threshold is met, the analysis continues to consider secondly whether such conduct, albeit within the general scope of such a duty, involved an unjustifiable use of powers associated with the duty. ...

At the first stage of the *Waterfield* test, police powers are recognized as deriving from the nature and scope of police duties, including, at common law, "the preservation of the peace, the prevention of crime, and the protection of life and property" (*Dedman*, [[1985] 2 SCR 2], at p. 32). The second stage of the test requires a balance between the competing interests of the police duty and of the liberty interests at stake. This aspect of the test requires a consideration of:

> whether an invasion of individual rights is necessary in order for the peace officers to perform their duty, and whether such invasion is reasonable in light of the public purposes served by effective control of criminal acts on the one hand and on the other respect for the liberty and fundamental dignity of individuals. (*Cloutier* [*v Langlois*, [1990] 1 SCR 158], at pp. 181-82)

The reasonable necessity or justification of the police conduct in the specific circumstances is highlighted at this stage. Specifically, in *Dedman*, *supra*, at p. 35, Le Dain J. provided that the necessity and reasonableness for the interference with liberty was to be assessed with regard to the nature of the liberty interfered with and the importance of the public purpose served. ...

With respect to terminology, I prefer to use the term "reasonable grounds to detain" rather than the U.S. phrase "articulable cause" since Canadian jurisprudence has employed reasonable grounds in analogous circumstances and has provided useful guidance to decide the issues in question. As I discuss below, the reasonable grounds are related to the police action involved, namely, detention, search or arrest.

The case law raises several guiding principles governing the use of a police power to detain for investigative purposes. The evolution of the *Waterfield* test, along with the *Simpson* articulable cause requirement, calls for investigative detentions to be premised upon reasonable grounds. The detention must be viewed as reasonably necessary on an objective view of the totality of the circumstances, informing the officer's suspicion that there is a clear nexus between the individual to be detained and a recent or on-going criminal offence. Reasonable grounds figures at the front-end of such an assessment, underlying the officer's reasonable suspicion that the particular individual is implicated in the criminal activity under investigation. The overall reasonableness of the decision to detain, however, must further be assessed against all of the circumstances, most notably the extent to which the interference with individual liberty is necessary to perform the officer's duty, the liberty interfered with, and the nature and extent of that interference, in order to meet the second prong of the *Waterfield* test.

Police powers and police duties are not necessarily correlative. While the police have a common law duty to investigate crime, they are not empowered to undertake any and all action in the exercise of that duty. Individual liberty interests are fundamental to the Canadian constitutional order. Consequently, any intrusion upon them must not be taken lightly and, as a result, police officers do not have *carte blanche* to detain. The power to detain cannot be exercised on the basis of a hunch, nor can it become a *de facto* arrest.

Search Powers Incident to Investigative Detention

. . .

I rely upon the *Waterfield* test discussed above to recognize that a power of search incidental to investigative detention does exist at common law. Under the first prong of the *Waterfield* test, the interference clearly falls within the general scope of a duty imposed by statute or recognized at common law. The duty at issue here is the protection of life and property, which was also at issue in *Dedman, supra*, at p. 32.

To continue in the *Waterfield* analysis, the conduct giving rise to the interference must involve a justified use of a police power associated with a general duty to search in relation to the protection of life and property. Put differently, the search must be reasonably necessary. The relevant considerations here include the duty being performed, the extent to which some interference with individual liberty is necessary in the performance of that duty, the importance of the performance of the duty to the public good, the nature of the liberty being interfered with, and the nature and extent of the interference: *Dedman, supra*, at pp. 35-36.

The general duty of officers to protect life may, in some circumstances, give rise to the power to conduct a pat-down search incident to an investigative detention. Such a search power does not exist as a matter of course; the officer must believe on reasonable grounds that his or her own safety, or the safety of others, is at risk. I disagree with the suggestion that the power to detain for investigative searches endorses an incidental search in all circumstances: see S. Coughlan, "Search Based on Articulable Cause: Proceed with Caution or Full Stop?" (2003), 2 C.R. (6th) 49, at p. 63. The officer's decision to search must also be reasonably necessary in light of the totality of the circumstances. It cannot be justified on the basis of a vague or non-existent concern for safety, nor can the search be premised upon hunches or mere intuition. …

To summarize, as discussed above, police officers may detain an individual for investigative purposes if there are reasonable grounds to suspect in all the circumstances that the individual is connected to a particular crime and that such a detention is necessary. In addition, where a police officer has reasonable grounds to believe that his or her safety or that of others is at risk, the officer may engage in a protective pat-down search of the detained individual. Both the detention and the pat-down search must be conducted in a reasonable manner. In this connection, I note that the investigative detention should be brief in duration and does not impose an obligation on the detained individual to answer questions posed by the police. The investigative detention and protective search power are to be distinguished from an arrest and the incidental power to search on arrest, which do not arise in this case.

Application to the Facts

Having set out the relevant considerations above, I turn to whether the detention and search of the appellant in this case has met the applicable standards.

The officers had reasonable grounds to detain the appellant. He closely matched the description of the suspect given by radio dispatch, and was only two or three blocks from the scene of the reported crime. These factors led the officers to reasonably suspect that the appellant was involved in recent criminal activity, and at the very least ought to be investigated further. The presence of an individual in a so-called high crime area is relevant only so far as it reflects his or her proximity to a particular crime. The high crime nature of a neighbourhood is not by itself a basis for detaining individuals.

Furthermore, there were reasonable grounds for a protective search of the appellant. There was a logical possibility that the appellant, suspected on reasonable grounds of having recently committed a break-and-enter, was in possession of break-and-enter tools, which could be used as weapons. The encounter also occurred just after midnight and there were no other people in the area. On balance, the officer was justified in conducting a pat-down search for protective purposes.

The officer's decision to go beyond this initial pat-down and reach into the appellant's pocket after feeling an admittedly soft object therein is problematic. The trial judge found that the officer had no reasonable basis for reaching into the pocket. This more intrusive part of the search was an unreasonable violation of the appellant's reasonable expectation of privacy in the contents of his pockets. The trial judge found as a fact that "there was nothing from which [he could] infer that it was reasonable to proceed beyond a pat down search for security reasons." The Court of Appeal did not give due deference to this important finding, which was largely based on the credibility of witnesses, an area strictly in the domain of the trial judge absent palpable and overriding error: *Housen v. Nikolaisen*, [2002] 2 S.C.R. 235, 2002 SCC 33. Moreover, the Crown has not discharged its burden to show on the balance of probabilities that the third aspect of the *Collins* test has been satisfied, namely that the search was carried out in a reasonable manner.

The seizure of the marijuana from the appellant was unlawful in this case. The admissibility of the evidence must accordingly be considered under s. 24(2) of the *Charter*.

[Iacobucci J concluded that the evidence obtained should be excluded under s 24(2) of the Charter. Major, Binnie, LeBel, and Fish JJ concurred. In a dissenting judgment, Deschamps J (Bastarache J concurring) agreed with the majority that an investigative detention power should be recognized at common law but favoured maintaining the operative standard as "articulable cause" rather than replacing it with "reasonable suspicion." Although concluding that the search violated s 8 of the Charter, Deschamps J would have admitted the evidence.]

Appeal allowed.

Mann has been widely criticized by commentators. A common complaint is that the case raises more questions than it answers about police detention powers. See P Healy, "Investigative Detention in Canada" [2005] Crim LR 98; JR Marin, "R v Mann: Further Down the Slippery Slope" (2005) 42 Alta L Rev 1123; J Stribopoulos, "In Search of Dialogue: The Supreme Court, Police Powers and the Charter" (2005) 31 Queen's LJ 1; C Skibinsky, "Regulating Mann in Canada" (2006) 69 Sask L Rev 197; and J Stribopoulos, "The Limits of Judicially Created Police Powers: Investigative Detention After Mann" (2007) 52 Crim LQ 299.

In addition, critics complain that in *Mann* the Court failed to adequately address the racial dimensions of police detention practices. For example, the now extensive empirical evidence documenting the disproportionate impact of police stop and frisk practices on black and native Canadians goes unmentioned and does not meaningfully inform the Court's analysis (see BL Berger, "Race and Erasure in Mann" (2004) 21 CR (6th) 58), as does the fact that Mann was Aboriginal (see DM Tanovich, "The Colourless World of Mann" (2004) 21 CR (6th) 47).

In *R v Clayton*, 2007 SCC 32, [2007] 2 SCR 725 the Supreme Court employed the ancillary powers doctrine to recognize a police power to conduct criminal investigative roadblock stops of vehicles and their occupants. By way of requirements, the Court recognized that such roadblocks must be tailored to the information possessed by police, the seriousness of the offence being investigated, and the temporal and geographic connection between the situation being investigated and the timing and location of the roadblock.

In *R v Suberu*, 2009 SCC 33, [2009] 2 SCR 460, the Supreme Court of Canada finally made clear that police have a duty to inform an individual who is subject to investigative detention regarding his or her right to retain and instruct counsel, and a duty to facilitate that right, *immediately* on such detention. McLachlin CJ and Charron J, writing for the majority, explained that "[t]he immediacy of this obligation is only subject to concerns for officer or public safety, or to reasonable limitations that are prescribed by law and justified under s. 1 of the Charter" (at para 2).

Arrest Powers

Section 494 of the *Criminal Code* sets out the arrest powers that anyone has without a judicial warrant and s 495 sets out the wider arrest powers of a peace officer without a warrant. Note that under s 495(2), the general rule is that a peace officer shall not arrest a person without warrant for less serious offences under the Code where the public interest in establishing the identity and securing the attendance of the person in court, securing evidence of the offence, and preventing the repetition of the offence or the commission of another offence can be satisfied by issuing an appearance notice or a summons.

A judicial warrant for an arrest can also be obtained. Under s 507(4) of the *Criminal Code*, if the justice of the peace considers that a case has been made out on oath for compelling an accused to answer the charge of the offence, then he or she will issue a summons unless the evidence presented discloses reasonable grounds to believe that it is necessary in the public interest to issue an arrest warrant. In this, as in many other of the arrest provisions in the *Criminal Code*, there is a distinct preference for the procedure that constitutes the least drastic interference with the accused's liberty.

In *R v Storrey*, [1990] 1 SCR 241, the Supreme Court examined s 495(1). Cory J stated that the section

> makes it clear that the police were required to have reasonable and probable grounds that the appellant had committed the offence of aggravated assault before they could arrest him. Without such an important protection, even the most democratic society could all too easily fall prey to the abuses and excesses of a police state. In order to safeguard the liberty of citizens, the *Criminal Code* requires the police, when attempting to obtain a warrant for an arrest, to demonstrate to a judicial officer that they have reasonable and probable grounds to believe that the person to be arrested has committed the offence. In the case of an arrest made without a warrant, it is even more important for the police to demonstrate that they have those same reasonable and probable grounds upon which they base the arrest.

> • • •

> There is an additional safeguard against arbitrary arrest. It is not sufficient for the police officer to personally believe that he or she has reasonable and probable grounds to make an arrest. Rather, it must be objectively established that those reasonable and probable grounds did in fact exist. That is to say a reasonable person, standing in the shoes of the police officer, would have believed that reasonable and probable grounds existed to make the arrest.

> In summary then, the *Criminal Code* requires that an arresting officer must subjectively have reasonable and probable grounds on which to base the arrest. Those grounds must, in addition, be justifiable from an objective point of view. That is to say, a reasonable person placed in the position of the officer must be able to conclude that there were indeed reasonable and probable grounds for the arrest. On the other hand, the police need not demonstrate anything more than reasonable and probable grounds. Specifically they are not required to establish a *prima facie* case for conviction before making the arrest. ...

> In the case at bar, the trial judge specifically stated that "Larkin had reasonable and probable grounds" to make the arrest. In my view there was ample evidence on which the trial judge could very properly make that finding. The reasonable grounds could be based subjectively on the testimony of Larkin and objectively upon the cumulative effect of the following items; (a) the possession and ownership by Storrey of a 1973 blue Thunderbird, which was a relatively unusual and uncommon car and was the type of car used in the infraction; (b) the fact that he had been stopped by the police on several occasions driving that car; (c) his past record of violence; (d) the fact that two of the victims picked out a picture of Cameron as someone who looked like their assailant; and (e) the remarkable resemblance of Storrey to Cameron. These factors taken together clearly were sufficient in their cumulative effect to constitute reasonable and probable grounds for Larkin to arrest the appellant.

> It should be noted, as well, that there is nothing to indicate that there was anything in the circumstances of the arrest which would make it suspect on any other ground. That is to say, there is no indication that the arrest was made because a police officer was biased towards a person of a different race, nationality or colour, or that there was a personal enmity between a

police officer directed towards the person arrested. These factors, if established, might have the effect of rendering invalid an otherwise lawful arrest. However, the arrest of the appellant was in every respect lawful and proper.

Powers Incident to Arrest

Cloutier v Langlois
Supreme Court of Canada
[1990] 1 SCR 158

[In this case, a lawyer charged two police officers with assault after he was frisked, before being placed in a police car, following his arrest for unpaid parking tickets. The Court held that the search of the lawyer, who was being verbally abusive, was justified for the police officers' safety and not conducted with excessive force or constraint. They dismissed the assault charges in the following opinion for the Court.]

L'HEUREUX-DUBÉ J: A "frisk" search incidental to a lawful arrest reconciles the public's interest in the effective and safe enforcement of the law on the one hand, and on the other its interest in ensuring the freedom and dignity of individuals. The minimal intrusion involved in the search is necessary to ensure that criminal justice is properly administered. I agree with the opinion of the Ontario Court of Appeal as stated in … *R. v. Morrison* [(1987), 35 CCC (3d) 437 (Ont CA)] … that the existence of reasonable and probable grounds is not a prerequisite to the existence of a police power to search. The exercise of this power is not, however, unlimited. Three propositions can be derived from the authorities and a consideration of the underlying interests.

1. This power does not impose a duty. The police have some discretion in conducting the search. Where they are satisfied that the law can be effectively and safely applied without a search, the police may see fit not to conduct a search. They must be in a position to assess the circumstances of each case so as to determine whether a search meets the underlying objectives.

2. The search must be for a valid objective in pursuit of the ends of criminal justice, such as the discovery of an object that may be a threat to the safety of the police, the accused or the public, or that may facilitate escape or act as evidence against the accused. The purpose of the search must not be unrelated to the objectives of the proper administration of justice, which would be the case, for example, if the purpose of the search was to intimidate, ridicule or pressure the accused in order to obtain admissions.

3. The search must not be conducted in an abusive fashion and, in particular, the use of physical or psychological constraint should be proportionate to the objectives sought and the other circumstances of the situation.

A search which does not meet these objectives could be characterized as unreasonable and unjustified at common law.

Should the police be able to seize hair or saliva samples for DNA testing as part of their search powers incident to arrest?

In *R v Stillman*, [1997] 1 SCR 607, a majority of the Supreme Court held that the taking of bodily samples for DNA testing without the accused's consent and without a warrant infringed ss 7 and 8 of the Charter and that the samples should be excluded under s 24(2). Cory J for the majority (Lamer CJ and La Forest, Sopinka, Iacobucci, and Major JJ concurring) stated:

> The power to search and seize incidental to arrest was a pragmatic extension to the power of arrest. Obviously the police must be able to protect themselves from attack by the accused who has weapons concealed on his person or close at hand. The police must be able to collect and preserve evidence located at the site of the arrest or in a nearby motor vehicle. ...
>
> The common law power cannot be so broad as to empower police officers to seize bodily samples. They are usually in no danger of disappearing. Here, there was no likelihood that the appellant's teeth impressions would change, nor that his hair follicles would present a different DNA profile with the passage of time. There was simply no possibility of the evidence sought being destroyed if it was not seized immediately. It should be remembered that one of the limitations to the common law power articulated in *Cloutier v. Langlois*, [*supra*], was the discretionary aspect of the power and that it should not be abusive. The common law power of search incidental to arrest cannot be so broad as to encompass the seizure without valid statutory authority of bodily samples in the face of a refusal to provide them. If it is, then the common law rule itself is unreasonable, since it is too broad and fails to properly balance the competing rights involved. ...
>
> The taking of the dental impressions, hair samples and buccal swabs from the accused also contravened the appellant's s. 7 Charter right to security of the person. The taking of the bodily samples was highly intrusive. It violated the sanctity of the body which is essential to the maintenance of human dignity. It was the ultimate invasion of the appellant's privacy. See *Pohoretsky* (1987), 33 C.C.C. (3d) 398 ... . In *Dyment* (1988), 45 C.C.C. (3d) 244 ... , La Forest J. emphasized that "the use of a person's body without his consent to obtain information about him, invades an area of personal privacy essential to the maintenance of his human dignity." Quite simply, the taking of the samples without authorization violated the appellant's right to security of his person and contravened the principles of fundamental justice.

See now ss 487.04 to 487.09 of the *Criminal Code*, which allow for the issuance of warrants to secure hair and blood for DNA testing.

L'Heureux-Dubé J (Gonthier J concurring) dissented and held that the seizures of the bodily samples were authorized by the common law powers of search incident to arrest because there was a minimal invasion of the accused's bodily integrity and no search warrant procedure for seizing samples for DNA analysis existed at the time.

When should the police be able to conduct a strip search as part of a search incident to arrest?

R v Golden
Supreme Court of Canada
2001 SCC 83, [2001] 3 SCR 679

IACOBUCCI and ARBOUR JJ (Major, Binnie, and LeBel JJ concurring): Since *Cloutier*, this Court has addressed the constitutionality of the seizure of bodily samples at common law in *Stillman*, supra. Cory J., speaking for the majority, held that the seizure of bodily samples, namely hair samples, buccal swabs and dental impressions, was not authorized by the common law power to search incident to arrest. Such a serious interference with a person's bodily integrity required statutory authorization and could not be justified under the common law power to search incident to arrest. Cory J. distinguished the situation in *Stillman* from other cases, such as *Cloutier*, supra, where searches incident to arrest had been found not to infringe the Charter on the basis that "completely different concerns arise where the search and seizure infringes upon a person's bodily integrity, which may constitute the ultimate affront to human dignity" (*Stillman*, supra, at para. 39). ...

Strip searches are thus inherently humiliating and degrading for detainees regardless of the manner in which they are carried out and for this reason they cannot be carried out simply as a matter of routine policy. The adjectives used by individuals to describe their experience of being strip searched give some sense of how a strip search, even one that is carried out in a reasonable manner, can affect detainees: "humiliating," "degrading," "demeaning," "upsetting," and "devastating." ... Some commentators have gone as far as to describe strip searches as "visual rape" (P.R. Shuldiner, "Visual Rape: A Look at the Dubious Legality of Strip Searches" (1979), 13 *J. Marshall L. Rev.* 273). Women and minorities in particular may have a real fear of strip searches and may experience such a search as equivalent to a sexual assault. ... The psychological effects of strip searches may also be particularly traumatic for individuals who have previously been subject to abuse (Commission of Inquiry into Certain Events at the Prison for Women in Kingston, *The Prison for Women in Kingston* (1996), at pp. 86-89). Routine strip searches may also be distasteful and difficult for the police officers conducting them. ...

The fact that the police have reasonable and probable grounds to carry out an arrest does not confer upon them the automatic authority to carry out a strip search, even where the strip search meets the definition of being "incident to lawful arrest" as discussed above. Rather, additional grounds pertaining to the purpose of the strip search are required. In *Cloutier*, supra, this Court concluded that a common law search incident to arrest does not require additional grounds beyond the reasonable and probable grounds necessary to justify the lawfulness of the arrest itself: *Cloutier*, supra, at pp. 185-86. However, this conclusion was reached in the context of a "frisk" search, which involved a minimal invasion of the detainee's privacy and personal integrity. In contrast, a strip search is a much more intrusive search and, accordingly, a higher degree of justification is required in order to support the higher degree of interference with individual freedom and dignity. In order to meet the constitutional standard of reasonableness that will justify a strip search, the police must establish that they have reasonable and probable grounds for concluding that a strip search is necessary in the particular circumstances of the arrest.

In light of the serious infringement of privacy and personal dignity that is an inevitable consequence of a strip search, such searches are only constitutionally valid at common law where they are conducted as an incident to a lawful arrest for the purpose of discovering weapons in the detainee's possession or evidence related to the reason for the arrest. In addition, the police must establish reasonable and probable grounds justifying the strip search in addition to reasonable and probable grounds justifying the arrest. Where these preconditions to conducting a strip search incident to arrest are met, it is also necessary that the strip search be conducted in a manner that does not infringe s. 8 of the Charter.

Parliament could require that strip searches be authorized by warrants or telewarrants, which would heighten compliance with the Charter. At a minimum, if there is no prior judicial authorization for the strip search, several factors should be considered by the authorities in deciding whether, and if so how, to conduct such a procedure.

In this connection, we find the guidelines contained in the English legislation, P.A.C.E. concerning the conduct of strip searches to be in accordance with the constitutional requirements of s. 8 of the Charter. The following questions, which draw upon the common law principles as well as the statutory requirements set out in the English legislation, provide a framework for the police in deciding how best to conduct a strip search incident to arrest in compliance with the Charter:

1. Can the strip search be conducted at the police station and, if not, why not?
2. Will the strip search be conducted in a manner that ensures the health and safety of all involved?
3. Will the strip search be authorized by a police officer acting in a supervisory capacity?
4. Has it been ensured that the police officer(s) carrying out the strip search are of the same gender as the individual being searched?
5. Will the number of police officers involved in the search be no more than is reasonably necessary in the circumstances?
6. What is the minimum of force necessary to conduct the strip search?
7. Will the strip search be carried out in a private area such that no one other than the individuals engaged in the search can observe the search?
8. Will the strip search be conducted as quickly as possible and in a way that ensures that the person is not completely undressed at any one time?
9. Will the strip search involve only a visual inspection of the arrestee's genital and anal areas without any physical contact?
10. If the visual inspection reveals the presence of a weapon or evidence in a body cavity (not including the mouth), will the detainee be given the option of removing the object himself or of having the object removed by a trained medical professional?
11. Will a proper record be kept of the reasons for and the manner in which the strip search was conducted?

Strip searches should generally only be conducted at the police station except where there are exigent circumstances requiring that the detainee be searched prior to being transported to the police station. Such exigent circumstances will only be established where the police have reasonable and probable grounds to believe that it is necessary to conduct the search in the field rather than at the police station. Strip searches conducted in the field could only be justified where there is a demonstrated necessity and urgency to search for weapons or objects that could be used to threaten the safety of the accused, the arresting officers or other individuals. The police would also have to show why it would have been unsafe to wait and conduct the strip search at the police station rather than in the field. Strip searches conducted in the field represent a much greater invasion of privacy and pose a greater threat to the detainee's bodily integrity and, for this reason, field strip searches can only be justified in exigent circumstances.

Having said all this, we believe that legislative intervention could be an important addition to the guidance set out in these reasons concerning the conduct of strip searches incident to arrest. Clear legislative prescription as to when and how strip searches should be conducted would be of assistance to the police and to the courts. ...

BASTARACHE J (McLachlin CJ and Gonthier and L'Heureux-Dubé JJ concurring) (dissenting): The same requirements justifying the conduct of a search incident to arrest apply regardless of whether the accused is subjected to a "frisk," a fingerprinting, the taking of a bodily sample or a strip search. These requirements ... include that the search be carried out for a valid objective in pursuit of the ends of criminal justice, such as the discovery of a weapon or evidence, and that it not be conducted in an abusive fashion. In addition, the power to search incident to arrest is a discretionary one and need not be exercised where police are satisfied that the law can be effectively and safely applied in its absence; see *Cloutier*, supra, at p. 186.

The unworkability of an approach that would create distinct categories of searches rests in the fact that all of the types of searches listed above may take many forms ranging from a low degree of intrusiveness to a high degree of intrusiveness, depending on the circumstances of the case. For example, on the facts of this case, the strip search of the accused which occurred in the stairwell was possibly not more intrusive than "pat-down" or frisk searches. By contrast, the search in the restaurant impacted more severely on the privacy and dignity of the accused. [The stairwell search involved looking down the suspect's pants while the restaurant search involved pulling drugs from his buttocks.] The standard of justification to which police will be held depends on the circumstances of the specific search in question, not upon the category into which it is placed.

An approach which would categorize searches according to the degree of intrusiveness also risks confusion. The taking of a hair or other easily obtainable bodily sample may seem no more intrusive than a full strip search. The taking of a hair sample in the absence of a warrant may nonetheless be found to violate s. 8 if police are not able to justify the search on the basis that it was for the purpose of discovering and preserving evidence or seizing weapons incident to arrest; see *R. v. Stillman*, [1997] 1 S.C.R. 607. By contrast, a strip search conducted in the absence of prior authorization may be lawful if it meets the common law requirements of a search incident to arrest even if the search was very intrusive.

In all cases, providing the arrest is lawful and the object of the search is related to the crime, the sole issue is the reasonability of the search. My colleagues assert that the fact that police have reasonable and probable grounds to carry out an arrest does not confer on them the authority to carry out a strip search, even where the strip search is related to the purpose of the arrest. They add an additional requirement in the case of strip searches that the police must establish reasonable and probable grounds justifying the conduct of the strip search itself. By placing strip searches in a category distinct from other types of searches, my colleagues have bypassed this Court's decision in *Cloutier*, supra, at pp. 185-86, that the existence of reasonable and probable grounds is not a prerequisite to the existence of a police power to search. I agree with my colleagues that the more intrusive the search and the higher the degree of infringement of personal privacy, the higher degree of justification; however, I disagree that the common law requires police to prove that they had reasonable and probable grounds to justify the strip search. Interpreting the common law in a manner consistent with Charter principles does not require the Court to redefine the common law right by adding this additional requirement. The existing common law rule that police demonstrate an objectively valid reason for the arrest rather than for the search is consistent with s. 8 of the Charter, provided that the strip search is for a valid objective and is not conducted in an abusive fashion.

Should the common law power of warrantless searches incident to arrest extend to a search of the accused's car? To a search conducted six hours after the arrest? See *R v Caslake*, [1998] 1 SCR 51, where the Supreme Court answers yes to both questions.

What about an arrestee's cellphone or smartphone? Should searching it be permitted incidental to arrest, or do the privacy implications of such a search demand a warrant? In *R v Fearon*, 2014 SCC 77, [2014] 3 SCR 621, the Supreme Court was sharply divided (4:3) on this question. The dissent concluded that absent exigent circumstances a warrant should be required. (This was also the view of an unusually unanimous United States Supreme Court when it decided the same question under the Fourth Amendment. See *Riley v California*, 134 S Ct 2473 (2014).) Although the majority in *Fearon* was alive to the privacy concerns involved in such searches, it concluded that the proper balance between the interests of privacy and effective law enforcement did not require a categorical warrant requirement as a precondition for all such searches. Instead, the majority employed its authority to develop the common law surrounding police powers to craft a set of rules to govern such searches. Cromwell J summarized the scheme developed by the majority as follows:

> [83] To summarize, police officers will not be justified in searching a cell phone or similar device incidental to every arrest. Rather, such a search will comply with s. 8 where:
>> (1) The arrest was lawful;
>> (2) The search is truly incidental to the arrest in that the police have a reason based on a valid law enforcement purpose to conduct the search, and that reason is objectively reasonable. The valid law enforcement purposes in this context are:
>>> (a) Protecting the police, the accused, or the public;
>>> (b) Preserving evidence; or
>>> (c) Discovering evidence, including locating additional suspects, in situations in which the investigation will be stymied or significantly hampered absent the ability to promptly search the cell phone incident to arrest;
>> (3) The nature and the extent of the search are tailored to the purpose of the search; and
>> (4) The police take detailed notes of what they have examined on the device and how it was searched.
>
> [84] In setting out these requirements for the common law police power, I do not suggest that these measures represent the only way to make searches of cell phones incident to arrest constitutionally compliant. This may be an area, as the Court concluded was the case in *Golden*, in which legislation may well be desirable. The law enforcement and privacy concerns may be balanced in many ways and my reasons are not intended to restrict the acceptable options.

Do you think it likely that Parliament will heed the majority's suggestion in *Fearon* and provide legislated guidance in this area? Before answering that question, you should note that although *Golden* was decided in 2001, Parliament has never taken up the Supreme Court's invitation to legislate on strip searches. This ties into a larger question regarding Canadian constitutional criminal procedure: which institution, Parliament or the Supreme Court, is the more appropriate source of new police powers? The next section introduces that ongoing debate.

VI. SOURCES OF POLICE POWERS AND THE ANCILLARY POWERS DEBATE

As the above should make apparent, police powers and their limits are derived from a variety of sources—constitutional, legislative, and common law. The most controversial source of new police powers is unquestionably the ancillary powers doctrine, which enables courts to recognize new police powers at "common law." It was that doctrine that the Supreme Court employed in *Mann* (above) to recognize the investigative detention power.

J Stribopoulos, "Sniffing Out the Ancillary Powers Implications of the Dog Sniff Cases"
(2009) 47 SCLR (2nd) 35 (references omitted)

Last Spring the Supreme Court of Canada released judgments in a pair of cases involving the use of drug sniffing dogs by police: *R. v. Kang-Brown*, and *R. v. A.M.* These decisions received considerable media attention, mostly for what they had to say about the constitutionality of the police employing drug-sniffing dogs. Lost in the media coverage, which was confused by the sheer length of the Court's opinions and the fact that the justices issued four separate sets of reasons in each case, was a larger controversy regarding the Court's continued use of the "ancillary powers doctrine" as a means of creating new common law police powers.

The ancillary powers doctrine allows for the recognition of police powers by deploying what is essentially a cost–benefit analysis. This law-making device has two parts. First, it begins with a query as to whether the impugned actions of a police officer fall within the scope of his or her broad duties. Assuming the answer is "yes," the second step involves a weighing of the apparent benefits, usually for law enforcement and public safety, as against any resulting interference with individual liberty interests. If the benefits are characterized as outweighing the costs, the action is said to be "justifiable" and a new police power is born.

Ever since the Supreme Court of Canada first used the ancillary powers doctrine to fashion a new police power in *Dedman*, criticism of the doctrine has been unrelenting. Originally, it came in the form of a scathing dissent by Chief Justice Dickson. He categorically rejected that *R. v. Waterfield*, the English decision that the majority fastened upon as supplying the authority for an ancillary powers doctrine, authorized courts to create new police powers. Chief Justice Dickson expressed serious reservations regarding this move, which he saw as "nothing short of fiat for illegality on the part of the police whenever the benefit of police action appeared to outweigh the infringement of individual rights." For him, it was "the function of the legislature, not the courts, to authorize ... police action that would otherwise be unlawful as a violation of rights traditionally protected at common law."

While members of the judiciary voiced initial criticism regarding the use of the ancillary powers doctrine to create new police powers, over the last twenty-five years skepticism has come almost exclusively from commentators. In the interim, the Supreme Court has uncritically accepted use of the ancillary powers doctrine as bases for recognizing a host of entirely unprecedented police powers. For example:

- a power to briefly detain motorists at sobriety checkstops [*R v Dedman*, [1985] 2 SCR 2];
- a power to enter premises in response to disconnected 911 calls [*R v Godoy*, [1999] 1 SCR 311];
- a power to briefly detain individuals who are reasonably suspected of involvement in recently committed or unfolding criminal activity, and to conduct protective weapons searches of such individuals where an officer has well-founded safety concerns [*R v Mann*, 2004 SCC 52, [2004] 3 SCR 59];
- a power to ask drivers questions about alcohol consumption and request their participation in sobriety tests without first complying with s. 10(b) of the *Charter* [*R v Orbanksi*; *R v Elias*, 2005 SCC 37, [2005] 2 SCR 3]; and
- a power to conduct criminal investigative roadblock stops where such a stop is tailored to the information possessed by police, the seriousness of the offence being investigated, and the temporal and geographic connection between the situation being investigated and the timing and location of the roadblock [*R v Clayton*, 2007 SCC 32, [2007] 2 SCR 725].

Kang-Brown and *A.M.* represent a continuation of this judicial law-making trend. ... these judgments effectively recognize that when reasonable grounds exist to suspect an individual is carrying narcotics, the police have the common law authority to use a drug detecting dog to sniff the individual suspect, as well as his or her belongings, in order to confirm or refute that suspicion. Although these judgments are noteworthy for what they say about police use of drug-sniffing dogs, they are far more significant for what they say about the ancillary powers doctrine.

In *Kang-Brown* and *A.M.*, for the first time since Chief Justice Dickson's dissent in *Dedman*, disagreement has broken out between the Supreme Court judges regarding the propriety of the Court using the ancillary powers doctrine to create new police powers. This disagreement strongly suggests that the fate of this doctrine as a future source of police powers may suddenly be in doubt. ...

No statute authorizes the use of drug sniffing dogs by police. As a result, legal authority for their use, if it exists, must be derived from the common law. If one were to examine the "common law" as it has been historically understood in England and throughout the Commonwealth, i.e. the written reasons of judges from previously decided cases, one will find no mention of drug sniffing dogs. I do not mean to suggest by this that the common law is somehow static. To the contrary, the great genius of the common law system is indeed its organic nature; specifically, the ability of judges to apply established tools of legal reasoning to *incrementally* expand existing principles in response to the changing needs of society.

Historically, when it came to government interfering with individual liberties, our courts were very reluctant to use their law-making authority to expand state powers. In fact, in this context, the common law courts traditionally showed much restraint. That restraint eventually became the bedrock of English constitutional law, taking the "principle of legality" as its label. Applying that principle, common law courts have long insisted that any interference with individual liberty or property rights be premised on clear legal authority. Absent such authority, the common law erred on the side of individual freedom. It is in this sense that the common law has been viewed, in the words of Justice LeBel, as "the law of liberty" [*Kang-Brown* at para 12].

In the search and seizure context the principle of legality has a very long lineage. It can be traced all the way back to *Entick v. Carrington*, one of England's earliest and most celebrated search cases. In that judgment the court refused a government request that it recognize, for the first time, an entirely unprecedented power on the part of the Secretary of State for the Northern Department to issue search warrants. In rejecting that request, Lord Chief Justice Camden remarked:

> What would the parliament say, if the judges should take upon themselves to mould an unlawful power into a convenient authority, by new restrictions? That would be, not judgment, but legislation.

This same approach carried forward to Canada. In the early years of the *Charter* there was only one anomalous exception: *Dedman*. In that case a slim (5 judge) majority of the Supreme Court seized on what was, up until that time, a relatively obscure decision of the English Court of Criminal Appeals in *Waterfield*, which had set down a two-part test for assessing whether a police officer was acting in "execution of his duty." (This was an element of the offence charged in that case.) In *Dedman*, however, the majority fastened on this test, and the cost–benefit analysis that it endorsed, transforming it into a basis for recognizing entirely new police powers. The power ultimately recognized in *Dedman* was the authority of police to conduct sobriety check-stops. As noted above, Justice Dickson wrote a scathing dissent, strikingly reminiscent of Justice Camden's opinion in *Entick v. Carrington*, in which he admonished the majority for taking on a law-making role that more appropriately belonged to Parliament.

For a while, at least, the law-making authority that *Dedman* recognized seemed to lay dormant. In the interim, the Supreme Court of Canada repeatedly refused to recognize new police powers in response to *Charter* challenges under s. 8, thereby engaging Parliament in a form of dialogue that led to the creation of a number of much needed legislated search powers. During this period, the Supreme Court sent strong signals that it would not again use the ancillary powers doctrine to create new police powers. As Justice La Forest explained, on behalf of the majority in *Wong*,

> The common law powers of search were extremely narrow, and the courts have left it to Parliament to extend them where need be … it does not sit well for the courts, as the protectors of our fundamental rights, to widen the possibility of encroachments on these personal liberties. It falls to Parliament to make incursions on fundamental rights if it is of the view that they are needed for the protection of the public in a properly balanced system of criminal justice.

This is how things remained throughout most of the nineteen-nineties under the Lamer Court, with only one isolated exception.

The turning point seemed to come in *Mann*, when the Supreme Court used the ancillary powers doctrine to recognize a police power to briefly detain an individual if a police officer has reasonable grounds to suspect that he is involved in recently committed or unfolding criminal activity. That power was combined with a limited protective pat-down search power, available where police have objectively based grounds to be concerned for their safety. Rather ironic was the Supreme Court's failure to acknowledge the extensive body of case law, cases that predated lower court developments that applied the *Waterfield* test to recognize an investigative detention power, which had clearly and consistently held that at *common law* there is no power to detain for investigative purposes short of actual arrest.

With few exceptions, *Mann* has been widely criticized by commentators ... . The chief complaint regarding the decision is that it tends to raise more questions than it answers, and in the process creates much confusion and thereby increases the chances of unjustified and abusive police stops. In this sense, it provides a textbook example of the problems inherent when the courts exceed their institutional capacities and begin creating entirely new and unprecedented police powers, taking on an almost legislative rather than judicial role.

Nevertheless, given the complexity of the issues raised by *Mann*, the case seemed to signal that any reluctance the Supreme Court had periodically expressed about creating new police powers had fallen to the wayside. Since *Mann* was decided the Supreme Court has used the ancillary powers doctrine to recognize some rather significant and entirely unprecedented police powers.

And then came the Supreme Court's decisions in *Kang-Brown* and *A.M.* Suddenly, for the first time since *Dedman*, a debate broke out amongst the justices regarding the legitimacy and efficacy of using the ancillary powers doctrine to create new police powers.

In a concurring judgment in *Kang-Brown*, Justice LeBel (joined by Justices Fish, Abella & Charron) refused to use the ancillary powers doctrine to recognize a "common law" power on the part of police to use drug-sniffing dogs. In a judgment strongly reminiscent of the Supreme Court's pronouncements in the late-eighties and early nineties, this group rejected the idea that it was the Court's role to fill the gaps in formal police powers. Justice LeBel wrote:

> The common law has long been viewed as a law of liberty. Should we move away from that tradition, which is still part of the ethos of our legal system and of our democracy? This case is about the freedom of individuals and the proper function of the courts as guardians of the Constitution. I doubt that it should lead us to depart from the common law tradition of freedom by changing the common law itself to restrict the freedoms protected by the Constitution under s. 8 of the Charter.

More practically, Justice LeBel explained this reluctance by noting: "the courts are ill-equipped to develop an adequate legal framework for the use of police dogs."

It is difficult to quarrel with these observations about the historic importance of the common law in protecting liberty and the need for courts to act with restraint before recognizing new police powers, especially where those powers would have complex and far-reaching consequences.

The only troubling aspect of Justice LeBel's analysis is his failure to convincingly explain why it was appropriate in *Mann* and *Clayton* to use the ancillary powers doctrine in this way, whereas it was inappropriate to do so in these cases. The complexity of the various issues raised by investigative detention power (for example, the use of force to effect such detentions, the temporal and geographic limits on them, the difficulty in reconciling this power with the right to counsel on detention found in s. 10(b), and what, if any, corresponding obligations the power might impose on those detained etc.) suggests that, if anything, the dog sniff power is better suited for recognition under the ancillary powers doctrine than were investigative detentions.

In his concurring reasons in *Kang-Brown*, Justice Binnie (joined by Chief Justice McLachlin) took exception to this sudden trepidation on the part of Justices LeBel, Fish, Abella and Charon. For Justice Binnie, the use of the ancillary powers doctrine to create new police powers is part of a long tradition of "incremental" expansion of the common law. That doctrine simply provides courts with a methodology, like many judge-created methodologies used by common law courts over time, to develop the law in a particular area.

With respect, the difficulty with this view is that it largely ignores the fact that there is nothing at all "incremental" about how new police powers are created under the cost–benefit analysis supplied by the ancillary powers doctrine. The truth is, our courts have used the doctrine to create police powers out of whole cloth. These new powers have no linkage to earlier judgments, and sometimes serve to implicitly overrule cases that pronounced on the absence of any such power (i.e. investigative detention providing the best example). This reality seems to contradict Justice Binnie's rather charitable characterization of the ancillary powers doctrine.

In addition, Justice Binnie's defence of the ancillary powers doctrine in *Kang-Brown* runs up against his rather frank acknowledgment in *Clayton*, where he agrees "with the critics that *Waterfield* is an odd godfather for common law police powers."

That said, Justice Binnie does seem to have the better argument at points. In his reasons in *Kang-Brown* he rightly complains that the approach advocated by Justice LeBel would breed even greater uncertainty. Litigants would have no way of knowing what approach the Court might be inclined to employ in a given case, one in which it is receptive to creating new police powers under the *Waterfield* test or one in which it insists on deferring such law-making responsibilities to Parliament.

For Justice Binnie the question was long ago settled. The only way forward, he insists, is for the courts to "proceed incrementally with the *Waterfield/Dedman* analysis of common law police powers rather than try to re-cross the Rubicon to retrieve the fallen flag of the *Dedman* dissent."

One is left to wonder, however, whether "crossing the Rubicon" is ever an appropriate analogy when it comes to judicial decision-making. For example, would it have answered the claim made in *Brown v. Board of Education* that the United States Supreme Court had already crossed the Rubicon when it decided in *Plessy v. Ferguson* that "separate but equal" was consistent with the equal protection clause of the Fourteenth Amendment? …

My point is, even questions that seem settled aren't always so. As I have argued elsewhere,

In part, the long-term viability of any common law constitutional system very much depends on the authority and willingness of its final court of appeal to revisit established doctrine when experience has demonstrated that one of its earlier judgments is either being misconstrued or was wrongly decided. This seems especially true in a system such as ours in Canada where the Constitution is considered to be a "living tree."

Just as important, for reasons going to its institutional integrity, the Court must proceed with great caution before substantially revamping established precedent or taking the drastic step of overruling an earlier judgment. If the Court appears too eager to revisit established principles then the authority of its judgments will be undermined and its institutional integrity will needlessly suffer. In other words, the institutional integrity of the Court would seem to depend both on its willingness to reconsider its past decisions when the reasons for doing so are compelling and the resolve to refrain from doing so when they are not.

As Justice Patrick Healy has correctly pointed out, the ancillary powers doctrine crept into our law like "something of a Trojan-horse for the expansion of police powers." As a result, the debate that has finally broken out amongst the justices at the Supreme Court of Canada on its continued use and utility is most welcome and long overdue.

In *Kang-Brown*, Justice Bastarache clearly had no difficulty with the idea of the Supreme Court taking the responsibility of filling gaps in police powers. He was quite willing to grant the police this new power based on little more than generalized suspicion. With his retirement, it remains to be determined how his replacement, Justice Cromwell, might feel about the place of the ancillary powers doctrine within our constitutional democracy. It is Justice Cromwell who would seem to hold the decisive vote on the future of this controversial source of new police powers. Unfortunately, there are no solid clues as to the position he might ultimately take on this important constitutional question.

On the controversy surrounding the ancillary powers doctrine, see G Luther, "Police Power and the Charter of Rights and Freedoms: Creation or Control" (1986) 51 Sask L Rev 117; RJ Delisle, "Judicial Creation of Police Powers" (1993) 20 CR (4th) 29; H Pringle, "The Smoke and Mirrors of Godoy: Creating Common Law Authority While Making Feeney Disappear" (1999) 21 CR (5th) 227; D Stuart, "The Unfortunate Dilution of Section 8 Protection: Some Teeth Remain" (1999) 25 Queen's LJ 65; D Stuart, "Godoy: The Supreme Reverts to the Ancillary Powers Doctrine to Fill a Gap in Police Power" (1999) 21 CR (5th) 225; S Coughlan, "Search Based on Articulable Cause: Proceed with Caution or Full Stop?" (2002) 2 CR (6th) 49; LA McCoy, "Liberty's Last Stand? Tracing the Limits of Investigative Detention" (2002) 46 Crim LQ 319; P Sankoff, "Articulable Cause Based Searches Incident to Detention—This Cooke May Spoil the Broth" (2002) 2 CR (6th) 41; J Stribopoulos, "A Failed Experiment? Investigative Detention: Ten Years Later" (2003) 41 Alta L Rev 335; LA McCoy, "Some Answers from the Supreme Court on Investigative Detention ... and Some More Questions" (2004) 49 Crim LQ 268; T Quigley, "Mann, It's a Disappointing Decision" (2004) 21 CR (6th) 41; T Quigley, "Brief Investigatory Detentions: A Critique of R v Simpson" (2004) 41 Alta L Rev 93; P Healy, "Investigative Detention in Canada" [2005] Crim LR 98; JR Marin, "R v Mann: Further Down the Slippery Slope" (2005) 42 Alta L Rev 1123; J Stribopoulos, "In Search of Dialogue: The Supreme Court, Police Powers and the Charter" (2005) 31 Queen's LJ 1; C Skibinsky, "Regulating Mann in Canada" (2006) 69 Sask L Rev 197; J Stribopoulos, "The Limits of Judicially Created Police

Powers: Investigative Detention After Mann" (2007) 52 Crim LQ 299; S Coughlan, "Common Law Police Powers and the Rule of Law" (2007) 47 CR (6th) 266; D Stuart, "Charter Standards for Investigative Powers: Have the Courts Got the Balance Right?" in J Cameron & J Stribopoulos, eds, *The Charter and Criminal Justice: Twenty-Five Years Later* (Toronto: LexisNexis, 2008) ch 4; S Coughlan, "Charter Protection Against Unlawful Police Action: Less Black and White Than It Seems" (2012) 57 SCLR (2nd) 205; V MacDonnell, "Assessing the Impact of the Ancillary Powers Doctrine on Three Decades of Charter Jurisprudence" (2012) 57 SCLR (2nd) 225; M Plaxton, "Police Powers After Dicey" (2012) 38 Queen's LJ 99; and J Stribopoulos, "The Rule of Law on Trial: Police Powers, Public Protest, and the G20" in ME Beare, N Des Rosiers & AC Deshman, eds, *Putting the State on Trial: The Policing of Protest During the G20 Summit* (Vancouver: University of British Columbia Press, 2015).

The Trial Process

This chapter is designed to present an overview of the criminal trial process with special attention to the constitutional and structural safeguards that are afforded the accused and to ethical issues confronting prosecutors, defence lawyers, and judges. The Donald Marshall Jr. case has been chosen as a case study because it provides an example of the frailty of the criminal process to neglect and improper motive and because it raises serious questions about the adequacy of our adversarial system of criminal justice, its treatment of the disadvantaged, and the recurring problem of miscarriages of justice. As ML Friedland stated in *The Trials of Israel Lipski* (London: Macmillan, 1984) at 204:

> A trial may in theory be an objective pursuit of truth, but in practice there are many subjective factors which influence the course of events. Justice may in theory be blind, but in practice she has altogether too human a perspective … . The case shows the inherent fallibility of the trial process and the constant danger of error. Society should think twice before shifting the balance too far in favour of the prosecution. Further, the case strengthens the arguments against capital punishment.

The first part of the chapter presents the *Marshall* case in its various aspects in some detail. The case is examined both as a case study of a wrongful conviction of an innocent person and with respect to the issues of racism and the treatment of Aboriginal people in the justice system. The second part examines legal and ethical issues concerning the distinctive roles of the prosecutor and defence counsel in a criminal trial including the constitutional obligation on the prosecutor to disclose relevant evidence to the accused. The third part examines the issue of pre-trial detention or bail. The fourth part examines how jurors are chosen in the small number of cases tried by jury. The final part examines the presumption of innocence and the burden and quantum of proof.

I. THE WRONGFUL CONVICTION OF DONALD MARSHALL JR.

Donald Marshall was convicted of murder by a judge and jury in 1971. He appealed his conviction to the Nova Scotia Supreme Court, Appellate Division in 1972 where his conviction was upheld. In 1983, his conviction was overturned by the same appeal court after a new appeal was ordered by the minister of justice when Marshall applied under a procedure then known as applying for the mercy of the Crown. (For the present procedure of applying to the minister of justice when a person's appeals have been exhausted, and the ability of the minister of justice to order a new trial or appeal if "there is a reasonable basis to conclude that a miscarriage of justice likely occurred," see ss 696.1 to 696.6 of the *Criminal Code*.)

Marshall's Appeals

R v Marshall
Nova Scotia Supreme Court, Appellate Division
(1972), 8 CCC (2d) 329

McKINNON CJNS (for the Court): The appellant Donald Marshall Jr. was charged in an indictment, that he, on or about the 28th day of May, 1971, at Sydney, in the County of Cape Breton, Province of Nova Scotia, did murder Sanford William (Sandy) Seale. …

After a trial by jury, presided over by Dubinsky, J., the appellant was found guilty and sentenced to serve a term of life imprisonment in Dorchester Penitentiary.

The grounds of appeal relied on by the appellant may be summarized as follows:

(1) that the learned trial judge erred in law in not adequately instructing the jury on the defence evidence, and in expressing opinions which were highly prejudicial to the accused;

(2) that the learned trial judge misdirected the jury on the meaning of reasonable doubt; that the evidence did not establish guilt beyond a reasonable doubt, the conviction was against the weight of evidence and was perverse;

(3) ground 3 relates to the evidence of the witnesses Pratico and Chant; also that the trial judge did not make proper inquiry as to whether or not they understood the nature of an oath;

(4) that the learned trial judge permitted the prosecuting officer to cross-examine the witness, Maynard Chant, before ruling that he was adverse; that the trial judge permitted the prosecuting officer, in the absence of the jury, while the witness Chant was on the witness stand, to read the evidence he gave at the preliminary hearing, thereby conditioning him for the evidence he would give before the jury;

(5) that the trial judge erred in instructing the jury they did not have to consider the question of manslaughter.

Briefly, the facts are that one, John Pratico, aged 16, was in the company of the deceased Seale and the appellant Marshall a very short time before Seale was stabbed. Pratico left the two men and stationed himself behind a bush in Wentworth Park, which is adjacent to Crescent Street, in Sydney, where he proceeded to consume a bottle of beer; while behind this bush, he observed Marshall and Seale.

Maynard Chant, aged 15, was in Wentworth Park at the same time, but not in the company of Pratico. Chant had attended church in Sydney and was attempting to get home to Louisbourg after having missed his bus. He was taking a shortcut through Wentworth Park when he noticed Pratico behind the bush. Pratico appeared to be watching something, and Chant decided to see what had drawn Pratico's attention.

They saw two men standing together and arguing in loud tones. One of the men, whom Pratico identified as the appellant Marshall, reached in his pocket and pulled out a "long shiny object" which he plunged into the "stomach" of the other, whom Pratico identified as Seale. Seale then collapsed.

Both Pratico and Chant fled the scene, but not together. In a nearby area, Chant was approached by the appellant Marshall who said, "look what they did to me" and displayed a cut on the inner part of his left forearm. M.D. Mattson, who lives at 103 Byng Avenue, overheard the conversation referred to, and called the police.

The appellant Marshall flagged down a car, and he and Chant had the operator drive to the spot where Seale was lying on the pavement of Crescent Street. Seale was taken to the Sydney City Hospital where he died as a result of his injuries on the following day, despite two surgical operations and massive blood transfusions.

According to the evidence of the appellant Marshall, he and Seale, who was a friend, were standing on the footbridge which spans two creeks in the park, when they were called to by two men who were on Crescent Street, and who wanted cigarettes or matches. The appellant and Seale walked up to the street and were met by two men dressed in long blue coats who identified themselves as priests from Manitoba. The strangers wanted to know if there were girls in the park and asked where they could find a bootlegger. According to the appellant, the older of the two men then made an unprovoked attack with a knife on Seale and the appellant, which resulted in Seale's fatal injury and the appellant being slashed on the arm.

According to the appellant Marshall, at the time of the attack, the man with the knife said he did not like niggers or Indians. The appellant is an Indian while the deceased was a negro. The appellant said that he then fled, being in fear of his life. …

The only issue before the Court at trial in relation to the charge against the appellant was whether or not he had committed the murder with which he was charged. His sole defence was a denial of that act, and the theory of the defence was based on his own evidence that the murder was committed by one of two strangers, who claimed to be priests from Manitoba.

In reviewing the evidence for the defence, the learned trial judge read fairly extensively from the testimony of the appellant, and commented on that evidence as follows:

> Now, gentlemen, you have to give very careful consideration to the story of the accused. I'm sure you will. As was his absolute right, he has gone on the stand and has given his version of the events that took place on that fateful night. Now contrary to what Pratico said, he said he was not in the vicinity of St. Joseph's Hall. And although he was with Mr. Seale, he had no dispute with him—those are the words I think—and he did not lay a hand on him. I repeat, he had no dispute with him and he did not lay a hand on him. And he told you how Seale came to get the injuries that he did receive. And I remind you, Mr. Foreman, that although the accused was subjected to a very vigorous and rigorous cross-examination, he adhered to his story that he told throughout. Now if you believe the version of the events that was told by Donald Marshall Jr., then it goes without saying that you must acquit him of this charge. Having gone on the stand he has become another witness in this case. You have the right to determine the credibility of him as a witness as you have the right to determine the credibility of any other witness. But you will bear in mind, Mr. Foreman—and I repeat, you will bear in mind—that Donald Marshall does not have to convince you of his innocence. He does not have to convince you of his innocence. It is the Crown, as I said over and over again, that must prove his guilt beyond a reasonable doubt. He does not have to convince you of his innocence!
>
> The Crown, of course, understandably, has attacked this story. There was some considerable discussion among counsel as to the nature of the wound that he had on his left arm, the depth of it, whether there was bleeding. Mrs. Davis said there was no bleeding, it's true. You saw the mark on his arm there. It's a pretty prominent mark even today after a number of months.

[When Marshall's arm was shown to the jury, it also revealed a tattoo that read "I hate cops."]

> You will bear in mind that he at the time showed Maynard Chant, "Look what they did to me." It was then and there at the that time he told Chant what was done to him. At that time he managed to stop a car and got into a car and went back to Crescent Street. I think it was Maynard Chant—your recollection would be better—who said that it was he, Donald Marshall, the accused, who flagged down a police car. And it was Donald Marshall who went to the hospital and to the police station with the police. I think you have to ask yourselves on the one hand, is that the action of a man who has just committed a crime, who will flag down

a police car, who will go with the police, who will do the things that he did and who maintains the consistency of his story. Keep in mind, as I said, that he does not have to prove his innocence.

On the other hand, Mr. Foreman, gentlemen on the other hand—in my opinion, you will have to assess very carefully the story that he told—two strangers who he says looked like priests, because they wore long coats and blue. He asked them, he said, whether they were priests and one of them said they were and said they were from Manitoba. They asked for cigarettes, smokes; they gave him the smokes. He and Seale gave smokes to these people, or he did. Then the man, one of these men asked him if there were any women and they said yes, there were lots of them in the park. And out of the blue comes this denunciation against blacks and Indians: "I don't like niggers and I don't like Indians." ...

In my opinion, the foregoing passages afford an adequate answer to the ground of objection that the learned trial judge did not adequately instruct the jury on the defence evidence and the theory of the defence. I am satisfied that he did so adequately, fairly and in a manner that was not capable of being understood by the jury as prejudicial to the accused.

... As to ground No. 2, counsel for the appellant contends that while the trial judge stated a number of times that the charge must be proved beyond a reasonable doubt, in other parts of his address, he used the words "satisfied" and "to your satisfaction" and this was misdirection. Further that he did not instruct the jury that if the evidence created a reasonable doubt, this would entitle them to acquit the accused.

This part of his charge reads as follows:

I said before that I would deal with the question of onus or burden of proof. The onus or burden of proving the guilt of an accused person beyond a reasonable doubt rests upon the Crown and never shifts. There is no burden on an accused person to prove his innocence. I repeat, there is no burden on an accused person to prove his innocence. Let me make that abundantly clear. If during the course of this trial, from beginning to end, during anything that may have been said by counsel during their speeches, that might in the slightest way be considered as suggestive of any burden on the accused to prove anything, let me tell you that there is no burden on the accused. The Crown must prove beyond a reasonable doubt that an accused is guilty of the offence with which he is charged before he can be convicted. If you have a reasonable doubt as to whether the accused committed the offence of non-capital murder, the offence with which he is charged, then it is your duty to give the accused the benefit of that doubt and to find him not guilty. In other words, if after considering all the evidence, the addresses of counsel and my charge to you, you come to the conclusion that the Crown has failed to prove to your satisfaction beyond a reasonable doubt that the accused, Marshall, committed the offence of non-capital murder, it is your duty to give this accused the benefit of the doubt and to find him not guilty.

The learned trial judge then proceeded to define "reasonable doubt" as an "honest doubt," a doubt which causes you to "say to yourselves, or any of you, 'I am not morally certain that he committed the offence,' then that would indicate to you—that would indicate there is a doubt in your mind and it would be a *reasonable* doubt which prevents you from arriving at the state of mind which would require you to find a verdict of guilty against this man."

Placing the instructions of the trial judge in their proper context, the jury could not, and were not, misled as to the proper application of the law regarding the "burden of proof." ...

Ground three relates to the evidence of the witnesses Pratico and Chant, counsel for the appellant contending that the trial judge did not make proper inquiry as to whether either witness understood the nature of an oath.

The record indicates that the trial judge declared himself satisfied that both Pratico, aged 16, and Chant, aged 15, understood the nature of an oath, and they were sworn without objection by the defence. This was a question of fact to be decided by the trial judge and I can see no good reason, under the circumstances, to interfere with that finding.

Counsel for the appellant also objects to the quality and sufficiency of the evidence given by Pratico and Chant.

Pratico testified that he saw the deceased Seale and the appellant Marshall at the scene of the crime and he gave direct evidence that he saw Marshall stab Seale. He was acquainted with both men. Under a rigorous cross-examination, he admitted to drinking on the night of the stabbing. The learned trial judge in his address to the jury reviewed this evidence and in clear language related Pratico's drinking to his credibility and left it for the jury to decide.

Regarding a conflict in his statements before and during trial, this is explained by the record which discloses that Pratico's life was threatened if he testified that the appellant stabbed Seale.

[The day before his testimony at Marshall's trial, Pratico told several people outside the courtroom, including Marshall's lawyer, the Crown prosecutor, and the investigating police officer, that Marshall did not stab Seale. Pratico had previously testified at the preliminary hearing that he had seen Marshall stab Seale. When Pratico testified, the trial judge prevented Marshall's defence lawyers from asking Pratico to explain why he had made these inconsistent statements. The Royal Commission examining the Marshall prosecution (*Royal Commission on the Donald Marshall Jr Prosecution* (1989)) subsequently concluded:

> We believe a full and complete cross-examination of John Pratico at this stage by Khattar [Marshall's lawyer] almost certainly would have resulted in his recanting evidence given during his examination-in-chief that he had seen Marshall stab Seale. In those circumstances, no jury would have convicted Donald Marshall Jr. (at 79)

On re-examination, the Crown prosecutor tried to introduce evidence that third parties had threatened Pratico (if he "squealed on Junior") shortly after Marshall was charged. The trial judge disallowed evidence of the alleged threats because the third parties were not before the court, but allowed the Crown prosecutor to ask Pratico why he had said outside the courtroom that Marshall did not stab Seale, when he had given testimony to the opposite effect. Pratico replied that he was "scared for his life." The trial judge then asked:

> Q. Now your being scared of your life, is that because of anything the accused said to you at the time?
>
> A. No.

(at 174 of the trial transcript).]

Chant's evidence corroborated in every material particular that of the witness Pratico. He testified that he saw a person crouched in the bushes at the place where Pratico said he witnessed the stabbing.

Chant, at first, declined to swear that the man who did the stabbing was the appellant Marshall, but this was inconsistent with a previous statement under oath made by him at the preliminary hearing. ...

Under ground No. 4, counsel for the appellant contends that when the jury was absent, the Crown prosecutor was permitted, while Chant was on the witness stand, to read the evidence he gave at the preliminary hearing, thereby conditioning him for the evidence he would give when the jury would return, this being highly improper and prejudicial to the appellant. ...

[The prosecutor read the transcript of Chant's testimony at the preliminary hearing in which Chant testified that he saw Marshall stab Seale. This was done in an attempt to have Chant, a Crown witness, declared an adverse witness who could be impeached with statements inconsistent with his previous testimony. After this, Chant was then questioned by both the prosecutor and the judge. The prosecutor asked (at 99-100):

Q. Who was the man that hauled out the object and drove it—

A. Donald Marshall.

After this the judge asked:

Q. But more, what do you say about the man that you recognized as Donald Marshall and the person who you saw doing something hauling out something and putting it into the stomach of the other person: what do you say about that?

A. The only thing I know is—

Q. Never mind—tell me, do you or don't you—what do you say as to who that person was?

A. I don't know who that person was.

Q. You say you don't know who the person was who pulled out the knife and stuck it in Seale's body?

A. No, I didn't.

Chant was read his testimony given at the preliminary hearing on two more occasions. After both readings Chant testified that he had seen Marshall stab Seale.

The Court of Appeal approved of this procedure, stating it was allowed because the prosecutor was alleging that his witness, Chant, had made a prior statement inconsistent with his original testimony under s 9(2) of the *Canada Evidence Act*, RSC 1970, c E-10 (now RSC 1985, c C-5, s 9(2)). McKinnon CJNS stated: "It does not appear to me that the appellant suffered any prejudice through Chant hearing the evidence he had previously given, for when the jury returned, the same evidence was read to him question by question." The Court of Appeal concluded: "if there was an error in the application of the section, no substantial wrong or miscarriage of justice resulted, and I would apply the provisions of s. 613(1)(b)(iii)" (now s 686(1)(b)(iii)). This provision allows an appeal court to sustain a conviction despite an error of law committed by the trial judge, but only if the appeal court concludes no substantial wrong or miscarriage of justice has occurred.]

The final ground of appeal is that the trial judge advised the jury their verdict was limited to "guilty" or "not guilty" of murder, and that they did not have to consider a verdict of manslaughter, although there was evidence that the deceased Seale had put up his fists.

In his instructions to the jury, the trial judge included the following:

> My opinion is that whoever caused these wounds committed non-capital murder ... the facts in this case as they came before you, gentlemen of the jury, from beginning of the case to the end, do *not* give rise to your having to consider the crime of manslaughter ...
>
> Now Mr. Foreman, the defence in this case is not self-defence. This is not a case of self-defence. This is a complete denial. The defence is, I didn't do it—complete denial! Not self-defence but even if it were self-defence, I would have to instruct you that if that were the evidence, the late Mr. Seale put up his fists, then to strike him with an instrument and stab him was something that would go far, far beyond the right of self-defence. That sort of defence would not be commensurate with the other man's act. That issue does not arise here because as I said, the defence here is a complete denial.

There was no suggestion at any time during trial by counsel for the appellant that the verdict of manslaughter should be left with the jury. I accept the Crown's contention that what the appellant now seeks is to completely discard the line of defence followed at the trial and argue that the trial judge should have told the jury that they might disbelieve substantially the whole of the evidence tendered by the Crown; that they might also disbelieve the appellant's evidence and find that the appellant stabbed Seale, but did so, in self-defence or as a result of provocation.

I am satisfied that the instruction of the learned trial judge excluding manslaughter from consideration by the jury was, on the evidence, a proper direction to place before them.

It is my opinion that the appeal should be dismissed.

Appeal dismissed.

Note on the Professional Responsibility of Defence Counsel

Marshall's counsel on appeal, by raising the possibility that Marshall was guilty of manslaughter as opposed to murder, seemed to suggest that Marshall killed Seale, but should be guilty of the less serious offence of manslaughter because he may have been provoked or acted at least subjectively in defence. Was such an argument by Marshall's appeal counsel ethical? Does it matter that Donald Marshall Jr. always maintained that he did not stab Sandy Seale?

In another case where a defence lawyer refused to pursue the accused's statement that another person committed the crime, an appeal court in allowing new evidence that another person did actually commit the crime observed that the accused's lawyer "totally misunderstood the role which was his, by setting himself up as the judge of his client, instead of respecting his client's instructions and truly defending his client's interests" [translation]: *R c Delisle* (1999), 133 CCC (3d) 541 at para 59 (Qc CA). See generally D Layton & M Proulx, *Ethics and Criminal Law*, 2nd ed (Toronto: Irwin Law, 2015) at 29-30.

The next case demonstrates an acceptance by the prosecutor, the defence lawyer, and somewhat reluctantly by the Nova Scotia Court of Appeal that Roy Ebsary, not Marshall, killed Sandy Seale.

R v Marshall

Nova Scotia Supreme Court, Appellate Division

(1983), 57 NSR (2d) 286

[This appeal was heard when the federal minister of justice on a petition for mercy ordered a new appeal in order to consider new evidence not heard at trial. Similar powers today are available on an application for ministerial review under s 696.3(3)(ii) if the federal minister of justice is satisfied "that there is a reasonable basis to conclude that a miscarriage of justice likely occurred." Note that the minister of justice, an elected official who sits in Cabinet, can also order a new trial under this section. Section 696.4 provides that the minister of justice should consider all relevant factors, including "new matters of significance that were not considered by the courts" and that an application for ministerial review "is not intended to serve as a further appeal and any remedy available on such an application is an extraordinary remedy." Practically, this often requires, as it did in Donald Marshall's wrongful conviction, the presentation of new evidence not previously considered by the court.]

BY THE COURT: Donald Marshall Jr. commenced serving his life sentence in prison November 5, 1971, having been confined to jail since June 20, 1971. He was paroled from penitentiary on August 29, 1981, and the Minister of Justice referred this matter to this court on June 16, 1982. The appellant contends that he never was guilty of the offence of murdering Sandy Seale, and that the fresh evidence taken before this court on December 1 and 2, 1982, when considered along with the prior record of the case, is of sufficient force to require the Appeal Division at this time to set aside the original conviction of the appellant and enter a verdict of acquittal.

We turn now to a consideration of the fresh evidence.

James W. MacNeil is a thirty-seven-year-old labourer, who was born in Sydney and lived there all his life. He testified that on the evening of May 28, 1971, he was at the State Tavern on George Street, in the city of Sydney, where he met by accident an older man by the name of Roy Ebsary, whom he had known for a period of months. He had visited Mr. Ebsary's home on Argyle Street several times, and when they had finished drinking together for the evening, near eleven o'clock, they were returning there once again. The two of them cut through Wentworth Park, crossed the bridge and arrived on Crescent Street on their way home.

Mr. MacNeil describes Mr. Ebsary as about sixty years of age, kind of stocky, not real tall, about 5'7", with a little hunch back. He was wearing a kind of black shawl and a sports coat. Mr. MacNeil's testimony then continues:

A. Then we went up and we went up to like the top of the hill. Like I said we were crossing over the street and we were—we were approached by this coloured youth and this Mr. Marshall. At that time I remember I recall that Mr. Marshall put my hand up behind my back like that, eh, and I remember I kinda like panicked because I—in a situation like that, you get "stensafied" or something like that but I remember the coloured fellow asking Roy Ebsary for money. He said, like, "Dig, man, dig," and he said, "I got something for you" and then he—I just heard the coloured fellow screaming and everything was so you know, like, "tensafied" and every darn thing and I seen him running and flopping. I seen him running and flopping.

His testimony continued:

A. ... The next day I went to Ebsary's house and I told him that that fellow died, I said. I said: "You didn't have to kill him." You know, "You should have give him the money." You know, and I told—I told his son that so his son just said, well, he said: "Well, if you say anything," well, he said—

Mr. MacNeil was then asked if he had ever communicated his story to the police, and in response he said:

A. Yeh, I told the police in Sydney.

Q. Sir?

A. I told the police in Sydney after I—after I heard that this fellow was in gaol, Mr. Marshall, for something he didn't do so I went and I told the police this and it bothered me because I wouldn't like to be in gaol for something I didn't do.

Q. When can you recall having spoken to Sergeant MacIntyre concerning that event?

A. It was about a week after you were sentenced.

Q. Are you able to explain why you waited that length of time before going to the police?

A. Well because like, ah, Roy's son told me, he said: "The whole family would be in trouble there." ...

Mr. Marshall was asked for an explanation of the difference between his testimony at the original trial and his recent testimony, and he said:

Q. Well in what way does your testimony differ in 1971 to today?

A. In 1971 I did not mention anything about hitting somebody or robbing somebody or something like that. I did not mention that.

Q. Why didn't you speak of that?

A. The robbery didn't happen. It wasn't even an attempt of a robbery. I wasn't dealing with a robbery and I was afraid that one way or the other they would put the finger at me saying—one way or the other they would have found a way—in my opinion, they would have found a way to put it on me whether I told them or not.

Q. To put what on you?

A. Attempted robbery. Maybe the murder probably—the robbery would have probably tried to cover up for the murder.

Q. Do you recall who the solicitors were who or the lawyers who acted for you at the 1971 trial?

A. C.M. Rosenblum and Simon Khattar.

Q. And were they aware of what—at the time in 1971, were they aware of what you said in court today?

A. No. ...

There was also evidence before us to the effect that counsel for Marshall at the time of his trial had no knowledge of the prior inconsistent statements given to the police by Chant, Pratico and Harris … .

Although Mr. Marshall now puts forward Mr. MacNeil as his chief witness, their evidence in the main is in conflict. The only material particular on which they agree is that Ebsary stabbed Seale … .

Mr. Marshall categorically denies jumping Mr. MacNeil from behind and putting his arm behind his back. He is obviously not prepared to admit at this stage that he was engaged in a robbery.

How two people could describe the same incident in such a conflicting manner has caused us great concern and casts doubt on the credibility of both men. However, the fact remains that Marshall's new evidence, despite his evasions, prevarications and outright lies, supports the essence of James MacNeil's story—namely, that Seale was *not* killed by Marshall but died at the hands of Roy Ebsary in the course of a struggle during the attempted robbery of Ebsary and MacNeil by Marshall and Seale. In our opinion, Marshall's evidence, old and new, if it stood alone, would hardly be capable of belief.

Even though the various members of this court may have varying degrees of belief as to some aspects of that evidence, we have no doubt that in the light of all the evidence now before this court no reasonable jury could, on that evidence, find Donald Marshall Jr. guilty of the murder of Sandy Seale. That evidence, even if much is not believed makes it impossible for a jury to avoid having a reasonable doubt as to whether the appellant had been proved to have killed Seale.

Putting it another way, the new evidence "causes us to doubt the correctness of the judgment at the trial."—Reference *Re Regina v. Truscott* (1967), 1 C.R.N.S. 1 (S.C.C.).

We must accordingly conclude that the verdict of guilt is not now supported by the evidence and is unreasonable and must order the conviction quashed. In such a case a new trial should ordinarily be required under s. 613(2)(b) of the *Criminal Code*. Here, however, no purpose would be served in so doing. The evidence now available, with the denials by Pratico and Chant that they saw anything, could not support a conviction of Marshall. Accordingly we must take the alternative course directed by s. 613(2)(a) and direct that a judgment of acquittal be entered in favour of the appellant.

This course accords with the following submission of counsel for the Crown as set forth in his factum:

> It is respectfully submitted that the appeal should be allowed, that the conviction should be quashed, and a direction made that a verdict of acquittal be entered.
>
> It is also submitted that the basis of the above disposition should be that, in light of the evidence now available, the conviction of the appellant cannot be supported by the evidence.

Donald Marshall Jr. was convicted of murder and served a lengthy period of incarceration. That conviction is now to be set aside. Any miscarriage of justice is, however, more apparent than real.

In attempting to defend himself against the charge of murder Mr. Marshall admittedly committed perjury for which he still could be charged.

By lying he helped secure his own conviction. He misled his lawyers and presented to the jury a version of the facts he now says is false, a version that was so far-fetched as to be incapable of belief.

By planning a robbery with the aid of Mr. Seale he triggered a series of events which unfortunately ended in the death of Mr. Seale.

By hiding the facts from his lawyers and the police Mr. Marshall effectively prevented development of the only defence available to him, namely, that during a robbery Seale was stabbed by one of the intended victims. He now says that he knew approximately where the man lived who stabbed Seale and had a pretty good description of him. With this information the truth of the matter might well have been uncovered by the police.

Even at the time of taking the fresh evidence, although he had little more to lose and much to gain if he could obtain his acquittal, Mr. Marshall was far from being straightforward on the stand. He continued to be evasive about the robbery and assault and even refused to answer questions until the court ordered him to do so. There can be no doubt but that Donald Marshall's untruthfulness through this whole affair contributed in large measure to his conviction.

We accordingly allow the appeal, quash the conviction and direct that a verdict of acquittal be entered.

Note on the Professional Responsibility of Prosecutors

The Crown prosecutor in the 1983 *Marshall* reference agreed that the conviction should be quashed in light of the new evidence. Is this an appropriate stance for a prosecutor to take in an adversarial system? As will be examined below, both jurisprudence and ethical codes stress that the Crown prosecutor is a "minister of justice" and not an adversary purely concerned with winning. In some miscarriage of justice cases, including many arising from the flawed testimony of forensic pathologist Dr. Charles Smith about non-accidental causes of baby deaths, the Crown has, in the face of new expert evidence revealing flaws in Dr. Smith's analysis, agreed that convictions should be quashed in the light of new evidence. See e.g. *Reference re Mullins-Johnson*, 2007 ONCA 720; *R v CM*, 2010 ONCA 690; *R v CF*, 2010 ONCA 691; *R v Kumar*, 2011 ONCA 120; and *R v Brant*, 2011 ONCA 362.

What other ethical duties should be placed on the Crown in relation to the evidence relied upon to obtain a conviction? On the basis of the widely accepted idea in common law jurisdictions that prosecutors should be ministers of justice concerned about truth and justice, Gary Edmond argues:

> The prosecutor should not, as a minister of justice, adduce insufficiently reliable evidence or permit forensic science and medicine evidence to be presented in terms stronger than empirical evidence will (or would) allow. The trial and trial safeguards—and their potential to address evidentiary infirmities—do not relieve the prosecutor of these fundamental responsibilities. Where there are serious doubts about opinions, and limited empirical support for techniques, prosecutors should not—regardless of historical practices—adduce the evidence. ...
>
> ... In all cases prosecutors should not wait for the defence to object before drawing the court's attention to issues that bear on the admissibility or evaluation of incriminating expert evidence. In practice, the prosecutor should not simply promote the positive case and leave the defence to contest admissibility and expose limitations. Where the prosecutor has a reasonable

belief that the techniques are reliable and there is evidence to support that contention, then they might lead the evidence but only on condition that any presentation is "warts and all" and the defence is able to make submissions or call appropriate witnesses.

Of particular relevance to the Dr. Smith cases in which many of the original convictions were the result of guilty pleas on less serious offences such as manslaughter and infanticide, Professor Edmond argues:

> Prosecutors should not rely on unreliable, speculative and "shaky" expert evidence in plea and charge negotiations and should not (mis)use insufficiently reliable opinions to secure admissions and bargains from those accused of criminal acts. On all occasions where incriminating expert evidence is relied upon, limitations with techniques and opinions should be disclosed.

G Edmond, "(Ad)ministering Justice: Expert Evidence and the Professional Responsibilities of Prosecutors" (2013) 37 UNSWLJ 921.

Do you agree with Professor Edmond's arguments? Of what significance is the role of defence lawyers and judges in the admissibility of potentially unreliable evidence?

If unreliable evidence is discovered in one case, does the Crown have an obligation to determine if similar errors occurred in other cases? Bruce MacFarlane, QC has argued that the Crown's "minister of justice" role justified Manitoba's actions, when he was its deputy attorney general, in reviewing all murder cases once it was discovered that in one case hair comparison evidence did not hold up when re-examined through DNA analysis. He explained:

> The starting point in this discussion necessarily involves an understanding of the role and responsibilities of prosecuting counsel. At law, Crown counsel in Canada, and more widely throughout the Commonwealth, have two separate and distinct roles. The first, that of "advocate," is well understood and publicly very visible. In respect of this role, the Supreme Court of Canada has observed that it is "both permissible and desirable" that the Crown "vigorously pursue a legitimate result to the best of its ability." "Indeed," the Court added, "this is a critical element of this country's criminal law mechanism." As a consequence, prosecuting counsel are expected to be firm and press the evidence to its legitimate strength.

The second role of Crown attorneys, seemingly at odds with that of advocate, is that of "minister of justice." The *locus classicus* concerning this responsibility was first described in 1954 by Rand J on behalf of the Supreme Court of Canada in *Boucher v The Queen*, [1955] SCR 16:

> It cannot be over-emphasized that the purpose of a criminal prosecution is not to obtain a conviction, it is to lay before a jury what the Crown considers to be credible evidence relevant to what is alleged to be a crime. Counsel have a duty to see that all available legal proof of the facts is presented: it should be done firmly and pressed to its legitimate strength but it must also be done fairly. The role of prosecutor excludes any notion of winning or losing; his function is a matter of public duty than which in civil life there can be none charged with greater personal responsibility. It is to be efficiently performed with an ingrained sense of the dignity, the seriousness and the justness of judicial proceedings.

In short, the prosecutor does not act in the largely partisan sense usually required of defence counsel by the adversarial system, but as a promoter of the public interest in achieving a just result. Significantly, the Supreme Court has noted that this role is not confined to the courtroom, but extends to all dealings with the accused.

Bruce MacFarlane makes the following observation in his article "Wrongful Convictions: Is It Proper for the Crown to Root Around Looking for Miscarriages of Justice?" (2012) 36 Man LJ 1 at 4:

> This legal framework provided Manitoba Justice with an appropriate basis for conducting a review designed to assess whether murder convictions entered in the Province may be insecure. The very prosecution service that urged conviction during the 1980s and 1990s on the basis of its role as advocate was, therefore, where the circumstances demanded, fully entitled to discharge its "minister of justice role" by doing a "double check" in the 21st century to ensure that justice had truly been served during the previous fifteen years.

MacFarlane also notes how the review revealed at least one wrongful conviction, that of Kyle Unger. On that case see MacFarlane, *supra* and "Kyle Unger" at <http://www.aidwyc.org/cases/historical/kyle-unger/>.

Note on the Professional Responsibility of Judges

The concluding passages of the Appellate Division's judgment in the 1983 *Marshall* reference created considerable controversy. The royal commission appointed to inquire into the causes of Marshall's wrongful conviction attempted to compel the judges who sat on the 1983 appeal to testify as to their reasons for making these comments. One of the judges on the 1983 panel, Justice Leonard Pace, had served as attorney general of Nova Scotia at the time of Marshall's conviction.

The Supreme Court of Canada decided that the principle of judicial independence gave the judges absolute immunity from testifying about the evidence before them and the meaning of their reasons. A majority also ruled that the chief justice of Nova Scotia could not be questioned as to why Justice Pace sat on the *Marshall* case. A minority would have allowed such questions, distinguishing them as concerning the administrative as opposed to the judicial function of the courts. See *Mackeigan v Hickman*, [1989] 2 SCR 796.

An inquiry committee appointed by the Canadian Judicial Council decided in 1990 not to recommend that the judges who sat on the 1983 Reference should be removed from office. Four members stated: "While their remarks in *obiter* were, in our view, in error, and inappropriate in failing to give recognition to manifest injustice, we do not feel that they are reflective of conduct so destructive that it renders the judges incapable of executing their office impartially and independently with continued public confidence." One member, McEachern CJBC, agreed but also stated that most of the criticisms of the judges in the 1983 reference by the royal commission "are not valid" because the appeal court had enough evidence before them to support their opinions about Marshall's conduct.

Note that the Canadian Judicial Council has since produced *Ethical Principles for Judges* <http://www.cjc-ccm.gc.ca/cmslib/general/news_pub_judicialconduct_Principles_en.pdf>, which addresses conflicts of interests in rule 6E as follows:

1. Judges should disqualify themselves in any case in which they believe they will be unable to judge impartially.
2. Judges should disqualify themselves in any case in which they believe that a reasonable, fair minded and informed person would have a reasoned suspicion of conflict between a judge's personal interest (or that of a judge's immediate family or close friends or associates) and a judge's duty.

3. Disqualification is not appropriate if: (a) the matter giving rise to the perception of a possibility of conflict is trifling or would not support a plausible argument in favour of disqualification, or (b) no other tribunal can be constituted to deal with the case or, because of urgent circumstances, failure to act could lead to a miscarriage of justice.

Given this, should someone in Justice Pace's position who had previously as attorney general been ultimately responsible for Marshall's conviction, though perhaps not personally involved, have sat as a judge on Marshall's second appeal?

The Aftermath of Marshall's Wrongful Conviction

Roy Ebsary was subsequently charged with the murder of Sandy Seale. A judge at a preliminary hearing determined there was insufficient evidence of Ebsary's intent to commit him for a trial for murder, so he was committed for trial for manslaughter. Ebsary's first trial ended in a hung jury because the jury apparently could not decide if he had acted in self-defence. He was convicted of manslaughter at a second trial. An appeal was allowed and a new trial ordered. At the third trial, Ebsary was again convicted of manslaughter. He was sentenced to three years' imprisonment but, on appeal, this sentence was reduced to a year's imprisonment.

Mr. Marshall received very little compensation after his wrongful conviction, in part because of the Nova Scotia Court of Appeal's remarks. Controversy continued around the case, and in 1986 the government of Nova Scotia appointed a public inquiry composed of three senior trial judges from outside the province. The following are extracts from its seven-volume 1989 report.

Royal Commission on the Donald Marshall Jr Prosecution
(1989)

Factual Findings

Late in the evening of May 28, 1971, Donald Marshall Jr. and Sandy Seale met by chance shortly after Seale left St. Joseph's Church Hall on George Street in Sydney. The two were walking through Wentworth Park when they met two other men, Roy Ebsary and James (Jimmy) MacNeil. Following a brief conversation initiated when Ebsary or MacNeil asked for a cigarette, Marshall and/or Seale asked Ebsary and MacNeil for money.

[The commission found that Seale said "Dig man, dig" to Ebsary and "this represented, at most, an expression of impatience or frustration by Seale, who wanted Ebsary to check more quickly to find out whether he had any money, and that the request was not accompanied by any verbal or physical threats from Marshall or Seale."]

This was a low-key, non-violent, non-criminal request, similar to the solicitations many of us routinely experience while walking the streets of any Canadian city. But this simple request triggered in the drunken and dangerous Ebsary a deadly over-reaction. Ebsary's intoxicated and irrational state likely made him believe he was under threat of attack when no such threat existed. Before their encounter that night, in fact, Ebsary had already decided—as he described it later—that "the next man that struck me would die in his tracks." (Exhibit 19, Page 145)

It has been suggested in some previous proceedings that the stabbing may have occurred in the course of an actual or attempted robbery, rolling or mugging, but these terms all imply some degree of criminality and we conclude Seale was not killed as a result of any such incident.

This is not merely an academic distinction. In its 1983 decision acquitting Marshall of Seale's murder, the Court of Appeal of Nova Scotia concluded Marshall and Seale had been involved in an attempted robbery at the time the stabbing took place and that Marshall, by failing to disclose this fact, had contributed in large measure to his own conviction. This conclusion adversely affected Marshall's later attempt to win compensation for his wrongful imprisonment.

Given Ebsary's history, it is conceivable that Ebsary's attack was totally unprovoked. But our view is that his volatility and his desire to be a heroic man of action led him to misinterpret a simple "panhandling" request, and then to overreact to an imagined threat of attack—with tragic consequences. ...

The criminal justice system failed Donald Marshall Jr. at virtually every turn, from his arrest and wrongful conviction in 1971 up to—and even beyond—his acquittal by the Court of Appeal in 1983. The tragedy of this failure is compounded by the evidence that this miscarriage of justice could have—and should have—been prevented, or at least corrected quickly, if those involved in the system had carried out their duties in a professional and/or competent manner.

If, for example, the Sergeant of Detectives of the Sydney City Police Department had not prematurely concluded—on the basis of no supporting evidence and in the face of compelling contradictory evidence—that Donald Marshall Jr. was responsible for the death of Sandy Seale, Marshall would almost certainly never have been charged with the crime. If the Crown prosecutor had provided full disclosure to Marshall's lawyers of the conflicting statements provided by alleged eyewitnesses; if Marshall's lawyers had conducted a more thorough defence, including pressing for such disclosure and conducting their own investigations into the killing; if the judge in the case had not made critical errors in law; Marshall would almost certainly not have been convicted.

When Marshall's wrongful conviction was finally discovered in the early 1980s, the Court of Appeal compounded the miscarriage of justice by describing Marshall as having contributed in large measure to his own conviction and by stating that any miscarriage of justice in the case was more apparent than real.

This Commission has concluded that Donald Marshall Jr. was not to blame for his own conviction and that the miscarriage of justice against him was real. ...

The Police Investigation

Sergeant of Detectives John MacIntyre ... very quickly decided that Marshall had stabbed Seale in the course of an argument, even though there was no evidence to support such a conclusion. MacIntyre discounted Marshall's version of events partly because he considered Marshall a troublemaker and partly because, in our view, he shared what we believe was a general sense in Sydney's White community at the time that Indians were not "worth" as much as Whites.

Regardless of the reasons for his conclusions, MacIntyre's investigation seemed designed to seek out only evidence to support his theory about the killing and to discount all evidence that challenged it.

The most damning evidence against Marshall came from two teenaged "eyewitnesses," Maynard Chant, a 14-year-old who was on probation in connection with a minor criminal offence, and John Pratico, a mentally unstable 16-year-old whose psychiatrist later testified that he was known to fantasize and invent stories to make himself the centre of attention.

Shortly after Seale died, both youths gave statements to MacIntyre. Chant, although he had seen nothing, generally corroborated Marshall's version of events, while Pratico claimed to have seen two men running away from the stabbing scene. A few days later, however, they both gave contradictory second statements to MacIntyre. Pratico claimed he had seen Marshall stab Seale during an argument. Chant said he had also heard the argument and seen the stabbing. He placed a "dark-haired fellow"—presumably Pratico— in the bushes near where the stabbing took place.

None of this, as we now know, was true. The information in these second statements came from Pratico and Chant accepting suggestions John MacIntyre made to them. His attempt to build a case against Marshall that conformed to his theory about what had happened went far beyond the bounds of acceptable police behaviour. MacIntyre took Pratico, an impressionable, unstable teenager, to a murder scene, offered the youth his own version of events and then persuaded Pratico to accept that version as the basis for what became Pratico's detailed and incriminating statement. MacIntyre then pressured Chant, who was on probation and frightened about being sent to jail, into not only corroborating Pratico's statement, but also into putting Pratico at the scene of the crime. MacIntyre's oppressive tactics in questioning these and other juvenile witnesses were totally unacceptable.

Largely because of the untrue statements MacIntyre had obtained, Donald Marshall Jr. was charged on June 4, 1971 with murdering Sandy Seale.

The Trial Process

In order for an accused to be committed for trial following a preliminary inquiry, the judge must be satisfied on the basis of what he or she has heard that there is admissible evidence which could, if it were believed, result in a conviction. Not surprisingly, Marshall was committed for trial before judge and jury on a charge of murder.

Trials are conducted under an adversarial system in which the interest of the State is represented by a Crown prosecutor and the interest of the accused is represented by defence counsel. In order for a person to be convicted of murder, a jury of the accused's peers must decide unanimously that the evidence establishes the person's guilt beyond reasonable doubt. The role of the defence counsel is to satisfy the jury that the Crown has failed to prove its case beyond a reasonable doubt. Defence counsel has a responsibility to the court not to mislead, but otherwise is responsible only to the accused.

The interest of the State, on the other hand, is to see that justice is done. The objectives of Crown counsel were put succinctly by Justice Rand in his judgment in the 1954 Supreme Court of Canada case of *Boucher v. The Queen*, [1955] S.C.R. 16:

> It cannot be over-emphasized that the purpose of a criminal prosecution is not to obtain a conviction, it is to lay before a jury what the Crown considers to be credible evidence relevant

to what is alleged to be a crime. Counsel have a duty to see that all available legal proof of the facts is presented; it should be done fairly. The role of prosecutor excludes any notion of winning or losing; his function is a matter of public duty than which in civil life there can be none charged with greater personal responsibility. It is to be efficiently performed with an ingrained sense of the dignity, the seriousness and the justness of judicial proceedings.

If Crown counsel is aware of evidence that could be helpful to the accused, they must disclose its existence to the accused, or the accused's counsel, before the trial takes place. In certain circumstances, it may even be incumbent upon Crown counsel to make such disclosures directly to the court. …

The Crown Prosecutor

Donald MacNeil was the chief Crown prosecutor in charge of this case. He presented the Crown's case at the preliminary inquiry and during the trial. …

[The commission found that MacNeil knew that Chant and Pratico had given inconsistent statements.]

Given the importance of these witnesses to the Crown's case, we believe he should have interviewed each of them separately in depth as part of what should be standard pre-trial preparation. That the witnesses were juveniles who had given conflicting statements made these interviews even more critical. MacNeil should have used these sessions to find out why they had made earlier, conflicting statements, and to satisfy himself that their later statements were truthful. We believe that if MacNeil had interviewed Chant [and] Pratico … separately, he might very well have learned that neither Chant nor Pratico had actually witnessed Marshall stabbing Sandy Seale.

MacNeil not only did not make the necessary effort to find out the reasons for those conflicting statements but he also—and just as importantly—did not disclose the existence of those earlier statements to Marshall's defence counsel.

According to the evidence before us, MacNeil generally did disclose the contents of statements of various witnesses to defence counsel if they asked for such information. If they did not, however, he would not make any disclosure. …

The evidence the Crown had in its possession in this particular case illustrates why the Crown must discharge this obligation to disclose. If defence counsel had been armed with the prior inconsistent statements by Chant [and] Pratico … , we believe they could have used them to raise at least a reasonable doubt about Marshall's guilt in the minds of the jury.

We believe MacNeil had an obligation prior to the preliminary inquiry to disclose to defence counsel the contents of the inconsistent statements given by Chant [and] Pratico … , and at least the names of George and Sandy MacNeil. His failure to discharge this obligation was a contributing factor leading to Donald Marshall Jr.'s wrongful conviction.

The Defence Counsel

Donald Marshall's defence was in the hands of counsel who were considered to be among the most experienced and competent in Cape Breton County. All the evidence indicates that C.M. Rosenblum, now deceased, was a skilled criminal defence lawyer and that Simon Khattar had a long and distinguished career at the Bar. Rosenblum and Khattar were retained by the Union of Nova Scotia Indians and the Department of Indian Affairs, and were paid substantial fees. They also had access to any funds they needed to do whatever they decided was necessary in order to provide for Marshall's defence. ...

Marshall was a young Native with no personal resources. He was in jail continuously from June 4 through the time of his preliminary inquiry and trial. He therefore had to depend exclusively on the efforts of Rosenblum and Khattar to meet the charges against him. They let him down. We consider their actions, or lack thereof, to be the antithesis of what one would expect from competent, skilled counsel.

Rosenblum and Khattar did not carry out or arrange for any independent investigation. They did not interview any of the witnesses for the Crown. ...

Defence counsel also did not ask the Crown to disclose the existence of statements or the details of the case against their client. ...

We conclude that Rosenblum and Khattar were aware Chant [and] Pratico ... had given statements to the police, although they likely did not know the details contained in such statements. For their own reasons, defence counsel elected not to attempt to obtain those statements. Eleven years later, in affidavits filed with the Court of Appeal in connection with the Reference hearing, they stated that "if evidence of the contents of the Statements ... had been adduced at trial, then the jury might reasonably have been induced to change its views regarding the guilt of Donald Marshall Jr." (Exhibit 134, Page 130) These statements, in their own words, faithfully describe the consequence of their failure to obtain copies of these crucial statements.

Why did they not obtain them? It is one of many questions we have concerning the role played by Marshall's defence counsel. Why, for example, did they not have an independent investigation conducted? Why did they not contact the Crown to learn the case to be met? Why did they not find out that Pratico, a key witness for the Crown, spent the time between the preliminary inquiry and the trial in the Nova Scotia Hospital being treated for mental illness?

Bernard Francis, a court worker in Sydney in 1971, testified that in his opinion Rosenblum did not work as hard for Native clients. We also heard evidence to suggest that Rosenblum and Khattar believed Marshall was guilty. Did those feelings influence the effort they put into mounting Marshall's defence?

We conclude that the fact that Marshall was a Native did indeed influence Rosenblum and Khattar. Given the reputation for competence they enjoyed in the Cape Breton legal community and the totally inadequate defence they provided to Marshall, the irresistible conclusion is that Marshall's race did influence the defence provided to him.

For whatever reason, Donald Marshall Jr. did not get the professional services to which any accused is entitled. Had defence counsel taken even the most rudimentary steps an accused should be entitled to expect from his or her counsel, it is difficult to believe Marshall would have been convicted.

[The commission found that Marshall's lawyer failed to bring fundamental errors of law to the Appellate Division's attention in 1972 and that his conduct amounted to a "serious breach of the standard of professional conduct expected and required of defence counsel."]

The Trial Judge

During the course of Donald Marshall Jr.'s trial, the trial judge, Mr. Justice Louis Dubinsky, made various incorrect rulings on evidence. While many of those errors may not have influenced the outcome of the trial when considered individually, some were indeed serious and may have had an effect on the verdict. In any case, the cumulative effect of the errors is such that we must conclude that Marshall did not receive a fair trial.

There is one particular error by the judge ... which we wish to comment as well. This concerns Mr. Justice Dubinsky's handling of John Pratico's attempt to recant his statement that Donald Marshall Jr. had killed Seale and that he had witnessed the stabbing. ...

In the corridor while he was waiting to testify, Pratico, of his own volition, approached Donald Marshall Sr. He told him that Donald Marshall Jr. did not kill Sandy Seale and that Pratico had lied when he testified at the preliminary inquiry that he had witnessed the stabbing.

When Pratico was sworn, MacNeil immediately attempted to introduce the evidence of what had been said outside the courtroom. The judge refused to permit it to be heard at that time. (Exhibit 1, Page 156) Subsequently, Khattar did bring out what Pratico said outside the courtroom during his cross-examination of Pratico, but MacNeil objected and the trial judge refused to permit a thorough and searching cross-examination about why Pratico had said what he did, why he had lied at the Preliminary and other matters. (Exhibit 1, Page 182). ...

We believe a full and complete cross-examination of John Pratico at this stage by Khattar almost certainly would have resulted in his recanting the evidence given during his examination-in-chief that he had seen Marshall stab Seale. In those circumstances, no jury would have convicted Donald Marshall Jr.

But that, unfortunately, is not what happened. Marshall was convicted and sentenced to life in prison. During the course of the trial, Justice Dubinsky made a comment that, in retrospect, now seems ironic in the extreme:

> Whether I am right—who is there in this world who can say that he never made mistakes, is a matter which may, may, if necessary, be looked into at some future time.

The 1972 Appeal

For our part, we believe a court of appeal has a duty to review the record of a criminal case placed before it. If the court becomes aware during this review of a significant error, which has not been raised by counsel, we believe the court has an obligation to raise the issue with counsel and to ensure that it is properly argued. If necessary, counsel should be recalled to deal with the issue. In this case, the Court of Appeal did not comment on the serious issues which were readily apparent on a reading of the trial transcript. These errors were so serious that a new trial should have been the inevitable result of any appeal.

We recognize that a duty such as we have outlined imposes a heavy burden on an appellate court, but it is important to remember that a provincial Court of Appeal is for all practical purposes the court of last resort for a convicted appellant. Since the possibility of a "routine" criminal matter being heard by the Supreme Court of Canada is virtually non-existent, provincial Courts of Appeal represent the final opportunity to make sure the law is properly applied according to accepted principles.

Our criminal justice system functions as an adversarial process, which is supposed to ensure that only the guilty are convicted. The overriding principle is the search for justice. There can be no justice if a conviction is sustained because of the inadequacy of counsel. The Appeal Courts must ensure that justice is done. When counsel fails, the courts must step in. …

The Correctional System

On July 29, 1982, the Court of Appeal granted an application for bail for Donald Marshall Jr. By that time, Marshall had been incarcerated, either in the Cape Breton County Jail, Dorchester Penitentiary, the Medium Security Facility at Springhill, Nova Scotia, or at the Carlton Centre halfway house in Halifax, Nova Scotia for approximately 11 years and one month. …

Having entered prison as a 17-year-old boy in 1971 and then having spent 11 years there for a crime he did not commit, Donald Marshall Jr., 28, was out on the street again in July 1982. Because he had been released on bail, however, he received none of the institutional assistance he would have been entitled to if he, in fact, had committed the crime for which he had been imprisoned and been released on parole. The bitter irony is that the system, which had failed Donald Marshall Jr. on so many occasions in the past, failed him again even as it sent him back into society.

This is not the fault of the corrections system, which is geared to assist offenders reintegrate into society but cannot logically exercise control over those who are not guilty of any crime. The system is simply not set up to deal with the unique situation in which Marshall found himself. While that is understandable, it is nonetheless difficult to imagine a more tragic circumstance. …

The 1983 Reference

[The commission concluded that the 1983 reference should have been established by the minister of justice as a broad-ranging inquiry into the miscarriage of justice under s 690(c) (see now s 696.3(2)) rather than as an appeal by Marshall from his conviction under s 690(b) (formerly s 617(b)) (see now s 696.3(3)(a)(ii)).]

As a practical matter, this decision to refer under Section 617(b) left Marshall with the burden of preparing and presenting the case to prove his own innocence. This reinforced the adversarial nature of an appeal, and it served to limit the issues canvassed before the Court. Although both governments felt that a full public airing was essential, the Section 617(b) appeal effectively confined the public hearing to the facts of the incident, and precluded a complete examination of why the wrongful conviction occurred. …

By using Section 617(b), the possibility of a new trial was raised, an outcome which no one wanted; of perhaps more importance, the evidence would be directed solely at guilt or innocence, and not to the factors leading to the wrongful conviction.

[The commission strongly criticized parts of the 1983 reference decision.]

This Commission has carefully examined the Court's judgment in the light of the record before the Court. We believe the Court made a serious and fundamental error when it placed the blame on Donald Marshall Jr. The Court reached conclusions unsupported by evidence and either ignored or refused to hear evidence that would have been critical of anyone other than Marshall. In so doing, the Court not only appeared to be acquitting Marshall with the greatest of reluctance, but it also absolved the criminal justice system of any responsibility for his wrongful conviction and imprisonment. ...

The Court of Appeal concluded that Donald Marshall Jr. had been engaged in an attempted robbery at the time Sandy Seale was murdered. From that initial finding, the Court drew a number of conclusions. The first was that Marshall was therefore guilty of "evasions, prevarications and outright lies." (Exhibit 4, Page 143) The Court did not indicate what Marshall's "outright lies" were, but presumably the Court accepted Jimmy MacNeil's evidence that the murder was the result of a struggle that occurred during an attempted robbery and rejected Marshall's evidence that no robbery or attempted robbery took place. If this, in fact, is the case, the Court took it upon itself to "convict" Marshall of an offence—committing a robbery—with which he was never charged. ...

Having concluded that Marshall was involved in a robbery attempt, the Court then took it upon itself to blame him for not confessing to this criminal offence—one with which he had not been charged—in order to win his freedom on another charge, of which he was not guilty ... .

The Court's characterization of the "robbery" as being the "only defence available" to Marshall is curious in the extreme. Surely in our criminal justice system there is no onus on an accused to develop a defence. Surely the onus and obligation on the part of the Crown is to bring forward truthful evidence which, if accepted, will support the conviction. How can an accused be blamed if he is convicted on the basis of perjured testimony? ...

We find it incomprehensible that the Court of Appeal failed to identify the perjured testimony and its source and the non-disclosure by the Crown of inconsistent statements as the key contributing factors to Donald Marshall Jr.'s conviction, and then suggested Marshall contributed "in large measure" to his own conviction. The thrust of the Court of Appeal's gratuitous comments in the last two pages of the judgment is to pin the blame on Marshall for his conviction and to ignore any evidence which would suggest fault on the part of the criminal justice system. The decision amounted to a defence of the system at Marshall's expense, notwithstanding overwhelming evidence to the contrary.

Righting the Wrong: Dealing with the Wrongfully Convicted

We believe an independent review mechanism needs to be established to deal with allegations of wrongful conviction. Its existence must be well publicized so that both those who claim to have been wrongfully convicted and those who have knowledge about a wrongful conviction will know who to approach with their concerns. The review mechanism must be independent so that those with information will be willing to come forward. Finally, if it is to be effective, this body will need to have investigative powers to look into the allegations and obtain access to all relevant information and interview all witnesses.

We recommend that the Attorney General take up the matter of establishing a review mechanism with his Federal and Provincial counterparts.

If it is determined that someone has been wrongfully convicted and imprisoned, we recommend that a judicial inquiry be constituted to consider any claim for compensation. Such an inquiry would also have the power to look into the factors that led to the wrongful conviction. We do not believe there should be any pre-set limit on the amount of appropriate compensation, nor do we believe that the person wrongfully convicted should be required to pay his or her legal fees out of whatever compensation they receive. Such expenses should be regarded as part of the expenses of the inquiry.

Visible Minorities and the Criminal Justice System

Having found that racism played a part in Donald Marshall Jr.'s wrongful conviction and imprisonment, we believed it was important to ensure that our justice system will not—and cannot—be influenced by the colour of a person's skin.

While we recognize that many of the causes of discrimination are rooted in institutions and social structures outside the criminal justice system, we believe there are specific steps that can—and should—be taken to reduce discrimination in the justice system itself.

In order to make sure that visible minorities are better represented at all levels of the criminal justice system, we recommend that the Department of Attorney General and Solicitor General adopt and publicize a Policy on Race Relations—with goals and timetables for implementation—based on a commitment to employment equity and the elimination of inequalities based on race. We also recommend that a Cabinet Committee on Race Relations, including both the Attorney General and the Solicitor General, be established, and that it meet regularly with representatives of minority groups to obtain their input on criminal justice matters.

To ensure that more minority group members have the opportunity to participate in the justice system as Crown prosecutors, defence counsel and judges, we recommend that the Governments of Canada and Nova Scotia, as well as the Nova Scotia Bar, financially support Dalhousie Law School's new special minority admissions program for Micmacs and indigenous Blacks.

We also recommend that the Government appoint qualified visible minority judges and administrative board members wherever possible.

In order to ensure that those involved in the criminal justice system are aware of—and sensitive to—the concerns of visible minorities, we recommend that the Dalhousie Law School, the Nova Scotia Barristers Society and the Judicial Councils support courses and programs dealing with legal issues facing visible minorities. We also recommend that the Attorney General establish continuing education programs for Crown prosecutors that will familiarize them with the problem of systemic discrimination and suggest ways in which they can reduce its impact. Similarly, we recommend that training for police officers include discussion of minority issues and encourage sensitivity to minority concerns.

To assist visible minority group members themselves to better understand their rights, we recommend that the Public Legal Education Society work with Native and Black groups to develop and provide appropriate materials and services. This activity should be financially supported by the Government ... .

Nova Scotia Micmac and the Criminal Justice System

Although we have dealt in the foregoing section with recommendations that would affect both Blacks and Natives, we recognize that, on a number of issues, Blacks and Natives regard the criminal justice system in different ways. There are historic, cultural and constitutional factors, for example, that have placed Natives in a special position in Canada. In the following two sections, we will address ourselves to recommendations relating more specifically to each of these groups.

In our view, Native Canadians have a right to a justice system that they respect and which has respect for them, and which dispenses justice in a manner consistent with and sensitive to their history, culture and language. To help achieve this, we recommend that a community controlled Native Criminal Court be established in Nova Scotia, initially as a five-year pilot project. This would involve, on one or more reserves, Native Justices of the Peace hearing summary conviction cases, the development of community diversion and mediation services and community work projects as alternatives to fines and imprisonment, the establishment of aftercare services and the provision of court worker services. Native communities would be entitled to choose to opt in or out of this pilot project model.

In order to facilitate this, as well as to deal with the questions of incorporating traditional Native customary law into the criminal and civil law as it applies to Native people and other important Native justice issues in Nova Scotia, we recommend that a Native Justice Institute be established with funding from the Federal and Provincial Governments. We also recommend that a tripartite forum involving Micmacs and federal and provincial governments be established to mediate and resolve outstanding issues between the Micmac and governments.

To improve the treatment of those Native accused who will continue to appear in our regular criminal courts, we recommend that Micmac interpreters be hired to work in all courts in the province; that the Provincial and Federal Governments, in consultation with Native communities, establish a Native court worker program in Nova Scotia; that the Chief Judge of the Provincial Court take steps to establish regular sittings of the Provincial Court on reserves; and that Judges seek the advice of Native Justice Committees composed of community leaders when sentencing Natives.

We also endorse a recommendation by counsel to the Attorney General that a study be done concerning proportional representation of visible minorities on juries.

To improve relations between Native accused and lawyers, we recommend that Nova Scotia Legal Aid be funded to assign sensitized lawyers to work specifically with Native clients and to hire a Native social worker/counsellor to act as a liaison between the Legal Aid service and Native people. At the same time, we recommend that the Nova Scotia

Barristers Society develop a continuing liaison program with Native people and educate its members regarding the special needs of Native clients.

To enhance the policing function in Native communities, we recommend that the RCMP and municipal police forces, where applicable, take immediate steps to recruit and hire Native Constables.

Blacks and the Criminal Justice System

The only legislation in Nova Scotia that specifically protects the rights of Blacks and other visible minorities is the Nova Scotia *Human Rights Act*. We believe it has not been as effective as it should be, so we recommend that the Act be amended to establish a Race Relations Division within the Commission, with at least one full time member who will be designated as Race Relations Commissioner.

We also recommend that the amended Act specifically state that those aspects of the criminal justice system that come under provincial jurisdiction are covered by the Act; that the Minister will (rather than may) appoint a Board of Inquiry if the Commission recommends it; and that the Commission be given the funds necessary to hire independent legal counsel rather than depending on the advice of the Department of Attorney General.

We also believe that in order to fulfill its education mandate, the Commission should be provided with the necessary funds to engage in an active public awareness program and that the Commission should produce an annual report of its activities.

In order to ensure that Blacks are more equitably treated in the courts, we recommend that the Province re-examine its funding of legal aid to ensure there are enough lawyers available to serve the needs of minority clients and, as well, that the Chief Justices and the Chief Judges of each court in the province exercise leadership to ensure fair treatment of minorities in the system.

Administration of Criminal Justice

As an important first step, we are recommending that a statutory office of Director of Public Prosecutions be established. He or she should have at least 10 years experience and would be appointed for a 10-year term by the Governor in Council, after consultation with the Nova Scotia Barristers Society and the two Chief Justices of the Supreme Court. The Director of Public Prosecutions would have the status of a Deputy Department head and would exercise all the functions of the Attorney General in relation to the administration of criminal justice, filing an annual report with the Attorney General.

To ensure equitable treatment before the courts, we recommend that the Attorney General—after consultation with the Director of Public Prosecutions—issue and then table in the legislature guidelines for the exercise of prosecutorial discretion.

Although the Attorney General would still be able to intervene in a prosecution, he or she would have to issue written instructions to that effect, which instructions would then be published at the appropriate time in the Royal Gazette.

To reinforce the police's unfettered right to lay charges, we recommend that the Solicitor General issue general instructions to the police informing them of their ultimate right and duty to determine the form and content of charges to be laid in a particular case, subject to the Crown's right to withdraw or stay charges after they have been laid.

Based on our findings concerning the lack of disclosure in the Marshall case, we recommend that the Attorney General urge the Federal Government to amend the *Criminal Code* to provide for full and timely disclosure of the evidence in possession of the Crown, including information that might mitigate or negate guilt. Judges would be required not to proceed with a case until they are satisfied such disclosure has taken place. Until such amendments are passed, we recommend that the Attorney General adopt and enforce similar provisions as policy. ...

Conclusion

Our purpose as Commissioners has been to review and assess the system of administration of criminal justice in Nova Scotia in the context of the wrongful conviction of Donald Marshall Jr.

Based on our review and assessment we have found that there were, and are, serious shortcomings in that system which must be addressed. Our recommendations are intended to remedy those shortcomings and to promote a system of administration of justice which responds appropriately and fairly in all cases.

While it is impossible to guarantee that there will never be another miscarriage of justice such as befell Donald Marshall Jr., it is imperative that those in authority act responsibly to reduce or eliminate such a possibility. It is to that end that we submit this Report.

See generally HA Kaiser, "The Aftermath of the Marshall Commission: A Preliminary Opinion" (1990) 13 Dal LJ 364; DH Wildsmith, "Getting at Racism: The Marshall Inquiry" (1990) 55 Sask L Rev 97; Forum, "Report to the Canadian Judicial Council" (1991) 40 UNBLJ 209; J Mannette, ed, *Elusive Justice: Beyond the Marshall Inquiry* (Halifax: Fernwood, 1992); K Roach, "Canadian Public Inquiries and Accountability" in P Stenning, ed, *Accountability for Criminal Justice* (Toronto: University of Toronto Press, 1995); and K Roach, "Wrongful Convictions in Canada" (2012) 80 U Cin L Rev 1465.

Racism and Court Dynamics

The insidious nature of racism often makes it difficult to identify and treat. This is true of systemic racism in the criminal justice system as well. Rarely, though not rarely enough, the criminal justice system will actually produce policies or decisions or treat individuals in overtly racist ways. More often, minorities report that they experience racism and exclusion through the combined effect of certain less apparent institutional practices of the criminal justice system. In its final report, the Commission on Systemic Racism in the Ontario Criminal Justice System (*Report of the Commission on Systemic Racism in the Ontario Criminal Justice System*, 1995) considered a number of ways in which the practices and process of courts create a racist atmosphere.

The commission met with defensiveness and cynicism in its work. One superior court judge stated the following:

I anticipate that the Commission, driven by the force of political correctness, will find that racism is rampant in the justice system—a conclusion that will not be based on hard evidence but ... on anecdote and unsubstantiated complaint. Failing all else the commission will find invisible racism—visible only to the commissioners.

Nevertheless, the commission argued that the *appearance* of racism is itself a dangerous phenomenon, keeping in mind the extent to which the court system relies upon the community's belief in the fairness of its processes. Research revealed that many Ontarians see courts as unfairly biased against members of visible minorities. The commission analyzed transcripts, reviewed submissions, observed trials, and conducted surveys and consultations in an effort to pinpoint practices that led to the appearance of racial inequity in the courts. Though, on their own, these practices may seem innocuous, their accumulated effect can produce an atmosphere of exclusion.

The commission found that the practice of swearing oaths on Christian Bibles produces a situation in which members of religious minorities or individuals who do not subscribe to a particular faith must declare in court their "deviance" from the Christian norm. Considering the religious diversity of the population and the secular nature of the Canadian state, the commission concluded that Ontario ought to abolish the religious oath and replace it with a promise to tell the truth combined with an acknowledgment of the legal consequences of lying. In the alternative, the commission suggested that the judiciary be educated as to the variety of oath requirements for a breadth of religious and secular groups.

Many members of racial minorities reported that the technical procedures, rapid pace, formality, and specialized language of the courts had the effect of excluding them from the legal process. While this experience is no doubt shared to some extent by most citizens that appear before the courts, power imbalances and relatively higher incidence of recent immigration and language difficulty intensify the problem among members of racial minorities. One means of attending to this problem is the expansion of programs to divert charges away from the criminal justice system. The commission also suggested that programs in which court workers, functioning as "cultural interpreters," support and inform accused persons and victims/witnesses should be strengthened and expanded.

Related to this last concern is the question of interpreter services in the criminal justice system. Section 14 of the Charter provides that "a party or witness in any proceedings who does not understand or speak the language in which the proceedings are conducted or who is deaf has the right to the assistance of an interpreter." In *R v Tran*, [1994] 2 SCR 951, the Supreme Court of Canada affirmed that, in the interests of a fair trial, the Charter guarantees access to continuous, precise, impartial, competent, and contemporaneous translation for an accused person who does not understand or speak the language of the Court. Nevertheless, the commission found serious problems with competence and impartiality on the part of court interpreters. As a system of redress, the commission recommended that a more systematized process of accreditation be implemented. The courts have subsequently held, however, that s 14 is not violated because an interpreter lacks formal training or because no interpreter is provided to facilitate communications between accused persons and their counsel: *R v R(AL)* (1999), 141 CCC (3d) 951 (Man CA) and *R v Rybak*, 2008 ONCA 354, 233 CCC (3d) 58.

The commission also recognized a racialized image of the justice system, which it called "the image of white justice." This image stems largely from the underrepresentation of "racialized persons" among judges, lawyers, and jury members. An accused person who is a member of a visible minority is most often met with a courtroom filled with white jurors, lawyers, and judges—an image that does not reflect the multiracial makeup of Canada. Interestingly, while recommending certain measures to expand juror eligibility to recent immigrants and minority groups, the commission provided no guidance as to what can be done to increase the numbers of judges and lawyers drawn from racial minorities.

Finally, the commission considered references to foreignness in court proceedings. In 28 percent of bail hearings and in one-third of other hearings and sentencing proceedings, judges or lawyers made reference to an accused's race or country of origin, whether relevant or not. Comments were grouped into three categories: "bad apple" cases, which involve references to an accused person's foreignness that are obviously hostile or suggesting bias; "hidden agenda" cases, in which comments, often made by Crown prosecutors, are made in hopes of prompting an adverse reaction to an individual on the part of a judge or jury; and, "apparently benign" cases where references to foreignness seem sympathetic. The commission recommended that the relevance of all references to race be scrutinized before they are introduced in court. As well, the commission counselled for a more effective complaints process combined with ethical and practical guidelines to guide judges and lawyers with respect to race issues.

This summary of the report of the Commission on Systemic Racism in the Ontario Criminal Justice System aimed to bring into focus some elements of the criminal process that create a racist or exclusionary atmosphere in courtrooms. Consider the following case in light of the commission's report.

R v S(RD)
Supreme Court of Canada
[1997] 3 SCR 484

[A consideration of the role of racism in the criminal process raises the issue of what constitutes impartiality and bias in the system. In the following case, a 15-year-old black youth was charged with assaulting a police officer. The only evidence in the case consisted of the conflicting testimony of the accused and the arresting officer, who was white. In the course of the trial, the trial judge, who was black, commented that police officers had been known to mislead the court in the past and to overreact with regard to non-white groups. The Crown successfully appealed the acquittal of the accused on the ground of reasonable apprehension of bias. The accused's further appeal to the Supreme Court was allowed in a 6:3 decision.]

L'HEUREUX-DUBÉ and McLACHLIN JJ (La Forest and Gonthier JJ concurring):
. . .

[29] In our view, the test for reasonable apprehension of bias established in the jurisprudence is reflective of the reality that while judges can never be neutral, in the sense of purely objective, they can and must strive for impartiality. It therefore recognizes as inevitable and appropriate that the differing experiences of judges assist them in their decision-making process and will be reflected in their judgments, so long as those experiences are relevant to the cases, are not based on inappropriate stereotypes, and do not prevent a fair and just determination of the cases based on the facts in evidence.

[30] We find that on the basis of these principles, there is no reasonable apprehension of bias in the case at bar. Like Cory J. we would, therefore, overturn the findings by the Nova Scotia Supreme Court (Trial Division) and the majority of the Nova Scotia Court of Appeal that a reasonable apprehension of bias arises in this case, and restore the acquittal of R.D.S. This said, we disagree with Cory J.'s position that the comments of Judge Sparks were unfortunate, unnecessary, or close to the line. Rather, we find them to reflect an entirely appropriate recognition of the facts in evidence in this case and of the context within which this case arose—a context known to Judge Sparks and to any well-informed member of the community.

. . .

[56] While it seems clear that Judge Sparks *did not in fact* relate the officer's probable overreaction to the race of the appellant R.D.S., it should be noted that if Judge Sparks *had* chosen to attribute the behaviour of Constable Stienburg to the racial dynamics of the situation, she would not necessarily have erred. As a member of the community, it was open to her to take into account the well-known presence of racism in that community and to evaluate the evidence as to what occurred against that background.

. . .

CORY J (Iacobucci J concurring) concurring in the majority decision:

. . .

[149] The history of anti-black racism in Nova Scotia was documented recently by the *Royal Commission on the Donald Marshall Jr. Prosecution* (1989). It suggests that there is a realistic possibility that the actions taken by the police in their relations with visible minorities demonstrate both prejudice and discrimination. ...

[150] However, there was *no* evidence before Judge Sparks that would suggest that anti-black bias influenced *this particular police officer's reactions.* Thus, although it may be incontrovertible that there is a history of racial tension between police officers and visible minorities, there was no evidence to link that generalization to the actions of Constable Stienburg. The reference to the fact that police officers may overreact in dealing with non-white groups may therefore be perfectly supportable, but it is nonetheless unfortunate in the circumstances of this case because of its potential to associate Judge Sparks's findings with the generalization, rather than the specific evidence. This effect is reinforced by the statement "[t]hat to me indicates a state of mind right there that is questionable" which immediately follows her observation.

[151] There is a further troubling comment. After accepting R.D.S.'s evidence that he was told to shut up, Judge Sparks added that "[i]t seems to be in keeping with the prevalent attitude of the day." Again, this comment may create a perception that the findings of credibility have been made on the basis of generalizations, rather than the conduct of the particular police officer. Indeed these comments standing alone come very close to indicating that Judge Sparks predetermined the issue of credibility of Constable Stienburg on the basis of her general perception of racist police attitudes, rather than on the basis of his demeanour and the substance of his testimony.

. . .

[158] A high standard must be met before a finding of reasonable apprehension of bias can be made. Troubling as Judge Sparks's remarks may be, the Crown has not satisfied its onus to provide the cogent evidence needed to impugn the impartiality of Judge Sparks.

Although her comments, viewed in isolation, were unfortunate and unnecessary, a reasonable, informed person, aware of all the circumstances, would not conclude that they gave rise to a reasonable apprehension of bias. Her remarks, viewed in their context, do not give rise to a perception that she prejudged the issue of credibility on the basis of generalizations, and they do not taint her earlier findings of credibility.

MAJOR J (Lamer CJ and Sopinka J concurring) in dissent:

. . .

[15] The bedrock of our jurisprudence is the adversary system. Criminal prosecutions are less adversarial because of the Crown's duty to present all the evidence fairly. The system depends on each side's producing facts by way of evidence from which the court decides the issues. Our system, unlike some others, does not permit a judge to become an independent investigator to seek out the facts.

[16] Canadian courts have, in recent years, criticized the stereotyping of people into what is said to be predictable behaviour patterns. If a judge in a sexual assault case instructed the jury or him- or herself that because the complainant was a prostitute he or she probably consented, or that prostitutes are likely to lie about such things as sexual assault, that decision would be reversed. Such presumptions have no place in a system of justice that treats all witnesses equally. Our jurisprudence prohibits tying credibility to something as irrelevant as gender, occupation or perceived group predisposition. ...

[18] It can hardly be seen as progress to stereotype police officer witnesses as likely to lie when dealing with non-whites. This would return us to a time in the history of the Canadian justice system that many thought had past. This reasoning, with respect to police officers, is no more legitimate than the stereotyping of women, children or minorities.

[19] In my opinion the comments of the trial judge fall into stereotyping the police officer. She said, among other things, that police officers have been known to mislead the courts, and that police officers overreact when dealing with non-white groups. She then held, in her evaluation of this particular police officer's evidence, that these factors led her to "a state of mind right there that is questionable." The trial judge erred in law by failing to base her conclusions on evidence.

Appeal allowed and acquittal by trial judge restored.

Aboriginal People and the Criminal Justice System

Public Inquiry into the Administration of Justice and Aboriginal People, *Report of the Aboriginal Justice Inquiry of Manitoba* (1991)

The Aboriginal Justice Inquiry was created in response to two specific incidents in late 1988.

The first of these was the November 1987 trial of two men for the 1971 murder of Helen Betty Osborne in The Pas, Manitoba. While the trial established that four men were present when the young Aboriginal woman was killed, only one of them ultimately was convicted of any crime. Following the trial, allegations were made that the identity of the four individuals who had been present at the killing was known widely in the local community shortly after the murder. Both the chief of The Pas Indian Band and the mayor of The Pas called for a judicial inquiry that would examine that and other questions related to the murder, including why it had taken 16 years to bring the case to trial.

On March 9, 1988 J.J. Harper, executive director of the Island Lake Tribal Council, died following an encounter with a City of Winnipeg police officer. The following day the police department exonerated the officer involved. Others, particularly those in the province's Aboriginal community, believed that there were many questions which had been left unanswered by the police department's internal investigation. In this case as well, numerous individuals requested the creation of a judicial inquiry.

These two incidents were seen by many as troubling examples of the manner in which Manitoba's justice system was failing Aboriginal people. The evidence of this failure has been apparent and abundant. While Aboriginal people comprise 11.8% of Manitoba's population, they represent at least 50% of the province's prison population. …

· · ·

The over-representation of Aboriginal people in our prisons has been getting significantly worse over the past 25 years. Prior to the Second World War, Aboriginal prison populations were no greater than Aboriginal representation in the population. By 1965, however, 22% of the inmates at the Stony Mountain penitentiary were Aboriginal. In the subsequent years this trend has continued and accelerated.

In 1984 Aboriginal people accounted for 33% of the population at Stony Mountain federal penitentiary and by 1989 they accounted for 46% of the penitentiary population. In 1983 Aboriginal people accounted for 37% of the population of the Headingley Correctional Institution; by 1989 they accounted for 41% of the institution's population. In 1989 Aboriginal people accounted for 67% of the inmate population at the Portage Correctional Institution for women. The Aboriginal population in institutions for young people in 1989 was 61%.

The Aboriginal population of all provincial correctional institutions in 1989 was 57%. The Aboriginal population of all correctional institutions in Manitoba (both federally and provincially administered) in 1989 was 56% (according to figures provided by the Manitoba Department of Justice and the Correctional Services of Canada).

[The overrepresentation of Aboriginal people in Canada's prisons has increased significantly since 1991. In 2011-12 Aboriginal people represented 28 percent of admissions to sentenced custody and 75 percent of admissions to sentenced custody in Manitoba, while making up 4 percent of the Canadian population: S Perreault, "Admissions to Adult Correctional Services in Canada, 2011/2012" (2014) *Juristat*. Aboriginal young persons under 18 constituted 49 percent of female admissions to youth correctional services and 36 percent of male admissions, while constituting 7 percent of the under-18-years-of-age population: S Perreault, "Admissions to Youth Correctional Services in Canada, 2011/2012" (2014) *Juristat*.]

Sentencing and Guilty Pleas

According to our analysis of Provincial Court study data, Aboriginal persons pleaded guilty in 60% of the cases, compared to 50% for non-Aboriginal persons.

Our analysis of the data also reveals that approximately 25% of Aboriginal persons received sentences that involved some degree of incarceration, compared to approximately 10% of non-Aboriginal persons, or 2.5 times more for Aboriginal persons.

In the sentencing of males between 18 and 34 years of age, Manitoba courts handed sentences involving some degree of incarceration to 29.5% of the Aboriginal offenders and 10.9% of the non-Aboriginal offenders. In the sentencing of females between 18 and 34 years of age, Manitoba courts handed sentences involving some degree of incarceration to 19.2% of the Aboriginal offenders and 3.7% of the non-Aboriginal offenders. ... These statistics are dramatic. There is something inherently wrong with a system which takes such harsh measures against an identifiable minority. It is also improbable that systemic discrimination has not played a major role in bringing this state of affairs into being. ...

Jails

None of the provincial institutions we visited, whether for males, females or youth, paid appropriate attention to the importance of elders and Aboriginal spirituality. As a result, Aboriginal inmates suffer. The absence of elders stands in stark contrast to the availability of Christian chaplains. Chaplains, often from a variety of denominations, are present in every provincial institution. Simply making identical provisions for elders as is made for chaplains is, however, not enough. The forms of religious observance are different. Participating in natural, outdoor surroundings is integral to Aboriginal spirituality and correctional institutions must adapt to that; having Aboriginal staff who share the inmate's and elder's spirituality, be it Cree, Ojibway or other, to escort inmates to such observances is one solution. This, of course, will require more Aboriginal staff. ...

There are other problems. A survey conducted by our Commission revealed that as many as 62% of Aboriginal inmates speak an Aboriginal language at home. There are, however, very few staff in the correctional institutions who speak an Aboriginal language and no programs are offered in an Aboriginal language. As a result, communication problems abound. Aboriginal inmates often do not understand institutional policies and programs. Many cannot read English and experience difficulty expressing themselves in a "foreign language."

Aboriginal Women

Aboriginal women come to the justice system with unique problems that arise from, or are related to, the fact that they face double discrimination in their lives. It is important that Aboriginal women be given positions of responsibility in the justice system. They should be involved as clerks, administrators, lawyers, judges, and so forth. They should be involved in the same way as men in law enforcement, in the administration of the courts, as probation officers and parole officers, and in the legal profession. Aboriginal women should be involved in substantial numbers in the RCMP and the City police forces, as well as in Aboriginal police forces.

While the role of Aboriginal women in Aboriginal society is not well understood in non-Aboriginal circles, we have been told, and accept, that a resumption of their traditional roles is the key to putting an end to Aboriginal female mistreatment.

The immediate need is for Aboriginal women to begin to heal from the decades of denigration they have experienced. But the ultimate objective is to encourage and assist Aboriginal women to regain and occupy their rightful place as equal partners in Aboriginal society.

We were moved by the situation of Aboriginal women. They suffer double discrimination: as women and as Aboriginal people; as victims and as offenders. We were convinced by arguments of Aboriginal women that a restoration of their traditional responsibility and position of equality in the family and community holds the key to resolving many of the problems we have identified.

[In examining the murder of Helen Betty Osborne the commission observed:

> It is intolerable that our society holds women, and Aboriginal women in particular, in a position of such low esteem. Violence against women has been thought for too long to be a private affair. Assaults on women have not been treated with the seriousness which they deserve. Betty Osborne was one of the victims of this despicable attitude towards women. … There is one fundamental fact: her murder was a racist and sexist act. Betty Osborne would be alive today had she not been an Aboriginal woman. … The four men who took her to her death from the streets of The Pas that night had gone looking for an Aboriginal girl with whom to "party." They found Betty Osborne. When she refused to party she was driven out of town and murdered. Those who abducted her showed a total lack of regard for her person or her rights as an individual. Those who stood by while the physical assault took place, while sexual advances were made and while she was being beaten to death showed their own racism, sexism and indifference. Those who knew the story and remained silent must share their guilt.]

A Strategy for Action

Aboriginal Justice Systems

We suggest that Aboriginal courts assume jurisdiction on a gradual basis, starting with summary conviction criminal cases, small claims and child welfare matters. Ultimately, there is no reason why Aboriginal courts and their justice systems cannot assume full jurisdiction over all matters at their own pace.

The law to be applied in such systems would ultimately be the criminal and civil codes of each Aboriginal community, and such part of federal and provincial laws as each community selects.

Police

We believe that the future of Aboriginal policing in Manitoba lies in the creation of Aboriginally controlled police forces for Aboriginal communities, and in increasing the numbers of Aboriginal police officers on existing forces. Increasing the level of awareness of the cultural uniqueness of Aboriginal people is also important. Each Aboriginal police force should ultimately assume responsibility for all law enforcement in their communities.

Metis communities also should develop regional Metis police forces, with their own police commissions.

All police forces within the province should increase the numbers of Aboriginal officers, strengthen cross-cultural education, improve relations with Aboriginal communities and change some of their practices.

Courts

The Court of Queen's Bench and the Provincial Court should be replaced with a new court to be known as the Manitoba Trial Court. Judges sitting in Aboriginal and other communities throughout the province would then have the jurisdiction to deal with any type of case. Various court practices should be altered to ensure the disposition of all types of cases within a reasonable time.

Juries

Systemic discrimination is clearly seen in the jury selection process. The right and responsibility of Aboriginal citizens to sit on a jury should be ensured by legislative and administrative change. The ease with which Aboriginal people can be excluded from the jury selection process should be stopped.

Sentencing

Incarceration should be used only as a last resort and only where a person poses a threat to another individual or to the community, or where other sanctions would not sufficiently reflect the gravity of the offence, or where the offender refuses to comply with the terms of another sentence that has been imposed upon him or her. Incarceration for non-payment of a fine should rarely occur. Other procedures for the collection of fines should be considered. If an individual wilfully refuses to pay a fine, and is able to do so, then incarceration can be considered after a show cause hearing.

Where incarceration is required for an Aboriginal person, it should be in a community-based facility in his or her home community, if one exists, or in a more culturally appropriate facility as close to that individual's home as possible.

Jails

The whole jail system should be reformed. Local community-based facilities in Aboriginal communities, staffed by Aboriginal correctional officers and designed to provide culturally appropriate programs for Aboriginal inmates, should be established.

. . .

The nature of institutions generally should change from purely custodial "prisons" to places where personal problems can be addressed and where work, education, job training and personal development programs are available. The number of Aboriginal people in jail should be substantially reduced. The overall capacity of the jail system should also be reduced.

Conclusion

With greater self-determination in their own territories, Aboriginal people can begin to feel they are being dealt with fairly. With their own justice system, they can assume responsibility and once again deal with their own problems in their own culturally appropriate manner.

For those Aboriginal people not living in an Aboriginal community, a restructuring of the existing justice system will enable them to be dealt with in a humane and positive manner. With Aboriginal people working in every aspect of that system, a sensitive, informed and positive approach to Aboriginal people will become possible.

ME Turpel, "On the Question of Adapting the Canadian Criminal Justice System for Aboriginal Peoples: Don't Fence Me In"
In *Aboriginal Peoples and the Justice System: Report of the National Round Table on Aboriginal Justice Issues* (Ottawa: Supply and Services Canada, 1993) at 174-79 (footnotes omitted)

I have isolated seven basic elements (or concepts) worth considering in light of this question of adaptation. The Aboriginal Justice Inquiry provides an excellent review of many points touched upon in the analysis to follow. I have hazarded this selection of seven but freely acknowledge that what is or is not fundamental to the criminal justice system is far from settled. … I should make one specific note regarding my own lack of understanding. I have not had extensive access to information regarding Inuit traditions, customs and experiences with the criminal justice system. On some of the contrasts brought out below, I must defer to Inuit to offer their perspective on these matters.

Crime as Against the State

An anti-social act or "crime" is considered in the Canadian criminal justice system to be an offence against society if it is against the person or possessions (property). Consequently the machinery of the Canadian state is invoked to examine the act and punish the offender. For Aboriginal peoples, anti-social acts against people or possessions are likely to be seen as a violation of one person by another. This does not mean that the community takes no interest or has no involvement in reacting to an anti-social act, but that it is seen within the context of the individuals, families, or accomplices to the event. When the offences are what might be called violations of responsibility and trust for others (by those in political office) or for the land, these would be seen as affecting all members of the community. This is relevant in terms of the broader requirement of restoration when an anti-social act is committed that demonstrates a violation of one's responsibility for others or for the land.

Adversarial System

The Supreme Court of Canada has opined that "[t]he principles of fundamental justice contemplate an accusatorial and adversarial system of criminal justice which is founded on respect for the autonomy and dignity of the person." The adversarial system is one of the most troubling aspects of the criminal justice system for Aboriginal peoples, and most Aboriginal people would say it exhibits little respect for their autonomy or dignity as persons. The notion of reaching truth (honesty) through combat, which infuses the rules of procedure that accompany the adversarial system, stand in sharp contrast to Aboriginal ethics and approaches. Specifically, it conflicts with the Aboriginal ethic of emotional restraint, which encourages people to be restrained in their interactions and responses and to avoid confrontation. This ethic is gravely compromised by the criminal trial process, which relies on words of indignation, hostility and angry rebuttal. All of this testimony is channelled through detailed formal rules and objections, which make the process very mystifying for Aboriginal people.

For an Aboriginal person, the information pertinent to understanding a criminal act would be shared openly without consideration of what is admissible, inadmissible, relevant or irrelevant, prejudicial or supportive. However, when this is filtered through the formal presentation of evidence and argument by counsel, an accused person or an Aboriginal witness would be extremely uncomfortable and indeed lost in the process. Those persons may also be deeply shamed by the accusation that their accounts may not be totally honest in that forum, even though this is simply a trial technique employed by counsel to test witnesses. Rather than compel the Aboriginal witness to a vigorous defence of his or her character and credibility, the witness may simply withdraw and refuse to participate in this exercise in so-called fact finding. This is a technique to avoid confrontation. It is a reaction to a system that is threatening and upsetting and that places one's credibility on the line to root out the lying witness.

Finally, the ethic of emotional restraint often means that public criticism of others is curtailed. The structure of the criminal trial process is that this is critical whether you are the accused person or a witness. However, a reluctance to criticize the conduct of others in the course of one's testimony would likely be interpreted by the court as meaning one is not certain of whether a specific person was at fault. The reluctance to criticize others is greatly exacerbated by the trial process, which is extremely intimidating and loaded with alien cultural baggage. Aboriginal witnesses tend to be soft-spoken and are often asked to speak up and admonished to behave better in court. ...

· · ·

Formal Written Offences/Defence

The Canadian criminal justice system relies upon formal and abstract definitions of crime in the *Criminal Code* and specifically defined defences (which may be set out legislatively or developed according to the common law). The definitions of crime include specific mental and physical elements (*mens rea* and *actus reus*). In many Aboriginal languages there is no separation of these two elements and indeed no equivalent concepts. This presents enormous problems for translation and undoubtedly many ill-informed guilty pleas. During the inquiry into the prosecution of Donald Marshall, Jr., Bernie Francis, a Micmac translator, was asked what the word "guilty" meant in Micmac. He said there was no equivalent word except the concept of "blame." Hence the question "Are you guilty?" would be translated as "Are you blamed?"

In addition to the language problem, the idea of guilt is troubling because it involves intent. Intent and guilt are not necessarily found in Aboriginal cultures, because notions of shame and acceptance of responsibility for situations are emphasized. Moreover, in relating the physical acts involved in an alleged crime, an Aboriginal person may not communicate details in the context of European notions of time and space.

Professional Class

Aboriginal justice systems did not for the most part (the Cherokee are an exception here) use professionally trained classes of persons like lawyers and judges to adjudicate disputes. Professionals are deeply distrusted in Aboriginal cultures because of the experiences with various experts—experts on education, experts on child welfare, etc. Professionals are respected in the dominant society because they have been educated for long periods at post-secondary institutions. This is in direct contrast with Aboriginal communities, where the degree of respect in the community is not premised necessarily on education in the formal system. The extent of life experience, faithfulness to Aboriginal culture and traditions, competence in one's language, and commitment to the community are most often the basis for respect in Aboriginal communities. Knowledge of sacred and spiritual traditions, ways and practices also commands special respect, even sometimes fear.

The idea of securing someone previously unknown to speak for you is quite alien. An Aboriginal person would have a representative of the family or clan speak for him or her but not a stranger who is a trained "talker." Also, it is seen as important that one have the opportunity to talk, uninterrupted, about important matters and that this be done publicly. The great Aboriginal tradition of public oratory stems from this responsibility to acknowledge one's accountability to the people and to find the best path for everyone, not simply oneself.

The concept of judging is also alien. A judge makes a win/lose decision. He or she is asked to do so based on knowing the rules and is accordingly respected within the legal profession. The only citizens of Aboriginal communities who may be comparable to judges are elders. The parallel is a weak one, however. Elders are respected because of their knowledge, commitment and wisdom. They are not simply educated, they are proven wise. Elders do not "judge." They see the whole person and find ways (through stories, meditations, prayers, and ceremonies) of helping an individual understand the shortcomings or problems that led to anti-social acts. They focus on harmony, rehabilitation, reintegration of an offender into the family, clan and community—not on guilt. They do not so much care whether an accused was at a certain place at a certain time. They want to know about the balance in their life and the fulfilment of individual responsibilities to others.

… The elders do not sit in judgement of you. They guide you on your own path of understanding and fulfillment of responsibilities. For Aboriginal peoples, the role of the judge is one of an outsider who knows nothing about you except regarding a specific incident and who is called to judge you. This is alien and terrifying.

Involvement of Strangers: Juries

The involvement of other strangers, in this case juries, in the criminal justice system is also problematic for Aboriginal people, although in a different way. The jury of one's peers in the criminal justice system is not an Aboriginal jury. Indeed the barriers to jury duty for Aboriginal people are considerable. Moreover, an Aboriginal person has no right to have Aboriginal people on the jury that deliberates on his or her case. The concept of juries is one that may have some compatibility with Aboriginal cultures. In the Aboriginal paradigm, however, your peers are not strangers to you; their knowledge of a person is precisely why they would be relevant to restoring harmony after an anti-social act or breach of personal responsibility. For example, if your offence is against a person of a different clan, it might be a jury from that clan that will decide on restoration of the victim and the community. They might deliberate with others from your clan.

Impartiality

The concept of impartiality in the criminal justice system, on the part of the judge, jury and criminal justice officials (the police), is contrary to the nature of Aboriginal experience in kinship communities. You value someone's participation and involvement in your problems not because they are strangers but because they know you, your family, your clan and your history. Obviously, impartiality may have a role in an impersonal pluralistic society, but within Aboriginal communities those who can help are often those who are wise and knowledgeable about family history.

Punishment

One of the biggest difficulties with the criminal justice system for Aboriginal people is the fact that it is oriented toward punishment of the offender in the interests of society by imposing a term of imprisonment, fines and, less often, forms of restitution and community service. The two cornerstones of punishment, imprisonment and fines, are both alien to Aboriginal peoples. The Canadian system is grounded in a retributive theory of punishment that hopes to match a measure of deprivation with a wrong-doing. Deterrence is also a central concern. Finally, rehabilitation of individuals is a goal of the Canadian criminal justice system. Realistically, efforts expended on rehabilitation consist mainly of ensuring that the severity of retribution will deter more wrong-doing.

The goal for Aboriginal communities after an incident of harm against a person or possessions was to resolve the immediate dispute through healing wounds, restoring social harmony and maintaining a balance among all people in the community. Harmony, balance and community welfare cannot be satisfied when an individual is imprisoned and taken out of the community. In very rare cases, Aboriginal persons may have been banished from the community, but imprisonment in the Canadian system is a harsh form of banishment and exclusion from what might be the offender's only avenue for healing and restoration. Also, when the offender is removed it may not be possible to restore the victim and the victim's family or clan to right the wrong. If the offender is paying a "debt to society" through a prison term, what about the repair of the debt to the victim and others in the community?

Too often in the criminal justice system the victim and the victim's family are simply forgotten. The case of Helen Betty Osborne's mother Justine is one in point. She was not kept informed of the police investigation into her daughter's murder, nor was her grief considered and community members involved to assist her with her loss. Her daughter's assailants were not required to make any reparations to her mother and family.

The Aboriginal experience in Canadian prisons has nothing to do with Aboriginal concepts of justice or Aboriginal culture, traditions and values. It is completely imposed and it does very little, if anything, for the rehabilitation of the offender and the healing of the community. The payment of fines is similarly alien. Paying the state for wrong-doing to an individual is alien to Aboriginal communities, where restitution and restoration require good conduct, exchange of gifts and compensation to the victim. The fact that Aboriginal communities are not structured as cash economies means that the payment of a monetary sum is particularly alien and especially burdensome to satisfy. Imprisonment for fine default, a problem that has been widely identified, stems from this context. These notions of punishment are not shared by Aboriginal peoples, even though they are mostly subject to them in the Canadian criminal justice system.

It is impossible to escape the conclusion that the Canadian criminal justice system is an alien system for Aboriginal peoples. It does not accord with the basic teachings and traditions of Aboriginal cultures, and it has never been agreed to explicitly by them. Even in the numbered treaties, such as Treaties 6, 7, and 8, the treaty signatories agreed to maintain peace and order between themselves and others of Her Majesty's subjects. This provision acknowledges the responsibility of Treaty First Nations to maintain peace and order in their communities, and it places upon those peoples an obligation to enforce adherence to the terms of their treaty among their citizens.

These seven basic elements or concepts in the Canadian criminal justice system are all problematic for Aboriginal peoples. Aboriginal peoples' approaches, as informed by Aboriginal culture and traditions, do not accord with the Canadian system. If Aboriginal peoples choose to abandon their traditional approaches and follow the path of the Canadian criminal justice system, that is their choice to make. However, to date I know of no Aboriginal people who have chosen this path. The history has been one of imposition of this system on Aboriginal peoples without regard to the fact that they do not share many of its elements, premises or concepts.

My answer to the question of whether the difficulty lies in fundamental elements of the Canadian criminal justice system is, *most definitely*. This is the problem, and it cannot be wished away simply by having Aboriginal people act as the administrators of a system that is not premised in Aboriginal culture and approaches.

Wrongful Convictions and the Death Penalty

What would have happened if the death penalty had been available in Marshall's case?

United States of America v Burns and Rafay
Supreme Court of Canada
2001 SCC 7, [2001] 1 SCR 283

THE COURT:

[1] Legal systems have to live with the possibility of error. The unique feature of capital punishment is that it puts beyond recall the possibility of correction. In recent years, aided by the advances in the forensic sciences, including DNA testing, the courts and governments in this country and elsewhere have come to acknowledge a number of instances of wrongful convictions for murder despite all of the careful safeguards put in place for the protection of the innocent. The instances in Canada are few, but if capital punishment had been carried out, the result could have been the killing by the government of innocent individuals. The names of Marshall, Milgaard, Morin, Sophonow and Parsons signal

prudence and caution in a murder case. Other countries have also experienced revelations of wrongful convictions, including states of the United States where the death penalty is still imposed and carried into execution.

[2] The possibility of a miscarriage of justice is but one of many factors in the balancing process which governs the decision by the Minister of Justice to extradite two Canadian citizens, Glen Sebastian Burns and Atif Ahmad Rafay, to the United States. A competing principle of fundamental justice is that Canadians who are accused of crimes in the United States can ordinarily expect to be dealt with under the law which the citizens of that jurisdiction have collectively determined to apply to offences committed within their territory, including the set punishment.

[3] Awareness of the potential for miscarriages of justice, together with broader public concerns about the taking of life by the state, as well as doubts about the effectiveness of the death penalty as a deterrent to murder in comparison with life in prison without parole for 25 years, led Canada to abolish the death penalty for all but a handful of military offences in 1976, and subsequently to abolish the death penalty for all offences in 1998. ...

The Principles of Fundamental Justice Are to Be Found in "The Basic Tenets of Our Legal System"

[70] The content of the "principles of fundamental justice" was initially explored by Lamer J. (as he then was) in *Re B.C. Motor Vehicle Act* [see Chapter 6], at p. 503:

> ... [T]he principles of fundamental justice are to be found in the basic tenets of our legal system. They do not lie in the realm of general public policy but in the inherent domain of the judiciary as guardian of the justice system. Such an approach to the interpretation of "principles of fundamental justice" is consistent with the wording and structure of s. 7, the context of the section, i.e., ss. 8 to 14, and the character and larger objects of the Charter itself. It provides meaningful content for the s. 7 guarantee all the while avoiding adjudication of policy matters. [Emphasis added.]

[71] The distinction between "general public policy" on the one hand and "the inherent domain of the judiciary as guardian of the justice system" is of particular importance in a death penalty case. The broader aspects of the death penalty controversy, including the role of retribution and deterrence in society, and the view that capital punishment is inconsistent with the sanctity of human life, are embedded in the basic tenets of our legal system, but they also reflect philosophic positions informed by beliefs and social science evidence outside "the inherent domain of the judiciary." The narrower aspects of the controversy are concerned with the investigation, prosecution, defence, appeal and sentencing of a person within the framework of the criminal law. They bear on the protection of the innocent, the avoidance of miscarriages of justice, and the rectification of miscarriages of justice where they are found to exist. These considerations are central to the preoccupation of the courts, and directly engage the responsibility of judges "as guardian[s] of the justice system." We regard the present controversy in Canada and the United States over possible miscarriages of justice in murder convictions (discussed more fully below) as falling within the second category, and therefore as engaging the special responsibility of the judiciary for the protection of the innocent. ...

[95] The avoidance of conviction and punishment of the innocent has long been in the forefront of "the basic tenets of our legal system." It is reflected in the presumption of innocence under s. 11(d) of the Charter and in the elaborate rules governing the collection and presentation of evidence, fair trial procedures, and the availability of appeals. The possibility of miscarriages of justice in murder cases has long been recognized as a legitimate objection to the death penalty, but our state of knowledge of the scope of this potential problem has grown to unanticipated and unprecedented proportions in the years since *Kindler* [[1991] 2 SCR 779] and *Ng* [[1991] 2 SCR 858] were decided. [These cases decided that it did not violate the Charter to extradite a fugitive to face the death penalty.] This expanding awareness compels increased recognition of the fact that the extradition decision of a Canadian Minister could pave the way, however unintentionally, to sending an innocent individual to his or her death in a foreign jurisdiction.

(a) The Canadian Experience

[96] Our concern begins at home. There have been well-publicized recent instances of miscarriages of justice in murder cases in Canada. Fortunately, because of the abolition of the death penalty, meaningful remedies for wrongful conviction are still possible in this country.

[97] The first of a disturbing Canadian series of wrongful murder convictions, whose ramifications were still being worked out when *Kindler* and *Ng* were decided, involved Donald Marshall, Jr. He was convicted in 1971 of murder by a Nova Scotia jury. He served 11 years of his sentence. He was eventually acquitted by the courts on the basis of new evidence. In 1989 he was exonerated by a Royal Commission which stated that:

> The criminal justice system failed Donald Marshall, Jr. at virtually every turn from his arrest and wrongful conviction for murder in 1971 up to, and even beyond, his acquittal by the Court of Appeal in 1983. The tragedy of the failure is compounded by evidence that this miscarriage of justice could—and should—have been prevented, or at least corrected quickly, if those involved in the system had carried out their duties in a professional and/or competent manner. That they did not is due, in part at least, to the fact that Donald Marshall, Jr. is a Native.

(Royal Commission on the Donald Marshall, Jr. Prosecution, *Digest of Findings and Recommendations* (1989), at p. 1)

In June 1990, a further commission of inquiry recommended that Marshall receive a compensation package consisting, among other things, of a payment for pain and suffering and monthly annuity payments guaranteed over a minimum period of 30 years, at the end of which he will have received in excess of $1 million. The miscarriage of justice in his case was known at the time *Kindler* and *Ng* were decided. What was not known was the number of other instances of miscarriages of justice in murder cases that would surface in subsequent years in both Canada and the United States.

[98] In 1970, David Milgaard was convicted of murder by a Saskatchewan jury and sentenced to life imprisonment. He served almost 23 years in jail. On two occasions separated by almost 22 years, it was held by Canadian courts that Milgaard was given the benefit of a fair trial, initially by the Saskatchewan Court of Appeal in January 1971 in *R. v. Milgaard* (1971), 2 C.C.C. (2d) 206, leave to appeal refused (1971), 4 C.C.C. (2d) 566n,

and subsequently by this Court in *Reference re Milgaard (Can.)*, [1992] 1 S.C.R. 866. There was no probative evidence that the police had acted improperly in the investigation or in their interviews with any of the witnesses, and no evidence that there had been inadequate disclosure in accordance with the practice prevailing at the time. Milgaard was represented by able and experienced counsel. No serious error in law or procedure occurred at the trial. Notwithstanding the fact that the conviction for murder followed a fair trial, new evidence surfaced years later. This Court, on a special reference, considered that "[t]he continued conviction of Milgaard would amount to a miscarriage of justice if an opportunity was not provided for a jury to consider the fresh evidence" (p. 873). In 1994, Milgaard commenced proceedings against the Government of Saskatchewan for wrongful conviction and in 1995 he sued the provincial Attorney General personally after the latter had told the media he believed Milgaard was guilty of the murder. DNA testing in 1997 ultimately satisfied the Saskatchewan government that Milgaard had been wrongfully convicted. In May 2000 another individual was prosecuted and convicted for the same murder. His appeal is pending before the Saskatchewan Court of Appeal. Compensation in the sum of $10 million was paid to Milgaard. The history of the wrongful conviction of David Milgaard shows that in Canada, as in the United States, a fair trial does not always guarantee a safe verdict.

[99] Of equal concern is the wrongful conviction for murder of Guy Paul Morin who was only 25 years old when he was arrested on April 22, 1985, and charged with the first degree murder of a child named Christine Jessop who was his next door neighbour. While initially acquitted by an Ontario jury, he was found guilty at a second jury trial in 1992. DNA testing carried out while the second appeal was pending before the Ontario Court of Appeal, more than 10 years after his initial arrest, exonerated him. His appeal was then uncontested, and he received an apology from the Attorney General of Ontario, compensation of $1.25 million, and the establishment of a commission (the Kaufman Inquiry) to look into the causes of the wrongful conviction. In his 1998 Report, the Commissioner, a former judge of the Quebec Court of Appeal, concluded:

> The case of Guy Paul Morin is not an aberration. By that, I do not mean that I can quantify the number of similar cases in Ontario or elsewhere, or that I can pass upon the frequency with which innocent persons are convicted in this province. We do not know. What I mean is that the causes of Mr. Morin's conviction are rooted in systemic problems, as well as the failings of individuals. It is no coincidence that the same systemic problems are those identified in wrongful convictions in other jurisdictions worldwide.

(Commission on Proceedings Involving Guy Paul Morin, *Report* (1998), vol. 2, at p. 1243)

[100] Thomas Sophonow was tried three times for the murder of Barbara Stoppel. He served 45 months in jail before his conviction was overturned in 1985 by the Manitoba Court of Appeal. It was not until June 2000 that the Winnipeg police exonerated Sophonow of the killing, almost 20 years after his original conviction. The Attorney General of Manitoba recently issued an apology to Mr. Sophonow and mandated the Honourable Peter Cory, recently retired from this Court, to head a commission of inquiry which is currently looking into the conduct of the investigation and the circumstances surrounding the criminal proceedings, both to understand the past and to prevent future miscarriages of justice. The commission will also examine the issue of compensation.

[101] In 1994, Gregory Parsons was convicted by a Newfoundland jury for the murder of his mother. He was sentenced to life imprisonment with no eligibility for parole for 15 years. Subsequently, the Newfoundland Court of Appeal overturned his conviction and ordered a new trial. Before that trial could be held, Parsons was cleared by DNA testing. The provincial Minister of Justice apologized to Parsons and his family and asked Nathaniel Noel, a retired judge, to conduct a review of the investigation and prosecution of the case and to make recommendations concerning the payment of compensation.

[102] These miscarriages of justice of course represent a tiny and wholly exceptional fraction of the workload of Canadian courts in murder cases. Still, where capital punishment is sought, the state's execution of even one innocent person is one too many.

[103] In all of these cases, had capital punishment been imposed, there would have been no one to whom an apology and compensation could be paid in respect of the miscarriage of justice (apart, possibly, from surviving family members), and no way in which Canadian society with the benefit of hindsight could have justified to itself the deprivation of human life in violation of the principles of fundamental justice.

[104] Accordingly, when Canada looks south to the present controversies in the United States associated with the investigation, defence, conviction, appeal and punishment in murder cases, it is with a sense of appreciation that many of the underlying criminal justice problems are similar. The difference is that imposition of the death penalty in the retentionist states inevitably deprives the legal system of the possibility of redress to wrongfully convicted individuals.

(b) The U.S. Experience

[105] Concerns in the United States have been raised by such authoritative bodies as the American Bar Association which in 1997 recommended a moratorium on the death penalty throughout the United States because, as stated in an ABA press release in October 2000:

> The adequacy of legal representation of those charged with capital crimes is a major concern. Many death penalty states have no working public defender systems, and many simply assign lawyers at random from a general list. The defendant's life ends up entrusted to an often underqualified and overburdened lawyer who may have no experience with criminal law at all, let alone with death penalty cases.
>
> The U.S. Supreme Court and the Congress have dramatically restricted the ability of our federal courts to review petitions of inmates who claim their state death sentences were imposed in violation of the Constitution or federal law.
>
> Studies show racial bias and poverty continue to play too great a role in determining who is sentenced to death. …

[107] On August 4, 2000, the Board of Governors of the Washington State Bar Association, being the state seeking the extradition of the respondents, unanimously adopted a resolution to review the death penalty process. The Governor was urged to obtain a comprehensive report addressing the concerns of the American Bar Association as they apply to the imposition of the death penalty in the State of Washington. In particular, the Governor was asked to determine "[w]hether the reversal of capital cases from our state by the federal courts indicates any systemic problems regarding how the death penalty is being implemented in Washington State."

[108]   Other retentionist jurisdictions in the United States have also expressed recent disquiet about the conduct of capital cases, and the imposition and the carrying out of the death penalty. These include:

(i) Early last year Governor George Ryan of Illinois, a known retentionist, declared a moratorium on executions in that state. The Governor noted that more than half the people sentenced to die there in the last 23 years were eventually exonerated of murder. Specifically, Illinois exonerated 13 death row inmates since 1977, one more than it actually executed. Governor Ryan said "I have grave concerns about our state's shameful record of convicting innocent people and putting them on death row." He remarked that he could not support a system that has come "so close to the ultimate nightmare, the state's taking of innocent life" (Governor Ryan Press Release, January 31, 2000).

(ii) The Illinois moratorium followed closely in the wake of a major study on wrongful convictions in death penalty cases by the Chicago Tribune newspaper, and a conference held at Northwestern University School of Law: see L.B. Bienen, "The Quality of Justice in Capital Cases: Illinois as a Case Study" (1998) 61 *Law & Contemp. Probs.* 193, at p. 213, fn. 103. The study examined the 285 death penalty cases that had occurred in Illinois since capital punishment was restored there. "The findings reveal a system so plagued by unprofessionalism, imprecision and bias that they have rendered the state's ultimate form of punishment its least credible" (*Chicago Tribune*, November 14, 1999, at p. C1).

(iii) One of the more significant exonerations in Illinois was the case of Anthony Porter who came within 48 hours of being executed for a crime he did not commit (*Chicago Tribune*, December 29, 2000, at p. 22N). ...

(vii) On September 12, 2000, the United States Justice Department released a study of the death penalty under federal law. It was the first comprehensive review of the federal death penalty since it was reinstated in 1988. The data shows that federal prosecutors were almost twice as likely to recommend the death penalty for black defendants when the victim was non-black than when he or she was black. Moreover, a white defendant was almost twice as likely to be given a plea agreement whereby the prosecution agreed not to seek the death penalty. The study also revealed that 43 percent of the 183 cases in which the death penalty was sought came from 9 of the 94 federal judicial districts. This has led to concerns about racial and geographical disparity. The then Attorney General Janet Reno said that she was "sorely troubled" by the data and requested further studies (*New York Times*, September 12, 2000, at p. 17).

[109]   Foremost among the concerns of the American Bar Association, the Washington State Bar Association and other bodies who possess "hands-on" knowledge of the criminal justice system, is the possibility of wrongful convictions and the potential state killing of the innocent. It has been reported that 43 wrongfully convicted people have been freed in the United States as a result of work undertaken by The Innocence Project, a clinical law program started in 1992 at the Cardozo School of Law in New York. See, generally, B. Scheck, P. Neufeld, and J. Dwyer, *Actual Innocence: Five Days to Execution and Other Dispatches from the Wrongly Convicted* (2000). One of the authors, Peter Neufeld testified to the House of Representatives Committee on the Judiciary that "DNA testing only helps correct conviction of the innocent in a narrow class of cases; most homicides do not involve biological evidence that can be determinative of guilt or innocence" .... .

[The Innocence Project in the United States reported 321 DNA exonerations in December 2014. See <http://www.innocenceproject.org>. A national US registry of exonerations that includes non-DNA cases reports more than 1,500 exonerations between 1989 and 2014. See <http://www.law.umich.edu/special/exoneration/Pages/about.aspx>.]

· · ·

[111] It will of course be for the United States to sort out the present controversy surrounding death penalty cases in that country. We have referred to some of the reports and some of the data, but there is much more that has been said on all sides of the issue. Much of the evidence of wrongful convictions relates to individuals who were saved prior to execution, and can thus be presented as evidence of the system's capacity to correct errors. The widespread expressions of concern suggest there are significant problems, but they also demonstrate a determination to address the problems that do exist. Our purpose is not to draw conclusions on the merits of the various criticisms, but simply to note the scale and recent escalation of the controversy, particularly in some of the retentionist states, including the State of Washington.

(c) The Experience in the United Kingdom

[112] Countries other than Canada and the United States have also experienced their share of disclosure of wrongful convictions in recent years. In the United Kingdom, in 1991, the then Home Secretary announced the establishment of a Royal Commission on Criminal Justice (the Runciman Commission) to examine the effectiveness of the criminal justice system in securing the conviction of the guilty and the acquittal of the innocent. In making the announcement, the Home Secretary referred to such cases as the "Birmingham Six" which had seriously undermined public confidence in the administration of criminal justice. The report of the Commission, pointing to potential sources of miscarriage of justice, was presented to the British Parliament in 1993. The new *Criminal Appeal Act*, adopted in 1995, created the Criminal Cases Review Commission, an independent body responsible for investigating suspected miscarriages of criminal justice in England, Wales and Northern Ireland and referring appropriate cases to the Court of Appeal.

[113] The Criminal Cases Review Commission started its casework in April 1997. As of November 30, 2000, it had referred 106 cases to the Court of Appeal. Of these, 51 had been heard, 39 convictions quashed, 11 upheld and one remained under reserve. The convictions overturned by the court as unsafe included 10 convictions for murder. In two of the overturned murder convictions, the prisoners had long since been hanged.

[114] In *R. v. Bentley (Deceased)*, [1998] E.W.J. No. 1165 (QL) (C.A.), the court posthumously quashed the murder conviction of Derek Bentley who was executed on January 28, 1953. The Crown had alleged that Bentley and an accomplice had embarked upon "a warehouse-breaking expedition" during which a police officer was killed. It was argued that the trial judge had erred in summing up to the jury. It was also argued that fresh evidence made the conviction unsafe. The Lord Chief Justice, Lord Bingham, said about the summing up in this case (at para. 78):

> It is with genuine diffidence that the members of this court direct criticism towards a trial judge widely recognised as one of the outstanding criminal judges of this century [Lord Goddard CJ]. But we cannot escape the duty of decision. In our judgment the summing up

on this case was such as to deny the appellant that fair trial which is the birthright of every British citizen.

After quashing the conviction on this basis, Lord Bingham C.J. said (at para. 95):

> It must be a matter of profound and continuing regret that this mistrial occurred and that the defects we have found were not recognised at the time.
>
> It does not appear that the Court of Appeal gave much weight to the fresh evidence, though one component of this evidence (dealing with the taking of the appellant's statement) was said to provide "additional support" (para. 130) for the conclusion that the conviction was unsafe.

[115]   Another recent case is *R. v. Mattan*, [1998] E.W.J. No. 4668 (QL) (C.A.). Mahmoud Hussein Mattan was convicted of murdering a Cardiff shopkeeper in 1952. The shopkeeper's throat had been cut. On August 19, 1952, the Court of Criminal Appeal refused his application for leave to appeal. He was hanged in Cardiff Prison on September 8, 1952. Fresh evidence came to light in 1969 but the Home Secretary declined in February 1970 to have the case re-opened. The Commission, however, referred the matter to the Court of Appeal, which found that the Crown had failed to disclose highly relevant evidence to the defence. In the result, the conviction was quashed. Near the end of its judgment, the Court of Appeal stated that "[i]t is, of course, a matter of very profound regret that in 1952 Mahmoud Mattan was convicted and hanged and it has taken 46 years for that conviction to be shown to be unsafe." It also observed that the case demonstrates that "capital punishment was not perhaps a prudent culmination for a criminal justice system which is human and therefore fallible" (para. 39).

[116]   The U.K. experience is relevant for the obvious reason that these men might be free today if the state had not taken their lives. But there is more. These convictions were quashed not on the basis of sophisticated DNA evidence but on the basis of frailties that perhaps may never be eliminated from our system of criminal justice. It is true, as the English Court of Appeal noted in *Mattan*, that the present rules require far more disclosure on the part of the Crown. And it is true that there was some blood on the shoes of Mattan that could now be shown by DNA testing not to have belonged to the victim. But there is always the potential that eyewitnesses will get it wrong, either innocently or, as it appears in the case of *Mattan*, purposefully in order to shift the blame onto another. And there is always the chance that the judicial system will fail an accused, as it apparently did in *Bentley*. These cases demonstrate that the concern about wrongful convictions is unlikely to be resolved by advances in the forensic sciences, welcome as those advances are from the perspective of protecting the innocent and punishing the guilty.

(d) Conclusion

[117]   The recent and continuing disclosures of wrongful convictions for murder in Canada, the United States and the United Kingdom provide tragic testimony to the fallibility of the legal system, despite its elaborate safeguards for the protection of the innocent. When fugitives are sought to be tried for murder by a retentionist state, however similar in other respects to our own legal system, this history weighs powerfully in the balance against extradition without assurances.

A Note on the Review of Convictions Once Appeals Have Been Exhausted

The Royal Commission on the Donald Marshall Jr. Prosecution, and six other commissions of inquiry that have examined various wrongful convictions, have all recommended or supported the creation of an independent body such as the British Criminal Cases Review Commission (CCRC), which has powers to investigate claims of wrongful convictions and refer them back to the courts on the basis that "there is a real possibility that the conviction, verdict or sentence would not be upheld were the reference to be made": *Criminal Appeal Act 1995* (UK), c 35, s 13.

As of July 2014, the CCRC has since its creation in 1997 considered over 18,000 applications and has referred 560 cases back to the Court of Appeal with 370 of the convictions referred being quashed. See <https://www.justice.gov.uk/about/criminal-cases-review-commission>.

The CCRC's performance has not been without controversy. Some argue that the CCRC should pay more attention to innocence. See M Naughton, "The Criminal Cases Review Commission: Innocence Versus Safety and the Integrity of the Criminal Justice System" (2012) 58 Crim LQ 207. On the performance of a commission in North Carolina limited to questions of factual innocence, see K Roach, "An Independent Commission to Review Claims of Wrongful Convictions: Lessons from North Carolina?" (2012) 58 Crim LQ 283. A UK parliamentary committee recommended that the CCRC be given more resources and powers to obtain information and that it be more aggressive in referring cases that appear to be incorrectly decided to the courts: Justice Committee, *Criminal Cases Review Commission*, 17 March 2015, HC 850.

In 2002, the *Criminal Code* was amended with respect to claims of miscarriages of justice after all appeals have been exhausted. The federal minister of justice, who is an elected official, retains the right to order a new trial or refer a case to a Court of Appeal if "satisfied that there is a reasonable basis to conclude that a miscarriage of justice likely occurred": *Criminal Code*, s 696.3(3). The minister of justice and people appointed by him or her may exercise investigative powers under s 696.2(2). For a more detailed description of the system, which also involves an independent special adviser to the minister of justice, see N Somji, "A Comparative Study of the Post-Conviction Review Process in Canada and the United Kingdom" (2012) 58 Crim LQ 137.

From 2002 to 2014, 105 applications were decided by the minister of justice, 13 of those cases being referred to the courts: *Annual Report Applications for Ministerial Review—Miscarriages of Justice* at <http://www.justice.gc.ca/eng/rp-pr/cj-jp/ccr-rc/index.html>. This means that the minister receives and decides far fewer applications for review than the CCRC but he or she grants relief in a higher percentage of cases.

The Question of Factual Innocence

Cases referred to the courts of appeal are, as in the *Marshall* appeal, decided under the regular appeal provisions under s 686. Should courts have additional jurisdiction to make declarations of innocence? In *Reference re Mullins-Johnson*, 2007 ONCA 720, the Ontario Court of Appeal concluded:

> [22] The fresh evidence shows that the appellant's conviction was the result of a rush to judgment based on flawed scientific opinion. With the entering of an acquittal, the appellant's legal innocence has been re-established. The fresh evidence is compelling in demonstrating that no

crime was committed against Valin Johnson and that the appellant did not commit any crime. For that reason, an acquittal is the proper result.

[23] There are not in Canadian law two kinds of acquittals: those based on the Crown having failed to prove its case beyond a reasonable doubt and those where the accused has been shown to be factually innocent. We adopt the comments of the former Chief Justice of Canada in *The Lamer Commission of Inquiry Pertaining to the Cases of: Ronald Dalton, Gregory Parsons, Randy Druken*, Annex 3, p. 342:

> [A] criminal trial does not address "factual innocence." The criminal trial is to determine whether the Crown has proven its case beyond a reasonable doubt. If so, the accused is guilty. If not, the accused is found not guilty. There is no finding of factual innocence since it would not fall within the ambit or purpose of criminal law.

[24] Just as the criminal trial is not a vehicle for declarations of factual innocence, so an appeal court, which obtains its jurisdiction from statute, has no jurisdiction to make a formal legal declaration of factual innocence. The fact that we are hearing this case as a Reference under s. 696.3(3)(a)(ii) of the *Criminal Code* does not expand that jurisdiction. The terms of the Reference to this court are clear: we are hearing this case "as if it were an appeal." While we are entitled to express our reasons for the result in clear and strong terms, as we have done, we cannot make a formal legal declaration of the appellant's factual innocence.

[25] In addition to the jurisdictional issue, there are important policy reasons for not, in effect, recognizing a third verdict, other than "guilty" or "not guilty," of "factually innocent." The most compelling, and, in our view, conclusive reason is the impact it would have on other persons found not guilty by criminal courts. As Professor Kent Roach observed in a report he prepared for the *Commission of Inquiry into Certain Aspects of the Trial and Conviction of James Driskell*, "there is a genuine concern that determinations and declarations of wrongful convictions could degrade the meaning of the not guilty verdict" (p. 39). To recognize a third verdict in the criminal trial process would, in effect, create two classes of people: those found to be factually innocent and those who benefited from the presumption of innocence and the high standard of proof beyond a reasonable doubt.

[26] Nothing we have said in these reasons should be taken as somehow qualifying the impact of the fresh evidence. That evidence, together with the other evidence, shows beyond question that the appellant's conviction was wrong and that he was the subject of a terrible miscarriage of justice. We conclude these reasons by paraphrasing what the president of the panel said to Mr. Mullins-Johnson at the conclusion of the oral argument after entering the verdict of acquittal: it is profoundly regrettable that as a result of what has been shown to be flawed pathological evidence Mr. Mullins-Johnson was wrongly convicted and has spent such a very long time in jail.

[27] We can only hope that these words, these reasons for judgment and the deep apology expressed by Ms. Fairburn on behalf of the Ministry of the Attorney General will provide solace to Mr. Mullins-Johnson, to his mother and to everyone who has been so terribly injured by these events.

Is this rejection of a factual innocence verdict appropriate? Note that the state of North Carolina has created a commission like the British CCRC with the power to investigate convictions when appeals have been exhausted and refer them back to an appellate court, but only in cases of "factual innocence" defined as "innocence of any criminal responsibility for the felony for which the person was convicted and for any other reduced level of criminal responsibility relating to the crime, and for which there is some credible, verifiable evidence of innocence that has not previously been presented at trial or considered at a hearing granted through post-conviction relief." See NC Gen Stat §§ 15 A-1460-75 (Supp 2006). The commission has considered over 1,500 applications since its creation, and eight persons have proven on "clear and convincing evidence" that they were factually innocent to three judges on a proceeding ordered by the commission. Note that both the commission and the three-judge panel have to be unanimous for a case to be referred or a conviction quashed under the North Carolina system. See <http://www.innocencecommission-nc.gov/stats.html>. See K Roach, "The Role of Innocence Commissions" (2010) 85 Chicago-Kent L Rev 89.

II. THE ROLE OF THE PROSECUTOR AND DEFENCE COUNSEL

In the Donald Marshall Jr. case, the prosecutor's failure to make full disclosure and the defence counsel's failure to press the case as hard as possible played important roles in the wrongful conviction.

As you read the following material, think about whether the criminal justice system is or should be based on an adversarial system of justice. If all the lawyers in the *Marshall* case had acted as competent and aggressive adversaries, could the miscarriage of justice have been prevented? Are there other problems?

Crown Counsel

The following case is a leading authority on the role of Crown counsel in a criminal trial.

Boucher v The Queen
Supreme Court of Canada
[1955] SCR 16

RAND J: ... There are finally the statements of counsel, which I confine to those dealing with the investigation by the Crown of the circumstances of a crime:

> (Translation) It is the duty of the Crown, when an affair like that happens, no matter what affair, and still more in a serious affair, to make every possible investigation, and if in the course of these investigations with our experts, the conclusion is come to that the accused is not guilty or that there is a reasonable doubt, it is the duty of the Crown, gentlemen, to say so, or if the conclusion is come to that he is not guilty, not to make an arrest. That is what was done here.
>
> When the Crown put in that evidence, it is not with the intention of bearing down on the accused, it was with the intention of rendering justice to him.

Many, if not the majority of, jurors acting, it may be, for the first time, unacquainted with the language and proceedings of Courts, and with no precise appreciation of the role of the prosecution other than as being associated with Government, would be extremely susceptible to the implications of such remarks. So to emphasize a neutral attitude on the part of Crown representatives in the investigation of the facts of a crime is to put the matter to unsophisticated minds as if there had already been an impartial determination of guilt by persons in authority. Little more likely to colour the consideration of the evidence by jurors could be suggested. It is the antithesis of the impression that should be given to them: they only are to pass on the issue and to do so only on what has been properly exhibited to them in the course of the proceedings. ...

It cannot be over-emphasized that the purpose of a criminal prosecution is not to obtain a conviction; it is to lay before a jury what the Crown considers to be credible evidence relevant to what is alleged to be a crime. Counsel have a duty to see that all available legal proof of the facts is presented: it should be done firmly and pressed to its legitimate strength, but it must also be done fairly. The role of prosecutor excludes any notion of winning or losing; his function is a matter of public duty than which in civil life there can be none charged with greater personal responsibility. It is to be efficiently performed with an ingrained sense of the dignity, the seriousness and the justness of judicial proceedings. ...

The conviction, therefore, must be set aside and a new trial directed.

[Four other judges wrote separate concurring opinions.]

In *Boucher v The Queen*, the Supreme Court of Canada emphasized that the role of the prosecutor is to adopt a neutral attitude, pressing credible evidence firmly but fairly. The prosecutor wields considerable power within the criminal justice system, as the following extract explains.

WJ Stuntz, "The Pathological Politics of Criminal Law"
(2001) 100 Mich L Rev 505 at 506 (footnotes omitted, emphasis as in original)

Substantive criminal law defines the conduct that the state punishes. Or does it? If the answer is yes, it should be possible, by reading criminal codes (perhaps with a few case annotations thrown in), to tell what conduct will land you in prison. Most discussions of criminal law, whether in law reviews, law school classrooms, or the popular press, proceed on the premise that the answer *is* yes. Law reform movements regularly seek to broaden or narrow the scope of some set of criminal liability rules, always on the assumption that by doing so they will broaden or narrow the range of behavior that is punished. Opponents of these movements operate on the same assumption—that the law determines who goes to prison and who doesn't, that the distribution of criminal punishment tracks criminal law as it is defined by code books and case reports. ...

But criminal law does not drive criminal punishment. It would be closer to the truth to say that criminal punishment drives criminal law. The definition of crimes and defenses plays a different and much smaller role in the allocation of criminal punishment that we usually suppose. In general, the role it plays is to empower prosecutors, who are the criminal justice system's real lawmakers. Anyone who reads criminal codes in search of a picture of what conduct leads to a prison term, or who reads sentencing rules in order to discover how severely different sorts of crimes are punished, will be seriously misled. ...

Courts make criminal law, when they do so, by interpreting criminal statutes in the context of criminal cases. Not all cases present interpretive opportunities. Few criminal cases go to trial, and of those that do, few raise serious questions about the meaning of the relevant criminal act or intent, or of some criminal defense. (The most common defense argument at trial is that the government has the wrong defendant, not that the defendant's behavior fails to satisfy the legal definition of the crime.) Courts' influence over the content of criminal law depends on the frequency and range of cases that do raise such issues. ...

Aside from homicide, rape, and a few other crimes (and only partially there), criminal law serves not as a means of separating those who are to be punished from those who are not, but as a grant of authority to prosecutors to do the separating. Criminal law is, in other words, not law at all, but a veil that hides a system that allocates criminal punishment discretionarily. Not quite—defendants can still go to trial, and sometimes win at trial, by arguing that someone else committed the crime charged, that the police arrested and the prosecution charged the wrong man. But rarely do defendants prevail, at trial or in any other setting, because the law does not criminalize their conduct. Prosecutors decide what is a crime, though juries occasionally—and *only* occasionally—get to decide whether defendants did the things prosecutors believe they did.

Prosecutorial Discretion

An important element of prosecutorial discretion is the number of charges laid and proceeded with in relation to any particular incident. The Manitoba Aboriginal Justice Inquiry reported:

> According to our analysis of the Provincial Court study statistics, 22% of Aboriginal persons appearing in Provincial Court faced four or more charges, compared to only 13% of non-Aboriginal persons. At the other end of the scale, while 50% of non-Aboriginal charged persons faced only one charge, this was true for only 37% of the Aboriginal persons.
>
> The data showed that Aboriginal persons who were charged faced 2.72 charges per person, compared to 2.19 for non-Aboriginal persons (almost 25% more charges per Aboriginal person).

Both the *Royal Commission on the Donald Marshall Jr Prosecution* (1989) and the Law Reform Commission of Canada in Working Paper 62, "Controlling Criminal Prosecutions: The Attorney General and the Crown Prosecutor" (1990) recommended that prosecutions be conducted under the supervision of a director of public prosecutions, subject only to public directives from the attorney general. The Law Reform Commission explained that such a reform was "[t]o ensure the independence of the prosecution service from partisan political influences, and reduce potential conflicts of interests within the Office of the Attorney General." Nova Scotia introduced such a system in 1990. See *Public Prosecutions Act*, SNS 1990, c 21.

Within contemporary Canadian criminal law, a key trend is toward increasing the number of offences that carry mandatory minimum sentences. In some instances, these minima apply automatically. In others, they require Crown counsel to decide whether to seek a minimum sentence. In the following case, the Supreme Court of Canada rejected the proposition that Crown counsel have a constitutional responsibility to consider the Aboriginal status of an accused when deciding whether to seek a mandatory minimum sentence.

R v Anderson
Supreme Court of Canada
2014 SCC 41, [2014] 2 SCR 167

MOLDAVER J:

I. Introduction

[1] This appeal raises the following question: Are Crown prosecutors constitutionally required to consider the Aboriginal status of an accused when deciding whether or not to seek a mandatory minimum sentence for impaired driving? The answer, in my view, must be no. There is no principle of fundamental justice that supports the existence of such a constitutional obligation. Absent such an obligation, the prosecutor's decision is a matter of prosecutorial discretion which is reviewable by the courts only for abuse of process.

[2] The present appeal involves a scheme of escalating, mandatory minimum sentences for impaired driving convictions. These mandatory minimums are set out in s. 255 of the *Criminal Code of Canada*, R.S.C. 1985, c. C-46 ("*Code*"). Section 727(1) of the *Code* states that the mandatory minimums set out in s. 255 are applicable only if the Crown, in advance of any plea, notifies the accused of its intention to seek a greater punishment by reason of previous convictions (the "Notice") and tenders proof at the sentencing hearing that the Notice was served. It is the Crown's discretionary decision to tender the Notice at the sentencing hearing that is the subject of the current debate.

[3] The respondent, Mr. Anderson, submits that the Crown is constitutionally obligated under s. 7 of the *Canadian Charter of Rights and Freedoms* to consider the accused's Aboriginal status in deciding whether or not to tender the Notice. According to Mr. Anderson, for sentencing purposes, consideration of Aboriginal status is a principle of fundamental justice. It follows that the Crown must consider it when making decisions that limit the sentencing options available to a judge.

[4] The Crown denies the existence of any such obligation. The Crown submits that the decision to tender the Notice is a matter of prosecutorial discretion. As such, it can only be reviewed for abuse of process. The Crown further submits that if mandatory minimum sentences within a statutory scheme prevent a judge from imposing a fit and just sentence that accords with the fundamental principle of proportionality, it is the scheme that should be challenged, not the exercise of prosecutorial discretion that has triggered it.

[5] For the reasons that follow, I conclude that Crown prosecutors are under no constitutional duty to consider the accused's Aboriginal status when tendering the Notice. As a matter of prosecutorial discretion, the decision is only reviewable for abuse of process.

. . .

[34] Having concluded that the Crown is not under a constitutional obligation to consider the accused's Aboriginal status when making a decision that limits the sentencing options available to a judge, the next question is whether the Crown's decision to tender the Notice is reviewable in some other way, and if so, under what standard.

(1) Review of Crown Decision Making

[35] There are two distinct avenues for judicial review of Crown decision making. The analysis will differ depending on which of the following is at issue: (1) exercises of prosecutorial discretion; or (2) tactics and conduct before the court.

[36] All Crown decision making is reviewable for abuse of process. However, as I will explain, exercises of prosecutorial discretion are *only* reviewable for abuse of process. In contrast, tactics and conduct before the court are subject to a wider range of review. The court may exercise its inherent jurisdiction to control its own processes even in the absence of abuse of process.

(a) Prosecutorial Discretion

[37] This Court has repeatedly affirmed that prosecutorial discretion is a necessary part of a properly functioning criminal justice system [citations omitted]. In *Miazga v. Kvello Estate*, 2009 SCC 51, [2009] 3 S.C.R. 339, at para. 47, the fundamental importance of prosecutorial discretion was said to lie, "not in protecting the interests of individual Crown attorneys, but in advancing the public interest by enabling prosecutors to make discretionary decisions in fulfilment of their professional obligations without fear of judicial or political interference, thus fulfilling their quasi-judicial role as 'ministers of justice.'" More recently, in *Sriskandarajah v. United States of America*, 2012 SCC 70, [2012] 3 S.C.R. 609, at para. 27, this Court observed that "[n]ot only does prosecutorial discretion accord with the principles of fundamental justice—it constitutes an indispensable device for the effective enforcement of the criminal law."

. . .

[39] In *Krieger*, this Court provided the following description of prosecutorial discretion:

> "Prosecutorial discretion" is a term of art. It does not simply refer to any discretionary decision made by a Crown prosecutor. Prosecutorial discretion refers to the use of those powers that constitute the core of the Attorney General's office and which are protected from the influence of improper political and other vitiating factors by the principle of independence. [para. 43]

[40] The Court went on to provide the following examples of prosecutorial discretion: whether to bring the prosecution of a charge laid by police; whether to enter a stay of proceedings in either a private or public prosecution; whether to accept a guilty plea to a lesser charge; whether to withdraw from criminal proceedings altogether; and whether to take control of a private prosecution (para. 46). The Court continued:

> Significantly, what is common to the various elements of prosecutorial discretion is that they involve the ultimate decisions as to whether a prosecution should be brought, continued or ceased, and what the prosecution ought to be for. *Put differently, prosecutorial discretion refers to decisions regarding the nature and extent of the prosecution and the Attorney General's participation in it.* Decisions that do not go to the nature and extent of the prosecution, i.e., the decisions that govern a Crown prosecutor's tactics or conduct before the court, do not fall within the scope of prosecutorial discretion. Rather, such decisions are governed by the

inherent jurisdiction of the court to control its own processes once the Attorney General has elected to enter into that forum. [Emphasis added; emphasis in original deleted; para. 47.]

. . .

[44] ... As this Court has repeatedly noted, "[p]rosecutorial discretion refers to the discretion exercised by the Attorney-General *in matters within his authority* in relation to the prosecution of criminal offences" (*Krieger*, at para. 44, citing *Power*, at p. 622, quoting D. Vanek, "Prosecutorial Discretion" (1988), 30 *Crim. L.Q.* 219, at p. 219 (emphasis added)). While it is likely impossible to create an exhaustive list of the decisions that fall within the nature and extent of a prosecution, further examples to those in *Krieger* include: the decision to repudiate a plea agreement (as in *R. v. Nixon*, 2011 SCC 34, [2011] 2 S.C.R. 566); the decision to pursue a dangerous offender application; the decision to prefer a direct indictment; the decision to charge multiple offences; the decision to negotiate a plea; the decision to proceed summarily or by indictment; and the decision to initiate an appeal. All pertain to the nature and extent of the prosecution. As can be seen, many stem from the provisions of the *Code* itself, including the decision in this case to tender the Notice.

[45] In sum, prosecutorial discretion applies to a wide range of prosecutorial decision making. That said, care must be taken to distinguish matters of prosecutorial discretion from constitutional obligations. The distinction between prosecutorial discretion and the constitutional obligations of the Crown was made in *Krieger*, where the prosecutor's duty to disclose relevant evidence to the accused was at issue:

> In *Stinchcombe* [[1991] 3 SCR 326], the Court held that the Crown has an obligation to disclose all relevant information to the defence. *While the Crown Attorney retains the discretion not to disclose irrelevant information, disclosure of relevant evidence is not, therefore, a matter of prosecutorial discretion but, rather, is a prosecutorial duty.* [Emphasis added; para. 54.]

Manifestly, the Crown possesses no discretion to breach the *Charter* rights of an accused. In other words, prosecutorial discretion provides no shield to a Crown prosecutor who has failed to fulfill his or her constitutional obligations such as the duty to provide proper disclosure to the defence.

(i) The Standard of Review for Prosecutorial Discretion

[46] The many decisions that Crown prosecutors are called upon to make in the exercise of their prosecutorial discretion must not be subjected to routine second-guessing by the courts. The courts have long recognized that decisions involving prosecutorial discretion are unlike other decisions made by the executive: see M. Code, "Judicial Review of Prosecutorial Decisions: A Short History of Costs and Benefits, in Response to Justice Rosenberg" (2009), 34 *Queen's L.J.* 863, at p. 867. Judicial non-interference with prosecutorial discretion has been referred to as a "matter of principle based on the doctrine of separation of powers as well as a matter of policy founded on the efficiency of the system of criminal justice" which also recognizes that prosecutorial discretion is "especially ill-suited to judicial review": *Power*, at p. 623. In *Krieger*, the Court discussed the separation of powers doctrine as a basis for judicial deference to prosecutorial discretion:

> In our theory of government, it is the sovereign who holds the power to prosecute his or her subjects. A decision of the Attorney General, or of his or her agents, within the authority

delegated to him or her by the sovereign is not subject to interference by other arms of government. An exercise of prosecutorial discretion will, therefore, be treated with deference by the courts and by other members of the executive. ... [para. 45]

[47] The Court also noted the more practical problems associated with regular review of prosecutorial discretion:

> The quasi-judicial function of the Attorney General cannot be subjected to interference from parties who are not as competent to consider the various factors involved in making a decision to prosecute. To subject such decisions to political interference, or to judicial supervision, could erode the integrity of our system of prosecution. [para. 32]

[48] Manifestly, prosecutorial discretion is entitled to considerable deference. It is not, however, immune from all judicial oversight. This Court has repeatedly affirmed that prosecutorial discretion is reviewable for abuse of process: *Krieger*, at para. 32; *Nixon*, at para. 31; *Miazga*, at para. 46.

[49] The jurisprudence pertaining to the review of prosecutorial discretion has employed a range of terminology to describe the type of prosecutorial conduct that constitutes abuse of process. In *Krieger*, this Court used the term "flagrant impropriety" (para. 49). In *Nixon*, the Court held that the abuse of process doctrine is available where there is evidence that the Crown's decision "undermines the integrity of the judicial process" or "results in trial unfairness" (para. 64). The Court also referred to "improper motive[s]" and "bad faith" in its discussion (para. 68).

[50] Regardless of the precise language used, the key point is this: abuse of process refers to Crown conduct that is egregious and seriously compromises trial fairness and/or the integrity of the justice system. Crown decisions motivated by prejudice against Aboriginal persons would certainly meet this standard.

· · ·

(ii) The Threshold Evidentiary Burden

[52] The burden of proof for establishing abuse of process lies on the claimant, who must prove it on a balance of probabilities: *Cook*, at para. 62; *R. v. O'Connor*, [1995] 4 S.C.R. 411, at para. 69, *per* L'Heureux-Dubé J.; *R. v. Jolivet*, 2000 SCC 29, [2000] 1 S.C.R. 751, at para. 19. However, given the unique nature of prosecutorial discretion—specifically, the fact that the Crown will typically (if not always) be the only party who will know *why* a particular decision was made, this Court in *Nixon* recognized that where prosecutorial discretion is challenged, the Crown may be required to provide reasons justifying its decision where the claimant establishes a proper evidentiary foundation: para. 60.

· · ·

(b) Tactics and Conduct Before the Court

[57] The second category in the framework for review of Crown activity was referred to in *Krieger* as "tactics or conduct before the court": para. 47. As stated in *Krieger*, "such decisions are governed by the inherent jurisdiction of the court to control its own processes once the Attorney General has elected to enter into that forum" (para. 47).

[58] Superior courts possess inherent jurisdiction to ensure that the machinery of the court functions in an orderly and effective manner: *R. v. Cunningham*, 2010 SCC 10,

[2010] 1 S.C.R. 331, at para. 18; *Ontario v. Criminal Lawyers' Association of Ontario*, 2013 SCC 43, [2013] 3 S.C.R. 3, at para. 26. Similarly, in order to function as courts of law, statutory courts have implicit powers that derive from the court's authority to control its own process: *Cunningham*, at para.18. This jurisdiction includes the power to penalize counsel for ignoring rulings or orders, or for inappropriate behaviour such as tardiness, incivility, abusive cross-examination, improper opening or closing addresses or inappropriate attire. Sanctions may include orders to comply, adjournments, extensions of time, warnings, cost awards, dismissals, and contempt proceedings.

[59] While deference is not owed to counsel who are behaving inappropriately in the courtroom, our adversarial system *does* accord a high degree of deference to the tactical decisions of counsel. In other words, while courts may sanction the conduct of the *litigants*, they should generally refrain from interfering with the conduct of the *litigation* itself. ...

[60] Crown counsel is entitled to have a trial strategy and to modify it as the trial unfolds, provided that the modification does not result in unfairness to the accused: *Jolivet*, at para. 21. Likewise, as this Court recently held in *R. v. Auclair*, 2014 SCC 6, [2014] 1 S.C.R. 83, a judge may exceptionally override a Crown tactical decision in order to prevent a *Charter* violation.

[61] Finally, as with all Crown decision making, courtroom tactics or conduct may amount to abuse of process, but abuse of process is not a precondition for judicial intervention as it is for matters of prosecutorial discretion.

VI. Conclusion

[62] Parliament has expressly conferred on the Crown the discretion to tender the Notice at the sentencing hearing through the governing provisions of the *Code*. This discretion is consistent with our constitutional traditions. As the Crown points out, tendering the Notice is not simply a decision as to what submissions will be made at a sentencing hearing (A.F., at para. 119). Tendering the Notice fundamentally alters the *extent* of prosecution—specifically, the extent of the jeopardy facing the accused. In this respect, the Crown's decision to tender the Notice is analogous to the decision to proceed with charges that attract a mandatory minimum sentence when other related offences have no mandatory minimum sentence; the decision to proceed by indictment rather than summary conviction when different mandatory minimum sentences are involved; and the decision to proceed by indictment rather than by summary conviction when that decision precludes certain sentencing options.

[63] For these reasons, I conclude that tendering the Notice is a matter of prosecutorial discretion. As a result, it is reviewable only for abuse of process. In the complete absence of any evidence to support it, Mr. Anderson's abuse of process argument must fail.

On the role of Crown counsel and the attorney general, see JLIJ Edwards, *The Law Officers of the Crown* (London: Sweet & Maxwell, 1964); JLIJ Edwards, *The Attorney-General, Politics and the Public Interest* (London: Sweet & Maxwell, 1984); P Stenning, *Appearing for the Crown* (Cowansville, Que: Brown Legal, 1986); I Scott, "Law, Policy, and the Role of the Attorney-General: Constancy and Change" (1989) 39 UTLJ 104; and K Roach, "The Attorney General and the Charter Revisited" (2002) 50 UTLJ 1.

Disclosure

Marshall's defence at his trial and his 1972 appeal was severely prejudiced by the fact that inconsistent statements that the "eyewitnesses" Pratico and Chant had made to the police and MacNeil's original 1971 statement to the police identifying Ebsary as the killer were not disclosed to the defence. If the same events occurred today, would there be disclosure?

Chapter IX, commentary 9 of the Canadian Bar Association's *Code of Professional Conduct* (Ottawa: CBA, 2009) outlines the ethical duties of the prosecutor:

> When engaged as a prosecutor, the lawyer's prime duty is not to seek a conviction, but to present before the trial court all available credible evidence relevant to the alleged crime in order that justice may be done through a fair trial upon the merits. The prosecutor exercises a public function involving much discretion and power and must act fairly and dispassionately. The prosecutor should not do anything that might prevent the accused from being represented by counsel or communicating with counsel and, to the extent required by law and accepted practice, should make timely disclosure to the accused or defence counsel (or to the court if the accused is not represented) of all relevant facts and known witnesses, whether tending to show guilt or innocence, or that would affect the punishment of the accused.

The Federation of Law Societies of Canada *Model Code of Professional Conduct* (Ottawa: FLSC, 2014) provides in rule 5.1-3 that "When acting as a prosecutor, a lawyer must act for the public and the administration of justice resolutely and honourably within the limits of the law while treating the tribunal with candour, fairness, courtesy and respect."

The Royal Commission on the Donald Marshall Jr. Prosecution recommended the enactment of *Criminal Code* provisions requiring disclosure. It stated:

> This decision of most American States to codify disclosure requirements is a good one. The approach reflected in current case law involves assessing each individual case of real or alleged non-disclosure to determine if it actually impairs the accused's constitutional right to make full answer and defence. We believe that such an *ad hoc* approach to disclosure means uncertainty and possible unfairness. The inability of an accused to adequately prepare a defence threatens the fairness of the criminal justice system, and it is desirable that as much discretion and subjectivity as possible be removed from decisions concerning disclosure.
>
> The fundamental interest in a fair trial of the accused requires that the accused receive from the Crown all information known to the Crown that might reasonably be considered useful to the accused. The Crown should have a positive and continuing duty to provide this information to the defence. It is immaterial whether or not defence counsel fails to request disclosure of the information in possession of the Crown, or indeed whether defence counsel is negligent in failing to do so. The circumstances of non-disclosure should not be permitted to affect adversely the fairness of the trial received by the accused. The focal point of the issue of fairness is the fact of disclosure of material evidence.
>
> We recommend that the Department of Attorney General of Nova Scotia urge the Federal Government to implement amendments to the *Criminal Code* of Canada as follows:
>
> 1. A justice shall not proceed with a criminal prosecution unless he is satisfied:
>   (a) that the accused has been given a copy of the information or indictment reciting the charge or charges against him in that prosecution; and
>   (b) that the accused has been advised of his right to disclosure.

2(1) Without request, the accused is entitled, before being called upon to elect the mode of trial or to plead to the charge of an indictable offence, whichever comes first, and thereafter:

(a) to receive a copy of his criminal record;

(b) to receive a copy of any statement made by him to a person in authority and recorded in writing or to inspect such a statement if it has been recorded by electronic means; and to be informed of the nature and content of any verbal statement alleged to have been made by the accused to a person in authority and to be supplied with any memoranda in existence pertaining thereto;

(c) to inspect anything that the prosecutor proposes to introduce as an exhibit and, where practicable, receive copies thereof;

(d) to receive a copy of any statement made by a person whom the prosecutor proposes to call as a witness or anyone who may be called as a witness, and recorded in writing or, in the absence of a statement, a written summary of the anticipated testimony of the proposed witness, or anyone who may be called as a witness;

(e) to receive any other material or information known to the Crown and which tends to mitigate or negate the defendant's guilt as to the offence charged, or which would tend to reduce his punishment therefore, notwithstanding that the Crown does not intend to introduce such material or information as evidence;

(f) to inspect the electronic recording of any statement made by a person whom the prosecutor proposes to call as a witness;

(g) to receive a copy of the criminal record of any proposed witness; and

(h) to receive, where not protected from disclosure by the law, the name and address of any other person who may have information useful to the accused, or other details enabling that person to be identified.

2(2) The disclosure contemplated in subsection (1), paragraphs (d), (e) and (h) shall be provided by the Crown and may be limited only where, upon an *inter partes* application by the prosecutor, supported by evidence showing a likelihood that such disclosure will endanger the life or safety of such person or interfere with the administration of justice, a justice having jurisdiction in the matter deems it just and proper.

2(3) Subsection (1) imposes a continuing obligation on the prosecutor to disclose the items as above provided.

3. Where a justice having jurisdiction in the matter is satisfied that there has not been compliance with the provisions of subsections 2(1) and 2(2) above, he shall, at the accused's request, adjourn the proceedings until, in his opinion, there has been compliance, and he may make such other order as he considers appropriate in the circumstances.

We recommend that until the proposed statutory amendments to the *Criminal Code* are effected, the Attorney General adopt and implement as a matter of policy the duties of disclosure reflected in the preceding recommendation.

The foregoing recommendations have not been enacted in the *Criminal Code*. The Supreme Court of Canada, however, has constitutionalized a broad right to disclosure under s 7 of the Charter in the following case.

R v Stinchcombe
Supreme Court of Canada
[1991] 3 SCR 326

SOPINKA J (La Forest, L'Heureux-Dubé, Gonthier, Cory, McLachlin, and Iacobucci JJ concurring): This appeal raises the issue of the Crown's obligation to make disclosure to the defence. A witness who gave evidence at the preliminary inquiry favourable to the accused was subsequently interviewed by agents for the Crown. Crown counsel decided not to call the witness and would not produce the statements obtained at the interview. The trial judge refused an application by the defence for disclosure on the ground that there was no obligation on the Crown to disclose the statements. The Court of Appeal affirmed the judgment at trial and the case is here with leave of this court.

It is difficult to justify the position which clings to the notion that the Crown has no legal duty to disclose all relevant information. The arguments against the existence of such a duty are groundless while those in favour, are, in my view, overwhelming. The suggestion that the duty should be reciprocal may deserve consideration by this court in the future but is not a valid reason for absolving the Crown of its duty. The contrary contention fails to take account of the fundamental difference in the respective roles of the prosecution and the defence. In *Boucher v. The Queen* (1955), 110 C.C.C. 263, [1955] S.C.R. 16, 20 C.R. 1, Rand J. states (at p. 270):

> It cannot be over-emphasized that the purpose of a criminal prosecution is not to obtain a conviction; it is to lay before a jury what the Crown considers to be credible evidence relevant to what is alleged to be a crime. Counsel have a duty to see that all available legal proof of the facts is presented: it should be done firmly and pressed to its legitimate strength, but it must also be done fairly. The role of prosecutor excludes any notion of winning or losing; his function is a matter of public duty than which in civil life there can be none charged with greater personal responsibility. It is to be efficiently performed with an ingrained sense of the dignity, the seriousness and the justness of judicial proceedings.

I would add that the fruits of the investigation which are in the possession of counsel for the Crown are not the property of the Crown for use in securing a conviction but the property of the public to be used to ensure that justice is done. In contrast, the defence has no obligation to assist the prosecution and is entitled to assume a purely adversarial role toward the prosecution. The absence of a duty to disclose can, therefore, be justified as being consistent with this role.

Other grounds advanced by advocates of the absence of a general duty to disclose all relevant information are that it would impose onerous new obligations on the Crown prosecutors resulting in increased delays in bringing accused persons to trial. This ground is not supported by the material in the record. As I have already observed, disclosure is presently being made on a voluntary basis. The extent of disclosure varies from province to province, from jurisdiction to jurisdiction and from prosecutor to prosecutor. The adoption of uniform, comprehensive rules for disclosure by the Crown would add to the work-load of some Crown counsel but this would be offset by the time saved which is now spent resolving disputes such as this one surrounding the extent of the Crown's obligation and dealing with matters that take the defence by surprise. In the latter case an adjournment is frequently the result of non-disclosure or more time is taken by a defence counsel who is not prepared. There is also compelling evidence that much time would be saved and, therefore, delays reduced by reason of the increase in guilty pleas, withdrawal of charges and shortening or waiver of preliminary hearings. ...

This review of the pros and cons with respect to disclosure by the Crown shows that there is no valid practical reason to support the position of the opponents of a broad duty of disclosure. Apart from the practical advantages to which I have referred, there is the overriding concern that failure to disclose impedes the ability of the accused to make full answer and defence. This common law right has acquired new vigour by virtue of its inclusion in s. 7 of the Canadian Charter of Rights and Freedoms as one of the principles of fundamental justice. ... The right to make full answer and defence is one of the pillars of criminal justice on which we heavily depend to ensure that the innocent are not convicted. Recent events have demonstrated that the erosion of this right due to non-disclosure was an important factor in the conviction and incarceration of an innocent person. In the Royal Commission on the Donald Marshall, Jr., Prosecution, Vol. 1: Findings and Recommendations (1989) (the "Marshall Commission Report"), the Commissioners found that prior inconsistent statements were not disclosed to the defence. This was an important contributing factor in the miscarriage of justice which occurred and led the Commission to state that "anything less than complete disclosure by the Crown falls short of decency and fair play" (Vol. 1 at p. 238). ...

With respect to what should be disclosed, the general principle to which I have referred is that all relevant information must be disclosed subject to the reviewable discretion of the Crown. The material must include not only that which the Crown intends to introduce into evidence but also that which it does not. No distinction should be made between inculpatory and exculpatory evidence. ... This obligation to disclose is not absolute. It is subject to the discretion of counsel for the Crown. This discretion extends both to the withholding of information and to the timing of disclosure. For example, counsel for the Crown has a duty to respect the rules of privilege. In the case of informers the Crown has a duty to protect their identity. In some cases serious prejudice or even harm may result to a person who has supplied evidence or information to the investigation. While it is a harsh reality of justice that ultimately any person with relevant evidence must appear to testify, the discretion extends to the timing and manner of disclosure in such circumstances. A discretion must also be exercised with respect to the relevance of information. While the Crown must err on the side of inclusion, it need not produce what is clearly irrelevant.

I am of the opinion that, subject to the discretion to which I have referred above, all statements obtained from persons who have provided relevant information to the authorities should be produced notwithstanding that they are not proposed as Crown witnesses. Where statements are not in existence, other information such as notes should be produced, and, if there are no notes, then in addition to the name, address and occupation of the witness, all information in the possession of the prosecution relating to any relevant evidence that the person could give should be supplied. ...

In this case, we are told that the witness gave evidence at the preliminary hearing favourable to the defence. The subsequent statements were not produced and, therefore, we have no indication from the trial judge as to whether they were favourable or unfavourable. Examination of the statements, which were tendered as fresh evidence in this court, should be carried out at trial so that counsel for the defence, in the context of the issues in the case and the other evidence, can explain what use might be made of them by the defence. In the circumstances, we must assume that non-production of the statements was an important factor in the decision not to call the witness. The absence of this evidence might very well have affected the outcome.

Accordingly, I would allow the appeal and direct a new trial at which the statements should be produced.

Plea Bargaining and Guilty Pleas

Because of Donald Marshall Jr.'s insistence on his innocence, plea bargaining was not a factor in the *Marshall* case. Is it possible Marshall's lawyers might have pleaded him guilty if they had been offered a manslaughter charge even if Marshall maintained his innocence? What should a court do in deciding whether to accept a guilty plea? In *Brosseau v The Queen*, [1969] SCR 181 at 185 the Supreme Court affirmed a guilty plea to non-capital murder even though the accused's own lawyer had to communicate with his client with a Cree interpreter and shockingly told the trial court when pleading his client guilty that "[t]he accused is describable only in terms of an absolute primitive. I don't pretend to have any particular understanding of his mind or of his intent." The accused sought to reopen the guilty plea on the basis that he had only pleaded guilty because he was scared of being hanged, but the Supreme Court ruled that because he was represented by counsel the trial judge was not required by law "to interrogate the accused" (at 190). In both that case and *R v Adgey*, [1975] 2 SCR 426 there were strong dissents maintaining that the trial judge should play a more active role in deciding whether to accept a guilty plea, a role that in some cases might involve an inquiry into not only whether a plea was voluntary but whether it was also factually accurate.

A number of wrongful convictions have been discovered following a guilty plea. For a case in which a guilty plea from a mentally disabled accused was accepted, and DNA subsequently revealed he was not guilty of the sexual assaults for which he was convicted, see *Marshall c R*, 2005 QCCA 852. In *R v Hanemaayer*, 2008 ONCA 580, a conviction of breaking and entering and assault, after an accused pleaded guilty when the homeowner identified him as the perpetrator, was overturned by the Court of Appeal on the basis of fresh evidence indicating that another person had committed the crime. In the latter case, Rosenberg JA explained that the accused had pleaded guilty because

> [11] … he lost his nerve. He found the homeowner to be a very convincing witness and he could tell that his lawyer was not making any headway in convincing the judge otherwise. Further, since his wife had left him and wanted nothing more to do with him, he had no one to support his story that he was home at the time of the offence. He says that his lawyer told him he would almost certainly be convicted and would be sentenced to six years imprisonment or more. However, if he changed his plea, his lawyer said he could get less than two years and would not go to the penitentiary. The appellant agreed to accept the deal even though he was innocent and had told his lawyer throughout that he was innocent.
>
> ⋯
>
> [17] … [T]o constitute a valid guilty plea, the plea must be voluntary, unequivocal and informed. There is no suggestion in this case that the appellant's plea almost twenty years ago did not meet these requirements. While the appellant speaks of advice from his lawyer to plead guilty, the fresh evidence makes clear that in the end the appellant came to his own decision. His

plea was unequivocal and he understood the nature of the charges he faced as well as the consequences of his plea.

[18] On the other hand, the court cannot ignore the terrible dilemma facing the appellant. He had spent eight months in jail awaiting trial and was facing the prospect of a further six years in the penitentiary if he was convicted. The estimate of six years was not unrealistic given the seriousness of the offence. The justice system held out to the appellant a powerful inducement that by pleading guilty he would not receive a penitentiary sentence.

· · ·

[30] ... I also repeat what we said to Mr. Hanemaayer at the conclusion of the hearing:

It is profoundly regrettable that errors in the justice system led to this miscarriage of justice and the devastating effect it has had on Mr. Hanemaayer and his family.

Other wrongful convictions following guilty pleas resulted from the faulty testimony of Dr. Charles Smith as to the cause of death of a number of infants, in cases in which prosecutors and judges accepted pleas to manslaughter or infanticide—which, unlike murder, do not carry a mandatory sentence of life imprisonment. See *R v Brant*, 2011 ONCA 362; *R v Sheratt-Robinson*, 2009 ONCA 886; *R v CM*, 2010 ONCA 690; and *R v CF*, 2010 ONCA 691. In *R v Kumar*, 2011 ONCA 120, the Court of Appeal concluded:

[34] [E]ven though an appellant's plea of guilty appears to meet all the traditional tests for a valid guilty plea, the court retains a discretion, to be exercised in the interests of justice, to receive fresh evidence to explain the circumstances that led to the guilty plea and that demonstrate a miscarriage of justice occurred. In our view, this is one of those cases. The circumstances are compelling. At the time he pleaded guilty, the appellant was facing a charge of second degree murder. He was relatively new to Canada and was unfamiliar with the language and the legal system. At the time of the infant's death, his wife had just returned from hospital after major surgery for a brain tumour. He was facing loss of his liberty for at least ten years, loss of custody of his remaining child and deportation. Competent counsel had been unable to obtain opinion evidence to refute the opinion of the then leading expert in the province [Dr. Smith] that the appellant had intentionally caused the death of his child. Like in *Hanemaayer*, the appellant faced a terrible dilemma. The justice system now held out a powerful inducement: a reduced charge, a much-reduced sentence (90 days instead of a minimum of ten years), all but the elimination of the possibility of deportation, and access to his surviving child. Given the persuasive value of the fresh expert evidence that shows that the conviction was unreasonable, this is a proper case to set aside the guilty plea to avoid a miscarriage of justice.

For a discussion of the complex scientific and cultural issues that can arise in baby death cases, especially those in which female caregivers are charged, see E Cunliffe, *Murder, Medicine and Motherhood* (Oxford: Hart, 2011). A number of the Dr. Smith cases are described at Association in Defence of the Wrongly Convicted, "Historical Cases," at <http://www.aidwyc .org/cases/historical/>. See also J Brockman, "An Offer You Can't Refuse: Pleading Guilty When Innocent" (2010) 56 Crim LQ 116. Plea bargaining in general is discussed in a special issue at (2005) 50 Crim LQ 1-212.

Would it have been proper in the face of Marshall's claims of innocence for the prosecutor to have offered him a plea bargain to a charge of manslaughter? Would it have been proper for defence counsel to have recommended that Marshall accept such a plea?

In the United States, an accused can plead guilty to a crime while maintaining innocence, something done in many cases to avoid a higher penalty. In *North Carolina v Alford*, 400 US 25 (1970), the US Supreme Court held it constitutionally permissible if there is a strong factual basis for the plea and it represents a voluntary and intelligent choice among the alternatives open to the accused. Should this sort of plea bargaining be allowed in Canada?

In *R v Hector* (2000), 146 CCC (3d) 81, the Ontario Court of Appeal refused to allow an accused to withdraw his guilty plea to three counts of first-degree murder even though he maintained his innocence, and even though the agreement provided that the Crown would not charge the accused's wife with obstruction of justice and would allow the accused to have a one-hour meeting with her. But the case was decided before the following provisions were added to the *Criminal Code*. Given these provisions, should *Hector* still be considered good law?

> 606(1.1) A court may accept a plea of guilty only if it is satisfied that the accused
>> (a) is making the plea voluntarily; and
>> (b) understands
>>> (i) that the plea is an admission of the essential elements of the offence,
>>> (ii) the nature and consequences of the plea, and
>>> (iii) that the court is not bound by any agreement made between the accused and the prosecutor.
>
> (1.2) The failure of the court to fully inquire whether the conditions set out in subsection (1.1) are met does not affect the validity of the plea.

No Contest or Nolo Contendere Pleas

Given the above, should courts allow an accused essentially to plead no contest? The Ontario Court of Appeal in *R v G(DM)* (2011), 275 CCC (3d) 295 reversed a conviction in a case in which a defence lawyer pleaded his hearing-impaired client not guilty, but also invited the court to convict on the basis of the Crown's reading in a summary of the allegations of sexual crimes, after which the accused and the Crown made joint submissions about the appropriate sentence. The Court of Appeal concluded:

> [118] A miscarriage of justice occurred in this case. The proceedings were encumbered by procedural unfairness. The practical effect of what occurred was that the appellant, who pleaded not guilty, essentially admitted the full sweep of the prosecutor's allegations that he had consistently denied since arrest. Yet none of the safeguards that we associate with either formal admissions or pleas of guilty were evident in the rush to judgment that occurred here. A hasty, ill-informed volte face from an outright denial to a veiled acceptance of everything alleged in the blink of an eye as trial proceedings were about to begin.
>
> [119] What occurred here also raises questions about the reliability of the conclusion of guilt that rests upon allegations untested in the crucible of cross-examination because of inadequate trial preparation by the appellant's former counsel.

In another case, however, the Ontario Court of Appeal distinguished *G(DM)* by stating that the fact that the accused "asserted innocence and did not admit guilt to his counsel does not invalidate these proceedings any more than it would vitiate a plea of guilty. Unlike the appellant in *G(DM)*, this appellant does not say he wanted to testify to deny the allegations, but the procedure followed denied him that opportunity. ... The flaw in *G(DM)* was in the execution": *R v RP*, 2013 ONCA 53, 295 CCC (3d) 28.

Aside from the legality or advisability of a no contest plea not provided for in the Code, what are the ethical implications of a defence lawyer pleading an accused who maintains his innocence guilty? Would this breach ethical rules against misleading the court and offering false evidence? Would it breach other ethical rules about providing competent and adversarial representation to clients?

The lawyer in *G(DM)* was subsequently disciplined by the Law Society in relation to the no contest matters and other matters involving inadequate preparation. The Disciplinary Tribunal found the lawyer guilty of misleading the court. The Appeal Division of the Disciplinary Tribunal in *Law Society of Upper Canada v Besant*, 2014 ONLSTA 50 reversed this finding, given the Ontario Court of Appeal's apparent acceptance of no contest pleas. Nevertheless it held that the lawyer had breached standards related to providing competent services in accepting the Crown's allegations by holding:

> [125] ... It was a serious lapse of Mr. Besant's [the defence lawyer] responsibility to give no consideration to what facts would form the basis of the *nolo-contendere* [no contest] procedure, or as the hearing panel stated, to take any steps to see that the allegations read in by the Crown were properly limited, and did not extend to 99 occurrences. It was a serious lapse of Mr. Besant's responsibility not to even discuss with the client what facts would be read into the record by the Crown, which would remain undisputed. ...

> [126] ... There was no guarantee that the joint submission [by the accused and Crown] would be accepted [by the trial judge]. But even if there was a high probability that the joint submission would be accepted, the allegations read into the record effectively became the facts in the case. The transcript of the proceedings would be available to the provincial parole board and potentially affect post-sentencing issues. The facts might be relevant in any subsequent legal proceedings involving DG. The hearing panel accurately reflected that an accused who is adamant as to his innocence and participates in a *nolo-contendere*-like process requires more, not less, protection than someone pleading guilty.

> • • •

> [130] Notwithstanding the existing jurisprudence, there are compelling reasons why a defence counsel should be extremely reluctant to assist with what is functionally a guilty plea when the client asserts his or her innocence. The potential for a wrongful conviction of a factually innocent client is obvious. Indeed, there have been a number of identified instances in the jurisprudence of individuals who have pleaded guilty or who did not contest criminal charges for pragmatic reasons, where their innocence was later demonstrated or where the basis for their guilt was subsequently undermined.

> [131] Second, although the Court of Appeal cited jurisprudence that countenanced even a guilty plea by an accused who maintains his or her innocence when the plea is voluntary, unequivocal and fully informed, we have doubts whether defence counsel should ever participate in such a plea. A court must be satisfied that the preconditions set out in s. 606(1.1) of the *Criminal Code*, earlier reproduced, exist. The difficulty in reconciling those preconditions with a guilty plea by someone asserting innocence has been addressed in the jurisprudence already cited. As well, the trial court conventionally asks the accused on a guilty plea whether the facts read in by the prosecutor are "substantially correct." Counsel will often answer affirmatively on the client's behalf or invite the accused to confirm that the facts are substantially correct. In our view, for the

purposes of possible Law Society disciplinary proceedings, it is potentially misleading for counsel to participate in advising a court that the facts are substantially correct, knowing that his or her client says that the facts are incorrect. That would arguably be an instance in which counsel is knowingly presenting the client's position to the court in a misleading way.

Although a judge may "conventionally" ask whether the facts behind a guilty plea are correct, this is not a requirement in s 606(1.1). Should it be? In addition to the ethical issues raised when a defence lawyer participates in a guilty plea by an accused who maintains innocence, what are the ethical implications for a Crown that offers such a plea and a judge who accepts such a plea?

Defence Counsel

Consider the role of the defence counsel. If Donald Marshall Jr. had told his lawyers that he and Seale were asking Ebsary and MacNeil for money, what should they have done? What if Marshall had told his lawyer (contrary to the royal commission's findings) that they planned to rob Ebsary and MacNeil?

The Manitoba Aboriginal Justice Inquiry concluded:

> Our survey of inmates revealed that Aboriginal inmates spend considerably less time with their lawyers. In fact, Aboriginal accused are more likely than non-Aboriginal accused to appear in court without a lawyer. While 61% of Aboriginal respondents saw their lawyers three or fewer times, 63% of non-Aboriginal respondents saw their lawyers four or more times. Forty-eight per cent of the Aboriginal respondents spent less than an hour in total with their lawyers, compared to 46% of non-Aboriginal inmates who saw their lawyers for three or more hours. The lack of time spent with a lawyer can have significant consequences for how an accused is dealt with in the system, because the lawyer may be less informed about the circumstances of the offence, the potential defences and the resources available as alternatives to detention.

Do you think the chances for effective representation are better under the "judicare" system used in some provinces in which a qualified accused obtains a certificate to pay for the lawyer he or she prefers, or a "public defender" system with full-time salaried defence lawyers? Another alternative is publicly funded legal aid clinics designed to service particular communities.

Chapter IX, commentaries 10 and 11 of the Canadian Bar Association's *Code of Professional Conduct* (2009) provide as follows:

Duties of Defence Counsel

10. When defending an accused person, the lawyer's duty is to protect the client as far as possible from being convicted except by a court of competent jurisdiction and upon legal evidence sufficient to support a conviction for the offence charged. Accordingly, and notwithstanding the lawyer's private opinion as to credibility or merits, the lawyer may properly rely upon all available evidence or defences including so-called technicalities not known to be false or fraudulent.

11. Admissions made by the accused to the lawyer may impose strict limitations on the conduct of the defence and the accused should be made aware of this. For example, if the accused clearly admits to the lawyer the factual and mental elements necessary to constitute the offence, the lawyer, if convinced that the admissions are true and voluntary, may properly take objection

to the jurisdiction of the court, or to the form of the indictment, or to the admissibility or suffi-ciency of the evidence, but must not suggest that some other person committed the offence, or call any evidence that, by reason of the admissions, the lawyer believes to be false. Nor may the lawyer set up an affirmative case inconsistent with such admissions, for example, by calling evi-dence in support of an alibi intended to show that the accused could not have done, or in fact had not done, the act. Such admissions will also impose a limit upon the extent to which the lawyer may attack the evidence for the prosecution. The lawyer is entitled to test the evidence given by each individual witness for the prosecution and argue that the evidence taken as a whole is insufficient to amount to proof that the accused is guilty of the offence charged, but the lawyer should go no further than that.

To similar effect see the commentary to rule 5.1-1 of the Federation of Law Societies of Can-ada *Model Code of Professional Conduct* (2014).

The following extract is dated, but it still demonstrates some of the ethical issues facing defence lawyers and how one lawyer failed to resolutely represent and keep the confidences of an Aboriginal accused in the Australian case of *Tuckiar v The King* (1934), 52 CLR 335.

Law Society of Upper Canada, "Defending a Criminal Case"
(1969)

CHIEF JUSTICE GALE: … What is the position of counsel when defending a client who has admitted his guilt?

1. What restrictions does this place upon the conduct of the trial by counsel?
2. Assume that counsel has explained the limitations which the client's admission imposes on counsel and the client agrees to permit counsel to defend him in accordance with these limitations but during the trial he insists upon giving evidence and gets into the witness box.

Mr. Sedgwick, would you take this on?

MR SEDGWICK: Yes sir.

The question is, as to a client who has admitted his guilt. Guilt is a question of mixed law and fact. …

The client who admits his guilt may only be saying that he did something and in law he may not be guilty of any offence, or at least he may not be guilty of the offence with which he is charged. However, assuming that the guilt of the accused seems reasonably clear, counsel is still entitled to put forward any defence available. As for instance such legal or technical defences as may go to the form of the indictment, limitations, etc. He may not, however, put forward a lying defence, such as an alibi, nor *a fortiori* may he put forward any defence that goes to prove that some person other than the accused is the guilty party. This he must explain to his client so that he will not misunderstand the eth-ical limitations to which counsel is subject, and he should get the client's concurrence to the proposed course of conduct.

As to the second part of the question, … [t]he accused has the right to give evidence and counsel has no right to prevent him although he may and, of course, should give his opinion as to the wisdom of that course. The case of *Tuckiar v. The King* (1934), 52 C.L.R.

335 is an illuminating one and in that case—it was a murder case—the defence called no evidence, and following a verdict of Guilty, counsel said in open court, and before sentence:

> I would like to state publicly that I have had an interview with the convicted prisoner, Tuckiar, in the presence of an interpreter. I asked him to tell the interpreter which was the true story. I asked him why he told the other story. He told me he was too much worried so he told a different story and that story was a lie. As an advocate, I did not deem it advisable to put the accused in the box.

That, I think, was bad enough but the trial judge made matters worse by following with this. He said:

> It did not occur to me at the time but I think I should have stated publicly that immediately on that confession being made to you, you and the protector of the Aborigines consulted me and asked my opinion as to the proper course for you, as counsel, to take and I then told you that if your client had been a white man—he was by the way an Aborigine—and had made a confession of guilt to you, I thought your proper course would have been to withdraw from the case; but as your client was an Aborigine and there might be some remnant of doubt as to whether his confession to you was any more reliable than any other confession he had made, the better course would be for you to continue to appear for him because if you had retired from the case it would have left it open to ignorant, malicious and irresponsible persons to say that this native had been abandoned and left without any proper defence.

It was an amazing performance. You will be pleased to know that the High Court of Australia quashed the conviction and discharged the accused and in doing so they made some very sensible comments about the duties and obligations of counsel. What that Court said was this:

> Counsel seems to have taken the course calculated to transfer to the judge the embarrassment which he appears to have so much felt. Why he should have conceived himself to have been in so grave a predicament, it is not easy for those experienced in advocacy to understand. Counsel had a plain duty both to his client and the court to press such rational considerations that the evidence fairly gave rise to in favour of complete acquittal or conviction of manslaughter only. Whether he be in fact guilty or not, a prisoner is, in point of law, entitled to acquittal from any charge which the evidence fails to establish he committed and it is not incumbent on his counsel by abandoning his defence to deprive him of the benefit of such rational arguments that fairly arise on the proofs submitted.

And then as to the subsequent disclosure of the communication made to him, the Court said:

> The subsequent action of the prisoner's counsel in openly disclosing the privileged communication of his client and acknowledging the correctness of more serious testimony against him is wholly indefensible. It was his paramount duty to respect the privilege attaching to the communication made to him as counsel, a duty the obligation of which was by no means weakened by the character of his client or the moment which he chose to make the disclosure. He was not entitled to divulge what he had learnt from the prisoner as his counsel. Our system

of administering justice fairly imposes on those who practise advocacy duties which have no analogies and the system cannot dispense with their strict observance.

A situation in point arose in Canada as recently as 1965 in the *Colpitts* case [1965] S.C.R. 739, and I quote very briefly from what Mr. Justice Spence said there. He said:

> It must be remembered that counsel for the appellant before calling the appellant as the only witness for the defence stated to the Learned Trial Judge in the presence of the jury ... "My Lord, yes, I am going to call one witness for the defence and that will be Reginald Colpitts, the accused. And Sir, I must, as a matter of professional ethics, do assert that this is going to happen against my better judgment and counsel. But Mr. Colpitts has decided to take the stand and I, of course, will act as examiner."

Of this Mr. Justice Spence said:

> As I have pointed out above, the learned trial judge in his charge gave to the jury two conclusions suggesting that they choose the more logical and one of them was framed in the words "and that after two months of deliberation he would have *concocted* the story that he insisted on telling you yesterday."

Mr. Justice Spence went on:

> I am of the opinion that that portion of the charge, when considered in the light of the remarks of the then counsel for the appellant which I have quoted could only suggest, and strongly suggest to the jury that they could place no reliance upon the evidence given by the appellant in his defence.

Reverting to my own voice, it is my view that counsel was ill-advised to make any such statement. He should merely have said the accused wishes to give evidence. Any reference to his own better judgment or to the advice that he had given his client was, in my view, improper and it was a breach of his obligations as counsel; and lastly, of course, what the client tells counsel may or may not be true. I have had clients tell me things and I have said, "For all I know, somebody may believe it—I can't." And you know, he may be merely trying it on for effect. But certainly he is not when talking to his counsel in any sense under oath and so if he elects to take the box and be sworn, you have no right to assume that he will commit perjury. I took longer than I should have done, Chief Justice, but that is at least my longest answer.

David Layton and Michel Proulx in *Ethics and Canadian Criminal Law*, 2nd ed (Toronto: Irwin Law, 2015) at 43-44 (footnotes omitted) deal with the case of *Colpitts* as follows:

> Counsel's knowledge concerning the guilt of the client frequently comes from confidential information, most often in the form of a client confession. In such a case, counsel is bound by the duty of confidentiality owed to the client and is prohibited from sharing the information with anyone. Sadly, this duty has not always been followed. The [lawyer] in ... *Tuckiar* ... acted improperly by sharing information of [his] client's guilt with the presiding judge and others. Taking such actions not only violates the client's confidence but may compromise the fact-finder's ability to try the case fairly.

It is equally unacceptable to reveal a client's incriminating confidences by way of suggestive comment or to make statements that imply impropriety on the part of the client. The resulting harm to the client can be seen in the Supreme Court of Canada case *R v Colpitts*. There, the accused had made inculpatory statements to the police in relation to a charge of murdering a prison guard. At trial, he testified that these statements to police were untrue, explaining that he had been trying to protect the real killer, who was a friend at the time. The accused's testimony was likely sabotaged in advance, however, by defence counsel's damning pronouncement to the judge and jury, made just prior to calling his client to the stand:

> My Lord, yes, I am going to call one witness for the defence, and that will be Reginald Colpitts, the accused. And sir, I must—as a matter of professional ethics—do assert that this is going to happen against my better judgment and counsel. ...

This pronouncement was ill-advised, raising the real possibility that the client had admitted guilt to counsel but was nonetheless insistent on taking the stand and committing perjury. Justice Spence, who penned the majority reasons in *Colpitts*, stated that these remarks in conjunction with the trial judge's charges "could only suggest, and strongly suggest, to the jury that they could place no reliance upon the evidence given by the appellant in his defence."

The authors go on to make recommendations about how lawyers should react to both anticipated and completed client perjury. They recommend that counsel should first attempt to convince the client not to engage in perjury and inform the client of the serious adverse consequences that can flow from perjury including the lawyer's remedies, which in their view may include withdrawal of the lawyer from the case and even disclosure by the lawyer if the client actually commits perjury and does not retract the false testimony. They conclude at 370-71 (footnotes omitted):

> There is good reason to deny a client the benefits of the duties of loyalty and confidentiality where he has abused the solicitor-client relationship in an effort to pervert the course of justice. In our opinion, disclosure is therefore justified *from a policy point of view* where perjury has occurred and where the client refuses to correct the falsehood. This is the position taken in the ABA Model Rules and the Third Restatement, both of which expressly require counsel to make disclosure of a client's completed perjury on a material matter.
>
> Yet the majority of Canadian ethical codes appear to preclude counsel from disclosing a completed client perjury to the court. ... [T]he confidentiality rules adopted by most governing bodies contain no exception that would allow disclosure for the purpose of remedying a client's perjury. In particular, these rules permit disclosure to prevent future harm but only where the harm involves death or serious bodily injury, a precondition that will almost never be met in the client-perjury scenario.

Although solicitor–client privilege is zealously protected, a number of exceptions have been recognized, including (1) when it must be revealed as the only means to demonstrate the innocence of the accused, (2) when the communications themselves are criminal in nature, and (3) for public safety reasons relating to a clear and serious risk of serious harm to an identifiable person or group of people. See *Smith v Jones*, [1999] 1 SCR 455 and *R v McClure*, 2001 SCC 14, [2001] 1 SCR 445.

For a further discussion of the ethical problems involved in defending a guilty person, see MM Orkin, "Defence of One Known to Be Guilty" (1958) 1 Crim LQ 170; WH Simon, "The Ethics of Criminal Defence" (1993) 91 Mich L Rev 1703; MH Freedman, "Professional Responsibility of the Criminal Defense Lawyer: The Three Hardest Questions" (1966) 64 Mich L Rev 1469; MH Freedman, *Lawyers' Ethics in an Adversary System* (Indianapolis, Ind: Bobbs Merrill, 1975), critically reviewed by RD Rotunda in (1976) 89 Harv L Rev 622; and MH Freedman, "Client Confidences and Client Perjury: Some Unanswered Questions" (1988) 136 U Pa L Rev 1939.

III. PRE-TRIAL RELEASE AND BAIL

Sandy Seale died May 29, 1971. Donald Marshall Jr. was arrested and charged with his murder on Friday, June 4, 1971. He was denied bail and held in jail during his preliminary hearing and trial. How might this have affected his trial? Marshall's pre-trial detention occurred before the introduction of the *Bail Reform Act*, RSC 1970 (2nd Supp), c 2, proclaimed in 1972 and now found in part XVI of the *Criminal Code*. In addition to the 1972 reforms, s 11(e) of the Charter now provides that those charged with an offence have the right not to be denied reasonable bail without just cause.

Would Marshall have been released under the current law? What conditions short of cash bail could have been designed to secure the goals of ensuring that the accused attend trial and not commit criminal offences in the time before trial? Could his release on bail have helped prevent his wrongful conviction? Because he was charged with murder, Marshall, not the Crown, would have to show cause why his detention was not justified, and he could only be released after a bail hearing in the superior court as opposed to regular bail hearings held before justices of the peace. See *Criminal Code*, s 522.

The Manitoba Aboriginal Justice Inquiry stated:

Studies of Provincial Court data reveal that:

- Aboriginal charged persons were 1.34 times more likely (55% versus 41% of non-Aboriginal charged persons) to be held in pre-trial detention.
- Of adult males between the ages of 18 and 34, Aboriginal persons spent approximately 1.5 times longer in pre-trial detention.
- Aboriginal charged women aged 18–34 were 2.4 times (48% compared to 20% of non-Aboriginal charged women) more likely to be held in pre-trial detention.
- In Winnipeg, Aboriginal detained persons spent more than twice as long in pre-trial detention as non-Aboriginal persons. Of persons held in pre-trial detention but subsequently released on bail, Aboriginal persons spent more time in custody before release.
- Aboriginal youth in pre-trial detention were detained an average of 29.3 days, compared to 10.8 days for non-Aboriginal youth.

The *Report of the Commission on Systemic Racism in the Ontario Criminal Justice System* (1995) found that

while white people were imprisoned before trial at about the same rate as after sentence (approximately 329 per 100,000 persons in the population before trial, and 334 after sentence), the pre-trial admission rate of black people was twice their sentenced admission rate (approximately 2,136 per 100,000 before trial, and 1,051 after sentence) ....

Excessive detention of untried accused was documented in Martin Friedland's 1965 study of Toronto courts [*Detention Before Trial* (Toronto: University of Toronto Press, 1965)], and subsequent *Criminal Code* amendments were intended to reduce imprisonment of untried persons. Nevertheless, every year in Ontario tens of thousands of untried accused spend time behind bars. In 1992/93, for example, 41,195 (49%) of a total of 83,405 admissions to Ontario prisons were unsentenced prisoners, of whom the vast majority had not been tried. By 1993/94, these remand admissions (46,151) amounted to 54% of total admissions (86,022) to provincial prisons ... .

In effect, these findings are evidence of the state exercising discretion as if it has more compelling reasons to imprison black adult males before their trials than white adult males charged with the same offences. This bias may reflect explicit beliefs that black men cannot be trusted to appear for trial, or are more dangerous or criminal than white men. But it could also arise from more implicit and subtle assumptions, since important characteristics of the release process are likely to promote stereotypical decision-making.

As presently organized, the bail system demands fast decisions, sometimes made within minutes, and it expects both the police and bail justices to make predictions based on vague criteria and information that is often inadequate. These features obviously do not compel decision-makers to rely on racial or other stereotypes, nor in any way excuse such reliance. But they establish conditions in which reliance on stereotypes, perhaps subconsciously, may make decisions easier. For example, a justice who assumes that police testimony about drug charges is seldom mistaken and that most black males charged with drug offences sell drugs for profit may quickly conclude at a bail hearing that a specific black male accused is likely to offend before trial. By drawing on such assumptions, the justice avoids the more difficult task of attempting to predict the likely behaviour of that individual.

The Commission's research suggests that in practice, the exception for charges laid under the *Narcotic Control Act* [see now *Controlled Drugs and Substances Act*] may be contributing significantly to disproportionate imprisonment of untried black accused. This exception arose out of a perceived need to strengthen law enforcement to combat the drug trade at the top of the drug distribution pyramid. In practice, however, the vast majority of trafficking and importing charges under the *Narcotic Control Act* are laid against minor actors in the drug trade. Most people charged with trafficking offences are petty "street traders" whose activities are a nuisance to local residents and business. A large proportion of persons charged with importing are small-scale couriers, often women, whose participation in the drug trade is likely limited. Because such people are easily replaced by those who control drug supplies, imprisonment of minor dealers and couriers has a negligible impact on the availability of illegal drugs to users.

The commission's recommendations concerning pre-trial detention included the following:

- require police officers and officers in charge to explain in writing why the accused was not released;
- require the relevance of any reference to the accused's immigration status, nationality, race, ethnicity, religion, place of origin, or birth to be explained to a Crown attorney;
- use legal aid to fund bail interview officers to help accused prepare for bail hearings;
- repeal the reverse onus for those charged with importing, trafficking, and related offences;
- direct Crown attorneys to eliminate irrelevant references to immigration and citizenship status and be aware of the dangers of inadvertent discrimination in relying on

factors such as residence and employment history to predict whether the accused will appear in court, and do not consider roots in the community with respect to the secondary ground for detention;

- direct Crown attorneys to ensure that cash bail is not set too high and that unnecessary and intrusive conditions such as "carry bail papers" are not imposed;
- provide increased training for justices of peace and judges regarding bail and how to avoid assumptions that may subtly discriminate against racialized people;
- make better use of interpreters at bail hearings and for the accused's meetings with counsel; and
- develop bail supervision programs.

Note that since this 1996 report, an increased percentage of accused have been denied bail.

The Canadian Civil Liberties Association in *Set Up to Fail: Bail and the Revolving Door of Pre-Trial Detention* (2014), available at <http://ccla.org/wordpress/wp-content/uploads/2014/07/Set-up-to-fail-FINAL.pdf>, noted that since 2005 more than half of those detained in provincial facilities for those serving sentences of less than two years were people awaiting trial. The study also found that people awaiting trial who are granted bail are increasingly subject to strict conditions and cash sureties. The association found that these practices had disproportionate effects on Aboriginal people, other racialized groups, the poor, and those suffering from mental illness.

Because Donald Marshall Jr. was charged with murder, an offence listed under s 469, he could not be released under the present s 522(2) (formerly s 457.7(2)) unless he was able to show cause why his continued detention was not justified. Section 522(2) provides:

> (2) Where an accused is charged with an offence listed in section 469, a judge of or a judge presiding in a superior court of criminal jurisdiction for the province in which the accused is charged shall order that the accused be detained in custody unless the accused, having been given a reasonable opportunity to do so, shows cause why his detention in custody is not justified within the meaning of subsection 515(10).

In the following cases, two courts of appeal reached opposite conclusions on whether this onus on the accused in s 522(2) violated s 11(e) of the Charter.

R v Bray
Ontario Court of Appeal
(1983), 2 CCC (3d) 325

MARTIN JA: The *Bail Reform Act*, 1970-71-72 (Can.), c. 37, introduced a liberal and enlightened system of pre-trial release. The object of the legislation clearly was to reduce pre-trial detention consistent with securing the attendance of the accused at his trial and the protection of the public interest. Counsel for the appellant stated that he was not challenging in this review that the primary and secondary grounds for detention specified in s. 457(7) [now s 515(10)] constitute "just cause" for the detention of an accused within s. 11(e) of the Charter.

In general, under the *Code*, the onus is on the prosecution to justify the detention of the accused on either the primary or secondary ground specified in s. 457(7). [The primary ground relates to the accused's attendance at trial while the secondary ground relates to the likelihood that the accused will commit offences if released pending trial.] However, after some four years of experience with the new legislation, Parliament, in response to concern by some segments of the public, by the *Criminal Law Amendment Act*, 1974-75-76 (Can.), c. 93, modified the original legislation by placing the onus on the accused in a limited number of offences, including murder, to show that his detention is not justified: see *R. v. Quinn* (1977), 34 C.C.C. (2d) 473 at p. 476, 34 N.S.R. (2d) 481.

In our view, the reverse onus provision in s. 457.7(2)(f) does not contravene the provisions of s. 11(e) of the Charter. Section 11(e) provides that a person charged with a criminal offence shall not be denied bail without "just cause." The primary and secondary grounds specified in s. 457(7) clearly constitute "just cause." Section 11(e) does not address the issue of onus and says nothing about onus. Further, the legal rights guaranteed by the Charter are not absolute and under s. 1 are subject to:

> … such reasonable limits prescribed by law as can be demonstrably justified in a free and democratic society.

The reverse onus provision in s. 457.7(2)(f) is a reasonable limitation even if, *prima facie*, it conflicts with s. 11(e); and we think that it does not. The reverse onus provision requires only that the accused satisfy the judge on a balance of probabilities that his detention is not justified on either the primary or secondary ground, a burden which it is rationally in his power to discharge. There is no burden cast upon him to disprove the offence or his implication in it, the onus is on the Crown to adduce evidence of the accused's implication in the offence.

R v Pugsley
Nova Scotia Court of Appeal
(1982), 2 CCC (3d) 266

PACE JA: Section 457.7(2)(f) places a very substantial burden on an accused person to show on a balance of probabilities that if he is released his attendance in court is ensured and his detention is not necessary in the public interest or for the protection and safety of the public.

Section 11 of the *Canadian Charter of Rights and Freedoms* reads in part as follows:

> 11. Any person charged with an offence has the right …
>
>   (e) not to be denied reasonable bail without just cause;

Under the Charter it seems clear to me that a person who is charged with an offence is entitled to reasonable bail unless the Crown can show just cause for a continuance of his detention. When one compares s. 457.7(2)(f) of the *Code* with s. 11(e) of the Charter it becomes obvious that there exists a glaring inconsistency which by the application of s. 52 of the *Constitution Act, 1982* renders the provision contained in the *Code* of no force or effect. However, this does not end the matter.

On the application before Grant J. the Crown, in opposing the release, showed facts which we considered relevant to this review. Those facts were that the accused was 42 years of age at the time of the alleged offence, unmarried and was self-employed on the family farm where he resided with his deceased father and stepmother. The offence was allegedly carried out by striking the father on the head with a stove poker and setting fire to the house in which both parents perished. The record reveals that the accused had a serious drinking problem and that he had at least two previous criminal convictions related to his addiction. However, both convictions were for driving offences and did not reveal any propensity for violence. There is evidence that at the time the present incident occurred the accused was drinking and that in the past he spent approximately $300 to $400 a week on alcoholic beverage. There is no evidence that his problem has been cured or that the accused is or was receiving active medical treatment for his illness. There is also evidence that the community in which the offence occurred would have a feeling of insecurity if the accused was released.

The denial of bail was affirmed.

In large part because of the next case, the Nova Scotia Court of Appeal in *R v Sanchez* (1999), 136 CCC (3d) 31 reversed *Pugsley* and held that the onus under s 522(2) on those charged with murder to show cause why they should not be subject to pre-trial detention is constitutional.

R v Pearson
Supreme Court of Canada
[1992] 3 SCR 665

LAMER CJ (L'Heureux-Dubé, Sopinka, Gonthier, and Iacobucci JJ concurring): The respondent Edwin Pearson was arrested in September, 1989, and charged with five counts of trafficking in narcotics, contrary to s. 4 of the *Narcotic Control Act*, R.S.C. 1985, c. N-1. A bail hearing was held shortly after his arrest. Pearson was denied bail and ordered detained in custody until trial.

Section 11(e) guarantees the right of any person charged with an offence "not to be denied reasonable bail without just cause." In my opinion, s. 11(e) contains two distinct elements, namely, the right to "reasonable bail" and the right not to be denied bail without "just cause." ...

Most of the current bail provisions in the *Criminal Code* were enacted in the *Bail Reform Act*, S.C. 1970-71-72, c. 37. The *Bail Reform Act* established a basic entitlement to bail. Bail must be granted unless pre-trial detention is justified by the prosecution. In *R. v. Bray* (1983), 2 C.C.C. (3d) 325 at p. 328, 144 D.L.R. (3d) 305, 32 C.R. (3d) 316, (Ont. C.A.), Martin J.A. described the *Bail Reform Act* as "a liberal and enlightened system of pre-trial release." In my view, s. 11(e) transforms the basic entitlement of this liberal and enlightened system into a constitutional right. Section 11(e) creates a basic entitlement to be granted reasonable bail unless there is just cause to do otherwise.

Section 515(6)(d) must be placed in context. In general, a person charged with an offence and produced before a justice, unless he or she pleads guilty, is to be released on an undertaking without conditions. However, the Crown is to be given a reasonable opportunity to show cause why either detention or some other order should be made: s. 515(1). Detention may be justified on the primary ground that "his detention is necessary to ensure his attendance in court" or, on the secondary ground that "detention is necessary in the public interest or for the protection or safety of the public ...": s. 515(10)(a) and (b).

Under s. 515(6)(d), where the accused is charged with an offence under the *Narcotic Control Act*, ss. 4 (trafficking or possession for the purpose of trafficking) or 5 (importing or exporting), or with conspiracy to commit any of these offences, the justice is to order the accused's detention. The accused, however, is to be afforded a reasonable opportunity to show cause why detention is not justified having regard to the primary and secondary grounds noted above. [The present s 515(6)(d) has a similar provision relating to the *Controlled Drugs and Substances Act*, SC 1996, c 19.]

The very specific characteristics of the offences subject to s. 515(6)(d) suggest that the special bail rules created by s. 515(6)(d) are necessary to create a bail system which will not be subverted by continuing criminal activity and by absconding accused. The offences subject to s. 515(6)(d) are undertaken in contexts in which criminal activity will tend to continue after arrest and bail, and they create the circumstances under which offenders are able to abscond rather than face trial. The special bail rules in s. 515(6)(d) combat these problems by requiring the accused to demonstrate that these problems will not arise.

The special bail rules in s. 515(6)(d) do not have any purpose extraneous to the bail system, but rather merely establish an effective bail system for specific offences for which the normal bail system would allow continuing criminal behaviour and an intolerable risk of absconding. The scope of these special rules is narrow and carefully tailored to achieve a properly functioning bail system. I therefore conclude that there is just cause for s. 515(6)(d) to depart from the basic entitlement of s. 11(e) and to deny bail in certain circumstances. Accordingly, I conclude that s. 515(6)(d) does not violate s. 11(e).

McLACHLIN J (La Forest J concurring (in dissent)): I have had the advantage of reading the reasons of the Chief Justice. I agree with them, save for his conclusion that s. 515(6)(d) of the *Criminal Code*, R.S.C. 1985, c. C-46, does not violate the constitutional right "not to be denied reasonable bail without just cause" guaranteed by s. 11(e) of the *Canadian Charter of Rights and Freedoms*. I share the Court of Appeal's concern that s. 515(6)(d) fails to distinguish between the large-scale commercial drug trafficker and the "small-time" drug trafficker. Were s. 515(6)(d) confined to the large-scale organized trafficker, there might be just cause for denying bail to people in this group. As the section stands, however, it can be used to deny bail to people when there is no reason or "just cause" for denying them bail. And where bail is denied without just cause, s. 11(e) of the Charter is infringed on its plain words.

[McLachlin J also found that s 515(6)(d) could not be justified under s 1 because it was not proportionate.]

R v Morales
Supreme Court of Canada
[1992] 3 SCR 711

LAMER CJ (La Forest, Sopinka, McLachlin, and Iacobucci JJ concurring): The respondent Maximo Morales was arrested in December, 1990. He was charged with trafficking in narcotics, possession of narcotics for the purpose of trafficking, importing narcotics and conspiracy to import narcotics, contrary to ss. 4 and 5 of the *Narcotic Control Act*, R.S.C. 1985, c. N-1, and s. 465(1)(c) of the *Criminal Code*. He is alleged to have participated in a major network to import cocaine into Canada. At the time of his arrest, Morales was awaiting trial for assault with a weapon, an indictable offence. He has subsequently been convicted of that offence.

A bail hearing was held shortly after Morales was arrested. Bail was denied and Morales was ordered detained in custody until trial.

[The accused appealed and challenged the constitutionality of the secondary grounds of detention under s 515(10)(b).]

As the appellant submits, the secondary ground contains two separate components. Detention can be justified either in the "public interest" or for the "protection or safety of the public." In my view each of these components entails very different constitutional considerations. As a result, the following analysis considers the public interest and public safety components of s. 515(10)(b) separately.

In my view, the criterion of "public interest" as a basis for pre-trial detention under s. 515(10)(b) violates s. 11(e) of the Charter because it authorizes detention in terms which are vague and imprecise. D. Kiselbach, "Pre-Trial Criminal Procedure: Preventive Detention and the Presumption of Innocence," 31 C.L.Q. 168 (1988-89), at p. 186, describes "public interest" as "the most nebulous basis for detention." I agree with this characterization of the public interest component of s. 515(10)(b) and view it as a fatal flaw in the provision.

... Since pre-trial detention is extraordinary in our system of criminal justice, vagueness in defining the terms of pre-trial detention may be even more invidious than is vagueness in defining an offence.

I am also unable to accept the submission of the intervener, the Attorney-General for Ontario, that the doctrine of vagueness should not apply to s. 515(10)(b) because it does not authorize arbitrary practices by law enforcement officials but rather merely authorizes judicial discretion. A standardless sweep does not become acceptable simply because it results from the whims of judges and justices of the peace rather than the whims of law enforcement officials. Cloaking whims in judicial robes is not sufficient to satisfy the principles of fundamental justice.

Nor would it be possible in my view to give the term "public interest" a constant or settled meaning. The term gives the courts unrestricted latitude to define any circumstances as sufficient to justify pre-trial detention. The term creates no criteria to define these circumstances. No amount of judicial interpretation of the term "public interest" would be capable of rendering it a provision which gives any guidance for legal debate.

As a result, the public interest component of s. 515(10)(b) violates ... s. 11(e) of the Charter because it authorizes a denial of bail without just cause.

[Chief Justice Lamer held that the public interest ground was not justified under s 1 of the Charter.]

... The vague and overbroad concept of public interest permits far more pre-trial detention than is required to meet the limited objectives of preventing crime and preventing interference with the administration of justice by those who are on bail. Accordingly, it does not constitute a minimal impairment of rights.

[He then held that the public safety ground did not violate s 11(e) of the Charter.]

In *Pearson*, I identified two factors which in my view are vital to a determination that there is just cause under s. 11(e). First, the denial of bail must occur only in a narrow set of circumstances. Secondly, the denial of bail must be necessary to promote the proper functioning of the bail system and must not be undertaken for any purpose extraneous to the bail system. In my opinion, the public safety component of s. 515(10)(b) provides just cause to deny bail within these criteria.

I am satisfied that the scope of the public safety component of s. 515(10)(b) is sufficiently narrow to satisfy the first requirement under s. 11(e). Bail is not denied for all individuals who pose a risk of committing an offence or interfering with the administration of justice while on bail. Bail is denied only for those who pose a "substantial likelihood" of committing an offence or interfering with the administration of justice, and only where this "substantial likelihood" endangers "the protection or safety of the public." Moreover, detention is justified only when it is "necessary" for public safety. It is not justified where detention would merely be convenient or advantageous. Such grounds are sufficiently narrow to fulfil the first requirement of just cause under s. 11(e).

I am also satisfied that the public safety component of s. 515(10)(b) is necessary to promote the proper functioning of the bail system and is not undertaken for any purpose extraneous to the bail system. In my view, the bail system does not function properly if an accused interferes with the administration of justice while on bail. The entire criminal justice system is subverted if an accused interferes with the administration of justice. If an accused is released on bail, it must be on condition that he or she will refrain from tampering with the administration of justice. If there is a substantial likelihood that the accused will not give this co-operation, it furthers the objectives of the bail system to deny bail.

In my view, the bail system also does not function properly if individuals commit crimes while on bail. One objective of the entire system of criminal justice is to stop criminal behaviour. The bail system releases individuals who have been accused but not convicted of criminal conduct, but in order to achieve the objective of stopping criminal behaviour, such release must be on condition that the accused will not engage in criminal activity pending trial. In *Pearson*, the reality that persons engaged in drug trafficking tend to continue their criminal behaviour even after an arrest was one basis for concluding that there is just cause to require persons charged with certain narcotics offences to justify bail. Similarly, if there is a substantial likelihood that the accused will engage in criminal activity pending trial, it furthers the objectives of the bail system to deny bail.

[GONTHIER J (L'Heureux-Dubé J concurring) in dissent held that the public interest ground was not inconsistent with the requirement of just cause under s 11(e). He stated:]

... [T]he concept of public interest is broader than that of protection or safety of the public, and includes interests which may not be properly included within the categories of public health or safety. The aim of avoiding interference with the administration of justice is one such example. Other examples of a public interest which have been mentioned as having been actually experienced are the protection of the accused himself from suicide or from the actions of others, the prevention of activities which involve the possession of or dealing in small quantities of illegal narcotics, or the preparation of reports for the court which require the presence of the accused. Also important is the consideration that the criterion of necessity in the public interest is capable of encompassing circumstances which have not been foreseen or, indeed, which may be unforeseeable, yet when they occur, albeit rarely, they obviously make the detention necessary and undoubtedly provide just cause for denying bail within the meaning of s. 11(e) of the Charter. The courts must be able to deal with such circumstances. The good governance of society and the rule of law itself require that Parliament be allowed to provide for social peace and order even in unforeseen circumstances. The appropriate instrument for doing this is through the administration of justice by the courts and allowing them a measure of discretion which they are bound to exercise judicially, that is, for reasons that are relevant, within the limits provided by law and in accordance with the Charter.

R v Hall
Supreme Court of Canada
2002 SCC 64, [2002] 3 SCR 309

[In this case, the Court dealt with the constitutionality of s 515(10)(c) added to the *Criminal Code* in 1997 and in response to the invalidation of the tertiary "public interest" ground for denial of bail in *R v Morales*.]

McLACHLIN CJ (L'Heureux-Dubé, Gonthier, Bastarache, and Binnie JJ concurring):

[1] On May 3, 1999, Peggy Jo Barkley-Dube's body was found on the kitchen floor of her home in the city of Sault Ste. Marie. The cause of death was massive hemorrhage from approximately 37 separate slash wounds to her hands, forearms, shoulder, neck and face. Her neck had been cut to the vertebrae and medical evidence indicated that the assailant intended to cut her head off.

[2] On June 4, 1999, the appellant, the victim's husband's second cousin, was charged with first degree murder. Compelling evidence linked him to the crime. Areas in the victim's home contained traces of the appellant's blood. Footprint impressions containing the victim's blood and matching the type of running shoes worn by the appellant were

found in her dining room and kitchen. The same footprint impressions had been left by the appellant in his parents' home. A surveillance video from a convenience store showed the appellant on the night of the homicide wearing shoes matching those seized from his parents' home. The appellant admitted to police that he had been in the convenience store that night but denied that he had been wearing the shoes.

[3] The murder received much media attention and caused significant public concern. A police officer testified that there was a general sense of fear that there was a killer at large, and the victim's father testified that his wife and three other daughters were very fearful.

[4] The appellant applied for bail. The *Criminal Code*, R.S.C. 1985, c. C-46, s. 515(10) provides that bail may be denied in three situations:

(a) Where the detention is necessary to ensure [the accused's] attendance in court in order to be dealt with according to law;

(b) Where the detention is necessary for the protection or safety of the public ... including any substantial likelihood that the accused will, if released from custody, commit a criminal offence or interfere with the administration of justice; and

(c) on any other just cause being shown and, without limiting the generality of the foregoing, *where the detention is necessary in order to maintain confidence in the administration of justice, having regard to all the circumstances, including the apparent strength of the prosecution's case, the gravity of the nature of the offence, the circumstances surrounding its commission and the potential for a lengthy term of imprisonment.* [Emphasis added.]

[5] Bolan J. held that the evidence did not support denying bail on the first two grounds. He was satisfied that the accused's community and family ties, plus the ample security proposed, would ensure that the accused would appear for his trial should he be released on bail. He was also satisfied that there was no reason to think the accused would commit an offence while on release and that bail conditions could be imposed which would eliminate this risk. He found, however, that the accused's detention was necessary to maintain confidence in the administration of justice in view of the highly charged aftermath of the murder, the strong evidence implicating the accused, and the other factors referred to in s. 515(10)(c). ...

[22] The first phrase of s. 515(10)(c) which permits denial of bail "on any other just cause being shown" is unconstitutional. Parliament cannot confer a broad discretion on judges to deny bail, but must lay out narrow and precise circumstances in which bail can be denied: *Pearson* and *Morales*, supra. This phrase does not specify any particular basis upon which bail could be denied. The denial of bail "on any other just cause" violates the requirements enunciated in *Morales*, supra, and therefore is inconsistent with the presumption of innocence and s. 11(e) of the Charter. Even assuming a pressing and substantial legislative objective for the phrase "on any other just cause being shown," the generality of the phrase impels its failure on the proportionality branch of the *Oakes* test (*R. v. Oakes*, [1986] 1 S.C.R. 103). Section 52 of the *Constitution Act, 1982*, provides that a law is void to the extent it is inconsistent with the Charter. It follows that this phrase fails. The next phrase in the provision, "without limiting the generality of the foregoing," is also void, since it serves only to confirm the generality of the phrase permitting a judge to deny bail "on any other just cause."

[23] However, this does not mean that all of s. 515(10)(c) is unconstitutional. The loss of the above phrases leaves intact the balance of s. 515(10)(c), which is capable of standing alone grammatically and in terms of Parliament's intention. Whatever the fate of the broad initial discretion para. (c) seems to convey, Parliament clearly intended to permit bail to be denied where necessary to maintain confidence in the administration of justice, having regard to the four specified factors. This leaves the question of whether this latter part of s. 515(10)(c), considered on its own, is unconstitutional. ...

[30] Bail denial to maintain confidence in the administration of justice is not a mere "catch-all" for cases where the first two grounds have failed. It represents a separate and distinct basis for bail denial not covered by the other two categories. The same facts may be relevant to all three heads. For example, an accused's implication in a terrorist ring or organized drug trafficking might be relevant to whether he is likely to appear at trial, whether he is likely to commit further offences or interfere with the administration of justice, and whether his detention is necessary to maintain confidence in the justice system. But that does not negate the distinctiveness of the three grounds. ...

IACOBUCCI J (Major, Arbour, and LeBel JJ concurring) in dissent: ...

[81] After the "public interest" component of s. 515(10)(b) was struck down by this Court in *Morales*, pre-trial detention could be justified only under one of the two traditional grounds, namely, ensuring the accused's attendance in court or protecting the safety of the public. As already mentioned, s. 515(10) was eventually amended to add the tertiary ground in dispute here. The other major change was the removal of the primary/secondary structure of the provision. As a result, bail can now be denied under any one of paras. (a), (b), or (c) of s. 515(10) without consideration of the other paragraphs.

[82] As noted above, Parliament waited five years before reacting to *Morales* by amending s. 515(10), and it is significant that the respondent was unable to point to any evidence that during these five years the pre-trial detention scheme was lacking in any way. Indeed, the only justification for the creation of the tertiary ground that the respondent was able to suggest was that "courts should have the exceptional power to deny bail in limited circumstances not covered by the existing legislation" (respondent's factum, at para. 21). However, in the absence of evidence of any deficiencies in the bail system during the five years after the *Morales* decision, the argument that bail judges require this residual category loses much of its force. Although the lack of an empirical foundation for the provision says nothing, in and of itself, as to its validity under s. 11(e) of the Charter (but it does arise in the s. 1 analysis), it is important to bear in mind the context underlying this appeal, namely, that for five years there was no indication that the bail system was in need of a tertiary ground in addition to the two traditional grounds for denying bail. ...

[99] The factors listed under s. 515(10)(c) are: "the apparent strength of the prosecution's case, the gravity of the nature of the offence, the circumstances surrounding its commission and the potential for a lengthy term of imprisonment." On their face, these factors seem relevant to a determination of whether bail should be granted or denied; however, one must assume here that the bail decision is not being made in order to ensure the accused attends court or to protect the public, otherwise the decision would be made under either s. 515(10)(a) or (b) which deal specifically with those grounds. As such, I find it difficult to see how these factors could promote the proper administration of justice

when it has already been concluded that it is not necessary to detain the accused in order to ensure the attendance of the accused at trial or to protect the safety of the public. ...

[106] Given this underpinning in public perceptions, s. 515(10)(c) is ripe for misuse, allowing for irrational public fears to be elevated above the Charter rights of the accused. In the face of a highly publicized serious crime and a strong *prima facie* case, the importance of the presumption of innocence or the right to bail will not be at the forefront of the minds of most members of the public. Many individuals will instead accept the factors listed in the provision to be a proxy for the accused's guilt, and the release of the accused may very well provoke outrage among certain members of the community. However, this outrage cannot be used by the bail judge as a justification for denying bail, whether or not it is dressed up in administration of justice language. Indeed, the case at bar aptly illustrates this very pitfall. Bolan J. said:

> This City, like any other small cities, looks to its courts for protection. The feelings of the community have been expressed by certain witnesses. Some people are afraid, and some people have voiced their concerns. This is a factor which I will accordingly take into consideration when I assess the third ground.

[107] With respect, the bail judge erred in considering the subjective fears of members of the public when he had already determined that the accused should not be denied bail for fear of flight or threat to the public. Although it may well be that the reaction of the public can play a role in determining the threat posed by the accused's release under the public safety ground, that is not what the bail judge decided in this case. It is the role of courts to guard the Charter rights of the accused when they conflict with irrational and subjective public views, even when sincerely held. The problem with s. 515(10)(c) is that, stripped to its essence, its very purpose is to allow these subjective fears to form the sole basis by which bail is denied. ...

[128] Finally, I emphasize that the role of this Court, and indeed of every court in our country, to staunchly uphold constitutional standards is of particular importance when the public mood is one which encourages increased punishment of those accused of criminal acts and where mounting pressure is placed on the liberty interest of these individuals. Courts must be bulwarks against the tides of public opinion that threaten to invade these cherished values. Although this may well cost courts popularity in some quarters, that can hardly justify a failure to uphold fundamental freedoms and liberty.

In *R v St-Cloud*, 2015 SCC 27, the Supreme Court held that it was an error to interpret s 515(10)(c) as a residual ground that would only justify pre-trial detention in rare or extraordinary cases. The Court indicated that judges who interpreted the section in this manner were wrongly favouring the minority judgment in *Hall*. The Court indicated that judges should consider all the circumstances of the case in light of the reaction of a reasonable, well-informed person, but not a "legal expert familiar with all the basic principles of the criminal justice system, the elements of criminal offences or the subtleties of criminal intent and of the defences that are available to accused persons" (at para 80). The Court also stated: "if the crime is serious or very violent, if there is overwhelming evidence against the accused and if the victim or victims were vulnerable, pre-trial detention will usually be ordered" (at para 88). Do you think this case will increase the already high levels of pre-trial detention in Canada?

How well do you think judges would balance competing interests in a case such as Donald Marshall's? How well do the grounds for the denial of bail in s 515(10)(c) sit with the presumption of innocence?

On pre-trial release, see GT Trotter, "Pearson and Morales: Distilling the Right to Bail" (1993) 17 CR (4th) 150; GT Trotter, *The Law of Bail in Canada*, 3rd ed (Toronto: Carswell, 2010); and D Stuart, *Charter Justice in Canadian Criminal Law*, 6th ed (Toronto: Carswell, 2014) at 493-506.

IV. THE JURY

The jury is composed of 12 people from the community in which the crime was alleged to have been committed, unless there has been a change of venue. The killing of Sandy Seale and the subsequent trial of Donald Marshall Jr. raised much emotion and controversy in Sydney, Nova Scotia. It was Sydney's first murder case in five years. (The last one involved the killing of a person from a minority group and had not been solved.) If you were the defence counsel in the *Marshall* case, would you have moved for a change of venue under s 599 (formerly s 527) of the *Criminal Code*? If you decided to do so, do you think the trial judge would have granted your request? Note that when Roy Ebsary was eventually charged with manslaughter in relation to Sandy Seale's death, he unsuccessfully argued that the pre-trial local and national publicity identifying him as "the killer" infringed his right under s 11(d) of the Charter to "be presumed innocent until proven guilty in a fair and public hearing by an independent and impartial tribunal." MacKeigan CJNS dismissed this argument in *R v Ebsary* (1984), 15 CCC (3d) 38 (NSCA). He concluded:

> In my opinion the jury was adequately instructed by the trial judge to disregard anything heard outside the courtroom and to base their verdict solely on the evidence. The usual jury selection process was properly followed. I am not prepared to say that a jury properly instructed, after a trial properly conducted on evidence properly admitted, would have been unable to give Ebsary a fair trial. The trial judge thus did not err in refusing to quash the indictment for violation of the Charter.

Requiring Trial by Jury

Donald Marshall Jr. was convicted by a judge and jury. Because he was charged with murder, he did not have a choice under the *Criminal Code* provisions then in force to elect a trial by judge alone. In *R v Turpin*, [1989] 1 SCR 1296 the accused were charged with the murder of the accused Turpin's husband. Under the same *Criminal Code* provisions that applied to Marshall, they were required to be tried by a judge and jury. They argued that their rights under s 11(f) of the Charter should be interpreted to give them a right to choose not to be tried by a jury. The Court rejected this argument, Wilson J stating:

> There is no constitutional right to a non-jury trial. There is a constitutional right to a jury trial and there may be a "right," using that term loosely, in an accused to waive the right to a jury trial. An accused may repudiate his or her s. 11(f) right but such repudiation does not, in my view, transform the constitutional right to a jury trial into a constitutional right to a non-jury trial so as to overcome the mandatory jury trial provisions of the *Criminal Code*.

The mandatory jury trial provisions that applied in the murder trials of both Donald Marshall Jr. and Sharon Turpin have been replaced by s 473 of the Code, which allows a person accused of murder to obtain a non-jury trial if both the accused and the attorney general consent. What considerations should govern the attorney general in the exercise of his or her veto over an accused's request for a non-jury trial?

Selecting the Jury

There are three main factors determining who sits on a jury. The first is the procedure used to summon a cross-section of the population for jury service. This selection is made under provincial or territorial legislation. In *R v Kokopenace*, 2015 SCC 28, the Supreme Court held that the underrepresentation of Aboriginal reserve residents on a jury roll in Kenora, Ontario did not violate the Charter because there was no deliberate exclusion, reasonable efforts had been made to include Aboriginal people, and there was no right to a jury roll or a jury that proportionately represented particular groups. Two judges dissented on the basis that Ontario had used inadequate lists and notices to send jury notices to reserve residents and had not made reasonable efforts to address the 10 percent return rate on jury notices from reserve residents or findings that only 4 percent of the jury roll were Aboriginal people living on reserves in a district where between 21.5 and 31.8 percent of residents lived on reserves.

The second is the limited number of peremptory challenges that can be used by both the accused and the prosecutor to challenge jurors without the need for any stated reason. Under s 634 of the *Criminal Code*, the accused and the prosecutor can make peremptory challenges of 4 to 20 prospective jurors depending on the seriousness of the charge.

The third is the availability of the challenge for cause procedure under s 638 of the Code, which allows both the accused and the prosecutor to challenge an unlimited number of potential jurors on various grounds, the most important being that they are not indifferent between the Crown and the accused.

The jury that tried Donald Marshall Jr. was composed of 12 white men. At the time, the jury pool was selected from those who paid taxes on property. The Royal Commission on the Donald Marshall Jr. Prosecution commented as follows:

> The lack of Natives on juries in Nova Scotia concerns members of the Native community. We know of no evidence that suggests Natives are deliberately excluded from jury duty in Nova Scotia. Nor can we argue definitively that the presence of a Native person on a jury in a case involving a Native accused will result in fairer treatment for the Native. Still, Native concerns are not unreasonable: Would a White person facing a Native prosecutor, defence lawyer, judge and jury, have some apprehension whether he would get as fair a hearing as if everyone were White?
>
> … It has been indicated to us that, in fact, no Native has ever been on a jury in Nova Scotia. We were given no explanation for this. We do, however, urge those involved in selecting juries for trials involving Native people—both prosecutors and defence counsel—not to automatically exclude Natives simply because they are of the same race as the accused.

The Manitoba Aboriginal Justice Inquiry stated:

> The purpose of the jury is to bring together 12 fair-minded representatives of the community to make a determination on the facts of a case. Counsel, however, see their role during jury selection as requiring them to try to select jurors likely to be supportive of their position. This attitude can distort the jury selection process. The ability, which both Crown and defence counsel have,

to dismiss jurors without stating any reason makes this distortion of the process almost inevitable. We believe that any 12 people not otherwise disqualified by the Act, who direct their minds to the evidence and apply the law given to them by the judge, and have heard the arguments and submissions of the lawyers, will bring in a reasonable verdict.

We have concerns about the manner in which peremptory challenges and stand-asides are used. While some defence lawyers and Crown attorneys make no distinction on the basis of race, we believe it is common practice for some Crown attorneys and defence counsel to exclude Aboriginal jurors through the use of stand-asides and peremptory challenges.

One example of such exclusion is the Helen Betty Osborne case in The Pas. There, the jury had no Aboriginal members. The six Aboriginal people who were called forward were peremptorily challenged by counsel for the defence. The lack of Aboriginal people on a jury in a case of that kind, in an area of the province where Aboriginal people make up at least 50% of the population, raises valid concerns about the manner in which our jury selection process operates.

The commission recommended that the *Criminal Code* be amended so that the only challenges to prospective jurors could be those made for an articulated cause, not peremptory challenges. A complex jurisprudence in the United States requires parties to provide "nondiscriminatory" reasons for the exercise of peremptory challenges. In Canada, challenges to Crown decisions to use peremptory challenges to remove African-Canadian jurors have been rejected largely on the basis that the accused does not have a right to a jury that includes "members having specific racial identities" (*R v Gayle* (2001), 154 CCC (3d) 221 at para 75 (Ont CA) and *R v Amos*, 2007 ONCA 672 at para 2) and on the basis of the "subjective" nature of peremptory challenges (*R v Cloutier*, [1979] 2 SCR 709).

See C Peterson, "Institutionalized Racism: The Need for Reform of the Criminal Jury Selection Process" (1993) 38 McGill LJ 147.

Challenges for Cause

Under s 638 of the *Criminal Code*, the prosecutor and the accused are entitled to any number of challenges for cause. The most common ground of a challenge for cause is that a juror is not indifferent between the Queen and the accused. The challenge for cause is decided by the last two members of the jury sworn or if two jurors have not been selected, by other members of the public present in the courtroom.

R v Parks
Ontario Court of Appeal
(1993), 84 CCC (3d) 353

[The accused was convicted by judge and jury of second-degree murder for killing a person during a cocaine deal. The accused wished to ask prospective jurors whether their ability to judge witnesses without bias, prejudice, or partiality would be affected by (1) the fact that the accused and the deceased were involved with drugs and (2) the fact that the accused is a black Jamaican immigrant and the deceased is a white man. The trial judge disallowed both questions and after conviction, the accused appealed.]

DOHERTY JA: On appeal, counsel for the appellant argued that both questions should have been allowed. I see no merit in the argument as it relates to the first question. The question implies that a witness's involvement in the drug trade and his or her personal use of illicit drugs should have no relevance in "judging witnesses." To the contrary, those factors could properly be considered by the jury in its assessment of the credibility and reliability of witnesses.

The propriety of the second question does require detailed consideration. The appellant does not challenge the proscription against challenges based on race, or the beliefs, opinions or prejudices of potential jurors set down in *Hubbert*, and reiterated in *R. v. Zundel*. Counsel did not seek to inquire into individual jurors' lifestyles, antecedents, or personal experiences with a view to exposing underlying racial prejudices. He did not propose the kind of wide-ranging personalized disclosure involved in *voir dire* inquiries into potential racial prejudice permitted in some American jurisdictions. Canadian courts have resisted that approach to jury selection. ...

A question directed at revealing those whose bias renders them partial does not "inject" racism into the trial, but seeks to prevent that bias from destroying the impartiality of the jury's deliberations.

In this case, the issue to be determined on a challenge for cause was not whether a particular potential juror was biased against blacks, but whether if that prejudice existed, it would cause that juror to discriminate against the black accused in arriving at his or her verdict. ...

In other words, the presumption that jurors will perform their duty according to their oath must be balanced against the threat of a verdict tainted by racial bias.

Racism, and in particular anti-black racism, is a part of our community's psyche. A significant segment of our community holds overtly racist views. A much larger segment subconsciously operates on the basis of negative racial stereotypes. Furthermore, our institutions, including the criminal justice system, reflect and perpetuate those negative stereotypes. These elements combine to infect our society as a whole with the evil of racism. Blacks are among the primary victims of that evil.

The criminal trial milieu may also accentuate the role of racial bias in the decision making process. Anti-black attitudes may connect blacks with crime and acts of violence. A juror with such attitudes who hears evidence describing a black accused as a drug dealer involved in an act of violence may regard his attitudes as having been validated by the evidence. That juror may then readily give effect to his or her preconceived negative attitudes towards blacks without regard to the evidence and legal principles essential to a determination of the specific accused's liability for the crime charged.

I am satisfied that in at least some cases involving a black accused there is a realistic possibility that one or more jurors will discriminate against that accused because of his or her colour. In my view, a trial judge, in the proper exercise of his or her discretion, could permit counsel to put the question posed in this case, in any trial held in Metropolitan Toronto involving a black accused. I would go further and hold that it would be the better course to permit that question in all such cases where the accused requests the inquiry.

The interracial nature of the violence involved in this case, and the fact that the alleged crime occurred in the course of the black accused's involvement in a criminal drug transaction, combined to provide circumstances in which it was essential to the conduct of a fair trial that counsel be permitted to put the question. With respect, I must conclude that the trial judge erred in refusing to allow counsel to ask the question.

Appeal allowed; new trial ordered.

The second question referred to here, known as "the *Parks* question," is accepted throughout Canada, and the Nova Scotia Court of Appeal held that an African-Canadian man charged with sexually touching a white student was denied his right to effective assistance of counsel in part because his lawyer did not seek to ask the question of jurors. The Court of Appeal concluded: "No informed discussion regarding challenge for cause in a potentially race-based case can occur without considering 'the *Parks* issue'": *R v Fraser*, 2011 NSCA 70 at para 58, 273 CCC (3d) 276. For a discussion of this case and its implications for trial judges dealing with unrepresented accused, see R Devlin & D Layton, "Culturally Incompetent Counsel and the Trial Level Judge: A Legal and Ethical Analysis" (2014) 60 Crim LQ 360.

R v Williams
Supreme Court of Canada
[1998] 1 SCR 1128

[The accused was an Aboriginal man charged with robbery. Relying on *Parks*, he sought to ask prospective jurors whether their ability to judge the case impartially would be affected by the fact that he was Aboriginal and that the complainant was white. The trial judge did not allow the question and the British Columbia Court of Appeal dismissed his appeal. An unanimous Supreme Court reversed.]

McLACHLIN J stated: ...

[14] A judge exercising the discretion to permit or refuse challenges for cause must act on the evidence and in a way that fulfills the purpose of s. 638(1)(b)—to prevent persons who are not indifferent between the Crown and the accused from serving on the jury. Stated otherwise, a trial judge, in the exercise of the discretion, cannot "effectively curtail the statutory right to challenge for cause": see *R. v. Zundel (No. 1)* (1987), 31 C.C.C. (3d) 97, at p. 135 (leave to appeal refused [1987] 1 S.C.R. xii). To guide judges in the exercise of their discretion, this Court formulated a rule in [*R v Sherratt*, [1991] 1 SCR 509], *supra*:

> the judge should permit challenges for cause where there is a "realistic potential" of the existence of partiality. *Sherratt* was concerned with the possibility of partiality arising from pre-trial publicity. However, as the courts in this case accepted, it applies to all requests for challenges based on bias, regardless of the origin of the apprehension of partiality.

[15] Applying *Sherratt* to the case at bar, the enquiry becomes whether in this case, the evidence of widespread bias against aboriginal people in the community raises a realistic potential of partiality.

. . .

[21] To suggest that all persons who possess racial prejudices will erase those prejudices from the mind when serving as jurors is to underestimate the insidious nature of

racial prejudice and the stereotyping that underlies it. … [R]acial prejudice interfering with jurors' impartiality is a form of discrimination. It involves making distinctions on the basis of class or category without regard to individual merit. It rests on preconceptions and unchallenged assumptions that unconsciously shape the daily behaviour of individuals. Buried deep in the human psyche, these preconceptions cannot be easily and effectively identified and set aside, even if one wishes to do so. For this reason, it cannot be assumed that judicial directions to act impartially will always effectively counter racial prejudice: see [SL Johnson, "Black Innocence and the White Jury" (1985) 83 Mich L Rev 1611], *supra*. Doherty J.A. recognized this in *Parks, supra*, at p. 371:

> In deciding whether the post-jury selection safeguards against partiality provide a reliable antidote to racial bias, the nature of that bias must be emphasized. For some people, anti-black biases rest on unstated and unchallenged assumptions learned over a lifetime. Those assumptions shape the daily behaviour of individuals, often without any conscious reference to them. In my opinion, attitudes which are engrained in an individual's subconscious, and reflected in both individual and institutional conduct within the community, will prove more resistant to judicial cleansing than will opinions based on yesterday's news and referable to a specific person or event.

[22] Racial prejudice and its effects are as invasive and elusive as they are corrosive. We should not assume that instructions from the judge or other safeguards will eliminate biases that may be deeply ingrained in the subconscious psyches of jurors. Rather, we should acknowledge the destructive potential of subconscious racial prejudice by recognizing that the post-jury selection safeguards may not suffice. Where doubts are raised, the better policy is to err on the side of caution and permit prejudices to be examined. Only then can we know with any certainty whether they exist and whether they can be set aside or not. It is better to risk allowing what are in fact unnecessary challenges, than to risk prohibiting challenges which are necessary. …

· · ·

[28] Racial prejudice against the accused may be detrimental to an accused in a variety of ways. The link between prejudice and verdict is clearest where there is an "interracial element" to the crime or a perceived link between those of the accused's race and the particular crime. But racial prejudice may play a role in other, less obvious ways. Racist stereotypes may affect how jurors assess the credibility of the accused. Bias can shape the information received during the course of the trial to conform with the bias: see *Parks, supra*, at p. 372. Jurors harbouring racial prejudices may consider those of the accused's race less worthy or perceive a link between those of the accused's race and crime in general. In this manner, subconscious racism may make it easier to conclude that a black or aboriginal accused engaged in the crime regardless of the race of the complainant: see Kent Roach, "Challenges for Cause and Racial Discrimination" (1995), 37 *Crim. L.Q.* 410, at p. 421.

· · ·

[30] Ultimately, it is within the discretion of the trial judge to determine whether widespread racial prejudice in the community, absent specific "links" to the trial, is sufficient to give an "air of reality" to the challenge in the particular circumstances of each case. The following excerpt from *Parks, supra*, at pp. 379-80, per Doherty J.A., states the law correctly:

I am satisfied that in at least some cases involving a black accused there is a realistic possibility that one or more jurors will discriminate against that accused because of his or her colour. In my view, a trial judge, in the proper exercise of his or her discretion, could permit counsel to put the question posed in this case, in any trial held in Metropolitan Toronto involving a black accused. I would go further and hold that it would be the better course to permit that question in all such cases where the accused requests the inquiry.

There will be circumstances in addition to the colour of the accused which will increase the possibility of racially prejudiced verdicts. It is impossible to provide an exhaustive catalogue of those circumstances. Where they exist, the trial judge must allow counsel to put the question suggested in this case.

. . .

[32] Section 638(2) requires two inquiries and entails two different decisions with two different tests. The first stage is the inquiry before the judge to determine whether challenges for cause should be permitted. The test at this stage is whether there is a realistic potential or possibility for partiality. The question is whether there is reason to suppose that the jury pool may contain people who are prejudiced and whose prejudice might not be capable of being set aside on directions from the judge. The operative verbs at the first stage are "may" and "might." Since this is a preliminary inquiry which may affect the accused's *Charter* rights (see below), a reasonably generous approach is appropriate.

[33] If the judge permits challenges for cause, a second inquiry occurs on the challenge itself. The defence may question potential jurors as to whether they harbour prejudices against people of the accused's race, and if so, whether they are able to set those prejudices aside and act as impartial jurors. The question at this stage is whether the candidate in question will be able to act impartially. To demand, at the preliminary stage of determining whether a challenge for cause should be permitted, proof that the jurors in the jury pool will not be able to set aside any prejudices they may harbour and act impartially, is to ask the question more appropriate for the second stage.

. . .

[41] A rule that accords an automatic right to challenge for cause on the basis that the accused is an aboriginal or member of a group that encounters discrimination conflicts from a methodological point of view with the approach in *Sherratt, supra,* that an accused may challenge for cause only upon establishing that there is a realistic potential for juror partiality. For example, it is difficult to see why women should have an automatic right to challenge for cause merely because they have been held to constitute a disadvantaged group under s. 15 of the *Charter.* Moreover, it is not correct to assume that membership in an aboriginal or minority group always implies a realistic potential for partiality. The relevant community for purposes of the rule is the community from which the jury pool is drawn. That community may or may not harbour prejudices against aboriginals. It likely would not, for example, in a community where aboriginals are in a majority position. That said, absent evidence to the contrary, where widespread prejudice against people of the accused's race is demonstrated at a national or provincial level, it will often be reasonable to infer that such prejudice is replicated at the community level.

[42] On the understanding that the jury pool is representative, one may safely insist that the accused demonstrate widespread or general prejudice against his or her race in the community as a condition of bringing a challenge for cause. It is at this point that bigoted or prejudiced people have the capacity to affect the impartiality of the jury.

[43] I add this. To say that widespread racial prejudice in the community can suffice to establish the right to challenge for cause in many cases is not to rule out the possibility that prejudice less than widespread might in some circumstances meet the *Sherratt* test. The ultimate question in each case is whether the *Sherratt* standard of a realistic potential for partiality is established.

. . .

[49] Section s. 638(1)(b) should be read in light of the fundamental rights to a fair trial by an impartial jury and to equality before and under the law. A principled exercise of discretion in accordance with *Charter* values is required: see *Sherratt, supra.*

[50] Although allowing challenges for cause in the face of widespread racial prejudice in the community will not eliminate the possibility of jury verdicts being affected by racial prejudice, it will have important benefits. Jurors who are honest or transparent about their racist views will be removed. All remaining jurors will be sensitized from the outset of the proceedings regarding the need to confront racial prejudice and will help ensure that it does not impact on the jury verdict. Finally, allowing such challenges will enhance the appearance of trial fairness in the eyes of the accused and other members of minority groups facing discrimination: see *Parks, supra.*

. . .

[57] There is a presumption that a jury pool is composed of persons who can serve impartially. However, where the accused establishes that there is a realistic potential for partiality, the accused should be permitted to challenge prospective jurors for cause under s. 638(1)(b) of the Code: see *Sherratt, supra.* Applying this rule to applications based on prejudice against persons of the accused's race, the judge should exercise his or her discretion to permit challenges for cause if the accused establishes widespread racial prejudice in the community.

[58] Although they acknowledged the existence of widespread bias against aboriginals, both Esson C.J. and the British Columbia Court of Appeal held that the evidence did not demonstrate a reasonable possibility that prospective jurors would be partial. In my view, there was ample evidence that this widespread prejudice included elements that could have affected the impartiality of jurors. Racism against aboriginals includes stereotypes that relate to credibility, worthiness and criminal propensity. As the Canadian Bar Association stated in *Locking Up Natives in Canada: A Report of the Committee of the Canadian Bar Association on Imprisonment and Release* (1988), at p. 5:

> Put at its baldest, there is an equation of being drunk, Indian and in prison. Like many stereotypes, this one has a dark underside. It reflects a view of native people as uncivilized and without a coherent social or moral order. The stereotype prevents us from seeing native people as equals.

There is evidence that this widespread racism has translated into systemic discrimination in the criminal justice system: see Royal Commission on Aboriginal Peoples, *Bridging the Cultural Divide: A Report on Aboriginal People and Criminal Justice in Canada,* at p. 33; *Royal Commission on the Donald Marshall Jr. Prosecution, Volume 1: Findings and Recommendations* (1989), at p. 162; *Report on the Cariboo-Chilcotin Justice Inquiry* (1993), at p. 11. Finally, as Esson C.J. noted, tensions between aboriginals and non-aboriginals have increased in recent years as a result of developments in such areas as land claims and fishing rights. These tensions increase the potential of racist jurors siding with the Crown as the perceived representative of the majority's interests.

[59] In these circumstances, the trial judge should have allowed the accused to challenge prospective jurors for cause. Notwithstanding the accused's defence that another aboriginal person committed the robbery, juror prejudice could have affected the trial in many other ways. Consequently, there was a realistic potential that some of the jurors might not have been indifferent between the Crown and the accused. The potential for prejudice was increased by the failure of the trial judge to instruct the jury to set aside any racial prejudices that they might have against aboriginals. It cannot be said that the accused had the fair trial by an impartial jury to which he was entitled.

[60] I would allow the appeal and direct a new trial.

If jurors can be asked about the possibility of racial prejudice and stereotypes influencing their deliberations, what about their attitudes toward specific crimes such as sexual abuse of young children? See *R v Find*, 2001 SCC 32, [2001] 1 SCR 863 rejecting such questions. In one wrongful conviction stemming from Dr. Charles Smith's flawed testimony about the cause of a child's death, the accused, Tammy Marquardt, unsuccessfully sought to question potential jurors whether they would be prejudiced by the fact that she was charged with killing her 2½-year-old son: *R v Marquardt* (1995), 44 CR (4th) 353 (Ont Gen Div), aff'd (1998), 124 CCC (3d) 375 (Ont CA). Marquardt was granted bail pending a fresh appeal in 2009, and her conviction was overturned with the consent of the Crown on the basis of fresh evidence about errors in Dr. Smith's testimony in 2011 ONCA 281. For an account of her case, see "Tammy Marquardt" at <http://www.aidwyc.org/cases/historical/tammy-marquardt/>.

Jury Unanimity

The jury deliberates in secret. Section 649 of the *Criminal Code* makes it a summary conviction offence for a juror to disclose any information relating to the proceedings of the jury unless in connection to the investigation and trial of the offence of obstruction of justice in relation to a juror. In the United States, jurors are routinely interviewed as to jury deliberations. One of the jurors who wrongfully convicted Donald Marshall Jr. in 1971 was reported in the press as giving an explanation for the verdict based on racist stereotypes (*Toronto Star*, 8 June 1986, A8). This issue was not examined in the royal commission report. In its report to Parliament, *The Jury* (1982), the Law Reform Commission of Canada recommended retaining this offence but making an exemption for "the furtherance of scientific research about juries which is approved by the Chief Justice of the Province." For a case affirming the constitutionality of the secrecy of the jury's deliberations and the constitutionality of s 649 of the Code in the face of an allegation that a juror made racist remarks, see *R v Pan; R v Sawyer*, 2001 SCC 42, [2001] 2 SCR 344.

V. QUANTUM AND BURDEN OF PROOF

Burden of Proof

The burden on the Crown to prove the guilt of an accused beyond a reasonable doubt is one of the most important safeguards in the criminal justice system. Reread the trial judge's instructions to the jury in the *Marshall* case concerning the quantum and burden of proof. Were they correct in light of the following cases?

Woolmington v DPP

House of Lords

[1935] AC 462

VISCOUNT SANKEY LC (for the Court): My Lords, the appellant, Reginald Woolmington, after a trial at the Somerset Assizes at Taunton on January 23, at which, after an absence of one hour and twenty-five minutes, the jury disagreed, was convicted at the Bristol Assizes on February 14 of the wilful murder of his wife on December 10, 1934, and was sentenced to death. He appealed to the Court of Criminal Appeal, substantially upon the ground that the learned judge had misdirected the jury by telling them that in the circumstances of the case he was presumed in law to be guilty of the murder unless he could satisfy the jury that his wife's death was due to an accident.

The appeal came before the Court of Criminal Appeal upon March 18 and was dismissed. The Court said "it may be that it might have been better" had the learned judge who tried the case said to the jury that if they entertained reasonable doubt whether they could accept his explanation they should either acquit him altogether or convict him of manslaughter only; but, relying upon s. 4, sub-s. 1, of the Criminal Appeal Act, 1907, which provides "that the court may, notwithstanding that they are of opinion that the point raised in the appeal might be decided in favour of the appellant, dismiss the appeal if they consider that no substantial miscarriage of justice has actually occurred," they dismissed the appeal.

Thereupon the Attorney-General gave his fiat certifying that the appeal of Reginald Woolmington involved a point of law of exceptional public importance and that in his opinion it was desirable in the public interest that a further appeal should be brought. The matter now comes before your Lordships' House.

The facts are as follows. Reginald Woolmington is 21½ years old. His wife, who was killed, was 17½ years old last December. They had known each other for some time and upon August 25 they were married. Upon October 14 she gave birth to a child. Shortly after that there appears to have been some quarrelling between them and she left him upon November 22 and went to live with her mother. Woolmington apparently was anxious to get her to come back, but she did not come. The prosecution proved that at about 9:15 in the morning of the 10th Mrs. Daisy Brine was hanging out her washing at the back of her house at 25 Newtown, Milborne Port. While she was engaged in that occupation, she heard voices from the next door house, No. 24. She knew that in that house her niece, Reginald Woolmington's wife, was living. She heard and could recognize the voice of Reginald Woolmington saying something to the effect "are you going to come back home?" She could not hear the answer. Then the back door in No. 24 was slammed. She heard a voice in the kitchen but could not tell what it said. Then she heard the sound of a gun. Upon that she looked out of the front window and she saw Reginald Woolmington, whose voice she had heard just before speaking in the kitchen, go out and get upon his bicycle, which had been left or was standing against the wall of her house, No. 25. She called out to him but he gave no reply. He looked at her hard and then he rode away.

According to Reginald Woolmington's own story, having brooded over and deliberated upon the position all through the night of December 9, he went on the morning of the 10th in the usual way to the milking at his employer's farm, and while milking conceived this idea that he would take the old gun which was in the barn and he would take it up that morning to his wife's mother's house where she was living, and that he would show her that gun and tell her that he was going to commit suicide if she did not come back. He would take the gun up for the purpose of frightening her into coming back to him by causing her to think that he was going to commit suicide. He finished his milking, went back to his father's house, had breakfast and then left, taking with him a hack saw. He returned to the farm, went into the barn, got the gun, which had been used for rook shooting, sawed off the barrels of it, then took the only two cartridges which were there and put them into the gun. He took the two pieces of the barrel which he had sawn off and the hack saw, crossed a field about 60 yards wide and dropped them into the brook. Having done that, he returned on his bicycle, with the gun in his overcoat pocket, to his father's house and changed his clothes. Then he got a piece of wire flex which he attached to the gun so that he could suspend it from his shoulder underneath his coat, and so went off to the house where his wife was living. He knocked at the door, went into the kitchen and asked her: "Are you coming back?" She made no answer. She came into the parlour, and on his asking her whether she would come back she replied she was going into service. He then, so he says, threatened he would shoot himself, and went on to show her the gun and brought it across his waist, when it somehow went off and his wife fell down and he went out of the house. He told the jury that it was an accident, that it was a pure accident; that whilst he was getting the gun from under his shoulder and was drawing it across his breast it accidentally went off and he was doing nothing unlawful, nothing wrong, and this was a pure accident. There was considerable controversy as to whether a letter in which he set out his grievances was written before or after the above events. But when he was arrested at 7:30 on the evening of the 10th and charged with having committed murder he said: "I want to say nothing, except I done it, and they can do what they like with me. It was jealousy I suppose. Her mother enticed her away from me. I done all I could to get her back. That's all."

The learned judge in summing-up the case to the jury said:

> If you accept his evidence, you will have little doubt that she died in consequence of a gunshot wound which was inflicted by a gun which he had taken to this house, and which was in his hands, or in his possession, at the time that it exploded. If you come to the conclusion that she died in consequence of injuries from the gun which he was carrying, you are put by the law of this country into this position: The killing of a human being is homicide, however he may be killed, and all homicide is presumed to be malicious and murder, unless the contrary appears from circumstances of alleviation, excuse, or justification. "In every charge of murder, the fact of killing being first proved, all the circumstances of accident, necessity, or infirmity

are to be satisfactorily proved by the prisoner, unless they arise out of the evidence produced against him: for the law will presume the fact to have been founded in malice until the contrary appeareth." That has been the law of this country for all time since we had law. Once it is shown to a jury that somebody has died through the act of another, that is presumed to be murder, unless the person who has been guilty of the act which causes the death can satisfy a jury that what happened was something less, something which might be alleviated, something which might be reduced to a charge of manslaughter, or was something which was accidental, or was something which could be justified.

At the end of his summing-up he added:

The Crown has got to satisfy you that this woman, Violet Woolmington, died at the prisoner's hands. They must satisfy you of that beyond any reasonable doubt. If they satisfy you of that, then he has to show that there are circumstances to be found in the evidence which has been given from the witness-box in this case which alleviate the crime so that it is only manslaughter or which excuse the homicide altogether by showing that it was a pure accident.

If at any period of a trial it was permissible for the judge to rule that the prosecution had established its case and that the onus was shifted on the prisoner to prove that he was not guilty and that unless he discharged that onus the prosecution was entitled to succeed, it would be enabling the judge in such a case to say that the jury must in law find the prisoner guilty and so make the judge decide the case and not the jury, which is not the common law. It would be an entirely different case from those exceptional instances of special verdicts where a judge asks the jury to find certain facts and directs them that on such facts the prosecution is entitled to succeed. Indeed, a consideration of such special verdict shows that it is not till the end of the evidence that a verdict can properly be found and that at the end of the evidence it is not for the prisoner to establish his innocence, but for the prosecution to establish his guilt. Just as there is evidence on behalf of the prosecution so there may be evidence on behalf of the prisoner which may cause a doubt as to his guilt. In either case, he is entitled to the benefit of the doubt. But while the prosecution must prove the guilt of the prisoner, there is no such burden laid on the prisoner to prove his innocence and it is sufficient for him to raise a doubt as to his guilt; he is not bound to satisfy the jury of his innocence.

… Throughout the web of the English Criminal Law one golden thread is always to be seen, that it is the duty of the prosecution to prove the prisoner's guilt subject to what I have already said as to the defence of insanity and subject also to any statutory exception. If, at the end of and on the whole of the case, there is a reasonable doubt, created by the evidence given by either the prosecution or the prisoner, as to whether the prisoner killed the deceased with a malicious intention, the prosecution has not made out the case and the prisoner is entitled to an acquittal. No matter what the charge or where the trial, the principle that the prosecution must prove the guilt of the prisoner is part of the common law of England and no attempt to whittle it down can be entertained. When dealing with a murder case the Crown must prove (a) death as a result of a voluntary act of the accused and (b) malice of the accused. It may prove malice either expressly or by implication. For malice may be implied where death occurs as the result of a voluntary act of the accused which is (i) intentional and (ii) unprovoked. When evidence of death and malice has been given (this is a question for the jury) the accused is entitled to show, by evidence or by examination of the circumstances adduced by the Crown that the act on his part which caused death was either unintentional or provoked. If the jury are either satisfied with his explanation or, upon a review of all the evidence, are left in reasonable doubt whether, even if his explanation be not accepted, the act was unintentional or provoked, the prisoner is entitled to be acquitted. It is not the law of England to say, as was said in the summing-up in the present case: "if the Crown satisfy you that this woman died at the prisoner's hands then he has to show that there are circumstances to be found in the evidence which has been given from the witness-box in this case which alleviate the crime so that it is only manslaughter or which excuse the homicide altogether by showing it was a pure accident." ...

We were then asked to follow the Court of Criminal Appeal and to apply the proviso of s. 4 of the Criminal Appeal Act, 1907, which says: "the Court may, notwithstanding that they are of opinion that the point raised in the appeal might be decided in favour of the appellant, dismiss the appeal if they consider that no substantial miscarriage of justice has actually occurred." There is no doubt that there is ample jurisdiction to apply that proviso in a case of murder. The Act makes no distinction between a capital case and any other case, but we think it impossible to apply it in the present case. We cannot say that if the jury had been properly directed they would have inevitably come to the same conclusion.

In the result we decline to apply the proviso and, as already stated, we order that the appeal should be allowed and the conviction quashed.

Appeal allowed; conviction quashed.

R v Oakes
Supreme Court of Canada
[1986] 1 SCR 103

DICKSON CJ: This appeal concerns the constitutionality of s. 8 of the *Narcotic Control Act*, R.S.C. 1970, c. N-1. The section provides, in brief, that if the court finds the accused in possession of a narcotic, he is presumed to be in possession for the purpose of trafficking. Unless the accused can establish the contrary, he must be convicted of trafficking. ...

The respondent, David Edwin Oakes, was charged with unlawful possession of a narcotic for the purpose of trafficking, contrary to s. 4(2) of the *Narcotic Control Act*. ... At trial, the Crown adduced evidence to establish that Mr. Oakes was found in possession of eight one gram vials of cannabis resin in the form of hashish oil. Upon a further search conducted at the police station, $619.45 was located. Mr. Oakes told the police that he had bought ten vials of hashish oil for $150 for his own use, and that the $619.45 was from a workers' compensation cheque. He elected not to call evidence as to possession of the narcotic. Pursuant to the procedural provisions of s. 8 of the *Narcotic Control Act*, the trial judge proceeded to make a finding that it was beyond a reasonable doubt that Mr. Oakes was in possession of the narcotic. Following this finding, Mr. Oakes brought a motion to challenge the constitutional validity of s. 8 of the *Narcotic Control Act*, which he maintained imposes a burden on an accused to prove that he or she was not in possession for the purpose of trafficking. He argued that s. 8 violates the presumption of innocence contained in s. 11(d) of the Charter. ... The relevant portions of s. 8 read:

> 8. ... if the court finds that the accused was in possession of the narcotic ... he shall be given an opportunity of establishing that he was not in possession of the narcotic for the purpose of trafficking ... if the accused fails to establish that he was not in possession of the narcotic for the purpose of trafficking, he shall be convicted of the offence as charged. ...

In determining the meaning of these words, it is helpful to consider in a general sense the nature of presumptions. ...

A permissive presumption leaves it optional as to whether the inference of the presumed fact is drawn following proof of the basic fact. A mandatory presumption requires that the inference be made.

Presumptions may also be either rebuttable or irrebuttable. If a presumption is rebuttable, there are three potential ways the presumed fact can be rebutted. First, the accused may be required merely to raise a reasonable doubt as to its existence. Secondly, the accused may have an evidentiary burden to adduce sufficient evidence to bring into question the truth of the presumed fact. Thirdly, the accused may have a legal or persuasive burden to prove on a balance of probabilities the non-existence of the presumed fact.

Finally, presumptions are often referred to as either presumptions of law or presumptions of fact. The latter entail "frequently recurring examples of circumstantial evidence" (*Cross on Evidence*, at p. 124) while the former involve actual legal rules. ...

I conclude that s. 8 of the *Narcotic Control Act* contains a reverse onus provision imposing a legal burden on an accused to prove on a balance of probabilities that he or she was not in possession of a narcotic for the purpose of trafficking. It is therefore necessary to determine whether s. 8 of the *Narcotic Control Act* offends the right to be "presumed innocent until proven guilty" as guaranteed by s. 11(d) of the Charter.

Section 11(d) of the Charter constitutionally entrenches the presumption of innocence as part of the supreme law of Canada. For ease of reference, I set out this provision again:

> 11. Any person charged with an offence has the right ...
>   (d) to be presumed innocent until proven guilty according to law in a fair and public hearing by an independent and impartial tribunal. ...

The presumption of innocence is a hallowed principle lying at the very heart of criminal law. Although protected expressly in s. 11(d) of the Charter, the presumption of innocence is referable and integral to the general protection of life, liberty and security of the person contained in s. 7 of the Charter (see *Re B.C. Motor Vehicle Act*, [1985] 2 S.C.R. 486, per Lamer J.). The presumption of innocence protects the fundamental liberty and human dignity of any and every person accused by the State of criminal conduct. An individual charged with a criminal offence faces grave social and personal consequences, including potential loss of physical liberty, subjection to social stigma and ostracism from the community as well as other social, psychological and economic harms. In light of the gravity of these consequences, the presumption of innocence is crucial. It ensures that until the State proves an accused's guilt beyond all reasonable doubt, he or she is innocent. This is essential in a society committed to fairness and social justice. The presumption of innocence confirms our faith in humankind; it reflects our belief that individuals are decent and law-abiding members of the community until proven otherwise. ...

To return to s. 8 of the *Narcotic Control Act*, it is my view that, upon a finding beyond a reasonable doubt of possession of a narcotic, the accused has the legal burden of proving on a balance of probabilities that he or she was not in possession of the narcotic for the purpose of trafficking. Once the basic fact of possession is proven, a mandatory presumption of law arises against the accused that he or she had the intention to traffic. Moreover, the accused will be found guilty of the offence of trafficking unless he or she can rebut this presumption on a balance of probabilities. ...

The Legislature, by using the word "establish" in s. 8 of the *Narcotic Control Act*, intended to impose a legal burden on the accused. This is most apparent in the words "if the accused fails to establish that he was not in possession of the narcotic for the purpose of trafficking, he shall be convicted of the offence as charged." ...

In general one must, I think, conclude that a provision which requires an accused to disprove on a balance of probabilities the existence of a presumed fact, which is an important element of the offence in question, violates the presumption of innocence in s. 11(d). If an accused bears the burden of disproving on a balance of probabilities an essential element of an offence, it would be possible for a conviction to occur despite the existence of a reasonable doubt. This would arise if the accused adduced sufficient evidence to raise a reasonable doubt as to his or her innocence but did not convince the jury on a balance of probabilities that the presumed fact was untrue.

The fact that the standard is only the civil one does not render a reverse onus clause constitutional. As Sir Rupert Cross commented in the [Wright Lecture], "The Golden Thread of the English Criminal Law: The Burden of Proof," delivered in 1976 at the University of Toronto, at pp. 11-3:

> It is sometimes said that exceptions to the Woolmington rule are acceptable because, whenever the burden of proof on any issue in a criminal case is borne by the accused, he only has to satisfy the jury on the balance of probabilities, whereas on issues on which the Crown bears the burden of proof the jury must be satisfied beyond a reasonable doubt. ... The fact that the standard is lower when the accused bears the burden of proof than it is when the burden of proof is borne by the prosecution is no answer to my objection to the existence of exceptions to the Woolmington rule as it does not alter the fact that a jury or bench of magistrates may have to convict the accused although they are far from sure of his guilt.

As we have seen, the potential for a rational connection between the basic fact and the presumed fact to justify a reverse onus provision has been elaborated in some of the cases discussed above and is now known as the "rational connection test." ... A basic fact may rationally tend to prove a presumed fact, but not prove its existence beyond a reasonable doubt. An accused person could thereby be convicted despite the presence of a reasonable doubt. This would violate the presumption of innocence. ...

I should add that this questioning of the constitutionality of the "rational connection test" as a guide to interpreting s. 11(d) does not minimize its importance. The appropriate stage for invoking the rational connection test, however, is under s. 1 of the Charter. This consideration did not arise under the Canadian Bill of Rights because of the absence of an equivalent to s. 1. ... To my mind, it is highly desirable to keep s. 1 and s. 11(d) analytically distinct. ...

To return to s. 8 of the *Narcotic Control Act*, I am in no doubt whatsoever that it violates s. 11(d) of the Charter by requiring the accused to prove on a balance of probabilities that he was not in possession of the narcotic for the purpose of trafficking. Mr. Oakes is compelled by s. 8 to prove he is *not* guilty of the offence of trafficking. He is thus denied his right to be presumed innocent and subjected to the potential penalty of life imprisonment unless he can rebut the presumption. This is radically and fundamentally inconsistent with the societal values of human dignity and liberty which we espouse, and is directly contrary to the presumption of innocence enshrined in s. 11(d). Let us turn now to s. 1 of the Charter. ...

The Crown submits that even if s. 8 of the *Narcotic Control Act* violates s. 11(d) of the Charter, it can still be upheld as a reasonable limit under s. 1 which, as has been mentioned, provides:

> 1. The Canadian Charter of Rights and Freedoms guarantees the rights and freedoms set out in it subject only to such reasonable limits prescribed by law as can be demonstrably justified in a free and democratic society.

The question whether the limit is "prescribed by law" is not contentious in the present case since s. 8 of the *Narcotic Control Act* is a duly enacted legislative provision. It is, however, necessary to determine if the limit on Mr. Oakes' right, as guaranteed by s. 11(d) of the Charter, is "reasonable" and "demonstrably justified in a free and democratic society" for the purpose of s. 1 of the Charter, and thereby saved from inconsistency with the Constitution.

It is important to observe at the outset that s. 1 has two functions: first, it constitutionally guarantees the rights and freedoms set out in the provisions which follow; and, second, it states explicitly the exclusive justificatory criteria (outside of s. 33 of the *Constitution Act, 1982*) against which limitations on those rights and freedoms must be measured. Accordingly, any s. 1 inquiry must be premised on an understanding that the impugned limit violates constitutional rights and freedoms—rights and freedoms which are part of the supreme law of Canada. As Wilson J. stated in *Singh v. Minister of Employment and Immigration* [[1985] 1 SCR 177], supra, at p. 218: "... it is important to remember that the courts are conducting this inquiry in light of a commitment to uphold the rights and freedoms set out in the other sections of the Charter."

A second contextual element of interpretation of s. 1 is provided by the words "free and democratic society." Inclusion of these words as the final standard of justification for limits on rights and freedoms refers the Court to the very purpose for which the Charter was originally entrenched in the Constitution: Canadian society is to be free and democratic. The Court must be guided by the values and principles essential to a free and democratic society which I believe embody, to name but a few, respect for the inherent dignity of the human person, commitment to social justice and equality, accommodation of a wide variety of beliefs, respect or cultural and group identity, and faith in social and political institutions which enhance the participation of individuals and groups in society. The underlying values and principles of a free and democratic society are the genesis of the rights and freedoms guaranteed by the Charter and the ultimate standard against which a limit on a right or freedom must be shown, despite its effect, to be reasonable and demonstrably justified.

The rights and freedoms guaranteed by the Charter are not, however, absolute. It may become necessary to limit rights and freedoms in circumstances where their exercise would be inimical to the realization of collective goals of fundamental importance. For this reason, s. 1 provides criteria of justification for limits on the rights and freedoms guaranteed by the Charter. These criteria impose a stringent standard of justification, especially when understood in terms of the two contextual considerations discussed above, namely, the violation of a constitutionally guaranteed right or freedom and the fundamental principles of a free and democratic society.

The onus of proving that a limit on a right or freedom guaranteed by the Charter is reasonable and demonstrably justified in a free and democratic society rests upon the party seeking to uphold the limitation. It is clear from the text of s. 1 that limits on the rights and freedoms enumerated in the Charter are exceptions to their general guarantee.

The presumption is that the rights and freedoms are guaranteed unless the party invoking s. 1 can bring itself within the exceptional criteria which justify their being limited. This is further substantiated by the use of the word "demonstrably" which clearly indicates that the onus of justification is on the party seeking to justify the limit.

The standard of proof under s. 1 is the civil standard, namely, proof by a preponderance of probability. The alternative criminal standard, proof beyond a reasonable doubt, would, in my view, be unduly onerous on the party seeking to limit. Concepts such as "reasonableness," "justifiability" and "free and democratic society" are simply not amenable to such a standard. Nevertheless, the preponderance of probability test must be applied rigorously. Indeed, the phrase "demonstrably justified" in s. 1 of the Charter supports this conclusion. ...

To establish that a limit is reasonable and demonstrably justified in a free and democratic society, two central criteria must be satisfied. First, the objective, which the measures responsible for a limit on a Charter right or freedom are designed to serve, must be "of sufficient importance to warrant overriding a constitutionally protected right or freedom." ... The standard must be high in order to ensure that objectives which are trivial or discordant with the principles integral to a free and democratic society do not gain s. 1 protection. It is necessary, at a minimum, that an objective relate to concerns which are pressing and substantial in a free and democratic society before it can be characterized as sufficiently important.

Second, once a sufficiently significant objective is recognized, then the party invoking s. 1 must show that the means chosen are reasonable and demonstrably justified. This involves "a form of proportionality test." Although the nature of the proportionality test will vary depending on the circumstances, in each case courts will be required to balance the interests of society with those of individuals and groups. There are, in my view, three important components of a proportionality test. First, the measures adopted must be carefully designed to achieve the objective in question. They must not be arbitrary, unfair or based on irrational considerations. In short, they must be rationally connected to the objective. Second, the means, even if rationally connected to the objective in this first sense, should impair "as little as possible" the right or freedom in question. Third, there must be a proportionality between the effects of the measures which are responsible for limiting the Charter right or freedom, and the objective which has been identified as of "sufficient importance." ...

Having outlined the general principles of a s. 1 inquiry, we must apply them to s. 8 of the *Narcotic Control Act*. Is the reverse onus provision in s. 8 a reasonable limit on the right to be presumed innocent until proven guilty beyond a reasonable doubt as can be demonstrably justified in a free and democratic society?

[The chief justice then concluded that the legislative objective of "curbing drug trafficking by facilitating the conviction of drug traffickers" was a substantial and pressing concern of sufficient importance to warrant overriding a constitutional right.]

As outlined above, this proportionality test should begin with a consideration of the rationality of the provision: is the reverse onus clause in s. 8 rationally related to the objective of curbing drug trafficking? At a minimum, this requires that s. 8 be internally rational; there must be a rational connection between the basic fact of possession and the presumed fact of possession for the purpose of trafficking. Otherwise, the reverse onus clause could give rise to unjustified and erroneous convictions for drug trafficking of persons guilty only of possession of narcotics.

In my view, s. 8 does not survive this rational connection test. As Martin J.A. of the Ontario Court of Appeal concluded, possession of a small or negligible quantity of narcotics does not support the inference of trafficking. In other words, it would be irrational to infer that a person had an intent to traffic on the basis of his or her possession of a very small quantity of narcotics. The presumption required under s. 8 of the *Narcotic Control Act* is overinclusive and could lead to results in certain cases which would defy both rationality and fairness. In light of the seriousness of the offence in question, which carries with it the possibility of imprisonment for life, I am further convinced that the first component of the proportionality test has not been satisfied by the Crown.

Having concluded that s. 8 does not satisfy this first component of proportionality, it is unnecessary to consider the other two components.

[Chouinard, Lamer, Wilson, and Le Dain JJ concurred with Dickson CJ. Estey and McIntyre JJ agreed with the result, stressing in their s 11(d) analysis the lack of a rational connection between the proved fact of possession and the presumed fact of an intention to traffic.]

Internal Rationality Between Proven and Presumed Facts No Longer Required Under Section 1

Note that the Court's strict holding in *Oakes* that there must be a rational connection between the proven and the presumed facts was disapproved of by the Court in *R v Laba*, [1994] 3 SCR 965. The Court decided in that case that there was no requirement of "internal rationality" between the proven and the presumed facts and that the proper issue under s 1 of the Charter was whether there was a rational connection between the limit on the presumption of innocence and the legislative objective. Even if such a connection existed, the Crown would still have to demonstrate under s 1 that the s 11(d) violation was the least restrictive means of achieving an objective and that there was an overall balance between the limitation of the right and the advancement of the legislative objective.

Presumption of Innocence Applies to Defence and to Elements of Offence

In *R v Whyte*, [1988] 2 SCR 3, the Supreme Court rejected a Crown argument that would have limited the presumption of innocence to the elements of the offence. Dickson CJ stated for the Court that

> the distinction between elements of the offence and other aspects of the charge is irrelevant to the s. 11(d) inquiry. The real concern is not whether the accused must disprove an element or prove an excuse, but that an accused may be convicted while a reasonable doubt exists. When that possibility exists, there is a breach of the presumption of innocence.
>
> The exact characterization of a factor as an essential element, a collateral factor, an excuse, or a defence should not affect the analysis of the presumption of innocence. It is the final effect of a provision on the verdict that is decisive. If an accused is required to prove some fact on the balance of probabilities to avoid conviction, the provision violates the presumption of innocence because it permits a conviction in spite of a reasonable doubt in the mind of the trier of fact as to the guilt of the accused.

R v Keegstra
Supreme Court of Canada
[1990] 3 SCR 697

DICKSON CJ [Wilson, L'Heureux-Dubé, and Gonthier JJ held for the Court that s 319(3)(a) infringed the presumption of innocence under s 11(d) of the Charter but that the infringement was a reasonable limit on the presumption of innocence that was justified under s 1 of the Charter.]

The judgments of the appeal courts in this case and in the accompanying appeal of [*R v Andrews* (1988), 65 OR (2d) 161, aff'd [1990] 3 SCR 870] reveal a divergence of opinion as to whether s. 11(d) of the Charter is infringed by the truth defence. In the Alberta Court of Appeal, Kerans J.A. viewed as crucial the possibility that an accused can be convicted of wilfully promoting hatred though there exists a reasonable doubt that the statements communicated are true. As the defence places an onus on the accused to prove truth on the balance of probabilities, he thus found it to infringe s. 11(d). In contrast to this conclusion, the Ontario Court of Appeal in *R. v. Andrews, supra,* found that s. 319(3)(a) does not place a true reverse onus upon the accused. Relying upon the majority judgment in *R. v. Holmes*, [1988] 1 S.C.R. 914, Grange J.A. felt that s. 319(3)(a) provides a defence which becomes applicable only after all elements of the offence have been proven beyond a reasonable doubt, a circumstance which was said to avoid infringing the presumption of innocence (p. 225). Grange J.A. distinguished this Court's decision in *R. v. Whyte*, [1988] 2 S.C.R. 3, on the grounds that the statutory presumption challenged in that case related to the proof of an essential element of the offence.

It is not overly difficult to settle the disagreement between the Alberta and Ontario Appeal Courts. Though some confusion may have existed after the decision of this Court in *Holmes*, since in *Whyte* it is clear that the presumption of innocence is infringed whenever the accused is liable to be convicted despite the existence of a reasonable doubt as to guilt in the mind of the trier of fact.

[He then held that the violation of s 11(d) by the reverse onus in the truth defence was justified under s 1.]

The reverse onus in the truth defence operates so as to make it more difficult to avoid conviction where the wilful promotion of hatred has been proven beyond a reasonable doubt. As the wilful promotion of hatred is hostile to Parliament's aims, placing such a burden upon the accused is rationally connected to a valid s. 1 objective. ...

To include falsity as a component of s. 319(2) for example, or even to require only that the accused raise a reasonable doubt as to the truthfulness of the statements, would excessively compromise the effectiveness of the offence in achieving its purpose. The former option would especially hinder Parliament's objective, for many statements are not susceptible to a true/false categorization. In either instance, however, where a reasonable doubt existed as to the falsity of an accused's statements an acquittal would be entered. To accept such a result it would have to be agreed that this relatively small possibility of truthfulness outweighs the harm caused through the wilful promotion of hatred. Yet to my mind the crucial objective of Parliament in this appeal justifies requiring a more convincing demonstration that a hate-monger's statements may be true, as a successful defence provides an excuse despite the presence of the harm sought to be eradicated (see Rauf, op. cit., at pp. 368-69). Having the accused prove truthfulness on the balance of probabilities is an understandable and valued precaution against too easily justifying such harm, and I hence conclude that the reverse onus provision in s. 319(3)(a) represents a minimal impairment of the presumption of innocence. ...

McLACHLIN J (Sopinka and La Forest JJ concurring) (in dissent): ... A rational connection between the aims of s. 319(3)(a) and its requirement that the accused prove the truth of his statements is difficult to discern. It is argued that without the reverse onus, it would be difficult if not impossible to obtain convictions for much speech promoting hate. If the objection is that it is merely difficult to prove the statements true or false, the answer is that the burden should be on the state because it has superior resources. If the objection is that it is impossible to know if the statements are true or false (i.e. true opinion), then the answer is that it cannot be ruled out that the statements may be more valuable than harmful, if we accept the ultimate value of the exchange of truthful ideas. The same considerations suggest that s. 319(3)(a)'s infringement of the presumption of innocence is neither minimal nor, given the importance of the infringement in the context of prosecutions under s. 319(2), sufficient to outweigh the dubious benefit of such a provision.

Similar considerations arise on the question of whether s. 319(3)(a) of the *Criminal Code* impairs the presumption of innocence under s. 11(d) as little as possible. It is said that hate promotion against identifiable groups is highly unlikely to be true. But that would be small comfort to a particular accused in the case where such a defence lay but he or she, because of restricted means or for whatever other reason, was unable to prove it. The presumption of innocence should not depend on the percentage of cases in which the defence in question may arise. ...

The final test of proportionality between the effects of the infringement and the objectives it promotes encounters other difficulties. We must start from the proposition that Parliament intended the truth to be a defence and that falsehood is an important element of the offence created by s. 319(2) of the *Criminal Code*. That fact, coupled with the centrality of the presumption of innocence in our criminal law, suggests that only a countervailing state interest of the most compelling kind could justify the infringement. But, as discussed in connection with the infringement of the guarantee of freedom of expression, it is difficult to see what benefits s. 319(2) in fact produces in terms of stemming hate propaganda and promoting social harmony and individual dignity. ... I conclude that s. 319(3)(a) is not saved by s. 1 of the Charter.

In *R v Downey*, [1992] 2 SCR 10, Cory J provided the following summary of the principles that emerged from the s 11(d) jurisprudence to date:

I. The presumption of innocence is infringed whenever the accused is liable to be convicted despite the existence of a reasonable doubt.

II. If by the provisions of a statutory presumption, an accused is required to establish, that is to say to prove or disprove, on a balance of probabilities either an element of an offence or an excuse, then it contravenes s. 11(d). Such a provision would permit a conviction in spite of a reasonable doubt.

III. Even if a rational connection exists between the established fact and the fact to be presumed, this would be insufficient to make valid a presumption requiring the accused to disprove an element of the offence.

IV. Legislation which substitutes proof of one element for proof of an essential element will not infringe the presumption of innocence if as a result of the proof of the substituted element, it would be unreasonable for the trier of fact not to be satisfied beyond a reasonable doubt of the existence of the other element. To put it another way, the statutory presumption will be valid if the proof of the substituted fact leads inexorably to the proof of the other. However, the statutory presumption will infringe s. 11(d) if it requires the trier of fact to convict in spite of a reasonable doubt.

V. A permissive assumption from which a trier of fact may but not must draw an inference of guilt will not infringe s. 11(d).

VI. A provision that might have been intended to play a minor role in providing relief from conviction will none the less contravene the Charter if the provision (such as the truth of a statement) must be established by the accused (see *Keegstra, supra*).

VII. It must of course be remembered that statutory presumptions which infringe s 11(d) may still be justified pursuant to s. 1 of the Charter. (As, for example, in *Keegstra, supra*.)

Quantum of Proof

At Donald Marshall Jr's trial, the judge defined reasonable doubt as "honest doubt" that would cause a juror to say "I am not morally certain that he committed the offence." Would such a definition be accepted today? Would the jury have acquitted Marshall had the judge instructed them in the terms of the following two cases?

R v Lifchus
Supreme Court of Canada
[1997] 3 SCR 320

[The trial judge told the jury to use the phrase "reasonable doubt" in its "ordinary, natural every day sense." The Supreme Court held this was an error.]

CORY J: …

[36] Perhaps a brief summary of what the definition should and should not contain may be helpful. It should be explained that:

- the standard of proof beyond a reasonable doubt is inextricably intertwined with that principle fundamental to all criminal trials, the presumption of innocence;
- the burden of proof rests on the prosecution throughout the trial and never shifts to the accused;
- a reasonable doubt is not a doubt based upon sympathy or prejudice;
- rather, it is based upon reason and common sense;
- it is logically connected to the evidence or absence of evidence;
- it does not involve proof to an absolute certainty; it is not proof beyond any doubt nor is it an imaginary or frivolous doubt; and
- more is required than proof that the accused is probably guilty
- a jury which concludes only that the accused is probably guilty must acquit.

[37] On the other hand, certain references to the required standard of proof should be avoided. For example:

- describing the term "reasonable doubt" as an ordinary expression which has no special meaning in the criminal law context;
- inviting jurors to apply to the task before them the same standard of proof that they apply to important, or even the most important, decisions in their own lives;
- equating proof "beyond a reasonable doubt" to proof "to a moral certainty";
- qualifying the word "doubt" with adjectives other than "reasonable," such as "serious," "substantial" or "haunting," which may mislead the jury; and
- instructing jurors that they may convict if they are "sure" that the accused is guilty, before providing them with a proper definition as to the meaning of the words "beyond a reasonable doubt."

[38] A charge which is consistent with the principles set out in these reasons will suffice regardless of the particular words used by the trial judge. Nevertheless, it may, as suggested in [*R v Girard* (1996), 109 CCC (3d) 545 (Qc CA)], *supra*, at p. 556, be useful to set out a "model charge" which could provide the necessary instructions as to the meaning of the phrase beyond a reasonable doubt.

[39] Instructions pertaining to the requisite standard of proof in a criminal trial of proof beyond a reasonable doubt might be given along these lines:

> The accused enters these proceedings presumed to be innocent. That presumption of innocence remains throughout the case until such time as the Crown has on the evidence put before you satisfied you beyond a reasonable doubt that the accused is guilty.

What does the expression "beyond a reasonable doubt" mean?

The term "beyond a reasonable doubt" has been used for a very long time and is a part of our history and traditions of justice. It is so engrained in our criminal law that some think it needs no explanation, yet something must be said regarding its meaning.

A reasonable doubt is not an imaginary or frivolous doubt. It must not be based upon sympathy or prejudice. Rather, it is based on reason and common sense. It is logically derived from the evidence or absence of evidence.

Even if you believe the accused is probably guilty or likely guilty, that is not sufficient. In those circumstances you must give the benefit of the doubt to the accused and acquit because the Crown has failed to satisfy you of the guilt of the accused beyond a reasonable doubt.

On the other hand you must remember that it is virtually impossible to prove anything to an absolute certainty and the Crown is not required to do so. Such a standard of proof is impossibly high.

In short if, based upon the evidence before the court, you are sure that the accused committed the offence you should convict since this demonstrates that you are satisfied of his guilt beyond a reasonable doubt.

[40] This is not a magic incantation that needs to be repeated word for word. It is nothing more than a suggested form that would not be faulted if it were used. For example, in cases where a reverse onus provision must be considered, it would be helpful to bring to the attention of the jury either the evidence which might satisfy that onus or the absence of evidence applicable to it. Any form of instruction that complied with the applicable principles and avoided the pitfalls referred to would be satisfactory.

R v Starr
Supreme Court of Canada
2000 SCC 40, [2000] 2 SCR 144

[The trial judge told the jury that the phrase "reasonable doubt" had no special connotation and it did not require proof of an absolute certainty. The Supreme Court held this was an error.]

IACOBUCCI J (Major, Binnie, Arbour, and LeBel JJ concurring): ...
   [107] With respect to the jury instructions on the phrase "beyond a reasonable doubt," as set out in *Lifchus, supra*, an instruction like the one in this case, which fails to explain that the beyond a reasonable doubt standard has special legal significance and requires a significantly higher quantum of proof than the balance of probabilities, will not satisfy the *Lifchus* standard. ...
   [239] The key difficulty with this instruction is that it was not made clear to the jury that the Crown was required to do more than prove the appellant's guilt on a balance of probabilities. The trial judge told the jury that they could convict on the basis of something less than absolute certainty of guilt, but did not explain, in essence, how much less. In

addition, rather than telling the jury that the words "reasonable doubt" have a specific meaning in the legal context, the trial judge expressly instructed the jury that the words have no "special connotation" and "no magic meaning that is peculiar to the law." By asserting that absolute certainty was not required, and then linking the standard of proof to the "ordinary everyday" meaning of the words "reasonable doubt," the trial judge could easily have been understood by the jury as asserting a probability standard as the applicable standard of proof.

[240] The trial judge did comply with some of the requirements discussed in *Lifchus*, *supra*. He explained that a reasonable doubt is not an imaginary or frivolous doubt resting on speculation or guess, and that a reasonable doubt is a real doubt based on reason and common sense upon a review of the evidence. He also explained, as mentioned, that the standard of proof beyond a reasonable doubt does not involve proof to an absolute certainty. However, the trial judge's adherence to these requirements would have benefited primarily the Crown, not the appellant.

[241] In the present case, the trial judge did refer to the Crown's onus and to the presumption of innocence, and he stated that the appellant should receive the benefit of any reasonable doubt. The error in the charge is that the jury was not told how a reasonable doubt is to be defined. As was emphasized repeatedly in *Lifchus* … , a jury must be instructed that the standard of proof in a criminal trial is higher than the probability standard used in making everyday decisions and in civil trials. Indeed, it is this very requirement to go beyond probability that meshes the standard of proof in criminal cases with the presumption of innocence and the Crown's onus. However, as Cory J. explained in these earlier decisions, it is generally inappropriate to define the meaning of the term "reasonable doubt" through examples from daily life, through the use of synonyms, or through analogy to moral choices. The criminal standard of proof has a special significance unique to the legal process. It is an exacting standard of proof rarely encountered in everyday life, and there is no universally intelligible illustration of the concept, such as the scales of justice with respect to the balance of probabilities standard. Unlike absolute certainty or the balance of probabilities, reasonable doubt is not an easily quantifiable standard. It cannot be measured or described by analogy. It must be explained. However, precisely because it is not quantifiable, it is difficult to explain.

[242] In my view, an effective way to define the reasonable doubt standard for a jury is to explain that it falls much closer to absolute certainty than to proof on a balance of probabilities. As stated in *Lifchus*, a trial judge is required to explain that something less than absolute certainty is required, and that something more than probable guilt is required, in order for the jury to convict. Both of these alternative standards are fairly and easily comprehensible. It will be of great assistance for a jury if the trial judge situates the reasonable doubt standard appropriately between these two standards. The additional instructions to the jury set out in *Lifchus* as to the meaning and appropriate manner of determining the existence of a reasonable doubt serve to define the space between absolute certainty and proof beyond a reasonable doubt. In this regard, I am in agreement with Twaddle J.A. in the court below, when he said, at p. 177:

> If standards of proof were marked on a measure, proof "beyond reasonable doubt" would lie much closer to "absolute certainty" than to "a balance of probabilities." Just as a judge has a duty to instruct the jury that absolute certainty is not required, he or she has a duty, in my

view, to instruct the jury that the criminal standard is more than a probability. The words he or she uses to convey this idea are of no significance, but the idea itself must be conveyed. ...

[243] In the appellant's case, with respect, the trial judge did not give instructions that could be construed as having located the reasonable doubt standard above the probability standard. Not only was the jury not told that something more than probability was required in order to convict, but nearly all of the instructions they were given (i.e., less than absolute certainty required, ordinary everyday words, no special meaning, more than a frivolous doubt required) weakened the content of the reasonable doubt standard in such a manner as to suggest that probability was indeed the requisite standard of proof. ... While obviously a mistake in the charge will not always be fatal, at no point did the instructions in this case cure the mistake. The fact that the trial judge repeatedly stated that the prosecution must prove guilt beyond a reasonable doubt is no cure given his failure to ever define reasonable doubt correctly. ... I reach this finding notwithstanding the fact that, like the jury charge in *Lifchus* when read as a whole, the jury charge in the present case was largely a model of fairness to the accused. The fact that other elements of the charge were fair to the accused cannot eliminate the prejudice caused by the improper instructions. Thus I conclude that there was not substantial compliance with the *Lifchus* principles. I would therefore allow the appeal on this ground. ...

L'HEUREUX-DUBÉ J (McLachlin CJ and Gonthier and Bastarache JJ concurring) in dissent:

[23] On the issue of the jury charge on reasonable doubt, the *Lifchus* standard provides guidelines for trial judges rather than an iron-clad roster of proscriptions and prohibitions. I do not read *Lifchus* as providing that the inclusion or exclusion of certain phrases automatically vitiates a jury charge. Instead, I read *Lifchus* as mandating that a charge be examined in its entirety to determine whether the jury properly understood the concept of proof beyond a reasonable doubt. I am of the opinion that the jury charge in this case properly communicated this concept to the jury. ...

[94] The trial judge's charge, however, was not flawless. Specifically, we must examine the effect of the trial judge's misstatement that the words "reasonable doubt" are used in their everyday, ordinary sense and have no special legal meaning. It is asserted that this flaw in the charge, together with the failure of the trial judge to state expressly that the Crown was required to do more than prove the appellant's guilt on a balance of probabilities, constitutes reversible error. With respect, I cannot agree.

[95] The verdict ought not to be disturbed because the charge, "when read as a whole, makes it clear that the jury could not have been under any misapprehension as to the correct burden and standard of proof to apply": *Lifchus*, at para. 41. While the judge told the jury that the words "reasonable doubt" had no special meaning, this was harmless error because he proceeded to give them all the legal information they required. The jury knew the accused was presumed innocent, they knew the standard of proof was very high—a standard just below absolute certainty—and they knew that they could not convict on a balance of probabilities. ...

[97] Moreover, the charge complied with *Lifchus*'s first principle that it must be made clear to the jury that the standard of proof beyond a reasonable doubt is inextricably

linked to the presumption of innocence and that this burden never shifts to the accused: *Lifchus*, at para. 27. The relevant portion of the trial judge's charge on this point is:

> Let me first emphasize the presumption of innocence. Simply put, the accused is presumed to be innocent and he continues to be and remain innocent unless and until the Crown has satisfied you beyond reasonable doubt of his guilt. This presumption remains with the accused and for his benefit from the beginning of the case until the end of the case. The onus of proving guilt rests upon the Crown from the beginning to the end of the case and it never shifts. There is no burden whatsoever on the accused to prove his innocence. The Crown must prove beyond a reasonable doubt that an accused person is guilty of the offence or offences with which he is charged before he can be convicted.

[98] In light of the trial judge's compliance with the bulk of the principles enunciated in *Lifchus*, I am loath to find that the charge was automatically vitiated by the failure to include a specific item mentioned in *Lifchus* or by the inclusion of an improper item. To do so would contravene our holding that "an error in the instructions as to the standard of proof may not constitute a reversible error": *Lifchus*, at para. 41.

[99] Jurors are sophisticated persons who are instructed to listen to and follow the entirety of the judge's charge to them. We must assume that they do so. It would ill behoove a reviewing court to do exactly what the jury is commanded not to do and isolate a phrase or a small section of the charge, ignoring the whole of it. I do not believe that is what Cory J. intended in *Lifchus*. Rather, he was attempting to provide guidance to trial judges in the extremely difficult task of articulating what is proof beyond a reasonable doubt and communicating this standard to the jury.

[100] *Lifchus* should be viewed as a broad template for trial judges to assist them in their difficult task. Cory J.'s suggestions provide a touchstone for comparison for courts in reviewing jury charges. However, reviewing courts must resist the temptation to use the *Lifchus* suggestions as a mandatory checklist. The tendency to do so is natural and understandable as it would make the task of reviewing a jury charge far easier. However, a jury charge is not a multiple choice exam that can be marked by a computer. Rather, it is akin to a work of literature that must be studied in its entirety in order to evaluate it as a whole.

[101] Examining the charge in its entirety, I do not find that a reasonable likelihood existed that the jury misapprehended the correct standard of proof. Accordingly, I would dismiss this ground of appeal.

New trial ordered.

ADDITIONAL READING

Berger, BL & J Stribopoulos, eds. *Unsettled Legacy: Thirty Years of Criminal Justice Under the Charter* (Toronto: LexisNexis, 2012).

Coughlan, S. *Criminal Procedure*, 2nd ed (Toronto: Irwin Law, 2012).

Cunliffe, E. *Murder, Medicine and Motherhood* (Oxford: Hart, 2011).

Garrett, B. *Convicting the Innocent* (Cambridge, Mass: Harvard University Press, 2010).

Huff, R & M Killas, eds. *Wrongful Convictions: Causes and Remedies* (New York: Routledge, 2013).

Penney, S, V Rondinelli & J Stribopoulos. *Criminal Procedure in Canada* (Toronto: LexisNexis, 2011).

Roach, K. *Due Process and Victims' Rights: The New Law and Politics of Criminal Justice* (Toronto: University of Toronto Press, 1999).

Stuart, D. *Charter Justice in Canadian Criminal Law*, 6th ed (Toronto: Carswell, 2014).

PART TWO

Principles of Criminal Liability

Conduct or Actus Reus

Criminal liability can exist only when there is a valid definition in law of criminal wrongdoing. This requirement may be justified, at least in part, by reference to the principle of legality. That principle excludes retroactive application of the criminal law and, according to Canadian constitutional jurisprudence examined in Chapter 1, it excludes the enforcement of offences that are impermissibly vague or overly broad. But what else is implied in the requirement for a valid definition of criminal wrongdoing? This chapter looks at the requirement for some forms of prohibited conduct, the *actus reus*.

One of the foundational principles of criminal liability is found in the maxim *actus non facit reum nisi mens sit rea*, which, translated, states that an act is not guilty unless there is also a guilty mind. It conveys the idea that there can be no criminally culpable act unless it is performed with a culpable mental state (see Chapter 7). The same might be said in reverse: there can be no criminal liability unless a guilty mind expresses itself in the performance of prohibited conduct. Just as the insistence on a culpable mind, or *mens rea*, prevents the criminalization of mere accidents, the requirement for criminal conduct is an important limitation on the ambit and the legitimacy of the criminal sanction. Without it, there would be no bar to the imposition of criminal liability for prohibited thoughts, which in itself would be intolerable in a free and democratic society, there being no principle of harm or utility that could justify this extension of the criminal law. Lord Mansfield said as much in 1784: "So long as an act rests in bare intention, it is not punishable by our laws" (*Rex v Scofield*, Caldecott's Rep 397).

It is important to recognize that the concept of *actus reus* refers to more than simply a prohibited action; *actus reus* comprises a bundle of components that, together, constitute the "guilty act." Put most helpfully, the *actus reus* requires a (1) physically voluntary (2) act or omission, (3) sometimes in certain prescribed circumstances, and (4) sometimes causing certain consequences. Each of these components is equally critical to defining the *actus reus* for a given offence, and the starting point is that a finding of guilt requires that the Crown prove each beyond a reasonable doubt. This chapter explores the principles governing these aspects of the *actus reus*.

The first section of this chapter looks at the concept of physical voluntariness, which is always a component of the *actus reus*. Section II considers the primary form of prohibited conduct, the act, but then takes up the fraught question of when one can be punished for omissions—failures to act. The section concludes with a brief consideration of so-called status offences. The third section addresses the need to examine particular circumstances that might be included in the definition of an offence, and the fourth section is concerned with offences that involve prohibited consequences, raising the issue of causation in criminal law. Having thus addressed the various components of the *actus reus*, the chapter concludes by examining a principle that governs the relationship between *actus reus* and *mens rea*, the principle of "contemporaneity," or "coincidence." Chapters 6 and 7 then turn to the issue of *mens rea* and fault requirements, with Chapter 6 also examining offences that are only based on the commission of the *actus reus*.

I. VOLUNTARINESS

The first of the elements of the *actus reus* is the requirement for voluntary conduct. Voluntariness is a requirement for every offence, whether a true crime or a quasi-criminal/regulatory offence. The requirement for voluntariness is best thought of as a demand that the prohibited conduct be a product of the will of the accused. Factual illustrations best reflect the distinction between the voluntary and involuntary performance of an act. If you fall on a slippery surface and in the course of falling strike the person next to you, is the application of force a voluntary act? If you have a statutory duty to maintain safe storage of dangerous products, does the destruction of your precautions by a third person or a natural force mean that you have voluntarily breached your duty? If you lose consciousness while driving due to a heart attack, is your dangerous driving a voluntary act?

As these examples suggest, physical involuntariness can cover a wide range of conduct, including reflexive action, sleepwalking, and accident. The essential characteristic of voluntariness is the conscious control of action. Consciousness alone, however, is not enough to establish voluntariness because a person might be conscious and yet still be incapable of controlling his or her conduct. The element of control is necessary in order to attribute responsibility for conduct. In sum, the voluntariness of a person's conduct will be established if his or her conduct is the product of conscious choice.

The criminal law thus views it as unjust to punish someone for conduct that is not truly their own, in the sense of not being fairly attributed to the accused's free choice. In this claim one finds a theory of human agency at play in the criminal law, a conception of agency that relies on a close relationship between moral blame and free choice. Consider the following extract from the writings of the great jurist and associate justice of the US Supreme Court, Oliver Wendell Holmes, in *The Common Law* (Boston: Little, Brown, and Company, 1881) at 54-55:

> The reason for requiring an act is, that an act implies a choice, and that it is felt to be impolitic and unjust to make a man answerable for harm, unless he might have chosen otherwise. But the choice must be made with a chance of contemplating the consequence complained of, or else it has no bearing on responsibility for that consequence. If this were not true, a man might be held

answerable for everything which would not have happened but for his choice at some past time. For instance, for having in a fit fallen on a man, which he would not have done had he not chosen to come to the city where he was taken ill.

With that statement in mind, consider the following case.

R v Larsonneur
Court of Criminal Appeal, England
(1933), 24 Cr App R 74

[On March 14, 1933, the appellant, who was a French citizen, landed at Folkestone with a French passport, which was endorsed with the condition that she not engage in any employment while in the United Kingdom. On March 22, 1933, the condition was varied by an undersecretary of state, requiring her to immediately leave the United Kingdom. On that day the appellant went to the Irish Free State. The Irish authorities ordered her deportation and, on April 20, 1933, the Irish Free State police brought her back to Holyhead, in the United Kingdom, and handed her over to the police there. She was detained and, on April 22, charged before a police magistrate. She was later convicted by a jury on a charge that she "being an alien to whom leave to land in the United Kingdom has been refused was found in the United Kingdom." The jury returned a verdict of "guilty through circumstances beyond her own control," and the chairman passed a sentence of three days' imprisonment and made an order recommending the appellant for deportation.]

HEWART LCJ: ... The fact is, as the evidence shows, that the appellant is an alien. She has a French passport, which bears this statement under the date March 14, 1933, "Leave to land granted at Folkestone this day on condition that the holder does not enter any employment, paid or unpaid, while in the United Kingdom," but on March 22, that condition was varied and one finds these words: "The condition attached to the grant of leave to land is hereby varied so as to require departure from the United Kingdom not later than March 22, 1933." Then follows the signature of an Under-Secretary of State. In fact, the appellant went to the Irish Free State and afterwards, in circumstances which are perfectly immaterial, so far as this appeal is concerned, came back to Holyhead. She was at Holyhead on April 21, 1944, a date after the day limited by the condition on her passport.

In these circumstances, it seems to be quite clear that Art. 1(4) of the *Aliens Order*, 1920 (as amended by the Orders of March 12, 1923, and August 11, 1931), applies. The Article is in the following terms: "An immigration officer, in accordance with general or special directions of the Secretary of State, may, by general order or notice or otherwise, attach such conditions as he may think fit to the grant of leave to land, and the Secretary of State may at any time vary such conditions in such manner as he things fit, and the alien shall comply with the conditions so attached or varied, and an alien who is found in the United Kingdom at any time after the expiration of the period limited by any such condition, shall for the purposes of this Order be deemed to be an alien to whom leave to land has been refused."

The appellant was, therefore, on April 21, 1933, in the position in which she would have been if she had been prohibited from landing by the Secretary of State and, that being so, there is no reason to interfere with the finding of the jury. She was found here and was, therefore, deemed to be in the class of persons whose landing had been prohibited by the Secretary of State, by reason of the fact that she had violated the condition on her passport. The appeal, therefore, is dismissed and the recommendation for deportation remains.

Appeal dismissed.

Larsonneur is now generally viewed as a case that improperly ignored the voluntariness component of the *actus reus*. A fine articulation of the common law principle of voluntariness is found in the following case from New Zealand. This case also helpfully demonstrates that the question of voluntariness, which is a component of the *actus reus*, is distinct from (and ought to be considered prior to) the issue of whether the accused had the requisite *mens rea*.

Kilbride v Lake
New Zealand Supreme Court
[1962] NZLR 590

WOODHOUSE J: On Thursday, 15 June 1961, the appellant drove his wife's car into Queen Street in the City of Auckland where he left it parked. He returned to it a short time later to find stuck to the inside of the windscreen a traffic offence notice drawing his attention to the fact that a current warrant of fitness was not displayed in terms of Reg. 52 of the Traffic Regulations 1956 (S.R. 1956/218). It was agreed before me that the warrant had been in its correct position when he left the vehicle, but that it could not be found upon his return. It was further agreed that during the period of his absence from the car the warrant had become detached from the windscreen in some way and been lost, or it had been removed by some person unknown. The fact that it was a current warrant was proved conclusively by records showing that on 13 April it had been issued by the Auckland Municipal Motor Vehicle Testing Station under No. 4513, and in respect of voucher No. 115456 … . Despite a written explanation to this general effect which he had forwarded on the same day, a prosecution followed and he was convicted before Justices on an information alleging that he "did operate a motor vehicle … and did fail to display in the prescribed manner a current warrant of fitness." …

The case for the appellant was that if he could show an absence of *mens rea*, then he could not be convicted, and he had succeeded in doing this as the warrant had disappeared without his knowledge during his absence from the car. On the other hand it was claimed for the respondent that this statutory offence was one which excluded *mens rea* as an ingredient to be proved. On this basis it was submitted that the offence was one of strict liability [what we would classify in Canada as "absolute liability"], and therefore the knowledge or the intention of the appellant was irrelevant. The issue thus raised on these simple facts directly poses the important question as to whether something done perfectly lawfully by the appellant could become an offence on his party by reasons of an intervening cause beyond his influence or control, and which produced an effect entirely outside his means of knowledge.

It has long been established, of course, that if there is an absolute prohibition, and the prohibited act is done by the defendant, then the absence of *mens rea* affords no defence. This principle derives its justification from the general public interest, and any consequential injustice which might seem to follow in individual cases has necessarily been accepted. In the present case the respondent has conceded that the appellant had no opportunity of dealing with the situations which arose. But, it is said, however unfair a conviction might be to him personally, this offence has been made one of absolute liability as it is essential to put strong pressure on drivers of motor vehicles to do their whole duty. He permitted the car to be on the road, it was found there without a warrant, and accordingly he is guilty of the offence. With all respect to the arguments of both counsel, however, I am of the opinion that the emphasis which has been put on the matter of *mens rea* has obscured the real issue in this case.

It is fundamental that quite apart from any need there might be to prove *mens rea*,

a person cannot be convicted of any crime unless he has committed an overt act prohibited by the law, or has made default in some act which there was a legal obligation to do. The act or omission must be voluntary (*10 Halsbury's Laws of England*, 3rd ed., 272).

He must be shown to be responsible for the physical ingredient of the crime or offence. This elementary principle obviously involves the proof of something which goes behind any subsequent and any additional inquiry that might become necessary as to whether *mens rea* must be proved as well. Until that initial proof exists arguments concerning *mens rea* are premature. ... The primary question arising on this appeal, in my opinion, is whether or not the physical element in the offence was produced by the appellant. This physical element may be described by the convenient term *acts reus*, in contrast to the mental element or *mens rea* which is also an ingredient of a crime or offence, unless expressly excluded by its statutory definition.

. . .

[I]n my opinion, it is a cardinal principle that, altogether apart from the mental element of intention or knowledge of the circumstances, a person cannot be made criminally responsible for an act or omission unless it was done or omitted in circumstances where there was some other course open to him. If this condition is absent, any act or omission must be involuntary, or unconscious, or unrelated to the forbidden event in any causal sense regarded by the law as involving responsibility. See for example, *Salmon on Jurisprudence*, 11th ed. 401, *Causation in the Law* by Hart and Honore 292, *et seq.*, and the passage in *10 Halsbury's Law of England* 3rd ed. 272 cited above. In my opinion a correct emphasis is now given by this last paragraph to the need for the act or omission making up the *actus reus* to be voluntary ... . Naturally the condition that there must be freedom to take one course or another involves free and conscious exercise of will in the case of an act, or the opportunity to choose to behave differently in the case of omissions. But this mental stimulus required to promote acts or available to promote omissions if the matter is adverted to, and consequently able to produce some forbidden condition, is entirely distinct from the mental element contained in the concept of *mens rea*. The latter is the intention or the knowledge behind or accompanying the exercise of will, while the former is simply the spark without which the *actus reus* cannot be produced at all. In the present case there was no opportunity at all to take a different course, and any inactivity on the part of the appellant after the warrant was removed was involuntary and unrelated to the offence. In these circumstances I do not think it can be said that the *actus reus* was in any sense the result of his conduct, whether intended or accidental. There was an act of the appellant which led up to the prohibited event (the *actus reus*), and that was to permit the car to be on the road. The second factual ingredient was not satisfied until the warrant disappeared during his absence. The resulting omission to carry the warrant was not within his conduct, knowledge or control. ...

For the foregoing reasons I am of the opinion that the physical ingredient of this charge was not proved against the appellant. Accordingly, I express no opinion on the submission that *mens rea* is excluded as an ingredient of the offence. On the view that I have taken of the case the point does not arise.

· · ·

Appeal allowed.

In *R v King*, [1962] SCR 746, the accused was charged with impaired driving having been injected with sodium pentothol, a fast-acting anaesthetic, by his dentist while having two teeth extracted. Upon awakening, the nurse warned him not to drive, but the accused testified that he did not hear that warning. He remembered getting into his car and, while driving, he fell unconscious. The accused's car then ran into the rear of a parked vehicle. Medical evidence suggested that his physical and mental condition at the time was consistent with the after-effects of sodium pentothol, which can induce a state of amnesia accompanied by a period during which an individual may feel competent to drive a car, only to suddenly lose conscious awareness. He was convicted of impaired driving but the Court of Appeal for Ontario quashed the conviction. The Supreme Court of Canada agreed, dismissing the Crown's appeal. Justice Taschereau, in separate concurring reasons, explained as follows: "It is my view that there can be no *actus reus* unless it is the result of a willing mind at liberty to make a definite choice or decision, or in other words, there must be a willpower to do an act whether the accused knew or not that it was prohibited by law" (at 749).

As you can see, the concept of free will and meaningful choice is central to the idea of voluntariness. As you study other areas of the criminal law, you will see that this concept of voluntariness reappears in a number of places, including specific defences such as intoxication (addressed in Chapter 16) and automatism (addressed in Chapter 15). You will also learn that the Supreme Court of Canada has built upon the concept of physical voluntariness to develop a broader conception of "moral" involuntariness applicable to defences such as the defence of duress. This expansion of the relevance of the idea of voluntariness took place in a case called *Ruzic*, which you will study when you consider the law of duress (Chapter 18). Although this expanded concept is not of concern in this chapter, the Court in *Ruzic* made some important statements about the concept of physical voluntariness, our current topic.

R v Ruzic
Supreme Court of Canada
2001 SCC 24, [2001] 1 SCR 687

LeBEL J: ...

[34] Even before the advent of the *Charter*, it became a basic concern of the criminal law that criminal responsibility be ascribed only to acts that resulted from the choice of a conscious mind and an autonomous will. In other words, only those persons acting in the knowledge of what they were doing, with the freedom to choose, would bear the burden and stigma of criminal responsibility. Although the element of voluntariness may sometimes overlap both *actus reus* and *mens rea* (see *R. v. Daviault*, [1994] 3 S.C.R. 63, at pp. 73-75, *per* Cory J.), the importance of *mens rea* and of the quality of voluntariness in it underscores the fact that criminal liability is founded on the premise that it will be borne only by those persons who knew what they were doing and willed it. ...

· · ·

[43] Let us examine the notion of "voluntariness" and its interplay with duress more closely. As Dickson J. stated in *R. v. Rabey*, [1980] 2 S.C.R. 513, at p. 522, "it is a basic principle that absence of volition in respect of the act involved is always a defence to a crime. A defence that the act is involuntary entitles the accused to a complete and unquali-fied acquittal." Dickson J.'s pronouncement was endorsed by the Court in *R. v. Parks*, [1992] 2 S.C.R. 871. The principle of voluntariness was given constitutional status in *Daviault*, *supra*, at pp. 102-3, where Cory J. held for the majority that it would infringe s. 7 of the *Charter* to convict an accused who was not acting voluntarily, as a fundamental aspect of the *actus reus* would be absent. More recently, in *R. v. Stone*, [1999] 2 S.C.R. 290, the crucial role of voluntariness as a condition of the attribution of criminal liability was again confirmed (at para. 1, *per* Binnie J., and paras. 155-58, *per* Bastarache J.) in an appeal concerning the defence of automatism.

· · ·

[45] What underpins ... these conceptions of voluntariness is the critical importance of autonomy in the attribution of criminal liability: *Perka* ... at pp. 250-51; Fletcher ... at p. 805. The treatment of criminal offenders as rational, autonomous and choosing agents is a fundamental organizing principle of our criminal law. ...

[46] Punishing a person whose actions are involuntary in the physical sense is unjust because it conflicts with the assumption in criminal law that individuals are autonomous and freely choosing agents.

II. ACTS, OMISSIONS, AND STATUS

The three subsections that follow are concerned, in turn, with acts of commission, omissions, and so-called status offences. It is already clear that the requirement for physical voluntari-ness applies irrespective of the offence charged. In defining the *actus reus* it is crucial to as-certain as precisely as possible the conduct that is prohibited. This section will make clear that the law generally favours criminal punishment only for actions, but that there are certain circumstances in which omissions or *failures* to act may be punishable in the criminal law. As you will see, status offences, which purport to punish in the complete absence of either an act or an omission, are deeply problematic but also exceedingly rare.

Acts

Most offences require proof of some positive act, such as stealing, driving, trespassing, or killing. The act is thus the "verb" in the definition of criminal liability, and it is "positive" in the sense that walking or running, as opposed to standing still, would be considered "positive." Offences premised on some such positive act—rather than mere passivity or omitting to do something—are the norm. Subject to the other elements of an offence being proven, punishing someone for something that they actively did poses no particular problems for the criminal law. Any complications related to the "act" tend to be definitional in nature. In some instances Parliament has provided definitions in an attempt to clarify what is meant by specific terms used in the definition of prohibited conduct. See, for example, the definitions for "break" (s 321), "communicating" (s 319(7)), "operate" (s 214), "sell" (ss 183 and 462.1), or "transfer" (s 84). See also s 2, the general section for definitions (consider the definition of "cattle"). Note that such words are often given a limited meaning in relation to specific offences. This means that words can mean different things for different parts of the criminal law, by virtue of express definition. Trafficking is given a specific definition in s 342(4) of the Code and another in s 2(1) of the *Controlled Drugs and Substances Act*, SC 1996, c 19. Other provisions perform the same function as conventional definitions but in a somewhat different form. For example, publication of a defamatory libel is an offence under s 301 of the Code but ss 303ff provide a long list of exceptions that restricts the *actus reus* of publication. In instances in which Parliament has offered no guidance or definition specifying what is contemplated by a particular act, one must look to the common law to find judicial interpretation of the term.

Omissions

The readiness of the criminal law to punish positive acts stands in stark contrast to the deep discomfort that the law manifests for criminalizing omissions—failures to act. Punishing a person for "doing nothing" raises far-reaching policy problems and, accordingly, the criminal law has been slow to impose criminal liability for omissions. Much of the controversy about liability for omissions relates to the extent to which the criminal law should create positive duties and then sanction non-compliance with them. To what extent should the criminal law enforce a duty to prevent the commission or continuation of an offence? Should the law punish the failure to report the commission of an offence? These questions have been vigorously debated for centuries. For a very long time there was an offence at common law, known as misprision of felony, consisting of a failure to report the commission of a serious offence. This offence was eventually abolished in favour of the position that inaction should only exceptionally be criminalized. It follows from this position that being a spectator to crime is not an offence. (For further discussion of this point, see Chapter 9.) There is no duty to intervene, prevent, or offer assistance unless the legislature specifically says so.

Thus, the starting point is that the criminal law will not punish for a mere failure to act. Yet there are certain circumstances under which the criminal law will overcome its reticence to punish for inaction. Put briefly, the law will only find someone criminally liable for an omission when that person was subject to a legal duty to act. As Dickson J (as he then was) explained in his dissenting opinion in *Moore v The Queen*, [1979] 1 SCR 195 at 206, "[o]mission to act in a particular way will give rise to criminal liability only where a duty to act arises at common law or is imposed by statute: 11 *Hals.* (4th ed) 15." On this account, liability for omissions is exceptional and reflects the policy choice that liability for inaction should not be generalized. Yet, as will be seen, even within this seemingly restrictive posture, it turns out that there is considerable scope for liability based on omissions in Canadian criminal law.

First, the *Criminal Code* includes certain offences that explicitly punish the failure to act in a certain fashion. These might be labelled "specific omission offences." Consider the following examples:

> 50. Every one commits an offence who ...
>
> (b) knowing that a person is about to commit high treason or treason does not, with all reasonable dispatch, inform a justice of the peace or other peace officer thereof or make other reasonable efforts to prevent that person from committing high treason or treason.

> 129. Every one who ...
>
> (b) omits, without reasonable excuse, to assist a public officer or peace officer in the execution of his duty in arresting a person or in preserving the peace, after having reasonable notice that he is required to do so ...
>
> is guilty of
>
> (d) an indictable offence and liable to imprisonment for a term not exceeding two years, or
>
> (e) an offence punishable on summary conviction.

> 252(1) Every person commits an offence who has the care, charge or control of a vehicle, vessel or aircraft that is involved in an accident with
>
> (a) another person,
>
> (b) a vehicle, vessel or aircraft, or
>
> (c) in the case of a vehicle, cattle in the charge of another person,
>
> and with intent to escape civil or criminal liability fails to stop the vehicle, vessel or, if possible, the aircraft, give his or her name and address and, where any person has been injured or appears to require assistance, offer assistance.

These offences are based on omissions and are, in a sense, "self-contained." They imply a legal duty and then punish for failure to discharge it. The legal duties implied by these offences are, respectively, the duty to report treason, the duty to assist a peace officer attempting to arrest a person, and the duty to stop your vehicle, identify yourself, and render assistance after an accident. Failure to perform any of these duties is an offence.

Yet the source of the greatest scope for the criminalization of omissions is in what we might call "general omission offences." Most notable in this regard is the crime of common nuisance and the definitions of "criminal negligence" and "duty" in s 219 of the Code.

> 180(1) Every one who commits a common nuisance and thereby
>
> (a) endangers the lives, safety or health of the public, or
>
> (b) causes physical injury to any person,
>
> is guilty of an indictable offence and liable to imprisonment for a term not exceeding two years.
>
> (2) For the purposes of this section, every one commits a common nuisance who does an unlawful act or fails to discharge a legal duty and thereby
>
> (a) endangers the lives, safety, health, property or comfort of the public; or
>
> (b) obstructs the public in the exercise or enjoyment of any right that is common to all the subjects of Her Majesty in Canada.

219(1) Every one is criminally negligent who

(a) in doing anything, or

(b) in omitting to do anything that it is his duty to do,

shows wanton or reckless disregard for the lives or safety of other persons.

(2) For the purposes of this section, "duty" means a duty imposed by law.

This definition applies, for example, in offences of criminal negligence causing death (s 220) or bodily harm (s 221).

Both common nuisance and criminal negligence (causing bodily harm or causing death, as the case may be) create the possibility for criminal punishment based on the failure to perform a legal duty. Neither specifies what legal duties might "plug in," referring instead generally to a "duty imposed by law" or a "legal duty."

What legal duties provide a sufficient basis for criminal liability? As explained by Justice Dickson in *Moore, supra,* there are two candidates: duties found in statutes and duties found in common law.

The *Criminal Code* sets out a number of legal duties that can serve to ground liability for a general omission offence. Some examples:

215(1) Every one is under a legal duty

(a) as a parent, foster parent, guardian or head of a family, to provide necessaries of life for a child under the age of sixteen years;

(b) to provide necessaries of life to their spouse or common-law partner; and

(c) to provide necessaries of life to a person under his charge if that person

(i) is unable, by reason of detention, age, illness, mental disorder or other cause, to withdraw himself from that charge, and

(ii) is unable to provide himself with necessaries of life.

216. Every one who undertakes to administer surgical or medical treatment to another person or to do any other lawful act that may endanger the life of another person is, except in cases of necessity, under a legal duty to have and to use reasonable knowledge, skill and care in so doing.

217. Every one who undertakes to do an act is under a legal duty to do it if an omission to do the act is or may be dangerous to life.

217.1. Every one who undertakes, or has the authority, to direct how another person does work or performs a task is under a legal duty to take reasonable steps to prevent bodily harm to that person, or any other person, arising from that work or task.

A person who fails to perform one of these federally legislated duties might then be liable for common nuisance or for criminal negligence causing bodily harm or death if the other elements of those offences are satisfied. (Note that s 215(2) of the *Criminal Code* creates a specific offence for failure to provide the necessaries of life.)

Consider the following case, which is an example of the interaction of the definition of criminal negligence and the duty imposed by s 217 of the *Criminal Code*, but also provides an interpretation of the word "undertakes" found in that section.

R v Browne
Ontario Court of Appeal
(1997), 116 CCC (3d) 183

ABELLA JA:

[1] The appellant, Dexter Browne, was charged with criminal negligence causing the death of Audrey Greiner by failing "to render assistance to [her] by failing to take her immediately to the hospital after undertaking to render such assistance." He was convicted and sentenced to 41½ years' imprisonment. The issue in this appeal is whether the trial judge erred in concluding that the appellant had caused Audrey Greiner's death by breaching a legal duty arising from an "undertaking" within the meaning of s. 217 of the *Criminal Code* to take her to the hospital. Only if the appellant can be found to have given an undertaking giving rise to a legal duty under s. 217 can he be found criminally negligent for "omitting to do anything that it is his duty to do" within the meaning of s. 219 of the *Code*.

Facts

[2] Audrey Greiner and Dexter Browne were drug dealers. At the time of her death, Greiner was 19 and Browne was 22. They had met several months earlier and sold crack cocaine together. They were also, the trial judge found, "at the very least close friends, probably boyfriend-girlfriend," though they did not live together.

[3] Just before 11:00 p.m. on April 13, 1994, Greiner and Browne were stopped by police on the street when they came out of a house being kept under surveillance. Both were arrested and strip-searched. No drugs were found. The police also searched the house Greiner and Browne had been in and, finding no drugs, released Greiner and Browne at about 11:30 p.m.

[4] Audrey Greiner had swallowed a plastic bag containing crack cocaine to avoid its detection by the police. After she and Browne were released, she tried unsuccessfully to throw up the bag. The two then spent almost an hour driving around Oshawa in a taxi looking for Browne's partner to warn him about the police raid.

[5] Between midnight and 1:00 a.m., Browne brought Greiner to the home he shared with his family. His 21-year-old brother, Marlon, was awake at the time and testified that he noticed nothing unusual about Greiner's behaviour. Browne took Greiner to his room in the basement, and left her alone for 10 or 15 minutes while he went upstairs to make something to eat. When the phone in his room rang unanswered, Browne went downstairs to find out why. He found Greiner shaking and sweating. The time was about 2:00 a.m.

[6] The trial judge described Browne's testimony on what happened next as follows. The statement found by the trial judge to constitute an "undertaking" by Browne is emphasized.

> … He called her name a couple of times and she did not answer at first, but then she said yes. He said, "*I'm going to take you to the hospital.*" He helped her up the stairs. He asked her if she could get up and there was no response. She sat up and she put her arm around him and he put his arm around her waist and they walked up the stairs. She could not walk on her own. He called a taxi. He testified she got heavy and he laid her on the floor by the front door and waited 10 to 15 minutes for the taxi. She was still sweating, shaking, and was

mumbling. The taxi arrived and he could not pick her up and asked his brother to help him take her to the taxi.

[7] The taxi driver's evidence was summarized by the trial judge as follows:

> … [T]he taxi driver testified he received a call from the dispatcher at 2:30 for 401 Sewells Road and he arrived ten or fifteen minutes later. He saw Audrey Greiner inside the house at the hallway, and she was not able to move. Her lips were purple, her mouth foaming, and her face was very pale. Dexter Browne and his brother put her in the taxi and Dexter Browne said to go to Centenary Hospital Emergency. He said nothing else and he went to the hospital immediately which took about 15 minutes.

[8] At about 2:45 a.m., the taxi arrived at the hospital and was met by three nurses who brought Greiner into the emergency unit by stretcher. Browne told the nurses that his friend needed her stomach pumped. He gave them Greiner's street name, "Carrie Norrie," rather than her real name. When specifically asked by one of the nurses if Greiner had consumed street drugs, he said at first that he did not know. Only after repeated requests by the nurses did he reveal that Greiner had taken drugs. The nurse said he seemed "genuinely perplexed."

[9] On her arrival at the hospital, Greiner had no pulse and no heartbeat. She was pronounced dead at 3:10 a.m.

[10] The trial judge found that the appellant told Ms. Greiner at about 2:00 a.m. that he would take her to the hospital and "immediately thereafter embarked on that act." She concluded that this statement was an "undertaking" within the meaning of s. 217 of the *Criminal Code*.

[11] The circumstances giving rise to a legal duty were summarized by the trial judge in the following passage:

> … By taking charge of Audrey Greiner after he knew that she had ingested crack, Dexter Browne undertook to care for her while the crack was in her body. That undertaking included rendering assistance to her which required taking her to the hospital immediately. On this basis, the legal duty to Audrey Greiner within the meaning of Section 217 arose just after 11:30 when the accused knew that Audrey Greiner had not vomited the crack cocaine. Although Dexter Browne testified that he did not say to Audrey Greiner that he would take care of her if something bad happened, he did admit that he would take care of her if she sold to someone who tried to rob her or anything like that. Given the frequency of swallowing drugs described by the accused and by Penny Marrotte, swallowing drugs was part of the activity and risk in dealing in drugs. His duty to his friend and co-dealer included seeing her through such times, and this included taking her to the hospital. Throughout all of these events, the accused was not a bystander. Whether the legal duty arose at 2:00 a.m. or earlier, I am satisfied beyond a reasonable doubt that Dexter Browne undertook to do the act alleged and such was an undertaking within the meaning of Section 217 of the *Criminal Code*.

[12] Using a taxi instead of calling 911 reflected, according to the trial judge, a "wanton and reckless disregard" for Audrey Greiner's life contrary to s. 219(1) of the *Criminal Code*.

Analysis

[13] The charge of criminal negligence against the appellant was particularized as follows, mirroring the language found in s. 217 of the *Criminal Code*:

> ... that he ... failed to render assistance to Audrey Greiner by failing to take her immediately to the hospital after undertaking to render such assistance and did thereby cause the death of Audrey Greiner ...

[14] The particularization of the charge in this way meant that to find a legal duty, there had first to be a finding of an undertaking. This flows from the language of s. 217 which states that everyone "who *undertakes* to do an act is under a legal duty to do it if an omission to do the act is or may be dangerous to life." In other words, the legal duty does not flow from the relationship between the parties, as it does in s. 215, which creates legal duties between spouses, between parents and children, and between dependants and their caregivers. Under s. 217, there is no pre-existing relationship or situation that creates a legal duty; there must be an undertaking before a legal duty is introduced into the relationship. The relationship or context is relevant only to the determination of whether the breach reflected a "wanton or reckless disregard" under s. 219(1), not to whether there was an undertaking under s. 217.

[15] What kind of an undertaking gives rise to a legal duty within the meaning of s. 217, the breach of which can result in criminal culpability? In my view, the ordinary dictionary definition of "undertaking" is of little assistance. There is no doubt that the definition embraces an interpretive continuum ranging from an assertion to a promise. But it seems to me that when we are deciding whether conduct is caught by the web of criminal liability, the threshold definition we apply must justify penal sanctions. A conviction for criminal negligence causing death carries a maximum penalty of life imprisonment. The word "undertaking" in s. 217 must be interpreted in this context. The threshold definition must be sufficiently high to justify such serious penal consequences. The mere expression of words indicating a willingness to do an act cannot trigger the legal duty. There must be something in the nature of a commitment, generally, though not necessarily, upon which reliance can reasonably be said to have been placed.

[16] Any other interpretation of "undertaking" imports theories of civil negligence, rendering individuals who breach civil standards of care susceptible to imprisonment. The criminal standard must be—and is—different and higher. Before someone is convicted of recklessly breaching a legal duty generated by his or her undertaking, that undertaking must have been clearly made, and with binding intent. Nothing short of such a binding commitment can give rise to the legal duty contemplated by s. 217.

[17] The trial judge found that the relationship between Dexter Browne and Audrey Greiner as partners in drug dealing gave rise to an implicit undertaking by Browne that he would take Audrey Greiner to the hospital whenever she swallowed cocaine. The fundamental error made by the trial judge was in reversing the analytical steps under s. 217 by starting her analysis with whether a duty of care existed, finding that it did, and then basing her finding of an undertaking on the existence of a legal duty. The inquiry should have begun with whether there was an undertaking. Only if there was an undertaking in the nature of a binding commitment could a legal duty have arisen under s. 217, regardless of the nature of the relationship between the appellant and Audrey Greiner.

[18] In my view, the evidence does not disclose any undertaking of a binding nature. These were two drug dealers who were used to swallowing bags of drugs to avoid detection by the police. There was no evidence that the appellant knew that Audrey Greiner was in a life-threatening situation until 2:00 a.m., when he immediately phoned for a taxi. His words to her at that time—"I'll take you to the hospital"—hardly constitute an undertaking creating a legal duty under s. 217. He said he would take her to the hospital when he saw the severity of her symptoms, and he did. There is no evidence either that a 911 call would have resulted in a significantly quicker arrival at the hospital at that hour or even that had she arrived earlier, Audrey Greiner's life could have been saved.

[19] There being no undertaking within the meaning of s. 217 of the *Criminal Code*, there can be no finding of a legal duty. There being no duty, there can be no breach contrary to s. 219 of the *Code*.

. . .

[22] Accordingly, I would allow the appeal, set aside the conviction, and enter an acquittal.

Appeal allowed; acquittal entered.

It would appear that duties established in provincial legislation can also serve as legal duties sufficient to ground liability in general omission offences. This creates an intriguing division of powers problem. As you have learned, the criminal law was intended to be uniform across the country and, accordingly, was assigned to the federal government as a head of power. If provincially legislated duties can be the basis for imposing criminal liability, the criminal law might punish certain omissions in some provinces while not in others. Does this not put at least some aspect of the substantive criminal law into the hands of provincial legislatures? Most interestingly, consider article 2 of Quebec's *Charter of Human Rights and Freedoms*, CQLR c C-12, which not only declares that every person in peril has the right to assistance but imposes a duty upon others to assist a person in peril. Despite the common law's longstanding position that there is no legal duty to be a good Samaritan, the existence of this legal duty in Quebec could be the basis for a prosecution for criminal negligence causing death.

The most fraught issue in this area is whether one can base criminal liability on failure to perform a common law duty. As you read in *Browne*, Justice Abella expressed concern about importing notions of civil negligence into the criminal law, which would "[render] individuals who breach civil standards of care susceptible to imprisonment." This is not merely a concern about the mixing of standards of fault but also about the structure of the criminal law and the idea of codification. Recall s 9 of the *Criminal Code*, which states, in part, that "no person shall be convicted or discharged under section 730 ... of an offence at common law."

R v Thornton
Ontario Court of Appeal
(1991), 3 CR (4th) 381

GALLIGAN JA:

[1] The presence in a person's blood of antibodies to Human Immunodeficiency Virus ("HIV") indicates that the person is probably infected with Acquired Immune Deficiency Syndrome ("AIDS"). AIDS is a grave illness which is usually fatal. It is infectious and particularly contagious through the blood.

[2] All of this is now well known. The appellant knew it in November 1987. In fact, he was well-informed about AIDS and its means of transmission. He knew as well that he was a member of a group which was highly at risk of contracting AIDS. Moreover, he knew that he had twice tested positive for HIV antibodies and that he was therefore infectious. He knew that the Canadian Red Cross collected blood for transfusion to persons in need of it, and that AIDS is transmitted by blood. He also knew that the Red Cross would not knowingly accept donations of blood from persons who had tested positive to HIV antibodies or who were members of his high-risk group. Nevertheless, on November 16, 1987, he donated blood to the Red Cross at a clinic in Ottawa. Fortunately, the Red Cross's screening process detected the contaminated blood and it was put aside.

[3] The appellant was charged with an offence contrary to s. 176(a) of the *Criminal Code* of Canada, R.S.C., c. C-34. That provision is now s. 180 and in these reasons for judgment reference will be made to the present provision. It was charged that he:

> [O]n or about the 16th day of November, 1987, at the City of Ottawa in the said Judicial District did commit a common nuisance endangering the lives or health of the public by donating to the Canadian Red Cross Society a quantity of his blood knowing that his blood had previously been found to contain antibodies to Human Immunodeficiency Virus and intentionally withholding the information from the Canadian Red Cross Society, contrary to Section 176(a) of the Criminal Code of Canada.

He was convicted of the charge by Flanigan J., sitting without a jury, and sentenced to a term of 15 months' imprisonment. He appeals both his conviction and his sentence.

[4] Counsel for the appellant attacked the conviction on three grounds:

1. That reprehensible as the appellant's conduct may have been, it did not amount to an offence known to the law.
2. That it was not proved that his conduct endangered the lives or health of the public or any member of it.
3. That the appellant did not have the necessary mens rea.

[5] The provisions of s. 180 of the Code are:

> 180.(1) Every one who commits a common nuisance and thereby
> (a) endangers the lives, safety or health of the public, or
> (b) causes physical injury to any person,
> is guilty of an indictable offence and liable to imprisonment for a term not exceeding two years.

(2) For the purposes of this section, every one commits a common nuisance who does an unlawful act or fails to discharge a legal duty and thereby

   (a) endangers the lives, safety, health, property or comfort of the public; or

   (b) obstructs the public in the exercise or enjoyment of any right that is common to all the subjects of Her Majesty in Canada.

[6] I will deal first with the argument that the appellant's conduct did not amount to an offence known to law. If, in the circumstances, the appellant's act of donating blood which he knew was HIV contaminated to the Red Cross was neither an unlawful act nor a failure to discharge a legal duty, then the indictment does not allege an offence known to law.

[7] Section 180(2)(a) provides that a common nuisance is committed by either the doing of an unlawful act, or the failure to discharge a legal duty which endangers the lives or health of the public. For the purposes of this appeal, I am prepared to assume the correctness of Mr. Greenspon's cogent argument that the words "unlawful act" must be taken to mean conduct which is specifically proscribed by legislation. The Code does not make it an offence to donate contaminated blood. Counsel were unable to refer the Court to any other statutory provision, federal or provincial, which does so. On the assumption, therefore, that the appellant's conduct could not constitute an "unlawful act," I will examine whether it amounted to a failure to discharge a "legal duty."

[8] I am unable to find any provision in the Code, or any other statute which I can read, as specifically imposing a legal duty upon a person to refrain from donating contaminated blood. The immediate issue therefore is two-fold. Can a "legal duty" within the meaning of s. 180(2) be one which arises at common law, or must it be one found in a statute? Is there a "legal duty" arising at common law the breach of which, assuming the other essential elements of the offence were proved, could be the basis of an offence under s. 180?

[9] There are no cases deciding whether the "legal duty" in s. 180(2) must be a duty imposed by statute or whether it can be a duty according to common law. However, the "duty imposed by law" which forms part of the definition of criminal negligence set out in s. 219 of the Code has been held to be either a duty imposed by statute or a duty arising at common law. The provisions of s. 219 are as follows:

219.(1) Every one is criminally negligent who

   (a) in doing anything, or

   (b) in omitting to do anything that it is his duty to do,

shows wanton or reckless disregard for the lives or safety of other persons.

   (2) For the purposes of this section, "duty" means a duty imposed by law.

[10] In *R. v. Coyne* (1958), 31 C.R. 335, 124 C.C.C. 176, the New Brunswick Supreme Court, Appeal Division, considered the criminal negligence provisions of the Code in relation to a hunting accident. Speaking for that Court, Ritchie J.A. held at pp. 179-180 [CCC, 338 CR]:

The "duty imposed by law" may be a duty arising by virtue of either the common law or by statute. Use of a firearm, in the absence of proper caution, may readily endanger the lives or safety of others. Under the common law anyone carrying such a dangerous weapon as a rifle is under the duty to take such precaution in its use as, in the circumstances, would be observed by a reasonably careful man. If he fails in that duty and his behaviour is of such a character as to show or display a wanton or reckless disregard for the lives or safety of other persons, then, by virtue of s. 191, his conduct amounts to criminal negligence.

[11] In *R. v. Popen* (1981), 60 C.C.C. (2d) 232, this Court also had occasion to consider the nature of the "duty imposed by law" contained in the definition of criminal negligence. It was a child abuse case. In giving the judgment of the Court, Martin J.A. said at p. 240:

> [A] parent is under a legal duty at common law to take reasonable steps to protect his or her child from illegal violence used by the other parent or by a third person towards the child which the parent foresees or ought to foresee.

The effect of that judgment is to hold that the common law duty, which was there described, was a "duty imposed by law" within the meaning of s. 219 because the Court held that its breach could amount to criminal negligence.

[12] These decisions lead me to the opinion that it is well settled that, for the purpose of defining criminal negligence, a "duty imposed by law" includes a duty which arises at common law.

[13] While the words "legal duty" in s. 180(2) are not the same as a "duty imposed by law" used in s. 219, they have exactly the same meaning. It follows therefore that the meaning given to a "duty imposed by law" in s. 219 should also be given to the "legal duty" contained in s. 180(2). Thus, I am of the opinion that the legal duty referred to in s. 180(2) is a duty which is imposed by statute or which arises at common law. It becomes necessary, then, to decide whether at common law there is a duty which would prohibit the donating of blood known to be HIV contaminated to the Red Cross.

[14] While this is not a civil case and the principles of tort law are not directly applicable to it, the jurisprudence on that subject is replete with discussions about the legal duties of one person to another which arise at common law. The jurisprudence is constant that those duties are legal ones: that is, they are ones which are imposed by law. Throughout this century and indeed since much earlier times, the common law has recognized a very fundamental duty, which while it has many qualifications, can be summed up as being a duty to refrain from conduct which could cause injury to another person.

[15] This is not the place to make a detailed examination of the jurisprudence on the subject of tort law but a few references to authority are in order. In *La Lievre and Dennes v. Gould*, [1893] 1 Q.B. 491 (C.A.), after a reference to *Heaven v. Pender* (1883), 11 Q.B.D. 503, [1881-5] All E.R. Rep. 35 (C.A.), Lord Esher M.R. said at p. 497:

> That case established that, under certain circumstances, one man may owe a duty to another, even though there is no contract between them. If one man is near to another, or is near to the property of another, *a duty lies upon him not to do that which may cause a person injury to that other*, or may injure his property. [Emphasis added.]

[16] In the course of his oft-quoted speech in the famous case of *M'Alister (or Donoghue) v. Stevenson*, [1932] A.C. 562 (sub nom. *Donoghue (or M'Alister v. Stevenson)*, [1932] All E.R. Rep. 1 (H.L.) Lord Atkin said at p. 580:

> The rule that you are to love your neighbour becomes in law, you must not injure your neighbour.

[17] The editors of *Bevan on Negligence*, 4th ed., vol. 1 at p. 8, have described the fundamental common law duty of one person toward another and the rationale for it:

> Before the law every man is entitled to the enjoyment of unfettered freedom so long as his conduct does not interfere with the equal liberty of all others. Where one man's sphere of activity impinges on another man's, a conflict of interests arises. The debateable land where these collisions may occur is taken possession of by the law, which lays down the rules of mutual intercourse. A liberty of action which is allowed therein is called a right, the obligation of restraint a duty, and these terms are purely relative, each implying the other. Duty, then, as a legal term indicates the obligation to limit freedom of action and to conform to a prescribed course of conduct. *The widest generalisation of duty is that each citizen "must do no act to injure another."* [Emphasis added.]

The authority which the editors give for their quoted statement of the duty is the judgment of Bramwell L.J. in *Foulkes v. Metropolitan District Ry. Co.* (1880), 5 C.P.D. 157 (C.A.).

[18] That brief reference to jurisprudence in civil matters shows that there is deeply embedded in the common law a broad fundamental duty which, although subject to many qualifications, requires everyone to refrain from conduct which could injure another. It is not necessary to decide in this case how far that duty extends. At the very least, however, it requires everyone to refrain from conduct which it is reasonably foreseeable could cause serious harm to other persons. Accepting, as I have, that a "legal duty" within the meaning of that term in s. 180(2) includes a duty arising at common law, I think that the common law duty to refrain from conduct which it is reasonably foreseeable could cause serious harm to other persons is a "legal duty" within the meaning of that term in s. 180(2).

[19] Donating blood which one knows to be HIV contaminated, to an organization whose purpose is to make the blood available for transfusion to other persons, clearly constitutes a breach of the common law duty to refrain from conduct which one foresees could cause serious harm to another person. It is thus a failure to discharge a "legal duty" within the contemplation of s. 180(2). It is therefore my conclusion that the indictment which alleges the commission of a nuisance by the donation of blood which the appellant knew to be HIV contaminated does allege an offence known to law. The first argument made by counsel for the appellant cannot be accepted.

[20] Counsel for the Crown referred to a number of cases where, at common law, the courts held that the exposing of others to the risk of becoming infected by a contagious disease constituted a common nuisance. Those cases are: *R. v. Vantandillo* (1815), 4 M. & S. 73, *R. v. Burnett* (1815), 4 M. & S. 272 and *R. v. Henson* (1852), Dears. 24. I have not cited them as authority in this case because s. 9(a) of the Code abolishes common law offences. They are, however, very helpful for two reasons. The first is they seem to be based upon the fundamental duty recognized by the common law to refrain from conduct which one can foresee could cause injury to others. The second reason is perhaps a stronger one. It has been said by the editor of *Tremeear's Annotated Criminal Code*, 6th ed. (Toronto: Carswell 1964) at p. 241 that the statutory definition of a common nuisance contained in the Code "does not differ from a criminal common nuisance at common law." Those cases show that the conduct of donating blood known to be HIV contaminated, if it exposed others to the risk of infection, is conduct very similar to that which the law has recognized to be a criminal common nuisance for almost 200 years. Finding that conduct to constitute

a common nuisance under s. 180 is consistent with the common law position and does not extend it.

[21] In turn now, consider the appellant's second argument, namely that it was not proved that the donation by the appellant of HIV contaminated blood endangered the lives or health of the public.

[22] In the course of his comprehensive reasons for judgment, Flanigan J. held:

> In the Court's view, upon the facts of this case as set out earlier, the public was in danger from the moment the accused donated his blood on the 16th day of November, 1987. The public, in general, was at risk and the fact that the effective screening by the Red Cross Society prevented injury or death, is of no assistance in the Court's view to this accused.

[23] There was ample evidence to support that finding. In order to show the magnitude of the risk to which the public was subjected by the conduct of the appellant, I will make brief reference to the evidence. Had it not been detected as contaminated by the screening process, the appellant's blood was destined for what is called "fractionation." That is a process whereby the blood from many individual donors is mixed together in order to produce blood products which then go out to hundreds or thousands of recipients. According to Dr. Gail Rock, the medical director of the Red Cross at Ottawa, the potential consequences of the unit of blood infected with the HIV virus getting into the fractionation process "are quite catastrophic."

[24] Fortunately, the Red Cross screening process is very good. But it is not perfect. The evidence is that the test is 99.3 per cent accurate. There are three reasons why the screening is not perfect. One of the reasons is not applicable in this case. The other two reasons are human error in the laboratory, and failure of the material used in the screening process.

[25] In addition to the risk of infection by recipients of the blood, there is another group of persons who are at risk of infection. They are health-care workers who are called upon to handle contaminated blood. The following question and answer are found in the transcript of Dr. Rock's evidence:

> Q. Apart from your concerns, as you expressed about infecting the blood pool, do you have any concerns with respect to staff at the Red Cross Centre who are actually involved in dealing with a donor, or dealing with any blood?

> A. Well of course we do have concerns and they are very real concerns because there are reported cases, well documented, of the transmission of AIDS to health care workers through handling blood samples. So any time that the nursing staff and the technologists are required to handle the blood samples which are contaminated, they run the risk of exposure.

[26] Section 180 requires that the conduct of a person "endanger" the lives or health of the public. It does not require actual injury or damage. The word "endanger" does not have any special technical meaning. Among the ordinary meanings of that word are the concepts of exposing someone to danger, harm or risk, or putting someone in danger of something untoward occurring (see Webster's *New World Dictionary*, 2d College ed., p. 461 and the *Shorter Oxford English Dictionary*, 3d ed., vol. 1 (Oxford: Clarendon Press), p. 654). The conduct of the appellant in donating his blood to the Red Cross obviously

put potential recipients and health-care workers at risk, or in danger of an untoward happening when he donated his blood.

[27] When the gravity of the potential harm is great—in this case "catastrophic"—the public is endangered even where the risk of harm actually occurring is slight, indeed even if it is minimal. I am therefore of the opinion that Flanigan J. was correct when he held that the public was in danger from the moment the appellant donated his blood. The second argument advanced by the appellant's counsel must fail.

[28] I now turn to consider his argument that the appellant did not have the mens rea necessary to have found a conviction. It was contended that the offence requires proof that the appellant actually knew of the danger created by his action, and that the trial Judge erroneously applied an objective standard when he decided that the appellant had mens rea.

[29] I am not convinced that Flanigan J. applied an objective test in this case. His finding respecting mens rea is as follows:

> In my view, by his actions, the accused has shown a rash want of care for the lives of others. *He did this knowing the full consequences of his blood being passed, in any form, to others.* [Emphasis added.]

[30] He clearly found that the appellant had personal knowledge of the consequences of his blood being passed to others. There was ample evidence to justify this finding. In his evidence, the appellant admitted that he had the following personal knowledge:

1. That prior to donating his blood on November 16, 1987, he had twice tested positive to HIV antibodies.

2. That his blood contained antibodies to the HIV virus.

3. That he was infectious at the time and that his blood must not be transferred to another person by any means.

4. That the reason the Red Cross collected blood was to give it to other persons.

5. That, according to Red Cross policies and procedures, he was not permitted to give blood.

6. That signs and a pamphlet which he had read made it clear that he was not permitted to give blood.

7. That there was no doubt in his mind that he was not to donate blood.

8. That he was well informed about AIDS, how it affected a person through the blood and that there was no known cure for it.

[31] He also admitted that he deliberately withheld from the Red Cross the information that he had tested positive for HIV antibodies and that he was in a high-risk group because he knew that, if he did so, his blood would not be accepted.

[32] The appellant testified that he donated his blood as a form of blood-letting to get rid of some of the contaminated blood, hoping that it would lessen the odds of his developing the fatal disease. He also said that he thought that the Red Cross screening system was foolproof and that his blood would not get through the system.

[33] Athena Munroe, a friend of the appellant, testified that in late November or early December 1987, she and the appellant discussed his giving of blood to the Red Cross. During her evidence in-chief, she said:

> Then I discussed with him the seriousness of what would happen if the blood got into the general population and he didn't seem all that concerned about that very much. He said: "I just wanted to see if I could get away with it. See if I get caught." That was pretty well it. I think we changed the subject after that.

In cross-examination, she gave the following evidence:

> Q. At least as far as you were concerned, his understanding was that it, to use your words, more than likely would be screened and he would be caught.

> A. More than likely, yes, but not absolutely.

In his evidence the appellant testified that, while that conversation did occur, he was just kidding in what he said to Ms. Munroe.

[34] Ms. Munroe testified that the appellant never told her that he gave blood as a form of blood-letting to help himself. She said that he made this up as a story after the event. The appellant testified that it was true and not made up.

[35] After a careful review of the evidence and of the appropriate factors to be taken into account in assessing the credibility of witnesses, Flanigan J. accepted the evidence of Ms. Munroe over that of the appellant where they were at variance. He also found that the appellant's evidence about blood-letting was concocted and that his explanation was neither true nor could it have reasonably been true.

[36] In the light of the findings of the trial Judge on the issue of credibility, and in the light of all of the other evidence, there can be no doubt that this appellant had personal knowledge that he should not donate his blood, that it was possible for it to get through the testing screen, and that it could cause serious damage to the life and health of members of the public. It follows that he knew that, by giving his blood to the Red Cross, he was endangering the lives and health of other members of the public. It therefore becomes unnecessary to decide whether some lesser form of mens rea could satisfy the requirements of s. 180. This appellant knew personally the danger to which the public was subjected by his donation of blood. He clearly had mens rea. Mr. Greenspon's third argument fails.

[37] It is my opinion that the appellant was properly convicted of the offence under s. 180. Accordingly, I would dismiss the appeal from conviction.

[38] With respect to sentence, the trial Judge did not impose the maximum sentence prescribed by law. The maximum sentence must be reserved for the worst offender committing the worst category of the offence. The sentence imposed took into account that, because of his prior good record, the appellant would not fall into the category of the worst offender. The offence, however, can certainly be categorized as among the worst offences. The appellant's conduct verges on the unspeakable. It cried out for a sentence which would act as a deterrent to others and which would express society's repudiation of what he did. One must have great compassion for this man. He faces a terrible future. Nevertheless, the sentence demonstrates no error in principle and is one that is eminently fit.

[39] While I would allow the application for leave to appeal sentence, I would dismiss the appeal from sentence.

Appeal dismissed.

[This case was appealed further to the Supreme Court of Canada, which dismissed the appeal with the following brief reasons:]

LAMER CJ:

[1] We are all of the view that this appeal fails. Section 216 imposed upon the appellant a duty of care in giving his blood to the Red Cross. This duty of care was breached by not disclosing that his blood contained HIV antibodies. This common nuisance obviously endangered the life, safety and health of the public.

[2] The appeal is dismissed.

In *Thornton* the Supreme Court said nothing of common law duties and ruled that the conviction could be sustained on the basis of s 216 of the Code. Reliance on this provision appears to distort the scope and content of that duty. In *R v Cuerrier*, [1998] 2 SCR 371, however, the Court created and imposed a duty of disclosure in a manner that resembles the creation of a common law duty. In effect, the Court decided that non-disclosure by the accused of his HIV-positive status foreclosed any possibility of a valid consent, thus enforcing a duty of disclosure in some circumstances. (See, now, *R v Mabior*, 2012 SCC 47, [2012] 2 SCR 584, discussed in Chapter 12.) There is no doubt room for judicial clarification of legislative uncertainty. It can be argued—and was by McLachlin J—that the result in *Cuerrier* exceeds that function and amounts to judicial legislation of a rule concerning valid consent.

Canadian criminal law remains surprisingly unsettled on the duties that might be invoked to establish liability for omissions. As a matter of principle, it seems that such liability should be limited to instances in which Parliament, acting under its authority to enact criminal law, has created a statutory duty. Only this is consistent with the abolition of common law crimes and the principle of legality, including the protection against vagueness or overbreadth. Statutory duties enacted by Parliament without reliance on its power over criminal law, and *a fortiori* duties enacted by provincial legislatures, are created for a purpose other than marking the boundary between criminal and non-criminal conduct. A breach of such duties in no way entails criminal sanction and there is no principled basis to say that it should. The only argument would be that breach of a civil (that is, non-criminal) duty is an unlawful act and as such merits criminal sanction when it causes a result that is prohibited by the criminal law. This might have been acceptable in a unified jurisdiction that allowed for common law crimes but today the case is weak. It would, in theory, allow a prosecution for manslaughter where a tort of civil negligence leads to death.

Criminal liability for non-compliance with legal duties should be restricted to statutory duties enacted by Parliament in reliance on s 91(27) of the *Constitution Act, 1867*.

Status

Historically, certain criminal offences appeared to punish when there was neither an act nor an omission. Such offences are often called "status offences" and they pose obvious principled problems for the criminal law. In the absence of an act or omission, status offences would effectively punish a state of being rather than what an individual did or did not do. To use the criminal law in such settings would amount to punishing an individual for *who he or she is* rather than how he or she chose to act. In cases in which that state of being is not chosen— as in the case of a crime that punished someone for "being tall" or belonging to a particular ethnic group—such an offence would also run afoul of our demand for voluntariness as a precondition to criminal liability.

For these reasons, the criminal law has always expressed a strong antipathy toward status offences. Although status may be an essential ingredient of some offences (for example, being a parent in the context of failing to provide the necessaries of life, or being an owner in the context of permitting the suffering of animals), "pure" status offences—offences in which there is truly no act or omission involved in the offence—do not seem to exist in contemporary Canadian criminal law. Some point to possession offences, being found in a common gaming or betting house (s 201(2)), and the offence of being nude in a public place (s 174) as possible modern status offences. Yet in each instance one can, without much difficulty, identify acts and/or omissions that underlie the offence. Perhaps the closest that the modern law has come to a status offence was the offence of vagrancy, pursuant to s 179(1)(b), until that offence was declared void for overbreadth in *R v Heywood*, [1994] 3 SCR 761.

The substantial concerns raised by punishment in the absence of an act or omission suggest that, if one encountered such an offence, a strong case could be made that criminal liability for a mere status offence offends s 7 of the Charter.

In an interesting contemporary appearance of status-like concerns in the criminal law, Parliament considered but rejected the option to create offences of being a member of a criminal organization or a terrorist organization. Instead Parliament created offences of *participation in the activities* of such organizations. Consider, for example, the following provisions:

83.18(1) Every one who knowingly participates in or contributes to, directly or indirectly, any activity of a terrorist group for the purpose of enhancing the ability of any terrorist group to facilitate or carry out a terrorist activity is guilty of an indictable offence and liable to imprisonment for a term not exceeding ten years.

(2) An offence may be committed under subsection (1) whether or not

(a) a terrorist group actually facilitates or carries out a terrorist activity;

(b) the participation or contribution of the accused actually enhances the ability of a terrorist group to facilitate or carry out a terrorist activity; or

(c) the accused knows the specific nature of any terrorist activity that may be facilitated or carried out by a terrorist group.

(3) Participating in or contributing to an activity of a terrorist group includes

(a) providing, receiving or recruiting a person to receive training;

(b) providing or offering to provide a skill or an expertise for the benefit of, at the direction of or in association with a terrorist group;

(c) recruiting a person in order to facilitate or commit

(i) a terrorism offence, or

(ii) an act or omission outside Canada that, if committed in Canada, would be a terrorism offence;

(d) entering or remaining in any country for the benefit of, at the direction of or in association with a terrorist group; and

(e) making oneself, in response to instructions from any of the persons who constitute a terrorist group, available to facilitate or commit

　·　　(i) a terrorism offence, or

(ii) an act or omission outside Canada that, if committed in Canada, would be a terrorism offence.

(4) In determining whether an accused participates in or contributes to any activity of a terrorist group, the court may consider, among other factors, whether the accused

(a) uses a name, word, symbol or other representation that identifies, or is associated with, the terrorist group;

(b) frequently associates with any of the persons who constitute the terrorist group;

(c) receives any benefit from the terrorist group; or

(d) repeatedly engages in activities at the instruction of any of the persons who constitute the terrorist group.

In your view, is this offence sufficiently different from a status offence to alleviate the concerns expressed above?

III. CIRCUMSTANCES

The *actus reus* of a given offence always involves voluntariness and either an act or an omission. There can, however, be more to the definition of the *actus reus*. It is common for the legislature to include specific circumstances among the elements of an offence. Wherever there are such elements, they are as much a part of the *actus reus* as the element of voluntary conduct, and failure by the Crown to prove such circumstances will lead to acquittal on the charge.

A critical point in the interpretation of offences is, therefore, to identify what circumstances, if any, are essential ingredients of the *actus reus*. Examples can be found readily. Consider the offence of impaired operation of a motor vehicle. Operating a motor vehicle—the voluntary action component of the *actus reus*—is not a crime. It is only when a circumstance is attached (here, that the individual operating the motor vehicle was impaired at the time) that the conduct becomes criminal. The same can be said of assault and all assault-related offences. It is only when a voluntary direct or indirect application of force is *unconsented to* that the *actus reus* for assault is complete. In a case of abduction in violation of a valid custody order, the existence of a valid order must be proved. When the charge is sexual interference with a person under 14 years, the age of the complainant must be proved. Assault of a police officer requires proof that the person assaulted was a police officer. And so on. Often the circumstances in question present little difficulty, whereas others, like consent, can be far more challenging.

Statutory definitions are sometimes provided to assist in clarifying relevant circumstances that might otherwise be ambiguous in large or small measure. Several of these can be found in the general section on definitions (s 2 of the *Criminal Code*) and others can be found elsewhere. Some circumstantial aspects of the *actus reus* might be clarified only through judicial interpretation.

For purposes of illustration, consider the following provisions of the *Criminal Code* and identify the relevant circumstances that form part of the *actus reus*.

Dangerous operation of motor vehicles, vessels and aircraft

249(1) Every one commits an offence who operates

(a) a motor vehicle in a manner that is dangerous to the public, having regard to all the circumstances, including the nature, condition and use of the place at which the motor vehicle is being operated and the amount of traffic that at the time is or might reasonably be expected to be at that place;

(b) a vessel or any water skis, surf-board, water sled or other towed object on or over any of the internal waters of Canada or the territorial sea of Canada, in a manner that is dangerous to the public, having regard to all the circumstances, including the nature and condition of those waters or sea and the use that at the time is or might reasonably be expected to be made of those waters or sea;

(c) an aircraft in a manner that is dangerous to the public, having regard to all the circumstances, including the nature and condition of that aircraft or the place or air space in or through which the aircraft is operated; or

(d) railway equipment in a manner that is dangerous to the public, having regard to all the circumstances, including the nature and condition of the equipment or the place in or through which the equipment is operated.

Punishment

249(2) Every one who commits an offence under subsection (1)

(a) is guilty of an indictable offence and liable to imprisonment for a term not exceeding five years; or

(b) is guilty of an offence punishable on summary conviction.

Dangerous operation causing bodily harm

249(3) Every one who commits an offence under subsection (1) and thereby causes bodily harm to any other person is guilty of an indictable offence and liable to imprisonment for a term not exceeding ten years.

Dangerous operation causing death

249(4) Every one who commits an offence under subsection (1) and thereby causes the death of any other person is guilty of an indictable offence and liable to imprisonment for a term not exceeding fourteen years.

Flight

249.1(1) Every one commits an offence who, operating a motor vehicle while being pursued by a peace officer operating a motor vehicle, fails, without reasonable excuse and in order to evade the peace officer, to stop the vehicle as soon as is reasonable in the circumstances.

Punishment

249.1(2) Every one who commits an offence under subsection (1)

(a) is guilty of an indictable offence and liable to imprisonment for a term not exceeding five years; or

(b) is guilty of an offence punishable on summary conviction.

Flight causing bodily harm or death

249.1(3) Every one commits an offence who causes bodily harm to or the death of another person by operating a motor vehicle in a manner described in paragraph 249(1)(a), if the person operating the motor vehicle was being pursued by a peace officer operating a motor vehicle and failed, without reasonable excuse and in order to evade the police officer, to stop the vehicle as soon as is reasonable in the circumstances.

Punishment

249.1(4) Every person who commits an offence under subsection (3)

(a) if bodily harm was caused, is guilty of an indictable offence and liable to imprisonment for a term not exceeding 14 years; and

(b) if death was caused, is guilty of an indictable offence and liable to imprisonment for life.

Assault

265(1) A person commits an assault when

(a) without the consent of another person, he applies force intentionally to that other person, directly or indirectly;

(b) he attempts or threatens, by an act or a gesture, to apply force to another person, if he has, or causes that other person to believe on reasonable grounds that he has, present ability to effect his purpose; or

(c) while openly wearing or carrying a weapon or an imitation thereof, he accosts or impedes another person or begs.

Application

265(2) This section applies to all forms of assault, including sexual assault, sexual assault with a weapon, threats to a third party or causing bodily harm and aggravated sexual assault.

Consent

265(3) For the purposes of this section, no consent is obtained where the complainant submits or does not resist by reason of

(a) the application of force to the complainant or to a person other than the complainant;

(b) threats or fear of the application of force to the complainant or to a person other than the complainant;

(c) fraud; or

(d) the exercise of authority.

Accused's belief as to consent

265(4) Where an accused alleges that he believed that the complainant consented to the conduct that is the subject-matter of the charge, a judge, if satisfied that there is sufficient evidence and that, if believed by the jury, the evidence would constitute a defence, shall instruct the jury, when reviewing all the evidence relating to the determination of the honesty of the accused's belief, to consider the presence or absence of reasonable grounds for that belief.

Assault with a weapon or causing bodily harm

267. Every one who, in committing an assault,

(a) carries, uses or threatens to use a weapon or an imitation thereof, or

(b) causes bodily harm to the complainant,

is guilty of an indictable offence and liable to imprisonment for a term not exceeding ten years or an offence punishable on summary conviction and liable to imprisonment for a term not exceeding eighteen months.

Aggravated assault

268(1) Every one commits an aggravated assault who wounds, maims, disfigures or endangers the life of the complainant.

Punishment

268(2) Every one who commits an aggravated assault is guilty of an indictable offence and liable to imprisonment for a term not exceeding fourteen years.

Arson—disregard for human life

433. Every person who intentionally or recklessly causes damage by fire or explosion to property, whether or not that person owns the property, is guilty of an indictable offence and liable to imprisonment for life where

(a) the person knows that or is reckless with respect to whether the property is inhabited or occupied; or

(b) the fire or explosion causes bodily harm to another person.

Arson—damage to property

434. Every person who intentionally or recklessly causes damage by fire or explosion to property that is not wholly owned by that person is guilty of an indictable offence and liable to imprisonment for a term not exceeding fourteen years.

Arson—own property

434.1 Every person who intentionally or recklessly causes damage by fire or explosion to property that is owned, in whole or in part, by that person is guilty of an indictable offence and liable to imprisonment for a term not exceeding fourteen years, where the fire or explosion seriously threatens the health, safety or property of another person.

IV. CONSEQUENCES AND CAUSATION

Many offences are defined in a way in which the existence of a voluntary act or omission, perhaps in certain circumstances, completes the *actus reus*. Many others include a specific outcome or consequence, such as causing death or bodily harm. Consider, for example, the offence of dangerous driving, which is complete when the manner of driving shows a marked departure from the standard that might be expected in the circumstances. This is distinguishable from dangerous driving causing death or dangerous driving causing bodily harm, which obviously require proof of those specific results.

As with specific circumstances that might be required by the definition of the offence, offences must be closely scrutinized to ascertain whether they require a particular consequence or result. This is usually not difficult to see but some instances are less obvious than others. Homicide requires proof that the act of the accused caused death. An unlawful act causing bodily harm requires proof of some harm that violates bodily integrity that is not trifling. Frightening the sovereign would appear to require proof that Her Majesty, and nobody else (including the governor general), was frightened. Sometimes the result that is prohibited is not a concrete event: the consequence might be a risk, as in fraud, in which the actions of the accused jeopardize the pecuniary interests of the victim.

When an offence specifies certain outcomes, the specified consequence itself generally poses little interpretive difficulty. Instead, the key issue tends to be whether the prescribed consequence was, indeed, *caused* by the accused's conduct. Accordingly, the cases in this section are concerned with basic principles of causation. The demand for causation does not typically raise problems of great difficulty. Conceptually, however, the subject of causation is rich and subtle, and when an issue of causation does arise, it can be thorny and complex to resolve. When an offence prohibits a specified result, proof of causation is plainly an essential element, without which the prosecution must fail.

Causation in the criminal law is actually composed of two elements: factual cause and legal cause. Factual cause asks merely whether some logical link can be drawn between the accused's conduct and the prohibited consequence. Although rarely an issue, as the following case demonstrates, if the Crown is unable to show such a link, causation is not established.

R v Winning
Ontario Court of Appeal
(1973), 12 CCC (2d) 449

GALE CJO (orally): This is an appeal by the appellant, who was convicted on May 16, 1972, of obtaining credit from T. Eaton Co. Limited (Eaton's) by false pretences. Following conviction she was sentenced to 14 days in jail.

We are all of the opinion that the conviction ought not to have been made and that the appeal should therefore be allowed.

Admittedly, the appellant applied for credit at Eaton's. She filled out an application for that purpose giving her proper name and address. In the particulars which she gave she made at least two false statements. Had Eaton's relied upon that application form then she would have been guilty of the offence charged, although it must be mentioned in passing that in fact she honoured her obligation and paid Eaton's on every occasion credit was advanced to her. However, the evidence clearly establishes that Eaton's did not rely upon the information contained in the application save for the name and address. This was made very clear by an Eaton's employee in this exchange:

Q. So the point I am making is you don't rely on this card except for anything other than the name and the address.

A. That's right.

Accordingly, in our view, the appellant did not obtain credit by a false pretence, because the credit was given not in reliance on her application, but rather in reliance on Eaton's investigation of her. The only matter upon which the company relied was her name and address, both of which were correctly given.

In the circumstances, the appeal will be allowed and the conviction quashed.

Appeal allowed.

As you can see, it will be the rare case that raises serious questions of factual causation. Having demonstrated that a line can be drawn connecting the accused's conduct to the prohibited consequence, the more difficult question is deciding whether this causal connection is *sufficiently strong* to support criminal liability. This is the question of legal causation and is the subject of the remainder of this section.

Despite the importance of this concept, the *Criminal Code* contains no general provisions governing the test for legal causation. Issues of causation frequently arise in homicide cases, and when Canada enacted its first *Criminal Code* in 1892 Parliament included specific provisions dealing with certain causation problems that arise when the prohibited consequence is death. You will see some of these provisions mentioned in some of the cases below and the key provisions are listed at the end of this section. In all other instances, however, one must turn to the common law to find the test and rules for legal causation.

Smithers v The Queen
Supreme Court of Canada
[1978] 1 SCR 506

DICKSON J:

[1] This is an appeal from a judgment of the Court of Appeal for Ontario [9 OR (2d) 127, 24 CCC (2d) 344] dismissing an appeal brought by the appellant from his conviction by judge and jury on a charge of manslaughter. The indictment alleges that the appellant did unlawfully kill Barrie Ross Cobby by kicking him.

[2] On 18th February 1973 a hockey game was played between the Applewood Midget Team and the Cooksville Midget Team at the Cawthra Park Arena in the town of Mississauga. The leading player on the Applewood team was the deceased, Barrie Cobby, 16 years of age; the leading player on the Cooksville team was the appellant. The game was rough, the players were aggressive and feelings ran high. The appellant, who is black, was subject to racial insults by Cobby and other members of the Applewood team. [Note that provocation in response to the racial taunts was not available as a defence to the manslaughter charge in this case because the defence of provocation is only applicable to a murder charge. See *Criminal Code*, s 232, as discussed in Chapter 14.] Following a heated and abusive exchange of profanities, both the appellant and Cobby were ejected from the game. The appellant made repeated threats that he was going to "get" Cobby. Cobby was very apprehensive and left the arena at the end of the game, some 45 minutes later, accompanied by eight or ten persons including friends, players, his coach and the team's manager. The appellant repeated his threats and challenges to fight as the group departed. Cobby did not take up the challenge. Instead, he hurried toward a waiting car. The appellant caught up with him at the bottom of the outside steps and directed one or two punches to Cobby's head. Several of Cobby's teammates grabbed the appellant and held him. Cobby, who had taken no steps to defend himself, was observed to double up and stand back while the appellant struggled to free himself from those holding him. While Cobby was thus bent over, and approximately two to four feet from the appellant, the appellant delivered what was described as a hard, fast kick to Cobby's stomach area. Only seconds elapsed between the punching and the kick. Following the kick, Cobby groaned, staggered towards his car, fell to the ground on his back, and gasped for air. Within five minutes he appeared to stop breathing. He was dead upon arrival at the Mississauga General Hospital.

[3] Dr. David Brunsdon, who performed an autopsy, testified that in his opinion death was due to the aspiration of foreign materials present from vomiting. He defined aspiration as the breathing, or taking in, of foreign material through the windpipe into the lungs. It appears from the medical evidence that aspiration is generally due to barbiturate overdosage, alcohol intoxication, motor vehicle accidents or epilepsy. One medical witness testified as to the possibility of spontaneous aspiration, whereby foreign material may be aspirated without any precipitating cause. This witness had seen three such cases out of the 900 to 1,000 cases of aspiration which he had experienced. In none of the three cases was the aspiration preceded by a blow. The consensus among the doctors was that spontaneous aspiration was a rare and unusual cause of death in the case of a healthy teenager such as Cobby. Normally, when a person vomits the epiglottis folds over to prevent the regurgitated stomach contents from entering the air passage. In the instant case this protective mechanism failed.

[4] In the Court of Appeal for Ontario three points were raised: (i) whether there was evidence of a causal connection between the kick and the death, upon which the jury was entitled to convict; (ii) whether the verdict was unreasonable; and (iii) whether the charge of the trial judge adequately delineated the essential issues and related the evidence to them. The majority of the Court (Evans and Martin JJ.A.) concluded that the issue of causation fell to be determined by the jury on the whole of the evidence, not the medical evidence alone. It was held that the charge, viewed in its totality, was adequate and contained no error in law. Houlden J.A., dissenting, noted that three doctors gave expert medical evidence for the prosecution as to the kick and the vomiting and all three doctors agreed that the kick probably caused the vomiting though they could not positively state that it did. He agreed that there was evidence upon which the jury could find beyond a reasonable doubt that the kick caused Cobby's death, but, in his opinion, the trial judge erred in failing to make clear to the jury that the Crown had to prove beyond a reasonable doubt that the kick caused the vomiting. In his view, by dealing generally with the law concerning manslaughter, assault and self-defence and then setting out at length the Crown and defence theories, the trial judge confused the jury. The judgment of the Ontario Court of Appeal dismissing the appeal specified the point of dissent in these terms: the trial judge failed to [at 349] "sufficiently delineate the issue as to the cause of death [of the deceased Cobby] and to relate the evidence to that issue."

[5] The ground of dissent in the Ontario Court of Appeal forms the first ground of appeal in this court. Counsel for the appellant submits that the trial judge, in emphasizing the act of assault as a constituent element in the crime of manslaughter, did not make it clear to the jury that the act of assault must also cause the death of the deceased and, secondly, that in giving his summation of the Crown and defence theories, the trial judge referred to the issue of causation as defence counsel's argument that the cause of death had not been proven beyond a reasonable doubt. It is contended that the effect of these remarks was to minimize this issue in the minds of the jury. The jury was never instructed, it is said, that as a matter of law one of the issues on which it had to be satisfied beyond a reasonable doubt was that the kick caused the vomiting.

[6] The trial judge commenced the general part of his charge with instruction as to onus of proof, presumption of innocence and reasonable doubt. He moved then to a discussion of circumstantial evidence and related that subject to what he referred to as "an important area, the cause of death," adding, "here no one saw inside Barry Cobby's

throat, or stomach or his lungs and here the evidence is circumstantial and indirect." Later in the charge, while discussing intent in relation to manslaughter, the trial judge said:

> Therefore, in this case, if you find the accused acted unlawfully in kicking Cobby and that death resulted therefrom, it is immaterial whether the accused intended, or did not intend, to cause death.

In giving his general directions on the law of manslaughter the trial judge stated:

> … manslaughter is the causing of death of a human being by an unlawful act, but not an intentional act.

Later he added:

> … any improper use of force, which is unlawful, if death results, is manslaughter.

The following passage of the charge is attacked by the appellant on the ground that it failed to emphasize that the act of assault must also cause the death of the accused:

> So that one difference between manslaughter and the act of assault is that in manslaughter the intent to kill is not necessary, whereas in assault the intent to apply force is necessary. Because a person commits assault without consent when he applies force intentional to the person of the other, directly or indirectly. So once you have an assault—the unlawful application of force—and a person dies as a result thereof, whether it is intended that he die or not, then you have the crime of manslaughter.

[7] It seems to me that this criticism is unwarranted because the judge stated plainly that in order to constitute the crime of manslaughter there must not only be an assault but a person must die as a result thereof.

. . .

[21] It is important in considering the issue of causation in homicide to distinguish between causation as a question of fact and causation as a question of law. The factual determination is whether A caused B. The answer to the factual question can only come from the evidence of witnesses. It has nothing to do with intention, foresight or risk. In certain types of homicide jurors need little help from medical experts. Thus if D shoots P or stabs him and death follows within moments, there being no intervening cause, jurors would have little difficulty in resolving the issue of causality from their own experience and knowledge.

[22] Expert evidence is admissible, of course, to establish factual cause. The work of expert witnesses in an issue of this sort, as Glanville Williams has pointed out ("Causation in Homicide," [1957] Crim LR 429 at 431), is "purely diagnostic and does not involve them in metaphysical subtleties"; it does not require them to distinguish between what is a "cause," i.e., a real and contributing cause of death, and what is merely a "condition," i.e., part of the background of the death. Nor should they be expected to say, where two or more causes combine to produce a result, which of these causes contributes the more.

[23] In the case at bar the Crown had the burden of showing factual causation—that beyond a reasonable doubt the kick caused the death. In my view, the trial judge did not err in failing to instruct the jury that in determining that issue they could consider only the medical evidence. The issue of causation is for the jury and not the experts. The weight to be given to the evidence of the experts was entirely for the jury. In the search for truth,

the jury was entitled to consider all of the evidence, expert and lay, and accept or reject any part of it. Non-medical testimony is available to both the Crown and the accused, and in the instant case lay evidence was vital to the defence raised by the appellant. That evidence tended to show that all the circumstances preceding the kick were such as to create in the deceased boy a highly emotional state which might well have given rise to spontaneous vomiting, unassociated with the kick.

[24] The second sub-question raised is whether there was evidence on the basis of which the jury was entitled to find that it had been established beyond a reasonable doubt that the kick caused the death. In answer to this question it may shortly be said that there was a very substantial body of evidence, both expert and lay, before the jury indicating that the kick was at least a contributing cause of death, outside the de minimis range, and that is all that the Crown was required to establish. It is immaterial that the death was in part caused by a malfunctioning epiglottis, to which malfunction the appellant may, or may not, have contributed. No question of remoteness or of incorrect treatment arises in this case.

[25] I should like to adopt two short passages from a case note on *Rex v. Larkin* (1942), 29 Cr. App. R. 18, by G.A. Martin, as he then was, which appeared in (1943), 21 Can. Bar. Rev. 503 at 504-505:

> There are many unlawful acts which are not dangerous in themselves and are not likely to cause injury which, nevertheless, if they cause death, render the actor guilty of culpable homicide, *e.g.*, the most trivial assault, if it should, through some unforeseen weakness in the deceased, cause death, will render the actor guilty of culpable homicide ...

> In the case of so-called intentional crimes where death is an unintended consequence the actor is always guilty of manslaughter at least. The act of the accused in *Rex v. Larkin* fell within the class of intentional crimes because he was engaged committing an assault upon Nielsen, and the fact that he caused a different type of harm to that which he intended did not free him from criminal responsibility.

The Crown was under no burden of proving intention to cause death or injury. The only intention necessary was that of delivering the kick to Cobby. Nor was foreseeability in issue. It is no defence to a manslaughter charge that the fatality was not anticipated or that death ordinarily would not result from the unlawful act.

[26] In *Regina v. Cato* (1975), 62 Cr. App. R. 41, the act supporting the manslaughter conviction was the injection by the accused into another person of morphine which the accused had unlawfully taken into his possession. Attention was directed to causation and the link alleged to exist between the injection of morphine and the death. The appellant's argument based on the medical evidence of causation and the rejection of that argument by the Court of Appeal are to be found in the following passage, pp. 44-45:

> First of all, he invited us to look at the evidence of causation, and he pointed out that the medical evidence did not at any point say "This morphine killed Farmer"; the actual link of that kind was not present. The witnesses were hesitant to express such a view and often recoiled from it, saying it was not for them to state the cause of death. It is perfectly true, as Mr. Blom-Cooper says, that the expert evidence did not in positive terms provide a link, but it was never intended to do so. The expert witnesses here spoke to factual situations, and the conclusions and deductions therefrom were for the jury. The first question was: was there

sufficient evidence upon which the jury could conclude, as they must have concluded, that adequate causation was present?

[27] The third sub-question is whether there was evidence from which the jury was entitled to find that it had been established beyond a reasonable doubt that the kick caused the aspiration. It is contended that the burden on the Crown was to prove beyond a reasonable doubt that the kick caused both the vomiting and the aggravated condition of aspiration. I do not agree. A person commits homicide, according to s. 205(1) of the Code, when directly or indirectly, by any means, he causes the death of a human being. Once evidence had been led concerning the relationship between the kick and the vomiting, leading to aspiration of stomach contents and asphyxia, the contributing condition of a malfunctioning epiglottis would not prevent conviction for manslaughter. Death may have been unexpected and the physical reactions of the victim unforeseen, but that does not relieve the appellant.

[28] In *Regina v. Garforth*, [1954] Crim. L.R. 936, a decision of the Court of Criminal Appeal of England, the accused, aged 16, and another young man, S., quarrelled with the deceased, aged 18, outside a dance hall. S. kicked the deceased and when he doubled up stabbed him in the neck and heart, then the accused kicked him on the body and legs and S. kicked him on the head. S. was found guilty of murder and the accused was found guilty of manslaughter. The accused appealed against his conviction on the grounds that there was no evidence that what he did was a cause of death. It was held, dismissing the appeal, that there was clear evidence that the accused unlawfully assaulted the deceased and inflicted minor injuries which contributed to the death. Had the jury found that the accused intended to do grievous bodily harm, he would have been guilty of murder.

[29] It is a well-recognized principle that one who assaults another must take his victim as he finds him. An extreme example of the application of the principle will be found in the English case of *Regina v. Blaue*, [1975] 1 W.L.R. 1411, [1975] 3 All E.R. 446, in which the court upheld a conviction for manslaughter where the victim's wounds were only fatal because of her refusal, on religious grounds, to accept a blood transfusion. The court rejected the argument that the victim's refusal had broken the chain of causation between the stabbing and the death.

[30] Although causation in civil cases differs from that in a criminal case, the "thin skulled man" may appear in the criminal law as in the civil law. The case of *R. v. Nicholson* (1926), 47 C.C.C. 113 (C.A.), will serve as an illustration. In that case, the accused dealt the deceased man two heavy blows. The man who was struck was in poor physical condition. His heart was abnormally small and he was suffering from Bright's disease. An eminent medical specialist was asked if the blow or blows could cause death, given the condition of the body which was described, and he said it was possible. The blow might be one of the causes. Over-indulgence in alcohol, bad health, and the blow and tussle combined, in his opinion, to account for the result. The appeal from conviction was dismissed. Even if the unlawful act, alone, would not have caused the death, it was still a legal cause so long as it contributed in some way to the death. I myself presided at a jury trial in which the accused, one Alan Canada, following an argument, struck his brother lightly on the head with a piece of firewood as a result of which the brother died some time later without regaining consciousness. The medical evidence showed that the bony structure of his skull

was unusually thin and fragile. The accused, on the advice of counsel, pleaded guilty to a charge of manslaughter and I have never considered that he was wrong in doing so.

[31] I would conclude this point by saying that although Dr. Hillsdon Smith thought that once vomiting had been induced, aspiration in these circumstances was no more than an accident; both Dr. Brunsdon and Dr. Butt acknowledged that the kick may have contributed to the epiglottal malfunction.

[32] That brings me to the third and final ground of appeal, namely, whether the trial judge's charge to the jury on the issue of self-defence amounted to misdirection. Although undoubtedly much upset by the actions and language of Cobby during the first ten minutes of play, thereafter the appellant alone was the aggressor. He relentlessly pursued Cobby some 45 minutes later for the purpose of carrying out his threat to "get" Cobby. Despite the frail factual underpinning for such a defence, the trial judge charged fully on self-defence and in a manner which, in my opinion, was not open to criticism.

[33] I would dismiss the appeal.

Smithers establishes a very low threshold for causation in the criminal law. It is, however, a pre-Charter case, decided in 1978. In 1994, with the Charter in hand, the Ontario Court of Appeal considered the constitutionality of the *Smithers* causation test in *R v Cribbin* (1994), 89 CCC (3d) 67 (Ont CA). The case concerned an accused who was involved in a beating that, although it inflicted non-life-threatening injuries, rendered the victim unconscious; then, left by the side of the road, he drowned in his own blood. Applying the *Smithers* test for causation, the accused was convicted, but appealed, arguing in part that the *Smithers* standard "sets the causation threshold in homicide so low as to infringe upon the principles of fundamental justice in s. 7 of the *Charter*" (at 81). The appellant's central argument was that the requirement for causation is a principle of fundamental justice and that the *de minimis* test does not satisfy this requirement, because it allows someone to be convicted of manslaughter when their acts are too causally remote from the death. Justice Arbour (who later sat on the Supreme Court of Canada) agreed that the requirement for causation "must be considered to be a principle of fundamental justice akin to the doctrine of mens rea" (at 87). Yet she found that, combined with the need for an appropriate level of fault, the causation standard set in *Smithers* was constitutionally compliant. She explained as follows (at 87-88):

> The principle of fundamental justice which is at stake in the jurisprudence dealing with the fault element in crime is the rule that the morally innocent should not be punished. This was the premise acceptable to all the judges in Creighton. McLachlin J. said, at pp. 60-61:
>
> > I agree with the Chief Justice that the rule that the morally innocent not be punished in the context of the objective test requires that the law refrain from holding a person criminally responsible if he or she is not capable of appreciating the risk.
> >
> > In my opinion, causation is embodied in the same principle of fundamental justice and it requires that the law should refrain from holding a person criminally responsible for consequences that should not be attributed to him or her. This is so because criminal causation as a legal rule is based on concepts of moral responsibility, rather than on demonstrable mechanical or scientific formulas. ...

Moral judgment is engaged when causation is used not merely as an explanation for the unfolding of events, but as a way of making people account for their contribution to a result. The morally innocent could be wrongly punished if criminal causation was reduced to a simple sine qua non requirement.

This link between causation and the fault element, both being based on the same notion of moral responsibility, leads me to conclude that the appellant's argument cannot succeed in light of Creighton. Not only must I consider that the approval of Smithers by McLachlin J., although obiter, disposes of the issue; more importantly, I think that the articulation of the fault element in unlawful act manslaughter in Creighton removes any danger that the de minimis causation test casts the net so broadly as to risk punishing the morally innocent. As the law of manslaughter stands, if a person commits an unlawful dangerous act, in circumstances where a reasonable person would have foreseen the risk of bodily harm which is neither trivial nor transitory, and the unlawful act is at least a contributing cause of the victim's death, outside the de minimis range, then the person is guilty of manslaughter. Both causation and the fault element must be proved beyond a reasonable doubt before the prosecution can succeed. Combined in that fashion, both requirements satisfy the principles of fundamental justice in that any risk that the de minimis test could engage the criminal responsibility of the morally innocent is removed by the additional requirement of objective foresight.

Therefore, in my opinion, the appellant's constitutional challenge fails.

The *Smithers* test governs analysis of legal causation for almost all crimes in Canada. There is, however, one area of the criminal law in which a different and more stringent causation test is used. The Supreme Court established this higher threshold for causation, applicable to a subset of the forms of first-degree murder, in the *Harbottle* decision.

R v Harbottle
Supreme Court of Canada
[1993] 3 SCR 306

[The following statement of facts is from the Supreme Court of Canada's headnote:] Appellant together with a companion forcibly confined a young woman. After his companion brutally sexually assaulted her and subjected her to a litany of atrocities while appellant watched, appellant and his companion discussed ways of killing her "nicely." When her struggling prevented their slashing her wrists, they decided to strangle her. Appellant held the victim's legs to prevent her from continuing to kick and struggle while his companion strangled her—her hands were tied. The trial judge told the jury that she had difficulty pointing to evidence of planning and deliberation and also charged them on the basis that murder in the first degree could have occurred while the victim was being sexually assaulted or forcibly confined. Since it was impossible to know on which basis the jury reached its verdict of guilty, the charge with respect to s. 214(5) (now s. 231(5)) of the *Criminal Code* had to be correct in order to obviate a new trial. The conviction was upheld at the Court of Appeal where it was conceded that appellant was a party to the murder while participating in her forcible confinement and sexual assault. At issue here was whether appellant's participation was such that he can be found guilty of first degree murder pursuant to s. 214(5).

CORY J: The appellant James Harbottle together with his friend Shawn Ross forcibly confined Elaine Bown. While she was still confined with her hands tied, Shawn Ross strangled her while Harbottle held her legs to prevent her from continuing to kick and struggle. What must be determined on this appeal is whether Harbottle's participation was such that he can be found guilty of first degree murder pursuant to the provisions of s. 214(5) of the *Criminal Code*, R.S.C. 1970, c. C-34, am. S.C. 1980-81-82-83, c. 125, s. 16 (and now R.S.C., 1985, c. C-46, s. 231(5)) (cited herein to R.S.C. 1970).

· · ·

Analysis

At the outset, I should express my complete agreement with Galligan J.A. speaking for the majority that there was ample evidence upon which the jury could have found that the murder of Elaine Bown was planned and premeditated by both Harbottle and Ross. Following the sexual assault, the two went out of the room and discussed the murder of the victim. They talked about slashing her wrists and Harbottle advocated that they kill her "nicely." Later, when slashing her wrists proved ineffective, they again discussed how best to kill her and determined that she should be strangled. Harbottle then carried her part way down the stairs until he fell. She walked the rest of the way. Ross and Harbottle then proceeded to carry out the planned strangulation. I would have thought that there would be no question that the jury's verdict of first degree murder could have been based upon the evidence of planning and premeditation.

However, the trial judge told the jury she had difficulty pointing to evidence of planning and deliberation. Therefore the jury was charged as well on the basis that the murder could have occurred while the victim was being sexually assaulted or forcibly confined and might thereby be found to be first degree murder. It is impossible to know on which basis the jury reached its verdict. It follows that if the charge with regard to s. 214(5) was not correct there must be a new trial. It is therefore essential that this issue be explored.

Section 214 is designed to impose the longest possible term of imprisonment without eligibility for parole upon those who commit the most grievous murders. It is concerned with contract killers, with those who murder police and correctional officers, with those who murder after due planning and premeditation, and with those who murder while committing crimes of domination.

To this effect, the portions of s. 214(5) [see now s 231(5)] relevant to this case provide that:

> 214. ...
> (5) Irrespective of whether a murder is planned and deliberate on the part of any person, murder is first degree murder in respect of a person when *the death is caused* by that person while committing or attempting to commit an offence under one of the following sections: ...
>   (b) section 246.1 (sexual assault);
>   (c) section 246.2 (sexual assault with a weapon, threats to a third party or causing bodily harm);
>   (d) section 246.3 (aggravated sexual assault); or
>   (e) section 247 (kidnapping and forcible confinement). [Emphasis added.]

At the outset I should state that I agree with Galligan J.A., at p. 391, that the question of causation under s. 214(5) "does not require a determination of who is a party to the commission of a particular offence" under s. 21. … What must be determined is the meaning of the words "when the death is caused by that person" as they appear in s. 214(5).

History of Section 214(5) and Its Present Wording

It was the position of the appellant, based upon the reasons of the minority in the Court of Appeal, that the legislative history of s. 214(5) compels an extremely narrow interpretation of the words "death is caused." It is contended that the subsection is applicable only to a person who diagnostically occasions the death of the victim. This reasoning is based upon the amendments resulting from the *Criminal Law Amendment Act (No. 2)*, 1976, S.C. 1974-75-76, c. 105, s. 4. That legislation changed the relevant wording of the section from "by his own act caused or assisted in causing the death" to "when the death is caused by that person," the wording which is still found in the current section. From this, it is argued that, since the new wording does not include "assisted," those who were simply parties to the murder could not be included. With respect I cannot accept that position.

The difficulties caused by such an interpretation can be readily appreciated when the old and new wording is juxtaposed:

Old—"by his own act caused or assisted in causing the death"
New—"when the death is caused by that person."

It can be seen that Parliament deleted both the words "his own act" and "caused or assisted in causing" and replaced them simply with the word "caused." That single word is, in my view, broad enough to include both perpetrators and those who assist in the murder and come within the purview of the substantial cause test I will set out later. Perhaps the error of the minority came about as a result of emphasizing the repeal of the words "assisted in causing" but leaving in, for purposes of interpretation, the old phrase "by his own act." This results in an interpretation of s. 214(5) as though it read "when death is caused by his own act" to the exclusion of the acts of other parties. On its face, the use of the wording "by that person" in the last version of the section cannot, in my view, have the same limiting effect as the previous formulation "by his own act."

On the other hand, the Crown contends that the phrase in s. 214(5) "when the death is caused by that person" is no more than an adoption by reference of the wording of s. 212(a) (now s. 229(a)) and not a distinct causation requirement. That provision states that culpable homicide is murder "where the person who causes the death of a human being" means to cause his death. (Emphasis added.) Neither can I accept that position. If Parliament had wished to accomplish this result it could have stated that murder was to be first degree murder "when the murder is committed by that person while committing" an offence of domination. Instead it reiterated a causation requirement within s. 214(5) and effect must be given to that additional phrase.

· · ·

The question which does arise is precisely what causal effect is required by the phrase "death … caused by that person." I think with respect, that the physically caused test advocated by the majority of the Court of Appeal is too restrictive. It would tend to raise the same impractical distinctions that Wilson J. warned against in *R. v. Paré*, supra, at p. 631, when she considered the phrase "while committing." She held that no sensible distinction existed between an accused who strangled his or her victim during the act of sexual assault and an accused who sexually assaulted and then shortly thereafter strangled the victim. In the case at bar, it would be unreasonable to suggest that, in order to be liable under s. 214(5), Harbottle must have pathologically caused the death of the victim by pulling one end of the brassiere strap while his co-accused pulled the other. I find it impossible to distinguish between the blameworthiness of an accused who holds the victim's legs thus allowing his co-accused to strangle her and the accused who performs the act of strangulation.

Object of the Section

In order to provide the appropriate distinctions pertaining to causation that must exist for the different homicide offences, it is necessary to examine the sections in their context while taking into account their aim and object.

At the outset, it is important to remember that when s. 214(5) comes into play it is in essence a sentencing provision. First degree murder is an aggravated form of murder and not a distinct substantive offence. … It is only to be considered after the jury has concluded that the accused is guilty of murder by causing the death of the victim. An accused found guilty of second degree murder will receive a mandatory life sentence. What the jury must then determine is whether such aggravating circumstances exist that they justify ineligibility for parole for a quarter of a century. It is at this point that the requirement of causation set out in s. 214(5) comes into play. The gravity of the crime and the severity of the sentence both indicate that a substantial and high degree of blameworthiness, above and beyond that of murder, must be established in order to convict an accused of first degree murder.

Substantial Cause Test

Accordingly, I suggest a restrictive test of substantial cause should be applied under s. 214(5). That test will take into account the consequences of a conviction, the present wording of the section, its history and its aim to protect society from the most heinous murderers.

The consequences of a conviction for first degree murder and the wording of the section are such that the test of causation for s. 214(5) must be a strict one. In my view, an accused may only be convicted under the subsection if the Crown establishes that the accused has committed an act or series of acts which are of such a nature that they must be regarded as a substantial and integral cause of the death. A case which considered and applied a substantial cause test from Australia is *R. v. Hallett*, [1969] S.A.S.R. 141 (S.C. in banco). In that case, the victim was left beaten and unconscious by the sea and was drowned by the incoming tide. The court formulated the following test of causation, at p. 149, which I find apposite:

> The question to be asked is whether an act or series of acts (in exceptional cases an omission or series of omissions) consciously performed by the accused is or are so connected with the event that it or they must be regarded as having a sufficiently substantial causal effect which

subsisted up to the happening of the event, without being spent or without being in the eyes of the law sufficiently interrupted by some other act or event.

The substantial causation test requires that the accused play a very active role—usually a physical role—in the killing. Under s. 214(5), the actions of the accused must form an essential, substantial and integral part of the killing of the victim. Obviously, this requirement is much higher than that described in *Smithers v. The Queen*, [1978] 1 S.C.R. 506, which dealt with the offence of manslaughter. There it was held at p. 519 that sufficient causation existed where the actions of the accused were "a contributing cause of death, outside the *de minimis* range." That case demonstrates the distinctions in the degree of causation required for the different homicide offences.

The majority of the Court of Appeal below expressed the view that the acts of the accused must physically result in death. In most cases, to cause physically the death of the victim will undoubtedly be required to obtain a conviction under s. 214(5). However, while the intervening act of another will often mean that the accused is no longer the substantial cause of the death under s. 214(5), there will be instances where an accused could well be the substantial cause of the death without physically causing it. For example, if one accused with intent to kill locked the victim in a cupboard while the other set fire to that cupboard, then the accused who confined the victim might be found to have caused the death of the victim pursuant to the provisions of s. 214(5). Similarly an accused who fought off rescuers in order to allow his accomplice to complete the strangulation of the victim might also be found to have been a substantial cause of the death.

Therefore, an accused may be found guilty of first degree murder pursuant to s. 214(5) if the Crown has established beyond a reasonable doubt that:

(1) the accused was guilty of the underlying crime of domination or of attempting to commit that crime;

(2) the accused was guilty of the murder of the victim;

(3) the accused participated in the murder in such a manner that he was a substantial cause of the death of the victim;

(4) there was no intervening act of another which resulted in the accused no longer being substantially connected to the death of the victim; and

(5) the crimes of domination and murder were part of the same transaction; that is to say, the death was caused while committing the offence of domination as part of the same series of events.

It would be appropriate to charge a jury in those terms.

Application of These Principles to This Case

· · ·

The evidence adduced clearly established all the elements of the test. The appellant was guilty (1) of at least one enumerated offence of domination (forcible confinement); (2) he participated in and was found guilty of the murder; (3) his participation in the murder was such that he was a substantial and integral cause of the death of the victim; (4) there was no intervening act of another which resulted in the accused's no longer being substantially connected to the death of the victim; and (5) the crimes of domination and murder were part of the same series of acts or transaction.

Further, after a careful review of the charge, I would agree with the majority of the Court of Appeal that the directions to the jury by the trial judge were eminently fair and adequately covered all the requisite elements of the offences of domination, murder and first degree murder.

Disposition

As the Court indicated at the conclusion of the hearing, the appeal must be dismissed.

Harbottle thus established a higher threshold of legal causation linked to certain words ("when the death is caused by that person") present in some of the definitions of first-degree murder. Although that decision concerned what is now s 231(5) of the *Criminal Code*, that same language is also found in ss 231(6), 231(6.01), 231(6.1), and 231(6.2). Based on the reasoning in *Harbottle*, this higher threshold for causation presumably applies to first-degree murder as defined in these subsections as well.

In the following case, the Supreme Court of Canada was asked to extend *Harbottle* causation to second-degree murder. Although it declined to do so, in answering this question the Court chose to address the issue of how the *Smithers* test ought to be explained to a jury. The division in the Court raises the question of whether the *Smithers* test remains intact or whether the threshold for causation has been subtly changed.

R v Nette
Supreme Court of Canada
2001 SCC 78, [2001] 3 SCR 488

[Note that, in the original reporting of the judgment, Justice L'Heureux-Dubé's minority opinion appeared first. In the following version the order of the opinions has been reversed for ease of reading.]

ARBOUR J (Iacobucci, Major, Binnie, and LeBel JJ concurring):

. . .

I. Introduction

[16] The present appeal raises the issue of causation in second degree murder. It requires a determination of the threshold test of causation that must be met before an accused may be held legally responsible for causing a victim's death in a charge of second degree murder. We must also examine how the applicable standard of causation should be conveyed to the jury.

II. *Factual Background*

[17] On Monday, August 21, 1995, Mrs. Clara Loski, a 95-year-old widow who lived alone in her house in Kelowna, British Columbia, was found dead in her bedroom. Her house had been robbed. Mrs. Loski was bound with electrical wire in a way that is referred to colloquially as "hog-tying." Her hands were bound behind her back, her legs were brought upwards behind her back and tied, and her hands and feet were bound together. A red garment was tied around her head and neck and entrapped her chin. This garment formed a moderately tight ligature around her neck, but did not obstruct her nose or mouth.

[18] One of Mrs. Loski's neighbours, Deanna Taylor, testified that she was standing in her backyard smoking on the afternoon of Friday, August 18, 1995 when she heard Mrs. Loski's door close and saw two male Caucasian youths leave through Mrs. Loski's back gate and run down the alley.

[19] Some 24 to 48 hours after Mrs. Loski was robbed and left hog-tied on her bed, she died. At some point she had fallen from the bed to the floor. The Crown's medical expert, Dr. Roy, was of the opinion that the cause of death was asphyxiation due to upper airway obstruction.

[20] The RCMP mounted an undercover operation with the appellant Nette as a target. In the course of this investigation, the appellant was induced to tell an undercover police officer, who was posing as a member of a criminal organization, about his involvement in the robbery and death of Mrs. Loski. This admission was recorded by the undercover officer and was put in evidence at trial.

[21] At trial, the appellant testified in his own defence. He stated that he went to Mrs. Loski's house alone on Saturday, August 19, 1995 just after midnight with the intention of breaking and entering her house. He testified that he knocked on the back door and it swung open on its own. He stated that it looked as if someone had already broken into the home. He testified that he found Mrs. Loski already dead in her bedroom and then left the home. With respect to the intercepted conversations obtained through the undercover operation, the appellant testified that he had made up the story about robbing and tying up Mrs. Loski in order to impress the undercover officer.

[22] The only medical evidence at trial on the issue of cause of death was the evidence of Dr. Roy, the forensic pathologist who investigated Mrs. Loski's death and who testified for the Crown. Dr. Roy concluded that Mrs. Loski died as a result of asphyxiation due to an upper airway obstruction. Dr. Roy could not isolate one factor from among the circumstances of Mrs. Loski's death and state that it alone caused her death by asphyxiation. In his view, a number of factors contributed to the asphyxial process, in particular, her hog-tied position, the ligature around her neck, as well as her age and corresponding lack of muscle tone. In cross-examination, Dr. Roy agreed that other factors, including Mrs. Loski's congestive heart failure and asthma may possibly have speeded up the process of asphyxiation.

[23] The appellant was charged with first degree murder on the basis that he had committed murder while committing the offence of unlawfully confining Mrs. Loski. The Crown's position at trial was that the act of causing death and the acts comprising the offence of unlawful confinement all formed part of one continuous sequence of events making up a single transaction, and that the appellant was therefore guilty of first degree murder pursuant to s. 231(5) of the *Criminal Code*. The appellant was tried before a judge

and jury. The jury returned a verdict of second degree murder and the Court of Appeal dismissed the appellant's appeal from that verdict. The only ground of appeal both before the Court of Appeal and before us concerns the test of causation applicable to second degree murder.

. . .

V. Issues

[39] The only issue on this appeal is the standard of causation for second degree murder and how the applicable standard should be explained to the jury.

VI. Analysis

A. Introduction

[40] There is no issue raised in this appeal with respect to the charge on first degree murder or manslaughter. The appellant's only ground of appeal is the propriety of the charge on second degree murder and, specifically, the applicable standard of causation for second degree murder. The appellant's position is that there is one standard of causation applicable to all forms of homicide and that the standard should be conveyed to the jury by using the words "substantial cause" that this Court said applied to the offence of first degree murder under s. 231(5) of the *Criminal Code* in *Harbottle*. The appellant says that the trial judge erred in effectively instructing the jury that the *Smithers* standard of "beyond *de minimis*" applied to the offence of second degree murder. Had the jurors been properly instructed on the standard of causation applicable to second degree murder, says the appellant, they might have acquitted the appellant on the second degree murder charge. The appellant therefore submits that the appeal should be allowed and a new trial ordered on the ground that the trial judge misdirected the jury on the standard of causation applicable to second degree murder.

[41] The respondent and the intervener Attorney General for Ontario submit that the applicable standard for second degree murder is the standard of "beyond *de minimis*" articulated in *Smithers, supra*. Their position is that the "substantial cause" test of causation is a higher standard of causation that only applies to the offence of first degree murder under s. 231(5) of the *Criminal Code*. As well, the Attorney General for Ontario submits that the higher *Harbottle* standard also applies to first degree murder under s. 231(6) of the *Criminal Code*, which uses the same terminology of "caused by that person" found in s. 231(5) in relation to murder committed in the course of criminal harassment. The respondent and intervener therefore say that the trial judge properly charged the jury on the applicable standard of causation in relation to second degree murder and that the appeal should accordingly be dismissed.

[42] While the standard of causation for second degree murder has not been raised squarely before this Court until now, it was before the Ontario Court of Appeal in *Cribbin, supra*, and *Meiler, supra*. In both of these cases, the *Smithers* standard of "beyond *de minimis*" was expressly approved of in relation to a charge of second degree murder.

B. *The Standard of Causation for Homicide Offences*

[43] The parties and intervener on this appeal characterize the decision required of this Court in the present case as a choice between the terminology of "beyond *de minimis*" on the one hand and "substantial cause" on the other in describing the standard of causation for second degree murder to the jury. In my view, this characterization does not properly reflect the decision that is required in this case. It confuses the question of what the standard of causation for second degree murder *is* with the question of how the standard of causation for second degree murder should be *expressed* in charging the jury. In my view, these two separate questions are best dealt with sequentially.

[44] In determining whether a person can be held responsible for causing a particular result, in this case death, it must be determined whether the person caused that result both in fact and in law. Factual causation, as the term implies, is concerned with an inquiry about how the victim came to his or her death, in a medical, mechanical, or physical sense, and with the contribution of the accused to that result. Where factual causation is established, the remaining issue is legal causation.

[45] Legal causation, which is also referred to as imputable causation, is concerned with the question of whether the accused person should be held responsible in law for the death that occurred. It is informed by legal considerations such as the wording of the section creating the offence and principles of interpretation. These legal considerations, in turn, reflect fundamental principles of criminal justice such as the principle that the morally innocent should not be punished … . In determining whether legal causation is established, the inquiry is directed at the question of whether the accused person should be held criminally responsible for the consequences that occurred … .

[46] In a given case, the jury does not engage in a two-part analysis of whether both factual and legal causation have been established. Rather, in the charge to the jury, the trial judge seeks to convey the requisite degree of factual and legal causation that must be found before the accused can be held criminally responsible for the victim's death.

[47] While causation is a distinct issue from *mens rea*, the proper standard of causation expresses an element of fault that is in law sufficient, in addition to the requisite mental element, to base criminal responsibility. The starting point in the chain of causation which seeks to attribute the prohibited consequences to an act of the accused is usually an unlawful act in itself. When that unlawful act is combined with the requisite mental element for the offence charged, causation is generally not an issue. For example, in the case of murder, where an accused intends to kill a person and performs an act which causes or contributes to that person's death, it is rare for an issue to arise as to whether the accused caused the victim's death. As I discussed in *Cribbin, supra*, where the jury is faced with a charge of murder and is satisfied that the accused intended to kill or intended to cause bodily harm that he knew was likely to cause death and was reckless as to whether death occurred, it will rarely be necessary for the trial judge to charge the jury on the standard of causation. In such a case, the *mens rea* requirement generally resolves any concerns about causation. It would be rare in a murder case where the intention to kill or to cause bodily harm likely to cause death is proven for the accused to be able to raise a doubt that, while he intended the result that occurred, he did not cause the intended result. Where it is established that the accused had the subjective foresight of death or serious bodily harm likely to cause death required to sustain a murder conviction, as

opposed to the lower manslaughter requirement of objective foreseeability of serious bodily harm, it would be unusual for an issue of causation to arise. Assuming a case arose where intention was established but causation was not proven, a proper verdict might be attempted murder: *Cribbin*, at p. 564.

[48] The law of causation is in large part judicially developed, but is also expressed, directly or indirectly, in provisions of the *Criminal Code*. For example, s. 225 of the *Code* provides that where a person causes bodily injury that is in itself dangerous and from which death results, that person causes the death notwithstanding that the immediate cause of death is proper or improper treatment. Similarly, ss. 222(5)(c) and 222(5)(d) provide that a person commits culpable homicide where he causes the death of a person by causing that person, by threats, fear of violence or by deception, to do anything that causes his death or by wilfully frightening a child or sick person. These statutory provisions and others like them in the *Code* preempt any speculation as to whether the act of the accused would be seen as too remote to have caused the result alleged, or whether the triggering of a chain of events was then interrupted by an intervening cause which serves to distance and exonerate the accused from any responsibility for the consequences. Where the factual situation does not fall within one of the statutory rules of causation in the *Code*, the common law general principles of criminal law apply to resolve any causation issues that may arise.

[49] In light of the statutory rules mentioned above, and in light of general principles of criminal responsibility, the civil law of causation is of limited assistance. The criminal law does not recognize contributory negligence, nor does it have any mechanism to apportion responsibility for the harm occasioned by criminal conduct, except as part of sentencing after sufficient causation has been found. In the same way it provides for the possibility of attributing responsibility through the law of attempt, which has no equivalent in the civil context. As a result, I do not find the appellant's submissions relating to the civil standard of causation to be helpful in elucidating the applicable criminal standard.

[50] In determining whether an accused is guilty of first or second degree murder, the first step for the trier of fact is to determine whether murder has been committed, pursuant to ss. 229 or 230 of the *Criminal Code*: *Farrant*, *supra*, at p. 141. Once this has been established, the remaining question is whether the offence should be classified as first or second degree murder in accordance with the criteria set out in s. 231 of the *Code*, which is, in essence, a sentencing provision: *Farrant*, *supra*; *R. v. Droste*, [1984] 1 S.C.R. 208; *R. v. Paré*, [1987] 2 S.C.R. 618; *R. v. Arkell*, [1990] 2 S.C.R. 695; *R. v. Luxton*, [1990] 2 S.C.R. 711, and *Harbottle*, *supra*. Where, as here, the Crown relies on s. 231(5) of the *Code*, the jury must first find that the accused is guilty of murder before moving on to a consideration of whether the accused's participation in the underlying offence and in the killing of the victim was so direct and substantial that a conviction for first degree murder is appropriate.

C. Did Harbottle Raise the Standard of Causation?

[51] This Court has previously examined the issue of causation in the homicide context in relation to manslaughter in *Smithers*, *supra*, and in relation to first degree murder under s. 231(5) of the *Code* in *Harbottle*, *supra*. In considering causation in relation to second degree murder in the present cause, it is helpful to first discuss the facts and legal

principles set out in *Smithers* and *Harbottle*, before moving on to a consideration of whether *Harbottle* raised the standard of causation for first degree murder under s. 231(5) of the *Code* only or for homicide offences generally.

[Justice Arbour then reviewed and discussed the Court's rulings in *Smithers* and *Harbottle*, concluding that the "substantial cause" test was confined to the special problems posed by, and language found in, s 231(5). (Justice Arbour also noted that similar language is found in s 231(6) of the *Code*.)]

• • •

[61] I agree with the appellant that what *Harbottle* really stresses is not solely or even primarily a higher causation requirement to raise murder to first degree murder under s. 231(5) of the *Code*, but rather the increased degree of participation required before the accused may be convicted of first degree murder under s. 231(5). However, I do not agree that the terminology of "substantial cause" should be used to describe the requisite degree of causation for all homicide offences.

• • •

[65] It is clear from a reading of *Harbottle* that the "substantial cause" test expresses the increased degree of moral culpability, as evidenced by the accused person's degree of participation in the killing, that is required before an accused can be found guilty under s. 231(5) of the *Criminal Code* of first degree murder. The increased degree of participation in the killing, coupled with a finding that the accused had the requisite *mens rea* for murder, justifies a verdict of guilty under s. 231(5) of the *Code*.

D. Explaining the Standard of Causation to the Jury

[66] As I discussed earlier, it is important to distinguish between what the legal standard of causation is and how that standard is conveyed to the jury. The difference between these two concepts has been obscured somewhat in the present case by the parties' focus on the terminology used to describe the standard of causation. I agree with the appellant's submission that there is only one standard of causation for all homicide offences, whether manslaughter or murder. However, I do not agree with the appellant that the standard must be expressed for all homicide offences, including second degree murder, as one of "substantial cause" as stated in *Harbottle*. Nor must the applicable standard be expressed with the terminology of "beyond *de minimis*" used in the *Smithers* standard.

[67] At para. 28, Lambert J.A. took note of the various terms used to describe the relevant standard of causation for homicide offences and emphasized the need to distinguish between the concept of causation and the terminology used to express it:

As can readily be seen, there is a diversity of terminology available to describe the relevant causal connection. It is important to be guided by the concepts relevant to causality rather than by the terminology.

[68] In his text *Canadian Criminal Law: A Treatise* (3rd ed. 1995), Professor D. Stuart quotes at p. 130 from the English case of *British Columbia Electric Railway v. Loach*, [1916] 1 A.C. 719 ([British Columbia] P.C.), in which the court expressed scepticism that special terminology could lead to an adequate approach to the issue of causation. While made

in the context of a civil action, I find the comments in that case to be applicable to the present context (at pp. 727-28):

> It is surprising how many epithets eminent judges have applied to the cause, which has to be ascertained for this judicial purpose of determining liability, and how many more to other acts and incidents, which for this purpose are not the cause at all. "Efficient or effective cause," "real cause," "proximate cause," "direct cause," "decisive cause," "immediate cause," "*causa causans*," on the one hand, as against, on the other, "*causa sine qua non*," "occasional cause," "remote cause," "contributory cause," "inducing cause," "condition," and so on. No doubt in the particular cases in which they occur they were thought to be useful or they would not have been used, but the repetition of terms without examination in other cases has often led to confusion, and it might be better, after pointing out that the inquiry is an investigation into responsibility, to be content with speaking of the cause of the injury simply and without qualification.

[69] In describing the *Smithers* standard of causation, Lambert J.A. concluded that the phrase "a contributing cause that is not trivial or insignificant" reflected the applicable standard without the need to resort to the use of the Latin expression "beyond *de minimis*." He further found that a cause that is "not insignificant" can be expressed positively as a cause that is "significant" and that it would therefore be correct to describe the *Smithers* standard as a "significant contributing cause" (para. 29).

[70] There is a semantic debate as to whether "not insignificant" expresses a degree of causation lower than "significant." This illustrates the difficulty in attempting to articulate nuances in this particular legal standard that are essentially meaningless. I agree with Lambert J.A. that even if it were desirable to formulate a causation test for second degree murder that is higher than the *Smithers* standard for manslaughter but less strict than the *Harbottle* standard for first degree murder under s. 231(5), which I conclude it is not, it would be difficult to formulate such a test in a meaningful way and even more difficult for a jury to grasp the subtle nuances and apply three different standards of causation.

[71] The causation standard expressed in *Smithers* is still valid and applicable to all forms of homicide. In addition, in the case of first degree murder under s. 231(5) of the *Code*, *Harbottle* requires additional instructions, to which I will return. The only potential shortcoming with the *Smithers* test is not in its substance, but in its articulation. Even though it causes little difficulty for lawyers and judges, the use of Latin expressions and the formulation of the test in the negative are not particularly useful means of conveying an abstract idea to a jury. In order to explain the standard as clearly as possible to the jury, it may be preferable to phrase the standard of causation in positive terms using a phrase such as "significant contributing cause" rather than using expressions phrased in the negative such as "not a trivial cause" or "not insignificant." Latin terms such as "*de minimis*" are rarely helpful.

[72] In deciding how the applicable standard of causation should be articulated to the jury, trial judges have a discretion in choosing the terminology they wish to use to explain the standard. Causation issues are case-specific and fact-driven. For that reason, it is important to afford a trial judge with the flexibility to put issues of causation to the jury in an intelligible fashion that is relevant to the circumstances of the case, including whether or not there are multiple accused persons or parties. As I discussed in *Cribbin*, *supra*, at pp. 565-66, while different terminology has been used to explain the applicable standard

in Canada, Australia and England, whether the terminology used is "beyond *de minimis*," "significant contribution" or "substantial cause," the standard of causation which this terminology seeks to articulate, within the context of causation in homicide, is essentially the same ... .

• • •

To the extent that trial judges may find it more useful to express the standard of causation in *Smithers* in a more direct and affirmative fashion, they may find it preferable to express the standard positively as a "significant contributing cause," to use the terminology of Lambert J.A. in the present appeal.

[73] In light of *Harbottle*, where the jury must be instructed on first degree murder under s. 231(5) of the *Code* in addition to manslaughter or second degree murder, the terminology of "substantial cause" should be used to describe the applicable standard for first degree murder so that the jury understands that something different is being conveyed by the instructions concerning s. 231(5) of the *Code* with respect to the requisite degree of participation of the accused in the offence. In such cases, it would make sense to instruct the jury that the acts of the accused have to have made a "significant" contribution to the victim's death to trigger culpability for the homicide while, to be guilty of first degree murder under s. 231(5), the accused's actions must have been an essential, substantial and integral part of the killing of the victim.

• • •

F. The Charge to the Jury and the Verdict

[85] As discussed above, I conclude that the test of causation is the same for all homicide offences and that it is not appropriate to apply a different standard of causation to the offences of manslaughter and murder. The applicable standard of causation has traditionally been articulated in this country on the basis of the language used in *Smithers* that the accused must be a cause of the death beyond *de minimis*. This standard has not been overruled in any subsequent decisions of this Court, including *Harbottle*.

[86] In this case, the charge to the jury was entirely satisfactory. The trial judge charged the jury on the elements of manslaughter, second degree murder and first degree murder under s. 231(5) of the *Criminal Code*. With respect to manslaughter and second degree murder, the trial judge told the jurors that they must find that the accused was "more than a trivial cause" of death in order to conclude that the accused caused Mrs. Loski's death. In essence, this reflects the test of causation set out in *Smithers*, and accurately states the correct standard of causation for second degree murder. On two occasions, once in the main charge and once in responding to a question from the jurors, Wilkinson J. misspoke in describing the appropriate test of causation for second degree murder, by contrasting the high standard of causation for first degree murder with the "slight or trivial cause necessary to find second degree murder." In my view, these errors, which reflect the difficulty of expressing a standard in the negative, would not have caused the jury to believe that the applicable standard of causation for second degree murder was lower than the *Smithers* standard of "more than a trivial cause." What the slips in the jury charge do illustrate is the fact that it is easier to express the standard of causation in positive terms, by referring to a "significant" contribution or cause, instead of using the negative phraseology

of "beyond *de minimis*" or "more than a slight or trivial cause" in explaining causation to the jury.

[87] Given that the jury found the accused guilty of second degree murder, we must conclude that the jury found that the appellant had the requisite intent for the offence of murder, namely subjective foresight of death. In light of the jury's conclusion with respect to intent, which in my view could not have been affected by the instructions on causation, it is clear that no reasonable jury could have had any doubt about whether the appellant's actions constituted a significant, operative cause of the victim's death. What is not clear from the verdict is the basis for the acquittal on the charge of first degree murder. The appellant suggests that the jury acquitted on first degree murder because it had a reasonable doubt as to whether the accused caused the victim's death on the *Harbottle* standard of causation, but convicted of second degree murder because it was satisfied the accused caused death on the lower *Smithers* standard. In my view, the conviction for second degree murder was amply supported on the evidence and the jury was correctly charged on the applicable legal requirements of causation. The jury was entitled to have a doubt as to whether the degree of participation of the accused in the underlying offence of unlawful confinement, combined with the need for his substantial contribution to the death of the victim, was sufficient to elevate the murder to first degree. Whatever the jury's reasons for acquitting the appellant of first degree murder, the jury's verdict of second degree murder is unimpeachable.

VII. Conclusion and Disposition

[88] For these reasons, I conclude that the trial judge correctly charged the jury on the applicable standard of causation for second degree murder in expressing the standard as one in which the accused must have been more than an insignificant or trivial cause of the victim's death. There is only one standard of causation for homicide offences, including second degree murder. That standard may be expressed using different terminology, but it remains the standard expressed by this Court in the case of *Smithers*, *supra*. The terminology of substantial cause in *Harbottle* is used to indicate the increased degree of participation in the killing that is required to raise the accused's culpability to first degree murder under s. 231(5) of the *Code. Harbottle* did not raise the standard of causation that applies to all homicide offences from the standard expressed in *Smithers*.

[89] … I would dismiss the appeal and uphold the jury's verdict of second degree murder.

Appeal dismissed.

L'HEUREUX-DUBÉ J (concurring in the result) (McLachlin CJ and Gonthier and Bastarache JJ concurring):

[1] I had the benefit of reading my colleague Madam Justice Arbour's reasons and while I concur in the result she reaches, I do not agree with her suggestion to rephrase the standard of causation for culpable homicide set out by this Court in *Smithers v. The Queen*, [1978] 1 S.C.R. 506. Writing for the Court, Dickson J. (as he then was) articulated the causation test in the following manner (at p. 519):

The second sub-question raised is whether there was evidence on the basis of which the jury was entitled to find that it had been established beyond a reasonable doubt that the kick caused the death. In answer to this question it may shortly be said that there was a very substantial body of evidence, both expert and lay, before the jury indicating that the kick was at least *a contributing cause of death, outside the* de minimis *range,* and that is all that the Crown was required to establish. [Emphasis added.]

[2] To avoid resorting to the Latin expression, Lambert J.A., in the Court of Appeal's ruling in this case ((1999), 141 C.C.C. (3d) 130 (B.C.C.A.)), suggested an English version that I believe adequately reflects *Smithers'* beyond *de minimis* standard (at para. 29):

In the *Smithers* case the relevant causal standard is described in the words "a contributing cause beyond *de minimis.*" If one were to avoid the Latin, which a jury may find confusing, the *Smithers* standard is "*a contributing cause that is not trivial or insignificant.*" See *Crimji* 6.45, para. 17. [Emphasis added.]

[3] In her reasons, my colleague also refers to the English translation of the *Smithers* test when she writes (at para. 54): "Since *Smithers,* the terminology of 'beyond *de minimis*' or 'more than a trivial cause' has been used interchangeably with 'outside the *de minimis* range' to charge juries as to the relevant standard of causation for all homicide offences, be it manslaughter or murder."

[4] The terms "not trivial" and "not insignificant" are accurate and do not alter the *Smithers* standard which, it is worth noting, has withstood the test of time. As one author points out, *Smithers* is "the generally authoritative test of causation for all criminal offences" (J. Presser, "All for a Good Cause: The Need for Overhaul of the *Smithers* Test of Causation" (1994), 28 C.R. (4th) 178, at p. 178). In that regard, my colleague also recognizes that the *Smithers* causation standard is valid and applicable to all forms of homicide (at paras. 85 and 88):

As discussed above, I conclude that the test of causation is the same for all homicide offences and that it is not appropriate to apply a different standard of causation to the offences of manslaughter and murder. *The applicable standard of causation has traditionally been articulated in this country on the basis of the language used in* Smithers *that the accused must be a* cause of the death beyond *de minimis.* This standard has not been overruled in any subsequent decisions of this Court, including *Harbottle.* ...

There is only one standard of causation for homicide offences, including second degree murder. That standard may be expressed using different terminology, *but it remains the standard expressed by this Court in the case of* Smithers, *supra.* [Emphasis added.]

[5] Having said so, my colleague suggests reformulating the *Smithers* beyond *de minimis* test, i.e., "a contributing cause [of death] that is not trivial or insignificant" in the language of a "significant contributing cause." She asserts that (at para. 70):

There is a semantic debate as to whether "not insignificant" expresses a degree of causation lower than "significant." This illustrates the difficulty in attempting to articulate nuances in this particular legal standard that are essentially meaningless.

[6] Evidently, my colleague considers that this rephrasing is merely a matter of semantics and, in her view, it does not alter the current test. I respectfully disagree. In my

opinion, this issue is a matter of substance, not semantics. There is a meaningful difference between expressing the standard as "a contributing cause that is not trivial or insignificant" and expressing it as a "significant contributing cause." Changing the terminology of the *Smithers* test in this manner would drastically change its substance. …

[7] To claim that something not unimportant is important would be a sophism. Likewise, to consider things that are not dissimilar to be similar would amount to an erroneous interpretation. In the same vein, a substantial difference exists between the terms "not insignificant" and "significant," and there is no doubt in my mind that to remove the double negative formulation from the *Smithers* causation test would effect a radical change to the law. I therefore agree with the position of both the respondent and the intervener that a "significant contributing cause" calls for a more direct causal relationship than the existing "not insignificant" or "not trivial" test, thus raising the standard from where it currently stands.

· · ·

[9] Accordingly, I find that recasting the *Smithers* "beyond *de minimis*" test in the language of a "significant contributing cause" is unwarranted because it raises the threshold of causation for culpable homicide without any reasons for doing so and none, of course, is given since my colleague indicates that the proposed reformulation does not modify the *Smithers* standard.

[10] Words have a meaning that should be given to them and different words often convey very different standards to the jury. In my view, describing a contributing cause as having a "significant" impact attaches a greater degree of influence or importance to it than do the words "not insignificant." …

· · ·

[14] In conclusion, I reiterate that the causation test in *Smithers* remains the law and to rephrase it in the language of a "significant contributing cause," as my colleague suggests, would draw the line at a different place, thus drastically changing the law. I have found no legitimate reason to reformulate the *Smithers* test, rather it is my opinion that such alteration should be strenuously proscribed since it will elevate the threshold of causation. As a result, I consider the current language of "a contributing cause [of death] that is not trivial or insignificant" to be the correct formulation that trial judges should use when expressing to the jury the standard of causation for all homicide offences.

[15] I would dismiss the appeal.

In your view, did the majority decision in *Nette* effectively raise the threshold for legal causation, as Justice L'Heureux-Dubé contends? For critical discussions of the *Nette* decision and its implications, see e.g. D Stuart, "Nette: Confusing Cause in Reformulating the Smithers Test" (2002) 46 CR (5th) 230 and S Anand, "Determining Causal Standards for First Degree Murder in the Wake of Nette: When Does the Substantial Cause Test Apply?" (2002) 46 Crim LQ 282.

By requiring only that the accused's conduct be a non-trivial (or significant) contributing cause, the *Smithers/Nette* test recognizes that there can be multiple causes of a proscribed consequence. Indeed, *Smithers* is itself a case in which the victim's death was brought about by more than one cause—the kick but also the malfunctioning epiglottis. When there are multiple causes, the prosecution must prove that the conduct of the accused contributed to the result within the standard defined in *Smithers* and *Nette*. A question arises, however: Can a subsequent event sever the causational link between the accused's conduct and the prohibited consequence? This introduces the question of so-called intervening causes. The following cases address this question, culminating in the Supreme Court of Canada's most recent statement on how to analyze whether an intervening cause breaks the chain of causation between the accused's acts and the proscribed consequence: *R v Maybin*, 2012 SCC 24, [2012] 2 SCR 30.

Pagett v The Queen
Court of Criminal Appeal, England
(1983), 76 Cr App R 279

[In the early hours of one morning on the first floor of a block of flats where he lived, the appellant, who was armed with a shotgun and cartridges, shot at police officers who were attempting to arrest him for various serious offences. The appellant had with him a 16-year-old girl who was pregnant by him, and against her will used her body to shield him from any retaliation by the officers. The officers in fact returned the appellant's fire and as a result the girl was killed. The appellant was charged, *inter alia*, with her murder. The jury acquitted the appellant of murder and convicted him of manslaughter.]

ROBERT GOFF LJ (for the court): ... [I]t was pressed upon us by Lord Gifford that ... as a matter of policy, no man should be convicted of homicide (or, we imagine, any crime of violence to another person) unless he himself, or another person acting in concert with him, fired the shot (or, we imagine, struck the blow) which was the immediate cause of the victim's death (or injury).

No English authority was cited to us in support of any such proposition, and we know of none. So far as we are aware, there is no such rule in English law; and, in the absence of any doctrine of constructive malice, we can see no basis in principle for any such rule in English law. Lord Gifford urged upon us that, in a case where the accused did not, for example, fire the shot which was the immediate cause of the victim's death, he will inevitably have committed some lesser crime, and that it would be sufficient that he should be convicted of that lesser crime. So, on the facts of the present case, it would be enough that the appellant was convicted of the crime of attempted murder of the two police officers, D.S. Sartain and D.C. Richards. We see no force in this submission. In point of fact, it is not difficult to imagine circumstances in which it would manifestly be inadequate for the accused merely to be convicted of a lesser offence; for example, a man besieged by armed terrorists in a house might attempt to make his escape by forcing some other person to act as a shield, knowing full well that that person would in all probability be shot, and possibly killed, in consequence. For that man merely to be convicted of an assault would, if the person he used as a shield were to be shot and killed, surely be inadequate in the circumstances; we can see no reason why he should not be convicted at least of manslaughter. But in any event there is, so far as we can discern, no basis of legal principle for Lord Gifford's submission. We are therefore unable to accept it.

In our judgment, the question whether an accused person can be held guilty of homicide, either murder or manslaughter, of a victim the immediate cause of whose death is the act of another person must be determined on the ordinary principles of causation, uninhibited by any such rule of policy as that for which Lord Gifford has contended. We therefore reject the second ground of appeal.

We turn to the first ground of appeal, which is that the learned judge erred in directing the jury that it was for him to decide *as a matter of law* whether by his unlawful and deliberate acts the appellant caused or was a cause of Gail Kinchen's death.

Now the whole subject of causation in the law has been the subject of a well-known and most distinguished treatise by Professors Hart and Honoré, *Causation in the Law*. Passages from this book were cited to the learned judge, and were plainly relied upon by him; we, too, wish to express our indebtedness to it. It would be quite wrong for us to consider in this judgment the wider issues discussed in that work. But, for present purposes, the passage which is of most immediate relevance is to be found in Chapter XII, in which the learned authors consider the circumstances in which the intervention of a third person, not acting in concert with the accused, may have the effect of relieving the accused of criminal responsibility. The criterion which they suggest should be applied in such circumstances is whether the intervention is voluntary, *i.e.* whether it is "free, deliberate and informed." We resist the temptation of expressing the judicial opinion whether we find ourselves in complete agreement with that definition; though we certainly consider it to be broadly correct and supported by authority. Among the examples which the authors give of non-voluntary conduct, which is not effective to relieve the accused of responsibility, are two which are germane to the present case, *viz.* a reasonable act performed for the purpose of self-preservation, and an act done in performance of a legal duty.

There can, we consider, be no doubt that a reasonable act performed for the purpose of self-preservation, being of course itself an act caused by the accused's own act, does not operate as a *novus actus interveniens*. If authority is needed for this almost self-evident proposition, it is to be found in such cases as *Pitts* (1842), C. & M. 284, and *Curley* (1909), 2 Cr. App. R. 96. In both these cases, the act performed for the purpose of self-preservation consisted of an act by the victim in attempting to escape from the violence of the accused, which in fact resulted in the victim's death. In each case it was held as a matter of law that, if the victim acted in a reasonable attempt to escape the violence of the accused, the death of the victim was caused by the act of the accused. Now one form of self-preservation is self-defence; for present purposes, we can see no distinction in principle between an attempt to escape the consequences of the accused's act, and a response which takes the form of self-defence. Furthermore, in our judgment, if a reasonable act of self-defence against the act of the accused causes the death of a third party, we can see no reason in principle why the act of self-defence, being an involuntary act caused by the act of the accused, should relieve the accused from criminal responsibility for the death of the third party. Of course, it does not necessarily follow that the accused will be guilty of the murder, or even of the manslaughter, of the third party; though in the majority of cases he is likely to be guilty at least of manslaughter. Whether he is guilty of murder or manslaughter will depend upon the question whether all the ingredients of the relevant offence have been proved; in particular, on a charge of murder, it will be necessary that the accused had the necessary intent, on the principles stated by the House of Lords in *Hyam v. D.P.P.* (1974), 59 Cr. App. R. 91; [1975] A.C. 55.

No English authority was cited to us, nor we think to the learned judge, in support of the proposition that an act done in the execution of a legal duty, again of course being an act itself caused by the act of the accused, does not operate as a *novus actus interveniens*.

Before the judge, the cases relied on by the prosecution in support of this proposition were the two Pennsylvanian cases already referred to, *Commonwealth v. Moyer (supra)* and *Commonwealth v. Almeida (supra)*. However, since the case of *Redline (supra)*, neither of these cases can be regarded as authority in the State of Pennsylvania: *Redline* was not cited to the learned judge, we suspect because it is not referred to in Hart and Honoré's *Causation in the Law*, almost certainly because the report of Redline was not available to the learned authors when their treatise went to the press. Even so, we agree with the learned judge that the proposition is sound in law, because as a matter of principle such an act cannot be regarded as a voluntary act independent of the wrongful act of the accused.

Appeal dismissed.

In *R v JSR*, 2008 ONCA 544, the Ontario Court of Appeal addressed a situation in many ways analogous to *Pagett*. The evidence in the case suggested that, while participating in a gunfight on busy Yonge Street in Toronto, the accused and one of his adversaries (call him "B") exchanged gunfire. B missed the accused, but hit and killed an innocent bystander, 15-year-old Jane Creba. The court held that the accused's conduct could constitute a contributing cause of the bystander's death under the common law test for causation. The court explained:

[29] Having concluded that the evidence is reasonably capable of supporting the mutual gun fight scenario, the causation issue in respect of Ms. Creba's death is analogous to causation questions in the car racing cases where one of the participants in the car race hits a bystander and causes injury or death. In such cases, both drivers may be held to have caused that injury or death: see *R. v. Rotundo* (1993), 47 M.V.R. (2d) 90 (Ont. C.A.); and *R. v. Menezes* (2002), 23 M.V.R. (4th) 185 (S.C.J.). In *Menezes* at para. 105, Hill J. described the causal responsibility of the participants in the car race in these terms:

Those at risk from the unreasonable and unjustified danger of an escapade of competitive driving, whether a spontaneous or planned event, include the occupants of other vehicles, cyclists, pedestrians, passengers in the racers' autos, and the co-participants themselves. *There is one danger. Each driver bears equal responsibility for its continued life span subject to withdrawal or [an] intervening event.* As each driver in effect induces the other to drive in an unlawfully unsafe manner, each is taken to assume any consequential risk objectively within the ambit of the danger created. [Emphasis added.]

[30] Borrowing the words of Hill J. and applying them to this case, a reasonable jury could find that each shooter induced the other to engage in a gun fight on a crowded street. "But for" the decision to engage in a gun fight on a crowded street and the resulting exchange of bullets, Ms. Creba would not have been killed.

The issue of causation has been raised in joint drag-racing situations in *R v Menezes* (2002), 50 CR (5th) 343 (Ont SC) and *R v Bhalru*, 2002 BCSC 1852, aff'd 2003 BCCA 644. These cases suggest that if A and B are drag racing and B crashes, killing or injuring himself or another, A is a joint cause of the injury or death. However, in *Menezes*, Justice Hill held that if A withdraws from or abandons the race before the crash and B is aware of this abandonment and does not slow down, A is not liable.

In *R v Blaue*, [1975] 1 WLR 1411 (Eng CA), the defendant stabbed an 18-year-old woman with a knife, which penetrated her lung. She was taken to hospital where she was told that a blood transfusion and surgery were necessary to save her life. She refused to have a blood transfusion on the ground that it was contrary to her religious beliefs as a Jehovah's Witness and she died the following day. The cause of death was bleeding into the pleural cavity, which would not have been fatal if she had accepted medical treatment when advised to do so. The defendant was charged with murder. The judge, in directing the jury on the issue of causation, said that they might think that they had little option but to find that the stab wounds were still an operative or substantial cause of death when the victim died. The defendant was convicted of manslaughter. The accused's appeal against conviction was dismissed. Lawton LJ, giving the judgment of the court, stated in part:

> It has long been the policy of the law that those who use violence on other people must take their victims as they find them. This in our judgment means the whole man, not just the physical man. It does not lie in the mouth of the assailant to say that his victim's religious beliefs which inhibited him from accepting certain kinds of treatment were unreasonable. The question for decision is what caused her death. The answer is the stab wound. The fact that the victim refused to stop this end coming about did not break the causal connection between the act and death.
>
> If a victim's personal representatives claim compensation for his death the concept of foreseeability can operate in favour of the wrongdoer in the assessment of such compensation: the wrongdoer is entitled to expect his victim to mitigate his damage by accepting treatment of a normal kind: see *Steele v. R. George & Co. (1937) Ltd.*, [1942] A.C. 497. As Mr. Herrod pointed out, the criminal law is concerned with the maintenance of law and order and the protection of the public generally. A policy of the common law applicable to the settlement of tortious liability between subjects may not be, and in our judgment is not, appropriate for the criminal law.
>
> The issue of the cause of death in a trial for either murder or manslaughter is one of fact for the jury to decide. But if, as in this case, there is no conflict of evidence and all the jury has to do is to apply the law to the admitted facts, the judge is entitled to tell the jury what the result of that application will be. In this case the judge would have been entitled to have told the jury that the defendant's stab wound was an operative cause of death. The appeal fails.

For an interesting discussion of the *Blaue* case, see D Klimchuk, "Causation, Thin Skulls and Equality" (1998) 11 Can JL & Jur 115.

In the following case the Supreme Court of Canada offered an approach for assessing intervening causes and whether a subsequent event has severed the chain of causation between the accused's acts and the proscribed consequence.

R v Maybin
Supreme Court of Canada
2012 SCC 24, [2012] 2 SCR 30

KARAKATSANIS J (for the Court):

[1] The causal link between an accused's actions and the victim's death is not always obvious in homicide cases. In cases involving multiple causes of death or intervening causes between an accused's action and the victim's death, determining causation is more challenging. An accused's unlawful actions need not be the only cause of death, or even the direct cause of death; the court must determine if the accused's actions are a significant contributing cause of death.

[2] This appeal raises the question of when an intervening act by another person severs the causal connection between the accused's act and the victim's death, thereby absolving the accused of legal responsibility for manslaughter.

[3] Late at night, in a busy bar, the appellants Timothy and Matthew Maybin, repeatedly punched the victim in the face and head. Timothy Maybin eventually struck a blow that rendered the victim unconscious. Arriving on the scene within seconds, a bar bouncer then struck the [unconscious] victim in the head. While the trial judge was not satisfied that Matthew Maybin's assault caused bodily harm, he found that he was a party to his brother's more serious assault. The medical evidence was inconclusive about which blows caused death. As a result, the trial judge acquitted the appellants and the bouncer. At issue is whether the trial judge could have concluded that the appellants caused the death in fact; and if so, whether the subsequent assault by another person constituted an intervening act that nonetheless broke the chain of legal causation.

[4] The British Columbia Court of Appeal (2010 BCCA 527, 295 B.C.A.C. 298) concluded that factual causation had been established: "but for" the actions of the appellants the victim would not have died. However, the judges used two different analytical approaches in addressing legal causation. Ryan J.A. writing for the majority (Huddart J.A. concurring) asked whether the risk of the harm caused by the intervening actor could have been reasonably foreseeable to the appellants. She concluded that it could have been. Ryan J.A. allowed the appeal, set aside the appellants' acquittals and ordered a new trial. Finch C.J.B.C., in dissent, did not agree that the appellants could have reasonably foreseen the conduct of the intervening actor, and concluded that the intentional act of a third party acting independently severed legal causation.

[5] In my view, both the "reasonable foreseeability" and the "intentional, independent act" approach may be useful in assessing legal causation depending on the specific factual matrix. However, neither is determinative of whether an intervening act severs the chain of causation so that an accused's act is not a significant contributing cause of death. They are tools to assist in addressing the test for legal causation set out by this Court in *Smithers v. The Queen*, [1978] 1 S.C.R. 506, and confirmed in *R. v. Nette*, 2001 SCC 78, [2001] 3 S.C.R. 488: Were the unlawful acts of the appellants a significant contributing cause of death?

· · ·

1. Background

[8] Late one night in a crowded bar, the victim apparently affronted the appellant Timothy Maybin by touching a pool ball on the appellant's table. Timothy Maybin then grabbed the victim and violently punched his face and head in quick succession. Timothy's brother, the appellant Matthew Maybin, helped his brother but was pulled away by bar staff. The victim did not defend himself, and after being hit a number of times, he staggered a few steps and fell face forward, unconscious, on the pool table. The commotion attracted the attention of a bar bouncer, who arrived within seconds on the scene. The bouncer asked who started the fight and after a patron pointed in the direction of the pool table, the bouncer immediately struck the unconscious victim in the back of the head with considerable force. The two assaults took place within less than a minute. The victim subsequently died as a result of bleeding in the brain.

[9] The trial judge (2008 BCSC 1277) concluded that all three accused had assaulted the victim and had either directly or indirectly caused bodily harm; but that the appellants on the one hand, and the bouncer on the other, acted independently of each other (para. 325). The trial judge found that there were three possible causes of death: the punches delivered by Timothy Maybin; the single blow struck by the bouncer; or a combination of the two. Because he was not satisfied beyond a reasonable doubt that either Timothy Maybin's punches or the bouncer's blow was the sole or a significant contributing cause of the fatal injury, he acquitted all three accused of manslaughter.

[10] On appeal, all three judges concluded that the trial judge erred in focussing narrowly upon the medical cause of death and failing to address the broader issues of factual and legal causation. The court was unanimous that the appellants' assaults were factually a contributing cause of death: "but for" their actions, the victim would not have died.

[11] In assessing legal causation, the majority and dissenting decisions accepted the standard set out by this Court in *Smithers* and confirmed in *Nette*. The court divided, however, in its analytical approach. The majority concluded that the risk of harm—from the intervention of bar staff in an escalating bar fight—was reasonably foreseeable. The dissenting decision concluded that the assault of the bouncer was not reasonably foreseeable and that the intentional act of an independent person severed legal causation.

[12] The court allowed the Crown appeals and ordered a new trial for the Maybin brothers; it dismissed the appeal from the acquittal of the bouncer. The Maybin brothers appeal to this Court as of right.

2. General Principles of Causation for Manslaughter

. . .

[15] In *Nette*, this Court affirmed the validity of the *de minimis* causation standard expressed in *Smithers* for culpable homicide. Writing for the majority, Arbour J. noted that causation in homicide cases involves two aspects: factual and legal causation. Factual causation is "an inquiry about how the victim came to his or her death, in a medical, mechanical, or physical sense, and with the contribution of the accused to that result" (*Nette*, at para. 44). The trier of fact usually asks: "But for" the action(s) of the accused, would the death have occurred? Factual causation is therefore inclusive in scope.

[16] Legal causation, however, is a narrowing concept which funnels a wider range of factual causes into those which are sufficiently connected to a harm to warrant legal

responsibility. Arbour J. noted that legal causation is "based on concepts of moral responsibility and is not a mechanical or mathematical exercise" (*Nette*, at para. 83). ...

[17] Further, this Court emphasized that causation issues are case-specific and fact-driven. The choice of terminology to put to a jury is discretionary in the context of the circumstances of the case (*Nette*, at para. 72). Implicit in *Nette* then, is the recognition that different approaches may be helpful in assessing legal causation, depending upon the specific factual context.

3. Factual Causation

[18] In this case all three judges of the Court of Appeal were satisfied that the appellants had factually caused the victim's death. As a result, the issue of factual causation was not strictly within the scope of this appeal. In oral submissions before this Court however, counsel for the appellants argued that factual causation was not established because the trial judge had a reasonable doubt as to who delivered the lethal blow. Counsel suggested that in such circumstances, it would be anomalous if the bouncer was acquitted and the appellants were convicted.

[19] As noted by the majority of the Court of Appeal, the bouncer was not in the same position as the Maybin brothers: the bouncer's assault was at the end of the chain of events leading to the victim's death (para. 46). Given the uncertainty of the medical evidence, the trial judge had a reasonable doubt about whether the bouncer's blow contributed to the death. As a result, he could not find that the actions of the bouncer were a factual cause of death (para. 51 of the Court of Appeal reasons). The court therefore dismissed the appeal from the acquittal of the bouncer for manslaughter.

[20] On the other hand, the appellants' unlawful acts not only seriously injured the victim, but also rendered him unconscious on the pool table where he was subsequently assaulted by the bouncer. Given these facts, the Court of Appeal concluded that even if the appellants' actions were not the direct and immediate cause of the victim's death, "but for" their actions, the victim would not have died. I agree. As *Smithers* and *Nette* made clear, factual causation is not limited to the direct and immediate cause, nor is it limited to the most significant cause. The Maybin brothers' assault was either the direct medical cause of death or it rendered the victim vulnerable to the bouncer's assault.

[21] For these reasons, I agree with the Court of Appeal that the trial judge erred in the factual causation inquiry in this case. He stopped with his assessment of the medical cause of death and did not consider the contribution of the appellants to that result by asking whether the deceased would have died "but for" the actions of the appellants. ...

[22] The fact that the bouncer's act may have been a *novus actus interveniens*, or an intervening act, is part of the analysis of whether *legal* causation has been established and whether the appellants should be held legally accountable for the death.

4. Legal Causation: Intervening Act

[23] The doctrine of intervening acts is used, when relevant, for the purpose of reducing the scope of acts which generate criminal liability. As Cromwell J.A. stated in *R. v. Tower*, 2008 NSCA 3, 261 N.S.R. (2d) 135, "the law recognizes that other causes may intervene to 'break the chain of causation' between the accused's acts and the death. This

is the concept of an 'intervening cause', that some new event or events result in the accused's actions not being a significant contributing cause of death" (para. 25).

· · ·

[25] The difficulty in formulating one test to determine when an intervening cause interrupts the chain of causation lies in the vast range of circumstances in which this issue arises. As mentioned, the majority and the dissent in the court below focussed on two different approaches to explain when an intervening act breaks the chain of causation.

[26] The first approach, applied by the majority, looks to whether the intervening act was objectively or reasonably foreseeable (see *R. v. Shilon* (2006), 240 C.C.C. (3d) 401 (Ont. C.A.)). The majority asked whether the risk of harm caused by the intervening actor was reasonably foreseeable to the appellants at the time they were committing the unlawful acts. It concluded that a trier of fact could find that it was reasonably foreseeable to the appellants that their assault on the victim, which occurred in a crowded bar, late at night, would provoke the intervention of others, perhaps the bar staff, with resulting non-trivial harm.

[27] The second approach, applied by the dissent, considers whether the intervening act is an independent factor that severs the impact of the accused's actions, making the intervening act, in law, the sole cause of the victim's death (see *R. v. Pagett* (1983), 76 Cr. App. R. 279 (C.A.); *R. v. Smith*, [1959] 2 Q.B. 35 (C.M.A.C.)). The dissent held that the bouncer's assault was just such an independent factor.

[28] In my view, both these approaches are analytical aids—not new standards of legal causation. I agree with the intervener, the Attorney General of Ontario, that while such approaches may be helpful, they do not create new tests that are dispositive. Neither an unforeseeable intervening act nor an independent intervening act is necessarily a sufficient condition to *break* the chain of legal causation. Similarly, the fact that the intervening act was reasonably foreseeable, or was not an independent act, is not necessarily a sufficient condition to *establish* legal causation. Even in cases where it is alleged that an intervening act has interrupted the chain of legal causation, the causation test articulated in *Smithers* and confirmed in *Nette* remains the same: Were the dangerous, unlawful acts of the accused a significant contributing cause of the victim's death?

[29] Depending on the circumstances, assessments of foreseeability or independence may be more or less helpful in determining whether an accused's unlawful acts were still a *significant contributing* cause at the time of death. Any assessment of legal causation should maintain focus on whether the accused should be held legally responsible for the consequences of his actions, or whether holding the accused responsible for the death would amount to punishing a moral innocent.

5. Reasonable Foreseeability

[30] An intervening act that is reasonably foreseeable will usually not break or rupture the chain of causation so as to relieve the offender of legal responsibility for the unintended result. This approach posits that an accused who undertakes a dangerous act, and in so doing contributes to a death, should bear the risk that other foreseeable acts may intervene and contribute to that death. Because the issue is whether the actions and consequences were reasonably foreseeable prospectively, at the time of the accused's objectively dangerous and unlawful act, it accords with our notions of moral accountability. This approach addresses the question: Is it fair to attribute the resulting death to the initial actor?

[31] Courts have sometimes couched the principle of foreseeability in different terms, asking whether the intervening act is so "extraordinary" or "unusual" that the accused should not be held responsible for the consequences of that act. In *R. v. Sinclair*, 2009 MBCA 71, 240 Man. R. (2d) 135, the accused beat the deceased and left him motionless in the roadway where he was struck by a passing motorist. The Manitoba Court of Appeal held that, in order for *novus actus interveniens* to apply to sever legal causation, the intervening act had to be, in some way, extraordinary or unusual. In *R. v. Hallett*, [1969] S.A.S.R. 141 (S.C. *in banco*), the victim was left unconscious on a beach; the Supreme Court of South Australia held that a natural event may break the chain of causation if it is "extraordinary" (a tidal wave), but not if it is the ordinary operation of natural forces (the tides).

[32] Objective foreseeability has thus been a useful tool in determining whether an intervening act severs the chain of legal causation. The more difficult question in applying such an approach is the scope of what has to be reasonably foreseeable. In this case, the parties disagree about whether the intervening act—the blow delivered by the bouncer— was reasonably foreseeable. While both the majority and dissent opinions apply a reasonable foreseeability framework, they arrive at different conclusions. This result is driven by their different views regarding what precisely must be reasonably foreseeable. Is it the specific assault by the intervening actor? Is it simply the risk of further bodily harm? Or is it the general nature of intervening acts and the accompanying risk of harm?

[33] The dissent took the narrow view that the specific scenario—the unprovoked assault by a bouncer of an unconscious patron—had to be reasonably foreseeable. The majority cast the net more broadly by concluding "that it was reasonably foreseeable that the [appellants'] assault would provoke the intervention of others, perhaps the bar staff, with resulting non-trivial harm" (para. 43).

[34] In my view, the chain of causation should not be broken only because the specific subsequent attack by the bouncer was not reasonably foreseeable. Because the time to assess reasonable foreseeability is at the time of the initial assault, rather than at the time of the intervening act, it is too restrictive to require that the precise details of the event be objectively foreseeable. In some cases, while the general nature of the ensuing acts and the risk of further harm may be reasonably likely, the specific manner in which it could occur may be entirely unpredictable. From the perspective of moral responsibility, it is sufficient if the general nature of the intervening act and the risk of non-trivial harm are objectively foreseeable at the time of the dangerous and unlawful acts.

. . .

[38] [It] is the general nature of the intervening acts and the accompanying risk of harm that needs to be reasonably foreseeable. Legal causation does not require that the accused must objectively foresee the precise future consequences of their conduct. Nor does it assist in addressing moral culpability to require merely that the risk of some non-trivial bodily harm is reasonably foreseeable. Rather, the intervening acts and the ensuing non-trivial harm must be reasonably foreseeable in the sense that the acts and the harm that actually transpired flowed reasonably from the conduct of the appellants. If so, then the accused's actions may remain a significant contributing cause of death.

[39] In this case, the appellants submit that the bouncer's assault of the unconscious victim was not reasonably foreseeable at all, unlike further injury to the victim by another patron joining in the fight or by bar staff attempting to impose order.

[40] I do not agree. If the physical intervention of the bar staff, with its risk of non-trivial harm was objectively foreseeable, then the specific details of that intervention did not themselves need to be foreseen. Focussing on the fact that the subsequent act was committed by a bouncer, as opposed to another patron, misplaces the focus on the actor, as opposed to the nature of the intervening act.

. . .

[42] In this case, the fight did escalate, with other patrons joining in, others calling for a bouncer, and bar staff hurrying to the area. Moreover, the bouncer in this case testified that he thought he *was* trying to impose order ("When asked to explain why he had punched [the victim], [the bouncer] said that the man had been identified to him as being the instigator of the fight and so he hit him to shock and disorient him, so as to gain control of the situation" (para. 131 of the trial judge's decision)). It was open to the trial judge to conclude that the risk of intervention by patrons and the bouncer was objectively foreseeable when the appellants commenced a one-sided fight in a crowded bar. Accordingly, I agree with the majority of the Court of Appeal that it was open to the judge to find that the intervening act was reasonably foreseeable in the circumstances of this case.

[43] One final point on this issue. The majority of the Court of Appeal stated that the reasonable foreseeability test is determinative on the issue of legal causation. ...

[44] The Court of Appeal in effect elevated this analytical approach to a new causation rule. I do not agree. The reasonable foreseeability approach is a useful tool and directly incorporates the notion of blameworthiness. However, as noted above, there may be other helpful analytical tools to assess whether legal responsibility should be imputed to the accused and whether the accused's acts were a significant contributing cause of death as required in *Smithers* and *Nette*.

6. Independent Acts

[45] In dissent, Finch C.J.B.C. agreed that "a person should not be held responsible for objectively unforeseeable consequences" and concluded that the actions of the bouncer were not reasonably foreseeable. He continued:

> However, persons should similarly not be held responsible *for intentional actions of a third party acting independently*. This was articulated by the Ontario Court of Appeal in *R. v. J.S.R.* (2008), ... 239 O.A.C. 42; 237 C.C.C. (3d) 305; 2008 ONCA 544, at para. 31:
>
> > [D]espite the existence of factual causation, it is said to be unfair to impute legal liability for the death to a person whose actions have been effectively overtaken by the more immediate causal action of another party acting independently. ...
> >
> > [The bouncer's] intentional conduct in striking the unconscious [victim] constitutes an intervening act in this case. He is an independent third party and the Maybin brothers should not be held morally or legally responsible for his acts, in the absence of a conclusion that the blows of Timothy Maybin and [the bouncer] in conjunction were the cause of death. [Emphasis in original; paras. 72-73.]

[46] Whether the effects of an accused's actions are "effectively overtaken by the more immediate causal action of another party acting independently" involves an assessment of the relative weight of the causes, looking retrospectively from the death.

[47] Courts have sought to articulate when the first cause ought to be overlooked because of the nature and effect of the subsequent causes, quite apart from whether or not the subsequent causes may have been foreseeable. In *Smith*, the victim died in hospital after being stabbed by the accused. It was later discovered that the victim had been improperly treated. When deciding whether the actions of medical staff constituted an intervening cause, the English Courts Martial Appeal Court declared that an intervening cause shields the accused from responsibility only if the accused's act is "merely the setting in which another cause operates" (p. 43). Or, put another way, only if the intervening cause "is so overwhelming as to make the original wound merely part of the history" leading to the victim's death (p. 43). Ultimately, the court articulated the standard as: "… if at the time of death the original wound is still an operating cause and a substantial cause, then the death can properly be said to be the result of the wound" (pp. 42-43). In *Hallett* when faced with the death of a man left unconscious on a beach who drowned as a result of "the ordinary operations of the tides" (p. 150), the court asked whether the original unlawful act was "so connected with the event that it … must be regarded as having a sufficiently substantial causal effect which subsisted up to the happening of the event" (p. 149).

. . .

[49] Whether an intervening act is independent is thus sometimes framed as a question of whether the intervening act is a response to the acts of the accused. In other words, did the act of the accused merely set the scene, allowing other circumstances to (coincidentally) intervene, or did the act of the accused trigger or provoke the action of the intervening party?

[50] When the intervening acts are natural events, they are more closely tied to the theory of foreseeability, and the courts ask whether the event was "extraordinary," as in *Hallett*. When the intervening acts are those of a person, exercising his or her free will, the focus is often on the independence of the actions.

. . .

[52] An intervening act by another person does not always sever the causal connection between the accused's act and the result: as mentioned, ss. 224 and 225 of the *Criminal Code* provide that the chain of causation is not broken if death could otherwise have been prevented by resorting to proper means (s. 224), or if the immediate cause of death is proper or improper treatment that is applied in good faith (s. 225). In addition, in this case, I need not consider the actions of a third party who acts in good faith, or under mistake, intimidation or similar pressure, or whose actions are not voluntary. Here, the bouncer criminally assaulted the unconscious victim causing bodily harm.

[53] What then, is the nature and degree of independence that may absolve the original actors of legal responsibility for the consequences of their actions? Turning to this case, was the act of the bouncer so independent of the actions of the appellants that his act should be regarded in law as the sole cause of the victim's death to the exclusion of the acts of the appellants?

. . .

[57] Was the bouncer's intentional assault an independent act? The answer depends upon whether the intervening act was so connected to the appellants' actions that it cannot be said to be independent. If the intervening act is a direct response or is directly linked to the appellants' actions, and does not by its nature overwhelm the original actions, then the appellants cannot be said to be morally innocent of the death.

[58] While the trial judge found the actions of the Maybin brothers and the actions of the bouncer to be separate and independent assaults, he also found these actions to be "an interrelated series of events" (para. 209). He found that the assaults took place in the same location and in the same manner, and from Timothy Maybin's first punch to the bouncer's blow, the elapsed time was less than a minute … .

[59] In this case, then, the trial judge could have found that the bouncer acted in direct and virtually immediate reaction to what the appellants did; that the bouncer acted after asking who had started the fight; and that his act was responsive and not coincidental conduct. It was open to the trial judge to find that the bouncer's act was closely connected in time, place, circumstance, nature and effect with the appellants' acts and that the effects of the appellants' actions were still "subsisting" and not "spent" at the time the bouncer acted (*R. v. Tower*, at para. 26). The evidence could support the conclusion that the blow delivered by the bouncer was not so "overwhelming" as to make the effect of the original assaults merely part of the history so that it can be said that the original assaults were not "operative" at the time of death (*R. v. Smith*). I conclude that it was open to the trial judge to find that the assault of the bouncer was not independent of the appellants' unlawful acts and that the appellants' actions remained a significant contributing cause of the victim's death. Arguably, the dangerous and unlawful acts of the appellants were not so remote to suggest that they were morally innocent of the death.

7. Conclusion

[60] Courts have used a number of analytical approaches to determine when an intervening act absolves the accused of legal responsibility for manslaughter. These approaches grapple with the issue of the moral connection between the accused's acts and the death; they acknowledge that an intervening act that is reasonably foreseeable to the accused may well not break the chain of causation, and that an independent and intentional act by a third party may in some cases make it unfair to hold the accused responsible. In my view, these approaches may be useful tools depending upon the factual context. However, the analysis must focus on first principles and recognize that these tools do not alter the standard of causation or substitute new tests. The dangerous and unlawful acts of the accused must be a significant contributing cause of the victim's death.

[61] I agree with the majority of the Court of Appeal that based upon the trial judge's findings of fact, it was open to him to conclude that the general nature of the intervening act and the accompanying risk of harm were reasonably foreseeable; and that the act was in direct response to the appellants' unlawful actions. The judge could have concluded that the bouncer's assault did not necessarily constitute an intervening act that severed the link between Timothy and Matthew Maybin's conduct and the victim's death, such that it would absolve them of moral and legal responsibility. The trial judge could have found that the appellants' actions remained a significant contributing cause of the death.

[62] For these reasons, I agree with the majority of the Court of Appeal that in the circumstances of this case, it was open to the trial judge to find that the appellants caused the death. I would dismiss the appeal.

Parliament can legislate causation requirements just as it can legislate other elements of the *actus reus*. Given the frequency with which causation issues arise in homicide cases, the *Criminal Code* includes a number of provisions dealing with certain issues of causation for offences involving death as a consequence. Some of these provisions were discussed in the cases above. Importantly, any causation test, whether created by Parliament or by the judges in their rulings, must comply with the Charter and, most specifically, with s 7, which ensures that "the principles of fundamental justice" will be observed when a person's life, liberty, or security of the person is infringed. As you have read, *Cribbin* addressed the constitutionality of the common law causation test. Are the following statutory rules governing causation in homicide cases fundamentally fair? To what extent have they been applied or challenged in the homicide cases that you read in this section?

Homicide

222(1) A person commits homicide when, directly or indirectly, by any means, he causes the death of a human being. ...

Idem

222(5) A person commits culpable homicide when he causes the death of a human being, ...

(c) by causing that human being, by threats or fear of violence or by deception, to do anything that causes his death; or

(d) by wilfully frightening that human being, in the case of a child or sick person.

Death that might have been prevented

224. Where a person, by an act or omission, does any thing that results in the death of a human being, he causes the death of that human being notwithstanding that death from that cause might have been prevented by resorting to proper means.

Death from treatment of injury

225. Where a person causes to a human being a bodily injury that is of itself of a dangerous nature and from which death results, he causes the death of that human being notwithstanding that the immediate cause of death is proper or improper treatment that is applied in good faith.

Acceleration of death

226. Where a person causes to a human being a bodily injury that results in death, he causes the death of that human being notwithstanding that the effect of the bodily injury is only to accelerate his death from a disease or disorder arising from some other cause.

Killing by influence on the mind

228. No person commits culpable homicide where he causes the death of a human being

(a) by any influence on the mind alone, or

(b) by any disorder or disease resulting from influence on the mind alone,

but this section does not apply where a person causes the death of a child or sick person by wilfully frightening him.

V. THE PRINCIPLE OF CONTEMPORANEITY

This chapter has addressed the various components of the *actus reus*: physical voluntariness, acts and omissions, circumstances, and consequences. The next two chapters turn to consider the mental element, or *mens rea*, required to establish guilt. By way of introduction to that substantial and interesting topic, this section explains a principle that concerns the relationship between the *actus reus* and *mens rea*: that of contemporaneity, sometimes called the principle of *coincidence* or *concurrence*. This principle holds that, with regard to all offences that require proof of fault, the offence cannot be proved unless the element of fault—the *mens rea*—and the *actus reus* coincide. In 1798, the Court of King's Bench made this pronouncement on the principle of contemporaneity in *Fowler v Padget*, 101 ER 1103 at 1106, 7 Term Rep 509:

> It is a principle of natural justice, and of our law, that *actus non facit reum nisi mens sit rea*. The intent and the act must concur to constitute the crime.

This principle of contemporaneity thus requires that there be a temporal overlap between the mental fault and the prohibited conduct. If the *mens rea* and the *actus reus* do not coincide in this way, the law would be punishing either for guilty conduct without the required fault or for guilty thoughts not expressed in guilty conduct. Contemporaneity does not pose a problem in most cases; yet, as the following cases show, a strict application of this principle would seem to risk unjust or even absurd results. You will see that, in response to these hard cases, the courts have resiled from an overly strict application of the contemporaneity requirement, preferring a more flexible application. Indeed, in *Fagan* and *Cooper*, below, you will see the courts toying with the idea of creating a new legal duty in order to solve difficult contemporaneity issues. The principle, however, remains an important component of our understanding of the prerequisites for criminal liability.

Fagan v Commissioner of Metropolitan Police
Court of Appeal, Criminal Division, England
[1969] 1 QB 439

JAMES J (with whom Lord Parker agreed): The appellant, Vincent Martel Fagan, was convicted by the Willesden magistrates of assaulting David Morris, a police constable, in the execution of his duty on August 31, 1967. He appealed to quarter sessions. On October 25, 1967, his appeal was heard by Middlesex Quarter Sessions and was dismissed. This matter now comes before the court on appeal by way of case stated from that decision of quarter sessions.

The sole question is whether the prosecution proved facts which in law amounted to an assault.

On August 31, 1967, the appellant was reversing a motor car in Fortunegate Road, London, N.W. 10, when Police Constable Morris directed him to drive the car forwards to the kerbside [so that he could ask the appellant to produce documents relating to the appellant's driving,] and standing in front of the car pointed out a suitable place in which to park. At first the appellant stopped the car too far from the kerb for the officer's liking. Morris asked him to park closer and indicated a precise spot. The appellant drove forward towards him and stopped it with the offside wheel on Morris's left foot. "Get off, you are on my foot," said the officer. "Fuck you, you can wait," said the appellant. The engine of the car stopped running. Morris repeated several times "Get off my foot." The appellant said reluctantly "Okay man, okay," and then slowly turned on the ignition of the vehicle and reversed it off the officer's foot. The appellant had either turned the ignition off to stop the engine or turned it off after the engine had stopped running.

The Justices at quarter sessions on those facts were left in doubt as to whether the mounting of the wheel on to the officer's foot was deliberate or accidental. They were satisfied, however, beyond all reasonable doubt that the appellant "knowingly, provocatively and unnecessarily allowed the wheel to remain on the foot after the officer said 'Get off, you are on my foot.'" They found that on those facts an assault was proved.

Mr. Abbas for the appellant relied upon the passage in *Stone's Justices' Manual* (1968), Vol. 1, p. 651, where assault is defined. He contends that on the finding of the justices the initial mounting of the wheel could not be an assault and that the act of the wheel mounting the foot came to an end without there being any *mens rea*. It is argued that thereafter there was no act on the part of the appellant which could constitute an *actus reus* but only the omission or failure to remove the wheel as soon as he was asked. That failure, it is said, could not in law be an assault, nor could it in law provide the necessary *mens rea* to convert the original act of mounting the foot into an assault.

Mr. Rant for the respondent argues that the first mounting of the foot was an *actus reus* which act continued until the moment of time at which the wheel was removed. During that continuing act, it is said, the appellant formed the necessary intention to constitute the element of *mens rea* and once that element was added to the continuing act, an assault took place. In the alternative, Mr. Rant argues that there can be situations in which there is a duty to act and that in such situations an omission to act in breach of duty would in law amount to an assault. It is unnecessary to formulate any concluded views on this alternative.

In our judgment the question arising, which has been argued on general principles, falls to be decided on the facts of the particular case. An assault is any act which intentionally—or possibly recklessly—causes another person to apprehend immediate and unlawful personal violence. Although "assault" is an independent crime and is to be treated as such, for practical purposes today "assault" is generally synonymous with the term "battery" and is a term used to mean the actual intended use of unlawful force to another person without his consent. On the facts of the present case the "assault" alleged involved a "battery." Where an assault involves a battery, it matters not, in our judgment, whether the battery is inflicted directly by the body of the offender or through the medium of some weapon or instrument controlled by the action of the offender. An assault may be committed by the laying of a hand upon another, and the action does not cease to be an assault if it is a stick held in the hand and not the hand itself which is laid on the person of the victim. For our part we see no difference in principle between the action of stepping on to a person's toe and maintaining that position and the action of driving a car on to a person's foot and sitting in the car whilst its position on the foot is maintained.

To constitute the offence of assault some intentional act must have been performed: a mere omission to act cannot amount to an assault. Without going into the question whether words alone can constitute an assault, it is clear that the words spoken by the appellant could not alone amount to an assault: they can only shed a light on the appellant's action. For our part we think the crucial question is whether in this case the act of the appellant can be said to be complete and spent at the moment of time when the car wheel came to rest on the foot or whether his act is to be regarded as a continuing act operating until the wheel was removed. In our judgment a distinction is to be drawn between acts which are complete—though results may continue to flow—and those acts which are continuing. Once the act is complete it cannot thereafter be said to be a threat to inflict unlawful force upon the victim. If the act, as distinct from the results thereof, is a continuing act there is a continuing threat to inflict unlawful force. If the assault involves a battery and that battery continues there is a continuing act of assault.

For an assault to be committed both the elements of *actus reus* and *mens rea* must be present at the same time. The "*actus reus*" is the action causing the effect on the victim's mind (see the observations of Park B. in *Regina v. St. George* [(1840), 9 C & P 483, 490, 493)]. The "*mens rea*" is the intention to cause that effect. It is not necessary that *mens rea* should be present at the inception of the *actus reus*: it can be superimposed upon an existing act. On the other hand the subsequent inception of *mens rea* cannot convert an act which has been completed without *mens rea* into an assault.

In our judgment the Willesden magistrates and quarter sessions were right in law. On the facts found the action of the appellant may have been initially unintentional, but the time came when knowing that the wheel was on the officer's foot the appellant (1) remained seated in the car so that his body through the medium of the car was in contact with the officer, (2) switched off the ignition of the car, (3) maintained the wheel of the car on the foot and (4) used words indicating the intention of keeping the wheel in that position. For our part we cannot regard such conduct as mere omission or inactivity.

There was an act constituting a battery which at its inception was not criminal because there was no element of intention but which became criminal from the moment the intention was formed to produce the apprehension which was flowing from the continuing act. The fallacy of the appellant's argument is that it seeks to equate the facts of this case with such a case as where a motorist has accidentally run over a person and, that action having been completed, fails to assist the victim with the intent that the victim should suffer.

We would dismiss this appeal.

BRIDGE J (dissenting): I fully agree with my Lords as to the relevant principles to be applied. No mere omission to act can amount to an assault. Both the elements of *actus reus* and *mens rea* must be present at the same time, but the one may be superimposed on the other. It is in the application of these principles to the highly unusual facts of this case that I have, with regret, reached a different conclusion from the majority of the court. I have no sympathy at all for the appellant, who behaved disgracefully. But I have been unable to find any way of regarding the facts which satisfies me that they amounted to the crime of assault. This has not been for want of trying. But at every attempt I have encountered the inescapable question: after the wheel of the appellant's car had accidentally come to rest on the constable's foot, what was it that the appellant did which constituted the act of assault? However the question is approached, the answer I feel obliged to give is: precisely nothing. The car rested on the foot by its own weight and remained stationary by its own inertia. The appellant's fault was that he omitted to manipulate the controls to set it in motion again.

Neither the fact that the appellant remained in the driver's seat nor that he switched off the ignition seem to me to be of any relevance. The constable's plight would have been no better, but might well have been worse, if the appellant had alighted from the car leaving the ignition switched on. Similarly I can get no help from the suggested analogies. If one man accidentally treads on another's toe or touches him with a stick, but deliberately maintains pressure with foot or stick after the victim protests, there is clearly an assault. But there is no true parallel between such cases and the present case. It is not, to my mind, a legitimate use of language to speak of the appellant "holding" or "maintaining" the car wheel on the constable's foot. The expression which corresponds to the reality is that used by the justices in the case stated. They say, quite rightly, that he "allowed" the wheel to remain.

With a reluctantly dissenting voice I would allow this appeal and quash the appellant's conviction.

Appeal dismissed.

R v Miller
Court of Appeal, Criminal Division, England
[1982] 2 All ER 386

[One night, while squatting in someone else's house, the appellant lit a cigarette and then lay down on a mattress in one of the rooms. He fell asleep before he had finished smoking and the cigarette dropped onto the mattress. When he woke up, he saw the mattress was smouldering. He did nothing about it; he merely moved to another room and went to sleep again. The house caught fire. The appellant was rescued and subsequently charged with arson, contrary to the *Criminal Damage Act 1971* (UK), c 48.]

MAY LJ (for the Court): … In both *Fagan's* case and the present, justice and good sense required that the defendant should not escape liability merely because the last thing that happened in the relevant story was an omission on his part. With respect to the Divisional Court in *Fagan's* case, we agree with Professor Glanville Williams's criticism of the reasoning of the majority of the court. In reality, driving the car wheel on to the policeman's foot was an act, was something which the driver did: the latter's failure thereafter to drive it off, despite the officer's request, was something which the driver did not do, it was an omission, and we think that it is unreal to describe it as any more than that.

On the other hand, in the driver's failure to release the officer's foot in the knowledge that he had just driven on to it, we think that there was clearly a substantial element of adoption by the driver, at the later stage, of what he had done a little earlier. We think that the conduct of the driver in that case can and should have been looked at as a whole and as the whole contained both the *actus reus* and *mens rea* they were sufficiently coincident to render the driver guilty of an assault, without having to resort to the somewhat artificial reasoning of the majority of the Divisional Court. In our opinion, an unintentional act followed by an intentional omission to rectify that act or its consequences can be regarded *in toto* as an intentional act. We do not seek to define the rule, if rule it be, any more precisely because each case must depend on its own facts and we prefer to leave it to the trial judge to give the jury what he considers to be the appropriate direction in any given case. We would only say that an unintentional act followed by an intentional omission to rectify it or its consequences, or a reckless omission to do so when recklessness is a sufficient *mens rea* for the particular case, should only be regarded *in toto* as an intentional or reckless act when reality and common sense so require: this may well be a matter to be left to the jury. Further, in the relevant analysis we think that whether or not there is on the facts an element of adoption on the part of the alleged offender of what he has done earlier by what he deliberately or recklessly fails to do later is an important consideration.

In these circumstances, although we doubt whether the recorder was correct in holding that when the appellant in the present case woke up there was any duty on him at criminal law to extinguish the smouldering mattress, nevertheless we do think that the whole of the appellant's conduct in relation to the mattress from the moment he lay on it with a lighted cigarette until the time he left it smouldering and moved to the adjoining room can and should be regarded as one act. Clearly his failure with knowledge to extinguish the incipient fire had in it a substantial element of adoption on his part of what he had unintentionally done earlier, namely set it on fire. ...

Appeal dismissed.

[A further appeal to the House of Lords was dismissed: [1983] 2 AC 161.]

LORD DIPLOCK: ... I see no rational ground for excluding from conduct capable of giving rise to criminal liability, conduct which consists of failing to take measures that lie within one's power to counteract a danger that one has oneself created, if at the time of such conduct one's state of mind is such as constitutes a necessary ingredient of the offence. I venture to think that the habit of lawyers to talk of "*actus reus*," suggestive as it is of action rather than inaction, is responsible for any erroneous notion that failure to act cannot give rise to criminal liability in English law.

• • •

I cannot see any good reason why, so far as liability under criminal law is concerned, it should matter at what point of time before the resultant damage is complete a person becomes aware that he has done a physical act which, whether or not he appreciated that it would at the time when he did it, does in fact create a risk that property of another will be damaged; provided that, at the moment of awareness, it lies within his power to take steps, either himself or by calling for the assistance of the fire brigade if this be necessary, to prevent or minimise the damage to the property at risk.

• • •

The recorder, in his lucid summing up to the jury (they took 22 minutes only to reach their verdict) told them that the accused having by [his] own act started a fire in the mattress which, when he became aware of its existence, presented an obvious risk of damaging the house, became under a duty to take some action to put it out. The Court of Appeal upheld the conviction, but their ratio decidendi appears to be somewhat different from that of the recorder. As I understand the judgment, in effect it treats the whole course of conduct of the accused, from the moment at which he fell asleep and dropped the cigarette on to the mattress until the time the damage to the house by fire was complete, as a continuous act of the accused, and holds that it is sufficient to constitute the statutory offence of arson if at any stage in that course of conduct the state of mind of the accused, when he fails to try to prevent or minimise the damage which will result from his initial act, although it lies within his power to do so, is that of being reckless as to whether property belonging to another would be damaged.

My Lords, these alternative ways of analysing the legal theory that justifies a decision which has received nothing but commendation for its accord with common-sense and justice, have, since the publication of the judgment of the Court of Appeal in the instant case, provoked academic controversy. Each theory has distinguished support. Professor J.C. Smith espouses the "duty theory"; Professor Glanville Williams who, after the decision of the Divisional Court in *Fagan v. Metropolitan Police Commissioner*, [1969] 1 Q.B. 439 appears to have been attracted by the duty theory, now prefers that of the continuous act. When applied to cases where a person has unknowingly done an act which sets in train events that, when he becomes aware of them, present an obvious risk that property belonging to another will be damaged, both theories lead to an identical result; and since what your Lordships are concerned with is to give guidance to trial judges in their task of summing up to juries, I would for this purpose adopt the duty theory as being the easier to explain to a jury, though I would commend the use of the word "responsibility," rather than "duty" which is more appropriate to civil than to criminal law since it suggests an obligation owed to another person, i.e., the person to whom the endangered property belongs, whereas a criminal statute defines combinations of conduct and state of mind which render a person liable to punishment by the state itself.

In *R v Cooper*, [1993] 1 SCR 146, the accused was charged with murder by manual strangulation and convicted. The accused testified that he became angry with the deceased and grabbed her by the throat with both hands and shook her. He then said that he could recall nothing else until he awoke in his car and found the body of the deceased beside him. The accused had no recollection of causing her death. There was evidence that the accused had consumed a considerable amount of alcohol. In directing the jury as to the accused's liability for murder under s 212(a)(ii) of the *Criminal Code*, the trial judge explained that once the accused had formed the intent to cause the deceased bodily harm, which he knew was likely to cause her death, he did not have to be aware of what he was doing at the moment she actually died. The Newfoundland Court of Appeal ordered a new trial, but the Supreme Court of Canada restored the conviction, Lamer CJ dissenting. Cory J stated for the Court:

> Not only must the guilty mind, intent or *mens rea* be present, it must also be concurrent with the impugned act. ...
>
> Yet, it is not always necessary for the guilty act and the intent to be completely concurrent: see, for example, *Fagan v. Metropolitan Police Commissioner*, [1968] 3 All E.R. 442 (Q.B.). In that case a motorist stopped his car on the foot of a police officer. This was apparently done by accident. When the officer, not unreasonably, asked the accused to move the car, he at first refused but eventually did move on. It was determined that while the first action of stopping was innocent of criminal intent, it acquired the necessary *mens rea* when the accused was made aware that the car was resting on the officer's foot and still refused to move. James J., concurring in the result, stated at p. 445: "It is not necessary that *mens rea* should be present at the inception of the *actus reus*; it can be superimposed on an existing act."
>
> There is, then, the classic rule that at some point the *actus reus* and the *mens rea* or intent must coincide. Further, I would agree with the conclusion of James J. that an act (*actus reus*) which may be innocent or no more than careless at the outset can become criminal at a later

stage when the accused acquires knowledge of the nature of the act and still refuses to change his course of action.

The determination of whether the guilty mind or *mens rea* coincides with the wrongful act will depend to a large extent upon the nature of the act. For example, if the accused shot the victim in the head or stabbed the victim in the chest with death ensuing a few minutes after the shooting or stabbing, then it would be relatively easy to infer that the requisite intent or *mens rea* coincided with the wrongful act (*actus reus*) of shooting or stabbing. As well, a series of acts may form part of the same transaction. For example the repeated blows of the baseball bat continuing over several minutes are all part of the same transaction. In those circumstances if the requisite intent coincides at any time with the sequence of blows then that could be sufficient to found a conviction.

An example of a series of acts that might be termed a continuous transaction appears in *Meli v. The Queen*, [1954] 1 W.L.R. 228 (P.C.). There the accused intended to kill the deceased, and to this end struck a number of blows. The effect of the blows was such that the accused thought the victim was dead and threw the body over a cliff. However, it was not the blows but rather the exposure suffered by the victim while he lay at the base of the cliff that resulted in the death. It was argued on behalf of the accused that when there was the requisite *mens rea* (during the beating) death did not ensue and when death did ensue there was no longer any intention to kill. The judicial committee of the Privy Council concluded that the entire episode was one continuing transaction that could not be subdivided in that way. At some point, the requisite *mens rea* coincided with the continuing series of wrongful acts that constituted the transaction. As a result, the conviction for murder was sustained. I agree with that conclusion.

· · ·

Did the accused possess such a mental state after he started strangling the victim? Here death occurred between 30 seconds and 2 minutes after he grabbed her by the neck. It could be reasonably inferred by the jury that, when the accused grabbed the victim by the neck and shook her, there was, at that moment, the necessary coincidence of the wrongful act of strangulation and the requisite intent to do bodily harm that the accused knew was likely to cause her death. Cooper was aware of these acts before he "blacked out." Thus although the jury was under no compulsion to do so, it was nonetheless open to them to infer that he knew that he was causing bodily harm and knew that it was so dangerous to the victim that it was likely to cause her death. It was sufficient that the intent and the act of strangulation coincided at some point. It was not necessary that the requisite intent continue throughout the entire two minutes required to cause the death of the victim.

Lamer CJ dissented:

[T]he intention to cause bodily harm by no means leads inexorably to the conclusion that the accused knew that the bodily harm was likely to cause death. It is, of course, this second aspect which is essential to a finding of guilt of murder under s. 212(a)(ii). Particularly with respect to an action such as grabbing by the neck, there may be a point at the outset when there is no intention to cause death and no knowledge that the action is likely to cause death. But there comes a point in time when the wrongful conduct becomes likely to cause death. It is, in my view, at that moment or thereafter, that the accused must have a conscious awareness of the likelihood of death. This awareness need not, however, continue until death ensues.

The Ontario Court of Appeal applied the "continuing transaction" approach to contemporaneity in *R v Bottineau*, 2011 ONCA 194, in which the court aptly described the circumstances giving rise to this case as "abhorrent beyond description" (at para 1). The accused were charged with the first-degree murder of their five-year-old grandson, Jeffrey, and the forcible confinement of their six-year-old granddaughter. The accused treated the grandchildren "like unloved and unwanted animals" (at para 18), confining them in an unheated room and ignoring the basic needs of the children. The grandson died of "terminal septicaemia brought on as a complication of prolonged starvation" (at para 20). One of the arguments that counsel for the appellants made on appeal was that they could not be convicted of murder because the Crown was unable to identify a specific point over this long period of neglect and abuse at which the accused possessed the requisite *mens rea*. Applying *Cooper*, the court rejected this argument, holding that "[t]his course of conduct was properly viewed as a single transaction. It was not incumbent on the Crown to point to the moment in time when it dawned on the appellants that their conduct would probably result in J.B.'s [Jeffrey's] death. It was sufficient if the Crown proved that at some point in time during that course of conduct, each accused knew that J.B.'s death was the probable consequence of the harm their abuse and neglect had caused and continued to cause to J.B." (at para 65).

Consider the case of *R v Williams*, 2003 SCC 41, [2003] 2 SCR 134. The accused had been in a relationship with the victim for 18 months and they had engaged in unprotected sex for approximately 5 months before he had learned of his HIV-positive status. At that point he was counselled about the risk of transmission and his duty to disclose his HIV status to sexual partners. Williams nevertheless continued to practise unprotected sex for over a year with the victim, who subsequently tested positive for HIV. He was charged with aggravated assault contrary to s 268 of the *Criminal Code*, which states that "every one commits an aggravated assault who wounds, maims, disfigures or endangers the life of the complainant." Although the sexual intercourse between the two might appear to have been consensual throughout, the law says that failure to disclose information that changes the nature and quality of an act vitiates consent. Accordingly, the Crown's position was that, after being in possession of knowledge of his HIV-positive status, and having failed to disclose that information to the victim, the accused had assaulted her and thereby endangered her life.

After the trial court found Williams guilty of aggravated assault, a majority of the Newfoundland Court of Appeal allowed the accused's appeal and substituted a conviction for *attempted* aggravated assault. At the Supreme Court of Canada, Justice Binnie, writing for the Court, stated that "[t]he respondent acted with a shocking level of recklessness and selfishness. There is no doubt that he committed a criminal assault on the complainant, and further that he was guilty of an *attempted* aggravated assault (as well as common nuisance)" (at para 2). However, on the medical evidence provided to it, the Court held there was a reasonable doubt as to whether, at such time as he was aware of his HIV-positive status (November 15, 1991), he was endangering the life of the victim. Justice Binnie reasoned that it was "at least doubtful that the complainant was free of HIV infection at the time the respondent first discovered, and then concealed, his HIV status" (at para 14). He explained the key problem in the case as follows (at para 35):

> To constitute a crime "at some point the *actus reus* and the *mens rea* or intent must coincide": *R. v. Cooper*, [1993] 1 S.C.R. 146, at p. 157. ... Here, however, before November 15, 1991, there was an endangerment but no intent; after November 15, 1991, there was an intent but at the very

least a reasonable doubt about the existence of any endangerment. Therein lies the essence of the Crown's problem in this case.

Justice Binnie also held that Wells CJN had erred in his dissent in the Court of Appeal when he had stated: "Clearly, if the evidence established, *with certainty*, that the complainant was infected by the [respondent] (or anyone else) prior to November 15, 1991, the [respondent] could not be found guilty on the charge because, being already infected, the complainant was no longer in a condition where she could be exposed to *risk* of such infection, subsequent to the [respondent] discovering he was HIV positive. She could not become more infected [emphasis in original]." Justice Binnie concluded (at para 53):

> [T]his amounts to saying that a reasonable doubt about the existence of the consequences required by s. 268(1) enures to the benefit of the Crown. An accused would be entitled to an acquittal only if it were established that the complainant was "with certainty" (Wells C.J.N.'s words) infected with HIV on November 15, 1991. This amounts to a reversal of the onus of proof on a central element of the *actus reus* of the offence, namely that the complainant was in fact put in harm's way by the assault in question rather than by antecedent sexual activities which, while lethal, were committed without the requisite *mens rea*.

The Court was careful to limit its findings to the facts established in the case at bar. In particular, Justice Binnie noted that one of the experts, Dr. Bowmer, had raised but not explored the possibility that unprotected sex between HIV-positive partners could pose a risk to the lives of those involved. Justice Binnie explained that "[n]othing in these reasons is intended to foreclose the possibility that in a future case the hypothesis raised by Dr. Bowmer could be properly explored in the evidence, and, depending on the findings of fact, lead to a different outcome with respect to a finding of endangerment" (at para 70).

The *actus reus* of attempted crimes will be discussed in detail in Chapter 10, but it is defined broadly in s 24 of the *Criminal Code* as doing or omitting to do anything that is not mere preparation to commit a crime, with the intent to commit the crime. Williams would have gone beyond mere preparation by having unprotected sexual intercourse with the victim when he knew that he was HIV-positive. The issue of whether the unprotected sex caused the victim to become HIV-positive—central to the question of whether Williams was guilty of aggravated assault—would not be relevant because of Parliament's broad definition of the *actus reus* of attempted aggravated assault. Justice Binnie concluded on this issue (at para 64):

> Failure to prove endangerment of life was fatal to the prosecution in this case of aggravated assault but it is not fatal to a conviction for *attempted* aggravated assault. Clearly, the respondent took more than preparatory steps. He did everything he could to achieve the infection of the complainant by repeated acts of intercourse for approximately one year between November 15, 1991 and November 1992 when the relationship ended. The reasonable doubt about the timing of her actual infection was the product of circumstances quite extraneous to the respondent's post-November 15, 1991 conduct.

The issue of consent and sexually transmitted diseases raises a set of extremely complex questions of law and public policy. The Supreme Court of Canada recently considered some of these issues in *R v Mabior*, 2012 SCC 47, [2012] 2 SCR 584 and *R v Hutchinson*, 2014 SCC 19, [2014] 1 SCR 346, which will be considered in Chapter 12. For further reading on this topic, see S Cowan, "Offences of Sex or Violence? Consent, Fraud, and HIV Transmission" (2014) 17

New Crim L Rev 135; L Vandervort, "HIV, Fraud, Non-Disclosure, Consent and a Stark Choice: Mabior or Sexual Autonomy" (2013) 60 Crim LQ 301; I Grant, "Rethinking Risk: The Relevance of Condoms and Viral Load in HIV Nondisclosure Prosecutions" (2009) 54 McGill LJ 389; and I Grant, "The Boundaries of the Criminal Law: The Criminalization of the Non-Disclosure of HIV" (2008) 31 Dal LJ 123.

The Supreme Court of Canada has never explicitly stated that the principle of contemporaneity is a principle of fundamental justice within the meaning of s 7 of the Charter, but a strong argument can be advanced for this conclusion.

ADDITIONAL READING

Brudner, A. "Owning Outcomes: On Intervening Causes, Thin Skulls, and Fault-Undifferentiated Crimes" (1998) 11 Can JL & Jur 89.

Colvin, E & S Anand. *Principles of Criminal Law*, 3rd ed (Toronto: Carswell, 2007) at 135-78.

Galloway, D. "Causation in Criminal Law: Interventions, Thin Skulls and Lost Chances" (1989) 14 Queen's LJ 71.

Hart, HLA & T Honoré. *Causation in the Law*, 2nd ed (Oxford: Clarendon Press, 1985).

Lynch, ACE. "The Mental Element in the Actus Reus" (1982) 98 Law Q Rev 109.

Manning, M & P Sankoff. *Manning, Mewett & Sankoff: Criminal Law*, 4th ed (Toronto: Lexis-Nexis, 2009) at 103-41.

Mewett, AW. "Causation and the Charter" (1994) 37 Crim LQ 1.

Moore, MS. *Act and Crime: The Philosophy of Action and Its Implications for Criminal Law* (Oxford: Oxford University Press, 2010).

Moore, MS. *Causation and Responsibility: An Essay in Law, Morals, and Metaphysics* (Oxford: Oxford University Press, 2009).

Patient, I. "Some Remarks About the Element of Voluntariness in Offences of Absolute Liability" [1968] Crim LR 23.

Roach, K. *Criminal Law*, 6th ed (Toronto: Irwin Law, 2015) ch 3.

Stuart, D. *Canadian Criminal Law*, 7th ed (Toronto: Carswell, 2014) at 81-170.

Absolute and Strict Liability

Is proof of a criminal act as discussed in the last chapter enough to impose liability? Does it make a difference whether the liability is for an offence found in the *Criminal Code* or for other offences that may be enacted by all levels of governments? What is the difference between regulatory and criminal offences? This chapter will address all of these questions.

The root issue is whether the criminal law should require proof of something more than a voluntary act or omission on the part of the accused in order to establish liability, or whether mere proof of the act or omission is sufficient for the purposes of censure and punishment. Is it justifiable for the state to impose punishment on someone who was morally blameless (at least in the sense of the person having committed the guilty act, but without any intention, knowledge, foresight, or carelessness in having done so)? See, generally, the classic book by HLA Hart, *Punishment and Responsibility: Essays in the Philosophy of Law* (Oxford: Oxford University Press, 1968).

The criminal law, especially since the entrenchment of the Charter, has required something more than proof of the criminal act in order to justify punishment. In other words, there must usually be proof of some guilty state of mind. The law presumes the requirement of some mental state with respect to "true criminal offences." This is a concept that is discussed below. However, with respect to other types of offences, often referred to as regulatory or public welfare offences, the Crown is not held to such a high standard. Subject to certain restraints imposed by the Charter, liability for regulatory or public welfare offences may be satisfied by proof of the act requirement, accompanied by no further fault requirement ("absolute liability") or a much-reduced fault requirement (referred to as "strict liability").

The cases in the first section of this chapter were decided when offences were classified as either "true criminal offences" (requiring a presumption of full *mens rea*) or "public welfare offences" (permitting no additional fault requirement at all). As revealed in the second section of this chapter, the Court in *R v Sault Ste Marie*, [1978] 2 SCR 1299 created a presumption that all public welfare or regulatory offences would require the prosecution to prove the prohibited act, but would then allow the accused to prove a defence of due diligence (or lack of negligence) or a reasonable mistake of fact on a balance of probabilities. This type of strict liability is particular to regulatory or public welfare offences and it constitutes a reduced fault requirement from the fault required for criminal offences as examined in the next chapter as well as a reversal of the burden of proof that is placed on the state to establish fault. The third section considers the constitutional challenges that have been made to absolute liability and strict liability offences as violating principles of fundamental justice protected under s 7 of the Charter and the presumption of innocence under s 11(d) of the Charter.

I. PUBLIC WELFARE OR TRUE CRIMINAL OFFENCES

Beaver v The Queen
Supreme Court of Canada
[1957] SCR 531

CARTWRIGHT J (with whom Rand and Locke JJ concurred): The appellant was tried jointly with one Max Beaver before His Honour Judge Forsyth and a jury in the Court of General Sessions of the Peace for the County of York on an indictment reading as follows:

> The jurors for our Lady the Queen present that
>
> LOUIS BEAVER and MAX BEAVER, at the City of Toronto, in the County of York, on or about the 12th day of March, in the year 1954, unlawfully did sell a drug, to wit, diacetylmorphine, without the authority of a licence from the Minister of National Health and Welfare or other lawful authority, contrary to Section 4(1)(f) of the Opium and Narcotic Drug Act, Revised Statutes of Canada, 1952, Chapter 201 and amendments thereto.
>
> The said jurors further present that the said LOUIS BEAVER and MAX BEAVER, at the City of Toronto, in the County of York, on or about the 12th day of March, in the year 1954, unlawfully did have in their possession a drug, to wit, diacetylmorphine, without the authority of a licence from the Minister of National Health and Welfare or other lawful authority, contrary to Section 4(1)(d) of the Opium and Narcotic Drug Act, Revised Statutes of Canada 1952, Chapter 201, and amendments thereto ...

On September 19, 1955, the accused were found guilty on both counts and on the same day the learned trial Judge found them to be habitual criminals. On October 17, 1955, the learned Judge sentenced them to 7 years' imprisonment on each count, the sentences to run concurrently, and also imposed sentences of preventive detention.

Max Beaver has since died and we are concerned only with the case of the appellant.

The appellant appealed to the Court of Appeal for Ontario against both convictions and against the finding that he was an habitual criminal. These appeals were dismissed.

On February 19, 1957, the appellant was given leave to appeal to this Court [117 Can CC 340, [1957] SCR 119] from the convictions on the two counts. ...

It is not necessary to set out the facts in detail. There was evidence on which it was open to the jury to find (i) that Max Beaver sold to a police officer, who was working under cover, a package which in fact contained diacetylmorphine, (ii) that the appellant was a party to the sale of the package, (iii) that while the appellant did not have the package on his person or in his physical possession he and Max Beaver were acting jointly in such circumstances that the possession which the latter had of the package was the possession of both of the accused, and (iv) that the appellant had no knowledge that the substance contained in the package was diacetylmorphine and believed it to be sugar of milk.

I do not mean to suggest that the jury would necessarily have made the fourth finding but there was evidence on which they might have done so, or which might have left them in a state of doubt as to whether or not the appellant knew that the package contained anything other than sugar of milk.

The learned trial Judge, against the protest of the appellant, charged the jury, in effect, that if they were satisfied that the appellant had in his possession a package and sold it, then, if in fact the substance contained in the package was diacetylmorphine, the appellant was guilty on both counts, and that the questions (i) whether he had any knowledge of what the substance was, or (ii) whether he entertained the honest but mistaken belief that it was a harmless substance were irrelevant and must not be considered. Laidlaw J.A. who delivered the unanimous judgment of the Court of Appeal, [116 Can CC 231], was of opinion that this charge was right in law and that the learned trial Judge was bound by the decision in *R. v. Lawrence*, 102 Can. C.C. 121, [1952] O.R. 149, to direct the jury as he did. The main question on this appeal is whether this view of the law is correct.

The problem is one of construction of the *Opium and Narcotic Drug Act*, R.S.C. 1952, c. 201, and particularly the following sections, which at the date of the offences charged read as follows:

4.(1) Every person who ...

(d) has in his possession any drug save and except under the authority of a licence from the Minister first had and obtained, or other lawful authority; ...

(f) manufactures, sells, gives away, delivers or distributes or makes any offer in respect of any drug, or any substance represented or held out by such person to be a drug, to any person without first obtaining a licence from the Minister, or without other lawful authority; ...

is guilty of an offence, and is liable

(i) upon indictment, to imprisonment for any term not exceeding seven years and not less than six months, and to a fine not exceeding one thousand dollars and not less than two hundred dollars, and, in addition, at the discretion of the judge, to be whipped; or

(ii) upon summary conviction, to imprisonment with or without hard labour for any term not exceeding eighteen months and not less than six months, and to a fine not exceeding one thousand dollars and not less than two hundred dollars.

(2) Notwithstanding the provisions of the *Criminal Code*, or of any other statute or law, the court has no power to impose less than the minimum penalties herein prescribed, and shall, in all cases of conviction, impose both fine and imprisonment.

15. Where any person is charged with an offence under paragraph (a), (d), (e), (f), or (g) of subsection (1) of section 4, it is not necessary for the prosecuting authority to establish that the accused had not a licence from the Minister or was not otherwise authorized to commit the act complained of, and if the accused pleads or alleges that he had such licence or other authority the burden of proof thereof shall be upon the person so charged.

17. Without limiting the generality of paragraph (d) of subsection (1) of section 4, any person who occupies, controls, or is in possession of any building, room, vessel, vehicle, enclosure or place, in or upon which any drug or any article mentioned in section 11 is found, shall, if charged with having such drug or article in possession without lawful authority, be deemed to have been so in possession unless he prove that the drug or article was there

without his authority, knowledge or consent, or that he was lawfully entitled to the possession thereof.

The judgment in appeal is supported by earlier decisions of Appellate Courts in Ontario, Quebec and Nova Scotia, but a directly contrary view has been expressed by the Court of Appeal for British Columbia. While this conflict has existed since 1948, this is the first occasion on which the question has been brought before this Court.

It may be of assistance in examining the problem to use a simple illustration. Suppose X goes to the shop of Y, a druggist, and asks Y to sell him some baking soda. Y hands him a sealed packet which he tells him contains baking soda and charges him a few cents. X honestly believes that the packet contains baking soda, but in fact it contains heroin. X puts the package in his pocket, takes it home and later puts it in a cupboard in his bathroom. There would seem to be no doubt that X has had actual manual and physical possession of the package and that he continues to have possession of the package while it is in his cupboard. The main question raised on this appeal is whether, in the supposed circumstances, X would be guilty of the crime of having heroin in his possession?

[A number of cases were then examined.]

When the decisions as to the construction of the *Opium and Narcotic Drug Act* on which the respondent relies are examined it appears that two main reasons are assigned for holding that *mens rea* is not an essential ingredient of the offence created by s. 4(1)(d), these being (i) the assumption that the subject-matter with which the Act deals is of the kind dealt with in the cases of which *Hobbs v. Winchester Corp.*, [1910] 2 K.B. 471, is typical and which are sometimes referred to as "public welfare offence cases," and (ii) by implication from the wording of s. 17 of the Act.

As to the first of these reasons, I can discern little similarity between a statute designed, by forbidding the sale of unsound meat, to ensure that the supply available to the public shall be wholesome, and a statute making it a serious crime to possess or deal in narcotics; the one is to ensure that a lawful and necessary trade shall be carried on in a manner not to endanger the public health, the other to forbid altogether conduct regarded as harmful in itself. As a necessary feature of his trade, the butcher holds himself out as selling meat fit for consumption; he warrants that quality; and it is part of his duty as trader to see that the merchandise is wholesome. The statute simply converts that civil personal duty into a public duty.

As to the second reason, the argument is put as follows. Using again the illustration I have taken above, it is said (i) that the words of s. 17 would require the conviction of X if the package was found in his bathroom cupboard "unless he prove that [it] was there without his authority, knowledge or consent," that is, he is *prima facie* presumed to be guilty but can exculpate himself by proving lack of knowledge, and (ii) that since no such words as "unless he prove that the drug was in his possession without his knowledge" are found in s. 4(1)(d) it must be held that Parliament intended that lack of knowledge should be no defence.

[Cartwright J then held that the wording of s 17 does not compel the Court to construe s 4 as not requiring *mens rea*.]

If the matter were otherwise doubtful I would be drawn to the conclusion that Parliament did not intend to enact that *mens rea* should not be an essential ingredient of the offence created by s. 4(1)(d) by the circumstance that on conviction a minimum sentence of 6 months' imprisonment plus a fine of $200 must be imposed. Counsel informed us that they have found no other statutory provision which has been held to create a crime of strict responsibility, that is to say, one in which the necessity for *mens rea* is excluded, on conviction for which a sentence of imprisonment is mandatory. The legislation dealt with in *Hobbs v. Winchester, supra*, provided that a sentence of imprisonment might, not must, be imposed on a convicted person.

It would, of course, be within the power of Parliament to enact that a person who, without any guilty knowledge, had in his physical possession a package which he honestly believed to contain a harmless substance such as baking soda but which in fact contained heroin, must on proof of such facts be convicted of a crime and sentenced to at least 6 months' imprisonment; but I would refuse to impute such an intention to Parliament unless the words of the statute were clear and admitted of no other interpretation. To borrow the words of Lord Kenyon in *Fowler v. Padget* (1798), 7 Term R. 509 at p. 514, 101 E.R. 1103: "I would adopt any construction of the statute that the words will bear, in order to avoid such monstrous consequences as would manifestly ensue from the construction contended for by the defendant."

For the above reasons I would quash the conviction on the charge of having possession of a drug.

As to the charge of selling, as is pointed out by my brother Fauteux, the appellant's version of the facts brings his actions within the provisions of s. 4(1)(f) since he and his brother jointly sold a substance represented or held out by them to be heroin; and I agree with the conclusion of my brother Fauteux that the conviction on the charge of selling must be affirmed.

For the above reasons, I would dismiss the appeal as to the first count (that is, of selling) but would direct that the time during which the appellant has been confined pending the determination of the appeal shall count as part of the term of imprisonment imposed pursuant to that conviction. As to the second count (that is, of having possession) I would allow the appeal, quash the conviction and direct a new trial. As leave to appeal from the finding that the appellant is an habitual criminal was granted conditionally upon the appeal from the convictions being successful, and as the appeal as to one conviction has failed, we are without jurisdiction to review the finding that the appellant is an habitual criminal and in the result that finding stands.

FAUTEUX J (with whom Abbott J concurred), dissenting in part: … The plain and apparent object of the Act is to prevent, by a rigid control of the possession of drugs, the danger to public health, and to guard society against the social evils which an uncontrolled traffic in drugs is bound to generate. The scheme of the Act is this: The importation, exportation, sale, manufacture, production and distribution of drugs are subject to the obtention of a licence which the Minister of National Health and Welfare may issue, with the approval of the Governor-General in Council, and in which the place where such operations may be carried on is stated. Under the same authority are indicated ports and places in Canada where drugs may be exported or imported, the manner in which they are to be packed and marked for export, the records to be kept for such export, import, receipt, sale, disposal and distribution. The Act also provides for the establishment of all other convenient and necessary regulations with respect to duration, terms and forms of the several licences therein provided. Without a licence, it is an offence to import or export from Canada and an offence for anyone who, not being a common carrier, takes or carries, or causes to be taken or carried from any place in Canada to any other place in Canada, any drug. Druggists, physicians, dentists and veterinary surgeons stand, of course, in a privileged class; but even their dealings in drugs for medicinal purposes are the object of a particular control. Under penalties of the law, some of them have to keep records of their operations, while others have the obligation to answer inquiries in respect thereto. Having in one's possession drugs without a licence or other lawful authority, is an offence. In brief, the principle underlying the Act is that possession of drugs covered by it is unlawful; and where any exception is made to the principle, the exceptions themselves are attended with particular controlling provisions and conditions.

The enforcement sections of the Act manifest the exceptional vigilance and firmness which Parliament thought of the essence to forestall the unlawful traffic in narcotic drugs and cope effectively with the unusual difficulties standing in the way of the realization of the object of the statute. Substantive and procedural principles generally prevailing under the *Criminal Code* in favour of the subject are being restricted or excepted. The power to search by day or by night, either premises or the person, is largely extended under s. 19. Special writs of assistance are provided for under s. 22. The consideration of the provisions of ss. 4 and 17 being deferred for the moment, the burden of proof is either alleviated or shifted to persons charged with violations under ss. 6, 11, 13, 16 and 18. Minimum sentences are provided or are made mandatory, under ss. 4 and 6. Deportation of aliens found guilty is also mandatory and this notwithstanding the provisions of the *Immigration Act* [RSC 1952, c 325] or any other Act, under s. 26. And the application of the *Identification of Criminals Act* [RSC 1952, c 144], ordinarily limited to the case of indictable offences, is, by s. 27, extended to any offence under the Act.

All of these provisions are indicative of the will of Parliament to give the most efficient protection to public health against the danger attending the uncontrolled use of drugs as well as against the social evils incidental thereto, by measures generally centred and directed to possession itself of the drugs covered by the Act. The subject-matter, the purpose and the scope of the Act are such that to subject its provisions to the narrow construction suggested on behalf of appellant would defeat the very object of the Act.

The main provisions to consider are those of s. 4(1)(d), reading as follows:

> 4.(1) Every person who ...
>   (d) has in his possession any drug save and except under the authority of a licence from the Minister first had and obtained, or other lawful authority; ... is guilty of an offence, and is liable.

On the plain, literal and grammatical meaning of the words of this section, there is an absolute prohibition to be in possession of drugs, whatever be the various meanings of which the word possession may be susceptible, unless the possession is under the authority of a licence from the Minister, first had and obtained, or under other lawful authority.

... Furthermore, and if it is argued that knowledge is of the essence of unlawful possession under both s. 4(1)(d) and s. 17, then one is at a loss to understand why Parliament should have, in the latter section, provided for a defence resting on the proof of lack of knowledge. A like interpretation of s. 17 strips this exculpatory provision of any meaning and effect. The language of the two sections can only be rationalized, I think, by interpreting s. 4(1)(d) as meaning what it says, i.e., as creating an absolute prohibition, and by interpreting s. 17 as extending the meaning of s. 4(1)(d), i.e., this absolute prohibition, to the circumstances described in s. 17, with however, and only in such circumstances, a defence resting on the proof of lack of knowledge.

As interpreted by most of the members of the Canadian Courts of Appeal since 1932, the provisions of s. 4(1)(d) are, like many other provisions of the Act, undoubtedly severe. The duty of the Courts is to give effect to the language of Parliament. And notwithstanding that the views expressed in *Morelli* and *Lawrence*, in particular, had been prevailing ever since 1932 and are still prevailing, Parliament has not seen fit to intervene. For all these reasons, I find it impossible to accede to the proposition that knowledge of the nature of the substance is of the essence of the offence of unlawful possession under the Act.

As to sale: Though the substance delivered to and paid for by Tassie was a drug, as admittedly it was represented and held out to be by appellant, it is said that the latter could not be guilty of the offence of sale under s. 4(1)(f) because, on his story, he intended and thought the substance sold to be sugar of milk. To this submission, the provisions of s. 4(1)(f) afford, I think, a complete answer:

> 4.(1) Every person who ...
>
> (f) ... sells, ... any drug, *or any substance represented or held out by such person to be a drug*, to any person without first obtaining a licence from the Minister, or without other lawful authority ... .

That the enforcement of the provisions of the Act may, in exceptional cases, lead to some injustice, is not an impossibility. But, to forestall this result as to such possible cases, there are remedies under the law, such as a stay of proceedings by the Attorney-General or a free pardon under the Royal Prerogative.

I would dismiss the appeal against the unanimous judgment of the Court of Appeal for Ontario affirming the conviction on the primary charges and, in view of this result, the unanimous judgment of the Court of Appeal, affirming the decision that appellant is an habitual criminal, remains undisturbed.

> *Appeal from conviction for possession of drug allowed; appeals from conviction for sale of a drug and finding of being an habitual criminal dismissed.*

R v Pierce Fisheries Ltd
Supreme Court of Canada
[1971] SCR 5

[The accused was charged with having undersized lobsters in its possession contrary to the *Lobster Fishery Regulations* made pursuant to the *Fisheries Act*, RSC 1952, c 119. The evidence showed that on the day in question the company would have bought or brought to its plant by truck and by boat 50,000 to 60,000 lbs of lobsters, and among these a fishery officer found 26 undersized lobsters. The Supreme Court of Canada allowed an appeal from an acquittal.]

RITCHIE J (for the majority): I agree with the submission made on behalf of the appellant, which appears to have received qualified approval in the reasons for judgment rendered on behalf of the Appeal Division by the Chief Justice of Nova Scotia, that the *Lobster Fishery Regulations* are obviously intended for the purpose of protecting lobster beds from depletion and thus conserving the source of supply for an important fishing industry which is of general public interest.

I do not think that a new crime was added to our criminal law by making regulations which prohibit persons from having undersized lobsters in their possession, nor do I think that the stigma of having been convicted of a criminal offence would attach to a person found to have been in breach of these regulations. The case of *Beaver v. The Queen*, ... affords an example of provisions of a federal statute other than the *Criminal Code* which were found to have created a truly criminal offence, but in the present case, to paraphrase the language used by the majority of this Court in the *Beaver* case, I can discern little similarity between a statute designed, by forbidding the possession of undersized lobsters to protect the lobster industry, and a statute making it a serious crime to possess or deal in narcotics.

In view of the above, it will be seen that I am of opinion that the offence created by s. 3(1)(b) of the Regulations falls within the first class of exceptions referred to by Wright J., in *Sherras v. De Rutzen*, ... and that it should be construed in accordance with the language in which it was enacted, free from any presumption as to the requirement of *mens rea*.

In considering the language of the Regulation, s. 3(1)(b), it is significant, though not conclusive, that it contains no such words as "knowingly," "wilfully," "with intent" or "without lawful excuse," whereas such words occur in a number of sections of the *Fisheries Act* itself which create offences for which *mens rea* is made an essential ingredient.

CARTWRIGHT CJ (dissenting): ... In my view a principle of construction of a statute which makes possession of a forbidden substance an offence was laid down by this Court in *Beaver v. The Queen*, [1957] S.C.R. 531, where it was said by the majority at p. 140:

> The essence of the crime is the possession of the forbidden substance and in a criminal case there is in law no possession without knowledge of the character of the forbidden substance.

Applying this principle to the words of the charge against the respondent in the case at bar, it appears to me that the express finding of fact that the respondent had no knowledge, factually or inferentially, that any of the lobsters on its premises and under its control were undersized necessarily leads to a finding of not guilty.

Parliament could, of course, provide by apt words that anyone having in fact an undersized lobster on his premises and under his control should be guilty of an offence although he had no knowledge that such lobster was undersized but, in my opinion, no such words have been used, and no such intention can be implied from the words which have been used considered in the light of all relevant circumstances.

In the decision of *R v Wholesale Travel Group Inc*, [1991] 3 SCR 154, parts of which are reproduced later in this chapter, the Court grappled again with the distinction between "true criminal offences" and "regulatory offences," in the context of a charging provision under the *Competition Act*, RSC 1970, c C-23. Justice Cory said the following in attempting to make this distinction:

Regulatory Offences and Strict Liability

A. The Distinction Between Crimes and Regulatory Offences

The common law has long acknowledged a distinction between truly criminal conduct and conduct, otherwise lawful, which is prohibited in the public interest. Earlier, the designations *mala in se* and *mala prohibita* were utilized; today prohibited acts are generally classified as either crimes or regulatory offences.

While some regulatory legislation such as that pertaining to the content of food and drink dates back to the Middle Ages, the number and significance of regulatory offences increased greatly with the onset of the Industrial Revolution. Unfettered industrialization had led to abuses. Regulations were, therefore, enacted to protect the vulnerable—particularly the children, men and women who laboured long hours in dangerous and unhealthy surroundings. Without these regulations many would have died. It later became necessary to regulate the manufactured products themselves and, still later, the discharge of effluent resulting from the manufacturing process. There is no doubt that regulatory offences were originally and still are designed to protect those who are unable to protect themselves.

English courts have for many years supported and given effect to the policy objectives animating regulatory legislation. In *Sherras v. De Rutzen*, [1895] 1 Q.B. 918 at p. 922, it was held that, while the *mens rea* presumption applied to true crimes because of the fault and moral culpability which they imply, that same presumption did not apply to offences "which ... are not criminal in any real sense, but are acts which in the public interest are prohibited under a penalty." This case illustrates the essential distinction in the legal treatment of regulatory as opposed to criminal offences—namely, the removal of the *mens rea* requirement.

The distinction between true crimes and regulatory offences was recognized in Canadian law prior to the adoption of the Charter. In *R. v. Pierce Fisheries Ltd.*, [1971] S.C.R. 5, at p. 13, Ritchie J. referred to "a wide category of offences created by statutes enacted for the regulation of individual conduct in the interests of health, convenience, safety and the general welfare of the public" which are not subject to the common law presumption of *mens rea* as an essential element to be proven by the Crown.

R. v. Sault Ste. Marie, [1978] 2 S.C.R. 1299, affirmed the distinction between regulatory offences and true crimes. There, on behalf of a unanimous court, Justice Dickson (as he then was) recognized public welfare offences as a distinct class. He held (at pp. 1302-3) that such offences, although enforced as penal laws through the machinery of the criminal law, "are in substance of a civil nature and might well be regarded as a branch of administrative law to which traditional principles of criminal law have but limited application."

The *Sault Ste. Marie* case recognized strict liability as a middle ground between full *mens rea* and absolute liability. Where the offence is one of strict liability, the Crown is required to prove neither *mens rea* nor negligence; conviction may follow merely upon proof beyond a reasonable doubt of the proscribed act. However, it is open to the defendant to avoid liability by proving on a balance of probabilities that all due care was taken. This is the hallmark of the strict liability offence: the defence of due diligence.

Thus, *Sault Ste. Marie* not only affirmed the distinction between regulatory and criminal offences, but also subdivided regulatory offences into categories of strict and absolute liability. The new category of strict liability represented a compromise which acknowledged the importance and essential objectives of regulatory offences but at the same time sought to mitigate the harshness of absolute liability which was found, at p. 1311, to "violate" fundamental principles of penal liability.

The Rationale for the Distinction

It has always been thought that there is a rational basis for distinguishing between crimes and regulatory offences. Acts or actions are criminal when they constitute conduct that is, in itself, so abhorrent to the basic values of human society that it ought to be prohibited completely. Murder, sexual assault, fraud, robbery and theft are all so repugnant to society that they are universally recognized as crimes. At the same time, some conduct is prohibited, not because it is inherently wrongful, but because unregulated activity would result in dangerous conditions being imposed upon members of society, especially those who are particularly vulnerable.

The objective of regulatory legislation is to protect the public or broad segments of the public (such as employees, consumers and motorists, to name but a few) from the potentially adverse effects of otherwise lawful activity. Regulatory legislation involves a shift of emphasis from the protection of individual interests and the deterrence and punishment of acts involving moral fault to the protection of public and societal interests. While criminal offences are usually designed to condemn and punish past, inherently wrongful conduct, regulatory measures are generally directed to the prevention of future harm through the enforcement of minimum standards of conduct and care.

It follows that regulatory offences and crimes embody different concepts of fault. Since regulatory offences are directed primarily not to conduct itself but to the consequences of conduct, conviction of a regulatory offence may be thought to import a significantly lesser degree of culpability than conviction of a true crime. The concept of fault in regulatory offences is based upon a reasonable care standard and, as such, does not imply moral blameworthiness in the same manner as criminal fault. Conviction for breach of a regulatory offence suggests nothing more than that the defendant has failed to meet a prescribed standard of care.

That is the theory but, like all theories, its application is difficult. For example, is the single mother who steals a loaf of bread to sustain her family more blameworthy than the employer who, through negligence, breaches regulations and thereby exposes his employees to dangerous working conditions, or the manufacturer who, as a result of negligence, sells dangerous products or pollutes the air and waters by its plant? At this stage it is sufficient to bear in mind that those who breach regulations may inflict serious harm on large segments of society. Therefore, the characterization of an offence as regulatory should not be thought to make light of either the potential harm to the vulnerable or the responsibility of those subject to regulation to ensure that the proscribed harm does not occur. It should also be remembered that, as social values change, the degree of moral blameworthiness attaching to certain conduct may change as well.

Nevertheless there remains, in my view, a sound basis for distinguishing between regulatory and criminal offences. The distinction has concrete theoretical and practical underpinnings and has proven to be a necessary and workable concept in our law. Since *Sault Ste. Marie*, this court has reaffirmed the distinction. Most recently, in *Thomson Newspapers Ltd. v. Canada (Director of Investigation and Research, Restrictive Trade Practices Commission)*, [1990] 1 S.C.R. 425, at pp. 510-11,

Justice La Forest adopted the following statement of the Law Reform Commission of Canada (Criminal Responsibility for Group Action, Working Paper No. 16, 1976, at p. 12):

> [The regulatory offence] is not primarily concerned with values, but with results. While values necessarily underlie all legal prescriptions, the regulatory offence really gives expression to the view that it is expedient for the protection of society and for the orderly use and sharing of society's resources that people act in a prescribed manner in prescribed situations, or that people take prescribed standards of care to avoid risks of injury. The object is to induce compliance with rules for the overall benefit of society.

B. The Fundamental Importance of Regulatory Offences in Canadian Society

Regulatory measures are the primary mechanisms employed by governments in Canada to implement public policy objectives. What is ultimately at stake in this appeal is the ability of federal and provincial governments to pursue social ends through the enactment and enforcement of public welfare legislation.

Some indication of the prevalence of regulatory offences in Canada is provided by a 1974 estimate by the Law Reform Commission of Canada. The commission estimated that there were, at that time, approximately 20,000 regulatory offences in an average province, plus an additional 20,000 regulatory offences at the federal level. By 1983, the commission's estimate of the federal total had reached 97,000. There is every reason to believe that the number of public welfare offences at both levels of government has continued to increase.

Statistics such as these make it obvious that government policy in Canada is pursued principally through regulation. It is through regulatory legislation that the community seeks to implement its larger objectives and to govern itself and the conduct of its members. The ability of the government effectively to regulate potentially harmful conduct must be maintained.

It is difficult to think of an aspect of our lives that is not regulated for our benefit and for the protection of society as a whole. From cradle to grave, we are protected by regulations; they apply to the doctors attending our entry into this world and to the morticians present at our departure. Every day, from waking to sleeping, we profit from regulatory measures which we often take for granted. On rising, we use various forms of energy whose safe distribution and use are governed by regulation. The trains, buses and other vehicles that get us to work are regulated for our safety. The food we eat and the beverages we drink are subject to regulation for the protection of our health.

In short, regulation is absolutely essential for our protection and well being as individuals, and for the effective functioning of society. It is properly present throughout our lives. The more complex the activity, the greater the need for and the greater our reliance upon regulation and its enforcement. For example, most people would have no idea what regulations are required for air transport or how they should be enforced. Of necessity, society relies on government regulation for its safety.

II. THE EMERGENCE OF STRICT LIABILITY

R v Sault Ste Marie
Supreme Court of Canada
[1978] 2 SCR 1299

DICKSON J (for the Court): In the present appeal the Court is concerned with offences variously referred to as "statutory," "public welfare," "regulatory," "absolute liability," or "strict responsibility," which are not criminal in any real sense, but are prohibited in the public interest: *Sherras v. De Rutzen*, [1895] 1 Q.B. 918. Although enforced as penal laws through the utilization of the machinery of the criminal law, the offences are in substance of a civil nature and might well be regarded as a branch of administrative law to which traditional principles of criminal law have but limited application. They relate to such everyday matters as traffic infractions, sales of impure food, violations of liquor laws, and the like. In this appeal we are concerned with pollution.

. . .

The Mens Rea Point

The distinction between the true criminal offence and the public welfare offence is one of the prime importance. Where the offence is criminal, the Crown must establish a mental element, namely, that the accused who committed the prohibited act did so intentionally or recklessly, with knowledge of the facts constituting the offence, or with wilful blindness toward them. Mere negligence is excluded from the concept of the mental element required for conviction. Within the context of a criminal prosecution a person who fails to make such enquiries as a reasonable and prudent person would make, or who fails to know facts he should have known, is innocent in the eyes of the law.

In sharp contrast, "absolute liability" entails conviction on proof merely that the defendant committed the prohibited act constituting the *actus reus* of the offence. There is no relevant mental element. It is no defence that the accused was entirely without fault. He may be morally innocent in every sense, yet be branded as a malefactor and punished as such.

Public welfare offences obviously lie in a field of conflicting values. It is essential for society to maintain, through effective enforcement, high standards of public health and safety. Potential victims of those who carry on latently pernicious activities have a strong claim to consideration. On the other hand, there is a generally held revulsion against punishment of the morally innocent. ...

Various arguments are advanced in justification of absolute liability in public welfare offences. Two predominate. Firstly, it is argued that the protection of social interests requires a high standard of care and attention on the part of those who follow certain pursuits and such persons are more likely to be stimulated to maintain those standards if they know that ignorance or mistake will not excuse them. The removal of any possible loophole acts, it is said, as an incentive to take precautionary measures beyond what would otherwise be taken, in order that mistakes and mishaps be avoided. The second main argument is one based on administrative efficiency. Having regard to both the difficulty of proving mental culpability and the number of petty cases which daily come before the

Court, proof of fault is just too great a burden in time and money to place upon the prosecution. To require proof of each person's individual intent would allow almost every violator to escape. This, together with the glut of work entailed in proving *mens rea* in every case would clutter the docket and impede adequate enforcement as virtually to nullify the regulatory statutes. In short, absolute liability, it is contended, is the most efficient and effective way of ensuring compliance with minor regulatory legislation and the social ends to be achieved are of such importance as to override the unfortunate by-product of punishing those who may be free of moral turpitude. In further justification, it is urged that slight penalties are usually imposed and that conviction for breach of a public welfare offence does not carry the stigma associated with conviction for a criminal offence.

Arguments of greater force are advanced against absolute liability. The most telling is that it violates fundamental principles of penal liability. It also rests upon assumptions which have not been, and cannot be, empirically established. There is no evidence that a higher standard of care results from absolute liability. If a person is already taking every reasonable precautionary measure, is he likely to take additional measures, knowing that however much care he takes, it will not serve as a defence in the event of breach? If he has exercised care and skill, will conviction have a deterrent effect upon him or others? Will the injustice of conviction lead to cynicism and disrespect for the law, on his part and on the part of others? These are among the questions asked. The argument that no stigma attaches does not withstand analysis, for the accused will have suffered loss of time, legal costs, exposure to the processes of the criminal law at trial and, however one may down-play it, the opprobrium of conviction. It is not sufficient to say that the public interest is engaged and, therefore, liability may be imposed without fault. In serious crimes, the public interest is involved and *mens rea* must be proven. The administrative argument has little force. In sentencing, evidence of due diligence is admissible and therefore the evidence might just as well be heard when considering guilt. Additionally, it may be noted that s. 198 of *The Highway Traffic Act of Alberta*, R.S.A. 1970, c. 169, provides that upon a person being charged with an offence under this Act, if the judge trying the case is of the opinion that the offence (a) was committed wholly by accident or misadventure and without negligence, and (b) could not by the exercise of reasonable care or precaution have been avoided, the judge may dismiss the case. See also s. 230(2) of the *Manitoba Highway Traffic Act*, R.S.M. 1970, c. H60, which has a similar effect. In these instances at least, the Legislature has indicated that administrative efficiency does not foreclose inquiry as to fault. It is also worthy of note that historically the penalty for breach of statutes enacted for the regulation of individual conduct in the interest of health and safety was minor, $20 or $25; today, it may amount to thousands of dollars and entail the possibility of imprisonment for a second conviction. The present case is an example.

The City of Sault Ste. Marie was charged that it did discharge, or cause to be discharged, or permitted to be discharged, or deposited materials into Cannon Creek and Root River, or on the shore or bank thereof, or in such place along the side that might impair the quality of the water in Cannon Creek and Root River, between March 13, 1972 and September 11, 1972. The charge was laid under s. 32(1) of the *Ontario Water Resources Act*, R.S.O. 1970, c. 332 [formerly *Ontario Water Resources Commission Act*, renamed by SO 1972, c 1, s 70(1)], which provides, so far as relevant, that every municipality or person that discharges, or deposits, or causes, or permits the discharge or deposit of any material of any kind into any water course, or on any shore or bank thereof, or in any place that may impair the quality of water, is guilty of an offence and, on summary conviction, is liable on first conviction to a fine of not more than $5,000 and on each subsequent conviction to a fine of not more than $10,000, or to imprisonment for a term of not more than one year, or to both fine and imprisonment.

Public welfare offences involve a shift of emphasis from the protection of individual interests to the protection of public and social interests: see F.B. Sayre, "Public Welfare Offenses," 33 *Columbia Law Rev.* 55 (1933); Hall, *General Principles of Criminal Law* (1947), c. 13, p. 427; R.M. Perkins, "Civil Offense," 100 *U. of Pa. L. Rev.* 832 (1952); Jobson, "Far from Clear," 18 *Crim. L.Q.* 294 (1975-76). The unfortunate tendency in many past cases has been to see the choice as between two stark alternatives: (i) full *mens rea*; or (ii) absolute liability. In respect of public welfare offences (within which category pollution offences fall) where full *mens rea* is not required, absolute liability has often been imposed. English jurisprudence has consistently maintained this dichotomy: see "Criminal Law, Evidence and Procedure," 11 Hals., 4th ed., pp. 20-22, para. 18. There has, however, been an attempt in Australia, in many Canadian Courts, and indeed in England, to seek a middle position, fulfilling the goals of public welfare offences while still not punishing the entirely blameless. There is an increasing and impressive stream of authority which holds that where an offence does not require full *mens rea*, it is nevertheless a good defence for the defendant to prove that he was not negligent.

Dr. Glanville Williams has written: "There is a half-way house between *mens rea* and strict responsibility which has not yet been properly utilized, and that is responsibility for negligence" (*Criminal Law: General Part*, 2nd ed. (1961), p. 262). Morris and Howard, in *Studies in Criminal Law* (1964), p. 200, suggest that strict responsibility might with advantage be replaced by a doctrine of responsibility for negligence strengthened by a shift in the burden of proof. The defendant would be allowed to exculpate himself by proving affirmatively that he was not negligent.

In the House of Lords case of *Sweet v. Parsley*, [1970] A.C. 132, Lord Reid noted the difficulty presented by the simplistic choice between *mens rea* in the full sense and an absolute offence. He looked approvingly at attempts to find a middle ground. Lord Pearce, in the same case, referred to the "sensible half-way house" which he thought the Courts should take in some so-called absolute offences. The difficulty, as Lord Pearce saw it, lay in the opinion of Viscount Sankey, L.C., in *Woolmington v. Director of Public Prosecutions*, [1935] A.C. 462, if the full width of that opinion were maintained. Lord Diplock, however, took a different and, in my opinion, a preferable view, at p. 164:

> *Woolmington's* case did not decide anything so irrational as that the prosecution must call evidence to prove the absence of any mistaken belief by the accused in the existence of facts which, if true, would make the act innocent, any more than it decided that the prosecution must call evidence to prove the absence of any claim of right in a charge of larceny. The jury is entitled to presume that the accused acted with knowledge of the facts, unless there is some evidence to the contrary originating from the accused who alone can know on what belief he acted and on what ground the belief, if mistaken, was held.

In *Woolmington's* case the question was whether the trial Judge was correct in directing the jury that the accused was required to prove his innocence. Viscount Sankey L.C., referred to the strength of the presumption of innocence in a criminal case and then made the statement, universally accepted in this country, that there is no burden on the prisoner to prove his innocence; it is sufficient for him to raise a doubt as to his guilt. I do not understand the case as standing for anything more than that. It is to be noted that the case is concerned with criminal offences in the true sense; it is not concerned with public welfare offences. It is somewhat ironic that *Woolmington's* case, which embodies a principle for the benefit of the accused, should be used to justify the rejection of a defence of reasonable care for public welfare offences and the retention of absolute liability, which affords the accused no defence at all. There is nothing in *Woolmington's* case, as I comprehend it, which stands in the way of adoption, in respect of regulatory offences, of a defence of due care, with burden of proof resting on the accused to establish the defence on the balance of probabilities.

There have been several cases in Ontario which open the way to acceptance of a defence of due diligence.

[A number of Ontario cases were then discussed.]

It is interesting to note the recommendations made by the Law Reform Commission to the Minister of Justice (*Our Criminal Law*) in March, 1976. The Commission advises (p. 32) that (i) every offence outside the *Criminal Code* be recognized as admitting of a defence of due diligence; (ii) in the case of any such offence for which intent or recklessness is not specifically required the onus of proof should lie on the defendant to establish such defence; (iii) the defendant would have to prove this on the preponderance or balance of probabilities. The recommendation endorsed a working paper (*Meaning of Guilt: Strict Liability*, June 20, 1974), in which it was stated that negligence should be the minimum standard of liability in regulatory offences, that such offences were (p. 32):

> ... to promote higher standards of care in business, trade and industry, higher standards of honesty in commerce and advertising, higher standards of respect for the ... environment and [therefore] the ... offence is basically and typically an offence of negligence;

that an accused should never be convicted of a regulatory offence if he establishes that he acted with due diligence, that is, that he was not negligent. In the working paper, the Commission further stated (p. 33), "... let us recognize the regulatory offence for what it is—an offence of negligence—and frame the law to ensure that guilt depends upon lack of reasonable care." The view is expressed that in regulatory law, to make the defendant disprove negligence—prove due diligence—would be both justifiable and desirable.

The decision of this Court in *The Queen v. Pierce Fisheries Ltd.*, [1971] S.C.R. 5, is not inconsistent with the concept of a "half-way house" between *mens rea* and absolute liability. In *Pierce Fisheries* the charge was that of having possession of undersized lobsters contrary to the Regulations under the *Fisheries Act*, R.S.C. 1952, c. 119. Two points arise in connection with the judgment of Ritchie J., who wrote for the majority of the Court. First, the adoption of what had been said by the Ontario Court of Appeal in *R. v. Pee-Kay Smallwares Ltd.* (1947), 90 C.C.C. 129 at p. 137:

> If on a prosecution for the offences created by the Act, the Crown had to prove the evil intent of the accused, or if the accused could escape by denying such evil intent, the statute, by which it was obviously intended that there should be complete control without the possibility

of any leaks, would have too many holes in it that in truth it would be nothing more than a legislative sieve.

Ritchie J. held that the offence was one in which the Crown, for the reason indicated in the *Pee-Kay Smallwares* case, did not have to prove *mens rea* in order to obtain a conviction. This, in my opinion, is the *ratio decidendi* of the case. Second, Ritchie J. did not, however, foreclose the possibility of a defence. The following passage from the judgment (at p. 21) suggests that a defence of reasonable care might have been open to the accused, but that in that case care had not been taken to acquire the knowledge of the facts constituting the offence:

> As employees of the company working on the premises in the shed "where fish is weighed and packed" were taking lobsters from boxes "preparatory for packing" in crates, and as some of the undersized lobsters were found "in crates ready for shipment," it would not appear to have been a difficult matter for some "officer or responsible employee" to acquire knowledge of their presence on the premises.

In a later passage Ritchie J. added (at p. 22):

> In this case the respondent knew that it had upwards of 60,000 lbs. of lobsters on its premises; it only lacked knowledge as to the small size of some of them, and I do not think that the failure of any of its responsible employees to acquire this knowledge affords any defence to a charge of violating the provisions of s. 3(1)(b) of the *Lobster Fishery Regulations*.

I do not read *Pierce Fisheries* as denying the accused all defences, in particular the defence that the company had done everything possible to acquire knowledge of the undersized lobsters. Ritchie J. concluded merely that the Crown did not have to prove knowledge.

We have the situation therefore in which many Courts of this country, at all levels, dealing with public welfare offences favour (i) *not* requiring the Crown to prove *mens rea*, (ii) rejecting the notion that liability inexorably follows upon mere proof of the *actus reus*, excluding any possible defence. The Courts are following the lead set in Australia many years ago and tentatively broached by several English Courts in recent years.

It may be suggested that the introduction of a defence based on due diligence and the shifting of the burden of proof might better be implemented by legislative act. In answer, it should be recalled that the concept of absolute liability and the creation of a jural category of public welfare offences are both the product of the judiciary and not of the Legislature. The development to date of this defence, in the numerous decisions I have referred to, of Courts in this country as well as in Australia and New Zealand, has also been the work of Judges. The present case offers the opportunity of consolidating and clarifying the doctrine.

The correct approach, in my opinion, is to relieve the Crown of the burden of proving *mens rea*, having regard to *Pierce Fisheries* and to the virtual impossibility in most regulatory cases of proving wrongful intention. In a normal case, the accused alone will have knowledge of what he has done to avoid the breach and it is not improper to expect him to come forward with the evidence of due diligence. This is particularly so when it is alleged, for example, that pollution was caused by the activities of a large and complex corporation. Equally, there is nothing wrong with rejecting absolute liability and admitting the defence of reasonable care.

In this doctrine it is not up to the prosecution to prove negligence. Instead, it is open to the defendant to prove that all due care has been taken. This burden falls upon the defendant as he is the only one who will generally have the means of proof. This would not seem unfair as the alternative is absolute liability which denies an accused any defence whatsoever. While the prosecution must prove beyond a reasonable doubt that the defendant committed the prohibited act, the defendant must only establish on the balance of probabilities that he has a defence of reasonable care.

I conclude, for the reasons which I have sought to express, that there are compelling grounds for the recognition of three categories of offences rather than the traditional two:

1. Offences in which *mens rea*, consisting of some positive state of mind such as intent, knowledge, or recklessness, must be proved by the prosecution either as an inference from the nature of the act committed, or by additional evidence.

2. Offences in which there is no necessity for the prosecution to prove the existence of *mens rea*; the doing of the prohibited act *prima facie* imports the offence, leaving it open to the accused to avoid liability by proving that he took all reasonable care. This involves consideration of what a reasonable man would have done in the circumstances. The defence will be available if the accused reasonably believed in a mistaken set of facts which, if true, would render the act or omission innocent, or if he took all reasonable steps to avoid the particular event. These offences may properly be called offences of strict liability. Mr. Justice Estey so referred to them in *Hickey's* case.

3. Offences of absolute liability where it is not open to the accused to exculpate himself by showing that he was free of fault.

Offences which are criminal in the true sense fall in the first category. Public welfare offences would, *prima facie*, be in the second category. They are not subject to the presumption of full *mens rea*. An offence of this type would fall in the first category only if such words as "wilfully," "with intent," "knowingly," or "intentionally" are contained in the statutory provision creating the offence. On the other hand, the principle that punishment should in general not be inflicted on those without fault applies. Offences of absolute liability would be those in respect of which the Legislature had made it clear that guilt would follow proof merely of the proscribed act. The over-all regulatory pattern adopted by the Legislature, the subject-matter of the legislation, the importance of the penalty, and the precision of the language used will be primary considerations in determining whether the offence falls into the third category.

Turning to the subject-matter of s. 32(1)—the prevention of pollution of lakes, rivers and streams—it is patent that this is of great public concern. Pollution has always been unlawful and, in itself, a nuisance: *Groat v. City of Edmonton*, [1928] S.C.R. 522. A riparian owner has an inherent right to have a stream of water "come to him in its natural state, in flow, quantity and quality": *Chasemore v. Richards* (1859), 7 H.L. Cas. 349 at p. 382. Natural streams which formerly afforded "pure and healthy" water for drinking or swimming purposes become little more than cesspools when riparian factory owners and municipal corporations discharge into them filth of all descriptions. Pollution offences are undoubtedly public welfare offences enacted in the interests of public health. There is thus no presumption of a full *mens rea*.

There is another reason, however, why this offence is not subject to a presumption of *mens rea*. The presumption applies only to offences which are "criminal in the true sense," as Ritchie J. said in *The Queen v. Pierce Fisheries, supra*, at p. 13. The Ontario *Water Resources Act* is a provincial statute. If it is valid provincial legislation (and no suggestion was made to the contrary), then it cannot possibly create an offence which is criminal in the true sense.

The present case concerns the interpretation of two troublesome words frequently found in public welfare statutes: "cause" and "permit." These two words are troublesome because neither denotes clearly either full *mens rea* nor absolute liability.

[A number of authorities were then cited.]

The Divisional Court of Ontario relied on these latter authorities in concluding that s. 32(1) created a *mens rea* offence.

The conflict in the above authorities, however, shows that in themselves the words "cause" and "permit" fit much better into an offence of strict liability than either full *mens rea* or absolute liability. Since s. 32(1) creates a public welfare offence, without a clear indication that liability is absolute, and without any words such as "knowingly" or "wilfully" expressly to import *mens rea*, application of the criteria which I have outlined above undoubtedly places the offence in the category of strict liability.

As I am of the view that a new trial is necessary, it would be inappropriate to discuss at this time the facts of the present case ... .

Appeal dismissed; cross-appeal dismissed.

When the *Sault Ste Marie* case was argued before the Supreme Court, the parties focused their arguments on whether the pollution offence required subjective fault and there was little discussion about whether there was a halfway house between subjective fault and non-fault. Robert J Sharpe and Kent Roach in their biography of Brian Dickson explain that, while Dickson had accepted the dichotomy in a case he decided in 1973 during his first year on the Supreme Court, he had become more accepting of the criticisms by academics and law reform commissions of the dichotomy. They suggest that Dickson as a former corporate lawyer "knew that any conviction could affect the reputation of a corporation and its managers." At the same time, they write that Dickson, who started each day riding his horse on his farm outside of Ottawa, "was concerned about pollution and the conservation of the natural environment. He was reluctant to allow corporations that polluted to escape unpunished simply because the government could not prove beyond a reasonable doubt that a high official in the corporation knew about the pollution. ... Corporate power, for Dickson, implied corporate responsibility." See RJ Sharpe & K Roach, *Brian Dickson: A Judge's Journey* (Toronto: University of Toronto Press, 2003) at 221-22.

In *Lévis (City) v Tétreault; Lévis (City) v 2629-4470 Québec inc*, 2006 SCC 12, [2006] 1 SCR 420, the Supreme Court affirmed that it would apply the "clear analytical framework and classification approach adopted in *Sault Ste. Marie"* and that while "[a]bsolute liability offences still exist … they have become an exception requiring clear proof of legislative intent."

III. CONSTITUTIONAL CONSIDERATIONS

Re BC Motor Vehicle Act
Supreme Court of Canada
[1985] 2 SCR 486

[The lieutenant governor in council of British Columbia referred the following question to the British Columbia Court of Appeal: "Is s. 94(2) of the *Motor Vehicle Act*, R.S.B.C. 1979, as amended by the *Motor Vehicle Amendment Act, 1982*, consistent with the *Canadian Charter of Rights and Freedoms*?" Section 94(2) provides that the offence created by s 94(1) "creates an absolute liability offence in which guilt is established by proof of driving, whether or not the defendant knew of the prohibition or suspension." Section 94(1) provides that a person who drives a motor vehicle while he or she is prohibited from driving or while his or her driver's licence is suspended commits an offence and is liable on first conviction to a fine and to imprisonment for not less than seven days and not more than six months. The British Columbia Court of Appeal answered the question in the negative.

The attorney general for British Columbia appealed to the Supreme Court of Canada. Lamer J delivered the judgment of the Court.]

LAMER J (Dickson CJ and Beetz, Chouinard, and Le Dain JJ concurring): A law that has the potential to convict a person who has not really done anything wrong offends the principles of fundamental justice and, if imprisonment is available as a penalty, such a law then violates a person's right to liberty under s. 7 of the *Canadian Charter of Rights and Freedoms* (Part I of the *Constitution Act, 1982*, as enacted by the *Canada Act*, 1982 (U.K.), c. 11).

In other words, absolute liability and imprisonment cannot be combined. …

In the framework of a purposive analysis, designed to ascertain the purpose of the s. 7 guarantee and "the interests it was meant to protect" (*R. v. Big M Drug Mart Ltd.*, [[1985] 1 SCR 295]), it is clear to me that the interests which are meant to be protected by the words "and the right not to be deprived thereof except in accordance with the principles of fundamental justice" of s. 7 are the life, liberty and security of the person. The principles of fundamental justice, on the other hand, are not a protected interest, but rather a qualifier of the right not to be deprived of life, liberty and security of the person.

Given that, as the Attorney-General for Ontario has acknowledged, "when one reads the phrase 'principles of fundamental justice,' a single incontrovertible meaning is not apparent," its meaning must, in my view, be determined by reference to the interests which those words of the section are designed to protect and the particular role of the phrase within the section. As a qualifier, the phrase serves to establish the parameters of the interests but it cannot be interpreted so narrowly as to frustrate or stultify them. For the narrower the meaning given to "principles of fundamental justice" the greater will be the possibility that individuals may be deprived of these most basic rights.

Sections 8 to 14, in other words, address specific deprivations of the "right" of life, liberty and security of the person in breach of the principles of fundamental justice, and as such, violations of s. 7. They are designed to protect, in a specific manner and setting, the right to life, liberty and security of the person set forth in s. 7. It would be incongruous to interpret s. 7 more narrowly than the rights in ss. 8 to 14. The alternative, which is to interpret all of ss. 8 to 14 in a "[n]arrow and technical" manner for the sake of congruity, is out of the question (*Law Society of Upper Canada v. Skapinker*, [[1984] 1 SCR 357], at p. 366).

Sections 8 to 14 are illustrative of deprivations of those rights to life, liberty and security of the person in breach of the principles of fundamental justice. For they, in effect, illustrate some of the parameters of the "right" to life, liberty and security of the person; they are examples of instances in which the "right" to life, liberty and security of the person would be violated in a manner which is not in accordance with the principles of fundamental justice. ...

Thus, ss. 8 to 14 provide an invaluable key to the meaning of "principles of fundamental justice." Many have been developed over time as presumptions of the common law, others have found expression in the international conventions on human rights. All have been recognized as essential elements of a system for the administration of justice which is founded upon a belief in "the dignity and worth of the human person" (preamble to the *Canadian Bill of Rights*, R.S.C. 1970, App. III), and on "the rule of law" (preamble to the *Canadian Charter of Rights and Freedoms*).

It is this common thread which, in my view, must guide us in determining the scope and content of "principles of fundamental justice." In other words, the principles of fundamental justice are to be found in the basic tenets of our legal system. They do not lie in the realm of general public policy but in the inherent domain of the judiciary as guardian of the justice system. Such an approach to the interpretation of "principles of fundamental justice" is consistent with the wording and structure of s. 7, the context of the section, *i.e.*, ss. 8 to 14, and the character and larger objects of the Charter itself. It provides meaningful content for the s. 7 guarantee all the while avoiding adjudication of policy matters.

. . .

Consequently, my conclusion may be summarized as follows:

The term "principles of fundamental justice" is not a right, but a qualifier of the right not to be deprived of life, liberty and security of the person; its function is to set the parameters of that right.

Sections 8 to 14 address specific deprivations of the "right" to life, liberty and security of the person in breach of the principles of fundamental justice, and as such, violations of s. 7. They are therefore illustrative of the meaning, in criminal or penal law, of "principles of fundamental justice"; they represent principles which have been recognized by the common law, the international conventions and by the very fact of entrenchment in the *Charter*, as essential elements of a system for the administration of justice which is founded upon the belief in the dignity and worth of the human person and the rule of law.

Consequently, the principles of fundamental justice are to be found in the basic tenets and principles, not only of our judicial process, but also of the other components of our legal system ... .

Whether any given principle may be said to be a principle of fundamental justice within the meaning of s. 7 will rest upon an analysis of the nature, sources, *rationale* and essential role of that principle within the judicial process and in our legal system, as it evolves ... .

I now turn to such an analysis of the principle of *mens rea* and absolute liability offences in order to determine the question which has been put to the Court in the present Reference.

Absolute Liability and Fundamental Justice in Penal Law

It has from time immemorial been part of our system of laws that the innocent not be punished. This principle has long been recognized as an essential element of a system for the administration of justice which is founded upon a belief in the dignity and worth of the human person and on the rule of law. It is so old that its first enunciation was in Latin *actus non facit reum nisi mens sit rea* ... .

This view has been adopted by this Court in unmistakable terms in many cases, amongst which the better known are *Beaver v. The Queen*, [1957] S.C.R. 531, and the most recent and often quoted judgment of Dickson J. writing for the Court in *R. v. City of Sault Ste. Marie, supra*.

This Court's decision in the latter case is predicated upon a certain number of postulates one of which, given the nature of the rules it elaborates, has to be to the effect that absolute liability in penal law offends the principles of fundamental justice. Those principles are, to use the words of Dickson J., to the effect that "there is a generally held revulsion against punishment of the morally innocent." He also stated that the argument that absolute liability "violates fundamental principles of penal liability" was the most telling argument against absolute liability and one of greater force than those advanced in support thereof.

In my view it is because absolute liability offends the principles of fundamental justice that this Court created presumptions against legislatures having intended to enact offences of a regulatory nature falling within that category. This is not to say, however, and to that extent I am in agreement with the Court of Appeal, that, as a result, absolute liability *per se* offends s. 7 of the *Charter*.

A law enacting an absolute liability offence will violate s. 7 of the *Charter* only if and to the extent that it has the potential of depriving of life, liberty, or security of the person.

Obviously, imprisonment (including probation orders) deprives persons of their liberty. An offence has that potential as of the moment it is open to the judge to impose imprisonment. There is no need that imprisonment, as in s. 94(2), be made mandatory. I am therefore of the view that the combination of imprisonment and of absolute liability violates s. 7 of the *Charter* and can only be salvaged if the authorities demonstrate under s. 1 that such a deprivation of liberty in breach of those principles of fundamental justice is, in a free and democratic society, under the circumstances, a justified reasonable limit to one's rights under s. 7.

As no one has addressed imprisonment as an alternative to the non-payment of a fine, I prefer not to express any views in relation to s. 7 as regards that eventuality as a result of a conviction for an absolute liability offence; nor do I need to address here, given the scope of my finding and the nature of this appeal, minimum imprisonment, whether it offends the *Charter per se* or whether such violation, if any, is dependent upon whether it be for a *mens rea* or strict liability offence. Those issues were not addressed by the court below and it would be unwise to attempt to address them here. It is sufficient and desirable for this appeal to make the findings I have and no more, that is, that no imprisonment may be imposed for an absolute liability offence, and, consequently, given the question put to us, an offence punishable by imprisonment cannot be an absolute liability offence.

Before considering s. 94(2) in the light of these findings, I feel we are however compelled to go somewhat further for the following reason. I would not want us to be taken by this conclusion as having inferentially decided that absolute liability may not offend s. 7 as long as imprisonment or probation orders are not available as a sentence. The answer to that question is dependent upon the content given to the words "security of the person." That issue was and is a live one. Indeed, though the question as framed focuses on absolute liability (s. 94(2)) in relation to the whole *Charter*, including the right to security of the person in s. 7, because of the presence of mandatory imprisonment in s. 94(1) only deprivation of liberty was considered. As the effect of imprisonment on the right to liberty is a foregone conclusion, *a fortiori* minimum imprisonment, everyone directed their arguments when discussing s. 7 to considering whether absolute liability violated the principles of fundamental justice, and then subsidiarily argued *pro* or *contra* the effect of s. 1 of the *Charter*.

Counsel for those opposing the validity of s. 94(2) took the position in this Court that absolute liability and severe punishment, always referring to imprisonment, violated s. 7 of the *Charter*. From the following passage of the judgment in the Court of Appeal it would appear that counsel for those opposing the validity of the section took the wider position in that Court that all absolute liability offences violated s. 7 because of "punishment of the morally innocent":

> In seeking to persuade the court to that conclusion counsel opposing the validity of s. 94(2) contended all absolute offences are now of no force and effect because of s. 7 of the Charter and that the provisions of s. 1 of the Charter should not be invoked to sustain them. In support of this submission counsel relied upon the view expressed by Dickson J. in *Sault Ste. Marie* that there was "a generally held revulsion against punishment of the morally innocent." They contended that had the Charter been in effect when *Sault Ste. Marie* was decided all absolute liability offences would have been struck down.

We accept without hesitation the statement expressed by the learned justice but do not think it necessarily follows that because of s. 7 of the Charter this category of offence can no longer be legislated. To the contrary, there are, and will remain, certain public welfare offences, e.g., air and water pollution offences, where the public interest requires that the offences be absolute liability offences.

While I agree with the Court of Appeal, as I have already mentioned, that absolute liability does not *per se* violate s. 7 of the *Charter*, I am somewhat concerned with leaving without comment the unqualified reference by the Court of Appeal to the requirements of the "public interest."

If, by reference to public interest, it was meant that the requirements of public interest for certain types of offences is a factor to be considered in determining whether absolute liability offends the principles of fundamental justice, then I would respectfully disagree; if the public interest is there referred to by the Court as a possible justification under s. 1 of a limitation to the rights protected at s. 7, then I do agree.

Indeed, as I said, in penal law, absolute liability always offends the principles of fundamental justice irrespective of the nature of the offence; it offends s. 7 of the *Charter* if as a result, anyone is deprived of his life, liberty or security of the person, irrespective of the requirement of public interest. In such cases it might only be salvaged for reasons of public interest under s. 1.

In this latter regard, something might be added. Administrative expediency, absolute liability's main supportive argument, will undoubtedly under s. 1 be invoked and occasionally succeed. Indeed, administrative expediency certainly has its place in administrative law. But when administrative law chooses to call in aid imprisonment through penal law, indeed sometimes criminal law and the added stigma attached to a conviction, exceptional, in my view, will be the case where the liberty or even the security of the person guaranteed under s. 7 should be sacrificed to administrative expediency. Section 1 may, for reasons of administrative expediency, successfully come to the rescue of an otherwise violation of s. 7, but only in cases arising out of exceptional conditions, such as natural disasters, the outbreak of war, epidemics, and the like.

Of course I understand the concern of many as regards corporate offences, specially, as was mentioned by the Court of Appeal, in certain sensitive areas such as the preservation of our vital environment and our natural resources. This concern might well be dispelled were it to be decided, given the proper case, that s. 7 affords protection to human persons only and does not extend to corporations.

[The Court subsequently held that corporations do not enjoy s 7 rights in *Irwin Toy Ltd v Quebec (Attorney-General)* (1989), 58 DLR (4th) 577. This means that an absolute liability offence that only applied to corporations would not violate s 7 of the Charter. At the same time, corporations charged with an offence that also applies to natural persons can still challenge the offence under s 7 as well as other rights under the Charter. See *R v Wholesale Travel Group Inc*, [1991] 3 SCR 154, excerpted later in this chapter.]

Even if it be decided that s. 7 does extend to corporations, I think the balancing under s. 1 of the public interest against the financial interests of a corporation would give very different results from that of balancing public interest and the liberty or security of the person of a human being.

Indeed, the public interest as regards "air and water pollution offences" requires that the guilty be dealt with firmly, but the seriousness of the offence does not in my respectful view support the proposition that the innocent *human* person be open to conviction, quite the contrary.

Section 94(2)

No doubt s. 94(2) enacts in the clearest of terms an absolute liability offence, the conviction for which a person will be deprived of his or her liberty, and little more, if anything, need be added … .

In the final analysis, it seems that both the appellant and the respondent agree that s. 94 will impact upon the right to liberty of a limited number of morally innocent persons. It creates an absolute liability offence which effects a deprivation of liberty for a limited number of persons. To me, that is sufficient for it to be in violation of s. 7.

Section 1

Having found that s. 94(2) offends s. 7 of the *Charter* there remains the question as to whether the appellants have demonstrated that the section is salvaged by the operation of s. 1 of the *Charter*. No evidence was adduced in the Court of Appeal or in this Court ... .

I do not take issue with the fact that it is highly desirable that "bad drivers" be kept off the road. I do not take issue either with the desirability of punishing severely bad drivers who are in contempt of prohibitions against driving. The bottom line of the question to be addressed here is: whether the Government of British Columbia has demonstrated as justifiable that the risk of imprisonment of a few innocent is, given the desirability of ridding the roads of British Columbia of bad drivers, a reasonable limit in a free and democratic society. That result is to be measured against the offence being one of strict liability open to a defence of due diligence, the success of which does nothing more than let those few who did nothing wrong remain free. As did the Court of Appeal, I find that this demonstration has not been satisfied, indeed, not in the least.

Having come to this conclusion [that s 94(2) violates s 7 of the Charter], I choose, as did the Court of Appeal, not to address whether the section violates the rights guaranteed under ss. 11(d) and 12 of the *Charter*.

[McIntyre and Wilson JJ delivered separate concurring judgments, limiting their decision to a case in which absolute liability is combined with a minimum term of imprisonment.]

Appeal dismissed.

The British Columbia legislature responded to this case by repealing s 94(2) of the BC *Motor Vehicle Act*, which had stated: "subsection (1) creates an absolute liability offence in which guilt is established by proof of driving, whether or not the defendant knew of the prohibition or suspension." Many thought that this would trigger the presumption outlined in *Sault Ste Marie* that all regulatory offences would be strict liability offences allowing a defence of due diligence or reasonable mistake of fact. In *R v Pontes*, [1995] 3 SCR 44, however, the Supreme Court held in a 5:4 decision that the offence of driving with a suspended licence was still an absolute liability offence because the only defence available to the accused was not available because of the principle that ignorance of the law is not an excuse. This principle and this case will be discussed in Chapter 8. In *Pontes*, however, the Supreme Court did not strike down the offence of driving with a suspended licence. Rather, it indicated that s 4.1 of the BC *Offence Act*, which was also amended in response to *Re BC Motor Vehicle Act*, would apply to those convicted of the offence. Section 4.1 provides that "no person is liable to imprisonment with respect to an absolute liability offence." Section 72 of the *Offence Act* also provides that failure to pay a fine will not result in a jail term. Thus the offence remained intact but imprisonment was not constitutionally available because the offence was classified as an absolute liability offence.

It is thus clear that imprisonment cannot be combined with an absolute liability offence. Interestingly enough, this was the approach taken by Justice Wilson in her sole concurring judgment in *Re BC Motor Vehicle Act, supra*. She concluded:

[128] Because of the absolute liability nature of the offence created by s. 94(2) of the *Motor Vehicle Act* a person can be convicted under the section even although he was unaware at the time he was driving that his licence was suspended and was unable to find this out despite the exercise of due diligence. While the legislature may as a matter of government policy make this an offence, and we cannot question its wisdom in this regard, the question is whether it can make it mandatory for the courts to deprive a person convicted of it of his liberty without violating s. 7. This, in turn, depends on whether attaching a mandatory term of imprisonment to an absolute liability offence such as this violates the principles of fundamental justice. I believe that it does. I think the conscience of the court would be shocked and the administration of justice brought into disrepute by such an unreasonable and extravagant penalty. It is totally disproportionate to the offence … .

[129] It is basic to any theory of punishment that the sentence imposed bear some relationship to the offence; it must be a "fit" sentence proportionate to the seriousness of the offence. Only if this is so can the public be satisfied that the offender "deserved" the punishment he received and feel a confidence in the fairness and rationality of the system. This is not to say that there is an inherently appropriate relationship between a particular offence and its punishment but rather that there is a scale of offences and punishments into which the particular offence and punishment must fit. Obviously this cannot be done with mathematical precision and many different factors will go into the assessment of the seriousness of a particular offence for purposes of determining the appropriate punishment but it does provide a workable conventional framework for sentencing. Indeed, judges in the exercise of their sentencing discretion have been employing such a scale for over a hundred years.

I believe that a mandatory term of imprisonment for an offence committed unknowingly and unwittingly and after the exercise of due diligence is grossly excessive and inhumane. It is not required to reduce the incidence of the offence. It is beyond anything required to satisfy the need for "atonement." And society, in my opinion, would not be abhorred by an unintentional and unknowing violation of the section. I believe, therefore, that such a sanction offends the principles of fundamental justice embodied in our penal system.

Would the combination of large fines and absolute liability offences violate s 7 of the Charter? The Ontario Court of Appeal considered this question in *R v 1260448 Ontario Inc (cob William Cameron Trucking); R v Transport Robert (1973) Ltée* (2003), 180 CCC (3d) 254 in the context of s 84.1 of the *Highway Traffic Act*, RSO 1990, c H.8, which provided a minimum $2,000 and maximum $50,000 fine whenever a wheel of a commercial motor vehicle became detached. The offence, enacted after several horrific traffic accidents, specifically applied regardless of the due diligence of the owner or operator of the commercial vehicle. The court concluded:

While the courts have not fully defined the limits of security of the person in s. 7, there are certain propositions established by the cases. In *Blencoe v. British Columbia (Human Rights Commission)*, [2000] 2 S.C.R. 307 at para. 57, Bastarache J. speaking for the majority held that, "[N]ot all state interference with an individual's psychological integrity will engage s. 7. Where the psychological integrity of a person is at issue, security of the person is restricted to 'serious state-imposed psychological stress.'" Thus, "[N]ot all forms of psychological prejudice caused by government will lead to automatic s. 7 violations." Further, there is no "generalized right to dignity, or more specifically, a right to free from stigma" (para. 57) and, "[d]ignity and reputation are not self-standing rights. Neither is freedom from stigma" (para. 80). …

[W]e are not convinced that a prosecution for the s. 84.1 offence engages the kind of exceptional state-induced psychological stress, even for an individual, that would trigger the security of the person guarantee in s. 7. The offence does not create a true crime, and like most regulatory offences, it focuses on the harmful consequences of otherwise lawful conduct rather than any moral turpitude. Thus, in *Wholesale Travel*, supra, at p. 224, Cory J. rejected the accused's claim that conviction for false advertising carried the stigma of dishonesty. In that case, where due diligence was available, the court characterized the fault element as one of "negligence rather than one involving moral turpitude" and thus, "any stigma that might flow from a conviction is very considerably diminished." The same can be said in this case. The s. 84.1 offence focuses on the unintended but harmful consequences of the commercial trucking industry. We reject the proposition that a defendant charged with this offence is stigmatized as a person operating in a wanton manner, heedless of the extreme dangers to life and limb posed by his or her operation. Conviction for the offence at most implies negligence and like the misleading advertising offence considered in *Wholesale Travel*, any stigma is very considerably diminished.

The diminished stigma attached to the s. 84.1 offence is not sufficient to trigger the security interest in s. 7 even when coupled with the possibility of a significant fine. This is simply not the kind of serious state-imposed psychological stress that is intended to be covered by security of the person. It is qualitatively different than the kinds of stresses that have been recognized in the cases. A review of those cases demonstrates a concern with state action that intrudes in an intimate and profound way as in *New Brunswick (Minister of Health and Community Services) v. G.(J.)*, [1999] 3 S.C.R. 46 (attempt to take a child away from its parents); *Rodriguez v. British Columbia (Attorney General)*, [1993] 3 S.C.R. 519 (criminal prohibition on assisting suicide for a desperately ill patient) and *R. v. Morgentaler*, [1988] 1 S.C.R. 30 (regulating abortion).

The right to security of the person does not protect the individual operating in the highly regulated context of commercial trucking for profit from the ordinary stress and anxieties that a reasonable person would suffer as a result of government regulation of that industry. As Lamer C.J.C. said in *G.(J.)* at para. 59, "[I]f the right were interpreted with such broad sweep, countless government initiatives could be challenged on the ground that they infringe the right to security of the person, massively expanding the scope of judicial review, and, in the process, trivializing what it means for a right to be constitutionally protected."

Accordingly, s. 84.1 of the HTA does not violate s. 7. It is therefore unnecessary to consider whether any violation could be saved by s. 1.

R v Wholesale Travel Group Inc
Supreme Court of Canada
[1991] 3 SCR 154

[The accused corporation was charged with several counts of false or misleading advertising, contrary to s 36(1)(a) of the *Competition Act*, RSC 1970, c C-23 on the basis that it wrongly advertised that its travel packages were "wholesale." These offences could be punished by up to one year's imprisonment as they were prosecuted. At trial, the court held that s 36 of the *Competition Act* and s 37.3, which creates a statutory due diligence defence, were inconsistent with ss 7 and 11(d) of the *Canadian Charter of Rights and Freedoms*, and therefore of no force and effect. The trial judge found that the statutory due diligence defence in ss 37.3(2)(a) and (b) was an unjustified violation of s 11(d) of the Charter and that a requirement for a timely retraction in ss 37.3(2)(c) and (d) imposed absolute liability in violation of s 7 of the Charter.

Section 37.3(2) of the *Competition Act* provided:

No person shall be convicted of an offence under section 36 or 36.1, if he establishes that,

(a) the act or omission giving rise to the offence with which he is charged was the result of error;

(b) he took reasonable precautions and exercised due diligence to prevent the occurrence of such error;

(c) he, or another person, took reasonable measures to bring the error to the attention of the class of persons likely to have been reached by the representation or testimonial; and

(d) the measures referred to in paragraph (c), except where the representation or testimonial related to a security, were taken forthwith after the representation was made or the testimonial was published.

The Supreme Court held that the accused company had standing to challenge the provision under ss 7 and 11(d).]

LAMER CJ (with whom six other members of the Court agreed) stated: In *Irwin Toy Ltd. v. Quebec (Attorney General)*, [1989] 1 S.C.R. 927, this Court held that only human beings can enjoy the right to life, liberty and security of the person guaranteed by s. 7 of the *Charter*, and that a corporation was therefore unable to seek a declaration that certain provisions of the *Consumer Protection Act* infringed s. 7 of the *Charter* and could not be upheld under s. 1 of the *Charter*. However, the majority was careful to note that there were no penal proceedings pending in the case and that the principle enunciated in *R. v. Big M Drug Mart Ltd.*, [1985] 1 S.C.R. 295, was therefore not involved ... .

A number of parties contended, in oral argument, that while this Court has held that a corporation which has been charged with a penal provision has standing to challenge the constitutionality of that provision, this does not necessarily mean that the corporation can *benefit* from a finding that the provision violates a *human being's* constitutional rights. In other words, when a corporation's constitutional challenge gives rise to a finding that a statutory provision violates a *human being's Charter* rights, the appropriate remedy under s. 52(1) of the *Constitution Act, 1982* is that the provision is of no force or effect with respect to human beings (because this is the extent of the inconsistency between the Constitution and the law), but the provision remains of force and effect with respect to corporations (because the provision as applied to corporations is *not* inconsistent with the Constitution).

Such an interpretation of the words "to the extent of the inconsistency" contained in s. 52(1) would be inconsistent with this Court's holding in *R. v. Big M Drug Mart Ltd., supra*, and would not accord with this Court's general approach to s. 52(1). For example, in *R. v. Morgentaler*, [1988] 1 S.C.R. 30, this Court restored Dr. Morgentaler's acquittal on the basis that s. 251 (the abortion provision) of the *Criminal Code*, R.S.C. 1970, c. C-34, limited women's rights under s. 7 of the *Charter*, could not be upheld under s. 1 and was therefore of no force or effect. Dr. Morgentaler, as an accused person, was entitled to challenge the constitutionality of s. 251 on the basis that it violated women's *Charter* rights. Moreover, he was entitled to *benefit* from the finding that the provision was inconsistent with the Constitution and was, therefore, of no force or effect. I am not prepared to depart from this approach to s. 52(1).

Thus, it is my view that Wholesale Travel does have standing to challenge the constitutionality of the false/misleading advertising provisions under ss. 7 and 11(d) of the *Charter* and may benefit from a finding that these provisions are unconstitutional. However, this is *not* to say that if the same provisions were enacted so as to apply *exclusively* to corporations, a corporation would be entitled to raise the *Charter* arguments which have been raised in the case at bar. The problem with ss. 36(1) and 37.3(2) of the *Competition Act* is that they are worded so as to encompass *both* individual and corporate accused; in this sense, they are "over-inclusive." Therefore, if the provisions violate an individual's *Charter* rights they must be struck down (to the extent of the inconsistency) under s. 52(1). Once the provisions are held to be of no force or effect, they cannot apply to *any* accused, whether corporate or individual.

[The Supreme Court unanimously held that the timely retraction requirement was a form of absolute liability that violated s 7 and could not be justified under s 1 of the Charter. Lamer CJ (with whom six other members of the Supreme Court, including La Forest J, agreed on this point) stated:]

In *Re B.C. Motor Vehicle Act*, *supra*, this Court held that the combination of absolute liability and possible imprisonment violates s. 7 of the *Charter* and will rarely be upheld under s. 1. This is because an absolute liability offence has the potential of convicting a person who really has done nothing wrong (that is, has acted neither intentionally nor negligently). In *R. v. Vaillancourt*, [*infra*], I stated that whenever the state resorts to the restriction of liberty, such as imprisonment, to assist in the enforcement of a law, even a mere provincial regulatory offence, there is, as a principle of fundamental justice, a minimum mental state (or fault requirement) which is an essential element of the offence. *Re B.C. Motor Vehicle Act* inferentially decided that even for a mere provincial regulatory offence *at least* negligence is required, in that *at least* a defence of due diligence must always be open to an accused *who risks imprisonment* upon conviction. The rationale for elevating *mens rea* from a presumed element in *R. v. City of Sault Ste. Marie*, [1978] 2 S.C.R. 1299, to a constitutionally required element, was that it is a principle of fundamental justice that the penalty imposed on an accused and the stigma which attaches to that penalty and/or to the conviction itself, necessitate a level of fault which reflects the particular nature of the crime … .

. . .

The Crown has conceded that the statutory defence afforded by s. 37.3(2) is "more restricted" than the common law defence of due diligence, but nonetheless argues that the limited nature of the statutory defence does not render it unconstitutional. Although paras. (a) and (b) of s. 37.3(2) refer specifically to an "error" and to the exercise of due diligence to prevent an "error," they, in my view, largely correspond to the usual due diligence defence. In other words, paras. (a) and (b) operate so as to provide a defence to an accused who has taken reasonable precautions to prevent false/misleading advertising and who has been duly diligent in ensuring that advertising is not false or misleading in nature. However, the additional requirement of "timely retraction" embodied in paras. (c) and (d) means that the statutory defence is considerably more narrow than the common law defence of due diligence.

An accused who did not realize, and could not reasonably have been expected to realize, that the representation in question was false or misleading until it was too late to comply with paras. (c) and (d) or who was, for some reason, unable to comply with paras. (c) and (d), but who had nonetheless taken reasonable precautions and who had exercised due diligence in preventing false/misleading advertising, would not fall within the statutory defence and would be convicted of false/misleading advertising. I agree with the majority of the Ontario Court of Appeal that paras. (c) and (d) of s. 37.3(2) could have the effect of depriving an accused of the defence of due diligence and could therefore require the conviction of an accused who was not negligent. Paragraphs (c) and (d) make the failure to undertake corrective advertising (a component of the offence of false/misleading advertising) an "offence" of absolute liability. Consequently, the constitutionally required fault level is not present in the false/misleading advertising provisions.

In light of the above discussion, I agree with the majority of the Court of Appeal that it is the presence of paras. (c) and (d) alone which offends s. 7 of the *Charter*. Thus, unless the limitation on s. 7 can be upheld under s. 1 of the *Charter*, these two paragraphs must be held to be of no force or effect, pursuant to s. 52(1) of the *Constitution Act, 1982*.

· · ·

It is not necessary to convict of false/misleading advertising those who did not undertake corrective advertising because they did not realize (and ought not to have realized) that the advertisement was false/misleading, in order to achieve the objectives set out above. If Parliament wished to encourage corrective advertising in order to meet the objectives set out above, it could have:

(a)   enacted a separate offence of "failure to correct false/misleading advertising" under which an accused who discovers or who ought to have discovered that an advertisement was false or misleading is required to be duly diligent in taking the corrective measures set out in paras. (c) and (d) in order to come within the statutory defence to this offence; or

(b)   maintained the component of "failure to correct false/misleading advertising" within the existing statutory defence to false advertising, but worded paras. (c) and (d) in such a way that the requirement for corrective advertising would arise upon the accused's discovery that the advertisement was false or misleading (or upon a finding that the accused ought to have discovered that the advertisement was false/misleading).

In my view, either of these alternative means would, without convicting the innocent, achieve the objective of encouraging advertisers to undertake corrective advertising and would therefore achieve the dual objectives of protecting consumers from the effects of false advertising and of preventing advertisers from benefiting from false/misleading representations. Given that these two alternatives were clearly open to Parliament, it can be seen that the existing paragraphs are unnecessarily intrusive on constitutional rights.

While an absolute liability component to the offence of false advertising would perhaps be more effective in facilitating convictions than would the alternatives proposed above, the simple answer to this contention is that Parliament could have retained the absolute liability component and, at the same time, infringed *Charter* rights to a much lesser extent, *had it not combined this absolute liability with the possibility of imprisonment.* In this sense, removing the possibility of imprisonment and leaving paras. (c) and (d) unchanged was a further less intrusive means which was available to Parliament.

[The Supreme Court also unanimously held that it is not an infringement of s 7 of the Charter to create an offence for which the mental element is negligence.]

LAMER CJ (with whom six other members of the Supreme Court, including La Forest J, agreed on this point) stated: Counsel for Wholesale Travel has argued that the offence of false/misleading advertising is one of those offences, contemplated by this Court in *Vaillancourt*, [1987] 2 S.C.R. 636, for which the special nature of the stigma attaching to a conviction and/or the severity of the available punishment is such that *subjective mens rea* is constitutionally required by s. 7.

Counsel for Wholesale Travel argued that the stigma attaching to a conviction of false/ misleading advertising is akin to the stigma of dishonesty which attaches to a conviction of theft. Given that the stigma attaching to theft was explicitly contemplated in *Vaillancourt* as one which may well necessitate a subjective *mens rea*, it was argued that the offence of false/misleading advertising also requires an element of subjective *mens rea* in order to comply with the principles of fundamental justice. In my view, while a conviction for false/misleading advertising carries some stigma, in the sense that it is not morally-neutral behaviour, it cannot be said that the stigma associated with this offence is analogous to the stigma of dishonesty which attaches to a conviction for theft. A conviction for false/misleading advertising will rest on a variety of facts, many of which will not reveal any dishonesty but, rather, carelessness and the conviction of same does not brand the accused as being dishonest. In my opinion, the same cannot be said for a conviction for theft.

While an aware state of mind may well be the most appropriate minimum standard of fault for imprisonment or for any offence included in the *Criminal Code*, a matter upon which I refrain from expressing any view, it does not follow that this standard of fault is entrenched in the *Charter*. As I stated in *Lippé v. Québec (Procureur général)*, (1991), 128 N.R. 1, at p. 34, "the *Constitution* does not always guarantee the ideal." As this Court stated in *Vaillancourt, supra*, the principles of fundamental justice dictate that negligence is the minimum fault requirement where an accused faces possible imprisonment upon conviction except for certain offences such as murder. For the reasons given above, it is my view that s. 7 of the *Charter* does not dictate the higher fault requirement contemplated by the Ontario Law Reform Commission for the offence of false/misleading advertising. Whether a fault requirement higher than this constitutional minimum ought to be adopted where an accused faces possible imprisonment or conviction of any offence under the *Criminal Code* is a question of public policy which must be determined by Parliament, and for the courts to pronounce upon this would be contrary to what this Court has said in *Re B.C. Motor Vehicle Act*, [1985] 2 S.C.R. 486, at p. 498-99: that we refrain from "adjudicating upon the merits or wisdom of enactments." It is not the role of this Court to "second guess" the policy decisions made by elected officials.

LA FOREST J added the following in his concurring judgment: For my part, I am prepared to accept the requirement of due diligence as sufficient for *Charter* purposes in the case of regulatory offences and some criminal offences having a significant regulatory base (e.g., gun control *R. v. Schwartz*, [1988] 2 S.C.R. 443). However, for most criminal offences I would be reluctant to accept a lower level of *mens rea* than criminal negligence.

CORY J (with whom L'Heureux-Dubé J concurred) stated: Those who argue against differential treatment for regulatory offences assert that there is no valid reason to distinguish between the criminal and regulatory accused. Each, it is said, is entitled in law to the same procedural and substantive protections. This view assumes equality of position between criminal and regulatory defendants; that is to say, it assumes that each starts out from a position of equal knowledge, volition and "innocence." The argument against differential treatment further suggests that differentiating between the regulatory and criminal defendants implies the subordination and sacrifice of the regulatory accused to the interests of the community at large. Such a position, it is argued, contravenes our basic concern for individual dignity and our fundamental belief in the importance of the individual. It is these assumptions which the licensing justification challenges.

The licensing concept rests on the view that those who choose to participate in regulated activities have, in doing so, placed themselves in a responsible relationship to the public generally and must accept the consequences of that responsibility. Therefore, it is said, those who engage in regulated activity should, as part of the burden of responsible conduct attending participation in the regulated field, be deemed to have accepted certain terms and conditions applicable to those who act within the regulated sphere. Foremost among these implied terms is an undertaking that the conduct of the regulated actor will comply with and maintain a certain minimum standard of care.

The licensing justification is based not only on the idea of a conscious choice being made to enter a regulated field but also on the concept of control. The concept is that those persons who enter a regulated field are in the best position to control the harm which may result, and that they should therefore be held responsible for it.

Does section 7 require in all cases that the Crown prove *mens rea* as an essential element of the offence? The resolution of this question requires that a contextual approach be taken to the meaning and scope of the s. 7 right. Certainly, there can be no doubt that s. 7 requires proof of some degree of fault. That fault may be demonstrated by proof of intent, whether subjective or objective, or by proof of negligent conduct, depending on the nature of the offence. While it is not necessary in this case to determine the requisite degree of fault necessary to prove the commission of particular crimes, I am of the view that with respect to regulatory offences, proof of negligence satisfies the requirement of fault demanded by s. 7. Although the element of fault may not be removed completely, the demands of s. 7 will be met in the regulatory context where liability is imposed for conduct which breaches the standard of reasonable care required of those operating in the regulated field.

Regulatory schemes can only be effective if they provide for significant penalties in the event of their breach. Indeed, although it may be rare that imprisonment is sought, it must be available as a sanction if there is to be effective enforcement of the regulatory measure. Nor is the imposition of imprisonment unreasonable in light of the danger that can accrue to the public from breaches of regulatory statutes. The spectre of tragedy evoked by such names as Thalidomide, Bhopal, Chernobyl and the *Exxon Valdez* can leave no doubt as to the potential human and environmental devastation which can result from the violation of regulatory measures. Strong sanctions including imprisonment are vital to the prevention of similar catastrophes. The potential for serious harm flowing from the breach of regulatory measures is too great for it to be said that imprisonment can never be imposed as a sanction.

[The Supreme Court was divided 5 to 4 on the question whether the shifting of the onus for the due diligence defence in s 37(2) violated s 11(d) of the Charter with the majority holding that the reverse onus to establish due diligence was constitutional.]

LAMER CJ [(with whom three other members of the Court concurred) stated that the provision violated s 11(d) and could not be upheld under s 1]: In *Vaillancourt, supra,* this Court held that s. 11(d) is offended when an accused may be convicted despite the existence of a reasonable doubt on an essential element of the offence (including those elements required by s. 7 of the *Charter*).

In *Whyte*, [1988] 2 S.C.R. 3, a majority of this Court held that the distinction between elements of the offence and other aspects of the charge is irrelevant to the s. 11(d) inquiry. Thus, the real concern is not whether the accused must disprove an element or prove an excuse, but that an accused may be convicted while a reasonable doubt exists.

Again, both the Crown and a number of interveners have argued that this interpretation of s. 11(d) should not apply in a regulatory setting. I can only reiterate my earlier comment that it is the fact that the state has resorted to the restriction of liberty through imprisonment for enforcement purposes which is determinative of the *Charter* analysis. A person whose liberty has been restricted by way of imprisonment has lost no *less* liberty because he or she is being punished for the commission of a regulatory offence as opposed to a criminal offence. A person whose liberty interest is imperilled is entitled to have the principles of fundamental justice fully observed. The presumption of innocence, guaranteed by s. 11(d), is clearly a principle of fundamental justice.

Given that I have determined, above, that paras. (c) and (d) of s. 37.3(2) must be held to be of no force or effect, the words "he establishes that" must be considered with respect to paras. (a) and (b) of s. 37.3(2). In this context, the words "he establishes that" place a burden on an accused to prove the two elements delineated thereafter *on a balance of probabilities* (see *R. v. Chaulk* [*and Morrissette,* [1990] 3 SCR 1303], at pp. 1317-18). Thus, if an accused fails to prove either of these elements on a balance of probabilities, (assuming the Crown has proved the *actus reus*) that accused will be convicted of false/misleading advertising. The *absence* of due diligence (presence of negligence) is clearly necessary for a finding of guilt. Thus, it seems clear to me that under s. 37.3(2) an accused could be convicted of false/misleading advertising despite the existence of a reasonable doubt as to whether the accused was duly diligent and, therefore, despite the existence of a reasonable doubt as to guilt.

[The reverse burden was not justified under s 1 because of the existence of less restrictive alternatives.]

Parliament clearly had the option of employing a mandatory presumption of negligence (following from proof of the *actus reus*) which could be rebutted by something *less* than an accused's establishing due diligence on a balance of probabilities. This option was, in fact, recommended by the Ontario Law Reform Commission in its *Report on the Basis of Liability for Provincial Offences* (1990). The Commission stated (at p. 48):

> With respect to the burden of proof for strict liability offences, the Commission proposes a compromise solution that balances the fundamental rights of the accused with the need for effective law enforcement. We recommend the enactment of a mandatory presumption rather than a reverse onus. In other words, *in the absence of evidence to the contrary, negligence will be presumed. The Crown will continue to bear the burden of establishing the physical element or actus reus beyond a reasonable doubt. However, in a strict liability case, it will be necessary that evidence of conduct capable of amounting to reasonable care be adduced, either by the testimony of the accused, through the examination or cross-examination of a Crown or defence witness, or in some other way. The accused will merely have an evidentiary burden and will no longer be required to satisfy the persuasive burden of establishing, on a balance of probabilities, that he was not negligent. Where evidence of reasonable care has been adduced, thereby rebutting the presumption, in order to secure a conviction the prosecution should be required to establish the accused's negligence beyond a reasonable doubt.* [Emphasis added.] ...

... The objective of incorporating a mandatory presumption and evidentiary burden into s. 37.3(2) would be to avoid placing an impossible burden on the Crown. Like most public welfare offences, false/misleading advertising is of such a nature that the accused will be in the best position to garner evidence of due diligence. In the absence of *some* explanation by the accused, it will nearly always be impossible for the Crown to prove the absence of due diligence. Indeed, without an evidentiary burden on the accused, the Crown may well be put in the difficult situation which was addressed in *R. v. Chaulk, supra*, whereby the burden of adducing evidence of negligence on an ongoing basis could give rise to intrusions of other *Charter* rights, such as the right to be free from unreasonable search and seizure (s. 8). Thus, the use of a mandatory presumption in s. 37.3(2) would be rationally connected to avoiding this impossible burden, would fall well within the range of means which impair *Charter* rights as little as is reasonably possible, and would be proportional in its effect on the presumption of innocence.

In summary, while the use of a mandatory presumption in s. 37.3(2) would also infringe s. 11(d), it constitutes a less intrusive alternative which would not violate the *Charter* (in that it would constitute a justifiable limit under s. 1).

In light of this alternative, it is my view that the words "he establishes that" do not limit constitutionally protected rights as little as is reasonably possible and that the persuasive burden cannot, therefore, be upheld as a reasonable limit under s. 1. However, even if it can be said that a mandatory presumption along with an evidentiary burden would not attain the objective *as effectively* as a persuasive burden and that the words in question therefore *do* limit *Charter* rights as little as is reasonably possible, it is my view that any marginal increase in the obtaining of the objective (via a persuasive burden on the accused) would be clearly outweighed by the detrimental effect on the presumption of innocence. In other words, if I am wrong in finding that the words in question do not pass the second branch of the proportionality test in *Oakes*, it is my view that the persuasive burden does not pass the third branch of the proportionality test in *Oakes* because the effect of the means chosen on *Charter* rights and freedoms is *not* proportional to the objective. Indeed, here we are postulating legislation enabling the imprisonment of those who were duly diligent but could not prove it on a balance of probabilities, even though there might well have existed a reasonable doubt thereof. Sending the innocent to jail is too high a price.

I also wish to point out that Parliament had the further option of maintaining the persuasive burden on the accused but removing the possibility of imprisonment. The use of a persuasive burden in circumstances where imprisonment was not a possible punishment would be far less intrusive on constitutional rights.

IACOBUCCI J [(with whom Gonthier and Stevenson JJ concurred) agreed that the section violated s 11(d), but held that it was valid under s 1]: At the outset, I would like to point out that it is now clear that a rigid or formalistic approach must be avoided when applying the various criteria of the *Oakes*, [1986] 1 S.C.R. 103, analysis, and that proper consideration must be given to the circumstances and context of a particular case: *R. v. Keegstra*, [1990] 3 S.C.R. 697, at pp. 737-38, *per* Chief Justice Dickson speaking for the majority. In the present case, the special nature of the legislation and offence in question must be kept in mind when applying s. 1 of the *Charter*. In this respect, I agree with Cory J. that what is ultimately involved in this appeal is the ability of federal and provincial governments to pursue social ends through the enactment and enforcement of public welfare legislation. While I abstain from commenting on the dichotomy articulated by Cory J. between "true crimes" and "regulatory offences," I agree with my colleague that the offence of false or misleading advertisement may properly be characterized as a public welfare offence and that the prohibition of such offences is of fundamental importance in Canadian society.

However, it is with respect to the third requirement of the *Oakes* analysis, that I respectfully disagree with the conclusions of Lamer C.J. This step requires a consideration of whether the means chosen impair the right or freedom in question *no more than is necessary to accomplish the desired objective.* Lamer C.J. is of the opinion that the use of a persuasive burden in s. 37.3(2) of the *Competition Act* cannot pass this third step of the *Oakes* analysis because of the presence of an alternative means open to Parliament that would be less intrusive on s. 11(d) of the *Charter* and would "go a long way" in achieving the objective. The alternative in question is the use of a "mandatory presumption of negligence" (following from the proof of the *actus reus*) which could be rebutted by something less than an accused establishing due diligence on a balance of probabilities, i.e., by raising a reasonable doubt as to due diligence. With respect, I cannot agree that such a means would achieve the stated objective as effectively nor would it go a long way in achieving it. Such a means would shift to the accused the burden of simply raising a reasonable doubt as to due diligence and would not thereby allow the effective pursuit of the regulatory objective. It would leave the Crown the legal burden of proving facts largely within the peculiar knowledge of the accused.

CORY J [(with whom L'Heureux-Dubé J concurred) held that the provision did not violate s 11(d)]: Wholesale Travel argues that the placing of a persuasive burden on the accused to establish due diligence on a balance of probabilities violates the presumption of innocence as guaranteed by s. 11(d) of the *Charter*. As the due diligence defence is the essential characteristic of strict liability offences as defined in *Sault Ste. Marie*, [1978] 2 S.C.R. 1299, the appellant's s. 11(d) claim represents a fundamental challenge to the entire regime of regulatory offences in Canada.

In *Sault Ste. Marie*, Dickson J. carefully considered the basic principles of criminal liability, including the presumption of innocence, and balanced them against the public goals sought to be achieved through regulatory measures. He determined that strict liability represented an appropriate compromise between the competing interests involved. This conclusion is no less valid today. The *Charter* was not enacted in a vacuum. The presumption of innocence which it guarantees had long been established and was well recognized at common law. The due diligence defence recognized in *Sault Ste. Marie* which is the target of the present challenge was itself a function of the presumption of innocence.

The reasons for ascribing a different content to the presumption of innocence in the regulatory context are persuasive and compelling. As with the *mens rea* issue, if regulatory mechanisms are to operate effectively, the Crown cannot be required to disprove due diligence beyond a reasonable doubt. Such a requirement would make it virtually impossible for the Crown to prove regulatory offences and would effectively prevent governments from seeking to implement public policy through regulatory means.

Quite simply, the enforcement of regulatory offences would be rendered virtually impossible if the Crown were required to prove negligence beyond a reasonable doubt. The means of proof of reasonable care will be peculiarly within the knowledge and ability of the regulated accused. Only the accused will be in a position to bring forward evidence relevant to the question of due diligence.

The conclusion that strict liability does not violate either s. 7 or s. 11(d) of the *Charter* is supported by the American approach to regulatory offences. Generally speaking, American courts have not recognized an intermediate category of strict liability. Rather, the U.S. Supreme Court has held that, where the person charged is aware of the regulated nature of the impugned conduct, it is constitutionally permissible to enact absolute liability offences, even where imprisonment is available as a penalty: see, for example, *United States v. Balint*, 258 U.S. 250 (1922); *United States v. Dotterweich*, 320 U.S. 277 (1943); *Morissette v. United States*, 342 U.S. 246 (1952); *Lambert v. California*, 355 U.S. 225 (1957). Furthermore, even in the case of serious criminal offences, it has been held that placing a persuasive burden on the accused to establish a defence does not violate the presumption of innocence: see *Patterson v. New York*, 432 U.S. 197 (1977); *Martin v. Ohio*, 480 U.S. 228 (1987). The constitutional validity of regulatory legislation which imposes strict liability would, under the American approach, seem to be beyond question.

[The result was 5:4 that the reverse onus provision should be upheld.]

In *R v Ellis-Don Ltd*, [1992] 1 SCR 840, (1990), 1 OR (3d) 193 (CA), the Supreme Court of Canada followed *Wholesale Travel* and allowed an appeal from an Ontario Court of Appeal decision that had held that s 37(2) of the *Occupational Health and Safety Act* as well as the reverse onus under *Sault Ste Marie* violated s 11(d) of the Charter. The majority of the Court of Appeal had held that the reversal could not be justified under s 1 of the Charter. Galligan JA stated:

It is now settled that s. 11(d) of the *Charter* implies proof of guilt beyond reasonable doubt. The effect of the onus, created by s. 37(2) of the Act and by the common law in *Sault Ste. Marie*, to prove the defence of due diligence on the balance of probabilities means that a court is required to convict an accused if it is not satisfied on the balance of probabilities that the accused has exercised due diligence even though it may have a reasonable doubt on the issue. It is a commonplace that it is unacceptable for someone to be convicted of an offence when there is a reasonable doubt about guilt. The constitutional issue is thus whether the statutory objective, significantly important as it is, justifies the imposition of that unsatisfactory situation. I am seriously troubled about how it could be said that the objective of this Act is so pressingly important that a risk should be taken of convicting someone who might be innocent. Important as the protection of workers' health and safety in the workplace may be I am unable to say that it is more important than protecting innocent citizens from homicide. Yet the law does not permit the conviction of a person charged with murder if the court has a doubt about his guilt. ...

I do not think that it is necessary to strike out the words in s. 37(2) or in the common law defence which impose upon the accused the burden of proving the defence of due diligence. It is sufficient that they be interpreted as imposing upon the accused only the evidential burden of showing some evidence which could raise a reasonable doubt on the issue of due diligence. The defence of due diligence both under s. 37(2) of the Act and at common law remains a viable defence. The defence of due diligence must be given effect to if at the end of all of the evidence the court is left in a state of reasonable doubt about whether in the particular circumstances the accused did in fact act with due diligence.

Houlden JA took the same approach:

When a person can be convicted and subjected to a heavy fine or imprisonment, even though the trier of fact has a reasonable doubt about whether the accused exercised due diligence, I believe there is a lack of proportionality between the effects and the objective. With respect, I would adopt the view of the Ontario Law Reform Commission in its "Report on the Basis of Liability for Provincial Offences," 1990, at pp. 47-48 on the necessity for preserving the presumption of innocence in strict liability offences.

Carthy JA dissented, stating:

Freedoms must live side by side with structure and order. Section 1 is where the balance is assessed. In my judgment the balance of probabilities test is a necessary, proper, fair and justified means of maintaining a structure that protects the safety of working persons and at the same time impinges modestly and to little account in practical application upon the employer. All rights and freedoms, once declared, tend to appear absolute. Section 1 provides a means of restraint and balance against that extreme to meet society's greater needs. Safety in the workplace is such a need.

Lamer CJ stated orally for the Supreme Court:

We are all of the view that this appeal must succeed. The existence of a restriction to s. 11(d) is governed by this court's decision in *R. v. Wholesale Travel Group Inc.*, [1991] 3 S.C.R. 154. The s. 1 analysis in *Wholesale* is applicable here, as there is no difference of substance between the nature of the legislation in that case and this one.

Accordingly, the appeal is allowed and the case is remitted to the Court of Appeal for disposal of the other grounds of appeal raised below and not dealt with by the Court of Appeal.

For a comment on the 1990 Ontario Law Reform Commission *Report on the Basis of Liability for Provincial Offences*, see K Roach (1990) 69 Can Bar Rev 802. For a contrasting view see BP Archibald, "Liability for Provincial Offences: Fault, Penalty and the Principles of Fundamental Justice in Canada" (1991) 14 Dal LJ 65. See also A Brudner, "Imprisonment and Strict Liability" (1990) 40 UTLJ 738; C Ruby & K Jull, "The Charter and Regulatory Offences: A Wholesale Revision" (1992) 14 CR (4th) 226; C Tollefson, "R v Wholesale Travel Group Inc" (1992) 71 Can Bar Rev 369; D Stuart, "The Supreme Court Drastically Reduces the Constitutional Requirement of Fault: A Triumph of Pragmatism and Law Enforcement Expediency" (1993) 15 CR (4th) 88; and J Keefe, "The Due Diligence Defence: A Wholesale Review" (1993) 35 Crim LQ 480.

ADDITIONAL READING

Colvin, E & S Anand. *Principles of Criminal Law*, 3rd ed (Toronto: Carswell, 2007) ch 6.

Jull, KE, TL Archibald & KW Roach. *Regulatory and Corporate Liability: From Due Diligence to Risk Management* (Aurora, Ont: Canada Law Book, as updated).

Manning, M & P Sankoff. *Manning, Mewett & Sankoff: Criminal Law*, 4th ed (Toronto: LexisNexis, 2009) ch 7.

Roach, K. *Criminal Law*, 6th ed (Toronto: Irwin Law, 2015) ch 5.

Sharpe, RJ. "Strict Liability and Due Diligence in Public Welfare Offences: R v City of Sault Ste Marie" (1979) 3 Can Bus LJ 453.

Stuart, D. *Canadian Criminal Law*, 7th ed (Toronto: Carswell, 2014) ch 3.

CHAPTER SEVEN

Fault or Mens Rea

The first essential element for criminal liability—the act or *actus reus* requirement—was introduced in Chapter 5. This chapter introduces the second essential element—the *mens rea* requirement. Described by various terms at different times, including "guilty mind," "mental element," "mental state," and, most recently, "fault," this requirement has a long lineage.

From the earliest days of the common law, *mens rea* has been a key precondition for attributing criminal liability. Early English commentators seized on a Latin legal maxim to state the rule, "*actus non facit reum nisi mens sit rea*," which translates literally as "an act does not become guilty unless the mind is guilty."

In Canada, there has long been a presumption of statutory interpretation that *mens rea* forms a part of all *criminal* offences. As Estey J explained in *Gaunt and Watts v The Queen*, [1953] 1 SCR 505 at 511:

> It is a general rule that *mens rea* is an essential ingredient of criminal offences. ... While an offence of which *mens rea* is not an essential ingredient may be created by legislation, in view of the general rule a section creating an offence ought not to be so construed unless Parliament has, by express language or necessary implication, disclosed such an intention.

Similar statements can be found in a number of Supreme Court of Canada decisions (see *Beaver v The Queen*, [1957] SCR 531 at 537-38, 542 and *R v Prue*, [1979] 2 SCR 547 at 551-54).

Just as long-standing as *mens rea* has been confusion regarding what it entails. As Stephen J observed in *R v Tolson* (1889), 23 QBD 168 (Ct for Cr Cases Reserved):

> Though this phrase is in common use, I think it most unfortunate, and not only likely to mislead, but actually misleading, on the following grounds. It naturally suggests that, apart from all particular definitions of crimes, such a thing exists as a "mens rea," or "guilty mind," which is always expressly or by implication involved in every definition. This is obviously not the case, for the

mental elements of different crimes differ widely. "Mens rea" means in the case of murder, malice aforethought; in the case of theft, an intention to steal; in the case of rape, an intention to have forcible connection with a woman without her consent; and in the case of receiving stolen goods, knowledge that the goods were stolen. In some cases it denotes mere inattention. For instance, in the case of manslaughter by negligence it may mean forgetting to notice a signal. It appears confusing to call so many dissimilar states of mind by one name. It seems contradictory indeed to describe a mere absence of mind as "mens rea," or guilty mind. The expression again is likely to and often does mislead. To an unlegal mind it suggests that by the law of England no act is a crime which is done from laudable motives, in other words, that immorality is essential to crime.

Like most legal Latin maxims, the maxim on mens rea appears to me to be too short and antithetical to be of much practical value. It is, indeed, more like the title of a treatise than a practical rule. ...

The principle involved appears to me, when fully considered, to amount to no more than this. The full definition of every crime contains expressly or by implication a proposition as to a state of mind. Therefore, if the mental element of any conduct alleged to be a crime is proved to have been absent in any given case, the crime so defined is not committed; or, again, if a crime is fully defined, nothing amounts to that crime which does not satisfy that definition. Crimes are in the present day much more accurately defined by statute or otherwise than they formerly were. The mental element of most crimes is marked by one of the words "maliciously," "fraudulently," "negligently," or "knowingly," but it is the general—I might, I think, say, the invariable—practice of the legislature to leave unexpressed some of the mental elements of crime. In all cases whatever, competent age, sanity, and some degree of freedom from some kinds of coercion are assumed to be essential to criminality, but I do not believe they are ever introduced into any statute by which any particular crime is defined.

The meanings of the words "malice," "negligence," and "fraud" in relation to particular crimes has been ascertained by numerous cases. Malice means one thing in relation to murder, another in relation to the *Malicious Mischief Act*, and a third in relation to libel, and so of fraud and negligence.

The English Law Commission Working Paper No 31, *The Mental Element in Crime* (1970), states:

One of the major stumbling blocks to the orderly development of English criminal law has been the confusion that has existed for the past 100 years or so over the question whether the language used in the creation of a statutory offence imports full *mens rea* (intention, knowledge or recklessness), some fault element short of *mens rea*, i.e., negligence, or some form of "absolute" or "strict" liability.

The Government of Canada document *The Criminal Law in Canadian Society* (1982) states at 48:

To summarize, it is vital to retain the standard of responsibility and fault for a finding of criminal liability, because of the significant meaning and impact of the criminal process and criminal sanctions. Second, it is important to clarify the ambiguities which currently exist as to the precise standard of culpability required for each criminal offence. Third, it is not necessary or desirable to confine the criminal law to acts committed by individuals against other individuals; rather, it is advisable to clarify and give greater consideration to the liability of organizations, and individuals acting within organizations, where serious harm to an individual or to the general good is caused or threatened.

These excerpts remind us that it is important to approach the issue of *mens rea* or fault with some care. There is no single type of fault applicable to crimes in general. To determine the fault requirement for a particular offence, the wording of the relevant enactment must be consulted along with principles of interpretation relating to fault developed by our courts over time. It is those principles that supply the focus of much of this chapter. It is also important to remember that many offences have more than one mental element and different types of fault might be applicable to different elements of the *actus reus*. A good example of this is the offence of criminal harassment (or "stalking"), which is found in s 264.1 of the *Criminal Code*. For a discussion of the complex fault requirements for that offence, see *R v Krushel* (2000), 142 CCC (3d) 1 (Ont CA). It is also necessary not only to identify the appropriate level of fault (that is, intent, knowledge, recklessness, wilful blindness, negligence, etc.), but also to describe the relationship of the particular fault element to the *actus reus* or prohibited act.

This chapter focuses on "true" criminal offences. As noted above, such offences are presumed to have a *mens rea* requirement. Indeed, as discussed below, the *Canadian Charter of Rights and Freedoms* requires that there be some fault element for all criminal offences and even demands subjective fault for a few crimes that carry a high degree of stigma—for example, murder.

In Section I, various legislative attempts to provide comprehensive fault definitions are considered. Section II introduces and explains the presumption in favour of subjective fault standards and the efforts necessary to displace it. Section III considers subjective and Section IV objective fault requirements. In Section V, constitutional considerations are raised once again. Finally, in Section VI, the mistake of fact defence is introduced and explained.

I. LEGISLATIVE DEFINITIONS OF FAULT

In Canada, there is no uniform definition of the fault requirements that apply to offences. For example, the *Criminal Code* does not include a comprehensive part (referred to by academics and law reformers as a "general part") that provides definitions of commonly used fault-related terms, like "intention," "knowledge," "wilful," "purpose," or "criminal negligence." The definitional enterprise is left largely to the courts to interpret terms on an offence-by-offence, term-by-term basis. This gives rise to a lack of clarity and to inconsistency between offences. This state of the law has led law reformers and others to call for the creation of a "general part." Efforts have been made by law reformers in Canada, the United Kingdom, and the United States. Despite a very respectable attempt at this endeavour by the now defunct Law Reform Commission of Canada (see *Recodifying Criminal Law*, below), Parliament has shown little interest in reshaping the *Criminal Code* in this way. The following excerpts explore this issue and provide some examples of attempts to codify general concepts.

American Law Institute, *Model Penal Code*
Proposed Official Draft, 1962

[The institute's *Model Penal Code* provides in the part on general principles of liability as follows:]

Section 2.02. General Requirements of Culpability.

(1) Minimum Requirements of Culpability.

Except as provided in Section 2.05, a person is not guilty of an offense unless he acted purposely, knowingly, recklessly or negligently, as the law may require, with respect to each material element of the offense.

(2) Kinds of Culpability Defined.

(a) Purposely.

A person acts purposely with respect to a material element of an offense when:

   (i)   if the element involves the nature of his conduct or a result thereof, it is his conscious object to engage in conduct of that nature or to cause such a result; and

   (ii) if the element involves the attendant circumstances, he is aware of the existence of such circumstances or he believes or hopes that they exist.

(b) Knowingly.

A person acts knowingly with respect to a material element of an offense when:

   (i)   if the element involves the nature of his conduct or the attendant circumstances, he is aware that his conduct is of that nature or that such circumstances exist; and

   (ii) if the element involves a result of his conduct, he is aware that it is practically certain that his conduct will cause such a result.

(c) Recklessly.

A person acts recklessly with respect to a material element of an offense when he consciously disregards a substantial and unjustifiable risk that the material element exists or will result from his conduct. The risk must be of such a nature and degree that, considering the nature and purpose of the actor's conduct and the circumstances known to him, its disregard involves a gross deviation from the standard of conduct that a law-abiding person would observe in the actor's situation.

(d) Negligently.

A person acts negligently with respect to a material element of an offense when he should be aware of a substantial and unjustifiable risk that the material element exists or will result from his conduct. The risk must be of such a nature and degree that the actor's failure to perceive it, considering the nature and purpose of his conduct and the circumstances known to him, involves a gross deviation from the standard of care that a reasonable person would observe in the actor's situation.

(3) Culpability Required Unless Otherwise Provided.

When the culpability sufficient to establish a material element of an offense is not prescribed by law, such element is established if a person acts purposely, knowingly or recklessly with respect thereto.

(4) Prescribed Culpability Requirement Applies to All Material Elements.

When the law defining an offense prescribes the kind of culpability that is sufficient for the commission of an offense, without distinguishing among the material elements thereof, such provisions shall apply to all the material elements of the offense, unless a contrary purpose plainly appears.

(5) Substitutes for Negligence, Recklessness and Knowledge.

When the law provides that negligence suffices to establish an element of an offense, such element also is established if a person acts purposely, knowingly or recklessly. When recklessness suffices to establish an element, such element also is established if a person acts purposely or knowingly. When acting knowingly suffices to establish an element, such element also is established if a person acts purposely.

(6) Requirement of Purpose Satisfied If Purpose Is Conditional.

When a particular purpose is an element of an offense, the element is established although such purpose is conditional, unless the condition negatives the harm or evil sought to be prevented by the law defining the offense.

(7) Requirement of Knowledge Satisfied by Knowledge of High Probability.

When knowledge of the existence of a particular fact is an element of an offense, such knowledge is established if a person is aware of a high probability of its existence, unless he actually believes that it does not exist.

(8) Requirement of Wilfulness Satisfied by Acting Knowingly.

A requirement that an offense be committed wilfully is satisfied if a person acts knowingly with respect to the material elements of the offense, unless a purpose to impose further requirements appears.

(9) Culpability as to Illegality of Conduct.

Neither knowledge nor recklessness or negligence as to whether conduct constitutes an offense or as to the existence, meaning or application of the law determining the elements of an offense is an element of such offense, unless the definition of the offense or the Code so provides.

(10) Culpability as Determinant of Grade of Offense.

When the grade or degree of an offense depends on whether the offense is committed purposely, knowingly, recklessly or negligently, its grade or degree shall be the lowest for which the determinative kind of culpability is established with respect to any material element of the offense.

_____

English Law Commission, *The Mental Element in Crime*
Working Paper No 31 (1970)

[The commission suggests the following legislative definitions for existing and future offences:]

Intention and knowledge

7.A.(1) a person intends an event not only
   (a) when his purpose is to cause that event but also
   (b) when he has no substantial doubt that that event will result from his conduct. (First alternative)
   (c) when he foresees that that event will probably result from his conduct. (Second alternative)
(2) a person is not by reason only of proposition 7A(1)(b) to be taken to intend the wrongdoing of others.
(3) a person knows of circumstances not only when he knows that they exist but also when
   (a) he has no substantial doubt that they exist. (First alternative)
   (b) he knows that they probably exist. (Second alternative)

Recklessness

B. a person is reckless if,
   (a) knowing that there is a risk that an event may result from his conduct or that a circumstance may exist, he takes that risk, and
   (b) it is unreasonable for him to take it having regard to the degree and nature of the risk which he knows to be present.

Negligence

C. a person is negligent if he fails to exercise such care, skill or foresight as a reasonable man in his situation would exercise.

Law Reform Commission of Canada, *Recodifying Criminal Law*
Report 31 (1987) at 143-44

2(4) Requirements for Culpability.

(a) General Requirements as to Level of Culpability.

Unless otherwise provided:

   (i) where the definition of a crime requires purpose, no one is liable unless as concerns its elements he acts
   (A) purposely as to the conduct specified by that definition,
   (B) purposely as to the consequences, if any, so specified, and

        (C) knowingly or recklessly as to the circumstances, if any, so specified;

(ii) where the definition of a crime requires recklessness, no one is liable unless as concerns its elements he acts

        (A) purposely as to the conduct specified by that definition,

        (B) recklessly as to the consequences, if any, so specified, and

        (C) recklessly as to the circumstances, whether specified or not;

(iii) where the definition of a crime requires negligence, no one is liable unless as concerns its elements he acts

        (A) negligently as to the conduct specified by that definition,

        (B) negligently as to the consequences, if any, so specified, and

        (C) negligently as to the circumstances, whether specified or not.

(b) Definitions.

"Purposely."

(i) A person acts purposely as to conduct if he means to engage in such conduct, and, in the case of an omission, if he also knows the circumstances giving rise to the duty to act or is reckless as to their existence.

(ii) A person acts purposely as to a consequence if he acts in order to effect:

        (A) that consequence; or

        (B) another consequence which he knows involves that consequence.

"Recklessly."

A person is reckless as to consequences or circumstances if, in acting as he does, he is conscious that such consequences will probably result or that such circumstances probably obtain.

[Alternative:]

"Recklessly."

A person is reckless as to consequences or circumstances if, in acting as he does, he consciously takes a risk, which in the circumstances known to him is highly unreasonable to take, that such consequences may result or that such circumstances may obtain.

"Negligently."

A person is negligent as to conduct, circumstances or consequences if it is a marked departure from the ordinary standard of reasonable care to engage in such conduct, to take the risk (conscious or otherwise) that such consequences will result, or to take the risk (conscious or otherwise) that such circumstances obtain.

(c) Greater Culpability Requirement Satisfies Lesser.

(i) Where the definition of a crime requires negligence, a person may be liable if he acts, or omits to act, purposely or recklessly as to one or more of the elements in that definition.

(ii)   Where the definition of a crime requires recklessness, a person may be liable if
       he acts, or omits to act, purposely as to one or more of the elements in that
       definition.

(d) Residual Rule.

Where the definition of a crime does not explicitly specify the requisite level of culpability,
it shall be interpreted as requiring purpose.

II. THE CHOICE BETWEEN A SUBJECTIVE AND
AN OBJECTIVE STANDARD

There are different ways of classifying the fault requirement for particular crimes. One fundamental distinction is between those aspects of fault that focus on what passed through the
mind of the accused at the relevant time (subjective fault) and those that are only concerned
with whether the accused measured up to some normative objective standard (objective
fault). This is one of the most important distinctions to be made in substantive criminal law.
As the excerpt from *R v ADH* below makes clear, there is a presumption in favour of subjective
fault that can only be displaced by Parliament through the use of clear language.

R v ADH
Supreme Court of Canada
2013 SCC 28, [2013] 2 SCR 269

[In this case, the Supreme Court had to decide whether the fault element for the offence
of child abandonment found in s 218 of the *Criminal Code* was to be assessed subjectively
or objectively. That provision provides that everyone "who unlawfully abandons or exposes a child who is under the age of ten years, so that its life is or is likely to be endangered or its health is or is likely to be permanently injured" is guilty of an offence. The
majority concluded that a subjective standard applied. In so concluding, they said the
following regarding the principles that govern the choice between a subjective or an objective standard for particular offences.]

CROMWELL J (McLachlin CJ and Fish, Abella, Cromwell, and Karakatsanis JJ concurring,
Rothstein and Moldaver JJ dissenting): ...
     [23] An important part of the context in which we must interpret s. 218 is the presump-
tion that Parliament intends crimes to have a subjective fault element. The Court has stated
and relied on this interpretative principle on many occasions: see, e.g., *Watts v. The Queen*,
[1953] 1 S.C.R. 505, at p. 511; *R. v. Rees*, [1956] S.C.R. 640, at p. 652; *Beaver v. The Queen*,
[1957] S.C.R. 531, at pp. 542-43; *R. v. Sault Ste. Marie*, [1978] 2 S.C.R. 1299, at pp. 1303
and 1309-10; *R. v. Prue*, [1979] 2 S.C.R. 547, at pp. 551 and 553; *R. v. Bernard*, [1988] 2
S.C.R. 833, at p. 871; *R. v. Martineau*, [1990] 2 S.C.R. 633, at p. 645; *R. v. Théroux*, [1993]
2 S.C.R. 5, at p. 18; *R. v. Lucas*, [1998] 1 S.C.R. 439, at para. 64. Perhaps the classic statement is that of Dickson J. (as he then was) for the Court in *Sault Ste. Marie*:

In the case of true crimes there is a presumption that a person should not be held liable for the wrongfulness of his act if that act is without *mens rea*. ...

... Where the offence is criminal, the Crown must establish a mental element, namely, that the accused who committed the prohibited act did so intentionally or recklessly, with knowledge of the facts constituting the offence, or with wilful blindness toward them. Mere negligence is excluded from the concept of the mental element required for conviction. Within the context of a criminal prosecution a person who fails to make such enquiries as a reasonable and prudent person would make, or who fails to know facts he should have known, is innocent in the eyes of the law. [Citations omitted; pp. 1303 and 1309-10.]

[24] Notwithstanding these many statements, the Crown in effect submits that there is no such presumption of legislative intent because it has not always been applied. The Crown notes that there are many offences in the *Code* that do not require subjective fault and further that there is no absolute rule requiring complete symmetry between the fault element and the prohibited consequences of the offence. In my view, however, these points do not negate the existence of the presumption of legislative intent. They show merely that the presumption does not invariably determine the outcome of a full contextual and purposive interpretation of a particular provision.

[25] Presumptions of legislative intent are not self-applying rules. They are instead principles of interpretation. They do not, on their own, prescribe the outcome of interpretation, but rather set out broad principles that ought to inform it. As Professor Sullivan has observed, presumptions of legislative intent, such as this one, serve as a way in which the courts recognize and incorporate important values into the legal context in which legislation is drafted and should be interpreted. These values both inform judicial understanding of legislation and play an important role in assessing competing interpretations: R. Sullivan, *Sullivan and Driedger on the Construction of Statutes* (4th ed. 2002), at p. 365.

[26] Professor Côté has described how these presumptions may inform the legal context in which legislation is drafted. He put it this way: "In some sense, presumptions of intent form part of the enactment's context, as they reflect ideas which can be assumed to have been both present in the mind of the legislature and sufficiently current as to render their explicit mention unnecessary": P.-A. Côté, in collaboration with S. Beaulac and M. Devinat, *The Interpretation of Legislation in Canada* (4th ed. 2011), at p. 470; see also R. Cross, *Statutory Interpretation* (3rd ed. 1995), by J. Bell and G. Engle, at pp. 165-67, and K. Roach, "Common Law Bills of Rights as Dialogue Between Courts and Legislatures" (2005), 55 *U.T.L.J.* 733. Parliament must be understood to know that this presumption will likely be applied unless some contrary intention is evident in the legislation.

[27] As for the role of the presumption of subjective fault in assessing competing interpretations, it sets out an important value underlying our criminal law. It has been aptly termed one of the "presumptive principles of criminal justice": *R. v. Beatty*, 2008 SCC 5, [2008] 1 S.C.R. 49, *per* Charron J., at paras. 22-23. While the presumption must—and often does—give way to clear expressions of a different legislative intent, it nonetheless incorporates an important value in our criminal law, that the morally innocent should not be punished. This has perhaps never been better expressed than it was by Dickson J. in *Pappajohn*, at pp. 138-39:

There rests now, at the foundation of our system of criminal justice, the precept that a man cannot be adjudged guilty and subjected to punishment, unless the commission of the crime was voluntarily directed by a willing mind. ... Parliament can, of course, by express words, create criminal offences for which a guilty intention is not an essential ingredient. Equally, *mens rea* is not requisite in a wide category of statutory offences which are concerned with public welfare, health and safety. Subject to these exceptions, *mens rea*, consisting of some positive states of mind, such as evil intention, or knowledge of the wrongfulness of the act, or reckless disregard of consequences, must be proved by the prosecution.

[28] Viewed in this way, the presumption of subjective fault is not an outdated rule of construction which is at odds with the modern approach to statutory interpretation repeatedly endorsed by the Court. On the contrary, the presumption forms part of the context which the modern approach requires to be considered.

[29] ... [T]here is nothing in the text or context of the child abandonment offence to suggest that Parliament intended to depart from requiring subjective fault. In fact, the text, scheme and purpose of the provision support the view that subjective fault is required. To the extent that Parliament's intent is unclear, the presumption of subjective fault ought to have its full operation in this case.

Appeal dismissed.

III. SUBJECTIVE STANDARDS OF FAULT

Given the presumption favouring them, subjective fault standards dominate in Canadian criminal law. However, merely because subjective fault is a formal requirement for an offence does not mean that objective considerations are irrelevant. What a reasonable person would have realized or known may be of value in the determination of what the accused actually thought. This point is made in the cases excerpted below.

R v Buzzanga and Durocher
Ontario Court of Appeal
(1979), 49 CCC (2d) 369

MARTIN JA: Since people are usually able to foresee the consequences of their acts, if a person does an act likely to produce certain consequences it is, in general, reasonable to assume that the accused also foresaw the probable consequences of his act and if he, nevertheless, acted so as to produce those consequences, that he intended them. The greater the likelihood of the relevant consequences ensuing from the accused's act, the easier it is to draw the inference that he intended those consequences. The purpose of this process, however, is to determine what the particular accused intended, not to fix him with the intention that a reasonable person might be assumed to have in the circumstances, where doubt exists as to the actual intention of the accused. The accused's testimony, if he gives evidence as to what was in his mind, is important material to be weighed with the other evidence in determining whether the necessary intent has been established. Indeed, Mr. Justice Devlin, in his charge to the jury in *R. v. Adams* (*The Times*, April 10, 1957), said that where the accused testified as to what was in his mind and the jury "thought he might be telling the truth," they would "have the best evidence available on what was in his own mind."

R v Tennant and Naccarato
Ontario Court of Appeal
(1975), 23 CCC (2d) 80

THE COURT: ... Where liability is imposed on a subjective basis, what a reasonable man ought to have anticipated is merely evidence from which a conclusion may be drawn that the accused anticipated the same consequences. On the other hand, where the test is objective, what a reasonable man should have anticipated constitutes the basis of liability.

Courts regularly refer to this idea as the "common sense inference." In short, a sane and sober person can usually be taken to intend the natural and probable consequences of his or her actions. In the *Model Jury Instructions* published by the Canadian Judicial Council, trial judges are advised to explain this idea to jurors in non-legalistic terms: "You may infer, as a matter of common sense, that a person usually knows what the predictable consequences of his or her actions are, and means to bring them about." The Supreme Court of Canada has specifically endorsed this very wording. (See *R v Walle*, 2012 SCC 41 at para 64, [2012] 2 SCR 438.) In doing so, it noted the importance of such an instruction, as it "provides the jury with a marker against which to measure the rather amorphous concept of intent. A proper instruction also sounds a cautionary note. The jurors are admonished that the inference is permissive, not presumptive, and that before acting on it, they must carefully consider the evidence that points away from it" (*ibid* at para 63).

What about the natural consequences of one's inaction? Is it permissible to draw an inference of intention from an accused's failure to take action? Much depends on context. In *R v Bottineau*, 2011 ONCA 194, the accused was charged with murdering her grandson who was in her care. The allegation was that over an extended period of time she denied him the necessaries of life (food and medical care) while subjectively realizing this would cause his death, which made her guilty of murder (as opposed to manslaughter for unlawfully causing the death by failing to provide the necessaries of life). On appeal, it was argued that the trial judge erred in drawing an inference of intention from her inaction, especially in light of evidence that suggested she was of diminished intellectual capacity. The Court of Appeal rejected this argument. Doherty JA explained:

[33] We cannot accept this submission. While it is true as a generalization that it is harder to infer a state of mind from a failure to act than from actions, the inference-drawing process is not governed by generalizations, but by the evidence and the findings of fact in the specific case.

[34] The distinction between an action and an omission is often one of semantics. Starving Jeffrey could be seen as an action (withholding adequate nutrition from him), or as an omission (failing to give Jeffrey adequate nutrition). The availability of the inference that a person intended or foresaw a certain result as a probable consequence of conduct will depend on the nature of that conduct and not its categorization as an act or omission.

[35] On the facts as found by the trial judge, the appellants' conduct consisted of the egregious, multi-faceted, long-term mistreatment of Jeffrey combined with the failure to seek medical assistance for Jeffrey in the final weeks and months of his life when his dire medical condition was obvious. A reasonable trier of fact could readily conclude that Jeffrey's death was the obvious and inevitable consequence of his mistreatment. A reasonable trier of fact could equally

infer that at some point during the mistreatment of Jeffrey the appellants appreciated that their continued abuse and neglect of Jeffrey would probably lead to his death.

[36] Whether the appellants' conduct is described as a series of omissions, a series of actions, or a blend of the two, their conduct was of a nature that readily permitted the inference that the appellants knew their conduct would probably bring about Jeffrey's death and yet they chose to persist in that conduct. The facts as found by the trial judge clearly justified the inferences he drew with respect to each appellant's state of mind.

Intention and Motive

This part of the chapter examines the two basic subjective fault requirements of intention and knowledge. They are at the core of subjective states of liability. Before looking at how the courts have analyzed these concepts, it is important to understand the difference between intention and the concept of motive.

It is sensible to begin with an important distinction, one that is not readily apparent to the layperson: the difference between motive and intention. Justice Dickson (as he then was) summed up the key differences in *R v Lewis*, [1979] 2 SCR 821:

> In ordinary parlance, the words "intent" and "motive" are frequently used interchangeably, but in the criminal law they are distinct. In most criminal trials, the mental element, the *mens rea* with which the Court is concerned, relates to "intent," i.e., the exercise of a free will to use particular means to produce a particular result, rather than with "motive," i.e., that which precedes and induces the exercise of the will. The mental element of a crime ordinarily involves no reference to motive: 11 Hals., 4th ed. (1976), p. 17, para. 11. . . .
>
> Accepting the term "motive" in a criminal law sense as meaning "ulterior intention," it is possible, I think, upon the authorities, to formulate a number of propositions.
>
> (1) As evidence, motive is always relevant and hence evidence of motive is admissible.
>
> This statement is drawn from Smith and Hogan where the authors state (p. 64):
>
> > This means simply that, if the prosecution can prove that D had a motive for committing the crime, they may do so since the existence of a motive makes it more likely that D in fact did commit it. Men do not usually act without a motive. . . .
>
> While evidence of motive is always relevant on the issue of intent or identity, motive must be evidenced by human acts and there are limits to the extent to which such acts may be introduced as motive: see *R. v. Barbour*, [1938] S.C.R. 465.
>
> (2) Motive is no part of the crime and is legally irrelevant to criminal responsibility. It is not an essential element of the prosecution's case as a matter of law.
>
> In language reminiscent of Smith and Hogan, Schroeder J.A. puts the matter this way in *R. v. Imrich* (1974), 6 O.R. (2d) 496:
>
> > When a defendant is indisputably shown to be the criminal, evidence of motive is immaterial. Motive relates to a consequence ulterior to the *mens rea* and the *actus reus* and, adopting this criterion, motive is irrelevant to criminal responsibility, viz., a man may be lawfully convicted of a crime whatever his motive may be or even if he has no motive. It is, of course, relevant as evidence for if the prosecution can prove that the defendant had a

motive for committing the crime it may do so, since the existence of a motive makes it more likely that the defendant did in fact commit it. ... All matters of motive are for the jury and are not to be dealt with as matters of law. Motive is never to be confused with intent and it is wholly inaccurate to say that without motive there can be no intent.

This majority view of the case was upheld upon subsequent appeal to this Court:

(3) Proved absence of motive is always an important fact in favour of the accused and ordinarily worthy of note in a charge to the jury.

In support of this proposition is the judgment of Davis J., in *Markadonis v. The King*, [1935] S.C.R. 657, at p. 665, who, prefacing his remarks with these words:

Moreover, I cannot escape from the view that the charge of the learned trial Judge did not present certain aspects of the case in favour of the accused that should have been dealt with and considered. ...

(4) Conversely, proved presence of motive may be an important factual ingredient in the Crown's case, notably on the issues of identity and intention, when the evidence is purely circumstantial.

This is, in effect, merely a restatement of Davis J.'s comments in *Markadonis*, supra. In *Barbour*, Mr. Justice Kerwin in dissent pointed out: "While the Crown is not obliged to adduce evidence of motive, the presence or absence of motive may be of very considerable importance." McWilliams, at pp. 299-300, refers to the opening statement of the Attorney-General in *Palmer*'s Case (1856) [see JF Stephen, *A History of the Criminal Law of England* (London: Macmillan, 1883) vol 3 at 389] that "if we find strong motives, the more readily shall we be led to believe in the probability of the crime having been committed; but if we find an absence of motive, the probability is the other way."

(5) Motive is therefore always a question of fact and evidence and the necessity of referring to motive in the charge to the jury falls within the general duty of the trial Judge "to not only outline the theories of the prosecution and defence but to give the jury matters of evidence essential in arriving at a just conclusion."

The latter portion of this proposition is drawn from the judgment of Mr. Justice Spence in *Colpitts v. The Queen*, [1965] S.C.R. 739, at p. 752, referred to by both Ritchie J., in *Imrich* at p. 626, and by Dubin J.A. at p. 509, in support of their differing views of that case. I think this latter conflict is instructive—in each case, there will clearly be differences of opinion as to whether certain matters of evidence are essential to the case for either party. A good deal of latitude should be allowed to the judgment of the trial Judge as to which matters of evidence are essential or not.

(6) Each case will turn on its own unique set of circumstances. The issue of motive is always a matter of degree.

Although motive is not usually a required element of criminal fault, Parliament has required proof of a religious or political objective or motive in addition to other intent requirements in its definition of terrorist activities in s 83.01(1)(b)(i)(A) of the *Criminal Code*. In *R v Khawaja*, 2012 SCC 69, [2012] 3 SCR 555, the Supreme Court rejected a claim that the motive clause violated freedom of expression and religion. It concluded:

Criminal liability should not be based on a person's political, religious or ideological views. Police should not target people as potential suspects solely because they hold or express particular views. Nor should the justice system employ improper stereotyping as a tool in legislation, investigation or prosecution. In the present case, the impugned provision is clearly drafted in a manner respectful of diversity, as it allows for the non-violent expression of political, religious or ideological views [see s 83.01(1.1)]. It raises no concerns with respect to improper stereotyping.

The following case demonstrates how the issue of intent can become easily confused with motive in specific contexts.

R v Steane
Court of Criminal Appeal, England
[1947] 1 KB 997

[Steane, a British subject, was an actor who had been employed in Germany prior to the outbreak of the Second World War. He was in Germany with his wife and two sons when the war commenced.

On July 5, 1945, following the cessation of hostilities, Steane gave a statement to an officer of the British Intelligence Service in which he admitted to working for the German broadcasting service during the war. He had apparently read "the news" on German radio and assisted with the production of films at the behest of the Nazi regime.

Based on his admission, Steane was charged with doing acts likely to assist the enemy, with intent to assist the enemy, contrary to regulation 2A of the *Defence (General) Regulations, 1939*. The regulation provided that: "If with intent to assist the enemy, any person does any act which is likely to assist the enemy ... then, without prejudice to the law relating to treason, he shall be guilty of an offence against this regulation and shall, on conviction on indictment, be liable to penal servitude for life."

At trial, Steane testified that in September 1939, shortly after the war commenced, he was arrested and questioned. At the completion of the interview he was ordered to "Say Heil Hitler, you dirty swine." When he refused, he was struck in the face and lost several teeth. He was thereafter imprisoned.

Steane testified that around Christmas 1939 he was sent for by Joseph Goebbels, propaganda minister for the Nazi regime, who asked him to participate in radio broadcasts. He refused. He was thereafter threatened to cooperate. He reluctantly participated in a voice test but deliberately tried to perform badly. Despite this, he was ordered to read the news and did so until April 1940, when he ultimately refused to cooperate any further. At that point members of the Gestapo visited him and told him: "If you don't obey, your wife and children will be put in a concentration camp." This was followed by a savage beating in May 1940, which resulted in one of his ears being partly torn off. As a result, he agreed to work with his old employers and helped in producing some films.

In his evidence, Steane insisted that the only reason he aided the Germans was because of his continual fear for his wife and children. He maintained, as he told British Intelligence in his original statement, that he never had the slightest idea or intention of assisting the enemy and that everything he did was done to save his wife and children.

Steane was tried before Henn-Collins J and a jury. He was convicted and sentenced to three years' penal servitude. Steane appealed.]

LORD GODDARD CJ (for the court): The difficult question that arises is in connexion with the direction to the jury with regard to whether these acts were done with the intention of assisting the enemy. The case as opened, and indeed, as put by the learned judge appears to this court to be this: A man is taken to intend the natural consequences of his acts; if, therefore, he does an act which is likely to assist the enemy, it must be assumed that he did it with the intention of assisting the enemy. Now, the first thing which the court would observe is that, where the essence of an offence or a necessary constituent of an offence is a particular intent, that intent must be proved by the Crown just as much as any other fact necessary to constitute the offence. The wording of the regulation itself shows that it is not enough merely to charge a prisoner with doing an act likely to assist the enemy; he must do it with the particular intent specified in the regulation. While no doubt the motive of a man's act and his intention in doing the act are, in law, different things, it is, none the less, true that in many offences a specific intention is a necessary ingredient and the jury have to be satisfied that a particular act was done with that specific intent, although the natural consequences of the act might, if nothing else were proved, be said to show the intent for which it was done. ...

In this case the court cannot but feel that some confusion arose with regard to the question of intent by so much being said in the case with regard to the subject of duress. Duress is a matter of defence where a prisoner is forced by fear of violence or imprisonment to do an act which in itself is criminal. If the act is a criminal act, the prisoner may be able to show that he was forced into doing it by violence, actual or threatened, and to save himself from the consequences of that violence. There is very little learning to be found in any of the books or cases on the subject of duress and it is by no means certain how far the doctrine extends, though we have the authority both of Hale and of Fitzjames Stephen, that while it does not apply to treason, murder and some other felonies, it does apply to misdemeanors; and offences against these regulations are misdemeanors. But here again, before any question of duress arises, a jury must be satisfied that the prisoner had the intention which is laid in the indictment. Duress is a matter of defence and the onus of proving it is on the accused. As we have already said, where an intent is charged on the indictment, it is for the prosecution to prove it, so the onus is the other way.

Now, another matter which is of considerable importance in this case, but does not seem to have been brought directly to the attention of the jury, is that very different considerations may apply where the accused at the time he did the acts is in subjection to an enemy power and where he is not. British soldiers who were set to work on the Burma road, or if invasion had unhappily taken place, British subjects who might have been set to work by the enemy digging trenches would undoubtedly be doing acts likely to assist the enemy. It would be unnecessary surely in their cases to consider any of the niceties of the law relating to duress, because no jury would find that merely by doing this work they were intending to assist the enemy. In our opinion it is impossible to say that where an act was done by a person in subjection to the power of others, especially if that other be a brutal enemy, an inference that he intended the natural consequences of his act must be drawn merely from the fact that he did it. The guilty intent cannot be presumed and must be proved. The proper direction to the jury in this case would have been that it was for the prosecution to prove the criminal intent, and that while the jury would be entitled to presume that intent if they thought that the act was done as a result of the free uncontrolled action of the accused, they would not be entitled to presume it, if the circumstances showed that the act was done in subjection to the power of the enemy, or was as consistent with an innocent intent as with a criminal intent, for example, the innocent intent of a desire to save his wife and children from a concentration camp. They should only convict if satisfied by the evidence that the act complained of was in fact done to assist the enemy, and if there was doubt about the matter, the prisoner was entitled to be acquitted.

It is to be observed also in this case that in summing-up the learned judge did not remind the jury of the various threats to which the prisoner swore he had been exposed. The jury might, of course, have disbelieved his evidence. The matters of these threats depended upon his evidence alone, and while it is fair to say that he does not appear to have been in any way shaken in cross-examination on these matters, the jury were not necessarily bound to believe it. But we do not think that the summing-up contained anything like a full enough direction as to the prisoner's defence. The defence must be fully put to the jury and we think they ought to have been reminded of various matters upon which the accused relied as negativing the intent. The jury may well have been left under the impression that, as they were told that a man must be taken to intend the natural consequences of his acts, these matters, as to which he had given evidence, were of no moment.

Appeal allowed; conviction quashed.

The word "purpose" is sometimes used to describe the culpable mental state necessary for criminal liability. In ordinary parlance, "purpose" is considered to be rather analogous to "motive" or "desire." As the next case illustrates, purpose does not necessarily have that meaning when used in criminal statutes.

R v Hibbert
Supreme Court of Canada
[1995] 2 SCR 973

[At his trial for attempted murder, the accused relied on the defence of duress. The victim of the offence was the accused's friend. The accused testified that he was forced by the principal offender to accompany him to the victim's apartment building and to lure the victim down to the lobby. The accused stood by while the principal offender then shot the victim. In the charge to the jury, the trial judge instructed the jury that if the accused joined in the common plot to shoot the victim under threats of death or grievous bodily harm, that would negate his having a common intention with the principal offender to shoot the victim and he must be found not guilty. The trial judge also instructed the jury that the accused could not rely on the common law defence of duress if a safe avenue of escape existed. The accused was acquitted of attempted murder, but convicted of the included offence of aggravated assault. The accused's appeal to the Ontario Court of Appeal was dismissed, but his further appeal to the Supreme Court of Canada was allowed and a new trial was ordered. The aspects of the case dealing with duress are set out in Chapter 18 of this casebook.]

LAMER CJ (for the Court): ... That threats of death or serious bodily harm can have an effect on a person's state of mind is indisputable. However, it is also readily apparent that a person who carries out the *actus reus* of a criminal offence in response to such threats will not necessarily lack the *mens rea* for that offence. Whether he or she does or not will depend both on what the mental element of the offence in question happens to be, and on the facts of the particular case. As a practical matter, though, situations where duress will operate to "negate" *mens rea* will be exceptional, for the simple reason that the types of mental states that are capable of being "negated" by duress are not often found in the definitions of criminal offences.

In general, a person who performs an action in response to a threat will *know* what he or she is doing, and will be aware of the probable consequences of his or her actions. Whether or not he or she *desires* the occurrence of these consequences will depend on the particular circumstances. For example, a person who is forced at gunpoint to drive a group of armed ruffians to a bank will usually know that the likely result of his or her actions will be that an attempt will be made to rob the bank, but he or she may not desire this result—indeed, he or she may strongly wish that the robbers' plans are ultimately foiled, if this could occur without risk to his or her own safety. In contrast, a person who is told that his or her child is being held hostage at another location and will be killed unless the robbery is successful will almost certainly have an active subjective desire that the robbery succeed. While the existence of threats clearly has a bearing on the *motive* underlying each actor's respective decision to assist in the robbery, only the first actor can be said not to *desire* that the robbery take place, and neither actor can be said not to have knowledge of the consequences of their actions.

[Lamer CJ first dealt with the meaning of the word "purpose" in s 21(1)(b) of the *Criminal Code*, which creates liability for a person who "does or omits to do anything for the purpose of aiding any person to commit" an offence. Lamer CJ then went on to discuss s 21(2) "in the interests of avoiding undue confusion in the law that applies to duress cases."]

It is impossible to ascribe a single fixed meaning to the term "purpose." In ordinary usage, the word is employed in two distinct senses. One can speak of an actor doing something "on purpose" (as opposed to by accident), thereby equating purpose with "immediate intention." The term is also used, however, to indicate the ultimate ends an actor seeks to achieve, which imports the idea of "desire" into the definition. This dual sense is apparent in the word's dictionary definition.

... Our task in the present case is to consider the meaning of "purpose" as it is employed in s. 21(1)(b) of the *Code* in light of the parliamentary objective underlying the subsection. It must be emphasized, however, that the word "purpose" is employed in many different sections of the *Criminal Code*, in a number of distinct contexts. My conclusions in the present case on the proper interpretation of the word "purpose" as it is employed in s. 21(1)(b) of the *Code* are thus restricted to this particular subsection. It may well be that in the context of some other statutory provision a different interpretation of the term will prove to be the most appropriate.

The problems associated with the "purpose equals desire" interpretation are several. First, incorporating the accused's feelings about the desirability of the commission of an offence by the principal into the definition of the *mens rea* for "aiding" can result in distinctions being made which appear arbitrary and unreasonable in light of the policy underlying s. 21(1)(b). As Professor Colvin notes, under the "purpose equals desire" interpretation, a person would not be guilty of aiding in the commission of an offence if he or she were "genuinely opposed or indifferent to it" (p. 123). The reason for the aider's indifference or opposition would be immaterial. The perverse consequences that flow from this are clearly illustrated by the following hypothetical situation described by Mewett and Manning:

> If a man is approached by a friend who tells him that he is going to rob a bank and would like to use his car as a getaway vehicle for which he will pay him $100, when that person is ... charged under s. 21 for doing something for the purpose of aiding his friend to commit the offence, can he say "My purpose was not to aid the robbery but to make $100"? His argument would be that while he knew that he was helping the robbery, his desire was to obtain the $100 and he did not care one way or the other whether the robbery was successful or not.

(*Criminal Law*, *supra*, at p. 112.) I agree with the authors' conclusion that "[t]hat would seem an absurd result" (p. 112).

The leading English case on the issue of whether duress negates the *mens rea* of parties to offences (under the common law governing party liability) is the House of Lords' decision in *Lynch*, *supra*. As Professor G. Williams observes in his *Textbook of Criminal Law*, 2nd ed. (London: Stevens & Sons, 1983), at p. 624: "The view taken by the majority of the House of Lords in *Lynch* was that duress is a defence on its own, and does not negative either the doing of the act charged or the *mens rea*. This is plainly right."

The position at common law, of course, does not in and of itself determine the meaning to be ascribed to the word "purpose" in the context of s. 21(1)(b) of the *Code*. It can, however, provide useful guidance when it comes to choosing between the two interpretations of the term that are available—one that accords with the common law position and the other that contradicts it. In the absence of reason to believe that Parliament intended its enactment of s. 21(1)(b) to radically alter the common law principles governing party liability, the interpretation that accords with the common law would seem to also be the most likely to accurately embody Parliament's intentions. This observation strengthens my conclusion that Parliament's use of the term "purpose" in s. 21(1)(b) should not be seen as incorporating the notion of "desire" into the mental state for party liability, and that the word should instead be understood as being essentially synonymous with "intention." ...

For these reasons, I conclude that the expression "for the purpose of aiding" in s. 21(1)(b), properly understood, does not require that the accused actively view the commission of the offence he or she is aiding as desirable in and of itself. As a result, the *mens rea* for aiding under s. 21(1)(b) is not susceptible of being "negated" by duress. ...

As was the case with the term "purpose" in s. 21(1)(b), the phrase "intention in common" [in s 21(2)] is capable of being understood in more than one sense. One possible interpretation is that "intention in common" means no more than that the two persons must have in mind the same unlawful purpose. Alternatively, however, it might be argued that the requirement of "commonality" requires that the two persons' intentions match in greater detail—in particular, that their motives or subjective views as to the desirability of the commission of the "unlawful purpose" match up. If this latter interpretation were adopted, it could be argued that although persons who assist others to commit criminal acts as a result of threats made by the others would "intend" to provide such assistance, their intention would not be "in common" with the intentions of the threatener, due to the different motives and, possibly, views as to the immediate desirability of the criminal activity at issue. In contrast, under the former interpretation a person would fall within the ambit of s. 21(2) if they intended to assist in the commission of the same offence envisioned by the principal, regardless of the fact that their intention might be due solely to the principal's threats. Of course, it would be open to such a person to avoid criminal liability through the common law defence of duress.

As noted earlier in *Paquette, supra*, Martland J. took the position that "intention in common" meant something more than "intention to commit or aid in the same offence," arguing (at p. 423) that:

> A person whose actions have been dictated by fear of death or of grievous bodily injury cannot be said to have formed a genuine common intention to carry out an unlawful purpose with the person who has threatened him with those consequences if he fails to co-operate.

The phrase "intention in common" is certainly open to being interpreted in this manner. However, notwithstanding the considerable weight I place on and the respect I have for the opinion of Martland J., I have come to the conclusion that, in the context of s. 21(2), the first interpretation discussed above is more consistent both with Parliament's intention and with the interpretation of s. 21(1)(b) I have adopted in these reasons. Many of the factors I considered earlier in the course of determining the meaning to be ascribed to the term "purpose" in s. 21(1)(b) apply with similar force to the problem of interpreting s. 21(2).

The conclusions that can be extracted from the discussion in the previous sections may be summarized as follows:

1. The fact that a person who commits a criminal act does so as a result of threats of death or bodily harm can in some instances be relevant to the question of whether he or she possessed the *mens rea* necessary to commit an offence. Whether or not this is so will depend, among other things, on the structure of the particular offence in question—that is, on whether or not the mental state specified by Parliament in its definition of the offence is such that the presence of coercion can, as a matter of logic, have a bearing on the existence of *mens rea*. If the offence is one where the presence of duress is of potential relevance to the existence of *mens rea*, the accused is entitled to point to the presence of threats when arguing that the Crown has not proven beyond a reasonable doubt that he or she possessed the mental state required for liability.

2. A person who commits a criminal act under threats of death or bodily harm may also be able to invoke an excuse-based defence (either the statutory defence set out in s. 17 or the common law defence of duress, depending on whether the accused is charged as a principal or as a party). This is so regardless of whether or not the offence at issue is one where the presence of coercion also has a bearing on the existence of *mens rea*.

3. The mental states specified in s. 21(1)(b) and (2) of the *Criminal Code* are not
    susceptible to being "negated" by duress. Consequently, it is not open to persons
    charged under these sections to argue that because their acts were coerced by
    threats they lacked the requisite *mens rea*. Such persons may, however, seek to have
    their conduct *excused* through the operation of the common law defence of duress.

It should be reiterated, however, that the holding in the present case is based on an interpretation of the particular terms of two specific offence-creating statutory provisions,
s. 21(1)(b) and (2) of the *Criminal Code*. The question of whether other offences can be
found, either in the *Code* or in some other statute, that are defined in such a way that the
presence of coercion *is* relevant to the existence of *mens rea*, remains open.

Appeal allowed; new trial ordered.

Chapter 18 of this casebook deals with the defence of duress.

R v Buzzanga and Durocher
Ontario Court of Appeal
(1979), 49 CCC (2d) 369

[The accused were charged with wilfully promoting hatred against francophones. They
both were sympathetic with the French community in which they lived, and had published
a pamphlet that was a satire of those who opposed bilingualism—in order, they said, to
combat apathy in the French-speaking community in relation to the building of a French-
language school.]

MARTIN JA: … The threshold question to be determined is the meaning of "wilfully" in
the term "wilfully promotes hatred" in s. 281.2(2) [see now s 319(2)] of the Criminal
Code. It will, of course, be observed that the word "wilfully" modifies the words "promotes
hatred," rather than the words "communicating statements."

• • •

As previously indicated, the word "wilfully" does not have a fixed meaning, but I am
satisfied that in the context of s. 281.2(2) it means with the intention of promoting hatred,
and does not include recklessness. The arrangement of the legislation proscribing the
incitement of hatred, in my view, leads to that conclusion.

Section 281.2(1) [see now s 319(1)], unlike s. 281.2(2), is restricted to the incitement
of hatred by communicating statements in a public place where such incitement is likely
to lead to a breach of the peace. Although no mental element is expressly mentioned in
s. 281.2(1), where the communication poses an immediate threat to public order, mens
rea is, none the less, required since the inclusion of an offence in the Criminal Code must
be taken to import mens rea in the absence of a clear intention to dispense with it: see
R. v. Prue; R. v. Baril (1979), 46 C.C.C. (2d) 257 at pp. 260-1, 96 D.L.R. 577 at pp. 580-1,
8 C.R. (3d) 68 at p. 73. The general mens rea which is required and which suffices for most
crimes where no mental element is mentioned in the definition of the crime, is either the

intentional or reckless bringing about of the result which the law, in creating the offence, seeks to prevent and, hence, under s. 281.2(1) [now s 319(1)] is either the intentional or reckless inciting of hatred in the specified circumstances.

The insertion of the word "wilfully" in s. 281.2(2) [now s 319(2)] was not necessary to import mens rea since that requirement would be implied in any event because of the serious nature of the offence: see R. v. Prue, supra. The statements, the communication of which are proscribed by s. 281.2(2), are not confined to statements communicated in a public place in circumstances likely to lead to a breach of the peace and they, consequently, do not pose such an immediate threat to public order as those falling under s. 281.2(1); it is reasonable to assume, therefore, that Parliament intended to limit the offence under s. 281.2(2) to the intentional promotion of hatred. It is evident that the use of the word "wilfully" in s. 281.2(2), and not in s. 281.2(1), reflects Parliament's policy to strike a balance in protecting the competing social interests of freedom of expression on the one hand, and public order and group reputation on the other hand.

· · ·

I conclude, therefore, that the appellants "wilfully" (intentionally) promoted hatred against the French Canadian community of Essex County only if: (a) their conscious purpose in distributing the document was to promote hatred against that group, or (b) they foresaw that the promotion of hatred against that group was certain or morally certain to result from the distribution of the pamphlet, but distributed it as a means of achieving their purpose of obtaining the French-language high school.

Whether the trial Judge misdirected himself as to the meaning of wilfully?

... I am of the view, however, that the learned trial Judge erred in holding that "wilfully" means only "intentional as opposed to accidental." Although, as previously indicated, "wilfully" has sometimes been used to mean that the accused's act, as distinct from its consequences, must be intended and not accidental (as in R. v. Senior, [1899] 1 Q.B. 283), it does not have that meaning in the provisions under consideration.

The learned trial Judge's view of the meaning of "wilfully" inevitably caused him to focus attention on the intentional nature of the appellants' conduct, rather than on the question whether they actually intended to produce the consequence of promoting hatred. ...

I am, with deference to the learned trial Judge, of the view that an intention to create "controversy, furor and an uproar" is not the same thing as an intention to promote hatred, and it was an error to equate them. I would, of course, agree that if the appellants intentionally promoted hatred against the French-speaking community of Essex County as a means of obtaining the French-language high school, they committed the offence charged. The appellants' evidence, if believed, does not, however, as the learned trial Judge appears to have thought, inevitably lead to that conclusion. The learned trial Judge, not having disbelieved the appellants' evidence, failed to give appropriate consideration to their evidence on the issue of intent and, in the circumstances, his failure so to do constituted self-misdirection.

Appeal allowed; new trial ordered.

The following case looks at the definition of "actual knowledge," a slightly lesser form of subjective fault than intentional or wilful conduct.

R v Théroux
Supreme Court of Canada
[1993] 2 SCR 5

[The accused was convicted of fraud for accepting deposits from investors in a building project, having told them that he had purchased deposit insurance when he in fact had not. The general fraud provision in the *Criminal Code* provides:

> 380(1) Every one who, by deceit, falsehood or other fraudulent means, whether or not it is a false pretence within the meaning of this Act, defrauds the public or any person, whether ascertained or not, of any property, money or valuable security … is guilty of an indictable offence … or … an offence punishable on summary conviction.]

McLACHLIN J (as she then was):

· · ·

3. *The Mens Rea of Fraud*

(i) *Doctrinal Considerations*

This brings us to the *mens rea* of fraud. What is the guilty mind of fraud? At this point, certain confusions inherent in the concept of *mens rea* itself become apparent. It is useful initially to distinguish between the mental element or elements of a crime and the *mens rea*. The term *mens rea*, properly understood, does not encompass all of the mental elements of a crime. The *actus reus* has its own mental element; the act must be the voluntary act of the accused for the *actus reus* to exist. *Mens rea*, on the other hand, refers to the guilty mind, the wrongful intention, of the accused. Its function in criminal law is to prevent the conviction of the morally innocent—those who do not understand or intend the consequences of their acts. Typically, *mens rea* is concerned with the consequences of the prohibited *actus reus*. Thus in the crimes of homicide, we speak of the consequences of the voluntary act—intention to cause death, or reckless and wilfully blind persistence in conduct which one knows is likely to cause death. In other offences, such as dangerous driving, the *mens rea* may relate to the failure to consider the consequences of inadvertence.

This brings me to the question of whether the test for *mens rea* is subjective or objective. Most scholars and jurists agree that, leaving aside offences where the *actus reus* is negligence or inadvertence and offences of absolute liability, the test for *mens rea* is subjective. The test is not whether a reasonable person would have foreseen the consequences of the prohibited act, but whether the accused subjectively appreciated those consequences at least as a possibility. In applying the subjective test, the court looks to the accused's intention and the facts as the accused believed them to be: G. Williams, Textbook of Criminal Law, 2nd ed. (1983), pp. 727-8.

Two collateral points must be made at this juncture. First, as Williams underlines, this inquiry has nothing to do with the accused's system of values. A person is not saved from conviction because he or she believes there is nothing wrong with what he or she is doing. The question is whether the accused subjectively appreciated that certain consequences would follow from his or her acts, not whether the accused believed the acts or their consequences to be moral. Just as the pathological killer would not be acquitted on the mere ground that he failed to see his act as morally reprehensible, so the defrauder will not be acquitted because he believed that what he was doing was honest.

The second collateral point is the oft-made observation that the Crown need not, in every case, show precisely what thought was in the accused's mind at the time of the criminal act. In certain cases, subjective awareness of the consequences can be inferred from the act itself, barring some explanation casting doubt on such inference. The fact that such an inference is made does not detract from the subjectivity of the test.

Having ventured these general comments on *mens rea*, I return to the offence of fraud. The prohibited act is deceit, falsehood, or some other dishonest act. The prohibited consequence is depriving another of what is or should be his, which may, as we have seen, consist in merely placing another's property at risk. The *mens rea* would then consist in the subjective awareness that one was undertaking a prohibited act (the deceit, falsehood or other dishonest act) which could cause deprivation in the sense of depriving another of property or putting that property at risk. If this is shown, the crime is complete. The fact that the accused may have hoped the deprivation would not take place, or may have felt there was nothing wrong with what he or she was doing, provides no defence. To put it another way, following the traditional criminal law principle that the mental state necessary to the offence must be determined by reference to the external acts which constitute the *actus* [*reus*] of the offence (see Williams, ibid., c. 3), the proper focus in determining the *mens rea* of fraud is to ask whether the accused intentionally committed the prohibited acts (deceit, falsehood, or other dishonest act) knowing or desiring the consequences proscribed by the offence (deprivation, including the risk of deprivation). The personal feeling of the accused about the morality or honesty of the act or its consequences is no more relevant to the analysis than is the accused's awareness that the particular acts undertaken constitute a criminal offence.

This applies as much to the third head of fraud, "other fraudulent means," as to lies and acts of deceit. Although other fraudulent means have been broadly defined as means which are "dishonest," it is not necessary that an accused personally consider these means to be dishonest in order that he or she be convicted of fraud for having undertaken them. The "dishonesty" of the means is relevant to the determination whether the conduct falls within the type of conduct caught by the offence of fraud; what reasonable people consider dishonest assists in the determination whether the *actus reus* of the offence can be made out on particular facts. That established, it need only be determined that an accused knowingly undertook the acts in question, aware that deprivation, or risk of deprivation, could follow as a likely consequence.

I have spoken of knowledge of the consequences of the fraudulent act. There appears to be no reason, however, why recklessness as to consequences might not also attract criminal responsibility. Recklessness presupposes knowledge of the likelihood of the prohibited consequences. It is established when it is shown that the accused, with such knowledge, commits acts which may bring about these prohibited consequences, while being reckless as to whether or not they ensue.

These doctrinal observations suggest that the *actus reus* of the offence of fraud will be established by proof of:

1. the prohibited act, be it an act of deceit, a falsehood or some other fraudulent means; and
2. deprivation caused by the prohibited act, which may consist in actual loss or the placing of the victim's pecuniary interests at risk.

Correspondingly, the *mens rea* of fraud is established by proof of:

1. Subjective knowledge of the prohibited act; and
2. Subjective knowledge that the prohibited act could have as a consequence the deprivation of another (which deprivation may consist in knowledge that the victim's pecuniary interests are put at risk).

Where the conduct and knowledge required by these definitions are established, the accused is guilty whether he actually intended the prohibited consequence or was reckless as to whether it would occur.

The inclusion of risk of deprivation in the concept of deprivation in *Olan* requires specific comment. The accused must have subjective awareness, at the very least, that his or her conduct will put the property or economic expectations of others at risk. As noted above, this does not mean that the Crown must provide the trier of fact with a mental snapshot proving exactly what was in the accused's mind at the moment the dishonest act was committed. Normally, the inference of subjective knowledge of the risk may be drawn from the facts as the accused believed them to be. The accused may introduce evidence negating that inference, such as evidence that his deceit was part of an innocent prank, or evidence of circumstances which led him to believe that no one would act on his lie or deceitful or dishonest act. But in cases like the present one, where the accused tells a lie knowing others will act on it and thereby puts their property at risk, the inference of subjective knowledge that the property of another would be put at risk is clear. ...

Pragmatic considerations support the view of *mens rea* proposed above. A person who deprives another person of what the latter has should not escape criminal responsibility merely because, according to his moral or her personal code, he or she was doing nothing wrong or because of a sanguine belief that all will come out right in the end. Many frauds are perpetrated by people who think there is nothing wrong in what they are doing or who sincerely believe that their act of placing other people's property at risk will not ultimately result in actual loss to those persons. If the offence of fraud is to catch those who actually practise fraud, its *mens rea* cannot be cast so narrowly as this. As stated in *R. v. Allsop*, ... approved by this court in *Olan*, at p. 150:

> Generally the primary objective of fraudsmen is to advantage themselves. The detriment that results to their victims is secondary to that purpose and incidental. It is "intended" only in the sense that it is a contemplated outcome of the fraud that is perpetrated.

The law of fraud must be sufficiently broad to catch this secondary incident of the defrauder's purpose or it will be of little avail.

This approach conforms to the conception of the offence of fraud which imbues this court's decision in *Olan*. *Olan* points the way to a conception of fraud broad enough in scope to encompass the entire panoply of dishonest commercial dealings. It defines the *actus reus* accordingly; the offence is committed whenever a person deceives, lies or otherwise acts dishonestly, and that act causes deprivation (including risk of deprivation) to another. To adopt a definition of *mens rea* which requires subjective awareness of dishonesty and a belief that actual deprivation (as opposed to risk of deprivation) will result, is inconsistent with *Olan*'s definition of the *actus reus*. The effect of such a test would be to negate the broad thrust of *Olan* and confine the offence of fraud to a narrow ambit, capable of catching only a small portion of the dishonest commercial dealing which *Olan* took as the target of the offence of fraud.

The question arises whether the definition of *mens rea* for fraud which I have proposed may catch conduct which does not warrant criminalization. I refer to the fear, reflected in the appellate decisions adopting a narrower definition of the required *mens rea*, that the reach of the offence of fraud may be extended beyond criminal dishonesty to catch sharp or improvident business practices which, although not to be encouraged, do not merit the stigma and loss of liberty that attends the criminal sanction. The concern is that any misrepresentation or practice which induces an incorrect understanding or belief in the minds of customers, or which causes deprivation, will become criminal. As Marshall J.A. put it in *Mugford, supra*, at pp. 175-6:

> ... it is not sufficient to base fraud merely upon a finding that the appellant induced a state of mind in his customers which was not correct. Any misrepresentation may have that effect. Criminal dishonesty extends further ...
>
> It would be a startling extension of criminal liability if every statement urging the public to purchase one's wares because only a limited supply remain were by itself to be visited with criminal sanction.

This poses starkly the critical question: does a view of the offence of fraud which catches a broad range of dishonest commercial dealing also catch conduct which should not be regarded as criminal, but rather left to the civil sanction?

In my view, the approach to the offence of fraud adopted in *Olan* and perused in these reasons does not take us out of the proper domain of the criminal sanction. To establish the *actus reus* of fraud, the Crown must establish beyond a reasonable doubt that the accused practised deceit, lied, or committed some other fraudulent act. Under the third head of the offence it will be necessary to show that the impugned act is one which a reasonable person would see as dishonest. Deprivation or the risk of deprivation must then be shown to have occurred as a matter of fact. To establish the *mens rea* of fraud the Crown must prove that the accused knowingly undertook the acts which constitute the falsehood, deceit or other fraudulent means, and that the accused was aware that deprivation could result from such conduct.

The requirement of intentional fraudulent action excludes mere negligent misrepresentation. It also excludes improvident business conduct or conduct which is sharp in the sense of taking advantage of a business opportunity to the detriment of someone less astute. The accused must intentionally deceive, lie or commit some other fraudulent act for the offence to be established. Neither a negligent misstatement, nor a sharp business practice, will suffice, because in neither case will the required intent to deprive by fraudulent means be present. A statement made carelessly, even if it is untrue, will not amount to an intentional falsehood, subjectively appreciated. Nor will any seizing of a business opportunity which is not motivated by a person's subjective intent to deprive by cheating or misleading others amount to an instance of fraud. Again, an act of deceit which is made carelessly without any expectation of consequences, as for example, an innocent prank or a statement made in debate which is not intended to be acted upon, would not amount to fraud because the accused would have no knowledge that the prank would put the property of those who heard it at risk. We are left then with deliberately practised fraudulent acts which, in the knowledge of the accused, actually put the property of others at risk. Such conduct may be appropriately criminalized, in my view.

Wilful Blindness

A state of wilful blindness, although controversial and sometimes confused with negligence, has been recognized as a form of fault equivalent to knowledge.

R v Briscoe
Supreme Court of Canada
2010 SCC 13, [2010] 1 SCR 411

[The accused, Briscoe, was charged with first-degree murder, kidnapping, and sexual assault. The Crown's theory was that the accused assisted in the crimes by driving a group to the crime scene, providing a weapon, and holding the victim and telling her to shut up. The trial judge acquitted on the basis that the accused did not know that the crimes would occur. The Crown's appeal to the Alberta Court of Appeal was allowed and a new trial was ordered on the basis that the trial judge erred by not considering wilful blindness. The accused appealed.]

CHARRON J (McLachlin CJ and Binnie, LeBel, Deschamps, Fish, Abella, Rothstein, and Cromwell JJ concurring): …

[21] Wilful blindness does not define the *mens rea* required for particular offences. Rather, it can substitute for actual knowledge whenever knowledge is a component of the *mens rea*. The doctrine of wilful blindness imputes knowledge to an accused whose suspicion is aroused to the point where he or she sees the need for further inquiries, but *deliberately chooses* not to make those inquiries. See *Sansregret v. The Queen*, [1985] 1 S.C.R. 570, and *R. v. Jorgensen*, [1995] 4 S.C.R. 55. As Sopinka J. succinctly put it in *Jorgensen* (at para. 103), "[a] finding of wilful blindness involves an affirmative answer to the question: Did the accused shut his eyes because he knew or strongly suspected that looking would fix him with knowledge?" …

[24] Professor Don Stuart makes the useful observation that the expression "deliberate ignorance" seems more descriptive than "wilful blindness," as it connotes "an actual process of suppressing a suspicion." Properly understood in this way, "the concept of wilful blindness is of narrow scope and involves no departure from the subjective focus on the workings of the accused's mind" (*Canadian Criminal Law: A Treatise* (5th ed. 2007), at p. 241). While a failure to inquire may be evidence of recklessness or criminal negligence,

as for example, where a failure to inquire is a marked departure from the conduct expected of a reasonable person, wilful blindness is not simply a failure to inquire but, to repeat Professor Stuart's words, "deliberate ignorance."

[25] In this case, I agree with Martin J.A. that the trial judge erred in law by failing to consider wilful blindness. As he noted, even Mr. Briscoe's own statements to the police suggest that he had a "strong, well-founded suspicion that someone would be killed at the golf course" (para. 30) and that he may have been wilfully blind to the kidnapping and prospect of sexual assault. His statements also show that he deliberately chose not to inquire about what the members of the group intended to do because he did not want to know. As he put it, "whatever you guys wanna do just do it. Don't do it around me. I don't want to see nothing. I don't know what the fuck you're gonna do." The trial judge relied heavily upon the statements in his reasons but did not refer to the doctrine of wilful blindness. Of course, whether Mr. Briscoe had the requisite *mens rea* for the three offences was a question for the trier of fact, and Mr. Briscoe is entitled to the benefit of any reasonable doubt on this issue. However, from a legal standpoint, it is my respectful view that the evidence cried out for an analysis on wilful blindness. In these circumstances, the Court of Appeal rightly concluded that the trial judge's failure to consider Mr. Briscoe's knowledge from that perspective constitutes a legal error which necessitates a new trial on all charges.

Appeal dismissed; new trial ordered.

Recklessness

As discussed in *Buzzanga and Durocher*, recklessness often forms the minimal subjective fault that can be read into offences that contain no explicit fault requirement. In *R v Sansregret* the Supreme Court discussed recklessness and its relation to wilful blindness as follows.

R v Sansregret
Supreme Court of Canada
[1985] 1 SCR 570

McINTYRE J: … The concept of recklessness as a basis for criminal liability has been the subject of much discussion. Negligence, the failure to take reasonable care, is a creature of the civil law and is not generally a concept having a place in determining criminal liability. Nevertheless, it is frequently confused with recklessness in the criminal sense and care should be taken to separate the two concepts. Negligence is tested by the objective standard of the reasonable man. A departure from his accustomed sober behaviour by an act or omission which reveals less than reasonable care will involve liability at civil law but forms no basis for the imposition of criminal penalties. In accordance with well-established principles for the determination of criminal liability, recklessness, to form a part of the criminal *mens rea*, must have an element of the subjective. It is found in the attitude of one who, aware that there is danger that his conduct could bring about the result prohibited by the criminal law, nevertheless persists, despite the risk. It is, in other words, the conduct of one who sees the risk and who takes the chance. It is in this sense that the term "recklessness" is used in the criminal law and it is clearly distinct from the concept of civil negligence.

. . .

The idea of wilful blindness in circumstances such as this has been said to be an aspect of recklessness. While this may well be true, it is wise to keep the two concepts separate because they result from different mental attitudes and lead to different legal results. A finding of recklessness in this case could not override the defence of mistake of fact. The appellant asserts an honest belief that the consent of the complainant was not caused by fear and threats. The trial judge found that such an honest belief existed. In the facts of this case, because of the reckless conduct of the appellant, it could not be said that such a belief was reasonable but, as held in *Pappajohn*, the mere honesty of the belief will support the "mistake of fact" defence, even where it is unreasonable. On the other hand, a finding of wilful blindness as to the very facts about which the honest belief is now asserted would leave no room for the application of the defence because, where wilful blindness is shown, the law presumes knowledge on the part of the accused, in this case knowledge that the consent had been induced by threats.

Wilful blindness is distinct from recklessness because, while recklessness involves knowledge of a danger or risk and persistence in a course of conduct which creates a risk that the prohibited result will occur, wilful blindness arises where a person who has become aware of the need for some inquiry declines to make the inquiry because he does not wish to know the truth. He would prefer to remain ignorant. The culpability in recklessness is justified by consciousness of the risk and by proceeding in the face of it, while in wilful blindness it is justified by the accused's fault in deliberately failing to inquire when he knows there is reason for inquiry.

IV. OBJECTIVE STANDARDS OF FAULT

This section examines fault requirements that deviate from a purely subjective inquiry into what passed through the mind of the accused person. It looks at standards of fault that focus on holding accused persons to an objective standard of conduct and the relation of such standards to subjective fault.

In *R v Hundal*, [1993] 1 SCR 867 the accused was charged with dangerous driving causing death. The accused, while driving an overloaded dump truck, proceeded into an intersection against a red light and killed the driver of a car which had moved into the intersection on a green light. The trial judge rejected the accused's explanation that he was only a short distance from the intersection when the light turned amber and because it was dangerous to try and stop he made a decision to go through the amber light. The accused's appeal to the Supreme Court of Canada was dismissed, Cory J stating for the Court (headings omitted):

> The appellant contends that the prison sentence which may be imposed for a breach of s. 233 (now s. 249) makes it evident that an accused cannot be convicted without proof beyond a reasonable doubt of a subjective mental element of an intention to drive dangerously. Certainly every crime requires proof of an act or failure to act, coupled with an element of fault which is termed the *mens rea*. ...

In my view, to insist on a subjective mental element in connection with driving offences would be to deny reality. It cannot be forgotten that the operation of a motor vehicle is, as I have said so very often, automatic and with little conscious thought. It is simply inappropriate to apply a subjective test in determining whether an accused is guilty of dangerous driving.

Although an objective test must be applied to the offence of dangerous driving, it will remain open to the accused to raise a reasonable doubt that a reasonable person would have been aware of the risks in the accused's conduct. The test must be applied with some measure of flexibility. That is to say the objective test should not be applied in a vacuum but rather in the context of the events surrounding the incident. ...

In summary, the *mens rea* for the offence of dangerous driving should be assessed objectively but in the context of all the events surrounding the incident. That approach will satisfy the dictates both of common sense and fairness. As a general rule, personal factors need not be taken into account. This flows from the licensing requirement for driving which assures that all who drive have a reasonable standard of physical health and capability, mental health and a knowledge of the reasonable standard required of all licensed drivers.

In light of the licensing requirement and the nature of driving offences, a modified objective test satisfies the constitutional minimum fault requirement for s. 233 (now s. 249) of the *Criminal Code* and is eminently well suited to that offence.

It follows then that a trier of fact may convict if satisfied beyond a reasonable doubt that, viewed objectively, the accused was, in the words of the section, driving in a manner that was "dangerous to the public, having regard to all the circumstances, including the nature, condition and use of such place and the amount of traffic that at the time is or might reasonably be expected to be on such place." In making the assessment, the trier of fact should be satisfied that the conduct amounted to a marked departure from the standard of care that a reasonable person would observe in the accused's situation.

Next, if an explanation is offered by the accused, such as a sudden and unexpected onset of illness, then in order to convict, the trier of fact must be satisfied that a reasonable person in similar circumstances ought to have been aware of the risk and of the danger involved in the conduct manifested by the accused. If a jury is determining the facts, they may be instructed with regard to dangerous driving along the lines set out above. There is no necessity for a long or complex charge. Neither the section nor the offence requires it. Certainly the instructions should not be unnecessarily confused by any references to advertent or inadvertent negligence. The offence can be readily assessed by jurors who can arrive at a conclusion based on common sense and their own everyday experiences.

Let us now consider whether the modified objective test was properly applied in this case. The trial judge carefully examined the circumstances of the accident. He took into account the busy downtown traffic, the weather conditions, and the mechanical conditions of the accused vehicle. He concluded, in my view very properly, that the appellant's manner of driving represented a gross departure from the standard of a reasonably prudent driver. No explanation was offered by the accused that could excuse his conduct. There is no reason for interfering with the trial judge's finding of fact and application of the law.

In the result the appeal must be dismissed.

R v Creighton
Supreme Court of Canada
[1993] 3 SCR 3

[The accused, an experienced drug user, was charged with manslaughter by means of the unlawful act of trafficking drugs when he injected cocaine into a friend who then died as a result of an overdose. The Court split 5:4 on a number of issues. In what follows the focus is on the nature of the objective test and reasonable person standard used in determining objective fault. Other issues raised in the case—namely, whether the use of objective as opposed to subjective fault was consistent with s 7 of the Charter and whether s 7 required that the fault element relate to all aspects of the *actus reus* including the causing of death—will be examined in a subsequent section.]

LAMER CJ (Sopinka, Iacobucci, and Major JJ concurring):

B. *The Objective Test*

An accused can only be held to the standard of a reasonable person if the accused was capable, in the circumstances of the offence, of attaining that standard. Consequently, in determining whether a reasonable person in the circumstances of the accused would have foreseen the risk of death arising from the unlawful act, the trier of fact must pay particular attention to any human frailties which might have rendered the accused incapable of having foreseen what the reasonable person would have foreseen. If the criminal law were to judge every accused by the inflexible standard of the monolithic "reasonable person," even where the accused could not possibly have attained that standard, the result, as Stuart notes, would be "absolute responsibility" for such persons: *Canadian Criminal Law: A Treatise* (2nd ed. 1987), at p. 192. H.L.A. Hart advanced a similar argument in "Negligence, *Mens Rea* and Criminal Responsibility" in *Punishment and Responsibility* (1968), at p. 154:

> If our conditions of liability are invariant and not flexible, i.e. if they are not adjusted to the capacities of the accused, then some individuals will be held liable for negligence though they could not have helped their failure to comply with the standard.
>
> · · ·

... [T]he reasonable person will be invested with any *enhanced* foresight the accused may have enjoyed by virtue of his or her membership in a group with special experience or knowledge related to the conduct giving rise to the offence. For example, in *Gosset* the accused police officer's experience and training in the handling of firearms is relevant to the standard of care under s. 86(2) of the *Criminal Code* concerning the careless use of firearms. In the present case, the reasonable person should be deemed to possess Mr. Creighton's considerable experience in drug use.

· · ·

It must be emphasized that this is *not* a subjective test: if a reasonable person with the frailties of the accused would nevertheless have appreciated the risk, and the accused did not in fact appreciate the risk, the accused must be convicted.

The rationale of incorporating capacity into the objective determination of fault is analogous to the rationale underlying the defence of mistake of fact in criminal law, where an accused who has an honest and reasonably held belief in an incorrect set of facts, and acts on the basis of those facts, is excused from punishment for the resulting harm. Human frailties which may affect the capacity of an accused to recognize the risks of unlawful conduct must be considered, however, not because they result in the accused believing in an incorrect set of facts, but rather because they render the accused incapable of perceiving the correct set of facts. It is, however, only those human frailties which relate to an accused's capacity to appreciate the risk in question that may be considered in this inquiry.

I shall now turn to elaborating what "human frailties" may factor into the objective test. It is perhaps best to begin by stating clearly what is not included. Intoxication or impairment through drug use which occurs as a result of voluntary consumption cannot serve to vitiate liability for the risks created by the negligent conduct of an accused. Additionally, a sudden and temporary incapacity to appreciate risk due to exigent circumstances (an emergency which diverts one's attention from an activity, for example) is not properly considered under the third part of the test, but may well result in an acquittal under the first part of the test, that is, would a reasonable person's attention in the same circumstances of the accused have been diverted from that activity.

Human frailties encompass personal characteristics habitually affecting an accused's awareness of the circumstances which create risk. Such characteristics must be relevant to the ability to perceive the particular risk. For example, while illiteracy may excuse the failure to take care with a hazardous substance identifiable only by a label, as the accused may be unable, in this case, to apprehend the relevant facts, illiteracy may not be relevant to the failure to take care with a firearm. This attention to the context of the offence and the nature of the activity is explored in greater detail below.

It should be emphasized that the relevant characteristics must be traits which the accused could not control or otherwise manage in the circumstances. For example, while a person with cataracts cannot be faulted for having reduced vision, he or she may be expected to avoid activity in which that limitation will either create risk or render him or her unable to manage risk which is inherent in an activity (driving, for example). The reasonable person is expected to compensate for his or her frailties, to the extent he or she is conscious of them and able to do so.

[Lamer CJ would have considered the fact that the accused was an experienced drug user in applying the reasonable person test, and held that an application of the objective standard was not necessary because the trial judge found that the accused subjectively appreciated the risk of death when injecting the deceased with cocaine.]

McLACHLIN J (L'Heureux-Dubé, Gonthier, and Cory JJ concurring):

B. The Nature of the Objective Test

I respectfully differ from the Chief Justice on the nature of the objective test used to determine the *mens rea* for crimes of negligence. In my view, the approach advocated by the Chief Justice personalizes the objective test to the point where it devolves into a subjective test, thus eroding the minimum standard of care which Parliament has laid down by the enactment of offences of manslaughter and penal negligence.

By way of background, it may be useful to restate what I understand the jurisprudence to date to have established regarding crimes of negligence and the objective test. The *mens rea* of a criminal offence may be either subjective or objective, subject to the principle of fundamental justice that the moral fault of the offence must be proportionate to its gravity and penalty. Subjective *mens rea* requires that the accused have intended the consequences of his or her acts, or that knowing of the probable consequences of those acts, the accused have proceeded recklessly in the face of the risk. The requisite intent or knowledge may be inferred directly from what the accused said or says about his or her mental state, or indirectly from the act and its circumstances. Even in the latter case, however, it is concerned with "what was actually going on in the mind of this particular accused at the time in question": L'Heureux-Dubé J. in *R. v. Martineau, supra,* at p. 655, quoting Stuart, *Canadian Criminal Law* (2nd ed. 1987), at p. 121.

Objective *mens rea*, on the other hand, is not concerned with what the accused intended or knew. Rather, the mental fault lies in failure to direct the mind to a risk which the reasonable person would have appreciated. Objective *mens rea* is not concerned with what was actually in the accused's mind, but with what should have been there, had the accused proceeded reasonably.

It is now established that a person may be held criminally responsible for negligent conduct on the objective test, and that this alone does not violate the principle of fundamental justice that the moral fault of the accused must be commensurate with the gravity of the offence and its penalty: *R. v. Hundal,* [1993] 1 S.C.R. 867.

However, as stated in *Martineau,* it is appropriate that those who cause harm intentionally should be punished more severely than those who cause harm inadvertently. Moreover, the constitutionality of crimes of negligence is also subject to the caveat that acts of ordinary negligence may not suffice to justify imprisonment: *R. v. City of Sault Ste. Marie,* [1978] 2 S.C.R. 1299; *R. v. Sansregret,* [1985] 1 S.C.R. 570. To put it in the terms used in *Hundal,* the negligence must constitute a "marked departure" from the standard of the reasonable person. The law does not lightly brand a person as a criminal. For this reason, I am in agreement with the Chief Justice in *R. v. Finlay, supra,* that the word "careless" in an underlying firearms offence must be read as requiring a marked departure from the constitutional norm.

It follows from this requirement, affirmed in *Hundal,* that in an offence based on unlawful conduct, a predicate offence involving carelessness or negligence must also be read as requiring a "marked departure" from the standard of the reasonable person. As pointed out in *DeSousa,* the underlying offence must be constitutionally sound.

To this point, the Chief Justice and I are not, as I perceive it, in disagreement. The difference between our approaches turns on the extent to which personal characteristics of the accused may affect liability under the objective test. Here we enter territory in large part uncharted. To date, debate has focused on whether an objective test for *mens rea* is ever available in the criminal law; little has been said about how, assuming it is applicable, it is to be applied. In *R. v. Hundal, supra,* it was said that the *mens rea* of dangerous driving should be assessed objectively in the context of all the events surrounding the incident. But the extent to which those circumstances include personal mental or psychological frailties of the accused was not explored in depth. In these circumstances, we must begin with the fundamental principles of criminal law.

• • •

I agree with the Chief Justice that the rule that the morally innocent not be punished in the context of the objective test requires that the law refrain from holding a person criminally responsible if he or she is not capable of appreciating the risk. Where I differ from the Chief Justice is in his designation of the sort of educational, experiential and so-called "habitual" factors personal to the accused which can be taken into account. The Chief Justice, while in principle advocating a uniform standard of care for all, in the result seems to contemplate a standard of care which varies with the background and predisposition of each accused. Thus an inexperienced, uneducated, young person, like the accused in R. v. Naglik, [1993] 3 S.C.R. 122, could be acquitted, even though she does not meet the standard of the reasonable person (reasons of the Lamer C.J. ...). On the other hand, a person with special experience, like Mr. Creighton in this case, or the appellant police officer in R. v. Gosset, supra, will be held to a higher standard than the ordinary reasonable person.

I must respectfully dissent from this extension of the objective test for criminal fault. In my view, considerations of principle and policy dictate the maintenance of a single, uniform legal standard of care for such offences, subject to one exception: incapacity to appreciate the nature of the risk which the activity in question entails.

This principle that the criminal law will not convict the morally innocent does not, in my view, require consideration of personal factors short of incapacity. The criminal law, while requiring mental fault as an element of a conviction, has steadfastly rejected the idea that a person's personal characteristics can (short of incapacity) excuse the person from meeting the standard of conduct imposed by the law.

· · ·

In summary, I can find no support in criminal theory for the conclusion that protection of the morally innocent requires a general consideration of individual excusing conditions. The principle comes into play only at the point where the person is shown to lack the capacity to appreciate the nature and quality or the consequences of his or her acts. Apart from this, we are all, rich and poor, wise and naive, held to the minimum standards of conduct prescribed by the criminal law. This conclusion is dictated by a fundamental proposition of social organization. As Justice Oliver Wendell Holmes wrote in The Common Law (1881), at p. 108: "when men live in society, a certain average of conduct, a sacrifice of individual peculiarities going beyond a certain point, is necessary to the general welfare."

The ambit of the principle that the morally innocent shall not be convicted has developed in large part in the context of crimes of subjective fault—crimes where the accused must be shown to have actually intended or foreseen the consequences of his or her conduct. In crimes of this type, personal characteristics of the accused have been held to be relevant only to the extent that they tend to prove or disprove an element of the offence. Since intention or knowledge of the risk is an element of such offences, personal factors can come into play. But beyond this, personal characteristics going to lack of capacity are considered under the introductory sections of the Code defining the conditions of criminal responsibility and have generally been regarded as irrelevant.

· · ·

To summarize, the fundamental premises upon which our criminal law rests mandate that personal characteristics not directly relevant to an element of the offence serve as excuses only at the point where they establish incapacity, whether the incapacity be the ability to appreciate the nature and quality of one's conduct in the context of intentional crimes, or the incapacity to appreciate the risk involved in one's conduct in the context of crimes of manslaughter or penal negligence. The principle that we eschew conviction of the morally innocent requires no more.

. . .

As I see it, the recognition that those lacking the capacity to perceive the risk should be exempted from criminal conviction and punishment does not entail the conclusion that the standard of care must be adjusted to take into account the accused's experience and education. The only actor-oriented question apposite to *mens rea* in these cases is whether the accused was capable of appreciating the risk, had he or she put her mind to it. If the answer is yes, as I believe it to be in all four cases before us—*Gosset, Creighton, Finlay* and *Naglik*—that is an end of the matter.

It may be that in some cases educational deficiencies, such as illiteracy on the part of a person handling a marked bottle of nitroglycerine in the Chief Justice's example, may preclude a person from being able to appreciate the risk entailed by his or her conduct. Problems of perception may have the same effect; regardless of the care taken, the person would have been incapable of assessing the risk, and hence been acquitted. But, in practice, such cases will arise only exceptionally. The question of *mens rea* will arise only where it has been shown that the accused's conduct (the *actus reus*) constitutes a dangerous and unlawful act (as in unlawful act manslaughter), or a marked departure from the standard of care of a reasonably prudent person (as in manslaughter by criminal negligence, or penal negligence offences). This established, conflict with the prohibition against punishing the morally innocent will arise only rarely. In unregulated activities, ordinary common sense is usually sufficient to permit anyone who directs his or her mind to the risk of the danger inherent in an activity to appreciate that risk and act accordingly—be the activity bottle throwing (as in *R. v. DeSousa*) or a barroom brawl. In many licensed activities, such as driving motor vehicles, there must be a basic amount of knowledge and experience before permission to engage in that activity will be granted (see *R. v. Hundal*). Where individuals engage in activities for which they lack sufficient knowledge, experience, or physical ability, they may be properly found to be at fault, not so much for their inability to properly carry out the activity, but for their decision to attempt the activity without having accounted for their deficiencies. The law expects people embarking on hazardous activities to ask questions or seek help before they venture beyond their depth. Thus even the inexperienced defendant may be properly found to be morally blameworthy for having embarked on a dangerous venture without taking the trouble to properly inform himself or herself. The criminal law imposes a single minimum standard which must be met by all people engaging in the activity in question, provided that they enjoy the requisite capacity to appreciate the danger, and judged in all the circumstances of the case, including unforeseen events and reasonably accepted misinformation. Without a constant minimum standard, the duty imposed by the law would be eroded and the criminal sanction trivialized.

Mental disabilities short of incapacity generally do not suffice to negative criminal liability for criminal negligence. The explanations for why a person fails to advert to the risk inherent in the activity he or she is undertaking are legion. They range from simple absent-mindedness to attributes related to age, education and culture. To permit such a subjective assessment would be "co-extensive with the judgment of each individual, which would be as variable as the length of the foot of each individual" leaving "so vague a line as to afford no rule at all, the degree of judgment belonging to each individual being infinitely various": *Vaughan v. Menlove* (1837), 3 Bing. (N.C.) 468, 132 E.R. 490, at p. 475;

see A.M. Linden, *Canadian Tort Law* (4th ed. 1988), at pp. 116-17. Provided the capacity to appreciate the risk is present, lack of education and psychological predispositions serve as no excuse for criminal conduct, although they may be important factors to consider in sentencing.]

This is not to say that the question of guilt is determined in a factual vacuum. While the legal duty of the accused is not particularized by his or her personal characteristics short of incapacity, it is particularized in application by the nature of the activity and the circumstances surrounding the accused's failure to take the requisite care. As McIntyre J. pointed out in *R. v. Tutton*, [1989] 1 S.C.R. 1392, the answer to the question of whether the accused took reasonable care must be founded on a consideration of all the circumstances of the case. The question is what the reasonably prudent person would have done in all the circumstances. Thus a welder who lights a torch causing an explosion may be excused if he has made an enquiry and been given advice upon which he was reasonably entitled to rely, that there was no explosive gas in the area. The necessity of taking into account all of the circumstances in applying the objective test in offences of penal negligence was affirmed in *R. v. Hundal, supra.*

. . .

The foregoing analysis suggests the following line of inquiry in cases of penal negligence. The first question is whether *actus reus* is established. This requires that the negligence constitute a marked departure from the standards of the reasonable person in all the circumstances of the case. This may consist in carrying out the activity in a dangerous fashion, or in embarking on the activity when in all the circumstances it is dangerous to do so.

The next question is whether the *mens rea* is established. As is the case with crimes of subjective *mens rea*, the *mens rea* for objective foresight of risking harm is normally inferred from the facts. The standard is that of the reasonable person in the circumstances of the accused. If a person has committed a manifestly dangerous act, it is reasonable, absent indications to the contrary, to infer that he or she failed to direct his or her mind to the risk and the need to take care. However, the normal inference may be negated by evidence raising a reasonable doubt as to lack of capacity to appreciate the risk. Thus, if a *prima facie* case for *actus reus* and *mens rea* is made out, it is necessary to ask a further question: did the accused possess the requisite capacity to appreciate the risk flowing from his conduct? If this further question is answered in the affirmative, the necessary moral fault is established and the accused is properly convicted. If not, the accused must be acquitted.

[McLachlin J affirmed the manslaughter conviction on the basis that a reasonable person in the circumstances would have been aware of the risk of non-trivial bodily harm. La Forest J wrote a separate judgment concurring with McLachlin J.]

Unfortunately, the certainty that emerged in the aftermath of the majority opinion in *Hundal* and *Creighton* on the permissibility of employing objective standards of liability and on the requirements for objective fault was relatively short-lived. In *Beatty*, a sharply divided Supreme Court reconsidered the *mens rea* required for the offence of dangerous driving causing death, the very crime at issue in *Hundal*.

R v Beatty
Supreme Court of Canada
2008 SCC 5, [2008] 1 SCR 49

[The accused was charged with three counts of dangerous driving causing death. The accident that gave rise to these charges occurred when the accused's pickup truck, for no apparent reason, suddenly crossed the solid centre line into the path of an oncoming vehicle, killing all three occupants. Witnesses driving behind the victims' car observed the accused's vehicle being driven in a proper manner prior to the accident. An expert inspection concluded that the accused's vehicle had not suffered from mechanical failure. Intoxicants were not a factor. The accused stated that he was not sure what happened but that he must have lost consciousness or fallen asleep and collided with the other vehicle. The question that divided the courts below was whether this momentary act of negligence was sufficient to constitute dangerous operation of a motor vehicle causing death within the meaning of s 249(4) of the *Criminal Code*. The trial judge acquitted the accused. The British Columbia Court of Appeal allowed an appeal by the Crown.]

CHARRON J (Bastarache, Deschamps, Abella, and Rothstein JJ concurring):

[6] … Unquestionably, conduct which constitutes a departure from the norm expected of a reasonably prudent person forms the basis of both civil and penal negligence. However, it is important not to conflate the civil standard of negligence with the test for penal negligence. Unlike civil negligence, which is concerned with the apportionment of loss, penal negligence is aimed at punishing *blameworthy* conduct. Fundamental principles of criminal justice require that the law on penal negligence concern itself not only with conduct that deviates from the norm, which establishes the *actus reus* of the offence, but with the offender's mental state. The onus lies on the Crown to prove both the *actus reus* and the *mens rea*. Moreover, where liability for penal negligence includes potential imprisonment, as is the case under s. 249 of the *Criminal Code*, the distinction between civil and penal negligence acquires a constitutional dimension.

[7] The *modified* objective test established by this Court's jurisprudence remains the appropriate test to determine the requisite *mens rea* for negligence-based criminal offences. As the label suggests, this test for penal negligence "modifies" the purely objective norm for determining civil negligence. It does so in two important respects. First, there must be a "marked departure" from the civil norm in the circumstances of the case. A mere departure from the standard expected of a reasonably prudent person will meet the threshold for civil negligence, but will not suffice to ground liability for penal negligence. The distinction between a mere departure and a marked departure from the norm is a question of degree. It is only when the conduct meets the higher threshold that the court may find, on the basis of that conduct alone, a blameworthy state of mind.

[8] Second, unlike the test for civil negligence which does not concern itself with the mental state of the driver, the modified objective test for penal negligence cannot ignore the actual mental state of the accused. Objective *mens rea* is based on the premise that a reasonable person in the accused's position would have been aware of the risks arising from the conduct. The fault lies in the absence of the requisite mental state of care. Hence, the accused cannot avoid a conviction by simply stating that he or she *was not thinking* about the manner of driving. However, where the accused raises a reasonable doubt

whether a reasonable person in his or her position would have been aware of the risks arising from the conduct, the premise for finding objective fault is no longer sound and there must be an acquittal. The analysis is thus contextualized, and allowances are made for defences such as incapacity and mistake of fact. This is necessary to ensure compliance with the fundamental principle of criminal justice that the innocent not be punished. ...

[Charron J reviewed the Court's earlier decision in *Hundal*.]

[40] Some of the language used in *Hundal* nonetheless left uncertainty about the degree to which personal characteristics could form part of the circumstances which must be taken into account in applying the modified objective test. (See for example the references to "certain personal factors" at p. 883 and to "human frailties" at p. 887.) This remaining uncertainty was later resolved in *Creighton*. Short of incapacity to appreciate the risk or incapacity to avoid creating it, personal attributes such as age, experience and education are not relevant. The standard against which the conduct must be measured is always the same—it is the conduct expected of the reasonably prudent person in the circumstances. The reasonable person, however, must be put in the *circumstances* the accused found himself in when the events occurred in order to assess the reasonableness of the conduct. To reiterate the example used above, the reasonable person becomes the one who "without prior warning, suffers a totally unexpected heart attack, epileptic seizure or detached retina" or becomes the one who "in the absence of any warning or knowledge of its possible effects, takes a prescribed medication which suddenly and unexpectedly" causes him to drive in a manner that is dangerous to the public. By so placing the reasonable person, the test is not personalized and the standard remains that of a reasonably prudent driver, but it is appropriately contextualized.

[41] In *Hundal*, Cory J. summarized the analytical framework for applying the modified objective test in the following oft-quoted passage (at pp. 888-89):

> It follows then that a trier of fact may convict if satisfied beyond a reasonable doubt that, viewed objectively, the accused was, in the words of the section, driving in a manner that was "dangerous to the public, having regard to all the circumstances, including the nature, condition and use of such place and the amount of traffic that at the time is or might reasonably be expected to be on such place." In making the assessment, the trier of fact should be satisfied that the conduct amounted to a marked departure from the standard of care that a reasonable person would observe in the accused's situation.
>
> Next, if an explanation is offered by the accused, such as a sudden and unexpected onset of illness, then in order to convict, the trier of fact must be satisfied that a reasonable person in similar circumstances ought to have been aware of the risk and of the danger involved in the conduct manifested by the accused.

[42] In reviewing a number of cases that have applied this test, I have observed two common difficulties. First, there appears to be some confusion on the distinction, if any, between "objectively dangerous driving" on one hand, and a "marked departure from the standard of care" on the other. This difficulty is quite understandable because some departures from the reasonable standard of care may not be "marked" or "significant" but are nonetheless undeniably dangerous. As we shall see, this case is one example. Second, there appears to be much uncertainty in the case law on how to deal with evidence about

the accused's mental state. In particular, when is evidence about the accused's actual mental state relevant? Is it relevant in determining whether the conduct constitutes a "marked departure" from the norm or, as the courts below in this case have done, should it be considered only as part of a distinct analysis on potential exculpatory defences?

[43] As we have seen, the requisite *mens rea* for the offence of dangerous driving was the sole issue before the Court in *Hundal*, and the test was expressed accordingly. In order to clarify the uncertainties I have mentioned, it may assist to restate the summary of the test in terms of both the *actus reus* and the *mens rea* of the offence. I respectfully disagree with the Chief Justice that the test for the *actus reus* is defined in terms of a marked departure from the normal manner of driving (para. 67). The *actus reus* must be defined, rather, by the words of the enactment. Of course, conduct that is found to depart markedly from the norm remains necessary to make out the offence because nothing less will support the conclusion that the accused acted with sufficient blameworthiness, in other words with the requisite *mens rea*, to warrant conviction. In addition, it may be useful to keep in mind that while the modified objective test calls for an objective assessment of the accused's manner of driving, evidence about the accused's actual state of mind, if any, may also be relevant in determining the presence of *sufficient mens rea*. I would therefore restate the test reproduced above as follows:

(a) The *Actus Reus*

The trier of fact must be satisfied beyond a reasonable doubt that, viewed objectively, the accused was, in the words of the section, driving in a manner that was "dangerous to the public, having regard to all the circumstances, including the nature, condition and use of the place at which the motor vehicle is being operated and the amount of traffic that at the time is or might reasonably be expected to be at that place."

(b) The *Mens Rea*

The trier of fact must also be satisfied beyond a reasonable doubt that the accused's objectively dangerous conduct was accompanied by the required *mens rea*. In making the objective assessment, the trier of fact should be satisfied on the basis of all the evidence, including evidence about the accused's actual state of mind, if any, that the conduct amounted to a marked departure from the standard of care that a reasonable person would observe in the accused's circumstances. Moreover, if an explanation is offered by the accused, then in order to convict, the trier of fact must be satisfied that a reasonable person in similar circumstances ought to have been aware of the risk and of the danger involved in the conduct manifested by the accused.

[44] I wish to elaborate on certain aspects of this test before applying it to the facts of this case.

3.4.1 Determining the Actus Reus

[45] I deal firstly with the *actus reus*. The offence is defined by the words of the legislative provision, not by the common law standard for civil negligence. In order to determine the *actus reus*, the conduct must therefore be measured as against the wording of s. 249.

Although the offence is negligence-based, this is an important distinction. As we have seen, conduct that constitutes dangerous operation of a motor vehicle as defined under s. 249 will necessarily fall below the standard expected of a reasonably prudent driver. The converse however is not necessarily true—not all negligent driving will constitute dangerous operation of a motor vehicle. If the court is satisfied beyond a reasonable doubt that the manner of driving was dangerous to the public within the meaning of s. 249, the *actus reus* of the offence has been made out. Nothing is gained by adding to the words of s. 249 at this stage of the analysis.

[46] As the words of the provision make plain, it is the *manner* in which the motor vehicle was operated that is at issue, not the consequence of the driving. The consequence, as here where death was caused, may make the offence a more serious one under s. 249(4), but it has no bearing on the question whether the offence of dangerous operation of a motor vehicle has been made out or not. Again, this is also an important distinction. If the focus is improperly placed on the consequence, it almost begs the question to then ask whether an act that killed someone was dangerous. The court must not leap to its conclusion about the manner of driving based on the consequence. There must be a meaningful inquiry into the manner of driving. The consequence, of course, may assist in assessing the risk involved, but it does not answer the question whether or not the vehicle was operated in a manner dangerous to the public. This Court explained this distinction in *R. v. Anderson*, [1990] 1 S.C.R. 265, as follows:

> In the circumstances of this case, the unfortunate fact that a person was killed added nothing to the conduct of the appellant. The degree of negligence proved against the appellant by means of the evidence that he drove after drinking and went through a red light was not increased by the fact that a collision occurred and death resulted. *If driving and drinking and running a red light was not a marked departure from the standard, it did not become so because a collision occurred.* In some circumstances, perhaps, the actions of the accused and the consequences flowing from them may be so interwoven that the consequences may be relevant in characterizing the conduct of the accused. That is not the case here. [Emphasis added; p. 273.]

3.4.2 Determining the Mens Rea

[47] In determining the question of *mens rea*, the court should consider the totality of the evidence, including evidence, if any, about the accused's actual state of mind. As discussed at length above, the *mens rea* requirement for the offence of dangerous driving will be satisfied by applying a modified objective test. This means that, unlike offences that can only be committed if the accused possesses a subjective form of *mens rea*, it is not necessary for the Crown to prove that the accused had a positive state of mind, such as intent, recklessness or wilful blindness. Of course, this does not mean that the actual state of mind of the accused is irrelevant. For example, if proof is made that a driver purposely drove into the path of an oncoming vehicle in an intentionally dangerous manner for the purpose of scaring the passengers of that vehicle or impressing someone in his own vehicle with his bravado, the requirement of *mens rea* will easily be met. One way of looking at it is to say that the subjective *mens rea* of intentionally creating a danger for other users of the highway within the meaning of s. 249 of the *Criminal Code* constitutes a "marked departure" from the standard expected of a reasonably prudent driver. ...

[48] However, subjective *mens rea* of the kind I have just described need not be proven to make out the offence because the mischief Parliament sought to address in enacting s. 249 encompasses a wider range of behaviour. Therefore, while proof of subjective *mens rea* will clearly suffice, it is not essential. In the case of negligence-based offences such as this one, doing the proscribed act with the absence of the appropriate mental state of care may instead suffice to constitute the requisite fault. The presence of objective *mens rea* is determined by assessing the dangerous conduct as against the standard expected of a reasonably prudent driver. If the dangerous conduct constitutes a "marked departure" from that norm, the offence will be made out. As stated earlier, what constitutes a "marked departure" from the standard expected of a reasonably prudent driver is a matter of degree. The lack of care must be serious enough to merit punishment. There is no doubt that conduct occurring in a few seconds can constitute a marked departure from the standard of a reasonable person. Nonetheless, as Doherty J.A. aptly remarked in *Willock*, "conduct that occurs in such a brief timeframe in the course of driving, which is otherwise proper in all respects, is more suggestive of the civil rather than the criminal end of the negligence continuum" (para. 31). Although *Willock* concerned the offence of criminal negligence, an offence which is higher on the continuum of negligent driving, this observation is equally apt with respect to the offence of dangerous operation of a motor vehicle.

[49] If the conduct does not constitute a marked departure from the standard expected of a reasonably prudent driver, there is no need to pursue the analysis. The offence will not have been made out. If, on the other hand, the trier of fact is convinced beyond a reasonable doubt that the objectively dangerous conduct constitutes a marked departure from the norm, the trier of fact must consider evidence about the actual state of mind of the accused, if any, to determine whether it raises a reasonable doubt about whether a reasonable person in the accused's position would have been aware of the risk created by this conduct. If there is no such evidence, the court may convict the accused.

4. Application to This Case

[50] First, did Mr. Beatty commit the *actus reus* of the offence? Did he operate his motor vehicle "in a manner that is dangerous to the public, having regard to all the circumstances, including the nature, condition and use of the place at which the motor vehicle is being operated and the amount of traffic that at the time is or might reasonably be expected to be at that place"? I repeat here the Court of Appeal's analysis of the circumstances for convenience:

> However, the evidence showed that there was only one lane for travel in each direction, the traffic was proceeding at or near the posted speed limit of 90 kilometres per hour, the highway was well-travelled, there was limited visibility approaching the curve, and the collision occurred within a split second of the respondent's crossing onto the oncoming lane of traffic.
>
> Viewed objectively, the respondent's failure to confine his vehicle to its own lane of travel was in "all the circumstances" highly dangerous to other persons lawfully using the highway, and in particular those approaching in a westerly direction on their own side of the road. [paras. 23-24]

[51] Up to this point in the analysis, I would agree with the Court of Appeal. In all the circumstances, Mr. Beatty's failure to confine his vehicle to his own lane of traffic was

dangerous to other users of the highway. Further, no suggestion was made at trial that Mr. Beatty was in a state of non-insane automatism at the time. However, this conclusion only answers the *actus reus* part of the offence. The more difficult question is whether Mr. Beatty had the necessary *mens rea*. There is no evidence here of any deliberate intention to create a danger for other users of the highway that could provide an easy answer to that question. Indeed, the limited evidence that was adduced about the actual state of mind of the driver suggested rather that the dangerous conduct was due to a momentary lapse of attention. Hence, the trial judge was correct in finding that the question of *mens rea* in this case turns on whether Mr. Beatty's manner of driving, viewed on an objective basis, constitutes a marked departure from the norm.

[52] In my respectful view, the Court of Appeal erred in faulting the trial judge for addressing her attention to Mr. Beatty's "momentary lack of attention" and his "few seconds of lapsed attention." The trial judge appropriately focused her analysis on Mr. Beatty's manner of driving in all the circumstances. She noted that there was no evidence of improper driving before the truck momentarily crossed the centre line and that the "few seconds of clearly negligent driving" was the only evidence about his manner of driving (para. 36). She appropriately considered the totality of the evidence in finding that "the only reasonable inference" was that "he experienced a loss of awareness" that caused him to drive straight instead of following the curve in the road (para. 36). In her view, this momentary lapse of attention was insufficient to found criminal culpability. She concluded that there was "insufficient evidence to support a finding of a *marked* departure from the standard of care of a prudent driver" (para. 37).

[53] Based on the totality of the evidence, I see no reason to interfere with the trial judge's assessment of Mr. Beatty's conduct in this case and her conclusion on Mr. Beatty's criminal liability. By contrast, it is my respectful view that the Court of Appeal leaped too quickly to the conclusion that the requisite *mens rea* could be made out from the simple fact of the accident occurring, leaving no room for any assessment of Mr. Beatty's conduct along the continuum of negligence.

[54] For these reasons, I would allow the appeal and restore the acquittals.

[55] McLACHLIN CJ (Binnie and LeBel JJ concurring): I agree with much of Justice Charron's analysis as well as with her disposition of the appeal. However, I take a different view on how the test for the offence of dangerous operation of a motor vehicle should be stated and how this impacts on cases of momentary lapse of attention, such as this case.

The Test for the Offence of Dangerous Driving

[56] At para. 43, my colleague describes the *actus reus* in terms of dangerous operation of a motor vehicle and the *mens rea* in terms of a marked departure from the standard of care that a reasonable person would observe in the accused's circumstances. In discussing the *actus reus*, my colleague observes that "[n]othing is gained by adding to the words of s. 249 at this stage of the analysis" (para. 45).

[57] With respect, I take a different view. A clear understanding of what is required to fulfill both the *actus reus* and *mens rea* of dangerous operation of a motor vehicle is important, and I see no impediment to judicial clarification of either element. Determining what constitutes dangerous driving without regard to the consequences—as the test

requires—is a difficult task, and one that has given rise to confusion. In my opinion the language of s. 249 of the *Criminal Code*, R.S.C. 1985, c. C-46, is consistent with requiring a marked departure as part of the *actus reus* of the offence.

[58] The jurisprudence of this Court offers assistance on what constitutes the *actus reus* and *mens rea* of dangerous driving and how the two elements of the offence should be described. *R. v. Hundal*, [1993] 1 S.C.R. 867, confirmed in *R. v. Creighton*, [1993] 3 S.C.R. 3, indicates that the characterization of "marked departure" from the norm applies to the *actus reus* of the offence, and that the *mens rea* of the offence flows by inference from that finding, absent an excuse casting a reasonable doubt on the accused's capacity.

[59] In *Hundal*, Cory J., writing for the majority, was concerned mainly with *mens rea*. However, after settling this matter, he stated the overall requirements of dangerous driving in terms of marked departure, without limiting them to *mens rea*:

> ... a trier of fact may convict if satisfied beyond a reasonable doubt that, viewed objectively, the accused was, in the words of the section, driving in a manner that was "dangerous to the public, having regard to all the circumstances, including the nature, condition and use of such place and the amount of traffic that at the time is or might reasonably be expected to be on such place." *In making the assessment, the trier of fact should be satisfied that the conduct amounted to a marked departure from the standard of care that a reasonable person would observe in the accused's situation.* [Emphasis added; p. 888.]

[60] Cory J. then went on to state that even where this is established, the accused may offer an excuse such as a sudden and unexpected onset of illness, thereby raising a reasonable doubt as to *mens rea*.

[61] In the absence of language in this passage confining the requirement of marked departure to the *mens rea* of the offence, it is reasonable to conclude that it was intended to apply to both the *actus reus* and the *mens rea* of the offence.

[62] Any doubt on the matter was removed by the majority decision of this Court in *Creighton*, in which Cory J. joined. At pp. 73-74, I wrote:

> The foregoing analysis suggests the following line of inquiry in cases of penal negligence. The first question is whether actus reus is established. This requires that the negligence constitute a marked departure from the standards of the reasonable person in all the circumstances of the case. ...
>
> The next question is whether the *mens rea* is established. As is the case with crimes of subjective *mens rea*, the *mens rea* for objective foresight of risking harm is normally inferred from the facts. The standard is that of the reasonable person in the circumstances of the accused. If a person has committed a manifestly dangerous act, it is reasonable, absent indications to the contrary, to infer that he or she failed to direct his or her mind to the risk and the need to take care. However, the normal inference may be negated by evidence raising a reasonable doubt as to lack of capacity to appreciate the risk. Thus, if a *prima facie* case for *actus reus* and *mens rea* is made out, it is necessary to ask a further question: did the accused possess the requisite capacity to appreciate the risk flowing from his conduct? If this further question is answered in the affirmative, the necessary moral fault is established and the accused is properly convicted. If not, the accused must be acquitted. [Emphasis added.]

[63] This analysis, which defines the *actus reus* in terms of a "marked departure" and the *mens rea* as the normal inference from that conduct, absent excuse, was penned only

a short time after *Hundal*, and concurred in by the majority of the Court, including Cory J. Justice Cory's decision in *Hundal* was cited and relied on in *Creighton* as a basis for this formulation. It follows that *Hundal* and *Creighton* should be seen as adopting the same test, and that any ambiguity in the discussion of dangerous driving in *Hundal* should be resolved in the manner suggested in *Creighton*.

[64] Requiring that the conduct alleged to constitute the *actus reus* of the offence constitute a marked departure from the standard of a reasonable person is consistent with the language of s. 249 of the *Criminal Code*. Section 249(1)(a) defines the *actus reus* in terms of operating a motor vehicle "in a manner that is dangerous to the public, having regard to all the circumstances," and goes on to provide a non-exhaustive list of circumstances to be taken into consideration. In this context, dangerousness is properly understood as requiring a marked departure from the conduct of a reasonable person, in the circumstances.

[65] If conduct not representing a marked departure is allowed to satisfy the *actus reus* requirement for dangerous driving, then it becomes unclear how *Criminal Code* dangerous driving is to be distinguished from a wide variety of provincial motor vehicle offences, at the level of the *actus reus*. Provincial motor vehicle legislation exists in part to manage and minimize the risks associated with the widespread use of motor vehicles. Thus in many cases, conduct representing a violation of provincial motor vehicle legislation will be "objectively dangerous" in comparison with strict compliance with the provisions of the legislation. Yet it would stretch the meaning of s. 249(1)(a) to suggest that such conduct would be sufficient to establish the *actus reus* of dangerous driving. The "marked departure" requirement provides a standard for determining what is objectively dangerous in the context of s. 249(1)(a), allowing relatively minor violations of provincial motor vehicle Acts to fall clearly outside the scope of conduct that Parliament intended to criminalize.

[66] I add that this formulation mirrors the theory on which the criminal law is founded—that the *actus reus* and *mens rea* of an offence represent two aspects of the criminal conduct. The *actus reus* is the act and the *mens rea*, or guilty mind, the intention to commit that act. If the *mens rea* of the offence requires a failure to take reasonable care which is inferred from the conduct of driving in a manner that represents a marked departure from the norm, then the *actus reus* must be the act of driving in a manner that represents a marked departure from the norm.

[67] I therefore conclude that the correct statement of the law is as follows:

1. The *actus reus* requires a marked departure from the normal manner of driving.

2. The *mens rea* is generally inferred from the marked departure in the nature of driving. Based on the finding of a marked departure, it is inferred that the accused lacked the requisite mental state of care of a reasonable person.

3. While generally the *mens rea* is inferred from the act constituting a marked departure committed by the accused, the evidence in a particular case may negate or cast a reasonable doubt on this inference.

The Problem of Momentary Lapse of Attention

[68] The problem at the heart of this case is whether acts of momentary lapse of attention can constitute the offence of dangerous driving. The accused was driving in an

entirely normal manner until his vehicle suddenly swerved over the centre line of the road, for reasons that remain unclear. Clearly there was momentary lapse of attention. The issue is whether this is capable of establishing the *actus reus* and *mens rea* of the offence.

[69] In my view, momentary lapse of attention without more cannot establish the *actus reus* or *mens rea* of the offence of dangerous driving. This flows from this Court's decision in *R. v. Mann*, [1966] S.C.R. 238, upholding the constitutionality of the provincial offence of careless driving. The constitutionality of the provincial offence was attacked on the ground that the field was occupied by the federal offence of dangerous driving. In order to resolve this issue, the Court was obliged to define the ambit of dangerous driving and careless driving, respectively. The Court concluded that the two offences were aimed at different conduct. In *Mann*, the distinction between the levels of negligence required for careless driving and dangerous driving was essential to upholding the constitutionality of the provincial offence of careless driving. Although some of the judges in *Mann* cast their reasoning in terms of inadvertent versus advertent negligence, concepts which are no longer the focus of the analysis in cases of dangerous driving (*Hundal*, at p. 889), what is clear is that the offence of dangerous driving requires a higher degree of negligence than careless driving. This Court affirmed the differing levels of negligence for careless driving and dangerous driving in *Hundal*.

[70] It follows that if the only evidence against the accused is evidence of momentary lapse of attention, the offence of dangerous driving is not established. This, in my view, is as it should be. The heavy sanctions and stigma that follow from a criminal offence should not be visited upon a person for a momentary lapse of attention. Provincial regulatory offences appropriately and adequately deal with this sort of conduct.

[71] In terms of the test for the offence outlined above, momentary lapse of attention does not establish the marked departure from the standard of care of a reasonably prudent driver required for the *actus reus* of the offence. As the case law teaches, one must consider the entire manner of driving of the accused, in all the circumstances. A moment of lapse of attention, in the context of totally normal driving, is insufficient to establish the marked departure required for the offence of dangerous driving. In order to avoid criminal liability, an accused's driving is not required to meet a standard of perfection. Even good drivers are occasionally subject to momentary lapses of attention. These may, depending on the circumstances, give rise to civil liability, or to a conviction for careless driving. But they generally will not rise to the level of a marked departure required for a conviction for dangerous driving.

[72] A momentary lapse of attention *without more* cannot establish the *actus reus* and *mens rea* of the offence of dangerous driving. However, additional evidence may show that the momentary lapse is part of a larger pattern that, considered as a whole, establishes the marked departure from the norm required for the offence of dangerous driving. For example, a momentary lapse might be caused by the consumption of alcohol or by carrying on an activity incompatible with maintaining proper control of the automobile. The trier of fact might conclude in such a case that considering the total driving pattern in all the circumstances, a marked departure from the norm is established.

· · ·

[77] On the test that I have suggested, the appropriate analysis in cases such as *Willock*, where momentary lapse of attention is all the Crown can prove, is the following. The starting point is that momentary lapse of attention cannot satisfy the requirements of the

offence of dangerous driving, and more particularly the requirement of a marked departure from the standard of care of a reasonably prudent driver required to establish the *actus reus*. A momentary lapse, without more, is therefore insufficient to establish the offence. However, additional elements in the proof may establish that the momentary lapse is part of a larger driving pattern that, considered as a whole, constitutes a marked departure from the standard of care of a reasonably prudent driver. It is for the trier of fact to consider all of the evidence objectively and determine if the *actus reus* of driving in a manner that constitutes a marked departure from the norm is established. If this is established, the *mens rea* will be inferred from the driving pattern, absent excuses presented by the accused such as a sudden and unexpected illness which raise a reasonable doubt as to criminal intent.

[78] Additional inquiry into the accused's actual state of mind is unnecessary. If the only evidence is of momentary lapse of attention, the *actus reus* is not established and the Crown's case fails, making further inquiry unnecessary. On the other hand, if the accused is driving in a manner that constitutes a marked departure from the norm, the inference will be that he lacked the requisite mental state of care of a reasonable person, absent an excuse, such as a sudden and unexpected onset of illness.

[79] The appellant in this case was charged with dangerous driving causing death. There has been some debate in lower courts, and among academic commentators, regarding the approach to *actus reus* and *mens rea* in driving cases where the offence charged is criminal negligence, rather than dangerous driving. In this case, the Court does not have to rule on the elements of the offence for a driving offence charged as criminal negligence, and these reasons should not be read as deciding that issue.

Application to This Case

[80] The only evidence adduced by the Crown in the case at bar was evidence of a momentary lapse of attention that caused the accused's vehicle to cross the centre line of the highway. In all other respects, the accused's driving was, on the evidence, entirely normal.

[81] It follows that all that has been established is momentary lapse of attention. The marked departure required for the offence of dangerous operation of a motor vehicle has not been made out. The Crown did not succeed in proving that the accused's manner of driving, viewed as a whole, constituted a marked departure from the standard of care of a reasonably prudent driver. It follows that it did not prove the *actus reus* of the offence, and its case must fail.

Conclusion

[82] I would allow the appeal and restore the acquittals.

· · ·

FISH J: ...

[84] I agree with Justice Charron that the *actus reus* of dangerous driving consists in the elements of that offence set out in s. 249(1) of the *Criminal Code*, R.S.C. 1985, c. C-46. Accordingly, in my view, anyone who commits that *actus reus* with the requisite *mens rea* is guilty of dangerous driving.

· · ·

[88] The fault element, however, is not the marked departure from the norm of a reasonably prudent driver but the fact that a reasonably prudent driver in the accused's circumstances would have been aware of the risk of that conduct, and if able to do so, would have acted to avert it. This requisite mental element may only be inferred where the impugned conduct represents a marked departure from the norm; it cannot be inferred from the mere fact that he or she operated the motor vehicle in a dangerous manner.

. . .

[90] The Chief Justice and Justice Charron, essentially for the same reasons, have concluded, correctly in my view, that the impugned conduct of the accused in this case did not amount to a marked departure from the norm. There may well be circumstances in which inattention, even transitory, will suffice to establish the fault element of dangerous driving. That was not the case here.

[91] I would for this reason, like my colleagues, allow the appeal and restore the acquittals entered by the trial judge.

Appeal allowed.

R v Roy
Supreme Court of Canada
2012 SCC 26, [2012] 2 SCR 60

[The accused brought his vehicle to a halt at a stop sign on a relatively steep unpaved back road, which was snow-covered and slippery. Visibility was extremely poor due to fog. After stopping, he proceeded to make a left turn onto the highway. By doing so, his vehicle came directly into the path of an oncoming tractor-trailer, which had the right of way, and the two vehicles collided, killing a passenger in his vehicle. The accused had no memory of the accident and could not explain why he pulled out to make the turn when he did. The accused was convicted of dangerous driving causing death prior to the Supreme Court delivering its judgment in *Beatty, supra*.]

CROMWELL J for the Court:

[1] Dangerous driving causing death is a serious criminal offence punishable by up to 14 years in prison. Like all criminal offences, it consists of two components: prohibited conduct—operating a motor vehicle in a dangerous manner resulting in death—and a required degree of fault—a marked departure from the standard of care that a reasonable person would observe in all the circumstances. The fault component is critical, as it ensures that criminal punishment is only imposed on those deserving the stigma of a criminal conviction. While a mere departure from the standard of care justifies imposing civil liability, only a marked departure justifies the fault requirement for this serious criminal offence.

[2] Defining and applying this fault element is important, but also challenging, given the inherently dangerous nature of driving. Even simple carelessness may result in tragic consequences which may tempt judges and juries to unduly extend the reach of the criminal law to those responsible. Yet, as the Court put it in *R. v. Beatty*, 2008 SCC 5, [2008] 1 S.C.R. 49, at para. 34, "If every departure from the civil norm is to be criminalized,

regardless of the degree, we risk casting the net too widely and branding as criminals persons who are in reality not morally blameworthy." Giving careful attention to the fault element of the offence is essential if we are to avoid making criminals out of the merely careless.

. . .

[4] In my view, the trial judge made a serious legal error in relation to the fault element: he simply inferred from the fact that the appellant had committed a dangerous act while driving that his conduct displayed a marked departure from the standard of care expected of a reasonable person in the circumstances. This error is not one that may be dismissed as harmless. I would allow the appeal and set aside the appellant's conviction for dangerous driving. As in my view the evidence in the record does not support a reasonable inference that the appellant exhibited a marked departure from the standard of care that a reasonable person would have exhibited in the circumstances, I would allow the appeal and enter an acquittal.

. . .

[36] The focus of the *mens rea* analysis is on whether the dangerous manner of driving was the result of a marked departure from the standard of care which a reasonable person would have exercised in the same circumstances (*Beatty*, at para. 48). It is helpful to approach the issue by asking two questions. The first is whether, in light of all the relevant evidence, a reasonable person would have foreseen the risk and taken steps to avoid it if possible. If so, the second question is whether the accused's failure to foresee the risk and take steps to avoid it, if possible, was a *marked departure* from the standard of care expected of a reasonable person in the accused's circumstances.

[37] Simple carelessness, to which even the most prudent drivers may occasionally succumb, is generally not criminal. As noted earlier, Charron J., for the majority in *Beatty*, put it this way: "If every departure from the civil norm is to be criminalized, regardless of the degree, we risk casting the net too widely and branding as criminals persons who are in reality not morally blameworthy" (para. 34). The Chief Justice expressed a similar view: "Even good drivers are occasionally subject to momentary lapses of attention. These may, depending on the circumstances, give rise to civil liability, or to a conviction for careless driving. But they generally will not rise to the level of a marked departure required for a conviction for dangerous driving" (para. 71).

[38] The marked departure from the standard expected of a reasonable person in the same circumstances—a modified objective standard—is the minimum fault requirement. The modified objective standard means that, while the reasonable person is placed in the accused's circumstances, evidence of the accused's personal attributes (such as age, experience and education) is irrelevant unless it goes to the accused's incapacity to appreciate or to avoid the risk (para. 40). Of course, proof of subjective *mens rea*—that is, deliberately dangerous driving—would support a conviction for dangerous driving, but proof of that is not required (Charron J., at para. 47; see also McLachlin C.J., at paras. 74-75, and Fish J., at para. 86).

. . .

[42] Driving which, objectively viewed, is simply dangerous, will not on its own support the inference that the accused departed markedly from the standard of care of a reasonable person in the circumstances (Charron J., at para. 49; see also McLachlin C.J., at para. 66, and Fish J., at para. 88). In other words, proof of the *actus reus* of the offence,

without more, does not support a reasonable inference that the required fault element was present. Only driving that constitutes a marked departure from the norm may reasonably support that inference.

. . .

[54] In my view, the record does not provide evidence on which a properly instructed trier of fact, acting reasonably, could conclude that the appellant's standard of care was a marked departure from that expected of a reasonable person in the circumstances. I accept that the driving, objectively viewed, was dangerous. But it must be noted that there was no evidence that the driving leading up to pulling into the path of oncoming traffic was other than normal and prudent driving. The focus, therefore, is on the momentary decision to pull onto the highway when it was not safe to do so. I do not think that the manner of driving, on its own, supports a reasonable inference that the appellant's standard of care was a marked departure from that expected of a reasonable driver in the same circumstances.

[55] Taking the Crown's case at its highest, the appellant pulled out from a stop sign at a difficult intersection and in poor visibility when it was not safe to do so. Although the trial judge did not make a specific finding on the point, Mr. McGinnis (the driver of the tractor-trailer) thought that the appellant's vehicle had stopped before proceeding onto the highway. Mr. McGinnis also testified that when he first saw the lights of the appellant's vehicle, he guessed that it was about 300-400 feet away but that it could have been as little as 100 feet. It is, of course, reasonable to assume that the appellant could have seen the McGinnis vehicle at least as soon as Mr. McGinnis was able to see the appellant's vehicle. Given the lighting on the tractor-trailer, it might be concluded that the tractor-trailer may have been visible somewhat sooner. However, on any realistic scenario consistent with the evidence, the time between visibility and impact would be only a few seconds. In my view, the appellant's decision to pull onto the highway is consistent with simple misjudgment of speed and distance in difficult conditions and poor visibility. The record here discloses a single and momentary error in judgment with tragic consequences. It does not support a reasonable inference that the appellant displayed a marked departure from the standard of care expected of a reasonable person in the same circumstances so as to justify conviction for the serious criminal offence of dangerous driving causing death.

V. Disposition

[56] I would allow the appeal, set aside the appellant's conviction and enter an acquittal.

V. CONSTITUTIONAL CONSIDERATIONS

As discussed at the end of the previous chapter, s 7 of the Charter has had a significant impact on minimal levels of fault for both criminal and quasi-criminal offences. *Re BC Motor Vehicle Act*, [1985] 2 SCR 486 [*Motor Vehicle Reference*] and *R v Pontes*, [1995] 3 SCR 44 established the proposition that some level of fault is required prior to the loss (or potential loss) of liberty by an accused person.

Section 7 of the Charter has also helped shape the fault requirement for true criminal offences. The cases of *R v Vaillancourt*, [1987] 2 SCR 636 and *R v Martineau*, [1990] 2 SCR 633 held that nothing less than subjective foresight of death is required before an accused person can be convicted of murder. *R v Logan*, [1990] 2 SCR 731 held that the phrase "ought to have known" in s 21(2) of the *Criminal Code* is of no force and effect when applied to the crimes of murder or attempted murder. These fault requirements for murder are addressed in Chapter 13. But short of murder, attempted murder, and crimes against humanity (discussed below), something less than subjective fault will suffice for most criminal offences. As long as there is a meaningful fault requirement, s 7 of the Charter may be satisfied by objective fault components. For example, in *R v Durham* (1992), 76 CCC (3d) 219, the Ontario Court of Appeal held that Parliament could use the civil standard of negligence for the offence of using a firearm in a careless manner or without reasonable precautions for the safety of others (s 86(2) of the Code). Arbour JA stated for the court:

> Generally speaking, there is likely to be more stigma attached to a criminal conviction than to the violation of a non-criminally related statute. Yet not all criminal offences carry the same amount of stigma. The stigma is proportional not only to the gravity of the conduct and of its consequences, but to the level of fault, represented by the mental element, with which the act or omission was performed. …
>
> It is constitutionally impermissible for Parliament to treat as murder a conduct devoid of the essential characteristic upon which the stigmatization of murderers came to be based, the moral turpitude represented by the intention to kill. In the same way, if it is his dishonesty that stigmatizes the convicted thief, Parliament will not be permitted, absent justification under s. 1 of the *Charter*, to brandish as a thief someone who has not been shown to be dishonest. In my opinion, this is the extent to which cases such as *Vaillancourt* … and *Reference re: s. 94(2) of Motor Vehicle Act* … compel the consideration of stigma as a factor from which compliance with s. 7 may be determined. Even though a person convicted of an offence under s. 86(2) of the *Code* will carry the stigma of having a criminal conviction, that is not sufficient to dictate that the offence must contain a subjective mental element.

The Supreme Court of Canada in *R v Finlay*, [1993] 3 SCR 103 agreed with Arbour JA's decision and held that an objective test satisfies the *mens rea* requirement for the offence of careless storage of firearms (s 86(2)). Lamer CJ stated for the Court: "there is not sufficient stigma arising from a conviction under s. 86(2) to require a subjective *mens rea*."

In *R v Peters* (1991), 69 CCC (3d) 461, the British Columbia Court of Appeal held that subjective foresight of consequences was not required by s 434(a) of the Code, which made it an offence to wilfully set fire to certain objects. McEachern CJBC stated:

> It is also apparent that the level of social stigma attaching to a conviction for some offences is a more important consideration than the range of sentence prescribed for that offence. The Supreme Court of Canada has particularized murder, and attempted murder which require an intent to cause death, and theft which requires a measure of dishonesty, as offences which require subjective *mens rea*. It has not provided a schedule of such offences, but it has frequently mentioned that this requirement applies "for only a very few offences" (*Logan*, p. 399). From time to time trial and appellate judges will have to categorize those few offences which require subjective foreseeability.
>
> While I confess I have some difficulty distinguishing levels of social stigma attached to theft as compared with other offences frequently committed for financial gain, I am content, for the purposes of this appeal, to conclude that subjective *mens rea* is not constitutionally required with

respect to consequences resulting from a wilful act other than murder or theft caused by a lack of care on the part of the accused.

In *R v DeSousa*, [1992] 2 SCR 944, the Supreme Court of Canada held that s 269 of the Code (unlawfully causing bodily harm), which requires *mens rea* for the underlying criminal act (which because of the *Motor Vehicle Reference* cannot be an absolute liability offence) and objective foreseeability of the risk of bodily harm that is neither trivial nor transitory, was constitutionally valid under s 7 of the Charter. Sopinka J stated for the Court:

> Although I have concluded by means of statutory interpretation that s. 269 requires objective foresight of the consequences of an accused's unlawful act, the appellant argues that s. 7 of the Charter requires subjective foresight of all consequences which comprise part of the *actus reus* of an offence. The appellant notes that in *R. v. Martineau*, [1990] 2 S.C.R. 633, Lamer C.J.C., speaking for the majority of the court, discussed (at p. 360) a ... "general principle that criminal liability for a particular result is not justified except where the actor possesses a culpable mental state in respect of that result." The appellant also relies on *R. v. Metro News Ltd.* (1986), 29 C.C.C. (3d) 35 (Ont. C.A.), leave to appeal refused [1986] 2 S.C.R. viii, for a similar proposition that (at pp. 54-55):
>
> > ... [t]he minimum and necessary mental element required for criminal liability for most crimes is knowledge of the circumstances which make up the *actus reus* of the crime and foresight or intention with respect to any consequence required to constitute the *actus reus* of the crime.
>
> The appellant submits that this authority supports a requirement that the minimum mental element required by s. 7 of the Charter for s. 269 includes an intention to cause bodily harm. ...
>
> Lamer C.J.C. stated in *Martineau* (at p. 647) that "[i]f Parliament wishes to deter persons from causing bodily harm during certain offences, then it should punish persons for causing the bodily harm." This is exactly what s. 269 attempts to do. In this particular provision the mental element requirement is composed of both the mental element of the underlying unlawful act and the additional requirement of objective foresight of bodily harm. There is, however, no constitutional requirement that intention, either on an objective or a subjective basis, extend to the consequences of unlawful acts in general.
>
> The absence of a constitutional requirement that intention extend to all aspects of an unlawful act was discussed by Wilson J. in *R. v. Bernard*, [1988] 2 S.C.R. 833, at pp. 888-89, where she concludes that the minimal element of the application of force is sufficient for a conviction for sexual assault causing bodily harm. She inferentially confirms that s. 7 of the *Charter* does not mandate intention in regard to all of the consequences required by the offence. The contrary position, that intention must extend to all of the required consequences of an offence, is not supported by the case law and should not be adopted as a constitutional requirement.
>
> There are many provisions where one need not intend all of the consequences of an action. ... there must be an element of personal fault in regard to a culpable aspect of the *actus reus*, but not necessarily in regard to each and every element of the *actus reus*. The requirement of fault in regard to a meaningful aspect of the *actus reus* is necessary to prevent punishing the mentally, and morally, innocent and is in keeping with a long line of cases of this Court including *Rees*, *supra*, and *Pappajohn*, *supra*. In many offences, such as assault or dangerous driving, the offence is made out regardless of the consequences of the act but the consequences can be used to aggravate liability for the offence. For example, both assault and assault causing bodily harm have identical *mens rea* requirements and the element of causing bodily harm is merely used to classify the

offence. No principle of fundamental justice prevents Parliament from treating crimes with certain consequences as more serious than crimes which lack those consequences.

A number of *Criminal Code* offences call for a more serious charge if certain consequences follow. To require intention in relation to each and every consequence would bring a large number of offences into question including manslaughter (s. 222(5)), criminal negligence causing bodily harm (s. 221), criminal negligence causing death (s. 220), dangerous operation causing bodily harm (s. 249(3)), dangerous operation causing death (s. 249(4)), impaired driving causing bodily harm (s. 255(2)), impaired driving causing death (s. 255(3)), assault causing bodily harm (s. 267(1)(b)), aggravated assault (s. 268), sexual assault causing bodily harm (s. 272(c)), aggravated sexual assault (s. 273), mischief causing danger to life (s. 430(2)) and arson causing bodily harm (s. 433(b)). As noted by Professor Colvin, "[i]t would, however, be an error to suppose that *actus reus* and *mens rea* always match in this neat way" (E. Colvin, *Principles of Criminal Law* (2nd ed. 1991), at p. 55).

Conduct may fortuitously result in more or less serious consequences depending on the circumstances in which the consequences arise. The same act of assault may injure one person but not another. The implicit rationale of the law in this area is that it is acceptable to distinguish between criminal responsibility for equally reprehensible acts on the basis of the harm that is actually caused. This is reflected in the creation of higher maximum penalties for offences with more serious consequences. Courts and legislators acknowledge the harm actually caused by concluding that in otherwise equal cases a more serious consequence will dictate a more serious response. …

To require fault in regard to each consequence of an action in order to establish liability for causing that consequence would substantially restructure current notions of criminal responsibility. Such a result cannot be founded on the constitutional aversion to punishing the morally innocent. One is not morally innocent simply because a particular consequence of an unlawful act was unforeseen by that actor. In punishing for unforeseen consequences the law is not punishing the morally innocent but those who cause injury through avoidable unlawful action. Neither basic principles of criminal law, nor the dictates of fundamental justice require, by necessity, intention in relation to the consequences of an otherwise blameworthy act.

In *R v Hundal*, [1993] 1 SCR 867, set out above in Section IV, the Supreme Court of Canada decided that dangerous driving under s 249 of the Code does not require a subjective awareness of risk. The Court's subsequent reconsideration of the *mens rea* requirement for dangerous driving in *R v Beatty*, 2008 SCC 5, [2008] 1 SCR 49 (set out above) did not overturn the holding from *Hundal* that s 7 does not require subjective fault for a dangerous driving conviction.

The Court in *R v Creighton*, [1993] 3 SCR 3 upheld the constitutionality of unlawful act manslaughter under s 222(5)(a). The Court was divided on the question whether objective foresight of the likelihood of *death* was required, with the majority of the Court (per McLachlin J) holding that the section required only the requisite *mens rea* for the underlying unlawful act and reasonable foreseeability of the risk of *bodily harm* that is neither trivial nor transitory. The entire Court agreed, however, that manslaughter was constitutional even though subjective fault is not required. Lamer CJ concluded:

The only basis upon which subjective foresight of death or the risk of death could be found to be constitutionally required in the case of unlawful act manslaughter, therefore, would be to find that the offence is one of those crimes for which "because of the special nature of the stigma attached to a conviction therefor or the available penalties, the principles of fundamental justice require a *mens rea* reflecting the particular nature of that crime": see *R. v. Vaillancourt*, per Lamer J., at p. 653. …

In my view, the stigma which attaches to a conviction for unlawful act manslaughter is significant, but does not approach the opprobrium reserved in our society for those who *knowingly* or
intentionally take the life of another. It is for this reason that manslaughter developed as a separate offence from murder at common law.

McLachlin J, for the majority, held that the *mens rea* requirement was only objective foresight of bodily harm (and not death) and indicated that there was no constitutional principle
that the fault element must include all elements of the *actus reus*. She concluded:

> The Chief Justice correctly observes that the criminal law has traditionally aimed at symmetry
> between the *mens rea* and the prohibited consequences of the offence. The *actus reus* generally
> consists of an act bringing about a prohibited consequence, e.g. death. Criminal law theory sug-
> gests that the accompanying *mens rea* must go to the prohibited consequence. The moral fault
> of the accused lies in the act of bringing about that consequence. The Chief Justice reasons from
> this proposition that since manslaughter is an offence involving the prohibited act of killing an-
> other, a *mens rea* of foreseeability of harm is insufficient; what is required is foreseeability of
> death. ...
>
> It is important to distinguish between criminal law theory, which seeks the ideal of absolute
> symmetry between *actus reus* and *mens rea*, and the constitutional requirements of the *Charter*.
> As the Chief Justice has stated several times, "the Constitution does not always guarantee the
> 'ideal'" (*R. v. Lippé*, [1991] 2 S.C.R. 114, at p. 142; *R. v. Wholesale Travel Group Inc.*, [1991] 3 S.C.R. 154,
> at p. 186; *R. v. Finlay*, [1993] 3 S.C.R. 103). ...
>
> I know of no authority for the proposition that the *mens rea* of an offence must always attach
> to the precise consequence which is prohibited as a matter of constitutional necessity. The rel-
> evant constitutional principles have been cast more broadly. No person can be sent to prison
> without *mens rea*, or a guilty mind, and the seriousness of the offence must not be disproportion-
> ate to the degree of moral fault. Provided an element of mental fault or moral culpability is pres-
> ent, and provided that it is proportionate to the seriousness and consequences of the offence
> charged, the principles of fundamental justice are satisfied. ...
>
> The foregoing considerations lead me to conclude that the fact that the *mens rea* of man-
> slaughter requires foreseeable risk of harm rather than foreseeable risk of death does not violate
> the principles of fundamental justice. In the final analysis, the moral fault required for man-
> slaughter is commensurate with the gravity of the offence and the penalties which it entails, and
> offends no principle of fundamental justice.

The Court in *R v Finta* addressed the constitutionalization of fault in the context of crimes
against humanity.

R v Finta
Supreme Court of Canada
[1994] 1 SCR 701

[The accused was charged under s 7(3.71) of the *Criminal Code* with committing unlawful
confinement, robbery, kidnapping, and manslaughter that constituted war crimes and
crimes against humanity as a result of his activities as a senior officer at a concentration
camp in Hungary. The trial judge ruled that the jury must determine that the accused was

aware of the circumstances that would bring his actions within the definition of war crimes or crimes against humanity. The accused was acquitted. The Crown appealed.]

CORY J (Lamer CJ and Gonthier and Major JJ concurring): The appellant contends that the deeming mechanism in the *Code* provision presently under consideration is such that an accused charged under s. 7(3.71) may be found guilty *not* of "war crimes" or "crimes against humanity" but of "ordinary" *Code* offences such as manslaughter, confinement or robbery. It is further argued that proof of the *mens rea* with respect to the domestic offences provides the element of personal fault required for offences under s. 7(3.71). Thus, it is submitted, proof of further moral culpability is not required, since once the necessary *mens rea* to confine forcibly, rob or commit manslaughter has been proved, it becomes impossible to maintain that the accused was morally innocent.

I cannot accept that argument. What distinguishes a crime against humanity from any other criminal offence under the Canadian *Criminal Code* is that the cruel and terrible actions which are essential elements of the offence were undertaken in pursuance of a policy of discrimination or persecution of an identifiable group or race. With respect to war crimes, the distinguishing feature is that the terrible actions constituted a violation of the laws of war. Although the term laws of war may appear to be an oxymoron, such laws do exist. War crimes, like crimes against humanity, shock the conscience of all right-thinking people. The offences described in s. 7(3.71) are thus very different from, and far more grievous than, any of the underlying offences.

For example, it cannot be denied that the crimes against humanity alleged in this case, which resulted in the cruel killing of thousands of people, are far more grievous than occasioning the death of a single person by an act which constitutes manslaughter in Canada. To be involved in the confinement, robbing and killing of thousands of people belonging to an identifiable group must, in any view of morality or criminality, be more serious than even the commission of an act which would constitute murder in Canada.

Therefore, while the underlying offences may constitute a base level of moral culpability, Parliament has added a further measure of blameworthiness by requiring that the act or omission constitute a crime against humanity or a war crime. If the jury is not satisfied that this additional element of culpability has been established beyond a reasonable doubt, then the accused cannot be found guilty of a war crime or a crime against humanity.

In *R. v. Vaillancourt*, … this court held that there are certain crimes where, because of the special nature of the unavoidable penalties or of the stigma attached to a conviction, the principles of fundamental justice require a mental blameworthiness or a *mens rea* reflecting the particular nature of that crime. It follows that the question which must be answered is not simply whether the accused is morally innocent, but rather, whether the conduct is sufficiently blameworthy to merit the punishment and stigma that will ensue upon conviction for that particular offence. In the present case there must be taken into account not only the stigma and punishment that will result upon a conviction for the domestic offence, but also the additional stigma and opprobrium that will be suffered by an individual whose conduct has been held to constitute crimes against humanity or war crimes. In reality, upon conviction, the accused will be labelled a war criminal and will suffer the particularly heavy public opprobrium that is reserved for these offences. Further, the sentence which will follow upon conviction will reflect the high degree of moral outrage that society very properly feels toward those convicted of these crimes. …

It cannot be inferred that someone who robs civilians of their valuables during a war has thereby committed a crime against humanity. To convict someone of an offence when it has not been established beyond a reasonable doubt that he or she was aware of conditions that would bring to his or her actions that requisite added dimension of cruelty and barbarism violates the principles of fundamental justice. The degree of moral turpitude that attaches to crimes against humanity and war crimes must exceed that of the domestic offences of manslaughter or robbery. It follows that the accused must be aware of the conditions which render his or her actions more blameworthy than the domestic offence.

I find support for this position in decisions of this court relating to the constitutional requirements for *mens rea*. In *R. v. Martineau*, [1990] 2 S.C.R. 633, the court struck down s. 213(a) of the *Criminal Code*, R.S.C. 1970, c. C-34. This section provided that the offence of murder would be committed in circumstances where a person caused the death of another while committing or attempting to commit certain named offences, and meant to cause bodily harm for the purpose of committing the underlying offence or to facilitate flight after committing the offence. Murder was deemed to have been committed regardless of whether the person meant to cause death and regardless of whether that person knew that death was likely to result from his or her actions. The majority of the Court (*per* Lamer C.J.C.) affirmed that in order to secure a conviction for murder, the principles of fundamental justice required subjective foresight of the consequences of death. As was noted in *R. v. DeSousa*, [1992] 2 S.C.R. 944, while it is not a principle of fundamental justice that fault or *mens rea* must be proved as to each separate element of the offence, there must be a meaningful mental element demonstrated relating to a *culpable aspect* of the *actus reus*: see also *R. v. Hess*[; *R v Nguyen*], [1990] 2 S.C.R. 906.

These cases make it clear that in order to constitute a crime against humanity or a war crime, there must be an element of subjective knowledge on the part of the accused of the factual conditions which render the actions a crime against humanity.

Thus, for all the reasons set out earlier, I am in agreement with the majority of the Court of Appeal's assessment that the mental element of a crime against humanity must involve an awareness of the facts or circumstances which would bring the acts within the definition of a crime against humanity. However, I emphasize it is *not* necessary to establish that the accused knew that his or her actions were inhumane. As the majority stated at p. 116:

> ... if the jury accepted the evidence of the various witnesses who described the conditions in the boxcars which transported the Jews away from Szeged, the jury would have no difficulty concluding that the treatment was "inhumane" within the definition of that word supplied by the trial judge. The jury would then have to determine whether Finta was aware of those conditions. If the jury decided that he was aware of the relevant conditions, the knowledge requirement was established regardless of whether Finta believed those conditions to be inhumane.

Similarly, for war crimes, the Crown would have to establish that the accused knew or was aware of the facts or circumstances that brought his or her actions within the definition of a war crime. That is to say the accused would have to be aware that the facts or circumstances of his or her actions were such that, viewed objectively, they would shock the conscience of all right thinking people.

Alternatively, the *mens rea* requirement of both crimes against humanity and war crimes would be met if it were established that the accused was wilfully blind to the facts or circumstances that would bring his or her actions within the provisions of these offences.

LA FOREST J (L'Heureux-Dubé and McLachlin JJ concurring): A *mens rea* need only be found in relation to the individually blameworthy elements of a war crime or crime against humanity, not every single circumstance surrounding it. This approach receives support in Canadian domestic law. In *R. v. DeSousa*, [1992] 2 S.C.R. 944, at pp. 964-65, this Court held that reading in such a requirement for every element of an offence misconstrues and overgeneralizes earlier decisions of this court. Rather, the proper approach, it noted, was that "there must be an element of personal *fault in regard to a culpable aspect* of the *actus reus*, but not necessarily in regard to each and every element of the *actus reus*" (emphasis added). ...

I would add that any stigma attached to being convicted under war crimes legislation does not come from the nature of the offence, but more from the surrounding circumstances of most war crimes. Often it is a question of the scale of the acts in terms of numbers, but that is reflected in the domestic offence; for example, a charge of the kidnapping or manslaughter of a hundred people in the domestic context itself raises a stigma because of the scale, but one that s. 7 is not concerned about. Similarly, the jurisprudence does not allow for stigma that may also result from being convicted of an offence in which the surrounding circumstances are legally irrelevant but public disapproval strong. Thus, one convicted of a planned and deliberate murder can face additional stigma because his or her actions were particularly repulsive or violent, but our system does not make any additional allowance for that.

Appeal dismissed.

See *Crimes Against Humanity and War Crimes Act*, SC 2000, c 24, ss 4 and 6, which incorporates the definitions of "genocide," "war crimes," and "crimes against humanity" from the *Rome Statute* establishing the International Criminal Court. See generally A Cassese, *International Criminal Law* (Oxford: Oxford University Press, 2003).

The final article addresses the relationship between the common law standards of subjective fault examined at the start of this chapter and the more limited constitutional standards of fault that have emerged in subsequent jurisprudence.

K Roach, "Mind the Gap: Canada's Different Criminal and Constitutional Standards of Fault"
(2011) 61 UTLJ 545 (footnotes omitted)

The Canadian experience with the constitutionalization of criminal law fault principles seems at first glance to be positive and robust. A closer examination of the Canadian experience, however, reveals that there has been significant slippage between criminal law standards of fault articulated in a series of common law cases before the *Charter* and the actual standards of fault that have been enforced by courts under the *Charter*. Common law presumptions of subjective fault for all criminal offences and for the extension of fault requirements to all aspects of the prohibited act articulated in pre-Charter cases such as *Gaunt and Watts*, *Beaver* and *Pappajohn* have been eclipsed by an acceptance under the *Charter* of negligence liability for all but a few crimes thought to carry such a special stigma that they require proof of subjective fault in relation to all aspects of the prohibited act. So far, the Court has only held that murder, attempted murder and war crimes have enough stigma to constitutionally require proof of subjective fault in relation to all aspects of the prohibited act. The Court has also in *DeSousa* and *Creighton* rejected the idea that fault should be established in reference to all aspects of the prohibited act even though there was some support for such a common law presumption before the *Charter*.

The gap that has emerged between Canadian criminal and constitutional law standards of fault is a fertile area for exploring the proper relationship between criminal and constitutional law. The gap can be defended on the basis that the courts have rightly been cautious and minimalistic when constitutionalizing fault principles as part of a supreme law that cannot easily be limited, overridden or amended. The Court has followed a case-by-case approach to constitutionalization defended by scholars such as Cass Sunstein who worry about the Court's capacities to formulate broad and deep theories of justice when enforcing the supreme law of the Constitution. The Court's caution in this area may be related to doubts about the project of interpreting the guarantees of the principles of fundamental justice in s. 7 of the *Charter* to include more than procedural fairness. The Court's approach has left plenty of room for courts and legislatures to develop negligence as a form of criminal fault and to experiment with blended forms of subjective and objective fault. As such, it recognizes that the principles of subjective fault no longer command the consensual support that they once did. The Court's acceptance of negligence liability and its attempts to ensure that negligence liability is adapted to the criminal context and adequately distinguished from civil negligence provides some evidence of its attraction to alternatives to subjective fault. Serious concerns have been raised that principles of subjective fault are inappropriate means to deal with pressing problems and Parliament has experimented with mixed subjective and objective forms of fault, most notably in the contexts of sexual assault and corporate crime. Viewed in this light, the Court's refusal to constitutionalize pre-*Charter* presumptions of subjective fault may represent a lack of confidence in the wisdom of the universal application of subjective fault in favour of a more contextual and selective approach.

On the other hand, the Court's cautious approach to constitutionalization of subjective fault and the gap that has emerged between constitutional and criminal law standards can be criticized. From the perspective of criminal law, it reveals a faint-hearted commitment to subjective principles of fault that were recognized before the *Charter* as a critical component of a just criminal justice system that held culpable individuals to account on the basis of their own perceptions and abilities. The court has had difficulties grappling with the difficulties of ensuring that negligence standards are applied fairly to the broad range of people who may commit criminal acts.

From the perspective of constitutional law, the Court's caution about constitutionalizing subjective fault principles under s. 7 of the *Charter* is likely related to its decisions to hold that once a right is recognized as a principle of fundamental justice, reasonable limits on the right can only be justified in exceptional circumstances such as emergencies. This unique and restrictive approach to s. 1 has tempered the Court's ability to constitutionalize subjective fault principles because of concerns that frequent exceptions to these principles would be difficult if not impossible to justify under s. 1. It has resulted in a truncated dialogue between courts and legislatures about whether departures from subjective fault principles can be justified. Unlike any other right in the *Charter*, the Supreme Court has held that s. 7 rights are close to absolute and should generally only be subject to reasonable limitation under s. 1 of the *Charter* in extraordinary emergency situations.

The unique treatment of s. 7 under s. 1 helps explain why the Court has been so reluctant to constitutionalize criminal law fault standards. The recognition of subjective fault principles under s. 7 of the *Charter* might have resulted in invalidation of the many criminal offences that only require criminal negligence or offences such as manslaughter that do not require the proof of fault in relation to all aspects of the prohibited act. The invalidation of such laws would have been the product of the Court's reluctance to accept reasonable limits on s. 7 rights even if some departures from common law fault standards could be justified by the government under an ordinary s. 1 test as reasonable limits on rights that are necessary to respond to the challenges presented by specific crimes such as sexual violence, corporate crime and harms caused by particularly dangerous activities such as unlawful acts including impaired and dangerous driving.

Some commentators have questioned the advisability of constitutionalizing fault requirements under s 7 of the Charter. See R Cairns Way, "Constitutionalizing Subjectivism: Another View" (1990) 79 CR (3d) 260 and J Stribopoulos, "The Constitutionalization of 'Fault' in Canada: A Normative Critique" (1999) 42 Crim LQ 227. Professor Cameron has argued that the entire enterprise of insisting on minimum constitutional fault requirements for those offences that carry a significant stigma, like murder, would have been better placed under s 12 of the Charter, the guarantee against cruel and unusual treatment or punishment. See J Cameron, "Fault and Punishment Under Sections 7 and 12 of the Charter" in J Cameron & J Stribopoulos, eds, *The Charter and Criminal Justice: Twenty-Five Years Later* (Toronto: LexisNexis, 2008). For arguments that constitutional principles should be but are not always central to criminal law, see BL Berger, "Constitutional Principles" in MD Dubber & T Hörnle, eds, *The Oxford Handbook of Criminal Law* (Oxford: Oxford University Press, 2014), where he argues:

> Criminal law is among the first arenas in which we see deeper constitutional commitments; it also reveals and tests the limits of the social justice that these commitments imagine. The poverty, illness, and social dislocation that continue to drive the criminal law point to the economic and social structures that are left largely undisturbed by constitutional law.

VI. MISTAKE OF FACT

In criminal law, mistake of fact is a difficult concept to categorize. It is a defence, but unlike most, it is not affirmative in nature. Rather, successfully raising the defence of mistake of fact involves a negation of *mens rea*.

Given its intimate connection to *mens rea*, mistake of fact has a comparatively long history. For example, in *R v Tolson* (1889), 23 QBD 168 (Ct for Cr Cases Reserved), Cave J noted:

> At common law an honest and reasonable belief in the existence of circumstances, which, if true, would make the act for which a prisoner is indicted an innocent act has always been held to be

a good defence. This doctrine is embodied in the somewhat uncouth maxim "actus non facit reum, nisi mens sit rea."

With the rise of subjective *mens rea* offences, the emphasis in the early cases on the need for an accused's belief to be "reasonable" soon fell away. In *R v Rees*, [1956] SCR 640, the accused was charged with contributing to the delinquency of a minor for having intercourse with a 16-year-old girl. The girl had apparently told the accused that she was 18. In a concurring judgment, Cartwright J explained:

> [T]he essential question is whether the belief entertained by the accused is an honest one and that the existence or non-existence of reasonable grounds for such belief is merely relevant evidence to be weighed by the tribunal of fact in determining such essential question.

In *Beaver v The Queen*, [1957] SCR 531 Cartwright J interpreted the offence of possession of morphine in the then *Opium and Narcotic Drug Act*, RSC 1952, c 201 as a true crime, but also held that the accused's honest but mistaken belief that the substance was "sugar of milk" and not morphine prevented a conviction. He concluded:

> [T]he essential question is whether the belief entertained by the accused is an honest one and that the existence or non-existence of reasonable grounds for such belief is merely relevant evidence to be weighed by the tribunal of fact in determining that essential question. ...
>
> Has X possession of heroin when he has in his hand or in his pocket or in his cupboard a package which in fact contains heroin but which he honestly believes contains only baking-soda? In my opinion that question must be answered in the negative. The essence of the crime is the possession of the forbidden substance and in a criminal case there is in law no possession without knowledge of the character of the forbidden substance. ...
>
> It would, of course, be within the power of Parliament to enact that a person who, without any guilty knowledge, had in his physical possession a package which he honestly believed to contain a harmless substance such as baking-soda but which in fact contained heroin, must on proof of such facts be convicted of a crime and sentenced to at least 6 months' imprisonment; but I would refuse to impute such an intention to Parliament unless the words of the statute were clear and admitted of no other interpretation.

What if an accused is mistaken about the nature of the illegal drugs possessed? In *R v Kundeus*, [1976] 2 SCR 272, the accused was convicted of trafficking LSD that he thought was mescaline on the basis that *mens rea* does not extend so far as to the knowledge of the precise type of illegal drug. Laskin CJ dissented on the basis that, while proof of the exact nature of the illegal drug may not be necessary, mescaline was treated in the law as a far less serious drug.

As is explained in more detail in Chapter 12, mistake of fact can also operate where an accused is charged with sexual assault and harbours a mistaken belief in consent. In *Pappajohn v The Queen*, [1980] 2 SCR 120, the accused was convicted of rape. The Court was divided on whether the defence arose on the facts in that case. The majority concluded that, given the diametrically opposing accounts offered by the accused and the complainant, it did not. Nevertheless, the entire Court agreed that on the right facts, the defence was indeed available to a charge of rape. Dickson J, dissenting in the result, provided the following very useful summary of the defence both historically and in contemporary Canadian criminal law:

Mistake is a defence, then, where it prevents an accused from having the *mens rea* which the law requires for the very crime with which he is charged. Mistake of fact is more accurately seen as a negation of guilty intention than as the affirmation of a positive defence. It avails an accused who acts innocently, pursuant to a flawed perception of the facts, and nonetheless commits the *actus reus* of an offence. Mistake is a defence though, in the sense that it is raised as an issue by an accused. The Crown is rarely possessed of knowledge of the subjective factors which may have caused an accused to entertain a belief in a fallacious set of facts. …

In principle, the defence should avail when there is an honest belief in consent, or an absence of knowledge that consent has been withheld. Whether the mistake is rooted in an accused's mistaken perception, or is based upon objective, but incorrect, facts confided to him by another, should be of no consequence. The kind of mistaken fact pleaded by the *Morgan* defendants, however, is more likely to be believed than a bald assertion of mistaken belief during a face to face encounter. In any event, it is clear that the defence is available only where there is sufficient evidence presented by an accused, by his testimony or by the circumstances in which the act occurred, to found the plea.

Honest and Reasonable Mistake

The next question which must be broached is whether a defence of honest, though mistaken, belief in consent must be based on reasonable grounds. A majority of the House of Lords in *Morgan* answered the question in the negative, and that view was affirmed by the Heilbron Committee. There can be no doubt this answer is consonant with principle. As Professor Keedy has written (22 *Harv. L. Rev.* 75, at p. 88), an act is reasonable in law when it is such as a man of ordinary care would do under similar circumstances; to require that the mistake be reasonable means that, if the accused is to have a defence, he must have acted up to the standard of an average man, whether the accused is himself such a man or not; this is the application of an outer standard to the individual; if the accused is to be punished because his mistake is one which an average man would not make, punishment will sometimes be inflicted when the criminal mind does not exist. …

In Canada, the *Tolson* rule has already been rejected by this Court in favour of the honest belief standard. Unless this Court wishes to overrule *Beaver v. The Queen*, it is difficult to see how the minority in *Morgan* can decide this appeal.

In *R. v. Rees*, the issue was whether there is *mens rea* for the offence of knowingly or wilfully contributing to juvenile delinquency. Cartwright J. set out the *Tolson* test and then held as follows:

> The first of the statements of Stephen J., quoted above should now be read in the light of the judgment of Lord Goddard C.J., concurred in by Lynskey and Devlin JJ. in *Wilson v. Inyang* which, in my opinion, rightly decides that the essential question *is* whether the belief entertained by the accused is an honest one and that the existence or non-existence of reasonable grounds for such belief is merely relevant evidence to be weighed by the tribunal of fact in determining such essential question. (at p. 651)

One year later, in *Beaver v. The Queen, supra*, a narcotics case, the opinion of Mr. Justice Cartwright was accepted by a majority of the Court. He adopted the paragraph quoted above from *Rees. Beaver* has since been regarded as an authoritative contribution to the law as to mental element, and mistaken belief, in true crimes.

It is not clear how one can properly relate reasonableness (an element in offences of negligence) to rape (a "true crime" and not an offence of negligence). To do so, one must, I think take the view that the *mens rea* goes only to the physical act of intercourse and not to non-consent, and acquittal comes only if the mistake is reasonable. This, upon the authorities, is not a correct view, the intent in rape being not merely to have intercourse, but to have it with a non-consenting woman. If the jury finds that mistake, whether reasonable or unreasonable, there should be no conviction. If, upon the entire record, there is evidence of mistake to cast a reasonable doubt upon the existence of a criminal mind, then the prosecution has failed to make its case.

As will be discussed in Chapter 12, *Pappajohn* was a controversial decision. In the specific context of sexual assault, Parliament ultimately intervened and legislated a requirement that in order to rely on a mistaken belief in consent, an accused person must have taken "reasonable steps, in the circumstances known to the accused at the time, to ascertain that the complainant was consenting" (see s 273.2(b)). This amendment is considered more fully in Chapter 12. Section 172.1(4) also denies a defence to those charged with online child luring if they claim they believed their interlocutor was over the age of majority "unless the accused took reasonable steps to ascertain the age of the person." Notice how such legislative provisions serve to combine subjective and objective fault elements.

With negligence-based offences—for example, strict liability offences in the "half-way house" between full *mens rea* and absolute liability offences recognized in *R v Sault Ste Marie*, [1978] 2 SCR 1299—mistake of fact is available but subject to a reasonableness requirement. As Dickson J explained in *Sault Ste Marie*, "The defence will be available if the accused reasonably believed in a mistaken set of facts which, if true, would render the act or omission innocent, or if he took all reasonable steps to avoid the particular event" (at 1326).

ADDITIONAL READING

Brudner, A. "Guilt Under the Charter: The Lure of Parliamentary Supremacy" (1998) 40 Crim LQ 287.

Cairns Way, R. "The Charter, the Supreme Court and the Invisible Politics of Fault" (1992) 12 Windsor YB Access Just 128.

Colvin, E & S Anand. *Principles of Criminal Law*, 3rd ed (Toronto: Thomson Carswell, 2007) at 179ff.

Manning, M & P Sankoff. *Manning, Mewett & Sankoff: Criminal Law*, 4th ed (Toronto: LexisNexis, 2009) at 143ff.

Roach, K. *Criminal Law*, 6th ed (Toronto: Irwin Law, 2015) ch 5.

Stuart, D. *Canadian Criminal Law*, 7th ed (Toronto: Carswell, 2014) ch 3.

Williams, G. *Criminal Law*, 2nd ed (London: Stevens and Sons, 1961) ch 2-5.

Williams, G. *The Mental Element in Crime* (Jerusalem: Magnes Press, 1965).

Williams, G. *Textbook of Criminal Law*, 2nd ed (London: Stevens and Sons, 1983) at 70ff.

Ignorance of the Law

Section 19 of the *Criminal Code* provides: "Ignorance of the law by a person who commits an offence is not an excuse for committing that offence." Although this is a traditional principle of criminal liability, it can be a harsh rule. Recall, as discussed in Chapter 1, the courts have been reluctant to hold that laws violate s 7 of the Charter because of excessive vagueness. Also note how the number of criminal offences, not to mention regulatory offences, as discussed in Chapter 6, has expanded in the modern age.

Although the principle that ignorance (or mistake) of the law is not an excuse appears simple and absolute, there are a number of complications. The first section of this chapter examines the relevance of the accused's belief about the legality of his or her actions to proof of the particular fault elements for particular offences such as theft. This section also throws some light on the nature of fault or *mens rea* standards.

The next section examines the related and sometimes illusive distinction between the accused's mistaken belief about the facts—a factor that is relevant to the proof of fault—and the accused's mistaken belief about the law—a factor that under s 19 of the Code is not an excuse for committing the offence.

The next section examines an exception to the ignorance of the law is not an excuse principle—namely, the defence of officially induced error. The Supreme Court has recently recognized the legitimacy of this defence and it now constitutes an exception, albeit a limited and tightly confined one, to the basic principle that ignorance of the law is not an excuse. As seen in the section that follows, however, the limited officially induced error defence has not been expanded to a more general defence based on a reasonable mistake of law.

The next section examines the possible direct and indirect effects of the Charter on s 19 through an examination of a case where a closely divided Supreme Court held that the operation of the ignorance of the law principle with respect to a regulatory offence had the effect of denying those charged with driving with a suspended licence their only possible defence. The Court then held that this meant that the regulatory offence should be treated as one of no fault and absolute liability as opposed to one of strict liability. The final section looks at possible statutory reforms of s 19.

I. MISTAKEN BELIEFS ABOUT THE LAW AND
PARTICULAR FAULT ELEMENTS

R v Howson
Ontario Court of Appeal
[1966] 3 CCC 348

[An employee of a towing service was charged with theft of a car when he refused to give a towed car back to its owner until the owner paid certain expenses. He was convicted at trial and appealed.]

PORTER CJO (with whom Evans JA concurred): … The relevant sections of the *Criminal Code* [s 269 is now s 322] read as follows:

> 269(1) Every one commits theft who fraudulently and without colour of right takes, or fraudulently and without colour of right converts to his use or to the use of another person, anything whether animate or inanimate, with intent,
>
>> (a) to deprive, temporarily or absolutely, the owner of it or a person who has a special property or interest in it, of the thing or of his property or interest in it …
>
> (3) A taking or conversion of anything may be fraudulent notwithstanding that it is effected without secrecy or attempt at concealment.
>
> (4) For the purposes of this Act the question whether anything that is converted is taken for the purpose of conversion, or whether it is, at the time it is converted, in the lawful possession of the person who converts it is not material.

In my view the word "right" should be construed broadly. The use of the word cannot be said to exclude a legal right. The word is in its ordinary sense charged with legal implications. I do not think that s. 19 affects s. 269. Section 19 only applies when there is an offence. There is no offence if there is colour of right. If upon all the evidence it may fairly be inferred that the accused acted under a genuine misconception of fact or law, there would be no offence of theft committed. The trial tribunal must satisfy itself that the accused has acted upon an honest, but mistaken belief that the right is based upon either fact or law, or mixed fact and law.

The learned trial Judge held that the removal of the vehicle to Merton St. was not an unreasonable thing to do. Under the circumstances, I would agree with this finding. The real question here is whether the accused had, under the circumstances, a colour of right sufficient to justify his refusal to release the vehicle. If not, upon the facts of this case, he would be guilty of theft.

The accused was an employee of his brother, Walter Howson, who was the owner of the towing company. The evidence indicates that the accused acted upon instructions from his brother. He stated that he believed he had a right to retain the car until the towing charges were paid. He produced a letter from the building superintendent which ostensibly gave him the right to retain the car. Because the accused was asked to give up the car and refused to do so without payment, the Magistrate said that he was wrongfully withholding the car, the company having no lien upon it. He thereupon convicted the accused. However, the Magistrate then proceeded to make certain comments. He said that the accused was not trying to steal a car or intending to steal one. He then said that the type of business was not one that he would encourage.

I think it is clear from this evidence that the Magistrate misdirected himself by failing to consider the question of colour of right. From what he said after the conviction, it was obvious that he did not believe that the accused was trying or intending to steal the car. Under these circumstances he should, I think, have acquitted the accused. There were other points raised in the argument, but since, upon the grounds stated, I would acquit, I do not think it necessary to deal with them.

I would, therefore, allow the appeal, quash the conviction, and direct that a verdict of acquittal be entered.

[For similar and other reasons Laskin JA also allowed the appeal.]

Appeal allowed; conviction quashed.

In *R v Docherty*, [1989] 2 SCR 941, the accused was charged with wilfully failing to comply with a probation order in the following circumstances. The accused was charged with and pleaded guilty to the offence of having care or control of a motor vehicle when his blood alcohol level exceeded 80 mg of alcohol in 100 ml of blood. At the time of the commission of the offence, the accused was bound by a probation order that required that he "keep the peace and be of good behaviour." It was the allegation of the Crown that the commission of the offence constituted the offence of wilful breach of a probation order. The accused testified that at the time he committed the offence of "over 80" he was unaware that he was breaking the law. The accused had been found in a parked vehicle in an intoxicated state and he testified that he did not think he was breaking the law because the car could not be started. The trial judge accepted the evidence of the accused and acquitted him of the offence. An appeal by the Crown by way of stated case to the Newfoundland Court of Appeal was dismissed as was the Crown's further appeal to the Supreme Court of Canada. Wilson J stated for the Court:

> I believe, in other words, [that the offence of wilful breach of a probation order] constitutes an exception to the general rule expressed in s. 19 in a case where the commission of a criminal offence is relied on as the *actus reus* under the section. An accused cannot have wilfully breached his probation order through the commission of a criminal offence unless he knew that what he did constituted a criminal offence. However, the conviction is evidence of the *mens rea* ... only to the extent that wilfulness can be inferred from the *actus reus* as indicated above. Such *mens rea* must be proved and s. 19 of the *Criminal Code* does not preclude the respondent from relying on his honest belief that he was not doing anything wrong to negate its presence. Where knowledge is itself a component of the requisite *mens rea*, the absence of knowledge provides a good defence.
>
> I would dismiss the appeal.

Note that subsequent to this case, Parliament amended the offence of breach of a probation order to delete the requirement that the breach be wilful. See s 733.1 of the *Criminal Code*. Is *Docherty* still good law?

The next case deals with an attempt to argue that a colour of right defence such as that in *Howson* is constitutionally required.

Jones and Pamajewon v The Queen
Supreme Court of Canada
[1991] 3 SCR 110

[The accused were charged with operating an unlawful bingo contrary to s 206 of the *Criminal Code*. The accused were members of an Indian band and were operating a bingo on an Indian reserve. They had been informed by the police that the *Criminal Code* prohibits lottery schemes unless operated under the auspices of a provincial licence. The accused, however, purported to renounce the jurisdiction of the federal and provincial governments in relation to gaming on reserves and to issue their own licences for operating bingos. The accused were convicted at trial and their appeal to the Ontario Court of Appeal was dismissed. They appealed to the Supreme Court of Canada.]

STEVENSON J stated for the Court: The appellants must be taken, for the purpose of this appeal, to acknowledge that they were mistaken in their belief that the *Criminal Code* did not apply to their activities on the reserve. They have not taken any proceedings to challenge the authority of Canada to enact laws applicable to those activities and have not made any such challenge here. In their factum, the appellants not only disclaim asking for such a determination, they ask the court not to make statements that may adversely affect legal issues concerning Indian self-government. That request will be respected.

There are, in my view, two clear barriers to this alleged defence. First, it is not a defence to this crime, secondly, any mistake is a mistake of law.

The appellants cited no authority for the proposition that colour of right is relevant to any crime which does not embrace the concept within its definition. They cited *R. v. Laybourn*, [1987] 1 S.C.R. 782; *R. v. DeMarco* (1973), 13 C.C.C. (2d) 369 (Ont. C.A.); *R. v. Howson*, [1966] 3 C.C.C. 348 (Ont. C.A.); *R. v. Johnson* (1904), 7 O.L.R. 525 (Div. Ct.). *Laybourn* is a case of mistake of fact as an issue in sexual assault. In the other cases the offences, such as theft, required the absence of a colour of right.

They argued that mistake of fact is a constitutionally mandated defence to criminal charges. Even assuming that proposition is correct, it can only apply to the *facts* which constitute the offence. There is no suggestion of any mistake relating to those facts here; the mistake is in believing that the law does not apply because it is inoperative on reserves.

Section 19 of the *Code* expresses the long-recognized principle that a mistake about the law is no defence to a charge of breaching it. No attack was made on the validity of that section. The argument here is that this legal mistake should be characterized as a mistake of fact and I find it impossible to characterize the mistaken belief put forward here as embracing any mistake of fact.

II. MISTAKE OF FACT AND MISTAKE OF LAW

In *R v Prue*, [1979] 2 SCR 547, the majority of the Supreme Court of Canada held that an accused's lack of knowledge that his licence had been automatically suspended under provincial law after a driving offence was a "question of fact" and not of law when the accused was charged under s 238 with driving while his licence was suspended (see now s 259(4)). Laskin CJ (with whom Spence, Dickson, and Estey JJ concurred) stated:

> So far as the operation of s. 238(3) is concerned, the existence of a suspension from driving is a question of fact underlying the invocation of that provision, and so too is proof that an accused charged thereunder drove while his licence to do so was under suspension. … I do not see how this position is affected by whether the provincial legislation operates to make a suspension automatic or whether it arises only upon some notice or other action to be taken thereunder. For the purpose of the *Criminal Code*, whether there has been an effective suspension is simply a question of fact.

Ritchie J (with whom Pigeon J concurred), dissenting, stated:

> These cases turn on the finding that the failure to give notice or to take such other administrative step as is required is a question of fact and that the accused's failure to know of the suspension is not a mistake of law.
>
> In the present case the respondents' lack of knowledge of the suspension of their licences was not occasioned by any mistake of fact but rather by ignorance of the law attendant upon failure to be aware of the automatic suspension for which provision is made in s. 86D of the *Motor-Vehicle Act*. …
>
> I am satisfied that the mistake made by the accused in the present cases is nothing more than a mistake as to the legal consequences of a conviction under s. 236 of the *Criminal Code* involving as they do the automatic suspension of the operator's licence under s. 86D of the *Motor-Vehicle Act*.

In *R v MacDougall*, [1982] 2 SCR 605, the accused was charged with driving a motor vehicle while his licence to do so was cancelled contrary to s 258(2) of the *Motor Vehicle Act*, RSNS 1967, c 191, in the following circumstances. Following his conviction of an offence contrary to s 233(2) of the *Criminal Code*, the accused was sent an "Order of Revocation of Licence" by the registrar of motor vehicles, but when he appealed this conviction he was sent a "Notice of Reinstatement" by the registrar. Subsequently, the accused's appeal was dismissed and he was so informed by his lawyer. Some time later, the registrar sent out another "Order of Revocation of Licence," which, however, the accused did not receive until after he was charged with the offence contrary to s 258(2). The accused testified that he believed he could drive until he was notified by the registrar that his licence had been revoked and this evidence was accepted by the trial judge. Section 250(3) of the *Motor Vehicle Act* provided that where an appeal is dismissed the driver's licence "shall be thereupon and hereby revoked and shall remain revoked." The accused was acquitted at trial and an appeal by the Crown to the county court was dismissed as was a further appeal by the Crown to the Appeal Division of the Supreme Court of Nova Scotia.

Ritchie J gave the unanimous judgment of the seven members of the Supreme Court of Canada (which included Laskin CJ):

His Honour Judge Sullivan and the majority of the Court of Appeal affirmed these findings and held that they disclosed a defence to the charge here laid on the ground that they disclosed a mistake of fact on the part of the accused within the meaning of *R. v. Sault Ste. Marie*, … whereas I am unable to treat the respondent's mistake otherwise than as a mistake of law in relation to his right, because of s. 250(3), to drive after his appeal had been dismissed. This was a mistake of law which does not afford the respondent a defence having regard to s. 19 of the *Criminal Code* which provides that:

> 19. Ignorance of the law by a person who commits an offence is not an excuse for committing that offence.

. . .

Before concluding, I should make mention of *R. v. Prue, R. v. Baril*, [1979] 2 S.C.R. 547, in which the majority of the court held that for the purposes of the *Criminal Code*, whether there has been an effective suspension is simply a question of fact. The case arose under s. 238(3) of the *Criminal Code* and the majority decision, delivered by the Chief Justice at p. 552, makes it clear that a distinction may be drawn between enforcement of a driving offence under the *Criminal Code* and one for the enforcement of a provincial enactment:

> In my opinion, the issue of ignorance of fact or ignorance of law is properly applicable to the enforcement of the provincial enactment under which the suspension from driving is made and not to the enforcement of s. 238(3) of the *Criminal Code*.

I am of the opinion that nothing in the foregoing reasons runs counter to the decision of the court in *Prue* and *Baril*.

For all these reasons I would allow this appeal and order a new trial.

Note that the majority of the Supreme Court in *R v Pontes*, [1995] 3 SCR 44 (below), disapproved of *MacDougall*, stressing that it was decided before the Charter. As will be seen, however, the majority of the Court in *Pontes* by characterizing the accused's lack of knowledge of a licence suspension as a mistake of law also did not follow *Prue*. The distinction between a mistake of law and a mistake of fact remains difficult to determine and will be discussed again in Chapter 12 on sexual assault.

III. THE DEFENCE OF OFFICIALLY INDUCED ERROR

Lévis (City) v Tétreault; Lévis (City) v 2629-4470 Québec inc
Supreme Court of Canada
2006 SCC 12, [2006] 1 SCR 420

[In this case, the Supreme Court unanimously recognized, for the first time, that officially induced error is available as a defence in Canadian criminal law. In *Lévis*, a numbered company was charged with operating a vehicle for which registration fees had not been paid, contrary to s 31.1 of the Quebec *Highway Safety Code*, CQLR c C-24.2. The company relied on the defence of officially induced error, arguing that it had been advised by an employee of the provincial insurance agency that a renewal notice would be mailed 30 days before the expiry of registration. This renewal notice never arrived. The company was acquitted in municipal court, which found that the offence was a strict liability offence and the company had exercised due diligence. The Superior Court dismissed the appeal of the City, and accepted an officially induced error defence. The City appealed to the Quebec Court of Appeal, which dismissed the application for leave to appeal in each case. The City further appealed to the Supreme Court of Canada.

LeBel J, for the Court, adopted the framework for the defence of officially induced error as set out by Lamer CJC in *R v Jorgensen*, [1995] 4 SCR 55. Although the offences in *Lévis* were regulatory, strict liability offences, the Court's adoption of Lamer CJC's framework in *Jorgensen*, which dealt with the defence with regard to the *Criminal Code* offence of selling obscene material, is a strong indication that the defence applies to true crimes as well. In discussing *Jorgensen*, LeBel J stated:]

[24] In Lamer C.J.'s view, this defence constituted a limited but necessary exception to the rule that ignorance of the law cannot excuse the commission of a criminal offence:

> Officially induced error of law exists as an exception to the rule that ignorance of the law does not excuse. As several of the cases where this rule has been discussed note, the complexity of contemporary regulation makes the assumption that a responsible citizen will have a comprehensive knowledge of the law unreasonable. This complexity, however, does not justify rejecting a rule which encourages a responsible citizenry, encourages government to publicize enactments, and is an essential foundation to the rule of law. Rather, extensive regulation is one motive for creating a limited exception to the rule that *ignorantia juris neminem excusat*. (*Jorgensen*, at para. 25)

[25] Lamer C.J. equated this defence with an excuse that has an effect similar to entrapment. The wrongfulness of the act is established. However, because of the circumstances leading up to the act, the person who committed it is not held liable for the act in criminal law. The accused is thus entitled to a stay of proceedings rather than an acquittal (*Jorgensen*, at para. 37).

[26] After his analysis of the case law, Lamer C.J. defined the constituent elements of the defence and the conditions under which it will be available. In his view, the accused must prove six elements:

(1) that an error of law or of mixed law and fact was made;
(2) that the person who committed the act considered the legal consequences of his or her actions;
(3) that the advice obtained came from an appropriate official;
(4) that the advice was reasonable;
(5) that the advice was erroneous; and
(6) that the person relied on the advice in committing the act (*Jorgensen*, at paras. 28-35).

[27] Although the Court did not rule on this issue in *Jorgensen*, I believe that this analytical framework has become established. Provincial appellate courts have followed this approach to consider and apply the defence of officially induced error (*R. c. Larivière* (2000), 38 C.R. (5th) 130 (Que. C.A.); *Maitland Valley Conservation Authority v. Cranbrook Swine Inc.* (2003), 64 O.R. (3d) 417 (Ont. C.A.)). ... It should be noted, as the Ontario Court of Appeal has done, that it is necessary to establish the objective reasonableness not only of the advice, but also of the reliance on the advice (*R. v. Cancoil Thermal*

Corp. (1986), 27 C.C.C. (3d) 295 (Ont. C.A.); *Cranbrook Swine*). Various factors will be taken into consideration in the course of this assessment, including the efforts made by the accused to obtain information, the clarity or obscurity of the law, the position and role of the official who gave the information or opinion, and the clarity, definitiveness and reasonableness of the information or opinion (*Cancoil Thermal*, at p. 303). It is not sufficient in such cases to conduct a purely subjective analysis of the reasonableness of the information. This aspect of the question must be considered from the perspective of a reasonable person in a situation similar to that of the accused.

[With the above test in mind, LeBel J held that the defence of officially induced error had not been established. He stated:]

[33] In my view, the respondent's allegations of fact do not show conduct that meets the standard of due diligence. The respondent was aware of the date when the fees relating to the registration of its vehicle would be due and, accordingly, the date when the registration would cease to be valid. It could and should have been concerned when it failed to receive a notice. Instead, it did nothing. It had a duty to do more. The acquittal was therefore unjustified.

[34] Nor has the respondent established that the conditions under which the defence or excuse of officially induced error is available have been met in this case and justified a stay of proceedings. The issues raised related at most to administrative practices, not to the legal obligation to pay the fees by the prescribed date. Two fundamental conditions that must be met for this defence to be available were therefore missing. In the circumstances, the respondent could not have considered the legal consequences of its conduct on the basis of advice from the official in question, nor could it have acted in reliance on that opinion, since no information regarding the nature and effects of the relevant legal obligations had been requested or obtained.

There are at least two questions that should be posed with regard to *Lévis* and *R v Jorgensen*, [1995] 4 SCR 55.

First, is it appropriate to analogize officially induced error to entrapment and therefore conclude that the proper remedy in the case of officially induced error is a stay of proceedings rather than an acquittal? It can be argued that the moral culpability of the accused persons in these two situations is very different. In the case of officially induced error, the accused has operated in a morally appropriate fashion and deserves to have the error treated as "an excuse," resulting in an acquittal.

Second, should the accused always have the burden of establishing the defence of officially induced error on a balance of probabilities? It can be argued that with respect to strict liability offences it is appropriate to require the accused to establish the defence on a balance of probabilities because officially induced error can be part of the due diligence inquiry and, as discussed in Chapter 6, the accused bears the burden of establishing due diligence on a balance of probabilities. But, where the offence is a criminal offence, with a presumption of subjective *mens rea* as it was in *Jorgensen*, it should not be automatically assumed that the burden of proof is on the accused on a balance of probabilities. Why shouldn't the normal criminal standard of reasonable doubt apply?

IV. A MORE GENERAL DEFENCE OF REASONABLE MISTAKE OF LAW?

In *Molis v The Queen*, [1980] 2 SCR 356, the accused was charged with trafficking in a restricted drug, MDMA, contrary to the federal *Food and Drugs Act*. When the accused first began manufacturing the drug it was not restricted; it was added to the Act by a regulation, which was properly published in the *Canada Gazette*. At his trial, the accused argued that he did not know it was illegal to manufacture the drug and that he had exercised due diligence in ascertaining the state of the law. The trial judge refused to leave this defence to the jury and he was convicted. The Supreme Court of Canada upheld the trial judge's decision, stating, per Lamer J, that "the defence of due diligence that was referred to in *Sault Ste. Marie* is that of due diligence in the relation to the fulfilment of a duty imposed by law and not in relation to the ascertainment of the existence of a prohibition or its interpretation."

Should the Court now decide a case like *Molis* differently? Would it matter what precise steps Molis had taken to ascertain the state of the law? Should the limited defence of officially induced error recognized in *Lévis* be expanded to include a defence of reasonable mistake of law? These questions were considered in the following case, in which the accused argued that a reasonable mistake of law should be a defence at least for a strict liability regulatory offence subject to a defence of due diligence.

**La Souveraine, Compagnie d'assurance générale v
Autorité des marchés financiers**
Supreme Court of Canada
2013 SCC 63, [2013] 3 SCR 756

WAGNER J (McLachlin CJ and Rothstein, Cromwell, Moldaver, Karakatsanis JJ concurring): ...

[56] The due diligence defence is available if the defendant reasonably believed in a mistaken set of facts that, if true, would have rendered his or her act or omission innocent. A defendant can also avoid liability by showing that he or she took all reasonable steps to avoid the particular event (*Sault Ste. Marie*, at p. 1326). The defence of due diligence is based on an objective standard: it requires consideration of what a reasonable person would have done in similar circumstances.

[57] However, this defence will not be available if the defendant relies solely on a mistake of law to explain the commission of the offence. Under Canadian law, a mistake of law can ground a valid defence only if the mistake was an officially induced error ... . A defendant can therefore gain nothing by showing that it made a reasonable effort to know the law or that it acted in good faith in ignorance of the law, since such evidence cannot exempt it from liability.

• • •

[65] ... [U]nder the law as it now stands in Canada, no matter how reasonable a mistake of law may be, it cannot—unlike a mistake of fact or an officially induced error—serve as a valid defence in the case of a strict liability offence. In *Molis v. The Queen*, [1980] 2 S.C.R. 356, Lamer J. noted:

[T]he defence of due diligence that was referred to in *Sault Ste. Marie* is that of due diligence in relation to the fulfilment of a duty imposed by law and not in relation to the ascertainment of the existence of a prohibition or its interpretation. [p. 364]

. . .

[68] This Court has held many a time that the fact that a defendant has exercised due diligence to find out and verify the nature of the applicable law is not a defence (*City of Lévis*, at para. 22). It has characterized the rule with respect to ignorance of the law as "an orienting principle of our criminal law which should not be lightly disturbed" (*Jorgensen*, at para. 5, *per* Lamer C.J.). In *City of Lévis*, at paras. 22-27, LeBel J. noted that this rule has the same weight in regulatory law.

[69] The rule with respect to ignorance of the law exists to ensure that the criminal justice system functions properly and that social order is preserved. G. Côté-Harper, P. Rainville and J. Turgeon explain this rule, conveyed by the maxim "ignorance of the law is no excuse," as follows (*Traité de droit pénal canadien* (4th ed. 1998), at p. 1098):

> [translation] The presumption of knowledge of the law becomes the *quid pro quo* for the principle of legality. The legislature assures citizens that it will not punish them without first telling them what is prohibited or required. But in exchange, it imposes on them an obligation to ask for information before acting … . Fear of social disorder and anarchy is the main argument of those who want to uphold the maxim. To accept an unrestricted possibility of hiding behind a subjective excuse of ignorance would be dangerous and improper.

. . .

[73] Despite the problems that flow from regulatory measures, the rise in the number of such measures and the commensurate multiplication of penal provisions designed to enforce them go hand in hand with the evolution of modern societies. These trends are well established. Regulatory measures are adopted to protect the public from dangers that can result from activities that are otherwise legitimate. The reason why penal sanctions are used in this context rather than civil law or administrative law sanctions lies in the deterrent power of penal law (H. Parent, *Traité de droit criminel*, vol. 2 (2nd ed. 2007), at paras. 496-500). Cory J. eloquently explained the importance of regulatory offences in *R. v. Wholesale Travel Group Inc.*, [1991] 3 S.C.R. 154, at pp. 221-22:

> It is difficult to think of an aspect of our lives that is not regulated for our benefit and for the protection of society as a whole. From cradle to grave, we are protected by regulations; they apply to the doctors attending our entry into this world and to the morticians present at our departure. Every day, from waking to sleeping, we profit from regulatory measures which we often take for granted. …
>
> In short, regulation is absolutely essential for our protection and well being as individuals, and for the effective functioning of society. It is properly present throughout our lives.

[74] The foregoing discussion underscores the conflicts that inevitably result from the constantly expanding presence of regulatory measures. Such measures play an essential role in the implementation of public policy. The rule that ignorance of the law is not a valid defence supports the state's duty in this regard. For this reason alone, it needs to be enforced.

[75] At the same time, the rise in the number of statutes coupled with their growing complexity increases the risk that a citizen will be punished in circumstances in which ignorance of the law might nevertheless be understandable.

[76] In light of all these considerations, I find that the objective of public protection that underlies the creation of regulatory offences militates strongly against accepting a *general* defence of reasonable mistake of law in this context. As Cory J. noted in *Wholesale Travel*, at p. 219,

> [r]egulatory legislation involves a shift of emphasis from the protection of individual interests and the deterrence and punishment of acts involving moral fault to the protection of public and societal interests.

[77] Moreover, it is incumbent on a regulated entity that engages in an activity requiring specific knowledge, including knowledge of the applicable law, to obtain that knowledge.

[Wagner J went on to find that there was no need for an exception to the ignorance of the law principle, even though the accused insurance company had written to the regulatory authority that charged it six months later setting out its erroneous understanding of the law and the regulatory authority had never replied. The authority's conduct was "of some concern" but not so "vexatious as to justify accepting a new exception to the rule with respect to ignorance of the law." Abella J, however, dissented and stated:]

[127] To date, officially induced error has only been used as a defence in circumstances where the official actually gave erroneous information to an accused. It has been seen, in other words, as requiring official conduct of an *active* kind. In my respectful view, however, there is no principled basis for excluding conduct of a more passive character, including silence from an official, which could, in some circumstances, reasonably be relied on as approval, or an "inducement." This is particularly the case if the silence occurs in a regulatory framework that demonstrably requires a degree of expedition. Punishing a regulated entity who is dependent on the regulator's timely response, and reasonably relies on its silence, perpetuates the very injustice that led to the development of the strict liability defences in the first place: finding the morally innocent culpable.

[128] Underlying the six elements of the defence of officially induced error is the broad principle that an individual not be held culpable when he or she is induced by an official's conduct into relying on a reasonable but incorrect understanding of the law. The analogous test in cases where official silence is relied on, will amount to determining whether that silence can be construed as an inducement to rely on a reasonable but incorrect understanding of the law. To paraphrase LeBel J. in *Lévis*, it will be necessary to demonstrate not only that the "advice" gleaned from the silence was reasonable, but also that reliance on it was reasonable in the circumstances. ...

· · ·

[137] I see in these facts all the requisite elements for officially induced error. La Souveraine took reasonable steps to satisfy itself that it was not violating the law. It based its conduct on a legal opinion from Flanders' lawyers, an opinion it could reasonably have concluded to be reliable based not only on the assumption that a lawyer's advice can be relied on as accurate, but also on the fact that that advice had proved to be accepted by the other provincial regulatory agencies. La Souveraine was entitled to assume that since Flanders was a national company, its lawyers would take the necessary steps to ensure compliance with respective provincial regulations. The jurisdiction in which the law firm was based is not relevant.

[138] The legal context was far from readily ascertainable. The AMF is responsible for regulating and being a resource for information about a highly complex financial sector. It has a duty to be diligent in performing its statutory role. Most of the entities it regulates require information in a timely way in order to carry on their businesses. This is certainly true in dealing with insurance, where the consequences of not having coverage can be catastrophic.

[In the result, Abella J would have stayed proceedings on the basis of officially induced error.]

V. MISTAKE OF LAW AND CONSTITUTIONAL CONSIDERATIONS

The following case revisits the divergence between the Court's decisions in *Prue* and *Mac-Dougall*. It also then examines the effect of a finding that the only possible defence open to the accused is one based on ignorance or mistake of the law on the classification of the offence as one of absolute or strict liability. (See Chapter 6 for further discussion of the distinction between these two types of regulatory offences.)

R v Pontes
Supreme Court of Canada
[1995] 3 SCR 44

[After *Re BC Motor Vehicle Act* discussed in Chapter 6, the British Columbia legislature deleted s 94(2) of the *Motor Vehicle Act*, which had provided that the offence of driving with a suspended licence was an absolute liability offence. As discussed in Chapter 6, the majority of the Court in this case held that the offence remained one of absolute liability, and for this reason imprisonment could not be constitutionally imposed for its violation. The focus in this extract is on the implications of the decision for the ignorance of the law is no excuse principle.]

CORY J (Lamer CJ and Sopinka, Iacobucci, and Major JJ concurring): ... Section 94(1)(a) still refers to s. 92 which, in turn, provides that a driver will "automatically and without notice" be prohibited from driving for a period of 12 months. ... Because the prohibition to drive in s. 92 is automatic and without notice, s. 94 effectively prevents an accused who is unaware of the prohibition from raising a defence of due diligence.

In determining whether either facet of the defence of due diligence is available in this case, it is important to remember the well-established principle, incorporated in s. 19 of the *Criminal Code*, R.S.C. 1985, c. C-46, that a mistake of law is no excuse. In other words, a mistake as to what the law is does not operate as a defence.

The application of this principle leads to the conclusion that an accused cannot put forward as a defence that he made diligent inquiries as to the legality of his actions or status. The submission of such a defence was specifically rejected in *R. v. Molis*, [1980] 2 S.C.R. 356. In that case, the accused was charged with trafficking in a drug restricted under the *Food and Drugs Act*. The drug which the accused had begun manufacturing had been unrestricted but later became restricted. At trial, the accused testified that he had exercised due diligence to ascertain the state of the law. This defence was rejected. At page 364 Lamer J. wrote:

> It is clear to me that we are dealing here with an offence that is not to be considered as one of absolute liability and, hence, a defence of due diligence is available to an accused. But I hasten to add that the defence of due diligence that was referred to in *Sault Ste. Marie* is that of due diligence in relation to the fulfilment of a duty imposed by law and not in relation to the ascertainment of the existence of a prohibition or its interpretation.

These principles must be kept in mind in the assessment of the Crown's contention that the decision of this court in *MacDougall, supra,* constitutes a complete answer to the characterization of the offence. In that case, following a conviction for failing to remain at the scene of an accident, the accused was prohibited from driving by the operation of s. 250(1) of the Nova Scotia *Motor Vehicle Act.* The accused subsequently drove while prohibited and was charged with that offence. At trial, he testified that he did not know of the prohibition. Ritchie J., on behalf of the court, held that the offence was one of strict liability, but that the defence of lack of knowledge of the prohibition was tantamount to a defence of ignorance of the law which, in light of the provision of s. 19 of the *Criminal Code,* could not provide a defence. ...

Two difficulties arise from the *MacDougall* decision. The first difficulty lies in its irreconcilability with the earlier decision of *R. v. Prue; R. v. Baril,* [1979] 2 S.C.R. 547. The second lies in the fact that *MacDougall* was rendered prior to the Charter, and that the jurisprudence on the minimal fault requirement has evolved since then.

In *Prue, supra,* the accused were convicted of an offence under the *Criminal Code.* As a result, their licences were automatically suspended under the provisions of the B.C. *Motor Vehicle Act.* They nonetheless drove their vehicles and were charged, not for a violation of the provincial statute under which the suspension was made, but rather under s. 238 of the *Criminal Code.* ... Laskin C.J.C. stated that as a result of the inclusion of the offence in the *Criminal Code,* it was necessary to import *mens rea.* He then considered the submission of the Crown that ignorance of the suspension was ignorance of the law, not a mistake of fact, and therefore could not be put forward as a defence. He then stated at p. 552:

> The effect, if this is a correct appraisal, is to make s. 238(3) an offence of absolute liability where the provincial suspension of a driving licence is automatic under the provincial enactment ... but not if the provincial suspension does not take effect without a requirement of notice.

Laskin C.J.C. thus implied that an offence which was automatic and without notice constituted an absolute liability offence. However, he went on to find that ignorance of the suspension of a licence, in that case, was a mistake of fact.

With respect to the ignorance of the suspension, these reasons simply cannot be reconciled with *MacDougall, supra.* It cannot be that a mistake as to the law under the *Criminal Code* constitutes a mistake of fact, whereas a mistake as to the provisions of the provincial statute constitutes a mistake of law. ...

It must be remembered that the *MacDougall* decision was rendered prior to the Charter. It thus did not consider the constitutionally required minimal fault component outlined by this court in cases such as *Reference re: Section 94(2) of the Motor Vehicle Act* [[1985] 2 SCR 486] and *Vaillancourt,* [[1987] 2 SCR 636]. The defence of due diligence must be available to defend a strict liability offence. If that defence is removed, the offence can no longer be classified as one of strict liability. When, as a result of the wording of the section, the only possible defence an accused can put forward is his ignorance of the fact that his licence had been suspended by the provisions of the provincial statute, which constitutes a mistake of law and therefore is not available as a defence, the accused is effectively denied the defence of due diligence. In those circumstances, the offence ought to be characterized as one of absolute liability.

It seems to be clear that the defence of due diligence is not available to an accused charged under ss. 92 and 94 of the B.C. *Motor Vehicle Act*. There are a number of examples which can illustrate this situation. First, take the situation of an accused charged with failure to give a sample of breath. After trial he is found guilty, fined and his licence suspended for three months. Apparently, in British Columbia, he would be given no notice of the automatic suspension of one year provided by the B.C. *Motor Vehicle Act*. Yet, he would be liable to conviction despite his honest and reasonable belief as a lay person that the total sentence imposed by the court was a fine and a suspension of his licence for a period of three months. Certainly, to most people "a court" is a court wherever it may be located and the sentence of that court is what is binding upon them. Even if an accused asked the court to confirm that this was the total extent of his sentence, this would not amount to a defence of due diligence since his error was as to the provisions of the B.C. *Motor Vehicle Act*, and this constitutes an error of law.

Similarly, if an accused is charged and convicted of impaired driving and sentenced to six months' prohibition from driving, he would leave the courtroom believing that this sentence constituted the entire penalty. However, by virtue of s. 92 of the Act, he is also, without any notice to him, automatically prohibited from driving for a period of 12 months from the date of conviction. If he drives after six months have expired and is stopped by the police, he would be charged with "driving while prohibited," despite the fact that he honestly and reasonably believed that he was no longer prohibited from driving. He would not be able to put this forward as a defence since ignorance of the law cannot be invoked as a defence, even if he took steps at his original trial to confirm before the convicting judge that this was the total extent of his penalty. Quite simply, the statute effectively deprives the accused of the defence of due diligence.

Significance of Notice

The legislature could readily convert this offence to one of strict liability by permitting the defence of due diligence to be raised. If there was any concern that those accused of the offence would defend on the basis that they had no knowledge of its effect, a provision requiring that notice be given of its consequences could be added. Notice could be given in many ways. The following are a few examples.

Upon the issuance or a renewal of a licence, notice could be given that upon conviction of the listed enumerated offences, there will be an automatic suspension of the licence for a 12-month period. Alternatively, notice of the consequences could be given with the serving of the summons or charge for the underlying offence. In still another manner, the notice could be given as a matter of course upon conviction for the underlying offence, and would thus form part of the record of the court proceedings. There is something so fundamentally fair about the giving of notice that I find it commendable. It must be remembered that regulatory offences number in the tens of thousands. There are federal regulations and provincial regulations that will vary in their terms and provisions from coast to coast. Surely it is not asking too much that the accused be given some form of notice.

GONTHIER J (with whom La Forest, L'Heureux-Dubé, and McLachlin JJ concurred) (in dissent): I do not believe that the "principles of fundamental justice" under s. 7 of the Charter require that an accused who is charged with a regulatory offence be entitled to claim due diligence in relation to the existence of the relevant statutory prohibition or its interpretation—that is, to avail himself of the defence of ignorance of the law. The defence of due diligence does not need to be expanded to meet the exigencies of the Charter. Indeed, to do so would eviscerate the ignorance of the law rule and render many of our laws unenforceable. To date, our court has refused to find that ignorance of the law is an excuse for breaking the law. Nor have we ever held that ignorance of the law should be viewed differently in the regulatory and criminal contexts. I respectfully suggest we refrain from doing so henceforth.

I would add that if the defence of due diligence has been expanded in light of s. 7 of the Charter to comprehend a defence of ignorance of the law, then it also appears that this court's ruling in *Molis, supra*, has been overturned. As already indicated, in *Molis*, Lamer J. stated unambiguously that the defence of due diligence refers to "due diligence in relation to the fulfilment of a duty imposed by law and not in relation to the ascertainment of the existence of a prohibition or its interpretation" (p. 364). To my mind, *Molis* should remain good law and is indistinguishable from the case at bar. It is no more necessary, as a principle of "fundamental justice," to allow the respondent to avail himself of his ignorance of a prohibition from driving by virtue of provincial legislation of general application, than it was to allow the accused drug traffickers in *Molis* to avail themselves of their ignorance that 3-4 methylenedioxy-N-methylamphetamine had been added as a prohibited substance to Sch. H of the *Food and Drugs Act*. ...

It is evident, then, that I disagree with Cory J.'s conclusion that a defence of due diligence is not available in relation to the impugned offence. Cory J. comes to this conclusion because he finds that the only defence effectively available to an accused who has been charged with driving while under a statutory prohibition is his ignorance of the fact that his licence has been suspended by the provisions of a provincial statute; but since this is mistake or ignorance of the law, it is not an available excuse. Furthermore, Cory J. suggests two examples to illustrate his claim that a due diligence defence is unavailable. In both examples, he suggests that an accused who is prohibited under a court order from driving for any period less than 12 months for having committed one of the underlying offences may be misled into believing that he is entitled to drive after the expiry of that prohibition, since he has had no notice of the continuing automatic prohibition effective by virtue of ss. 92 and 94(1). He suggests that such a person would be liable to conviction "despite his honest and reasonable belief as a lay person that the total sentence imposed by the court was a fine and a suspension of his licence for a period of" less than 12 months (at para. 43).

I agree that Cory J.'s examples are within the realm of possibility, and also that there may be a sense in which they can be considered as giving rise to some unfairness. But if this is so, it is an unfairness which our legal system has long countenanced in refusing to allow ignorance of the law to serve as a valid excuse. As a matter of principle, it is no more unfair to convict the accused in this case than it was in *Molis, supra*, for the trafficking of a substance he honestly and reasonably believed was not prohibited, or to disallow the accused in *Forster*, [[1992] 1 SCR 339], from relying on her letter of resignation to demonstrate that she lacked the intent for being absent without leave.

Of course, this is not to say that ignorance of the law cannot be successfully pleaded as a factor in mitigation of sentence (Clayton Ruby, *Sentencing*, 4th ed. (Toronto: Butterworths, 1994), at p. 196. In such a case, it may well be appropriate to sentence an offender to the minimum fine of $300 and to seven days' imprisonment under s. 92(1)(c) of the *Motor Vehicle Act*.

Finally, I note that the appellant raised the possibility that a driver whose licence is suspended and who is prohibited from driving by operation of law may also be able to avail himself of the defence of "officially induced error." This defence was not raised here and has yet to be formally recognized by this court, though it was referred to in obiter by Ritchie J. in *R. v. MacDougall, supra*. ... Assuming without deciding that such a defence would be available if an accused were misled by the Superintendent of Motor Vehicles or by some other official responsible for the administration of the *Motor Vehicle Act*, such a defence would not demonstrate absence of negligence in relation to the *actus reus* of driving while under a statutory prohibition, but rather would be an additional defence thereto, operating as an exception to the rule that ignorance of the law does not excuse. As a result, the potential availability of such a defence does not assist in the characterization of the impugned provisions as being of strict liability.

Appeal dismissed.

VI. STATUTORY REFORM

Law Reform Commission of Canada, *Recodifying Criminal Law*, Report 31 (1987) at 34-35 (footnotes omitted), provides:

> 3(7) Mistake or Ignorance of Law. No one is liable for a crime committed by reason of mistake or ignorance of law:
> (a) concerning private rights relevant to that crime; or
> (b) reasonably resulting from
>   (i) non-publication of the law in question,
>   (ii) reliance on a decision of a court of appeal in the province having jurisdiction over the crime charged, or
>   (iii) reliance on competent administrative authority.

Comment

Mistake of law in general is no defence. This is the position at common law, under section 19 of the *Criminal Code* and under clause 3(7) of this Code. It is up to the citizen to find out what the law is and comply with it.

On the other hand no one can fairly be punished for breaking a law which he has no reasonable chance of ascertaining. For this reason present law has created two exceptions to the general rule. Ignorance of law owing to non-publication of regulations is a defence. Mistake of law resulting from officially induced error may also be a defence.

Clause 3(7)(b) codifies these two exceptions, extending one of them and adding another. It extends the first exception to non-publication of any law. It adds an exception in the case of mistake resulting from reliance on the law as stated by the court of appeal in the province where the charge is tried. No one can reasonably be expected to be wiser than the highest court in his jurisdiction; rather he is entitled to assume the law is what that court says it is until the Supreme Court of Canada states otherwise.

In addition there are certain crimes, such as theft and fraud, where honest but erroneous belief in a claim of right negatives criminal liability. Insofar as such belief is based on error of law, mistake of law will operate as a defence. This is the position under present law and also under clause 3(7)(a) of this Code.

Clause 3(7)(b) then provides three exceptions to the general rule, but all three relate solely to mistakes *reasonably* resulting from the factors specified.

The June 1993 *Federal Proposals to Amend the Criminal Code (General Principles)* provides that s 19 should be repealed and the following section be added to the *Criminal Code*:

> 34(1) Neither ignorance of the law nor mistake of law is a defence to an offence unless
>
>   (a) the description of the offence provides a defence of claim of right or colour of right, or otherwise provides a defence of ignorance of the law or mistake of law, and the ignorance or mistake relates to that defence;
>
>   (b) the description of the offence includes an element that concerns a matter of private rights, and the ignorance or mistake relates to that matter of private rights; or
>
>   (c) the offence was committed under an officially induced mistake of law.
>
> (2) For the purpose of paragraph (1)(b), ignorance or mistake relating to the existence or interpretation of an Act or of regulations made thereunder does not constitute ignorance or mistake that relates to a matter of private rights.
>
> (3) For the purpose of paragraph (1)(c), an officially induced mistake of law is a defence only if
>
>   (a) the mistake is in respect of the existence or interpretation of a law and results from information or advice given by an official responsible for the administration or enforcement of that law,
>
>   (b) the person relied in good faith on that information or advice, and
>
>   (c) it was reasonable for the person to have relied on that information or advice,
>
> but information or advice given by an official mentioned in paragraph (a) to the effect that the law will not be enforced in a particular case or in particular circumstances does not provide a basis for the defence of officially induced mistake of law.
>
> (4) Nothing in this section affects the defence of non-publication of regulations that is provided by subsection 11(2) of the *Statutory Instruments Act*.

ADDITIONAL READING

Boisvert, A-M. "Innocence Morale, Diligence Raisonnable and Erreur de Droit" (1995) 41 CR (4th) 243.

Manning, M & P Sankoff. *Manning, Mewett & Sankoff: Criminal Law*, 4th ed (Toronto: Lexis-Nexis, 2009) at 356-78.

Roach, K. *Criminal Law*, 6th ed (Toronto: Irwin Law, 2015) ch 2.

Stewart, H. "Mistake of Law Under the Charter" (1998) 40 Crim LQ 476.

Stuart, D. *Canadian Criminal Law*, 7th ed (Toronto: Carswell, 2014) at 366-98.

PART THREE

Extensions of Criminal Liability

Participation

Criminal offences can at times be committed by two or more people together. When more than one person is involved, each might be involved in a different way or to a different degree. Thus a central topic among the general principles of criminal liability is the matter of participation. On what basis is a person's involvement in the commission of a criminal offence sufficient for him or her to be held liable as a party to the offence? Between the actual perpetrator of the offence and an innocent bystander lies a broad margin of connection or involvement in the commission of an offence. The law relating to participation defines the principles on which the actual perpetrator (or perpetrators) and persons other than the actual perpetrator(s) can be held accountable as parties to an offence.

There are five modes of participation identified in ss 21 and 22 of the *Criminal Code*.

Parties to offence

21(1) Every one is a party to an offence who

(a) actually commits it;

(b) does or omits to do anything for the purpose of aiding any person to commit it; or

(c) abets any person in committing it.

Common intention

21(2) Where two or more persons form an intention in common to carry out an unlawful purpose and to assist each other therein and any one of them, in carrying out the common purpose, commits an offence, each of them who knew or ought to have known that the commission of the offence would be a probable consequence of carrying out the common purpose is a party to that offence.

Person counselling offence

22(1) Where a person counsels another person to be a party to an offence and that other person is afterwards a party to that offence, the person who counselled is a party to that offence, notwithstanding that the offence was committed in a way different from that which was counselled.

Idem

22(2) Every one who counsels another person to be a party to an offence is a party to every offence that the other commits in consequence of the counselling that the person who coun-selled knew or ought to have known was likely to be committed in consequence of the counselling.

Definition of "counsel"

22(3) For the purposes of this Act, "counsel" includes procure, solicit or incite.

This chapter looks at actual commission, aiding, abetting, common intention, and coun-selling. These are all distinct modes of participation in a criminal offence and a person found guilty by any one of them is a party to the substantive offence. By contrast, an accessory after the fact is not a party to the offence but is nonetheless liable for facilitating a party's escape. Although an accessory is not a party, the principles relating to accessoryship are considered in the last section of this chapter.

Before beginning with principals, it is appropriate to note here that Parliament has recently created a new type of offence with regard to organized crime and terrorism, one in which the element of conduct is defined as *facilitation*. At first glance, this might appear to be a form of aiding or abetting commission of a substantive offence; but actually, facilitation *is* a substan-tive offence in itself. Similarly, acts of facilitation cannot be construed as inchoate offences in the nature of attempt or incitement. They are complete offences in and of themselves.

I. MODES OF PARTICIPATION

Section 21(1) of the Code puts an aider or abettor on the same legal footing as a principal (*R v Thatcher*, [1987] 1 SCR 652). Each of these parties will be convicted of the offence in which they are proven to have participated. Nonetheless, it is analytically important to understand the differences between the modes of participation specified in s 21 and especially to attend to the elements of each mode.

Section 21(1)(a) refers to the person who "actually commits" the offence. The person who actually commits the offence is often referred to as the principal. Subject to proof of identifi-cation, this mode of participation seldom poses difficult challenges. More than one person can commit a single offence, as when two or more strike blows on a victim with the requisite *mens rea* and the beating causes the victim's death. (*R v McMaster*, [1996] 1 SCR 740 at 753). A more difficult task arises when it is unclear on the evidence whether the accused actually committed the charged offence, or alternatively acted as an aider or abettor. In *R v Thatcher*, the Supreme Court of Canada held that a jury can convict an accused if every member of the jury is satisfied beyond a reasonable doubt that the accused was either a principal or an aider or abettor. It is not necessary for the jury to reach unanimity about which mode of participa-tion applies.

R v Thatcher
Supreme Court of Canada
[1987] 1 SCR 652

DICKSON CJ (Beetz, Estey, Wilson, and Le Dain JJ concurring):

[1] On 7th May 1984 Colin Thatcher was arrested and charged with causing the death of his ex-wife, JoAnn Kay Wilson. After a 14-day trial before judge and jury, he was convicted of first degree murder and sentenced to life imprisonment without eligibility for parole for 25 years. An appeal to the Saskatchewan Court of Appeal was dismissed (Vancise J.A. dissenting). Colin Thatcher now appears before this court requesting that the jury's guilty verdict be set aside.

[2] The position of the Crown throughout the trial was that Mr. Thatcher had murdered Mrs. Wilson or alternatively that he caused someone else to do so and was therefore guilty as a party to the offence pursuant to s. 21 of the *Criminal Code*. ...

[3] Another ground of appeal, in my view of more substance than those just described, was also argued by counsel for Mr. Thatcher. It was not the subject of a dissent in the Court of Appeal and was unanimously dismissed by that court. Leave to argue this ground was sought from this court and was granted. Counsel contended that the trial judge erred in failing to instruct the jury that a verdict of guilty must be unanimous in relation to one or other of the alternative means of committing the offence of murder. The effect of the argument, in the circumstances of this case, was that in order to find Mr. Thatcher guilty of murder the jury had to be unanimous that he intentionally killed his former wife or, alternatively, that he aided or abetted another person or persons in her killing; it was simply not sufficient that some members of the jury would hold to one theory and other members would hold to the other theory. That, as I see it, is the principal issue in this appeal.

· · ·

[5] On the evening of Sunday, 17th May 1981, JoAnn Wilson was shot and wounded while in the kitchen of her home. A bullet fired from a high powered rifle passed through a triple glaze glass window and struck her in the shoulder. She was hospitalized for about three weeks. The evidence was that JoAnn Wilson was terrified by this attempt on her life. After the shooting she gave up her right to custody of Regan and, a year later, agreed to accept approximately one half of the original court award, spread over five years. No one was charged with the 17th May 1981 incident.

(iii) 21st January 1983

[6] At about six o'clock in the evening of 21st January 1983 JoAnn Wilson came home, drove into the garage of her home and was ferociously beaten and then shot to death. Twenty-seven wounds were inflicted on her head, neck, hands and lower legs. The injuries included a broken arm, a fracture of the wrist and a severed little left finger. A single bullet entered her skull causing death.

[7] Mr. Craig Dotson testified as to the finding of the body. He stated that he left work at the Legislative Buildings shortly before 6:00 p.m. on 21st January 1983 and was walking home when he noted a green car with a female driver turn into the garage at the Wilson residence. He continued walking for about a block. He heard loud shrill screams behind him. He turned back to investigate. He heard a single loud sharp noise and then silence. As

he approached a lane near the Wilson garage he saw a man emerge from the garage. He did not pay any particular attention. It was dark. He was 30 to 40 feet from the individual. He walked a little further and saw a body in a pool of blood on the floor of the garage.

[8] Mr. Dotson told the police he thought the man he momentarily observed had a beard, was about 30 years old, 5 foot 9 inches to 5 foot 11 inches in height and of medium build. A composite sketch prepared by the police with Mr. Dotson's aid did not fit Colin Thatcher, whom Mr. Dotson knew as a member of the Saskatchewan Legislative Assembly.

· · ·

The Charge and the Verdict

[53] In his charge to the jury, despite objection from counsel for the defence, the trial judge indicated to the jury the following direction on potential culpability:

> At the outset I should explain to you that there are two ways in which the offence of murder could have been committed by this accused. If you find on the evidence and are satisfied beyond a reasonable doubt that Colin Thatcher did that act or actions himself that caused the death of JoAnn Wilson, it is open to you to find him guilty of murder. Alternatively, if you find that acts done or performed by the accused resulted in the death of JoAnn Wilson and were done with the intent that they cause her death, even though the actual killing was done by another or others, it is open to you to find this accused guilty of murder.

[54] The trial judge also referred the jury to s. 21(1) of the Criminal Code and further commented:

> Colin Thatcher is charged with committing the offence of murder. If you do not find that he did the act of murder himself, he is equally guilty if you find and are satisfied that he either aided or abetted another or others in its commission.

During the charge the trial judge alluded to the argument of defence counsel that if the jury accepted the evidence of even one of the witnesses who said he was in Moose Jaw at the time of the murder, Thatcher could not have committed the murder. Counsel also told the jury that as the Crown had not produced any evidence that anyone else killed JoAnn Wilson it was the duty of the jury to find him not guilty. The trial judge said:

> With respect, I am unable to agree with this argument. I tell you as a matter of law that the fact that the Crown cannot adduce evidence that another individual or individuals actually did the act does not preclude you from finding that the killing was done on behalf of Colin Thatcher and it is still open to you to return a finding of guilty of murder if you so find.

· · ·

(ii) Failure to Relate the Law to the Facts Regarding the Crown's Alternative Theory

· · ·

[64] The trial judge read the contents of s. 21(1) to the jury and referred, correctly, to what was meant by the term "aiding" or "abetting": "intentional encouragement or assistance in the commission of the offence." As stated, he pointed out that the actual perpetrator need not be identified. He thus accurately stated the law as to s. 21(1).

· · ·

[72] Thus, s. 21 has been designed to alleviate the necessity for the Crown choosing between two different forms of participation in a criminal offence. The law stipulates that both forms of participation are not only equally culpable, but should be treated as one single mode of incurring criminal liability. The Crown is not under a duty to separate the different forms of participation in a criminal offence into different counts. Obviously, if the charge against Thatcher had been separated into different counts, he might well have been acquitted on each count notwithstanding that each and every juror was certain beyond a reasonable doubt either that Thatcher personally killed his ex-wife or that he aided and abetted someone else who killed his ex-wife. This is precisely what s. 21 is designed to prevent.

. . .

[79] … In the present case, Thatcher was charged that he did "unlawfully cause the death of JoAnn Kay Wilson and did thereby commit first degree murder." The charge was carefully worded, and there is no injustice in his conviction on the indictment irrespective of whether the jurors shared the same view as to the most likely manner in which Thatcher committed the murder.

[80] When one considers the implications of the appellant's submission, it becomes even clearer that it is without merit. In the present case there were doubtless three alternatives in the minds of each of the jurors:

    (a)   Thatcher personally killed his ex-wife;
    (b)   he aided and abetted someone else to do so;
    (c)   he is innocent of the crime.

[81] The jurors were told that if any of them had a reasonable doubt regarding (c), Thatcher should be acquitted. Every single juror was, evidently, solidly convinced that (c) was simply not what occurred. Each one was certain that the true statement of affairs was (a) or (b). Even if we suppose, as the appellant would have us do, that the jurors individually went beyond thinking in terms of (a) or (b) and specifically opted for one theory, and that some jurors thought only (a) could have occurred and others thought only (b) could have occurred, I am far from convinced that there would have been any injustice from convicting Thatcher. As stated, there is no legal difference between the two. Much is made of the fact that (a) and (b) are *factually* inconsistent theories, in the sense that evidence proving (a) tends to disprove (b). But this is really only true of one category of evidence, namely identification and alibi evidence. The overwhelming mass of evidence against Thatcher was consistent with *either* theory. In particular, the evidence tracing the murder weapon to Thatcher was highly probative, as were his statements to various witnesses (prior to the murder) of his intention to kill JoAnn Wilson, and his statement to Lynn Mendell (after the murder) that he had "blown away" his wife.

[82] The appellant's suggestion would fail to achieve justice in a significant number of cases. Suppose the evidence in a case is absolutely crystal clear that when X and Y entered Z's house, Z was alive, and when X and Y left, Z was dead. Suppose that in their evidence each of X and Y says that the other of them murdered Z but each admits to having aided and abetted. Are X and Y each to be acquitted if some of the jurors differ as to which of X and Y actually committed the offence? I can see absolutely no reason in policy or law to uphold such an egregious conclusion. The appellant's submission ignores the very reason why Parliament abolished the old common law distinctions: namely, they

permitted guilty persons to go free. As Professor Peter MacKinnon points out in "Jury Unanimity: A Reply to Gelowitz and Stuart" (1986), 51 C.R. (3d) 134, at p. 135, if an accused is to be acquitted in situations when every juror is convinced that the accused committed a murder in one of two ways, merely because the jury cannot agree on *which* of the two ways, "it is difficult to imagine a situation more likely to bring the administration of justice into disrepute—and deservedly so."

In *R v Pickton*, 2010 SCC 32, [2010] 2 SCR 198, the Supreme Court of Canada considered how to apply the *Thatcher* principle in a case in which the Crown's theory at trial was that the accused actually committed the *actus reus* of murder.

R v Pickton
Supreme Court of Canada
2010 SCC 32, [2010] 2 SCR 198

CHARRON J (McLachlin CJ and Deschamps, Abella, Rothstein, and Cromwell JJ concurring):

1. Overview

[1] Robert William Pickton became a person of interest to the police in early 2001 when a task force began collecting the DNA of women missing from the downtown eastside of Vancouver. All the missing women were drug-dependent sex-trade workers who had frequently worked in that area. Mr. Pickton operated a pig butchering business adjacent to his residence on his family's property in Port Coquitlam, east of Vancouver. The investigation culminated in the discovery of the dismembered remains of many of the women on Mr. Pickton's property, some in buckets in a freezer in his workshop, some in a garbage pail in the piggery near the slaughterhouse, others elsewhere on the property.

[2] Mr. Pickton was charged with 27 counts of first degree murder.

[3] In pre-trial rulings, the trial judge quashed one count and severed 20 others and the trial proceeded on the remaining six counts of first degree murder. At the conclusion of what was a lengthy trial, the jury returned a verdict of not guilty of first degree murder, but guilty of second degree murder on each of the six counts.

· · ·

[5] Mr. Pickton appealed from his convictions of second degree murder. His appeal essentially turned on whether the trial judge's responses to a question by the jury undermined the fairness of the trial by introducing, as the defence contended, an alternate, ill-defined route to conviction at this late stage of the trial. Mr. Pickton based this contention on the following course of events.

[6] Throughout the trial, the Crown maintained that Mr. Pickton actually shot/killed the six women. The defence took the position that the Crown failed to prove that Mr. Pickton was the sole perpetrator, suggesting the potential involvement of others to the exclusion of Mr. Pickton. On the fourth and last day of instructions to the jury, the defence requested that the trial judge specifically instruct the jury in accordance with the respective theories of the parties by adding what has been referred to as the "actual shooter"

instruction. The Crown consented to the request, and the trial judge accordingly gave the following jury instruction in respect of the first three counts, each relating to a victim who, it was accepted by both counsel, died as a result of a gunshot wound to the head (the Crown relied on a similar-fact inference to prove that the other three women had also been murdered by Mr. Pickton):

> If you find that Mr. Pickton shot [name of victim], you should find that the Crown has proven [element 3, the identity of the killer]. On the other hand, *if you have a reasonable doubt about whether or not he shot her, you must return a verdict of not guilty* on the charge of murdering her. [Emphasis added.]

Mr. Pickton argued that for the trial judge to later retract from this instruction on the sixth day of deliberations, by instructing the jury that they could also find that he was the killer if he "was otherwise an active participant" in the killings, occasioned a miscarriage of justice.

. . .

2. Analysis

[13] … The central issue in this appeal is whether, in the context of the main charge and the trial as a whole, the trial judge's response to the sole question posed by the jury effectively changed the "goal posts," as Mr. Pickton's counsel put it, thereby adversely impacting on the fairness of the trial. A subsidiary issue arises whether the instructions as a whole, including the response to the jury question, adequately conveyed the law on the potential routes to criminal liability.

. . .

[17] The Crown took and maintained the position throughout the trial that Mr. Pickton was the sole perpetrator of all six murders. The defence relentlessly tried to discredit the Crown's theory by suggesting the potential involvement of others, some named and others not, to the exclusion of Mr. Pickton. Mr. Pickton's counsel took great pains to demonstrate how the Crown's sole perpetrator theory permeated each step of the proceedings and, likewise, how the defence strategy was reflected at each of those steps, from the defence's opening statement to the jury to its submissions on the jury question.

. . .

[21] The fallacy of Mr. Pickton's argument lies in the fact that the *defence theory itself* put the participation of others at issue. Throughout the trial, the defence by its approach urged the jury to consider that others may have actually killed the victims. An inevitable consequence of going down that road is that the jury would have to be instructed on how this could, if at all, impact on Mr. Pickton's own criminal liability.

. . .

[23] Accordingly, the trial judge did not confine his instructions to the Crown's sole perpetrator theory, but explained to the jury what effect any finding that others may have participated in the commission of the offences would have on the question of Mr. Pickton's criminal liability. I will refer to these instructions compendiously as the "other suspects instructions." Low J.A. reviewed the relevant parts of the jury charge at some length at paras. 140-44 and 156. This analysis need not be repeated here. Suffice it to note that the other suspects instructions in question went along the same lines as the following

instruction given to the jury immediately following the trial judge's explanation of the elements of the offence of first degree murder:

> [8] A person commits an offence if he, *alone or along with somebody else or others*, personally does everything necessary to constitute the offence. Accordingly, *it is not necessary for you to find that Mr. Pickton acted alone in order to find him guilty of the offence.* You may find that Mr. Pickton *acted in concert with other persons*, although you may not know who they are. It is sufficient if you are satisfied beyond a reasonable doubt, having considered all the evidence, that he *actively participated in the killing* of the victim. It is not sufficient that he was merely present or took a minor role. The issue for you to decide is whether you are satisfied that it has been proven that he was involved to the extent that the law requires [to] establish his criminal liability. [Emphasis added.]

[24] The other suspects instructions were responsive to the evidence and the central issues raised at trial, and they are entirely correct in law. More importantly, on the question that occupies us, the record reveals that it was known throughout the trial to both Crown and defence counsel that the jury would be instructed along these lines. … As we shall see, the impugned answer to the jury question was consistent with this instruction. In answer to the question whether they could find that Mr. Pickton was the killer if they inferred that he "acted indirectly," the members of the jury were ultimately instructed that they could do so, provided they found that he "was otherwise an active participant" in the killings. The contention that the defence was somehow taken by surprise by this course of events is not, therefore, borne out on the record.

· · ·

[28] As events turned out, the inconsistency occasioned by the addition of the actual shooter instruction was not lost on the jury, nor ultimately on the trial judge. On the sixth day of deliberations, the jury submitted the following question:

> When considering Element 3 [the identity of the killer] on one or more of the counts, are we able to say "Yes," if we infer that the accused acted indirectly?

… [A]fter hearing submissions from counsel about the question, the trial judge recharged the jury by essentially repeating some of the other suspects instructions and the actual shooter instruction. Shortly after the recharge, however, and as he later explained in his written reasons for the ruling, the trial judge became concerned that the actual shooter paragraphs were inconsistent with the other suspects instructions and were not responsive to the evidence and the central issues of the trial. The trial judge therefore asked the jury to suspend their deliberations temporarily, and, after advising counsel of his intention, he re-instructed the jury by changing the actual shooter instruction so that it was consistent with the other suspects instructions. The corrected paragraph, which applied to the victims of counts 1 to 3, read as follows:

> If you find that Mr. Pickton shot [name of victim] *or was otherwise an active participant in her killing*, you should find that the Crown has proven this element. On the other hand, if you have a reasonable doubt about whether or not he was *an active participant in her killing*, you must return a verdict of not guilty. [Emphasis added.]

· · ·

[30] On the central issue in this appeal, I therefore conclude that the trial judge's response to the question posed by the jury did not adversely impact on the fairness of the trial as the appellant contends.

. . .

LeBEL J (Binnie and Fish JJ concurring):

I. Introduction

[37] The primary issue in this appeal is the adequacy of jury instructions given at the end of a long and disturbing six-count murder trial which lasted almost a full year. Although we must necessarily conduct a careful review of those trial proceedings with a view to ensuring that justice is done on the particular facts of this case, it is also important that the applicable law be carefully delineated and clarified for future cases. I am reminded of the words of Doherty J.A. in *R. v. Bernardo* (1997), 121 C.C.C. (3d) 123 (Ont. C.A.), at para. 19: "[D]etached and reflective appellate review of the trial process is perhaps most important in notorious, emotion-charged cases involving the least deserving accused."

. . .

III. Analysis

A. Forms of Party Liability Under the Criminal Code

[51] Generally speaking, there are two forms of liability for *Criminal Code* offences, primary or principal liability (actually or personally committing the offence), and secondary liability (also known as party liability), both codified in s. 21 of the *Criminal Code*. Whether an accused is found guilty either as a principal offender or as a party to the offence, the result is the same in law: the accused will be convicted of the substantive offence. It is for this reason that it is sometimes said that it is "a matter of indifference" at law whether an accused personally committed a crime, or alternatively, aided and/or abetted another to commit the offence: *R. v. Thatcher*, [1987] 1 S.C.R. 652, at p. 694; *Chow Bew v. The Queen*, [1956] S.C.R. 124, at p. 127. This is also why the Crown need not specify in an indictment the nature of an accused's participation in an offence: *R. v. Harder*, [1956] S.C.R. 489; *Thatcher*, at p. 694.

[52] Section 21 of the *Criminal Code*, which codifies both co-principal and party modes of liability, provides as follows:

21(1) Every one is a party to an offence who

(a) actually commits it;

(b) does or omits to do anything for the purpose of aiding any person to commit it; or

(c) abets any person in committing it.

(2) Where two or more persons form an intention in common to carry out an unlawful purpose and to assist each other therein and any one of them, in carrying out the common purpose, commits an offence, each of them who knew or ought to have known that the commission of the offence would be a probable consequence of carrying out the common purpose is a party to that offence.

[53] Section 21 makes it clear that an accused cannot escape liability simply because one or more other persons could also be found liable for the same offence. Thus, under s. 21(1)(a), every person who commits all of the elements of an offence will face criminal liability as a co-principal along with any others who also committed all elements of that offence. Under s. 21(1)(b) and (c), an accused will be found liable for an offence even if he or she did not commit all elements of that offence, but provided aid or encouragement, with the requisite *mens rea*, to another person who did commit the offence.

[54] Where, as here, an accused is charged with murder, the law of party liability under s. 21 therefore provides for the various ways in which an accused can be found guilty of murder under s. 229 of the *Criminal Code*, notwithstanding that under some of the modes of participation, the accused has not actually caused the death of the victim according to the standard set out in that offence. In essence, though it may not be the case that the accused actually did not kill the victim, he or she can still be held liable for the murder.

B. Instructions About Party Liability

[55] Where a trial is by judge and jury, the relevant principles of party liability must be carefully explained so that they can be properly applied to the evidence, and correctly set out in the jury instructions. This is particularly important where there is potential involvement of third parties in the offence, but that involvement is unclear, and the accused is the only person being tried in the trial. ...

[56] The decision of this Court in *Thatcher* provides some guidance as to the relevant principles of party liability and how they might be incorporated into jury instructions. The trial judge in *Thatcher* had read the contents of s. 21(1) to the jury and described what was meant by the term "aiding" or "abetting" by stating that it meant "intentional encouragement or assistance in the commission of the offence," and noting that the actual perpetrator need not be identified.

. . .

[58] Three principles from the decision in *Thatcher* are relevant here. First, if there is evidence admitted at trial which properly supports an alternate mode of liability under s. 21, an instruction on that section should be left with the jury, even though the identity of the other participant or participants is unknown, and even though the precise part played by each participant may be uncertain. Second, it is not necessary for the trial judge to relate the law to the evidence which could support the alternate theory of aiding and abetting where evidence adduced by the Crown relates to either mode of participation, and evidence adduced by the defence relates to either the accused's innocence or the accused's guilt under the relevant subsection(s) of s. 21. Finally, a jury need not be unanimous on the nature of the accused's participation in the offence, so long as it is satisfied that the accused either committed the offence personally or, alternatively, aided and abetted another to commit the offence, provided the jury is satisfied beyond a reasonable doubt that the accused did one or the other.

. . .

[63] In certain circumstances, uncertainty as to the involvement of known or unknown third parties as co-principals in the offence may also be legally irrelevant. Co-principal liability is codified in s. 21(1)(a) of the *Criminal Code*: "Every one is a party to an offence who actually commits it." It therefore arises whenever two or more people

"actually commit" an offence to make both people individually liable for that crime. It also arises where two or more persons together form an intention to commit an offence, are present at the commission of the crime, and contribute to it, although they do not personally commit all of the essential elements of that offence (*R. v. Mena* (1987), 34 C.C.C. (3d) 304 (Ont. C.A.), at p. 316). If the trier of fact is satisfied beyond a reasonable doubt that the accused committed all elements of the crime, it does not matter whether another person may also have committed it.

. . .

C. Application to the Record

. . .

[74] It was necessary on the evidence for the trier of fact to decide that Mr. Pickton was either liable for the murders as the actual shooter, or that he was liable through his assistance to an unknown third party who was the actual shooter. It was not relevant for the jury to direct their minds to the possibility that Mr. Pickton and a third party both caused the victims' deaths as co-principals, and not helpful to provide them with an instruction which opened up party liability, but stopped short of setting out its relevant principles as they applied to the evidence. The possibility that Mr. Pickton only aided and abetted the murders *was* legally relevant on the evidence in this case.

. . .

D. Aiding and Abetting

[76] The main focus of s. 21(1)(b) and (c) is on the intention with which the aid or encouragement has been provided. The act or omission relied upon must in fact aid or abet, and it must also have been done with the particular intention to facilitate or encourage the principal's commission of the offence, with knowledge that the principal intends to commit the crime: *R. v. Briscoe*, [2010] 1 S.C.R. 411, at paras. 14 and 16-18. To be found liable for first degree murder as an aider and abettor of a planned and deliberate murder, an accused must have knowledge that the murder was planned and deliberate: *Briscoe*, at para. 17. Wilful blindness will satisfy the knowledge component of s. 21(1)(b) or (c): *Briscoe*, at para. 21.

[77] On the record in this case, the acts of aiding or abetting relied upon to make Mr. Pickton liable for the murders could have included many things, from the "luring" of the victims to the farm, to providing them with drugs or subduing them, to encouraging a third party killer by making it known that Mr. Pickton would help dismember and dispose of the bodies so that the killer would not get caught. This same evidence could similarly have provided the necessary evidence of intention and knowledge, including knowledge of the planned and deliberate nature of the murders.

. . .

[80] ... Given that there was no evidence in any of the counts that there was more than one operative cause of death, the instructions should have made it clear that the jury could only convict Mr. Pickton of the killings if they were satisfied beyond a reasonable doubt, having considered all the evidence, that he *either* personally shot the victims *or* aided and abetted another person in the killings.

. . .

F. The Curative Proviso

. . .

[86] The trial was all about the participation of Mr. Pickton in the murders of the six victims. I will not attempt to review here all of the evidence offered by the Crown during what was a very long trial. However, on a review of the record, in my opinion, the Crown presented compelling, overwhelming evidence of the participation of Mr. Pickton in the murders. From whichever perspective we consider the participation of Mr. Pickton, on the evidence, he was necessarily either a principal or an aider or abettor. It would surpass belief that a properly instructed jury would not have found him guilty of murder in the presence of such cogent evidence of his involvement. Indeed, this properly instructed jury would likely have convicted Mr. Pickton of first degree rather than second degree murder.

[87] Certainly, this was a long and difficult trial—but it was also a fair one. Despite the errors set out above, there was no miscarriage of justice occasioned by the trial proceedings. Mr. Pickton was entitled to the same measure of justice as any other person in this country. He received it. He is not entitled to more.

While s 21(1) puts principals, aiders, and abettors on the same legal footing, other modes of participation also arise. Section 21(2) extends party liability when two or more persons act with a common intention to carry out an unlawful purpose. Section 22 establishes that a person who counsels the commission of an offence will become a party if the offence is subsequently committed. Aiding, abetting, common intention, and counselling an offence that is ultimately committed are the forms of secondary (or party) liability alluded to in LeBel J's decision in *Pickton*. The ensuing sections of this chapter explore the elements of each of these forms of secondary liability before turning to accessoryship.

II. AIDING AND ABETTING

Sections 21(1)(b) and 21(1)(c) respectively provide that those who aid or abet the commission of an offence will be convicted of the primary offence. The courts have frequently said that aiding and abetting are definitionally distinct. Aiding is typically associated with some form of material assistance in the commission of an offence, whereas abetting is usually associated with verbal encouragement or comparable forms of incitement.

Defining the Scope of Liability

Given that ss 21(1)(b) and 21(1)(c) extend party liability to those who do not commit the full offence, it is particularly important to define what actions or encouragement constitute aiding and abetting. As with any form of criminal liability, a further question specifically concerns the inculpatory elements of participation as an aider or abettor. What is the element of fault required for proof of these modes of participation? In *R v Greyeyes*, the Supreme Court of Canada considered the definition of aiding and abetting and the circumstances in which party liability for trafficking in narcotics would be extended to a person who assists a prospective purchaser of narcotics to find a source from which they might buy.

R v Greyeyes
Supreme Court of Canada
[1997] 2 SCR 825

[Constable Morgan, an undercover RCMP officer, bought five "joints" of marijuana from Greyeyes. The following day, Morgan asked the appellant if he knew where he could get some cocaine. The appellant stated that he knew a source, and if Morgan would drive him, he would attempt to get some. The appellant directed Morgan to an apartment building. Greyeyes went inside alone and returned to say that the people he was hoping to talk to were out but would be back later that evening.

Morgan and the appellant returned to the apartment building that evening and entered together. Greyeyes identified himself over the intercom and they both went up to the apartment door. Greyeyes again identified himself. A voice from inside asked what they wanted. The appellant said "cocaine." The voice asked how much, and the appellant looked at Morgan, who indicated "one." The appellant replied "one." Morgan asked the appellant how much it would cost, and the appellant told him it would be $40. At this point the people in the apartment encountered difficulty opening the door and after a few minutes the person inside said to slide the money under the door, which the appellant did. Immediately a small pink flap containing two-tenths of a gram of cocaine was passed back under the door. The appellant picked it up, handed it to Morgan, and then started walking toward the exit. When they left the building, Morgan drove the appellant home and gave him $10 for helping him obtain the cocaine.

At trial the accused was acquitted of trafficking in cocaine on the basis that his actions did not amount to aiding and abetting. On appeal, the Court of Appeal overturned the acquittal and entered a conviction. A further appeal was taken to the Supreme Court, which dismissed the appeal and upheld the conviction of trafficking on the facts. The Court, however, disagreed about the question of whether someone who simply assists the purchaser of drugs would be guilty of aiding and abetting the trafficking of the drugs.]

CORY J (McLachlin and Major JJ concurring): …

[25] Can someone either acting as an agent for a purchaser of narcotics or assisting a purchaser to buy narcotics be found to be a party to the offence of trafficking under s. 21(1) of the *Code*, by aiding or abetting in the sale of narcotics? In my view, the response to the question must be that such a person can indeed be found to be a party to the offence.

Aiding and Abetting

[26] The terms "aiding" and "abetting" are often used together in the context of determining whether persons are parties to an offence. Although the meanings of these terms are similar, they are separate concepts: *R. v. Meston* (1975), 28 C.C.C. (2d) 497 (Ont. C.A.), at pp. 503-4. To aid under s. 21(1)(b) means to assist or help the actor: *Mewett & Manning on Criminal Law* (3rd ed. 1994), at p. 272; E.G. Ewaschuk, *Criminal Pleadings & Practice in Canada* (2nd ed. 1987 (loose-leaf)), at p. 15-7, para. 15:2020 (release May 1997). To abet within the meaning of s. 21(1)(c) includes encouraging, instigating, promoting or procuring the crime to be committed: *Mewett & Manning on Criminal Law*, *supra*, at p. 272; *Criminal Pleadings & Practice in Canada*, *supra*, at p. 15-11, para. 15:3010 (release December 1996).

Liability of an Agent for the Purchaser

[27] The appellant claims that he cannot be a party to the offence of trafficking since he was acting exclusively on behalf of the purchaser of the drugs and not the seller. He contends that since a purchaser of a narcotic cannot be convicted of aiding and abetting the seller's offence of trafficking, then someone who extends assistance only to the purchaser should not be found to be a party either.

[28] In *Meston*, *supra*, the Ontario Court of Appeal considered whether a purchaser of drugs aids or abets the seller. In that case the charge of trafficking arose from the sale of approximately three-quarters of a pound of marijuana. Martin J.A. for the Court accepted that, on principle, the conduct of a purchaser who encourages the sale of a substance which he knows it is illegal for the vendor to sell falls within the ordinary meaning of the word "abets" used in s. 21(1)(c) of the *Code*. Thus, a purchaser should be a party to the offence of selling.

[29] However, Martin J.A. then went on to consider this Court's decision in *Poitras v. The Queen*, [1974] S.C.R. 649. The reasons in that case persuaded him that a purchaser should not, by reason of the purchase alone, be found to be a party to the offence of trafficking. Martin J.A. referred at p. 507 to the following passage from the dissenting reasons of Laskin J. (as he then was) at 655 of *Poitras*:

> ... [S]ince possession of a narcotic is an offence, and there is an onus on an accused who pleads not guilty to a charge under s. 4(2) to establish that his possession was not for the purpose of trafficking (see s. 8 of the Act), it would, in my opinion, be incongruous to turn a mere purchaser into a trafficker by using s. 21 of the *Criminal Code* to supply the want of definition.

He went on to conclude that it is implicit from the reasons of Dickson J. (as he then was) for the majority in *Poitras* that he too accepted the proposition that the purchaser of a narcotic does not by that act alone engage in trafficking. I agree with that conclusion.

· · ·

[31] Certainly there can be no doubt that someone who purchases a narcotic must assist the vendor in completing the sale. Without a purchaser, there could be no sale of the narcotic. However, Parliament has chosen to address the culpability of purchasers in a different fashion. As soon as someone obtains possession of a narcotic, he or she may be charged with possession or possession for the purpose of trafficking. Yet it is clear that that person does not come within the definition of trafficking. Nor can he or she be found guilty of aiding or abetting the offence of trafficking on the basis of the purchase alone. Parliament has created other offences under which a purchaser may be charged as a result of the purchase.

[32] It must be emphasized that there is no legislative intention similar to that which exists for purchasers to be found for those who assist or act as agents for a purchaser. Drug trafficking by its very nature is a business which involves and is dependent upon many "middle men." If the same exception which applies to purchasers were extended to agents for the purchaser, then the agents could escape culpability entirely. They should not. Quite simply there is no reason to extend the exception for purchasers to those who assist or encourage purchasers in an illegal sale. The activities of an agent for a purchaser or one who assists a purchaser to buy narcotics certainly come within the definition of "aiding" or "abetting" under s. 21(1) of the *Code*. By bringing together the source of supply

and the prospective purchaser, these persons obviously assist in the sale of narcotics. Acting as a spokesperson for a purchaser has the effect of assisting both the purchaser and the vendor to complete the transaction. It follows that an agent for a purchaser or one who assists the purchaser to buy the drugs can properly be found guilty as a party to the offence of trafficking under s. 21(1) of the *Code*.

. . .

Application of the Principle to the Case at Bar

[36] Let us apply that principle to the facts of this case. It must be determined whether the accused actually aided or abetted the sale of narcotics. There is no doubt in my mind that he did. The trial judge found as a fact that the appellant acted as a spokesperson for the purchaser. He was the one who brought the customer to the seller. He was the connection between the buyer and the seller. He escorted the buyer to the seller's apartment, negotiated with the seller to purchase the drug, and accepted $10 from the buyer for facilitating the deal. The buyer had tried to purchase drugs from the very same apartment earlier in the week, but was denied access, apparently because he was unknown to the seller. It was only as a result of the appellant's assistance that the prospective buyer was able to get into the apartment building. These facts are sufficient to establish that the appellant aided in the sale of narcotics within the meaning of s. 21(1)(b) of the *Code* and encouraged the sale within the meaning of s. 21(1)(c) of the *Code*.

[37] Next it must be determined whether the appellant had the requisite *mens rea* or guilty mind to satisfy s. 21(b). That section provides that any person who does anything *for the purpose of aiding* a person to commit an offence is a party to the offence. The term "for the purpose of" was considered in *R. v. Hibbert*, [1995] 2 S.C.R. 973. Writing for a unanimous Court, Lamer C.J. acknowledged at p. 995 that the term "purpose" could be interpreted in two different ways:

> One can speak of an actor doing something "on purpose" (as opposed to by accident) thereby equating purpose with "immediate intention." The term is also used, however, to indicate the ultimate ends an actor seeks to achieve, which imports the idea of "desire" into the definition.

After reviewing the pertinent case law and academic commentary, Lamer C.J. concluded that the former definition must have been that intended by Parliament when it drafted s. 21(1)(b) of the *Code*. For the purposes of this section, he said, "purpose" should be equated with "intention" and not "desire." In other words, in order to satisfy the purpose requirement under s. 21(1)(b), the Crown is required to prove only that the accused intended the consequences that flowed from his or her aid to the principal offender, and need not show that he or she desired or approved of the consequences.

[38] Section 21(1)(c) simply provides that any person who abets any person in committing an offence is a party to that offence. In order to secure a conviction, the Crown must prove not only that the accused encouraged the principal with his or her words or acts, but also that the accused intended to do so: *R. v. Curran* (1977), 38 C.C.C. (2d) 151 (Alta. C.A.); *R. v. Jones* (1977), 65 Cr. App. R. 250 (C.A.). It is the establishment by the Crown of that intention which satisfies the *mens rea* or guilty mind requirement of s. 21(1)(c).

[39] Did the appellant intend to assist or encourage the sale? There can be no doubt that the appellant knew he was assisting in the illegal sale of narcotics, and that he intended to do so. His words and actions demonstrate that he deliberately set out to bring together the parties to the transaction and acted as the conduit for delivering the drugs from the seller to the buyer. The appellant may have been *motivated* solely by a desire to help the buyer, but what he *intended* to do was to facilitate the sale of narcotics, and this is a culpable intention. Since the appellant actually encouraged and assisted in the illegal sale of narcotics, and since he had the intention of doing so, he was guilty of trafficking as a party pursuant to s. 21(1)(b) and (c) of the *Code*.

. . .

L'HEUREUX-DUBÉ J (La Forest, Sopinka, and Gonthier JJ concurring):

[1] I have had the advantage of reading the reasons of my colleague Justice Cory. While I agree with much of his analysis as well as the conclusion he reaches, I have difficulty with one aspect of his reasons. Specifically, I believe that his interpretation of s. 21 of the *Criminal Code*, R.S.C., 1985, c. C-46, and the manner in which it applies to the offence of drug trafficking under s. 4(1) of the *Narcotic Control Act*, R.S.C., 1985, c. N-1, leads to a broad scope of liability which is unwarranted.

[2] The thrust of my colleague's reasons (at para. 32) is that "one who assists a purchaser to buy narcotics ... come[s] within the definition of 'aiding' or 'abetting' under s. 21(1) of the *Code*." By assisting the purchaser, this person makes the sale of narcotics possible, and thus is a party to the offence of trafficking. My colleague recognizes, however, that a purchaser, through the act of buying alone, cannot be convicted of trafficking, but feels that *any act* of the person offering assistance to the purchaser, no matter how trivial, can lead (assuming the requisite knowledge and intent are also present) to a finding of guilt for this offence.

[3] This reasoning is based, in part, upon the idea that Parliament has specifically excluded purchasers from the offence of trafficking yet never intended to extend that immunity to persons assisting the purchase. I do not share my colleague's view of Parliament's intent in this regard. Moreover, I am deeply concerned that the adoption of his approach would lead to convictions for trafficking in situations that were never intended to come within that definition.

[4] Merely as an example of the breadth of my colleague's approach, I offer the following scenario. Ms. A wishes to buy drugs and warns her boyfriend, Mr. B, that she will walk over, through a dangerous neighbourhood, unless he drives her there. He agrees, and upon arrival, she enters and makes the purchase alone. Despite his minimal participation, Mr. B has assisted the sale because he has conveyed the purchaser to the designated sale location. As a result, while Ms. A, as a purchaser, will receive the lesser possession conviction, Mr. B will be guilty of trafficking.

[5] In my view, such a result is unacceptable. In this regard, while I express no opinion about the particular situation to which he was referring, I agree with the general sentiment expressed by Seaton J.A. in *R. v. Eccleston* (1975), 24 C.C.C. (2d) 564 (B.C.C.A.), at p. 568, who observed that extending "the definition of trafficking so as to encompass conduct that right-minded people would say is not trafficking is damaging and to be avoided"; see also Bruce A. MacFarlane, Robert J. Frater and Chantal Proulx, *Drug Offences in Canada* (3rd ed. 1996 (loose-leaf)), at p. 5-22; *R. v. Lauze* (1980), 17 C.R. (3d) 90 (Que. C.A.), *per* Monet J.A.

· · ·

[8] ... [D]espite his or her crucial assistance in helping to complete the sale of narcotics, the purchaser cannot *by this action alone* be found guilty of the offence of aiding or abetting the offence of trafficking. Frankly, I see no reason why this reasoning should not be extended to third parties as well. In situations where the facts reveal no more than incidental assistance of the sale through rendering aid to the purchaser, it stands to reason that these persons should be treated as purchasers, and not as traffickers. The proper charge in these circumstances would be aiding or abetting the possession of a narcotic, and not trafficking.

[9] The offence of aiding or abetting possession of a narcotic is a permissible legal result and has occurred on many occasions: see, for example, *R. v. Miller*, 12 C.C.C. (3d) 54 (B.C.C.A.), at p. 87; *Re Chambers and The Queen*, 20 C.C.C. (3d) 440 (Ont. C.A.); *Zanini v. The Queen*, [1967] S.C.R. 715.

[10] In my view, this approach also offers a number of advantages. First, I believe it accords with the general notion that the "punishment" should be in accord with the crime: Eric Colvin, *Principles of Criminal Law* (2nd ed. 1991), at p. 28. A trafficking conviction, in the circumstances indicated above, is quite harsh, carries with it considerable stigma and has negative consequences for the repute of justice. In this regard, it is also worth noting that the sentencing structure for these offences is rather disparate. A trafficking conviction is punishable by up to life imprisonment, while a possession conviction carries a maximum seven-year sentence.

[11] Perhaps more importantly, I believe this approach benefits from a certain symmetry. It is clear that someone whose acts are designed to aid a purchaser, yet incidentally benefit the seller, has assisted much more in the purchase of the narcotic than in the sale. As such, it is only fitting that this person share the culpability and stigma of the purchaser rather than that of the vendor.

· · ·

[13] In the case at bar, however, I have no difficulty concluding that the appellant did far more than act as a purchaser. My colleague has described the nature of the appellant's participation in the sale in detail, and these facts demonstrate a concerted effort on his part to effect the transfer of narcotics. The appellant located the seller, brought the buyer to the site and introduced the parties. It is clear that without this assistance, the purchase would never have taken place. Moreover, he acted as a spokesperson, negotiated the price of the drugs, and passed the money over to the seller. He also accepted money for having facilitated the deal. As my colleague points out, without the appellant's assistance, the buyer would never have been able to enter the apartment building and contact the seller. These are not the acts of a mere purchaser, and as a result it is clear that the appellant aided the traffic of narcotics.

[14] With respect to the required intention to commit such an offence under s. 21(1)(b) of the *Code*, and whether it was established in this case, I am in complete agreement with the approach taken by my colleague.

· · ·

Appeal dismissed and conviction for trafficking upheld.

In *R v Briscoe* the Supreme Court of Canada expanded upon the mental element of aiding and abetting.

R v Briscoe
Supreme Court of Canada
2010 SCC 13, [2010] 1 SCR 411

[Briscoe was acquitted of kidnapping, aggravated sexual assault, and first-degree murder. On the Crown's case, a man named Laboucan had formed a plan with others to kill some-one. The 13-year-old victim, Courtepatte, was lured from a shopping mall to a secluded golf course on the false pretext of joining a party. At the golf course, she was raped and killed by numerous principal actors. Briscoe drove the car from the mall to the golf course, handed a weapon to one principal, and at one point held the victim and told her angrily to shut up or be quiet. Briscoe gave a statement to police in which he said he was fearful for himself and his girlfriend, and that he "didn't want to know" what Laboucan and the others planned to do to Courtepatte. Although Briscoe admitted hearing Laboucan and the others talk about killing people, he denied knowing "definitely, for sure" what they intended to do with Courtepatte.]

CHARRON J (for the Court): ...

2. Background

. . .

[7] What happened to Ms. Courtepatte was not the main question at trial. There was no real question about whether she had been a victim of a kidnapping, aggravated sexual assault, or culpable homicide. There was also no serious question that the homicide fell within the category of first degree murder, either because it was planned and deliberate, or because it was committed during the commission of a crime of domination within the meaning of s. 231(5) of the *Criminal Code*, R.S.C. 1985, c. C-46. The issue was whether each accused was involved and, if so, whether criminal liability flowed from this involvement.

[8] The Crown's theory was that Mr. Laboucan was "the mastermind behind these offences" who had formulated the plan, selected the victim, and communicated the plan to the others. Mr. Briscoe's actions, carried out with knowledge of Mr. Laboucan's plan, made him a party to the offences. His participation included driving the group to and from the crime scene, choosing a secluded location, providing and transporting weapons, and taking "an active role" by holding Ms. Courtepatte and telling her to shut up, and threatening Ms. K.B. The Crown argued that Mr. Briscoe had actual knowledge of or was wilfully blind to the plan. The Crown also submitted that, even apart from Mr. Briscoe's acts of assistance, his presence coupled with his knowledge of the plan made him an abettor. His presence could lend courage to the attackers, discourage rescue, and give Ms. Courtepatte "one more reason to feel helpless and lost and futile" (J.R., vol. XIII, at pp. 169-73).

[9] The trial judge essentially accepted the Crown's theory. He found that Mr. Laboucan had committed the offences as a principal offender and that Mr. Briscoe had aided in the commission of the crimes by doing four things: he "drove the group to the place" where the crimes were committed; he "selected a place to stop the characteristics of which facilitated" the commission of the crimes; he "opened the trunk of the car at Mr. Laboucan's request" and "gave him one of the tools that was taken to the grassy area, albeit a tool apparently not used to murder Ms. Courtepatte"; and he "angrily told Ms. Courtepatte to be quiet when she was screaming after Ms. S.B. hit her and before Mr. Laboucan sexually assaulted and murdered her" (para. 277). Therefore, the *actus reus* for being a party to the offences was proven.

[10] The trial judge then examined whether Mr. Briscoe had the requisite *mens rea* for any of the offences. Did he intend to assist Mr. Laboucan in the commission of the crimes? In order to have such intention, he would have to have known of Mr. Laboucan's intention to commit each of the crimes. The crucial question then became whether he had such knowledge. The trial judge concluded that Mr. Briscoe did not have the requisite knowledge. Although Mr. Briscoe did not testify at trial, the Crown introduced statements he had made to the police following his arrest. The trial judge ruled the statements voluntary and relied heavily on their contents in concluding that Mr. Briscoe lacked the requisite knowledge. ...

[11] In brief, the trial judge's conclusions on *mens rea* were the following. On the charge of kidnapping, despite finding that Mr. Briscoe knew that Mr. Laboucan intended to at least seriously scare Ms. Courtepatte, the trial judge determined that the evidence did not support the conclusion that Mr. Briscoe knew "Ms. Courtepatte and Ms. KB had been lured by fraud into his car" (paras. 283-84). On the charge of aggravated sexual assault, although Mr. Briscoe's "statement does suggest that he understood Mr. Laboucan anticipated to be sexually intimate with Ms. Courtepatte," there was "nothing to indicate he understood that Mr. Laboucan intended to sexually assault Ms. Courtepatte" (para. 285). Finally, on the charge of first degree murder, the trial judge held that "the evidence does not establish that he knew Mr. Laboucan in fact intended to kill Ms. Courtepatte. Further the evidence certainly does not establish that he himself had the requisite intent for murder" (para. 286). The trial judge concluded that, in these circumstances, the evidence was not sufficient to prove beyond a reasonable doubt "that Mr. Briscoe did any of the assistive things he did knowing, much less intending, that they would assist Mr. Laboucan" to commit any of the crimes (para. 287). The trial judge did not consider whether Mr. Briscoe was wilfully blind, despite the Crown's submissions. He acquitted Mr. Briscoe on all charges.

[12] The Crown appealed Mr. Briscoe's acquittals to the Court of Appeal of Alberta. Writing for a unanimous court, Martin J.A. held that the trial judge erred in law by failing to consider whether Mr. Briscoe was "wilfully blind to the harm his cohorts intended to cause the victim" and that, "[b]ut for this error, the verdicts may well have been different" on all three charges (para. 41). The Court of Appeal set aside the acquittals and ordered a new trial on all charges. Mr. Briscoe now appeals to this Court.

3. Analysis

[13] Canadian criminal law does not distinguish between the principal offender and parties to an offence in determining criminal liability. Section 21(1) of the *Criminal Code* makes perpetrators, aiders, and abettors equally liable:

> 21(1) Every one is a party to an offence who
>
> (a) actually commits it;
>
> (b) does or omits to do anything for the purpose of aiding any person to commit it;
> or
> (c) abets any person in committing it.

The person who provides the gun, therefore, may be found guilty of the same offence as the one who pulls the trigger. The *actus reus* and *mens rea* for aiding or abetting, however, are distinct from those of the principal offence.

[14] The *actus reus* of aiding or abetting is doing (or, in some circumstances, omitting to do) something that assists or encourages the perpetrator to commit the offence. While it is common to speak of aiding and abetting together, the two concepts are distinct, and liability can flow from either one. Broadly speaking, "[t]o aid under s. 21(1)(b) means to assist or help the actor ... . To abet within the meaning of s. 21(1)(c) includes encouraging, instigating, promoting or procuring the crime to be committed": *R. v. Greyeyes*, [1997] 2 S.C.R. 825, at para. 26. The *actus reus* is not at issue in this appeal. As noted earlier, the Crown argued at trial that Mr. Briscoe was both an aider and an abettor. The trial judge's finding that Mr. Briscoe performed the four acts of assistance described above is not disputed.

[15] Of course, doing or omitting to do something that resulted in assisting another in committing a crime is not sufficient to attract criminal liability. As the Court of Appeal for Ontario wrote in *R. v. F. W. Woolworth Co.* (1974), 3 O.R. (2d) 629, "one does not render himself liable by renting or loaning a car for some legitimate business or recreational activity merely because the person to whom it is loaned or rented chooses in the course of his use to transport some stolen goods, or by renting a house for residential purposes to a tenant who surreptitiously uses it to store drugs" (p. 640). The aider or abettor must also have the requisite mental state or *mens rea*. Specifically, in the words of s. 21(1)(b), the person must have rendered the assistance *for the purpose* of aiding the principal offender to commit the crime.

[16] The *mens rea* requirement reflected in the word "purpose" under s. 21(1)(b) has two components: intent and knowledge. For the intent component, it was settled in *R. v. Hibbert*, [1995] 2 S.C.R. 973, that "purpose" in s. 21(1)(b) should be understood as essentially synonymous with "intention." The Crown must prove that the accused intended to assist the principal in the commission of the offence. The Court emphasized that "purpose" should not be interpreted as incorporating the notion of "desire" into the fault requirement for party liability. It is therefore not required that the accused desired that the offence be successfully committed (*Hibbert*, at para. 35). The Court held, at para. 32, that the perverse consequences that would flow from a "purpose equals desire" interpretation of s. 21(1)(b) were clearly illustrated by the following hypothetical situation described by Mewett and Manning:

If a man is approached by a friend who tells him that he is going to rob a bank and would like to use his car as the getaway vehicle for which he will pay him $100, when that person is … charged under s. 21 for doing something for the purpose of aiding his friend to commit the offence, can he say "My purpose was not to aid the robbery but to make $100"? His argument would be that while he knew that he was helping the robbery, his desire was to obtain $100 and he did not care one way or the other whether the robbery was successful or not.

(A.W. Mewett and M. Manning, *Criminal Law* (2nd ed. 1985), at p. 112.)

The same rationale applies regardless of the principal offence in question. Even in respect of murder, there is no "additional requirement that an aider or abettor subjectively approve of or desire the victim's death" (*Hibbert*, at para. 37 (emphasis deleted)).

[17] As for knowledge, in order to have the intention to assist in the commission of an offence, the aider must know that the perpetrator intends to commit the crime, although he or she need not know precisely how it will be committed. That sufficient knowledge is a prerequisite for intention is simply a matter of common sense. Doherty J.A. in *R. v. Maciel*, 2007 ONCA 196, 219 C.C.C. (3d) 516, provides the following useful explanation of the knowledge requirement which is entirely apposite to this case (at paras. 88-89):

… a person who is alleged to have aided in a murder must be shown to have known that the perpetrator had the intent required for murder under s. 229 (a): *R. v. Kirkness* (1990), 60 C.C.C. (3d) 97 (S.C.C.) at 127.

The same analysis applies where it is alleged that the accused aided a perpetrator in the commission of a first degree murder that was planned and deliberate. The accused is liable as an aider only if the accused did something to assist the perpetrator in the planned and deliberate murder and if, when the aider rendered the assistance, he did so for the purpose of aiding the perpetrator in the commission of a planned and deliberate murder. Before the aider could be said to have the requisite purpose, the Crown must prove that the aider knew the murder was planned and deliberate. Whether the aider acquired that knowledge through actual involvement in the planning and deliberation or through some other means, is irrelevant to his or her culpability under s. 21(1).

[18] It is important to note that Doherty J.A., in referring to this Court's decision in *R. v. Kirkness*, [1990] 3 S.C.R. 74, rightly states that the aider to a murder must "have known that the perpetrator had the intent required for murder." While some of the language in *Kirkness* may be read as requiring that the aider share the murderer's intention to kill the victim, the case must now be read in the light of the above-noted analysis in *Hibbert*. The perpetrator's intention to kill the victim must be known to the aider or abettor; it need not be shared. *Kirkness* should not be interpreted as requiring that the aider and abettor of a murder have the same *mens rea* as the actual killer. It is sufficient that he or she, armed with *knowledge* of the perpetrator's intention to commit the crime, acts with the intention of assisting the perpetrator in its commission. It is only in this sense that it can be said that the aider and abettor must intend that the principal offence be committed.

• • •

[25] In this case, I agree with Martin J.A. that the trial judge erred in law by failing to consider wilful blindness. As he noted, even Mr. Briscoe's own statements to the police suggest that he had a "strong, well-founded suspicion that someone would be killed at the golf course" (para. 30) and that he may have been wilfully blind to the kidnapping

and prospect of sexual assault. His statements also show that he deliberately chose not to inquire about what the members of the group intended to do because he did not want to know. As he put it, "whatever you guys wanna do just do it. Don't do it around me I don't want to see nothing I don't know what the fuck you're gonna do." The trial judge relied heavily upon the statements in his reasons but did not refer to the doctrine of wilful blindness. Of course, whether Mr. Briscoe had the requisite *mens rea* for the three offences was a question for the trier of fact, and Mr. Briscoe is entitled to the benefit of any reasonable doubt on this issue. However, from a legal standpoint, it is my respectful view that the evidence cried out for an analysis on wilful blindness. In these circumstances, the Court of Appeal rightly concluded that the trial judge's failure to consider Mr. Briscoe's knowledge from that perspective constitutes a legal error which necessitates a new trial on all charges.

The facts in *R v Briscoe* bear some similarities to those in *Dunlop and Sylvester v The Queen*. However, there are also important differences in the judicial accounts of the facts in these two cases. As you read *Dunlop and Sylvester*, note that the dissenting judges adopt a different view of the evidence from that of the majority.

Dunlop and Sylvester v The Queen
Supreme Court of Canada
[1979] 2 SCR 881

[The appellants were tried and convicted by a judge and jury of rape for their part in a mass rape of a 16-year-old complainant by members of a motorcycle gang at an abandoned dump. The complainant testified that the two appellants had raped her. The appellants denied this. One of the appellants testified he had met with the motorcycle gang earlier in the night at the dump and was with the complainant at a bar before the rape. The appellants also testified that they arrived at the dump site, saw a woman having intercourse with a gang member, delivered four cases of beer, and left after three minutes.]

DICKSON J (Laskin CJ and Spence and Estey JJ concurring): ... On s. 21(1) of the *Code*, the jury was instructed as follows:

Secondly, I should also instruct you on the law relating to parties to an offence. Section 21(1) of the *Criminal Code* reads as follows:

Everyone is a party to an offence who:
(a) actually commits it,
(b) does or omits to do anything for the purpose of aiding any person to commit it,
or
(c) abets any person in committing it.

Abets, that word abets means encourages, supports, upholds. It is another way of expressing a person giving assistance to someone committing the offence. Everyone who aids and encourages the person in the commission of the offence is as guilty as the person who commits the actual criminal act.

To find that the accused is guilty of aiding or abetting the commission of an offence by another person, it is only necessary to show that he understood what was being done and by some act on his part assisted or encouraged the attainment of that act.

Mere presence at the scene of a crime is not sufficient to ground culpability. Something more is needed: encouragement of the principal offender; an act which facilitates the commission of the offence, such as keeping watch on [or] enticing the victim away, or an act which tends to prevent or hinder interference with accomplishment of the criminal act, such as preventing the intended victim from escaping or being ready to assist the prime culprit. Thus, in an early work, *Foster's Crown Law*, p. 350, we read:

> ... in order to render a person an accomplice and a principal in felony, he must be aiding and abetting at the fact, or ready to afford assistance if necessary, and therefore if A. happeneth to be present at a murder, for instance, and taketh no part in it, nor endeavoureth to prevent it, nor apprehendeth the murderer, nor levyeth hue and cry after him, this strange behaviour of his, though highly criminal, will not of itself render him either principal or accessory.

. . .

In this Court the question of aiding and abetting was canvassed in *Preston v. R.* [[1949] SCR 156]. The appellant and another were accused of having set fire to a school. Mr. Justice Estey delivered the majority judgment in this Court, in the course of which he stated (p. 159) that in order to find the appellant guilty of aiding, abetting, counselling or procuring, it was only necessary to show that he understood what was taking place and by some act on his part encouraged or assisted in the attainment thereof. Later he said (p. 160) that mere presence does not constitute aiding and abetting, but presence under certain circumstances may itself be evidence thereof. He proceeded to review the evidence and concluded, p. 161:

> If appellant's explanation was not believed by the jury there was *evidence in addition to his mere presence* upon which they might well conclude that he was guilty of aiding, abetting, counselling or procuring. (Emphasis added.)

Two Canadian cases make the distinction between presence with prior knowledge, and accidental presence. In *R. v. Dick* [(1947), 2 CR 417 (Ont CA)], the accused was charged with the murder of her husband. According to her own statement, she met her husband and Bohozuk, a friend, and they went with her in a borrowed car, her husband in the front seat and Bohozuk in the back. The two men began to quarrel, both were drinking; Bohozuk pulled a gun and shot Mr. Dick. It was not a happy marriage, nor were Mr. Dick and Bohozuk on best of terms. There was some surrounding evidence casting doubt upon the non-involvement of the accused. As Chief Justice Robertson noted, she did not admit that there was any design, nor that she knew Bohozuk intended to shoot Dick, nor even that she knew Bohozuk had a weapon with him. Yet the trial judge gave only general directions on aiding and abetting to the jury. Robertson C.J.O. concluded at pp. 432-3:

Now, while it may be that a jury might infer from the evidence a good deal that is not expressly admitted, it is not at all certain that this jury did infer that the appellant knew more than she admits knowing of Bohozuk's then present purpose. This jury should have been instructed that if they found that the appellant was no more than passively acquiescent at the time of the shooting and that she had no reason to expect that there would be any shooting until it actually occurred, then s. 69 did not apply.

In the result, a new trial was ordered.

In *R. v. Hoggan* [(1965), 47 CR 256 (Alta SC (AD))], the charge was that the accused aided and abetted in wilfully attempting to defeat the course of justice by attempting to dissuade a witness from giving evidence. Johnson J.A. concluded at p. 260:

> There are two things that must be proved before an accused can be convinced of being a party by aiding and abetting. It must be proved that he had knowledge that the principal intended to commit the offence and that the accused aided and abetted him. Where there is no knowledge that an offence is to be committed, the presence of an accused at the scene of the crime cannot be a circumstance which could be evidence of aiding and abetting.

The basis for Johnson J.A.'s approach to aiding and abetting is found in *Preston* and *Coney* [(1882), 8 QBD 534], both of which he cites.

The case of *R. v. Salajko* [[1970] 1 CCC 352 (Ont CA)] is like the instant case in many respects. A girl was raped by fifteen young men in a lonely field. Three were charged. Two of these were identified as having had intercourse with the girl. She admitted, however, that the third accused, Salajko, though seen to be near the girl with his pants down while she was being raped by others, did not have intercourse with her. The Crown placed its case against him on s. 21(1)(b) and (c) of the *Criminal Code*. One might be forgiven for thinking that it was open to the jury to infer encouragement by conduct, but the Ontario Court of Appeal thought otherwise. Chief Justice Gale, delivering the judgment of the Court, stated that in the absence of evidence to suggest something in the way of aiding, or counselling, or encouraging on the part of the accused with respect to that which was being done by the others, there was simply no evidence upon which a jury could properly arrive at a verdict of guilty against the particular accused. The learned Chief Justice also found error in the trial judge's charge which seemed to indicate that a person could abet another in the commission of an offence if, knowingly, he stood by while the offence was being committed.

. . .

In the case at bar I have great difficulty in finding any evidence of anything more than mere presence and passive acquiescence. Presence at the commission of an offence can be evidence of aiding and abetting if accompanied by other factors, such as prior knowledge of the principal offender's intention to commit the offence or attendance for the purpose of encouragement. There was no evidence that while the crime was being committed either of the accused rendered aid, assistance or encouragement to the rape of Brenda Ross. There was no evidence of any positive act or omission to facilitate the unlawful purpose. One can infer that the two accused knew that a party was to be held, and that their presence at the dump was not accidental or in the nature of casual passers-by, but that is not sufficient. A person cannot properly be convicted of aiding or abetting in the commission of acts which he does not know may be or are intended: *per* Viscount

Dilhorne in *Director of Public Prosecutions for Northern Ireland v. Maxwell*, [1978] 3 All E.R. 1140 at p. 1144 (H.L.). One must be able to infer that the accused had prior knowledge that an offence of the type committed was planned i.e., that their presence was with knowledge of the intended rape. On this issue, the Crown elicited no evidence.

· · ·

A person is not guilty merely because he is present at the scene of a crime and does nothing to prevent it: Smith & Hogan, *Criminal Law*, 4th ed. (1978), p. 117. If there is no evidence of encouragement by him, a man's presence at the scene of the crime will not suffice to render him liable as aider and abettor. A person who, aware of a rape taking place in his presence, looks on and does nothing is not, as a matter of law, an accomplice. The classic case is the hardened urbanite who stands around in a subway station when an individual is murdered.

[Dickson J also held that the trial judge erred in not responding to the jury's question: "If the accused were aware of a rape taking place in their presence and did nothing to prevent or persuade the discontinuance of the act, are they considered as an accomplice to the act under law?" with an unequivocal "no."

The appeals were allowed and the appellants were acquitted on the ground that the verdict would not necessarily have been the same in the absence of the trial judge's error. Dickson J stated that the jury's question indicated that they had not accepted evidence of the appellants' direct participation and it was in the interest of justice to acquit the appellants, who had already been subjected to two trials.]

MARTLAND J (dissenting) (Ritchie and Pigeon JJ concurring):

· · ·

It is not disputed that mere presence at the scene of a crime is not, in itself, sufficient to establish aiding and abetting the commission of an offence, but the trial Judge did not instruct the jury that it was. He charged the jury that "it is only necessary to show that he understood what was being done and by some act on his part assisted or encouraged the attainment of the act."

· · ·

… But the statement that the appellants were merely present at the dump and were passive observers of an act of sexual intercourse has to be based upon the evidence of the appellants. It was for the jury to decide whether or not to accept that evidence. The statement overlooks entirely the other evidence which was before the jury and which is summarized in the following passage from the reasons of Matas J.A.:

> Appellants' argument is made on the basis of accepting the accuseds' evidence that they were merely delivery men for a quantity of beer, they arrived late, saw intercourse taking place and left within a few minutes without investigating the incident. But it is impossible for this court to base its decision solely on acceptance of appellants' version of the night's events.
>
> The jury was entitled to consider all the evidence, including the earlier meeting of the Spartans at the dump (with Sylvester and Dunlop present) when Douglas was introduced as a prospect, the presence of members of the group at the Waldorf beverage room where the complainant and her friend were spending some time, bringing of the complainant by Douglas to the dump, the reappearance of a group of Spartans at the same location (where

the gang rape took place), the arrival of the accused with a substantial quantity of beer, the observation by both accused of intercourse taking place by the complainant and one male but with other men nearby.

The evidence, of which the above constitutes a bare outline, was of a nature which would permit the jury to draw an inference that the accused were more than merely present at a crime and had done nothing about it. The jury could conclude, beyond a reasonable doubt, that the accused had assumed a role which would qualify them as aiders or abettors under sec. 21(2) *(sic)* of the *Code*.

In my opinion there was evidence on which the jury could conclude that the appellants had aided and abetted the commission of the offence. The jury had been properly instructed as to what was necessary in order to establish aiding and abetting. The sufficiency of that evidence was solely a matter for the determination of the jury and was not a matter to be decided by the Court of Appeal.

The trial judge has been criticized for his response to the question asked by the jury, which is referred to in the passage from the reasons of Hall J.A. which I have cited. It is said that the answer to that question should have been a flat "no."

In answer to that criticism I would adopt what was said by Matas J.A. as follows:

> Counsel for appellants argued that at one stage, in the absence of the jury, during discussion of the question put by the jury, Crown counsel and the trial judge seemed to think that a simple "no" would suffice as an answer to the juror's question. But a reading of the entire discussion discloses that Crown counsel thought this would not meet the case and that the trial judge on consideration decided, correctly in my opinion, that he would have to expand his answer.
>
> Wright J. was not being asked a question as part of an academic exercise but in the context of the evidence of the events of that evening. We must assume that the jury were reasonably intelligent and understood the definitions which had been given to them. They were not asking [i]f a casual passerby, who by coincidence was delivering beer and observed a girl having intercourse with one man while other men were in the vicinity, would become a party. The question was asked in the light of all the evidence which the jury had heard and it is in this light that the question and answer must be examined.
>
> As well, the final paragraph of the answer deals specifically with knowledge and intention. For convenience I repeat it here:
>
> > "So that if you find an accused person knew that an offence was being committed and intentionally omitted to do something, for the purpose of aiding another to commit the offence, that if he had done it might have hindered or actually prevented the offence, then presumably you can find that the person was a party to the offence. But unless it reaches that level, then you cannot find him a party."
>
> It seems to me that this comment put the situation fairly to the jury.
>
> In my view the Crown has satisfied the onus of showing that the learned trial judge had not erred in either the instructions or the answer on the question of the applicability of sec. 21(2) *(sic)* of the *Code*.

· · ·

Appeal allowed and acquittal entered.

In *R v Nixon* (1990), 57 CCC (3d) 97 (BCCA), the accused was the senior officer in charge of the Vancouver police lockup. He was convicted of aggravated assault of a prisoner, Jacobsen, who was beaten after giving a false name. His appeal was dismissed by the British Columbia Court of Appeal with Legg JA stating:

> After concluding that she was satisfied beyond a reasonable doubt that the appellant was present at the time of the assault and knew what happened, the trial judge reasoned that under the *Police Act*, R.S.B.C. 1979, c. 331, and ss. 27 and 37 of the *Criminal Code* of Canada, the appellant had a duty to protect Jacobsen. By failing to act to prevent the assault on Jacobsen the appellant failed to discharge this duty and, on the basis of this omission, was guilty of aiding and abetting the commission of the assault.
>
> ...
>
> With reference to *Dunlop and Sylvester* she stated:
>
> This case indicates something more than mere presence was needed. In the circumstances of the case at bar there was more than mere presence. But assuming there was only mere presence, this case has one very important aspect that was not present in ... the *Dunlop and Sylvester v. The Queen* case. That is the fact that Nixon is a police officer and has the obligation to protect his charges. He has that duty by legislation. He cannot say he was not involved. He was there, he had a duty to involve himself.
>
> ...
>
> I am unable to accept an argument advanced by the appellant that the appellant cannot be convicted of an assault by reason of a failure to act because assault requires the intentional application of force. The appellant was not convicted of assault as a principal but as a party under s. 21 of the *Criminal Code* on the ground that he aided and abetted the commission of the assault by others. ...
>
> The question is whether the appellant aided or abetted the commission of the assault by reason of his failure to protect Jacobsen who was under his care.
>
> The appellant relied on the judgment of Mr. Justice Dickson in *Dunlop and Sylvester v. The Queen, supra,* and submitted that something more than mere presence was needed.
>
> Counsel for the appellant argued that the presence of the appellant at the scene of the assault, without any active steps on his part to aid or encourage its commission, must be interpreted as no more than "mere presence" and is thus not capable of making the appellant a party to the offence.
>
> I am unable to accept that submission. An accused who is present at the scene of an offence and who carries out no overt acts to aid or encourage the commission of the offence may none the less be convicted as a party if his purpose in failing to act was to aid in the commission of the offence. Section 21(1)(b) extends by its very terms to such an omission in that it makes a person a party to an offence who "omits to do anything for the purpose of aiding [in the commission of the offence]." A failure to act in accordance with a duty to act may be an omission to do something for the purpose of aiding or abetting.
>
> In some circumstances the presence of an accused will, in itself, be held to have encouraged the commission of the offence. In this situation there will be more than "mere presence" on the part of the accused and the accused will be liable as a party.

Apart from issues relating to the *actus reus* in various forms of participation by parties, there are also questions concerning the mental element. These issues were introduced in the extract from *R v Briscoe*, which makes clear that the reference to purpose in s 21(1)(b) requires intent and that wilful blindness could be substituted for the additional knowledge requirement. In *R v Helsdon*, 2007 ONCA 54, the Ontario Court of Appeal rejected an argument that s 21(1)(b) does not require subjective *mens rea* in a case in which the principal offender might be guilty on the basis of objective fault in part on the basis that "[i]mporting an interpretation that would require a lesser [degree of] mens rea for an aider so as to mirror the mens rea for the principal offence would require ignoring or reading down the plain language contained in s. 21(1)(b)."

In *R v Popen* (1981), 60 CCC (2d) 232 (Ont CA), the accused was charged with manslaughter of his infant daughter as a result of mistreatment on a number of occasions by his wife. The jury convicted after the trial judge directed the jury that the accused could be convicted as a party to the wife's offence pursuant to s 21(1)(b). The Ontario Court of Appeal sent the case back for a new trial. Martin JA stated as follows:

> After giving this matter our most careful consideration, we are of the view that there was no evidence that the appellant had done or omitted to do anything *for the purpose of* aiding his wife inflict the injuries to the child. Even if the appellant's omission to take action to prevent his wife mistreating the child had the effect of assisting the wife, we are all of the view that there was no evidence upon which a jury could reasonably find that the appellant's inaction was for the purpose of assisting his wife and there was, consequently, no basis for the application of s. 21(1)(b).
>
> Although as previously mentioned, the trial Judge did not leave s. 21(1)(c) with the jury we think that he did not err in this respect and that there is no basis for the application of s. 21(1)(c). In some circumstances, a person who is present at the commission by another of an illegal act, which he has a duty to prevent, may by mere inactivity encourage the illegal act. The law, in our view, is correctly stated in Smith and Hogan, *Criminal Law*, 4th ed. (1978), at pp. 118-9:
>
> > Where D has a right to control the actions of another and he deliberately refrains from exercising it, his inactivity may be a positive encouragement to the other to perform an illegal act, and, therefore, an aiding and abetting.

Martin JA then set out a number of cases and continued:

> In the above cases, the person having a right and a duty to control the actions of another was present when the illegal acts occurred.
>
> As previously mentioned, the appellant was not shown to have been present on any occasion when his wife mistreated the child and we do not think the authorities referred to by Smith and Hogan in the passage previously quoted, or by Robertson C.J.O. in *R. v. Halmo* (1941), 76 C.C.C. 116 can be applied to the present case in these circumstances.
>
> We think, however, that it would have been open to a jury, properly charged, to find that the appellant was criminally negligent in failing to protect his child from his wife's mistreatment, when under a duty to do so, and that such failure contributed to the child's death. If the jury reached the conclusion that the appellant was criminally negligent in failing to take proper steps to protect the child, and that his criminal negligence contributed to her death, he would, of course, be independently guilty of manslaughter, as distinct from being a party to his wife's offence.

III. COMMON INTENTION

Section 21(2) of the Code extends liability beyond that contemplated in s 21(1). For s 21(2) to apply, the accused must form a common intention with another person or persons to carry out an unlawful purpose and to assist them with that purpose. When such a common intention is found, the accused will be held responsible for criminal acts that are a probable consequence of the common intention, if the accused knew or ought to have known that the criminal acts were a probable consequence. In *R v Kirkness*, the Supreme Court considered the elements of liability under s 21(2).

R v Kirkness
Supreme Court of Canada
[1990] 3 SCR 74

CORY J (Lamer CJ and La Forest, Sopinka, and Gonthier JJ concurring): ...

The appellant and his friend, Alexander Snowbird, came from God's Lake Narrows. On December 31, 1987 they were in Winnipeg. That evening they went to a number of bars and undoubtedly drank a good deal. In the early morning hours of New Year's Day, Snowbird took the appellant to the alley behind the residence of Elizabeth Johnson and suggested that they break into her house. The appellant readily agreed. They opened a window through which the appellant entered and opened the back door for Snowbird.

Elizabeth Johnson was a slight, frail woman of eighty-three years. She was asleep in her bed when the two men broke into her house. Snowbird saw her. He went into her bedroom, removed her clothes and sexually assaulted her. The appellant, on the instructions of Snowbird, remained outside. He sat in a chair in the hallway on the other side of the bedroom door for some time and otherwise occupied himself by stealing various things from the house. The appellant also placed a chair against the front door of the house while Snowbird was in the bedroom sexually assaulting Mrs. Johnson. In the long and detailed statement which the appellant gave to the police he explained that he had taken this action because he thought someone might come into the residence while he and Snowbird were there.

Subsequent to the sexual assault, Alexander Snowbird dragged Elizabeth Johnson from the bedroom into the hallway where, according to the appellant, she "just laid there." The appellant then entered the bedroom and there proceeded to steal various items. Upon leaving the bedroom, the appellant saw Snowbird begin to choke the victim. The appellant told Snowbird "not to do that because he (Snowbird) was going to kill her." According to the appellant, Snowbird then placed a plastic bag over the head of Elizabeth Johnson, dragged her into the bathroom, dumped her into the bathtub and turned on the hot water.

In all of his statements to the police the appellant denied ever touching Elizabeth Johnson or that he had participated in either the sexual assault, the choking or the suffocation of the victim.

· · ·

Both the appellant and Snowbird were charged with first degree murder. Snowbird was convicted of that crime while the appellant was acquitted.

· · ·

The facts of this case are depressing and sordid in the extreme. Their simple recitation incites feelings of anger and utter revulsion. That sense of disgust is bound to strengthen the very natural tendency to closely associate the appellant with the perpetrator of this particularly despicable crime. The almost inevitable result is to think that the appellant must be guilty because of his association with Snowbird. Nevertheless, principles of criminal law and fairness require that the guilt or innocence of Kirkness be determined solely on the evidence which implicates him in the killing of the victim. Both the despicable and the personable are entitled to be judged guilty or innocent solely on the basis of the evidence relating to the crime with which they are charged.

It must be remembered that the twelve members of the jury heard all the evidence and were for several days immersed in this tale of brutish violence and cruel insensitivity. Indeed, they were complimented by counsel for the Crown for the careful attention that they had given to all the witnesses throughout the trial. They listened to and obviously assessed the lengthy and detailed statement given by Kirkness to the police. At the conclusion of the trial, the jury, acting as judges of the facts, acquitted the appellant. They reached this decision as representatives of their community, no doubt carrying with them all of that community's natural sympathy for a frail, helpless, elderly lady brutally murdered in her own home. The verdict of the jury constitutes, in a very real way, the verdict of the community. Trial by jury in criminal cases is a process that functions exceedingly well and constitutes a fundamentally important aspect of our democratic society. It is not members of the judiciary, but rather the members of the jury, sitting as members of the community, who make the decision as to guilt or innocence which is so vitally important both to the individual accused and the community.

· · ·

Kirkness could only be implicated, pursuant to the provisions of s. 21 of the *Code*, as a party to the sexual assault. He was not the prime mover in the crime. He neither sexually assaulted, strangled nor suffocated the victim. …

[It cannot] be said that the appellant, who had formed an intent in common with Snowbird to carry out the unlawful purpose of breaking and entering, knew before entering that Snowbird would either commit a sexual assault or kill the victim. It will be recalled that in this case the only evidence against the appellant was that contained in his statement that he placed a chair against the front door knowing that a sexual assault was taking place in the bedroom. There is no indication that he knew that death or bodily harm short of death might result from the sexual assault. He did not enter into the bedroom. Indeed, it appears that the bedroom door was closed for some period of time so that he could not be aware of everything that was taking place. Further, it is apparent from the verdict of the jury, which was obviously based upon the expert's testimony, that the bodily harm causing death resulted from suffocation. The strangulation and suffocation of the victim occurred after the sexual assault.

There is no evidence that the appellant was a party to the suffocation of Elizabeth Johnson. Rather, he told Snowbird not to strangle the victim as he was going to kill her. His statement makes it clear that he was not aiding or abetting Snowbird in the strangulation or suffocation of Mrs. Johnson.

· · ·

To determine the adequacy of the charge on the issue of manslaughter, it is necessary to once more consider the evidence. Again the appellant could only be found guilty of either murder or manslaughter if he was found to be a party to the sexual assault. The sole evidence which implicated him in the sexual assault was contained in the portion of his statement in which he said that he had placed a chair against the front door of the house when he knew Snowbird was assaulting the victim in her bedroom. I would observe that this action could have been taken as much to prevent the apprehension of the two accused while they stole articles from the house as to facilitate the sexual assault by Snowbird. Nonetheless, it was evidence upon which the jury could have found the appellant to be a party to murder or manslaughter as a result of being a party to the sexual assault if that assault had resulted in the death of the victim.

However, there was no evidence that the appellant knew or had any reason to believe that death was likely to result from the sexual assault. Nor did the death result from the sexual assault. Rather, as stated above, the jury must have found that the death occurred due to strangulation. There was no evidence that the appellant was a party to Snowbird's strangulation and suffocation of Mrs. Johnson. Once again, the only evidence was that of his statement in which he denied any participation in those acts. The fact that he told Snowbird to stop when he saw him strangling the victim indicates that if the appellant ever had been a party to any offences, from that point on he had removed himself from any joint enterprise with Snowbird that involved the killing of Mrs. Johnson.

• • •

WILSON J (L'Heureux-Dubé J concurring) (dissenting):

• • •

As with any other criminal offence an accused may not be held criminally responsible unless the essential elements of the offence have been proved by the Crown. In the context of party liability these elements take a somewhat different form from the form they take in the case of principal offenders. The reason for this is that the acts and intent of a party must be examined in relation to the acts and intent of the principal.

• • •

[Wilson J explained the facts and reasoning in *Dunlop and Sylvester v The Queen*, then turned to *R v Salajko*, which was described in the extract from Dickson J's judgment in *Dunlop and Sylvester*, above. In *Salajko*, the accused had stood with his pants down while another party raped the victim.]

> … In *Dunlop and Sylvester, supra*, Dickson J. commented at p. 894 that: "One might be forgiven for thinking that it was open to the jury to infer encouragement by conduct." I agree with the statement of Professor Stuart in his text *Canadian Criminal Law: A Treatise* (Toronto 1982) that "This is surely the better view." (at p. 493). I find it difficult to view such behaviour as "passive acquiescence." In my view, the decision in *Salajko* is anomalous and should not be followed.

To be convicted as an aider or abettor one must also possess the necessary state of mind. Dickson J. addressed this issue also in *Dunlop and Sylvester*. He found that there must be evidence supporting an inference that the accused had prior knowledge that an offence of the type committed was planned.

• • •

The first step in establishing liability under s. 21(2) is to show that the accused formed an intention in common with others to carry out an unlawful purpose and to assist them in achieving that purpose. This common intention need not be pre-planned in any way. It is sufficient, and the case law supports this proposition, that such intention arise just prior to or at the time of the commission of the offence. ...

In my opinion, there is no question that a common purpose was shared by Snowbird and Kirkness in this case. Where one has aided or abetted in the commission of an offence, there can be little doubt that a shared intention to effect an unlawful purpose existed. In this case Kirkness was a principal in the break and enter. By his own admission Snowbird asked him to come along in the plan to rob the house. He agreed. Moreover, it was he who effected the break and enter by prying open a window at the back of the house with a handle off a garden tool. It was he who first entered and let Snowbird in through the back door. There is not a scintilla of evidence to suggest that the accused did not share an intention in common with Snowbird.

· · ·

Section 21(2) of the *Code* deems a party criminally liable for the acts of the principal offender when the accused knew or ought to have known of the probable commission of the acts which constitute the offence. There are two elements to this last branch of s. 21(2): (i) the commission of the ultimate offence has to be probable; and (ii) the accused must know or ought to have known of this probability.

The first question to be asked is whether the killing of the victim was a probable consequence of the unlawful purpose. If the jury determined that the unlawful purpose encompassed only the breaking and entering, it would be hard to justify a finding that the death of the occupant was a probable consequence of that purpose. If, however, the jury determined that the unlawful purpose encompassed also acts of physical violence against the occupant, then the route to party liability on the part of Kirkness is much clearer. Apart from the particular circumstances surrounding this series of events, it seems to me that violence so often accompanies sexual crimes that it is implicit in the very nature of the offence that some harm short of death is probable. This is so, in my opinion, whenever the common unlawful purpose contemplates physical interference with a person. There may, of course, be situations where the level of physical violence contemplated is so minimal that serious bodily harm is merely a possibility rather than a probability. And it may indeed be the case that this observation would hold true even in some situations where the unlawful purpose is an assault of a sexual nature. While I personally would not have thought that what occurred in this case is one of those instances, the question whether the causing of bodily harm short of death was a probable consequence of the sexual offence committed against Elizabeth Johnson was for the jury to decide.

· · ·

5. Abandonment

· · ·

In this case it was open to the jury to find that the participation of Kirkness went beyond mere encouragement. He had physically placed a chair in front of the door to prevent their activities in the house from being discovered. What evidence could the jury have relied upon to support a conclusion that he had effectively withdrawn himself? Kirkness took no steps to remove the chair or to otherwise intervene in Snowbird's domination of the victim. The only action upon which the accused relies to demonstrate his withdrawal is his act of saying to Snowbird, "stop that, you'll kill her." The question for the jury is whether this statement, if believed, is sufficient to negate Kirkness's participation in the crime.

6. *Distinguishing Subs. 21(1) from Subs. 21(2)*

. . .

The two subsections of s. 21 deal with different circumstances. Subsection (1) applies to make everyone a party to an offence who commits it or who aids and abets in its commission. Subsection (2) covers the case where, in the absence of aiding and abetting, a person may become a party to an offence committed by another which he knew or ought to have known was a probable consequence of carrying out an unlawful purpose in common with the actual perpetrator.

Rose put the matter similarly at p. 65:

[Section 21(2)] is quite plainly intended to provide liability in the case of *consequential* offences which were not committed nor aided or abetted by the accused, but which *resulted* from the prosecution of the *original* offence. ... [Emphasis original.]

It is my view that since aiders and abettors have been treated differently from common intenders by Parliament, some difference between these two subsections must be recognized.

On the other hand, circumstances may undoubtedly arise in which it will be difficult to distinguish the applicability of the two subsections. Where an accused has aided or abetted the commission of some crime, party liability under subs. (1) follows where the crime which is ultimately committed is of the same type as the one in which the accused has assisted. Under subs. (2), on the other hand, party liability follows upon a finding that the offence actually committed was one which the accused knew or ought to have known would be a probable consequence of the commission of the contemplated offence in which he assisted. The difficult task for the jury in such cases is to distinguish between when the crime actually committed is of a similar type to that contemplated, and when the crime actually committed is a probable consequence of the crime contemplated.

In my view, the difference between the two is that the doctrine of similarity was not intended to include situations where the principal committed another offence, even a probable one, in order to cover up his crime or to facilitate his escape. I believe that, in order to be an offence "of the type" within the meaning of s. 21(1), the committed offence must not only be similar but must be sufficiently contemporaneous with the contemplated offence. Section 21(2) is, in my view, reserved for those instances where there has been a break in time between the two offences, and the offence actually committed follows after, but as a consequence of the offence originally planned.

. . .

Liability under s. 21(2) does not require the accused to assist directly in the act causing the death. It is sufficient, with certain limitations, that manslaughter was a probable *consequence* of the offence in which the accused aided or abetted. The trial judge, by posing the question in terms of whether the sexual assault caused the death, improperly implied that if Kirkness did not directly assist in the act which caused the death of the victim, i.e., the suffocation, then he could not be held responsible for the death of the victim.

My colleague appears to agree with this. I do not. In my respectful view, the question for the jury never was whether the sexual assault caused the death. Rather the question was whether Kirkness aided or abetted Snowbird in a crime which was of the type which could have caused *bodily harm* or whether bodily harm could have resulted as a consequence of carrying out the sexual assault. This is a point of fundamental importance which I believe was lost on the jury because of the trial judge's misdirection.

In *R v Gauthier* the Supreme Court of Canada considered when the jury should be instructed to consider the defence of abandonment.

R v Gauthier
Supreme Court of Canada
2013 SCC 32, [2013] 2 SCR 403

[In this case, the accused had entered into a pact with her husband to murder their children and commit suicide. There was evidence that, after having supplied her husband with pills to kill the children, the accused had communicated to him that they should not go through with their plan. She was convicted of aiding and abetting in the murder of her three children. The issue on appeal was whether there was sufficient evidence of abandonment.]

WAGNER J (LeBel, Abella, Rothstein, Moldaver, and Karakatsanis JJ concurring): …
    [40] The reasons for recognizing the defence of abandonment in Canadian law bear repeating. There are two policy reasons in criminal law for making this defence available to parties to offences. First, there is a need to ensure that only morally culpable persons are punished; second, there is a benefit to society in encouraging individuals involved in criminal activities to withdraw from those activities and report them … .

. . .

    [50] One who is a party to an offence on the basis that he or she did or omitted to do anything for the purpose of aiding any person to commit the offence, or abetted any person in committing it (s. 21(1) of the *Criminal Code*), or on the basis that he or she had formed with other persons an intention to carry out an unlawful purpose and to assist each other therein and that an offence was committed in carrying out the common purpose (s. 21(2) of the *Criminal Code*), may raise the defence of abandonment if the evidence shows

    (1) that there was an intention to abandon or withdraw from the unlawful purpose;

    (2) that there was timely communication of this abandonment or withdrawal from the person in question to those who wished to continue;

    (3) that the communication served unequivocal notice upon those who wished to continue; and

    (4) that the accused took, in a manner proportional to his or her participation in the commission of the planned offence, reasonable steps in the circumstances either to neutralize or otherwise cancel out the effects of his or her participation or to prevent the commission of the offence.

[51] I recognize that there will be circumstances, even where the accused is a party within the meaning of s. 21(1) of the *Criminal Code*, in which timely and unequivocal communication by the accused of his or her intention to abandon the unlawful purpose will be considered sufficient to neutralize the effects of his or her participation in the crime. But there will be other circumstances, primarily where a person has aided in the commission of the offence, in which it is hard to see how timely communication to the principal offender of the person's intention to withdraw from the unlawful purpose will on its own be considered reasonable, and sufficient to meet the test set out in the preceding paragraph.

[52] In conclusion, and more specifically in the context of s. 21(1) of the *Criminal Code*, the defence of abandonment should be put to the jury only if there is evidence in the record that is capable of supporting a finding that a person who was initially a party to the carrying out of an unlawful purpose subsequently took reasonable steps in the circumstances either to neutralize the effects of his or her participation or to prevent the commission of the offence.

2. *Application to the Case at Bar*

[53] In the case at bar, the defence of abandonment did not have an air of reality.

. . .

[62] … [E]ven if it were assumed that the evidence the appellant relies upon would be sufficient for a jury to reasonably conclude that she had communicated her intention to withdraw from the plan and that her communication was timely and unequivocal, that communication would not on its own have sufficed, in the circumstances of this case, for the judge to put the defence of abandonment to the jury.

[63] The appellant did more than merely promise to take part in the murder-suicide pact. She supplied her spouse with the intoxicants he used to cause the children's deaths. She therefore had to do more either to neutralize the effects of her participation or to prevent the commission of the offence. For example, she could have hidden or destroyed the medication she had purchased, remained watchful and taken the children to a safe place for the evening, insisted that her spouse give her verbal confirmation of what he intended to do, or simply called the authorities.

[64] I conclude that the record did not contain evidence upon which a properly instructed jury acting reasonably could have found that the appellant had abandoned the common unlawful purpose, and could accordingly have acquitted her, if it believed the evidence to be true. The defence of abandonment therefore did not meet the air of reality test, and the trial judge was not required to put the defence to the jury.

. . .

FISH J (dissenting):

. . .

[71] On the law as it was then understood, the trial judge was bound to put abandonment to the jury if there was evidence that the appellant (a) had changed—or "abandoned"—her earlier intention to aid or abet the murder of her children, and (b) had adequately communicated to her husband that she had withdrawn from their pact.

[72] This Court has repeatedly held that the defence of abandonment includes *no other essential elements*. And our attention has not been drawn to a single Canadian decision to the contrary, at any level.

[73] In my view, there *was* evidence at Ms. Gauthier's trial upon which a properly instructed jury might well have found that she had abandoned the suicide pact in respect of which she was charged and convicted of murder. Or at least have been left with a reasonable doubt on this issue, which would of course have sufficed to warrant Ms. Gauthier's acquittal.

. . .

[82] Justice Wagner would impose additional requirements on the defence of abandonment, particularly with respect to liability under s. 21(1), where the accused would need to adduce evidence that he or she took steps to neutralize any prior contribution to the commission of the offence or, in the alternative, to prevent the commission of the offence.

. . .

[94] These authorities all make clear that the defence of abandonment does not require that the accused take steps to neutralize prior participation in the criminal enterprise or to prevent the commission of the offence. While such evidence may strengthen a defence of abandonment, failure to take neutralizing or preventative steps is not fatal. Thus, for example, in *R. v. Edwards*, 2001 BCSC 275, at para. 186, the accused's efforts to stop the commission of the offence were treated as evidence that the *Whitehouse* requirements were met—not as additional requirements of the defence.

[95] If we were to accept that the defence of abandonment now requires that an accused take steps to neutralize previous assistance or to prevent the commission of the crime, I am inclined to believe that this change should only be given prospective effect—at least in this case. As Don Stuart explains in *Canadian Criminal Law: A Treatise* (6th ed. 2011), at p. 9: "It is almost universally accepted that the view that judges merely declare existing law rather than create new law is outmoded and wrong."

[96] But on any view of the matter, in light of the state of the law universally accepted in Canada at the time of the appellant's trial, it would be fundamentally unfair at this stage to fault the appellant for failing to demonstrate anything more than a change of intention, plus timely and unequivocal notice of withdrawal from the murder-suicide pact. Since the appellant's testimony provided some evidence on these two essential elements, there was an air of reality to the defence. The trial judge therefore erred by withholding the defence of abandonment from the jury.

The Court's decision in *Canadian Foundation for Children, Youth and the Law v Canada*, 2004 SCC 4, [2004] 1 SCR 76, discussed in Chapter 1, provides some precedent for restricting a defence, but not necessarily for the Court to impose that restriction retroactively on the accused. Do you agree with Justice Fish that the restriction of the defence should have, at most, been prospective only? For a discussion of prospective law making by courts, see ML Friedland, "Prospective and Retrospective Judicial Lawmaking" (1974) 24 UTLJ 170.

In *R v Logan*, the Supreme Court of Canada considered the constitutionality of the objective mental element in s 21(2) of the Code, in relation to attempted murder. The issue of the *mens rea* for attempted murder is dealt with in Chapter 7.

R v Logan
Supreme Court of Canada
[1990] 2 SCR 731

[The accused were charged with a number of offences relating to the robbery of a Becker's convenience store and the serious wounding of the cashier, Barbara Turnbull. Two of the accused were convicted of attempted murder and appealed to the Ontario Court of Appeal (1988), 46 CCC (3d) 354. The Court of Appeal held that the objective test in s 21(2) of the Code is inoperative in relation to attempted murder, stating:

> As previously noted, on a charge of attempted murder, the necessary *mens rea* must be that of an intention to kill. In our opinion, in so far as s. 21(2) permits a conviction of a party for the offence of attempted murder on the basis of objective foreseeability, a lesser degree of *mens rea* than is required for the principal, it is contrary to the principles of fundamental justice. Nor do we think that this departure from the principles of fundamental justice can be saved by s. 1 of the *Charter*.
>
> · · ·
>
> Consistent with what was stated by Lamer J., it is unnecessary, in order to deter others, to convict of attempted murder a person who did not know but ought to have known that the principal would shoot with intent to kill. Under such circumstances, a person who forms an intention with one or more other persons to carry out an armed robbery while armed with a firearm and to assist each other therein would be guilty of armed robbery and of using a firearm in the commission of such an indictable offence.
>
> Severe sentences are imposed for armed robbery where all aggravating factors, such as a severe injury to the person who was robbed, are entitled to be considered. Such a severe sentence should sufficiently deter others from engaging in such criminal conduct.
>
> Thus, on a charge of attempted murder, where s. 21(2) is invoked to determine the liability of a party to the offence, the words of s. 21(2), "ought to have known," must be held to be inoperative and cannot be resorted to by the trier of fact to determine the guilt of such an accused person.
>
> It follows that the conviction of Sutcliffe Logan and Warren Johnson for the attempted murder of Barbara Turnbull cannot stand.
>
> Sutcliffe Logan and Warren Johnson were, however, also found guilty of the armed robbery of Barbara Turnbull (count 10) and of using a firearm while committing that indictable offence (count 11).
>
> Because the jury had also convicted them of the attempted murder of Barbara Turnbull, the learned trial judge stayed the robbery count. With respect, we think that he erred in so doing since the count for attempted murder was a separate and distinct delict from that of the robbery, including separate and additional factors, and there was no reason why both convictions could not stand. In any event, since the conviction for attempted murder cannot stand, there is now no basis for the stay.
>
> · · ·
>
> The matter should be remitted to the learned trial judge to sentence both of them for the offence of armed robbery, and in doing so he will, of course, take into consideration the very serious aggravating factors which relate to that offence.
>
> In summary, all of the appeals before us are dismissed save, with respect to the appeals by Sutcliffe Logan and Warren Johnson from their convictions for attempted murder, convictions

for the robbery of Barbara Turnbull are substituted. The matter of the sentence on these convictions is remitted to the trial judge.

The Supreme Court of Canada dismissed a further appeal.]

LAMER CJ stated for the Court (Sopinka and L'Heureux-Dubé JJ concurring): ... The appellant is challenging the constitutionality of s. 21(2) in general and, in particular, of the objective component of the section ("ought to have known"). However, the Court of Appeal, quite correctly, did not declare the objective component of s. 21(2) inoperative for all offences. They dealt specifically with the operation of the provision in relation to the offence of attempted murder and the possibility that a party to an attempted murder could be convicted upon proof of objective intent, whereas a conviction of the principal would require proof of subjective intent. More generally, as a basis for their decision, the court determined that it is a principle of fundamental justice that a party to *any* offence cannot be found guilty of the offence based on a lower standard of requisite *mens rea* than that required for convicting the principal.

For this proposition, the court relied on our judgment in *Vaillancourt*. In that case, this Court held that for a few offences the principles of fundamental justice require that a conviction cannot stand unless there is proof beyond a reasonable doubt of a minimum degree of *mens rea*, and that legislation providing for any lesser degree violates the *Charter* and is inoperative. Murder was one of those offences.

With respect, I cannot construe *Vaillancourt* as saying that, as a general proposition, Parliament cannot ever enact provisions requiring different levels of guilt for principal offenders and parties. Although I readily admit that, as a matter of policy, the proposition seems more equitable than not, I am not ready to characterize it as a principle of fundamental justice. It must be remembered that within many offences there are varying degrees of guilt and it remains the function of the sentencing process to adjust the punishment for each individual offender accordingly. The argument that the principles of fundamental justice prohibit the conviction of a party to an offence on the basis of a lesser degree of *mens rea* than that required to convict the principal could only be supported, if at all, in a situation where the sentence for a particular offence is fixed. However, currently in Canada, the sentencing scheme is flexible enough to accommodate the varying degrees of culpability resulting from the operation of ss. 21 and 22.

That said, however, there are a few offences with respect to which the operation of the objective component of s. 21(2) will restrict the rights of an accused under s. 7. If an offence is one of the few for which s. 7 requires a minimum degree of *mens rea*, *Vaillancourt* does preclude Parliament from providing for the conviction of a party to that offence on the basis of a degree of *mens rea* below the constitutionally required minimum.

· · ·

Having completed the initial step of the inquiry, one can proceed to the second step in determining the requisite *mens rea* for the conviction of a party pursuant to s. 21(2) on a charge of attempted murder. When the principles of fundamental justice require *subjective* foresight in order to convict a principal of attempted murder, that same minimum degree of *mens rea* is constitutionally required to convict a party to the offence of attempted murder. Any conviction for attempted murder, whether of the principal directly or of a party pursuant to s. 21(2), will carry enough stigma to trigger the constitutional requirement. To the extent that s. 21(2) would allow for the conviction of a party to the offence of attempted murder on the basis of objective foresight, its operation restricts s. 7 of the *Charter*. ...

[T]he objective of [s 21(2)] is to deter joint criminal enterprises and to encourage persons who do participate to ensure that their accomplices do not commit offences beyond the planned unlawful purpose. This is a legislative objective of sufficient importance to justify overriding the rights of an accused under s. 7 of the *Charter*.

· · ·

The objective component of s. 21(2) unduly impairs rights under s. 7 of the *Charter* when it operates with respect to an offence for which a conviction carries severe stigma and for which, therefore, there is a constitutionally required minimum degree of *mens rea*. The words "ought to know" allow for the possibility that while a party may not have considered and accepted the risk that an accomplice may do something with the intent to kill in furtherance of the common purpose, the party, through this negligence, could still be found guilty of attempted murder. In other words, parties could be held to be criminally negligent with respect to the behaviour of someone else. For most offences under the *Criminal Code*, a person is only convicted for criminal negligence if consequences have ensued from their actions. While a person may be convicted, absent consequences, for criminal negligence (*e.g.*, dangerous operation of a motor vehicle), none of these forms of criminal negligence carry with them the stigma of being labelled a "killer." In a situation where s. 21(2) is operating in relation to the offence of attempted murder, no consequences have resulted from the actions of the party and yet the party could be convicted of this offence and suffer severe accompanying stigma and penalty.

Because of the importance of the legislative purpose, the objective component of s. 21(2) can be justified with respect to most offences. However, with respect to the few offences for which the Constitution requires subjective intent, the stigma renders the infringement too serious and outweighs the legislative objective which, therefore, cannot be justified under s. 1.

I would, therefore, as did the Court of Appeal, declare inoperative the words "or ought to have known" when considering under s. 21(2) whether a person is a party to any offence where it is a constitutional requirement for a conviction that foresight of the consequences be subjective, which is the case for attempted murder. Once these words are deleted, the remaining section requires, in the context of attempted murder, that the party to the common venture know that it is probable that his accomplice would do something with the intent to kill in carrying out the common purpose.

Appeal dismissed.

In *R v Jackson*, [1993] 4 SCR 573, the Supreme Court of Canada dealt with the combination of s 21(2) and manslaughter. McLachlin J stated for the Court:

> This leaves the question of the *mens rea* required to sustain a conviction for manslaughter under s. 21(2) of the *Criminal Code*. The Court of Appeal held that to be convicted of manslaughter under s. 21(2) of the *Code*, the Crown must establish that the accused knew or ought to have known that *killing* short of murder was a probable consequence of the pursuit of the common unlawful purpose. However, as was previously noted, since the date of the Court of Appeal's decision, this court has held that manslaughter does not require that a risk of death be foreseeable;

foreseeability of the risk of harm is sufficient: *Creighton, supra*. This court's decision in *R. v. Trin-neer*, [1970] S.C.R. 638, suggests that there is nothing inherent in s. 21(2) which requires a higher *mens rea* than would otherwise be required for a conviction for manslaughter. There the court held unanimously that an accused could be convicted of constructive murder as a party to that offence under the combination of ss. 21(2) and 230 (then s. 202) of the *Criminal Code*, without the Crown proving that the accused knew or ought to have known that it was probable death would ensue from the execution of the common unlawful purpose. While it would no longer be possible to convict for murder under s. 21(2) without proof of subjective awareness of the risk of death (*R. v. Logan*, [1990] 2 S.C.R. 731), the reasoning in *Trinneer*, coupled with *Creighton, supra*, suggests that the appropriate *mens rea* for manslaughter under s. 21(2) is objective awareness of the risk of harm. It must follow that a conviction for manslaughter under s. 21(2) does not require foreseeability of death, but only foreseeability of harm, which in fact results in death.

IV. COUNSELLING AS A FORM OF PARTICIPATION

The case below deals with counselling a crime that was committed under s 22 of the *Criminal Code*. A person found guilty under this provision is a party to the offence. In Chapter 10, we discuss the separate offence of counselling a crime that is not committed under s 464 of the Code.

R v O'Brien
Nova Scotia Court of Appeal
2007 NSCA 3

[The appellant, Marty David O'Brien, was convicted by Justice Scanlan of counselling Brandy Lynn Richard to rob a convenience store on December 10, 2004. Richard was a drug addict who bought illegal drugs from O'Brien from time to time. By the time of O'Brien's trial, Richard had confessed to robbing Elliott's convenience store in Amherst, Nova Scotia on both November 16 and December 10, 2004 to get money to buy drugs.]

HAMILTON JA: ...

[5] Shortly before the robbery took place, Mr. O'Brien and William Lank were with Ms. Richard at her residence, according to the testimony of Ms. Richard and the police statement of the appellant. At different places in her evidence, Ms. Richard testified about the discussions that took place at that time about the proposed robbery. She testified that during these discussions Mr. O'Brien said that with only a young girl working at the store at that time a robbery would be easy, that the robbery would not be hard, that Ms. Richard did not have to worry, that no one would put themself at risk for minimum wage, and that he agreed with Mr. Lank that she should "paint" her face.

· · ·

[7] The judge convicted Mr. O'Brien of counselling Ms. Richard with respect to the December robbery because of the corroborating evidence he found in Mr. O'Brien's police statement:

[10] Marty O'Brien offered words of encouragement for her to continue with the robbery. He said he heard it was just going to be a young girl, it would be easy, not to worry about it. Those, I am satisfied, are words of encouragement.

[11] Again, as to the face painting, clearly Mr. Lank was present and made a statement in relation to the makeup, but Ms. Richard, and I accept her evidence in this regard, says Mr. O'Brien agreed with the face painting, and again echoed the words that nobody would jeopardize themselves for minimum wage. *I am satisfied Mr. O'Brien, based on his own evidence together with the evidence of Ms. Richard, that he was there, he was offering those words of encouragement, that reassurance, all in furtherance of his undertaking or enterprise.* He knew if she got some money, she could buy drugs from him. He was prepared to sell the drugs once she got the money, and it was going to be easy. ... [Emphasis added]

· · ·

[15] During Ms. Richard's testimony about her discussions with Mr. O'Brien in her residence prior to the December robbery, she testified:

Q. Okay. So you mentioned that Marty dropped in. Did you have any discussions with him about some pills?
A. No, not at this time.
Q. Well, what ...
A. Just more about me and Will were ... Me and Will had talked about the robbery *and I told Will that I don't think a second one will be good so close, because they already know about it. Thinking, you know, that cops already know that it's robbed.* And that Will said that he knew that there was another kid there and that there was nobody there. And then [the appellant] said, Well, it wouldn't be that hard then. ... [Emphasis added]

[16] This suggests Ms. Richard had not made up her mind to rob Elliott's, that she was still in the process of deciding what to do at the time Mr. O'Brien made this and his various other comments to her, contrary to Mr. O'Brien's submission that the robbery would have occurred with or without his comments.

[17] The appellant also argued that the judge erred in finding that he had a motive to counsel Ms. Richard to rob the store; namely, that he would make money from subsequently selling drugs to her. He pointed to the fact that he did not sell drugs to her following the December robbery. While motive is not an element of counselling, it may be taken into account by the trier of fact in making findings with respect to the element of intent. This is what the judge did and I am not satisfied that he erred in doing so.

[18] The appellant has not satisfied me that the judge erred in concluding that his words, considered in context, were encouragement and hence counselling. Mr. O'Brien was a drug trafficker who made money selling drugs to addicts such as Ms. Richard. He had sold drugs to Ms. Richard previously, including following the November robbery. When he met Ms. Richard prior to the December robbery she was in the process of deciding whether to commit the robbery to get money to buy drugs. His discussion with her prior to the robbery was supportive. He was not available to sell drugs to her following the December robbery because he had been picked up by the police and was at the police station being questioned. In this context I am not satisfied the judge made an error of law or a palpable and overriding error of fact when he concluded that Mr. O'Brien counselled Ms. Richard to commit the December robbery. I would dismiss this ground of appeal.

V. ACCESSORY AFTER THE FACT

The modes of participation reviewed previously are all concerned with ways in which a person might be considered a party to an offence. The criminal liability of an accessory after the fact is defined in ss 23, 23.1, and 463 of the Code.

As with modes of participation, accessoryship contemplates some relation between the conduct of the accessory after the fact and the commission of a criminal offence. The accessory is not a party to the offence, however, but a principal party in a distinct offence that consists of facilitating the escape of another person who was a party to the offence. Conviction of an accessory is not contingent upon conviction of a party to the offence: *R v Shalaan*, [1998] 1 SCR 88.

R v Duong
Ontario Court of Appeal
(1998), 124 CCC (3d) 392

DOHERTY JA:

[1] The appellant was convicted of being an accessory after the fact to a murder committed by one Chinh Lam.

. . .

II

[3] The facts are straightforward and come principally from statements given by the appellant to the police immediately after his arrest. ...

[4] Two people were killed in December 1993. There were reports in the newspapers and on television connecting Lam to the homicides. The appellant and Lam had been friends for five or six years. Lam called the appellant and asked if he could stay at the appellant's apartment. Lam indicated he was "in trouble for murder" and had no place to go. The appellant had seen the media reports of the homicides and knew that Lam was in trouble. The appellant allowed Lam to hide in his apartment for about two weeks. After receiving information that Lam was in the apartment, the police raided the apartment and found Lam hiding in the bedroom. They arrested Lam and the appellant who was also present in the apartment.

[5] The appellant was specifically asked by the police what Lam told him about the homicides. He replied:

> He just came to me and told me he was in trouble for it but I didn't want to know anything because I knew I would be in trouble for helping him hide, so I didn't want to know anymore. Like my brother doesn't know anything. He told me not to hide him but I said we would.

[6] The appellant was also asked whether he was afraid of Lam and he replied:

> No. I told you he's a friend, so I wanted to help. I knew I would get in trouble but I did—but I did it anyways.

[7] Lam was charged with two counts of first degree murder and three counts of attempted murder. He pled not guilty and after a lengthy trial he was convicted of two counts of second degree murder and two counts of attempted murder. ...

[8] The appellant did not call any evidence at trial.

[9] The trial judge held that the Crown had to prove that the appellant knew that Lam was a party to a murder when the appellant agreed to hide him from the authorities, and that wilful blindness of that fact would suffice to establish the necessary culpable mental state. In finding that the appellant was wilfully blind, he said:

> ... The accused gave a statement admitting that he knew Lam was wanted for murder. In that statement he admitted that he knew he would be in trouble for harbouring Lam and deliberately elected not to inquire of Lam [as to] his involvement in the homicide.
>
> I found this was a classic case of wilful blindness, fixing the accused with knowledge.

· · ·

[11] At trial, the Crown and defence agreed that the appellant could only be convicted if he knew that Lam had been a party to murder. They agreed that wilful blindness of that fact would suffice. On appeal, both the Crown and the defence retreated somewhat from the positions taken at trial. The Crown argues that it was only necessary to show that the appellant knew or was wilfully blind to the fact that Lam had committed "a criminal offence." The appellant argues that the appellant could only be convicted if he knew that Lam had been a party to murder and that wilful blindness has no application to this case.

[12] The Crown's submission that it need only show that the appellant had knowledge that Lam had committed "a criminal offence" runs aground on the language of s. 23(1) of the *Criminal Code*:

> *An accessory after the fact to an offence is one who, knowing that a person has been a party to the offence*, receives, comforts or assists that person for the purpose of enabling that person to escape. [Emphasis added.]

[13] Section 23(1) contemplates aid given to someone who has committed an offence (the principal) by a person who knew that principal had committed that offence when the assistance was provided. This indictment reflects the language of s. 23(1) and charges that the appellant "knowing that Chinh Lam was a party to the offence of murder, did assist Chinh Lam."

[14] It is also significant that the crime of being an accessory after the fact to murder has its own penalty provision (s. 240) which is more severe than the penalty provision applicable to those who are accessories to other crimes (s. 463). This is a further indication that where the Crown chooses to charge someone with being an accessory after the fact to murder, it cannot gain a conviction based on a more generalized knowledge that the principal had committed some crime.

[15] There is little Canadian case law dealing with the knowledge requirement in s. 23(1), perhaps because the language of s. 23(1) is unambiguous. In *R. v. Vinette* (1974), 19 C.C.C. (2d) 1 (S.C.C.), the accused was charged with being an accessory after the fact to manslaughter. Both the majority (per Pigeon J. at p. 7) and the dissent (per Laskin C.J.C. at pp. 2-3) accepted that the Crown had to prove that an accused charged with being an accessory after the fact to a homicide had knowledge of "the unlawful killing." Similarly, in *R. v. A.(M.)*, released March 22, 1996, this court proceeded on the basis that

knowledge of the offence committed by the person aided was an essential element of the charge of being an accessory after the fact. See, also, D. Watt, Accesssoryship After the Fact: Substantive Procedural and Evidentiary Considerations (1981), 21 C.R. (3d) 307 at 308, 318-19; V. Rose, Parties to an Offence (1982) at pp. 164-66, 194.

[16] In other jurisdictions where provisions like s. 23(1) were in effect, or the common law prevailed, courts required that the Crown prove that the accessory after the fact knew of the specific offence committed by the person assisted: *R. v. Levy*, [1912] 1 K.B. 158 at 160 (C.C.A.); *R. v. Tevendale*, [1955] V.L.R. 95 (Vict. S.C.); *R. v. Carter and Savage* (1990), 47 A. Crim. R. 55 at 63 (Queensland C.A.); P. Gillies, Criminal Law (1990) at 765-66. For example, in *R. v. Carter and Savage, supra*, Carter J. said at p. 63:

> It follows that in this case it was incumbent upon the Crown to establish the fact that the principal offender had done the acts said to constitute the offence of murder, that the accused knew that and, with that knowledge, received or assisted Carter in order to enable him to escape punishment.

[17] The authorities referred to by Crown counsel rely on statutory language which is very different from that found in s. 23(1). These statutes create a more generic offence involving the hindering of an investigation, or interference with the apprehension or conviction of a person. For example, in *R. v. Morgan*, [1972] 1 Q.B. 436 (C.A.), the relevant statutory provision provided:

> Where a person has committed an arrestable offence, any other person who, *knowing or believing him to be guilty of the offence or of some other arrestable offence*, does without lawful authority or reasonable excuse any act with intent to impede his apprehension or prosecution shall be guilty of an offence. [Emphasis added.]

[18] Parliament could have enacted similar legislation. It has not, however, done so and it is beyond the authority of the courts to enact such legislation by judicial fiat. I am not moved by the Crown's further contention that the requirement that the Crown prove that the accessory had knowledge of the offence committed by the person aided will allow individuals to escape justice when they aid someone believing that person has committed crime "x" when in fact the person has committed crime "y." If that is the effect of the present legislation, it is for Parliament to decide whether the statutory prohibition should be expanded. Moreover, it seems to me that the circumstances posited by the Crown would give rise to a charge of obstructing justice under s. 139(2) of the *Criminal Code*.

[19] A charge a laid under s. 23(1) must allege the commission of a specific offence (or offences) and the Crown must prove that the alleged accessory knew that the person assisted was a party to that offence. The Crown will meet its burden if it proves that the accused had actual knowledge of the offence committed. Whether wilful blindness will suffice is addressed below. The further question of whether recklessness as to the offence committed by the principal would be sufficient need not be decided in this case.

[20] The appellant argues that wilful blindness can only be relied on by the Crown if the Crown proves that an accused whose suspicions were aroused had the means available to verify the accuracy of those suspicions. The appellant goes on to contend that he could have turned only to Lam to verify his suspicions and that the record does not suggest that Lam would have admitted his culpability in the murders. It follows, says the appellant, that he did not have the means available to him to verify his suspicions and should not,

therefore, be held culpable on the basis of wilful blindness. The appellant cites no authority for this proposition.

[21] Wilful blindness is explained in *R. v. Sansregret*, (1985), 18 C.C.C. (3d) 223 at 235 (S.C.C.):

> ... [W]ilful blindness arises where a person who has become aware of the need for some inquiry declines to make the inquiry because he does not wish to know the truth. He would prefer to remain ignorant. The culpability in recklessness is justified by consciousness of the risk and by proceeding in the face of it, *while in wilful blindness it is justified by the accused's fault in deliberately failing to inquire when he knows there is reason for inquiry.* [Emphasis added.]

[22] More recently, in *R. v. Jorgensen*, (1995), 102 C.C.C. (3d) 97 at 135 (S.C.C.), Sopinka J. described wilful blindness in these terms in reference to a charge of selling obscene material:

> ... *It is well established in criminal law that wilful blindness will also fulfil a mens rea requirement.* If the retailer becomes aware of the need to make further inquiries about the nature of the videos he was selling yet deliberately chooses to ignore these indications and does not make any further inquiries, then the retailer can be nonetheless charged under s. 163(2)(a) for "knowingly" selling obscene materials. *Deliberately choosing not to know something when given reason to believe further inquiry is necessary can satisfy the mental element of the offence.* ...
>
> A finding of wilful blindness involves an affirmative answer to the question: Did the accused shut his eyes because he knew or strongly suspected that looking would fix him with knowledge? [Emphasis added.]

[23] These authorities make it clear that where the Crown proves the existence of a fact in issue and knowledge of that fact is a component of the fault requirement of the crime charged, wilful blindness as to the existence of that fact is sufficient to establish a culpable state of mind. Liability based on wilful blindness is subjective. Wilful blindness refers to a state of mind which is aptly described as "deliberate ignorance" (D. Stuart, Canadian Criminal Law, 3rd ed. (1995) at 209). Actual suspicion, combined with a conscious decision not to make inquiries which could confirm that suspicion, is equated in the eyes of the criminal law with actual knowledge. Both are subjective and both are sufficiently blameworthy to justify the imposition of criminal liability.

[24] The appellant's submission misunderstands the basis upon which liability is imposed where wilful blindness exists. Liability turns on the decision not to inquire once real suspicions arise and not on the hypothetical result of inquiries which were never made. Where an accused chooses to make no inquiries, preferring to remain "deliberately ignorant," speculation as to what the accused would have learned had he chosen to make the necessary inquiries is irrelevant to the determination of the blameworthiness of that accused's state of mind.

[25] The appellant also submits that even if wilful blindness has application in the circumstances of this case, the trial judge erred in finding that the appellant was wilfully blind to the fact that Lam was a party to murder. This is in essence an argument that the trial judge's finding is unreasonable. It was urged that the appellant's statements to the police suggested only that he suspected that Lam had some connection, perhaps as a witness, to the homicides. The appellant submits that a finding of knowledge that Lam

was a party to murder based on those statements was more speculation than reasonable inference.

[26] It was certainly open to trial counsel to advance the argument now urged upon this court. I cannot say, however, that the trial judge's rejection of that argument and his conclusion that the appellant's suspicions extended to a suspicion that Lam had been a party to murder was unreasonable. It was open to him to infer that the appellant's statements revealed a state of mind which encompassed the suspicion that Lam was in trouble because he had been a party to murder. The fact that the appellant may have contemplated other possible connections between Lam and the murders afforded no bar to a finding that he was wilfully blind to the fact that Lam was a party to murder.

ADDITIONAL READING

Colvin, E & S Anand. *Principles of Criminal Law*, 3rd ed (Toronto: Carswell, 2007) ch 10.

Manning, M & P Sankoff. *Manning, Mewett & Sankoff: Criminal Law*, 4th ed (Toronto: Lexis-Nexis, 2009) ch 8.

Roach, K. *Criminal Law*, 6th ed (Toronto: Irwin Law, 2015) ch 4.

Stuart, D. *Canadian Criminal Law*, 7th ed (Toronto: Carswell, 2014) ch 9.

Inchoate Offences

Just as people do not always act alone in the commission of criminal offences, they do not always achieve their unlawful objectives. This chapter is concerned with criminal liability for incomplete offences, of which there are three types having general application in Canadian criminal law: attempt, incitement (also called counselling), and conspiracy. These types are examined in the first three sections of this chapter. They are described as *inchoate* because the full offences are not completed; like all criminal offences, however, they require proof of both a prohibited act and fault.

There are two overarching questions of principle regarding the nature and outer limits of inchoate liability. First, how does the criminal law mark the boundary between a thought to commit an unlawful act and preliminary conduct that attracts the legitimate imposition of the criminal sanction? This question is explored in several of the cases extracted in Section I of this chapter. Second, when and how should the criminal law distinguish between unsuccessful and successful efforts to engage in criminal activity?

In Chapter 2, the harm principle was introduced and discussed primarily in the context of moral offences. In this chapter, the harm principle becomes relevant in a different way. The premise for creating inchoate offences is that criminality does not lie solely in the completion of an offence. Indeed, the prohibited act in inchoate offences may not in itself be harmful or criminal. Rather, the most defensible justification for prosecution of inchoate offences is that the prohibited act gives rise to a culpable risk of criminal behaviour, and is coupled with an intention on the part of the wrongdoer to engage in the criminal act. When a wrongdoer attempts to bring about a criminal consequence, but fails, there is a very real question about how their moral blameworthiness compares with that of the wrongdoer who succeeds.

The American criminal law scholar Sanford Kadish, among others, has argued that it is irrational to punish inchoate offences differently from completed crimes.

SH Kadish, "The Criminal Law and the Luck of the Draw"
(1994) 84 J Crim L & Criminology 679 at 679, 681-82 (footnotes omitted)

I propose to consider what to make of a doctrine of the criminal law that seems to me not rationally supportable notwithstanding its near universal acceptance in Western law, the support of many jurists and philosophers, and its resonance with the intuitions of lawyers and lay people alike. This is the doctrine—the harm doctrine, I'll call it—that reduces punishment for intentional wrongdoers (and often precludes punishment for negligent and reckless wrongdoers) if by chance the harm they intended or risked does not occur.

· · ·

I will begin by setting out the law that most clearly exhibits the harm doctrine at work. This is the law governing the punishment of failed efforts to do some prohibited harm (the law of attempts). ...

Consider the case of a man who stabbed his son in anger, pleaded guilty and was convicted of a crime equivalent for our purposes to attempted murder. After serving several months of a two year sentence he was paroled. However, three months later his son, who had been hospitalized since the attack, took a turn for the worse and died, whereupon the prosecutor, quite within the law, charged the father with murder, a crime punishable with life imprisonment or death.

What did the father do in jail or on parole that merited the greater punishment? Not a thing. If a good constitution or a good surgeon had saved the son, the father could not have been further punished. The occurrence of the resulting death alone raises the crime and the punishment. In most jurisdictions this same principle operates for all crimes, not just homicidal crimes. In California, for example, an attempt to commit a crime is punishable with half the punishment for the completed crime. Thus, the reward for failing, no matter how hard you try to succeed or how close you come, is a lesser punishment.

Arguably, the culpable creation of risk, rather than the imposition of harm, should dictate the law's treatment of inchoate offences. However, focusing on the risk inherent in the offender's actions to the exclusion of consequences is inconsistent with most people's intuitive sense of justice. Arguments about the proper basis for allocating criminal liability can draw strength from many quarters, but determining the extent of liability for inchoate offences remains difficult.

There are also many other questions that arise concerning inchoate liability, some of which conjure up entertaining logic puzzles that rarely surface in practice. One such puzzle is impossibility. Does it matter to the principles of inchoate liability that it may be impossible to commit the commission of the completed offence, for example, because the police are running a sting operation as discussed in relation to *United States of America v Dynar*, [1997] 2 SCR 462, excerpted below?

A further issue is how do the forms of inchoate liability relate among themselves and to the modes of participation? Can there be an attempted conspiracy or, conversely, a conspiracy or agreement to attempt? Can there be incitement to attempt or conspiracy? The issue of the combination of various forms of inchoate liability is examined in the fourth section of this chapter.

Finally, there are many complete offences that are similar to inchoate liability because they punish conduct in advance and in preparation of ultimate crimes. For example, many of the offences part II.1 added to the *Criminal Code* after the terrorist attacks of September 11, 2001 can be seen as punishing conduct in preparation for terrorism such as financing terrorism and participation in a terrorist group for the purpose of enhancing its ability to facilitate or carry out a terrorist act. See *Criminal Code*, ss 83.03 and 83.18. The last section of this chapter will consider the degree to which such complete offences should be interpreted in a manner consistent with the principles that govern the inchoate crimes of attempt, counselling, and conspiracy.

I. ATTEMPT

A person who tries to commit a criminal offence but does not succeed can nevertheless be found guilty of attempting the offence if his or her conduct falls within the terms of s 24:

Attempts

24(1) Every one who, having an intent to commit an offence, does or omits to do anything for the purpose of carrying out his intention is guilty of an attempt to commit the offence whether or not it was possible under the circumstances to commit the offence.

Question of law

24(2) The question whether an act or omission by a person who has an intent to commit an offence is or is not mere preparation to commit the offence, and too remote to constitute an attempt to commit the offence, is a question of law.

Actus Reus

It is clear that there must be some act that goes beyond preparation but what that is has often raised difficulty.

R v Cline
Ontario Court of Appeal
(1956), 115 CCC 18

LAIDLAW JA: … [T]heories and tests have been formulated with a view to finding an answer to the question whether or not an act is sufficient in law to constitute an *actus reus*. It is my respectful opinion that there is no theory or test applicable in all cases, and I doubt whether a satisfactory one can be formulated. Each case must be determined on its own facts, having due regard to the nature of the offence and the particular acts in question. Much of the difficulty and confusion is attributable, in my humble opinion, to an insufficient understanding of the nature and gist of the crime of criminal attempt; and arises also in respect of the vexed question whether a particular act is an act of preparation only, or is an attempt. Perhaps, therefore, it will be helpful to observe carefully certain features of a criminal attempt as the doctrine of that offence was developed and established in the common law.

. . .

The consummation of a crime usually comprises a series of acts which have their genesis in an idea to do a criminal act; the idea develops to a decision to do that act; a plan may be made for putting that decision into effect; the next step may be preparation only for carrying out the intention and plan; but when that preparation is in fact fully completed, the next step in the series of acts done by the accused for the purpose and with the intention of committing the crime as planned cannot, in my opinion, be regarded as remote in its connection with that crime. The connection is in fact proximate. ...

After considering the nature of a criminal attempt and the principles as they were developed and established in the common law, together with the cases to which I have referred, and others, I state these propositions in my own words to guide me in the instant case: (1) There must be *mens rea* and also an *actus reus* to constitute a criminal attempt, but the criminality of misconduct lies mainly in the intention of the accused. (2) Evidence of similar acts done by the accused before the offence with which he is charged, and also afterwards if such acts are not too remote in time, is admissible to establish a pattern of conduct from which the Court may properly find *mens rea*. (3) Such evidence may be advanced in the case for the prosecution without waiting for the defence to raise a specific issue. (4) It is not essential that the *actus reus* be a crime or a tort or even a moral wrong or social mischief. (5) The *actus reus* must be more than mere preparation to commit a crime. But (6) when the preparation to commit a crime is in fact fully complete and ended, the next step done by the accused for the purpose and with the intention of committing a specific crime constitutes an *actus reus* sufficient in law to establish a criminal attempt to commit that crime.

Deutsch v The Queen
Supreme Court of Canada
[1986] 2 SCR 2

[The accused was charged with attempting to procure female persons to have illicit sexual intercourse with another person contrary to s 195(1)(a) (see now s 212(1)(a)) of the *Criminal Code*. The accused had placed an advertisement in a newspaper for a secretary/sales assistant and the evidence of three women who responded to the advertisement, and of a policewoman, was that during each job interview the accused indicated that as part of the job the woman would be required to have sexual intercourse with clients or potential clients of the company where that appeared to be necessary to conclude a contract. He also mentioned that the women could earn up to $100,000 a year.

The trial judge acquitted the accused on the basis that his acts had not gone beyond mere preparation because he had not offered the job to the women. An appeal by the Crown to the Ontario Court of Appeal from the acquittal was allowed. The Supreme Court dismissed the accused's subsequent appeal.]

LE DAIN J (for the Court): ... It has been frequently observed that no satisfactory general criterion has been, or can be, formulated for drawing the line between preparation and attempt, and that the application of this distinction to the facts of a particular case must be left to common sense judgment. ... Despite academic appeals for greater clarity and certainty in this area of the law I find myself in essential agreement with this conclusion.

In my opinion the distinction between preparation and attempt is essentially a qualitative one, involving the relationship between the nature and quality of the act in question and the nature of the complete offence, although consideration must necessarily be given, in making that qualitative distinction, to the relative proximity of the act in question to what would have been the completed offence, in terms of time, location and acts under the control of the accused remaining to be accomplished.

. . .

I agree with the Court of Appeal that if the appellant had the necessary intent to induce or persuade the women to seek employment that would require them to have sexual intercourse with prospective clients, then the holding out of the large financial rewards in the course of the interviews, in which the necessity of having sexual intercourse with prospective clients was disclosed, could constitute the *actus reus* of an attempt to procure. It would clearly be a step, and an important step, in the commission of the offence. Before an offer of employment could be made in such circumstances an applicant would have to seek the position, despite its special requirement. Thus such inducement or persuasion would be the decisive act in the procuring. There would be little else that the appellant would be required to do towards the completion of the offence other than to make the formal offer of employment. I am further of the opinion that the holding out of the large financial rewards in the course of the interviews would not lose its quality as a step in the commission of the offence, and thus as an *actus reus* of attempt, because a considerable period of time might elapse before a person engaged for the position had sexual intercourse with prospective clients or because of the otherwise contingent nature of such sexual intercourse.

For these reasons I would dismiss the appeal. I agree with the Court of Appeal that because the trial judge did not make a finding as to whether or not there was the necessary intent to procure there must be a new trial.

Appeal dismissed.

Note that the breadth of the *actus reus* of an attempted crime means that an attempted crime may be an alternative to a completed crime. In this regard recall *R v Williams*, 2003 SCC 41, [2003] 2 SCR 134, discussed in Chapter 5, in which a conviction for attempted aggravated assault was substituted for a conviction for aggravated assault in a case in which there was reasonable doubt that the accused's actions had caused the victim to become HIV-positive.

Mens Rea

Is the *mens rea* for an attempt the intent to commit the complete offence or could it be something less?

R v Ancio
Supreme Court of Canada
[1984] 1 SCR 225

[Ancio, who wanted to speak with his estranged wife, broke into an apartment building with a loaded sawed-off shotgun. Kurely, the man with whom Ancio's wife had been living, went to investigate the sound of breaking glass and threw the chair he was carrying at Ancio when he saw him climbing the stairs. The gun discharged, missing Kurely, and a struggle followed. The trial judge found that Ancio had broken into the apartment building with the intent to use the weapon to force his wife to leave and convicted him of attempted murder by combining ss 24 and 213(d) (now s 230(d)). The Court of Appeal overturned the conviction and ordered a new trial. The Crown appealed to the Supreme Court of Canada.]

McINTYRE J (for the Court): … The common law recognition of the fundamental importance of intent in the crime of attempt is carried forward into the *Criminal Code*. A reading of s. 24 of the *Code* and all its predecessors since the enactment of the first *Code* in 1892 confirms that the intent to commit the desired offence is a basic element of the offence of attempt. Indeed, because the crime of attempt may be complete without the actual commission of any other offence and even without the performance of any act unlawful in itself, it is abundantly clear that the criminal element of the offence of attempt may lie solely in the intent. As noted by Glanville Williams, *Criminal Law: The General Part*, 2nd ed. (1961), part 207, p. 642, in discussing attempts: "An *actus reus* … need not be a crime apart from the state of mind. It need not even be a tort, or a moral wrong, or a social mischief." The question now arises: What is the intent required for an attempt to commit murder? As has been indicated earlier, the Crown's position is that the intent required for a conviction on a charge of attempt to murder is the intent to do that which will, if death is caused, constitute the commission of murder as defined in ss. 212 [now s 229] and 213 of the *Code*, so that a combination of ss. 24 and 213(d) can form the basis for a conviction of attempted murder. The respondent, on the other hand, argues that although the authorities presently limit the intent to that which would constitute murder as defined in s. 212 of the *Code*, logic and principle dictate that the intent should be limited to the specific intent to kill described in s. 212(a)(i) … .

The completed offence of murder involves a killing. The intention to commit the complete offence of murder must therefore include an intention to kill. I find it impossible to conclude that a person may intend to commit the unintentional killings described in ss. 212 and 213 of the *Code*. I am then of the view that the *mens rea* for an attempted murder cannot be less than the specific intent to kill.

As I have said earlier, there is a division of opinion upon this point and strong arguments have been raised in favour of the Crown's position that a "lesser intent," such as that provided in s. 212(a)(ii) or even no intent at all relating to the causing of death as provided in s. 213(d), may suffice to found a conviction for attempted murder. This view is supported in [*R v Lajoie*, [1974] SCR 399]. In my view, with the utmost respect for those who differ, the sections of the *Criminal Code* relied on in that case do not support that position.

. . .

It was argued, and it has been suggested in some of the cases and academic writings on the question, that it is illogical to insist upon a higher degree of *mens rea* for attempted murder, while accepting a lower degree amounting to recklessness for murder. I see no merit in this argument. The intent to kill is the highest intent in murder and there is no reason in logic why an attempt to murder, aimed at the completion of the full crime of murder, should have any lesser intent. If there is any illogic in this matter, it is in the statutory characterization of unintentional killing as murder. The *mens rea* for attempted murder is, in my view, the specific intent to kill. A mental state falling short of that level may well lead to conviction for other offences, for example, one or other of the various aggravated assaults, but not a conviction for an attempt at murder. For these reasons, it is my view that *Lajoie* should no longer be followed.

I would accordingly dismiss the Crown's appeal and confirm the Court of Appeal's order for a new trial.

R v Logan
Supreme Court of Canada
[1990] 2 SCR 731

[The accused were charged with a number of offences relating to the robbery of a Becker's convenience store and the serious wounding of the cashier, Barbara Turnbull. Two of the accused were convicted of attempted murder and appealed to the Ontario Court of Appeal (1988), 46 CCC (3d) 354, which set aside the conviction. The Supreme Court of Canada dealt as follows with the issue of the *mens rea* for attempted murder. Other aspects of the case are set out in Chapter 9 of this casebook dealing with participation.]

LAMER CJ (for the Court, Sopinka and L'Heureux-Dubé JJ concurring in the result): ... With respect to the case at bar, then, the first question which must be answered is whether the principles of fundamental justice require a minimum degree of *mens rea* in order to convict an accused of attempted murder. *Ancio* established that a specific intent to kill is the *mens rea* required for a principal on the charge of attempted murder. However, as the constitutional question was not raised or argued in that case, it did not decide whether that requisite *mens rea* was a *constitutional* requirement. The case simply interpreted the offence as currently legislated.

In *R. v. Martineau* (1990), 58 C.C.C. (3d) 353, a judgment handed down this day, this court has decided, as a constitutional requirement, that no one can be convicted of murder unless the Crown proves beyond a reasonable doubt that the person had *subjective* foresight of that fact that the death of the victim was likely to ensue. Because of both the stigma and the severe penal consequences which result from a conviction for murder, the *Constitution Act, 1982* requires at least that degree of intent.

As defined in *Ancio*, the elements of *mens rea* for attempted murder are identical to those for the most severe form of murder, murder under s. 212(a)(i). For each, the accused must have had the specific intent to kill. All that differs is the "consequences" component of the *actus reus*. Quite simply, an attempted murderer is, if caught and convicted, a "lucky murderer." Therefore, it would seem logical that the requisite *mens rea* for a murder conviction, as described in *Martineau*, must be the same for a conviction of attempted murder. However, logic is not sufficient reason to label something a "constitutional requirement." As I have stated in *Vaillancourt*, the principles of fundamental justice require a minimum degree of *mens rea* for only a very few offences. The criteria by which these offences can be identified are, primarily, the stigma associated with a conviction and, as a secondary consideration, the penalties available.

The stigma associated with a conviction for attempted murder is the same as it is for murder. Such a conviction reveals that although no death ensued from the actions of the accused, the intent to kill was still present in his or her mind. The attempted murderer is no less a killer than a murderer: he may be lucky—the ambulance arrived early, or some other fortuitous circumstance—but he still has the same killer instinct. Secondly, while a conviction for attempted murder does not automatically result in a life sentence, the offence is punishable by life and the usual penalty is very severe.

… The sentencing range available to the judge is not conclusive of the level of *mens rea* constitutionally required. Instead, the crucial consideration is whether there is a continuing serious social stigma which will be imposed on the accused upon conviction … .

For these reasons, the *mens rea* for attempted murder cannot, without restricting s. 7 of the *Charter*, require of the accused less of a mental element than that required of a murderer under s. 212(a)(i) [now s 229(a)(i)], that is, *subjective* foresight of the consequences. While Parliament, as I have already implied, could well extend our definition of attempted murder in *Ancio* to include the unsuccessful murderers of s. 212(a)(ii), it cannot go further and include objective foresight as being sufficient for a conviction without restricting s. 7 of the *Charter*.

[L'Heureux-Dubé J dissented and held that an intent to murder as in *Ancio* should be the constitutionally required intent for attempted murder as opposed to the slightly lower knowledge requirement contemplated as a constitutional minimum by the majority.]

As this Court held in *R. v. Ancio*, [1984] 1 S.C.R. 225, a conviction for attempted murder requires proof of the specific intent to kill. No lesser *mens rea* will suffice. Parliament has decided to create a distinct offence for attempted murder, recognizing that the results of criminal acts are not to be ignored … . When the attempt does not result in death, logic as well as principles of fundamental justice enshrined in the *Canadian Charter of Rights and Freedoms*, dictate that the specific intent to commit the attempted murder crime must be conclusively proven. As I said in *Martineau*: "If both components, *actus reus* as well as *mens rea*, are not considered when assessing the level of fault attributable to an offender, we would see manslaughter and assault causing bodily harm as no more worthy of condemnation than an assault. Mere attempts would become as serious as full offences."

When mere attempts are at issue, *mens rea* assumes a dominant role. The rationale for invoking a test of subjective foresight for attempted murder does not stem from the crime's relationship to the crime of completed murder, but rather from its connection to crimes of attempt generally. Therefore, I do not choose to follow my colleague's dialectic on the impact of fundamental justice, or of constitutional compulsion upon Parliamentary sovereignty when legislating with respect to these crimes. The motivation for requiring subjective foresight for attempt crimes radiates from the primacy of the *mens rea* component, not from any potential penalties or social stigma that might attend conviction for the completed offence.

Appeal dismissed.

In *R v Sorrell and Bondett* (1978), 41 CCC (2d) 9 (Ont CA), the accused were charged with attempted robbery of the manager of a takeout food store in Kingston ("Aunt Lucy's Fried Chicken") and were tried by a judge without a jury. They were acquitted and the Crown appealed. On the night of the incident, the manager had closed the store 15 minutes early. Several minutes after this, the accused came to the door of the store and knocked on it. The manager said "Sorry we are closed" and returned to his work. The accused then left. At this time the accused had balaclavas over their heads and another store employee noticed that one of the accused had a gun in his hand. The police were called and arrested the accused a short distance from the store. By this time, they had thrown away the balaclavas but one accused was found in possession of a loaded revolver.

The Court of Appeal dismissed the appeal, stating:

> In our view, the trial Judge's reasons are more consistent with a finding that the necessary intent to commit robbery was not proved beyond a reasonable doubt, than with a finding that such intent was established by the evidence. In any event, the Crown has not satisfied us that the trial Judge found the existence of an intent to rob.
>
> If the trial Judge had found that the respondents intended to rob the store, the acts done by them clearly had advanced beyond mere preparation, and were sufficiently proximate to constitute an attempt ... . If the trial Judge had found that the respondents had the necessary intent his finding that the acts done by the respondents did not go beyond mere preparation and did not constitute attempted robbery, would constitute an error of law that would not only warrant, but require our intervention.
>
> The prosecution in this case was forced to rely exclusively upon the acts of the accused, not only to constitute the *actus reus*, but to supply the evidence of the necessary *mens rea*. This Court in *R. v. Cline* rejected the so-called "unequivocal act" test for determining when the stage of attempt has been reached. That test excludes resort to evidence *aliunde*, such as admissions, and holds that the stage of attempt has been reached only when the acts of the accused show unequivocally on their face the criminal intent with which the acts were performed. We are of the view that where the accused's intention is otherwise proved, acts which on their face are equivocal, may none the less, be sufficiently proximate to constitute an attempt. Where, however, there is no extrinsic evidence of the intent with which accused's acts were done, acts of the accused, which on their face are equivocal, may be insufficient to show that the acts were done with the intent to commit the crime that the accused is alleged to have attempted to commit, and hence insufficient to establish the offence of attempt.

Impossibility

Can a person be guilty of an attempt when completion of the offence is for some reason impossible?

United States of America v Dynar
Supreme Court of Canada
[1997] 2 SCR 462

CORY and IACOBUCCI JJ (Lamer CJ and La Forest, L'Heureux-Dubé, and Gonthier JJ concurring):

[1] The issue in this appeal is whether the respondent's conduct in the United States would constitute a crime if carried out in this country, thereby meeting the requirement of "double criminality" which is the pre-condition for the surrender of a Canadian fugitive for trial in a foreign jurisdiction. This issue requires the Court to consider the scope of the liability for attempted offences and conspiracy under Canadian criminal law, specifically, whether impossibility constitutes a defence to a charge of attempt or conspiracy in Canada. ...

[3] Arye Dynar, a Canadian citizen, was the subject of a failed "sting" operation attempted by the Federal Bureau of Investigation in the United States. Mr. Dynar was indicted together with Maurice Cohen, who is also a Canadian citizen, in the United States District Court of Nevada. The United States indictment charged both Mr. Dynar and Mr. Cohen with one count of attempting to launder money in violation of Title 18, *United States Code*, § 1956(a)(3), and one count of conspiracy to violate Title 18, *United States Code*, § 1956(a)(3), contrary to Title 18, *United States Code*, § 371. The Government of the United States requested their extradition by Diplomatic Note dated November 30, 1992. This appeal relates to the request for the extradition of Mr. Dynar.

[4] The events that formed the basis of the indictment began with a telephone call placed on January 2, 1990, from Canada, by Mr. Dynar to a former associate, Lucky Simone, who was living in Nevada. The call was apparently made to seek investors for a business operation in the United States. Lucky Simone had, unbeknownst to Mr. Dynar, become a confidential informant working for FBI agent William Matthews. He informed Agent Matthews of Mr. Dynar's call, and Agent Matthews requested that Mr. Simone return the call. Mr. Simone gave his consent for Agent Matthews to record the conversation.

[5] Affidavit evidence filed by the Requesting State indicates that, during the 1980s, Mr. Dynar was the subject of investigations in the United States pertaining to the laundering of substantial amounts of money originating in the State of Nevada. Agent Matthews' involvement in the investigation of Mr. Dynar's activities began in 1988. When Mr. Dynar made contact with Lucky Simone in 1990, Agent Matthews deposed that he decided to determine whether or not Mr. Dynar was still involved in laundering money which was the proceeds of crime. He had Mr. Simone introduce a second confidential informant, known as "Anthony," to Mr. Dynar. Anthony was instructed to ask if Mr. Dynar would be willing to launder large sums obtained as a result of illegal trafficking. When asked, Mr. Dynar agreed with alacrity to launder money for Anthony.

[6] A great many conversations between the two men were recorded over the course of some months. On all of these occasions, Anthony was in Las Vegas, Nevada and Mr. Dynar was in Canada. Eventually, Mr. Dynar and Anthony arranged an initial meeting. The meeting was purportedly to allow Anthony to give money to Mr. Dynar for laundering as a first step towards developing a relationship in which Mr. Dynar would regularly launder money for him. During several of the conversations, it was made clear that the money to be laundered was "drug money." Mr. Dynar insisted more than once that the

amounts had to be large in order to make his efforts worthwhile. The conversations also disclosed that Mr. Dynar had an associate named "Moe," who was subsequently identified as Maurice Cohen. Agent Matthews recorded all of the conversations in Las Vegas pursuant to the applicable law of the United States, which only requires the consent of one party for the lawful interception of the conversation. Special Agent Charles Pine of the Internal Revenue Service (IRS) was able to identify the voice of Maurice Cohen in the background of several of the conversations.

[7] The initial plan of the American authorities was to set up the transfer of funds to Mr. Dynar in the United States. However, Mr. Dynar believed that he was the subject of a sealed indictment in the United States charging him with laundering very large sums of money and that if he travelled to that country, he would be arrested. It was accordingly agreed that Mr. Dynar's associate, Maurice Cohen, would meet Anthony's associate in Buffalo. Mr. Cohen was to take the money to Toronto where it would be laundered by Mr. Dynar. It would then be taken back to Buffalo by Mr. Cohen on the following day, after a commission for Mr. Dynar had been deducted.

[8] In Buffalo, Mr. Cohen met with Special Agent Dennis McCarthy of the IRS, who was posing as Anthony's associate. The conversations that took place between them in preparation for the transfer of funds were recorded by Agent McCarthy. They contain several statements to the effect that Mr. Cohen was working for Mr. Dynar, as well as some explanations of the logistics of the laundering scheme. In the end, however, the money was not transferred to Mr. Cohen. The FBI aborted the operation by pretending to arrest Agent McCarthy just prior to the transfer of the money. Mr. Cohen was allowed to return to Canada. ...

[49] The *Criminal Code* creates the crime of attempt to commit an offence:

> 24.(1) Every one who, having an intent to commit an offence, does or omits to do anything for the purpose of carrying out the intention is guilty of an attempt to commit the offence *whether or not it was possible under the circumstances to commit the offence.* [Emphasis added.]

On its face, the statute is indifferent about whether or not the attempt might possibly have succeeded. Therefore it would seem, at first blush, not to matter that Mr. Dynar could not possibly have succeeded in laundering money known to be the proceeds of crime. So long as he attempted to do so, he is guilty of a crime.

[50] In our view, s. 24(1) is clear: the crime of attempt consists of an intent to commit the completed offence together with some act more than merely preparatory taken in furtherance of the attempt. This proposition finds support in a long line of authority. See, e.g., *R. v. Cline* (1956), 115 C.C.C. 18 (Ont. C.A.), at p. 29; *R. v. Ancio*, [1984] 1 S.C.R. 225, at p. 247; *R. v. Deutsch*, [1986] 2 S.C.R. 2, at pp. 19-26; *R. v. Gladstone*, [1996] 2 S.C.R. 723, at para. 19. In this case, sufficient evidence was produced to show that Mr. Dynar intended to commit the money-laundering offences, and that he took steps more than merely preparatory in order to realize his intention. That is enough to establish that he attempted to launder money contrary to s. 24(1) of the *Criminal Code*.

[51] However, the respondent argues that Parliament did not intend by s. 24(1) to criminalize all attempts to do the impossible, but only those attempts that the common law has classified as "factually impossible." An attempt to do the factually impossible, according to the respondent, is an attempt that runs up against some intervening obstacle and for that reason cannot be completed. The classic example involves a pick-pocket who

puts his hand into a man's pocket intending to remove the wallet, only to find that there is no wallet to remove.

[52] Traditionally, this sort of impossibility has been contrasted with "legal impossibility." An attempt to do the legally impossible is, according to those who draw the distinction, an attempt that must fail because, even if it were completed, no crime would have been committed. See Eric Colvin, *Principles of Criminal Law* (2nd ed. 1991), at pp. 355-56.

[53] According to the respondent, the *Criminal Code* criminalizes only attempts to do the factually impossible. An attempt to do the legally impossible, in the absence of an express legislative reference to that variety of impossibility, is not a crime.

[54] As support for this interpretation, the respondent offers two arguments. The first is that Parliament based s. 24(1) on an English provision whose purpose was to overrule a decision of the House of Lords that had made factual impossibility a defence. See Barry Brown, "'The attempt, and not the deed, Confounds us': Section 24 and Impossible Attempts" (1981), 19 *U.W.O.L. Rev.* 225, at pp. 228-29. On the strength of this argument, the New Zealand Court of Appeal accepted that New Zealand's equivalent to s. 24(1) criminalizes attempts whose completion is factually impossible but not those whose completion is legally impossible. See *R. v. Donnelly*, [1970] N.Z.L.R. 980 (New Zealand C.A.), at pp. 984, 988.

[55] The respondent's second argument is that Parliament, had it intended to criminalize attempts to do the legally impossible, would have used the words "whether or not it was factually or legally impossible" in s. 24(1). As examples of statutes that were intended to criminalize attempts to do the legally impossible, the respondent cites provisions of statutes from the United Kingdom and from the United States:

> (1) If, with intent to commit an offence to which this section applies, a person does an act which is more than merely preparatory to the commission of the offence, he is guilty of attempting to commit the offence.
>
> (2) A person may be guilty of attempting to commit an offence to which this section applies even though the facts are such that the commission of the offence is impossible.
>
> (3) In any case where—
>
>> (a) apart from this subsection a person's intention would not be regarded as having amounted to an intent to commit an offence; but
>>
>> (b) if the facts of the case had been as he believed them to be, his intention would be so regarded,
>
> then, for the purposes of subsection (1) above, he shall be regarded as having had an intent to commit that offence. (*Criminal Attempts Act 1981* (U.K.), 1981, c. 47.)

If the conduct in which a person engages otherwise constitutes an attempt to commit a crime pursuant to section 110.00, it is no defense to a prosecution for such attempt that the crime charged to have been attempted was, under the attendant circumstances, factually or legally impossible of commission, if such crime could have been committed had the attendant circumstances been as such person believed them to be. (*N.Y. Penal Law* § 110.10 (Consol. 1984).)

[56] A third argument, which the respondent does not advance, is that the words "under the circumstances" restrict the scope of s. 24(1) to attempts to do the factually impossible. An attempt that is not possible "under the circumstances," according to this argument, is by implication possible under some other set of circumstances. Otherwise,

there would be no need to mention circumstances—the mere mention of impossibility would suffice. President North of the New Zealand Court of Appeal made this very argument in *Donnelly, supra*, at p. 988:

> In my opinion the significant words in s. 72(1) [New Zealand's equivalent to s. 24(1) of the *Criminal Code*] are "in the circumstances," which seem to me to imply that in other circumstances it might be possible to commit the offence. This I think points to the conclusion that s. 72(1) went no further than to ensure that a person who had the necessary criminal intent and did an act for the purpose of accomplishing his object was guilty of an attempt even although it so happened that it was not possible to commit the full offence.

[57] In addition there is another way of turning the same language to the respondent's advantage. "Circumstances," in ordinary parlance, are facts. Laws, by contrast, are not circumstances. Accordingly, applying the rule that *expressio unius est exclusio alterius*, the mention in s. 24(1) of attempts that are circumstantially or factually impossible may be taken to exclude attempts that are legally impossible. The question, as one Canadian writer has framed it, is whether " 'the circumstances' referred to in [s 24(1)] include the legal status of the actor's conduct." Brown, *supra*, at p. 229.

[58] Still another argument in favour of the respondent's position, though one that reflects judicial policy rather than the strict ascertainment of legislative intent, is that penal statutes, if ambiguous, should be construed narrowly, in favour of the rights of the accused. "[T]he overriding principle governing the interpretation of penal provisions is that ambiguity should be resolved in a manner most favourable to accused persons." *R. v. McIntosh*, [1995] 1 S.C.R. 686, at p. 705.

[59] Although some of these arguments have a certain force, what force they have is greatly attenuated when it is realized that the conventional distinction between factual and legal impossibility is not tenable. The only relevant distinction for purposes of s. 24(1) of the *Criminal Code* is between imaginary crimes and attempts to do the factually impossible. The criminal law of Canada recognizes no middle category called "legal impossibility." Because Mr. Dynar attempted to do the impossible but did not attempt to commit an imaginary crime, he can only have attempted to do the "factually impossible." For this reason, Mr. Dynar's proposal that s. 24(1) criminalizes only attempts to do the factually impossible does not help him.

[60] As we have already indicated, an attempt to do the factually impossible is considered to be one whose completion is thwarted by mere happenstance. In theory at least, an accused who attempts to do the factually impossible could succeed but for the intervention of some fortuity. A legally impossible attempt, by contrast, is considered to be one which, even if it were completed, still would not be a crime. One scholar has described impossible attempts in these terms:

> Three main forms of impossibility have set the framework for contemporary debate. First, there is impossibility due to inadequate means (Type I). For example, A tries to kill B by shooting at him from too great a distance or by administering too small a dose of poison; C tries to break into a house without the equipment which would be necessary to force the windows or doors. ...
>
> The second form of impossibility arises where an actor is prevented from completing the offence because some element of its *actus reus* cannot be brought within the criminal design

(Type II). For example, A tries to kill B by shooting him when he is asleep in bed, but in fact B has already died of natural causes; C tries to steal money from a safe which is empty. ...

The third form of impossibility arises where the actor's design is completed but the offence is still not committed because some element of the *actus reus* is missing (Type III). For example, A may take possession of property believing it to have been stolen when it has not been; B may smuggle a substance for reward believing it to be a narcotic when it is sugar. ...

Colvin, *supra*, at pp. 355-56.

[61] According to Professor Colvin, factually impossible attempts are those that fall into either of the first two categories. Legally impossible attempts are those that fall into the third category.

[62] Colvin's schema appears attractive. But in fact it draws distinctions that do not stand up on closer inspection. There is no legally relevant difference between the pickpocket who reaches into the empty pocket and the man who takes his own umbrella from a stand believing it to be some other person's umbrella. Both have the *mens rea* of a thief. The first intends to take a wallet that he believes is not his own. The second intends to take an umbrella that he believes is not his own. Each takes some steps in the direction of consummating his design. And each is thwarted by a defect in the attendant circumstances, by an objective reality over which he has no control: the first by the absence of a wallet, the second by the accident of owning the thing that he seeks to steal. It is true that the latter seems to consummate his design and still not to complete an offence; but the semblance is misleading. The truth is that the second man does not consummate his design, because his intention is not simply to take the particular umbrella that he takes, but to take an umbrella that is not his own. That this man's design is premised on a mistaken understanding of the facts does not make it any less his design. A mistaken belief cannot be eliminated from the description of a person's mental state simply because it is mistaken.

[63] If it were otherwise, the effect would be to eliminate from our criminal law the defence of mistaken belief. If mistaken beliefs did not form part of an actor's intent—if an actor's intent were merely to do what he in fact does—then a man who honestly but mistakenly believed that a woman had consented to have sexual relations with him and who on that basis actually had sexual relations with that woman, would have no defence to the crime of sexual assault. His intention, on this limited understanding of intention, would have been to sleep with the particular woman with whom he slept; and that particular woman, by hypothesis, is one who did not consent to sleep with him. Substituting the one description ("a woman who did not consent to sleep with him") for the other ("the particular woman with whom he slept"), it would follow that his intention was to sleep with a woman who had not consented to sleep with him. But of course, and as we have already strenuously urged, intention is one thing and the truth is another. Intention has to do with how one sees the world and not necessarily with the reality of the world.

[64] Accordingly, there is no difference between an act thwarted by a "physical impossibility" and one thwarted "following completion." Both are thwarted by an attendant circumstance, by a fact: for example, by the fact of there being no wallet to steal or by the fact of there being no umbrella to steal. The distinction between them is a distinction without a difference. Professor Colvin himself agrees that "[t]he better view is that impossibility of execution is never a defence to inchoate liability in Canada" (p. 358).

[65] There is, however, a relevant difference between a failed attempt to do something that is a crime and an imaginary crime. See Pierre Rainville, "La gradation de la culpabilité morale et des formes de risque de préjudice dans le cadre de la répression de la tentative" (1996), 37 *C. de D.* 909, at pp. 954-55. It is one thing to attempt to steal a wallet, believing such thievery to be a crime, and quite another thing to bring sugar into Canada, believing the importation of sugar to be a crime. In the former case, the would-be thief has the *mens rea* associated with thievery. In the latter case, the would-be smuggler has no *mens rea* known to law. Because s. 24(1) clearly provides that it is an element of the offence of attempt to have "an intent to commit an offence," the latter sort of attempt is not a crime.

[66] Nor should it be. A major purpose of the law of attempt is to discourage the commission of subsequent offences. See Williams' *Textbook of Criminal Law, supra*, at pp. 404-5. See also Brown, *supra*, at p. 232; Eugene Meehan, "Attempt—Some Rational Thoughts on Its Rationale" (1976-77), 19 *Crim. L.Q.* 215, at p. 238; Don Stuart, *Canadian Criminal Law* (3rd ed. 1995), at p. 594. But one who attempts to do something that is not a crime or even one who actually does something that is not a crime, believing that what he has done or has attempted to do is a crime, has not displayed any propensity to commit crimes in the future, unless perhaps he has betrayed a vague willingness to break the law. Probably all he has shown is that he might be inclined to do the same sort of thing in the future; and from a societal point of view, that is not a very worrisome prospect, because by hypothesis what he attempted to do is perfectly legal.

[67] Therefore, we conclude that s. 24(1) draws no distinction between attempts to do the possible but by inadequate means, attempts to do the physically impossible, and attempts to do something that turns out to be impossible "following completion." All are varieties of attempts to do the "factually impossible" and all are crimes. Only attempts to commit imaginary crimes fall outside the scope of the provision. Because what Mr. Dynar attempted to do falls squarely into the category of the factually impossible—he attempted to commit crimes known to law and was thwarted only by chance—it was a criminal attempt within the meaning of s. 24(1). The evidence suggests that Mr. Dynar is a criminal within the contemplation of the Canadian law and so the double criminality rule should be no bar to his extradition to the United States.

[68] Notwithstanding the difficulties associated with the conventional distinction between factual and legal impossibility, a certain reluctance to embrace our conclusion persists in some quarters. It seems to us that this is in part due to a misunderstanding of the elements of the money-laundering offences. Both s. 462.31(1) of the *Criminal Code* and s. 19.2(1) of the *Narcotic Control Act* require knowledge that the property being laundered is the proceeds of crime. It is tempting to think that knowledge is therefore the *mens rea* of these offences. But "*mens rea*" denotes a mental state. *Mens rea* is the subjective element of a crime. See Williams' *Textbook of Criminal Law, supra*, at p. 71. Knowledge is not subjective, or, more accurately, it is not entirely subjective.

[69] As we have already said, knowledge, for legal purposes, is true belief. Knowledge therefore has two components—truth and belief—and of these, only belief is mental or subjective. Truth is objective, or at least consists in the correspondence of a proposition or mental state to objective reality. Accordingly, truth, which is a state of affairs in the external world that does not vary with the intention of the accused, cannot be a part of *mens rea*. As one Canadian academic has said, [translation] "[t]he truth of the accused's

belief is not part of the *mens rea* of s. 24(1) Cr.C." See Rainville, *supra*, at p. 963. Know-ledge as such is not then the *mens rea* of the money-laundering offences. Belief is.

[70] The truth of an actor's belief that certain monies are the proceeds of crime is something different from the belief itself. That the belief be true is one of the attendant circumstances that is required if the *actus reus* is to be completed. In other words, the act of converting the proceeds of crime presupposes the existence of some money that is in truth the proceeds of crime.

[71] In this, the money-laundering offences are no different from other offences. Murder is the intentional killing of a person. Because a person cannot be killed who is not alive, and because a killing, if is to be murder, must be intentional, it follows that a successful murderer must believe that his victim is alive. An insane man who kills another believing that the one he kills is a manikin does not have the *mens rea* needed for murder. Thus, the successful commission of the offence of murder presupposes both a belief that the victim is alive just before the deadly act occurs and the actual vitality of the victim at that moment. Both truth and belief are required. Therefore, knowledge is required. But this does not mean that the vitality of the victim is part of the *mens rea* of the offence of murder. Instead, it is an attendant circumstance that makes possible the completion of the *actus reus*, which is the killing of a person.

[72] In general, the successful commission of any offence presupposes a certain co-incidence of circumstances. But these circumstances do not enter into the *mens rea* of the offence. As one author observes, it is important "to keep separate the intention of the accused and the circumstances as they really were" (Brown, *supra*, at p. 232).

[73] The absence of an attendant circumstance is irrelevant from the point of view of the law of attempt. An accused is guilty of an attempt if he intends to commit a crime and takes legally sufficient steps towards its commission. Because an attempt is in its very nature an incomplete substantive offence, it will always be the case that the *actus reus* of the completed offence will be deficient, and sometimes this will be because an attendant circumstance is lacking. In *Ancio*, *supra*, at pp. 247-48, McIntyre J. said:

> As with any other crime, the Crown must prove a *mens rea*, that is, the intent to commit the offence in question and the *actus reus*, that is, some step towards the commission of the of-fence attempted going beyond mere acts of preparation. Of the two elements the more sig-nificant is the *mens rea*. ...
>
> Indeed, because the crime of attempt may be complete without the actual commission of any other offence and even without the performance of any act unlawful in itself, it is abun-dantly clear that the criminal element of the offence of attempt may lie solely in the intent.

[74] So it should not be troubling that what Mr. Dynar did does not constitute the *actus reus* of the money-laundering offences. If his actions did constitute the *actus reus*, then he would be guilty of the completed offences described in s. 462.31 of the *Criminal Code* and s. 19.2 of the *Narcotic Control Act*. There would be no need even to consider the law of attempt. The law of attempt is engaged only when, as in this case, the *mens rea* of the completed offence is present entirely and the *actus reus* of it is present in an incomplete but more-than-merely-preparatory way.

[75] The respondent argues that, even accepting that the truth of a belief is not a part of the *mens rea*, nevertheless he did not have the requisite *mens rea*. In particular, the respondent suggests that, in determining whether an accused has the requisite *mens rea*

for attempt, a court should consider only those mental states that supply the accused's motivation to act.

[76] This proposal is a way of overlooking an accused's mistaken beliefs. Thus, the respondent argues that he did not have the requisite *mens rea* because he desired only to make money by doing a service to Anthony, the undercover agent. It did not matter to Mr. Dynar whether the money was the proceeds of crime or not. He would have been just as happy to convert funds for the United States Government as for some drug kingpin. Mr. Dynar's only concern was that he should receive a commission for his services.

[77] The theoretical basis for this thinking appears in Professor George Fletcher's attempted defence of the distinction between factual impossibility and legal impossibility (in *Rethinking Criminal Law* (1978)). Fletcher, on whom the respondent relies, says that an accused's legally relevant intention comprises only those mental states that move the accused to act as he does (at p. 161):

> [M]istaken beliefs are relevant to what the actor is trying to do if they affect his incentive in acting. They affect his incentive if knowing of the mistake would give him a good reason for changing his course of conduct.
>
> Because most facts are, from the accused's point of view, of no consequence, what the accused thinks about most facts is legally irrelevant.

[78] Thus, to take one of Fletcher's examples, it does not matter what day a criminal thought it was when he committed a crime, because whatever he might have thought the day was, he would still have acted as he did. In Fletcher's view, similar reasoning explains why it is not a crime to deal with "legitimate" property thinking that one is dealing with the proceeds of crime (at p. 162):

> [I]t seems fairly clear that the fact that the [goods were] stolen does not affect the actor's incentive in paying the price at which [they were] offered to him by the police. If he were told that the goods were not stolen, that would not have provided him with a reason for turning down the offer. If they were not stolen, so much the better. It follows, therefore, that it is inappropriate to describe his conduct as attempting to receive stolen [goods].

[79] But this view confounds motivation and intention. If attention were paid only to the former, then the number of crimes would be greatly, if not very satisfactorily, reduced, because what moves many criminals to crime is some desire relatively more benign than the desire to commit a crime. We suspect that only the most hardened criminals commit crimes just for the sake of breaking the law. To at least many malefactors, it must be a matter of indifference whether their actions constitute crimes. Probably most thieves would not turn up their noses at the opportunity to loot a house simply because it has been abandoned and so is the property of no one. The goal is the making of a quick dollar, not the flouting of the law. In this, we again agree completely with Glanville Williams, who said:

> Normally, motivation is irrelevant for intention. Every receiver of stolen goods would prefer to have non-stolen goods at the same price, if given the choice; but if he knows or believes the goods are stolen, he intends to receive stolen goods. We have to say that a person intends his act in the circumstances that he knows or believes to exist. This being the rule for con-summated crimes, no good reason can be suggested why it should differ for attempts. ("The

Lords and Impossible Attempts, or *Quis Custodiet Ipsos Custodes*?," [1986] *Cambridge L.J.* 33, at p. 78.)

[80] In this case, it is almost certainly true that Mr. Dynar would have been content to convert the United States Government's money even if he had known that it had nothing to do with the sale of drugs. Presumably his only concern was to collect his percentage. The provenance of the money must have been, for him, largely irrelevant. But, from the point of view of the criminal law, what is important is not what moved Mr. Dynar, but what Mr. Dynar believed he was doing. "We have to say that a person intends his act in the circumstances that he knows or believes to exist." And the evidence is clear that Mr. Dynar believed that he was embarked upon a scheme to convert "drug money" from New York City.

[81] Looking to intent rather than motive accords with the purpose of the criminal law in general and of the law of attempt in particular. Society imposes criminal sanctions in order to punish and deter undesirable conduct. It does not matter to society, in its efforts to secure social peace and order, what an accused's motive was, but only what the accused intended to do. It is no consolation to one whose car has been stolen that the thief stole the car intending to sell it to purchase food for a food bank. Similarly, the purpose of the law of attempt is universally acknowledged to be the deterrence of subsequent attempts. A person who has intended to do something that the law forbids and who has actually taken steps towards the completion of an offence is apt to try the same sort of thing in the future; and there is no assurance that next time his attempt will fail.

[82] Applying this rationale to impossible attempts, we conclude that such attempts are no less menacing than are other attempts. After all, the only difference between an attempt to do the possible and an attempt to do the impossible is chance. A person who enters a bedroom and stabs a corpse thinking that he is stabbing a living person has the same intention as a person who enters a bedroom and stabs someone who is alive. In the former instance, by some chance, the intended victim expired in his sleep perhaps only moments before the would-be assassin acted. It is difficult to see why this circumstance, of which the tardy killer has no knowledge and over which he has no control, should in any way mitigate his culpability. Next time, the intended victim might be alive. Similarly, even if Mr. Dynar could not actually have laundered the proceeds of crime this time around, there is hardly any guarantee that his next customer might not be someone other than an agent of the United States Government.

[83] The import of all of this is that Mr. Dynar committed the crime of attempt; and for having done so he should be extradited to the United States. The facts disclose an intent to launder money and acts taken in furtherance of that design. Section 24(1) of the *Criminal Code* requires no more.

[The dissenting opinion of Major J (Sopinka and McLachlin JJ concurring) has been omitted.]

Appeal allowed and cross-appeal dismissed

II. INCITEMENT

Criminal liability for incitement, or counselling, exists in two forms in Canadian law. The first is incitement of an offence that is actually committed (s 22) and the second is incitement of an offence that is not committed (s 464). The first is a mode of participation in the commission of the offence because the inciter, in effect, causes the commission of an offence through another person. This form of incitement is considered in Chapter 9. The second is an independent offence of inchoate liability, which is considered here.

Under s 464 of the *Criminal Code*, incitement of an offence that is not completed is criminalized on the theory that, by inciting another, the inciter has already taken affirmative steps toward the completion of an offence. At what point is this offence complete? What *mens rea* should be required of the inciter? In particular, is a fault below an intent to commit the completed offence sufficient to convict a person of incitement to commit an offence not completed?

R v Hamilton
Supreme Court of Canada
2005 SCC 47, [2005] 2 SCR 432

FISH J (McLachlin CJ and Bastarache, Binnie, LeBel, and Deschamps JJ concurring):

[1] The respondent, Luther Hamilton, offered for sale through the Internet access to a "credit card number generator"—in terms that extolled its use for fraudulent purposes. As part of the same package of "Top Secret" files, he also offered for sale bomb "recipes" and information on how to commit burglaries.

[2] Mr. Hamilton was charged under s. 464(a) of the *Criminal Code*, R.S.C. 1985, c. C-46, in four separate counts, with counselling the commission of indictable offences that were not in fact committed.

[3] The trial judge was not satisfied that Mr. Hamilton had acted with the requisite *mens rea*, or culpable intent, and she therefore acquitted him on all four counts: (2002), 3 Alta. L.R. (4th) 147, 2002 ABQB 15. The Court of Appeal for Alberta dismissed the Crown's appeal: (2003), 25 Alta. L.R. (4th) 1, 2003 ABCA 255.

[4] The Crown now appeals to this Court on the ground that the trial judge erred as to the *mens rea* of counselling. In the Crown's view, it is unnecessary to prove that the person who counselled the offence intended that it be committed; recklessness is sufficient.

[5] The Crown contends that even if recklessness is insufficient, the trial judge erred in confounding "motive" and "intent." With respect, I agree that the trial judge erred in this regard and that her verdict, but for this error, might very well have been different, at least on the count for counselling fraud. She acquitted Mr. Hamilton of that offence because, in her own words, "[h]is *motivation* was monetary" (para. 53 (emphasis added)).

[6] I would therefore allow the Crown's appeal, order a new trial on the count for counselling fraud and dismiss the appeal with respect to the three remaining counts.

• • •

[13] The Crown contends that recklessness satisfies the fault requirement of counselling and that, even if intent (as opposed to recklessness) must be proved, the trial judge erred in grafting onto the required element of intention an additional requirement of motive. ...

[14] At common law, counselling or procuring a felony was a substantive offence, whether or not the felony was subsequently committed: *Brousseau v. The King* (1917), 56 S.C.R. 22. The charges that concern us here are now codified in s. 464(a) of the *Criminal Code*, which provides:

> 464. …
>
>   (a) every one who counsels another person to commit an indictable offence is, if the offence is not committed, guilty of an indictable offence and liable to the same punishment to which a person who attempts to commit that offence is liable;

[15] The *actus reus* for counselling will be established where the materials or statements made or transmitted by the accused *actively induce* or *advocate*—and do not merely *describe*—the commission of an offence: *R. v. Sharpe*, [2001] 1 S.C.R. 45, 2001 SCC 2, at para. 57, *per* McLachlin C.J.

· · ·

[21] Our concern here is with the imposition of criminal liability on those who counsel others to commit crimes. In this context, "counsel" includes "procure, solicit or incite": see s. 22(3) of the *Criminal Code*.

· · ·

[23] Those who encourage the commission of crimes in any of these ways are criminally responsible for their conduct by way of "secondary liability."

[24] The rationale underlying secondary liability was described by the Law Reform Commission of Canada as "straightforward, obvious and justifiable"—in principle, though not always in practice: Working Paper 45, *Secondary Liability: Participation in Crime and Inchoate Offences* (1985), at p. 5.

[25] According to the Commission (at pp. 5-6):

> … the rationale for secondary liability is the same as that for primary liability. Primary liability attaches to the commission of acts which are outlawed as being harmful, as infringing important human interests and as violating basic social values. Secondary liability attaches on the same ground to their attempted commission, to counselling their commission and to assisting their commission.
>
> This is clear with participation. If the primary act (for example, killing) is harmful, then doing it becomes objectionable. But if doing it is objectionable, it is also objectionable to get another person to do it, or help him do it. For while killing is objectionable because it causes actual harm (namely, death), so too inducing and assisting killing are objectionable because of the potential harm: *they increase the likelihood of death occurring.*
>
> The same arguments hold for inchoate crimes. Again, if the primary act (for example, killing), is harmful, society will want people not to do it. Equally, it will not want them even to try to do it, or to counsel or incite others to do it. *For while the act itself causes actual harm, attempting to do it, or counselling, inciting or procuring someone else to do it, are sources of potential harm—they increase the likelihood of that particular harm's occurrence.* Accordingly, society is justified in taking certain measures in respect of them: outlawing them with sanctions, and authorizing intervention to prevent the harm from materializing. [Emphasis added.]

[26] These passages, in my view, aptly explain why Parliament has imposed criminal responsibility on those who counsel, procure, solicit or incite others to commit crimes, whether or not the crimes are in fact committed.

[27] And it seems to me that the plain meaning of the terms used by Parliament to achieve this purpose point to a fault element that combines advertent conduct with a "conscious disregard of *unjustified* (and substantial) risk" that it entails: L. Alexander and K.D. Kessler, "Mens Rea and Inchoate Crimes" (1997), 87 J. *Crim. L. & Criminology* 1138, at p. 1175 (emphasis in original).

[28] The "substantial and unjustified risk" standard of recklessness has venerable roots in Canada and in other common law jurisdictions as well: see, for example, *Leary v. The Queen*, [1978] 1 S.C.R. 29, at p. 35 (Dickson J., as he then was, dissenting on other grounds); and, generally, M.L. Friedland and K. Roach, *Criminal Law and Procedure: Cases and Materials* (8th ed. 1997), at pp. 508 ff., where Herbert Wechsler explains, at pp. 510-11, why the American Law Institute required in its *Model Penal Code* that the risk consciously disregarded be both "substantial" and "unjustifiable."

[29] In short, the actus reus for counselling is the deliberate encouragement or active inducement of the commission of a criminal offence. And the mens rea consists in nothing less than an accompanying intent or conscious disregard of the substantial and unjustified risk inherent in the counselling: that is, it must be shown that the accused either intended that the offence counselled be committed, or knowingly counselled the commission of the offence while aware of the unjustified risk that the offence counselled was in fact likely to be committed as a result of the accused's conduct.

. . .

[39] The trial judge ... acquitted Mr. Hamilton on the charge of counselling fraud because she had "a doubt that Mr. Hamilton had subjective intent to counsel fraud" (para. 53). And she explained her conclusion this way:

> His *motivation* was monetary, and he sought to pique the curiosity of readers who might acquire the information in the same way that he was initially attracted to the information. Further, he struck me as utterly unsophisticated and naïve to the point that he cannot be said to have been wilfully blind or reckless. [Emphasis added; para. 53.]

[40] Essentially, on my reading of this passage, the trial judge acquitted Mr. Hamilton on this count because his *motivation* was mercenary as opposed to malevolent.

[41] In my respectful view, this was an error of law requiring our intervention.

[42] The distinction between motive and intent has been well understood by Canadian courts since at least 1979, when Dickson J. stated:

> In ordinary parlance, the words "intent" and "motive" are frequently used interchangeably, but in the criminal law they are distinct. In most criminal trials, the mental element, the *mens rea* with which the court is concerned, relates to "intent," *i.e.* the exercise of a free will to use particular means to produce a particular result, rather than with "motive," *i.e.* that which precedes and induces the exercise of the will. The mental element of a crime ordinarily involves no reference to motive. ...

(*Lewis v. The Queen*, [1979] 2 S.C.R. 821, at p. 831)

[43] Cory and Iacobucci JJ. also underlined this distinction in *United States of America v. Dynar*, [1997] 2 S.C.R. 462, emphasizing the importance, as a matter of legal policy, of maintaining it with vigilance: "It does not matter to society, in its efforts to secure social peace and order, what an accused's motive was, but only what the accused intended to do. It is no consolation to one whose car has been stolen that the thief stole the car intending

to sell it to purchase food for a food bank" (para. 81). See also *R. v. Hibbert*, [1995] 2 S.C.R. 973.

[44] In this case, of course, the motive attributed to the accused was far less laudable. He sought to make "a quick buck" by encouraging the intended recipients of his Internet solicitation to purchase a device that generated credit card numbers easily put to fraudulent use.

[45] The trial judge's conclusion that Mr. Hamilton did not intend to induce the recipients to use those numbers is incompatible with the plain meaning of the "teaser" e-mail and with her other findings of fact, including her finding that Mr. Hamilton well understood that use of the generated numbers was illegal. Her assertion that "[h]is motivation was monetary" immediately after her reference to these facts demonstrates an error of law as to the *mens rea* for counselling the commission of a crime, and warrants a new trial.

V

[46] I would for these reasons allow the appeal on the count for counselling fraud and order a new trial on that count, but dismiss the appeal in relation to the three remaining counts.

CHARRON J (dissenting) (Major and Abella JJ concurring):

[47] At issue in this appeal is the requisite mental element for the offence of counselling the commission of an indictable offence which is not committed. More specifically, must the counsellor intend that the counselled offence be committed or is it sufficient to show recklessness as to the consequences? As we shall see, the debate concerns not so much language as it does the limits of criminal liability.

· · ·

[76] The requisite *mens rea* is not expressly set out in s. 464. However, this is not unusual. The mental element of an offence is not always described in the enactment. Often it must be inferred from the nature of the prohibited activity and the harm it is meant to guard against. In this case, because of the nature of the offence, our earlier discussion on the requisite *actus reus* can largely inform the determination of the necessary *mens rea*. As we have seen, it is not sufficient that the communication simply raise the possibility of affecting its recipient; it must actively seek to persuade that person to commit the crime. It follows that the counsellor must, at the very least, *intend to persuade* the person counselled to commit the offence. In this respect, it is my view that mere recklessness as to the counselled person's reaction to the communication is insufficient. In other words, it is not enough that the counsellor, knowing that the communication is objectively capable of persuading a person to commit an offence, goes ahead and does the act anyway. If mere recklessness as to the communication's potential power of persuasion were to suffice, some may argue that the publication of Shakespeare's *Henry VI*, with its famous phrase "let's kill all the lawyers," should be subject to state scrutiny!

[77] Hence, the counsellor must intend to persuade the person counselled to commit the offence. Simply intending the communication, as advocated by the Crown at trial, is not sufficient. An additional question has been posed, mostly in academic writings: must the counsellor also intend that the offence be committed? This is often referred to as a "dual *mens rea*" requirement. In my view, in all but the most unusual circumstances, it is not necessary to adopt a distinct "two-step" approach to determine whether the accused

possesses the necessary *mens rea*. It is logical to infer that the counsellor who intends to persuade the person counselled to commit an offence intends that the offence be committed. However, unusual circumstances did arise in *R. v. Janeteas* (2003), 172 C.C.C. (3d) 97 (Ont. C.A.), and it became necessary for the court to examine whether the counsellor must also intend the commission of the counselled offence. The question was fully canvassed by Moldaver J.A. who concluded that such an intent was required. I agree with his analysis.

[78] The peculiar facts of *Janeteas* are as follows. Mr. Janeteas came to befriend J.B. and her mother B.G., subsequently learning of J.B.'s marital difficulties with her husband Dr. M.B. According to Mr. Janeteas, he began to fear for Dr. M.B.'s safety as a result of conversations with J.B. and B.G. in which they made it known that they wanted to have Dr. M.B. harmed or even killed. He felt that Dr. M.B. should be warned, and in an attempt to obtain hard evidence, tape-recorded a conversation with J.B. and B.G. in which he actively encouraged them to have Dr. M.B. harmed or killed and expressed his willingness to make the necessary arrangements. He then met with Dr. M.B., and over the next few months was able to obtain $35,000 from him. Moldaver J.A. found that Mr. Janeteas did not possess the requisite *mens rea*, stating, at para. 43:

> The present case is one of those rare instances where, despite the appellant's intention that his words be taken seriously, the Crown does not maintain that he intended the commission of the crimes counselled. While the appellant's actions were reprehensible, I am not convinced that the reach of the criminal law should be extended, at the expense of established principle, to ensnare the likes of the appellant ... .

[80] Although the offence in question was a different one, the reasoning of the Court in *Keegstra* on the requisite mental element is nonetheless instructive, because much the same concerns about the potential breadth of the prohibition against acts of communication informed the analysis of the Court on the question of *mens rea*. The Court adopted a stringent standard, noting that the limitation on the *mens rea* required to convict for "wilfully promoting hatred" was a key factor in minimizing the impairment of freedom of expression caused by that provision. Dickson C.J. noted that the requirement that the speaker subjectively intend that his speech promote hatred "significantly restricts the reach of the provision, and thereby reduces the scope of the targeted expression" (p. 775). This was seen to be "an invaluable means of limiting the incursion of s. 319(2) into the realm of acceptable (though perhaps offensive and controversial) expression" (p. 775). Of course, the word "wilfully" is not found in s. 464 as it was in s. 319(2). However, the restricted meaning of the word "counsel," as an *active* inducing, procuring or encouraging the commission of an offence, connotes the same requirement that there be a subjective intent to persuade the person counselled *to commit the offence*. This requirement, from a logical standpoint, can only be met if the counsellor intends that the offence be committed. Recklessness alone cannot suffice. Since the *mens rea* is largely inferred from the *actus reus* itself, the application of the lesser standard of recklessness, in my view, would result in widening the scope of prohibited activity beyond that accepted by this Court in *Sharpe*.

[81] There is no question that the Crown is correct in saying that the Internet poses particular risks because of the ease with which mass communications may be disseminated worldwide. The particular nature of communications through cyberspace may well provide justification to limit the diffusion of the most dangerous expression on a lesser standard, even on objective grounds alone. However, it is my view that the remedy does not lie in an expansive interpretation of the offence of counselling. The offence of counselling,

applying as it does to all crimes, is too blunt an instrument to address this situation without imperiling a range of harmless and/or valuable expression.

[82] For these reasons, I agree with the Court of Appeal that the more demanding standard of subjective *mens rea* should apply: the counsellor must intend that the counselled offence be committed for the offence to be made out. As noted by the Ontario Court of Appeal in *Janeteas* and the Alberta Court of Appeal in this case, this approach has the support of many in the legal community. For Canadian writings, see: D. Stuart, *Canadian Criminal Law: A Treatise* (4th ed. 2001), at pp. 227 and 703; K. Roach, *Criminal Law* (3rd ed. 2004), at pp. 125-26; E. Colvin, *Principles of Criminal Law* (2nd ed. 1991), at p. 377. For American academic support, see: W.R. LaFave, *Substantive Criminal Law* (2nd ed. 2003), vol. 2, at pp. 194-95; J. Dressler, *Understanding Criminal Law* (3rd ed. 2001), at pp. 415-16. For British support, see: A. Ashworth, *Principles of Criminal Law* (4th ed. 2003), at p. 466; G. Williams, *Textbook of Criminal Law* (2nd ed. 1983), at p. 442; *Smith & Hogan Criminal Law* (9th ed. 1999), at p. 271.

E. Application to This Case

[83] As noted earlier, the trial judge concluded that the *actus reus* of the offence had been proven in respect of each of the four counts. While this conclusion in respect of the fraud count appears well founded, it is difficult to find support on the record in respect of the three remaining counts. As discussed earlier, a simple "how to" recipe for committing a crime, without more, does not appear to meet the test adopted in *Sharpe*. However, no issue was raised with respect to the trial judge's conclusion on the *actus reus* and it is not necessary to decide the matter to dispose of this appeal.

[84] The trial judge concluded that Mr. Hamilton did not have the necessary *mens rea* on any standard. The Court of Appeal saw no reason to interfere with her conclusion. Nor do I. My colleague Fish J. is of the view that the trial judge erred by confounding "motive" and "intent." He rests this conclusion on the trial judge's finding that Mr. Hamilton's motivation was monetary. With respect, I disagree. The trial judge's consideration of Mr. Hamilton's motivation must be examined in the context of the evidence before her, and her reasons must be read as a whole ... .

[85] ... The trial judge was entitled to consider motive. It is a piece of circumstantial evidence that may assist in determining an accused's state of mind. In reading her reasons as a whole, I see no reason to interfere with the conclusion reached by the Court of Appeal on this issue, at para. 44:

> The trial judge did not err as alleged by the Crown. As she was entitled to do, the trial judge considered motive as part of her fact findings. But her decision was based on other facts relating to the respondent's knowledge. She found, for example, that the respondent had not read most of the "Top Secret" files. She also found that he was not interested in their contents and that he was, overall, "naive, lazy or ignorant." Dealing with the credit card number generator, the trial judge accepted the respondent's testimony that he did not think any generated numbers could be used because they lacked an expiry date. On the basis of these facts, she found the respondent lacked sufficient knowledge of the consequences of his actions to satisfy the *mens rea* requirement. It is clear that she understood the nature of the test she was bound to apply and did not err in law.

Appeal allowed; new trial ordered.

III. CONSPIRACY

A conspiracy exists when two or more people agree to commit a criminal offence and the offence of conspiracy is complete upon their agreement. Difficulties can arise on several points. Was there an agreement and, if so, on what? Does it matter if it was impossible to commit the completed offence?

United States of America v Dynar
Supreme Court of Canada
[1997] 2 SCR 462

CORY and IACOBUCCI JJ: …

(a) What Is a Criminal Conspiracy?

[86] In *R. v. O'Brien*, [1954] S.C.R. 666, at pp. 668-69, this Court adopted the definition of conspiracy from the English case of *Mulcahy v. R.* (1868), L.R. 3 H.L. 306 (U.K. H.L.), at p. 317:

> A conspiracy consists not merely in the intention of two or more, but in the agreement of two or more to do an unlawful act, or to do a lawful act by unlawful means. So long as such a design rests in intention only, it is not indictable. When two agree to carry it into effect, the very plot is an act in itself, and the act of each of the parties … punishable if for a criminal object. …

There must be an intention to agree, the completion of an agreement, and a common design. Taschereau J., in *O'Brien*, *supra*, at p. 668, added that:

> Although it is not necessary that there should be an overt act in furtherance of the conspiracy, to complete the crime, I have no doubt that there must exist *an intention to put the common design into effect*. A common design necessarily involves an intention. Both are synonymous. The intention cannot be anything else but the will to attain the object of the agreement. [Emphasis in original.]

[87] In *R. v. Cotroni*, [1979] 2 S.C.R. 256, at p. 276, Dickson J. (as he then was) described the offence of conspiracy as "an inchoate or preliminary crime." In setting out the necessary elements of the offence, he noted at pp. 276-77 that:

> The word "conspire" derives from two Latin words, "con" and "spirare," meaning "to breathe together." To conspire is to agree. The essence of criminal conspiracy is proof of agreement. On a charge of conspiracy the agreement itself is the gist of the offence: *Paradis v. R.*, at p. 168. The *actus reus* is the fact of agreement: *D.P.P. v. Nock*, at p. 66. The agreement reached by the co-conspirators may contemplate a number of acts or offences. Any number of persons may be privy to it. Additional persons may join the ongoing scheme while others may drop out. So long as there is a continuing overall, dominant plan there may be changes in methods of operation, personnel, or victims, without bringing the conspiracy to an end. *The important inquiry is not as to the acts done in pursuance of the agreement, but whether there was, in fact,*

a common agreement to which the acts are referable and to which all of the alleged offenders were privy. [Emphasis added.]

Conspiracy is in fact a more "preliminary" crime than attempt, since the offence is considered to be complete before any acts are taken that go beyond mere preparation to put the common design into effect. The Crown is simply required to prove a meeting of the minds with regard to a common design to do something unlawful, specifically the commission of an indictable offence. See s. 465(1)(c) of the *Criminal Code*.

[88]   A conspiracy must involve more than one person, even though all the conspirators may not either be identified, or be capable of being convicted. See for example *O'Brien, supra*; *R. v. Guimond*, [1979] 1 S.C.R. 960. Further, each of the conspirators must have a genuine intention to participate in the agreement. A person cannot be a conspirator if he or she merely pretends to agree. In *O'Brien*, Rand J. held at p. 670 that

a conspiracy requires an actual intention in both parties at the moment of exchanging the words of agreement to participate in the act proposed; mere words purporting agreement without an assenting mind to the act proposed are not sufficient.

Where one member of a so-called conspiracy is a police informant who never intends to carry out the common design, there can be no conspiracy involving that person. Nonetheless, a conspiracy can still exist between other parties to the same agreement. It is for this reason that the conspiracy in this case is alleged to involve Mr. Dynar and Mr. Cohen, and not the confidential informant "Anthony."

[89]   There can be no doubt that a criminal conspiracy constitutes a serious offence that is properly extraditable. Indeed, it was so recognized in the 1976 treaty between Canada and the U.S. in force at the time of the sting operation. The crime has a long and malevolent history. Conspirators have plotted to overthrow monarchs from biblical times through the time of the Plantaganets and Tudors. Guy Fawkes conspired with others to blow up the parliament buildings. Today conspirators plot to carry out terrorist acts, to commit murders or to import forbidden drugs. Society is properly concerned with conspiracies since two or more persons working together can achieve evil results that would be impossible for an individual working alone. For example, it usually takes two or more conspirators to manufacture and secrete explosives or to arrange for the purchase, importation and sale of heroin. The very fact that several persons in combination agree to do something has for many years been considered to constitute "a menace to society": *O'Brien, supra*, at p. 669. In fact, the scale of injury that might be caused to the fabric of society can be far greater when two or more persons conspire to commit a crime than when an individual sets out alone to do an unlawful act.

[90]   As a result, it is obvious that the reason for punishing conspiracy before any steps are taken towards attaining the object of the agreement is to prevent the unlawful object from being attained, and therefore to prevent this serious harm from occurring. See Glanville Williams, *Criminal Law: The General Part* (2nd ed. 1961), at p. 710. It is also desirable to deter similar conduct in the future. Those who conspire to do something that turns out to be impossible betray by their actions a propensity and aptitude to commit criminal acts; and there is no reason to believe that schemers who are thwarted on one occasion will not be successful on the next. Thus, the rationale for punishing conspirators coincides with the rationale for punishing persons for attempted crimes. Not only is the

offence itself seen to be harmful to society, but it is clearly in society's best interests to make it possible for law enforcement officials to intervene before the harm occurs that would be occasioned by a successful conspiracy or, if the conspiracy is incapable of completion, by a subsequent and more successful conspiracy to commit a similar offence.

(b) Is Impossibility a Defence to Conspiracy?

[91] By virtue of the "preliminary" nature of the offence of criminal conspiracy, the mere fact that money was not transferred to Mr. Cohen for laundering by Mr. Dynar would not preclude a finding that a conspiracy existed between them. Criminal liability will still ensue, as long as the agreement and the common intention can be proved. Does it make any difference to the potential liability of the conspirators that they could not have committed the substantive offence even if they had done everything that they set out to do? Put another way, should conspirators escape liability because, owing to matters entirely outside their control, they are mistaken with regard to an attendant circumstance that must exist for their plan to be successful? Such a result would defy logic and could not be justified.

[92] Impossibility as a defence to a charge of criminal conspiracy has received comparatively little attention by courts or academic writers. *Director of Public Prosecutions v. Nock*, [1978] 2 All E.R. 654 (U.K. H.L.), is the leading English case which considered the applicability of the defence of impossibility in a charge of conspiracy. In that case, the conspiracy was found to consist of an agreement to produce cocaine on a particular occasion from a specific substance. The agreement was impossible to carry out because the substance chosen was incapable of producing cocaine. The impossibility of carrying out this agreement was the basis for the conclusion that the same distinction between factual and legal impossibility that we have criticized in the law of attempt ought to apply to the law of conspiracy. The respondent relies upon *Nock*, and urges the adoption of legal impossibility as a defence to criminal conspiracy in Canada. This submission cannot be accepted.

[93] In England, *Nock* has been specifically overtaken by the *Criminal Attempts Act 1981*, s. 5, which now makes criminal liability for conspiracy possible where the accused are mistaken as to an attendant circumstance that is necessary to prove the full offence. Effectively, this precludes the defence of legal impossibility as understood in *Nock*, *supra*, but preserves the defence for "imaginary crimes." As we have seen, the latter term encompasses situations where individuals do something they believe contravenes the law when it does not. Thus, for example, in England it is not a crime to conspire to purchase Scotch whisky, because the purchase of that whisky is not a crime known to English law.

[94] Section 465(1)(c) of the Canadian *Criminal Code* does not specifically state that criminal liability for conspiracy can ensue where the substantive offence is impossible to commit. However, even in the absence of such an explicit legislative direction, the analysis of the House of Lords in *Nock* should not be accepted. The case has been rightly subjected to both academic and judicial criticism, and to the extent that it is based on the same distinction between factual and legal impossibility that has been applied in the law of attempt, it too is conceptually untenable.

[95] In England, the acceptance of legal impossibility as a defence to conspiracy in *Nock* was predicated on the adoption by the House of Lords of the same position regarding the law of attempt: see *Haughton v. Smith*, [1973] 3 All E.R. 1109 (Eng. C.A.). The

House of Lords has now expressly overruled the *Haughton* decision in *R. v. Shivpuri*, [1986] 2 All E.R. 334 (U.K. H.L.). They did so on the basis that quite apart from the provisions of the *Criminal Attempts Act*, the distinction between factual and legal impossibility is untenable in the law of attempt. The application of the distinction in *Nock* must now be questioned as well, even in the absence of legislative amendment. Accordingly, the desirability of using the *Nock* principles in Canada has been appropriately doubted by Cadsby Prov. Ct. J. in *R. v. Atkinson* (April 13, 1987), Cadsby Prov. J. (Ont. Prov. Ct.). The New Zealand Court of Appeal has also rejected *Nock*, except perhaps in the case of "imaginary crimes": *R. v. Sew Hoy*, [1994] 1 N.Z.L.R. 257 (New Zealand C.A.).

[96]   A number of Canadian academic authorities have also been justly critical of the use of the distinction between factual and legal impossibility in the law of conspiracy, and in particular, have criticized the *Nock* case for this reason. Most writers take the position that if the distinction between factual and legal impossibility is rejected in the case of attempt, it should *a fortiori* be rejected for conspiracy. Thus, for example, Colvin in *Principles of Criminal Law, supra*, at p. 358, indicates, in a discussion that deals primarily with the law of attempt, that he prefers the view that "impossibility of execution is never a defence to inchoate liability in Canada." Since this position is clear in the *Criminal Code* with regard to attempt, "there is no good reason to treat conspiracy and other forms of inchoate liability any differently."

[97]   Professor Stuart in *Canadian Criminal Law, supra*, at pp. 644-45, convincingly contends that the same rationale for rejecting the distinction between factual and legal impossibility in the law of attempt should apply to the law of conspiracy. He puts his position in this way (at p. 644):

> If conspiracy is considered, as it has been suggested that it should, as a preventive crime owing its existence to the fact that it is a step, even though a limited one, towards the commission of a full offence, it is difficult to see why the approach to impossibility should differ.

[98]   According to Professor Alan Mewett and Morris Manning in *Mewett & Manning on Criminal Law* (3rd ed. 1994), at p. 341, if it were not for the decision in *Nock*, the question as to whether impossibility should constitute a defence to the offence of conspiracy ought not to arise at all. In *Nock*, the House of Lords held that because the offence can never materialize, "[t]here was no *actus reus* because there was no act of agreeing to commit an offence." Mewett and Manning criticize this reasoning as unsound because "[i]t is wrong to think that there is something that can, in the abstract, be called an *actus reus*." It is the agreement that is the *actus*, and the intention to do the act that is unlawful (the *mens rea*) that turns the agreement into an *actus reus*, or a "guilty act." These authors would restrict the availability of the defence of impossibility to situations of "true" legal impossibility (which we have referred to as imaginary crimes), where persons conspire to do something that is not a crime known to law regardless of whether the facts are as the accused believe them to be.

[99]   Canadian courts have only rarely considered this issue. In *R. v. Wah*, [1964] 1 C.C.C. 313 (Ont. C.A.), the Ontario Court of Appeal, in a case involving conspiracy to commit forgery, held at p. 315 that "[i]n a prosecution for conspiracy a conviction may not be registered if the operation for the commission of which the accused allegedly conspired would, if accomplished, not have made the accused guilty of the substantive offence." The respondent obviously finds comfort in this case.

[100] Although some of the language in *Wah* suggests a more general acceptance of the defence of legal impossibility in a case of conspiracy, the case was decided on a much narrower basis. There the substantive offence was defined as involving the making of a false document, knowing it to be false. The resolution of the case turned on the definition of "false document." Kelly J.A. held that the photograph of the false document was not itself a false document. Therefore, the crime could not be committed regardless of the intention of the accused. There was no issue as to mistaken belief regarding particular circumstances. The accused simply intended to do something which was not prohibited by law. In addition, Kelly J.A. found that the Crown had not established that the photograph was intended to be used to induce anyone to believe that the reproduced document was genuine.

[101] *Wah* should only be accepted as authority for the proposition that impossibility can be a defence to a charge of conspiracy where the conspirators intend to commit an "imaginary crime." This approach to impossibility and conspiracy has also been taken in older cases dealing with economic conspiracies: see for example *R. v. Howard Smith Paper Mills Ltd.*, [1957] S.C.R. 403, at p. 406, citing *R. v. Whitchurch* (1890), 24 Q.B.D. 420 (Eng. Q.B.).

[102] None of these authorities stands in the way of a conclusion that, from a purely conceptual perspective, the distinction between factual and legal impossibility is as unsound in the law of conspiracy as it is in the law of attempt. As we concluded in discussing impossible attempts, cases of so-called "legal" impossibility turn out to be cases of factual impossibility and the distinction collapses, except in cases of "imaginary crimes." Conspiracy to commit such fanciful offences of course cannot give rise to criminal liability.

[103] Furthermore, like attempt, conspiracy is a crime of intention. The factual element—or *actus reus*—of the offence is satisfied by the establishment of the agreement to commit the predicate offence. This factual element does not have to correspond with the factual elements of the substantive offence. The goal of the agreement, namely the commission of the substantive offence, is part of the mental element—or *mens rea*—of the offence of conspiracy.

[104] The conspiracy alleged in the case at bar involves the commission of an offence that requires knowledge of a circumstance as one of its essential elements. When a substantive offence requires knowledge of a particular circumstance, the Crown is required to prove a subjective element, which is best described as belief that the particular circumstance exists. The Crown is also required to prove an objective element, namely the truth of the circumstance. It is the presence of the objective circumstance that translates the subjective belief into knowledge or "true belief."

[105] However, since the offence of conspiracy only requires an *intention* to commit the substantive offence, and not the commission of the offence itself, it does not matter that, from an objective point of view, commission of the offence may be impossible. It is the subjective point of view that is important, and from a subjective perspective, conspirators who intend to commit an indictable offence intend to do everything necessary to satisfy the conditions of the offence. The fact that they cannot do so because an objective circumstance is not as they believe it to be does not in any way affect this intention. The intention of the conspirators remains the same, regardless of the absence of the circumstance that would make the realization of that intention possible. It is only in retrospect that the impossibility of accomplishing the common design becomes apparent.

[106] If the failure of a conspiracy as a result of some defect in the attendant circumstances were to be considered to constitute "legal" impossibility and as such a defence to a charge of conspiracy, the fact that the conspirators are not culpable becomes a matter of pure luck, divorced from their true intentions. This result is unacceptable. Rather it would be consistent with the law of conspiracy to hold that the absence of the attendant circumstance has no bearing on the intention of the parties, and therefore no bearing on their liability.

[107] It has long been accepted that conspirators can be punished for their agreement (*actus reus*) and their intention to commit the offence (*mens rea*). This is true even though the police intervene to prevent the conspirators from committing the substantive offence which was the aim of the conspiracy. By the same token, it should make no difference to the culpability of the conspirators if the police intervene in a way that makes the offence impossible to commit because, for example, the money to be laundered is not derived from crime. The conspirators could still be properly convicted on the basis that the agreement to do the unlawful object is considered dangerous to society and reprehensible in itself.

[108] This approach does not substitute a different mental element for the offence of conspiracy from that required for the substantive offence of money laundering. In those offences that require knowledge, the mental element is belief. Therefore, the subjective state of mind of a money launderer is the belief that the money is derived from an illicit source. Similarly, the subjective state of mind of the person who conspires with others to launder money is also the belief that the money is derived from an illicit source. For the substantive offence to be committed, the objective circumstance—the existence of actual proceeds of crime—must also exist. But this is *not* the objective element of the offence of conspiracy. The essential element of conspiracy is the existence of the agreement to put the intention of the conspirators into effect.

[109] It follows from all that has been said above that a conspiracy to commit a crime which cannot be carried out because an objective circumstance is not as the conspirators believed it to be is still capable of giving rise to criminal liability in Canada. Legal impossibility cannot be invoked as a defence to the charge.

IV. OTHER FORMS OF INCHOATE LIABILITY

Combining Inchoate Forms of Liability

R v Déry
Supreme Court of Canada
2006 SCC 53, [2006] 2 SCR 669

FISH J (McLachlin CJ and Binnie, LeBel, Deschamps, Abella, and Charron JJ concurring):
[1] Jacques Déry stands convicted of attempting to conspire to commit theft, and of attempting to conspire to unlawfully possess the proceeds.

[2] Never before has anyone been convicted in Canada of an attempt to conspire to commit a substantive offence of any sort. That should come as no surprise: Attempting

to conspire to commit a substantive offence has never previously been recognized as a crime under Canadian law.

[3] I would decline to do so now. ...

[5] December brings with it, in Canada and elsewhere, a holiday season widely and joyously celebrated by "raising a glass." Liquor merchants must frequently replenish their shelves to keep the glasses filled. In the Quebec City region, the Société des alcools du Québec ("SAQ") is forced by the increased demand to stock more of its products than its secure warehouses can contain. The inevitable overflow is stored temporarily in trailers parked outdoors at an SAQ compound.

[6] An unrelated investigation resulted in the interception of discussions between Mr. Déry, Daniel Savard and others, concerning the possibility of stealing this liquor stored outdoors. On the strength of the intercepted conversations, Messrs. Déry and Savard were both charged with conspiracy to commit theft and conspiracy to possess stolen goods.

[7] There was no evidence that either accused had taken any steps to carry out the proposed theft, and the trial judge was not persuaded that they had at any point agreed to steal or possess the liquor that was the object of their covetous musings: (2002), 7 C.R. (6th) 325. In the absence of a proven agreement, the judge quite properly felt bound to acquit the accused of the conspiracies charged. On each count, however, he convicted both co-accused of *attempting* to conspire, which he believed to be an included offence.

• • •

[30] To conflate counselling and attempt to conspire is to rely on semantics where principle fails. While it may well be true that to counsel another to conspire is, in the ordinary sense of the word, to "attempt" (or *try*) to form a conspiracy, not all efforts to conspire amount, in law, to counselling. Yet we are urged by the Crown in this case to recognize attempted conspiracy as an offence different from, and wider than, the established offence of counselling.

[31] In *R. v. Hamilton*, [2005] 2 S.C.R. 432, 2005 SCC 47, this Court held that "the *actus reus* for counselling is the *deliberate encouragement or active inducement of the commission of a criminal offence*" (para. 29 (emphasis in original)): see also *R. v. Sharpe*, [2001] 1 S.C.R. 45, 2001 SCC 2, at para. 57, *per* McLachlin C.J. This relatively high threshold for the *actus reus* of incitement is an essential safeguard. As Charron J. (dissenting, but not on this point) observed at para. 72, "[i]t is th[e] concern of potential overbreadth that informed this Court's adoption in *Sharpe* of a more restricted meaning of counselling." Charron J. noted as well that counselling an offence not committed is rarely prosecuted (para. 48).

• • •

[36] Recognition of attempted conspiracy as a crime might well capture cases of feigned agreement, but this sort of change in the law is best left to Parliament. Moreover, the evil targeted by criminalizing unilateral conspiracies will in any event normally be caught under our law by the offence of "counselling an offence not committed." That offence, to which I referred earlier, is set out in s. 464 of the *Criminal Code*:

> 464. Except where otherwise expressly provided by law, the following provisions apply in respect of persons who counsel other persons to commit offences, namely,

(a) every one who counsels another person to commit an indictable offence is, if the offence is not committed, guilty of an indictable offence and liable to the same punishment to which a person who attempts to commit that offence is liable; and

(b) every one who counsels another person to commit an offence punishable on summary conviction is, if the offence is not committed, guilty of an offence punishable on summary conviction.

[37] It seems to me as well that this would be an inappropriate occasion for this Court to recognize attempt to conspire as a crime for unilateral conspiracies, even if it were within our power and we were inclined on principle to do so. This is not a case with only one willing party. Nor was there *any* agreement, bogus *or* bona fide, for Mr. Déry to join. The appeal turns entirely on whether criminal liability attaches to fruitless discussions in contemplation of a substantive crime that is never committed, nor even attempted, by any of the parties to the discussions. I am satisfied that it does not.

· · ·

[47] Given that conspiracy is essentially a crime of intention, and "[c]riminal law should not patrol people's thoughts" (*Dynar*, at para. 169, *per* Major J.), it is difficult to reach further than the law of conspiracy already allows. Even if it were possible, it has never been the goal of the criminal law to catch all crime [TRANSLATION] "in the egg," as the Attorney General for Canada has put it in this case (factum, at para. 58). In this sense, conspiracies are criminalized when hatched. And they can only be hatched by agreement.

[48] This basic element of conspiracy—agreement—exposes the otherwise hidden criminal intentions of the parties to it. This demonstrates their commitment to a prohibited act. By contrast, the criminal law intervenes later in the progression from thought to deed where someone acts alone. Overt steps are then thought necessary to disclose and establish with sufficient certainty the criminal intention that is an essential element of the attempt to commit an offence.

[49] By its very nature, moreover, an agreement to commit a crime in concert with others enhances the risk of its commission. Early intervention through the criminalization of conspiracy is therefore both principled and practical.

[50] Likewise, the criminalization of attempt is warranted because its purpose is to prevent harm by punishing behaviour that demonstrates a substantial risk of harm. When applied to conspiracy, the justification for criminalizing attempt is lost, since an attempt to conspire amounts, at best, to a risk that a risk will materialize.

[51] Finally, though Mr. Déry discussed a crime hoping eventually to commit it with others, neither he nor they committed, or even agreed to commit, the crimes they had discussed. The criminal law does not punish bad thoughts of this sort that were abandoned before an agreement was reached, or an attempt made, to act upon them.

[52] For these reasons, I would allow the appeal, set aside Mr. Déry's convictions and order that acquittals be entered instead.

New Statutory Forms of Inchoate Liability

Various offences such as those relating to the financing of terrorism, participation in a terrorist group, or luring a child on a computer for the purpose of facilitating a sexual offence are defined as complete crimes in themselves but are similar to inchoate crimes such as attempts, conspiracy, or counselling because they criminalize preliminary acts. The next case deals with the issue of how the *actus reus* and *mens rea* requirements of complete offences based on inchoate liability should be interpreted.

R v Legare
Supreme Court of Canada
2009 SCC 56, [2009] 3 SCR 551

[The accused was charged under s 172.1(1)(c) (now s 172.1(1)(b)) with using a computer to lure a child for the purpose of facilitating a sexual offence including sexual interference and sexual touching with an underage child. The accused was told on the computer that the child was 13 years of age (she was actually 12 years of age) and subsequently phoned her "to talk dirty" and engaged in a sexual conversation before the child hung up. The accused did not admit that he intended to commit or facilitate a sexual assault with the girl and did not make any efforts to contact her further or meet with her. The trial judge acquitted on the basis that the accused's conduct had failed to facilitate the conduct of the underlying offences and the Crown had failed to prove that the accused intended to lure the girl for the purpose of one of the underlying offences. The Crown's appeal was allowed and the accused appealed to the Supreme Court.]

FISH J (Binnie, LeBel, Abella, Charron, Rothstein, and Cromwell JJ concurring):

. . .

[24] At the time of the appellant's trial, s. 172.1(1)(c) of the *Criminal Code* provided:

172.1(1) Every person commits an offence who, by means of a computer system within the meaning of subsection 342.1(2), communicates with

. . .

(c) a person who is, or who the accused believes is, under the age of fourteen years, for the purpose of facilitating the commission of an offence under section 151 [sexual interference] or 152 [invitation to touching], subsection 160(3) [bestiality] or 173(2) [exposure of genitals] or section 281 [abduction] with respect to that person. [s 172.1(1)(b) now has raised the relevant age to 16 years of age]

[25] It will immediately be seen that s. 172.1(1)(c) creates an incipient or "inchoate" offence, that is, a preparatory crime that captures otherwise legal conduct meant to culminate in the commission of a completed crime. It criminalizes conduct that *precedes* the commission of the sexual offences to which it refers, and even an attempt to commit them. Nor, indeed, must the offender meet or intend to meet the victim with a view to committing any of the specified secondary offences. This is in keeping with Parliament's objective to close the cyberspace door before the predator gets in to prey.

[28] Section 172.1(1) makes it a crime to communicate by computer with underage children or adolescents for the purpose of *facilitating* the commission of the offences mentioned in its constituent paragraphs. In this context, "facilitating" includes *helping to bring about* and *making easier or more probable*—for example, by "luring" or "grooming" young persons to commit or participate in the prohibited conduct; by reducing their

inhibitions; or by prurient discourse that exploits a young person's curiosity, immaturity or precocious sexuality.

[29] I hasten to add that sexually explicit language is not an essential element of the offences created by s. 172.1. Its focus is on the intention of the accused at the time of the communication by computer. Sexually explicit comments may suffice to establish the criminal purpose of the accused. But those who use their computers to lure children for sexual purposes often groom them online by first gaining their trust through conversations about their home life, their personal interests or other innocuous topics.

[30] As Hill J. explained in *R. v. Pengelley*, [2009] O.J. No. 1682 (QL) (S.C.J.), at para. 96:

> ... computer communications may serve to sexualize or groom or trick a child toward being receptive to a sexual encounter, to cultivate a relationship of trust, or to undertake a process of relinquishing inhibitions, all with a view to advancing a plan or desire to physical sexual exploitation of a young person.

[31] Accordingly, the content of the communication is not necessarily determinative: what matters is whether the evidence as a whole establishes beyond a reasonable doubt that the accused communicated by computer with an underage victim *for the purpose of facilitating* the commission of a specified secondary offence in respect of that victim.

[32] The italicized words in the preceding paragraph, drawn textually from 172.1(1)(c), make clear that the intention of the accused must be determined *subjectively*. I agree in this regard with the Attorney General of Ontario. As Doherty J.A. stated in *Alicandro*, at para. 31, the accused must be shown to have "engage[d] in the prohibited communication with the *specific intent* of facilitating the commission of one of the designated offences" with respect to the underage person who was the intended recipient of communication (emphasis added).

[33] This view is commanded not only by the plain meaning of s. 172.1(1)(c) but also by precedent regarding other "for the purpose" offences in the *Criminal Code*, and policy considerations governing preparatory offences of this kind. As Andrew Ashworth puts it:

> ... inchoate crimes are an extension of the criminal sanction, and the more remote an offence becomes from the actual infliction of harm, the higher the degree of fault necessary to justify criminalization.

(*Principles of Criminal Law* (6th ed. 2009) at p. 456)

[34] As mentioned earlier, this policy consideration is particularly relevant to s. 172.1 of the *Code*, which criminalizes preparatory conduct even more remote from the infliction of harm than other incipient or inchoate crimes, such as attempt and counselling or procuring the commission of an offence.

[35] The application of a subjective standard of fault is appropriate as well in light of the broad nature of the act component of s. 172.1. Requiring the Crown to prove that the accused communicated by computer with the specific intent mandated by the plain language of the provision helps to ensure that innocent communication will not be unintentionally captured by the *Code*.

[36] To sum up, then, I reiterate that s. 172.1(1)(c) comprises three elements: (1) an intentional communication by computer; (2) with a person whom the accused knows or believes to be under 14 years of age [Parliament now has raised this to 16 years of age]; (3) for the specific purpose of facilitating the commission of a specified secondary offence—

that is, abduction or one of the sexual offences mentioned in s. 172.1(1)(c)—with respect to the underage person.

[37] All three elements must, of course, be established by the Crown beyond a reasonable doubt.

[38] In determining whether the Crown has discharged its burden under s. 172.1, it is neither necessary nor particularly helpful for trial judges to recast every element of the offence in terms of its *actus reus*, or "act" component, and its *mens rea*, or requisite mental element. As in the case of attempt, s. 172.1 criminalizes otherwise lawful conduct when its specific purpose is to facilitate the commission of a specified secondary offence with respect to an underage person. Separately considered, neither the conduct itself nor the purpose alone is sufficient to establish guilt: It is not an offence under s. 172.1 *to communicate by computer with an underage person*, nor is it an offence under s. 172.1 to facilitate the commission of a specified secondary offence in respect of that person *without communicating by computer*.

[39] In this unusual context, determining whether each of the essential elements I have set out constitutes all or part of the *actus reus* or *mens rea* of s. 172.1(1)(c) is of no assistance in reaching the appropriate verdict on a charge under that provision. More specifically, forcibly compartmentalizing the underage requirement of s. 172.1(1)(c)—"a person who is, or who the accused believes is, under the age of fourteen years"—as either part of the *actus reus* or part of the *mens rea*, may well introduce an element of confusion in respect of both concepts.

[40] Is it part of the *actus reus* that the accused communicated with a person of *any age* whom the accused *believed to be* under 14? Is it part of the *mens rea* that the person was *in fact* under 14? I see no conceptual or practical advantage in attempting to resolve these questions. It seems to me preferable, in setting out the elements of s. 172.1, to adopt "language which accurately conveys the effect of the law without in itself imposing an unnecessary burden of translation and explanation": *Howard's Criminal Law* (5th ed. 1990), p. 11.

[41] I believe that the elements of the offence, as I have set them out, achieve that objective: They satisfy the principle of legality by affording the required degree of certainty, respecting the will of Parliament, and reflecting "the overall need to use the criminal law with restraint": see D. Stuart, *Canadian Criminal Law: A Treatise* (5th ed. 2007), p. 86.

[42] Finally, it is neither necessary nor necessarily sufficient for the impugned acts of the accused to be *objectively capable* of facilitating the commission of the specified secondary offence with respect to the underage person concerned. Accordingly, the content of the communication is not necessarily determinative: What matters, I repeat, is whether *the evidence as a whole* establishes beyond a reasonable doubt that the accused communicated by computer with an underage victim for the purpose of facilitating the commission of a specified secondary offence with respect to that victim.

[43] For all of these reasons, I would dismiss Mr. Legare's appeal.

[44] As mentioned at the outset, the trial judge, in acquitting Mr. Legare, adopted an unduly restrictive construction of s. 172.1(1)(c) and misapprehended the essential elements of the offence. Understandably, he therefore did not make the findings of fact necessary to warrant either an acquittal or a conviction on a proper understanding of the section.

[45] In these circumstances, I agree with the Court of Appeal that Mr. Legare's acquittal must be set aside and a new trial must be had.

In *R v Khawaja*, the Supreme Court of Canada considered the proper interpretation and constitutionality of inchoate offences established by Parliament in the wake of the September
11, 2001 terrorist attacks. *Khawaja* deals with the combination of different inchoate forms of
liability and raises important questions about the outer limits of criminal liability for the culpable creation of risk.

R v Khawaja

Supreme Court of Canada

2012 SCC 69, [2012] 3 SCR 555

McLACHLIN CJ (for the Court):

[1] The appellant, Mohammad Momin Khawaja, was convicted of five offences under
Part II.1 of the *Criminal Code*, R.S.C. 1985, c. C-46, the Terrorism section. He faces a life
sentence and a concurrent sentence of 24 years of imprisonment, with a 10-year period
of parole ineligibility.

. . .

II. *The Evidence*

[3] The facts underlying the offences were largely undisputed. Voluminous email
correspondence attested in graphic detail to the appellant's ideological commitment to
violent "jihad" and to his acts in Canada and elsewhere to further jihad-inspired terrorist
activities.

[4] While living with his siblings in Canada, the appellant became obsessed with
Osama Bin Laden and his cause. The appellant began communicating with other people
committed to violence in the name of Islam, some of whom he referred to as "the bros."
He entered into covert email correspondence with Junaid Babar, an American of Pakistani
descent who eventually pled guilty in New York City to five counts of providing material
support or resources to Al Qaeda. He also communicated extensively with Omar Khyam,
the leader of a terrorist cell based in London, England, who was convicted along with
several co-conspirators of a plot to bomb targets in the U.K. and elsewhere in Europe.

[5] The appellant repeatedly offered Khyam and Babar support. He gave Khyam
money for an explosives operation in the United Kingdom or elsewhere in Europe. He
gave Babar cash, supplies and SIM cards so that Babar could contact Khyam when transporting detonators to Europe. He provided funds to support Babar, Khyam and "the bros"
in their jihadist efforts. He designed a remote arming device for explosives that he referred
to as the "hifidigimonster," and offered to smuggle it into the U.K. and train the U.K. cell
on its use. He recruited a woman in Ottawa to facilitate transfers of money. He also offered
to procure night goggles for use by the group.

[6] The appellant travelled to Pakistan alone and with Khyam, and attended Babar's
small arms training camp. He made his parents' home in Pakistan available to the "bros."
He suggested members of the U.K. group travel to Canada for weapons training. He also
proposed to Khyam via email that a supporter of the Khyam group be sent to Israel on a
suicide mission.

[7] On March 29, 2004, the RCMP arrested the appellant and searched his house in Orleans, Ottawa. They seized the "hifidigimonster," electronic components and devices, parts suitable for constructing more remote arming devices, documents corroborating the assembly process for the device, instructional literature and tools, military calibre rifles and ammunition, other weapons, hard drives, $10,300 in one-hundred dollar bills, military books and jihad-related books. No blasting caps, other detonators or explosives components were discovered.

III. Judicial History

[8] By direct indictment, the appellant was charged with seven offences under the Terrorism section of the *Criminal Code*. The appellant brought a preliminary constitutional motion (allowed in part) and a motion for a directed verdict of acquittal (dismissed). He elected to be tried by judge alone, and was convicted on five counts and found guilty of two included offences.

A. The Pre-Trial Charter Challenge (2006), 214 C.C.C. (3d) 399

[9] Prior to trial, the appellant sought a declaration that several terrorism provisions of the *Criminal Code* ... are unconstitutional. The motion judge found that the impugned provisions are neither unconstitutionally vague nor overbroad.

[10] However, the motion judge held that s. 83.01(1)(b)(i)(A), which provides that a terrorist activity must be an act or omission committed in whole or in part "for a political, religious or ideological purpose, objective or cause" was a *prima facie* infringement of s. 2(a), (b) and (d) of the *Charter*. He found that the effect of this "motive clause" would be "to focus investigative and prosecutorial scrutiny on the political, religious and ideological beliefs, opinions and expressions of persons and groups," which in turn would produce a chilling effect on the expression of beliefs and opinions (para. 58). He found that the infringement could not be justified under s. 1 and accordingly severed the motive clause from s. 83.01(1).

B. The Trial (2008), 238 C.C.C. (3d) 114

[11] The trial proceeded on the basis that the motive clause was severed from the legislation. The trial judge found the appellant guilty of seven offences.

...

IV. The Legislation

[21] The *Anti-terrorism Act*, S.C. 2001, c. 41, part of which now forms Part II.1 of the *Criminal Code*, was passed in 2001, in the aftermath of the Al Qaeda attacks in the United States and Resolution 1373 of the United Nations Security Council, which called on member states to take steps to prevent and suppress terrorist activity (U.N. Doc. S/RES/1373). The purpose of the legislation is to provide a means by which terrorism may be prosecuted and prevented: *Application under s. 83.28 of the Criminal Code (Re)*, 2004 SCC 42, [2004] 2 S.C.R. 248.

[22] While the immediate impetus for the legislation may have been concern following the terrorist attacks of September 11, 2001, the legislation has a much broader history

and context. As the recitals to the U.N. Resolution make clear, these events were part of an unfolding and escalating international problem. Canada, which had experienced the Air India and Narita bombings, was no stranger to this problem. The legislation is not emergency legislation, but a permanent part of the criminal law of this country: *Application under s. 83.28 of the Criminal Code (Re)*, at para. 39.

[23] The appellant says that the definition section of the legislation, s. 83.01(1), offends *Charter* guarantees, notably freedom of religion and freedom of expression. ... [The section relevantly defines "terrorist activity" to mean an act, omission, conspiracy, attempt, or threat to cause one of the consequences listed in ss 83.01(1)(b)(ii)(A) to (E), if committed with the necessary mental state. However, conduct that falls within an exception for armed conduct conducted in accordance with international law is excluded.]

. . .

[25] Furthermore, the act or omission that causes one of the consequences enumerated in 83.01(1)(b)(ii)(A) to (E) only constitutes "terrorist activity" if it is accompanied by the requisite mental state. The act or omission must be done with the intention of causing one of the enumerated consequences. In addition, the act or omission must be done with the ulterior intention of intimidating the public or a segment of the public as regards its security, or to compel a person, a government or an organization—whether inside or outside of Canada—to do or refrain from doing any act (s. 83.01(1)(b)(i)(B)). Finally, the act or omission must be done in whole or in part for a political, religious or ideological purpose, objective or cause (s. 83.01(1)(b)(i)(A)).

[26] "Terrorist group" is defined as a person or group that has as one of its purposes or activities the facilitation or carrying out of any "terrorist activity," or a person or group identified in a regulation adopted under s. 83.05.

[27] Based on these definitions, the legislation goes on to create a number of offences, including:

- Providing or making available property or services for terrorist purposes (s. 83.03) (maximum term of imprisonment of 10 years);
- Participating in or contributing to the activity of a terrorist group (s. 83.18) (maximum term of imprisonment of 10 years);
- Facilitating a terrorist activity (s. 83.19) (maximum term of imprisonment of 14 years);
- Instructing people to carry out an activity for a terrorist group (s. 83.21) (liable to imprisonment for life).

[28] The counts on which the appellant was convicted variously engage all of these offences.

. . .

[33] The appellant challenges the constitutionality of the legislation only on one ground: that its chilling effect violates s. 2 of the *Charter*. The appellants in the companion appeals also allege a violation of s. 2 of the *Charter*, and additionally challenge the constitutionality of s. 83.18 for overbreadth pursuant to s. 7 of the *Charter*. [As a reminder, the concept of overbreadth was introduced in Chapter 1.]

. . .

(b) The Scope of the Law

[41] Section 83.18(1) criminalizes participation in or contributions to the activities of a terrorist group. It requires for conviction that the accused (a) knowingly (b) participate in or contribute to, (c) directly or indirectly, (d) any activity of a terrorist group, (e) for the purpose of enhancing the ability of any terrorist group to facilitate or carry out a terrorist activity. Subsection (2) specifies that, in order to secure a conviction, the Crown does not have to prove that (a) the terrorist group actually facilitated or carried out a terrorist activity, that (b) the accused's acts actually enhanced the ability of a terrorist group to do so, or that (c) the accused knew the specific nature of any terrorist activity facilitated or carried out by a terrorist group. As the Ontario Court of Appeal found in *United States of America v. Nadarajah (No. 1)*, 2010 ONCA 859, 109 O.R. (3d) 662:

> ... s. 83.18 applies to persons who, by their acts, contribute to or participate in what they know to be activities of what they know to be a terrorist group. In addition, those acts must be done for the specific purpose of enhancing the ability of that terrorist group to facilitate or carry out activity that falls within the definition of terrorist activity. [para. 28]

[42] The appellants argue that s. 83.18 is overbroad because it captures conduct that does not contribute materially to the creation of a risk of terrorism, such as direct and indirect participation in legitimate, innocent and charitable activities carried out by a terrorist group. They contend that, "[i]n the absence of some explicit disassociation from the group's terrorist ideology, participating in *any activity* of the group could be viewed as intending to enhance the group's abilities to carry out terrorist activities" (Nadarajah factum, at para. 35 (emphasis added)). Thus, innocent individuals, who may or may not sympathize with the cause of a terrorist group, could be convicted under s. 83.18 purely on the basis of attending a visibility-enhancing event held by the charitable arm of a group that also engages in terrorist activity. Professor Roach has opined that even lawyers and doctors who legitimately provide their professional services to a known terrorist could be convicted under s. 83.18: see K. Roach, "The New Terrorism Offences and the Criminal Law," in R. J. Daniels, P. Macklem and K. Roach, eds., *The Security of Freedom: Essays on Canada's Anti-Terrorism Bill* (2001), 151, at p. 161. According to the appellants, these scenarios demonstrate that the law is overbroad.

[43] The first step in assessing the validity of this argument is to interpret s. 83.18 to determine its true scope: *Ontario v. Canadian Pacific Ltd.*, [1995] 2 S.C.R. 1031, *per* Lamer C.J., at para. 10.

[44] The Terrorism section of the *Criminal Code*, like any statutory provision, must be interpreted with regard to its legislative purpose. That purpose is "to provide means by which terrorism may be prosecuted and prevented" (*Application under s. 83.28 of the Criminal Code (Re)*, at para. 39)—*not* to punish individuals for innocent, socially useful or casual acts which, absent any intent, indirectly contribute to a terrorist activity.

[45] This purpose commands a high *mens rea* threshold. To be convicted, an individual must not only participate in or contribute to a terrorist activity "*knowingly*," his or her actions must also be undertaken "*for the purpose*" of enhancing the abilities of a terrorist group to facilitate or carry out a terrorist activity. The use of the words "for the purpose of" in s. 83.18 may be interpreted as requiring a "higher subjective purpose of enhancing the ability of any terrorist group to carry out a terrorist activity": K. Roach, "Terrorism

Offences and the Charter: A Comment on R. v. Khawaja" (2007), 11 *Can. Crim. L.R.* 271, at p. 285.

[46] To have the *subjective* purpose of enhancing the ability of a terrorist group to facilitate or carry out a terrorist activity, the accused must *specifically intend* his actions to have this general effect. The specific nature of the terrorist activity, for example the death of a person from a bombing, need not be intended (s. 83.18(2)(c)); all that need be intended is that his action will enhance the ability of the terrorist group to carry out or facilitate a terrorist activity.

[47] The effect of this heightened *mens rea* is to exempt those who may unwittingly assist terrorists or who do so for a valid reason. Social and professional contact with terrorists—for example, such as occurs in normal interactions with friends and family members—will not, absent the specific intent to enhance the abilities of a terrorist group, permit a conviction under s. 83.18. The provision requires subjective fault, as opposed to mere negligent failure to take reasonable steps to avoid unwittingly assisting terrorists: see K. Roach, "Terrorism Offences and the Charter: A Comment on R. v. Khawaja," at p. 285. For example, a lawyer who represents a known terrorist may know that, if successful at trial, his client will thereafter pursue his contributions to terrorism. However, the lawyer could only be convicted under s. 83.18 if his intent was specifically to enable the client to pursue further terrorist activities, as opposed to simply affording his client a full defence at law.

[48] To convict under s. 83.18, the judge must be satisfied beyond a reasonable doubt that the accused intended to enhance the ability of a terrorist group to facilitate or carry out a terrorist activity. There may be direct evidence of this intention. Or the intention may be inferred from evidence of the knowledge of the accused and the nature of his actions.

[49] The appellants argue that, even if the scope of s. 83.18 is narrowed by the high *mens rea* requirement, it is still overbroad because it captures conduct that, while perhaps animated by the intent to enhance the abilities of a terrorist group, is essentially harmless. For example, a person who marches in a non-violent rally held by the charitable arm of a terrorist group, with the specific intention of lending credibility to the group and thereby enhancing the group's ability to carry out terrorist activities, is not necessarily contributing to terrorism in any meaningful way. Yet, on the basis of the plain meaning of s. 83.18, that person could be convicted for participating in terrorism.

[50] This argument relies on an incorrect interpretation of s. 83.18. The *actus reus* of s. 83.18 does not capture conduct that discloses, at most, a negligible risk of enhancing the abilities of a terrorist group to facilitate or carry out a terrorist activity. Although s. 83.18(1) punishes an individual who "participates in or contributes to ... *any activity* of a terrorist group," the context makes clear that Parliament did not intend for the provision to capture conduct that creates no risk or a negligible risk of harm. Indeed, the offence carries with it a sentence of up to 10 years of imprisonment and significant stigma. This provision is meant to criminalize conduct that presents a real risk for Canadian society.

[51] A purposive and contextual reading of the provision confines "participat[ion] in" and "contribut[ion] to" a terrorist activity to conduct that creates a risk of harm that rises beyond a *de minimis* threshold. While nearly every interaction with a terrorist group carries some risk of indirectly enhancing the abilities of the group, the scope of s. 83.18

excludes conduct that a reasonable person would not view as capable of materially enhancing the abilities of a terrorist group *to facilitate or carry out a terrorist activity*.

[52] The determination of whether a reasonable person would view conduct as capable of materially enhancing the abilities of a terrorist group to facilitate or carry out a terrorist activity hinges on the nature of the conduct and the relevant circumstances. For example, the conduct of a restaurant owner who cooks a single meal for a known terrorist is not of a nature to materially enhance the abilities of a terrorist group to facilitate or carry out a terrorist activity: K. E. Davis, "Cutting off the Flow of Funds to Terrorists: Whose Funds? Which Funds? Who Decides?," in *The Security of Freedom: Essays on Canada's Anti-Terrorism Bill*, 299, at p. 301. By contrast, giving flight lessons to a known terrorist is clearly conduct of a nature to materially enhance the abilities of a terrorist group to facilitate or carry out a terrorist activity: *House of Commons Debates*, Vol. 137, No. 95, 1st Sess., 37th Parl., October 16, 2001, at p. 6165 (Hon. Anne McLellan).

[53] I conclude that a purposive interpretation of the *actus reus* and *mens rea* requirements of s. 83.18 excludes convictions (i) for innocent or socially useful conduct that is undertaken absent any intent to enhance the abilities of a terrorist group to facilitate or carry out a terrorist activity, and (ii) for conduct that a reasonable person would not view as capable of materially enhancing the abilities of a terrorist group to facilitate or carry out a terrorist activity.

[54] Having determined that the scope of the law is narrower than was argued by the appellants, I turn to the second step of the analysis, the objective of the law.

(c) The Objective of the Law

[55] The parties agree that the objective of the terrorism provisions is to prosecute *and prevent* terrorism. The need to prosecute acts that support or assist terrorist activity that may never materialize into acts of terrorism flows from the great harm resulting from terrorism offences, the Crown contends. The appellants agree that it is legitimate for the state to prevent terrorist acts from taking place.

(d) Are the Impugned Provisions Broader Than Necessary or Is Their Impact Disproportionate?

[56] Finally, I must ask whether the impugned provisions are broader than necessary to prevent and prosecute terrorism, or have an impact that is grossly disproportionate to that objective.

[57] The appellants argue that, in relation to its objective, s. 83.18 is broader than necessary and has a grossly disproportionate impact because it criminalizes acts (1) which do not disclose a risk of harm, (2) which are not connected to a real or contemplated terrorist act, and (3) which are preliminary to the commission of an inchoate offence. The first two arguments are answered by the limited scope of s. 83.18. As we have seen, conviction under s. 83.18 entails (1) an *actus reus* that excludes conduct that a reasonable person would not view as capable of materially enhancing the abilities of a terrorist group to facilitate or carry out a terrorist activity, and (2) a high *mens rea* (specific intent to enhance the abilities of a terrorist group to facilitate or carry out a terrorist activity). The Crown must prove both these elements beyond a reasonable doubt. Conduct that meets

both these requirements discloses a non-negligible risk of harm and is sufficiently connected to real or contemplated terrorist activity.

[58] As stated above, the appellants' third argument is that the impact of s. 83.18 is grossly disproportionate to Parliament's objective of curbing terrorism because it criminalizes acts that are preliminary to the commission of an inchoate offence. The appellants agree that stopping a terrorist act before it takes place is a legitimate legislative objective. However, they argue that the existing crimes of conspiracy and attempt are sufficient to achieve this objective, and that it is unnecessary and disproportionate to reach back further and criminalize activity that is preliminary or ancillary to those preparatory acts.

[59] The appellants rely on this Court's statement in *R. v. Déry*, 2006 SCC 53, [2006] 2 S.C.R. 669, *per* Fish J., that criminal liability does not attach "to fruitless discussions in contemplation of a substantive crime that is never committed, nor even attempted, by any of the parties to the discussions" (para. 37). They argue that s. 83.18 goes even further and criminalizes "indirect and fruitless contributions to non-terrorist activities where the intention is to enhance the ability of a group to commit such preliminary acts as conspiring or counselling, even where no terrorist act is facilitated or carried out and the accused is unaware of the specific nature of the act contemplated" (Nadarajah factum, at para. 43).

[60] In my opinion, *Déry* does not assist the appellants. First, *Déry* was concerned with interpretation, not constitutional boundaries. Indeed, the reasons contemplate that Parliament could, if it wished, create an offence of attempted conspiracy: "Recognition of attempted conspiracy as a crime might well capture cases of feigned agreement, but this sort of change in the law is best left to Parliament" (para. 36).

[61] Second, the reason given in *Déry* for not punishing acts preceding the commission of an inchoate offence is that such acts would not be sufficiently proximate to a substantive offence and the harmful conduct that it seeks to address (see paras. 43-46). Here, there is no problem of remoteness from a substantive offence because Parliament has defined the substantive offence, not as a terrorist act, but as acting in ways that enhance the ability of a terrorist group to carry out a terrorist activity.

[62] I return to the central question: Is s. 83.18 broader than necessary or does it have a grossly disproportionate impact, considering that the state objective is the prevention and prosecution of terrorism? It is true that s. 83.18 captures a wide range of conduct. However, as we have seen, the scope of that conduct is reduced by the requirement of specific intent and the exclusion of conduct that a reasonable person would not view as capable of materially enhancing the abilities of a terrorist group to facilitate or carry out a terrorist activity. On the other side of the scale lies the objective of preventing the devastating harm that may result from terrorist activity. When the tailored reach of the section is weighed against the objective, it cannot be said that the selected means are broader than necessary or that the impact of the section is disproportionate.

[63] I add this. The breadth of the impugned provisions reflects Parliament's determination that "there is substantive harm inherent in all aspects of preparation for a terrorist act because of the great harm that flows from the completion of terrorist acts": *R. v. Ahmad* (2009), 257 C.C.C. (3d) 199 (Ont. S.C.J.), at para. 60. In the context of the present analysis, it is appropriate to exhibit due deference to this determination. The criminalization under s. 83.18 of a broad range of interactions that have the potential to—and are intended to—materially enhance the abilities of terrorist groups is not grossly disproportionate nor

overbroad in relation to the objective of prosecuting and, in particular, of preventing terrorism.

[64] For the foregoing reasons, I conclude that s. 83.18 does not violate s. 7 of the *Charter*.

[McLachlin CJ held that it had not been demonstrated in this case that the terrorism section breached s 2(b) of the Charter in purpose or effect, but left open the possibility that s 83.01(1)(b)(ii)(E) may in a future case be found to capture protected expressive activity.]

. . .

VII. *Conclusion*

[132] I would dismiss the appeal and affirm the convictions and the sentence imposed by the Court of Appeal.

Has the Supreme Court in *Khawaja* adequately responded to the dangers that a statutory inchoate offence such as s 83.18 would "make a terrorist out of nothing"? For arguments that British courts have not adequately responded to these dangers when interpreting even broader terrorism offences such as possession of an item which gives rise to a reasonable suspicion that it will be used for a terrorist purpose, see J Hodgson & V Tadros, "How to Make a Terrorist Out of Nothing" (2009) 72 Mod L Rev 984. Conversely, if the Supreme Court has cured legislative overbreadth by reading down the s 83.18 offence, has it sufficiently respected Parliament's intent to enact such a broad crime in an attempt to prevent terrorism?

ADDITIONAL READING

Colvin, E & S Anand. *Principles of Criminal Liability*, 3rd ed (Toronto: Carswell, 2007), ch 9.

Goode, MR. *Criminal Conspiracy in Canada* (Toronto: Carswell, 1975).

Kadish, SH. "The Criminal Law and the Luck of the Draw" (1994) 84 J Crim L & Criminology 679.

Manning, M & P Sankoff. *Manning, Mewett & Sankoff: Criminal Law*, 4th ed (Toronto: Lexis-Nexis, 2009) ch 9.

Meehan, E & JH Currie. *The Law of Criminal Attempt*, 2nd ed (Toronto: Carswell, 2000).

Roach, K. *Criminal Law*, 6th ed (Toronto: Irwin Law, 2015) ch 3.

Stewart, H. "The Centrality of the Act Requirement for Criminal Attempts" (2001) 51 UTLJ 399.

Stuart, D. *Canadian Criminal Law*, 7th ed (Toronto: Carswell, 2014) ch 10.

Corporate Liability

Late in 2003, the law concerning corporate liability under the *Criminal Code* was fundamentally changed by the statutory amendments found in ss 2, 22.1, and 22.2 of the *Criminal Code*. To understand these changes, it is necessary to understand the common law that existed before these amendments were passed. The first section of this chapter examines the common law concept of the directing minds whose fault could be attributed to the corporation on the basis of their authority to direct the corporation and, in particular, to set its policies. The second section of this chapter explores the new statutory regime and, in particular, how it has replaced the common law concept of "directing minds" with a new and broader statutory concept of "senior officer." It also examines how s 22.1 of the *Criminal Code* provides for organizational liability for criminal offences of negligence and how s 22.2 provides for organizational liability for criminal offences of subjective intent.

I. THE OLD COMMON LAW OF DIRECTING MINDS

R v Waterloo Mercury Sales Ltd
Alberta District Court
(1974), 18 CCC (2d) 248

LEGG DCJ: Waterloo Mercury Sales Ltd. is charged with two counts of fraud under s. 338(1) of the *Criminal Code*.

The accused corporation through its used-car sales manager, Walter Golinuwski, purchased some 26 automobiles in Ontario and shipped them to Alberta. After the vehicles were unloaded, but before being placed on the used-car sales lot, the odometers of some of these vehicles were turned back so that the odometer reading showed that the vehicle had been driven a substantially smaller number of miles than it had in fact been driven.

The vehicles which are the subject-matter of the two counts of fraud in the indictment were two of the vehicles purchased in Ontario on which the odometers were turned back.

The odometers were altered by a third party on the instructions of the used car sales manager, Golinuwski, and when the vehicles were offered for sale the odometer reading was incorrect. ...

The main issue in this trial is whether the accused corporation can be held criminally liable for the act of its used-car sales manager if such act is done within the scope of his authority.

In the case at bar the used-car sales manager, Golinuwski, was not an officer or director of the accused company. He operated two used car lots for the accused, which were situated close to, but did not form part of the main offices of the accused. His responsibilities were to buy used cars, clean them up, do minor reconditioning on them, fix the sales price, arrange advertising and promotion, demonstrate them to and makes sales to the public. In these duties he was assisted by a sales and other staff consisting of 12 people. He approved all sales made by the salesmen. ...

In my opinion, Golinuwski was not a lesser employee. I find that it was the policy of the accused corporation to delegate to him "the sole active and directing will" of the corporation in all matters relating to the used car operation of the company, and as such he was its directing mind and will. His actions and intent were those of the accused itself and his conduct renders the company criminally liable. ...

I am mindful of the fact that the findings I have arrived at may be a further extension of the criminal liability of a corporation. None the less, having regard to the facts of this particular case I am of the opinion that it is in line with the judgments of Ford J.A. in *R. v. Fane Robinson Ltd.*, [[1941] 2 WWR 235 (Alta CA)], and that of Jessup J. in *R. v. J.J. Beamish Construction Co. Ltd.*, [1967] 1 C.C.C. 301.

I accept the evidence of Mr. Purvis [the president of the company] that he had no personal knowledge of the circumstances which led to these charges being laid and that he had circulated written instructions to all segments of his company not to alter odometers on the vehicles. However, this is not, in my opinion, a defence in light of the findings I have made.

Waterloo Mercury Sales Ltd. is guilty on both counts in the indictment.

Accused convicted.

Canadian Dredge & Dock Co v The Queen
Supreme Court of Canada
[1985] 1 SCR 662

[Four corporations appealed their convictions for bid rigging after a 15-month trial. They argued that the managers in charge of the bids acted in fraud of the corporation, for their own benefit, contrary to corporate instructions and outside the scope of their authority.]

ESTEY J for the Court:
... The position of the corporation in criminal law must first be examined. Inasmuch as all criminal and *quasi*-criminal offences are creatures of statute the amenability of the corporation to prosecution necessarily depends in part upon the terminology employed in the statute. In recent years there has developed a system of classification which segregates the offences according to the degree of intent, if any, required to create culpability.

(a) Absolute Liability Offences

Where the Legislature by the clearest intendment establishes an offence where liability arises instantly upon the breach of the statutory prohibition, no particular state of mind is a prerequisite to guilt. Corporations and individual persons stand on the same footing in the face of such a statutory offence. It is a case of automatic primary responsibility. Accordingly, there is no need to establish a rule for corporate liability nor a *rationale* therefor. The corporation is treated as a natural person.

(b) Offences of Strict Liability

Where the terminology employed by the Legislature is such as to reveal an intent that guilt shall not be predicated upon the automatic breach of the statute but rather upon the establishment of the *actus reus*, subject to the defence of due diligence, an offence of strict liability arises: see *R. v. City of Sault Ste. Marie*, [1978] 2 S.C.R. 1299. As in the case of an absolute liability offence, it matters not whether the accused is corporate or unincorporate, because the liability is primary and arises in the accused according to the terms of the statute in the same way as in the case of absolute offences. It is not dependent upon the attribution to the accused of the misconduct of others. This is so when the statute, properly construed, shows a clear contemplation by the Legislature that a breach of the statute itself leads to guilt, subject to the limited defence above noted. In this category, the corporation and the natural defendant are in the same position. In both cases liability is not vicarious but primary.

(c) Offences Requiring Mens Rea

These are the traditional criminal offences for which an accused may be convicted only if the requisite *mens rea* is demonstrated by the prosecution. ...

The route which was taken in this country and in the United Kingdom is not that which has been followed by the federal courts of the United States. Criminal responsibility in the corporation has for many years, in those courts, been placed upon the basis of the doctrine of *respondeat superior*. The resultant vicarious liability seems to arise in the corporation out of the criminal acts of any employee, supervisory, menial or otherwise. The United States Supreme Court expounded this principle as far back as *New York Central and Hudson R. v. U.S.* (1909), 212 U.S. 481. Although the statute there before the court specifically imposed liability in the corporation for the acts of its employees (without limitation), the courts have construed the case as establishing vicarious criminal liability in a corporation for the wrongful acts of its employees of all grades and classes. The rule was restated by the Court of Appeal of the 8th Circuit in *Egan v. U.S.* (1943), 137 F. 2d 369 at p. 379, *per* Thomas J.:

> The test of corporate responsibility for the acts of its officers and agents, whether such acts be criminal or tortious, is whether the agent or officer in doing the thing complained of was engaged in "employing the corporate powers actually authorized" for the benefit of the corporation "while acting within the scope of his employment in the business of the principal."
> If the act was so done it will be imputed to the corporation whether covered by the agent or officer's instructions, whether contrary to his instructions, and whether lawful or unlawful. Such acts under such circumstances are not ultra vires even though unlawful. There is no

longer any distinction in essence between the civil and criminal liability of corporations, based upon the element of intent or wrongful purpose. Malfeasance of their agents is not ultra vires.

These principles have been restated as recently as the judgment in *U.S. v. Basic Construction et al.* (1983), 711 F. 2d 570 (5th C.C.A.).

The state courts have not as consistently pursued the course of vicarious liability of corporations in the criminal law. In *People v. Canadian Fur Trappers Corp.* (1928), 248 N.Y. 159, the New York Court of Appeals, Crane J., speaking for a court that included Chief Justice Cardozo, rejected vicarious liability as a basis for corporate criminal responsibility and seemed to adopt, at pp. 163 and 169, something akin to the identification theory. To the same effect is *State of Idaho v. Adjustment Department Credit Bureau Inc.* (1971), 483 P. 2d 687 at p. 691, where corporate liability was found only if:

> ... the commission of the offense was authorized, requested, commanded or performed (i) by the board of directors, or (ii) by an agent having responsibility for formation of corporate policy or (iii) by a "high managerial agent" having supervisory responsibility over the subject matter of the offense and acting within the scope of his employment in behalf of the corporation.

State of Louisiana v. Chapman Dodge Center Inc. (1983), 428 S. 2d 413 at pp. 419-20, is to the same general effect. For a position midway between the *Canadian Fur Trappers, supra,* and these cases, see *Commonwealth of Massachusetts v. Beneficial Finance Co., et al.* (1917), 275 N.E. 2d 33.

At the present time, therefore, the common law in the United States seems to be based, in the federal courts on the doctrine of vicarious liability, and in many of the state courts on something akin to the identification doctrine. Court decisions are not a complete guide to the state law on this matter, however, as some states have adopted the American Law Institute Model Penal Code, which at para. 2.07 attributes criminal liability to the corporation on much the same basis as did the court in *State of Idaho v. Adjustment Department Credit Bureau Inc., supra*. On the other hand, at least one state has by statute applied the doctrine of vicarious liability without a limitation as to the level of responsibility of the employee or agent: see State of Maine, Rev. Stats. Anns. 17-A, s. 60. ...

[The *Model Penal Code* provides:

> 2.07(1) A corporation may be convicted of the commission of an offense if: ...
>   (c) the commission of the offense was authorized, requested, commanded, performed or recklessly tolerated by the board of directors or by a high managerial agent acting in behalf of the corporation within the scope of his office or employment.

Section 2.07(4)(c) defines "high managerial agent" to mean an officer of a corporation, or any other agent of a corporation "having duties of such responsibility that his conduct may fairly be assumed to represent the policy of the corporation or association."]

In summary, therefore, the courts in this country can be said to this date to have declined generally to apply the principle of *respondeat superior* in the determination of corporate criminal responsibility. Criminal responsibility in our courts thus far has been achieved in the *mens rea* offences by the attribution of the corporation of the acts of its employees and agents on the more limited basis of the doctrine of the directing mind or identification. Corporate responsibility in both strict and absolute liability offences has been found to arise on the direct imposition of a primary duty in the corporation in the statute in question, as construed by the court. By what appears to be the same purely pragmatic reasoning, the courts of the United Kingdom find criminal liability in a corporation only by the attribution to it of the conduct of its employees and agents where those natural persons represent the core, mind and spirit of the corporation. The United States federal courts are inclined, as we have seen, to find criminal liability in the corporation by vicarious liability where any employee-agent commits, in the course of his employment, the criminal act.

The criticisms of the United States federal court doctrine are manifold. The net is flung too widely, it is said. Corporations are punished in instances where there is neither moral turpitude nor negligence. No public policy is served by punishing shareholders where the corporate governing body has been guilty of no unlawful act. The disparity between the treatment of the corporate employer and the natural employer is wide and wholly without a basis in justice or political science. The test as applied in the United States federal courts may be on the broad basis above indicated because so many of the federal statutory crimes are regulatory in nature: see Leigh, p. 267, footnote 134.

In the criminal law, a natural person is responsible only for those crimes in which he is the primary actor either actually or by express or implied authorization. There is no vicarious liability in the pure sense in the case of the natural person. That is to say that the doctrine of *respondeat superior* is unknown in the criminal law where the defendant is an individual. Lord Diplock, in *Tesco Supermarkets Ltd. v. Nattrass*, [1972] A.C. 153 at p. 199, stated:

> Save in cases of strict liability where a criminal statute, exceptionally, makes the doing of an act a crime irrespective of the state of mind in which it is done, criminal law regards a person as responsible for his own crimes only. It does not recognise the liability of a principal for the criminal acts of his agent: because it does not ascribe to him his agent's state of mind. *Qui peccat per alium peccat* per se is not a maxim of criminal law.

On the other hand, the corporate vehicle now occupies such a large portion of the industrial, commercial and sociological sectors that amenability of the corporation to our criminal law is as essential in the case of the corporation as in the case of the natural person.

Thus where the defendant is corporate the common law has become pragmatic, as we have seen, and a modified and limited "vicarious liability" through the identification doctrine has emerged. ...

The identity doctrine merges the board of directors, the managing director, the superintendent, the manager or anyone else delegated by the board of directors to whom is delegated the governing executive authority of the corporation, and the conduct of any of the merged entities is thereby attributed to the corporation. In [*R v St Lawrence Corp*, [1969] 2 OR 305 (CA)], and other authorities, a corporation may, by this means, have more than one directing mind. This must be particularly so in a country such as Canada where corporate operations are frequently geographically widespread. The transportation companies, for example, must of necessity operate by the delegation and subdelegation of authority from the corporate centre; by the division and subdivision of the corporate brain, and by decentralizing by delegation the guiding forces in the corporate undertaking. The application of the identification rule in *Tesco, supra*, may not accord with the realities of life in our country, however appropriate we may find to be the enunciation of the abstract principles of law there made. ...

The identification theory was inspired in the common law in order to find some pragmatic, acceptable middle ground which would see a corporation under the umbrella of the criminal law of the community but which would not saddle the corporation with the criminal wrongs of all of its employees and agents. If there were to be no outer limit on the reach of the doctrine, the common law would have established criminal corporate liability by the doctrine of *respondeat superior*. What then is the appropriate outer limit of the attribution of criminal conduct of a directing mind when he undertakes activities in fraud of the corporation or for his own benefit? ...

Were the charge in question a charge of fraud, there would clearly be no benefit to the corporation, and indeed the design of the dishonest employee was aimed squarely at reducing the financial stature of the employer. It can hardly be said with any reality that a person designing and executing such a scheme could be, while doing so, the directing mind and the *ego* of the company itself. That being so, no longer would we be faced with the logical conundrum that a person however dishonest cannot defraud himself. Once the *ego* is split into its original two parts that problem disappears. The employee would be guilty of fraud and the victim of that fraud would be the company. The victim would, in all logic, have a defence against a charge that it too had committed fraud in its own right. Were the criminal law otherwise, it would not provide protection of any interest in the community. Punishment of the corporation for such acts of its employee would not advantage society by advancing law and order. It is otherwise, however, where there is benefit to the corporation, in whole or in part, from the unlawful acts of its directing mind. ...

In my view, the outer limit of the delegation doctrine is reached and exceeded when the directing mind ceases completely to act, in fact or in substance, in the interests of the corporation. Where this entails fraudulent action, nothing is gained from speaking of fraud in whole or in part because fraud is fraud. What I take to be the distinction raised by the question is where all of the activities of the directing mind are directed against the interests of the corporation with a view to damaging that corporation, whether or not the result is beneficial economically to the directing mind, that may be said to be fraud on the corporation. Similarly, but not so importantly, a benefit to the directing mind in single transactions or in a minor part of the activities of the directing mind is in reality quite different from benefit in the sense that the directing mind intended that the corporation should not benefit from any of its activities in its undertaking. A benefit of course can, unlike fraud, be in whole or in part, but the better standard, in my view, is established when benefit is associated with fraud. The same test then applies. Where the directing mind conceives and designs a plan and then executes it whereby the corporation is intentionally defrauded, and when this is the substantial part of the regular activities of the directing mind in his office, then it is unrealistic in the extreme to consider that the manager is the directing mind of the corporation. His entire energies are, in such a case, directed to the destruction of the undertaking of the corporation. When he crosses that line he ceases to be the directing mind and the doctrine of identification ceases to operate. The same reasoning and terminology can be applied to the concept of benefits.

Where the criminal act is totally in fraud of the corporate employer and where the act is intended to and does result in benefit exclusively to the employee-manager, the employee-directing mind, from the outset of the design and execution of the criminal plan, ceases to be a directing mind of the corporation and consequently his acts could not be attributed to the corporation under the identification doctrine. This might be true as well on the American approach through *respondeat superior*. Whether this is so or not, in my view, the identification doctrine only operates where the Crown demonstrates that the action taken by the directing mind (a) was within the field of operation assigned to him; (b) was not totally in fraud of the corporation, and (c) was by design or result partly for the benefit of the company. ...

I therefore would answer both questions as they relate to the defences of "acting wholly or partly in fraud of the corporation," and "in whole or in part for the benefit of the directing mind," as follows:

1. On the evidence in these records, the respective directing minds of the appellants did not act wholly in fraud of their respective corporate employers.
2. Neither did the four directing minds act wholly for their own benefit in the sense that no benefit from their actions would accrue to the appellants, and in any event the record clearly reveals an intention on their part to benefit their respective corporations.
3. Express or implied instructions prohibiting the unlawful acts specifically, or unlawful conduct generally, are not a defence whether the corporate liability springs from authorization of the acts of an agent or the unlawful acts of a directing mind. In any case, only in the record relating to CD is there any evidence of any such prohibition. ...

I would therefore dismiss all four appeals.

Appeals dismissed.

R v Safety-Kleen Canada Inc
Ontario Court of Appeal
(1997), 114 CCC (3d) 214

[The corporate accused was convicted of knowingly giving false information to a provincial officer contrary to s 145 of the *Environmental Protection Act*, RSO 1980, c 141. It appealed on the basis that the individual driver who made the false statement was not the directing mind of the corporation.]

DOHERTY JA: ... This appeal concerns the liability of the appellant, a corporate employer, for the misconduct of Mr. Howard, its employee. The appeal from the conviction on count 2 involves a consideration of the scope of corporate responsibility for offences which require proof of a culpable state of mind. ...

Count 2 alleged that the appellant knowingly gave false information in a return to a provincial officer. Section 145 of the Act provided:

> 145. No person shall knowingly give false information in any application, return or statement made to the Minister, a provincial officer or any employee of the Ministry in respect of any matter under this Act or the regulations.

Assuming that the manifest was a return, it is clear that the offence was made out against Mr. Howard. The manifest was false and Mr. Howard knew it was false. In determining the appellant's liability it is necessary to begin by placing the offence created by s. 145 into one of the three categories identified in *R. v. Sault Ste. Marie (City)*, [1978] 2 S.C.R. 1299, 40 C.C.C. (2d) 353. The parties agree that this offence falls into the first category (*mens rea* offences) as it is an offence which requires proof of a culpable state of mind. Specifically, the prosecution had to prove that Mr. Howard knew the document was false.

Corporations can be convicted of crimes involving a culpable mental state. Absent a statutory basis for that liability, corporate liability for such crimes is determined by the application of the identification theory set down in *R. v. Canadian Dredge & Dock Co. Ltd.*, [1985] 1 S.C.R. 662, 19 C.C.C. (3d) 1, and developed in *"Rhône" (The) v. "Peter A.B. Widener" (The)*, [1993] 1 S.C.R. 497. In *Rhône*, Iacobucci J. succinctly summarized the inquiry demanded by the identification theory at pp. 520-21:

> ... the focus of [the] inquiry must be whether the impugned individual has been delegated the "governing executive authority" of the company within the scope of his or her authority. I interpret this to mean that one must determine whether the discretion conferred on an employee amounts to an express or implied delegation of executive authority to design and supervise the implementation of corporate policy rather than simply to carry out such policy. In other words, the Courts must consider who has been left with the decision-making power in a relevant sphere of corporate activity.

The inquiry described by Iacobucci J. is a fact-driven one which looks beyond titles and job descriptions to the reality of any given situation. Mr. Howard was a truck driver for the appellant. He was also the appellant's sole representative in a very large geographical area. He was responsible for collecting waste, completing necessary documentation, maintaining the appellant's property in the region, billing, and responding to calls from customers and regulators. When Mr. Howard was on holidays, the appellant did not do business in the region. Mr. Howard did not, however, have any managerial or supervisory function. He took no role in shaping any aspect of the appellant's corporate policies.

Unlike the judge at the first level of appeal, I do not read the trial judge's reasons as including a finding that Mr. Howard was a directing mind of the appellant for the relevant purpose. The trial judge clearly rejected the characterization of Mr. Howard as a "low level employee" and found that he had wide authority in his region. Beyond this, she made no finding. Rather, she based her conviction on this count on a finding that the company did not take all reasonable steps to avoid the event. In my view, since the offence alleged in count 2 requires proof of a culpable mental state, a finding of a lack of due diligence is irrelevant. The determinative question of whether Mr. Howard's actual authority was sufficient to justify attributing his culpable mind to the appellant was never addressed.

Consequently, no finding on the crucial question of whether Mr. Howard was the directing mind of the appellant for the relevant purpose exists.

There is no doubt that Mr. Howard had many responsibilities and was given wide discretion in the exercise of those responsibilities. It is equally clear that those, like Mr. Corcoran, who dealt with the appellant in the area, equated Mr. Howard with the appellant corporation. Neither of these facts establish the kind of governing executive authority which must exist before the identification theory will impose liability on the corporation. Mr. Howard had authority over matters arising out of the performance of the task he was employed to do. It was his job to collect and transport waste to its eventual destination in Breslau. His authority extended over all matters, like the preparation of necessary documentation, arising out of the performance of those functions. I find no evidence, however, that he had authority to devise or develop corporate policy or make corporate decisions which went beyond those arising out of the transfer and transportation of waste. In my opinion, Mr. Howard's position is much like that of the tugboat captain in The *Rhône, supra*. Both had extensive responsibilities and discretion, but neither had the power to design and supervise the implementation of corporate policy. The majority of the Supreme Court of Canada concluded that the captain was not a directing mind of his corporate employer. I reach the same conclusion with respect to Mr. Howard.

A NOTE ON VICARIOUS LIABILITY AND THE CHARTER

Vicarious liability occurs when the acts and fault of one person are attributed to another. Although widely used in tort law, it is disfavoured under the criminal law and required a clear statement by Parliament before the enactment of the Charter. The Saskatchewan Court of Appeal in *R v Burt* (1987), 38 CCC (3d) 299 at 311 held that "the principles of fundamental justice simply do not recognize the ascribing to one person of another's state of mind. Accordingly, where a statute purports to make one person vicariously liable for another's *mens rea* offence the statute may be said to offend … the principles of fundamental justice." Note, however, that a statute that applies only to corporations may be immune from challenge under s 7 of the Charter because corporations are not protected under s 7 as persons that enjoy the right to life, liberty, and security of the person and the right not to be deprived of those rights except in accordance with the principles of fundamental justice.

II. THE NEW STATUTORY PROVISIONS FOR ORGANIZATIONAL LIABILITY

Three key definitions are now contained in s 2 of the *Criminal Code*:

"organization" means

(a) a public body, body corporate, society, company, firm, partnership, trade union or municipality, or

(b) an association of persons that
(i) is created for a common purpose,
(ii) has an operational structure, and
(iii) holds itself out to the public as an association of persons;

"representative," in respect of an organization, means a director, partner, employee, member, agent or contractor of the organization;

"senior officer" means a representative who plays an important role in the establishment of an organization's policies or is responsible for managing an important aspect of the organization's activities and, in the case of a body corporate, includes a director, its chief executive officer and its chief financial officer.

Section 22.1 of the *Criminal Code* provides for organizational liability for negligence-based offences:

In respect of an offence that requires the prosecution to prove negligence, an organization is a party to the offence if
    (a) acting within the scope of their authority
        (i) one of its representatives is a party to the offence, or
        (ii) two or more of its representatives engage in conduct, whether by act or omission, such that, if it had been the conduct of only one representative, that representative would have been a party to the offence; and
    (b) the senior officer who is responsible for the aspect of the organization's activities that is relevant to the offence departs—or the senior officers, collectively, depart—markedly from the standard of care that, in the circumstances, could reasonably be expected to prevent a representative of the organization from being a party to the offence.

Section 22.2 of the *Criminal Code* provides for organizational liability for subjective intent offences:

In respect of an offence that requires the prosecution to prove fault—other than negligence—an organization is a party to the offence if, with the intent at least in part to benefit the organization, one of its senior officers
    (a) acting within the scope of their authority, is a party to the offence;
    (b) having the mental state required to be a party to the offence and acting within the scope of their authority, directs the work of other representatives of the organization so that they do the act or make the omission specified in the offence; or
    (c) knowing that a representative of the organization is or is about to be a party to the offence, does not take all reasonable measures to stop them from being a party to the offence.

Note that s 718.21 sets out sentencing principles for organizations and s 732.1(3.1) provides for probation orders against organizations.

The following article provides a preliminary overview and assessment of the new law concerning organizational liability.

T Archibald, K Jull & K Roach, "The Changed Face of Corporate Criminal Liability"
(2004) 48 Crim LQ 367

In the dying days of the last parliamentary session of 2003, Parliament enacted Bill C-45 amending the *Criminal Code* with respect to the liability of corporations and other organizations. The bill had all party approval. It was also supported by the families of 26 miners who died in the Westray mine explosion in 1992, a disaster that might have been prevented by corporate compliance with health and safety regulations. In that case, manslaughter charges were laid against two Westray managers, but were dropped after especially protracted legal proceedings. Bill C-45 was held out by the government as a response to Westray—a response that seems even more pressing after subsequent disasters such as the poisoning of water in Walkerton and the Enron scandal. The wide support for the bill was cited by the *Halifax Herald* as

> witness to the rightness of the cause. … Holding corporations responsible for their decisions may not be the kind of redress Westray family members had in mind when they began their journey for justice, but they can take comfort in the fact that the measure should be a strong deterrent to the recurrence of such a tragedy in workplaces across the nation. It is only too bad it took so long to bring justice to Westray families.

Bill C-45 constitutes a fundamental change, if not a revolution, in corporate criminal liability. It creates a new regime of criminal liability that applies not only to corporations, but unions, municipalities, partnerships and other associations of persons. It replaces the traditional legal concept of corporate liability based on the fault of the corporation's "directing mind(s)," the board of directors and those with the power to set corporate policy, with liability tied to the fault of all of the corporation's "senior officers." That definition includes all those employees, agents or contractors who play "an important role in the establishment of an organization's policies" or who have responsibility "for managing an important aspect of the organization's activities." It will no longer be necessary for prosecutors to prove fault in the boardrooms or at the highest levels of corporation: the fault of even middle managers may suffice. It also provides that the conduct of the organization's "representatives" will be attributed to the organization and defines a representative to include not only directors, employees and partners but also agents and contractors. In a word, Bill C-45 significantly expands the net of corporate and organizational liability.

In many ways, the expansion of the corporate liability is overdue. The legal concept of the "directing mind" within the corporate boardroom has become outdated by new forms of organic management. In addition, organizations should not escape responsibility for work that they contract out to those who are not their employees. The new sentencing provisions of Bill C-45 also allow a judge to place a corporation on probation and to take steps to repair harms that it has caused and to prevent similar harms in the future. It is also sensible that the new law sets a lower standard for corporate criminal liability based on crimes of negligence as opposed to crimes of subjective fault. To this extent, the law preserves important gradations of liability.

There are, however, some aspects of Bill C-45 that are more troubling. The new law blurs the traditional and important distinction between regulatory and criminal liability. A corporation could be found guilty of a subjective intent offence because its senior officers (including some managers) knew that a representative of a corporation was or was about to become a party to the offence, but did not take all reasonable measures to stop that representative—an employee, agent or contractor—from being a party to the offence. The distinction between criminal and regulatory liability is also blurred with respect to criminal offences based on negligence. To be sure, prosecutors who bring criminal charges based on negligence will still bear the onus of proving both the *actus reus* and fault beyond a reasonable doubt. The new law also acknowledges that the standard of negligence in criminal law requires proof of not simple negligence but of a marked departure from the reasonable standard of care. In contrast, regulatory offences will only require the prosecutor to prove the commission of the prohibited act or *actus reus* beyond a reasonable doubt, while requiring the corporation to establish due diligence on a balance of probabilities to escape liability. Although these differences are important in a court of law, they may not seem so significant in the wake of some tragedy.

Lawyers will likely advise corporate officers, including middle managers, that their explanations for tragedies may be used against the corporation for both regulatory or criminal charges. A criminal charge—even one based on negligence—may expose corporations and their shareholders to significant publicity and stigma. A manslaughter or criminal negligence charge against a corporation, let alone a murder or a fraud charge, will often be front page news. The expansion of corporate criminal liability in Bill C-45 is bound to make relations between corporations and regulatory investigators far more adversarial than at present.

Greater reliance on criminal liability might be worth it if the result was genuine deterrence and reparation for the harms caused. But there is some reason to doubt that this will be the case. Some corporations facing serious criminal charges may simply declare bankruptcy, ending the promise of Bill C-45 that the criminal law can be used to reform their practice and achieve some reparation for the victims. Moreover, there is reason to be concerned that the threat of criminal liability will lead those in regulated industries to more frequently invoke their right to silence and other *Charter* protections that are routinely available for those facing criminal changes, and less likely to apply to regulatory charges. Finally, the difficulties of securing criminal convictions even under the enhanced law should not be underestimated and the advantages of a regulatory prosecution which requires the corporation to establish due diligence should not be forgotten. The exact consequences of expanded criminal liability can only be determined by empirical research, but the blurring of criminal and regulatory liability should be carefully monitored. ...

II. The New Law of Expanded Organizational Criminal Liability

(1) Expanded Definition of "Organization"

One of the more important yet neglected changes in the new law is that it extends far beyond the corporate world to include all "organizations." An organization is now defined in s. 2 of the *Criminal Code* to include a "public body, body corporate, society, company, firm, partnership, trade union or municipality." An organization also includes less formal associations of persons that are "created for a common purpose, has an operational structure and hold itself out to the public as an association of persons." By this definition, some organized criminal gangs could be prosecuted under these provisions, and if convicted, fined and/or placed on probation. The intent appears to widen criminal liability beyond mere structure to include various types of collective organizations. In principle, this makes some sense. In the short term, it will require organizations, such as partnerships, to reconsider their executive structure and to acquire insurance coverage with respect to a much wider potential criminal liability.

The real effect of these changes, if implemented, will be felt in circles outside of the corporation (which was already subject to criminal charges under the common law of *Canadian Dredge*). Governmental institutions may be faced with criminal (and not just regulatory) prosecutions. Charitable organizations, or trade unions, may face criminal prosecutions. While it may have been previously possible under the common law to charge such organizations, the explicit reference to them in this legislation sends a green light to policing bodies and private complainants that they may now become potential targets.

(2) Expanded Definition of "Representative"

Under the new law, organizations are held responsible not only for the actions of their senior officers, but also of their "representatives." Representatives are defined broadly to include not only directors, partners, employees and members, but also agents or contractors. In principle, this approach also makes sense given that modern organizations frequently contract out work in order to achieve efficiencies. In some cases, the actions of agents or contractors might have been attributed to the corporation under the common law. Nevertheless, the clarity of the new statutory definition makes it more likely that organizations could be charged on the basis of actions taken on their behalf by "agents" or "contractors." This reality may require organizations to re-think issues such as insurance and the supervision of the activities of agents and contractors.

(3) New Definition of "Senior Officer"

The Department of Justice was critical of the doctrine that restricted the concept of directing mind to policy making functions at the highest level. The new law now requires the prosecution to prove only that those who controlled the operation of the organization were criminally liable, and not those who set policy in head office either on the board of directors or as senior executives. The linchpin to the new legislative framework is the concept of a "senior officer." It is the mind of the senior officer that will bind the corporation. "Senior officer" is now defined in s. 2 of the *Criminal Code* as follows:

> "Senior officer" means a representative who plays an important role in the establishment of the organization's policies *or* is responsible for managing an important aspect of the organization's activities and, in the case of a body corporate, includes a director, its chief executive officer and its chief financial officer.

The key distinction in the above definition is the disjunctive test that is established by the use of the word "or." A senior officer may play an important role in the framing of policies *or* is responsible for managing an important aspect of the organization's activities. This new test clearly overrules *The Rhone* [[1993] 1 SCR 497], as it widens the liability of the corporation beyond the boardroom to encompass activities that are operational in nature, at the managerial level. The corporation can be liable if senior managers either created policies or managed an important aspect of the organization's activities that resulted in violations of the law. The policy/operational distinction has been eliminated, as far as organizational liability is concerned.

As to the resolution of what an "important role" will mean, this will be the subject of intense litigation in the future. The test will require the court to inquire into the organizational structure of a particular defendant. It may require either inside testimony from a whistleblower or expert evidence with respect to comparative positions in other companies or industries.

It might be argued that the words "important role" are unconstitutionally vague under s. 7 of the Charter. A threshold problem with such an argument will be whether a corporation charged with a new offence even has standing to challenge a law that applies only to corporations that are not entitled to rights to life, liberty and security of the person under s. 7 of the Charter. [See *Irwin Toy Ltd v Quebec*, [1989] 1 SCR 927.] Although corporations have been able to defend criminal and even civil cases on the basis that the law might violate the right of natural persons, the definition of "senior officer" in s. 2 of the *Criminal Code* can only be applied in prosecutions of corporations that are not entitled to s. 7 rights of the Charter.

Some commentators have observed that "a legislature that wanted to insulate a law from section 7 review would thus have to make that law only applicable to corporations, something that is not commonly done." [See RJ Sharpe, K Swinton & K Roach, *The Canadian Charter of Rights and Freedoms*, 2nd ed (Toronto: Irwin Law, 2002) at 182.] The new definition of "senior officer" in Bill C-45 is one of those rare laws that applies only to corporations. Even if a corporation has standing to challenge the definition of "senior officer" as unduly vague, the jurisprudence has been characterized by judicial deference. In other words, courts will consider that vague statutory language such as "an important role" is subject to subsequent interpretation by the courts that will make its meaning more precise.

Although the definition of "senior officer" is undoubtedly broader than the old common law definition of "directing mind," the onus remains on the Crown to prove beyond a reasonable doubt that a senior officer had an "important role" either in establishing an organization's policies or managing an important aspect of its activities. Consistent with the principles of strict and purposive construction of the criminal law, courts may give the new concept a narrower reading in cases in which it is not fair and does not make sense to attribute the fault of an employee, low level manager, agent or contractor back to the corporation. The Crown's burden of proof, as well as the uncertainty as to the exact meaning of senior officer, highlights the continued advantage of a regulatory offence prosecution.

In regulatory offences, all the Crown must prove beyond a reasonable doubt is the commission of the prohibited act. The defence must show, as part of due diligence, that it designed and implemented systems to prevent the particular problem without the need to define either the corporation's directing mind or, now, its senior officer. ...

In the *Westray* example, the prosecution would be required to prove only that those who controlled the operation of the mine were criminally negligent. Again, this is logical. Why should the entire organization be excused from criminal liability (as is presently the case) because senior policy-makers were insulated from the negligence of operational managers? Modern corporate management no longer resembles the old pyramid, and the organization should not be exempt as a result of the evolution of corporate structures.

The impact of the new definition of "senior officer" varies between subjective intent offences and negligence offences, and as a result these require separate treatment in our analysis.

(4) Subjective Intent Offences

The case of *Canadian Dredge* dealt with the subjective intent offence of bid-rigging. This offence can be classified as a type of fraud. In Canada, charges against corporations for subjective intent offences are relatively rare. Post-Enron, it is perhaps easier to envisage a corporation being charged with such a crime. This scenario is reflected in the language used by the government in describing its reform initiative:

> The most obvious way for an organization to be criminally responsible is if the senior officer actually committed the crime for the direct benefit of the organization. For example, if the CEO fudges financial reports and records, leading others to provide funds to the organization, both the organization and the CEO will be guilty of fraud.
>
> However, senior officers may direct others to undertake such dishonest work. The Bill therefore makes it clear that the organization is guilty if the senior officer has the necessary intent, but subordinates carry out the actual physical act. For example, a senior officer may be benefiting the organization by instructing employees to deal in goods that are stolen. The senior officer may instruct employees to buy from the supplier offering the lowest price, knowing that the person who offers to sell the goods at the lowest price can only make such an offer because the goods are stolen. The employees themselves have no criminal intent but the senior officer and the organization could be found guilty.

The newly enacted s. 22.2 of the *Criminal Code* sets out three separate ways in which the organization can be found to have committed a crime requiring fault other than negligence:

> 22.2 In respect of an offence that requires the prosecution to prove fault—other than negligence—an organization is a party to the offence if, with the intent at least in part to benefit the organization, one of its senior officers
>
> (a) acting within the scope of their authority, is a party to the offence;
>
> (b) having the mental state required to be a party to the offence and acting within the scope of their authority, directs the work of other representatives of the organization so that they do the act or make the omission specified in the offences; or
>
> (c) knowing that a representative of the organization is or is about to be a party to the offence, does not take all reasonable measures to stop them from being a party to the offence.

The above definition preserves the common law to the extent that it allows the fault of a senior officer who is the directing mind and acting within the scope of his authority to be attributed to the organization. The evolution in the law is that senior officers who are not directing minds can also have their conduct attributed to the corporation. Section 22.2 requires however that the senior officers act "with intent at least in part to benefit the organization." This means that the fault of a senior officer who has absolutely no intent to benefit the organization will not be attributed to the organization even though his or her actions may have unintentionally benefited the organization. This language may be an important protection for organizations when senior officers act in a rogue fashion for their own gain and with no intent to even partially benefit the organization.

Crimes such as fraud or money laundering have high levels of stigma. It is for this reason that subjective intent is generally a requirement for crimes with high stigma. In the area of fraud, the Supreme Court of Canada [in *Zlatic v The Queen*, [1993] 2 SCR 29] has maintained the requirement of subjective awareness of the risk to others, although this principle does not require a subjective appreciation of each element:

Fraud by "other fraudulent means" does not require that the accused subjectively appreciate the dishonesty of his acts. The accused must knowingly, i.e. subjectively, undertake the conduct which constitutes the dishonest act, and must subjectively appreciate that the consequences of such conduct could be deprivation, in the sense of causing another to lose his pecuniary interest in certain property or in placing that interest at risk.

The government's legislation has spread the stigma of a conviction to the entire corporation, even if only one part of the corporation was at fault. This approach is consistent with the new organic corporate structures that have extended decision-making powers beyond the boardroom to diverse sectors. There is, however, something about the application of this approach to subjective criminal law intent offences that is troublesome. Subjective intent offences are more blameworthy and ought to be punished as such. The new law could dilute this notion.

Our Supreme Court has always restricted the notion of a corporation's mind to a policy-making function while appreciating that there could be more than one mind that exercises this function. The new provisions extend the corporation's mind to important aspects of the corporation's activities outside of the boardroom. (Recall that the definition of "senior officer" includes someone who is responsible for managing an important aspect of the organization's activities.) To extend the notion to management at the operational level intuitively seems better suited to crimes of criminal negligence than subjective intent crimes that require some element of "thinking." The corporate mind will now encompass policy and important operational decisions. The following law school exam example shows the difficulty with this doctrine when pushed to the extreme limits, particularly, where the crime is one of the most serious.

Suppose the captain of *The Rhone* is a malevolent person who dislikes the competition so much that he purposely decides to ram another boat with the intent of sinking it, and then decides to run over the stricken sailors who are in the water. If several sailors died, then the Captain could be properly charged with the subjective intent offence of murder. Under the old definition, the company that employed the captain could not be charged with murder, unless there was evidence that it was board policy to ram competitors' ships or harm their workers. Under the new definition, the company could conceivably be charged with murder, since the Captain would qualify as a "senior officer" who was responsible for managing an important aspect of the organization's activities and because his actions were committed with the "intent in part to benefit the organization." The company could become a party to the offence of murder, as the criminal act was done with intent in part to benefit the corporation.

What is troubling in this example is the stigma specifically related to the crime of murder, a subjective intent offence. The company's real fault lies in the domain of negligence in failing to perform the appropriate background checks on the captain (perhaps he has a criminal record for acts of violence). The legislation elevates corporate liability from negligence to the subjective crime of murder by virtue of the result. While this is not pure vicarious liability (as it only applies to senior officers), it borders on that principle. …

Section 22.2(b) makes the organization liable if the senior officer "having the mental state required to be party to the offence and acting within the scope of their authority, directs the work of other representatives of the organization so that they do the act or make the omission specified in the offence." The requirement that the senior officer has the mental state required under the parties provision of s. 21 of the *Criminal Code* will generally ensure some degree of subjective fault in relation to the crime. Section 21(2) does contemplate liability on the basis that the senior officer ought to have known that the commission of the offence would be a probable consequence of carrying out an unlawful purpose that he or she formed with some person. In such a case, a corporation could be convicted of a subjective fault offence in part on the basis of objective foresight of that particular offence by the senior officer. It should also be recalled that although the senior officer must be at fault under s. 22.2(b), the actual offence could be committed by any "representative" of the organization. That is a broad term encompassing not only all employees but also all agents and contractors of the organization.

Section 22.2(c) even more directly than 22.2(b) makes it possible for an organization to be convicted of a subjective fault offence in part because of a failure of its senior officer to act in a reasonable fashion. Section 22.2(c) is a curious combination of a *mens rea* standard of knowingly being aware that a representative is or is about to be party to the offence, with the objective standard that the corporation is at fault if the senior officer "does not take all reasonable measures to stop [the representatives] from being a party to the offence." The rationale for this preventative section is described by the Department of Justice as follows:

> Finally, an organization would be guilty of a crime if a senior officer knows employees are going to commit an offence but does not stop them because he wants the organization to benefit from the crime. Using the stolen goods example, the senior officer may become aware that an employee is going to get a kickback from the thieves for getting the organization to buy the stolen goods. The senior officer has done nothing to set up the transaction. But, if he does nothing to stop it because the organization will benefit from the lower price, the organization would be responsible.

As an intuitive sentiment, it makes sense that managers ought not to condone illegal conduct of their employees, and if they do, the corporation ought to be responsible. Yet the requirement to take remedial action, and the attachment of criminal liability for the omission to do so, is anomalous for a subjective fault offence. The result is that the corporation may be punished for a subjective fault offence in large part because its senior officer, knowing that a representative of the corporation is or is about to become a party to an offence, did not take all reasonable steps to prevent the offence.

In the case of *Wholesale Travel* [[1991] 3 SCR 154], the court upheld the provision placing the legal onus on the defendant to show that he took all reasonable precautions and exercised due diligence in the context of a regulatory offence. Bill C-45 does not shift the legal onus: the prosecution would still have to prove that the accused did not take all reasonable measures. A parallel can be drawn to recent legislation in the area of sexual assault requiring the accused to take reasonable steps, in the circumstances known to the accused at the time, to ascertain that the complainant was consenting. This legislation has been upheld as meeting minimum constitutional standards in the context that sexual assault is an offence requiring proof of subjective *mens rea*. The courts have pointed out in this context that the accused is not under an obligation to determine all relevant circumstances and is not required to have taken all reasonable steps. [See *R v Darrach* (1998), 122 CCC (3d) 225 (Ont CA), aff'd on other grounds [2000] 2 SCR 443.] The issue is what the accused actually knew, not what he or she ought to have known. In contrast, s. 22.2(c) requires senior officers not only to stop themselves, but also to take all reasonable measures to actively stop someone else from acting. The assumption seems to be that senior officers, including managers, will have enough legal knowledge and business acumen to recognize that conduct of lower level officials is criminal. There is a further assumption that they will have sufficient control over their employees, as well as contractors, to stop the conduct. The intent is to require senior officers and managers who know there is a problem in a mine or a problem with fraudulent records to do all that can reasonably be expected to stop the commission of offences. This is a laudable requirement, but one that has traditionally been placed on those charged with regulatory offences and required to prove that they exercised due diligence to prevent the commission of the prohibited act. In contrast, the "all reasonable steps" requirement of s. 22.2(c) applies to a wide range of fault offences, ranging from murder to fraud. In the end, the corporation could be convicted of the most serious offences because of a senior officer's failure to take all reasonable steps to stop or prevent an offence that he or she knows is being committed.

With respect to offences recognized by the courts to have sufficient stigma to require proof of subjective fault in relation to all elements of the prohibited act, there are parts of s. 22.2(b) and (c) that may violate ss. 7 and 11(d) of the Charter. As discussed, a corporation may not have standing to raise a s. 7 challenge given that s. 22.2 only applies to corporations. With respect to s. 11(d) of the Charter it could, however, be argued that the legislative substitution of an "all reasonable steps" requirement for subjective fault in relation to the commission of the prohibited act may violate the presumption of innocence. At the same time, the Crown can argue that the corporation will only be convicted of a subjective fault offence if one of its senior officers has subjective and guilty knowledge that a representative of the organization is or is about to be a party to the offence.

How will courts determine what senior officers should do to satisfy the new and onerous "all reasonable steps" requirement in s. 22.2(c)? Here the blurring of lines between regulatory offences and criminal offences of subjective fault becomes obvious. Courts will look to industry standards, risk management techniques and other factors that have traditionally been relevant to the determination of the due diligence defence. Many of the same factors and evidence of corporate conduct that determines the due diligence defence now will be relevant when the corporation is charged with a serious criminal offence of subjective fault.

(5) Negligence Offences

Section 22.1 of the *Criminal Code* holds organizations liable for crimes of negligence where the acts and omissions of its representatives, taken as a whole, constitute an offence and the responsible senior officer or manager departs "markedly from the standard of care that, in the circumstances, could reasonably be expected to prevent a representative of the organization from being a party to the offence." As with s. 22.2, this new section brings issues normally associated with the due diligence defence for regulatory offences, into the centre of the determination of the criminal liability of a corporation or other organization. The intent of s. 22.2 to extend corporate criminal liability is clear from the government's explanation of the section:

With respect to the physical element of the crime, Bill C-45 (proposed s. 22.1 of the *Criminal Code*) provides that an organization is responsible for the negligent acts or omissions of its representative. The Bill provides that the conduct of two or more representatives can be combined to constitute the offence. It is not therefore necessary that a single representative commit the entire act.

For example, in a factory, an employee who turned off three separate safety systems would probably be prosecuted for causing death by criminal negligence if employees were killed as a result of an accident that the safety systems would have prevented. The employee acted negligently. On the other hand, if three employees each turned off one of the safety systems each thinking that it was not a problem because the other two systems would still be in place, they would probably not be subject to criminal prosecution because each one alone might not have shown reckless disregard for the lives of other employees. However, the fact that the individual employees might escape prosecution should not mean that their employer necessarily would not be prosecuted. After all, the organization, through its three employees, turned off the three systems.

The legislation implements the cumulative concept by permitting collective action to ground corporate liability provided that senior officers have departed markedly from the standards reasonably expected to police and prevent such action.

Section 22.1 provides:

> 22.1 In respect of an offence that requires the prosecution to prove negligence, an organization is a party to the offence if:
>   (a) acting within the scope of their authority
>   (i) one of its representatives is a party to the offence, or
>   (ii) two or more of its representatives engage in conduct, whether by act or omission, such that, if it had been the conduct of only one representative, that representative would have been a party to the offence; and
>   (b) the senior officer who is responsible for the aspect of the organization's activities that is relevant to the offence departs—or the senior officers, collectively, depart—markedly from the standard of care that, in the circumstances, could reasonably be expected to prevent a representative of the organization from being a party to the offence.

As a first point, the cumulative or collective concept in s. 22.1(a)(ii) makes good sense in the context of negligence offences. It should not make a difference to corporate criminal liability if the conduct of one, two or ten representatives of the corporation must combine to produce the prohibited act. The heart of these offences relates to a failure of the organization as a whole to properly implement risk management systems to prevent negligence. The new definition recognizes the organic structure of modern corporations.

Some crimes, such as unlawful act manslaughter, have been interpreted by the Supreme Court of Canada as having stigma sufficient only to require the Crown to prove a marked departure from the norm. This standard nonetheless exceeds mere notions of negligence as found in the regulatory defence of due diligence. In fact, for true crimes, regardless of language employed in the Code that is suggestive of the standard of *mere* negligence, the application of the Charter forces these offences to be "read up" to require a marked departure from the norm. [See *R v Creighton*, [1993] 3 SCR 3.]

The wording that will be the subject of heated litigation is "could reasonably be expected to prevent." This wording could blur the line between the standard of due diligence in regulatory offences and the new criminal offences. The only difference would be the onus of proof. The Crown would still have the legal onus in the criminal case of proving beyond a reasonable doubt that the corporation departed from reasonable diligence. The practical result would likely be an evidentiary onus on the corporate accused to show that the violation could not have been reasonably prevented in light of industry standards.

In determining what could reasonably be expected to prevent the offence, there is a risk that hindsight bias will be a factor. In other words, what might have been done to prevent the commission of the offence may only emerge with the clarity of hindsight after the commission of the offence. At the same time, a finding that the senior officer did not do all that could reasonably have been expected to have prevented the offence will not be enough for liability under s. 22.1. The Crown will still have to prove beyond a reasonable doubt that the senior officer was criminally negligent in the form of a marked departure from the standard of care that could reasonably have been expected to have prevented the crime. Unlike a regulatory prosecution, the Crown will have to prove both the negligence fault elements of marked departure and breach of a reasonable standard of care beyond a reasonable doubt. Although there is a convergence, especially in evidential and practical terms, between criminal liability under s. 22.1 and regulatory liability, some legal distinctions remain.

A decade after they were enacted, there are still few cases applying the new corporate liability provisions. The following case involved a successful Crown appeal from a $250,000 fine of a corporation for four counts of criminal negligence causing death.

R v Metron Construction Corporation
Ontario Court of Appeal
2013 ONCA 541

PEPALL JA for the court:

[1] On Christmas Eve, 2009, three workers and a site supervisor employed by the respondent, Metron Construction Corporation, plunged to their deaths. Together with two others, they had boarded a swing stage that collapsed as it descended from the exterior of the fourteenth floor of a high-rise construction site. The respondent pleaded guilty to one count of criminal negligence causing death and was sentenced to a fine of $200,000. The Crown seeks leave to appeal this sentence on the grounds that it is manifestly unfit.

. . .

[3] The respondent is an Ontario company which carries on business in the construction industry. At the time of the accident, in addition to the site at which the incident underlying this appeal took place, it was working on three small to medium size construction projects in southern Ontario. Joel Swartz is the President and sole director of the respondent.

[4] In September of 2009, the respondent entered into an agreement to restore concrete balconies on two high-rise buildings located on Kipling Avenue in the City of Toronto.

The respondent retained a project manager who, on behalf of the respondent, hired Fayzullo Fazilov as site supervisor.

[5] The project was to be completed by November 30, 2009. Delays arose prior to its commencement and, in December, the appellant was offered a $50,000 bonus if the project were to be completed by the end of December, 2009.

· · ·

[14] Subsequent forensic examination of the swing stage revealed that a significant cause of the collapse was its defective design and inability to withstand the combined weight of the six men and their equipment. Moreover, had six lifelines been available, and had each of the workers been attached to a lifeline as required by both s. 141 of O. Reg. 213/91 and industry standards, the men would have survived. To the respondent's knowledge, at any given time all workers on a swing stage were hooked up to lifelines. The respondent did not know why, on December 24th, 2009, there was a departure from this practice.

[15] It was agreed by the parties that Fazilov had failed to take reasonable steps to prevent bodily harm and death by: (1) directing and or permitting six workers to work on the swing stage when he knew or should have known that it was unsafe to do so; (2) directing and/or permitting six workers to board the swing stage knowing that only two lifelines were available; and (3) permitting persons under the influence of a drug to work on the project.

[16] As a result of the acts and omissions of Fazilov, a "senior officer" within the meaning of s. 2 of the *Criminal Code*, the respondent pled guilty to criminal negligence causing death pursuant to s. 22.1(b), s. 217.1, and s. 219 of the *Code*.

· · ·

[54] In 1992, 26 miners were killed at the Westray coal mine in Nova Scotia after methane gas ignited. A public inquiry into the explosion was established with Justice K. Peter Richard serving as its Commissioner. In his report entitled "The Westray Story: a Predictable Path to Disaster" (November 1997 Province of Nova Scotia), Commissioner Richard concluded, at pp. vii-ix, that the loss of the miners was not the result of an isolated error but showed instead an operating philosophy that consistently prioritized economic expediency over concerns for workers' safety. At p. ix, he described the Westray explosion as "a story of incompetence, of mismanagement, of bureaucratic bungling, of deceit, of ruthlessness, of cover-up, of apathy, of expediency, and of cynical indifference." He placed responsibility, in part, on the owner/operator of the mine, Curragh Resources Inc.

[55] Ultimately a prosecution of two managers of the mine was abandoned.

[56] Bill C-45, *An Act to amend the Criminal Code (Criminal Liability of Organizations)*, 2nd Sess., 37th Parl., 2003 (assented to 7 November 2003), S.C. 2003, c. 21, flowed from the incidents described in the Report.

[57] Prior to the enactment of Bill C-45, corporate criminal liability was established through the actions or omissions and the state of mind of a directing mind of the corporation. A directing mind could cause the corporation to be criminally liable for his or her acts or omissions. At common law, a directing mind was defined as a person with:

> authority to design and supervise the implementation of corporate policy rather than simply to carry out such policy. In other words, the courts must consider who has been left with the decision making power in a relevant sphere of corporate activity: *Rhône (The) v. Peter A.B. Widener (The)*, [1993] 1 S.C.R. 497 at 521.

[58] This was known as the identification doctrine: *Canadian Dredge & Dock Co. v. The Queen*, [1985] 1 S.C.R. 662.

[59] Some authors suggested that this model failed to respond to the reality of the modern corporation where much of the policy-making is delegated throughout the corporation and responsibility is diffuse: see for example, James Gobert, "Corporate Criminality: Four Models of Fault" (1994), 14 Legal Studies 393 at pp. 395-6.

[60] The amendments embodied in Bill C-45 were intended to ameliorate this difficulty. The definition of "senior officer" in s. 2 of the *Code* served to broaden the scope of those whose conduct could establish the criminal liability of the organization.

· · ·

[79] The *Criminal Code* offence engaged in this appeal is criminal negligence causing death. It is one of the most serious offences in the *Code*. As stated by this court in *R. v. L.(J.)* (2006), 204 C.C.C. (3d) 324 at para. 14, the offence of criminal negligence causing death is "at the high end of a continuum of moral blameworthiness." A conviction for such an offence requires a marked and substantial departure from the conduct of a reasonably prudent person in the circumstances: *R. v. J.F.*, 3 S.C.R. 215, at para. 16 and *R. v. R.(M.)*, (2012) 275 C.C.C. (3d) 45, at para. 28.

[80] The seriousness of the offence of criminal negligence causing death is reflected in the maximum punishment for such an offence—life imprisonment for an individual: s. 220(b). If an offender is an organization, the quantum of the fine is unlimited: s. 735(1)(a). This contrasts significantly with the *OHSA* [*Occupational Health and Safety Act*] provisions.

[81] The presence of corporate criminal liability for criminal negligence in the *Criminal Code* is not intended to duplicate, replace, or interfere with provincial health and safety legislation. Rather, it is intended to provide additional deterrence for morally blameworthy conduct that amounts to a wanton and reckless disregard for the lives or safety of others: Minister of Justice, "Government Response to the Fifteenth Report of the Standing Committee on Justice and Human Rights," Sessional Paper No. 8512-372-178 (2002).

[82] In the United Kingdom, the *Corporate Manslaughter and Corporate Homicide Act, 2007* (UK), c. 19 broadened the scope for criminal liability for certain organizations. The sentencing guidelines promulgated by the Sentencing Guidelines Council recognized the greater moral blameworthiness that attaches to a conviction for corporate manslaughter, as the offence is named in the United Kingdom, and that fines must not only deter but must also be punitive: Sentencing Guidelines Council, *Corporate Manslaughter & Health and Safety Offences Causing Death, Definitive Guideline* (2010) ("UK Sentencing Guidelines"). Indeed, at s. 24, they provide:

> The offence of corporate manslaughter, because it requires a gross breach at the senior level, will ordinarily involve a level of seriousness significantly greater than a health and safety offence. The appropriate fine will seldom be less than £500,000 and may be measured in millions of pounds.

[83] While these guidelines are obviously inapplicable in Canada, they do provide a comparative approach to a comparable offence.

· · ·

[118] The respondent was convicted of a very serious offence. It is a different and more serious offence than those found under the *OHSA*. As mentioned, the site supervisor's role should not serve to diminish the gravity of the offence. The intent of Bill C-45 is to trigger responsibility by the corporation for the conduct and supervision of its representative.

[119] The criminal negligence of Fazilov, for which the respondent is criminally liable, was extreme. Three times as many workers were on the swing stage when it collapsed than was usual practice. In addition, three times as many workers were on the swing stage than there were lifelines available, and even then only one of the lifelines was properly engaged.

[120] Having regard to the nature and gravity of the offence, the victims, the principles set forth in s. 718 and the specific factors described in 718.2(1), I am of the view that a fine $750,000 is a fit fine in the circumstances.

ADDITIONAL READING

Archibald, T, K Jull & K Roach. "Corporate Criminal Liability: Myriad Complexity in the Scope of Senior Officer" (2013) 60 Crim LQ 386.

Archibald, TL, KE Jull & K Roach. *Regulatory and Corporate Liability: From Due Diligence to Risk Management* (Aurora, Ont: Canada Law Book, 2014) (loose-leaf).

Bittle, S. "Cracking Down on Corporate Crime? The Disappearance of Corporate Criminal Liability Legislation in Canada" (2013) 11:2 Pol'y & Pract in Health & Safety 45.

Bittle, S. *Still Dying for a Living* (Vancouver: University of British Columbia Press, 2012).

Colvin, E & S Anand. *Principles of Criminal Law*, 3rd ed (Toronto: Carswell, 2007) at 122-30.

MacPherson, DL. "Extending Corporate Criminal Liability" (2004) 30 Man LJ 253.

Roach, K. *Criminal Law*, 6th ed (Toronto: Irwin Law, 2015) ch 6.

Stuart, D. *Canadian Criminal Law*, 7th ed (Toronto: Carswell, 2014) at 751-65.

Stuart, D. "Punishing Corporate Criminals with Restraint" (1995) 6 Crim LF 219.

Wells, C. *Corporations and Criminal Responsibility*, 2nd ed (Oxford: Oxford University Press, 2001).

PART FOUR

The Special Part: Sexual Assault and Homicide

Sexual Assault

I. INTRODUCTION

Victimization surveys reveal that an alarming number of Canadians are (and will be) victims of sexual violence, and that these crimes disproportionately victimize women, children, and transgendered individuals. In the not too distant past, antiquated laws and rules of evidence, that in hindsight seem strikingly misogynistic, worsened the trauma occasioned by such crimes.

Today, offences relating to sexual violence are found primarily in part VIII of the *Criminal Code*, which deals with offences against the person. These crimes were substantially re-formed in 1983. The old offences of rape, attempted rape, sexual intercourse with the feeble-minded, and indecent assault were repealed and replaced by offences of sexual assault (s 271); sexual assault with a weapon, causing bodily harm, with threats, or with accomplices (s 272); and aggravated sexual assault (s 273). This part of the Code was also amended to reform other aspects of substantive law, procedure, and evidence in the prosecution of sex-ual offences. In particular, Parliament has attempted on several occasions to clarify the law relating to consent and mistaken belief in consent: see now ss 273.1 and 273.2. It has three times attempted to control the admissibility of evidence concerning a complainant's previ-ous sexual conduct (see now s 276), and it has enacted measures to regulate the extent to which a complainant's confidential records (medical, psychiatric, etc.) can be disclosed: see ss 278.1 through 278.9. In the following extract, Melanie Randall appraises these reforms and considers how well they have been translated into "the actual processing of crimes."

> **M Randall, "Sexual Assault Law, Credibility, and 'Ideal Victims':**
> **Consent, Resistance, and Victim Blaming"**
> (2010) 22 CJWL 397 at 398-99 (footnotes omitted)

The archetype of the ideal sexual assault victim, which has been expanded somewhat over the years in response to increased social and legal awareness of violence against women, nevertheless still functions to disqualify many complainants' accounts of their sexual assault experiences. To this extent, the "ideal victim" myth often works to undermine the credibility of those women who are seen to deviate too far from stereotypical notions of "authentic" victims, and from what are assumed to be "reasonable" victim responses. Credibility assessments remain absolutely pivotal in sexual assault trials. These assessments of credibility remain deeply influenced by myths and stereotypes surrounding "ideal," "real," or "genuine" victims of sexual assault.

Paradoxically, perhaps, I also argue that sexual assault law reform has, in some important ways, been overwhelmingly successful in the past few decades in Canada. In response to many years of intensive feminist legal scholarship and advocacy, revisions to the *Criminal Code* of Canada have addressed some of the major and traditional legal problems surrounding definitions and prosecutions of the crime of sexual assault. These *Criminal Code* amendments have also sought to excise legally embedded rape myths and to revise evidentiary rules to ensure fairer trials.

Positive amendments within the area of sexual assault law include, for example, the removal of spousal immunity for sexual assault, the development of statutory limits on examining a complainant's past sexual history, the redefinition of consent, and the invigorated legal requirement that an accused demonstrate having taken "reasonable steps" to obtain consent in order to have his "mistake" excused. These promising advances in sexual assault law mean that the law pertaining to the crime of sexual assault appears, on its surface at least, to have been cleansed of its most problematic excesses. In short, the criminal law of sexual assault in Canada looks pretty good, statutorily speaking.

Despite these successes in law reform, however, serious and troubling difficulties persist within the Canadian legal landscape, especially pertaining to the actual processing of crimes of sexual assault in the criminal justice system. Revisions to the *Criminal Code* notwithstanding, these difficulties have yet to be meaningfully remedied. Put differently, with regard to sexual assault in Canada, the law on the books and the law in action are two very different things—or, to engage a well-worn expression in relation to the law on sexual assault, "*plus ça change, plus c'est la même chose.*"

According to figures supplied by Statistics Canada, only 8 percent of adult women victimized by sexual assault in 2004 reported the crime to police. Holly Johnson reports that only 42 percent of cases reported to police result in charges being laid, and no more than 11 percent of cases result in sexual assault convictions. This attrition is what Randall has in mind when she points out the difference between sexual assault law on the books and the law in action: H Johnson, "Limits of a Criminal Justice Response: Trends in Police and Court Processing of Sexual Assault" in E Sheehy, ed, *Sexual Assault Law in Canada: Law, Legal Practice and Women's Activism* (Ottawa: University of Ottawa Press, 2012) 613. Another element of the law in action is how the trier of fact determines the facts, including the credibility of witnesses. This was discussed in Chapter 4 in relation to the trial process and the Donald Marshall Jr. wrongful conviction; but it also presents distinct issues in the context of sexual assault law involving credibility contests between largely female complainants and male accused.

At the core of the reformed approach to sexual assault is recognition that sexual violence is a serious form of assault and should be approached as such. On this view, sexual assault captures a range of harmful conduct that can extend from an unwanted kiss or touch to forcible intercourse with life-threatening violence. Escalating offences, starting with sexual assault and building to aggravated sexual assault, allow for more severe forms of sexual violence to be addressed directly.

Section II of this chapter offers a lengthy extract from the leading Supreme Court of Canada decision on sexual assault, *R v Ewanchuk*. *Ewanchuk* establishes the fundamental elements of sexual assault. Section III elaborates on the elements identified in *Ewanchuk*, containing several cases that define the *actus reus* of sexual assault, and particularly consider how sexual assault is distinguished from assault more generally and what constitutes valid consent to sexual activity. Section IV turns to the mental element of fault, and further considers what mental element will suffice in respect of absence of consent, and when an accused can claim a defence of mistaken belief in consent.

II. THE LEGAL ELEMENTS OF SEXUAL ASSAULT

The leading decision on the elements of sexual assault is *R v Ewanchuk*, [1999] 1 SCR 330. As you read this lengthy extract, pay attention to the *actus reus* and required mental elements. In particular, consider the manner in which consent has both *actus reus* and *mens rea* dimensions. The case also serves to illustrate, especially in the review and critique of the reasoning in the lower courts, that this area of the law is far from free of pernicious myths and stereotypes.

R v Ewanchuk
Supreme Court of Canada
[1999] 1 SCR 330

MAJOR J (Lamer CJ and Cory, Iacobucci, Bastarache, and Binnie JJ concurring):

[1] In the present appeal the accused was acquitted of sexual assault. The trial judge relied on the defence of implied consent. This was a mistake of law as no such defence is available in assault cases in Canada. This mistake of law is reviewable by appellate courts, and for the reasons that follow the appeal is allowed.

I. Facts

[2] The complainant was a 17-year-old woman living in the city of Edmonton. She met the accused respondent Ewanchuk on the afternoon of June 2, 1994, while walking through the parking lot of the Heritage Shopping Mall with her roommate. The accused, driving a red van towing a trailer, approached the two young women. He struck up a conversation with them. He related that he was in the custom wood-working business and explained that he displayed his work at retail booths in several shopping malls. He said that he was looking for staff to attend his displays, and asked whether the young women were looking for work. The complainant's friend answered that they were, at which point the accused asked to interview her friend privately. She declined, but spoke with the accused beside his van for some period of time about the sort of work he required, and eventually exchanged telephone numbers with the accused.

[3]   The following morning the accused telephoned the apartment where the complainant and her friend resided with their boyfriends. The complainant answered the phone. She told the accused that her friend was still asleep. When he learned this, the accused asked the complainant if she was interested in a job. She indicated that she was, and they met a short time later, again in the Heritage Mall parking lot. At the accused's suggestion, the interview took place in his van. In the words of the complainant, a "very business-like, polite" conversation took place. Some time later, the complainant asked if she could smoke a cigarette, and the accused suggested that they move outside since he was allergic to cigarette smoke. Once outside the van, he asked the complainant if she would like to see some of his work, which was kept inside the trailer attached to his van, and she indicated that she would.

[4]   The complainant entered the trailer, purposely leaving the door open behind her. The accused followed her in, and closed the door in a way which made the complainant think that he had locked it. There is no evidence whether the door was actually locked, but the complainant stated that she became frightened at this point. Once inside the trailer, the complainant and the accused sat down side-by-side on the floor of the trailer. They spoke and looked through a portfolio of his work. This lasted 10 to 15 minutes, after which the conversation turned to more personal matters.

[5]   During the time in the trailer the accused was quite tactile with the complainant, touching her hand, arms and shoulder as he spoke. At some point the accused said that he was feeling tense and asked the complainant to give him a massage. The complainant complied, massaging the accused's shoulders for a few minutes. After she stopped, he asked her to move in front of him so that he could massage her, which she did. The accused then massaged the complainant's shoulders and arms while they continued talking. During this mutual massaging the accused repeatedly told the complainant to relax, and that she should not be afraid. As the massage progressed, the accused attempted to initiate more intimate contact. The complainant stated that, "he started to try to massage around my stomach, and he brought his hands up around—or underneath my breasts, and he started to get quite close up there, so I used my elbows to push in between, and I said, No."

[6]   The accused stopped immediately, but shortly thereafter resumed non-sexual massaging, to which the complainant also said, "No." The accused again stopped, and said, "See, I'm a nice guy. It's okay."

[7]   The accused then asked the complainant to turn and face him. She did so, and he began massaging her feet. His touching progressed from her feet up to her inner thigh and pelvic area. The complainant did not want the accused to touch her in this way, but said nothing as she said she was afraid that any resistance would prompt the accused to become violent. Although the accused never used or threatened any force, the complainant testified that she did not want to "egg [him] on." As the contact progressed, the accused laid himself heavily on top of the complainant and began grinding his pelvic area against hers. The complainant testified that the accused asserted, "that he could get me so horny so that I would want it so bad, and he wouldn't give it to me because he had self-control."

[8]   The complainant did not move or reciprocate the contact. The accused asked her to put her hands across his back, but she did not; instead she lay "bone straight." After less than a minute of this the complainant asked the accused to stop. "I said, Just please stop. And so he stopped." The accused again told the complainant not to be afraid, and

asked her if she trusted that he wouldn't hurt her. In her words, the complainant said, "Yes, I trust that you won't hurt me." On the stand she stated that she was afraid throughout, and only responded to the accused in this way because she was fearful that a negative answer would provoke him to use force.

[9] After this brief exchange, the accused went to hug the complainant and, as he did so, he laid on top of her again, continuing the pelvic grinding. He also began moving his hands on the complainant's inner thigh, inside her shorts, for a short time. While still on top of her the accused began to fumble with his shorts and took out his penis. At this point the complainant again asked the accused to desist, saying, "No, stop."

[10] Again, the accused stopped immediately, got off the complainant, smiled at her and said something to the effect of, "It's okay. See, I'm a nice guy, I stopped." At this point the accused again hugged the complainant lightly before opening up his wallet and removing a $100 bill, which he gave to the complainant. She testified that the accused said that the $100 was for the massage and that he told her not to tell anyone about it. He made some reference to another female employee with whom he also had a very close and friendly relationship, and said that he hoped to get together with the complainant again.

[11] Shortly after the exchange of the money the complainant said that she had to go. The accused opened the door and the complainant stepped out. Some further conversation ensued outside the trailer before the complainant finally left and walked home. On her return home the complainant was emotionally distraught and contacted the police.

[12] At some point during the encounter the accused provided the complainant with a brochure describing his woodwork and gave her his name and address, which she wrote on the brochure. The investigating officer used this information to locate the accused at his home, where he was arrested. He was subsequently charged with sexual assault and tried before a judge sitting alone.

[13] The accused did not testify, leaving only the complainant's evidence as to what took place between them. The trial judge found her to be a credible witness and her version of events was not contradicted or disputed. In cross-examination the complainant testified that, although she was extremely afraid throughout the encounter, she had done everything possible to project a confident demeanour, in the belief that this would improve her chances of avoiding a violent assault. The following passage is illustrative of her evidence:

Q You didn't want to show any discomfort, right?

A No.

Q Okay. In fact, you wanted to project the picture that you were quite happy to be with him and everything was fine, right?

A Not that I was happy, but that I was comfortable.

Q Comfortable, all right. And relaxed?

A Yes.

Q And you did your best to do that, right?

A Yes.

[14] Later in cross-examination, counsel for the accused again asked the complainant about the image she sought to convey to the complainant by her behaviour:

Q And you wanted to make sure that he didn't sense any fear on your part, right?

A Yes.

II. Judicial History

A. Court of Queen's Bench

[15] The trial judge made a number of findings of fact in his oral judgement. He found that the complainant was a credible witness. He found as facts: that in her mind she had not consented to any of the sexual touching which took place; that she had been fearful throughout the encounter; that she didn't want the accused to know she was afraid; and that she had actively projected a relaxed and unafraid visage. He concluded that the failure of the complainant to communicate her fear, including her active efforts to the contrary, rendered her subjective feelings irrelevant.

[16] The trial judge then considered the question of whether the accused had raised the defence of honest but mistaken belief in consent, and concluded that he had not. The trial judge characterized the defence position as being a failure by the Crown to discharge its onus of proving "beyond a reasonable doubt that there was an absence of consent." That is, he took the defence to be asserting that the Crown had failed to prove one of the components of the *actus reus* of the offence. This led the trial judge to characterize the defence as one of "*implied consent*." In so doing he concluded that the complainant's conduct was such that it could be *objectively* construed as constituting consent to sexual touching of the type performed by the accused.

[17] The trial judge treated consent as a question of the complainant's behaviour in the encounter. As a result of that conclusion he found that the defence of honest but mistaken belief in consent had no application since the accused made no claims as to his mental state. On the totality of the evidence, provided solely by the Crown's witnesses, the trial judge concluded that the Crown had not proven the absence of consent beyond a reasonable doubt and acquitted the accused.

B. Alberta Court of Appeal (1998), 57 Alta. L.R. (3d) 235

[18] Each of the three justices of the Court of Appeal issued separate reasons. McClung and Foisy JJ.A. both dismissed the appeal on the basis that it was a fact-driven acquittal from which the Crown could not properly appeal. In addition, McClung J.A. concluded that the Crown had failed to prove the accused possessed the requisite criminal intent. He found that the Crown had failed to prove beyond a reasonable doubt that the accused had intended to commit an assault upon the complainant.

[19] Fraser C.J. dissented. She found that the trial judge erred in a number of ways. Specifically, she found that:

- The trial judge erred in his interpretation of the term "consent" as that term is applied to the offence of sexual assault.
- There is no defence of "implied consent," independent of the provisions of ss. 273.1 and 273.2 of the *Criminal Code*.

- It was an error to employ an objective test to determine whether a complainant's "consent" was induced by fear.
- The trial judge erred in the legal effect he ascribed:

    – to the complainant's silence when subjected to sexual contact by the respondent;
    – to the complainant's non-disclosure of her fear when subjected to sexual contact by the respondent;
    – to the complainant's expressed lack of agreement to sexual contact;
    – to the fact that there was no basis for a defence of "implied consent" or "consent by conduct";
    – to the fact that there was no consent to sexual activity.

- The defence of mistake of fact had no application to the issue of "consent" in this case.
- The trial judge erred when he failed to consider whether the respondent had been wilfully blind or reckless as to whether the complainant consented.

[20] Fraser C.J. held that the only defence available to the accused was that of honest but mistaken belief in consent, and concluded that this defence could not be sustained on the facts as found. Accordingly, she would have allowed the appeal and substituted a verdict of guilty.

III. Analysis

A. Appealable Questions of Law

[21] The majority of the Court of Appeal dismissed the appeal on the ground that the Crown raised no question of law but sought to overturn the trial judge's finding of fact that reasonable doubt existed as to the presence or absence of consent. If the trial judge misdirected himself as to the legal meaning or definition of consent, then his conclusion is one of law, and is reviewable. ...

[22] It properly falls to this Court to determine whether the trial judge erred in his understanding of consent in sexual assault, and to determine whether his conclusion that the defence of "implied consent" exists in Canadian law was correct.

B. The Components of Sexual Assault

[23] A conviction for sexual assault requires proof beyond reasonable doubt of two basic elements, that the accused committed the *actus reus* and that he had the necessary *mens rea*. The *actus reus* of assault is unwanted sexual touching. The *mens rea* is the intention to touch, knowing of, or being reckless of or wilfully blind to, a lack of consent, either by words or actions, from the person being touched.

(1) Actus Reus

[24] The crime of sexual assault is only indirectly defined in the *Criminal Code*, R.S.C. 1985, c. C-46. The offence is comprised of an assault within any one of the definitions in s. 265(1) of the *Code*, which is committed in circumstances of a sexual nature, such that the sexual integrity of the victim is violated: see *R. v. S.(P.L.)*, [1991] 1 S.C.R. 909. ... [Sections 265(1) and (2) were then reproduced.]

[25] The *actus reus* of sexual assault is established by the proof of three elements: (i) touching, (ii) the sexual nature of the contact, and (iii) the absence of consent. The first two of these elements are objective. It is sufficient for the Crown to prove that the accused's actions were voluntary. The sexual nature of the assault is determined objectively; the Crown need not prove that the accused had any *mens rea* with respect to the sexual nature of his or her behaviour: see *R. v. Litchfield*, [1993] 4 S.C.R. 333, and *R. v. Chase*, [1987] 2 S.C.R. 293.

[26] The absence of consent, however, is subjective and determined by reference to the complainant's subjective internal state of mind towards the touching, at the time it occurred: see *R. v. Jensen* (1996), 106 C.C.C. (3d) 430 (Ont. C.A.), at pp. 437-38, aff'd [1997] 1 S.C.R. 304, *R. v. Park*, [1995] 2 S.C.R. 836, at p. 850, *per* L'Heureux-Dubé J., and D. Stuart, *Canadian Criminal Law* (3rd ed. 1995), at p. 513.

[27] Confusion has arisen from time to time on the meaning of consent as an element of the *actus reus* of sexual assault. Some of this confusion has been caused by the word "consent" itself. A number of commentators have observed that the notion of consent connotes active behaviour: see, for example, N. Brett, "Sexual Offenses and Consent" (1998), 11 *Can. J. Law & Jur.* 69, at p. 73. While this may be true in the general use of the word, for the purposes of determining the absence of consent as an element of the *actus reus*, the actual state of mind of the complainant is determinative. At this point, the trier of fact is only concerned with the complainant's perspective. The approach is purely subjective.

[28] The rationale underlying the criminalization of assault explains this. Society is committed to protecting the personal integrity, both physical and psychological, of every individual. Having control over who touches one's body, and how, lies at the core of human dignity and autonomy. The inclusion of assault and sexual assault in the *Code* expresses society's determination to protect the security of the person from any non-consensual contact or threats of force. The common law has recognized for centuries that the individual's right to physical integrity is a fundamental principle, "every man's person being sacred, and no other having a right to meddle with it in any the slightest manner": see Blackstone's *Commentaries on the Laws of England* (4th ed. 1770), Book III, at p. 120. It follows that any intentional but unwanted touching is criminal.

[29] While the complainant's testimony is the only source of direct evidence as to her state of mind, credibility must still be assessed by the trial judge, or jury, in light of all the evidence. It is open to the accused to claim that the complainant's words and actions, before and during the incident, raise a reasonable doubt against her assertion that she, in her mind, did not want the sexual touching to take place. If, however, as occurred in this case, the trial judge believes the complainant that she subjectively did not consent, the Crown has discharged its obligation to prove the absence of consent.

[30] The complainant's statement that she did not consent is a matter of credibility to be weighed in light of all the evidence including any ambiguous conduct. The question at this stage is purely one of credibility, and whether the totality of the complainant's conduct is consistent with her claim of non-consent. The accused's perception of the complainant's state of mind is not relevant. That perception only arises when a defence of honest but mistaken belief in consent is raised in the *mens rea* stage of the inquiry.

(a) "Implied Consent"

[31] Counsel for the respondent submitted that the trier of fact may believe the complainant when she says she did not consent, but still acquit the accused on the basis that her conduct raised a reasonable doubt. Both he and the trial judge refer to this as "implied consent." It follows from the foregoing, however, that the trier of fact may only come to one of two conclusions: the complainant either consented or not. There is no third option. If the trier of fact accepts the complainant's testimony that she did not consent, no matter how strongly her conduct may contradict that claim, the absence of consent is established and the third component of the *actus reus* of sexual assault is proven. The doctrine of implied consent has been recognized in our common law jurisprudence in a variety of contexts but sexual assault is not one of them. There is no defence of implied consent to sexual assault in Canadian law.

(b) Application to the Present Case

[32] In this case, the trial judge accepted the evidence of the complainant that she did not consent. That being so, he then misdirected himself when he considered the actions of the complainant, and not her subjective mental state, in determining the question of consent. As a result, he disregarded his previous finding that all the accused's sexual touching was unwanted. Instead he treated what he perceived as her ambiguous conduct as a failure by the Crown to prove the absence of consent.

[33] As previously mentioned, the trial judge accepted the complainant's testimony that she did not want the accused to touch her, but then treated her conduct as raising a reasonable doubt about consent, described by him as "implied consent." This conclusion was an error. ...

[34] The finding that the complainant did not want or consent to the sexual touching cannot co-exist with a finding that reasonable doubt exists on the question of consent. The trial judge's acceptance of the complainant's testimony regarding her own state of mind was the end of the matter on this point.

[35] This error was compounded somewhat by the trial judge's holding that the complainant's subjective and self-contained fear would not have changed his mind as to whether she consented. Although he needn't have considered this question, having already found that she did not in fact consent, any residual doubt raised by her ambiguous conduct was accounted for by what he accepted as an honest and pervasive fear held by the complainant.

(c) Effect of the Complainant's Fear

[36] To be legally effective, consent must be freely given. Therefore, even if the complainant consented, or her conduct raises a reasonable doubt about her non-consent, circumstances may arise which call into question what factors prompted her apparent consent. The *Code* defines a series of conditions under which the law will deem an absence of consent in cases of assault, notwithstanding the complainant's ostensible consent or participation. As enumerated in s. 265(3), these include submission by reason of force, fear, threats, fraud or the exercise of authority, and codify the longstanding common law rule that consent given under fear or duress is ineffective: see G. Williams, *Textbook of Criminal Law* (2nd ed. 1983), at pp. 551-61. ... [Section 265(3) was then reproduced.]

[37] The words of Fish J.A. in [*St-Laurent c Québec (Juge de Cour du Québec)* (1993), [1994] RJQ 69 (Que CA)], at p. 82, aptly describe the concern which the trier of fact must bear in mind when evaluating the actions of a complainant who claims to have been under fear, fraud or duress:

> "Consent" is ... stripped of its defining characteristics when it is applied to the submission, non-resistance, non-objection, or even the apparent agreement, of a deceived, unconscious or compelled will.

[38] In these instances the law is interested in a complainant's reasons for choosing to participate in, or ostensibly consent to, the touching in question. In practice, this translates into an examination of the choice the complainant believed she faced. The courts' concern is whether she *freely* made up her mind about the conduct in question. The relevant section of the *Code* is s. 265(3)(b), which states that there is no consent as a matter of law where the complainant believed that she was choosing between permitting herself to be touched sexually or risking being subject to the application of force.

[39] The question is not whether the complainant would have preferred not to engage in the sexual activity, but whether she believed herself to have only two choices: to comply or to be harmed. If a complainant agrees to sexual activity solely because she honestly believes that she will otherwise suffer physical violence, the law deems an absence of consent, and the third component of the *actus reus* of sexual assault is established. The trier of fact has to find that the complainant did not want to be touched sexually and made her decision to permit or participate in sexual activity as a result of an honestly held fear. The complainant's fear need not be reasonable, nor must it be communicated to the accused in order for consent to be vitiated. While the plausibility of the alleged fear, and any overt expressions of it, are obviously relevant to assessing the credibility of the complainant's claim that she consented out of fear, the approach is subjective.

[40] Section 265(3) identifies an additional set of circumstances in which the accused's conduct will be culpable. The trial judge only has to consult s. 265(3) in those cases where the complainant has actually chosen to participate in sexual activity, or her ambiguous conduct or submission has given rise to doubt as to the absence of consent. If, as in this case, the complainant's testimony establishes the absence of consent beyond a reasonable doubt, the *actus reus* analysis is complete, and the trial judge should have turned his attention to the accused's perception of the encounter and the question of whether the accused possessed the requisite *mens rea*.

(2) Mens Rea

[41] Sexual assault is a crime of general intent. Therefore, the Crown need only prove that the accused intended to touch the complainant in order to satisfy the basic *mens rea* requirement. See *R. c. Daviault*, [1994] 3 S.C.R. 63.

[42] However, since sexual assault only becomes a crime in the absence of the complainant's consent, the common law recognizes a defence of mistake of fact which removes culpability for those who honestly but mistakenly believed that they had consent to touch the complainant. To do otherwise would result in the injustice of convicting individuals who are morally innocent: see *R. v. Creighton*, [1993] 3 S.C.R. 3. As such, the *mens rea* of sexual assault contains two elements: intention to touch and knowing of, or being reckless

of or wilfully blind to, a lack of consent on the part of the person touched. See *Park, supra*, at para. 39.

[43] The accused may challenge the Crown's evidence of *mens rea* by asserting an honest but mistaken belief in consent. The nature of this defence was described in *R. v. Pappajohn*, [1980] 2 S.C.R. 120, at p. 148, by Dickson J. (as he then was) (dissenting in the result):

> Mistake is a defence ... where it prevents an accused from having the *mens rea* which the law requires for the very crime with which he is charged. Mistake of fact is more accurately seen as a negation of guilty intention than as the affirmation of a positive defence. It avails an accused who acts innocently, pursuant to a flawed perception of the facts, and nonetheless commits the *actus reus* of an offence. Mistake is a defence though, in the sense that it is raised as an issue by an accused. The Crown is rarely possessed of knowledge of the subjective factors which may have caused an accused to entertain a belief in a fallacious set of facts.

[44] The defence of mistake is simply a denial of *mens rea*. It does not impose any burden of proof upon the accused (see *R. v. Robertson*, [1987] 1 S.C.R. 918, at p. 936) and it is not necessary for the accused to testify in order to raise the issue. Support for the defence may stem from any of the evidence before the court, including, the Crown's case-in-chief and the testimony of the complainant. However, as a practical matter, this defence will usually arise in the evidence called by the accused.

(a) Meaning of "Consent" in the Context of an Honest but Mistaken Belief in Consent

[45] As with the *actus reus* of the offence, consent is an integral component of the *mens rea*, only this time it is considered from the perspective of the accused. Speaking of the *mens rea* of sexual assault in *Park, supra*, at para. 30, L'Heureux-Dubé J. (in her concurring reasons) stated that:

> ... the *mens rea* of sexual assault is not only satisfied when it is shown that the accused knew that the complainant was essentially saying "no," but is also satisfied when it is shown that the accused knew that the complainant was essentially not saying "yes."

[46] In order to cloak the accused's actions in moral innocence, the evidence must show that he believed that the complainant *communicated consent to engage in the sexual activity in question*. A belief by the accused that the complainant, in her own mind wanted him to touch her but did not express that desire, is not a defence. The accused's speculation as to what was going on in the complainant's mind provides no defence.

[47] For the purposes of the *mens rea* analysis, the question is whether the accused believed that he had obtained consent. What matters is whether the accused believed that the complainant effectively said "yes" through her words and/or actions. The statutory definition added to the *Code* by Parliament in 1992 is consistent with the common law:

> 273.1(1) Subject to subsection (2) and subsection 265(3), "consent" means, for the purposes of sections 271, 272 and 273, the voluntary agreement of the complainant to engage in the sexual activity in question.

[48] There is a difference in the concept of "consent" as it relates to the state of mind of the complainant *vis-à-vis* the *actus reus* of the offence and the state of mind of the accused in respect of the *mens rea*. For the purposes of the *actus reus*, "consent" means that the complainant in her mind wanted the sexual touching to take place.

[49] In the context of *mens rea*—specifically for the purposes of the honest but mistaken belief in consent—"consent" means that the complainant had affirmatively communicated by words or conduct her agreement to engage in sexual activity with the accused. This distinction should always be borne in mind and the two parts of the analysis kept separate.

(b) Limits on Honest but Mistaken Belief in Consent

[50] Not all beliefs upon which an accused might rely will exculpate him. Consent in relation to the *mens rea* of the accused is limited by both the common law and the provisions of ss. 273.1(2) and 273.2 of the *Code*. ... [These sections are then reproduced.]

[51] For instance, a belief that silence, passivity or ambiguous conduct constitutes consent is a mistake of law, and provides no defence: see *R. v. M.(M.L.)*, [1994] 2 S.C.R. 3. Similarly, an accused cannot rely upon his purported belief that the complainant's expressed lack of agreement to sexual touching in fact constituted an invitation to more persistent or aggressive contact. An accused cannot say that he thought "no meant yes." As Fraser C.J. stated at p. 272 of her dissenting reasons below:

> One "No" will do to put the other person on notice that there is then a problem with "consent." *Once a woman says "No" during the course of sexual activity, the person intent on continued sexual activity with her must then obtain a clear and unequivocal "Yes" before he again touches her in a sexual manner.* [Emphasis in original.]

I take the reasons of Fraser C.J. to mean that an unequivocal "yes" may be given by either the spoken word or by conduct.

[52] Common sense should dictate that, once the complainant has expressed her unwillingness to engage in sexual contact, the accused should make certain that she has truly changed her mind before proceeding with further intimacies. The accused cannot rely on the mere lapse of time or the complainant's silence or equivocal conduct to indicate that there has been a change of heart and that consent now exists, nor can he engage in further sexual touching to "test the waters." Continuing sexual contact after someone has said "No" is, at a minimum, reckless conduct which is not excusable. In *R. v. Esau*, [1997] 2 S.C.R. 777, at para. 79, the Court stated:

> An accused who, due to wilful blindness or recklessness, believes that a complainant ... in fact consented to the sexual activity at issue is precluded from relying on a defence of honest but mistaken belief in consent, a fact that Parliament has codified: *Criminal Code*, s. 273.2(a)(ii).

(c) Application to the Facts

[53] In this appeal the accused does not submit that the complainant's clearly articulated "No's" were ambiguous or carried some other meaning. In fact, the accused places great reliance on his having stopped immediately each time the complainant said "no" in

order to show that he had no intention to force himself upon her. He therefore knew that the complainant was not consenting on four separate occasions during their encounter.

[54] The question which the trial judge ought to have considered was whether anything occurred between the communication of non-consent and the subsequent sexual touching which the accused could honestly have believed constituted consent.

[55] The trial judge explicitly chose not to consider whether the accused had the defence of honest but mistaken belief in consent, and concluded that the defence was probably not available unless the accused testified. This conclusion ignores the right of the accused to have this defence considered solely on the Crown's case. The trial judge paid only passing interest to this defence undoubtedly because he had concluded that the defence of implied consent exonerated the accused. The accused is entitled to have all available defences founded on a proper basis considered by the court, whether he raises them or not: see *R. v. Bulmer*, [1987] 1 S.C.R. 782, at p. 789.

[56] In *Esau, supra*, at para. 15, the Court stated that, "before a court should consider honest but mistaken belief or instruct a jury on it there must be some plausible evidence in support so as to give an air of reality to the defence." See also *R. v. Osolin*, [1993] 4 S.C.R. 595. All that is required is for the accused to adduce some evidence, or refer to evidence already adduced, upon which a properly instructed trier of fact could form a reasonable doubt as to his *mens rea*: see *Osolin, supra*, at pp. 653-54, and p. 687.

[57] The analysis in this appeal makes no attempt to weigh the evidence. At this point we are concerned only with the facial plausibility of the defence of honest but mistaken belief and should avoid the risk of turning the air of reality test into a substantive evaluation of the merits of the defence.

[58] As the accused did not testify, the only evidence before the Court was that of the complainant. She stated that she immediately said "NO" every time the accused touched her sexually, and that she did nothing to encourage him. Her evidence was accepted by the trial judge as credible and sincere. Indeed, the accused relies on the fact that he momentarily stopped his advances each time the complainant said "NO" as evidence of his good intentions. This demonstrates that he understood the complainant's "NO's" to mean precisely that. Therefore, there is nothing on the record to support the accused's claim that he continued to believe her to be consenting, or that he re-established consent before resuming physical contact. The accused did not raise nor does the evidence disclose an air of reality to the defence of honest but mistaken belief in consent to this sexual touching.

[59] The trial record conclusively establishes that the accused's persistent and increasingly serious advances constituted a sexual assault for which he had no defence. But for his errors of law, the trial judge would necessarily have found the accused guilty. In this case, a new trial would not be in the interests of justice. Therefore, it is proper for this Court to exercise its discretion under s. 686(4) of the *Code* and enter a conviction: see *R. v. Cassidy*, [1989] 2 S.C.R. 345, at pp. 354-55.

[60] In her reasons, Justice L'Heureux-Dubé makes reference to s. 273.2(b) of the *Code*. Whether the accused took reasonable steps is a question of fact to be determined by the trier of fact only after the air of reality test has been met. In view of the way the trial and appeal were argued, s. 273.2(b) did not have to be considered.

· · ·

V. Disposition

[67] The appeal is allowed, a conviction is entered and the matter is remanded to the trial judge for sentencing.

L'HEUREUX-DUBÉ J (Gonthier J concurring):

[68] Violence against women takes many forms: sexual assault is one of them. In Canada, one-half of all women are said to have experienced at least one incident of physical or sexual violence since the age of 16 (Statistics Canada, "The Violence Against Women Survey," *The Daily*, November 18, 1993). The statistics demonstrate that 99 percent of the offenders in sexual assault cases are men and 90 percent of the victims are women (*Gender Equality in the Canadian Justice System: Summary Document and Proposals for Action* (April 1992), at p. 13, also cited in *R. v. Osolin*, [1993] 4 S.C.R. 595, at p. 669).

[69] Violence against women is as much a matter of equality as it is an offence against human dignity and a violation of human rights. As Cory J. wrote in *Osolin, supra*, at p. 669, sexual assault "is an assault upon human dignity and constitutes a denial of any concept of equality for women." These human rights are protected by ss. 7 and 15 of the *Canadian Charter of Rights and Freedoms* and their violation constitutes an offence under the assault provisions of s. 265 and under the more specific sexual assault provisions of ss. 271, 272 and 273 of the *Criminal Code*, R.S.C. 1985, c. C-46.

[70] So pervasive is violence against women throughout the world that the international community adopted in December 18, 1979 (Res. 34/180), in addition to all other human rights instruments, the *Convention on the Elimination of All Forms of Discrimination Against Women*, Can. T.S. 1982 No. 31, entered into force on September 3, 1981, to which Canada is a party, which has been described as "the definitive international legal instrument requiring respect for and observance of the human rights of women." (R. Cook, "Reservations to the Convention on the Elimination of All Forms of Discrimination Against Women" (1990), 30 *Va. J. Int'l L.* 643, at p. 643.) ...

[Relevant provisions from the *Convention on the Elimination of All Forms of Discrimination Against Women* were reproduced, followed by analogous provisions from a number of other international human rights instruments.]

• • •

[73] Our *Charter* is the primary vehicle through which international human rights achieve a domestic effect (see *Slaight Communications Inc. v. Davidson*, [1989] 1 S.C.R. 1038; *R. v. Keegstra*, [1990] 3 S.C.R. 697). In particular, s. 15 (the equality provision) and s. 7 (which guarantees the right to life, security and liberty of the person) embody the notion of respect of human dignity and integrity.

[74] It is within that larger framework that, in 1983, Canada revamped the sexual assault provisions of the *Code* (S.C. 1980-81-82-83, c. 125), formerly ss. 143, 149 and 244 (R.S.C. 1970, c. C-34) which are now contained in the general assault provisions of s. 265. Together with the 1992 amendments of the *Code* (*An Act to amend the Criminal Code (sexual assault)*, S.C. 1992, c. 38), mainly ss. 273.1 and 273.2, they govern the issue of consent in the context of sexual assault. In the preamble to the 1992 Act, Parliament expressed its concern about the "prevalence of sexual assault against women and children"

and stated its intention to "promote and help to ensure the full protection of the rights guaranteed under sections 7 and 15 of the *Canadian Charter of Rights and Freedoms*."

[75] Fraser C.J., in her dissenting reasons in this case, has set out the legislative history of those provisions. In *R. v. Cuerrier*, [1998] 2 S.C.R. 371, Cory J. and I both noted the significant reform of sexual assault provisions undertaken by Parliament. (See C. Boyle, *Sexual Assault* (1984), at pp. 27-29.) I observed in *R. v. Park*, [1995] 2 S.C.R. 836, at para. 42, that:

> ... the primary concern animating and underlying the present offence of sexual assault is the belief that women have an inherent right to exercise full control over their own bodies, and to engage only in sexual activity that they wish to engage in. If this is the case, then our approach to consent must evolve accordingly, for it may be out of phase with that conceptualization of the law.

See also *R. v. Seaboyer*, [1991] 2 S.C.R. 577.

[76] In the present case, the respondent was charged with sexual assault under s. 271 of the *Criminal Code*. The applicable notions of "assault" and "consent" are defined in ss. 265, 273.1 and 273.2 of the *Criminal Code*. ... [The sections were then reproduced.]

[78] I have had the benefit of the reasons of Justice Major in this appeal and I agree generally with his reasons on most issues and with the result that he reaches. However, I wish to add some comments and discuss some of the reasoning of the trial judge and of the majority of the Court of Appeal.

· · ·

[82] This case is not about consent, since none was given. It is about myths and stereotypes, which have been identified by many authors and succinctly described by D. Archard, *Sexual Consent* (1998), at p. 131:

> Myths of rape include the view that women fantasise about being rape victims; that women mean "yes" even when they say "no"; that any woman could successfully resist a rapist if she really wished to; that the sexually experienced do not suffer harms when raped (or at least suffer lesser harms than the sexually "innocent"); that women often deserve to be raped on account of their conduct, dress, and demeanour; that rape by a stranger is worse than one by an acquaintance. Stereotypes of sexuality include the view of women as passive, disposed submissively to surrender to the sexual advances of active men, the view that sexual love consists in the "possession" by a man of a woman, and that heterosexual sexual activity is paradigmatically penetrative coitus.

· · ·

[83] The trial judge believed the complainant and accepted her testimony that she was afraid and he acknowledged her unwillingness to engage in any sexual activity. In addition, there is no doubt that the respondent was aware that the complainant was afraid since he told her repeatedly not to be afraid. The complainant clearly articulated her absence of consent: she said no. Not only did the accused not stop, but after a brief pause, as Fraser C.J. puts it, he went on to an "increased level of sexual activity" to which twice the complainant said no. What could be clearer?

[84] The trial judge gave no legal effect to his conclusion that the complainant submitted to sexual activity out of fear that the accused would apply force to her. Section 265(3)(b) states that no consent is obtained where the complainant submits by reason of threats or

fear of the application of force. Therefore, s. 265(3)(b) applies and operates to further establish the lack of consent: see *Cuerrier, supra*.

· · ·

[88] In the Court of Appeal, McClung J.A. compounded the error made by the trial judge. At the outset of his opinion, he stated at p. 245 that "it must be pointed out that the complainant did not present herself to Ewanchuk or enter his trailer in a bonnet and crinolines." He noted, at pp. 245-46, that "she was the mother of a six-month-old baby and that, along with her boyfriend, she shared an apartment with another couple."

[89] Even though McClung J.A. asserted that he had no intention of denigrating the complainant, one might wonder why he felt necessary to point out these aspects of the trial record. Could it be to express that the complainant is not a virgin? Or that she is a person of questionable moral character because she is not married and lives with her boyfriend and another couple? These comments made by an appellate judge help reinforce the myth that under such circumstances, either the complainant is less worthy of belief, she invited the sexual assault, or her sexual experience signals probable consent to further sexual activity. Based on those attributed assumptions, the implication is that if the complainant articulates her lack of consent by saying "no," she really does not mean it and even if she does, her refusal cannot be taken as seriously as if she were a girl of "good" moral character. "Inviting" sexual assault, according to those myths, lessens the guilt of the accused as Archard, *supra*, notes at p. 139:

> … the more that a person contributes by her behaviour or negligence to bringing about the circumstances in which she is a victim of a crime, the less responsible is the criminal for the crime he commits. A crime is no less unwelcome or serious in its effects, or need it be any the less deliberate or malicious in its commission, for occurring in circumstances which the victim helped to realise. Yet judges who spoke of women "inviting" or "provoking" a rape would go on to cite such contributory behaviour as a reason for regarding the rape as less grave or the rapist as less culpable. It adds judicial insult to criminal injury to be told that one is the part author of a crime one did not seek and which in consequence is supposed to be a lesser one.

[90] McClung J.A. writes, at p. 247:

> There is no room to suggest that Ewanchuk knew, yet disregarded, her underlying state of mind as he furthered his *romantic intentions*. He was not aware of her true state of mind. Indeed, his ignorance about that was what she wanted. The facts, set forth by the trial judge, provide support for the overriding trial finding, couched in terms of consent by implication, that the accused had no proven preparedness to assault the complainant to get what he wanted. [Emphasis added.]

On the contrary, both the fact that Ewanchuk was aware of the complainant's state of mind, as he did indeed stop each time she expressly stated "no," and the trial judge's findings reinforce the obvious conclusion that the accused knew there was no consent. These were two strangers, a young 17-year-old woman attracted by a job offer who found herself trapped in a trailer and a man approximately twice her age and size. This is hardly a scenario one would characterize as reflective of "romantic intentions." It was nothing more than an effort by Ewanchuk to engage the complainant sexually, not romantically.

[91] The expressions used by McClung J.A. to describe the accused's sexual assault, such as "clumsy passes" (p. 246) or "would hardly raise Ewanchuk's stature in the pantheon of chivalric behaviour" (p. 248), are plainly inappropriate in that context as they minimize the importance of the accused's conduct and the reality of sexual aggression against women.

[92] McClung J.A. also concluded that "the sum of the evidence indicates that Ewanchuk's advances to the complainant were far less criminal than hormonal" (p. 250) having found earlier that "every advance he made to her stopped when she spoke against it" and that "[t]here was no evidence of an assault or even its threat" (p. 249). According to this analysis, a man would be free from criminal responsibility for having non-consensual sexual activity whenever he cannot control his hormonal urges. Furthermore, the fact that the accused ignored the complainant's verbal objections to any sexual activity and persisted in escalated sexual contact, grinding his pelvis against hers repeatedly, is more evidence than needed to determine that there was an assault.

[93] Finally, McClung J.A. made this point: "In a less litigious age going too far in the boyfriend's car was better dealt with on site—a well-chosen expletive, a slap in the face or, if necessary, a well directed knee" (p. 250). According to this stereotype, women should use physical force, not resort to courts to "deal with" sexual assaults and it is not the perpetrator's responsibility to ascertain consent, as required by s. 273.2(b), but the women's not only to express an unequivocal "no," but also to fight her way out of such a situation. In that sense, Susan Estrich has noted that "rape is most assuredly not the only crime in which consent is a defense; but it is the only crime that has required the victim to resist physically in order to establish nonconsent" ("Rape" (1986), 95 *Yale L.J.* 1087, at p. 1090).

[94] Cory J. referred to the inappropriate use of rape myths by courts in *Osolin, supra,* at p. 670:

> A number of rape myths have in the past improperly formed the background for considering evidentiary issues in sexual assault trials. These include the false concepts that: women cannot be raped against their will; only "bad girls" are raped; anyone not clearly of "good character" is more likely to have consented.

[95] This case has not dispelled any of the fears I expressed in *Seaboyer, supra,* about the use of myths and stereotypes in dealing with sexual assault complaints (see also Bertha Wilson, "Will Women Judges Really Make a Difference?" (1990), 28 *Osgoode Hall L.J.* 507). Complainants should be able to rely on a system free from myths and stereotypes, and on a judiciary whose impartiality is not compromised by these biased assumptions. The *Code* was amended in 1983 and in 1992 to eradicate reliance on those assumptions; they should not be permitted to resurface through the stereotypes reflected in the reasons of the majority of the Court of Appeal. It is part of the role of this Court to denounce this kind of language, unfortunately still used today, which not only perpetuates archaic myths and stereotypes about the nature of sexual assaults but also ignores the law.

[96] In "The Standard of Social Justice as a Research Process" (1997), 38 *Can. Psychology* 91, K.E. Renner, C. Alksnis and L. Park make a strong indictment of the current criminal justice process, at p. 100:

The more general indictment of the current criminal justice process is that the law and legal doctrines concerning sexual assault have acted as the principle [*sic*] systemic mechanisms for invalidating the experiences of women and children. *Given this state of affairs, the traditional view of the legal system as neutral, objective and gender-blind is not defensible.* Since the system is ineffective in protecting the rights of women and children, it is necessary to re-examine the existing doctrines which reflect the cultural and social limitations that have preserved dominant male interests at the expense of women and children. [Emphasis added.]

[97] This being said, turning to the facts of the present case, I agree with Major J. that the findings necessary to support a verdict of guilty on the charge of sexual assault have been made. In particular, there is, on the record, no evidence that would give an air of reality to an honest belief in consent for any of the sexual activity which took place in this case. One cannot imply that once the complainant does not object to the massage in the context of a job interview, there is "sufficient evidence" to support that the accused could honestly believe he had permission to initiate sexual contact. This would mean that complying to receive a massage is consent to sexual touching. It would reflect the myth that women are presumptively sexually accessible until they resist. McLachlin J. has recognized in *R. v. Esau*, [1997] 2 S.C.R. 777, at para. 82, that reliance on rape myths cannot ground a defence of mistaken belief in consent:

> Care must be taken to avoid the false assumptions or "myths" that may mislead us in determining whether the conduct of the complainant affords a sufficient basis for putting the defence of honest mistake on consent to the jury. One of these is the stereotypical notion that women who resist or say no may in fact be consenting.

Furthermore, I agree with Fraser C.J. at p. 278 that there is no air of reality to a defence of mistaken belief in consent "in the face of the complainant's clearly stated verbal objections."

• • •

Disposition

[102] Like my colleague Major J., I would allow the appeal, enter a conviction and send the matter back to the trial judge for sentencing.

McLACHLIN J:

[103] I agree with the reasons of Justice Major. I also agree with Justice L'Heureux-Dubé that stereotypical assumptions lie at the heart of what went wrong in this case. The specious defence of implied consent (consent implied by law), as applied in this case, rests on the assumption that unless a woman protests or resists, she should be "deemed" to consent (see L'Heureux-Dubé J.). On appeal, the idea also surfaced that if a woman is not modestly dressed, she is deemed to consent. Such stereotypical assumptions find their roots in many cultures, including our own. They no longer, however, find a place in Canadian law.

[104] I join my colleagues in rejecting them.

Appeal allowed.

III. THE ACTUS REUS OF SEXUAL ASSAULT

The cases in this part focus on interpreting s 265 and ss 271 to 273.1 of the *Criminal Code* in order to establish the *actus reus* of sexual assault. First, what is a *sexual* assault?

R v Chase
Supreme Court of Canada
[1987] 2 SCR 293

McINTYRE J: ... The facts may be briefly described. The respondent, Chase, was a neighbour of the complainant, a 15-year-old girl. They lived in a small hamlet near Fredericton, New Brunswick. On 22nd October 1983 Chase entered the home of the complainant without invitation. The complainant and her 11-year-old brother were in the downstairs portion of the house, playing pool. Their 83-year-old grandfather was upstairs sleeping. Their parents were absent. The respondent seized the complainant around the shoulders and arms and grabbed her breasts. When she fought back, he said: "Come on, dear, don't hit me, I know you want it." The complainant said at trial that: "He tried to grab for my private, but he didn't succeed because my hands were too fast." Eventually, the complainant and her brother were able to make a telephone call to a neighbour and the respondent left. Prior to leaving, he said that he was going to tell everybody that she had raped him. The whole episode lasted little more than half an hour. The respondent was charged with the offence of sexual assault and was found guilty after trial in the Provincial Court. He appealed to the Court of Appeal for New Brunswick, where his appeal was dismissed, a verdict of guilty of the included offence of common assault under s. 245(1) of the *Criminal Code* was substituted, and a sentence of six months' imprisonment was imposed. ...

Sexual assault is an assault, within any one of the definitions of that concept in s. 244(1) [now s 265(1)] of the *Criminal Code*, which is committed in circumstances of a sexual nature, such that the sexual integrity of the victim is violated. The test to be applied in determining whether the impugned conduct has the requisite sexual nature is an objective one: "Viewed in the light of all the circumstances, is the sexual or carnal context of the assault visible to a reasonable observer?": *Taylor*, ... per Laycraft C.J.A., at p. 269. The part of the body touched, the nature of the contact, the situation in which it occurred, the words and gestures accompanying the act, and all other circumstances surrounding the conduct, including threats, which may or may not be accompanied by force, will be relevant: see S.J. Usprich, "A New Crime in Old Battles: Definitional Problems with Sexual Assault" (1987), 29 Cr. L.Q. 200, at p. 204. The intent or purpose of the person committing the act, to the extent that this may appear from the evidence, may also be a factor in considering whether the conduct is sexual. If the motive of the accused is sexual gratification, to the extent that this may appear from the evidence it may be a factor in determining whether the conduct is sexual. It must be emphasized, however, that the existence of such a motive is simply one of many factors to be considered, the importance of which will vary depending on the circumstances. ...

Turning to the case at bar, I have no difficulty in concluding, on the basis of the principles I have discussed above, that there was ample evidence before the trial judge upon which he could find that sexual assault was committed. Viewed objectively, in the light of all the circumstances, it is clear that the conduct of the respondent in grabbing the complainant's breasts constituted an assault of a sexual nature. I would therefore allow the appeal, set aside the conviction of common assault recorded by the Court of Appeal and restore the conviction of sexual assault made at trial. The sentence of six months should stand.

Appeal allowed; conviction restored.

In *R v V(KB)*, [1993] 2 SCR 857 the Court applied *Chase* in upholding a conviction for sexual assault in a case involving a father who had grabbed his three-year-old son's genital area as a disciplinary response to the child's having done this to others. Although the father's purpose was clearly not sexual gratification, Iacobucci J reasoned that "it was clearly open to the trial judge to conclude from all the circumstances that the assault was one of a sexual nature and that the assault was such that the sexual integrity of the appellant's son was violated." Sopinka J, dissenting, concluded that the father's lack of intention for sexual gratification was a decisive factor weighing against finding a sexual assault on these facts.

As you have read in the *Ewanchuk* decision, "consent" appears in two analytical places in the offence of sexual assault: in the *actus reus* (when we ask whether the complainant in fact consented) and, if the complainant did not consent, in the *mens rea* (when we ask whether the accused was aware that there was no consent). Section IV of this chapter concerns the second question, the *mens rea* dimension of consent. But in recent years the Supreme Court has issued important decisions regarding the question of when, at law, a complainant is able to consent and when that consent, if given, may be vitiated (or made legally "void"). These decisions relate to complicated social and empirical issues, as well as to difficult normative questions.

The first decision, *R v JA*, involves the question of whether a complainant can provide "advance consent" in circumstances in which she knows she will be rendered unconscious by virtue of the sexual activity. This case is useful not only for exploring that complicated issue, but also for explaining the relationship between the *actus reus* and the *mens rea*. Crucially, Chief Justice McLachlin's first line provides the fundamental principle that must guide analysis of consent in the law of sexual assault.

R v JA
Supreme Court of Canada
2011 SCC 28, [2011] 2 SCR 440

McLACHLIN CJ (Deschamps, Abella, Charron, Rothstein, and Cromwell JJ concurring):
   [1] It is a fundamental principle of Canadian law that a person is entitled to refuse sexual contact. From this, it follows that sexual acts performed without consent and without an honest belief in consent constitute the crime of sexual assault. The issue raised by this appeal is whether a person can perform sexual acts on an unconscious person if the person consented to those acts in advance of being rendered unconscious.
   [2] The Crown argues that consent in advance of being rendered unconscious does not change the fact that the person, while unconscious, does not have an operating mind

and is therefore incapable of consenting to sexual acts performed on her while uncon-scious. It argues that this is what the *Criminal Code*, R.S.C. 1985, c. C-46, requires, and that to hold otherwise would be to condone non-consensual sex and sexual exploitation. The respondent, J.A., on the other hand, argues that he may engage in sexual activity with an unconscious person, provided he does not exceed the bounds of what the unconscious person expected. To hold otherwise, the respondent says, is to criminalize benign and essentially consensual sexual activity.

[3] Our task on this appeal is to determine whether the *Criminal Code* defines consent as requiring a conscious, operating mind throughout the sexual activity. I conclude that the *Code* makes it clear that an individual must be conscious throughout the sexual activity in order to provide the requisite consent. Parliament requires ongoing, conscious consent to ensure that women and men are not the victims of sexual exploitation, and to ensure that individuals engaging in sexual activity are capable of asking their partners to stop at any point. I would therefore allow the appeal and restore the conviction of the respondent.

I. Facts

[4] On May 22, 2007, the respondent J.A. and his long-time partner K.D. spent an evening together at home. While watching a movie on the couch, they started to kiss and engage in foreplay. After some time, they went upstairs to their bedroom and became more intimate. They both undressed, and started kissing on the bed.

[5] While K.D. was lying on her back, J.A. placed his hands around her throat and choked her until she was unconscious. At trial, K.D. estimated that she was unconscious for "less than three minutes." She testified that she consented to J.A. choking her, and understood that she might lose consciousness. She stated that she and J.A. had experi-mented with erotic asphyxiation, and that she had lost consciousness before.

[6] When K.D. regained consciousness, she was on her knees at the edge of the bed with her hands tied behind her back, and J.A. was inserting a dildo into her anus.

· · ·

[8] K.D. testified that J.A. removed the dildo ten seconds after she regained conscious-ness. The two then had vaginal intercourse. When they had finished, J.A. cut K.D.'s hands loose.

[9] K.D. made a complaint to the police on July 11. In a videotaped statement, she told the police that she had not consented to the sexual activity that had occurred. She later recanted her allegation, and claimed that she made a false complaint to the police because J.A. had threatened to seek sole custody of their two-year-old son. J.A. was charged with aggravated assault, sexual assault, attempting to render the complainant unconscious in order to sexually assault her, and with breaching his probation order.

[Note: By the time it reached the Supreme Court of Canada, the case proceeded on the assumption that, before she went unconscious, K.D. had consented to all of the activity that took place while she was unconscious. That is, J.A. had not acted "beyond the scope" of K.D.'s consent. The only question was whether that consent was valid in law.]

· · ·

III. Analysis

A. Issue on Appeal

[21] The only question before this Court is whether consent for the purposes of sexual assault requires the complainant to be conscious throughout the sexual activity. This is because the Crown appeals to this Court as of right on the basis of "any question of law on which a judge of the court of appeal dissents": *Criminal Code*, s. 693(1)(a). Accordingly, whether the complainant consented in fact or suffered bodily harm are not at issue; nor is the Court of Appeal's holding that, for reasons of procedural fairness, the Crown in this case cannot rely on bodily harm to vitiate consent since it did not formally allege that bodily harm occurred. Since the issue of bodily harm is not before this Court, I take no position on whether or in which circumstances individuals may consent to bodily harm during sexual activity. In my view, it would be inappropriate to decide the matter without the benefit of submissions from interested groups.

B. Framework of Sexual Assault

[22] Before turning to the issue in this case, it is useful to consider the framework of the law of sexual assault.

[23] A conviction for sexual assault under s. 271(1) of the *Criminal Code* requires proof beyond a reasonable doubt of the *actus reus* and the *mens rea* of the offence. A person commits the *actus reus* if he touches another person in a sexual way without her consent. Consent for this purpose is actual subjective consent in the mind of the complainant at the time of the sexual activity in question: *Ewanchuk*. As discussed below, the *Criminal Code*, s. 273.1(2), limits this definition by stipulating circumstances where consent is not obtained.

[24] A person has the required mental state, or *mens rea* of the offence, when he or she knew that the complainant was not consenting to the sexual act in question, or was reckless or wilfully blind to the absence of consent. The accused may raise the defence of honest but mistaken belief in consent if he believed that the complainant communicated consent to engage in the sexual activity. However, as discussed below, ss. 273.1(2) and 273.2 limit the cases in which the accused may rely on this defence. For instance, the accused cannot argue that he misinterpreted the complainant saying "no" as meaning "yes" (*Ewanchuk*, at para. 51).

[25] The issue in this case is whether the complainant consented, which is relevant to the *actus reus*; the Crown must prove the absence of consent to fulfill the requirements of the wrongful act. However, the provisions of the *Criminal Code* with respect to the *mens rea* defence of honest but mistaken belief also shed light on the issue of whether consent requires the complainant to have been conscious throughout the duration of the sexual activity.

· · ·

C. The Concept of Consent Under the Criminal Code

· · ·

[34] Consent for the purposes of sexual assault is defined in s. 273.1(1) as "the voluntary agreement of the complainant to engage in the sexual activity in question." This

suggests that the consent of the complainant must be specifically directed to each and every sexual act, negating the argument that broad advance consent is what Parliament had in mind. As discussed below, this Court has also interpreted this provision as requiring the complainant to consent to the activity "at the time it occur[s]" (*Ewanchuk*, at para. 26).

[35] Section 273.1(2) provides a non-exhaustive list of circumstances in which no consent is obtained. These examples shed further light on Parliament's understanding of consent.

[36] Section 273.1(2)(b) provides that no consent is obtained if "the complainant is incapable of consenting to the activity." Parliament was concerned that sexual acts might be perpetrated on persons who do not have the mental capacity to give meaningful consent. This might be because of mental impairment. It also might arise from unconsciousness .... .

[37] The provisions of the *Criminal Code* that relate to the *mens rea* of sexual assault confirm that individuals must be conscious throughout the sexual activity. Before considering these provisions, however, it is important to keep in mind the differences between the meaning of consent under the *actus reus* and under the *mens rea*: *Ewanchuk*, at paras. 48-49. Under the *mens rea* defence, the issue is whether the accused believed that the complainant *communicated consent*. Conversely, the only question for the *actus reus* is whether the complainant was subjectively consenting in her mind. The complainant is not required to *express* her lack of consent or her revocation of consent for the *actus reus* to be established.

. . .

[40] Section 273.1(2)(e) establishes that it is an error of law for the accused to believe that the complainant is still consenting after she "expresses ... a lack of agreement to continue to engage in the activity." Since this provision refers to the expression of consent, it is clear that it can only apply to the accused's *mens rea*. Nonetheless, it indicates that Parliament wanted people to be capable of revoking their consent at any time during the sexual activity. This in turn supports the view that Parliament viewed consent as the product of a conscious mind, since a person who has been rendered unconscious cannot revoke her consent. As a result, the protection afforded by s. 273.1(2)(e) would not be available to her.

[41] According to my colleague, Fish J., s. 273.1(2)(e) "suggests that the complainant's consent *can* be given in advance, and remains operative unless and until it is subsequently revoked" (para. 104 (emphasis in original)). With respect, I cannot accept this interpretation. The provision in question establishes that the accused must halt all sexual contact once the complainant expresses that she no longer consents. This does not mean that a failure to tell the accused to stop means that the complainant must have been consenting. As this Court has repeatedly held, the complainant is not required to express her lack of consent for the *actus reus* to be established. Rather, the question is whether the complainant subjectively consented in her mind: *Ewanchuk*; *R. v. M.(M.L.)*, [1994] 2 S.C.R. 3.

[42] Section 273.2 sheds further light on Parliament's conception of consent. Section 273.2(b) states that a person wishing to avail himself of the *mens rea* defence must not only believe that the complainant communicated her consent (or in French, "*l'accusé croyait que le plaignant avait consenti*" (s. 273.2)), but must also have taken reasonable steps to ascertain whether she "was consenting" to engage in the sexual activity in question at the time it occurred. How can one take reasonable steps to ascertain whether a person is consenting to sexual activity while it is occurring if that person is unconscious?

Once again, the provision is grounded in the assumption that the complainant must consciously consent to each and every sexual act. Further, by requiring the accused to take reasonable steps to ensure that the complainant "was consenting," Parliament has indicated that the consent of the complainant must be an ongoing state of mind.

[43] The question in this case is whether Parliament defined consent in a way that extends to advance consent to sexual acts committed while the complainant is unconscious. In my view, it did not. J.A.'s contention that advance consent can be given to sexual acts taking place during unconsciousness is not in harmony with the provisions of the *Code* and their underlying policies. These provisions indicate that Parliament viewed consent as requiring a "capable" or operating mind, able to evaluate each and every sexual act committed. To hold otherwise runs counter to Parliament's clear intent that a person has the right to consent to particular acts and to revoke her consent at any time. Reading these provisions together, I cannot accept the respondent's contention that an individual may consent in advance to sexual activity taking place while she is unconscious.

· · ·

[58] The respondent ... argues that requiring conscious consent to sexual activity may result in absurd outcomes. He cites the example of a person who kisses his sleeping partner. In that situation, he argues, the accused would be guilty of sexual assault unless he is permitted to argue that his sleeping partner consented to the kiss in advance.

· · ·

[Chief Justice McLachlin canvassed a number of reasons not to alter the definition of consent to deal with this asserted problem, before arriving at the following conclusion:]

[63] The Crown suggested that this Court could allow for mild sexual touching that occurs while a person is unconscious by relying on the *de minimis* doctrine, based on the Latin phrase *de minimis non curat lex*, or the "law does not care for small or trifling matters": *Canadian Foundation for Children, Youth and the Law v. Canada (Attorney General)*, 2004 SCC 4, [2004] 1 S.C.R. 76, at para. 200, *per* Arbour J., dissenting. Without suggesting that the *de minimis* principle has no place in the law of sexual assault, it should be noted that even mild non-consensual touching of a sexual nature can have profound implications for the complainant.

[64] Running through the arguments in favour of carving out particular circumstances as exceptions to the conscious consent paradigm of the *Criminal Code* is the suggestion that the strict approach Parliament has adopted toward consent in the context of sexual assault has no place in relationships of mutual trust, like marriage. However, accepting this view would run counter to Parliament's clear rejection of defences to sexual assault based on the nature of the relationship. The *Criminal Code* does not establish a different inquiry into consent depending on the relationship between the accused and the complainant. Their relationship may be evidence for both the *actus reus* and the *mens rea*, but it does not change the nature of the inquiry into whether the complainant consented, as conceived by the *Criminal Code*.

[65] In the end, we are left with this. Parliament has defined sexual assault as sexual touching without consent. It has dealt with consent in a way that makes it clear that ongoing, conscious and present consent to "the sexual activity in question" is required. This concept of consent produces just results in the vast majority of cases. It has proved of

great value in combating the stereotypes that historically have surrounded consent to sexual relations and undermined the law's ability to address the crime of sexual assault. In some situations, the concept of consent Parliament has adopted may seem unrealistic. However, it is inappropriate for this Court to carve out exceptions when they undermine Parliament's choice. In the absence of a constitutional challenge, the appropriate body to alter the law on consent in relation to sexual assault is Parliament, should it deem this necessary.

IV. Summary

[66] The definition of consent for sexual assault requires the complainant to provide actual active consent throughout every phase of the sexual activity. It is not possible for an unconscious person to satisfy this requirement, even if she expresses her consent in advance. Any sexual activity with an individual who is incapable of consciously evaluating whether she is consenting is therefore not consensual within the meaning of the *Criminal Code*.

V. Disposition

[67] I would allow the appeal, and restore the respondent's conviction for sexual assault.

FISH J (Binnie and LeBel JJ concurring) (dissenting):

[68] It is a fundamental principle of the law governing sexual assault in Canada that no means "no" and only yes means "yes."

[69] K.D., the complainant in this case, said yes, not no. She consented to her erotic asphyxiation by the respondent, J.A., her partner at the time. Their shared purpose was to render K.D. unconscious and to engage in sexual conduct while she remained in that state. It is undisputed that K.D.'s consent was freely and voluntarily given—in advance and while the conduct was still in progress. Immediately afterward, K.D. had intercourse with J.A., again consensually.

[70] K.D. first complained to the police nearly two months later when J.A. threatened to seek sole custody of their two-year-old child. She later recanted.

[71] We are nonetheless urged by the Crown to find that the complainant's *yes in fact* means *no in law*. With respect for those who are of a different view, I would decline to do so.

[72] The provisions of the *Criminal Code*, R.S.C. 1985, c. C-46, regarding consent to sexual contact and the case law (including *R. v. Ewanchuk*, [1999] 1 S.C.R. 330) relied on by the Crown were intended to protect women against abuse by others. Their mission is not to "protect" women *against themselves* by limiting their freedom to determine autonomously when and with whom they will engage in the sexual relations of their choice. Put differently, they aim to safeguard and enhance the sexual autonomy of women, and not to make choices for them.

[73] The Crown's position, if adopted by the Court, would achieve exactly the opposite result. It would deprive women of their freedom to engage by choice in sexual adventures that involve no proven harm to them or to others. That is what happened here.

[74] Adopting the Crown's position would also require us to find that cohabiting partners across Canada, including spouses, commit a sexual assault when either one of

them, *even with express prior consent*, kisses or caresses the other while the latter is asleep. The absurdity of this consequence makes plain that it is the product of an unintended and unacceptable extension of the *Criminal Code* provisions upon which the Crown would cause this appeal to rest.

[75] Lest I be misunderstood to suggest otherwise, I agree that consent will be vitiated where the contemplated sexual activity involves a degree of bodily harm or risk of fatal injury that cannot be condoned under the common law, or on grounds of public policy. Asphyxiation to the point of unconsciousness may well rise to that level, but the contours of this limitation on consent have not been addressed by the parties. Nor has the matter been previously considered by the Court. For procedural reasons as well, the issue of bodily harm must be left for another day.

[76] I agree as well that prior consent affords no defence where it is later revoked or where the ensuing conduct does not comply with the consent given.

[77] Applying these principles here, I would dismiss the appeal.

[78] Finally, I think it helpful to set out succinctly the issue on this appeal.

[79] According to the Chief Justice, the question is "whether an unconscious person can qualify as consenting [to sexual activity]" (para. 33). With respect, that is not the question at all: *No one* has suggested in this case that an unconscious person can validly consent to sexual activity.

[80] Rather, the question is whether a *conscious* person can freely and voluntarily consent in advance to agreed sexual activity that will occur while he or she is briefly and consensually rendered unconscious. My colleague would answer that question in the negative; I would answer that question in the affirmative, absent a clear prohibition in the *Criminal Code*, absent proven bodily harm that would vitiate consent at common law, and absent any evidence that the conscious partner subjected the unconscious partner to sexual activity beyond their agreement.

[81] In this case, J.A. engaged with K.D. in sexual activity to which K.D. freely consented while conscious. The Chief Justice would nonetheless convict J.A. of sexual assault, a serious crime. I oppose this result. In my respectful view, it is unwarranted as a matter of statutory interpretation, prior decisions of the Court, or considerations of policy. And it is wrong on the facts of this case.

[82] That is what divides us. The rest is commentary.

· · ·

[103] I agree that prior consent to sexual activity can later be revoked. And I agree that a person cannot while unconscious consent or revoke consent. It hardly follows, in my respectful view, that consenting adults cannot, as a matter of law, willingly and consciously agree to engage in a sexual practice involving transitory unconsciousness—on the ground that, during the brief period of that consensually induced mental state, they will be unable to consent to doing what they have already consented to do.

[104] If anything, the wording of s. 273.1(2)(e) suggests that the complainant's consent *can* be given in advance, and remains operative unless and until it is subsequently revoked: It provides that "the complainant, *having consented* to engage in sexual activity," may later revoke his or her consent. I agree with the respondent that revocation is a question of fact. In this regard, I again mention that the complainant, upon regaining consciousness, did not revoke her prior consent to the sexual conduct in issue—which was then still

ongoing. And it has not been suggested that she had earlier revoked her consent by words or conduct, or even in her own mind.

[105] With respect, there is no factual or legal basis for holding that K.D.'s prior consent, otherwise operative throughout, was temporarily rendered inoperative during the few minutes of her voluntary unconsciousness. In my view, it was not suspended by the fact that she had rendered herself incapable of revoking the consent she had chosen, freely and consciously, *not to revoke* either immediately before or immediately after the brief interval of her unconsciousness. Nothing in s. 273.1(2)(e) creates a legal requirement, or a binding legal fiction, that warrants convicting the complainant's partner of sexual assault in these circumstances.

$\cdots$

[108] Lest I be misunderstood in this regard, I hasten to add that K.D.'s prior consent to the "activity in question" constituted a valid consent only to the contemplated activity. In the absence of any evidence that J.A.'s conduct exceeded the scope of K.D.'s consent, I am unable to find in the mentioned provisions of the *Criminal Code* any basis for concluding that K.D.'s consent in fact was not a valid consent in law.

$\cdots$

[116] Respect for the privacy and sexual autonomy of consenting adults has long been embraced by Parliament as a fundamental social value and an overarching statutory objective: "Keeping the state out of the bedrooms of the nation" is a legislative policy, and not just a political slogan.

[117] The approach advocated by the Chief Justice would also result in the criminalization of a broad range of conduct that Parliament cannot have intended to capture in its definition of the offence of sexual assault. Notably, it would criminalize kissing or caressing a sleeping partner, however gently and affectionately. The absence of contemporaneous consent, and therefore the *actus reus*, would be conclusively established by accepted evidence that the complainant was asleep at the time. Prior consent, or even an explicit request—"kiss me before you leave for work"—would not spare the accused from conviction.

[The Crown argued that this outcome would be avoided using prosecutorial discretion and the principle of *de minimis non curat lex*. Justice Fish rejected both of these as adequate or appropriate responses to this problem, and went on to address certain other arguments advanced by the Crown and the majority.]

$\cdots$

[145] For all of these reasons, I would affirm the judgment of the Court of Appeal and dismiss the present appeal to this Court.

This next case addresses the issue of "fraud vitiating consent." Read s 265(3)(c); it is the provision at the heart of this case. As you will see in Chief Justice McLachlin's decision (for a unanimous Court), this case is, in a sense, a "sequel" to the 1998 one of *Cuerrier*, which the chief justice explains briefly below. Consider also *Hutchinson*, summarized in a note following this case.

R v Mabior
2012 SCC 47, [2012] 2 SCR 584

McLACHLIN CJ (LeBel, Deschamps, Fish, Abella, Rothstein, Cromwell, Moldaver, and Karakatsanis JJ concurring):

I. Overview

[1] This case raises the issue of whether an HIV-positive person who engages in sexual relations without disclosing his condition commits aggravated sexual assault.

[2] Sex without consent is sexual assault under s. 265 of the *Criminal Code*, R.S.C. 1985, c. C-46. *R. v. Cuerrier*, [1998] 2 S.C.R. 371, establishes that failure to advise a partner of one's HIV status may constitute fraud vitiating consent. Because HIV poses a risk of serious bodily harm, the operative offence is one of aggravated sexual assault, attracting a maximum sentence of life imprisonment: *Cuerrier*, at para. 95; ss. 265, 268 and 273 *Cr. C.*

[3] While *Cuerrier* laid down the basic requirements for the offence, the precise circumstances when failure to disclose HIV status vitiates consent and converts sexual activity into a criminal act remain unclear. The parties ask this Court for clarification.

[4] I conclude that a person may be found guilty of aggravated sexual assault under s. 273 of the *Criminal Code* if he fails to disclose HIV-positive status before intercourse and there is a realistic possibility that HIV will be transmitted. If the HIV-positive person has a low viral count as a result of treatment and there is condom protection, the threshold of a realistic possibility of transmission is not met, on the evidence before us.

II. Background

[5] The respondent, Mr. Mabior, lived in Winnipeg. His house was a party place. People came in and out, including a variety of young women. Alcohol and drugs were freely dispensed. From time to time, Mr. Mabior had sex with women who came to his house, including the nine complainants in this case.

[6] Mr. Mabior did not tell the complainants that he was HIV-positive before having sex with them; indeed, he told one of them that he had no STDs. On some occasions, he wore condoms, on others he did not. Sometimes the condoms broke or were removed, and in some cases, the precise nature of the protections taken is unclear. Eight of the nine complainants testified that they would not have consented to sex with Mr. Mabior had they known he was HIV-positive. None of the complainants contracted HIV.

[7] Mr. Mabior was charged with nine counts of aggravated sexual assault (and other related offences), based on his failure to disclose to the complainants that he was HIV-positive. In defence, Mr. Mabior called evidence that he was under treatment, and that he was not infectious or presented only a low risk of infection at the relevant times.

[8] The trial judge convicted Mr. Mabior of six counts of aggravated sexual assault (2008 MBQB 201, 230 Man. R. (2d) 184). She acquitted him on the other three, on the basis that sexual intercourse using a condom when viral loads are undetectable does not place a sexual partner at "significant risk of serious bodily harm," as required by *Cuerrier*.

[9] Mr. Mabior appealed from these six convictions; the Crown did not appeal from the three acquittals. The Manitoba Court of Appeal varied the trial judge's decision, holding

that *either* low viral loads *or* condom use could negate significant risk (2010 MBCA 93, 258 Man. R. (2d) 166). This reduced to two the counts on which Mr. Mabior could be convicted, and the Court of Appeal entered acquittals on the four remaining counts. The Crown appeals these acquittals. Mr. Mabior has not cross-appealed against the two convictions upheld by the Court of Appeal.

. . .

[In *Cuerrier*, the Supreme Court of Canada held that fraud sufficient to vitiate consent under s 265(3)(c) has two elements, which Chief Justice McLachlin summarized in *Mabior* as follows: "(1) *a dishonest act* (either falsehoods or failure to disclose HIV status); and (2) *deprivation* (denying the complainant knowledge which would have caused her to refuse sexual relations that exposed her to a significant risk of serious bodily harm)." These are the two "branches" of the *Cuerrier* test. The parties in this case invited the Court to revisit this test on the basis that it was ill-defined and uncertain: What is a "significant risk"? What is "serious bodily harm"? The Court in *Mabior* concluded that these uncertainties could be overcome, and offered guidance in cases involving the failure to disclose HIV-positive status:]

[56] We have discussed the need for a clear and appropriately tailored test for fraud vitiating consent in s. 265(3)(c) of the *Criminal Code*, in the context of failure to disclose HIV-positive status. With a view to meeting that need, we have canvassed four guides to construing the provision—the proper ambit of the criminal law, the common law and statutory background of the concept of fraud, *Charter* values and the approach to non-disclosure of HIV status adopted in other countries. This brings us to the nub of the question before us—when, precisely, should non-disclosure of HIV status amount to fraud vitiating consent under s. 265(3)(c)?

. . .

[58] While it may be difficult to apply, the *Cuerrier* approach is in principle valid. It carves out an appropriate area for the criminal law—one restricted to "significant risk of serious bodily harm." It reflects the *Charter* values of autonomy, liberty and equality, and the evolution of the common law ... . The test's approach to consent accepts the wisdom of the common law that not every deception that leads to sexual intercourse should be criminalized, while still according consent meaningful scope. While *Cuerrier* takes the criminal law further than courts in other common law jurisdictions have, it can be argued other courts have not gone far enough: see L.H. Leigh, "Two cases on consent in rape" (2007), 5 *Arch. News* 6.

[59] Some interveners challenge the use of the criminal law in the case of HIV on the ground that it may deter people from seeking treatment or disclosing their condition, thereby increasing the health risk to the carrier and those he has sex with. On the record before us, I cannot accept this argument. The only "evidence" was studies presented by interveners suggesting that criminalization "probably" acts as a deterrent to HIV testing: see, e.g., M.A. Wainberg, "Criminalizing HIV transmission may be a mistake" (2009), 180 *C.M.A.J.* 688. Other studies suggest little difference in reporting rates in states that criminalized and did not criminalize behaviour: S. Burris, et al., "Do Criminal Laws Influence HIV Risk Behavior? An Empirical Trial" (2007), 39 *Ariz. St. L.J.* 467, at p. 501. The conclusions in these studies are tentative, and the studies were not placed in evidence and not

tested by cross-examination. They fail to provide an adequate basis to justify judicial reversal of the accepted place of the criminal law in this domain.

[60] It follows that *Cuerrier* should not be jettisoned. The problems of uncertainty and appropriate reach that have emerged in its application should be addressed, but to the extent possible within the general framework of *Cuerrier*. This brings us to the suggestions for dealing with the problems of uncertainty and overbreadth that have arisen in applying *Cuerrier*.

. . .

[Chief Justice McLachlin canvassed several possible approaches, settling on the Court's favoured approach:]

[84] In my view, a "significant risk of serious bodily harm" connotes a position between the extremes of no risk (the trial judge's test) and "high risk" (the Court of Appeal's test). Where there is a *realistic possibility of transmission of HIV*, a significant risk of serious bodily harm is established, and the deprivation element of the *Cuerrier* test is met. This approach is supported by the following considerations.

[85] First, "significant risk of serious bodily harm" cannot mean any risk, however small. That would come down to adopting the absolute disclosure approach, with its numerous shortcomings, and would effectively read the word "significant" out of the *Cuerrier* test.

[86] Second, a standard of "high" risk does not give adequate weight to the nature of the harm involved in HIV transmission. "Significant risk" in *Cuerrier* is informed both by the risk of contraction of HIV and the seriousness of the disease if contracted. These factors vary inversely. The more serious the nature of the harm, the lower the probability of transmission need be to amount to a "significant risk of serious bodily harm."

[87] Third, as discussed earlier in considering guides to interpretation, a standard of realistic possibility of transmission of HIV avoids setting the bar for criminal conviction too high or too low. A standard of any risk, however small, would arguably set the threshold for criminal conduct too low. On the other hand, to limit s. 265(3)(c) to cases where the risk is "high" might condone irresponsible, reprehensible conduct.

[88] Fourth, the common law and statutory history of fraud vitiating consent to sexual relations supports viewing "significant risk of serious bodily harm" as requiring a realistic possibility of transmission of HIV. This history suggests that only serious deceptions with serious consequences are capable of vitiating consent to sexual relations. Interpreting "significant risk of serious bodily harm" in *Cuerrier* as extending to any risk of transmission would be inconsistent with this. A realistic possibility of transmission arguably strikes the right balance for a disease with the life-altering consequences of HIV.

[89] Fifth, the values of autonomy and equality enshrined in the *Charter* support an approach to fraud vitiating consent that respects the interest of a person to choose whether to consent to sex with a particular person or not. The law must strike a balance between this interest and the need to confine the criminal law to conduct associated with serious wrongs and serious harms. Drawing the line between criminal and non-criminal misconduct at a realistic possibility of transmission arguably strikes an appropriate balance between the complainant's interest in autonomy and equality and the need to prevent over-extension of criminal sanctions.

[90] Finally, interpreting "significant risk of serious bodily harm" as entailing a realistic possibility of transmission of HIV is supported by a number of cases. ...

[91] These considerations lead me to conclude that the *Cuerrier* requirement of "significant risk of serious bodily harm" should be read as requiring disclosure of HIV status if there is a realistic possibility of transmission of HIV. If there is no realistic possibility of transmission of HIV, failure to disclose that one has HIV will not constitute fraud vitiating consent to sexual relations under s. 265(3)(c).

[92] The test of realistic possibility of transmission proposed in these reasons is specific to HIV. As discussed above, "significant risk" depends both on the degree of the harm and risk of transmission. These two factors vary inversely. A treatable sexually transmitted disease that does not seriously alter a person's life or life-expectancy might well not rise to the level of constituting "serious bodily harm," and would also fail to meet the requirement of endangerment of life for aggravated sexual assault under s. 273(1). Where the line should be drawn with respect to diseases other than HIV is not before us. It is enough to note that HIV is indisputably serious and life-endangering. Although it can be controlled by medication, HIV remains an incurable chronic infection that, if untreated, can result in death. As such, the failure to advise a sexual partner of one's HIV status may lead to a conviction for aggravated sexual assault under s. 273(1) of the *Criminal Code*. (This said, it may be that with further medical advances, the death rate may decline to the point where the risk of death is virtually eliminated, reducing the offence to sexual assault *simpliciter* under s. 271(1) of the *Criminal Code*. Similarly, the day may come when researchers will find a cure for HIV, with the possible effect that HIV will cease to cause "serious bodily harm" and the failure to disclose will no longer fall under the category of fraud vitiating consent for the purposes of sexual assault.)

. . .

(4) Realistic Possibility of HIV Transmission

. . .

[94] This leaves the question of when there is a realistic possibility of transmission of HIV. The evidence adduced here satisfies me that, as a general matter, a realistic possibility of transmission of HIV is negated if (i) the accused's viral load at the time of sexual relations was low, *and* (ii) condom protection was used.

[95] The conclusion that low viral count coupled with condom use precludes a realistic possibility of transmission of HIV, and hence does not constitute a "significant risk of serious bodily harm" on the *Cuerrier* test, flows from the evidence in this case. This general proposition does not preclude the common law from adapting to future advances in treatment and to circumstances where risk factors other than those considered in this case are at play.

[Chief Justice McLachlin reviewed the evidence regarding the baseline risk of transmission of HIV per act of vaginal intercourse with an infected male partner (between 0.05 percent and 0.1 percent), the effectiveness of condom use (reducing the risk of transmission by 80 percent), and antiretroviral therapy (reducing the risk of transmission by 89 to 96 percent). She concluded that "on the evidence before us, the ultimate percentage risk of transmission resulting from the combined effect of condom use *and* low viral load is clearly extremely low—so low that the risk is reduced to a speculative possibility rather than a realistic possibility" (para 101).]

. . .

[103] This leads to the conclusion that on the evidence before us, the combined effect of condom use *and* low viral load precludes a realistic possibility of transmission of HIV. In these circumstances, the *Cuerrier* requirement of significant risk of serious bodily harm is not met. There is no deprivation within the meaning of *Cuerrier* and failure to disclose HIV status will not constitute fraud vitiating consent under s. 265(3)(c) of the *Criminal Code*.

(5) Summary

[104] To summarize, to obtain a conviction under ss. 265(3)(c) and 273, the Crown must show that the complainant's consent to sexual intercourse was vitiated by the accused's fraud as to his HIV status. Failure to disclose (*the dishonest act*) amounts to fraud where the complainant would not have consented had he or she known the accused was HIV-positive, and where sexual contact poses a significant risk of or causes actual serious bodily harm (*deprivation*). A significant risk of serious bodily harm is established by a realistic possibility of transmission of HIV. On the evidence before us, a realistic possibility of transmission is negated by evidence that the accused's viral load was low at the time of intercourse and that condom protection was used. However, the general proposition that a low viral load combined with condom use negates a realistic possibility of transmission of HIV does not preclude the common law from adapting to future advances in treatment and to circumstances where risk factors other than those considered in the present case are at play.

[105] The usual rules of evidence and proof apply. The Crown bears the burden of establishing the elements of the offence—a dishonest act and deprivation—beyond a reasonable doubt. Where the Crown has made a *prima facie* case of deception and deprivation as described in these reasons, a tactical burden may fall on the accused to raise a reasonable doubt, by calling evidence that he had a low viral load at the time and that condom protection was used.

B. Application

[106] With respect to the four counts before us, the complainants all consented to sexual intercourse with the accused. Each of the complainants testified that they would not have had sex with the accused had they known that he was HIV-positive. The only issue is whether their consent was vitiated because he did not tell them that he had HIV.

[107] The trial judge found the accused guilty of aggravated sexual assault on the four counts where it was established that his viral load was not undetectable or no condom was used. The Court of Appeal set aside the convictions on the basis that *either* an undetectable viral load *or* condom protection would suffice.

[108] As set out above, at this point in the development of the common law, a clear test can be laid down. The absence of a realistic possibility of HIV transmission precludes a finding of fraud vitiating consent under s. 265(3)(c) of the *Criminal Code*. In the case at hand, no realistic possibility of transmission was established when the accused had a

low viral load and wore a condom. It follows that the appeal should be allowed insofar as the decision of the Court of Appeal conflicts with this conclusion.

[109] The accused had a low viral load at the time of intercourse with each of S.H., D.C.S. and D.H., but did not use a condom. Consequently, the trial judge's convictions on these counts should be maintained. This leaves K.G. The trial judge convicted on the ground that, although the accused used a condom at the time of the encounter, his viral load "was not suppressed" (para. 128). As discussed, the combination of a low viral load—as opposed to an *undetectable* viral load—and of condom use negates a realistic possibility of transmission, on the evidence in this case. The record shows that the accused's viral load was low at the time of sexual relations with K.G. When combined with condom protection, this low viral load did not expose K.G. to a significant risk of serious bodily harm. The trial judge's conviction on this count must be reversed.

[110] I would allow the appeal in part and restore the convictions in respect of the complaints by S.H., D.C.S. and D.H. I would dismiss the appeal in respect of the complaint by K.G.

In *R v Hutchinson*, 2014 SCC 19, [2014] 1 SCR 346, the Court unanimously upheld a conviction for sexual assault. In this case, Hutchinson had poked holes into condoms he used when having sexual intercourse with his girlfriend. The girlfriend, who had previously refused to have unprotected sex, became pregnant. As in *Mabior*, the Court approached this case as raising a question of statutory interpretation and, in particular, as requiring the Court to consider how to draw a clear line between criminal and non-criminal conduct, while avoiding the risk of over-criminalization.

Two issues were raised by these facts: (1) had the complainant even consented and (2) was her consent vitiated by fraud, according to the *Mabior/Cuerrier* analysis? The majority concluded that the complainant had consented to the specific physical act of sexual intercourse, but that her consent was vitiated by fraud. Specifically, for the first part of the test set out in *Mabior/Cuerrier*, Hutchinson's decision to use sabotaged condoms constituted dishonesty. The second part of the *Mabior/Cuerrier* test for fraud asks if there was "deprivation," specifically interpreted in the HIV cases to require a significant risk of serious bodily harm. In *Hutchinson*, the majority held that the deprivation, or "harm," risked by Hutchinson's actions was depriving a woman of the capacity to choose to protect herself from an increased risk of pregnancy by using effective birth control. Given that pregnancy causes "profound changes in a woman's body," this constituted a deprivation that was as serious as the "significant risk of serious bodily harm" required in *Cuerrier* and *Mabior*.

Justices Abella, Moldaver, and Karakatsanis would also have convicted Hutchinson, but on the basis that the complainant had never consented; rather, she had consented to a different sexual activity. These justices characterized the relevant consent as being consent to sexual intercourse with a condom, which they saw as different from consenting to unprotected sexual intercourse.

IV. THE MENTAL ELEMENT

The prosecution of sexual assault can be fraught with evidentiary difficulties because events usually occur in private between the accused and the complainant. The following case deals with two matters. One is an important issue of substantive law: Can the accused raise a defence of mistaken belief in consent if he or she honestly but unreasonably believed that the complainant was consenting? (Mistake of fact was considered more generally in Chapter 7.) The second question concerns the evidentiary threshold that must be met before a defence may be considered by the trier of fact and whether that threshold was met in this case. On the first issue the Court was unanimous but on the second it was divided.

Pappajohn v The Queen
Supreme Court of Canada
[1980] 2 SCR 120

[The accused, a businessman, met with the complainant, a real estate agent, to discuss the pending sale of his house. After a three-hour lunch during which much liquor was consumed, the accused took the complainant to his house. Some three hours later the complainant ran naked out of the house with a bow-tie round her neck and her hands tied tightly behind her back. At trial the complainant denied any form of consent, testifying that she had physically and mentally resisted throughout. Pappajohn's testimony was the opposite: according to him, there had been preliminary sexual activity with her consent and acts of intercourse, again with her consent; the gagging and binding was done to stimulate sexual activity, and it was only then that she suddenly became hysterical and screamed.

The trial judge refused to instruct the jury that if the accused honestly believed that the complainant consented, whether or not she did in fact consent, then he should be acquitted. The sole issue left with the jury was whether she did in fact consent. An appeal by the accused from his conviction to the British Columbia Court of Appeal was dismissed. Lambert JA dissented (holding that the defence of honest and reasonable mistake of fact should have been left to the jury).]

DICKSON J (Estey J concurring) (dissenting): ... Is the accused's perception of consent relevant to a charge under s. 143 of the *Criminal Code*? The argument against the application of *Director of Public Prosecutions v. Morgan*, [1976] A.C. 182, in Canada, is that the *Code* creates a statutory offence of rape which does not expressly advert to, or require, that there be a state of mind or intent to proceed in the absence of consent.

[A number of cases were then examined.]

. . .

Counsel for the Crown in the instant appeal reviewed and compared s. 143 of the *Code* with other Part IV *Code* offences, to make the point that the subjective belief of an accused is no part of the case to be proved by the Crown. It was contended that, since reference to intention to proceed in the absence of consent is lacking in s. 143, the statutory wording prevails over case authorities which consider the mental element in terms of the common law definition. Section 148 of the *Code* was cited in comparison. This section specifies as an ingredient of the offence, knowledge or reason for belief that the female person is, by reason of her mental condition, incapable of giving a reasonable consent. Knowledge of the existence of a blood-relationship is a constituent element of the crime of incest, spelled out in s. 150 of the *Code*.

One cannot assume, on the strength of these two sections, that there is no *mens rea* element relating to consent, for crimes of rape. Parliament does not consistently employ wording which indicates express levels of intention (such as knowingly, intentionally, wilfully) for all offences which undoubtedly import a mental element. Even within Part IV, there is no consistency in the wording of the offences. I do not think the determination of the mental element for rape turns, in any way, on a comparative analysis of the wording for Part IV offences.

… In summary, intention or recklessness must be proved in relation to all elements of the offence, including absence of consent. This simply extends to rape the same general order of intention as in other crimes. …

Mistake is a defence, then, where it prevents an accused from having the *mens rea* which the law requires for the very crime with which he is charged. Mistake of fact is more accurately seen as a negation of guilty intention than as the affirmation of a positive defence. It avails an accused who acts innocently, pursuant to a flawed perception of the facts, and nonetheless commits the *actus reus* of an offence. Mistake is a defence though, in the sense that it is raised as an issue by an accused. The Crown is rarely possessed of knowledge of the subjective factors which may have caused an accused to entertain a belief in a fallacious set of facts.

If I am correct that: (i) s. 143 of the *Criminal Code* imports a *mens rea* requirement, and (ii) the *mens rea* of rape includes intention, or recklessness as to non-consent of the complainant, a mistake that negatives intention or recklessness entitles the accused to an acquittal. Glanville Williams notes (*Criminal Law, The General Part*, 2nd ed. (1961), p. 173, para. 65):

> It is impossible to assert that a crime requiring intention or recklessness can be committed although the accused laboured under a mistake negativing the requisite intention or recklessness. Such an assertion carries its own refutation. …

I do not think the defence of mistaken belief can be restricted to those situations in which the belief has been induced by information received from a third party. That was the situation in the *Morgan* case. In *Morgan*, the belief in consent was induced by information related by the complainant's husband, who spoke of his wife's sexual propensities. The foundation for the defence, incredible as it turned out to be, in view of the violence, was the misinformation of the husband. Had the defendants believed that information, and had the wife's overt conduct been relatively consistent with it, the defendants would have had a defence. That is the effect of the *dicta* of the House of Lords in the *Morgan* case.

In principle, the defence should avail when there is an honest belief in consent, or an absence of knowledge that consent has been withheld. Whether the mistake is rooted in an accused's mistaken perception, or is based upon objective, but incorrect, facts confided to him by another, should be of no consequence. The kind of mistaken fact pleaded by the *Morgan* defendants, however, is more likely to be believed than a bald assertion of mistaken belief during a face-to-face encounter. In any event, it is clear that the defence is available only where there is sufficient evidence presented by an accused, by his testimony or by the circumstances in which the act occurred, to found the plea. …

The next question which must be broached is whether a defence of honest, though mistaken, belief in consent must be based on reasonable grounds. A majority of the House of Lords in *Morgan* answered the question in the negative, and that view was affirmed by the Heilbron Committee. There can be no doubt this answer is consonant with principle.

[A number of cases and authorities in other jurisdictions were then set out.]

. . .

In Canada, the *Tolson* rule has already been rejected by this Court in favour of the honest belief standard. Unless this Court wishes to overrule *Beaver v. The Queen*, [1957] S.C.R. 531, it is difficult to see how the minority in *Morgan* can decide this appeal.

. . .

It is not clear how one can properly relate reasonableness (an element in offences of negligence) to rape (a "true crime" and not an offence of negligence). To do so, one must, I think, take the view that the *mens rea* goes only to the physical act of intercourse and not to non-consent, and acquittal comes only if the mistake is reasonable. This, upon the authorities, is not a correct view, the intent in rape being not merely to have intercourse, but to have it with a nonconsenting woman. If the jury finds that mistake, whether reasonable or unreasonable, there should be no conviction. If, upon the entire record, there is evidence of mistake to cast a reasonable doubt upon the existence of a criminal mind, then the prosecution has failed to make its case. In an article by Professor Colin Howard, "The Reasonableness of Mistake in the Criminal Law," 4 *U. Queensland L.J.* 45 (1961-64), the following is offered (p. 47):

> To crimes of *mens rea* or elements of a crime which requires *mens rea*, mistake of fact *simpliciter* is a defence; to crimes of negligence, or elements of an offence which requires only negligence, mistake of fact is a defence only if the mistake was in all the circumstances a reasonable one to make.

. . .

I am not unaware of the policy considerations advanced in support of the view that if mistake is to afford a defence to a charge of rape, it should, at the very least, be one a reasonable man might make in the circumstances. There is justifiable concern over the position of the woman who alleges she has been subjected to a non-consensual sexual act; fear is expressed that subjective orthodoxy should not enable her alleged assailant to escape accountability by advancing some cock-and-bull story. The usual response of persons accused of rape is—"she consented." Are such persons now to be acquitted, simply by saying: "even if she did not consent, I believed she consented"? The concern is legitimate and real. It must, however, be placed in the balance with other relevant considerations. First, cases in which mistake can be advanced in answer to a charge of rape must be few in number. People do not normally commit rape *per incuriam*. An evidential case must exist to support the plea. Secondly, if the woman in her own mind withholds consent, but her conduct and other circumstances lend credence to belief on the part of the accused that she was consenting, it may be that it is unjust to convict. I do not think it will do to say that in those circumstances she, in fact, consented. In fact, she did not, and it would be open to a jury to so find. Thirdly, it is unfair to the jury, and to the accused, to speak in terms of two beliefs, one entertained by the accused, the other by a reasonable man, and to ask the jury to ignore an actual belief in favour of an attributed belief. The mind with which the jury is concerned is that of the accused. By importing a standard external to the accused, there is created an incompatible mix of subjective and objective factors. If an honest lack of knowledge is shown, then the subjective element of the offence is not proved. ...

Perpetuation of fictions does little for the jury system or the integrity of criminal justice. The ongoing debate in the Courts and learned journals as to whether mistake must be reasonable is conceptually important in the orderly development of the criminal law, but in my view, practically unimportant because the accused's statement that he was mistaken is not likely to be believed unless the mistake is, to the jury, reasonable. The jury will be concerned to consider the reasonableness of any grounds found, or asserted to be available, to support the defence of mistake. Although "reasonable grounds" is not a precondition to the availability of a plea of honest belief in consent, those grounds determine the weight to be given the defence. The reasonableness, or otherwise, of the accused's belief is only evidence for, or against, the view that the belief was actually held and the intent was, therefore, lacking.

Canadian juries, in my experience, display a high degree of common sense, and an uncanny ability to distinguish between the genuine and the specious.

· · ·

I come now to what is perhaps the most difficult part of this case, namely, whether there was an evidential base sufficient to require the trial Judge to place before the jury the defence of mistaken belief in consent. The trial Judge and two Judges of the Court of Appeal concluded no such base existed. Chief Justice Farris, in dismissing the appeal, was strongly influenced by the fact that "at no time did the appellant suggest in his evidence that while there was resistance on the part of the complainant nonetheless he honestly believed that she was in fact consenting. He did testify that there was resistance after acts of bondage but from then on there was no intercourse." With respect, it is not necessary that an accused specifically plead mistake. The issue to which an accused's state of mind is relevant is *mens rea* and that issue is always before the jury, the onus being on the prosecution. Nor is a defence of honest belief necessarily inconsistent with a defence of consent. In raising the latter, an accused is challenging the factual aspect of the offence. Did the complainant or did she not consent? If she did, the *actus reus* was not committed. The defence of honest belief is different in nature, for it rests upon an accused's subjective perception of that factual situation.

· · ·

If there was "some" evidence to "convey a sense of reality" to a defence of mistake as to consent, then the jury ought to have been instructed to consider that plea. ...

· · ·

There is circumstantial evidence supportive of a plea of belief in consent: (1) Her necklace and car keys were found in the living-room. (2) She confirmed his testimony that her blouse was neatly hung in the clothes closet. (3) Other items of folded clothing were found at the foot of the bed. (4) None of her clothes were damaged in the slightest way. (5) She was in the house for a number of hours. (6) By her version, when she entered the house, the appellant said he was going to break her. She made no attempt to leave. (7) She did not leave while he undressed. (8) There was no evidence of struggle, and (9) she suffered no physical injuries, aside from three scratches.

· · ·

… The possibility of a mistaken belief in consent in the pre-bondage phase was an issue that should have been placed before the jury: the Judge's failure to do so makes it imperative, in my opinion, in the interests of justice, that there be a new trial. It was open to the jury to find only token resistance prior to the "bondage" incident, which the appellant may not have perceived as a withholding of consent. The accused was convicted of that which, perhaps, he did not intend to do had he known of no consent. It does not follow that, by simply disbelieving the appellant on consent, in fact, the jury thereby found that there was no belief in consent, and that the appellant could not reasonably have believed in consent.

I would allow the appeal, set aside the judgment of the British Columbia Court of Appeal and direct a new trial.

McINTYRE J (Martland, Pigeon, Beetz, and Chouinard JJ concurring): In a dissenting judgment, Lambert J.A. was of the opinion that there was sufficient evidence to put the defence to the jury. He would have directed the jury that the accused was entitled to an acquittal if the jury found that he entertained an honest and reasonably held mistaken belief in the existence of consent. This is a view which I cannot share in view of the pronouncement in this Court in *Beaver v. The Queen*, [1957] S.C.R. 531 at p. 538.

… Before any obligation arises to put defences, there must be in the evidence some basis upon which the defence can rest and it is only where such an evidentiary basis is present that a trial Judge must put a defence. Indeed, where it is not present he should not put a defence for to do so would only be to confuse.

· · ·

In relating the law to the facts of any case, we must keep in mind what it is that the trial Judge must look for in the evidence in deciding whether there is, in the words of Fauteux J., "some evidence or matter apt to convey a sense of reality in the argument, and in the grievance." In this case, to convey such a sense of reality, there must be some evidence which if believed would support the existence of a mistaken but honest belief that the complainant was in fact consenting to the acts of intercourse which admittedly occurred. This requires a more detailed recital of the evidence than would ordinarily be necessary.

[The facts were then examined.]

· · ·

With that thought in mind and, bearing in mind that the object of the judicial search must be evidence of a mistaken but honest belief in the consent of the complainant, one must first ask the question "Where is this evidence to be found?" It cannot be found in the evidence of the complainant. She denies actual consent and her evidence cannot provide any support for a mistaken belief in consent. Her conduct, according to her description, is that of a terrified, hysterical, non-consenting woman who resisted the appellant's advances, albeit unsuccessfully, and when able fled from his house in search of assistance. Turning then to the evidence of the appellant, it immediately becomes apparent that his evidence speaks of actual consent, even co-operation, and leaves little if any room for the suggestion that she may not have been consenting but he thought she was. The two stories are, as has been noted before, diametrically opposed on this vital issue. It is not for the trial Judge to weigh them and prefer one to the other. It is for him in this situation, however, to recognize the issue which arises on the evidence for the purpose of deciding what defences are open. In this situation the only realistic issue which can arise is the simple issue of consent or no consent. In my opinion, the trial Judge was correct in concluding that there simply was not sufficient evidence to justify the putting of the defence of mistake of fact to the jury. He left the issue of consent and that was the only one arising on the evidence.

In reaching this conclusion, I am not unmindful of the evidence of surrounding circumstances which were said to support the appellant's contention. I refer to the absence of serious injury suffered by the complainant and the absence of damage to clothing, as well as to the long period of time during which the parties remained in the bedroom. These matters may indeed be cogent on the issue of actual consent but, in my view, they cannot by themselves advance a suggestion of a mistaken belief. The finding of the clothes at the foot of the bed, the necklace and the keys in the living-room, are equally relevant on the issue of actual consent and, in my view, cannot affect the issue which was clearly framed by the opposing assertions of consent and non-consent.

It would seem to me that if it is considered necessary in this case to charge the jury on the defence of mistake of fact, it would be necessary to do so in all cases where the complainant denies consent and an accused asserts it. To require the putting of the alternative defence of mistaken belief in consent, there must be, in my opinion, some evidence beyond the mere assertion of belief in consent by counsel for the appellant. This evidence must appear from or be supported by sources other than the appellant in order to give it any air of reality. In *R. v. Plummer and Brown* (1975), 24 C.C.C. (2d) 497, Evans J.A. (as he then was), speaking for the Ontario Court of Appeal, considered that there was such evidence as far as Brown was concerned and directed a new trial because the defence had not been put. In that case, the complainant had gone to Plummer's "pad" where she had been raped by Plummer. Brown entered the room where the rape occurred after Plummer had gone. Apparently, he had arrived at the house separately from Plummer. It was open on the evidence to find that he was unaware then that Plummer had threatened the complainant and terrorized her into submission. He had intercourse with her and she said that because of continuing fear from Plummer's threats, she submitted without protest. In these special circumstances, the defence was required. The facts clearly established at least an air of reality to Brown's defence. In *Morgan*, there was evidence of an invitation by the complainant's husband to have intercourse with his wife and his assurance that her show of resistance would be a sham. In other words, there was evidence explaining, however preposterous the explanation might be, a basis for the mistaken belief. In the case at bar, there is no such evidence.

Where the complainant says rape and the accused says consent, and where on the whole of the evidence, including that of the complainant, the accused, and the surrounding circumstances, there is a clear issue on this point, and where as here the accused makes no assertion of a belief in consent as opposed to an actual consent, it is unrealistic in the absence of some other circumstance or circumstances, such as are found in the *Plummer and Brown* and *Morgan* cases, to consider the Judge bound to put the mistake of fact defence. In my opinion, the trial Judge was correct in refusing to put the defence on the evidence before him.

I might add that I have had the advantage of reading the reasons of my brother Dickson J. and, while it is apparent that I am unable to accept his view on the evidentiary question, I am in agreement with that part of his judgment dealing with the availability as a defence to a charge of rape in Canada of what is generally termed the defence of mistake of fact.

I would dismiss the appeal.

[Martland J agreed with McIntyre J, but would leave undecided the question whether the accused's belief need be "honest" or "honest and reasonable."]

Appeal dismissed.

Section 265(4) of the Code, which came into force in 1983, provides:

> Where an accused alleges that he believed that the complainant consented to the conduct that is the subject-matter of the charge, a judge, if satisfied that there is sufficient evidence and that, if believed by the jury, the evidence would constitute a defence, shall instruct the jury, when reviewing all the evidence relating to the determination of the honesty of the accused's belief, to consider the presence or absence of reasonable grounds for that belief.

Does this change the law as stated by the Court in *Pappajohn*?

Judges continue to be divided on what constitutes an "air of reality" in a particular case. See e.g. *Reddick v The Queen*, [1991] 1 SCR 1086. In *R v Bulmer*, [1987] 1 SCR 782, McIntyre J stated for the Court: "The statement of the accused alleging a mistaken belief will be a factor but will not by itself be decisive, and even in its total absence, other circumstances might dictate the putting of the defence." Lamer J added: "If this means that the trial judge is not required to put the defence to the jury merely because the accused's lawyer has referred to the defence in argument, then I agree. … However, I must respectfully take issue with the 'air of reality' norm if it is to be understood as going so far as enabling the trial judge to choose not to leave the defence of honest belief with the jury even in a case where the accused has taken the stand and asserted under oath that he or she honestly believed in consent."

In *Osolin v The Queen*, [1993] 4 SCR 595, the issue was, *inter alia*, whether s 265(4) infringed s 11(d) (presumption of innocence) or s 11(f) (right to trial by jury) of the Charter. The Supreme Court unanimously held that it did not. All judges agreed with Cory J's analysis of the constitutionality of the provision. Cory J stated:

> Section 265(4) of the *Criminal Code* is applicable to all assaults, not just sexual assaults. It appears to be no more than the codification of the common law defence of mistake of fact. …
>
> It is trite law that a trial judge must instruct the jury only upon those defences for which there is a real factual basis. A defence for which there is no evidentiary foundation should not be put to the jury. This rule extends well beyond the defence of mistaken belief in consent and is of long standing. In *Kelsey v. The Queen*, [1953] 1 S.C.R. 220, at p. 226, Fauteux J., writing for the majority, held:
>
>> The allotment of any substance to an argument or of any value to a grievance resting on the omission of the trial Judge from mentioning such argument must be conditioned on the existence in the record of some evidence or matter apt to convey *a sense of reality* in the argument and in the grievance. [Emphasis added.]

• • •

In the realm of sexual assault cases the requirement of sufficient evidence has caused some confusion. Yet in my view these words require no more than the application of the principles that have been set out above. In *Pappajohn, supra,* it was held that the defence of mistaken belief in consent should only be put to the jury if there was an adequate and evidentiary foundation found for it.

· · ·

The question that arises is whether this means that in order for the defence to be put to the jury there must be some evidence of mistaken belief in consent emanating from a source other than the accused. In my view, this proposition cannot be correct. There is no requirement that there be evidence independent of the accused in order to have the defence put to the jury. However, the mere assertion by the accused that "I believed she was consenting" will not be sufficient. What is required is that the defence of mistaken belief be supported by evidence beyond the mere assertion of a mistaken belief.

· · ·

The distinction between a burden of proof with regard to an offence or an element of the offence, and an evidentiary burden is critical. It must be remembered that the accused only bears the evidentiary burden of raising the issue of mistake, and in fact, only bears that burden if sufficient evidence has not already been raised by the prosecution's case.

· · ·

Section 265(4) does not create a statutory presumption. The accused seeking to raise the defence of mistaken belief only bears a tactical evidentiary burden.

· · ·

Section 265(4) leaves the burden on the Crown in regard to all the essential elements of the offence. The prosecution must prove both the *mens rea* and the *actus reus* beyond a reasonable doubt: that the accused engaged in sexual intercourse with a woman who was not consenting, and that he intended to engage in sexual intercourse without the consent of the woman.

Cory J added with respect to the trial by jury issue:

The appellant was provided with a trial by jury. The only elements of the trial that were decided by the trial judge were those things properly within his realm, namely those issues pertaining to trial process and questions of law. There is consequently no violation of the appellant's right to a trial by jury.

Five members of the Court, however, did not agree with Cory J on the question whether there can be an "air of reality" when the complainant and the accused have given "diametrically opposed" versions of the facts. Three other members of the Court (L'Heureux-Dubé, Iacobucci, and Major JJ) agreed with Cory J's view that in such circumstances there cannot be an "air of reality." Cory J stated:

In what circumstances will it be appropriate to consider a defence of mistaken belief in consent? It is the position of the intervener, the Attorney General for Ontario, that the defence cannot arise in situations where the evidence of the complainant and the accused are diametrically opposed. For example, if the accused states that there was willing consent and the complainant denies any consent then the defence simply cannot arise. In such circumstances for a jury to accept the defence of mistaken belief in consent it would have to reject all the evidence given at the trial including that tendered by both the complainant (no consent) and that of the accused (willing consent). Indeed in order to give effect to the defence a jury would have to speculate upon and give effect to a third version of events which was not in evidence.

• • •

I agree with this position. The defence of mistake may arise when the accused and the complainant tell essentially the same story and then argue that they interpreted it differently. Realistically it can only arise when the facts described by the complainant and the accused generally correspond but the interpretation of those facts leads to a different state of mind for each of the parties. In a situation where the evidence given is directly opposed as to whether there was consent, the defence of mistake as to consent simply cannot exist. However, even in the absence of that defence, the jury will nonetheless be bound to acquit if it has a reasonable doubt as to whether there was consent in light of the conflicting evidence on the issue. Lack of consent is an integral element of the offence. In cases where there is conflicting evidence on the issue the trial judge will always direct the jury that they must be satisfied beyond a reasonable doubt that consent was lacking.

The majority of the Court, however, took the same position as McLachlin J, who stated:

Before leaving this question, I should comment on two points. The first is the argument that the divergent stories of the complainant and the accused on consent, as a matter of law, necessarily preclude a third alternative, the defence of honest but mistaken belief. I am not so convinced as my colleagues that where the evidence consists of two diametrically opposed stories, one alleging lack of consent and the other consent, it is logically impossible to conceive of the defence of honest but mistaken belief arising. While it may rarely occur, it seems to me possible for a jury to accept parts of the testimonies of both the complainant and the accused, concluding that notwithstanding lack of actual consent, the accused honestly believed in consent. As A.W. Bryant states:

> … the removal of this alternative plea on the basis that the testimony of the complainant and the accused are diametrically opposed, and that there is a lack of common ground for the defence is based, in part, on the premise that the complainant's version is complete—a questionable assumption in some cases. Moreover, a requirement for corroboration may wrongly encourage an accused to dovetail partially his testimony with that of the complainant in order to supply the necessary common ground for the defence.

The test for an "air of reality" applies with respect to any matter of defence that is raised by the evidence and that does not carry a legal burden with it. It means that no matter of defence can be considered by the trier of fact unless it meets this standard. In *R v Cinous*, 2002 SCC 29, [2002] 2 SCR 3, the Supreme Court of Canada again reviewed this standard and repeated that the test is whether "a properly instructed jury acting reasonably could acquit." This is a question of law for the trial judge and, in effect, it asks whether the trier of fact, acting reasonably, could entertain a reasonable doubt. The Court also repeated that this is a principle of general application.

The following case turns on the findings of fact made by the trial judge. The Supreme Court nevertheless concludes that the trial judge made an error of law in her disposition of the case. What are the essential findings of fact by the trial judge and what, according to the Supreme Court, was the mistake of law in her disposition? Can these be reconciled?

Sansregret v The Queen
Supreme Court of Canada
[1985] 1 SCR 570

McINTYRE J: ... The appellant, a man in his early twenties, and the complainant, a woman of thirty-one years, had lived together in the complainant's house for about a year before the events of October 15, 1982. Their relationship had been one of contention and discord with violence on the part of the appellant; "slapping" or "roughing up" in his description, "blows" in hers. The appellant had left the house for short periods and in September of 1982 the complainant decided to end the affair. She told the appellant to leave and he did.

On September 23, 1982, some days after his dismissal, the appellant broke into the house at about 4:30 a.m. He was "raging" at her and furious because of his expulsion. He terrorized her with a file-like instrument with which he was armed. She was fearful of what might occur, and in order to calm him down she held out some hope of a reconciliation and they had intercourse. A report was made to the police of this incident, the complainant asserting she had been raped, but no proceedings were taken. The appellant's probation officer became involved and there was evidence that he had asked the complainant not to press the matter, presumably because it would interfere with the appellant's probation.

On October 15, 1982, again at about 4:30 a.m., the appellant broke into the complainant's house through a basement window. She was alone, and, awakened by the entry, she seized the bedroom telephone in an effort to call the police. The appellant picked up a butcher knife in the kitchen and came into the bedroom. He was furious and violent. He accused her of having another boyfriend; pulled the cord of the telephone out of the jack and threw it into the living-room; threatened her with the knife and ordered her to take off her nightdress and made her stand in the kitchen doorway, naked save for a jacket over her shoulders, so he could be sure where she was while he repaired the window to conceal his entry from the police, should they arrive. He struck her on the mouth with sufficient force to draw blood, and on three occasions rammed the knife blade into the wall with great force, once very close to her. He told her that if the police came he would put the knife through her, and added that if he had found her with a boyfriend he would have killed them both. At one point he tied her hands behind her back with a scarf. The complainant said she was in fear for her life and sanity.

By about 5:30 a.m., after an hour of such behaviour by the appellant, she tried to calm him down. She pretended again that there was some hope of a reconciliation if the appellant would settle down and get a job. This had the desired effect. He calmed down and after some conversation he joined her on the bed and they had intercourse. The complainant swore that her consent to the intercourse was solely for the purpose of calming him down, to protect herself from further violence. This, she said, was something she had learned from earlier experience with him. In her evidence she said:

> I didn't consent at any time.
>
> I was very afraid. My whole body was trembling. I was sure I would have a nervous breakdown. I came very, very close to losing my mind. All I knew was I had to keep this man calm or he would kill me.

. . .

[The trial judge had made the following findings:

> As I said, no rational person could have been under any honest mistake of fact. However, people have an uncanny ability to blind themselves to much that they don't want to see, and to believe in the existence of facts as they would wish them to be. The accused says that, notwithstanding the reign of terror which preceded their chat, notwithstanding that he held a knife while they talked, notwithstanding that he did most of the talking and that the complainant's answers were clearly equivocal, he presumed and believed that everything between them was peachy. This, notwithstanding that three weeks earlier, on a replay of the same sort of evening, his probation officer became involved and the complainant moved out of her house. Very honestly, despite my confidence in the ability of people to blind themselves to reality, and even if the accused had not lied about other parts of his testimony, I would have been hard-pressed to credit the honesty of his belief.
>
> However, his honest belief finds support in the testimony of the complainant. She knows him and in her opinion, notwithstanding all the objective facts to the contrary, he did believe that everything was back to normal between them by the time of the sexual encounter. His subsequent behaviour as well, attests to that fact.
>
> I do not like the conclusion which this leads me to. There was no real consent. There was submission as a result of a very real and justifiable fear. No one in his right mind could have believed that the complainant's dramatic about-face stemmed from anything other than fear. But the accused did. He saw what he wanted to see, heard what he wanted to hear, believed what he wanted to believe.
>
> The facts in *Pappajohn v. R.*, [1980] 2 S.C.R. 120, are quite dissimilar to those in this case. The dictum of the Supreme Court of Canada, however, is clear and broad and in no way seems to limit itself to the peculiar circumstances of that case. Perhaps the Crown will appeal this decision to obtain some direction from the Supreme Court on whether it was that court's intention to cover situations where an accused, who demonstrates the clarity and shrewdness this accused showed in securing his own safety at the outset can turn around and because it does not suit his wishes, can go wilfully blind to the obvious shortly thereafter. In any event, the ratio of *Pappajohn* is clear and it leaves me no alternative but to acquit.

The Manitoba Court of Appeal had allowed a Crown appeal and substituted a conviction.]

It is evident that the trial judge would have convicted the appellant of rape had it not been for the defence of mistake of fact. She considered that the belief in the consent expressed by the appellant was an honest one and therefore on the basis of *Pappajohn* [*v The Queen*, [1980] 2 SCR 120], even if it were unreasonably held, as it is clear she thought it was, he was entitled to his acquittal. This application of the defence of mistake of fact would be supportable were it not for the fact that the trial judge found in addition that the appellant had been wilfully blind to reality in his behaviour on October 15th. Such a finding would preclude the application of the defence and lead to a different result. It is my opinion then that the trial judge erred in this matter in that though she made the requisite findings of fact that the appellant was wilfully blind to the consequences of his acts she did not apply them according to law. ...

Wilful blindness is distinct from recklessness because, while recklessness involves knowledge of a danger or risk and persistence in a course of conduct which creates a risk that the prohibited result will occur, wilful blindness arises where a person who has become aware of the need for some inquiry declines to make the inquiry because he does not wish to know the truth. He would prefer to remain ignorant. The culpability in recklessness is justified by consciousness of the risk and by proceeding in the face of it, while in wilful blindness it is justified by the accused's fault in deliberately failing to inquire when he knows there is reason for inquiry. ...

This case reveals, in my view, an appropriate set of circumstances for the application of the "wilful blindness" rule. I have outlined the circumstances which form the background. I have referred to the findings of the trial judge that the appellant blinded himself to the obvious and made no inquiry as to the nature of the consent which was given. If the evidence before the court was limited to the events of October 15th, it would be difficult indeed to infer wilful blindness. To attribute criminal liability on the basis of this one incident would come close to applying a constructive test to the effect that he should have known she was consenting out of fear. The position, however, is changed when the evidence reveals the earlier episode and the complaint of rape which it caused, knowledge of which, as I have said, had clearly reached the accused. Considering the whole of the evidence then, no constructive test of knowledge is required. The appellant was aware of the likelihood of the complainant's reaction to his threats. To proceed with intercourse in such circumstances constitutes, in my view, self-deception to the point of wilful blindness.

In my view, it was error on the part of the trial judge to give effect to the "mistake of fact" defence in these circumstances where she had found that the complainant consented out of fear and the appellant was wilfully blind to the existing circumstances, seeing only what he wished to see. Where the accused is deliberately ignorant as a result of blinding himself to reality the law presumes knowledge, in this case knowledge of the nature of the consent. There was therefore no room for the operation of this defence.

This is not to be taken as a retreat from the position taken in *Pappajohn* that the honest belief need not be reasonable. It is not to be thought that any time an accused forms an honest though unreasonable belief he will be deprived of the defence of mistake of fact. This case rests on a different proposition. Having wilfully blinded himself to the facts before him, the fact that an accused may be enabled to preserve what could be called an honest belief, in the sense that he has no specific knowledge to the contrary, will not afford a defence because, where the accused becomes deliberately blind to the existing facts, he is fixed by law with actual knowledge and his belief in another state of facts is irrelevant.

I would dismiss the appeal.

An important feature of the 1983 reforms was an amendment of the Code that excluded evidence of the complainant's previous sexual conduct. In the past, the law had permitted the admission of this evidence on the basis that it had probative value on the issue of consent and regarding the credibility of the complainant. Parliament rejected these ideas, but the Supreme Court of Canada held in *R v Seaboyer; R v Gayme*, [1991] 2 SCR 577 that by excluding sexual history evidence without regard to the use to which that evidence would be put, the 1983 exclusionary rule went too far. Justice McLachlin for the majority alluded to *Pappajohn* when she stated that "[t]he basis of the accused's honest belief in the complainant's consent may be sexual acts performed by the complainant at some other time or place" and that such evidence would be inappropriately precluded by the rule. Parliament responded to *Seaboyer* in Bill C-49. As enacted, the Bill provides as follows:

An Act to amend the Criminal Code (sexual assault)

WHEREAS the Parliament of Canada is gravely concerned about the incidence of sexual violence and abuse in Canadian society and, in particular, the prevalence of sexual assault against women and children;

WHEREAS the Parliament of Canada recognizes the unique character of the offence of sexual assault and how sexual assault and, more particularly, the fear of sexual assault affects the lives of the people of Canada;

WHEREAS the Parliament of Canada intends to promote and help to ensure the full protection of the rights guaranteed under sections 7 and 15 of the *Canadian Charter of Rights and Freedoms*;

WHEREAS the Parliament of Canada wishes to encourage the reporting of incidents of sexual violence or abuse, and to provide for the prosecution of offences within a framework of laws that are consistent with the principles of fundamental justice and that are fair to complainants as well as to accused persons;

WHEREAS the Supreme Court of Canada has declared the existing section 276 of the *Criminal Code* to be of no force and effect;

AND WHEREAS the Parliament of Canada believes that at trials of sexual offences, evidence of the complainant's sexual history is rarely relevant and that its admission should be subject to particular scrutiny, bearing in mind the inherently prejudicial character of such evidence;

1. The *Criminal Code* is amended by adding thereto, immediately after section 273 thereof, the following sections:

273.1(1) Subject to subsection (2) and subsection 265(3), "consent" means, for the purposes of sections 271, 272 and 273, the voluntary agreement of the complainant to engage in the sexual activity in question.

(2) No consent is obtained, for the purposes of sections 271, 272 and 273, where

(a) the agreement is expressed by the words or conduct of a person other than the complainant;

(b) the complainant is incapable of consenting to the activity;

(c) the accused induces the complainant to engage in the activity by abusing a position of trust, power or authority;

(d) the complainant expresses, by words or conduct, a lack of agreement to engage in the activity; or

(e) the complainant, having consented to engage in sexual activity, expresses, by words or conduct, a lack of agreement to continue to engage in the activity.

(3) Nothing in subsection (2) shall be construed as limiting the circumstances in which no consent is obtained.

273.2 It is not a defence to a charge under section 271, 272 or 273 that the accused believed that the complainant consented to the activity that forms the subject-matter of the charge, where

(a) the accused's belief arose from the accused's

(i) self-induced intoxication, or

(ii) recklessness or wilful blindness; or

(b) the accused did not take reasonable steps, in the circumstances known to the accused at the time, to ascertain that the complainant was consenting.

2. Section 276 of the said Act is repealed and the following substituted therefor:

276.(1) In proceedings in respect of an offence under section 151, 152, 153, 155 or 159, subsection 160(2) or (3) or section 170, 171, 172, 173, 271, 272 or 273, evidence that the complainant has engaged in sexual activity, whether with the accused or with any other person, is not admissible to support an inference that, by reason of the sexual nature of that activity, the complainant

(a) is more likely to have consented to the sexual activity that forms the subject-matter of the charge; or

(b) is less worthy of belief.

(2) In proceedings in respect of an offence referred to in subsection (1), no evidence shall be adduced by or on behalf of the accused that the complainant has engaged in sexual activity other than the sexual activity that forms the subject-matter of the charge, whether with the accused or with any other person, unless the judge, provincial court judge or justice determines, in accordance with the procedures set out in sections 276.1 and 276.2, that the evidence

(a) is of specific instances of sexual activity;

(b) is relevant to an issue at trial; and

(c) has significant probative value that is not substantially outweighed by the danger of prejudice to the proper administration of justice.

(3) In determining whether evidence is admissible under subsection (2), the judge, provincial court judge or justice shall take into account

(a) the interests of justice, including the right of the accused to make a full answer and defence;

(b) society's interest in encouraging the reporting of sexual assault offences;

(c) whether there is a reasonable prospect that the evidence will assist in arriving at a just determination in the case;

(d) the need to remove from the fact-finding process any discriminatory belief or bias;

(e) the risk that the evidence may unduly arouse sentiments of prejudice, sympathy or hostility in the jury;

(f) the potential prejudice to the complainant's personal dignity and right of privacy;

(g) the right of the complainant and of every individual to personal security and to the full protection and benefit of the law; and

(h) any other factor that the judge, provincial court judge or justice considers relevant.

Perhaps not surprisingly, these amendments were also challenged and so the dialogue continued between the Supreme Court and Parliament. At issue was whether Bill C-49 provided sufficient constitutional protection for both the accused and the complainant.

In *R v Darrach* (1998), 122 CCC (3d) 225 (Ont CA) these new provisions were upheld as constitutional. The accused unsuccessfully argued that s 273.2 violated ss 7 and 11(c) of the Charter by employing objective forms of *mens rea* and requiring the accused to demonstrate that he took reasonable steps to ascertain whether the complainant consented. Morden ACJO stated:

[85] With respect to the challenge based on s. 7, I am far from satisfied that sexual assault is one of those "very few" offences (*R. v. Vaillancourt*, [1987] 2 S.C.R. 636 at 653, 39 C.C.C. (3d) 118),

which carries such a stigma that its *mens rea* component must be one of subjectivity. See Hogg, *Constitutional Law of Canada* (1992), looseleaf ed., vol. 2 at pp. 44-34 to 44-35. I say this because: it is an offence of general intent; it can be prosecuted by way of summary conviction; it is a generic offence which covers a broad range of conduct, some of which may be very minor compared to other offences; there is no minimum penalty, the maximum penalty is 10 years, and within this range the sentence can be tailored to reflect the moral opprobrium of both the offence and the offender. See *R. v. Creighton*, [1993] 3 S.C.R. 3, 83 C.C.C. (3d) 346, particularly at pp. 48-49, with respect to the offence of manslaughter.

[86] Further, I accept that the stigma characterization has been fairly criticized as being a most unstable one for making important constitutional decisions on the applicability of s. 7 of the *Charter* to the substantive elements of offences. See, for example, Hogg, *Constitutional Law of Canada* (1992) loose-leaf ed., at p. 44-35 and Stuart, *Charter Justice in Canadian Criminal Law*, 2nd ed. (Scarborough, ON: Carswell, 1996) at p. 74.

[87] Notwithstanding the foregoing reservations, I am prepared to decide this issue on the basis that the offence of sexual assault carries with it a sufficient social stigma as to require a subjective fault requirement on the part of the accused person. In my view, notwithstanding s. 273.2(b), the offence is still largely one based on subjective fault—at least to a level that would satisfy constitutional requirements.

[88] No doubt, the provision can be regarded as introducing an objective component into the mental element of the offence but it is one which, in itself, is a modified one. It is personalized according to the subjective awareness of the accused at the time. The accused is to "take reasonable steps, *in the circumstances known to the accused at the time*, to ascertain that the complainant was consenting." In other words, the accused is not under an obligation to determine all the relevant circumstances—the issue is what he actually knew, not what he ought to have known.

[89] In addition, while the provision requires reasonable steps, it does not require that *all* reasonable steps be taken, as it did in the first version of the bill (Bill C-49, s. 1) that resulted in s. 273.2 and as does s. 150.1(4) of the *Criminal Code*, which is referred to in the judgment of the Supreme Court of Canada in *R. v. Hess; R. v. Nguyen*, [1990] 2 S.C.R. 906 at 922 and 925. Clearly, "all reasonable steps" imposes a more onerous burden than that in s. 273.2(b). I, of course, do not intend to express any view on the constitutionality of s. 150.1(4).

[90] The subjective *mens rea* component of the offence remains largely intact. The provision does not require that a mistaken belief in consent must be reasonable in order to exculpate. The provision merely requires that a person about to engage in sexual activity take "reasonable steps ... to ascertain that the complainant was consenting." Were a person to take reasonable steps, and nonetheless make an unreasonable mistake about the presence of consent, he or she would be entitled to ask the trier of fact to acquit on this basis.

[91] The extent to which the provision alters principles of liability underlying the offence of sexual assault is indicated in the reasons of McLachlin J. in *R. v. Esau* (1997), 116 C.C.C. (3d) 289 (S.C.C.) at 314. Although the statement is in a dissenting judgment I do not think that there is any proposition in the majority judgment of Major J. at variance with it. McLachlin J. said:

> A person is not entitled to take ambiguity as the equivalent of consent. If a person, acting honestly and without wilful blindness, perceives his companion's conduct as ambiguous or unclear, his duty is to abstain or obtain clarification on the issue of consent. This appears to be the rule at common law. In this situation, to use the words of Lord Cross of Chelsea in *Morgan, supra*, [[1976] AC 182] at p. 203, "it is only fair to the woman and not in the least

unfair to the man that he should be under a duty to take reasonable care to ascertain that she is consenting to the intercourse and be at risk of a prosecution if he fails to take such care." As Glanville Williams, *Textbook of Criminal Law* (London: Stevens & Sons, 1978), at p. 101, put it: "the defendant is guilty if he realized the woman might not be consenting and took no steps to find out."

[92] Following this quotation, she said at pp. 314-15:

I note that Parliament has affirmed this common sense proposition in enacting s. 273.2 of the *Criminal Code* of Canada which states that "[i]t is not a defence to a charge [of sexual assault] that the accused believed that the complainant consented to the activity that forms the subject-matter of the charge, where … the accused did not take reasonable steps, in the circumstances known to the accused at the time, to ascertain that the complainant was consenting." See also *R. v. Darrach* (1994), 17 O.R. (3d) 481 (Prov. Div.) [the judgment under appeal before this court]. The question is whether the defendant at bar, properly attentive to the issue of consent (i.e., not wilfully blind), could have, in light of the ambiguity, honestly concluded that the complainant had the capacity and was consenting to the sexual activity.

[93] Finally, having regard to the basic rationale underlying constitutionally mandated fault requirements that it is wrong to punish a person who is "morally innocent" (*Reference re Section 94(2) of the Motor Vehicle Act* (1985), 23 C.C.C. (3d) 289 (S.C.C.) at 311), it is difficult to contemplate that a man who has sexual intercourse with a woman who has not consented is morally innocent if he has not taken reasonable steps to ascertain that she was consenting.

The accused in *Darrach* appealed further to the Supreme Court with respect to the constitutionality of the amended s 276. The Court concluded that the amended provision is consistent with ss 7, 11(c), and 11(d) of the Charter and is therefore constitutional. The Court did not address the constitutionality of ss 273.1 and 273.2. See *R v Darrach*, 2000 SCC 46, [2000] 2 SCR 443.

Although the Court of Appeal for Ontario upheld ss 273.1 and 273.2, as this next excerpt illustrates, the manner by which it chose to do so has attracted criticism.

C Boyle & M MacCrimmon, "The Constitutionality of Bill C-49: Analyzing Sexual Assault as if Equality Really Mattered" (1999) 41 Crim LQ 198 at 214-17

It is difficult to characterize the "reasonable steps" provision in terms of traditional criminal law concepts, in part because the mistaken belief defence is in itself a hybrid. On the one hand it is a denial of *mens rea*. On the other, it is similar to a defence proper such as self-defence, in that it will not be addressed unless it has an "air of reality" on the evidence. "Reasonable steps" with its linkage to the *mens rea* concept of mistaken belief but its wording in terms of behaviour rather than belief, muddies the waters further. …

Turning then to its equality underpinnings … however the provision is characterized, it is well supported by s. 15, as intended by Parliament. The men who are most dangerous to women and children, that is those men who are indifferent to the sexual autonomy of others, those who genuinely believe that women are in a perpetual state of consent which can only be withdrawn, if at all, by vigorous resistance, those who believe that resistance is the signal of consent disguised as virtue by a member of a group culturally constructed as mendacious in this context, and those who are not prepared to take no at its face value, are labeled as morally innocent by a rule which insists on subjective mistaken belief in consent defence. If willingness to entertain such beliefs is privileged by the law as a defence then women belong to a group the members of which can be harmed with impunity as long as self-interested misconceptions about women's sexual accessibility are maintained.

The Court of Appeal in *Darrach* addressed the constitutionality of the "reasonable steps" provision in the following way. First, on the basis of an implicit assumption that the provision relates to the *mens rea* of sexual assault, it was "far from satisfied" that sexual assault is a stigma offence. Second, however, on the assumption that it is, enough subjective fault is still required to satisfy constitutional standards. Thus it was noted that the test is a modified, that is, personalized, objective one, and the accused need not take "all" reasonable steps. Further, the court was of the view that the accused who has taken reasonable steps but nevertheless makes an unreasonable mistake about consent, is entitled to an acquittal. This is startling. It would seem sensible to interpret reasonable steps to mean those steps that a person would take to avoid making an unreasonable mistake. Why would the Court of Appeal wish to read the provision down to require a lower level of care? This seems all the more puzzling when it is followed by the comment that "it is difficult to contemplate that a man who has sexual intercourse with a woman who has not consented is morally innocent if he has not taken reasonable steps to ascertain that she was consenting." Why would the man who does not take sufficient steps to avoid an unreasonable mistake be construed as morally innocent? Here we believe that attention to equality arguments might at the very least have prevented the court from reading down the meaning of reasonable steps in a case where there was no factual context to give practical significance to the issue. When this point is combined with the fact that the court quoted with approval from McLachlin J.'s dissenting judgment in *R. v. Esau*, which does not clearly distinguish the failure to take reasonable steps from recklessness, it is hard to avoid the conclusion that the court is giving minimal content to the provision following an incomplete constitutional analysis. Before one has sexual contact with another person whom the law clothes with a constitutional right to equality, one must take some steps to ascertain consent, but not enough steps to avoid an unreasonable mistake!

The interrelationship between ss 273.1 and 273.2 was addressed by the Manitoba Court of Appeal in *R v Malcolm*, 2000 MBCA 77, 147 CCC (3d) 34, leave to appeal to SCC refused, [2001] 1 SCR xiv. Writing for the court, Helper JA indicated:

> In *R. v. Sansregret*, [1985] 1 S.C.R. 570 (S.C.C.), McIntyre J., for the Court, explained the concept of recklessness and then distinguished wilful blindness (pp. 581 and 584 respectively). Recklessness will arise where an accused subjectively perceives a danger or risk that consent is not present, but proceeds in any event. Wilful blindness, on the other hand, will arise in situations where it is obvious in the circumstances that there is no true consent (not just a risk that there may not be a consent), but the accused does not confirm that lack of consent because he wants to be able to say that he did not "know" that there was no consent.

Section 273.2(b), however, injects an objective standard for unreasonable sexual behaviour. In his article entitled "The Pendulum Has Been Pushed Too Far" (1993) 42 U.N.B.L.J. 349, Don Stuart states at p. 352:

> The most significant change [in the passage of Bill C-49] is the declaration in s. 273.2(b) that the accused will not have a mistaken belief defence where he did not take reasonable steps in the circumstances known to him to ascertain whether the complainant was consenting. This expressly reverses the substantive ruling in *R. v. Pappajohn* [[1980] 2 SCR 120] that an honest belief in consent will excuse even if it was unreasonable.

Mr. Stuart envisions that s. 273.2(b) will capture those cases where, although the accused did not perceive that there was a danger that the complainant might not be consenting, he was aware of the presence of certain circumstances, which circumstances would have led a reasonable person to take further steps to ascertain consent.

That viewpoint is endorsed by Rosemary Cairns Way in her article "Bill C-49 and the Politics of Constitutionalized Fault" (1993) 42 U.N.B.L.J. 325, where she states at pp. 329-30 in regard to s. 273.2:

> The intent of the section is twofold. Subsection (a) clarifies the existing law on the mistaken belief defence; that is, i) sexual assault is a general intent offence in which the "defence" of intoxication does not apply, and, ii) a mistake which is either reckless or wilfully blind is no defence. Subsection (b) changes the current law. It overrules the result in *R. v. Pappajohn* that a mistaken belief in consent need only be honestly held to afford a complete defence. Subsection (b) provides that, in order to rely on an honest mistake, an accused must take reasonable steps, in the circumstances known to him at the time, to ascertain if consent exists. In other words, subsection (b) relocates the culpability in sexual assault. *It explicitly shifts the focus, in a limited number of cases, away from the self-conscious wrongdoing of the accused.*
>
> The new focus is on the culpability inherent in the accused's failure to take reasonable steps to determine if the act he is about to engage in is in fact mutual and consensual. *The provision creates a form of objective liability in that the accused is held up to a standard of reasonable conduct which is assessed on the basis of the circumstances known to the accused at the time of the assault.* The provision does not require that the belief in consent itself be reasonable, but rather that the accused make a reasonable effort to ascertain if consent in fact exists. [emphasis added]

See also "Judging Sexual Assault Law Against a Standard of Equality" (1995) 29 U.B.C.L. Rev. 341, wherein John McInnes & Christine Boyle make the following comment about the application of s. 273.2(b) at pp. 361-62:

> This ... provision ... modifies rather than supplants *Pappajohn*. The entirety of its effect is to limit the ambit of the *Pappajohn* defence of honest belief in consent by the imposition of what can be called a "somewhat objective" standard. Since it is settled law that the accused must point to evidence to give a claim of mistaken belief in consent an air of reality before it can be left with the jury, the provision merely adds the requirement that in the circumstances known to the accused, he took reasonable steps to ascertain consent. The "reasonable steps" requirement thus effectively imposes a positive duty on those who undertake the activity of sexual relations to be reasonable in the circumstances known to

them in ensuring that their partner consents. This in no way alters the fact that the mistake alleged by the accused may still be unreasonable. The standard is really only quasi-objective because the ostensibly objective standard of reasonableness with respect to the steps taken to ascertain consent will be coloured by whatever "circumstances known to the accused" is interpreted to mean.

Finally, in "The Constitutionality of Bill C-49: Analyzing Sexual Assault as if Equality Really Mattered" (1998) 41 C.L.Q. 198, Christine Boyle & Marilyn MacCrimmon discuss s. 273.2(b), stating at p. 214:

> … [T]his provision could be seen as changing the *mens rea* of sexual assault by introducing a *quasi*-objective standard for fault. Section 273.2(b) creates a mixed objective/subjective test. In order to argue that he mistakenly believed that a non-consenting woman was consenting the accused must have taken reasonable steps (objective) in the circumstances known to him at the time (subjective).

After reviewing some of the case law, the court summed up the effect of these provisions:

> Considering all of the case law reviewed above, it appears that s. 273.2(b) must be considered in situations where there is an air of reality to the accused's assertion of honest belief in consent and the accused is neither wilfully blind nor reckless in that belief, but circumstances exist which call into question the reasonableness of the accused's actions.
>
> Section 273.2(b) requires the court to apply a quasi-objective test to the situation. First, the circumstances known to the accused must be ascertained. Then, the issue which arises is, if a reasonable man was aware of the same circumstances, would he take further steps before proceeding with the sexual activity? If the answer is yes, and the accused has not taken further steps, then the accused is not entitled to the defence of honest belief in consent. If the answer is no, or even maybe, then the accused would not be required to take further steps and the defence will apply.

ADDITIONAL READING

Criminal Justice Division. *Best Practices for Investigating and Prosecuting Sexual Assault* (Edmonton: Alberta Justice and Solicitor General, 2013).

Cunliffe, E. "Sexual Assault Cases in the Supreme Court of Canada: Losing Sight of Substantive Equality?" (2012) 57 SCLR (2nd) 295.

Manning, M & P Sankoff. *Manning, Mewett & Sankoff: Criminal Law*, 4th ed (Toronto: LexisNexis, 2009) ch 21.

McGlynn, C & VE Munro. *Rethinking Rape Law: Comparative and International Perspectives* (London: Routledge, 2011).

Roach, K. *Criminal Law*, 6th ed (Toronto: Irwin Law, 2015) ch 10.

Sheehy, EA, ed. *Sexual Assault Law in Canada: Law, Legal Practice and Women's Activism* (Ottawa: University of Ottawa Press, 2012).

Stuart, D. *Canadian Criminal Law*, 7th ed (Toronto: Carswell, 2014) at 319-53. Many additional readings are cited by Stuart in his treatise.

Homicide

This chapter gives special attention to homicide offences. Some forms of homicide—in particular, murder—are regarded as the most serious of offences in Canada, and in most other countries. In Canada, a conviction for murder automatically results in a life sentence (*Criminal Code*, s 235), although the period of parole ineligibility depends on a number of variables (see *Criminal Code*, ss 745-745.51). For historical reasons associated with the social and cultural status of murder, and due to the enhanced sanctions that accompanied a conviction for murder (which until 1976 included the death penalty), the provisions in the *Criminal Code* that concern murder are unique and somewhat complicated. Moreover, the application of the *Charter of Rights and Freedoms* to this area of the law has had a dramatic impact on the formal requirements for murder.

Section 222 of the *Criminal Code* defines, in broad terms, the parameters of homicide:

222(1) A person commits homicide when, directly or indirectly, by any means, he causes the death of a human being.

(2) Homicide is culpable or not culpable.

(3) Homicide that is not culpable is not an offence.

(4) Culpable homicide is murder or manslaughter or infanticide.

(5) A person commits culpable homicide when he causes the death of a human being,

(a) by means of an unlawful act;

(b) by criminal negligence;

(c) by causing that human being, by threats or fear of violence or by deception, to do anything that causes his death; or

(d) by wilfully frightening that human being, in the case of a child or sick person.

Read in conjunction with s 229, which defines murder, all culpable homicides that are not murder are infanticide or manslaughter. Infanticide, defined in s 233 of the *Criminal Code*, is rather unique, both a freestanding offence and a defence to a charge of murder. Consequently, we will consider it last, at the very end of this chapter, after we have considered the elements of murder.

In most cases involving a homicide, the relevant gateway for criminal responsibility is the offence of manslaughter. Therefore, manslaughter provides the focus of Section I of this chapter. In Section II we consider the requirement for murder in s 229 of the *Criminal Code*, including the impact of the Charter on this offence. Section III deals with first-degree murder and the various ways in which it can be committed. Finally, Section IV deals briefly with infanticide.

I. MANSLAUGHTER

A homicide occurs whenever a person causes the death of another human being (s 222(1)). Not every homicide, however, is culpable (s 222(2)). Imagine that a motorist is travelling within the speed limit. A child darts into the road in pursuit of an errant ball and is struck and killed. Such an event is a tragedy. It is even a "homicide," but it is not a crime. In the language of the Code, it is not "culpable" (s 222(3)).

Manslaughter involves the killing of another human in one of the culpable ways specified by s 222(5) (set out above), most commonly either by means of an unlawful act (typically, an assault) or by criminal negligence. Continuing with the hypothetical from the last paragraph, imagine that the driver had been drinking, was speeding, and that these factors played a significant contributing role in his inability to stop prior to striking and killing the child. On such facts, a case of criminal negligence is likely established and the killing moves into the category of a "culpable homicide," manslaughter.

More common, however, is manslaughter by means of an unlawful act (s 222(5)(a)). Typically, a violent act is the cause—for example, a beating, a stabbing, or a shooting. Many manslaughter cases begin as murder prosecutions that fail because the Crown is unable to establish that at the time of the killing the accused intended, or subjectively foresaw, the likelihood of causing the victim's death. Indeed, this is what most contested murder trials are about—determining whether the accused is guilty of murder or manslaughter. The distinction is hugely important because the punishment for manslaughter is greatly reduced when compared with murder. Section 236 provides:

> 236. Every person who commits manslaughter is guilty of an indictable offence and liable
>> (a) where a firearm is used in the commission of the offence, to imprisonment for life and
> to a minimum punishment of imprisonment for a term of four years; and
>> (b) in any other case, to imprisonment for life.

Note that life imprisonment is available as the maximum potential punishment for manslaughter. Unlike murder, which carries an *automatic* sentence of life imprisonment, there is no minimum punishment for manslaughter, except in those cases where a firearm is involved.

The murder/manslaughter issue will arise in a number of ways in the chapters that follow dealing with defences. The issue comes up often in the context of intoxication, where the accused alleges that he or she did not have the specific intent for murder, due to the distorting influence of alcohol. Manslaughter may also emerge as a final verdict by virtue of provocation in s 232 of the *Criminal Code*, addressed in Chapter 14.

The fault requirements with respect to manslaughter were addressed in Chapter 7. In *R v Creighton*, [1993] 3 SCR 3 the Supreme Court held that the fault requirement for unlawful act manslaughter requires *mens rea* for the underlying unlawful act (which cannot be an absolute liability offence) and objective foreseeability that the unlawful act gives rise to a risk of bodily harm that is neither trivial nor transitory. This was held to meet the requirements of s 7 of the Charter, as developed through previous cases like *Vaillancourt* and *Martineau*, reproduced below. Justice McLachlin (as she then was) made the following comments in *Creighton* in rejecting a claim that s 7 of the Charter requires subjective fault for manslaughter:

> Before venturing on analysis, I think it appropriate to introduce a note of caution. We are here concerned with a common law offence virtually as old as our system of criminal law. It has been applied in innumerable cases around the world. And it has been honed and refined over the centuries. Because of its residual nature, it may lack the logical symmetry of more modern statutory offences, but it has stood the practical test of time. Could all this be the case, one asks, if the law violates our fundamental notions of justice, themselves grounded in the history of the common law? Perhaps. Nevertheless, it must be with considerable caution that a twentieth century court approaches the invitation which has been put before us: to strike out, or alternatively, rewrite, the offence of manslaughter on the ground that this is necessary to bring the law into conformity with the principles of fundamental justice. ...
>
> To the extent that stigma is relied on as requiring foreseeability of the risk of death in the offence of manslaughter, I find it unconvincing. The most important feature of the stigma of manslaughter is the stigma which is *not* attached to it. The *Criminal Code* confines manslaughter to non-intentional homicide. A person convicted of manslaughter is *not* a murderer. He or she did *not* intend to kill someone. A person has been killed through the fault of another, and that is always serious. But by the very act of calling the killing *manslaughter* the law indicates that the killing is less blameworthy than murder. It may arise from negligence, or it may arise as the unintended result of a lesser unlawful act. The conduct is blameworthy and must be punished, but its stigma does not approach that of murder.
>
> To put it another way, the stigma attached to manslaughter is an appropriate stigma. Manslaughter is not like constructive murder, where one could say that a person who did not in fact commit murder might be inappropriately branded with the stigma of murder. The stigma associated with manslaughter is arguably exactly what it should be for an unintentional killing in circumstances where risk of bodily harm was foreseeable. There is much common sense in the following observation: The offender has killed, and it does not seem wrong in principle that, when he is far from blameless, he should be convicted of an offence of homicide. To some extent it must be an intuitive conclusion, but it does not seem too difficult to argue that those who kill, and who are going to be convicted of something, should be convicted of homicide. That, after all, is what they have done. (Adrian Briggs, "In Defence of Manslaughter," [1983] *Crim. L.R.* 764 at p. 765.)
>
> It would shock the public's conscience to think that a person could be convicted of manslaughter absent any moral fault based on foreseeability of harm. Conversely, it might well shock the public's conscience to convict a person who has killed another only of aggravated assault—the result of requiring foreseeability of death—on the sole basis that the risk of death was not reasonably foreseeable. The terrible consequence of death demands more. In short, the *mens rea*

requirement which the common law has adopted—foreseeability of harm—is entirely appropriate to the stigma associated with the offence of manslaughter. To change the *mens rea* requirement would be to risk the very disparity between *mens rea* and stigma of which the appellant complains.

I come then to the second factor mentioned in *Martineau*, the relationship between the punishment for the offence and the *mens rea* requirement. Here again, the offence of manslaughter stands in sharp contrast to the offence of murder. Murder entails a mandatory life sentence; manslaughter carries with it no minimum sentence. This is appropriate. Because manslaughter can occur in a wide variety of circumstances, the penalties must be flexible. An unintentional killing while committing a minor offence, for example, properly attracts a much lighter sentence than an unintentional killing where the circumstances indicate an awareness of risk of death just short of what would be required to infer the intent required for murder. The point is, the sentence can be and is tailored to suit the degree of moral fault of the offender. This court acknowledged this in *Martineau*, at p. 362: "The more flexible sentencing scheme under a conviction for manslaughter is in accord with the principle that punishment be meted out with regard to the level of moral blameworthiness of the offender." It follows that the sentence attached to manslaughter does not require elevation of the degree of *mens rea* for the offence.

This brings me to the third factor relating to the gravity of the offence set out in *Martineau*, the principle that those causing harm intentionally must be punished more severely than those causing harm unintentionally. As noted, this principle is strictly observed in the case of manslaughter. It is by definition an unintentional crime. Accordingly, the penalties imposed are typically less than for its intentional counterpart, murder.

I conclude that the standard of *mens rea* required for manslaughter is appropriately tailored to the seriousness of the offence. ...

I have suggested that jurisprudential and historic considerations confirm a test for the *mens rea* of manslaughter based on foreseeability of the risk of bodily injury, rather than death. I have also argued that the considerations of the gravity of the offence and symmetry between the *mens rea* of the offence and its consequences do not entail the conclusion that the offence of manslaughter as it has been historically defined in terms of foreseeability of the risk of bodily harm is unconstitutional. It is my view that policy considerations support the same conclusion. In looking at whether a long-standing offence violates the principles of fundamental justice, it is not amiss, in my view, to look at such considerations.

First, the need to deter dangerous conduct which may injure others and in fact may kill the peculiarly vulnerable supports the view that death need not be objectively foreseeable, only bodily injury. To tell people that if they embark on dangerous conduct which foreseeably may cause bodily harm which is neither trivial nor transient, and which in fact results in death, that they will not be held responsible for the death but only for aggravated assault, is less likely to deter such conduct than a message that they will be held responsible for the death, albeit under manslaughter not murder. Given the finality of death and the absolute unacceptability of killing another human being, it is not amiss to preserve the test which promises the greatest measure of deterrence, provided the penal consequences of the offence are not disproportionate. This is achieved by retaining the test of foreseeability of bodily harm in the offence of manslaughter.

Secondly, retention of the test based on foreseeability of bodily harm accords best with our sense of justice. I have earlier alluded to the view, attested to by the history of the offence of manslaughter, that causing the death of another through negligence or a dangerous unlawful act should be met by a special sanction reflecting the fact that a death occurred, even though death was not objectively foreseeable. This is supported by the sentiment that a person who engages in dangerous conduct that breaches the bodily integrity of another and puts that person at risk may properly be held responsible for an unforeseen death attributable to that person's peculiar vulnerability; the aggressor takes the victim as he finds him. The criminal law must reflect not only the concerns of the accused, but the concerns of the victim and, where the victim is killed, the concerns of society for the victim's fate. Both go into the equation of justice.

Finally, the traditional test founded on foreseeability of the risk of bodily harm provides, in my belief, a workable test which avoids troubling judges and juries about the fine distinction between foreseeability of the risk of bodily injury and foreseeability of the risk of death—a distinction which, as argued earlier, reduces to a formalistic technicality when put in the context of the thin-skull rule and the fact that death has in fact been inflicted by the accused's dangerous act. The traditional common law test permits a principled approach to the offence which meets the concerns of society, provides fairness to the accused, and facilitates a just and workable trial process.

Writing in dissent, former Chief Justice Lamer would have required proof of objective foresight of death for a manslaughter conviction. Note that in 1993, as Justice McLachlin observed, there was no mandatory minimum penalty of imprisonment for manslaughter. As noted above, due to amendments introduced in 1995, there is now a mandatory minimum penalty of four years' imprisonment for manslaughter if committed with a firearm. Should this development affect the fault requirements for a manslaughter conviction?

Note that the Supreme Court has upheld this new mandatory minimum penalty in a number of cases. In one case, it held that the penalty was not cruel and unusual punishment when applied to an accused who accidentally killed his friend. The Court observed:

> While holding the rifle which he knew to be loaded, the appellant jumped up to the lower bunk in order to shake Mr. Teed—either to awaken him, or to get his attention. As might be expected in this state of intoxication, the appellant lost his footing while he jumped, and he fell. The gun discharged, and the bullet struck Mr. Teed in the head, killing him instantly. The gun was not susceptible to shock discharge. There was no evidence that the appellant intended to aim the gun at the victim.

R v Morrisey, 2000 SCC 39 at para 5, [2000] 2 SCR 90. See also *R v Ferguson*, 2008 SCC 6, [2008] 1 SCR 96, which upheld the four-year minimum sentence in a case in which an RCMP officer was convicted of manslaughter for shooting a person in a police cell.

II. SECOND-DEGREE MURDER

The *actus reus* for manslaughter and murder is exactly the same: directly or indirectly causing the death of another human being, usually by means of an unlawful act. The key difference between the two offences is the *mens rea*. Section 229 of the *Criminal Code* is at the heart of the offence of murder. It sets out three basic ways in which a culpable homicide can be classified as murder. Section 229 states:

229. Culpable homicide is murder

(a) where the person who causes the death of a human being

(i) means to cause his death, or

(ii) means to cause him bodily harm that he knows is likely to cause his death, and is reckless whether death ensues or not;

(b) where a person, meaning to cause death to a human being or meaning to cause him bodily harm that he knows is likely to cause his death, and being reckless whether death ensues or not, by accident or mistake causes death to another human being, notwithstanding that he does not mean to cause death or bodily harm to that human being; or

(c) where a person, for an unlawful object, does anything that he knows or ought to know is likely to cause death, and thereby causes death to a human being, notwithstanding that he desires to effect his object without causing death or bodily harm to any human being.

The fault requirements under each of these sections are dealt with below.

Section 229(a): Intentional or Reckless Killing

R v Simpson
Ontario Court of Appeal
(1981), 58 CCC (2d) 122

[This case involved two counts of attempted murder. The accused met one victim in a bar and had sex with her in his apartment, following which he strangled her to the point of unconsciousness. The accused attacked the second victim after she left the same bar where the accused met the first victim. The appeal concerned the accuracy of the trial judge's instructions to the jury on the definition of murder in the context of trying to explain the offence of attempted murder.]

MARTIN JA: …

Misdirection as to Intent Required to Constitute Attempted Murder

Following the argument of the appeal, and while the decision of the Court was under reserve, the Court requested counsel to submit argument with respect to the effect of a passage in the Judge's charge defining the intent requisite for attempted murder, to which no objection was taken at the trial, and which was not a ground of appeal. The Court reconvened on February 12, 1981, and heard argument with respect to the passage in question.

The learned trial Judge charged the jury as follows:

Under the *Criminal Code*, anyone who attempts by any means to commit murder is guilty of an indictable offence. In this case neither victim died, most fortunately. So the charge isn't murder but attempted murder. What is murder? It is defined in Section 212 [now s 229] of the *Criminal Code*, in part, as follows:

"Culpable homicide is murder
(a) where the person who causes the death of a human being (1) means to cause his death, or (2) means to cause him bodily harm that he knows is likely to cause his death and is reckless whether death ensues or not."

Now culpable means blameworthy. Culpable homicide is death of a human being for which some person may be blamed in law. The definition that I have just read to you then is one of murder; and the charge we are dealing with here is attempt to murder. I have earlier told you that proof of the intention of the accused is an essential element in the offence of attempt to murder. The Crown must satisfy you beyond a reasonable doubt that the accused stabbed the victim and that he did so intending to cause the death, or intending to cause the victim bodily harm that he knew or ought to have known was likely to cause death and was reckless whether death ensued or not. I repeat the second part of that definition: If the Crown has, on the evidence, satisfied you beyond a reasonable doubt that the accused was the stabber and that in stabbing he intended so cause bodily harm that he knew or ought to have known was likely to cause death and was reckless whether death ensued or not, then the offence of attempted murder has been proved.

It has now been authoritatively decided that either of the intents specified in s. 212(a)(i) and (ii) suffices to constitute the intent required for the offence of attempted murder; see *Lajoie v. The Queen* (1973), 10 C.C.C. (2d) 313; *R. v. Ritchie*, [1970] 5 C.C.C. 336. Unfortunately, the learned trial Judge, in paraphrasing the intent specified in s. 212(a)(ii)—namely, an intention to cause bodily harm that the offender knows is likely to cause death—substituted for the requisite intent an intention to cause bodily harm that offender knows or ought to know is likely to cause death. This incorrect summary of the provision of s. 212(a)(ii) constituted a serious error. Liability under s. 212(a)(ii) is subjective and the requisite knowledge that the intended injury is likely to cause death must be brought home to the accused subjectively. To substitute for that state of mind an intention to cause bodily harm that the accused knows or ought to know is likely to cause death is to impose liability on an objective basis. An intention to cause bodily harm that the offender ought to have known was likely to cause death is merely evidence from which, along with all the other circumstances, the jury may infer that the accused actually had the requisite intention and knowledge required by s. 212(a)(ii). It does not, however, constitute the requisite state of mind. ...

The error was never corrected by the learned trial Judge. It is true that in putting the case for the Crown he said:

> The Crown suggests to you that if you are satisfied that Simpson was the attacker, you should in the circumstances have no doubt that he intended to kill or cause bodily harm knowing that it might result in death and being reckless as to whether death ensued or not.

It is to be observed that even this passage is not entirely correct as it refers to an intention to cause bodily harm knowing that it might result in death, as distinct from an intention to inflict bodily harm that the offender knows is likely to cause bodily harm. In any event, the jury would rely on the Judge's instruction, as they had previously been told they must, with respect to the elements of the offence of attempted murder.

In my view, the seriousness of the error requires a new trial unless it is proper to invoke the curative provisions of s. 613(1)(b)(iii). ... I have not been persuaded, even by Mr. Watt's able argument, that it is appropriate to invoke the provisions of s. 613(1)(b)(iii) in relation to the conviction of the appellant on count 2 relating to Cathy Wagenaar. I am not satisfied that a reasonable jury properly instructed, having found that the appellant was Cathy Wagenaar's assailant, would inevitably have found that he intended to kill her or intended to inflict an injury upon her that he knew was likely to kill her. Although it would be open to a properly-instructed jury to conclude that the requisite intent to constitute attempted murder had been established, the accompanying circumstances and the assailant's utterances are not such as to inevitably require a reasonable jury to reach that conclusion. ...

Appeal allowed.

R v Cooper
Supreme Court of Canada
[1993] 1 SCR 146

[The accused was charged with murdering his female acquaintance. He had been drinking with her and they got into an argument. The accused said that the victim had hit him. He testified to remembering strangling the victim, but had no recollection after that until he awoke to find the victim dead. The medical evidence confirmed that the victim had been strangled to death and that the pressure to her throat would have been applied for between 30 seconds and two minutes, and probably closer to two minutes. The trial judge instructed the jury that, once the accused had formed the intent to cause the victim bodily harm, which he knew would likely cause her death, he need not be aware of what he was doing at the moment she actually died. The accused was convicted, but the Court of Appeal found that this instruction was erroneous.]

CORY J: ...

The Nature of the Intent Required to Secure a Conviction Under s. 212(a)(ii)

Section 212(a)(ii) [now s 229(a)(ii)] provides:

> s. 212 Culpable homicide is murder
> (a) where the person who causes the death of a human being ...
> (ii) means to cause him bodily harm that he knows is likely to cause his death, and is reckless whether death ensues or not.

This section was considered in *R. v. Nygaard*, [[1989] 2 SCR 1074]. On the issue of the requisite intent the court was unanimous. At pages 1087-88, it was said:

> The essential element is that of intending to cause bodily harm of such a grave and serious nature that the accused knew that it was likely to result in the death of the victim. The aspect of recklessness is almost an afterthought ... .

The aspect of recklessness can be considered an afterthought since to secure a conviction under this section it must be established that the accused had the intent to cause such grievous bodily harm that he knew it was likely to cause death. One who causes bodily harm that he knows is likely to cause death must, in those circumstances, have a deliberate disregard for the fatal consequences which are known to be likely to occur. That is to say he must, of necessity, be reckless whether death ensues or not.

The concept of recklessness was considered by this court in *R. v. Sansregret*, [1985] 1 S.C.R. 570. At page 582 it was said:

> [Recklessness] is found in the attitude of one who, aware that there is danger that his conduct could bring about the result prohibited by the criminal law, nevertheless persists, despite the risk. It is, in other words, the conduct of one who sees the risk and who takes the chance.

The same words can apply to s. 212(a)(ii) with this important addition: it is not sufficient that the accused foresee simply a danger of death; the accused must foresee a likelihood of death flowing from the bodily harm that he is occasioning the victim.

It is for this reason that it was said in *Nygaard* that there is only a "slight relaxation" in the *mens rea* required for a conviction for murder under s. 212(a)(ii) as compared to s. 212(a)(i). The position was put in this way at p. 1089:

> ... [where] two accused form the intent to repeatedly and viciously strike a person in the head with a baseball bat realizing full well that the victim will probably die as a result. None the less they continue with the bone-splintering, skull-shattering assault. The accused ... must have committed as grave a crime as the accused who specifically intends to kill. ... I would conclude that the crime defined in s. 212(a)(ii) can properly be described as murder and on a "culpability scale" it varies so little from s. 212(a)(i) as to be indistinguishable.

The intent that must be demonstrated in order to convict under s. 212(a)(ii) has two aspects. There must be (a) subjective intent to cause bodily harm; (b) subjective knowledge that the bodily harm is of such a nature that it is likely to result in death. It is only when those two elements of intent are established that a conviction can properly follow.

What Degree of Concurrency Is Required Between the Wrongful Act and the Requisite Mens Rea?

There can be no doubt that under the classical approach to criminal law it is the intent of the accused that makes the wrongful act illegal. It is that intent which brings the accused within the sphere of blameworthiness and justifies the penalty or punishment which is imposed upon him for the infraction of the criminal law. The essential aspect of *mens rea* and the absolute necessity that it be present in the case of murder was emphasized by Lamer J. (as he then was) in *R. v. Vaillancourt*, [1987] 2 S.C.R. 636. At p. 653 he stated:

> It may well be that, as a general rule, the principles of fundamental justice require proof of a subjective *mens rea* with respect to the prohibited act, in order to avoid punishing the "morally innocent."

The essential element of a subjectively guilty mind in order to convict a person of murder was again emphasized in *R. v. Martineau*, [1990] 2 S.C.R. 633.

However, not only must the guilty mind, intent or *mens rea* be present, it must also be concurrent with the impugned act. Professor D. Stuart has referred to this as "the simultaneous principle": see *Canadian Criminal Law*, 2nd ed. (1987), p. 305. The principle has been stressed in a number of cases. For example in *R. v. Droste* (1979), 49 C.C.C. (2d) 52 (Ont. C.A.), the accused had intended to murder his wife by pouring gasoline over the interior of the car and setting fire to it while she was within it. Before he could light the gasoline the car crashed into a bridge and ignited prematurely. As a result both his children were killed rather than his wife. He was charged with their murder and convicted. On appeal Arnup J.A., speaking for the Court of Appeal in directing a new trial, stated at pp. 53-54:

> ... the trial Judge did not instruct the jury of the necessity of the Crown showing that at the time of the occurrence at the bridge, the appellant, intending to kill his wife, had done an act with that intention, and in the course of doing so his children were killed. *In short, he did not tell them that the mens rea and the actus reus must be concurrent.* ... (Emphasis added.)

Yet, it is not always necessary for the guilty act and the intent to be completely concurrent: see, for example, *Fagan v. Metropolitan Police Commissioner*, [1968] 3 All E.R. 442 (Q.B.). ... James J., concurring in the result, stated at p. 445:

It is not necessary that *mens rea* should be present at the inception of the *actus reus*; it can be superimposed on an existing act.

There is, then, the classic rule that at some point the *actus reus* and the *mens rea* or intent must coincide. Further, I would agree with the conclusion of James J. that an act (*actus reus*) which may be innocent or no more than careless at the outset can become criminal at a later stage when the accused acquires knowledge of the nature of the act and still refuses to change his course of action.

The determination of whether the guilty mind or *mens rea* coincides with the wrongful act will depend to a large extent upon the nature of the act. For example, if the accused shot the victim in the head or stabbed the victim in the chest with death ensuing a few minutes after the shooting or stabbing, then it would be relatively easy to infer that the requisite intent or *mens rea* coincided with the wrongful act (*actus reus*) of shooting or stabbing. As well, a series of acts may form part of the same transaction. For example the repeated blows of the baseball bat continuing over several minutes are all part of the same transaction. In those circumstances if the requisite intent coincides at any time with the sequence of blows then that could be sufficient to found a conviction.

An example of a series of acts that might be termed a continuous transaction appears in *Meli v. The Queen*, [1954] 1 W.L.R. 228 (P.C.). There the accused intended to kill the deceased, and to this end struck a number of blows. The effect of the blows was such that the accused thought the victim was dead and threw the body over a cliff. However, it was not the blows but rather the exposure suffered by the victim while he lay at the base of the cliff that resulted in the death. It was argued on behalf of the accused that when there was the requisite *mens rea* (during the beating) death did not ensue and when death did ensue there was no longer any intention to kill. The judicial committee of the Privy Council concluded that the entire episode was one continuing transaction that could not be subdivided in that way. At some point, the requisite *mens rea* coincided with the continuing series of wrongful acts that constituted the transaction. As a result, the conviction for murder was sustained. I agree with that conclusion.

Application of the "Contemporaneous" Principles to This Case

...

There is no question that in order to obtain a conviction the Crown must demonstrate that the accused intended to cause bodily harm that he knew was ultimately so dangerous and serious that it was likely to result in the death of the victim. But that intent need not persist throughout the entire act of strangulation. When Cooper testified that he seized the victim by the neck, it was open to the jury to infer that by those actions he intended to cause her bodily harm that he knew that was likely to cause her death. Since breathing is essential to life, it would be reasonable to infer the accused knew that strangulation was likely to result in death. I would stress that the jury was, of course, not required to make such an inference but, on the evidence presented, it was open to them to do so.

Did the accused possess such a mental state after he started strangling the victim? Here death occurred between 30 seconds and two minutes after he grabbed her by the neck. It could be reasonably inferred by the jury, that when the accused grabbed the victim by the neck and shook her that there was, at that moment, the necessary coincidence of the wrongful act of strangulation and the requisite intent to do bodily harm that the accused knew was likely to cause her death. Cooper was aware of these acts before he "blacked out." Thus although the jury was under no compulsion to do so, it was none the less open to them to infer that he knew that he was causing bodily harm and knew that it was so dangerous to the victim that it was likely to cause her death. It was sufficient that the intent and the act of strangulation coincided at some point. It was not necessary that the requisite intent continue throughout the entire two minutes required to cause the death of the victim. …

The Court of Appeal asked … whether "continuing awareness on his part of what he was doing and its probable result [was] established." The accused argued that in using this expression the Court of Appeal was not going so far as to require the presence of a continuous intent up to the moment of death. Rather, he contended that the court was merely stating that in order for there to be a conviction under this section the *mens rea* must be present at or after the point at which it becomes likely the death will ensue. It was his position that if the intent to cause bodily harm that the accused knew was likely to cause death should disappear before the point was reached at which death became likely then the accused could not be found guilty. He stated that it was only at this point that the *mens rea* and *actus reus* could coalesce into the crime described in s. 212(a)(ii).

This argument should not be accepted. It would require the Crown to provide expert evidence as to the moment at which death physiologically became a likelihood. It would be impossible to fix the time of the "likelihood" of death and difficult to provide evidence as to the duration of the requisite intent of the accused. That cannot be the meaning of this section. Neither the plain wording of this section nor any concept of fairness require the Crown to demonstrate such a complex chronological sequence. In order to obtain a conviction under s. 212(a)(ii), the Crown must prove that the accused caused and intended to cause bodily harm that he knew was likely to cause the death of the victim. If death results from a series of wrongful acts that are part of a single transaction then it must be established that the requisite intent coincided at some point with the wrongful acts. …

Appeal allowed; conviction restored.

Section 229(b): Transferred Intent

R v Fontaine
Manitoba Court of Appeal
2002 MBCA 107, 168 CCC (3d) 263

[The accused was convicted of one count of first-degree murder, two counts of attempted murder, one count of criminal negligence causing death, and one count of criminal negligence causing bodily harm. The accused was intent on committing suicide and during the course of a high-speed chase, deliberately drove his car into a parked semi-trailer in the oncoming lane. At the time of the collision, there were three individuals in the vehicle being driven by the accused. The accused survived the collision, but one passenger in his car was killed.]

STEEL JA: ...

Section 229(b) of the Criminal Code

[10] Murder is a crime of specific intent. By virtue of s. 229(b) of the *Criminal Code*, a person will be deemed to have that specific intent when, intending to kill one person, he mistakenly kills another person. Section 229(b) of the *Criminal Code* states:

> 229. Culpable homicide is murder ...
>
> (b) where a person, meaning to cause death to a human being or meaning to cause him bodily harm that he knows is likely to cause his death, and being reckless whether death ensues or not, by accident or mistake causes death to another human being, notwithstanding that he does not mean to cause death or bodily harm to that human being; ...

[11] The question in the case at bar is whether the above section transfers the specific intent necessary for a charge of murder when, instead of the accused attempting to murder someone else, he attempts to commit suicide and kills another in the process.

[12] The only reported case which raises this issue is that of *R. v. Brown* (1983), 4 C.C.C. (3d) 571 (Ont. H.C.) interpreted the words "cause death to a human being" in s. 229(b) of the *Criminal Code* to read "cause death to any human being (himself included)." This is the interpretation urged upon us by the Crown.

· · ·

[15] In order to determine whether an intent to commit suicide is properly transferred pursuant to s. 229(b) of the *Criminal Code*, it will be necessary to examine the nature of suicide and how it differs, conceptually, from murder.

[16] Although there are some comments to the contrary, the majority of early English jurisprudence discusses suicide as something different than murder in that murder requires the killing of another person.

· · ·

[24] With respect to Canadian jurisprudence, this case is very much one of first impression. Counsel has referred our court to a single decision, that being the decision of the Ontario High Court of Justice in Brown. In that case, without reference to any history or case law, O'Brien J. accepted the argument of the Crown that the words "cause death to a human being" in s. 229(b) of the *Criminal Code* (then s. 212(b)) "should be read and construed in their ordinary meaning, and that being so those words would include the accused himself."

[25] While the above decision appears to be the only one that purports to directly consider the issue of transferred intent in suicide, there are several other cases which may offer us some guidance. ...

[27] Several cases have referred to murder as the intentional killing of "another." One well-known example is *R. v. Creighton*, [1993] 3 S.C.R. 3. McLachlin J., as she then was, wrote (at pp. 41-42):

> The *Criminal Code* defines three general types of culpable homicide. There is murder, the intentional killing of *another* human being. There is infanticide, the intentional killing of a child. All other culpable homicides fall into the residual category of manslaughter. ... [Emphasis in original.]

[28] A review of the principles of statutory interpretation as they relate to penal statutes is also instructive in our attempt to interpret s. 229(b) in the context of these facts.

[29] The original definition of "homicide" in the *Criminal Code*, 1892, 55-56 Vict., c. 29, stated as follows:

> 218. Homicide is the killing of a human being by another, directly or indirectly, by any means whatsoever.

[30] In the *Criminal Code*, S.C. 1953-54, c. 51, the above section (then numbered s. 250) was combined and re-enacted as s. 194. Subsection (1) of s. 194 then read:

> (1) A person commits homicide when, directly or indirectly, by any means, he causes the death of a human being.

Thus, the 1954 amendment deleted the reference to the killing of a human being by another.

[31] A well-known principle of statutory interpretation is the presumption that change is purposeful. Ruth Sullivan, *Driedger on the Construction of Statutes*, 3rd ed. (Toronto: Butterworths, 1994), writes on this principle (at p. 450):

> It is presumed that amendments to the wording of a legislative provision are made for some intelligible purpose: to clarify the meaning, to correct a mistake, to change the law.

· · ·

[33] In our case, language polishing may indeed have been intended as s. 250 [RSC 1927, c 36] (the former s. 218) was not amended by itself. Rather, s. 250 was combined and re-enacted with ss. 252 (which defined culpable homicide) and 253. A study of this process of amendment leads me to the conclusion that the legislature did not turn its mind to the fact that the definition of "homicide" changed from the killing of a human being "by another" to "causes the death of a human being." They were merely combining three sections and the result, at the end of the day, spoke of the death of a human being.

[34] Moreover, another principle of statutory interpretation, that of the strict construction rule in penal legislation, mitigates in favour of the accused. Penal legislation that create offences punishable by fines, loss of freedom, or curtailment of a privilege or right are strictly construed. Section 229(b) is ambiguous in its interpretation as to whether it is intended to be limited to the killing of another or to include the killing of oneself. Where ambiguity is present in a piece of penal legislation, the statutory interpretation rule of strict construction should be applied because of the potential for serious interference with individual rights. ...

[36] I am aware that there is now one overriding principle of statutory interpretation. All other principles are subservient to the contextual and purposeful interpretation of statutes, where the words of an Act are read in their entire context and in their grammatical and ordinary sense harmoniously with the scheme of the Act, the object of the Act, and the intention of Parliament. See *R. v. Loscerbo (A.)* (1994), 89 C.C.C. (3d) 203 (C.A.), at para. 18, per Scott C.J.M. Most recently, the Supreme Court of Canada had occasion to confirm this one overarching approach to statutory interpretation in *Bell ExpressVu Ltd. Partnership v. Rex*, [2002] 5 W.W.R. 1, at para. 26, per Iacobucci J.

[37] I also agree that this is true, even when struggling with the interpretation of penal statutes. The first step is always to attempt to determine the real intention of the legislature

and the meaning of the statute compatible with its goals. However, when attempts at interpretation still leave doubt as to the meaning or scope of the text of the statute, the rule of strict construction of penal statutes can become applicable. See *R. v. Hasselwander*, [1993] 2 S.C.R. 398.

[38] In *Bell ExpressVu*, Iacobucci J., writing for a unanimous court, recognized the exception for penal statutes (at paras. 28-29):

> Other principles of interpretation—such as the strict construction of penal statutes and the "Charter values" presumption—only receive application where there is ambiguity as to the meaning of a provision. ...

What, then, in law is an ambiguity? To answer, an ambiguity must be "real" (*Marcotte* ... , at p. 115). The words of the provision must be "reasonably capable of more than one meaning" (*Westminster Bank Ltd. v. Zang* (1965), [1966] A.C. 182 (U.K.H.L.), at p. 222, per Lord Reid). By necessity, however, one must consider the "entire context" of a provision before one can determine if it is reasonably capable of multiple interpretations. In this regard, Major J.'s statement in *Canadian Oxy Chemicals Ltd. v. Canada (Attorney General)*, [1999] 1 S.C.R. 743 (S.C.C.), at para. 14, is apposite: "It is only when genuine ambiguity arises between two or more plausible readings, *each equally in accordance with the intentions of the statute*, that the courts need to resort to external interpretive aids" [emphasis in original], to which I would add, "including other principles of interpretation."

[39] Furthermore, the resolution of the ambiguity in favour of the accused in this case is reinforced when one considers the present differing social attitudes toward murder as opposed to suicide.

[40] In *Creighton*, the Supreme Court of Canada reaffirmed the legal principles relevant to determining the constitutionality of a *mens rea* requirement. Three of those principles are (at p. 46):

1. The stigma attached to the offence, and the available penalties requiring a *mens rea* reflecting the particular nature of the crime;
2. Whether the punishment is proportionate to the moral blameworthiness of the offender; and
3. The idea that those causing harm intentionally must be punished more severely than those causing harm unintentionally.

[41] Thus, the guiding principle underlying the constitutional analysis of fault in criminal law is that the state cannot punish a person as morally blameworthy unless such blameworthiness has been established. The gravity of the conduct itself, as well as the moral blameworthiness of the offender, must be analyzed in order to determine the extent of the social stigma to be attached to the crime.

[42] First degree murder is perhaps the most stigmatizing offence known to law. It carries with it the most draconian minimum sentence of life imprisonment with no parole for 25 years. It is normally associated with the act of one who plans and deliberates to take the life of another person. Society as a whole condemns this crime.

[43] Suicide on the other hand is normally seen as an act of desperation, often impulsive, and the act of a person who is ill and in need of treatment. By removing the crime of attempted suicide from the *Criminal Code*, Parliament recognized society's desire to see individuals who attempt suicide treated instead of criminalized.

[44] To accept the definition proposed by Brown and equate the *mens rea* for suicide with murder would offend all three principles enumerated by the Supreme Court of Canada. It is not consistent with the stigma and available penalties, and it is not proportionate to the moral blameworthiness of the offender.

[45] Given the early English treatment of murder and suicide as different crimes, the fact that suicide in Canada is no longer a crime, and the high moral culpability attached to the crime of murder, I conclude that the words of the provision in s. 229(b) of the *Criminal Code* are reasonably capable of more than one meaning. Given that ambiguity, the statutory interpretation rule of strictly construing penal legislation in favour of the accused would result in a conclusion that s. 229(b) refers to the killing of another and not the killing of oneself.

· · ·

Summary

[84] Section 229(b) is ambiguous in its interpretation. A review of English, American, and Canadian jurisprudence leads me to the conclusion that suicide and murder are two different conceptual entities. They have been treated differently historically. Moreover, where one act is legal and the other act is illegal, the transfer of intent from one to another should not necessarily follow.

[85] There are good policy reasons to differentiate between the two in terms of culpability. Suicide is not currently an offence pursuant to the *Criminal Code*. We can contrast this with murder, which is recognized as the most serious crime in our *Criminal Code* and a crime that requires specific intent. ...

Appeal allowed.

Section 229(c): Unlawful Object

Section 229(c) provides:

> 229. Culpable homicide is murder ...
>
>   (c) where a person, for an unlawful object, does anything that he knows or ought to know is likely to cause death, and thereby causes death to a human being, notwithstanding that he desires to effect his object without causing death or bodily harm to any human being.

On its face, s 229(c) appears to allow a murder conviction to rest on objective foreseeability of death. In a number of pre-Charter decisions, the courts evidenced considerable discomfort with this possibility and deliberately interpreted the provision as narrowly as reason would allow. In *R v Vasil*, [1981] 1 SCR 469 at 500, the Supreme Court held that the unlawful object must be "clearly distinct from the immediate object of the dangerous (unlawful) act."

In *R v Martineau*, [1990] 2 SCR 633 at 645-46 (excerpted more fully in the next section), Lamer CJ indicated that the reference to "ought to know" in s 229(c) was inconsistent with the constitutionally required *mens rea* for murder—namely, subjective knowledge of the likelihood of death. He concluded:

> The rationale underlying the principle that subjective foresight of death is required before a person is labelled and punished as a murderer is linked to the more general principle that criminal liability for a particular result is not justified except where the actor possesses a culpable mental

state in respect of that result. ... In my view, in a free and democratic society that values the autonomy and free will of the individual, the stigma and punishment attaching to the most serious of crimes, murder, should be reserved for those who choose to intentionally cause death or who choose to inflict bodily harm that *they know is likely to cause death*. The essential role of requiring subjective foresight of death in the context of murder is to maintain a proportionality between the stigma and punishment attached to a murder conviction and the moral blameworthiness of the offender. [Emphasis added.]

As a result, s 229(c) must now be read as though the "ought to know" language is not there. Unfortunately, despite the passage of 25 years, Parliament has still not amended s 229(c) to remove the objective arm of the subsection. Moreover, trial judges have in a surprising number of cases erred by either reading or allowing the jury to read s 229(c) as it is written in the *Criminal Code* and with the unconstitutional "ought to know" intact. See *R v H(DA)* (1997), 120 CCC (3d) 533 at para 42 (BCCA); *R v Salt*, 2007 ONCA 263 at paras 17-19; and *R v Winmill*, 2008 NBCA 88 at para 48, 239 CCC (3d) 1.

For a few years after *Martineau*, s 229(c) seemed to fall into disuse, but it has been resorted to extensively in more recent years, especially in Ontario. It is often used in cases where the accused does not intend to harm the victim, but is engaged in the pursuit of an unlawful object. The next case involves an application of s 229(c) in the post-*Martineau* era.

R v Shand
Ontario Court of Appeal
2011 ONCA 5, 104 OR (3d) 491

[The appellant, along with two other individuals (JB and JH), attended at the home of a local drug dealer in order to rob him. At some point after the appellant entered the home he produced a loaded gun, which discharged and killed one of the occupants of the home. At that trial, the appellant did not testify. There was conflicting evidence on how the gun came to be discharged. The judge charged the jury on s 229(c), which then found the appellant guilty of breaking and entering with intent to commit an indictable offence (robbery while using a firearm) and second-degree murder. He was sentenced to life imprisonment with parole ineligibility set at 15 years.]

ROULEAU JA (for the court): ...

[30] The trial judge informed the parties that he would charge the jury on s. 229(c), and subsequently provided the following instruction to the jury:

When committing robbery, Mr. Shand also committed an unlawful act which caused the death of Mr. Fraser. You may find any of the following to be an unlawful act—an assault, careless use of a firearm, pointing a firearm. This is for the purpose of furthering the commission of robbery. It is not necessary for the Crown to prove that Mr. Shand intended to kill or cause harm to Mr. Fraser. Further, Mr. Shand must have actually known that clubbing someone and the gun discharging in the presence of other people in a small room was likely to cause death to another human being. Mr. Shand does not have to foresee the actual situation or the developing events leading to the death. Section 229(c) considerations apply to the confrontation between Mr. Shand and Mr. Blow where either he clubbed Christopher

Blow and somehow the gun discharged or during the confrontation the trigger was jarred and squeezed or jarred so that the gun went off. It is the unlawful activity with the defendant being found to know that such activity is likely to result in a person being killed that counts.

· · ·

[The appellant raised a number of grounds of appeal, including a claim that s 229(c) is unconstitutional because it is inconsistent with s 7 of the Charter. Before addressing the Charter argument, the court addressed the proper interpretation of s 229(c). It ultimately concluded that, properly construed, s 229(c) is constitutional.]

[123] Before considering whether s. 229(c) is constitutional, I must determine the proper interpretation and application of the section. Though the wording of the section has undergone little change in over one hundred years, its context has changed greatly. There have been amendments to the Criminal Code, the phrase "ought to know" was read out of s. 229(c) in *Martineau* and the Charter has led to broader changes in what is required to constitute murder. This compels me, in a sense, to re-evaluate and interpret the section afresh.

[124] As previously noted, the Supreme Court of Canada in *R. v. Vaillancourt* and *R. v. Martineau* found that the constructive murder provisions of the Criminal Code, which permitted conviction with objective foresight of death, were unconstitutional. As a result, both the operative portion and the context of s. 229(c) are different from when the section was previously considered in *Tennant* and *Vasil*.

[125] As I will explain, the new context is one which dictates a narrower reading of s. 229(c), one that is clearly focused on the requirement that, when the act causing the death is carried out, the accused subjectively foresaw that some person's death was likely.

[126] There are two basic components to s. 229(c). The first is relatively straightforward. It requires that the perpetrator be pursuing an unlawful object. The second component is the doing of anything that the person knows is likely to cause someone's death. For simplicity, I will refer to this second component as the "dangerous act." Generally, it is the interpretation of this component that has been problematic.

[127] As stated in *R. v. Vasil*, at p. 490 S.C.R., the unlawful object must be "conduct which, if prosecuted fully, would amount to a serious crime, that is an indictable offence requiring mens rea."

[128] Similar to the "unlawful purpose" in s. 21(2), the unlawful object is what the accused set out to do—his or her purpose or goal. Put otherwise, the unlawful object is the end that the accused seeks to achieve. The accused may have more than one object, his or her objects may change and new objects may be added during the commission of the offence. However, any unlawful act an accused may commit or seek to commit in order to achieve his or her object does not necessarily constitute an unlawful object as required under s. 229(c). If, for example, you intend to shoot someone, pointing a firearm constitutes an unlawful act, but would not constitute an unlawful object for the purposes of s. 229(c).

[129] In accordance with the principles of statutory interpretation, s. 229(c) must be interpreted so as not to make s. 229(a) redundant. Parliament created two separate routes to establish murder and each must be given meaning. The difference between ss. 229(a) and 229(c) is that s. 229(c) requires more than proof of an unlawful object. The Crown must also prove that, when the dangerous act was committed, the person knew that death was likely. As a result, where the intention is causing the death of the victim or causing

bodily harm to the victim knowing that death is likely, s. 229(a) applies. This is because there is no need to carry out a further analysis focusing on the state of mind of the accused when the dangerous act causing death was committed. Because the two-part analysis prescribed by s. 229(c) is not required in these circumstances, it is apparent that s. 229(a) and not s. 229(c) applies. The situation is similar when s. 229(b) is at play, except that the attempt to cause the death of a person or to cause bodily harm to a person knowing that death is likely results in the mistaken death of another victim.

[130] However, this is not to say that s. 229(c) could not apply where the unlawful object is to kill someone. For example, if an accused, seeking to obtain access to a location in order to assassinate someone, sets off a diversionary explosion at a nearby location, and this explosion kills a passerby or a security guard, s. 229(c) could be applicable, with the unlawful object being the murder of the intended victim and the dangerous act being the explosion. ...

[131] The appellant argues that the dangerous act must be distinct from the unlawful object. In the appellant's submission, this principle has been established by this court in *R. v. Desmoulin* and *R. v. DeWolfe*, and by the Supreme Court of Canada in *R. v. Vasil*.

[132] However, these cases were decided before *R. v. Vaillancourt* and *R. v. Martineau* effectively amended s. 229(c) by striking out the phrase "ought to know." As explained above, the pre-*Vaillancourt* jurisprudence was largely driven by concern over the objective foresight component of s. 229(c). Specifically, the courts were concerned that s. 229(a) would be subsumed by s. 229(c), which established murder through negligent risk-taking: see, e.g., *Tennant*, at p. 92 C.C.C. Following *Martineau*, that concern no longer exists.

[133] Since the phrase "ought to know" has now been removed from s. 229(c), the provision is now more closely related to s. 229(a)(ii), and there is no longer a concern that the objective foresight of s. 229(c) will subsume the subjective intent requirement of s. 229(a). The notion that the two provisions should be kept clearly distinct to ensure that the mens rea for murder was not overly relaxed has disappeared.

[134] In the post-*Vaillancourt* period, the need to distinguish between the dangerous act and the unlawful object was addressed by this court in *R. v. Meiler*, [1999] O.J. No. 1506, 136 C.C.C. (3d) 11 (C.A.). As explained, at para. 48 of that decision, "s. 229(c) contemplates some act or conduct by the offender done to bring about some further unlawful object other than the injury that causes the death. Put another way, the unlawful object must be a different object than the assault upon the deceased that gives rise to the charge under s. 229(c)." The requirement that the dangerous act be distinct from the unlawful object is simply a requirement that there be an unlawful object, other than the assault on the deceased, in pursuance of which the accused committed the act or acts that caused the death.

[135] Approached in this way, s. 229(c) is distinct from s. 229(a)(i) or (ii). If the accused intends to kill or cause serious bodily harm to the deceased, the conduct will almost invariably come within either s. 229(a)(i) or (ii), and s. 229(c) will not apply.

[136] I see no reason to draw the somewhat arbitrary distinction between the unlawful object and the dangerous act in the manner suggested by the appellant. Imposing such a requirement might well lead courts to make artificial and strained definitions of the dangerous act and the unlawful object. Section 229(c) requires that the unlawful object be something other than the harm that is foreseen as a consequence of the dangerous act. In other words, if the accused's purpose—the unlawful object—was something other than

to cause the death of the victim or bodily harm to the victim knowing that death is likely, then it will be sufficiently distinct from the dangerous act to engage s. 229(c). In contrast, if the unlawful object was the death of the victim or to cause bodily harm to the victim knowing death was likely, s. 229(c) would not apply. The requirement of distinctness would not be met, as the unlawful object would be the very harm foreseen as a consequence of the dangerous act.

. . .

[138] … In *DeWolfe*, this court commented that courts must be careful about engaging in the unrealistic dissection of the unlawful object in order to fit the facts of the case into s. 229(c). This will arise in situations in which the accused commits an act or series of acts with one general purpose, and the fundamental question facing the trier of fact is whether or not the accused intended to kill or to cause grievous bodily harm to the victim. In these cases, decision makers should be careful not to search out additional and tenuous unlawful objects that the accused carried out, in order to apply s. 229(c).

. . .

[141] As gatekeeper, the trial judge must be cautious not to instruct juries on s. 229(c) in situations which fit squarely within s. 229(a) or (b). The unlawful object must be a genuine object, and not simply one aspect of the same "general purpose" of causing death or bodily harm that is likely to cause death. Put otherwise, there must be an "air of reality" to the unlawful object that forms the basis of s. 229(c). In *DeWolfe*, the appellant was shooting at the victim, and the question facing the jury was whether or not he possessed the intent required under s. 229(a) (then s. 212(a)). In that situation, this court was right to find that s. 229(c) did not apply and should not have been put to the jury.

[142] This caution also addresses the concern that s. 229(c) might be used by the Crown as a substitute to s. 229(a) or (b) in an attempt to somehow lessen the burden of proving intent. In the apt words of Zuber J.A. in *DeWolfe*, at para. 24, we should "prevent [s 229(c)] from overflowing its banks and making murder of almost every unlawful homicide." While this concern was more acute when s. 229(c) had an objective component, it still remains today.

[143] Precisely how the distinct purpose or harm requirement is to be interpreted will have to be developed over time and need not be decided in the present case. As I will explain, on the facts of this case, the unlawful object and the harm foreseen as a consequence of the dangerous act are clearly distinct.

. . .

[145] The first requirement of s. 229(c) is that the dangerous act must be clearly identified and defined. It must also be something that is done in furtherance of the unlawful object, though it need not constitute an offence in itself: see *Vasil*, at pp. 482-83 S.C.R.

[146] Further, the dangerous act must be a specific act that results in death. In referring to a specific act, I include a series of closely related acts, as some allowance must be made for a continuing transaction: see *R. v. Cooper*, [1993] 1 S.C.R. 146, [1993] S.C.J. No. 8. However, a general course of conduct only loosely connected to the killing could not be considered a single transaction for the purpose of defining the dangerous act.

[147] Using *Vasil* as an example, the unlawful object was the destruction of the furniture which, if prosecuted, would have constituted a full mens rea offence pursuant to what is now s. 430 of the Criminal Code. The dangerous act was setting the furniture on fire. The perpetrator's evidence, as well as common sense, established that the dangerous

act was done as a means of achieving the unlawful object. It was also proven that the ensuing fire caused the death of the two children who were sleeping in the house.

[148] In *Vasil*, the unlawful object and the dangerous act were closely related. This will generally be the case, as s. 229(c) requires that the dangerous act be carried out in order to achieve the unlawful object. However, as noted earlier, the harm foreseen by the dangerous act in *Vasil*, the likelihood of the death of the children, was different than the unlawful object, the destruction of the furniture.

[149] The importance of identifying the specific dangerous act or series of dangerous acts as distinct from the other steps taken to carry out the unlawful object becomes apparent once we turn to the need to prove that the accused knew death was likely. The intention to carry out the unlawful object is not sufficient to meet the requirements of s. 229(c). If this were the only state of mind required, s. 229(c) would become a new constructive murder provision. Although the presence of the intent with respect to the unlawful object is a necessary component of the offence, it is not sufficient. The Crown must also establish an additional component of mens rea—the intent to commit the dangerous act knowing that it is likely to cause death.

[150] Again, using *Vasil* as an example, the question was whether the perpetrator, at the time that he set the fire, knew that this dangerous act was likely to cause death. The trier of fact must focus on the specific moment when the act was committed and determine the perpetrator's subjective foresight at that point. In doing so, the trier of fact must consider the perpetrator's state of knowledge and all of the surrounding circumstances as well as the actions and statements of the perpetrator at and around that point in time.

[151] Several questions may be relevant to this inquiry. For example, was the dangerous act done in a moment of panic? Did the perpetrator know that people were in the house sleeping? Did the perpetrator understand what would happen once the fire was set? Once again, it is the perpetrator's state of knowledge "at that time" that must be determined.

[152] Vague realization that death is possible will not be sufficient. Similarly, if the dangerous act was done as a reaction, and out of panic, this may tend to show that the required subjective foresight of death was not present at the time that the act was committed.

[153] For the act to constitute murder, the appellant must have known that death was "likely." In this context, "likely" has to be understood as being something more than an awareness of risk or a possibility or chance of death. It is not sufficient that the accused foresee a danger of death: *Cooper*, at p. 155 S.C.R. In *Cooper*, Cory J. also referred to *R. v. Nygaard*, [1989] 2 S.C.R. 1074, [1989] S.C.J. No. 110, where the court had explained that there was only a "slight relaxation" of the mens rea required for a conviction for murder under ss. 229(a)(i) and 229(a)(ii). What is necessary is subjective knowledge that death is likely, which must be present at some point during the acts committed by the appellant that caused the death.

· · ·

[188] As explained earlier, s. 229(c) will be satisfied where the following elements are present:

    (a)   the accused must pursue an unlawful object other than to cause the death of the victim or bodily harm to the victim knowing that death is likely;

    (b)   the unlawful object must itself be an indictable offence requiring mens rea;

   (c)   in furtherance of the unlawful object, the accused must intentionally commit a dangerous act;

   (d)   the dangerous act must be distinct from the unlawful object, but as stated above, only in the sense that the unlawful object must be something other than the likelihood of death, which is the harm that is foreseen as a consequence of the dangerous act;

   (e)   the dangerous act must be a specific act, or a series of closely related acts, that in fact results in death, though the dangerous act need not itself constitute an offence; and

   (f)   when the dangerous act is committed, the accused must have subjective knowledge that death is likely to result.

[189] In applying the principles outlined above to the facts of this case, the unlawful object was robbery. Although the appellant carried a gun to the robbery, and this is also unlawful, this was not his purpose or goal, so it is not an unlawful object in the sense used in s. 229(c). In all probability, the appellant was hoping to carry out the theft with little violence and no likelihood of death.

[190] In identifying the dangerous act, as explained earlier, it is important not to frame the dangerous act too broadly. A broad and vague characterization of what constitutes the dangerous act does not fit well into the causation framework and may skew the subsequent mens rea analysis.

[191] It would, for example, be wrong to frame the dangerous act as entering a home with a loaded gun or engaging in a home invasion with a gun. Although these "acts," in a sense, led to the events in the basement bedroom, they were not the acts that actually caused the death.

[192] When Brisbois fled to the basement with the marijuana and the appellant and J.B. pursued her, the situation changed significantly.

[193] In my view, it is upon entering the basement bedroom that the appellant committed the dangerous act. The act was drawing and using his gun in an attempt to subdue the occupants of the room. This act was clearly done in furtherance of the unlawful object, being the robbery. Whether the gun was intentionally or accidently discharged, it was the choice to use the gun in order to subdue the occupants that caused the death.

[194] The critical issue, then, is whether the appellant possessed the necessary mens rea at the time that he committed the dangerous act. If, when he pulled out the gun and used it in the confined space of the basement bedroom, the appellant knew that it was likely to cause death, but did so nonetheless in pursuance of the theft, this would satisfy the mens rea component of s. 229(c).

[195] If, however, he did not then know that death was likely, the necessary mens rea would be absent. It is critical that the appellant's state of mind at this particular point in time is ascertained. That determination is a subjective one. The question is not what he ought to have known. The question is what he actually knew and foresaw. Surrounding facts, including the appellant's prior conduct, can be considered to determine what the appellant actually knew. What his state of mind may have been before or after committing the dangerous act is not determinative.

[196] In determining the appellant's subjective knowledge, relevant facts could include the appellant's knowledge of whether the gun was loaded and whether the safety of the

gun was on or off; the appellant's knowledge of the presence and location of a person or persons who could be hurt if the gun discharged; whether the appellant was acting in panic or out of fear; the conduct of the appellant as observed by others; whether the appellant drew the gun or had already drawn it; and whether the appellant was using the gun to press or force others to submit or using it in an attempt to extricate himself from a dangerous situation. All of these facts may shed light on the mental state of the appellant at the critical moment in time.

[197] The appellant argues that s. 229(c) had no application to the facts of this case, as it requires that there be a dangerous act distinct from the unlawful object. At trial, the theory of the defence was that the appellant brought the gun in order to carry out the robbery and that it discharged accidently, killing the victim. On the appellant's view, there was no dangerous act separate and distinct from the unlawful object of robbery, as the gun and its use were an integral part of the robbery. In other words, this was a robbery gone wrong.

[198] As I explained earlier, the dangerous act need not be distinct in the sense of being unrelated to the acts carrying out the unlawful object. In fact, as the text of s. 229(c) requires that the dangerous act be committed for or in pursuance of the unlawful object, the dangerous act must be associated with the unlawful object to fall within the provision. In the present case, the dangerous act was the choice to draw and use the gun in order to subdue the occupants of the basement bedroom and take the bag of marijuana. The fact that the gun may have discharged accidently while being used to that end does not remove these facts from the ambit of s. 229(c).

[199] In my view, therefore, there was an adequate factual basis for the trial judge to charge the jury on s. 229(c).

· · ·

[The court went on to reject the appellant's claim that the trial judge erred in his instruction to the jury regarding s 229(c). In coming to this conclusion, it provided further insight on the meaning of s 229(c).]

[209] ... [D]etermining whether a person knew that an act was "likely to cause death" is, of course, a fact-specific question. In some s. 229(c) cases, an elaboration of the term may be desirable. It may, for example, be of assistance to a jury faced with applying s. 229(c) to be told that "likely" requires more than knowledge that death was a possibility or that there was a chance of death. As Cory J. stated in *Cooper*, at p. 155 S.C.R., when discussing similar language in s. 212(a) (ii) (now s. 229(a)(ii)), "it is not sufficient that the accused foresee simply a danger of death, the accused must foresee a likelihood of death flowing from the bodily harm that he is occasioning the victim" (emphasis in original).

[210] The jury could also be instructed to avoid reasoning backwards. That is, they should avoid the logical fallacy of assuming that, because the victim died, the appellant must have known that death was likely. This type of analysis essentially amounts to the constitutionally prohibited reasoning that the accused "ought to have known" that his or her act was likely to cause death.

· · ·

[224] For these reasons, I would find s. 229(c) to be constitutional and would dismiss the appeal.

Appeal dismissed.

Given the complexity inherent in a proper s 229(c) instruction, do you think the provision creates an undue risk that a jury might wrongly find an accidental killing to be murder even in circumstances in which the accused did not actually subjectively foresee the likelihood of death? See generally K Roach, "The Problematic Revival of Murder Under Section 229(c) of the Criminal Code" (2010) 47 Alta L Rev 675.

Constitutional Considerations

After the Charter came into force, the Supreme Court decided a number of cases that measured statutory fault requirements against the principles of fundamental justice in s 7 of the Charter. As discussed in Chapter 6, the case of *Re BC Motor Vehicle Act*, [1985] 2 SCR 486 established that it is constitutionally impermissible for an offence to carry the potential for imprisonment without some minimum level of *mens rea* or fault. To permit otherwise, reasoned the Supreme Court of Canada, would offend the principles of fundamental justice because it would allow for the punishment of the morally innocent. The Court built upon and extended the constitutionalization of fault in the context of murder. The prime target was s 213 (now s 230) of the *Criminal Code*, the "constructive murder" or "felony murder" provision, which made it possible for an individual who did not necessarily foresee the subjective likelihood of death to be convicted of murder. In fact, with respect to s 213(d), which was at issue in *Vaillancourt*, the Crown was under no obligation to establish any fault requirement in relation to death.

As will be seen, s 213 has been invalidated by the Court in its entirety. It provided:

213. Culpable homicide is murder where a person causes the death of a human being while committing or attempting to commit high treason or treason or an offence mentioned in section 52 (sabotage), 76 (piratical acts), 76.1 (hijacking an aircraft), 132 or subsection 133(1) or sections 134 to 136 (escape or rescue from prison or lawful custody), 143 or 145 (rape or attempt to commit rape), 149 or 156 (indecent assault), subsection 246(2) (resisting lawful arrest), 247 (kidnapping and forcible confinement), 302 (robbery), 306 (breaking and entering) or 389 or 390 (arson), whether or not the person means to cause death to any human being and whether or not he knows that death is likely to be caused to any human being, if

(a) he means to cause bodily harm for the purpose of
(i) facilitating the commission of the offence, or
(ii) facilitating his flight after committing or attempting to commit the offence,
and the death ensues from the bodily harm;
(b) he administers a stupefying or overpowering thing for a purpose mentioned in paragraph (a), and the death ensues therefrom;
(c) he wilfully stops, by any means, the breath of a human being for a purpose mentioned in paragraph (a), and the death ensues therefrom; or
(d) he uses a weapon or has it upon his person
(i) during or at the time he commits or attempts to commit the offence, or
(ii) during or at the time of his flight after committing or attempting to commit the offence,
and the death ensues as a consequence.

Vaillancourt v The Queen
Supreme Court of Canada
[1987] 2 SCR 636

LAMER J (Dickson CJ and Estey and Wilson JJ concurring): Vaillancourt was convicted
of second degree murder following a trial before a Sessions Court judge and jury in Montreal. He appealed to the Quebec Court of Appeal, arguing that the judge's charge to the
jury on the combined operation of ss. 213(d) and 21(2) of the *Criminal Code*, R.S.C. 1970,
c. C-34, was incorrect. His appeal was dismissed and the conviction was affirmed: (1984),
31 C.C.C. (3d) 75. Before this court, he has challenged the constitutional validity of
s. 213(d) alone and in combination with s. 21(2) under the *Canadian Charter of Rights
and Freedoms*.

The appellant and his accomplice committed an armed robbery in a pool-hall. The
appellant was armed with a knife and his accomplice with a gun. During the robbery, the
appellant remained near the front of the hall while the accomplice went to the back. There
was a struggle between the accomplice and a client. A shot was fired and the client was
killed. The accomplice managed to escape and has never been found. The appellant was
arrested at the scene.

In the course of his testimony, the appellant said that he and his accomplice had agreed
to commit this robbery armed only with knives. On the night of the robbery, however,
the accomplice arrived at their meeting place with a gun. The appellant said that he objected because, on a previous armed robbery, his gun had discharged accidentally, and he
did not want that to happen again. He insisted that the gun be unloaded. The accomplice
removed three bullets from the gun and gave them to the appellant. The appellant then
went to the bathroom and placed the bullets in his glove. The glove was recovered by the
police at the scene of the crime and was found at trial to contain three bullets. The appellant testified that, at the time of the robbery, he was certain that the gun was unloaded.

Before this court, the following constitutional questions were formulated:

1. Is s. 213(d) of the *Criminal Code* inconsistent with the provisions of either s. 7
   or s. 11(d) of the *Canadian Charter of Rights and Freedoms*, and, therefore, of
   no force or effect?

2. If not, is the combination of s. 21 and s. 213(d) of the *Criminal Code* inconsistent
   with the provisions of either s. 7 or s. 11(d) of the *Canadian Charter of Rights
   and Freedoms* and is s. 21 of the *Criminal Code* therefore of no force or effect in
   the case of a charge under s. 213(d) of the *Criminal Code*?

The appellant has framed his attack on s. 213(d) of the Code in very wide terms. He
has argued that the principles of fundamental justice require that, before Parliament can
impose any criminal liability for causing a particular result, there must be some degree
of subjective *mens rea* in respect of that result. This is a fundamental question with far-
reaching consequences. If this case were decided on that basis, doubt would be cast on
the constitutional validity of many provisions throughout our *Criminal Code*, in particular
s. 205(5)(a) [now s 222(5)(a)], whereby causing death by means of an unlawful act is
culpable homicide, and s. 212(c) [now s 229(c)] whereby objective foreseeability of the
likelihood of death is sufficient for a murder conviction in certain circumstances.

However, the appellant was convicted under s. 213(d) and the constitutional question is limited to this provision. In my opinion, the validity of s. 213(d) can be decided on somewhat narrower grounds. In addition, the Attorney-General of Canada has seen fit not to intervene to support the constitutionality of s. 213(d), which is clearly in jeopardy in this case, though he may have intervened to support ss. 205(5)(a) and 212(c) and other similar provisions. I will thus endeavour not to make pronouncements the effect of which will be to predispose in *obiter* of other issues more properly dealt with if and when the constitutionality of the other provisions is in issue. I do, however, find it virtually impossible to make comments as regards s. 213(d) that will not have some effect on the validity of the rest of s. 213 or that will not reveal to some extent my views as regards s. 212(c). However, the validity of those sections and of paras. (a) to (c) of s. 213 is not in issue here and I will attempt to limit my comments to s. 213(d).

The appellant has also challenged the combined operation of ss. 21(2) and 213(d). Given my decision on the validity of s. 213(d) and in view of the importance of s. 21(2) and the absence of the Attorney-General of Canada, I do not find it necessary or advisable to deal with s. 21(2) in this appeal.

It is first necessary to analyze s. 213(d) in the context of the other murder provisions in the Code in order to determine its true nature and scope. Murder is defined as a culpable homicide committed in the circumstances set out at ss. 212 and 213 of the Code. There is a very interesting progression through s. 212 to s. 213 with respect to the mental state that must be proven.

The starting point is s. 212(a)(i) [see now s 229(a)(i)], which provides:

> 212. Culpable homicide is murder
>   (a) where the person who causes the death of a human being
>   (i) means to cause his death …

This clearly requires that the accused have actual subjective foresight of the likelihood of causing the death coupled with the intention to cause that death. This is the most morally blameworthy state of mind in our system.

There is a slight relaxation of this requirement in s. 212(a)(ii) [see now s 229(a)(ii)], which provides:

> 212. Culpable homicide is murder
>   (a) Where the person who causes the death of a human being …
>   (ii) means to cause him bodily harm that he knows is likely to cause his death, and is reckless whether death ensues or not;

Here again the accused must have actual subjective foresight of the likelihood of death. However, the Crown need no longer prove that he intended to cause the death but only that he was reckless whether death ensued or not. It should also be noted that s. 212(a)(ii) is limited to cases where the accused intended to cause bodily harm to the victim.

Section 212(c) [see now s 229(c)] provides:

> 212. Culpable homicide is murder …
>   (c) where a person, for an unlawful object, does anything that he knows or ought to know is likely to cause death, and thereby causes death to a human being, notwithstanding that he desires to effect his object without causing death or bodily harm to any human being.

In part, this is simply a more general form of recklessness and thus the logical extension of s. 212(a)(ii), in that it applies when the accused "does *anything* ... he knows ... is likely to cause death" (emphasis added). However, there is also a further relaxation of the mental element required for murder in that it is also murder where the accused "does *anything that he ... ought to know* is likely to cause death" (emphasis added). This eliminates the requirement of actual subjective foresight and replaces it with objective foreseeability or negligence.

Although the concept of felony murder has a long history at common law, a brief review of the historical development of s. 213 [see now s 230] indicates that its legitimacy is questionable. ...

Finally, the Law Reform Commission of Canada criticized s. 213 in *Homicide* (1984), Working Paper 33, at pp. 47-51, and excluded the notion of constructive murder from its Draft Criminal Code (*Recodifying Criminal Law* (1986), Report 30, cl. 6(3), p. 54).

Prior to the enactment of the Charter, Parliament had full legislative power with respect to "The Criminal Law" (*Constitution Act, 1867*, s. 91(27)), including the determination of the essential elements of any given crime.

However, federal and provincial legislatures have chosen to restrict through the Charter this power with respect to criminal law. Under s. 7, if a conviction, given either the stigma attached to the offence or the available penalties, will result in a deprivation of the life, liberty or security of the person of the accused, then Parliament must respect the principles of fundamental justice. It has been argued that the principles of fundamental justice in s. 7 are only procedural guarantees. However, in *Re B.C. Motor Vehicle Act*, [1985] 2 S.C.R. 486, this Court rejected that argument and used s. 7 to review the substance of the legislation. As a result, while Parliament retains the power to define the elements of a crime, the courts now have the jurisdiction and, more important, the duty, when called upon to do so, to review that definition to ensure that it is in accordance with the principles of fundamental justice. ...

It may well be that as, a general rule, the principles of fundamental justice require proof of a subjective *mens rea* with respect to the prohibited act, in order to avoid punishing the "morally innocent." ...

There are many provisions in the Code requiring only objective foreseeability of the result or even only a causal link between the act and the result. As I would prefer not to cast doubt on the validity of such provisions *in this case*, I will assume, but only for the purposes of this appeal, that something less than subjective foresight of the result may, sometimes, suffice for the imposition of criminal liability for causing that result through intentional criminal conduct.

But, whatever the minimum *mens rea* for the act or the result may be, there are, though very few in number, certain crimes where, because of the special nature of the stigma attached to a conviction therefor or the available penalties, the principles of fundamental justice require a *mens rea* reflecting the particular nature of that crime. Such is theft, where, in my view, a conviction requires proof of some dishonesty. Murder is another such offence. The punishment for murder is the most severe in our society and the stigma that attaches to a conviction for murder is similarly extreme. In addition, murder is distinguished from manslaughter only by the mental element with respect to the death. It is thus clear that there must be some special mental element with respect to the death before a culpable homicide can be treated as a murder. That special mental element gives rise to the moral blameworthiness which justifies the stigma and sentence attached to a murder conviction. I am presently of the view that it is a principle of fundamental justice that a conviction for murder cannot rest on anything less than proof beyond a reasonable doubt of subjective foresight. Given the effect of this view on part of s. 212(c), for the reasons I have already given for deciding this case more narrowly, I need not and will not rest my finding that s. 213(d) violates the Charter on this view, because s. 213(d) does not, for reasons I will set out hereinafter, even meet the lower threshold test of objective foreseeability. I will therefore, for the sole purpose of this appeal, go no further than say that it is a principle of fundamental justice that, absent proof beyond a reasonable doubt of at least objective foreseeability, there surely cannot be a murder conviction.

[Lamer J then discussed s 11(d) of the Charter and stated, *inter alia*:]

What offends the presumption of innocence is the fact that an accused may be convicted despite the existence of a reasonable doubt on an essential element of the offence, and I do not think that it matters whether this results from the existence of a reverse onus provision or from the elimination of the need to prove an essential element.

The *mens rea* required for s. 213 consists of the *mens rea* for the underlying offence and the intent to commit one of the acts set forth in paras. (a) to (d) (*Swietlinski v. The Queen*, [1980] 2 S.C.R. 956). Section 213 does not impose on the accused the burden of disproving objective foreseeability. Further, it does not completely exclude the need to prove any objective foreseeability. Rather, s. 213 has substituted for proof beyond a reasonable doubt of objective foreseeability, if that is the essential element, proof beyond a reasonable doubt of certain forms of intentional dangerous conduct causing death.

The question is, therefore, can Parliament make this substitution without violating ss. 7 and 11(d)? As I have discussed earlier, if Parliament frames the section so that, upon proof of the conduct, it would be unreasonable for a jury not to conclude beyond a reasonable doubt that the accused ought to have known that death was likely to ensue, then I think that Parliament has enacted a crime which is tantamount to one which has objective foreseeability as an essential element, and, if objective foreseeability is sufficient, then it would not be in violation of s. 7 or s. 11(d) in doing so in that way. The acid test of the constitutionality of s. 213 is this ultimate question: *Would it be possible for a conviction for murder to occur under s. 213 despite the jury having a reasonable doubt as to whether the accused ought to have known that death was likely to ensue?* If the answer is yes, then the section is *prima facie* in violation of ss. 7 and 11(d). I should add in passing that if the answer is no, then it would be necessary to decide whether objective foreseeability is sufficient for a murder conviction. However, because in my view the answer is yes and because I do not want to pass upon the constitutionality of s. 212(c) in this case, I will not address that issue. ...

Notwithstanding proof beyond a reasonable doubt of the matters set forth in paras. (a) to (d) a jury could reasonably be left in doubt as regards objective foreseeability of the likelihood that death be caused. In other words, s. 213 will catch an accused who performs one of the acts in paras. (a) to (d) and thereby causes a death but who otherwise would have been acquitted of murder because he did not foresee and could not reasonably have foreseen that death would be likely to result. For that reason, s. 213 *prima facie* violates ss. 7 and 11(d). It is thus not necessary to decide whether objective foreseeability is sufficient for murder as s. 213 does not even meet that standard. This takes us to s. 1 for the second phase of the constitutional inquiry.

Finding that s. 213 [see now s 230] of the *Criminal Code* infringes ss. 7 and 11(d) of the Charter does not end the inquiry on the constitutional validity of s. 213. Any or all of paras. (a) to (d) of s. 213 can still be upheld as a reasonable limit "demonstrably justified in a free and democratic society" under s. 1 of the Charter.

In this case and at this stage of the inquiry, we need only consider para. (d) of s. 213. The criteria to be assessed under s. 1 have been set out by this court in several cases, particularly *R. v. Big M Drug Mart Ltd.*, [1985] 1 S.C.R. 295, and *R. v. Oakes*, [1986] 1 S.C.R. 103. First, the objective which the measures are designed to serve must be "of sufficient importance to warrant overriding a constitutionally protected right or freedom" (*Big M Drug Mart, supra*, at p. 352). Through s. 213(d) of the Code, Parliament intended to deter the use or carrying of a weapon in the commission of certain offences, because of the increased risk of death. In my view, it is clear that this objective is sufficiently important.

In addition, the measures adopted must be reasonable and demonstrably justified. The measures adopted appear to be rationally connected to the objective: indiscriminately punishing for murder all those who cause a death by using or carrying a weapon, whether the death was intentional or accidental, might well be thought to discourage the use and the carrying of weapons. I believe, however, that the measures adopted would unduly impair the rights and freedoms in question (see *Big M Drug Mart, supra*, at p. 352). It is not necessary to convict of murder persons who did not intend or foresee the death and who could not even have foreseen the death in order to deter others from using or carrying weapons. If Parliament wishes to deter the use or carrying of weapons, it should punish the use or carrying of weapons. A good example of this is the minimum imprisonment for using a firearm in the commission of an indictable offence under s. 83 of the *Criminal Code*. In any event, the conviction for manslaughter which would result instead of a conviction for murder is punishable by, from a day in jail, to confinement for life in a penitentiary. Very stiff sentences when weapons are involved in the commission of the crime of manslaughter would sufficiently deter the use or carrying of weapons in the commission of crimes. But stigmatizing the crime as murder unnecessarily impairs the Charter right.

In my view, therefore, s. 213(d) is not saved by s. 1.

[La Forest J issued separate concurring reasons, as did Beetz J, with whom Le Dain J joined; they refrained from addressing whether the principles of fundamental justice required subjective foresight of death as a precondition for a murder conviction.]

McINTYRE J (dissenting): I am not prepared to accept the proposition that s. 213(d) of the *Criminal Code* admits of a conviction for murder without proof of objective foreseeability of death or the likelihood of death, but in the view I take of this case it is not necessary to reach a firm conclusion on that point.

. . .

The principal complaint in this case is not that the accused should not have been convicted of a serious crime deserving of severe punishment, but simply that Parliament should not have chosen to call that crime "murder." No objection could be taken if Parliament classified the offence as manslaughter or a killing during the commission of an offence, or in some other manner. As I have observed before (see *R. v. Ancio*, [1984] 1 S.C.R. 225, at p. 251), while it may be illogical to characterize an unintentional killing as murder, no principle of fundamental justice is offended only because serious criminal conduct, involving the commission of a crime of violence resulting in the killing of a human being, is classified as murder and not in some other manner. As Martin J.A. said in *R. v. Munro and Munro, supra*, at p. 301: "This legislation has frequently been criticized as being harsh, but that is a matter for Parliament and not for the courts."

As has been noted, the appellant's conviction is based on a combination of s. 21(2) and s. 213(d) of the *Criminal Code*. There was in this case evidence of active participation in the commission of the robbery, the underlying offence, and the terms of s. 21(2) were fully met. It must be accepted that the section gives expression to a principle of joint criminal liability long accepted and applied in the criminal law. I am unable to say upon what basis one could exempt conduct which attracts criminal liability, under s. 213 of the *Criminal Code*, from the application of that principle. In *R. v. Munro and Munro, supra*, Martin J.A. said, at p. 301:

> Patently, Parliament has decided that the carrying of weapons during the commission of certain crimes, such as robbery, so manifestly endangers the lives of others, that one who joins a common purpose to commit one of the specified offences and who knows or ought to know that his accomplice has upon his person a weapon which he will use if needed, must bear the risk if death, in fact, ensues as a consequence of the use or possession of the weapon during the commission of one of the specified offences or during the flight of the offender after the commission or attempted commission of the underlying offence. ...

In my view, Martin J.A. has stated the policy considerations which have motivated Parliament in this connection and I would not interfere with the Parliamentary decision. I would, therefore, dismiss the appeal and answer the two constitutional questions in the negative.

R v Martineau
Supreme Court of Canada
[1990] 2 SCR 633

[In this case, the Court struck down s 213(a) (now s 230(a)). The deceased were deliberately shot by Martineau's accomplice during a robbery.]

LAMER CJ [at the time of the judgment] (Dickson CJ [at the time of hearing] and Wilson, Gonthier, and Cory JJ concurring): ... Thirty witnesses gave evidence including the accused. The evidence revealed that Martineau and his friend, Tremblay, had set out one evening armed with a pellet pistol and rifle respectively. Martineau testified that he knew that they were going to commit a crime, but that he thought it would only be a "b and e." After robbing the trailer and its occupants, Martineau's friend Tremblay shot and killed the McLeans. As they left the trailer, Martineau asked Tremblay why he killed them and Tremblay answered, "they saw our faces." Martineau responded, "But they couldn't see mine 'cause I had a mask on." ...

Parliament, of course, decides what a crime is to be, and has the power to define the elements of a crime. With the advent of the *Charter* in 1982, Parliament also has, however, directed the courts to review those definitions to ensure that they are in accordance with the principles of fundamental justice. We, as a court, would be remiss not to heed this command of Parliament. This is an unassailable proposition since the decision of Parliament to entrench into our constitutional framework a *Charter of Rights and Freedoms* and also the principle that the Constitution is the supreme law of the land. Since 1982, this court has consistently assumed its duty to measure the content of legislation against the guarantees in our *Charter* designed to protect individual rights and freedoms: see for example *Singh v. Minister of Employment and Immigration*, [1985] 1 S.C.R. 177; *Re B.C. Motor Vehicle Act*, [1985] 2 S.C.R. 486; and *R. v. Oakes*, [1986] 1 S.C.R. 103.

. . .

Section 213(a) [now s 230(a)] of the *Code* defines culpable homicide as murder where a person causes the death of a human being while committing or attempting to commit a range of listed offences, whether or not the person means to cause death or whether or not he or she knows that death is likely to ensue if that person means to cause bodily harm for the purpose of facilitating the commission of the offence or flight after committing or attempting to commit the offence. The introductory paragraph of the section, therefore, expressly removes from the Crown the burden of proving beyond a reasonable doubt that the accused had subjective foresight of death. This section stands as an anomaly as regards the other murder provisions, especially in light of the common law presumption against convicting a person of a true crime without proof of intent or recklessness.

A conviction for murder carries with it the most severe stigma and punishment of any crime in our society. The principles of fundamental justice require, because of the special nature of the stigma attached to a conviction for murder, and the available penalties, a *mens rea* reflecting the particular nature of that crime. The effect of s. 213 is to violate the principle that punishment must be proportionate to the moral blameworthiness of the offender, or as Professor Hart puts it in *Punishment and Responsibility* (1968), at p. 162, the fundamental principle of a morally based system of law that those causing harm intentionally be punished more severely than those causing harm unintentionally. The rationale underlying the principle that subjective foresight of death is required before a person is labelled and punished as a murderer is linked to the more general principle that criminal liability for a particular result is not justified except where the actor possesses a culpable mental state in respect of that result.

In my view, in a free and democratic society that values the autonomy and free will of the individual, the stigma and punishment attaching to the most serious of crimes, murder, should be reserved for those who choose to intentionally cause death or who choose to inflict bodily harm that they know is likely to cause death. The essential role of requiring subjective foresight of death in the context of murder is to maintain a proportionality between the stigma and punishment attached to a murder conviction and the moral blameworthiness of the offender. Murder has long been recognized as the "worst" and most heinous of peace time crimes. It is, therefore, essential that to satisfy the principles of fundamental justice, the stigma and punishment attaching to a murder conviction must be reserved for those who either intend to cause death or who intend to cause bodily harm that they know will likely cause death. ...

As regards s. 1 of the *Charter*, there is no doubt that the objective of deterring the infliction of bodily harm during the commission of certain offences because of the increased risk of death is of sufficient importance to warrant overriding a *Charter* right. Further, indiscriminately punishing for murder all those who cause death irrespective of whether they intended to cause death might well be thought to discourage the infliction of bodily harm during the commission of certain offences because of the increased risk of death. But it is not necessary in order to achieve this objective to convict of murder persons who do not intend or foresee the death. In this regard the section unduly impairs the *Charter* rights. If Parliament wishes to deter persons from causing bodily harm during certain offences, then it should punish persons for causing the bodily harm. Indeed, the conviction for manslaughter that would result instead of a conviction for murder is punishable by, from a day in jail, to confinement for life. Very stiff sentences for the infliction of bodily harm leading to death in appropriate cases would sufficiently meet any deterrence objective that Parliament might have in mind. The more flexible sentencing scheme under a conviction for manslaughter is in accord with the principle that punishment be meted out with regard to the level of moral blameworthiness of the offender. To label and punish a person as a murderer who did not intend or foresee death unnecessarily stigmatizes and punishes those whose moral blameworthiness is not that of a murderer, and thereby unnecessarily impairs the rights guaranteed by ss. 7 and 11(d) of the *Charter*. In my view then, s. 213(a), indeed all of s. 213, cannot be saved by s. 1 of the *Charter*.

L'HEUREUX-DUBÉ J (dissenting): … This notion of "subjective mental element" from the reasons of Lamer J. in *Vaillancourt* is neither constitutionally mandated nor necessitated by elemental principles of the criminal law. The insistence on a subjective foresight requirement was not germane to the decision in *Vaillancourt*. The *obiter* statements were endorsed by only four of the eight Justices who participated in *Vaillancourt*.

· · ·

It should be noted that in the present case the underlying offence was committed, and the intent to inflict bodily harm was clear. Moreover, this amalgamation of indispensable prerequisites establishes that this crime, as phrased by Lamer J. in *Vaillancourt*, is "tantamount to one which has objective foreseeability as an essential element, and, if objective foreseeability is sufficient, then it would not be in violation of s. 7 or s. 11(d) in doing so in that way." I am of the view that in light of these requirements, the test of objective foreseeability is sufficient, and that if that test has been met, then no *Charter* violation has taken place. The above list requires that the accused specifically intend to, and actually commit the underlying offence, and specifically intend to, and actually inflict bodily harm. In my view, the inexorable conclusion is that the resulting death is objectively foreseeable.

Those who are critical of all forms of the "felony-murder" rule base their denunciation on the premise that *mens rea* is the exclusive determinant of the level of "stigma" that is properly applied to an offender. This appears to me to confuse some very fundamental principles of criminal law and ignores the pivotal contribution of *actus reus* to the definition and appropriate response to proscribed criminal offences. If both components, *actus reus* as well as *mens rea*, are not considered when assessing the level of fault attributable to an offender, we would see manslaughter and assault causing bodily harm as no more worthy of condemnation than an assault. Mere attempts would become as serious as full offences. The whole correlation between the consequences of a criminal act and its

retributive repercussions would become obscured by a stringent and exclusive examination of the accused's own asserted intentions.

· · ·

In the United States the common law notion of felony-murder continues to exist in a
modified form in all but three states. Gilbert, "Degrees of Felony Murder" (1983), 40
Wash. and Lee L. Rev. 1601. While a number of jurisdictions have limited the rule by
requiring the felony to be inherently violent or by requiring violent means to be used
during the course of the felony, the rule still contains no requirement of subjective foresight of death. Apart from certain limits *when combined with the death penalty*, the United
States Supreme Court has consistently upheld the constitutional validity of the felony-
murder rule. *Tison v. Arizona*, 107 S.Ct. 1676 (1987); *Gregg v. Georgia*, 428 U.S. 153 (1976).

· · ·

I find this concentration on social "stigma" to be overemphasized, and, in the great
majority of cases, completely inapplicable. The facts in the present appeals reveal the truly
heinous nature of the criminal acts at issue. The concern that these offenders not endure
the mark of Cain is, in my view, an egregious example of misplaced compassion. If the
apprehension is that the offenders in question will suffer from their "murderer" label, I
suspect they will fare little better tagged as "manslaughterers." Accidental killings cannot,
after *Vaillancourt*, result in murder prosecutions. Only killings resulting from circumstances in which death is, at a minimum, objectively foreseeable will be prosecuted under
s. 213(a). Furthermore, the duration of imprisonment, if at all different, will not attenuate
the "stigma." To the extent that any such "stigma" can be said to exist, it is at least as palpable
upon release to the outside world as it is within the prison environment itself.

· · ·

Section 213(a) does not deal with accidental killings, but rather with killings that are
objectively foreseeable as a result of the abominable nature of the predicate crimes, committed with specific intent, coupled with the intentional infliction of bodily harm. Given
the dual subjective requirement already in place, the deterrence factor is most cogent in
these circumstances. Whatever the competing arguments may be with respect to deterring
the merely negligent, here we are dealing with those who have already expressly acted
with the intent to commit at least two underlying serious crimes. If deterrence is to ever
have any application to the criminal law, and in my view it should, this is the place.

· · ·

Policy considerations in Canada as well as in other jurisdictions have inspired legislation that considers objective foreseeability sufficient as the minimum *mens rea* requirement for murder. While it may not be the very best test for all cases, it is certainly a
constitutionally valid one. Parliament did not have to enact s. 213(a), but that is not the
question before this Court. The issue is whether it could. In my view, the answer rests on
what level of foreseeability will be required before a conviction for murder can be returned.
Based on this Court's precedents, and the principles of fundamental justice, I believe that
the objective foreseeability of death test for the crime of murder is constitutionally valid.
The additional mandatory elements demanded by s. 213(a) lend even greater force to this
conclusion.

Striking down the legislation simply because some other scheme may be preferable
would be an unwarranted intrusion into Parliament's prerogative, and would undermine
the means it has chosen to protect its citizens. The *Charter* is not designed to allow this

Court to substitute preferable provisions for those already in place in the absence of a clear constitutional violation. Such a task should be reserved for the Law Reform Commission or other advisory bodies. This Court's province is to pronounce upon the constitutionality of those provisions properly before it. The *Charter* does not infuse the courts with the power to declare legislation to be of no force or effect on the basis that they believe the statute to be undesirable as a matter of criminal law policy. For the aforementioned reasons, I do not believe that s. 213(a) offends the *Canadian Charter of Rights and Freedoms*.

[Sopinka J also struck down the section but did so on the basis that the section does not require even an objective foreseeability of death and would have limited the Court's decision to this narrower holding: "Overbroad statements of principle are inimical to the tradition of incremental development of the common law. Likewise, the development of law under the *Canadian Charter of Rights and Freedoms* is best served by deciding cases before the courts, not by anticipating the results of future cases."]

See also *R v Sit*, [1991] 3 SCR 124, which deals with the constitutional validity of s 213(c) (now s 230(c)) of the Code. The cause of death was strangulation by one of the accused's accomplices. Lamer CJ stated for the Court:

The respondent argued before this court that the finding of the majority in *Martineau* that subjective foreseeability of death is the minimum constitutional *mens rea* requirement for murder is *obiter dictum*. The respondent emphasized that, under s. 213(a) of the *Code*, an accused could be convicted of murder in the absence of proof that he had *objective* foresight of the death of his victim. Section 213(a), therefore, could have been found to violate ss. 7 and 11(d) of the Charter on the basis that the provision did not require objective foresight of death as an essential element of the offence. In this light, our findings regarding subjective foresight of death were arguably unnecessary to the resolution of the case.

In my opinion, a correct reading of *Martineau* does not support the respondent's submission. In *Martineau*, as I noted above, this court was asked to pronounce on the constitutional validity of s. 213(a) of the *Criminal Code*. To answer this question, it was necessary to determine the minimum degree of *mens rea* required by the Charter for the offence of murder. The determination of this minimum constitutional *mens rea* requirement was, therefore, the live issue before this court. Consequently, our finding in *Martineau* that proof of subjective foresight of death is necessary in order to sustain a conviction for murder and that s. 213(a) of the *Criminal Code* violated the Charter since it did not embrace this requirement, was not *obiter dictum*. This finding was the *ratio decidendi* of the decision.

To a certain extent, Parliament has responded to the Court's decisions in this area by enacting a number of mandatory minimum sentencing provisions. In particular, s 236, reproduced in Section I above, establishes a minimum sentence of four years' imprisonment (and a maximum of life imprisonment) for manslaughter committed with the use of a firearm. In *R v Morrisey*, 2000 SCC 39, [2000] 2 SCR 90, the Court upheld the constitutional validity of a related provision that mandates a four-year minimum sentence for criminal negligence causing death when a firearm is used in the commission of the offence.

III. FIRST-DEGREE MURDER

In 1976, when the law of murder was vastly reformed, Parliament made a distinction be-tween first-degree murder and second-degree murder. While both categories of murder carry a mandatory sentence of life imprisonment, with second-degree murder the trial judge may set parole ineligibility between 10 and 25 years, whereas with first-degree murder pa-role ineligibility must be set at 25 years. (In the case of multiple murders, the sentencing judge now has the discretion to order that the periods of parole ineligibility apply consecu-tively.) Given all of this, the consequences of a conviction for first-degree, as opposed to second-degree, murder are dramatic.

Section 231 of the *Criminal Code* establishes the categories of first-degree murder as follows:

231(1) Murder is first degree murder or second degree murder.

(2) Murder is first degree murder when it is planned and deliberate.

(3) Without limiting the generality of subsection (2), murder is planned and deliberate when it is committed pursuant to an arrangement under which money or anything of value passes or is intended to pass from one person to another, or is promised by one person to another, as con-sideration for that other's causing or assisting in causing the death of anyone or counselling an-other person to do any act causing or assisting in causing that death.

(4) Irrespective of whether a murder is planned and deliberate on the part of any person, murder is first degree murder when the victim is

(a) a police officer, police constable, constable, sheriff, deputy sheriff, sheriff's officer or other person employed for the preservation and maintenance of the public peace, acting in the course of his duties;

(b) a warden, deputy warden, instructor, keeper, jailer, guard or other officer or a perma-nent employee of a prison, acting in the course of his duties; or

(c) a person working in a prison with the permission of the prison authorities and acting in the course of his work therein.

(5) Irrespective of whether a murder is planned and deliberate on the part of any person, murder is first degree murder in respect of a person when the death is caused by that person while committing or attempting to commit an offence under one of the following sections:

(a) section 76 (hijacking an aircraft);

(b) section 271 (sexual assault);

(c) section 272 (sexual assault with a weapon, threats to a third party or causing bodily harm);

(d) section 273 (aggravated sexual assault);

(e) section 279 (kidnapping and forcible confinement); or

(f) section 279.1 (hostage taking).

(6) Irrespective of whether a murder is planned and deliberate on the part of any person, murder is first degree murder when the death is caused by that person while committing or attempting to commit an offence under section 264 and the person committing that offence intended to cause the person murdered to fear for the safety of the person murdered or the safety of anyone known to the person murdered.

(6.01) Irrespective of whether a murder is planned and deliberate on the part of a person, murder is first degree murder when the death is caused by that person while committing or attempting to commit an indictable offence under this or any other Act of Parliament if the act or omission constituting the offence also constitutes a terrorist activity.

(6.1) Irrespective of whether a murder is planned and deliberate on the part of a person, murder is first degree murder when

(a) the death is caused by that person for the benefit of, at the direction of or in association with a criminal organization; or

(b) the death is caused by that person while committing or attempting to commit an indictable offence under this or any other Act of Parliament for the benefit of, at the direction of or in association with a criminal organization.

(6.2) Irrespective of whether a murder is planned and deliberate on the part of a person, murder is first degree murder when the death is caused by that person while committing or attempting to commit an offence under section 423.1.

(7) All murder that is not first degree murder is second degree murder.

We examine the formal requirements of some of these categories of first-degree murder in the cases below.

Section 231(2): "Planned and Deliberate"

R v More
Supreme Court of Canada
[1963] SCR 522, [1963] 3 CCC 289

[The accused was depressed over his financial affairs. Fearful that their disclosure would be upsetting to his wife, he planned to kill her and then kill himself. The accused succeeded in killing his wife, but failed at his attempted suicide and was charged with capital murder under previous *Criminal Code* provisions, which required proof that the murder was "planned and deliberate." The accused led psychiatric evidence in an attempt to raise a reasonable doubt as to whether he meant to kill his wife and whether the murder was planned and deliberate. The case turned on the trial judge's directions to the jury on the use that could be made of psychiatric evidence. The Court also expressed an opinion on the meaning of planned and deliberate murder.]

CARTWRIGHT J: … In the circumstances of this case, the defence of insanity having been expressly disclaimed, there were really only two questions for the jury. The first was whether the appellant meant to cause the death of his wife; if this was answered in the affirmative he was guilty of murder. The second, which arises under s. 202A(2)(a) [enacted 1960-61, c 44, s 1] of the *Criminal Code*, 1953-54 (Can.), c. 51, was whether this murder was planned and deliberate on his part; if this was answered in the affirmative he was guilty of capital murder.

The evidence that the murder was planned was very strong, but, as was properly pointed out to the jury by the learned trial Judge, they could not find the accused guilty of capital murder unless they were satisfied beyond a reasonable doubt not only that the murder was planned but also that it was deliberate. The learned trial Judge also rightly instructed the jury that the word "deliberate," as used in s. 202A(2)(a), means "considered, not impulsive."

Other meanings of the adjective given in the *Oxford Dictionary* are "not hasty in decision," "slow in deciding" and "intentional." The word as used in the subsection cannot have simply the meaning "intentional" because it is only if the accused's act was intentional that he can be guilty of murder and the subsection is creating an additional ingredient to be proved as a condition of an accused being convicted of capital murder.

The recital of the facts and the evidence of the appellant as to what occurred at the moment of the discharge of the rifle, set out in the reasons of my brother Judson, show that it was open to the jury to take the view that the act of the appellant in pulling the trigger was impulsive rather than considered and therefore was not deliberate. The evidence of the two doctors and particularly that of Dr. Adamson, also quoted by my brother Judson, that, in his opinion, at the critical moment the appellant was suffering from a depressive psychosis resulting in "impairment of ability to decide even inconsequential things, inability to make a decision in a normal kind of a way" would have a direct bearing on the question whether the appellant's act was deliberate in the sense defined above; its weight was a matter for the jury.

The case of *R v Widdifield* (1961), 6 Crim LQ 152 (Ont SC) has stood the test of time as an authoritative pronouncement on the content of the expression "planned and deliberate." The following is the reported excerpt from the charge to the jury by Gale J (later Gale CJO):

> I think that in the Code "planned" is to be assigned, I think, its natural meaning of a calculated scheme or design which has been carefully thought out, and the nature and consequences of which have been considered and weighed. But that does not mean, of course, to say that the plan need be a complicated one. It may be a very simple one, and the simpler it is perhaps the easier it is to formulate.
>
> The important element, it seems to me, so far as time is concerned, is the time involved in developing the plan, not the time between the development of the plan and the doing of the act. One can carefully prepare and plan and immediately it is prepared set out to do the planned act, or, alternatively, you can wait an appreciable time to do it once it has been formed.
>
> As far as the word "deliberate" is concerned, I think that the Code means that it should also carry its natural meaning of "considered," "not impulsive," "slow in deciding," "cautious," implying that the accused must take time to weigh the advantages and disadvantages of his intended action.

In *R v Nygaard*, [1989] 2 SCR 1074 the Court held that it was possible for a murder to be classified as first-degree murder on the basis of the secondary intent in s 229(a)(ii)—a reckless killing. The case involved two accused who planned to beat the victim with baseball bats in relation to a relatively minor dispute over money and property. The victim died. Writing for the majority, Cory J held in part:

> In my view, the vital element of the requisite intent is that of causing such bodily harm that the perpetrator knows that it is likely to cause death and yet persists in the assault. There can be no doubt that a person can plan and deliberate to cause terrible bodily harm that he knows is likely to result in death. Nothing is added to the aspect of planning and deliberation by the requirement that the fatal assault be carried out in a reckless manner, that is to say by heedlessly proceeding with the deadly assault in the face of the knowledge of the obvious risks. The planning and

deliberation to cause the bodily harm which is likely to be fatal must of necessity include the planning and deliberating to continue and to persist in that conduct despite the knowledge of the risk. The element of recklessness does not exist in a vacuum as a sole *mens rea* requirement, but rather it must act in conjunction with the intentional infliction of terrible bodily harm. I, therefore, conclude that planning and deliberation may well be coupled with the *mens rea* requirement of s. 212(a)(ii) and that a first degree murder conviction can be sustained by virtue of the combined operation of s. 214(2) and s. 212(a)(ii) [now ss 231(2) and 229(a)(ii)].

As well, the appellant argued it was wrong to label an offence under s. 212(a)(ii) as murder. It was said that the requisite *mens rea* is such that it is not as grave a crime as that defined in s. 212(a)(i) where the requisite intent is to cause the death of someone. I cannot accept that contention. The variation in the degree of culpability is too slight to take into account. Let us consider the gravity of the crime described by s. 212(a)(ii) in the light of three examples which, pursuant to the section, would be murder. First, an accused forms the intent to inflict multiple stab wounds in the abdomen and chest of a person knowing that the wounds are likely to kill the victim and, heedless of the known probable result, proceeds with the stabbing. Secondly, an accused forms the intent to shoot a former associate in the chest knowing that death is likely to ensue and, uncaring of the result, shoots the victim in the chest. Thirdly, two accused form the intent to repeatedly and viciously strike a person in the head with a baseball bat realizing full well that the victim will probably die as a result. None the less they continue with the bone-splintering, skull-shattering assault. The accused in all these examples must have committed as grave a crime as the accused who specifically intends to kill. Society would, I think, find the drawing of any differentiation in the degree of culpability an exercise in futility. The difference in the calibration on the scale of culpability is too minute to merit a distinction. I would conclude that the crime defined in s. 212(a)(ii) can properly be described as murder and on a "culpability scale" it varies so little from s. 212(a)(i) as to be indistinguishable.

Section 231(4): Murder of Police Officer, Etc.

R v Collins
Ontario Court of Appeal
(1989), 48 CCC (3d) 343

[The accused was charged with first-degree murder for killing a police officer. At the time he was killed, the officer was on duty and in uniform. He was shot by the accused at very close range. The accused was convicted of first-degree murder on the basis of s 214(4)(a) (now s 231(4)(a)) of the *Criminal Code*, which provides that irrespective of whether a murder is planned and deliberate, murder is first-degree murder when the victim is "a police officer, police constable, constable, sheriff, deputy sheriff, sheriff's officer or other person employed for the preservation and maintenance of the public peace, acting in the course of his duties." The accused argued that s 214(4)(a) was unconstitutional and infringed s 7 of the Charter because an accused could be convicted of first-degree murder without the need to prove planning and deliberation.]

GOODMAN JA: … Is s. 214(4)(a) of the *Criminal Code* of Canada (now R.S.C. 1985 c. C-46, s. 231(4)(a)) constitutionally invalid because it is contrary to the provisions of s. 7 of the Charter?

. . .

The constitutionality of s. 214(4) (now s. 231(4)) was not argued at trial. On this appeal, counsel for the appellant took the position that the stigma associated with first degree murder and the stricter penalty (mandatory non-eligibility for parole for a period of twenty-five years as opposed to a possible ten-year minimum non-eligibility for parole period for second degree murder) for such offence can only be justified on the basis of a higher degree of moral blameworthiness. It was his submission that only the provisions of s. 214(2) (now s. 231(2)) satisfies this requirement. ... Section 214(1) and (2) (now s. 231(1) and (2)) read as follows:

> 214(1) Murder is first degree murder or second degree murder.
> (2) Murder is first degree murder when it is planned and deliberate.

The added degree of blameworthiness required for first degree murder under s-s. (2) consists of the planning and deliberation of a killing. Under s. 214(4)(a) there is no need to prove planning and deliberation. It is sufficient for the Crown to prove that the victim is one of the persons designated in s-s. (4)(a) acting in the course of his duties.

He relied on the decision of the Supreme Court of Canada in *R. v. Vaillancourt* 60 C.R. (3d) 289 and on a decision of this Court in *R. v. Munro and Munro* (1983), 8 C.C.C. (3d) 260. In *Vaillancourt* it was held that it is a principle of fundamental justice that, absent proof beyond a reasonable doubt of at least objective foreseeability of death this cannot be a murder conviction. The court held that s. 213(d) of the Code [now s 230(d)] had substituted for proof beyond a reasonable doubt of objective foreseeability proof beyond a reasonable doubt of certain forms of intentional dangerous conduct causing death. A person could be convicted under s. 213(d) although the jury had a reasonable doubt as to whether the accused ought to have known that death was likely to ensue. An accused in such circumstances, who might otherwise be convicted of a lesser offence, would bear the stigma of a murder notwithstanding his lack of intention to kill or objective foreseeability. Accordingly the court found s. 213(d) to be in violation of ss. 7 and 11(d) of the Charter.

In the case at bar the argument with respect to stigma is much less relevant. Before an accused can be convicted of first degree murder the Crown must prove all of the elements required for a conviction of second degree murder. The stigma of a murder conviction carrying with it a mandatory sentence of life imprisonment attaches to such an accused even if the Crown failed to prove the additional ingredients required for a conviction of first degree murder.

. . .

Subsection 5 of s. 214, like subsection 4, provides that irrespective of whether the murder is planned or deliberate, it is classified as first degree murder when the death is caused by an accused while committing or attempting to commit certain offences as set forth in s-s. (5). The rationale behind s. 214(5) would appear to be that Parliament regards the offences therein enumerated, which involves an accused exercising dominion and control over other persons of so serious a nature as to require a heavier sentence by way of additional deterrent. It must be noted, however, that in addition to the element of added moral culpability being present, the offender would have full knowledge of the existence of the state of facts which render him liable to the heavier penalty for the commission of a murder in those circumstances.

There can be little doubt that the rationale behind the provisions of s. 214(4) is to provide additional protection to the persons designated in s. 214(4)(a) while acting in the course of their duties. Their occupations are extremely dangerous having regard to the persons with whom they are in frequent contact by reason of the nature of their occupations. The classification of the murder of such persons as first degree murder with the heavier penalty consequent thereon is obviously designed as an additional deterrent to potential murderers. It might be rationalized that the murder of a person whose obligation it is to maintain law and order carries with it an added moral culpability and requires a heavier deterrent to protect the public interest.

It was the position of counsel for the appellant that s. 214(4)(a) does not require the Crown to prove that accused had knowledge of the identity of the victim as one of the persons designated in s-s. (4) and that he was acting in the course of his duties. His submission was that in those circumstances there was no additional moral culpability justifying a heavier penalty upon a conviction for murder and accordingly subsection (4) is constitutionally invalid. He further submitted that if the conviction for first degree murder, as opposed to second degree murder, was registered on the basis of the provisions of subsection 4(a), it cannot stand even though the trial judge charged the jury that it was incumbent on the Crown to prove that the appellant knew the victim was a police constable acting in the course of his duty and there was evidence upon which the jury could so find.

Counsel for the Attorney-General for Canada who appeared on the appeal as an intervener took the position that in s. 214(4)(a) Parliament had identified an aggravating element which would justify the classification of a murder as a first degree murder. It was his submission that the element of *mens rea* is a matter relevant only to the determination whether murder had been committed under ss. 212 and 213 of the Code and that there is no *mens rea* element associated with the inquiry contemplated by s. 214. He submitted that once the Crown has satisfied the jury beyond a reasonable doubt that the accused was guilty of murder under ss. 212 or 213, then the offence of murder will be properly characterized as first degree murder upon proof beyond a reasonable doubt of the aggravating elements set forth in s. 214(4)(a) and no element of *mens rea* is involved in such determination.

. . .

There can be no doubt that the onus was on the Crown to establish beyond a reasonable doubt the *actus reus* and *mens rea* of the substantive offence of murder under s. 212. I am of the view, however, that under s. 214(4)(a) there is an onus on the Crown to establish beyond a reasonable doubt that the victim was a person who falls within the designation of the occupations set forth in that subsection acting in the course of his duties to the knowledge of the accused or with recklessness on his part as to whether the victim was such a person so acting.

In my opinion there is no binding authority to the contrary. It seems clear to me that the object of the classification of first degree murder in s. 214 is to require a more severe punishment for the offence of murder in circumstances that involve an added degree of moral culpability or to act as a more effective deterrent in the prevention of the murder of persons engaged in the preservation, prevention of infringement and enforcement of the law or of persons who have fallen under the domination of an offender.

It is my view that s. 214(4)(a) should be interpreted in such a manner that requires proof of the facts which give rise to the added moral culpability or which would act as an additional deterrent. It is clear to me that to fulfill such interpretation it is necessary that the Crown prove that the murderer had knowledge of the identity of the victim as one of the persons designated in the subsection and that such person was acting in the course of his duties or was reckless as to such identity and acts of the victim.

The section could, of course, be interpreted to simply require that the Crown prove that the occupation of the victim was one of those set forth in the subsection and that the person was acting in the course of his duties without proof of knowledge thereof on the part of the murderer. The subsection does not refer to proof of such knowledge.

I am satisfied that if the latter interpretation is adopted, it would offend s. 7 of the Charter. If, for example, a gunman sees two persons on the street dressed in plain clothes of whom one is a merchant walking home and the other is a detective on his way to investigate or in the process of investigating a break-in and if the gunman decides without planning and deliberation to shoot and kill one of them and does so he would be guilty of murder no matter which person he killed. In the case of the killing of the ordinary citizen he would be guilty of second degree murder with a sentence of life imprisonment with a possibility of parole eligibility after ten years but in the case of the killing of the detective he would be guilty of first degree murder with a sentence of life imprisonment with a possibility of parole in no less than twenty-five years being the minimum period before parole eligibility (subject of course to the provisions of s. 745 of the Code (formerly s. 672).

Although the crime of murder is deserving of the heavy sentence involved, it seems to me that there would be no difference in moral culpability in the example set forth above no matter which person was the victim nor would there be any additional deterrent provided under s. 214(4)(a) in those circumstances if proof of knowledge that the detective was indeed a detective acting in the course of his duty were not required. There would then be no rational or logical reason for imposing a heavier penalty in the case where the murderer killed the person who he did not know and had no reason to know was a police officer acting in the course of his duties.

On the other hand, if s. 214(4)(a) is interpreted to require proof of such knowledge before the murder can be classified as first degree murder then a heavier sentence can be justified on the basis of added moral culpability or as additional deterrent on the grounds of public policy. In such event, it is my opinion that the subsection would not contravene the provisions of s. 7 of the Charter.

I am of the opinion that where a statutory provision is open to two interpretations, one of which will contravene the Charter and the other of which will not, the provision should be interpreted in such a manner as will not contravene the Charter (see *R. v. Corbett* 64 C.R. (3d) 1 per Beetz J. at p. 23).

I conclude that the onus is on the Crown to prove that the appellant knew that the victim was a police officer who was acting in the course of his duty and I find, accordingly, that the provisions of s. 214(4)(a) do not contravene s. 7 of the Charter. In the present case the trial judge charged the jury in accordance with this conclusion. There was evidence to support a finding of knowledge on the part of the appellant.

Appeal dismissed.

Section 231(5): "While Committing"

The leading decision on the requirements of s 231(5) is *R v Paré*, [1987] 2 SCR 618. In that case, the Court faced the question of what the phrase "while committing" means in the context of the identical predecessor provision (s 214(5)), in a case where the accused killed a young boy shortly after having indecently assaulted him. *Paré* is substantially reproduced in Chapter 1.

R v Russell

Supreme Court of Canada

2001 SCC 53, [2001] 2 SCR 804

[The accused was charged with first-degree murder on the basis that he caused the death of the victim while forcibly confining another individual, contrary to s 231(5)(e). It was alleged that the accused tied and gagged his girlfriend in her bed, forced her to have sexual intercourse, left her tied in the bedroom, and then went to the basement and beat and stabbed the deceased to death. The preliminary inquiry judge concluded that the deceased did not have to be the victim of the underlying offence of forcible confinement in order to sustain a charge of first-degree murder under s 231(5). The Superior Court judge quashed the committal for first-degree murder and substituted a committal for second-degree murder, on the theory that s 231(5) requires the victim of the murder and the enumerated offence to be the same person. The Court of Appeal reversed, holding that, even if the preliminary inquiry judge erred in his interpretation of s 231(5)(e), the error constituted an error within his jurisdiction and was not reviewable.]

McLACHLIN CJ: ...

2. Section 231(5)

I turn now to the question of whether the preliminary inquiry judge erred in holding that s. 231(5) may apply even if the victim of the murder and the victim of the enumerated offence are not the same.

The question is first and foremost one of statutory interpretation. As such, the governing principles are well-settled: the words in question should be considered in the context in which they are used, and read in a manner consistent with the purpose of the provision and the intention of the legislature: see *R. v. Heywood*, [1994] 3 S.C.R. 761 (citing Elmer A. Driedger, *Construction of Statutes* (2nd ed. 1983), at p. 87; *R. v. Hasselwander*, [1993] 2 S.C.R. 398). "If the ordinary meaning of the words is consistent with the context in which the words are used and with the object of the act, then that is the interpretation which should govern": *Heywood*, supra, at p. 784.

The language of s. 231(5) is clear. The provision does not state that the victim of the murder and the victim of the enumerated offence must be one and the same. It requires only that the accused have killed "while committing or attempting to commit" one of the enumerated offences. Nothing in that phrase suggests that the provision's application is limited to cases in which the victim of the murder and the victim of the enumerated offence are the same. An interpretation of the provision that recognized such a limitation would effectively read into the provision a restriction that is not stated.

Other provisions of the *Criminal Code* indicate that, where Parliament intends to limit the phrase "while committing or attempting to commit," it does so in express language. Section 231(6), for example, provides that "Irrespective of whether a murder is planned and deliberate on the part of any person, murder is first degree murder when the death is caused by that person while committing or attempting to commit an offence under section 264 [Criminal Harassment] and the person committing that offence intended to cause the person murdered to fear for the safety of the person murdered or the safety of anyone known to the person murdered."

Without the limitation, s. 231(6) would apply to a person who had murdered one person while criminally harassing another. The limitation restricts the application of the provision to those who murder the person they are criminally harassing. No analogous limitation is stated in s. 231(5).

Still other provisions of the *Criminal Code* suggest that Parliament's use of the phrase "while committing or attempting to commit" does not in itself reflect an intention to create a same-victim requirement. Section 231(6.1), for example, provides that "[M]urder is first degree murder when the death is caused while committing or attempting to commit an offence under section 81 [using explosives] for the benefit of ... a criminal organization."

Section 81 proscribes conduct that includes using explosives against property: see s. 81(1)(c) ("Every one commits an offence who ... with intent to destroy or damage property without lawful excuse, places or throws an explosive substance anywhere ..."). Parliament must have contemplated, therefore, that s. 231(6.1) might be applied even where there is no "victim" at all to the underlying crime. It would be senseless to say that the victim of the murder and the explosives offence must be one and the same where the latter crime might have no victim at all. Section 231(6.1) suggests that the use of the phrase "while committing or attempting to commit" does not itself create a same-victim requirement.

If Parliament had intended to restrict the scope of s. 231(5), it could have done so explicitly, as it did in s. 231(6). That Parliament did not incorporate such a restriction suggests that it intended "while committing or attempting to commit" to apply even where the victim of the murder and the victim of the enumerated offence are not the same. Indeed, several of the offences enumerated in s. 231(5) quite clearly raise the possibility that the person murdered will not be the same as the victim of the enumerated crime, and it would be difficult to conclude that this possibility did not occur to the drafters of the provision. A hijacker might kill a person on the runway; a kidnapper might kill the parent of the child he means to kidnap; a hostage-taker might kill an innocent bystander or a would-be rescuer. It is difficult to conclude that Parliament did not envision such possibilities.

The fact that s. 231(5) reaches not only successfully executed offences but also attempts raises similar concerns. Many attempt charges stem from crimes that were thwarted or aborted, often because of the intervention of a third party. Parliament surely envisioned such scenarios when it drafted the provision. Had Parliament not wanted the provision to reach these circumstances, it could easily have attached an explicit restriction to the provision's language.

In arguing that s. 231(5) applies only where the victim of the murder and the victim of the enumerated offence are the same, the appellant relies principally on this Court's judgment in *Paré*, [[1987] 2 SCR 618]. In *Paré*, the accused had murdered a boy two minutes after indecently assaulting him. The question was whether the accused had committed the murder "while committing" the indecent assault. Wilson J. quoting Martin J.A. answered the question in the affirmative, holding that a death is caused "while committing" an offence enumerated under s. 231(5) "where the act causing death and the acts constituting the [enumerated offence] all form part of one continuous sequence of events forming a single transaction": *Paré*, at p. 632. Wilson J. reasoned that this understanding of the provision best reflects the underlying policy concerns, which she characterized as follows at p. 633:

> The offences listed in s. 214(5) [now s. 231(5)] are all offences involving the unlawful domination of people by other people. Thus an organizing principle for s. 214(5) can be found. This principle is that where a murder is committed by someone already abusing his power by illegally dominating another, the murder should be treated as an exceptionally serious crime.

While that passage does not in itself suggest that s. 231(5) applies only where the victim of the murder and the enumerated offence are the same, Wilson J. went on to write: "it is the continuing illegal domination of the victim which gives continuity to the sequence of events culminating in the murder. The murder represents an exploitation of the position of power created by the underlying crime and makes the entire course of conduct a 'single transaction'": *Paré*, *supra*, at p. 633. The appellant's argument is that Parliament "never intended that the existence of unlawful domination, in and of itself, [would be] sufficient to warrant classifying a murder as first degree murder." Rather, as Wilson J. recognized, "it is the unlawful domination *of the victim* that justified this classification" (appellant's factum, at p. 20 (emphasis in original)).

There is some support for the appellant's interpretation of s. 231(5) in this Court's other judgments dealing with s. 231(5). In *R. v. Arkell*, [1990] 2 S.C.R. 695, we considered whether s. 214(5) (now s. 231(5)) violates s. 7 of the Charter because it results in punishment that is not proportionate to the seriousness of the offences. In rejecting that contention, Lamer C.J. wrote: "Parliament's decision to treat more seriously murders that have been committed while the offender is exploiting a position of power through illegal domination *of the victim* accords with the principle that there must be proportionality between a sentence and the moral blameworthiness of the offender and other considerations such as deterrence and societal condemnation of the acts of the offender": *Arkell*, supra, at p. 704 (emphasis added).

In *Luxton*, [[1990] 2 SCR 711] we addressed the related question of whether the combined effect of s. 214(5) and s. 669(a) infringes s. 7 of the Charter by foreclosing individualized sentences and thereby violating the principle that the severity of a sentence should reflect the degree of moral blameworthiness associated with the crime. Section 669(a) (now s. 745(a)) provides that an accused convicted of first degree murder must be sentenced to life in prison without the possibility of parole until he has served 25 years of his sentence. In finding that the impugned provisions did not infringe s. 7, Lamer C.J. wrote: "Murders that are done while committing offences which involve the illegal domination *of the victim* by the offender have been classified as first degree murder": *Luxton*, at p. 721 (emphasis added).

I am not persuaded, however, that this Court intended in *Paré*, *Arkell*, or *Luxton*, ... to foreclose the application of s. 231(5) to multiple-victim scenarios. None of those cases involved multiple-victim scenarios, and the issue was simply not addressed by the Court. In my view, the references to the "victim" simply reflect the facts of those cases. The essential thrust of Wilson J.'s reasoning in *Paré*, *supra*, was that the offences enumerated in s. 231(5) are singled out because they are crimes involving the domination of one person by another. The essence of the reasoning was that s. 231(5) reflects Parliament's determination that murders committed in connection with crimes of domination are particularly blameworthy and deserving of more severe punishment. In many cases, such murders will be committed as the culmination of the accused's domination of the victim of the enumerated offence. This was the case in *Paré*, supra, *Arkell*, *supra*, and *Luxton* … . In other cases, however, the accused will have murdered one person in connection with the domination of another. I cannot conclude that Wilson J.'s judgment in *Paré*, or Lamer C.J.'s judgments in *Arkell* or *Luxton* foreclose the application of s. 231(5) in such cases.

In my view the appellant states the organizing principle of s. 231(5) too narrowly. The provision reflects Parliament's determination that murders committed in connection with crimes of domination are particularly blameworthy and deserving of more severe punishment. "While committing or attempting to commit" requires the killing to be closely connected, temporally and causally, with an enumerated offence. As long as that connection exists, however, it is immaterial that the victim of the killing and the victim of the enumerated offence are not the same.

In oral argument, the appellant relied heavily on the fact that murder is not itself an offence enumerated under s. 231(5). On the appellant's theory, if Parliament had contemplated that the provision might be applied to multiple-victim scenarios, it would surely have included murder on the list of offences, because murder committed to facilitate another, or other, murder is obviously as morally blameworthy as murder committed to facilitate any of the enumerated offences. In the appellant's view, the absence of murder from the list of offences can only be explained by the fact that Parliament did not contemplate that the provision might be applied to situations in which the victim of the murder and the victim of the enumerated offence are not the same.

I think the more likely explanation for the exclusion of murder from the list of enumerated offences under s. 231(5) is simply that, in most situations in which an accused has killed two or more people and there is a temporal and causal nexus between the killings, s. 231(2) will apply. That provision states that "[m]urder is first degree murder when it is planned and deliberate." While one can imagine situations in which an accused might have killed two or more people spontaneously, without planning or deliberation, such scenarios are surely the exception rather than the rule. In all likelihood, the reason that Parliament did not include murder as an enumerated offence under s. 231(5) is that it concluded that most multiple murders would engage s. 231(2).

The appellant rightly points out that s. 231(5) imposes a severe penalty—indeed, the most severe penalty imposed under our *Criminal Code*—and accordingly it is particularly important that the provision be strictly construed. While this principle is unimpeachable, it cannot in itself justify restricting the ordinary meaning of the provision's words. The cases of this Court dealing with s. 231(5) make clear that an accused commits a murder "while committing or attempting to commit" an enumerated offence only if there is a close temporal and causal connection between the murder and the enumerated offence: see, e.g., *Paré*, supra, at p. 632 (stating that a murder is committed "while committing" an enumerated offence only "where the act causing death and the acts constituting [the enumerated offence] all form part of one continuous sequence of events forming a single transaction"); *R. v. Kirkness*, [1990] 3 S.C.R. 74. In my view this requirement appropriately restricts the application of s. 231(5) to contexts within the intended scope of the provision.

Appeal dismissed.

The Supreme Court addressed the constitutionality of s 231(5) in *R v Arkell*, [1990] 2 SCR 695. *Arkell* was a decision released concurrently with *Martineau*. In it, the Court rejected a claim that s 231(5) violates s 7 of the Charter because it results in punishment that is not proportionate to the seriousness of the offence committed. In coming to this conclusion, Lamer CJ provided the following explanation on behalf of the Court:

> … All murders are serious crimes. Some murders, however, are so threatening to the public that Parliament has chosen to impose exceptional penalties on the perpetrators. One such class of murders is that found in s. 214(5), murders done while committing a hijacking, a kidnapping and forcible confinement, a rape, or an indecent assault.
>
> The offences listed in s. 214(5) are all offences involving the unlawful domination of people by other people. Thus an organizing principle for s. 214(5) can be found. This principle is that where a murder is committed by someone already abusing his power by illegally dominating another, the murder should be treated as an exceptionally serious crime. Parliament has chosen to treat these murders as murders in the first degree. I can find no principle of fundamental justice that prevents Parliament, guided by the organizing principle identified by this court in *Paré*, from classifying murders done while committing certain underlying offences as more serious, and thereby attaching more serious penalties to them. In the case of the distinction between first and second degree murder, the difference is a maximum extra 15 years that must be served before one is eligible for parole. This distinction is neither arbitrary nor irrational. The section is based on an organizing principle that treats murders committed while the perpetrator is illegally dominating another person as more serious than other murders. Further, the relationship between the classification and the moral blameworthiness of the offender clearly exists. Section 214 only comes into play when murder has been proven beyond a reasonable doubt. In light of *Martineau*, this means that the offender has been proven to have had subjective foresight of death. Parliament's decision to treat more seriously murders that have been committed while the offender is exploiting a position of power through illegal domination of the victim accords with the principle that there must be a proportionality between a sentence and the moral blameworthiness of the offender and other considerations such as deterrence and societal condemnation of the acts of the offender. Therefore, I conclude that, in so far as s. 214(5) is neither arbitrary nor irrational, it does not infringe upon s. 7 of the Charter. I note that in this appeal there was no argument made as regards s. 12 of the Charter, although that issue was raised in a case heard and disposed of concurrently, *R. v. Luxton* [[1990] 2 SCR 711]. …

In *R v Luxton*, [1990] 2 SCR 711, released concurrently with *Martineau*, the Supreme Court also dealt with a constitutional challenge aimed at what were then ss 214(5)(e) and 669 (and are now ss 231(5)(e) and 745(a)). The basis for the challenge included ss 7, 9, and 12 of the Charter. The appellant argued that these guarantees were offended by the combined effect of the impugned sections, which the appellant claimed failed to accord with the constitutional requirement that a just sentencing system contain a gradation of punishments differentiated according to the malignity of offences and that sentencing be individualized. In rejecting the appellant's s 7 claim, Lamer CJ wrote for the Court:

> In my view the combination of ss. 214(5)(e) and 669 clearly demonstrates a proportionality be-tween the moral turpitude of the offender and the malignity of the offence, and moreover it is in accord with the other objectives of a system of sentencing ... . As I have stated, we are dealing with individuals that have committed murder and have done so with the now constitutionally mandated *mens rea* of subjective foresight of death. Parliament has chosen, once it has been proven that an offender has committed murder, to classify certain of those murders as first degree. Murders that are done while committing offences which involve the illegal domination of the victim by the offender have been classified as first degree murder. Forcible confinement is one of those offences involving illegal domination. The added element of forcible confinement, in the context of the commission of a murder, markedly enhances the moral blameworthiness of an offender. Indeed, forcible confinement is punishable by up to 10 years in prison. The decision of Parliament to elevate murders done while the offender commits forcible confinement to the level of first degree murder is consonant with the principle of proportionality between the blame-worthiness of the offender and the punishment. Further, it is consistent with the individualization of sentencing especially since only those who have killed with subjective foresight of death while also committing the offence of forcible confinement are subjected to that punishment. I, therefore, can find no principle of fundamental justice that has been violated by the combination of ss. 214(5)(e) and 669 of the *Criminal Code*. Equally, for these same reasons, I conclude that there is no violation of s. 2(e) of the *Canadian Bill of Rights*.

With respect to the s 9 Charter argument, Lamer CJ indicated:

> The combined effect of the impugned sections does not demonstrate arbitrariness on the part of Parliament. Indeed, as I noted above, Parliament has narrowly defined a class of murderers under an organizing principle of illegal domination and has specifically defined the conditions under which the offender can be found guilty of first degree murder. In order to be found guilty of first degree murder under s. 214(5)(e), the offender must have committed murder with subjec-tive foresight of death and must have committed the murder "while committing or attempting to commit ... forcible confinement." Where the act causing death and the acts constituting the forcible confinement all form part of one continuous sequence of events forming a single trans-action, the death is caused "while committing" an offence for the purposes of s. 214(5): see *Paré* ... , at p. 107. To commit the underlying offence of forcible confinement, the offender must use "physical restraint, contrary to the wishes of the person restrained, but to which the victim submits unwillingly, thereby depriving the person of his or her liberty to move from one place to another": quote from *R. v. Dollan and Newstead* (1980), 53 C.C.C. (2d) 146 (Ont. H.C.J.) at p. 154, as cited with approval in *R. v. Gratton* (1985), 18 C.C.C. (3d) 462, 13 W.C.B. 368 (C.A.). It is true that the definition of forcible confinement adopted by the courts allows for varying circumstances in each individual case. But this alone is not a sign of arbitrariness. The offence of forcible confine-ment as defined falls clearly under the rubric of the organizing principle enunciated by Wilson J. in *Paré*, namely, that of the illegal domination of one person by another. The decision of Parlia-ment to attach a minimum 25-year sentence without eligibility for parole in cases of first degree murder, having regard to all these circumstances, cannot be said to be arbitrary within the mean-ing of s. 9 of the Charter.

Regarding the claim that the combined effect of ss 231(5)(e) and 745(a) offended the guarantee in s 12 of the Charter against cruel and unusual punishment, Lamer CJ concluded as follows:

> In my view, the combination of ss. 214(5)(e) and 669 does not constitute cruel and unusual punishment. These sections provide for punishment of the most serious crime in our criminal law, that of first degree murder. This is a crime that carries with it the most serious level of moral blameworthiness, namely, subjective foresight of death. The penalty is severe and deservedly so. The minimum 25 years to be served before eligibility for parole reflects society's condemnation of a person who has exploited a position of power and dominance to the gravest extent possible by murdering the person that he or she is forcibly confining. The punishment is not excessive and clearly does not outrage our standards of decency. In my view, it is within the purview of Parliament, in order to meet the objectives of a rational system of sentencing, to treat our most serious crime with an appropriate degree of certainty and severity.

See also *R v Sand*, 2003 MBQB 45, 172 Man R (2d) 274, in which *Arkell*, *Luxton*, and *Collins* were followed in a case involving a challenge to s 231(4)(a) of the *Criminal Code*, where the victim was a police officer.

IV. INFANTICIDE

Section 233 of the *Criminal Code* provides as follows:

> A female person commits infanticide when by a wilful act or omission she causes the death of her newly-born child, if at the time of the act or omission she is not fully recovered from the effects of giving birth to the child and by reason thereof or of the effect of lactation consequent on the birth of the child her mind is then disturbed.

Although this provision has been a part of the Code for 60 years, until the following case was decided there was a fair amount of uncertainty surrounding the status of infanticide in Canadian criminal law.

R v LB
Ontario Court of Appeal
2011 ONCA 153

[LB was charged with two counts of first-degree murder. She admitted to killing two of her children: the first in 1998 (when LB was still a youth) and the second in 2002 (as an adult). LB had a history of psychiatric problems. The evidence established that LB smothered her first child when he was six weeks old. Initially, the authorities had concluded the death had resulted from sudden infant death syndrome. Four years later LB had a second child, whom she smothered in his crib when he was ten weeks old. At the time, the death was attributed to sudden unexplained death syndrome.

In 2004, when seeking help for her ongoing psychiatric difficulties, LB confessed to killing her two infants to a physician. She was arrested and charged with two counts of murder. She gave a full confession to police, explaining her actions as the result of being "really confused" and "fighting with her thoughts" when she smothered her two babies.

LB insisted that she did not want to hurt her children, but wanted to help them. LB's own childhood had been difficult; her mother had been an alcoholic who abused her, and LB had been involved with the child welfare authorities when she was growing up and had been homeless for a time.

The trial judge had the benefit of psychiatric expert evidence. The psychiatrists agreed that LB suffered from a serious personality disorder prior to her pregnancies. According to one of the psychiatrists, Dr. Gojer, whose evidence the trial judged preferred, LB suffered from a personality disorder with prominent borderline traits stemming from issues of rejection and abandonment. Both psychiatrists agreed that the respondent's personality features predisposed her to postpartum mood disturbance. Dr. Gojer was of the opinion that LB was suffering from a mixed affective disorder at the time of both homicides. In his report, he said: "It is likely that her mental state at the time of both homicides was impacted on or associated with mood and behavioural changes as a consequence of the effects of child birth, from which she had not fully recovered." The second psychiatrist acknowledged the presence of postpartum depression, but could not quantify the role played by that depression in LB's mental state at the relevant time.

The trial judge ultimately concluded he was satisfied that at the time of the homicides LB's mind was disturbed as a result of her not having fully recovered from the biological effects of giving birth or perhaps the effects of lactation at the time she killed her children. He determined that the disturbance caused by the effects of giving birth and perhaps lactation was sufficient to afford the respondent the defence of infanticide.

The trial judge acquitted LB on the murder charges and convicted her of the included offence of infanticide on both charges. The Crown appealed against the acquittals on the murder charges, submitting that, as the trial judge had found that the Crown had established all the essential elements of first-degree murder on both charges, he had erred in law in acquitting on those charges and convicting on the charges of infanticide. The Crown sought a new trial on the murder charges.]

DOHERTY JA (Moldaver and Cronk JJA concurring):

[1]   Infanticide has been part of the criminal law of Canada for over 60 years. Homicides for which a conviction for infanticide is a possible verdict are rare. Most of the few convictions for infanticide are the product of guilty pleas. There is no Canadian appellate decision that has examined the infanticide provisions in the *Criminal Code*, R.S.C. 1985, c. C-46 in any detail. This appeal raises an issue that goes to the very nature of those provisions. Is infanticide both a substantive offence and a partial defence to a murder charge, or is it exclusively a substantive offence that may in appropriate cases be an included offence in a murder charge to be considered by the trier of fact if, and only if, the Crown fails to prove murder?

[2]   Choosing between the two characterizations of infanticide has profound importance in a case like this one where a mother is charged with murdering her child. If infanticide provides a partial defence to murder, the mother will escape a murder conviction if the homicide falls within the purview of infanticide even though the Crown may prove all the essential elements of the crime of murder. If, however, infanticide operates only as a potential included offence on a murder charge, and if the Crown proves the essential elements of murder, the mother must be convicted of murder even though the homicide falls within the meaning of infanticide.

[3] The two interpretations lead to dramatically different sentencing options. If the mother can raise infanticide as a partial defence, and if she is successful and convicted of infanticide, she is liable to a maximum penalty of five years. Existing sentencing patterns suggest she could receive a non-custodial sentence: see G. Fitch, "Infanticide" (Paper presented to the National Criminal Law Program: Substantive Criminal Law, Halifax, Nova Scotia, July 2004) Federation of Law Societies of Canada, 2004, section 11.5, at p. 17. However, if infanticide serves only as a potential included offence if murder is not proved and the mother is found to have committed murder, she must be sentenced to life imprisonment.

[4] The submissions made by the Crown, respondent and intervener also raise two additional issues that affect the operation of the provisions:

- What is the *mens rea* or fault requirement for infanticide?
- If an accused can raise a "defence" of infanticide to a murder charge, does the Crown have the onus of negating that defence, or is the accused required to establish on a balance of probabilities that the homicide constitutes infanticide?

· · ·

[58] Infanticide, as defined in s. 233, targets a very particularized form of culpable homicide. The section has potential application only where a mother kills her newborn child, defined in the *Criminal Code* as a child under one year of age. The potential application of infanticide is further limited by requiring that at the time of the homicide, the mother's mind must be "disturbed," either because she is not fully recovered from the effects of giving birth or by reason of the effect of lactation.

[59] The definition of infanticide focuses on two things. First, it requires a mother–child relationship between the perpetrator and the victim. Second, the mental state of the perpetrator/mother must be disturbed and that disturbance must be connected to the effects of giving birth or lactation. Unlike other mental states that may mitigate criminal responsibility, infanticide does not require any causal connection between the disturbance of the mother's mind and the decision to do the thing that caused her child's death: *R. v. Guimont* (1999), 141 C.C.C. (3d) 314 (Q.C.A.), at p. 317; E. Cunliffe, "Infanticide: Legislative History and Current Questions" (2009) 55 Crim. L.Q. 94, at pp. 112-113; I. Grant, D. Chunn & C. Boyle, *The Law of Homicide*, loose-leaf (Scarborough: Carswell, 1995), at p. 4-91. Because the mother's mental "disturbance" is not connected to the decision to kill, that "disturbance" is better considered as part of the *actus reus* and not a *mens rea* component of the crime of infanticide.

[60] The drastically different penalties available upon conviction for murder, manslaughter or infanticide reflect the very different levels of moral blameworthiness attached to each offence. Clearly murder is regarded as the most blameworthy and infanticide as the least blameworthy. Manslaughter occupies that vast middle ground of blameworthiness between the two extremes of murder and infanticide. The very different penalties prescribed by Parliament for the offences of murder and infanticide leave no doubt that a mother who commits a culpable homicide that constitutes infanticide is regarded as having committed a much less serious crime than someone who committed murder.

[61] Section 222(4) declares that "culpable homicide is murder or manslaughter or infanticide." Section 222(4) suggests that the three categories of culpable homicide are alternatives to each other, such that any specific culpable homicide will fit within one and

only one of the three categories. To properly place a particular culpable homicide in its appropriate category one must look to the definitions of murder and infanticide. If the homicide does not fit within either of those specific definitions, by operation of s. 234, the homicide is categorized as manslaughter.

[62] Infanticide is clearly a much more specific form of culpable homicide than murder. In my view, it is arguable that, in categorizing a culpable homicide, one must begin with the narrower and more specific definition of infanticide. If a homicide fits within that definition it is excluded by the operation of s. 222(4) from the broader category of culpable homicides defined as murder. On this approach, a culpable homicide that is infanticide is not murder. For the purpose of s. 662(3), the Crown fails to prove murder if the homicide is infanticide, thereby allowing a jury to return a verdict on the included offence of infanticide. Counsel for the respondent and the intervener, in their helpful submissions, advance this interpretation.

[63] I do not go so far as to agree with counsel that the reading of the homicide provisions as a whole compels the interpretation they have advanced as summarized immediately above. I am satisfied, however, that placing s. 233 and s. 662(3) in the broader context of the homicide regime renders the interpretation urged by Crown counsel considerably less obvious than it appears to be when those two sections are considered in isolation. The exercise in statutory interpretation must go beyond the words of those sections even as read in the context of the other homicide provisions.

. . .

[The court carefully reviewed the legislative history relating to infanticide in Canada, before continuing.]

[98] Treating infanticide as a partial defence to murder is consistent with the distinction drawn between infanticide and murder by Parliament. It allows juries to draw that distinction in cases where mothers are charged with murdering their children and evidence brings the homicide within the very narrow factual confines of infanticide. Eliminating infanticide as a partial defence effectively allows the Crown to remove the distinction between infanticide and murder through the exercise of its charging discretion.

[99] My application of the "modern principle" of statutory interpretation leads me to conclude that Parliament intended to make infanticide a partial defence to murder when it introduced infanticide into the *Criminal Code* in 1948. Parliament did not intend to alter the status of infanticide by the 1954 amendments. Infanticide was initially, and still is, both a stand alone indictable offence and a partial defence to a charge of murder.

. . .

[104] It has been the accepted wisdom in Canada since infanticide became part of the criminal law that it operates as both an offence and a partial defence to murder. There is merit to the Crown's claim that infanticide has operated in this dual capacity more by way of assumption than as a result of any critical analysis of the relevant *Criminal Code* provisions. This appeal has forced that critical analysis. I am satisfied that the analysis supports the long held assumption. Infanticide is both a discrete indictable offence and a partial defence to murder under the terms of the present *Criminal Code*. Whether it should continue to so operate, and if so under what terms, raises difficult policy questions. Those questions are for Parliament and not the court.

. . .

[107] Counsel for the respondent and the intervener submit that infanticide requires proof of the same *mens rea* required to prove murder under s. 229(a); that is an intention to kill, or an intention to cause bodily harm knowing that it is likely to cause death and being reckless as to that result. In making this argument, counsel rely on the word "wilful" in s. 233, the language of the 1948 provision, an *obiter* statement in *Creighton*, and trial decisions, *e.g. R. v. Smith* (1976), 32 C.C.C. (2d) 224 (Nfld. Dist. Ct.), at pp. 230-31; *R. v. Del Rio*, [1979] O.J. No. 16 (H.C.), at para. 46. Most of the Canadian academic literature also favours a *mens rea* for infanticide akin to that required for murder: see Cunliffe, at pp. 113-16; Anand, at pp. 716-18; Boyle et al., at 4-91 to 4-93.

[108] The respondent's and intervener's reliance on the word "wilful" in s. 233 is understandable. "Wilful" is a strong *mens rea* word and can be understood to require proof of an intention to bring about the prohibited consequence, *e.g.* death, even where, as in s. 233, on a plain grammatical reading "wilful" modifies the phrase "act or omission" and not the phrase "causes death": *R. v. Docherty*, [1989] 2 S.C.R. 941, at pp. 949-50; M. Manning & P. Sankoff, *Manning, Mewett & Sankoff: Criminal Law*, 4th ed. (Markham: LexisNexis, 2009), at p. 173. However, the *Criminal Code* is notoriously inconsistent in the manner in which it uses *mens rea* words. This court has recognized that "wilful" can have different meanings in different sections of the *Criminal Code*: *R. v. Buzzanga and Durocher* (1979), 25 O.R. (2d) 705 (C.A.), at p. 717.

[109] In *Buzzanga*, this court stressed that the meaning of "wilful" in one section of the *Criminal Code* could be influenced by the *mens rea* language of clearly related *Criminal Code* provisions. The *mens rea* for murder is expressly set out in the language of s. 229(a). The word "wilful" is not used. The use of very different *mens rea* language in s. 229, as compared to the word "wilful" in s. 233, suggests that Parliament did not intend to equate the *mens rea* required for murder (s. 229) with the *mens rea* required for infanticide (s. 233). While the word "wilful" figures in any analysis of the *mens rea* for infanticide, I do not think that word alone is determinative of the *mens rea* required for infanticide.

· · ·

[114] Considering the homicide provisions as a whole and the obvious hierarchy created by those provisions, I do not think that the infanticide provision can be read as requiring proof of the same *mens rea* as that required for murder. Instead, a *mens rea* for infanticide akin to that for manslaughter is much more consistent with the hierarchy of culpable homicides established in the *Criminal Code*. In my view, infanticide as a form of culpable homicide, should require the *mens rea* required for manslaughter. There is nothing inherent in the seriousness of the offence or the stigma attached to it which requires the imposition of a higher *mens rea* like that required for murder. That, of course, is not to say that a mother who intends to kill her child is, therefore, not guilty of infanticide. Clearly, a person who intends to kill foresees the risk of bodily harm to the child and, therefore, has the required *mens rea* for either manslaughter or infanticide.

[115] If infanticide was read as requiring proof of the same *mens rea* as murder, circumstances could produce anomalous results. For example, if infanticide requires the *mens rea* for murder, a mother who intends to kill her child but whose conduct comes within the meaning of infanticide would be convicted of infanticide, the least culpable form of culpable homicide. A second mother, whose conduct also comes within the meaning of infanticide, but who was so emotionally distraught as to be incapable of forming the intention for murder, could not be convicted of infanticide but would instead be

convicted of manslaughter, a more serious offence. Surely, a mother who does not intend to kill her child should not be regarded as having committed a more culpable homicide than the mother who did have that intention. This anomaly disappears if the *mens rea* for infanticide captures both the mother who intends to kill and the mother who unlawfully assaults her child in circumstances where bodily harm to the child is foreseeable.

[116] There is a second, and I think significant, practical problem with treating the *mens rea* for infanticide as the same as that required for murder. Infanticide requires evidence that the mother's mind was "disturbed" at the time of the homicide. Evidence proffered by the defence to meet the evidentiary burden on that issue will, in some cases, cast doubt on whether the mother intended to kill her child. If infanticide operates as a partial defence to murder only where the *mens rea* for murder exists, the very same evidence offered to bring the mother within the infanticide defence could push her outside of that defence by negating the intention to kill or the existence of foresight as to the likelihood of death. If the *mens rea* for infanticide is interpreted as including the *mens rea* required for murder or manslaughter, the defence is not put in the position of offering evidence of the mother's mental state that could simultaneously support and undermine the infanticide defence.

[117] I think treating the *mens rea* for infanticide as reaching not only an intention to kill, but also objective foresight of bodily harm, provides a coherent and comprehensive reading of the homicide provisions that best reflects the relative seriousness of the three levels of culpable homicide created in the *Criminal Code*. This approach does give the word "wilful" a meaning that is somewhat inconsistent with its customary meaning. I am satisfied, however, that a coherent and workable reading of s. 233 in the context of the homicide provisions supports my interpretation of the word "wilful" in this context.

· · ·

[121] For the reasons set out above, I do not think that the *mens rea* for infanticide can be equated with the *mens rea* for murder. In my view, to prove infanticide, the Crown must establish the *mens rea* associated with the unlawful act that caused the child's death and objective foreseeability of the risk of bodily harm to the child from that assault. On this approach, it is the unique *actus reus* of infanticide that distinguishes it from murder and manslaughter. Those distinctions are what caused Parliament to treat infanticide as a culpable homicide, but one that was significantly less culpable than murder and even manslaughter. The presence of the *mens rea* for murder, while not negating the partial defence of infanticide, is not a condition precedent to the existence of that partial defence.

· · ·

[125] The presumption of innocence, constitutionally protected by s. 11(d) of the *Canadian Charter of Rights and Freedoms*, requires that the Crown prove the essential elements of the crime alleged beyond a reasonable doubt. It also requires that the Crown negate potential defences to the same standard of proof … .

[126] As the trial judge appreciated, any deviation from the requirement that the Crown bear the burden of proof is a *prima facie* violation of s. 11(d), and is constitutional only if justified under s. 1 of the *Charter* … .

[127] Placing the burden on the accused to establish infanticide can pass constitutional scrutiny only if the reallocation of the burden is "prescribed by law." The trial judge did not address this issue.

[128] In *R. v. Effert* (2009), 244 C.C.C. (3d) 510 (Alta. Q.B.), Veit J. declined to follow the trial judge's ruling in this case and held that the Crown bore the burden to disprove the partial defence of infanticide. In her analysis (paras. 13-18), she doubted whether a judge-made requirement that the accused establish the necessary disturbance of the mind on the balance of probabilities could be said to be a limit on the presumption of innocence "prescribed by law." I share her doubts.

[129] A limit on a *Charter* right may be found in a statute or other legislative instrument either expressly or by necessary implication: *R. v. Swain*, [1991] 1 S.C.R. 933, at p. 968; *R. v. Thomsen*, [1988] 1 S.C.R. 640, at pp. 650-55. The infanticide provisions do not contain any express reversal of the burden of proof or otherwise purport to limit the application of s. 11(d) of the *Charter*. Nor can any limit be read by necessary implication into any statutory provision relevant to infanticide. Section 16(4), which reverses the onus where an accused raises an "insanity" defence, has no application to infanticide. As Veit J. explains, infanticide is *"sui generis"* and cannot be viewed as a variation on the mental disorder requirement of the "insanity" defence: *Effert*, at para. 17. The reversal of the burden where "insanity" is raised does not imply anything about the appropriate burden where infanticide is raised.

[130] A s. 1 limit on a constitutional right may also "result from the application of the common law": *R. v. Therens*, [1985] 1 S.C.R. 613, at p. 645. Potential common law limits on *Charter* rights must be approached cautiously, particularly where the common law limit is created post-*Charter*. A cautious approach is dictated because judge-made common law limitations are not the product of the same considered and public weighing and balancing of competing interests and values that should be reflected in legislative provisions limiting constitutional rights.

[131] I find it particularly difficult to resort to the common law to overlay a constitutional limit on what is a statutory defence. I would have thought that if a reversal of the onus in relation to the partial defence of infanticide was viewed as a justifiable limit on the presumption of innocence, Parliament would have taken steps to write that limit into the statutory defence. To analogize to the caution sounded by Binnie J., speaking in dissent, in *R. v. Stone*, [1999] 2 S.C.R. 290, at para. 50, a court should not organize its own s. 1 justification for a *Charter* violation where Parliament in crafting a statutory defence did not see fit to create one.

. . .

[133] Even if the court could invoke the common law to limit the presumption of innocence as it applies to the statutory defence of infanticide, I see no justification for doing so. My research reveals that in every jurisdiction in which the partial defence of infanticide is recognized, neither the legislature nor the courts have seen fit to relieve the Crown of its customary burden of proof. There is no suggestion in the case law or commentary from those jurisdictions that bearing the burden of proof has posed a difficult, much less insurmountable, burden for the Crown. Indeed, I do not understand the Crown on this appeal to have argued that it cannot realistically be expected to meet the customary burden of proof where the defence of infanticide is in play.

[134] No doubt if the defence advances infanticide as a partial defence to murder and the Crown resists that defence, the Crown may have a difficult task in establishing beyond a reasonable doubt that the mother's mind was not "disturbed" in the sense required for the infanticide defence. That problem arises whenever the Crown must prove or disprove

a certain state of mind. It should not be viewed as an impediment to the conviction of the accused, but rather as a reflection of the premium placed on individual freedom, the value underlying the constitutional right to be presumed innocent.

[135] In any event, as observed by Veit J. in *Effert*, at para. 20, any disadvantage potentially suffered by the Crown is largely overcome where the court makes an assessment order under s. 672.11(c) and the accused cooperates in that assessment. The respondent cooperated with the assessment order made in this case, and Dr. Klassen who did the assessment was able to provide a detailed report and give valuable evidence at the trial.

· · ·

[137] I see no justification for limiting the respondent's constitutional right to be presumed innocent of the charge of murder. Assuming a sufficient evidentiary basis to give the infanticide claim an air of reality, the respondent was entitled to be acquitted on the murder charge and convicted of the included offence of infanticide unless the Crown could negate the defence of infanticide beyond a reasonable doubt.

· · ·

[140] Applying the approach outlined above to the facts of this case, it was conceded that the respondent caused her children's deaths and that in doing so she committed a culpable homicide. Those concessions take one to the point where the culpable homicide must be categorized. The trial judge found on the balance of probabilities that the respondent met the criteria for infanticide in respect of both homicides. That finding negated any argument that the Crown had proven beyond a reasonable doubt that at least one of the elements of infanticide was not present. The trial judge, therefore, returned the proper verdicts—not guilty of murder but guilty of infanticide.

· · ·

[141] I would dismiss the appeal.

ADDITIONAL READING

Archibald, BP. "The Constitutionalization of the General Part of the Criminal Law" (1988) 67 Can Bar Rev 403.

Brudner, A. "Proportionality, Stigma and Discretion" (1996) 38 Crim LQ 302.

Grant, I. "Rethinking the Sentencing Regime for Murder" (2001) 39 Osgoode Hall LJ 655.

Manning, M & P Sankoff. *Manning, Mewett & Sankoff: Criminal Law*, 4th ed (Toronto: Lexis-Nexis, 2009) ch 19.

Mewett, AW. "First Degree Murder" (1978-79) 21 Crim LQ 82.

Roach, K. *Criminal Law*, 6th ed (Toronto: Irwin Law, 2015) ch 10.

Stuart, D. *Canadian Criminal Law*, 7th ed (Toronto: Carswell, 2014) at 217-29.

Stuart, D. "Further Progress on the Constitutional Requirement of Fault, but Stigma Is Not Enough" (1990) 79 CR (3rd) 247.

PART FIVE

Principles of Exculpation

CHAPTER FOURTEEN

Provocation

I. INTRODUCTION

Provocation is a partial defence to the offence of murder only. If this defence is successful, it has the effect of reducing murder to manslaughter, but cannot result in a complete acquittal. Practically, then, the accused who successfully pleads provocation escapes the mandatory minimum sentence for murder: life imprisonment (with a period of parole ineligibility for 10 to 25 years in the case of second-degree murder and a mandatory parole ineligibility period of 25 years in the case of first-degree murder). Manslaughter is punishable by up to life imprisonment, but the *Criminal Code* imposes no minimum sentence (unless a firearm is used in the commission of the offence, in which case the statutory minimum is four years' imprisonment).

Provocation is codified in s 232 of the *Criminal Code*:

232(1) Culpable homicide that otherwise would be murder may be reduced to manslaughter if the person who committed it did so in the heat of passion caused by sudden provocation.

(2) A wrongful act or insult that is of such a nature as to be sufficient to deprive an ordinary person of the power of self-control is provocation for the purposes of this section if the accused acted on it on the sudden and before there was time for his passion to cool.

(3) For the purposes of this section, the questions

(a) whether a particular wrongful act or insult amounted to provocation, and

(b) whether the accused was deprived of the power of self-control by the provocation that he alleges he received,

are questions of fact, but no one shall be deemed to have given provocation to another by doing anything that he had a legal right to do, or by doing anything that the accused incited him to do in order to provide the accused with an excuse for causing death or bodily harm to any human being.

(4) Culpable homicide that otherwise would be murder is not necessarily manslaughter by reason only that it was committed by a person who was being arrested illegally, but the fact that the illegality of the arrest was known to the accused may be evidence of provocation for the purpose of this section.

As with all defences, before the matter can be left to the jury, there must be an air of reality to the claim that the accused acted with provocation: see *R v Tran*, 2010 SCC 58, [2010] 3

SCR 350 and *R v Mayuran*, 2012 SCC 31, [2012] 2 SCR 162. If an air of reality is established and the defence is left with the jury, the Crown must disprove the existence of provocation beyond a reasonable doubt.

The defence of provocation has deep roots in the common law, taking shape as a distinct doctrine in the criminal law in the 17th century (see J Horder, *Provocation and Responsibility* (Oxford: Oxford University Press, 1992) at 5-42). The defence was a very narrow one tied to prevailing conceptions of male honour; in *DPP v Camplin*, [1978] 1 AC 705 at 713-14, Lord Diplock explained that the defence historically applied to three situations—"chance medley or a sudden falling out" between men, "the discovery by a husband of his wife in the act of committing adultery and the discovery by a father of someone committing sodomy on his son." Today, it has become a problematic and highly controversial defence. Criticisms are levied against the defence on a number of grounds. Some point to the manner in which it privileges the emotion of anger as a potentially excusatory factor in the law of homicide, while not recognizing other intense emotions (such as compassion or mercy). Others question the defence's apparent acceptance that the loss of "the power of self-control" and sudden violence is an expected response to certain forms of affront for which, as a so-called concession to human frailty, one may be partially excused. Some of the most powerful attacks on the defence focus on the strongly gendered dimensions of the defence. Commentators note that, in its application, provocation primarily serves to partially excuse men for murdering women. The defence supports dangerous patterns of male violence against women and remains very much informed by the criminal law's historical protection of male norms of honour and offence. These forceful critiques and the perceived overuse of the defence in the context of spousal homicide have led to calls to abolish the defence.

The following three excerpts give a sense of the criticisms levied against provocation on these related bases: provocation's privileging of anger or rage, its understanding of intense emotion and the responses that it can produce, and the deeply gendered nature of the defence. This chapter then examines the interpretation and application of this provision, returning throughout to these critical themes, and concludes with a brief consideration of the relationship between provocation and *mens rea*.

I Grant, D Chunn & C Boyle, *The Law of Homicide*
(Toronto: Carswell, 1999) at 6-3 (footnotes omitted)

It is often said that the defence functions as a concession to human frailty. Hence, the fundamental question is when an uncontrolled impulse to kill another should be seen as frailty justifying at least some compassion. A preliminary point to note is the human emotion to which compassion is directed. In provocation, a special defence, albeit a partial one, has been created to deal with homicidal rage. The contrast between the legal treatment of this and other emotions will be drawn in this chapter. There is no defence where the emotion is compassion. There is not even a partial defence with respect to euthanasia ... . Thus, if the accused was moved not by rage, but by pity, (s)he is still guilty of murder. Necessity is probably not a defence to murder—the impulse toward self-preservation is not an emotion privileged by law (except in the context of self-defence). Section 17 has excluded duress as a defence to murder, even where the accused killed to save the threatened life of a loved one. So love is not an emotion privileged by this area of the law .... Despair is not a defence to murder. A battered woman may kill in despair, not in rage. If provocation as a defence is a compassionate response to human frailty, why is rage the privileged emotion?

In the following excerpt, the author questions the criminal law's handling of emotion in the law of defences and its "voluntarist" focus on whether intense emotion has resulted in the loss of the accused's "power of self-control" or capacity to choose one's actions. The concept of "moral involuntariness" in the law of criminal defences will arise again in Chapter 18, which considers the defence of duress.

BL Berger, "Emotions and the Veil of Voluntarism:
The Loss of Judgment in Canadian Criminal Defences"
(2006) 51 McGill LJ 99 at 111-12, 114-17, 126 (footnotes omitted)

In this mechanistic/descriptive account, circumstances produce emotions that bear down on the person, resulting in particular actions. But are these emotional responses that we want the law to recognize as legitimate or even tolerable? Are the emotions conditioned by a set of social norms that we find unacceptable? In the voluntarist account that the Court has now installed at the base of criminal defences, these questions do not figure into the analysis. The result is a criminal law with considerable conservative inertia because the prevailing norms and social arrangements are taken as given, like cogs in the machine of human agency, rather than as contestable subjects that both the individual and society have a moral obligation to inquire into and to judge.

· · ·

An evaluative understanding of emotion treats emotions as themselves sites for thought and reflection, rather than simply forces levelled upon the individual. ... To view emotions in this evaluative way involves recognizing that emotions are themselves always already based in assessments of and judgments about the world. Emotions are, therefore, themselves open to judgment.

This vision of emotions carries three implications essential to the argument in this article: two conceptual and one juridical. The first conceptual implication is that emotions involve thought on the part of the actor. Emotions are, as Nussbaum puts it, intelligent. The kind of thought involved in emotions is a critical engagement with the prevailing norms and social structures that suggest particular emotional responses. Emotions are responses to thoughtful reflection on what is good or bad, high or low, in the world around us. As a corollary, this view of thoughtful emotions includes the idea that societal structures have something to do with the emotions that we feel. Normative reflection and emotion cannot be meaningfully disaggregated. As such, embedded in each emotion is a value-based commitment that is open to examination and, potentially, condemnation. ...

The second implication of the evaluative view of emotions, flowing directly from this last point, is that emotions can be mistaken—we can err in our emotions. This conclusion flies in the face not just of the mechanistic view of human agency, but of the folksy wisdom peddled by the likes of Oprah and Dr. Phil who would tell us that "it's not a matter of right and wrong, it's about feelings." If emotions are a product of our critical, if often less-than-conscious, reflection about the norms and assumptions in the world around us, then we can fall into error—we can be wrong in our emotions. This means that emotions are, in fact, open to outside scrutiny and criticism; emotions can be evaluated ... . That is, we can critique emotions because we object to the value judgments upon which they are based. The normative basis for the emotions is abject and, therefore, the emotion ought to be condemned, not tolerated.

These two conclusions—that emotions involve reflection or thought and that emotions can be wrong, so are open to criticism—give rise to a third implication particularly germane to the juridical context with which I am concerned. When the law turns its attention to the human actions that flow from emotion, as is the case in defences such as duress, it ought not to ignore the thoughtful element of emotions and the possibility of value-errors. Indeed, this is the true moment of judgment. When faced with a circumstance in which a person reacts to strong emotion, it is insufficient to state simply that the individual's choice was constrained and, therefore, his conduct was not morally voluntary. This approach dodges the difficult question. It is based on a reductionistic view of both emotion and human agency. Most significantly, this approach retreats from the moment of judgment. The evaluative view would require the law to ask whether we accept the bases for this emotion—whether, in a case of provocation, we accept the notion that homosexuals are to be feared more than heterosexuals or whether, when it comes to duress, a threat to a loved one fairly withdrew the accused's responsibility to show respect and care for others.

. . .

A more transparent idiom would allow debate and contestation on what we understand to be desirable reactions to legitimate social norms. This is good. It is good because it allows the law to ferret out regressive social structures, and it is good because it keeps the law sensitive to the evolution of social norms.

. . .

[A]ny examination of the values and norms being expressed by the criminal law must operate with a baseline assumption: whatever the criminal law is expressing, it must be in the service of diversity, antisubordination, and equality. Norms inconsistent with these baseline commitments are simply not tolerable aspects of our legal culture and must not be given force by the criminal law. That is, what can legitimately count as a basis for blame in the criminal law must be devoid of both discriminatory reasoning (on the part of the justice system or the accused) and subordinating effects ... . Happily, this last point is supported by the Canadian constitutional mandate to develop criminal common law and statute in accordance with *Charter* values, which privilege precisely these principles.

J Horder, *Provocation and Responsibility*
(Oxford: Clarendon Press, 1992) at 192-94 (footnotes omitted)

As noted above, the vast majority of killers are male. Even in the domestic context, men are much more likely to have been the serious aggressors whether they are ultimately killers or victims. These grim facts might at one time have been regarded as part of the natural order of things which it is the function of the law to reflect. One must now ask whether the doctrine of provocation, under the cover of an alleged compassion for human infirmity, simply reinforces the conditions in which men are perceived and perceive themselves as natural aggressors, and in particular *women's* natural aggressors. Unfortunately, the answer to that question is yes.

· · ·

... I am presently concerned with the values commonly thought by men, in particular, to be central to their conceptions of self-worth. For it is threats to these values which are most likely to produce the desire for retaliatory suffering, and thus the violence that is characteristically a male response to provocation.

One way to approach this is to look through the wrong end of the telescope, working backwards to the relevant values by analyzing the common causes of angry male violence. In an important study of the nature and antecedents of violent events, Dobash and Dobash questioned battered women about the sources of the conflicts leading to violent episodes with their partners. On the accounts these women gave, the typical violent episode is prompted by possessiveness or sexual jealousy (45 per cent of cases; in 30 per cent of cases this cause led to the worst episode of violence). A further 15 per cent of case where the partner was described as typically seeing a reason to argue and attack involved expectations about domestic work. A significant proportion of women said that an attempt made by them to leave their partner was either or both the last (15 per cent of cases) and the worst (7 per cent of cases) episode of violence.

What we learn from Dobash and Dobash's account is the centrality to men's conception of self-worth of *possessiveness* with regard to women who are partners and wives. It is absolute possession of a woman's sexual fidelity, of her labour, and of (on demand) her presence, love, and attention in general that lies at the heart of many men's conceptions of their self-worth. ...

The use of the provocation defence is dominated by men, for whom the use of violence (as often in the first as in the last resort) to secure what Tov-Ruach calls a women's "unconditional, unjudgmental attentive acceptance" is all too commonly regarded as natural or understandable—perhaps even appropriate. It is thus largely from a male-centred perspective that the reduction of an intentional killing from murder to manslaughter is capable of being regarded as a compassion to human infirmity. From a feminist perspective the existence of such mitigation simply reinforces in the law that which public institutions ought in fact to be seeking to eradicate, namely, the acceptance that there is something natural, inevitable, and hence in some (legal) sense-to-be-recognized forgivable about men's violence against women, and their violence in general.

The gendered impact of the defence of provocation has been the subject of considerable commentary and criticism. See e.g. JM Maher et al, "Honouring White Masculinity: Culture, Terror, Provocation and the Law" (2005) 23 Austl Feminist LJ 147; A Howe, "Provocation in Crisis—Law's Passion at the Crossroads? New Directions for Feminist Strategists" (2004) 21 Austl Feminist LJ 53; S Yeo, "The Role of Gender in the Law of Provocation" (1997) 26 Anglo-Am L Rev 431; RE Dobash & RP Dobash, *Women, Violence, and Social Change* (London: Routledge, 1992); and S Lees, "Naggers, Whores, and Libbers: Provoking Men to Kill" in J Radford & DEH Russell, eds, *Femicide: The Politics of Woman Killing* (New York: Twayne, 1992) 267.

II. INTERPRETING AND APPLYING THE PROVISIONS

The text of s 232 leaves a large set of questions open for debate and interpretation. What kinds of acts or words can serve as a "wrongful act or insult"? What is meant by the exclusion of "doing anything that [one] had a legal right to do" from the scope of potentially provocative conduct? What role does the requirement that the accused must have acted "on the sudden" play in the application of the defence? As you will see, perhaps the most fraught and contentious question is how the "ordinary person" should be imagined when applying the defence of provocation. Over the years, the courts have wrestled with all of these questions and, increasingly, with the critiques of the defence that you read in the previous section. The current approach to provocation is best set out in the Supreme Court's 2010 decision in *R v Tran*, 2010 SCC 58, [2010] 3 SCR 350, which appears later in this section. To understand how the defence of provocation is understood in Canadian law, and how it has developed and changed through judicial interpretation, this section begins with some earlier cases that lay bare the central interpretive challenges and social policy dimensions of the defence.

In the following decision, Chief Justice Dickson provides a helpful overview and history of the defence, while setting out the Canadian approach to provocation. Both the facts and the reasoning in this case also raise the question central to the development of the law of provocation: What attributes, beliefs, and characteristics should be ascribed to the "ordinary person" when applying the provocation defence?

R v Hill
Supreme Court of Canada
[1986] 1 SCR 313

DICKSON CJ (Beetz, Estey, Chouinard, and La Forest JJ concurring): Gordon James Elmer Hill was charged with committing first degree murder at the City of Belleville, County of Hastings, on the person of Verne Pegg, contrary to s. 218(1) of the *Criminal Code*, R.S.C. 1970, c. C-34. He was found by the jury not guilty of first degree murder but guilty of second degree murder. He was sentenced to imprisonment for life without eligibility for parole until 10 years of his sentence had been served.

Hill appealed his conviction to the Court of Appeal of Ontario. He raised many grounds of appeal, but the Court of Appeal called upon the Crown with respect to one ground only, relating to the charge on the issue of provocation. The ground of appeal was that the trial judge failed to instruct the jury properly as to the "ordinary person" in s. 215(2) [now s 232(2)] of the *Criminal Code*. ...

These two subsections, given their plain meaning, produce three sequential questions for answer by the tribunal:

1. Would an ordinary person be deprived of self-control by the act or insult?
2. Did the accused in fact act in response to those "provocative" acts; in short, was he or she provoked by them whether or not an ordinary person would have been?
3. Was the accused's response sudden and before there was time for his or her passion to cool? ...

At the time of the killing, Hill was a male, 16 years of age. The narrow question in this appeal is whether the trial judge erred in law in failing to instruct the jury that if they found a wrongful act or insult they should consider whether it was sufficient to deprive an ordinary person "of the age and sex of the appellant" of his power of self-control. Was it incumbent in law on the trial judge to add that gloss to the section? That is the issue.

I. The Facts

At trial both parties agreed that it was the acts of Hill which caused the death of Pegg but disagreed otherwise. The position of the Crown at trial was that Hill and Pegg were homosexual lovers and that Hill had decided to murder Pegg after a falling-out between them. The Crown argued that Hill deliberately struck Pegg in the head while Pegg lay in bed. This did not kill Pegg who immediately ran from the bedroom into the bathroom to try to and stop the flow of blood from his head. Realizing he had been unsuccessful, Hill took two knives from the kitchen and stabbed Pegg to death.

Hill's version of the events was very different. He admitted to causing the death of Pegg but put forward two defences: self-defence and provocation. Hill testified that he had known Pegg for about a year through the latter's involvement with the "Big Brother" organization. Hill stated that on the night in question he had been the subject of unexpected and unwelcome homosexual advances by Pegg while asleep on the couch in Pegg's apartment. Pegg pursued Hill to the bathroom and grabbed him, at which time Hill picked up a nearby hatchet and swung it at Pegg in an attempt to scare him. The hatchet struck Pegg in the head. Hill then ran from the apartment but returned shortly afterward. Upon re-entering the apartment, he was confronted by Pegg who threatened to kill him. At this point, Hill obtained two knives from the kitchen and stabbed Pegg to death.

. . .

[The trial judge instructed the jury that when they were assessing whether an ordinary person would be deprived of self-control by the act or insult, the personal characteristics of the accused should not be taken into account. Counsel for Hill objected that the "ordinary person" should be defined as an ordinary person *of the same age and sex of the accused*. The trial judge did not recharge the jury and the accused appealed his conviction. The Court of Appeal allowed the appeal, set aside the conviction, and ordered a new trial on the charge of second-degree murder, finding that the trial judge failed to properly instruct the jury on the attributes that ought to be ascribed to the "ordinary person."]

IV. The Issue

The issue in this appeal is whether the Ontario Court of Appeal erred in law in holding that the trial judge erred in law with respect to the elements of the objective test relevant to the defence of provocation in failing to direct the jury that the "ordinary person" within the meaning of that term in s. 215(2) of the *Criminal Code* was an "ordinary person of the same age and sex as the accused."

V. The Defence of Provocation

The defence of provocation appears to have first developed in the early 1800's. Tindal C.J. in *R. v. Hayward* (1833), 6 Car. & p. 157 at p. 158, told the jury that the defence of provocation was derived from the law's "compassion to human infirmity." It acknowledged that all human beings are subject to uncontrollable outbursts of passion and anger which may lead them to do violent acts. In such instances, the law would lessen the severity of criminal liability.

Nevertheless, not all acts done in the heat of passion were to be subject to the doctrine of provocation. By the middle of the 19th century, it became clear that the provoking act had to be sufficient to excite an ordinary or reasonable person under the circumstances. As Keating J. stated in *R. v. Welsh* (1869), 11 Cox C.C. 336 at p. 338:

> The law is, that there must exist such an amount of provocation as would be excited by the circumstances in the mind of a reasonable man, and so as to lead the jury to ascribe the act to the influence of that passion.

The *Criminal Code* codified this approach to provocation by including under s. 215 [now s 232] three general requirements for the defence of provocation. First, the provoking wrongful act or insult must be of such a nature that it would deprive an ordinary person of the power of self-control. That is the initial threshold which must be surmounted. Secondly, the accused must actually have been provoked. As I have earlier indicated, these two elements are often referred to as the objective and subjective tests of provocation respectively. Thirdly, the accused must have acted on the provocation on the sudden and before there was time for his or her passion to cool.

(a)   The Objective Test of Provocation and the Ordinary Person Standard

In considering the precise meaning and application of the ordinary person standard or objective test, it is important to identify its underlying rationale. Lord Simon of Glaisdale has perhaps stated it most succinctly when he suggested in Camplin, at p. 726, that

> the reason for importing into this branch of the law the concept of the reasonable man [was] … to avoid the injustice of a man being entitled to rely on his exceptional excitability or pugnacity or ill-temper or on his drunkenness.

If there were no objective test to the defence of provocation, anomalous results could occur. A well-tempered, reasonable person would not be entitled to benefit from the provocation defence and would be guilty of culpable homicide amounting to murder, while an ill-tempered or exceptionally excitable person would find his or her culpability mitigated by provocation and would be guilty only of manslaughter. It is society's concern that reasonable and non-violent behaviour be encouraged that prompts the law to endorse the objective standard. The criminal law is concerned among other things with fixing standards for human behaviour. We seek to encourage conduct that complies with certain societal standards of reasonableness and responsibility. In doing this, the law quite logically employs the objective standard of the reasonable person.

With this general purpose in mind, we must ascertain the meaning of the ordinary person standard. What are the characteristics of the "ordinary person"? To what extent should the attributes and circumstances of the accused be ascribed to the ordinary person? To answer these questions, it is helpful to review the English and Canadian jurisprudence. Since Canadian courts have relied heavily on English developments, I shall begin with the English cases.

· · ·

[After reviewing the development of the English case law, Chief Justice Dickson turned to the Canadian jurisprudence:]

(ii) Canadian Case Law

The Supreme Court of Canada has also had occasion to provide guidance on the ordinary person standard for provocation. In *Taylor v. The King*, [1947] S.C.R. 462, a case in which the accused was drunk at the time of his alleged provocation, Kerwin J. made clear that for the purposes of the objective test of provocation, the "criterion is the effect on an ordinary person ... the jury is not entitled to take into consideration any alleged drunkenness on the part of the accused."

This Court again rejected a consideration of the drunkenness of the accused in connection with the objective test in *Salamon v. The Queen*, [1959] S.C.R. 404, Fauteux J., as he then was, endorsed the trial judge's instruction to the jury not to consider "the character, background, temperament, or condition of the accused" in relation to the objective test of provocation. Similarly, Cartwright J. (dissenting on another issue) wrote that the trial judge correctly "made it plain that on this [objective] branch of the inquiry no account should be taken of the idiosyncrasies of the appellant and that the standard to be applied was that of an ordinary person."

Finally, in *Wright v. The Queen*, [1969] S.C.R. 335, a son was charged with the shooting death of his father. The evidence suggested that there had been some difficulties in their relationship. The father was said to have been a bad-tempered and violent man who had mistreated his son on a number of occasions. The accused had not seen his father for a period of about five years until a few days prior to the fatal incident. On the evening of the shooting, the accused had spent most of the day drinking with his friends. In considering the objective test of provocation, the court rejected the relevance of the quality of the accused's relationship with his father, the mentality of the accused or his possible drunkenness. ... The Court went on to state, at p. 340:

> While the character, background, temperament, idiosyncrasies, or the drunkenness of the accused are matters to be considered in the second branch of the enquiry, they are excluded from the consideration in the first branch. A contrary view would denude of any sense the objective test. ...

What lessons are to be drawn from this review of the case law? I think it is clear that there is widespread agreement that the ordinary or reasonable person has a normal temperament and level of self-control. It follows that the ordinary person is not exceptionally excitable, pugnacious or in a state of drunkenness.

In terms of other characteristics of the ordinary person, it seems to me that the "collective good sense" of the jury will naturally lead it to ascribe to the ordinary person any general characteristics relevant to the provocation in question. For example, if the provocation is a racial slur, the jury will think of an ordinary person with the racial background that forms the substance of the insult. To this extent, particular characteristics will be ascribed to the ordinary person. Indeed, it would be impossible to conceptualize a sexless or ageless ordinary person. Features such as sex, age or race do not detract from a person's characterization as ordinary. Thus particular characteristics that are not peculiar or idiosyncratic can be ascribed to an ordinary person without subverting the logic of the objective test of provocation. ...

It is important to note that, in some instances, certain characteristics will be irrelevant. For example, the race of a person will be irrelevant if the provocation involves an insult regarding a physical disability. Similarly, the sex of an accused will be irrelevant if the provocation relates to a racial insult. Thus the central criterion is the relevance of the particular feature to the provocation in question. With this in mind, I think it is fair to conclude that age will be a relevant consideration when we are dealing with a young accused person. For a jury to assess what an ordinary person would have done if subjected to the same circumstances as the accused, the young age of an accused will be an important contextual consideration.

I should also add that my conclusion that certain attributes can be ascribed to the ordinary person is not meant to suggest that a trial judge must in each case tell the jury what specific attributes it is to ascribe to the ordinary person. The point I wish to emphasize is simply that in applying their common sense to the factual determination of the objective test, jury members will quite naturally and properly ascribe certain characteristics to the "ordinary person."

· · ·

I have the greatest of confidence in the level of intelligence and plain common sense of the average Canadian jury sitting on a criminal case. Juries are perfectly capable of sizing the matter up. In my experience as a trial judge I cannot recall a single instance in which a jury returned to the court-room to ask for further instructions on the provocation portion of a murder charge. A jury frequently seeks further guidance on the distinction between first degree murder, second degree murder and manslaughter, but rarely, if ever, on provocation. It seems to be common ground that the trial judge would not have been in error if he had simply read s. 215 of the *Code* and left it at that, without embellishment. I am loath to complicate the task of the trial judge, in cases such as the case at bar, by requiring him or her as a matter of law to point out to the members of the jury that in applying the objective test they must conceptualize an "ordinary person" who is male and young. The accused is before them. He is male and young. I cannot conceive of a Canadian jury conjuring up the concept of an "ordinary person" who would be either female or elderly, or banishing from their minds the possibility that an "ordinary person" might be both young and male. I do not think anything said by the judge in the case at bar would have led the jury to such an absurdity.

VII. *Conclusion*

I find that the trial judge's charge to the jury on the ordinary person standard in the defence of provocation was consistent with the requirements of the *Criminal Code* and correct in law. It was not necessary to direct the jury that the ordinary person means an ordinary person of the same age and sex as the accused. I would, therefore, allow the appeal and restore the conviction.

[Justices Lamer, Wilson, and Le Dain agreed with Chief Justice Dickson's general articulation of the law of provocation, but dissented on the basis that the trial judge should have drawn specific attention to the age (and, for Justice Wilson, sex) of the accused in this case. Justice Wilson's view was that "[t]he jury must be directed to consider any facts which make the wrongful act or insult comprehensible to them in the same way as it was comprehended by the accused and then, having appreciated the factual context in which the wrongful act or insult took place, must measure the accused's response to this insult against the objective standard of the ordinary person similarly situated and similarly insulted." She explained that the law should take account of Hill's age of 16 because "the law does not attribute to individuals in the developmental stage of their youth the same degree of responsibility as is attributed to fully adult actors." She also stated that Hill's sex should be considered "not because different standards of self-control are attributable to the two sexes, but in order to put the wrongful act or insult into context for purposes of assessing its gravity. In assessing the reaction of the ordinary person to a sexual assault it is the ordinary person who is a male subjected to a homosexual assault which must be considered." Accordingly, she reasoned that "the appropriate formulation of the objective standard against which the respondent's reaction to the wrongful act must be measured in this case is the standard of the ordinary sixteen year old male subjected to a homosexual assault."]

———————————

Think back to the excerpt in the previous section of this chapter entitled "Emotions and the Veil of Voluntarism: The Loss of Judgment in Canadian Criminal Defences." Is there a risk that Justice Wilson's approach would give force to a form of panic and violence in responses to same-sex sexual advances that is at odds with norms of "diversity, antisubordination, and equality"? Does Chief Justice Dickson's majority approach—which approved of a simple instruction about whether the act or insult would cause "the ordinary person" to lose self-control—present lesser danger in this respect, or is any such risk an inherent aspect of a defence of provocation?

As the next case shows, the question of how to approach and contextualize the ordinary person for the purposes of the defence of provocation has remained a significant issue and the law on this point has continued to develop. The following decision addresses another set of difficult interpretive issues arising from s 232, including the meaning of "wrongful act or insult" and "legal right." Importantly, this case also clearly displays the gendered dimensions of the defence, discussed in the prior section of this chapter.

R v Thibert
Supreme Court of Canada
[1996] 1 SCR 37

[The defence of provocation was the central issue in this controversial case in which the accused killed his wife's lover. A majority of three judges held that the defence of provocation should have been left with the jury in the circumstances. The essential facts, which appeared in Justice Major's dissent, were as follows and have been placed here for ease of reference.]

[37] The appellant Norman Eugene Thibert was charged with first degree murder in the shooting death of his estranged wife's lover, Alan Sherren. Norman Eugene Thibert married his wife, Joan Thibert, in July, 1970. The couple had two children, Michelle, and Catrina, aged 22 and 19 respectively, at the time of the trial.

[38] The Thiberts' marriage had its share of problems. Early on in the marriage, Mr. Thibert admitted to his wife that he had had three extramarital affairs. In September, 1990, Mrs. Thibert began an intimate relationship with the deceased, a co-worker. She disclosed this relationship to her husband in April, 1991. He was distraught and eventually convinced his wife to remain with him and attempt to make their marriage work.

[39] On July 2, 1991, Mrs. Thibert decided to leave her husband. She took a hotel room rather than returning home. The appellant drove around the city that evening, unsuccessfully searching for the hotel where his wife was staying. When he returned home, he removed a rifle and a shotgun from the basement of the house to the garage. He testified that he thought about killing the deceased, his wife, or himself. He loaded the rifle, and then left the guns in a corner of the garage, having at that point abandoned his violent thoughts.

[40] The daughter, Catrina arrived home to find her father very upset. He told her of her mother's affair. At approximately 11:00 p.m., Mrs. Thibert telephoned her husband at home to tell him of her decision to leave him. At his request, she agreed to meet him the next morning, at Smitty's Restaurant in St. Albert, a suburb of Edmonton at 7:00 a.m.

[41] The next morning Mr. Thibert and Catrina went to the restaurant to meet Mrs. Thibert who arrived at the meeting with the deceased. The appellant attempted to persuade her to return home with him, but she refused. The meeting at Smitty's lasted approximately one hour. At the end of the meeting, Mr. Thibert promised not to bother his wife at work, and in return, she promised to think about coming home that night to again talk to him. Outside the restaurant, while waiting for Mrs. Thibert to finish talking with Catrina, the appellant told the deceased, "I hope you intend on moving back east or living under assumed names. ... Because as long as I have got breath in my body I am not going to give up trying to get my wife back from you, and I will find you wherever you go."

[42] The appellant testified that, when he returned home, he thought about killing himself, and so returned to the garage and retrieved the guns. He sawed off the barrel of the shotgun, but then discovered that the gun was inoperable since the firing pin was broken.

[43] He telephoned his wife at work several times in an effort to persuade her to return to him.

[44] During one afternoon call, she asked him to stop phoning her and told him that she was leaving work to make a bank deposit. The appellant then drove into the city, planning to find his wife while she was at the bank, and away from the influence of the deceased, and again attempt to convince her to give the marriage another try.

[45] He put the loaded rifle in the back of his car before departing, thinking that he might have to kill the deceased. He testified that a few miles from home he abandoned that thought, but instead planned to use the rifle as a final bluff to get his wife to come with him. The police later seized a box of shells from the vehicle, although the appellant stated that he did not remember placing the ammunition in the car.

[46] At approximately 2:45 p.m., the appellant parked across the street from his wife's place of work. When he saw Mrs. Thibert depart for the bank, he followed her. She noticed him at a stoplight, at which time he attempted to persuade her to get into his car so they could talk. The appellant followed Mrs. Thibert to the bank, and insisted that they go some place private to talk. Mrs. Thibert agreed to meet him in a vacant lot but instead, out of fear returned to her workplace. The appellant followed her into the parking-lot.

The appellant again tried to persuade Mrs. Thibert to go some place with him to talk, but she continued to refuse.

[47] The appellant told Mrs. Thibert that he had a high powered rifle in his car, but claimed that it was not loaded. He suggested that he would have to go into Mrs. Thibert's workplace and use the gun. At that time, the deceased came out of the building and began to lead Mrs. Thibert back into the office. The appellant then removed the rifle from the car.

[48] The appellant's evidence was that the deceased began walking towards him, with his hands on Mrs. Thibert's shoulders swinging her back and forth, saying, "You want to shoot me? Go ahead and shoot me." and "Come on big fellow, shoot me. You want to shoot me? Go ahead and shoot me." At some point, Mrs. Thibert either moved, or was moved aside. The appellant testified that the deceased kept coming towards him, ignoring the appellant's instructions to stay back. The appellant testified that his eyes were closed as he tried to retreat inward and the gun discharged.

[49] After the shot, Mrs. Thibert ran into the office building. At some point, the appellant put the gun down, entered the office building, and calmly said that he wanted to talk to his wife. He then exited the building, picked up the gun, put more ammunition in it, and said he was not going to hurt anyone. He placed the gun in his car and drove away.

[50] While he was driving, the appellant noticed a police car following him. He pulled off onto a side road, and surrendered to the police. At the time of his arrest, Constable Baumgartner recorded that the appellant stated "It's out of me now. He was fooling around with my wife." Constable Turner recorded the appellant's statement as "For what it's worth, I was just after him. For what it's worth, it's out of me now. He was fooling around with my wife."

CORY J (Sopinka and McLachlin JJ concurring):

[1] The sole question to be considered on this appeal is whether the trial judge was correct in leaving the defence of provocation with the jury. Put another way, the issue is whether there was any evidence upon which a reasonable jury acting judicially and properly instructed could find that there had been provocation.

[2] If the trial judge was correct in leaving provocation with the jury, then it is conceded that there must be a new trial. This is the result of the failure to instruct the jury that there was no onus resting upon the appellant to establish the defence but rather that it rested upon the Crown to establish beyond a reasonable doubt that there had not been provocation. The necessity of giving these instructions has been emphasized by this court in *Latour v. The King*, [1951] S.C.R. 19, and in *Linney v. The Queen* (1977), [1978] 1 S.C.R. 646. If on the other hand it was inappropriate for the trial judge to leave the defence of provocation to the jury, then the fact that he erred in the instructions pertaining to provocation was immaterial and it would be appropriate to find that no substantial wrong or miscarriage had been occasioned by the error.

• • •

[4] The section specifies that there is both an objective and a subjective element to the defence. Both must be satisfied if the defence is to be invoked. First, there must be a wrongful act or insult of such a nature that it is sufficient to deprive an ordinary person of the power of self-control as the objective element. Second, the subjective element requires that the accused act upon that insult on the sudden and before there was time for

his passion to cool. The objective aspect would at first reading appear to be contradictory for, as legal writers have noted, the "ordinary" person does not kill. Yet, I think the objective element should be taken as an attempt to weigh in the balance those very human frailties which sometimes lead people to act irrationally and impulsively against the need to protect society by discouraging acts of homicidal violence.

When Should the Defence of Provocation Be Left to the Jury?

. . .

[6] ... [B]efore the defence of provocation is left to the jury, the trial judge must be satisfied (a) that there is *some* evidence to suggest that the particular wrongful act or insult alleged by the accused would have caused an ordinary person to be deprived of self-control, and (b) that there is some evidence showing that the accused was actually deprived of his or her self-control by that act or insult. This threshold test can be readily met, so long as there is some evidence that the objective and subjective elements may be satisfied. If there is, the defence must then be left with the jury.

. . .

The Wrongful Act or Insult

[8] *Taylor v. The King*, [1947] S.C.R. 462, adopted the *Oxford English Dictionary* definition of "insult," and found it to mean:

> ... an act, or the action, of attacking or assailing; an open and sudden attack or assault without formal preparations; injuriously contemptuous speech or behaviour; scornful utterance or action intended to wound self-respect; an affront; indignity.

The Objective Element of the Test: How Ordinary Is the "Ordinary Person" and Would That Person Have Been Provoked by the Wrongful Act or Insult?

. . .

[15] The problem was considered by this court in *R. v. Hill*, [1986] 1 S.C.R. 313. There a 16-year-old male fought off the homosexual advances of an older man who was his "Big Brother." The narrow "ordinary person" test was rejected and a more contextual one adopted. Dickson C.J.C., writing for the majority of the court, held that the age and sex of the accused are important considerations in the objective branch of the test. At page 331, he noted that "particular characteristics that are not peculiar or idiosyncratic can be ascribed to an ordinary person without subverting the logic of the objective test of provocation." Although it was not necessary in the circumstances of that case to go beyond a consideration of the age and sex of the accused, Dickson C.J.C. did state that the jury should "assess what an ordinary person would have done if subjected to the same circumstances as the accused" (p. 332). Thus, although characteristics such as a propensity to drunken rages or short-tempered violence cannot be taken into account, other characteristics may properly be considered without in any way demeaning or subverting the aim of the objective test to encourage responsible behaviour. So too, it is proper for the jury to consider the background of the relationship between the deceased and the accused,

including earlier insults which culminated in the final provocative actions or words. For a jury to take this into account would not adversely affect the objective aspect of the test.

[16] The provincial courts of appeal have widened, I believe correctly, the approach to the objective element in order to consider the background relationship between the deceased and the accused. In *R. v. Daniels* (1983), 7 C.C.C. (3d) 542 (N.W.T.C.A.), Laycraft J.A., for the court, acknowledged that the personal attributes of an accused should be excluded from the objective test but held that the background events should be taken into consideration. ...

[17] In *R. v. Conway* (1985), 17 C.C.C. (3d) 481, 14 W.C.B. 7 (Ont. C.A.), Howland C.J.O. concluded that the history and background of the relationship between the victim and the accused is relevant and pertinent to the "ordinary person" test. He stated at p. 487:

> [The trial judge] should have told [the jury] present acts or insults, in themselves insufficient to cause an ordinary man to lose self-control, may indeed cause such loss of self-control when they are connected with past events and external pressures of insult by acts or words and accordingly in considering whether an ordinary man would have lost self-control they must consider an ordinary man who had experienced the same series of acts or insults as experienced by the appellant. ...

[18] In my view, so long as the provocation section remains in the *Criminal Code* in its present form, certain characteristics will have to be assigned to the "ordinary person" in assessing the objective element. The "ordinary person" must be of the same age, and sex, and share with the accused such other factors as would give the act or insult in question a special significance and have experienced the same series of acts or insults as those experienced by the accused.

[19] In summary then, the wrongful act or insult must be one which could, in light of the past history of the relationship between the accused and the deceased, deprive an ordinary person, of the same age, and sex, and sharing with the accused such other factors as would give the act or insult in question a special significance, of the power of self-control.

The Subjective Element

[20] In *R. v. Tripodi*, [1955] S.C.R. 438, Rand J. interpreted "sudden provocation" to mean that "the wrongful act or insult must strike upon a mind unprepared for it, that it must make an unexpected impact that takes the understanding by surprise and sets the passions aflame" (p. 443). To this definition, I would add that the background and history of the relationship between the accused and the deceased should be taken into consideration. This is particularly appropriate if it reveals a long history of insults, levelled at the accused by the deceased. This is so even if the insults might induce a desire for revenge so long as immediately before the last insult, the accused did not intend to kill. Glanville Williams adopts this position in his *Textbook of Criminal Law*, 2nd ed. (London: Stevens & Sons, 1983). At p. 530, he puts it in this way: "affronts over a long period of time inducing the desire for revenge do not preclude the defence of provocation, if immediately before the last affront the defendant did not intend to kill." He adds further that, "the last affront may be comparatively trivial, merely the last straw that makes the worm turn, so to speak."

[21] … These then are the considerations which the trial judge must take into account in making assessment as to whether or not there was any evidence upon which a reasonable jury acting judicially and properly instructed could find that the defence of provocation could be applicable in the circumstances of this case.

Bearing in Mind the Principles Pertaining to Provocation, Was There Any Evidence Adduced in This Case Which Required the Trial Judge to Leave That Defence with the Jury?

[22] In this case, there is no doubt that the relationship of the wife of the accused with the deceased was the dominating factor in the tragic killing. Obviously, events leading to the breakup of the marriage can never warrant taking the life of another. Affairs cannot justify murder. Yet the provocation defence section has always been and is presently a part of the *Criminal Code*. Any recognition of human frailties must take into account that these very situations may lead to insults that could give rise to provocation. Some European penal codes recognize "crimes of passion" as falling within a special category. Indeed, many of the Canadian cases which have considered the applicability of the defence arise from such situations: see, for example, the cases of *Daniels* and *Conway*, supra. The defence of provocation does no more than recognize human frailties. Reality and the past experience of the ages recognize that this sort of situation may lead to acts of provocation. Each case must be considered in the context of its particular facts to determine if the evidence meets the requisite threshold test necessary to establish provocation.

The Objective Element of the Test

[23] In this case, it is appropriate to take into account the history of the relationship between the accused and the deceased. The accused's wife had, on a prior occasion, planned to leave him for the deceased but he had managed to convince her to return to him. He hoped to accomplish the same result when his wife left him for the deceased on this second occasion. At the time of the shooting he was distraught and had been without sleep for some 34 hours. When he turned into the parking-lot of his wife's employer he still wished to talk to her in private. Later, when the deceased held his wife by her shoulders in a proprietary and possessive manner and moved her back and forth in front of him while he taunted the accused to shoot him, a situation was created in which the accused could have believed that the deceased was mocking him and preventing him from his having the private conversation with his wife which was so vitally important to him.

[24] Taking into account the past history between the deceased and the accused, a jury could find the actions of the deceased to be taunting and insulting. It might be found that, under the same circumstances, an ordinary person who was a married man, faced with the breakup of his marriage, would have been provoked by the actions of the deceased so as to cause him to lose his power of self-control. There was some evidence, therefore, that would satisfy the objective element of the test. Next, it remains to be seen whether there was evidence that could fulfil the subjective element of the test.

The Subjective Element of the Test

[25] It must be determined whether there was evidence that the appellant was actually provoked. Once again it is necessary to take into account the past history involving the accused, the deceased and his wife. Further, it cannot be forgotten that the accused had not slept for some 34 hours and that he described himself as being devastated, stressed out and suicidal. He emphasized how important it was to him to talk to his wife in private, away from the deceased. It was in this manner that he successfully persuaded his wife to stay with him on the earlier occasion. When his wife returned to her employer's parking-lot and the deceased came out of the building, he testified that his thoughts were "here is the man that won't give me a half hour alone with my wife after 21 years and he has had her for 24 hours the night before."

[26] It was when the deceased put his arm around his wife's waist and started leading her back towards the building that the appellant removed the rifle from the car. He testified that he did so as a bluff. He hoped it would make them take him more seriously and succeed in convincing his wife to accompany him so that they could talk privately. From this point, the deceased's actions could be construed as a conscious attempt to test the appellant's limits. When he saw that the appellant had a gun, he advanced towards him. The appellant's wife was in front of the deceased and the deceased had his hands on her shoulders. The appellant recalled that the deceased was swinging Mrs. Thibert from side to side like a moving target. While doing this, the deceased was laughing and grinning at the appellant. He also dared the appellant to fire and taunted him by saying: "Come on big fellow, shoot me. You want to shoot me? Go ahead and shoot me." The deceased continued to approach the appellant, proceeding as fast as he could. In turn, the appellant kept backing up and told the deceased to "stay back," but the deceased continued to approach him. The appellant testified that he remembered wanting to scream because the deceased would not stop coming towards him. The appellant's eyes were tightly closed when he fired the gun. The time the appellant held the gun until he fired was not long. The events unfolded very quickly, in a matter of moments, seconds, not minutes.

[27] The respondent submitted that "[r]ejection in the context of a romantic relationship will not constitute a basis for the provocation defence." This is correct. If the appellant had simply brooded over the unhappy situation, put a rifle in his car and gone looking for the deceased, then the history of the deceased's relationship with the wife of the accused could not be used as a basis for a defence of provocation because the necessary final act of provocation was missing. However, in this case, rejection is not the most significant or overriding factor. The appellant sought to avoid the deceased in order to talk privately with his wife. The evidence indicates that the confrontation with the deceased in the parking-lot was unexpected. The appellant had gone to some lengths to avoid meeting the deceased.

[28] In my view, there was evidence upon which a reasonable jury acting judicially and properly instructed could have concluded that the defence of provocation was applicable. Next, it must be considered whether the acts of the deceased were those which he had a legal right to do and thus within the exemption described in s. 232(3).

Were the Acts of the Deceased Ones Which He Had a Legal Right to Do but Which Were Nevertheless Insulting?

[29] It will be remembered that s. 232(3) provides that "no one shall be deemed to have given provocation to another by doing anything that he had a legal right to do." In the context of the provocation defence, the phrase "legal right" has been defined as meaning a right which is sanctioned by law as distinct from something which a person may do without incurring legal liability. Thus, the defence of provocation is open to someone who is "insulted." The words or act put forward as provocation need not be words or act which are specifically prohibited by the law. ...

[30] Thus, while the actions of the deceased in the parking-lot were clearly not prohibited by law, they could none the less be found by a jury to constitute insulting behaviour. In light of the past history, possessive or affectionate behaviour by the deceased towards the appellant's wife coupled with his taunting remarks could be considered to be insulting. Nor can it be said that these actions really constituted self-defence. The deceased was told by the appellant's wife that the gun was unloaded and he may have believed her. In any event, he continued to advance towards the appellant and to goad him to shoot despite the request to stop. In the circumstances, the actions of the deceased could well be found not to be acts of self-defence. A jury could infer that it was the taunting of the appellant by the deceased who was preventing him from talking privately with his wife which was the last straw that led him to fire the rifle suddenly before his passion had cooled. While the deceased's conduct might not have been specifically prohibited nor susceptible to a remedy it was not sanctioned by any legal right.

[31] In summary, there was some evidence upon which a reasonable jury acting judicially and properly instructed could find that the defence of provocation was applicable. It was appropriate for the trial judge to leave this defence with the jury. Once it was determined the defence should be left, then the trial judge was required to correctly relate the principles of reasonable doubt as they applied to that defence. ...

Disposition

[35] In the result, I would allow the appeal, set aside the decision of the Court of Appeal and direct a new trial on the charge of second degree murder.

MAJOR J (Iacobucci J concurring) (dissenting):

· · ·

A. Was the Defence of Provocation Properly Left with the Jury?

· · ·

[63] In my opinion, in this case there is no evidence of a wrongful act or insult sufficient to deprive an ordinary person of the power of self-control. That the deceased may have positioned Mrs. Thibert between himself and the appellant cannot constitute a wrongful act or insult. Nor can the statements "You want to shoot me? Go ahead and shoot me" and "Come on big fellow, shoot me" be considered a wrongful act or insult. Those actions are not contemptuous or scornful; they are legitimate reactions to a dangerous situation. It would be improper to require victims to respond in a certain way when

faced with armed, threatening individuals. The defence claim that the wrongful act or insult came from the appellant's evidence that the deceased used Joan Thibert as a shield while taunting him to shoot is ironic. The appellant had control of the only true weapon involved in this situation, the rifle.

[64] Further, that the deceased had a personal relationship with Mrs. Thibert is not a wrongful act or insult sufficient to cause an ordinary person to lose the power of self-control. The breakup of a marriage due to an extramarital affair cannot constitute such a wrongful act or insult. I agree with the statement of Freeman J.A. in *R. v. Young* (1993), 78 C.C.C. (3d) 538 (N.S.C.A.), at p. 542 that:

> It would set a dangerous precedent to characterize terminating a relationship as an insult or wrong act capable of constituting provocation to kill. The appellant may have been feeling anger, frustration and a sense of loss, particularly if he was in a position of emotional dependency on the victim as his counsel asserts, but that is not provocation of a kind to reduce murder to manslaughter.

[65] Similarly, it would be a dangerous precedent to characterize involvement in an extramarital affair as conduct capable of grounding provocation, even when coupled with the deceased's reactions to the dangerous situation he faced. At law, no one has either an emotional or proprietary right or interest in a spouse that would justify the loss of self-control that the appellant exhibited.

[66] In that connection, Cory J. states that the events leading to the breakup of a relationship are not factors going to provocation but I wonder whether the effect of his reasons is such that these factors have been taken into account in the context of provocation. My colleague emphasizes that the accused still wished to see his wife alone after the end of the relationship. However, in my view, she had made it clear on a number of occasions that she did not wish to be alone with him. This was a choice that Joan Thibert was free to make. The accused had no right or entitlement to speak with his wife in private. The fact that the accused believed that the deceased was preventing him from doing so is not, with respect, a fact that ought to be taken into account when considering the defence of provocation.

[67] If I am wrong and the objective threshold test for provocation is met, the appeal would fail on the subjective element of the test. The appellant had known of his wife's involvement with the deceased for some time. He knew his wife wanted to leave him, and had seen the deceased with his wife earlier that day. It cannot be said that the appellant's mind was unprepared for the sight of his wife with the deceased such that he was taken by surprise and his passions were set aflame. There was no element of suddenness on the facts of this case.

[68] For these reasons, I am of the opinion that neither the objective branch nor the subjective branch of the threshold test for leaving the defence of provocation with the jury has been met. There is no evidence on which a reasonable jury, acting judicially could find a wrongful act or insult sufficient to deprive the ordinary person of the power of self-control. Neither is there any evidence that the appellant acted on the sudden. The defence should not have been left with the jury. This was an error that did not prejudice the appellant.

· · ·

[70] I would dismiss the appeal.

Thibert was the Supreme Court of Canada's leading decision on the law of provocation for 14 years. As you have seen, the Court developed a kind of "mixed" approach to constructing the reasonable person for the purposes of the defence of provocation. Although we take a strictly objective approach to determining what standard of self-control we require of the accused, when we consider the gravity of the provoking insult, those attributes that give the insult its particular significance are ascribed to the "ordinary person." You will recall also that the Court in *Hill* said that the judge may, but need not, instruct the jury about such features.

In the years since *Thibert*, one consequential and thorny question for the law has been whether—if the accused claims that the insult was particularly provoking to (usually) him because of the conventions, assumptions, and norms of his cultural community—the reasonable person should be thought of as belonging to that particular culture or as holding those beliefs. On the one hand, the law should seek to take account of Canada's multicultural nature and might, therefore, recognize that some cultural beliefs will render a particular act or insult particularly grave. On the other hand, as you have seen, the defence of provocation works disproportionately to mitigate the punishment of men who murder women. If a given culture or subculture holds views that are antithetical to egalitarian aspirations and Canadian constitutional commitments regarding gender equality, should the law "support" such views by treating them as mitigating of punishment? Two provincial appellate courts arrived at very different answers to this question.

The BC Court of Appeal addressed the issue in 2004 in *R v Nahar*, 2004 BCCA 77. In *Nahar*, the accused was convicted by a judge alone of second-degree murder of his wife. His sole defence was provocation. The accused had immigrated to Canada from the Punjab in 1995. Some years later he returned to participate in an arranged marriage, bringing his new wife back to Canada. After arriving in Canada, Ms. Nahar "is said to have smoked, consumed alcohol, and socialized with other men, generally behaving in a manner that was completely at odds with the culture and traditions of the Sikh community in which they were raised" (at para 2). This behaviour caused heated arguments and persistent conflict between Mr. and Ms. Nahar: "The relationship was tumultuous. Ms. Nahar's behaviour and her defiance persisted. Arguments over her conduct were frequent and at times they became violent" (at para 7). On the night of the killing, the accused testified that "his wife was trying to push him out the door of [her] suite defiantly insisting that he could not stop her and that she would 'keep on going'" (at para 8). The accused testified that at that stage his "brain became numb" and, although he said he did not remember doing so, he picked up a kitchen knife and fatally stabbed his wife once in the neck and once in the heart. The trial judge held that the defence of provocation was not satisfied because the insults or behaviour of the wife would not have caused an ordinary person to lose the power of self-control. On appeal, the accused argued that the trial judge had erred by failing to take into account "the implications of Mr. Nahar having been raised in the Sikh culture where behaviour of a married woman such as is attributed to Ms. Nahar is said to be particularly intolerable and embarrassing to a married man" (at para 30). The Court of Appeal held that such considerations should, indeed, factor into the provocation analysis but dismissed the appeal, concluding that the trial judge had, in fact, taken the accused's cultural background into account. Justice Lowry explained as follows:

[37] … It appears to be accepted that, based on Cory J.'s discussion of the objective element in *R. v. Thibert*, the ordinary person must have been one who shared Mr. Nahar's cultural background so that the implications of his being a Sikh, and having been raised in the Sikh tradition, were to be taken into account in measuring the gravity of the insult which is said to have caused him to stab his wife.

[38] That being so, the question the trial judge was required to consider was not merely whether an ordinary married man would be severely distressed by the behaviour attributed to Ms. Nahar and her conduct just before she was stabbed. It was rather whether, having regard for the cause and duration of the couple's troubled relationship, an insult that carried the same emotional impact for an ordinary young married man of the same cultural background as it apparently carried for Mr. Nahar, would cause such a man to lose his power of self-control.

[39] In my view, it was certainly open to the trial judge to conclude there was no reasonable doubt that, even taking into account Mr. Nahar's cultural background, the ordinary person would not in the circumstances have lost his power of self-control. Indeed, I consider that was the only sound conclusion. Further, from what Fraser J. said was central to the case at the outset, it appears clear to me that, in assessing the objective element, he was mindful of the evidence that bore on Mr. Nahar's cultural background.

By contrast, in *R v Humaid* (2006), 208 CCC (3d) 43 (Ont CA), the court questioned the relevance of culture, ethnicity, or religious beliefs to the reasonable person test. In *Humaid*, a jury convicted the accused of first-degree murder for killing his wife. At trial, the defence theory was that his wife's alleged admission to him of sexual infidelity amounted to a psychological blow that threw the accused into a state of dissociation in which he did not form the intent to murder, or that it constituted provocation whereby he temporarily lost the power of self-control. In respect to the provocation defence, the accused, who was a practising Muslim, led evidence from an expert on Islamic religion and culture. The expert testified that Islamic culture was male-dominated, that it put great significance on family honour, and that infidelity, especially by females, "was considered a very serious violation of the family's honour and worthy of harsh punishment by the male members of the family" (at para 67). However, the expert acknowledged that individual Muslims would have different views on these matters, depending on their experiences and background, and that there was no evidence from the accused or the expert on whether the accused shared strong views on infidelity and family honour. The trial judge instructed the jury that "the 'ordinary person' should be regarded as a person of the same age, sex and with the same marital background and relationship history as the appellant, but should not be taken as a person sharing the appellant's religion, culture or customs" (at para 76). On appeal, Mr. Humaid argued, in part, that this had been a misdirection on the law of provocation. The Court of Appeal upheld the conviction for first-degree murder. The court held that there was no air of reality to the defence, and therefore it should not have been put to the jury. The court reasoned (at paras 82-84) that given there was no evidence the accused actually shared the religious and cultural beliefs relating to infidelity that the expert attributed to some Muslims, the expert testimony could not assist in raising an air of reality for provocation. Furthermore, Justice Doherty noted that "[p]rovocation does not shield an accused who has not lost self-control, but has instead acted out of a sense of revenge or a culturally driven sense of the appropriate response to someone else's misconduct" (at para 85). Addressing the broader issue of whether religious and cultural characteristics are relevant to the ordinary person test, Justice Doherty offered the following *obiter* comments:

> [92] [*Hill*, *supra*], and *Thibert*, *supra*, establish that the "ordinary person" inquiry is a blend of subjective and objective considerations. In some situations, there can be no doubt that the accused's religious or cultural beliefs will be attributed to the "ordinary person" to properly apply the "ordinary person" test as described in the authorities. To borrow the language of *Thibert*, one's religious and cultural beliefs can give "a special significance" to the acts or insult said to have constituted the provocation. For example, where the alleged provocative insult demeans or otherwise targets the religious or cultural beliefs of an accused, it seems beyond question that those beliefs must be factored into the "ordinary person" test to determine whether the insults were capable of causing an "ordinary person" to lose self-control.
>
> [93] In this case, however, the appellant's religious and cultural beliefs are not the target of the alleged insult. Rather, the appellant's religious and cultural beliefs are said to render the words spoken by Aysar [his wife] highly insulting. The difficult problem, as I see it, is that the alleged beliefs which give the insult added gravity are premised on the notion that women are inferior to men and that violence against women is in some circumstances accepted, if not encouraged. These beliefs are antithetical to fundamental Canadian values, including gender equality. It is arguable that as a matter of criminal law policy, the "ordinary person" cannot be fixed with beliefs that are irreconcilable with fundamental Canadian values. Criminal law may simply not accept that a belief system which is contrary to those fundamental values should somehow provide the basis for a partial defence to murder.

The question of how cultural difference should be addressed in the criminal law, and more specifically in the context of criminal defences, has been the subject of much recent academic debate in Canada and abroad. Much of this discussion explores the complex interrelationship among multiculturalism, gender equality, and criminal law. See e.g. BL Berger, "Moral Judgment, Criminal Law and the Constitutional Protection of Religion" (2008) 40 SCLR (2nd) 513; H Power, "Provocation and Culture" (2006) Crim L Rev 871; S Coughlan, "Annotation to Humaid" (2006) 37 CR (6th) 349; A Dundes Renteln, "The Use and Abuse of the Cultural Defence" (2005) 20 CJLS 47; A Phillips, "When Culture Meets Gender: Issues of Cultural Defence in the English Courts" (2004) 66 Mod L Rev 510; A Dundes Renteln, *The Cultural Defense* (Oxford and New York: Oxford University Press, 2004); S Moller Okin, "Feminism and Multiculturalism: Some Tensions" (1998) 108 Ethics 661; and S Yeo, "Sex, Ethnicity, Power of Self-Control and Provocation Revisited" (1996) 18 Sydney L Rev 304.

The Supreme Court of Canada's decision in *R v Tran* is now the leading case on the defence of provocation. In it, the Court summarized and clarified the Canadian approach to provocation, returned to the issue of how to approach the objective component of the provocation test, and set some important limits on the kinds of beliefs and values that can be ascribed to the ordinary person. In so doing, it also settled the question raised in the *Nahar* and *Humaid* decisions.

R v Tran

Supreme Court of Canada

2010 SCC 58, [2010] 3 SCR 350

CHARRON J:

[1] In the early afternoon of February 10, 2004, the appellant Thieu Kham Tran entered the locked apartment of his estranged wife, Hoa Le Duong, unexpected and uninvited. The couple had separated a few months earlier and the appellant had purportedly relinquished his keys to the former matrimonial home. Unbeknownst to her, however, he had kept a set of keys in his possession. Ms. Duong was in her bedroom, in her bed with her boyfriend, An Quoc Tran, when they heard the door open.

[2] The appellant entered Ms. Duong's bedroom through the half-closed door. Ms. Duong and Mr. An Tran stood up, naked. The appellant immediately attacked Mr. An Tran, scratching at his eyes, kicking and punching him. He then attacked Ms. Duong in the same fashion. Suddenly, the appellant ran out of the room to the kitchen. While he was gone, Ms. Duong and Mr. An Tran tried hastily to get dressed. Although the appellant had come to the apartment with a sheathed knife in the pocket of his coat, he came back into the bedroom armed with two butcher knives taken from the kitchen. He stabbed Mr. An Tran one time in the chest. Mr. An Tran asked to talk but the appellant was yelling and angry. The appellant then stepped back to the bedroom door, used his own phone and called his godfather. He told his godfather: "I caught them."

[3] At this point, Mr. An Tran was having trouble breathing. He tried to walk to the window. The appellant then turned to Ms. Duong and chopped her hand. When she showed him the wound he said he would kill her. With Mr. An Tran standing behind her at the window, Ms. Duong tried to block the knives that were still coming from the appellant towards Mr. An Tran and received two additional cuts to her forearm. The appellant then asked Ms. Duong: "Are you beautiful?" Pulling her head up, he slashed her face with a deep cut from her right ear across her right cheek.

[4] Mr. An Tran finally managed to exit the bedroom. He was on the ground crawling into the living room. The appellant followed him and repeatedly stabbed him with both knives. Ms. Duong stayed in the bedroom. She went to the window and was yelling for help when she saw the appellant's godfather arriving. She then tried to close the bedroom door, but the appellant forced himself back in. The appellant looked out the window, and, returning to the living room, stepped on Mr. An Tran's face and stomach on his way out. With the two knives, the appellant proceeded to repeatedly stab Mr. An Tran's chest and then stepped on his face. According to the autopsy, Mr. An Tran was stabbed a total of 17 times, of which six were lethal wounds. The appellant cut his own hand and arm with one of the knives and put that knife in the hand of Mr. An Tran, who was now lying motionless on the living room floor.

[5] The appellant was tried before a judge sitting without a jury for five offences arising out of these tragic events. This appeal is only concerned with the charge of second degree murder of Mr. An Tran. The sole defence raised at trial was whether the murder should be reduced to manslaughter due to provocation. The trial judge accepted the defence, holding that the Crown had failed to disprove the elements of provocation. She therefore acquitted the appellant of second degree murder and convicted him of manslaughter. On appeal by the Crown, the Court of Appeal of Alberta unanimously held that the defence

of provocation had no air of reality (2008 ABCA 209, 91 Alta. L.R. (4th) 113). The court therefore set aside the verdict, substituted a conviction for second degree murder, and remitted the matter back to the trial court for sentencing. The appellant appeals to this Court as of right.

[6] The preceding overview of the facts reflects the trial judge's findings and uncontested items of evidence. I agree with the Court of Appeal that, on those facts, there was no air of reality to the defence of provocation. In my respectful view, the trial judge proceeded on wrong legal principles concerning the requirements for the defence of provocation and, as a result, erred in law in finding that there was an evidential basis in this record for that defence.

[7] Specifically, there was no "insult" within the meaning of s. 232 of the *Criminal Code*, R.S.C. 1985, c. C-46. As rightly concluded by the Court of Appeal, the appellant's view of his estranged wife's sexual involvement with another man after the couple had separated—found at trial to be the "insult"—cannot in law be sufficient to excuse "a loss of control in the form of a homicidal rage" and constitute "an excuse for the ordinary person of whatever personal circumstances or background" (Watson J.A., at para. 64). In addition, the uncontradicted evidence about the appellant's knowledge that his wife was involved with another man and his own conduct in entering her home and bedroom, unexpected and uninvited, belied any notion that this supposed "insult" would have struck "upon a mind unprepared for it" as required by law (Hunt J.A., at para. 18). Finally, there was no air of reality to the appellant "acting on the sudden at the time of the killing" (Watson J.A., at para. 77).

[8] As a conviction for murder was inevitable, both on the law and on the trial judge's essential findings of fact, the Court of Appeal properly substituted a verdict of second degree murder and remitted the matter for sentencing. I would dismiss the appeal.

2. Analysis

[9] Provocation is the only defence which is exclusive to homicide. As a partial defence, it serves to reduce murder to manslaughter when certain requirements are met. The defence, which originated at common law, is codified in s. 232 of the *Criminal Code*. The focal point for any analysis on the nature of the defence therefore lies in the wording of the statute:

> 232.(1) Culpable homicide that otherwise would be murder may be reduced to manslaughter if the person who committed it did so in the heat of passion caused by sudden provocation.
>
> (2) A wrongful act or an insult that is of such a nature as to be sufficient to deprive an ordinary person of the power of self-control is provocation for the purposes of this section if the accused acted on it on the sudden and before there was time for his passion to cool.
>
> (3) For the purposes of this section, the questions
>
> > (a) whether a particular wrongful act or insult amounted to provocation, and
> >
> > (b) whether the accused was deprived of the power of self-control by the provocation
> > that he alleges he received,
>
> are questions of fact, but no one shall be deemed to have given provocation to another by doing anything that he had a legal right to do, or by doing anything that the accused incited

him to do in order to provide the accused with an excuse for causing death or bodily harm to any human being.

(4) Culpable homicide that otherwise would be murder is not necessarily manslaughter by reason only that it was committed by a person who was being arrested illegally, but the fact that the illegality of the arrest was known to the accused may be evidence of provocation for the purpose of this section.

[10] As the opening words of the provision make plain, the defence will only apply where the accused had the necessary intent for murder and acted upon this intent. Parliament thus carefully limited the application of the defence. The requirements of the defence contained in s. 232 have been described variously by the Court as comprising either two, three or four elements. For example, in *R. v. Hill*, [1986] 1 S.C.R. 313, Dickson C.J. identified three general requirements for the defence of provocation:

First, the provoking wrongful act or insult must be of such a nature that it would deprive an ordinary person of the power of self-control. That is the initial threshold which must be surmounted. Secondly, the accused must actually have been provoked. As I have earlier indicated, these two elements are often referred to as the objective and subjective tests of provocation respectively. Thirdly, the accused must have acted on the provocation on the sudden and before there was time for his or her passion to cool. [p. 324]

In *R. v. Thibert*, [1996] 1 S.C.R. 37, Cory J. for the majority of the Court collapsed these three requirements into two elements, one objective and the other subjective, describing them as follows:

First, there must be a wrongful act or insult of such a nature that it is sufficient to deprive an ordinary person of the power of self-control as the objective element. Second, the subjective element requires that the accused act upon that insult on the sudden and before there was time for his passion to cool. [Emphasis in original deleted; para. 4.]

Subsequently, in *R. v. Parent*, 2001 SCC 30, [2001] 1 S.C.R. 761, the Court reiterated the test in *Thibert* but framed it in terms of four required elements:

... (1) a wrongful act or insult that would have caused an ordinary person to be deprived of his or her self-control; (2) which is sudden and unexpected; (3) which in fact caused the accused to act in anger; (4) before having recovered his or her normal control ... . [para. 10]

[11] These various formulations do not differ in substance. While it may be conceptually convenient in any given case to formulate the requirements of the defence in terms of distinct elements and to treat each of these elements separately, it is important to recognize that the various components of the defence may overlap and that s. 232 must be considered in its entirety.

• • •

[18] The common law defence of provocation was adopted and codified in the Canadian *Criminal Code* from its inception in 1892. The wording of s. 232 remains substantially unaltered. The same cannot be said of the social context in which it is embedded. The continued appropriateness of the defence has been a source of controversy, both in Canada and abroad. Some commentators and reviewing bodies have recommended that the defence be abandoned altogether, leaving provocation, when relevant, as a factor to

be considered in sentencing. For a discussion of such reform proposals in Canada and elsewhere, see D.E. Ives, "Provocation, Excessive Force in Self-Defence and Diminished Responsibility," in Law Commission of Great Britain, *Partial Defences to Murder: Overseas Studies*, Consultation Paper 173 (App. B) (2003), 73, at pp. 78-81; Australia, Victorian Law Reform Commission, *Defences to Homicide: Final Report* (2004); New Zealand Law Commission, *The Partial Defence of Provocation*, Report 98 (2007).

[19] Parliament has not chosen this course and the defence continues to exist in Canada. This does not mean, however, that the defence in its present articulation should not continue to evolve to reflect contemporary social norms, and in particular, *Charter* values. Just as at common law the notion of an "insult ... sufficient to deprive an ordinary person of the power of self-control," now codified under s. 232, is not frozen in time. By incorporating this objective element, the defence of provocation is necessarily informed by contemporary social norms and values. These include society's changed views regarding the nature of marital relationships and the present reality that a high percentage of them end in separation.

[20] It is with these considerations in mind that I turn to an examination of the defence as contained in s. 232 of the *Criminal Code*.

2.2 Provocation Under Section 232 of the Criminal Code

[21] Viewing the provision as a whole, I offer some preliminary comments about the juridical nature of the defence. A criminal law defence is usually characterized as providing either an excuse or a justification for the impugned conduct. As Professor K. Roach rightly observes: "As a partial defence that reduces murder to manslaughter, provocation does not fit easily into the excuse/justification framework" (*Criminal Law* (4th ed. 2009), at p. 358). In *R. v. Manchuk*, [1938] S.C.R. 18, at pp. 19-20, this Court explained that "provocation ... neither justifies nor excuses the act of homicide. But the law accounts the act and the violent feelings which prompted it less blameable because of the passion aroused by the provocation, ... though still sufficiently blameable to merit punishment— and it may be punishment of high severity—but not the extreme punishment of death."

[22] Thus, the accused's conduct is partially *excused* out of a compassion to human frailty. While the call for compassion was particularly compelling in times when the alternative was the death penalty, the rationale subsists today, given the serious consequences to the offender flowing from a conviction for murder. It is not sufficient, however, that an accused's sudden reaction to a wrongful act or insult may be explained from a purely subjective standpoint. The provision incorporates an objective standard against which the accused's reaction must be measured—that which may be expected of the "ordinary person" in like circumstances. Not all instances of loss of self-control will be excused. Rather, the requisite elements of the defence, taken together, make clear that the accused must have a *justifiable* sense of being wronged. This does not mean, and in no way should be taken as suggesting, that the victim is to be blamed for the accused's act, nor that he or she deserved the consequences of the provocation. Nor does it mean that the law sanctions the accused's conduct. Instead, the law recognizes that, as a result of human frailties, the accused reacted inappropriately and disproportionately, but understandably to a sufficiently serious wrongful act or insult.

[23] In my view, the requirements of s. 232 are most usefully described as comprising two elements, one objective and the other subjective. As Cory J. for the majority of the Court put it in *Thibert*:

> First, there must be a wrongful act or insult of such a nature that it is sufficient to deprive an ordinary person of the power of self-control as the objective element. Second, the subjective element requires that the accused act upon that insult on the sudden and before there was time for his passion to cool. [Emphasis in original deleted; para. 4.]

[24] I will review each element in turn.

2.2.1 The Objective Element: A Wrongful Act or Insult Sufficient to Deprive an Ordinary Person of the Power of Self-Control

[25] For the purpose of discussion, the objective element may be viewed as two-fold: (1) there must be a wrongful act or insult; and (2) the wrongful act or insult must be sufficient to deprive an ordinary person of the power of self-control.

[26] While the concepts "wrongful act" and "insult" are not defined, the following limitation is set out in s. 232(3):

> 232. ...
>
> > (3) For the purposes of this section, the questions
> >
> > > (a) whether a particular wrongful act or insult amounted to provocation, and
> > > (b) whether the accused was deprived of the power of self-control by the provocation that he alleges he received,
> >
> > are questions of fact, but no one shall be deemed to have given provocation to another by doing anything that he had a legal right to do, or by doing anything that the accused incited him to do in order to provide the accused with an excuse for causing death or bodily harm to any human being.

The second branch of s. 232(3) is not at issue in this case and I do not propose to discuss the limitation on the defence in circumstances where the accused himself incites the act of provocation with a view to providing himself with an excuse for committing the offence. The "legal right" limitation on the defence, however, merits further discussion in the context of this case.

[27] It is well established that the phrase "legal right" does not include all conduct not specifically prohibited by law. For example, the fact that a person may not be subject to legal liability for an insult directed at the accused does not mean that he or she has the "legal right" to make the insult within the meaning of s. 232(3) and that provocation is not open to the accused. To require that an insult be specifically prohibited by law would effectively render the word "insult" under s. 232(2) redundant, as any such "insult" would necessarily be a "wrongful act." The phrase "legal right" has been defined, rather, as meaning a right which is sanctioned by law, such as a sheriff proceeding to execute a legal warrant, or a person acting in justified self-defence (*Thibert*, at para. 29, citing *R. v. Haight* (1976), 30 C.C.C. (2d) 168 (Ont. C.A.), at p. 175, and *R. v. Galgay*, [1972] 2 O.R. 630 (C.A.), at p. 649). Interpreted in this manner, the notion of legal right serves to carve out from the ambit of s. 232 legally sanctioned conduct which otherwise could amount in fact, to an "insult."

[28] There has been academic criticism of this approach. Professor Roach argues, for example, that the concept of legal right could be rethought in the context of domestic violence. He writes: "It could be argued that people have a legal right to leave relationships and even to make disparaging comments about ex-partners. The Court's continued refusal to recognize this broader interpretation of a legal right could deny women the equal protection and benefit of the law" (p. 359).

[29] In my view, these concerns, while legitimate, are better addressed at the stage when the gravity of the "insult" is objectively measured as against the ordinary person standard. In other words, while one spouse undoubtedly has a legal right to leave his or her partner, in some circumstances the means by which that spouse communicates this decision may amount *in fact* to an "insult," within the ordinary meaning of the word. However, to be recognized *at law*, the insult must be of sufficient gravity to cause a loss of self-control, as objectively determined. The fact that the victim has the "legal right," in the broad sense of the term, to leave the relationship is an important consideration in the assessment of this objective standard.

[30] The "ordinary person," as a legal concept, has generally been assimilated in the case law to the well-known "reasonable person" and the two terms are often used interchangeably: e.g., *Hill*, at p. 331. While I believe that the two fictional entities share the same attributes, at first blush some may question this as a logical inconsistency, given that a "reasonable" person would not commit culpable homicide in the first place. Indeed, "reasonableness" often defines the standard of conduct which is expected at law, and conduct which meets this standard, as a general rule, does not attract legal liability. The inconsistency is resolved when it is recalled that the defence is only a partial one, and that the defendant, even if successful, will still be guilty of manslaughter. The use of the term "ordinary person" therefore reflects the normative dimensions of the defence; that is, behaviour which comports with contemporary society's norms and values will attract the law's compassion. Meeting the standard, however, will only provide a *partial* defence. In this context, it seems to me that the label "ordinary person" is more suitable and this may explain Parliament's choice of words. Cory J. for the majority of the Court in *Thibert* explained how the ordinary person standard should be interpreted:

> Yet, I think the objective element should be taken as an attempt to weigh in the balance those very human frailties which sometimes lead people to act irrationally and impulsively against the need to protect society by discouraging acts of homicidal violence. [para. 4]

[31] Applying this objective standard has not been without difficulty. A central concern has been the extent to which the accused's personal characteristics and circumstances should be considered when applying the "ordinary person" test. Traditionally, Canadian courts, endorsing the approach of their English counterparts, adopted a restrictive approach, prohibiting any reference to the accused's characteristics or circumstances (*Bedder v. Director of Public Prosecutions*, [1954] 1 W.L.R. 1119 (H.L.); *Salamon v. The Queen*, [1959] S.C.R. 404; *Wright v. The Queen*, [1969] S.C.R. 335). However, this approach required the court to completely ignore relevant contextual circumstances in making its determinations.

[32] Recognizing this deficiency, a broader approach was eventually adopted in conceptualizing the "ordinary person" so as to account for some, but not all, of the individual characteristics of the accused. As Dickson C.J. explained in *Hill*, this more flexible approach is essentially a matter of common sense:

... the "collective good sense" of the jury will naturally lead it to ascribe to the ordinary person any general characteristics relevant to the provocation in question. For example, if the provocation is a racial slur, the jury will think of an ordinary person with the racial background that forms the substance of the insult. To this extent, particular characteristics will be ascribed to the ordinary person. Indeed, it would be impossible to conceptualize a sexless or ageless ordinary person. Features such as sex, age, or race, do not detract from a person's characterization as ordinary. Thus particular characteristics that are not peculiar or idiosyncratic can be ascribed to an ordinary person *without subverting the logic of the objective test of provocation.* [Emphasis added; p. 331.]

[33] I emphasize the words of caution that, in adopting this more flexible approach, care must be taken not to subvert the logic of the objective test. Indeed, if all of the accused's characteristics are taken into account, the ordinary person *becomes* the accused. As Dickson C.J. noted, this approach would lead to the anomalous result that "[a] well-tempered, reasonable person would not be entitled to benefit from the provocation defence ... while an ill-tempered or exceptionally excitable person would find his or her culpability mitigated by provocation and would be guilty only of manslaughter" (p. 324).

[34] Further, an individualized approach ignores the cardinal principle that criminal law is concerned with setting standards of human behaviour. As Dickson C.J. put it: "It is society's concern that reasonable and non-violent behaviour be encouraged that prompts the law to endorse the objective standard" (p. 324). Similarly, McIntyre J. in concurring reasons expanded upon this purpose, stating:

> The law fixes a standard for all which must be met before reliance may be placed on the provocation defence. Everyone, whatever his or her idiosyncrasies, is expected to observe that standard. It is not every insult or injury that will be sufficient to relieve a person from what would otherwise be murder. The "ordinary person" standard is adopted to fix the degree of self-control and restraint expected of all in society. [p. 336]

It follows that the ordinary person standard must be informed by contemporary norms of behaviour, including fundamental values such as the commitment to equality provided for in the *Canadian Charter of Rights and Freedoms*. For example, it would be appropriate to ascribe to the ordinary person relevant racial characteristics if the accused were the recipient of a racial slur, but it would not be appropriate to ascribe to the ordinary person the characteristic of being homophobic if the accused were the recipient of a homosexual advance. Similarly, there can be no place in this objective standard for antiquated beliefs such as "adultery is the highest invasion of property" (*Mawgridge*, at p. 1115), nor indeed for any form of killing based on such inappropriate conceptualizations of "honour."

[35] Finally, the particular circumstances in which the accused finds himself will also be relevant in determining the appropriate standard against which to measure the accused's conduct. This is also a matter of common sense, as it would be impossible to conceptualize how the ordinary person might be expected to react without considering the relevant context. Again here, however, care must be taken not to "subver[t] the logic of the objective [inquiry]" and assimilate circumstances that are peculiar to the individual accused into the objective standard (*Hill*, at p. 331). For example, in determining the appropriate objective standard, it will be relevant for the trier of fact to know that the alleged provocation occurred in circumstances where the deceased was wrongfully firing the

accused from his long-term employment. This context is necessary to set the appropriate standard. But the standard does not vary depending on the accused's peculiar relationship or particular feelings about his employer or his employment. Personal circumstances may be relevant to determining whether the accused was in fact provoked—the subjective element of the defence—but they do not shift the ordinary person standard to suit the individual accused. In other words, there is an important distinction between contextualizing the objective standard, which is necessary and proper, and individualizing it, which only serves to defeat its purpose.

2.2.2 The Subjective Element: The Provocation Must Have Caused the Accused to Lose Self-Control and Act While out of Control

[36] Once it is established that the wrongful act or insult was sufficient to deprive an ordinary person of the power of self-control, the inquiry turns to a consideration of the subjective element of the defence. The subjective element can also be usefully described as two-fold: (1) the accused must have acted in response to the provocation; and (2) on the sudden before there was time for his or her passion to cool.

[37] The inquiry into whether the accused was in fact acting in response to the provocation focuses on the accused's subjective perceptions of the circumstances, including what the accused believed, intended or knew. In other words, the accused must have killed because he was provoked and not because the provocation existed (*R. v. Faid*, [1983] 1 S.C.R. 265, at p. 277, citing Professor G. L. Williams in his *Textbook of Criminal Law* (1978), at p. 480).

[38] The requirement of suddenness was introduced into the defence as a way of distinguishing a response taken in vengeance from one that was provoked. Therefore, suddenness applies to both the act of provocation and the accused's reaction to it. The wrongful act or insult must itself be sudden, in the sense that it "must strike upon a mind unprepared for it, that it must make an unexpected impact that takes the understanding by surprise and sets the passions aflame" (*R. v. Tripodi*, [1955] S.C.R. 438, at p. 443). Further, the intentional killing must have been committed by the accused "before there was time for his passion to cool": s. 232(2) of the *Criminal Code*.

2.3 The Role of the Judge and Jury

[39] As noted earlier, s. 232(3) provides that determining whether a particular wrongful act or insult amounted to provocation and whether the accused was deprived of the power of self-control by the provocation are questions of fact. Consistent with the wording of this provision, it remains with the jury, and not the trial judge, to weigh the evidence in order to determine whether the Crown has discharged its burden of disproving that the killing was caused by provocation (*R. v. Fontaine*, 2004 SCC 27, [2004] 1 S.C.R. 702, at para. 56, citing *R. v. Schwartz*, [1988] 2 S.C.R. 443).

[40] However, the interpretation of a legal standard (the elements of the defence) and the determination of whether there is an air of reality to a defence constitute questions of law, reviewable on a standard of correctness. The term "air of reality" refers to the inquiry into whether there is an evidential foundation for a defence. Statements that there is or is not an air of reality express a legal conclusion about the presence or absence of an evidential foundation for a defence: *R. v. Cinous*, 2002 SCC 29, [2002] 2 S.C.R. 3, at

paras. 50 and 55; *R. v. Osolin*, [1993] 4 S.C.R. 595, at p. 682; *Parnerkar v. The Queen*, [1974] S.C.R. 449, at p. 461. Thus, this inquiry is not a review of the trial judge's assessment of the evidence but of the judge's legal conclusions in relation to the defence of provocation: *R. v. Ewanchuk*, [1999] 1 S.C.R. 330, at para. 21.

[41] In a jury trial, the judge is the gatekeeper and judge of the law and must therefore put the defence to the jury only where there is evidence upon which a "reasonable jury acting judicially" could find that the defence succeeds (*Faid*, at p. 278). For the defence to succeed, the jury must have a reasonable doubt about whether each of the elements of provocation was present. This necessarily requires that there be a sufficient evidential basis in respect of each component of the defence before it is left to the jury: the evidence must be reasonably capable of supporting the inferences necessary to make out the defence before there is an air of reality to the defence (*Fontaine*, at para. 56; *R. v. Reddick*, [1991] 1 S.C.R. 1086, at p. 1088, citing *Pappajohn v. The Queen*, [1980] 2 S.C.R. 120, at p. 133). In a trial by judge alone, the trial judge must instruct himself or herself accordingly. Therefore, the trial judge errs in law if he or she gives effect to the defence of provocation in circumstances where the defence should not have been left to a jury, had the accused been tried by a jury.

3. Application to the Case

[42] As stated at the outset, I agree with the Court of Appeal that there was no air of reality to the defence of provocation in this case. The conduct in question does not amount to an "insult"; nor does it meet the requirement of suddenness.

[43] As for the objective element of the defence, the appellant does not suggest that he was provoked by a "wrongful act." Rather, his contention is that, in the context of his relationship with Ms. Duong, his discovery of her sexual involvement with Mr. An Tran amounted to an insult at law. The facts do not support this contention.

[44] First, it is difficult to see how the conduct of Ms. Duong and Mr. An Tran could constitute an insult on any ordinary meaning of the word. The general meaning of the noun "insult" as defined in the *Shorter Oxford English Dictionary on Historical Principles* (6th ed. 2007), vol. 1, at p. 1400, is "[a]n act or the action of attacking; (an) attack, (an) assault." Likewise, the action of insulting means to "[s]how arrogance or scorn; boast, exult, esp. insolently or contemptuously ... . Treat with scornful abuse; subject to indignity; ... offend the modesty or self-respect of." Here, Ms. Duong and Mr. An Tran were alone in the privacy of her bedroom, neither wanting nor expecting the appellant to show up. In these circumstances, I agree with Hunt J.A. that "[n]othing done by the complainant or the victim comes close to meeting the definition of insult. Their behaviour was not only lawful, it was discreet and private and entirely passive vis-à-vis the [appellant]. They took pains to keep their relationship hidden ... . Their behaviour came to his attention only because he gained access to the building by falsely saying he was there to pick up his mail" (para. 17).

[45] Further, there was nothing sudden about the discovery. The appellant is the one whose appearance came as a total surprise to Ms. Duong and Mr. An Tran, not the other way around. On the factual findings made by the trial judge, the appellant had not only suspected his wife's relationship with another man, but he made deliberate attempts to surveillance her activity, including by eavesdropping on her conversations. The night

before the tragic events, the appellant told his godmother that he now knew who the man was whom his wife was seeing (trial judge's reasons, at p. 26). Therefore, it cannot be said that his discovery, upon entering Ms. Duong's bedroom unannounced and uninvited, "str[uck] upon a mind unprepared for it."

[46] Finally, I also agree with Watson J.A. that on "the subjective side of the question," the trial judge's findings of "[o]utward excitement and anger" could not be decisive (para. 76). The appellant did not testify about his state of mind. The evidence shows, as Watson J.A. notes, that he

> was measuring his actions on what he was saying and doing. The trial judge should have addressed whether he could have regained his self control by the time he went into the living room and finished off the victim—not merely whether he was still angry and excited. The trial judge found his anger continued but she failed to direct herself to consider whether the continuation of his anger amounted to a continuing lack of the power of self control without an opportunity to recover it. [para. 76]

As Watson J.A. rightly concluded, "there was on the trial judge's fact findings no air of reality to his acting on the sudden at the time of the killing" (para. 77).

4. Disposition

[47] The Court of Appeal properly substituted a conviction for second degree murder and returned the matter to the trial court for sentencing. As Watson J.A. stated: "In light of the law, and of the trial judge's findings of fact, and of the overwhelming evidence, a conviction for murder was unavoidable" (para. 81). I would dismiss the appeal.

With the *Tran* decision, the trend at the Supreme Court of Canada seems to have been a narrowing in the defence of provocation. This narrowing has occurred, in large measure, through judgments in which the Court held that there was no "air of reality" to the defence. Consider, for example, the following case.

R v Mayuran
Supreme Court of Canada
2012 SCC 31, [2012] 2 SCR 162

ABELLA J:

[1] Suganthini Mayuran (Suganthini) immigrated to Canada from Sri Lanka in 2004. She had married Mayuran Thangarajah (Mayuran) in an arranged marriage earlier that year. When she arrived in Canada, she moved into an apartment in Montréal with her husband, his father, his mother, his younger sister, his brother Manchutan and Manchutan's wife Dayani.

[2] On December 3, 2004, Suganthini was arrested for the murder of her sister-in-law Dayani. Dayani had been stabbed 45 times.

[3] The Crown's case at the jury trial was that Suganthini was alone in the apartment with Dayani at the time of death and therefore had the exclusive opportunity to commit

the offence. The Crown relied on the testimony of the Thangarajah family to establish its case, supported by independent evidence corroborating their story and linking Suganthini to the murder.

$\cdots$

[7] Of particular relevance to this appeal, Suganthini's husband Mayuran and her mother-in-law testified that while Suganthini was in prison, she confessed to the murder in several telephone conversations with them. She told them she killed Dayani because Dayani had ridiculed her about her learning ability and her level of education. They said that a few phone calls later, however, Suganthini denied having killed Dayani. Her newer version was that she had been threatened by the real murderer, whose name she would not reveal.

$\cdots$

[10] An autopsy found 45 stab wounds in Dayani's body. The pathologist, Dr. André Lauzon, testified that given their lack of depth, the wounds had likely been inflicted by a knife with a broken tip. A knife with a broken tip was in fact found at the scene, and François Julien, the DNA expert called by the Crown, testified that he found both Dayani's and Suganthini's blood on the blade of the knife. Only Suganthini's DNA was found on the handle. Dr. Lauzon also said that the cuts Suganthini received on her hand were consistent with an injury that could have been caused by stabbing someone.

$\cdots$

[18] The primary issue in this appeal is whether the Court of Appeal erred in concluding that there was a sufficient evidentiary foundation for the defence of provocation to have been put to the jury notwithstanding that it was not raised by the defence at trial.

$\cdots$

[20] This Court has held that a defence should only be put to the jury if it has an "air of reality" (*R. v. Cinous*, [2002] 2 S.C.R. 3, at para. 50). The air of reality test imposes two duties on the trial judge: to "put to the jury all defences that arise on the facts, whether or not they have been specifically raised by an accused"; and "to keep from the jury defences lacking an evidential foundation" (*Cinous*, at para. 51). Whether a defence arises on the evidence of the accused or of the Crown, the trial judge must put the defence to the jury if it has an air of reality (*Cinous*, at para. 53; *R. v. Osolin*, [1993] 4 S.C.R. 595).

[21] In determining whether a defence has an air of reality, there must be an examination into the sufficiency of the evidence. It is not enough for there to be "some evidence" supporting the defence (*Cinous*, at para. 83). The test is "whether there is (1) evidence (2) upon which a properly instructed jury acting reasonably could acquit if it believed the evidence to be true" (*Cinous*, at para. 65). For defences that rely on indirect evidence or defences like provocation that include an objective reasonableness component, the trial judge must examine the "field of factual inferences" that can reasonably be drawn from the evidence (*Cinous*, at para. 91).

[22] The relationship between the air of reality and the defence of provocation was recently considered by this Court in *R v. Tran*, [2010] 3 S.C.R. 350, where Charron J. explained that

[f]or the defence to succeed, the jury must have a reasonable doubt about whether each of the elements of provocation was present. This necessarily requires that there be a sufficient evidential basis in respect of each component of the defence before it is left to the jury: the

evidence must be reasonably capable of supporting the inferences necessary to make out the defence before there is an air of reality to the defence ... . [para. 41]

• • •

[24] In order for the defence of provocation to have an air of reality in this case, the evidence must be capable of giving rise to a reasonable doubt that an ordinary person in Suganthini's circumstances would be deprived of the power of self-control when hearing insults about his or her level of education. In my respectful opinion, that conclusion is simply untenable.

[25] The majority in the Court of Appeal found that the defence of provocation had an air of reality based on the alleged prison conversation in which Suganthini confessed that she killed Dayani because she had made fun of her. The fact that there were 45 stab wounds, the court concluded, supported the inference that the murder had "occurred in the heat of passion caused by sudden provocation." But, the majority did not in any way address whether the objective element of the defence was met.

• • •

[30] ... Suganthini argued that her particular circumstances were relevant in assessing her reaction, including the fact that she was a new immigrant who was attempting to integrate into the community as quickly as possible, which heightened her sensitivity to insults relating to her level of education and ability to learn. These considerations, however, while relevant, do not transform her conduct into an act that an ordinary person would have committed. As Charron J. noted in *Tran*, this would "individualize" the objective element of the test and defeat its purpose.

[31] Based on this record, a properly instructed jury could not conclude that an ordinary person in Suganthini's circumstances would be deprived of self-control when "scolded" about her level of education to such a degree that she would stab the person 45 times in a responsive rage. This, it seems to me, has absolutely no air of reality. There was, as a result, no duty on the trial judge to instruct the jury on the defence of provocation.

• • •

[51] I would allow the appeal and restore the conviction.

For an excellent critical commentary on the air of reality test as articulated in *Mayuran*, see G Ferguson, "Provocation: Air of Reality and the Ordinary Person Test" (2012) 94 CR (6th) 32. Ferguson also argues that the Court was wrong to conclude that the accused's status as a new immigrant should not be factored into the ordinary person test because to do so "'would individualize' the objective element of the test and defeat its purpose" (at para 30). He argues that, rather than a "peculiar and idiosyncratic" characteristic, "[i]t is the type of circumstance that should be considered relevant in determining whether an ordinary, newly arrived immigrant woman facing those same circumstances of cultural and economic isolation might lose the power of self-control if ridiculed about her ability to learn and fit in to her new country" (at para 43). Do you agree?

The Supreme Court similarly held that there was no air of reality to the defence of provocation in *R v Cairney*, 2013 SCC 55, [2013] 3 SCR 420 and *R v Pappas*, 2013 SCC 56, [2013] 3 SCR 452. In *Cairney*, the accused was living with the deceased, Ferguson, and Ferguson's common law spouse, Rosenthal. Rosenthal was also the accused's cousin. On the day in question, the three were together when Ferguson became angry with Rosenthal and started to verbally abuse her. Cairney heard Ferguson tell Rosenthal "that if her back had not been sore, he would have thrown her across the kitchen" (at para 4). Cairney left the room, retrieved a loaded shotgun, and came back with the intention of scaring Ferguson to deter future mistreatment of Rosenthal. He walked up to Ferguson, smashed the phone with the shotgun, and began to lecture Ferguson on his abuse of Rosenthal. Ferguson responded by saying, "What are you gonna do, shoot me? You don't have the guts to shoot me," and then turned to leave the apartment. Cairney called after Ferguson, at which point the deceased responded with the alleged provocation: "Fuck you, you goof. This is none of your business, I'll do with [Rosenthal] whatever I want." He then left the apartment, at which point Cairney followed him into the stairwell and shot him. The trial judge left the defence of provocation with the jury, which acquitted Cairney of second-degree murder and convicted him of manslaughter. The Court of Appeal held that there was no air of reality to the defence and ordered a new trial. The Crown appealed to the Supreme Court of Canada. Chief Justice McLachlin, writing for a majority of the Court (Abella and Fish JJ dissenting), held that although there is no hard-and-fast rule that provocation is unavailable when the accused initiates or invites the provocative act or insult (so-called self-induced provocation), in these circumstances there was no air of reality to the defence of provocation. She reasoned as follows: "An ordinary person who seeks to extract a promise at gunpoint would not be surprised if the person confronted rebuffs the overture, in words like those used by the victim here. Ferguson's response fell within a range of predictable responses. There is nothing on the record to support the element of sudden shock required to cause an ordinary person to lose self-control" (at para 61).

In *Pappas*, the accused claimed that the deceased, Kullman, had been extorting money from him for approximately 18 months. The threats included revealing details of Pappas' offshore investments to the tax authorities and threatening to harm Pappas' mother if he stopped paying or went to the police. Pappas "decided that he had had enough" (at para 4) and went to Kullman's condominium with a 9mm handgun loaded with hollow-point bullets. He told the police that he brought the gun only to intimidate Kullman; on the other hand, he also explained that he selected the ammunition because it was particularly lethal. At the condominium he appealed to Kullman to stop the extortion, to which the deceased replied, "Buddy, why the fuck should I? You're the best cash out I have and I got great fucking insurance" (at para 5). Pappas, who understood the reference to "insurance" as a threat against his mother, claimed that at this point he "snapped." He pulled out the gun and shot Kullman twice in the back and then again in the head at close range. The trial judge left the defence of provocation with the jury, which nevertheless found Pappas guilty of second-degree murder. Pappas appealed to the Court of Appeal, and subsequently to the Supreme Court, on the basis of errors in the trial judge's jury instruction on provocation. Chief Justice McLachlin, writing for a majority of the Court, held that there was no air of reality to the defence of provocation because there was no evidence supporting the "suddenness" requirement. Although the killing itself was sudden,

> [t]he contention that Pappas was caught unprepared by Kullman's comments is outside the range of reasonable inferences that can be drawn from [the] evidence. ... Accepting Pappas' evidence that he "snapped" as true, this was not the result of a sudden insult striking an unprepared mind. It was simply the final stage of doing what he had come to do—killing Kullman if that was necessary to stop the extortion and threats. [para 41]

For academic commentary voicing concern about the narrowing of the defence of provocation, see D Stuart, "The Supreme Court Strangles the Defence of Provocation" (2014) 5 CR (7th) 249 and P Sankoff, "R v Cairney: Predictable Responses and the Shrinking Defence of Provocation" (2014) 5 CR (7th) 254.

III. PROVOCATION AND INTENT

This last section considers the relationship between the partial defence of provocation and the intent for murder in s 229(a) of the *Criminal Code* (see Chapter 13). The central issue is whether provocation is a defence that vitiates or compromises the intent for murder, or whether it operates outside the scope of the positive fault requirements for murder as an independent, or "free-standing," excuse.

In the following case, the accused argued that the objective element of the provocation defence conflicted with the constitutional principle that the *mens rea* for murder must be subjective. The Ontario Court of Appeal's answer turns on properly understanding the relationship between provocation and intent.

R v Cameron
Ontario Court of Appeal
(1992), 71 CCC (3d) 272

DOHERTY JA: The appellant was convicted of second degree murder. He was sentenced to life imprisonment without eligibility for parole for 10 years. He appeals his conviction alleging that the statutory defence of provocation set out in s. 232 of the *Criminal Code* contravenes ss. 7 and 11(d) of the *Canadian Charter of Rights and Freedoms*. ...

I. The Constitutional Challenge

The appellant contends that the "defence of provocation operates by negativing an essential element of the *mens rea* for murder." He goes on to argue that as provocation is premised in part on an objective standard, the statutory definition of provocation cannot stand in light of the authorities which hold that liability for murder cannot be determined by reference to an objective fault standard: see *R. v. Martineau* (1990), 58 C.C.C. (3d) 353 (S.C.C.).

The argument misconceives the effect of s. 232. The section does not detract from or negative the fault requirement for murder, but serves as a partial excuse for those who commit what would be murder but for the existence of the partial defence created by s. 232. As the opening words of s. 232 plainly indicate, the defence only need be considered where the Crown has proved beyond a reasonable doubt that the accused committed murder: see *R. v. Campbell* (1977), 38 C.C.C. (2d) 6 at p. 15; *R. v. Oickle* (1984), 11 C.C.C. (3d) 180 at p. 190 (S.C. App. Div.).

The statutory defence of provocation does not detract from the *mens rea* required to establish murder, but rather, where applicable, serves to reduce homicides committed with the *mens rea* necessary to establish murder to manslaughter.

The appellant also argues that, even if the statutory defence of provocation stands apart from the *mens rea* required for murder, ss. 7 and 11(d) of the Charter render the section inoperative in so far as it imposes an objective standard on the availability of the defence. He argues that for constitutional purposes there could be no distinction between a statutory provision which imposes liability for murder on an objective basis (e.g., s. 230(d)) and a statutory provision like s. 232 which limits the availability of a defence to murder according to an objective criterion.

I disagree. The former imposes liability in the absence of a constitutionally mandated minimum level of fault. The latter provides a partial excuse despite the existence of the constitutionally required level of fault. Section 232 does not impose liability where subjective fault does not exist but reduces the liability even when that fault exists.

The objective component of the statutory defence of provocation serves a valid societal purpose (see *R. v. Hill* (1986), 25 C.C.C. (3d) 322 at pp. 330-1), and cannot be said to be contrary to the principles of fundamental justice.

Resort to s. 11(d) of the Charter does not assist the appellant. Section 232 does not place any burden of proof on an accused to disprove anything essential to the establishing of his culpability. Indeed, the onus is on the Crown to negate provocation beyond a reasonable doubt: *Linney v. The Queen* (1977), 32 C.C.C. (2d) 294 (S.C.C.). Nor, for the reasons set out above, does s. 232 modify the statutory definition of murder so as to eliminate an element of the offence required by s. 7 of the Charter.

The constitutional argument fails.

In the following decision, the Supreme Court of Canada confirmed this understanding of the relationship between provocation and *mens rea*. The case again underscores the gendered dimensions of the law of provocation, and Chief Justice McLachlin's decision is illuminating in its specific attention to the role of anger in the law of provocation and intent.

R v Parent
Supreme Court of Canada
2001 SCC 30, [2001] 1 SCR 761

McLACHLIN CJ:

[1] On September 24, 1996, the respondent, Réjean Parent, shot and killed his estranged wife. She had initiated divorce proceedings four years earlier and they were involved in litigation over the division of their assets, some of which were held in a corporation. In the meantime, their financial situation deteriorated, to the point that Mr. Parent's shares were seized and put up for sale. The wife attended the sale, allegedly intending to buy the shares. Mr. Parent also attended. He carried a loaded gun with a locked security catch in his pocket. There, she suggested they speak and they retired into a nearby room. Shortly after, shots were heard. Mr. Parent had shot his wife six times. She died from the wounds later that night.

[2] Mr. Parent was charged with first degree murder. At trial, he testified that when they proceeded to the room his wife had said, in effect: "I told you that I would wipe you out completely." He then felt a hot flush rising and shot. He said he "didn't know what [he] was doing any more" and was aiming in front of him. He said he did not intend to kill his

wife. After doing so, he left the building and spent the afternoon in a strip club before giving himself up to police that evening.

[3] At trial, Mr. Parent argued that the verdict should be reduced to manslaughter on the basis of lack of criminal intent or provocation. The jury found him guilty of manslaughter. He was sentenced to 16 years' imprisonment, and a lifetime prohibition on possessing firearms, ammunition and explosives. ...

[4] The Crown appealed the verdict of manslaughter, and Parent appealed the sentence. The Quebec Court of Appeal dismissed the appeal from the verdict without reasons, but in separate proceedings ((1999), 142 C.C.C. (3d) 82) reduced the sentence to six years' imprisonment, after giving Mr. Parent credit of two years for time served. In this Court, the appellant raised one point only: that the judge had erred in his instructions to the jury on the effect of anger, creating a "defence of anger" (défense de colère) distinct from the defence of provocation. The respondent, for his part, argued that any difficulties in the judge's directions to the jury were cleared up in his redirection on provocation in answer to jury questions and that the jury properly convicted the accused of manslaughter on the basis of provocation.

[5] Two issues are raised: (1) whether the trial judge erred in his charge to the jury on intention, and (2) if so, whether that error was cured by the redirection. I conclude that the trial judge erred in his direction on intention and that the recharge did not eliminate the possibility that this error led the jury wrongly to find the respondent guilty of manslaughter. Accordingly, the conviction must be set aside and a new trial ordered.

1. Did the Trial Judge Err in His Charge to the Jury on Intention?

[6] The jury had three possible offences before it: first degree murder, second degree murder and manslaughter. All three offences require proof of an act of killing (*actus reus*) and the corresponding criminal intention (*mens rea*). In relation to murder, the defence of provocation does not eliminate the need for proof of intention to kill, but operates as an excuse that has the effect of reducing murder to manslaughter.

[7] The Crown argues that the trial judge erred in suggesting that anger is capable of negating the intention to kill and that the jury could reduce the offence to manslaughter on this basis. More particularly, the Crown suggests that the judge's directions wrongly treated anger as a matter that could negate the criminal intent or *mens rea* of the offence; wrongly suggested that negation of intent can reduce the offence to manslaughter; and wrongly left open the suggestion that anger alone can establish provocation, when in fact other requirements must be met pursuant to s. 232 of the *Criminal Code*, R.S.C. 1985, c. C-46. The gravamen of the Crown's submission is that the trial judge's direction on intention was confusing and wrong and left it open to the jury to convict the accused of manslaughter, not on the basis of provocation (which the trial judge correctly defined), but on the erroneous basis that a high degree of anger short of provocation, as defined in law, could negate the criminal intent or *mens rea* of the offence.

[8] The Crown objects to the portions of the jury charge in which the trial judge stated that the jury must take into account [TRANSLATION] "evidence surrounding the defence of provocation raised by the accused" in determining the accused's intent to kill. The Crown also objects to the trial judge's treatment of *mens rea* in the following passages:

For example, murder may be reduced to manslaughter where a person's state of mind is affected by alcohol consumption, drug consumption or where a person's state of mind is obscured or diminished by an outside force, by an incident like, for example, *a fit of anger*.

You no doubt appreciate that we are not talking about an arbitrary reduction.

In other words, it is not sufficient for a person to simply say "I was drinking" or "I took some drugs" or "I was really angry."

That alone, that's not enough, and all that always depends on the circumstances. It always depends on the nature of the facts at issue, of external influences, or outside influences capable of affecting one's state of mind.

It depends on the nature of the fact at issue, of its importance, its seriousness, its intensity in relation to the action that was taken by the person who committed the crime, all the while taking into account the evidence as a whole and all the circumstances.

So, you must look at the accused's state of mind when he killed Suzanne Bédard, you look at the entire evidence, including the elements surrounding the provocation defence with a view to determining whether he acted with the criminal intention that I defined earlier.

Here, the accused, when he testified, described to you his state of mind when Suzanne Bédard said the words in question.

You must then decide if this incident was sufficiently serious, important, intense so as to cause him to lose his faculties to the point of reducing the crime of murder to manslaughter.

You will ask yourselves if his state of mind was affected, diminished, and if so, the intensity, the degree to which, taking into account all the circumstances at the time when he did what he did.

To reduce murder to manslaughter, you must come to the conclusion that the influence of the events that occurred was *strong enough, important enough, intense enough to cause the accused to not know or not want what he was doing by reason of his state of mind, that his faculties were too diminished to fully assess the situation, or that raise a reasonable doubt in his favour, in this respect.* [Emphasis added.]

[9] The Crown argues that this passage creates a halfway house defence of anger, between non-mental disorder automatism and provocation. I agree. This passage suggests that anger, if sufficiently serious or intense, but not amounting to the defence of provocation, may reduce murder to manslaughter. It also suggests that anger, if sufficiently intense, may negate the criminal intention for murder. These connected propositions are not legally correct. Intense anger alone is insufficient to reduce murder to manslaughter.

[10] The passage cited overstates the effect of anger. Anger can play a role in reducing murder to manslaughter in connection with the defence of provocation. Anger is not a stand-alone defence. It may form part of the defence of provocation when all the requirements of that defence are met: (1) a wrongful act or insult that would have caused an ordinary person to be deprived of his or her self-control; (2) which is sudden and unexpected; (3) which in fact caused the accused to act in anger; (4) before having recovered his or her normal control: *R. v. Thibert*, [1996] 1 S.C.R. 37. Again, anger conceivably could, in extreme circumstances, cause someone to enter a state of automatism in which that person does not know what he or she is doing, thus negating the voluntary component of the *actus reus*: *R. v. Stone*, [1999] 2 S.C.R. 290. However, the accused did not assert this defence. In any event, the defence if successful would result in acquittal, not reduction to manslaughter.

[11] So it seems clear that the trial judge misdirected the jury on the effect of anger in relation to manslaughter. His directions left it open to the jury to find the accused guilty of manslaughter, on the basis of the anger felt by the accused, even if they concluded that the conditions required for the defence of provocation were not met. The directions raise the possibility that the jury's verdict of manslaughter may have been based on erroneous legal principles, unless they were corrected in the recharge to the jury. ...

3. Conclusion

[18] The trial judge erred in his charge to the jury on the effect of anger on criminal intent or *mens rea* and its relationship to manslaughter. This error was not corrected on the recharge and we cannot infer from the way the trial proceeded that the jury's verdict of manslaughter was not based on the erroneous initial direction. It follows that the conviction for manslaughter must be set aside and a new trial directed.

[19] As indicated earlier, the Crown in this appeal, relied solely on the trial judge's misdirections on anger and criminal intent. It is therefore unnecessary to comment further on the applicability of the defence of provocation as it may be tendered at the new trial. It will be for the judge on the new trial to determine whether, on the evidence there presented, the defence of provocation should be put to the jury.

[20] I would allow the appeal and direct a new trial on second degree murder.

For commentaries on this case, see GT Trotter, "Provocation, Anger and the Intent for Murder: A Comment on R v Parent" (2002) 47 McGill LJ 669 and J Klineberg, "Anger and Intent for Murder: The Supreme Court Decision in R v Parent" (2003) 41 Osgoode Hall LJ 37.

Interestingly, in a recent three-paragraph judgment in *R v Bouchard*, 2014 SCC 64, the Supreme Court affirmed an Ontario Court of Appeal judgment that had ordered a new trial on the basis that the trial judge's instruction had not clearly indicated that provocation could be relevant to the intent to murder under s 229(a), even if it did not qualify as a partial defence under s 232. Doherty JA, for the majority in the Ontario Court of Appeal, stated:

> [54] The appellant's evidence that Mr. Nicholson kissed him and said "I love you" and his evidence describing his reaction to Mr. Nicholson's actions were relevant both to the *mens rea* issue and to the statutory defence of provocation. The evidence was relevant to the *mens rea* issue because the appellant testified that the actions of Mr. Nicholson caused him to "lose it" and assault Mr. Nicholson without regard to the consequences of his actions. The jury had to consider that evidence in determining whether the Crown had proved beyond a reasonable doubt that the appellant intended to kill Mr. Nicholson or foresaw his death as the probable consequence of the assault.
>
>   . . .
>
> [60] The statutory definition of provocation in s. 232 has no application when considering the impact of a deceased's conduct on an accused's state of mind for the purpose of determining whether the Crown has established the requisite *mens rea* ... .
>
> [61] The distinction between conduct of a deceased relevant to an accused's state of mind and conduct that may qualify as provocation under s. 232 is especially important where there is evidence of intoxication. To qualify as provocation under s. 232, the jury must be satisfied that the conduct was sufficient to deprive an ordinary person of self-control. In making that assessment,

the jury does not take into consideration the alcohol consumption of the particular accused, but instead looks at the hypothetical ordinary sober person's response to the alleged provocation: see *Hill*, at pp. 328-29. If the alleged provocation could not deprive an ordinary person of self-control, the conduct cannot meet the statutory definition of provocation.

[62] However, potentially provocative conduct that fails the ordinary person test and, there-fore, cannot qualify as provocation under s. 232, must still be considered by a jury in assessing whether an accused had the necessary *mens rea*. In the context of the *mens rea* inquiry, the accused's intoxication could potentially play a significant role in support of the claim that a deceased's conduct caused the accused to act without regard to the consequences and without the necessary *mens rea*.

This case recalls many of the same contextual issues raised in the first case extracted in this chapter, *R v Hill*. Specifically, it raises the risk of violent responses to same-sex sexual advances, where those reactions are informed by discriminatory beliefs. In *R v Tran*, the Supreme Court of Canada seemed to address this concern by holding that, given that the ordinary person standard should be informed by fundamental Charter values such as equality, "it would not be appropriate to ascribe to the ordinary person the characteristic of being homophobic if the accused were the recipient of a homosexual advance" (at para 34). Here, however, the focus on subjective *mens rea* means that a court does not need to ask itself whether "an ordinary person" would lose self-control, but only whether the accused had the subjective *mens rea* required for the offence charged.

ADDITIONAL READING

Colvin, E & S Anand. *Principles of Criminal Law*, 3rd ed (Toronto: Carswell, 2007) at 371-87.

Dressler, J. "Provocation: Partial Justification or Partial Excuse?" (1988) 51 Mod L Rev 487.

Forell, C. "Gender Equality, Social Values and Provocation Law in the United States, Canada, and Australia" (2006) 14 Am UJ Gender Soc Pol'y & L 27.

Klimchuk, D. "Outrage, Self-Control and Culpability" (1994) 44 UTLJ 441.

Manning, M & P Sankoff. *Manning, Mewett & Sankoff: Criminal Law*, 4th ed (Toronto: Lexis-Nexis, 2009) at 747-76.

Mousourakis, G. "Reason, Passion and Self-Control: Understanding the Moral Basis of the Provocation Defence" (2007) 28 RDUS 215.

Nourse, VF. "Passion's Progress: Modern Law Reform and the Provocation Defense" (1997) 106 Yale LJ 1331.

Quigley, T. "Battered Women and the Defence of Provocation" (1991) 55 Sask L Rev 223.

Roach, K. *Criminal Law*, 6th ed (Toronto: Irwin Law, 2015) ch 10.

Stuart, D. *Canadian Criminal Law*, 7th ed (Toronto: Carswell, 2014) at 580-99.

Trotter, GT. "Anger, Provocation and the Intent for Murder: A Comment on R v Parent" (2002) 47 McGill LJ 669.

CHAPTER FIFTEEN

Mental Disorder and Automatism

I. INTRODUCTION

The mental disorder defence has the potential to apply to an accused person whose psychiatric or developmental condition renders them unable to appreciate the nature and consequences of their actions or unable to know that their actions are wrong. Traditionally this defence was rarely raised in proceedings, because the consequence of its acceptance was automatic indefinite detention. Such detention was found by the Supreme Court in *R v Swain*, [1991] 1 SCR 933 to be an unjustified violation of ss 7 and 9 of the *Charter of Rights and Freedoms*. As Benjamin Berger identifies in the following extract, Parliament responded to *Swain* by amending the *Criminal Code* in relation to the disposition of an accused. However, in other important ways the mental disorder defence remains narrow and particular, failing to capture many aspects of psychiatric conditions that one might think would bear upon criminal responsibility.

BL Berger, "Mental Disorder and the Instability of Blame in Criminal Law"
in F Tanguay-Renaud & J Stribopoulos, eds, *Rethinking Criminal Law Theory:*
New Canadian Perspectives in the Philosophy of Domestic, Transnational, and
International Criminal Law
(Portland, Or: Hart, 2012) 117 at 117, 121, 131 (footnotes omitted)

The Canadian law of mental disorder was substantially revised in 1991 by means of a raft of legislative amendments to the Criminal Code. One feature of the new legislation was the shift in language of "insanity" to "mental disorder." No doubt the key change was in disposition. Rather than an accused being found not guilty by reason of insanity, at which point the accused would be held at the pleasure of the Lieutenant-Governor, an accused who is declared NCRMD [not criminally responsible by reason of mental disorder] is now moved through a disposition hearing before a review board comprised of legal and psychiatric experts who decide on the appropriate treatment and control options, a decision driven largely by assessments of dangerousness. ...

The words "a mental disorder" in s 16 of the Criminal Code are defined as "a disease of the mind" and the courts have given this concept an expansive construction. Courts have emphasized that reference to "a disease of the mind" is not a delegation to psychiatric authority—the term is a legal one, to be defined and applied by judges. ...

Consider the salient features of what we might call the "*M'Naghten* paradigm" as reflected in the Canadian test for mental disorder. First, and perhaps most prominent, is the emphasis that these tests place on the capacity for practical reasoning and cognition. ... This highly rational and narrowly cognitive approach to mental disorder excludes certain conditions that would appear to bear on our sense of the justice of attributing criminal responsibility. As commonly noted, the cognitive focus of the test excludes *volitional* impairments from the defence of mental disorder, as it does the issue of emotional appreciation. Furthermore, the threshold for disruption is a high one, requiring "extreme cognitive impairments," a test that is "rarely met by even the most psychotic of defendants." Another prominent (and associated) feature of this approach to mental disorder is the exclusion of *emotional* appreciation from the measure of criminal responsibility. This exclusion draws the boundary around NCRMD in such a way as to remove the defence from those suffering extreme forms of personality disorder such as psychopathy or sociopathy. These various features of the doctrine yield a defence that is chiefly concerned with a narrow band of mental disorders: indeed, the defence is shaped in such a way as to be most responsive to and largely focused on extreme forms of paranoid schizophrenia that involve powerful delusions. ...

The core of the defence still turns on the presence of a disease of the mind with two possible branches of cognitive effects: incapacity to appreciate the nature and consequences of the act, or to know that the act was wrong. This stability in the legal doctrine stands in stark contrast to the degree of change in our appreciation of the incidence and nature of various psychological and developmental disorders afflicting those who find themselves involved in the criminal justice system. Whereas the shape of the mental disorder defence might have once enjoyed a degree of fit with social knowledge as to the facts of forensically relevant psychiatric conditions, there is mounting evidence that the legal test for mental disorder is inhospitable or even actively hostile to certain mental disorders found with surprising frequency in our growing penal population. ...

The picture painted is of a criminal law chronically detached from or comfortably ignorant of situations that raise serious concerns within the best accounts of the conditions for criminal responsibility. And this leads us to the question: "what is the function of a criminal law doctrine so unconcerned with facts that bear on its own theoretical preoccupations?"

Berger ultimately suggests that "the under-inclusive doctrine of mental disorder serves as a mechanism for the elision of collective blame for a complex social problem" (at 136), allowing us to disregard the difficult issues of collective, social, and political responsibility that arise at the meeting of mental health, social disadvantage, and crime. Consider these claims as you study the cases in this chapter.

Section II of this chapter examines the important preliminary procedural matters affecting the mental disorder defence, including fitness to stand trial, restrictions on the ability of the Crown to raise the mental disorder issue, the burden of proof placed on the proponent of the mental disorder issue, and the consequences of a successful defence.

Section III examines the constituent elements of the mental disorder defence—the first element being the threshold requirement that the accused has a mental disorder or disease of the mind. It also examines the two alternative arms of the second element of the mental disorder defence—namely, whether the mental disorder rendered the person incapable of appreciating the nature and quality of the act or omission, or whether the mental disorder rendered the person incapable of knowing that the act or omission was wrong.

Section IV examines the defence of automatism. Automatism refers to a specific condition of disassociation between the mind and body in which a person acts in an involuntary manner. The issue of automatism has been briefly discussed in Chapter 5 relating to the voluntariness of conduct. It is discussed in this chapter because a critical issue in most automatism cases is whether the cause of the automatism is classified as a mental disorder. If the cause is so classified, then the mental disorder defence will generally apply because those who act involuntarily will not be capable of appreciating the nature and quality of their actions or knowing that they are wrong. As will be seen, concerns about social protection loom large in decisions about whether automatism should be included in the mental disorder defence.

II. PROCEDURAL ELEMENTS OF THE MENTAL DISORDER DEFENCE

Fitness to Stand Trial

The mental disorder defence is directed toward the accused's condition at the time that the offence was alleged to have been committed. Nevertheless, a mental disorder may persist or arise after the alleged offence. Moreover, it may be of such an extent that the accused will be found unfit to stand trial. Section 2 of the *Criminal Code* provides that:

> "unfit to stand trial" means unable on account of mental disorder to conduct a defence at any stage of the proceedings before a verdict is rendered or to instruct counsel to do so, and, in particular, unable on account of mental disorder to
> (a) understand the nature or object of the proceedings,
> (b) understand the possible consequences of the proceedings, or
> (c) communicate with counsel.

The following provisions are among those that govern the determination of the fitness-to-stand-trial issue:

672.22 An accused is presumed fit to stand trial unless the court is satisfied on the balance of probabilities that the accused is unfit to stand trial.

672.23(1) Where the court has reasonable grounds, at any stage of the proceedings before a verdict is rendered, to believe that the accused is unfit to stand trial, the court may direct, of its own motion or on application of the accused or the prosecutor, that the issue of fitness of the accused be tried.

(2) An accused or a prosecutor who makes an application under subsection (1) has the burden of proof that the accused is unfit to stand trial.

. . .

672.32(1) A verdict of unfit to stand trial shall not prevent the accused from being tried subsequently where the accused becomes fit to stand trial.

(2) The burden of proof that the accused has subsequently become fit to stand trial is on the party who asserts it, and is discharged by proof on the balance of probabilities.

R v Whittle
Supreme Court of Canada
[1994] 2 SCR 914

SOPINKA J observed for the Court: ... By virtue of s. 16 of the *Criminal Code*, persons suffering a disease of the mind in the circumstances defined in that section are exempted from criminal liability and punishment. The section embodies the policy of the law that such persons are sick as opposed to blameworthy and should be treated rather than punished: see *R. v. Chaulk*, [1990] 3 S.C.R. 1303, at p. 1336. These persons are not, however, exempt from being tried. Part XX.1 of the *Criminal Code* contains detailed provisions providing for mental assessments by physicians and for determination of the fitness of persons suffering from mental disorders to stand trial. Section 672.23 provides that where, at any stage of the proceedings, the court believes on reasonable grounds that the accused is unfit to stand trial, it may direct the trial of that issue. The application can be made on the court's own motion or by the accused or the prosecutor. Many accused persons who are found not guilty by reason of a mental disorder are fit to stand trial. The fact that an accused is not criminally responsible within the meaning of s. 16, does not mean that he or she is unfit to stand trial. If the contrary were true there would be little purpose in providing for the plea authorized by s. 16. Most persons who suffered from the mental disorder defined in the section would be exempted from trial and would not get to plead until they had recovered subsequent to the date of the offence.

The test for fitness to stand trial is quite different from the definition of mental disorder in s. 16. It is predicated on the existence of a mental disorder and focuses on the ability to instruct counsel and conduct a defence. That test which was developed under the common law is now codified in s. 2 of the Code. ... It requires limited cognitive capacity to understand the process and to communicate with counsel. In *R. v. Taylor* (1992), 77 C.C.C. (3d) 551, 17 C.R. (4th) 371, the Ontario Court of Appeal, after reviewing the authorities, held that the trial judge erred in concluding that the accused must be capable of making rational decisions beneficial to him. At page 567, Lacourcière J.A., on behalf of the court, stated:

> The "limited cognitive capacity" test strikes an effective balance between the objectives of the fitness rules and the constitutional right of the accused to choose his own defence and to have a trial within a reasonable time.

Accordingly, provided the accused possesses this limited capacity, it is not a prerequisite that he or she be capable of exercising analytical reasoning in making a choice to accept the advice of counsel or in coming to a decision that best serves her interests.

As a result of the Supreme Court's decision in *R v Demers*, 2004 SCC 46, [2004] 2 SCR 489, s 672.851 of the Code now provides for the possibility that proceedings against an accused found unfit to stand trial could be permanently stayed if the person is not likely to ever become fit to stand trial and does not pose a significant threat to the safety of the public.

On the limitations of the test for determining fitness to stand trial for people with permanent mental disabilities such as fetal alcohol spectrum disorder see K Roach & A Bailey, "The Relevance of Fetal Alcohol Spectrum Disorder in Canadian Criminal Law from Investigation to Sentencing" (2009) 42 UBC L Rev 1.

Who Can Raise the Mental Disorder Issue?

R v Swain

Supreme Court of Canada

[1991] 1 SCR 933

LAMER CJ (Sopinka and Cory JJ concurring) stated: ... I agree that it would be "manifestly" wrong if evidence of insanity were to influence the jury's decision on the issue of whether the accused committed the alleged act, but, with respect, I fail to see how the discretion of the trial judge to refuse to allow the Crown to raise insanity unless there is "convincing evidence" that the accused committed the alleged act will prevent this from happening. In my opinion, while the Ontario Court of Appeal [in *Simpson*] has recognized the prejudicial effect of allowing the Crown to raise evidence of insanity, it has not formulated a mechanism which adequately safeguards the right of the accused to control his or her defence.

In my view, the ability of the Crown to raise evidence of insanity over and above the accused's wishes, under the existing common law rule, does interfere with the accused's control over the conduct of his or her defence. However, this is not to say that if an accused chooses to raise evidence which tends to put his or her mental capacity for criminal intent into question but falls short of raising the defence of insanity (within s. 16), the Crown will be unable to raise its own evidence of insanity. In circumstances where the accused's own evidence tends to put his or her mental capacity for criminal intent into question, the Crown will be entitled to put forward its own evidence of insanity and the trial judge will be entitled to charge the jury on s. 16. ...

In my view, the objective of the common law rule which allows the Crown, in some cases, to raise evidence of insanity over and above the accused's wishes is twofold. One of the objectives was identified by Martin J.A. in *Simpson*, [(1977), 35 CCC (2d) 337 (Ont CA)], at p. 362:

> ... to avoid the conviction of an accused who may not be responsible on account of insanity, but who refuses to adduce cogent evidence that he was insane.

The common law rule is aimed not only at avoiding the unfair treatment of the accused but also at maintaining the integrity of the criminal justice system itself. The accused is not the only person who has an interest in the outcome of the trial; society itself has an interest in ensuring that the system does not incorrectly label insane people as criminals.

The second objective was aptly characterized by the appellant as the protection of the public from presently dangerous persons requiring hospitalization. This objective arises from the fact that the Crown's option to simply discontinue the prosecution of an accused, whom it suspects was insane at the time of the offence, does not address the concern that such a person may well be presently dangerous and may therefore bring him or herself into contact with the criminal justice system once again. ...

The dual objectives discussed above could be met without unnecessarily limiting Charter rights if the existing common law rule were replaced with a rule which would allow the Crown to raise independently the issue of insanity only after the trier of fact had concluded that the accused was otherwise guilty of the offence charged. Under this scheme, the issue of insanity would be tried after a verdict of guilty had been reached, but prior to a conviction being entered. If the trier of fact then subsequently found that the accused was insane at the time of the offence, the verdict of not guilty by reason of insanity would be entered. Conversely, if the trier of fact found that the accused was not insane, within the meaning of s. 16, at the time of the offence a conviction would then be entered.

Such a rule would safeguard an accused's right to control his or her defence and would achieve both the objective of avoiding the conviction of a person who was insane at the time of the offence and the objective of protecting the public from a person who may be presently dangerous. Of course, an accused would also be entitled, under this scheme, to raise his s. 7 right not to be found guilty if he was insane at the time of the offence. An accused would, if he chooses not to do so earlier, raise the issue of insanity after the trier of fact has concluded that he or she was guilty of the offence charged, but before a verdict of guilty was entered. This is consistent with the accused's right, under our criminal justice system, to force the Crown to discharge its full burden of proof on the elements of *actus reus* and *mens rea* before raising other matters. However, this does not mean that the accused can raise insanity only after both *actus reus* and *mens rea* have been proven. While the Crown would be limited to raising evidence of insanity only after the trier of fact was satisfied that the full burden of proof on *actus reus* and *mens rea* had been discharged or after the accused's own defence has somehow put his or her mental capacity for criminal intent in issue, the accused would have the option of raising evidence of insanity at any time during the trial. ...

In my view, the new common law rule achieves the dual objectives enunciated above without limiting an accused's rights under s. 7 of the Charter. Under the new common law rule, there will only be two instances in which the Crown will be entitled to lead evidence of insanity. First, the Crown may raise evidence of insanity after the trier of fact has concluded that the accused is otherwise guilty of the offence charged. In these circumstances the Crown's ability to raise evidence of insanity cannot interfere with the conduct of the accused's defence because the Crown's ability to do so will not be triggered until after the accused has concluded his or her defence. Second, the Crown may raise evidence of insanity if the accused's own defence has (in the view of the trial judge) put the accused's capacity for criminal intent in issue. In these circumstances the Crown's ability to raise evidence of insanity is not inconsistent with the accused's right to control the conduct of his or her defence because the very issue has been raised by the accused's conduct of his or her defence. Furthermore, as was stated above, the Crown's ability to raise evidence of insanity only after an accused has put his or her mental capacity for criminal intent in issue does not raise the problem of the Crown's being able to place an accused in a position where inconsistent defences must be advanced.

[LA FOREST J (Gonthier J concurring) wrote an opinion substantially concurring with Lamer CJ. WILSON J concurred in the result but disagreed with Lamer CJ as to the "second instance" in which the Crown can introduce evidence of insanity. She stated:]

While I agree with the Chief Justice that modifying the existing common law rule so as to give the prosecution only a conditional right to introduce evidence of insanity during the course of the trial, i.e., in circumstances where the accused has himself put his mental capacity in issue, is a less intrusive means of achieving the government objective, I am not sure that such modified common law rule can itself survive full Charter scrutiny. In my view, permitting the Crown to raise insanity during the course of the trial, even if that permission is conditional, still infringes upon the accused's right to control his defences. ... Nor can it satisfy the minimal impairment branch of the *Oakes* test because, although it is a less intrusive means of accomplishing the government's objective, it is not the least intrusive means of doing so.

I believe, moreover, that conferring on the prosecution a conditional right to raise the issue of insanity during the course of the trial infringes upon the equality rights of the mentally disabled under s. 15 of the Charter. It denies the mentally disabled, a group in our society which has been negatively stereotyped and historically disadvantaged, the control over their defences reposed in other accused persons and does so in a way which is discriminatory. In denying the mentally disabled personal autonomy in decision-making it reinforces the stereotype that they are incapable of rational thought and the ability to look after their own interests. In a word, it denies them equality with other accused persons under the guise, putting it at its best, of a benign paternalism. The prosecution's conditional right will only pass constitutional muster, in my view, if it can be shown that there exists no alternative that achieves the same objective without limiting the accused's s. 7 or s. 15 rights or at least limiting them to a significantly lesser degree.

It seems to me that the principle advanced in support of the prosecution's right to introduce evidence of insanity can be effectively implemented by having the issue of the accused's insanity raised at the conclusion of the trial in cases where the defences put forward by the accused have been rejected and the essential elements of the offence have been established by the prosecution beyond a reasonable doubt. At that point I think either party should be free to raise the issue of the accused's insanity. I realize, of course, that there is an element of circularity involved in this approach in that insanity has a direct bearing on proof of *mens rea*. However, I prefer this approach since it both respects the accused's right to waive the defence of insanity and ensures that any resultant prejudice he suffers in the finding of guilt flows from his own decision not to avail himself of the defence and not as a consequence of the prosecution's having raised the issue in the middle of the trial process.

Burden of Proof

R v Chaulk
Supreme Court of Canada
[1990] 3 SCR 1303

[In this case, the majority of the Court held that the former s 16(4) of the *Criminal Code*, which provided that "Everyone shall, until the contrary is proven, be presumed to be and to have been sane," violated s 11(d) of the Charter, but was a "reasonable limit" under s 1.]

LAMER CJ (Dickson CJ, La Forest, Sopinka, and Cory JJ concurring): In my view, the principles enunciated in *Whyte* [briefly extracted in Chapter 4] are applicable to this case and establish that the presumption of sanity embodied in s. 16(4) violates the presumption of innocence. If an accused is found to have been insane at the time of the offence, he will not be found guilty; thus the "fact" of insanity precludes a verdict of guilty. Whether the claim of insanity is characterized as a denial of *mens rea*, an excusing defence or, more generally, as an exemption based on criminal incapacity, the fact remains that sanity is essential for guilt. Section 16(4) allows a factor which is essential for guilt to be presumed, rather than proven by the Crown beyond a reasonable doubt. Moreover, it requires an accused to disprove sanity (or prove insanity) on a balance of probabilities; it therefore violates the presumption of innocence because it permits a conviction in spite of a reasonable doubt in the mind of the trier of fact as to the guilt of the accused. ...

Accordingly, the objective of s. 16(4) is to avoid placing an impossible burden of proof on the Crown and to thereby secure the conviction of the guilty. In my view, this objective is sufficiently important to warrant limiting constitutionally protected rights and s. 16(4) passes the first branch of the *Oakes* test. ...

It is not the role of this Court to second-guess the wisdom of policy choices made by Parliament. In enacting s. 16(4), Parliament may not have chosen the absolutely least intrusive means of meeting its objective, but it has chosen from a range of means which impair s. 11(d) as little as is reasonably possible. Within this range of means it is virtually impossible to know, let alone be sure, which means violate Charter rights *the least*. ...

As I have mentioned above, the Charter does not require Parliament to "roll the dice" in its effort to achieve "pressing and substantial" objectives in order to adopt the absolutely least intrusive legislative provision.

While the effect of s. 16(4) on the presumption of innocence is clearly detrimental, given the importance of the objective that the Crown not be encumbered with an unworkable burden and given that I have concluded above that s. 16(4) limits s. 11(d) as little as is reasonably possible, it is my view that there is proportionality between the effects of the measure and the objective.

Accordingly, s. 16(4) is a reasonable limit on the presumption of innocence which can be upheld under s. 1 of the Charter.

[McLACHLIN J (L'Heureux-Dubé and Gonthier JJ concurring) held that s 16(4) did not violate s 11(d) of the Charter:]

I arrive then at this conclusion. To conceive the insanity provisions of the *Criminal Code* narrowly in terms of the essential elements of criminal offences or exculpatory defences ignores the historical and philosophical origins of the fundamental precept that sanity is a pre-condition of criminal responsibility. It violates the language of s. 16 of the Code, which refers to capacity for criminal responsibility rather than actual states of mind. It is at odds with the fact that insanity in s. 16 can be raised by the Crown in circumstances where neither the elements of the offence nor a defence are at issue. And it confuses true acquittal, the result of the absence of an essential element of an offence or the presence of a defence to it, with formal acquittal coupled with alternative coercive measures because mental impairment renders the imposition of true penal responsibility inappropriate. Rather than straining to confine the insanity provisions in the dual strait-jacket of the "elements" of or "exculpatory defences" to an offence, I prefer to view s. 16 as referring to a more basic precept of the criminal law system—the notion that the attribution of criminal responsibility and punishment is morally and legally justifiable only for those who have the capacity to reason and thus to choose right from wrong.

The next question is whether the presumption of sanity, viewed as the fundamental pre-condition of criminal responsibility, offends the presumption of innocence embodied in s. 11(d) of the Charter. The answer to this question must be negative. The presumption of innocence found in s. 11(d) of the Charter is merely another way of expressing the principle that the Crown must prove an accused's guilt beyond a reasonable doubt. That being the purpose of the presumption of innocence, it follows that the presumption of sanity cannot be contrary to s. 11(d) because, as Professor Mewett observed in the passage set out earlier, the issue of insanity "does not affect the prosecution's burden to prove beyond a reasonable doubt everything that constitutes guilt." The presumption of sanity in s. 16(4) of the *Criminal Code* merely relieves the Crown from establishing that the accused has the capacity for rational choice which makes attribution of criminal responsibility and punishment morally justifiable. The Crown must still prove the guilt of the accused—i.e., the *actus reus*, the *mens rea*, and the absence of exculpatory defences raised on the evidence—beyond a reasonable doubt.

[WILSON J, dissenting on this issue, held that the provision violated s 11(d) and could not be justified under s 1.]

I start from the premise that the government must have been of the view that it was necessary to impose a persuasive burden on the accused to prove his insanity on a balance of probabilities in order to prevent perfectly sane persons who had committed crimes from escaping criminal liability on tenuous insanity pleas. In other words, the government must have concluded that the imposition of a purely evidentiary burden on the accused, i.e., the burden of adducing sufficient evidence to raise a reasonable doubt in the minds of the jury as to his sanity was not enough. Hence the presumption of sanity and the reverse onus on the accused to prove insanity, bringing s. 16(4) into conflict with s. 11(d) of the Charter as explained in *Whyte*.

If I am correct in my starting premise, then it would appear that under the first branch of *Oakes* the government would have to adduce evidence under s. 1 to show that this was a real social problem, that perfectly sane persons who had committed crimes were in significant numbers escaping criminal liability on tenuous insanity pleas and that something had to be done about it.

There is, however, a difficulty here because s. 16(4) merely reflects what, as we have seen, was already the common law and had been the common law for some time prior even to the enactment of the original section in Canada's first *Criminal Code*. There is therefore no historic experience in our jurisdiction with a purely evidentiary burden in order to show that such a burden was not adequate to achieve the government's objective. ...

It would appear that in the United States the evidentiary burden has not resulted in a flood of accused persons being found not guilty by reason of insanity. Nor have the Americans witnessed a great rush of insanity pleas. As the American Psychiatric Association notes in *Statement on the Insanity Defence* (1982):

> Successful invocation of the (insanity) defence is rare (probably involving a fraction of 1% of all felony cases). While philosophically important for the criminal law, the insanity defence is empirically unimportant.

The respondent, for the reasons discussed above, has not been able to establish that s. 16(4) of the *Criminal Code* was aimed at an existing pressing and substantial concern and, while it may be that the legislature need not necessarily wait until such a concern has arisen, I do not believe that the respondent has succeeded in establishing even a likelihood of its arising. I would conclude therefore that the first requirement of the *Oakes* test has not been met.

Consequences of Mental Disorder as a Defence

Winko v British Columbia (Forensic Psychiatric Institute)
Supreme Court of Canada
[1999] 2 SCR 625

McLACHLIN J (Lamer CJ and Cory, Iacobucci, Major, Bastarache, and Binnie JJ concurring):

[1] In every society there are those who commit criminal acts because of mental illness. The criminal law must find a way to deal with these people fairly, while protecting the public against further harms. The task is not an easy one.

[2] In 1991 Parliament provided its answer to this challenge: Part XX.1 of the *Criminal Code*, R.S.C. 1985, c. C-46. The appellant Winko submits that Part XX.1 violates his rights to liberty, security of the person and equality under the *Canadian Charter of Rights and Freedoms*. ...

[3] I conclude that Part XX.1 of the *Criminal Code* protects the liberty, security of the person, and equality interests of those accused who are not criminally responsible ("NCR") on account of a mental disorder by requiring that an absolute discharge be

granted unless the court or Review Board is able to conclude that they pose a significant risk to the safety of the public. It follows that Part XX.1 does not deprive mentally ill accused of their liberty or security of the person in a manner contrary to the principles of fundamental justice. Nor does it violate their right to equal treatment under the law. ...

[17] Historically at common law, those who committed criminal acts while mentally ill were charged and required to stand trial like other offenders. At the end of the trial, they were either acquitted or convicted and sentenced accordingly. The common law permitted no special verdict or disposition. The only concession made to the illness that induced the offence was the accused's right to raise the defence that he or she was unable to understand the nature and quality of the act, the *M'Naghten Rules*: see *M'Naghten's Case* (1843), 10 Cl. & Fin. 200, 8 E.R. 718 (H.L.). The law held that such incapacity deprived the mentally ill accused person of the criminal intent or *mens rea* required for the offence. Sanity, however, was presumed; it was up to the accused to demonstrate the contrary.

[18] Until 1990, the provisions of the *Criminal Code* dealing with criminal acts committed as a result of mental illness reflected the common law approach of treating those offences like any others, subject to the special defence of not understanding the nature and quality of the act. The only verdicts available under the *Criminal Code* were conviction or acquittal. However, even where the accused was acquitted on the basis of mental illness, he or she was not released, but was automatically detained at the pleasure of the Lieutenant Governor in Council: *Criminal Code*, s. 614(2) (formerly s. 542(2)) (repealed S.C. 1991, c. 43, s. 3).

[19] The first *Charter* challenge against this system came in *R. v. Chaulk*, [1990] 3 S.C.R. 1303, where a majority of this Court ruled that the requirement that the accused prove an inability to understand the nature and quality of his or her act violated the accused's right to be presumed innocent, but that the burden was constitutionally saved under s. 1. A second *Charter* challenge came in *R. v. Swain*, [1991] 1 S.C.R. 933, where this Court struck down the provision for automatic, indefinite detention of an NCR accused on the basis that it violated the accused's s. 7 liberty rights.

[20] In response to *Swain*, Parliament introduced sweeping changes by enacting Part XX.1 of the *Criminal Code* in 1991. ... Part XX.1 reflected an entirely new approach to the problem of the mentally ill offender, based on a growing appreciation that treating mentally ill offenders like other offenders failed to address properly the interests of either the offenders or the public. The mentally ill offender who is imprisoned and denied treatment is ill-served by being punished for an offence for which he or she should not in fairness be held morally responsible. At the same time, the public facing the unconditional release of the untreated mentally ill offender was equally ill-served. To achieve the twin goals of fair treatment and public safety, a new approach was required.

[21] Part XX.1 rejects the notion that the only alternatives for mentally ill people charged with an offence are conviction or acquittal; it proposes a third alternative. Under the new scheme, once an accused person is found to have committed a crime while suffering from a mental disorder that deprived him or her of the ability to understand the nature of the act or that it was wrong, that individual is diverted into a special stream. Thereafter, the court or a Review Board conducts a hearing to decide whether the person should be kept in a secure institution, released on conditions, or unconditionally discharged. The emphasis is on achieving the twin goals of protecting the public and treating the mentally ill offender fairly and appropriately. ...

[27] Any disposition regarding an NCR accused must be made in accordance with s. 672.54. The court or Review Board may order that the NCR accused be discharged absolutely, that he or she be discharged on conditions, or that he or she be detained in a hospital and subject to the conditions the court or Review Board considers appropriate. Although the court or Review Board has a wide latitude in determining the appropriate conditions to be imposed, it can only order that psychiatric or other treatment be carried out if the NCR accused consents to that condition, and the court or Review Board considers it to be reasonable and necessary: s. 672.55(1).

[28] The Review Board must hold a further hearing within 12 months of making any disposition other than an absolute discharge and further reviews must be conducted at least every 12 months thereafter: s. 672.81(1). A further hearing also must be held as soon as practicable when the restrictions on the liberty of the NCR accused are increased significantly, or upon the request of the person in charge of the place where the accused is detained or directed to attend: s. 672.81(2). Apart from these mandatory reviews, the Review Board may review any of its dispositions at any time, on the request of the accused or any other party: s. 672.82(1). Any party may appeal against a disposition by a court or the Review Board to the Court of Appeal on a question of law or fact or a question of mixed law and fact: s. 672.72(1). ...

[35] If the NCR verdict is not a verdict of guilt or an acquittal, neither is it a verdict that the NCR accused poses a significant threat to society. Part XX.1 does not presume the NCR accused to pose such a threat. Rather, it requires the court or the Review Board to assess whether such a threat exists in each case. Part XX.1 thus recognizes that, contrary to the stereotypical notions that some may still harbour, the mentally ill are not inherently dangerous. The mentally ill have long been subject to negative stereotyping and social prejudice in our society based on an assumption of dangerousness. ...

[38] In *Swain, supra*, at p. 1015, this Court, *per* Lamer C.J.C., recognized that the NCR accused cannot be presumed to be dangerous:

> ... [W]hile the assumption that persons found not guilty by reason of insanity pose a threat to society may well be *rational*, I hasten to add that I recognize that it is not *always* valid. While past violent conduct and previous mental disorder may indicate a greater possibility of future dangerous conduct, this will not necessarily be so. Furthermore, not every individual found not guilty by reason of insanity will have such a personal history. (Emphasis in original.)

[39] In the spirit of supplanting the old stereotypes about mentally ill offenders, Part XX.1 supplements the traditional guilt-innocence dichotomy of the criminal law with a new alternative for NCR accused—an alternative of assessment to determine whether the person poses a continuing threat to society coupled with an emphasis on providing opportunities to receive appropriate treatment. The twin branches of the new system—assessment and treatment—are intimately related. Treatment, not incarceration, is necessary to stabilize the mental condition of a dangerous NCR accused and reduce the threat to public safety created by that condition. As Macfarlane J.A. stated regarding the predecessor scheme in *Re Rebic and The Queen* (1986), 28 C.C.C. (3d) 154 (B.C.C.A.) at p. 171, quoted with approval by Lamer C.J.C. in *Swain*, at p. 1004:

> The *objective* of the legislation is to protect society and the accused until the mental health of the latter has been restored. The objective *is to be achieved by treatment* of the patient in a hospital, rather than in a prison environment. [Emphasis added by Lamer C.J.C.]

[40] Part XX.1 protects society. If society is to be protected on a long-term basis, it must address the cause of the offending behaviour—the mental illness. It cannot content itself with locking the ill offender up for a term of imprisonment and then releasing him or her into society, without having provided any opportunities for psychiatric or other treatment. Public safety will only be ensured by stabilizing the mental condition of dangerous NCR accused.

[41] Part XX.1 also protects the NCR offender. The assessment-treatment model introduced by Part XX.1 of the *Criminal Code* is fairer to the NCR offender than the traditional common law model. The NCR offender is not criminally responsible, but ill. Providing opportunities to receive treatment, not imposing punishment, is the just and appropriate response.

[McLachlin J went on to conclude that the new regime did not violate s 7 or s 15 of the Charter. Section 672.54 did not create a burden or presumption of dangerousness on the accused, its reference to a significant threat to the safety of the public was not vague, and it was not based on stereotypes about mentally disordered offenders but rather required an "individualized process" that was "the antithesis of the logic of the stereotype."]

Note that when *Winko* was decided, s 672.54 governing dispositions provided:

Where a court or Review Board makes a disposition under subsection 672.45(2) or section 672.47 or 672.83, it shall, taking into consideration the need to protect the public from dangerous persons, the mental condition of the accused, the reintegration of the accused into society and the other needs of the accused, make one of the following dispositions that is the least onerous and least restrictive to the accused:

(a) where a verdict of not criminally responsible on account of mental disorder has been rendered in respect of the accused and, in the opinion of the court or Review Board, the accused is not a significant threat to the safety of the public, by order, direct that the accused be discharged absolutely;

(b) by order, direct that the accused be discharged subject to such conditions as the court or Review Board considers appropriate; or

(c) by order, direct that the accused be detained in custody in a hospital, subject to such conditions as the court or Review Board considers appropriate.

This provision was amended by SC 2014, c 6, s 9 to put more emphasis on public safety. It now provides:

When a court or Review Board makes a disposition under subsection 672.45(2), section 672.47, subsection 672.64(3) or section 672.83 or 672.84, it shall, taking into account the safety of the public, which is the paramount consideration, the mental condition of the accused, the reintegration of the accused into society and the other needs of the accused, make one of the following dispositions that is necessary and appropriate in the circumstances:

(a) where a verdict of not criminally responsible on account of mental disorder has been rendered in respect of the accused and, in the opinion of the court or Review Board, the accused is not a significant threat to the safety of the public, by order, direct that the accused be discharged absolutely;

(b) by order, direct that the accused be discharged subject to such conditions as the court or Review Board considers appropriate; or

(c) by order, direct that the accused be detained in custody in a hospital, subject to such conditions as the court or Review Board considers appropriate.

Will or should this new provision make a difference to the constitutionality of the disposition of those found not guilty on account of mental disorder? For a background to the amendments that led to the above amendment and the creation of a new regime for high-risk NCR accused, and a prediction that the new provision will be challenged under the Charter, see Rebecca Sutton, "Canada's Not Criminally Responsible Reform Act: Mental Disorder and the Danger of Public Safety" (2014) 60 Crim LQ 41.

In *R v Conway*, 2010 SCC 22, [2010] 1 SCR 765, the Supreme Court of Canada considered the mental health review board's jurisdiction to grant Charter remedies to rectify a breach of a mentally disordered offender's Charter rights and freedoms. Justice Abella characterized the Ontario Review Board as "a quasi-judicial body with significant authority over a vulnerable population." She held, on behalf of a unanimous Court, that review boards must comply with the Charter in exercising their decision-making power under part XX.1 of the *Criminal Code*, and that they have jurisdiction to grant Charter remedies under s 24(1) of the Charter. She offered the following explanation of the review boards' composition and expertise:

> The Board's task calls for "significant expertise" (*Owen*, at paras. 29-30) and the Board's membership, which sits in five-member panels comprised of the chairperson (a judge or a person qualified for or retired from appointment to the bench), a second legal member, a psychiatrist, a second psychiatrist or psychologist and one public member (ss. 672.39 and 672.4(1)), guarantees that the requisite experts perform the Board's challenging task (*Owen*, at para. 29; s. 672.39). Further, as almost one-quarter of NCR patients and accused found unfit to stand trial spend at least 10 years in the review board system, with some, like Mr. Conway, spending significantly longer … , review boards become intimately familiar with the patients under their supervision.

III. MENTAL DISORDER AS A DEFENCE

Section 16 of the *Criminal Code* provides:

16(1) No person is criminally responsible for an act committed or an omission made while suffering from a mental disorder that rendered the person incapable of appreciating the nature and quality of the act or omission or of knowing that it was wrong.

(2) Every person is presumed not to suffer from a mental disorder so as to be exempt from criminal responsibility by virtue of subsection (1), until the contrary is proved on the balance of probabilities.

(3) The burden of proof that an accused was suffering from a mental disorder so as to be exempt from criminal responsibility is on the party that raises the issue.

Note that mental disorder is defined in s 2 as a disease of the mind, preserving the pre-1992 jurisprudence on this issue.

Mental Disorder or Disease of the Mind

Cooper v The Queen
Supreme Court of Canada
[1980] 1 SCR 1149

DICKSON J (Laskin CJ and Beetz, Estey, and McIntyre JJ concurring): … Let me say by way of commencement that, to date, the phrase "disease of the mind" has proven intractable, and has eluded satisfactory definition by both medical and legal disciplines. It is not a term of art in either law or psychiatry, Indeed, Glanville Williams, *Textbook of Criminal Law* (1978), p. 592, says that the phrase is no longer in medical use: "It is a mere working concept, a mere abstraction, like sin."

In *R. v. Kemp*, [1957] 1 Q.B. 399, an oft-cited decision, the primary issue was whether arteriosclerosis came within the meaning of "disease of the mind." Devlin J. agreed that there was an absence of medical opinion as to the categories of malfunction properly to be termed "diseases of the mind," and rejected the idea that for legal purposes, a distinction should be made between diseases physical and mental in origin. In his view, arteriosclerosis is a disease of the mind and can provide a defence to a criminal charge. He reviewed the relationship between medical evidence and the legal conclusions to be drawn therefrom (p. 406):

> Doctors' personal views, of course, are not binding upon me. I have to interpret the rules according to the ordinary principles of interpretation, but I derive help from their interpretations inasmuch as they illustrate the nature of the disease and the matters which from the medical point of view have to be considered in determining whether or not it is a disease of the mind.

In *Bratty v. A.-G. Northern Ireland*, [1963] A.C. 386, Lord Denning agreed that the question of whether an accused suffers from a disease of the mind is properly resolved by the judge. He acknowledged that "the major mental diseases, which the doctors call psychoses … are clearly diseases of the mind," and that "any mental disorder which has manifested itself in violence and is prone to recur is a disease of the mind" (p. 412).

. . .

Support for a broad and liberal legal construction of the words "disease of the mind" will be found in the writings of the renowned jurist, formerly Chief Justice of Australia, Sir Owen Dixon, who wrote:

> The reason why it is required that the defect of reason should be "from disease of the mind," in the classic phrase used by Sir Nicholas Tindal, seems to me no more than to exclude drunkenness, conditions of intense passion and other transient states attributable either to the fault or to the nature of man. In the advice delivered by Sir Nicholas Tindal no doubt the words "disease of the mind" were chosen because it was considered that they had the widest possible meaning. He would hardly have supposed it possible that the expression would be treated as one containing words of the law to be weighed like diamonds. I have taken it to include, as well as all forms of physical or material change or deterioration, every recognizable disorder or derangement of the understanding whether or not its nature, in our present

state of knowledge, is capable of explanation or determination. (A Legacy of Hadfield, M'Naghten and Maclean, 31 A.L.J. 255 at 260 (1957-58).)

Recently, in Canada, the Ontario Court of Appeal contributed judicial direction in this area of the law, in the cases of *R. v. Rabey* (1977), 37 C.C.C. (2d) 461, 79 D.L.R. (3d) 414, 17 O.R. (2d) 1, and *R. v. Simpson* (1977), 35 C.C.C. (2d) 337, 77 D.L.R. (3d) 507, 16 O.R. (2d) 129, both of which were decided subsequent to the trial of the appellant. ...

Simpson has greater significance for the present appeal. There, the accused appealed the finding of not guilty by reason of insanity on two charges of attempted murder. The facts, which indicate two incidents of stabbing, are not remarkable. As framed by Martin J.A., the issue was whether a personality disorder is a disease of the mind within the meaning of s. 16 of the Code. He held that, notwithstanding the psychiatric evidence, the question raised must be resolved as a question of law. But the legal position, as I understand it, is properly expressed in the following passage (at pp. 349-50):

> The term "disease of the mind" is a legal concept, although it includes a medical component, and what is meant by that term is a question of law for the judge. ... It is the function of the psychiatrist to describe the accused's mental condition and how it is considered from the medical point of view. It is for the judge to decide whether the condition described is comprehended by the term "disease of the mind."

As a matter of practice, the trial judge can permit the psychiatrist to be asked directly whether or not the condition in question constitutes a disease of the mind. Concerning the controversy over the classification of a "psychopathic personality," Martin J.A. found implicit recognition in Canadian and British authorities for the proposition that such a disorder can constitute a disease.

The general principles, not in issue on the further appeal to this Court, were reiterated by Mr. Justice Martin in *R. v. Rabey, supra*. Disease of the mind is a legal term. It is within the province of the judge to determine what mental conditions are within the meaning of that phrase and whether there is any evidence that an accused suffers from an abnormal mental condition comprehended by that term. More importantly, he held that if there is any evidence the accused did suffer such a disease in legal terms, the question of fact must be left with the jury.

· · ·

What is interesting in these two cases for our purposes is the maintenance of a clear distinction between the weight to be given medical opinions expressed in evidence, however relevant, and the task of the trial judge to form an independent conclusion as to whether the mental condition falls within the legal concept.

In summary, one might say that in a legal sense "disease of the mind" embraces any illness, disorder or abnormal condition which impairs the human mind and its functioning, excluding however, self-induced states caused by alcohol or drugs, as well as transitory mental states such as hysteria or concussion. In order to support a defence of insanity the disease must, of course, be of such intensity as to render the accused incapable of appreciating the nature and quality of the violent act or of knowing that it is wrong.

R v Bouchard-Lebrun
Supreme Court of Canada
2011 SCC 58, [2011] 3 SCR 575

LeBEL J:

[1] In this appeal, the Court must decide whether a toxic psychosis that results from a state of self-induced intoxication caused by an accused person's use of chemical drugs constitutes a "mental disorder" within the meaning of s. 16 of the *Criminal Code*, R.S.C. 1985, c. C-46 ("*Cr. C.*"), and thus exempts the appellant from criminal responsibility for an offence involving interference with the bodily integrity of another person. In general, this case also gives the Court an opportunity to review the respective scopes of the insanity defence and the defence of self-induced intoxication. [Self-induced intoxication is considered in Chapter 16 of this casebook.]

[2] The appellant brutally assaulted two individuals while he was in a psychotic condition caused by chemical drugs he had taken a few hours earlier. He seriously injured one of the individuals by stomping on his head. The victim suffered serious and permanent harm. After being convicted by the Court of Québec on two counts of aggravated assault and assault (2008 QCCQ 5844), the appellant tried unsuccessfully on appeal to obtain a verdict of not criminally responsible on account of mental disorder (2010 QCCA 402, 260 C.C.C. (3d) 548). With leave of this Court, the appellant is now appealing the judgment of the Quebec Court of Appeal, which rejected the argument that a toxic psychosis resulting from the voluntary consumption of drugs is a "mental disorder" within the meaning of s. 16 *Cr. C.*

· · ·

[8] At the time of the assault, the appellant was highly intoxicated because of the effects of the "*poire bleue*" pill he had taken a few hours earlier. In addition to the "normal" symptoms of intoxication resulting from the use of that drug, the highly toxic pill had produced a striking and, according to the appellant, unanticipated effect on him, as it caused a complete dissociation between the appellant's subjective perceptions and the objective reality. To put it bluntly, he was [TRANSLATION] "on another planet." Two witnesses at the trial stated that he [TRANSLATION] "started acting weird" and was "completely out of it" after taking the "*poire bleue*" pill.

[9] In actual fact, the appellant experienced an episode that might be described as religious delirium in light of its symptoms. It was after taking the drug that he became obsessed with the "upside-down cross" supposedly worn by Mr. Lévesque. During the attack, he made statements of a religious nature that, although coherent, were basically absurd. For example, he said that the Apocalypse was coming. At one point, he raised his arms in the air and asked the victims and the helpless witnesses to the attack whether they believed in him. After referring a few times to God and the Devil once the attack was over, he blessed Mr. Dumas's spouse by making the sign of the cross on her forehead. Mr. Dumas was still lying on the floor when the appellant then left the scene very calmly as if nothing had just happened.

[10] It has never been in dispute, in any of the courts, that the appellant was in a serious psychotic condition at the time of the offences and that the effects of that condition diminished gradually until they disappeared on October 28, 2005. The essential issue in this appeal is instead how that psychosis affects the appellant's criminal responsibility. I

will consider this issue later in these reasons. For now, it will suffice to note that, according to the evidence, the appellant had never experienced a psychotic episode such as this prior to the incidents in question. He had no underlying disease of the mind, nor was he addicted to a particular substance. Although he described himself at trial as an [TRANSLATION] "occasional user" of drugs, the evidence does not establish that he "abused" drugs—if it can be said that occasional drug use does not constitute abuse, that is.

· · ·

[26] [T]he appellant is arguing indirectly that the toxic psychosis he developed after taking a "*poire bleue*" pill resulted from an underlying disease of the mind that became apparent as a result of his intoxication. But because of the obstacles presented by the evidence in the record and the trial judge's findings of fact in relation to this argument, the appellant does not focus on his personal situation. Instead, he relies on an argument of general application. According to him, *any* toxic psychosis, even one that results, as the trial judge found in this case, from a single episode of intoxication, must be considered a "mental disorder" within the meaning of s. 16 *Cr. C.* (A.F., at para. 48). The appellant's reasoning therefore rests on the premise that intoxication can never be the real or underlying cause of toxic psychosis and that toxic psychosis must originate in a pre-existing mental condition.

· · ·

[38] This general principle does not seem particularly contentious. If the accused was intoxicated and in a psychotic condition at the material time, the problem the court faces is to identify a specific source for his or her mental condition, namely self-induced intoxication or a disease of the mind, and determine whether it falls within the scope of s. 33.1 or s. 16 *Cr. C.* This appears to be all the more difficult to do in cases in which the mental health of the accused was already precarious prior to the incident in question, even if his or her problems had not yet been diagnosed at the time, and in which the psychosis emerged while the accused was highly intoxicated. Yet this identification of the source of the psychosis plays a key role, since it will ultimately determine whether the accused will be held criminally responsible for his or her actions.

[39] The law, as it now stands, includes a fairly general framework for resolving this difficult question. The starting point must be the legal concept of "disease of the mind" as defined by Dickson J. in *Cooper*, the leading case:

> In summary, one might say that in a legal sense "disease of the mind" embraces any illness, disorder or abnormal condition which impairs the human mind and its functioning, *excluding however, self-induced states caused by alcohol or drugs*, as well as transitory mental states such as hysteria or concussion. [Emphasis added; p. 1159.]

· · ·

C. Defence Provided for in Section 16 Cr. C.: An Exception to the General Principle of Criminal Responsibility

[44] The defence of not criminally responsible on account of mental disorder, which Parliament codified in s. 16 *Cr. C.*, addresses concerns that are very legitimate in a democratic society. Insofar as the principles governing this defence are properly applied, a verdict of not criminally responsible on account of mental disorder protects the integrity of our country's criminal justice system and the collective interest in ensuring respect for

its fundamental principles. A review of the fundamental principles of criminal law that underlie the defence of mental disorder confirms the importance of this defence in Canadian criminal law.

[45] According to a traditional fundamental principle of the common law, criminal responsibility can result only from the commission of a voluntary act. This important principle is based on a recognition that it would be unfair in a democratic society to impose the consequences and stigma of criminal responsibility on an accused who did not voluntarily commit an act that constitutes a criminal offence.

[46] For an act to be considered voluntary in the criminal law, it must be the product of the accused person's free will. As Taschereau J. stated in *R. v. King*, [1962] S.C.R. 746, "there can be no *actus reus* unless it is the result of a willing mind at liberty to make a definite choice or decision, or in other words, there must be a willpower to do an act whether the accused knew or not that it was prohibited by law" (p. 749). This means that no one can be found criminally responsible for an involuntary act (see Dickson J.'s dissenting reasons in *Rabey v. The Queen*, [1980] 2 S.C.R. 513, which were endorsed on this point in *R. v. Parks*, [1992] 2 S.C.R. 871).

[47] An individual's will is expressed through conscious control exerted by the individual over his or her body (*Perka v. The Queen*, [1984] 2 S.C.R. 232, at p. 249). The control may be physical, in which case voluntariness relates to the muscle movements of a person exerting physical control over his or her body. The exercise of a person's will may also involve moral control over actions the person wants to take, in which case a voluntary act is a carefully thought out act that is performed freely by an individual with at least a minimum level of intelligence (see H. Parent, *Responsabilité pénale et troubles mentaux: Histoire de la folie en droit pénal français, anglais et canadien* (1999), at pp. 266-71). Will is also a product of reason.

[48] The moral dimension of the voluntary act, which this Court recognized in *Perka*, thus reflects the idea that the criminal law views individuals as autonomous and rational beings. Indeed, this idea can be seen as the cornerstone of the principles governing the attribution of criminal responsibility (L. Alexander and K.K. Ferzan with contributions by S.J. Morse, *Crime and Culpability: A Theory of Criminal Law* (2009), at p. 155). When considered from this perspective, human behaviour will trigger criminal responsibility only if it results from a "true choice" or from the person's "free will." This principle signals the importance of autonomy and reason in the system of criminal responsibility. ...

[49] This essential basis for attributing criminal responsibility thus gives rise to a presumption that each individual can distinguish right from wrong. The criminal law relies on a presumption that every person is an autonomous and rational being whose acts and omissions can attract liability. This presumption is not absolute, however: it can be rebutted by proving that the accused did not at the material time have the level of autonomy or rationality required to attract criminal liability. Thus, criminal responsibility will not be imposed if the accused gives an excuse for his or her act that is accepted in our society, in which there is "a fundamental conviction that criminal responsibility is appropriate only where the actor is a discerning moral agent, capable of making choices between right and wrong" (*R. v. Chaulk*, [1990] 3 S.C.R. 1303, at p. 1397). In *Ruzic*, the Court recognized the existence of a principle of fundamental justice that "only voluntary conduct—behaviour that is the product of a free will and controlled body, unhindered by external constraints—should attract the penalty and stigma of criminal liability" (para. 47).

[50] Insanity is an exception to the general criminal law principle that an accused is deemed to be autonomous and rational. A person suffering from a mental disorder within the meaning of s. 16 *Cr. C.* is not considered to be capable of appreciating the nature of his or her acts or understanding that they are inherently wrong. This is why Lamer C.J. stated in *Chaulk* that the insanity provisions of the *Criminal Code* "operate, at the most fundamental level, as an exemption from criminal liability which is predicated on an incapacity for criminal intent" (p. 1321 (emphasis deleted)).

[51] The logic of *Ruzic* is that it can also be said that an insane person is incapable of morally voluntary conduct. The person's actions are not actually the product of his or her free will. It is therefore consistent with the principles of fundamental justice for a person whose mental condition at the relevant time is covered by s. 16 *Cr. C.* not to be criminally responsible under Canadian law. Convicting a person who acted involuntarily would undermine the foundations of the criminal law and the integrity of the judicial system.

[52] However, the defence of mental disorder remains unique. It does not result in acquittal of the accused, but instead leads to a verdict of not criminally responsible. That verdict triggers an administrative process whose purpose is to determine whether the accused is a significant threat to the safety of the public, to take any necessary action to control that threat and, if necessary, to provide the accused with appropriate care. A verdict of not criminally responsible on account of mental disorder thus gives effect to society's interest in ensuring that morally innocent offenders are treated rather than punished, while protecting the public as fully as possible.

· · ·

D. Requirements of the Defence of Not Criminally Responsible on Account of Mental Disorder

[55] Section 16(2) *Cr. C.* provides that "[e]very person is presumed not to suffer from a mental disorder so as to be exempt from criminal responsibility." An accused who seeks to avoid criminal responsibility on this ground must prove on a balance of probabilities that, at the material time, he or she was suffering from "a mental disorder that rendered the person incapable of appreciating the nature and quality of the act or omission or of knowing that it was wrong" (s. 16(1) *Cr. C.*). ...

[56] An accused who wishes to successfully raise the defence of mental disorder must therefore meet the requirements of a two-stage statutory test. The first stage involves *characterizing* the mental state of the accused. The key issue to be decided at trial at this stage is whether the accused was suffering from a mental disorder in the legal sense at the time of the alleged events. The second stage of the defence provided for in s. 16 *Cr. C.* concerns the *effects of the mental disorder*. At this stage, it must be determined whether, owing to his or her mental condition, the accused was incapable of "knowing that [the act or omission] was wrong" (s. 16(1) *Cr. C.*).

[57] In the instant case, it is not in dispute that the appellant was incapable of distinguishing right from wrong at the material time. The trial judge wrote that [TRANSLATION] "[a]t the time the criminal acts were committed, the accused did not realize what he was doing and was in a serious psychotic condition; there is no real dispute about this" (para. 2). Therefore, the only issue in this appeal is whether the psychosis resulted from a "mental disorder" within the meaning of s. 16 *Cr. C.*

(1) Incapacity Must Result from a Disease of the Mind

[58] The *Criminal Code* does not contain a precise definition of the "mental disorder" concept for the purposes of s. 16 *Cr. C.* Section 2 *Cr. C.* simply provides that the term "mental disorder" means "a disease of the mind" ("*toute maladie mentale*" in French). Because of the circular nature of this definition, the courts have had to gradually delineate this legal concept over time.

[59] The line of authority based on *Cooper* clearly confirms that the scope of the legal concept of "mental disorder" is very broad. In *Cooper*, Dickson J. stated that the "disease of the mind" concept includes "any illness, disorder or abnormal condition which impairs the human mind and its functioning" (p. 1159). In *Rabey*, Dickson J. explained that "the concept is broad, embracing mental disorders of organic and functional origin, whether curable or incurable, temporary or not, recurring or non-recurring" (p. 533). While it must be borne in mind that a verdict of not criminally responsible triggers a special mechanism for the management of the accused, the inclusive nature of the definition of "mental disorder" can be explained in particular by Parliament's wish to give the public a high level of protection from persons who could be a threat to others (J. Barrett and R. Shandler, *Mental Disorder in Canadian Criminal Law* (loose-leaf), at p. 4-12).

[60] The "mental disorder" concept continues to evolve, which means that it can be adapted continually to advances in medical science (*R. v. Simpson* (1977), 35 C.C.C. (2d) 337 (Ont. C.A.)). As a result, it will undoubtedly never be possible to define and draw up an exhaustive list of the mental conditions that constitute "disease[s] of the mind" within the meaning of s. 2 *Cr. C.* As Martin J.A., writing for the Ontario Court of Appeal, stated in *R. v. Rabey* (1977), 17 O.R. (2d) 1, this concept "is not capable of precise definition" (p. 12). It is thus flexible enough to apply to any mental condition that, according to medical science in its current or future state, is indicative of a disorder that impairs the human mind or its functioning, and the recognition of which is compatible with the policy considerations that underlie the defence provided for in s. 16 *Cr. C.*

(2) Characterizing a Mental Condition as a "Mental Disorder" Is a Legal Exercise with a Medical and Scientific Substratum

[61] For the purposes of the *Criminal Code*, "disease of the mind" is a legal concept with a medical dimension. Although medical expertise plays an essential part in the legal characterization exercise, it has long been established in positive law that whether a particular mental condition can be characterized as a "mental disorder" is a question of law to be decided by the trial judge. In a jury trial, the judge decides this question, not the jury. As Martin J.A. stated in an oft-quoted passage from *Simpson*, "[i]t is the function of the psychiatrist to describe the accused's mental condition and how it is considered from the medical point of view. It is for the Judge to decide whether the condition described is comprehended by the term 'disease of the mind'" (p. 350). If the judge finds as a matter of law that the mental condition of the accused is a "mental disorder," it will ultimately be up to the jury to decide whether, on the facts, the accused was suffering from such a mental disorder at the time of the offence.

[62] Thus, the trial judge is not bound by the medical evidence, since medical experts generally take no account of the policy component of the analysis required by s. 16 *Cr. C.* (*Parks*, at pp. 899-900). Moreover, an expert's opinion on the legal issue of whether the

mental condition of the accused constitutes a "mental disorder" within the meaning of the *Criminal Code* has "little or no evidentiary value" (*R. v. Luedecke*, 2008 ONCA 716, 269 O.A.C. 1, at para. 113).

[63] The respective roles of the expert, the judge and the jury were summarized in *R. v. Stone*, [1999] 2 S.C.R. 290. Writing for the majority, Bastarache J. stated the following:

> Taken alone, the question of what mental conditions are included in the term "disease of the mind" is a question of law. However, the trial judge must also determine whether the condition the accused claims to have suffered from satisfies the legal test for disease of the mind. This involves an assessment of the particular evidence in the case rather than a general principle of law and is thus a question of mixed law and fact. ... The question of whether the accused actually suffered from a disease of the mind is a question of fact to be determined by the trier of fact. [Citation omitted; para. 197.]

[64] The central issue in this appeal is a question of law within the meaning of *Stone*. It is common ground that the appellant was in a psychotic condition that prevented him from distinguishing right from wrong. The main issue is whether a toxic psychosis caused exclusively by a single episode of intoxication constitutes a "mental disorder" within the meaning of s. 16 *Cr. C.*

[65] It can be seen at this point that the appellant's position poses a serious problem. To argue that toxic psychosis must always be considered a "mental disorder" is to say that the legal characterization exercise under s. 16 *Cr. C.* depends exclusively on a medical diagnosis. If the appellant's position were accepted, psychiatric experts would thus be responsible for determining the scope of the defence of not criminally responsible on account of mental disorder. This argument conflicts directly with this Court's consistent case law over the past three decades and cannot succeed. It would shift the responsibility for deciding whether the accused is guilty from the judge or jury to the expert.

E. Specific Problem of a Toxic Psychosis That Results from the Voluntary Consumption of Alcohol or Drugs

[66] An additional reason for rejecting the appellant's central argument has to do with the very diverse reality encompassed by the term "toxic psychosis." In the case law, this term usually refers to the symptoms of the accused as diagnosed by psychiatrists. However, medical science does not always identify the causes of toxic psychosis as precisely as is required in law. Although toxic psychosis is always related to exposure to a toxic substance, the circumstances in which it may arise can vary a great deal. This is readily apparent from a review of the case law on this point [citations omitted].

[67] Many factors might contribute to a state of substance-induced psychosis, including the fact that symptoms of a paranoid personality disorder are active at the time drugs are taken (*Mailloux*), the combined effect of exposure to toxic vapours and a period of intense stress (*Oakley*), dependence on certain drugs, such as cocaine (*Moroz* and *Snelgrove*), heavy drug use during the days and hours leading up to the commission of the crime (*Lauv* and *Paul*), and withdrawal following a period of excessive drinking (*R. v. Malcolm* (1989), 50 C.C.C. (3d) 172 (Man. C.A.)). It seems that this diversity of circumstances can be attributed to variations in psychological makeup and psychological histories from one accused to another, as well as in the nature of the drug use that contributed

to their psychoses. The quantity and toxicity of the drugs taken also seem to have a significant effect in this regard. As a result, in each new situation, the case turns on its own facts and cannot always be fitted easily into the existing case law.

[68] Because of the heterogeneous nature of the circumstances in which a toxic psychosis at the material time may be medically diagnosed, I consider it unwise to adopt an approach as broad as the one proposed by the appellant. In *Cooper*, this Court instead urged the courts to exercise particular caution where an accused person's mental condition was closely related to an episode of intoxication contemporaneous with the offence. In my opinion, the Court, in its decision in *Cooper*, recommended a contextual approach that was intended to strike a fair balance between the need to protect the public from persons whose mental state is inherently dangerous and the desire to impose criminal liability solely on persons who are responsible for the state they were in at the time of the offence. Since this contextual approach means that a court must base its analysis on the particular circumstances of the case before it, I cannot accept the recent decisions or opinions that seem to suggest that toxic psychosis is always a disease of the mind within the meaning of the *Criminal Code* [citations omitted].

[69] When confronted with a difficult fact situation involving a state of toxic psychosis that emerged while the accused was intoxicated, a court should start from the general principle that temporary psychosis is covered by the exclusion from *Cooper*. This principle is not absolute, however: the accused can rebut the presumption provided for in s. 16(2) *Cr. C.* by showing that, at the material time, he or she was suffering from a disease of the mind that was unrelated to the intoxication-related symptoms. To determine whether an accused has discharged the burden of proof in this respect, the court should adopt the "more holistic approach" described by Bastarache J. in *Stone* (para. 203). As the Attorney General of Ontario suggested in this Court, it is ultimately this "more holistic approach" that will enable a court to determine whether the mental condition of an accused at the material time constitutes a "mental disorder" for the purposes of s. 16 *Cr. C.* (Factum, at paras. 22-23).

[70] In *Stone*, Bastarache J. proposed a flexible approach structured around two analytical tools and certain policy considerations. The purpose of the approach is to help the courts distinguish mental conditions that fall within the scope of s. 16 *Cr. C.* from those covered by *Cooper*'s exclusion of "self-induced states caused by alcohol or drugs" (p. 1159). In other words, a court should use this approach to determine whether a medically diagnosed disease of the mind constitutes a mental disorder in the legal sense.

· · ·

[77] Although the courts can seek assistance from the existing case law, it would be preferable for them to engage in an individualized analysis that takes account of the specific circumstances of each case. This means that the courts should determine on a case-by-case basis, applying the "more holistic approach" from *Stone*, whether the mental condition of each accused is included in or excluded from the definition of "disease of the mind" proposed by Dickson J. in *Cooper*. This approach is consistent with the line of authority based on *Rabey*, in which this Court endorsed Martin J.A.'s opinion that "[p]articular transient mental disturbances may not … be capable of being properly categorized in relation to whether they constitute 'disease of the mind' on the basis of a generalized statement and must be decided on a case-by-case basis" (pp. 519-20).

F. Application of the Principles to This Appeal

. . .

[85] In this context, I conclude that the appellant was not suffering from a "mental disorder" for the purposes of s. 16 *Cr. C.* at the time he committed the assault. He has failed to rebut the presumption that his toxic psychosis was a "self-induced stat[e] caused by alcohol or drugs" in accordance with the definition in *Cooper*. A malfunctioning of the mind that results *exclusively* from self-induced intoxication cannot be considered a disease of the mind in the legal sense, since it is not a product of the individual's inherent psychological makeup. This is true even though medical science may tend to consider such conditions to be diseases of the mind. In circumstances like those of the case at bar, toxic psychosis seems to be nothing more than a symptom, albeit an extreme one, of the accused person's state of self-induced intoxication. Such a state cannot justify exempting an accused from criminal responsibility under s. 16 *Cr. C.*

[86] This conclusion takes account of the policy considerations referred to by Dickson J. in *Cooper*. In light of Dr. Faucher's expert assessment of the frequency of toxic psychosis in circumstances analogous to the ones in the instant case, the appellant's position, if adopted, would affect the integrity of the criminal justice system in ways that would be difficult to accept. If everyone who committed a violent offence while suffering from toxic psychosis were to be found not criminally responsible on account of mental disorder regardless of the origin or cause of the psychosis, the scope of the defence provided for in s. 16 *Cr. C.* would become much broader than Parliament intended. These considerations reinforce the conclusion that the toxic psychosis of the appellant in this case is covered by *Cooper*'s exclusion of "self-induced states caused by alcohol or drugs."

Appeal dismissed.

The determination of whether the accused suffers from a disease of the mind is often crucial in cases of automatism or involuntary conduct, because an accused who acts in an involuntary manner will satisfy one or both of the arms of the mental disorder defence—namely, he or she will be incapable of (1) appreciating the nature and quality of the act or (2) knowing that the act is wrong. Automatism is discussed in Section IV of this chapter. The two alternative arms of the second element of the mental disorder defence will now be explored.

Appreciating the Nature and Quality of the Act

Cooper v The Queen
Supreme Court of Canada
[1980] 1 SCR 1149

DICKSON J (Laskin CJ and Beetz, Estey, and McIntyre JJ concurring): ... In contrast to the position in England under the M'Naghten rules, where the words used are "knows the nature and quality of his act," s. 16 of the *Code* uses the phrase "appreciating the nature and quality of an act or omission." The two are not synonymous. The draftsman of the *Code*, as originally enacted, made a deliberate change in language from the common law rule in order to broaden the legal and medical considerations bearing upon the mental state of the accused and to make it clear that cognition was not to be the sole criterion. Emotional, as well as intellectual, awareness of the significance of the conduct, is in issue. The *Report of the Royal Commission on the Law of Insanity as a Defence in Criminal Cases* (McRuer Report) (Canada, Queen's Printer (1956)), contains a useful discussion on the point (p. 12):

> ... An examination of the civil law of England and Canada shows that there is an important difference between "know" or "knowledge" on the one hand and "appreciate" or "appreciation" on the other when used and applied to a given set of circumstances. This is best illustrated by the principles of law underlying those cases in which the maxim *volenti non fit injuria* is involved. There is a clear distinction between mere knowledge of the risk and appreciation of both the risk and the danger.

To "know" the nature and quality of an act may mean merely to be aware of the physical act, while to "appreciate" may involve estimation and understanding of the consequences of that act. In the case of the appellant, as an example, in using his hands to choke the deceased, he may well have known the nature and quality of that physical act of choking. It is entirely different to suggest, however, that in performing the physical act of choking, he was able to appreciate its nature and quality in the sense of being aware that it could lead to or result in her death. In the opinion of the medical expert who testified at the trial, the appellant could have been capable of intending bodily harm and of choking the girl, but not of having intended her death.

Our *Code* postulates an independent test, requiring a level of understanding of the act which is more than mere knowledge that it is taking place; in short, a capacity to apprehend the nature of the act and its consequences. The position in law is well expressed in the McRuer Report at p. 12:

> Under the Canadian statute law a disease of the mind that renders the accused person incapable of an appreciation of the nature and quality of the act must necessarily involve more than mere knowledge that the act is being committed, there must be an appreciation of the factors involved in the act and a mental capacity to measure and foresee the consequences of the violent conduct.

· · ·

The test proposed in the McRuer Report, which I would adopt (save for deletion of the word "fully" in the fourth line), is this (p. 13):

> The true test necessarily is, was the accused person at the very time of the offence—not before or after, but at the moment of the offence—by reason of disease of the mind, unable fully to appreciate not only the nature of the act but the natural consequences that would flow from it? In other words was the accused person, by reason of disease of the mind, deprived of the mental capacity to foresee and measure the consequences of the act?

The legally relevant time is the time when the act was committed.

In the *Simpson* decision, Martin J.A. offered the view that s. 16(2) exempts from liability an accused who, due to a disease of the mind, has no real understanding of the nature, character and consequences of the act at the time of its commission. I agree. With respect, I accept the view that the first branch of the test, in employing the word "appreciates," imports an additional requirement to mere knowledge of the physical quality of the act. The requirement, unique to Canada, is that of perception, an ability to perceive the consequences, impact, and results of a physical act. An accused may be aware of the physical character of his action (i.e., in choking) without necessarily having the capacity to appreciate that, in nature and quality, that act will result in the death of a human being. This is simply a restatement, specific to the defence of insanity, of the principle that *mens rea*, or intention as to the consequences of an act, is a requisite element in the commission of a crime.

See also, to the same effect, the unanimous judgments of the Supreme Court of Canada in *R v Barnier*, [1980] 1 SCR 1124, per Estey J, and *Kjeldsen v The Queen*, [1981] 2 SCR 617, per McIntyre J. In *Kjeldsen*, the Court stated:

> To be capable of "appreciating" the nature and quality of his acts, an accused person must have the capacity to know what he is doing; in the case at bar, for example, to know that he was hitting the woman on the head with the rock, with great force, and in addition he must have the capacity to estimate and to understand the physical consequences which would flow from his act, in this case that he was causing physical injury which could result in death.

The Court adopted the reasoning in the following statement by Martin JA in *Regina v Simpson* (1977), 35 CCC (2d) 337 (Ont CA):

> While I am of the view that s. 16(2) exempts from liability an accused who by reason of disease of the mind has no real understanding of the nature, character and consequences of the act at the time of its commission, I do not think the exemption provided by the section extends to one who has the necessary understanding of the nature, character and consequences of the act, but merely lacks appropriate feelings for the victim or lacks feelings of remorse or guilt for what he has done, even though such lack of feeling stems from "disease of the mind." Appreciation of the nature and quality of the act does not import a requirement that the act be accompanied by appropriate feeling about the effect of the act on other people: see *Willgoss v. The Queen* (1960), 105 C.L.R. 295; *R. v. Leech* (1972), 10 C.C.C. (2d) 149, 21 C.R.N.S. 1, [1973] 1 W.W.R. 744; *R. v. Craig* (1974), 22 C.C.C. (2d) 212, [1975] 2 W.W.R. 314 [affirmed 28 C.C.C. (2d) 311]. No doubt the absence of such feelings is a common characteristic of many persons who engage in repeated and serious criminal conduct.

R v Abbey
Supreme Court of Canada
[1982] 2 SCR 24

[The accused was charged with importing cocaine and possession of cocaine for the purpose of trafficking contrary to ss 5 and 4(2) of the *Narcotic Control Act*, RSC 1970, c N-1, and at a trial before a judge without a jury relied on the defence of insanity. The accused had agreed to buy cocaine in Peru for himself and some friends and upon his return the drug was located in a cursory check by customs officials. At the time that he went through customs and in the following period when he was arrested, the accused appeared normal.

The accused did not testify and the only defence evidence called was that of a psychiatrist who based his opinion on interviews he had with the accused and with the accused's mother and on other psychiatric reports. Both the defence psychiatrist and the Crown psychiatrist who was called in reply agreed that the accused suffered from a disease of the mind known as hypomania, but they differed as to whether he was incapable of appreciating the nature and quality of his acts. They did agree, however, that he knew what he was doing and that it was wrong. In giving effect to the defence, the trial judge found that the accused had a delusion that he was in receipt of power from a source external to himself and that he was protected from punishment by the mysterious external force. The trial judge found that the accused's ability to appreciate the nature and quality of the act was incapacitated to the degree required by s 16 of the *Criminal Code* in that he failed to appreciate the consequences of punishment for his acts. The trial judge also referred to a closely related delusion that the accused was irrevocably committed to importing the cocaine by reason of a force acting upon him. An appeal by the Crown from the finding of not guilty by reason of insanity was dismissed by the British Columbia Court of Appeal.]

DICKSON J (for the Court): … Dr. Vallance's opinion was that Abbey, at all material times, was suffering from a disease of the mind, a manic illness, known as hypomania. While Abbey appreciated that he was bringing cocaine into Canada and knew that what he was doing was wrong, he believed that, if caught, he would not be punished. Dr. Vallance said:

> He had a considerable disturbance of mood. He had delusional ideas. He had hallucinatory experiences. It's difficult under circumstances like that to fully appreciate what you are doing, particularly when the feelings and delusional ideas are tangled up with what you are doing. If you feel that you are for some delusional idea inordinately powerful or safe, then that impairs good judgment. I am sure he had some appreciation of what he was doing.

Dr. Vallance further testified that, while Abbey was not rendered totally incapable of appreciating the nature and quality of his acts by reason of the disease of mind from which he suffered, there was a degree of impairment of judgment. He had the feeling that he was being looked after by some outside force that was feeding him strength and that no harm would come to him and even if he did get caught it did not matter because somehow he would be looked after. Dr. Vallance made reference to Abbey's delusional belief that he was committed to a particular path of action which he could not change and his further delusional idea, while in Lima, Peru, that he had "astro-travelled" back to Vancouver already and that in getting on the plane in Lima to fly home he was simply having the body follow where the "rest" had already gone.

… In finding Abbey not guilty by reason of insanity the judge concluded that "one, who like Abbey suffers from the delusion that he is protected from punishment by some mysterious external force which comes to him as described in the evidence of Dr. Vallance, has his ability to appreciate the nature and quality of his acts incapacitated to the degree required to meet the test of s. 16(2). He is, by disease of the mind, deprived of the ability to assess an important consequence of his act. He is deprived of the effect of the penal sanctions. …"

… Taggart J.A., speaking for the Court of Appeal, said that *Cooper v. The Queen*, [[1980] 1 SCR 1149], and *R. v. Barnier*, [1980] 1 S.C.R. 1124 made it clear that there is a distinction between "know" and "appreciate" and that the words "appreciate the nature and quality of his acts" connote more than a mere knowledge of the physical nature of the acts being committed. With respect, I agree. The British Columbia Court of Appeal failed, however, to deal with the question of what it is an accused must fail to "appreciate" before he can be found legally insane. The court simply accepted the trial judge's conclusion that somebody who, because of a disease of the mind, has the delusion that he is protected from punishment by some mysterious external force, is incapacitated from appreciating the nature and quality of his acts.

... "Consequences" in *Cooper v. The Queen, R. v. Barnier* and *Kjeldsen v. The Queen* refer to the physical consequences of the act. All three cases were murder cases, violent crimes in which there was a victim who suffered the "consequences" of the accused's actions ... (*Cooper v. The Queen*, at pp. 1162-63).

· · ·

Although there is some controversy in academic circles, I adopt the more traditional view espoused by Glanville Williams, *Criminal Law, The General Part*, 2nd ed. (1961), para. 166, p. 525, that a delusion falling under the "first arm" of the insanity defence negatives an element of the crime, the *mens rea*.

... A delusion which renders an accused "incapable of appreciating the nature and quality of his act" goes to the *mens rea* of the offence and brings into operation the "first arm" of s. 16(2): he is not guilty by reason of insanity. A delusion which renders an accused incapable of appreciating that the penal sanctions attaching to the commission of the crime are applicable to him does not go to the *mens rea* of the offence, does not render him incapable of appreciating the nature and quality of the act, and does not bring into operation the "first arm" of the insanity defence.

· · ·

I am of the view that the trial judge erred in law in holding that a person who by reason of disease of the mind does not "appreciate" the penal consequences of his actions is insane within the meaning of s. 16(2) of the *Criminal Code*.

Appeal allowed; new trial ordered.

Knowing That the Act Is Wrong

R v Chaulk
Supreme Court of Canada
[1990] 3 SCR 1303

[The accused appealed from the judgment of the Manitoba Court of Appeal, which had dismissed their appeals from convictions for first-degree murder. The Supreme Court's decision upholding the reverse onus provision under s 1 of the Charter was set out earlier in this chapter.]

LAMER CJ (Dickson CJ and Wilson, La Forest, Gonthier, and Cory JJ concurring): ... This Court has also been asked to revisit its interpretation of the meaning of the word "wrong" found in s. 16(2). There are other issues specific to the appeal which are set out further on in these reasons.

On September 3, 1985, the appellants Chaulk and Morrissette entered a home in Winnipeg, plundered it for valuables and then stabbed and bludgeoned its sole occupant to death. A week later they turned themselves in, making full confessions.

After a transfer proceeding in the Youth Court (Chaulk and Morrissette were 15 and 16 years of age, respectively), the appellants were tried and convicted of first degree murder by a jury in the Manitoba Court of Queen's Bench. The only defence raised was insanity within the meaning of s. 16 of the Code. Expert evidence was given at trial that the appellants suffered from a paranoid psychosis which made them believe that they had the power to rule the world and that the killing was a necessary means to that end. They knew the laws of Canada existed, but believed that they were above the ordinary law; they thought the law was irrelevant to them. They thought they had a right to kill the victim because he was "a loser." ...

In his directions to the jury, Ferg J. clearly stated the meaning that was to be given to the term "wrong" for the purposes of s. 16(2). He directed:

> Next as an alternative even if the accused did appreciate the nature and quality of what he was doing and it's for you to decide, as I've said, is also insanity if the accused was laboring under a disease of the mind that rendered him incapable of knowing that his act was wrong. [sic] By wrong I mean that it was a criminal act or legally wrong.

[The trial judge repeated these instructions when the jury, after deliberating for some time, asked the following:

> Re: Knowledge of the laws of Canada:
>   (a) does this refer to simple knowledge of the rules as evidenced by recognition of the consequences, i.e.: police and jail term or;
>   (b) does it refer to their awareness of whether the laws apply to them at the time of the murder ... ?]

Ferg J. answered their question by repeating substantially what he had stated in his original direction. He summarized:

> This part is the alternative, the second part, and this has to do with knowledge capable of knowing his act was wrong. As an alternative even if the accused did—if you find that it's for you to decide—did appreciate the nature and quality of what he was doing, and it's for you to decide as I just said, it is also insanity if the accused was laboring under a disease of the mind that rendered him incapable of knowing that his act was wrong and by the word wrong I mean that it was a criminal act or illegally wrong, if you will, the laws of Canada.

The Court of Appeal found no error on the part of the trial judge in directing the jury, stating that it was clear that the appellants "knew and fully appreciated the nature and consequences of their acts and they knew that what they were doing was legally wrong."

... The appellants submit that the term "wrong" for the purposes of s. 16(2) should be interpreted to mean "morally" wrong and not "legally" wrong. The respondent made no submission with respect to this issue in its factum, but argued orally that, regardless of the meaning that is to be given to the word "wrong" in this case, the difference between morally wrong and legally wrong where a very serious offence such as murder is involved "is so narrow as to be hardly worth the effort of deciding between them." It was further argued in oral pleadings that the meaning of "wrong" in s. 16(2), having its source in the seminal judgment of the House of Lords in *M'Naghten's Case* (1843), 10 Cl. & Fin. 200, 8 E.R. 718, incorporates not only a moral but also a legal dimension in such a way that the two cannot be divorced, with the result that a person who knows that an act is legally wrong must also comprehend that the act is morally wrong.

The meaning of the term "wrong" for the purposes of s. 16(2) was determined by this court in *Schwartz v. The Queen*, [1977] 1 S.C.R. 673. Speaking for the majority, Martland J. held that the capacity to know that an act is wrong in this context means no more than the capacity to know that what one is doing is against the law of the land.

. . .

Dickson J., as he then was, dissented in *Schwartz*. He noted that the word "wrong" as used in s. 16(2) is ambiguous and is capable of meaning either "legally" or "morally" wrong. He also noted that the issue had given rise to conflicting lines of authority in England, Australia and Canada.

In order to resolve this question, Dickson J. first examined the internal structure of the Code in order to determine the meaning that Parliament intended to give the term. It would have been internally coherent, he submitted, for Parliament to use the word "unlawful" if it had intended "wrong" to mean "contrary to law." Furthermore, the use of the word "mauvais" in the French version of s. 16(2) suggests that Parliament intended the term to have a meaning broader than merely "unlawful." Lastly, s. 13 formerly provided that no child between seven and thirteen years of age could be convicted of a criminal offence "unless he was competent to know the nature and consequences of his conduct and to appreciate that it was wrong"; it would be insupportable, in this context, to equate knowledge that an act is wrong with the knowledge that the act is contrary to law.

Dickson J. then considered jurisprudential and doctrinal authorities antedating *M'Naghten's Case* and concluded that the historical common law test to determine the criminal responsibility of insane persons was whether the particular accused had the capacity to distinguish between conduct that was good or evil, right or wrong. *M'Naghten's Case*, in his view, did not depart from this standard. In fact, the case drew a clear line between knowledge that an act is illegal and knowledge that the act is one that a person ought not do; this distinction is revealed in the following passage in *M'Naghten's Case* (at p. 723 [ER]):

> If the accused was conscious that the act was one which he ought not to do, and if that act was at the same time contrary to the law of the land, he is punishable.

This passage indicates clearly that an accused will only be convicted if he commits an act which he knows he ought not do and which, at the same time, is contrary to law. ...

More fundamentally, Dickson J. concluded that a reading of s. 16(2) as a whole leads to the conclusion that "wrong" must mean contrary to the ordinary moral standards of reasonable men and women. The object of s. 16(2) is to protect individuals who do not have the capacity to judge whether an act is wrong; the inquiry as to the capacity of an accused to reason must not end simply because it is determined that the accused knew that the act was a crime. He argued that this would not serve to protect amoral persons since any incapacity must result from a disease of the mind (at p. 22):

Section 16(2) must be read *in toto*. One looks at capacity to reason and to reach rational decisions as to whether the act is morally wrong. If wrong simply means "illegal" this virtually forecloses any inquiry as to capacity. The question for the jury is whether mental illness so obstructed the thought processes of the accused as to make him incapable of knowing that his acts were morally wrong. The argument is sometimes advanced that a moral test favours the amoral offender and that the most favoured will be he who had rid himself of all moral compunction. This argument overlooks the factor of disease of the mind. If, as a result of disease of the mind, the offender has lost completely the ability to make moral distinctions and acts under an insane delusion, it can well be said that he should not be criminally accountable.

The interpretation of "wrong" as meaning "morally wrong" would not, in his opinion, have the effect of opening up the insanity defence to a far greater number of accused persons. First, what is illegal and what breaches society's moral standards does not often differ. Secondly, " '[m]oral wrong' is not to be judged by the personal standards of the offender but by his awareness that society regards the act as wrong" (p. 13). He concluded that an accused is not therefore free, as a result of such interpretation, to substitute at will his own sense of morality for that of society, but is to be acquitted by reason of insanity if, by reason of disease of the mind, he is incapable of knowing that society generally considers a particular act to be immoral.

With respect for contrary views, it is my opinion that *Schwartz* was wrongly decided by this Court and that the dissenting opinion of Dickson J. (concurred in by Laskin C.J., Spence and Beetz JJ.) is to be preferred. The majority judgment fails, in my respectful view, to appreciate the manner in which insanity renders our normal principles of criminal responsibility inapplicable to an individual as well as the particular objectives of s. 16 of the Code. ...

In my view, *Schwartz* had the effect of expanding the scope of criminal responsibility unacceptably to include persons who, by reason of disease of the mind, were incapable of knowing that an act was wrong according to the normal and reasonable standards of society even though they were aware that the act was formally a crime. It is now necessary for this Court to reconsider its decision in *Schwartz* in order to redefine the scope of criminal liability in a manner that will bring it into accordance with the basic principles of our criminal law.

The rationale underlying the defence of insanity in Canada, as discussed above under the rubric "The Nature of the Insanity Provisions," rests on the belief that persons suffering from insanity should not be subject to standard criminal culpability with its resulting punishment and stigmatization. This belief, in turn, flows from the principle that individuals are held responsible for the commission of criminal offences because they possess the capacity to distinguish between what is right and what is wrong.

Section 16(2) of the Code embodies this conception of criminal responsibility by providing that no person shall be convicted of an offence who, at the time of committing the act in question, is in a state of "natural imbecility" or has disease of the mind to such a degree as to render him incapable of "knowing that an act or omission is wrong." The principal issue in this regard is the capacity of the accused person to know that a particular act or omission is wrong. As such, to ask simply what is the meaning of the word "wrong" for the purposes of s. 16(2) is to frame the question too narrowly. To paraphrase the words of the House of Lords in *M'Naghten's Case*, the courts must determine in any particular case *whether an accused was rendered incapable, by the fact of his mental disorder, of knowing that the act committed was one that he ought not have done.*

Viewed from this perspective, it is plain to me that the term "wrong" as used in s. 16(2) must mean more than simply legally wrong. In considering the capacity of a person to know whether an act is one that he ought or ought not to do, the inquiry cannot terminate with the discovery that the accused knew that the act was contrary to the formal law. A person may well be aware that an act is contrary to law but, by reason of "natural imbecility" or disease of the mind, is at the same time incapable of knowing that the act is morally wrong in the circumstances according to the moral standards of society. This would be the case, for example, if the person suffered from a disease of the mind to such a degree as to know that it is legally wrong to kill but, as described by Dickson J. in *Schwartz*, kills "in the belief that it is in response to a divine order and therefore not morally wrong" (p. 678).

In applying s. 16(2) to a particular set of facts, it may be established that the accused who attempts to invoke the insanity defence is capable of knowing that he ought not do the act because he knows, first, that the act is contrary to the formal law or, secondly, that the act breaches the standard of moral conduct that society expects of its members. ...

An interpretation of s. 16(2) that makes the defence available to an accused who knew that he or she was committing a crime but was unable to comprehend that the act was a moral wrong will not open the floodgates to amoral offenders or to offenders who relieve themselves of all moral considerations. First, the incapacity to make moral judgments must be causally linked to a disease of the mind; if the presence of a serious mental disorder is not established, criminal responsibility cannot be avoided. Secondly, as was pointed out by Dickson J. in *Schwartz, supra,* "'[m]oral wrong' is not to be judged by the personal standards of the offender but by his awareness that society regards the act as wrong" (p. 678). The accused will not benefit from substituting his own moral code for that of society. Instead, he will be protected by s. 16(2) if he is incapable of understanding that the act is wrong according to the ordinary moral standards of reasonable members of society.

In the case at bar, the trial judge directed the jury that the insanity defence was not available to the appellants pursuant to the second branch of the test set out in s. 16(2) if it reached the conclusion that the appellants knew, at the time of committing the offence, that the act was contrary to the laws of Canada. Of course, he cannot be faulted for having followed the decision of this Court in *Schwartz*. Nevertheless, for the reasons discussed above, our interpretation of s. 16(2) in *Schwartz* was not correct. As a result, I would order a new trial. ...

McLACHLIN J (L'Heureux-Dubé and Sopinka JJ concurring) (dissenting): ... Lamer C.J. has accepted the appellants' invitation to reconsider this Court's earlier conclusion that the capacity to know the act or omission was legally wrong suffices. In his view, an accused who is capable of knowing an act or omission is legally wrong is not subject to the criminal process if mental illness rendered him or her incapable of knowing the act or omission was morally wrong. I, on the other hand, take the view that it does not matter whether the capacity relates to legal wrongness or moral wrongness—all that is required is that the accused be capable of knowing that the act was in some sense "wrong." If the accused has this capacity, then it is neither unfair nor unjust to submit the accused to criminal responsibility and penal sanction.

The latter position is supported in my view by: (a) the plain language of s. 16(2); (b) an historical view of our insanity provisions; (c) the purpose and theory underlying our insanity provisions; and (d) by practical difficulties related to the problem of determining what is "morally wrong." I will consider each of these arguments in turn. ...

... I turn now to the purpose and theory underlying the insanity provisions. In my view, they too support the view that "wrong" in s. 16(2) of the Code means simply that which one "ought not to do." The rationale behind the insanity provisions, as discussed earlier in these reasons, is that it is unfair and unjust to make a person who is not capable of conscious choice between right or wrong criminally responsible. Penal sanctions are appropriate only for those who have the ability to reason right from wrong, people capable of appreciating what they ought and ought not to do. A person may conclude that he or she ought not to do an act for a variety of reasons. One may be that it is illegal. Another may be that it is immoral. The reasons for which one concludes that one ought not to do an act are collateral to the fundamental rationale behind the insanity provisions—that criminal conviction is appropriate only where the person is capable of understanding that he or she ought not to do the act in question.

The wider rationale underlying the criminal law generally supports the same view. While other factors may figure, two main mechanisms function to keep people's conduct within the appropriate legal parameters: (1) a sense of morality, and (2) a desire to obey the law. In most cases, law and morality are coextensive, but exceptionally they are different. Where morality fails, the legal sanction should not be removed as well. To do so is to open the door to arguments that absence of moral discernment should excuse a person from the sanction of the criminal law, and thus remove one of the factors which deters inappropriate and destructive conduct. That should not be done lightly. The fact that such arguments could not be entertained without establishing a "disease of the mind" is small comfort when one takes account of the difficulty of defining or diagnosing "disease of the mind." Recent research seems to suggest that the vast majority of forensic psychiatrists and psychologists, including those who have given evidence with respect to legal insanity in a large number of cases, have no effective understanding of the legal test about which they are expressing an opinion: R. Rogers and R.E. Turner, "Understanding of Insanity: A National Survey of Forensic Psychiatrists and Psychologists" (1987), 7 *Health L. Can.* 71. See also J. Ziskin, D. Faust, *Coping with Psychiatric and Psychological Testimony* (4th ed. 1988), vol. I, at pp. 389-408.

To hold that absence of moral discernment due to mental illnesses should exempt a person who knows that legally he or she ought not do to a certain act is, moreover, to introduce a lack of parallelism into the criminal law; generally absence of moral appreciation is no excuse for criminal conduct. When the moral mechanism breaks down in the case of an individual who is sane, we do not treat that as an excuse for disobeying the law; for example, in the case of a psychopath. The rationale is that an individual either knows or is presumed to know the law, and the fact that his or her moral standards are at variance with those of society is not an excuse. Why, if the moral mechanism breaks down because of disease of the mind, should it exempt the accused from criminal responsibility where he or she knows, or was capable of knowing, that the act was illegal and hence one which he or she "ought not to do." Why should deficiency of moral appreciation due to mental illness have a different consequence than deficiency of moral appreciation due to a morally-impoverished upbringing, for example? I see no reason why the policy of the law should differ in the two cases. ...

The problem with making capacity to appreciate moral wrong the test for criminal responsibility where the incapacity is caused by mental illness is that of determining what society's moral judgment will be in every situation. What result is to obtain on those occasions where an accused claims an incapacity to know that his or her unlawful act was morally wrong and, objectively, the act was one for which the moral wrongfulness can be disputed? Certainly a court is in no position to make determinations on questions of morality, nor is it fair to expect a jury to be able to agree on what is morally right or morally wrong. The prospect of greater certainty, and the avoidance of metaphysical arguments on right and wrong is the chief advantage of adhering to the traditional *M'Naghten* test for criminal responsibility where causative disease of the mind exists—whether the accused, for whatever reason, was capable of appreciating that his or her act is wrong.

Appeal allowed; new trial ordered.

R v Oommen
Supreme Court of Canada
[1994] 2 SCR 507

[The accused suffered from a paranoid delusion and believed that the woman he repeatedly shot was part of a conspiracy that was coming into his house to kill him. The trial judge held that the accused was not entitled to the mental disorder defence because he had the capacity to know that society in general would regard his acts as wrong even though "subjectively the accused did not believe his act to be wrong" and "he believed that he had no choice to do anything but what he did."

The Supreme Court reversed his murder conviction and ordered a new trial in which the accused could raise the mental disorder defence.]

McLACHLIN J (for the Court): In the early morning hours of March 24, 1991, Mathew Oommen killed Gina Lynn Beaton as she lay sleeping on a mattress in his apartment by firing 9 to 13 shots at her from a .22 calibre rimfire semi-automatic repeating rifle. On February 26, 1992, he was convicted of second degree murder before a judge alone and sentenced to life imprisonment without eligibility for parole for 10 years. The Alberta Court of Appeal set aside the conviction and ordered a new trial on the ground that the trial judge had erred in his interpretation of the insanity provision of s. 16(1) of the *Criminal Code*, R.S.C., 1985, c. C-46. The Crown appeals to this court against that order, seeking reinstatement of the conviction for murder.

The Evidence

The evidence disclosed no rational motive for the killing. To understand it, we must delve into the disordered workings of Mr. Oommen's mind.

For a number of years Mr. Oommen had been suffering from a mental disorder described as a psychosis of a paranoid delusional type. As a result, he harboured false and fixed beliefs that he was the butt of conspiracies and situations that endangered him. Mr. Oommen's disorder had led to hospitalization in 1984, 1988 and in February, 1991, shortly before he killed Ms. Beaton.

At the time of the killing, Mr. Oommen's paranoia was fixed on a belief that the members of a local union were conspiring to destroy him. In November, 1986, he had been struck on the head and robbed while driving a taxi-cab. Mr. Oommen attributed this incident to the fact that he had transported certain individuals during labour disputes at one of the local plants. His friends and doctors testified that he became paranoid that there would be further attacks on his life.

At this point, Gina Lynn Beaton came into Mr. Oommen's life and tragically became part of his delusion. The two met prior to Christmas, 1990. Ms. Beaton needed a place to stay. Mr. Oommen let her stay in his apartment for a period of time, in return for some cooking and cleaning. Mr. Oommen sought the advice of both friends and a local police officer as to the propriety of his sheltering Ms. Beaton. He seemed to be concerned that the relationship might be misapprehended as sexual. After a while, Ms. Beaton left the apartment and moved to Edmonton. Shortly before her death, she returned to Fort Mc-Murray and Mr. Oommen's apartment.

Mr. Oommen became fixated with the notion that his assailants and enemies had incorporated Ms. Beaton and commissioned her to kill him. On the evening of the killing he became convinced that members of the conspiracy had surrounded his apartment building with the intention of moving in on him and killing him. This delusion, combined with his belief that Ms. Beaton was one of the conspirators, convinced him that he was obliged to kill her to prevent her from killing him. So he shot her while she lay sleeping on the floor.

It was established that about the time of the killing, Mr. Oommen called a taxi dispatcher several times to request the police. It was also established that someone had rung the buzzers or doorbells of all the apartments. Mr. Oommen said that this was the signal from the conspirators outside to Ms. Beaton to kill him. A tenant, awakened by the doorbell, saw Mr. Oommen outside the building twice soon afterward, apparently putting liquor containers in the garbage. Another tenant, similarly awakened, went out into the hall and met Mr. Oommen, who asked him to call the police because he had just killed someone who had come at him with a knife. When the police arrived Mr. Oommen told the officer: "I called the caretaker. I shot and killed a girl inside. She thought I was sleeping. She came with a knife. I had no other choice, so I shot her, okay." Mr. Oommen repeated this story to the lawyer a friend found for him, Mr. George. He explained that he had shot and killed the girl who had been staying with him. Mr. George asked why. Mr. Oommen replied that she had tried to come with a knife and kill him. He said he saw something, a shiny object, in her hand and "instead [of] she killing me, I went and lowered the gun and killed her."

Mr. Oommen repeated this story at 5:27 a.m. in his statement to the police. Constable Bazowski observed that during the interview, Mr. Oommen vacillated between quiet and animated behaviour. Sometimes his voice would drop to a whisper; sometimes he would pound his fist on the table to emphasize his points. He seemed eager to offer an explanation of what had happened. He explained that he had seen the deceased pass his bedroom door with a knife in her hand as she went to the washroom on more than one occasion during the night. He knew that she was going to kill him, he thought on the instructions of others, and he "opened fire" on her as she lay pretending to be asleep. He had no choice or he would have been killed. Constable Bazowski gained the impression that Mr. Oommen believed the constable was investigating or ought to investigate why the girl was trying to kill him.

There was no question at trial that Mr. Oommen had killed Ms. Beaton. Nor was there much doubt that Mr. Oommen's insane delusions provoked the killing. As Dr. Trichard testified:

> He, on that very night of the assault, was convinced that there were people outside the building that had staked out the building and were coming to attack him. He had, in fact, heard the buzzers being rung throughout the building and had incorporated this into the idea that he was being pursued.
>
> On the night in question, he also became convinced that his assailants had incorporated the unfortunate deceased and had given her the commission that she was to kill him. So that on that night, it was him alone with her in this apartment, and it was either she was going to kill him, or he had to stop her. I believe that he was therefore acting under a delusion at the time that he committed this offence.

The only issue was whether this delusion exempted Mr. Oommen from criminal responsibility under s. 16(1) of the *Criminal Code* on the ground that he lacked the capacity at the relevant time to know the difference between right and wrong. Dr. Trichard testified that a person suffering from this mental disorder would not lose the intellectual capacity to understand right from wrong and would know that to kill a person is wrong. However, the person's delusions would affect the person's interpretation of events so that the individual would honestly believe killing to be justified under the circumstances. In the abstract, the person would know killing was wrong. But his delusion would cause him to believe that killing was justified under the circumstances as he perceived them. In Crown cross-examination Dr. Trichard stated:

> Q. You have a person suffering from the disease that you have described. He kills someone and does not believe he has done wrong, or does not at the time he is doing the killing believe he is doing wrong. In this disorder as opposed to others, that cannot be because he thinks killing is not wrong in any abstract sense, but because he has some particular delusion or belief, or maybe some actual information—maybe his killing really is justified in a particular situation—but he has some believe [sic] that justifies it to him.
>
> A. I believe that would be so, yes.

And again:

> Q. Dr. Trichard, if you could address yourself then to the account you received of Mr. Oommen's case and the killing that he did, it would be your belief that he, in his own mind at the time of doing it, would, because of his delusions and his fear, feel he was justified in doing what he was doing?
>
> A. Yes, I do believe that.

In other words, Mr. Oommen possessed the general capacity to distinguish right from wrong. However, on the night of the killing, his delusions deprived him of the capacity to know that killing Ms. Beaton was wrong. On the contrary, those delusions led him to believe that killing was necessary and justified. ...

The trial judge found that the accused was acting under the influence of a paranoid delusion at the time of the killing and that this was the cause of the killing: "When I consider what caused the murder, I find that I have very little doubt that it was caused and, indeed, compelled by the mental disorder suffered by [Mr. Oommen] and described by the psychiatrists as a psychosis of a delusional paranoid type." The trial judge found that on a balance of probabilities Mr. Oommen "was capable of knowing that what he was doing was wrong according to moral standards of society. ... [H]e was capable of knowing that society in general would regard it as wrong."

Despite this general capacity to distinguish right from wrong, the trial judge found as a fact that "subjectively the accused did not believe his act to be wrong." Whether because of this subjective belief in the rightness of his act or confusion engendered by the delusion, the trial judge found that Mr. Oommen was unable to apply his general ability to distinguish right from wrong to the act of killing Ms. Beaton: "I must say that I'm certain that the fact of that knowledge could not have in any way assisted the accused in refraining from committing the act because in his own mind he believed he had no choice to do anything but what he did." The trial judge concluded that in view of the accused's general capacity to know right from wrong, he was not relieved from criminal responsibility under s. 16(1), notwithstanding his subjective belief that what he did was right and his inability to apply his general knowledge of right and wrong. ...

Section 16(1) affirms that a person who lacks the capacity to know that the act he is committing is wrong is exempt from criminal responsibility.

This appeal poses the following legal issue. What is meant by the phrase "knowing that [the act] was wrong" in s. 16(1)? Does it refer only to abstract knowledge that the act of killing would be viewed as wrong by society? Or does it extend to the inability to rationally apply knowledge of right and wrong and hence to conclude that the act in question is one which one ought not to do?

A review of the history of our insanity provision and the cases indicates that the inquiry focuses not on general capacity to know right from wrong, but rather on the ability to know that a particular act was wrong in the circumstances. The accused must possess the intellectual ability to know right from wrong in an abstract sense. But he or she must also possess the ability to apply that knowledge in a rational way to the alleged criminal act.

The wording of s. 16(1) suggests this result. It proclaims that the focus is not a general capacity to understand that the act, say of killing, is wrong, but rather the act "committed" or omission "made," i.e., the particular act or omission at issue in the criminal proceedings.

The history of s. 16(1) confirms this. The provision finds its origin in the "*M'Naghten Rules*": *M'Naghten's Case* (1843), 10 Cl. & Fin. 200, 8 E.R. 718. The House of Lords put the following questions, inter alia, to the judges (at p. 203 Cl. & Fin., p. 720 E.R.):

> 2d. What are the proper questions to be submitted to the jury, when a person alleged to be afflicted with insane delusion respecting one or more particular subjects or persons, is charged with the commission of a crime (murder, for example), and insanity is set up as a defence?
>
> 3d. In what terms ought the question to be left to the jury, as to the prisoner's state of mind at the time when the act was committed?

Lord Chief Justice Tindal replied (at p. 210 Cl. & Fin., p. 722 E.R.), that the judges thought that these two questions could be answered together:

> [W]e have to submit our opinion to be, that the jurors ought to be told in all cases that every man is to be presumed to be sane, and to possess a sufficient degree of reason to be responsible for his crimes, until the contrary be proved to their satisfaction; and that to establish a defence on the ground of insanity, it must be clearly proved that, *at the time of the committing of the act, the party accused was labouring under such a defect of reason,* from disease of the mind, as not to know the nature and quality of the act he was doing; or, if he did know it, *that he did not know he was doing what was wrong.* (Emphasis added.)

Both the question and answer demonstrate that the rule focuses not on a general capacity to understand right and wrong in some abstract sense, but on the particular capacity of the accused to understand that his or her act was wrong at the time of committing the act. Lord Chief Justice Tindal added an explanation of the word "wrong" (at pp. 210-1 Cl. & Fin., p. 723 E.R.):

> If the accused was conscious that the act was one which he ought not to do, and if that act was at the same time contrary to the law of the land, he is punishable; and the usual course therefore has been to leave the question to the jury, *whether the party accused had a sufficient degree of reason to know that he was doing an act that was wrong.* ... (Emphasis added.)

Tollefson and Starkman, *Mental Disorder in Criminal Proceedings* (1993), p. 30, suggest that what the judges were saying was this:

> We agree with you that the meaning to be conveyed to the jury is that the exemption is based on whether the accused is capable of knowing that the act was contrary to the law. But for practical reasons, the jury cannot be told that in so many words. We therefore use the word "wrong," and make it as clear as possible that the jurors must view the act in the context of the specific charge and not in some general sense.

In *Chaulk, supra,* this court affirmed that the focus must be on capacity to know that the act committed was wrong, and not merely on a general capacity to distinguish right from wrong. Lamer C.J.C., writing for the majority, stated (at p. 1354):

> The principal issue in this regard is the capacity of the accused person to know that a particular act or omission is wrong. As such, to ask simply what is the meaning of the word "wrong" for the purposes of s. 16(2) is to frame the question too narrowly. To paraphrase the words of the House of Lords in *M'Naghten's Case,* the courts must determine in any particular case whether an accused was rendered incapable, by the fact of his mental disorder, of knowing that the act committed was one that he ought not have done.

The crux of the inquiry is whether the accused lacks the capacity to rationally decide whether the act is right or wrong and hence to make a rational choice about whether to do it or not. The inability to make a rational choice may result from a variety of mental disfunctions; as the following passages indicate, these include at a minimum the states to which the psychiatrists testified in this case—delusions which make the accused perceive an act which is wrong as right or justifiable, and a disordered condition of the mind which deprives the accused of the ability to rationally evaluate what he is doing.

• • •

Finally, it should be noted that we are not here concerned with the psychopath or the person who follows a personal and deviant code of right and wrong. The accused in the case at bar accepted society's views on right and wrong. The suggestion is that, accepting those views, he was unable because of his delusion to perceive that his act of killing was wrong in the particular circumstances of the case. On the contrary, as the psychiatrists testified, he viewed it as right. This is different from the psychopath or person following a deviant moral code. Such a person is capable of knowing that his or her acts are wrong in the eyes of society, and despite such knowledge, chooses to commit them. To quote Herbert Fingarette, *The Meaning of Criminal Insanity* (1972), pp. 200-1:

> It should be evident that we are not here reverting to the thesis that "knew it was wrong" means "judged it wrong in the light of his own conscience." … such a definition could never be acceptable in a viable criminal law. As the courts have rightly insisted, it is a public standard of wrong that must be used, whether public law or community morality.
>
> What we are saying here is that "knowing the nature and quality of the act or that it is wrong" in the context of insanity (and thus, rationality) means "having the capacity to rationally assess—define and evaluate—his own particular act in the light of the relevant public standards of wrong." …
>
> The preceding comments should not be taken to mean that a person is not responsible if he holds irrational beliefs, for that is not the case. … The point is that if the person has a mental makeup which is such that he lacks even the capacity for rationality, then responsibility is vitiated. If he has the capacity but simply fails to use it, responsibility is not precluded.

Application of the Law to This Appeal

The evidence indicated that the accused was suffering from a mental disorder causing paranoid delusion at the time of the killing. The trial judge found that this mental disorder "compelled" the killing. The remaining question was whether the disorder "rendered [the accused] incapable of appreciating the nature and quality of the act or omission or of knowing that it was wrong."

The evidence was capable of supporting an affirmative answer to the question of whether the accused was deprived of the capacity to know his act was wrong. First, there was evidence that the accused honestly felt that he was under imminent danger of being killed by Ms. Beaton if he did not kill her first, and that for this reason, believed that the act of killing her was justified. This delusion would have deprived the accused of the ability to know that his act was wrong; in his eyes, it was right. Secondly (and this may be to say the same thing), there was evidence capable of supporting the conclusion that the accused's mental state was so disordered that he was unable to rationally consider whether his act was right or wrong in the way a normal person would.

The trial judge found that while the accused was generally capable of knowing that the act of killing was wrong, he could not apply that capacity for distinguishing right from wrong at the time of the killing because of his mental disorder. He further found that because of that disorder, Mr. Oommen was deluded into believing that he had no choice but to kill. These findings are consistent with the conclusion that Mr. Oommen's mental disorder deprived him of the capacity to know his act was wrong by the standards of the ordinary person. As the cases make clear, s. 16(1) of the *Criminal Code* embraces not only the intellectual ability to know right from wrong, but the capacity to apply that knowledge to the situation at hand.

Appeal dismissed.

Considering the Two Alternative Arms of the Mental Disorder Defence Together

In *R c Landry* (1988), 48 CCC (3d) 552 (Que CA), the accused was charged with first-degree murder as a result of the killing of a person who had formerly been his friend. The evidence established that the accused had the serious mental illness of paranoid schizophrenia and over a number of years had come to believe that his former friend was Satan and that he, the accused, was God. The accused came to believe that it was necessary for him to kill the deceased so as to save the world from destruction. In explaining the defence of insanity under s 16 of the *Criminal Code*, the trial judge directed the jury to the effect that that defence was available only if the disease of the mind affected the accused to the extent that he was incapable of knowing that he was killing the deceased or incapable of knowing that killing was unlawful.

On appeal by the accused from his conviction for first-degree murder the Quebec Court of Appeal allowed the appeal and substituted a verdict of not guilty by reason of insanity. Beauregard JA stated for the court:

> I see a difference between, on one hand, the accused who, because of a mental disorder, killed believing that he was killing Satan on the orders of God and, on the other hand, the accused who killed because his mental disorder prevented him from having sympathy for his victim or remorse for his act, or the accused who killed because his mental disorder made him believe that he would not be arrested by the police or that, if he were arrested, he would not be charged. In the first case, the accused's mental state directly affects the accused's *mens rea*; in the other two cases, it does not.
>
> If s. 7 of the *Canadian Charter of Rights and Freedoms* prevents Parliament from permitting a person to be stigmatized by a conviction for murder other than under a legal provision which is in conformity with the principles of fundamental justice, and if one must necessarily interpret laws in conformity with our Constitution, I am of the opinion that s. 16 must be interpreted in a sufficiently broad manner in order to offer a defence to the appellant in the present case.
>
> Landry who knew that he was killing Fortin and who knew that it was unlawful, is guilty of murder despite his mental disorder. But, even if Landry knew the nature and the consequences of his act and even if he knew that it was unlawful, he was incapable of appreciating the nature and quality of his act if, at that moment, he thought that he was God and that Fortin was Satan. This is an error in judgment arising from the confusion between Landry and God, and Fortin and Satan.
>
> As the additional instructions given by the judge were in my opinion insufficient in the present case and as the jury most probably relied on these final instructions in rendering its verdict, assuming that they believed the appellant, the verdict cannot stand.

The Crown appealed to the Supreme Court of Canada, which dismissed the appeal. Lamer CJ stated for the majority of the Court, [1991] 1 SCR 99:

> In *Chaulk*, this court reconsidered its interpretation of the word "wrong" in s. 16(2). In *Schwartz*, ... the majority of this court held that "wrong" for the purposes of s. 16(2) means "legally wrong." The

trial judge and the Court of Appeal in the case at bar relied on our decision in *Schwartz* in interpreting the second arm of s. 16(2) and thus applied that test in a restrictive manner that excluded any consideration of the respondent's capacity to know the *moral* wrongfulness of his act. As a result, Nichols J.A. felt compelled to take into account the respondent's inability to know the moral wrongfulness of the act under the first branch of the test, that is, as part of appreciating the "nature or quality" of the act. Furthermore, Beauregard J.A. invoked s. 7 of the Charter in order to extend the scope at s. 16(2) to protect an accused who is incapable of appreciating the moral wrongfulness of an act.

I am unable to support the reasoning that led to the Court of Appeal's conclusion. The Court of Appeal interpreted s. 16(2) in a manner that clearly contradicted prior judgments of this court. In accordance with our decisions in *R. v. Cooper, supra, R. v. Kjeldsen*, [1981] 2 S.C.R. 617, and *R. v. Abbey*, [1982] 2 S.C.R. 24, the first branch of the s. 16(2) test protects an accused who, because of a disease of the mind, was incapable of appreciating the *physical* consequences of his act. The Court of Appeal erred in using s. 7 of the Charter to modify the established interpretation of this statutory provision.

Despite my disagreement with the reasons of the Court of Appeal, I believe that it reached the correct result. It is my opinion that if the Court of Appeal had had the benefit of this court's judgment in *Chaulk*, it would have reached the identical conclusion for different reasons. It was established at trial and accepted by the Court of Appeal that the respondent in this case suffered from a disease of the mind to the extent that he was rendered incapable of knowing that the act was morally wrong in the circumstances. He suffered from the delusion that he was God and that he had a divine mission to kill the victim.

IV. MENTAL DISORDER AND NON-MENTAL DISORDER AUTOMATISM

Automatism is unconscious and involuntary behaviour. In cases where the cause of automatism is not a mental disorder, a successful claim of automatism will result in a not guilty verdict and the freedom of the accused.

R v Parks
Supreme Court of Canada
[1992] 2 SCR 871

LAMER CJ (Cory J concurring) (dissenting in part): In the small hours of the morning of May 24, 1987 the respondent, aged 23, attacked his parents-in-law, Barbara Ann and Denis Woods, killing his mother-in-law with a kitchen knife and seriously injuring his father-in-law. The incident occurred at the home of his parents-in-law while they were both asleep in bed. Their residence was 23 km. from that of the respondent, who went there by car. Immediately after the incident, the respondent went to the nearby police station, again driving his own car. He told the police:

> I just killed someone with my bare hands; Oh my God, I just killed someone; I've just killed two people; My God, I've just killed two people with my hands; My God, I've just killed two people. My hands; I just killed two people. I killed them; I just killed two people; I've just killed my mother- and father-in-law. I stabbed and beat them to death. It's all my fault.

At the trial the respondent presented a defence of automatism, stating that at the time the incidents took place he was sleepwalking. The respondent has always slept very deeply and has always had a lot of trouble waking up. The year prior to the events was particularly stressful for the respondent. His job as a project coordinator for Revere Electric required him to work ten hours a day. In addition, during the preceding summer the respondent had placed bets on horse races which caused him financial problems. To obtain money he also stole some $30,000 from his employer. The following March his boss discovered the theft and dismissed him. Court proceedings were brought against him in this regard. His personal life suffered from all of this. However, his parents-in-law, who were aware of the situation, always supported him. He had excellent relations with them: he got on particularly well with his mother-in-law, who referred to him as the "gentle giant." His relations with his father-in-law were more distant, but still very good. In fact, a supper at their home was planned for May 24 to discuss the respondent's problems and the solutions he intended to suggest. Additionally, several members of his family suffer or have suffered from sleep problems such as sleepwalking, adult enuresis, nightmares and sleeptalking.

The respondent was charged with the first degree murder of Barbara Ann Woods and the attempted murder of Denis Woods.

The trial judge chose to put only the defence of automatism to the jury, which first acquitted the respondent of first degree murder and then of second degree murder. The judge also acquitted the respondent of the charge of attempted murder for the same reasons. The Court of Appeal unanimously upheld the acquittal.

· · ·

This Court has only ruled on sleepwalking in an *obiter dictum* in *Rabey v. The Queen*, [1980] 2 S.C.R. 513. The Court found that sleepwalking was not a "disease of the mind" in the legal sense of the term and gave rise to a defence of automatism. Should the Court maintain this position?

In *Black's Law Dictionary* (5th ed. 1979) automatism is defined as follows:

> Behavior performed in a state of mental unconsciousness or dissociation without full awareness, *i.e.*, somnambulism, fugues. Term is applied to actions or conduct of an individual apparently occurring without will, purpose, or reasoned intention on his part; a condition sometimes observed in persons who, without being actually insane, suffer from an obscuration of the mental faculties, loss of volition or of memory, or kindred affections. ...

[Lamer CJ reviewed the expert evidence called at trial.]

Three very important points emerge from this testimony: (1) the respondent was sleepwalking at the time of the incident; (2) sleepwalking is not a neurological, psychiatric or other illness: it is a sleep disorder very common in children and also found in adults; (3) there is no medical treatment as such, apart from good health practices, especially as regards sleep. It is important to note that this expert evidence was not in any way contradicted by the prosecution, which as the trial judge observed did have the advice of experts who were present during the testimony given by the defence experts and whom it chose not to call.

[Lamer CJ held that the trial judge had not erred by leaving the jury with non-mental disorder automatism and affirmed the conviction. He would, however, have referred the matter back to the trial judge to impose some conditions on the accused to prevent a recurrence of the behaviour. The rest of the Court held that the courts were not equipped to devise a permanent peace bond to respond to Parks's sleepwalking.]

LA FOREST J (concurring):

. . .

It may be that some will regard the exoneration of an accused through a defence of somnambulism as an impairment of the credibility of our justice system. Those who hold this view would also reject insane automatism as an excuse from criminal responsibility. However, these views are contrary to certain fundamental precepts of our criminal law: only those who act voluntarily with the requisite intent to commit an offence should be punished by criminal sanction. The concerns of those who reject these underlying values of our system of criminal justice must accordingly be discounted.

In the end, there are no compelling policy factors that preclude a finding that the accused's condition was one of non-insane automatism. I noted earlier that it is for the Crown to prove that somnambulism stems from a disease of the mind; neither the evidence nor the policy considerations in this case overcome the Crown's burden in that regard.

[The Crown's appeal from the acquittal was dismissed.]

R v Stone
Supreme Court of Canada
[1999] 2 SCR 290

[This case involved an accused charged with murder and convicted by a jury of manslaughter for stabbing his wife 47 times after she had made various insulting comments about the accused including statements that his children with his prior wife were not his and he was a bad lover, and she would not sleep with him again. The accused raised defences of both non-mental disorder automatism and mental disorder automatism (as well as provocation) but the judge only left the defence of mental disorder automatism to the jury. The accused appealed on this issue.]

BASTARACHE J (L'Heureux-Dubé, Gonthier, Cory, and McLachlin JJ concurring):

[101] The present case involves automatism, and more specifically, "psychological blow" automatism. The appellant claims that nothing more than his wife's words caused him to enter an automatistic state in which his actions, which include stabbing his wife 47 times, were involuntary. How can an accused demonstrate that mere words caused him to enter an automatistic state such that his actions were involuntary and thus do not attract criminal law sanction? This is the issue raised in this appeal.

. . .

A. *The Nature of Automatism*

[155] The legal term "automatism" has been defined on many occasions by many courts. In *Rabey, supra*, Ritchie J., speaking for the majority of this Court, at p. 518, adopted the following definition of the Ontario High Court of Justice in *R. v. K.* (1970), 3 C.C.C. (2d) 84 (Ont. H.C.), at p. 84:

> Automatism is a term used to describe unconscious, involuntary behaviour, the state of a person who, though capable of action is not conscious of what he is doing. It means an unconscious involuntary act where the mind does not go with what is being done.

[156] The reference to unconsciousness in the definition of automatism has been the source of some criticism. In her article "Automatism and Criminal Responsibility" (1982-83), 25 *Crim. L.Q.* 95, W.H. Holland points out that this reference to unconsciousness reveals that the law assumes that a person is necessarily either conscious or unconscious. However, the medical literature speaks of different levels of consciousness (p. 96). Indeed, the expert evidence in the present case reveals that medically speaking, unconscious means "flat on the floor," that is, in a comatose-type state. I therefore prefer to define automatism as a state of impaired consciousness, rather than unconsciousness, in which an individual, though capable of action, has no voluntary control over that action.

[157] Two forms of automatism are recognized at law: insane automatism and non-insane automatism. Involuntary action which does not stem from a disease of the mind gives rise to a claim of non-insane automatism. If successful, a claim of non-insane automatism entitles the accused to an acquittal. In *Parks, supra*, La Forest J. cited with approval, at p. 896, the following words of Dickson J. speaking in dissent in *Rabey, supra*, at p. 522:

> Although the word "automatism" made its way but lately to the legal stage, it is basic principle that absence of volition in respect of the act involved is always a defence to a crime. A defence that the act is involuntary entitles the accused to a complete and unqualified acquittal. That the defence of automatism exists as a middle ground between criminal responsibility and legal insanity is beyond question.

[158] On the other hand, involuntary action which is found, at law, to result from a disease of the mind gives rise to a claim of insane automatism. It has long been recognized that insane automatism is subsumed by the defence of mental disorder, formerly referred to as the defence of insanity. For example, in *Rabey, supra*, Ritchie J. adopted the reasoning of Martin J.A. of the Ontario Court of Appeal. In *R. v. Rabey* (1977), 17 O.R. (2d) 1 (Ont. C.A.), Martin J.A. stated, at p. 12:

> Automatism caused by disease of the mind is subsumed under the defence of insanity leading to the special verdict of not guilty on account of insanity, whereas automatism not resulting from disease of the mind leads to an absolute acquittal. ...

[159] Likewise, in dissent in *Rabey* (S.C.C.), Dickson J. noted, at p. 524:

> Automatism may be subsumed in the defence of insanity in cases in which the unconscious action of an accused can be traced to, or rooted in, a disease of the mind. Where that is so, the defence of insanity prevails.

[160] More recently, in *Parks, supra*, La Forest J. confirmed that insane automatism falls within the scope of the defence of mental disorder as set out in s. 16 of the *Code* when he noted that where automatism stems from a disease of the mind, the accused is entitled to a verdict of insanity rather than an acquittal (p. 896). See also *R. v. Chaulk*, [1990] 3 S.C.R. 1303, at p. 1321. This classification is consistent with the wording of s. 16, which makes no distinction between voluntary and involuntary acts. Furthermore, the inclusion of mental disorder automatism within the ambit of s. 16 provides courts with an appropriate framework for protecting the public from offenders whose involuntarily criminal acts are rooted in diseases of the mind. ...

[161] Accordingly, a successful claim of insane automatism will trigger s. 16 of the *Code* and result in a verdict of not criminally responsible on account of mental disorder. Thus, although courts to date have spoken of insane "automatism" and non-insane "automatism" for purposes of consistency, it is important to recognize that in actuality true "automatism" only includes involuntary behaviour which does not stem from a disease of the mind. Involuntary behaviour which results from a disease of the mind is more correctly labelled a s. 16 mental disorder rather than insane automatism. For purposes of consistency, I will continue to refer to both as "automatism." However, I believe the terms "mental disorder" automatism and "non-mental disorder" automatism rather than "insane" automatism and "non-insane" automatism more accurately reflect the recent changes to s. 16 of the *Code*, and the addition of Part XX.1 of the *Code*. ...

C. Step 1: Establishing a Proper Foundation for a Defence of Automatism

· · ·

[174] In her 1993 *Proposals to amend the Criminal Code (general principles)*, the Minister of Justice recommended that the legal burden of proof in all cases of automatism be on the party that raises the issue on a balance of probabilities. This is the same legal burden that this Court applied to a claim of extreme intoxication akin to a state of automatism in *Daviault*, [[1994] 3 SCR 63]. It is also the legal burden Parliament assigned to the defence of mental disorder in s. 16 of the *Code*, which, as mentioned above, is equally applicable to voluntary and involuntary actions stemming from a disease of the mind and therefore applies to mental disorder automatism. As I explained above, different legal approaches to claims of automatism, whether based on the context in which the alleged automatism arose or on the distinction between mental disorder and non-mental disorder automatism, is problematic and should be avoided. Indeed, counsel for the appellant in the present case recognized as much in oral argument before this Court:

> No, I think that the—the conflict arises in a slightly different situation, which I'm going to come to in a moment, and that is that, when one deals with insanity, the evidentiary burden is upon the accused to establish that on the balance of probabilities.
>
> When one comes now, pursuant to this Court's decision in *Daviault*, to drunkenness akin to automatism, again, the onus is upon the accused, and the evidentiary burden as well.
>
> Whereas in non-insane automatism, the onus simply is upon the defence to raise it and for the Crown to then disprove it beyond a reasonable doubt in essence.
>
> So that is where I concede that there is a contradiction and that there may be some merit in having the same test and the same process applied to each of the different kinds of mental disorder, to use the term loosely.

[175] An appropriate legal burden applicable to all cases involving claims of automatism must reflect the policy concerns which surround claims of automatism. The words of Schroeder J.A. in *R. v. Szymusiak*, [1972] 3 O.R. 602 (Ont. C.A.), at p. 608, come to mind:

> … a defence which in a true and proper case may be the only one open to an honest man, but it may just as readily be the last refuge of a scoundrel.

[176] The recognition that policy considerations are relevant is nothing new to this area of criminal law. In *Rabey* (Ont. C.A.), *supra*, Martin J.A., whose reasons were adopted by the majority of this Court, recognized that the term "disease of the mind" contains both a medical component and legal or policy component (p. 425). Dickson J., dissenting in *Rabey* (S.C.C.), noted, at p. 546, that specific policy considerations were involved in determining whether a claim of automatism should be categorized as mental disorder or non-mental disorder:

> There are undoubtedly policy considerations to be considered. Automatism as a defence is easily feigned. It is said the credibility of our criminal justice system will be severely strained if a person who has committed a violent act is allowed an absolute acquittal on a plea of automatism arising from a psychological blow. The argument is made that the success of the defence depends upon the semantic ability of psychiatrists, tracing a narrow path between the twin shoals of criminal responsibility and an insanity verdict. Added to these concerns is the *in terrorem* argument that the floodgates will be raised if psychological blow automatism is recognized in law.

[177] Likewise, in *Parks*, *supra*, La Forest J. considered policy to be a relevant consideration for trial judges in distinguishing between mental disorder and non-mental disorder automatism (p. 896 and pp. 907-908).

[178] In both *Rabey* and *Parks*, policy considerations were relegated to the second stage of the automatism analysis to determine whether the condition alleged by the accused was mental disorder or non-mental disorder automatism. In neither case is there any indication that this Court intended to preclude the consideration of policy in the determination of an appropriate legal burden for cases involving claims of automatism.

[179] The foregoing leads me to the conclusion that the legal burden in cases involving claims of automatism must be on the defence to prove involuntariness on a balance of probabilities to the trier of fact. …

[180] In *Chaulk*, *supra*, and *Daviault*, *supra*, this Court recognized that although placing a balance of probabilities burden on the defence with respect to an element of the offence constitutes a limitation of an accused person's rights under s. 11(d) of the *Charter*, it can be justified under s. 1. In my opinion, the burden is also justified in the present case. The law presumes that people act voluntarily in order to avoid placing the onerous burden of proving voluntariness beyond a reasonable doubt on the Crown. Like extreme drunkenness akin to automatism, genuine cases of automatism will be extremely rare. However, because automatism is easily feigned and all knowledge of its occurrence rests with the accused, putting a legal burden on the accused to prove involuntariness on a balance of probabilities is necessary to further the objective behind the presumption of voluntariness. In contrast, saddling the Crown with the legal burden of proving voluntariness beyond a reasonable doubt actually defeats the purpose of the presumption of voluntariness. Thus, requiring that an accused bear the legal burden of proving involuntariness on

a balance of probabilities is justified under s. 1. There is therefore no violation of the Constitution.

· · ·

F. Step 2: Determining Whether to Leave Mental Disorder or Non-Mental Disorder Automatism with the Trier of Fact

· · ·

[194] The determination of whether mental disorder or non-mental disorder automatism should be left with the trier of fact must be undertaken very carefully since it will have serious ramifications for both the individual accused and society in general. As mentioned above, mental disorder automatism is subsumed by the defence of mental disorder as set out in the *Code*. Accordingly, a successful defence of mental disorder automatism will result in a verdict of not criminally responsible on account of mental disorder as dictated by s. 672.34 of the *Code*. Under s. 672.54, an accused who receives this qualified acquittal may be discharged absolutely, discharged conditionally or detained in a hospital. In contrast, a successful defence of non-mental disorder automatism will always result in an absolute acquittal.

[195] The assessment of which form of automatism should be left with the trier of fact comes down to the question of whether or not the condition alleged by the accused is a mental disorder. Mental disorder is a legal term. It is defined in s. 2 of the *Code* as "a disease of the mind." In *Parks, supra*, at pp. 898-99, the majority of this Court adopted the reasons of Martin J.A. in *Rabey* (Ont. C.A.), *supra*, which included the following explanation of the term "disease of the mind," at pp. 12-13:

> Although the term "disease of the mind" is not capable of precise definition, certain propositions may, I think, be asserted with respect to it. "Disease of the mind" is a legal term, not a medical term of art; although a legal concept, it contains a substantial medical component as well as a legal or policy component. …
>
> The evidence of medical witnesses with respect to the cause, nature and symptoms of the abnormal mental condition from which the accused is alleged to suffer, and how that condition is viewed and characterized from the medical point of view, is highly relevant to the judicial determination of whether such a condition is capable of constituting a "disease of the mind." The opinions of medical witnesses as to whether an abnormal mental state does or does not constitute a disease of the mind are not, however, determinative, since what is a disease of the mind is a legal question. …

[196] In *Rabey* (Ont. C.A.), Martin J.A. described the task of the trial judge in determining the disease of the mind issue as follows, at p. 13:

> I take the true principle to be this: It is for the Judge to determine what mental conditions are included within the term "disease of the mind," and whether there is any evidence that the accused suffered from an abnormal mental condition comprehended by that term. …

G. Determining Whether the Condition the Accused Claims to Have Suffered from Is a Disease of the Mind

[203] In *Parks*, La Forest J. recognized that there are two distinct approaches to the disease of the mind inquiry: the internal cause theory and the continuing danger theory.

He recognized the internal cause theory as the dominant approach in Canadian jurisprudence but concluded, at p. 902, that this theory "is really meant to be used only as an analytical tool, and not as an all-encompassing methodology." This conclusion stemmed from a finding that somnambulism, the alleged trigger of the automatism in *Parks*, raises unique problems which are not well-suited to analysis under the internal cause theory. I agree that the internal cause theory cannot be regarded as a universal classificatory scheme for "disease of the mind." There will be cases in which the approach is not helpful because, in the words of La Forest J., at p. 903, "the dichotomy between internal and external causes becomes blurred." Accordingly, a new approach to the disease of the mind inquiry is in order. As I will explain below, a more holistic approach, like that developed by La Forest J. in *Parks*, must be available to trial judges in dealing with the disease of the mind question. This approach must be informed by the internal cause theory, the continuing danger theory and the policy concerns raised in this Court's decisions in *Rabey* and *Parks*.

(1) The Internal Cause Theory

. . .

[208] Given that the present case involves psychological blow automatism, I believe it is appropriate to express my opinion that the position of the majority in *Rabey* on this issue is preferable. The point of undertaking the comparison is to determine whether a normal person might have reacted to the alleged trigger by entering an automatistic state as the accused claims to have done. In cases involving claims of psychological blow automatism, evidence of an extremely shocking trigger will be required to establish that a normal person might have reacted to the trigger by entering an automatistic state, as the accused claims to have done. …

[210] The comparison involved in the disease of the mind inquiry is thus a contextual objective test. The accused's automatistic reaction to the alleged trigger must be assessed from the perspective of a similarly situated individual. This requires that the circumstances of the case be taken into account. However, I emphasize that this is not a subjective test.

[211] The appellant argues that the objective element of the internal cause theory violates ss. 7 and 11(d) of the *Charter*. According to the appellant, the *Charter* requires that the focus of the disease of the mind inquiry be on the actual, subjective response of the accused rather than that of a normal person. With respect, this argument fails to recognize that the objective inquiry into whether the condition claimed by the accused is a disease of the mind is applied only after a subjective inquiry into whether there is evidence upon which a properly instructed jury could find that the accused acted involuntarily on a balance of probabilities has been completed by the trial judge. That is, the objective standard affects only the classification of the defence rather than the assessment of whether the *actus reus* of the offence has been established. A similar objective standard was applied to the defence of provocation in *R. v. Cameron* (1992), 71 C.C.C. (3d) 272 (Ont. C.A.), where the Ontario Court of Appeal held that the objective standard involved in the defence of provocation does not violate ss. 7 and 11(d) because it does not detract from the *mens rea* required to establish murder. The point I wish to make here is that the objective component of the internal cause theory does not affect the burden of proof on the issue of whether the accused voluntarily committed the offence. Moreover, the impact of the objective comparison is limited even with regard to the disease of the mind inquiry. As

noted above, I agree with La Forest J. in *Parks* that the internal cause theory is only an analytical tool. It is not being held out as the definitive answer to the disease of the mind question. In each case, the trial judge must determine whether and to what extent the theory is useful given the facts of the case. Indeed, he or she has the discretion to disregard the theory if its application would not accord with the policy concerns which underlie the disease of the mind inquiry. In this way, the internal cause approach attempts to strike an appropriate balance between the objectives of providing an exemption from criminal liability for morally innocent offenders and protecting the public. In these circumstances, the objective component of the internal cause theory does not limit either s. 7 or s. 11(d) of the *Charter*. I would add that consideration of the subjective psychological make-up of the accused in the internal cause theory would frustrate the very purpose of making the comparison, which is of course to determine whether the accused was suffering from a disease of the mind in a legal sense.

(2) The Continuing Danger Theory

[212] As mentioned above, both the majority and dissenting judges of this Court in *Rabey*, as well as La Forest J. in *Parks*, recognized that policy considerations are relevant to the determination of whether a claim of automatism is the result of a disease of the mind. One policy factor which is central to the disease of the mind inquiry is the need to ensure public safety. Indeed, as mentioned above, La Forest J. recognized in *Parks* that the second dominant approach to the disease of the mind question is the continuing danger theory. This theory holds that any condition which is likely to present a recurring danger to the public should be treated as a disease of the mind. In other words, the likelihood of recurrence of violence is a factor to be considered in the disease of the mind inquiry. This approach must be qualified to recognize that while a continuing danger suggests a disease of the mind, a finding of no continuing danger does not preclude a finding of a disease of the mind. See *Rabey*, *supra*, at p. 15 (Ont. C.A.), *per* Martin J.A., and at pp. 533 and 551 (S.C.C.), *per* Dickson J.; *Parks*, *supra*, at p. 907, *per* La Forest J.

[213] In my opinion, trial judges should continue to consider the continuing danger theory as a factor in the determination of whether a condition should be classified as a disease of the mind. However, I emphasize that the continuing danger factor should not be viewed as an alternative or mutually exclusive approach to the internal cause factor. Although different, both of these approaches are relevant factors in the disease of the mind inquiry. As such, in any given case, a trial judge may find one, the other or both of these approaches of assistance. To reflect this unified, holistic approach to the disease of the mind question, it is therefore more appropriate to refer to the internal cause factor and the continuing danger factor, rather than the internal cause theory and the continuing danger theory. ...

(3) Other Policy Factors

[218] There may be cases in which consideration of the internal cause and continuing danger factors alone does not permit a conclusive answer to the disease of the mind question. Such will be the case, for example, where the internal cause factor is not helpful because it is impossible to classify the alleged cause of the automatism as internal or external, and the continuing danger factor is inconclusive because there is no continuing

danger of violence. Accordingly, a holistic approach to disease of the mind must also permit trial judges to consider other policy concerns which underlie this inquiry. As mentioned above, in *Rabey* and *Parks*, this Court outlined some of the policy concerns which surround automatism. I have already referred to those specific policy concerns earlier in these reasons. I repeat that I do not view those policy concerns as a closed category. In any given automatism case, a trial judge may identify a policy factor which this Court has not expressly recognized. Any such valid policy concern can be considered by the trial judge in order to determine whether the condition the accused claims to have suffered from is a disease of the mind. In determining this issue, policy concerns assist trial judges in answering the fundamental question of mixed law and fact which is at the centre of the disease of the mind inquiry: whether society requires protection from the accused and, consequently, whether the accused should be subject to evaluation under the regime contained in Part XX.1 of the Code. …

Application to the Present Case

[223] At trial, the appellant claimed both mental disorder and non-mental disorder automatism. The learned trial judge concluded that the appellant had established a proper foundation for a defence of automatism, but that only mental disorder automatism should be left with the jury. In coming to these conclusions, the trial judge did not have the benefit of these reasons to guide him. Nevertheless, this does not warrant allowing the appeal because, as I explain below, the approach taken by the trial judge did not impair the appellant's position.

[224] In determining whether the appellant had established a proper foundation for a defence of automatism, the trial judge stated that there must be evidence of unconsciousness throughout the commission of the crime. As I have explained above, automatism is more properly defined as impaired consciousness, rather than unconsciousness. Furthermore, lack of voluntariness, rather than consciousness, is the key legal element of automatism. Accordingly, the trial judge should have concerned himself with assessing whether there was evidence that the appellant experienced a state of impaired consciousness in which he had no voluntary control over his actions rather than whether there was evidence that the appellant was unconscious throughout the commission of the crime. Obviously, unconsciousness as defined by the trial judge supposes involuntariness. However, his finding that there was evidence of unconsciousness throughout the commission of the crime may have been based on a misunderstanding of the nature of the evidentiary burden on the accused at the proper foundation stage.

[225] In accordance with much of the jurisprudence at the time, the trial judge may have found that a proper foundation for automatism had been established because the defence had met an evidentiary burden which amounted to no more than the appellant's claim of involuntariness and confirming expert psychiatric evidence. There is no indication that he assessed whether the defence had raised evidence on which a properly instructed jury could find that the appellant acted involuntarily on a balance of probabilities. Likewise, there is no indication that the trial judge recognized the limited weight to be accorded to the psychiatric evidence in this case, which only served to confirm that the appellant's claim of automatism was plausible provided the account of events he provided to Dr. Janke was accurate and truthful. Nor did the trial judge discuss the relevance of

motive or corroborating evidence on his conclusion that a proper foundation for automatism had been established.

[226] Turning to the disease of the mind stage of the automatism analysis, I note that the evidence in this case raised *only one alleged cause* of automatism, Donna Stone's words. Based on this evidence, the trial judge found that only mental disorder automatism should be left with the jury. This conclusion was based primarily on a finding that the present case is indistinguishable from *MacLeod* [(1980), 52 CCC (2d) 193 (BCCA)]. Such reliance on precedent fails to reveal what effect, if any, the internal cause factor, the continuing danger factor and other policy factors had on the decision to leave only mental disorder automatism with the jury. This is not in accordance with the holistic approach to the disease of the mind question set out in these reasons. However, the internal cause factor and the continuing danger factor, as well as the other policy factors set out in this Court's decisions in *Rabey* and *Parks* all support the trial judge's finding that the condition the appellant alleges to have suffered from is a disease of the mind in the legal sense. In particular, the trigger in this case was not, in the words of Martin J.A. quoted in this Court's decision in *Rabey*, at p. 520, "extraordinary external events" that would amount to an extreme shock or psychological blow that would cause a normal person, in the circumstances of the accused, to suffer a dissociation in the absence of a disease of the mind. Accordingly, I find that the trial judge nevertheless reached the correct result on the disease of the mind question. As previously noted, in such a case, only mental disorder automatism must be put to the jury. There is no reason to go beyond the facts of this case in applying the rules discussed above.

[227] In the end, I must conclude that no substantial wrong or miscarriage of justice occurred in the present case. Even if I had found that the trial judge erred in applying the evidentiary burden at the proper foundation stage of the automatism analysis, this error could only have benefitted the appellant. Although the trial judge did not apply the holistic approach to disease of the mind established in these reasons, he reached the correct result on this issue. There is no reasonable possibility that the verdict would have been different had the errors not been made; see *R. v. Bevan*, [1993] 2 S.C.R. 599. I would therefore dismiss this ground of appeal.

BINNIE J (dissenting) (Lamer CJ and Iacobucci and Major JJ concurring):

[1] A fundamental principle of the criminal law is that no act can be a criminal offence unless it is performed or omitted voluntarily. In this case the appellant acknowledges that he killed his wife. He stabbed her 47 times with his knife in a frenzy. His defence was that he lost consciousness when his mind snapped under the weight of verbal abuse which the defence psychiatrist characterized as "exceptionally cruel" and "psychologically sadistic." The trial judge ruled in favour of the appellant that "there is evidence of unconsciousness throughout the commission of the crime," and the British Columbia Court of Appeal agreed ((1997), 86 B.C.A.C. 169 (B.C. C.A.), at p. 173) that "a properly instructed jury, acting reasonably, could find some form of automatism."

[2] The appellant had elected trial by jury. He says he was entitled to have the issue of voluntariness, thus properly raised, determined by the jury. He says that there was no proper legal basis for the courts in British Columbia to deprive him of the benefit of an evidentiary ruling which put in issue the Crown's ability to prove the *actus reus* of the offence.

[3] The trial judge ruled that the evidence of involuntariness was only relevant (if at all) to a defence of not criminally responsible by reason of mental disorder (NCRMD). This was upheld by the Court of Appeal. When it is appreciated that all of the experts agreed the appellant did not suffer from any condition that medicine would classify as a disease of the mind, it is perhaps not surprising that the jury found the accused to be sane. He was convicted of manslaughter. The contention of the appellant that the act of killing, while not the product of a mentally disordered mind, was nevertheless involuntary, was never put to the jury.

[4] The appellant argues that the judicial reasoning that effectively took the issue of voluntariness away from the jury violates the presumption of his innocence and his entitlement to the benefit of a jury trial guaranteed by s. 11(d) and (f) and is not saved by s. 1 of the *Canadian Charter of Rights and Freedoms*. ...

[6] In my view, it follows from the concurrent findings in the courts below (that the appellant successfully put in issue his consciousness at the time of the offence) that he was entitled to the jury's verdict on whether or not his conduct, though sane, was involuntary. That issue having been withdrawn from the jury, and the Crown thereby having been relieved of the one real challenge to its proof, the appellant is entitled to a new trial.

. . .

(III) ONUS OF PROOF

[44] My colleague Bastarache J. proposes, at para. 179, that the Court take this opportunity to add to the evidential burden on the accused a second and more onerous obstacle, namely the persuasive or legal burden on the accused to establish automatism on a balance of probabilities. The onus issue does not truly arise on the facts of the appeal. The issue of non-mental disorder automatism was not put to the jury at all, and it is superfluous to consider what *ought* to have been said about onus had the trial judge done what he didn't do and, as the appeal is to be dismissed, he will never have to do in this case.

. . .

[74] It follows, I think, that once the trial judge exercised his gatekeeper function to screen frivolous or feigned claims, it was for the jury to make up its mind on the credibility of the plea of automatism. This jurisdiction should not be removed by "judicially created policy." It is to be expected that the jury will subject the evidence of involuntariness to appropriate scrutiny. There was discussion in *Rabey* about the need to maintain the credibility of the justice system. In my view, the jury is as well placed as anyone in the justice system to uphold its credibility. The bottom line is, after all, that the task of weighing the credibility of such defences was confined by Parliament to the jury. The Court should respect the allocation of that responsibility.

(c) Ground 3: The Contention That the Mental Disorder Provisions of the
     Criminal Code Were Appropriate to Resolve the Automatism Issue on
     the Facts of This Case

[75] The third major submission on behalf of the Crown was that quite apart from this Court's decision in *Rabey* the present case was correctly subjected to the NCRMD provisions of s. 16 of the *Code*. The Crown says that here the operating cause of the dissociation was a "disease of the mind," giving that concept its full *legal* scope, and in such

situations questions of involuntariness are properly subsumed into the NCRMD analysis. This is despite the fact that in this case all the experts were agreed that the appellant did not suffer from any "disease of the mind" known to medicine. I accept, as stated, that "disease of the mind" is a legal concept, but nevertheless a significant disconnection between law and medicine on this point will often impose a measure of artificiality to create the medical equivalent of trying to pound square pegs into round holes. ...

[83] The s. 16 question has an air of artificiality in the case of someone who claims to have been unconscious at the material time. If true, he or she not only failed to appreciate "the nature and quality of the act" but also failed to appreciate that the act was taking place at all. If false, the accused is simply untruthful. Nevertheless, the presence of a "disease of the mind" does trigger the application of s. 16, and an accused whose automatism is a product of a disease of the mind should be found NCRMD instead of being acquitted. The concept of "disease of the mind" is, and should continue to be, controlled by legal considerations rather than purely medical considerations.

[84] At the same time, where as here medical experts for the prosecution and the defence agree that there is no "disease of the mind" known to medicine, and the only justification offered in support of attributing the conduct to mental disorder is the inability of an accused to identify an "external" cause, there is, in my view, an insufficient basis for (i) shifting the persuasive burden of proof from the Crown to the defence under s. 16, and (ii) taking the issue of non-mental disorder automatism away from the jury. ...

[86] It is open to the Crown or defence to establish on a balance of probabilities a mental disorder. The Crown, of course, must follow the rule in *R. v. Swain*, [1991] 1 S.C.R. 933, which prevents the admission of evidence relating to mental disorder by the Crown until the defence puts in issue the mental capacity of the accused for criminal intent, as explained by Lamer C.J., at p. 976:

> Thus, although it is a principle of fundamental justice that an accused has the right to control his or her own defence, this is not an "absolute" right. If an accused chooses to conduct his or her defence in such a way that *that accused's mental capacity for criminal intent is somehow put into question*, then the Crown will be entitled to "complete the picture" by raising its own evidence of insanity and the trial judge will be entitled to charge the jury on s. 16. [Emphasis added.]

The same point was made by La Forest J. in *Parks, supra*, at p. 898, in relation to automatism:

> If the accused pleads automatism, the Crown is then entitled to raise the issue of insanity, but the prosecution then bears the burden of proving that the condition in question stems from a disease of the mind; see *Rabey, supra*, at pp. 544-45.

If the jury were satisfied that the s. 16 requirements were met, that would end the matter: the appellant would have been found not criminally responsible on account of mental disorder (NCRMD). He or she would not be permitted to ignore NCRMD status and seek a full acquittal on the basis of involuntariness. However, in my view, if the jury rejects NCRMD status, it should still be left with the elementary instruction that the accused is entitled to an acquittal if the Crown fails to establish beyond a reasonable doubt all of the elements of the offence, including voluntariness. ...

(5) Conclusion on the Automatism Issue

[90] In the result, I believe the appellant was entitled to have the plea of non-mental disorder automatism left to the jury in this case in light of the trial judge's evidentiary ruling that there was evidence the appellant was unconscious throughout the commission of the offence, for the following reasons.

[91] Firstly, I do not accept the Crown's argument that a judge-made classification of situations into mental disorder automatism and non-mental disorder automatism can relieve the Crown of the obligation to prove all of the elements of the offence, including voluntariness. As stated, such an interpretation encounters strong objections under s. 7 and s. 11(d) of the *Charter*, and there has been no attempt in this case to provide a s. 1 justification.

[92] Secondly, imposition of a persuasive burden of proof on the appellant to establish "involuntariness" on a balance of probabilities, in substitution for the present evidential burden, runs into the same *Charter* problems, and no attempt has been made in the record to justify it.

[93] Thirdly, the "internal cause" theory, on which the Crown rested its argument, cannot be used to deprive the appellant of the benefit of the jury's consideration of the voluntariness of his action, once he had met the evidential onus, without risking a violation of s. 11(f) of the *Charter*. *Rabey*'s treatment of the internal cause theory has to be looked at in light of the decision of this Court in *Parks, supra*, which signalled some serious reservations about the usefulness of the "internal cause" theory, except as an "analytical tool." *Rabey*, as clarified in *Parks*, does not impose a presumption that a lack of voluntariness must be attributed to the existence of a mental disorder any time there is no identification of a convincing external cause. Once the appellant in this case had discharged his evidential onus, he was entitled to have the issue of voluntariness go to the jury.

[94] Fourthly, it was wrong of the courts to require the appellant to substitute for his chosen defence of involuntariness the conceptually quite different plea of insanity. One of the few points of agreement between the defence and Crown experts at trial was that the appellant did not suffer from anything that could be described medically as a disease of the mind. He was either unconscious at the time of the killing or he was not telling the truth at the time of the trial. This was a question for the jury. The statutory inquiry into whether he was "suffering from a mental disorder" that rendered him "incapable of appreciating the nature and quality of the act of omission or knowing that it was wrong" are qualitative questions that are not really responsive to his allegation that he was not conscious of having acted at all.

[95] Finally, the evidence established that there *are* states of automatism where perfectly sane people lose conscious control over their actions. At that point, it was up to the jury, not the judge, to decide if the appellant had brought himself within the physical and mental condition thus identified. As Dickson C.J. observed in *Bernard, supra*, at p. 848, the jurors were "perfectly capable of sizing the matter up." ...

IV. Disposition

[100] In the result, I would have allowed the appeal, set aside the order of the British Columbia Court of Appeal and directed a new trial. Had I shared the conclusion of

Bastarache J. to dismiss the appeal against conviction, I would also have concurred in the dismissal of the Crown's appeal on sentence for the reasons he gives.

For comments on this case, see A Brudner, "Insane Automatism: A Proposal for Reform" (2000) 45 McGill LJ 65; P Healy, "Automatism Confined" (2000) 45 McGill LJ 87; and DM Paciocco, "Death by Stone-ing: The Demise of the Defence of Simple Automatism" (1999) 26 CR (5th) 273.

What is the status of the Court's decision in *R v Parks* that sleepwalking could produce non-mental disorder automatism? In *R v Luedecke*, below, the Ontario Court of Appeal held that a trial judge had erred when he acquitted an accused who committed a sexual assault while he was asleep and had a history of such behaviour.

R v Luedecke
Ontario Court of Appeal
2008 ONCA 716, 236 CCC (3d) 317

DOHERTY JA (for the court):

. . .

[90] *Stone* alters the approach to the characterization of automatism as non-mental disorder automatism or mental disorder automatism in at least two significant ways. First, after *Stone* the trial judge must begin from the premise that the automatism is caused by a disease of the mind and look to the evidence to determine whether it convinces him or her that the condition is not a "disease of the mind." This approach is in direct contrast with *Parks* where the non-mental disorder automatism claim succeeded because the Crown failed to prove that the condition was caused by a disease of the mind.

[91] Second, although *Stone* accepts the multi-factored approach to the policy component of the characterization of the automatism set out in *Parks*, it refocuses the continuing danger aspect of that approach. After *Stone*, in evaluating the risk of repetition and hence the danger to the public, trial judges must not limit their inquiry only to the risk of further violence while in an automatistic state. Commenting on this refinement of the continuing danger inquiry Professor Paciocco observes in "Death by Stone-ing: The Demise of the Defence of Simple Automatism" at p. 281:

> This part of the judgment effectively reverses *Parks*. The triggers for Parks' somnambulism or sleep-walking included stress, fatigue, insomnia and exercise. There is no point in speaking of the likelihood of such triggers being present in the future. It is a veritable certainty that they will be. *It is clear that had* Parks *been tried using the* Stone *test, the only defence that would have been left to the jury would be* "mental disorder automatism." [Emphasis added.]

[92] Professor Paciocco's prediction is largely borne out by the Canadian parasomnia cases that post-date *Stone*. I am aware of five including this case. In the other four cases, the automatistic states flowing from the parasomnia were held to constitute diseases of the mind: see *Canada v. Campbell* (2000), 35 C.R. (5th) 314 (Ont. S.C); *R. v. Balenko*, [2000] Q.J. No. 717 (C.Q. (Crim. Div.)); *R. v. Romas* (2002), 6 M.V.R. (5th) 101 (B.C. Prov. Ct.); and *R. v. Churchyard*, an unreported decision of Smith J. released November 19, 2003 (Ont. S.C.).

[93] The majority position in *Stone* signals a strong preference for a finding of NCR-MD in cases where an accused establishes that he or she was in a disassociative state and acted involuntarily. Social defence concerns, inevitably present in such cases, must to a large degree drive the analysis in automatism cases after *Stone*.

[94] The strong preference for an NCR-MD verdict expressed in *Stone* is explained in part by the very different treatment accorded those found NCR-MD compared to the historical treatment provided to those found not guilty by reason of insanity, as was the case at the time of the trial in *Parks*. Prior to 1991, persons found not guilty by reason of insanity were detained indefinitely at the pleasure of the Lieutenant Governor in Council. The provisions of Part XX.I of the *Criminal Code* not only disposed of the insanity nomenclature but completely changed the post-verdict treatment of those found NCR-MD: S.C. 1991, c. 43.

[95] I do not think it is coincidental that *Stone* and *Winko*, the leading case on the interpretation of Part XX.I of the *Criminal Code*, were heard by the same nine judges about ten days apart, and decided about three weeks apart several months later. It is hard to resist the inference that *Stone* was written having in mind what the court would say three weeks later when it released its decision in *Winko*. ...

[97] ... As interpreted in *Winko*, s. 672.54 requires the absolute discharge of anyone found NCR-MD unless the court or the Review Board determines that the individual poses "a significant threat to the public." McLachlin J. said at para. 52:

> This interpretation of s. 672.54 eliminates any need for the NCR accused to prove lack of dangerousness and relieves him or her of any legal or evidentiary burden. If the evidence does not support the conclusion that the NCR accused is a significant risk, the NCR accused need do nothing; the only possible order is an absolute discharge.

[98] The risk determination required by s. 672.54 cannot not be based on speculation or assumptions about how persons with mental disorders behave. There must be evidence establishing the significant risk. That risk must be a real risk of criminal conduct involving physical or psychological harm to individuals in the community. A risk of trivial harm or miniscule risk of significant harm will not suffice to deprive the individual of his or her liberty: *Winko*, at para. 57. ...

[100] A combined reading of *Stone* and *Winko* yields a comprehensive response to automatism claims. At the pre-verdict stage, social defence concerns dominate. Those concerns focus on the risk posed by the potential recurrence of the conduct in issue. Where that risk exists, the risk combined with the occurrence of the conduct that led to the criminal proceedings will almost always justify further inquiry into the accused's dangerousness so as to properly protect the public.

[101] In the post-verdict stage, however, the emphasis shifts to an individualized assessment of the actual dangerousness of the person found NCR-MD. Where that personalized assessment does not demonstrate the requisite significant risk, the person found NCR-MD must receive an absolute discharge. Even where a significant risk exists, the disposition order must be tailored to the specific circumstances of the individual and must, to the extent possible, minimize the interference with that individual's liberty.

[A new trial for sexual assault was ordered and Luedecke consented to a verdict of not criminally responsible by reason of mental disorder, given that the Court of Appeal determined that his sleepwalking constituted a mental disorder or disease of the mind. He subsequently received an absolute discharge under s 672.54 of the *Criminal Code* as interpreted in *Winko*, above, on the basis that he was not a significant threat to the safety of the public. Note that this case was decided before s 672.54 was amended in 2014 as discussed above.]

ADDITIONAL READING

Berger, BL. "Mental Disorder and the Instability of Blame in Criminal Law" in F Tanguay-Renaud & J Stribopoulos, eds, *Rethinking Criminal Law Theory: New Canadian Perspectives in the Philosophy of Domestic, Transnational, and International Criminal Law* (Portland, Or: Hart, 2012) 117.

Boisvert, A-M. "Psychanalyse d'une défense: réflexions sur l'aliénation mentale" (1990) 69 Can Bar Rev 46.

Colvin, E & S Anand. *Principles of Criminal Law*, 3rd ed (Toronto: Thomson, 2007) ch 7.

Healy, P. "R v Chaulk: Some Answers and Some Questions on Insanity" (1991) 2 CR (4th) 95.

Healy, P. "Automatism Confined" (2000) 45 McGill LJ 87.

Manning, M & P Sankoff. *Manning, Mewett & Sankoff: Criminal Law*, 4th ed (Toronto: LexisNexis, 2009) ch 13, 14.

Martin, GA. "The Insanity Defence" (1989) 10 Criminal Lawyers' Association Newsletter 19.

Roach, K. *Criminal Law*, 6th ed (Toronto: Irwin Law, 2015) ch 8.

Stuart, D. *Canadian Criminal Law*, 7th ed (Toronto: Carswell, 2014) at 109-41, 411-57.

Sutton, R. "Canada's Not Criminally Responsible Reform Act: Mental Disorder and the Danger of Public Safety" (2013) 60 Crim LQ 41.

Intoxication

To what extent should voluntary, self-induced intoxication by alcohol or another drug afford a defence to the prosecution's case in the sense of negating proof of a voluntary *actus reus* or the *mens rea* of the offence? This question has long been a matter of controversy.

If an intoxicant can negate the mental element required for an offence, or the voluntariness of the *actus reus*, the logic of the law seems to compel an acquittal. Conversely, if a person can become irresponsible by self-induced intoxication, there is a compelling argument that, for reasons of policy, the law should deny him or her a defence and even substitute the fault of being intoxicated for the fault element as defined in the particular offence. Apart from the logic or the policy of the law, there is also an important empirical question: what is the effect of particular intoxicants, given the nature and quantity of the drugs consumed, the time of consumption, and the condition of the person who consumed them?

This chapter focuses on the manner in which the law addresses the competing claims of logic and policy. Section I examines the common law decision that is the genesis of the modern intoxication defence. Section II examines the controversial common law distinction between offences of "specific intent," for which evidence of intoxication can raise a reasonable doubt as to the accused's intent, and offences of "general intent," for which the defence of intoxication has generally been excluded. Section III examines the controversial case of *R v Daviault*, which recognized that extreme intoxication proven by the accused on a balance of probabilities and with expert evidence could be a defence to offences of general intent such as sexual assault. It examines s 33.1 of the *Criminal Code*, which was enacted within a year of *Daviault* and which precludes—subject to Charter challenge—the use of the *Daviault* defence for general-intent offences that infringe bodily integrity. Section IV considers how the courts define involuntary intoxication, and what consequences ensue when an accused is involuntarily intoxicated.

I. THE COMMON LAW DEFENCE OF INTOXICATION

DPP v Beard
House of Lords
[1920] AC 479

LORD BIRKENHEAD LC: … Under the law of England as it prevailed until early in the nineteenth century voluntary drunkenness was never an excuse for criminal misconduct; and indeed the classic authorities broadly assert that voluntary drunkenness must be considered rather an aggravation than a defence. This view was in terms based upon the principle that a man who by his own voluntary act debauches and destroys his will power shall be no better situated in regard to criminal acts than a sober man. An early statement of the law is to be found in *Reniger v. Fogossa* (1 Plowd. 1, 19). "If a person that is drunk kills another, this shall be felony, and he shall be hanged for it, and yet he did it through ignorance, for when he was drunk he had no understanding nor memory; but inasmuch as that ignorance was occasioned by his own act and folly, and he might have avoided it, he shall not be privileged thereby." In Hale's Pleas of the Crown, vol. i., p. 32, the learned author says:

> This vice (drunkenness) doth deprive men of the use of reason, and puts many men into a perfect, but temporary phrenzy; and therefore, according to some civilians, such a person committing homicide shall not be punished simply for the crime of homicide, but shall suffer for his drunkenness answerable to the nature of the crime occasioned thereby; so that yet the formal cause of his punishment is rather the drunkenness than the crime committed in it: but by the laws of England such a person shall have no privilege by this voluntary contracted madness, but shall have the same judgment as if he were in his right senses.

Blackstone, in his Commentaries, Book IV., c. 2, s. III., 25, states: "As to artificial, voluntarily contracted madness, by drunkenness or intoxication, which, depriving men of their reason, puts them in a temporary phrenzy; our law looks upon this as an aggravation of the offence, rather than as an excuse for any criminal misbehaviour."

Judicial decisions extending over a period of nearly one hundred years make it plain that the rigidity of this rule was gradually relaxed in the nineteenth century, though this mitigation cannot for a long time be affiliated upon a single or very intelligible principle.

[A number of cases decided in the 19th century were then examined.]

Notwithstanding the difference in the language used I come to the conclusion that (except in cases where insanity is pleaded) these decisions establish that where a specific intent is an essential element in the offence, evidence of a state of drunkenness rendering the accused incapable of forming such an intent should be taken into consideration in order to determine whether he had in fact formed the intent necessary to constitute the particular crime. If he was so drunk that he was incapable of forming the intent required he could not be convicted of a crime which was committed only if the intent was proved. This does not mean that the drunkenness in itself is an excuse for the crime but that the state of drunkenness may be incompatible with the actual crime charged and may therefore negative the commission of that crime. In a charge of murder based upon intention to kill or to do grievous bodily harm, if the jury are satisfied that the accused was, by reason of his drunken condition, incapable of forming the intent to kill or to do grievous bodily harm, unlawful homicide with malice aforethought is not established and he cannot be convicted of murder. But nevertheless unlawful homicide has been committed by the accused, and consequently he is guilty of unlawful homicide without malice aforethought, and that is manslaughter: per Stephen J. in *Doherty's Case* (16 Cox C.C. 307). This reasoning may be sound or unsound; but whether the principle be truly expressed in this view, or whether its origin is traceable to that older view of the law held by some civilians (as expressed by Hale) that, in truth, it may be that the cause of the punishment is the drunkenness which has led to the crime, rather than the crime itself; the law is plain beyond all question that in cases falling short of insanity a condition of drunkenness at the time of committing an offence causing death can only, when it is available at all, have the effect of reducing the crime from murder to manslaughter.

The conclusions to be drawn from these cases may be stated under three heads:

1. That insanity, whether produced by drunkenness or otherwise, is a defence to the crime charged. The distinction between the defence of insanity in the true sense caused by excessive drinking, and the defence of drunkenness which produces a condition such that the drunken man's mind becomes incapable of forming a specific intention, has been preserved throughout the cases. The insane person cannot be convicted of a crime: *Felstead v. The King* ([1914] A.C. 534); but, upon a verdict of insanity, is ordered to be detained during His Majesty's pleasure. The law takes no note of the cause of the insanity. If actual insanity in fact supervenes, as the result of alcoholic excess, it furnishes as complete an answer to a criminal charge as insanity induced by any other cause. In the early cases of *Burrow* (1 Lewin 75) and *Rennie* (1 Lewin 76) Holroyd J. refused to regard drunkenness as an excuse unless it had induced a continuing and lasting condition of insanity. But in *Reg. v. Davis* (14 Cox C.C. 563), where the prisoner was charged with wounding with intent to murder, Stephen J. thought (and I agree with him) that insanity, even though temporary, was an answer. The defence was that the prisoner was of unsound mind at the time of the commission of the act, and the evidence established that he was suffering from delirium tremens resulting from overindulgence in drink. Stephen J. said:

   > But drunkenness is one thing and the diseases to which drunkenness leads are different things; and if a man by drunkenness brings on a state of disease which causes such a degree of madness, even for a time, which would have relieved him from responsibility if it had been caused in any other way, then he would not be criminally responsible. In my opinion, in such a case the man is a madman, and is to be treated as such, although his madness is only temporary … . If you think there was a distinct disease caused by drinking, but differing from drunkenness, and that by reason thereof he did not know that the act was wrong, you will find a verdict of not guilty on the ground of insanity.

2. That evidence of drunkenness which renders the accused incapable of forming the specific intent essential to constitute the crime should be taken into consideration with the other facts proved in order to determine whether or not he had this intent.

3. That evidence of drunkenness falling short of a proved incapacity in the accused to form the intent necessary to constitute the crime, and merely establishing that his mind was affected by drink so that he more readily gave way to some violent passion, does not rebut the presumption that a man intends the natural consequences of his acts.

Would a trial judge today be correct in adopting the three propositions set out in *Beard*, above? What objections could you make to a judge's charge that did so? *Beard* has been interpreted as restricting the intoxication defence to "specific intent" offences. What is the meaning of the term "specific intent" as used in *Beard*? Does *Beard* distinguish "general intent" offences from those of "specific intent"?

In *DPP v Beard*, Lord Birkenhead states three conclusions that may be drawn from the English law as it stood in 1920 in respect of intoxication. In Canada, the law in respect of mental disorders and their relationship with intoxication has developed since *Beard* was decided. The leading case, *R v Bouchard-Lebrun*, was introduced in Chapter 15 with reference to the interplay between mental disorder and intoxication. In the following extract, LeBel J explains how the Canadian approach to the intoxication defence has developed since *Beard*.

R v Bouchard-Lebrun
2011 SCC 58, [2011] 3 SCR 575

LeBEL J: ...

[30] In *Beard*, therefore, the House of Lords stated the principle that intoxication can be raised as a defence in respect of a specific intent offence in certain circumstances. This principle still represents the state of the law in Canada on this question, although it is subject to the qualification of Lord Birkenhead's third rule in *R. v. Robinson*, [1996] 1 S.C.R. 683 (*Daley*, at para. 40). In *Robinson*, this Court held that the third of the rules from *Beard*, which was based on the *capacity* of the accused to form a specific intent, violated ss. 7 and 11(d) of the *Canadian Charter of Rights and Freedoms*, because it required a jury to convict even if there was a reasonable doubt that the accused possessed *actual intent*. The Court therefore replaced this rule with one to the effect that intoxication can be a defence if it prevented the accused from forming the actual specific intent to commit the offence.

[31] Since *Beard*, it has thus been possible to apply the intoxication defence to acquit an accused charged with a specific intent offence or, where the nature of the offence so permits, to convict the accused of a lesser included offence requiring only general intent. Another question that subsequently arose was whether an accused could also use the defence of self-induced intoxication to raise a reasonable doubt about *mens rea* where the offence required only general intent. In *Leary v The Queen*, [1978] 1 S.C.R. 29, this Court answered this question in the negative. In that case, the Court established the principle that the recklessness shown by an accused in becoming voluntarily intoxicated can constitute the fault element needed to find that a general intent offence has been committed (*Daley*, at para. 36; see also the reasons of McIntyre J. in *R. v. Bernard*, [1988] 2 S.C.R. 833).

[32] In *Daviault*, however, a majority of the Court held that the "substituted *mens rea*" rule from *Leary* was contrary to ss. 7 and 11(d) of the *Charter*. Cory J. stated that "[a]

person intending to drink cannot be said to be intending to commit a sexual assault" (p. 92). He added that "to deny that even a very minimal mental element is required for sexual assault offends the *Charter* in a manner that is so drastic and so contrary to the principles of fundamental justice that it cannot be justified under s. 1 of the *Charter*" [*idem*]. The Court thus cast aside the *Leary* rule in *Daviault* and established the principle that accused persons who were in a "state akin to automatism or insanity" at the time they committed an act constituting a general intent offence would be legally entitled to raise a reasonable doubt concerning the required mental element [at 100].

[33] Sopinka J. wrote a strong dissent in *Daviault*. In his view, there was no reason to abandon the *Leary* rule, since the application of that rule did not relieve the Crown of the responsibility of proving "the existence of a *mens rea* or any of the other elements of the offence of sexual assault which are required by the principles of fundamental justice" (p. 115). He felt that the validity of the *Leary* rule was also reinforced by sound policy considerations, including society's right "to punish those who of their own free will render themselves so intoxicated as to pose a threat to other members of the community" (p. 114).

[34] Less than a year after *Daviault*, Parliament enacted s. 33.1 *Cr. C.* to ensure that "intoxication may never be used as a defence against general intent violent crimes such as sexual assault and assault" (*House of Commons Debates*, vol. 133, 1st Sess., 35th Parl., June 22, 1995, at p. 14470).

[*Daviault* and s 33.1 of the *Criminal Code* are discussed in Section III of this chapter.]

. . .

[40] There is of course some correlation between "self-induced states caused by alcohol or drugs," which the Court, in *Cooper*, excluded from the definition of the legal concept of "disease of the mind" for the purposes of s. 16 *Cr. C.*, and the states of intoxication now covered by s. 33.1 *Cr. C.* However, where an accused raises a defence of mental disorder, it [is] important that the legal analysis of the situation follow a logical order. The court must not begin its analysis by considering whether the mental condition of the accused at the material time is covered by s. 33.1 *Cr. C.* Such an approach would reverse the steps of the appropriate analytical process and disregard the nature of the defence raised by the accused. And as a result of it, the legal characterization exercise required by s. 16 *Cr. C.* would depend on the interpretation of the concept of causation in issue in s. 33.1 *Cr. C.* The court must instead consider the specific principles that govern the insanity defence in order to determine whether s. 16 *Cr. C.* is applicable. If that defence does not apply, the court can then consider whether s. 33.1 *Cr. C.* is applicable if it is appropriate to do so on the facts of the case.

Three key points arise from this passage. First, if a party raises mental disorder on the basis of intoxication, the court must initially consider whether the accused meets the requirements in s 16 of the *Criminal Code*—in particular, whether he or she suffered from a mental disorder or disease of the mind as legally defined at the time of the alleged act. The court should only consider the intoxication defence if s 16 does not apply. Second, where s 16 does not apply, the court must consider whether s 33.1 of the *Criminal Code* governs the case. As further explained in Section III, the constitutionality of s 33.1 is in some question and the provision has already been challenged in trial courts. It seems likely that, at some point, an appeal court will need to resolve this issue. Finally, Canadian case law offers an important clarification to the third *Beard* principle.

Beard speaks of whether a person is so intoxicated that he or she cannot form the intent. For many years courts in Canada followed this formulation of the intoxication defence. However, in *R v Robinson*, [1996] 1 SCR 683 the Court reconsidered, and, for the majority, Lamer CJ concluded that a jury should be charged "that their overall duty is to determine whether or not the accused possessed the requisite intent for the crime." The rules that govern the instructions a trial judge should give to the jury are somewhat complex: see *R v Daley*, 2007 SCC 53, [2007] 3 SCR 523 and *R v Walle*, 2012 SCC 41, [2012] 2 SCR 438. Nevertheless, they are necessary for implementing the principle that an accused should not be convicted of an offence unless the Crown has proven beyond a reasonable doubt that he or she possessed the necessary *mens rea*: this requires a focus on the accused's actual intent, not simply on whether he or she had the capacity (but perhaps did not exercise it) for the intent.

As the following sections demonstrate, this principle operates differently in relation to specific intent offences than it does in relation to offences classified as requiring general intent. It is therefore important as a preliminary step to distinguishing specific intent offences from those of general intent. This distinction is explained in *R v George*, [1960] SCR 871 and was further considered in subsequent cases.

II. INTOXICATION AND SPECIFIC INTENT

The distinction between specific and general intent exists solely for the purpose of determining whether there is a defence of intoxication at common law. The distinction has been criticized by some as not grounded in principle; but it has been praised by others as based on sound policy. Intuitively, specific intent connotes a more focused, concentrated, or complicated form of *mens rea*, but this idea has never been coherently developed.

R v George
Supreme Court of Canada
[1960] SCR 871

RITCHIE J (with whom Martland J concurred): This is an appeal from a judgment of the Court of Appeal of British Columbia affirming the acquittal of the respondent by Morrow Co. Ct. J. of the charge that he did "unlawfully and by violence steal from the person of Nicholas Avgeris the sum of Twenty-two Dollars."

The learned trial Judge has found that: "A man of 84, was violently manhandled by an Indian on the date noted in the Indictment ... as a result of which he was in hospital for a month. During this scuffle he was badly injured, dumped into a bathtub and pulled out again when he agreed to give the Indian what money he had, $22," and he has also "reached the conclusion ... without any doubt that it was the accused who committed the offence on the night in question." The learned trial Judge continued: "The first statement perhaps should be considered. It was obviously written in the words of someone who has not had too much education. In his second paragraph after recalling the drinking period, he said: 'Then I came to and I was in house and I remember hitting man and I don't remember where I went after.'"

Notwithstanding these findings, the learned trial Judge acquitted the respondent, saying: "To me it is very much a border line case. That being so it is my duty to give the accused the benefit of the doubt on the defence of drunkenness that has been set up in my mind."

After acquitting him, the learned trial Judge addressed the accused in part as follows: "You are being acquitted not because you didn't do it—there is no doubt in my mind that you did do it—you are being acquitted because I have found that you were so drunk on the night in question that you were unable to form an intent to do it." From this acquittal the Crown appealed to the Court of Appeal of British Columbia, and in rendering the decision of the majority of that Court Mr. Justice O'Halloran said:

> I am unable with respect to accept Crown counsel's submission that in failing to convict respondent of assault upon this charge of robbery, the learned trial Judge omitted to instruct himself regarding any difference between the intent to commit the robbery and a specific intent to commit assault as one of the essential ingredients of the robbery with which he was charged.
>
> In my judgment, with respect, a sufficient answer thereto is; that having found the respondent so incapacitated by liquor that he could not form an intent to commit the robbery, it follows rationally in the circumstances here, that he must also be deemed to have found that respondent was equally incapable for the same reason of having an intent to commit the assault. If he could not have the intent to commit the robbery, *viz.*, to assault and steal as charged, then he could not have the intent either to assault or to steal when both occurred together as charged; the charge reads "by violence steal."

Leave to appeal to this Court was granted pursuant to an application made on behalf of the Attorney-General of British Columbia. No appeal was taken from the acquittal of the respondent on the charge of robbery and the grounds of appeal are, in large measure, devoted to the question of whether a distinction should be drawn "between the degree of drunkenness required to negative the existence of" that intent which is, under the *Cr. Code*, an essential ingredient of the crime of robbery and the degree of drunkenness which is necessary to negative such intent as is an ingredient of common assault.

Pursuant to s. 569 [now s 662] of the *Cr. Code*, the learned trial Judge was under a duty to direct his mind to the "included offence" of assault. ...

In my opinion, the duty which rests upon the trial Judge to direct himself with respect to all included offences of which there is evidence can, in no way, be affected by the fact that the Crown Prosecutor has omitted to make reference to such offences. It follows, in my view, that in a case where the trial Judge has wrongly applied the law applicable to such an offence the Crown is not deprived of its statutory right of appeal because of the omission of its agent at the trial to address the Court on the matter.

The fact that the learned trial Judge found, as I think he did, that the respondent had "violently manhandled" an old man but was not guilty of assault because he was drunk at the time raises the question of law posed by the appellant as to whether, under the circumstances as found by the trial Judge, drunkenness is a valid defence to common assault.

In considering the question of *mens rea*, a distinction is to be drawn between "intention" as applied to acts done to achieve an immediate end on the one hand and acts done with the specific and ulterior motive and intention of furthering or achieving an illegal object on the other hand. Illegal acts of the former kind are done "intentionally" in the sense that they are not done by accident or through honest mistake, but acts of the latter kind are the product of preconception and are deliberate steps taken towards an illegal goal. The former acts may be the purely physical products of momentary passion, whereas the latter involve the mental process of formulating a specific intent. A man, far advanced in drink, may intentionally strike his fellow in the former sense at a time when his mind is so befogged with liquor as to be unable to formulate a specific intent in the latter sense. The offence of robbery, as defined by the *Cr. Code*, requires the presence of the kind of intent and purpose specified in ss. 269 [now s 322] and 288 [now s 343], but the use of the word "intentionally" in defining "common assault" in s. 230(a) [now s 265(1)(a)] of the *Cr. Code* is exclusively referable to the physical act of applying force to the person of another.

I would adopt the following passage from Kenny's Outlines of Criminal Law, 17th ed., pp. 58-9, para. 42, as an authoritative statement on this subject. He there says:

> In *Director of Public Prosecutions v. Beard*, [1920] A.C. 479 ... it was laid down that evidence of such drunkenness as "renders the accused incapable of forming the specific intent, essential to constitute the crime, should be taken into consideration, with the other facts proved, in order to determine whether or not he had this intent." In such a case the drunkenness, if it negatives the existence of the indispensable mental element of the crime, "negatives the commission of that crime." Thus a drunken man's inability to form an intention to kill, or to do grievous bodily harm involving the risk of killing, at the time of committing a homicide, may reduce his offence from murder to manslaughter (which latter crime requires no more than a realization that some bodily harm may be caused). Drunkenness may likewise show that a supposed burglar had no intention of stealing, or that wounds were inflicted without any "intent to do grievous bodily harm," or that a false pretence was made with no "intent to defraud." But it must be remembered that a man may be so drunk as not to form an intention to kill or do grievous bodily harm while yet in sufficient control of his senses to be able to contemplate some harm and so to be guilty of manslaughter or of an unlawful wounding.

The decision of the learned trial Judge, in my opinion, constitutes a finding that the respondent violently manhandled a man and knew that he was hitting him. Under these circumstances, evidence that the accused was in a state of voluntary drunkenness cannot be treated as a defence to a charge of common assault because there is no suggestion that the drink which had been consumed had produced permanent or temporary insanity and the respondent's own statement indicates that he knew that he was applying force to the person of another.

In view of the above, I would allow the appeal. ...

FAUTEUX J (with whom Taschereau J concurred): ... In considering the question of *mens rea*, a distinction is to be made between (i) intention as applied to acts considered in relation to their purposes and (ii) intention as applied to acts considered apart from their purposes. A general intent attending the commission of an act is, in some cases, the only intent required to constitute the crime while, in others, there must be, in addition to that general intent, a specific intent attending the purpose for the commission of the act.

Contrary to what is the case in the crime of robbery, where, with respect to theft, a specific intent must be proved by the Crown as one of the constituent elements of the offence, there is no specific intent necessary to constitute the offence of common assault, which is defined as follows in s. 230, *Cr. Code*:

.A person commits an assault when, without the consent of another person or with consent, where it is obtained by fraud,

(a) he applies force intentionally to the person of the other, directly or indirectly, or

(b) he attempts or threatens, by an act or gesture, to apply force to the person of the other, if he has or causes the other to believe upon reasonable grounds that he has present ability to effect his purpose.

The word "intentionally" appearing in s. 230(a) is exclusively related to the application of force or to the manner in which force is applied. This, indeed, is also made clear in the French version, reading:

230. Commet des voies de fait, ou se livre à une attaque, quiconque, sans le consentement d'autrui, ou avec son consentement, s'il est obtenu par fraude,

(a) *d'une manière intentionnelle*, applique, directement ou indirectement, la force ou la violence contre la personne d'autrui, ou

(b) tente ou menace, par un acte ou un geste, d'appliquer la force ou la violence contre la personne d'autrui, s'il est en mesure actuelle, ou s'il porte cette personne à croire, pour des motifs raisonnables, qu'il est en mesure actuelle d'accomplir son dessein. [The italics are mine.]

There can be no pretence, in this case, that the manner in which force was applied by the respondent to his victim was accidental or—excluding at the moment, from the consideration, the defence of drunkenness—unintentional.

On this finding of fact, the accused was guilty of common assault unless there was evidence indicating a degree of drunkenness affording, under the law, a valid defence.

The trial Judge entertained a doubt on the question whether the Crown had proved, as part of its case, that the accused had, owing to drunkenness, the capacity to form the *specific intent* required in the offence of robbery, *i.e.*, the intent to steal. ... [Note that this should now be read subject to subsequent decisions such as *R v Robinson*, *supra*, that hold the ultimate issue should now be intent, not capacity to have the specific intent.]

Hence, the question is whether, owing to drunkenness, respondent's condition was such that he was incapable of applying force intentionally. I do not know that, short of a degree of drunkenness creating a condition tantamount to insanity, such a situation could be metaphysically conceived in an assault of the kind here involved. It is certain that, on the facts found by the trial Judge, this situation did not exist in this case.

The accused was acquitted of the offence of robbery, not on the ground that he could not have applied force intentionally, but because of the doubt entertained by the trial Judge on the question whether he had the capacity to form the specific intent required as a constituent element for the offence of theft.

In these views, the finding of the trial Judge that the accused had not the capacity to form the specific intent to commit robbery did not justify the conclusion reached in appeal that he could not then have committed the offence of common assault; nor is it shown that, had the trial Judge considered common assault, the verdict would necessarily have been the same.

In these circumstances, the Court of Appeal should have allowed the appeal from the acquittal and should have proceeded to make an order pursuant to its authority under s. 592(4)(b) [now s 686(4)(b)], to wit, either enter a verdict of guilty with respect to the offence of which, in its opinion, formed in the light of the law applicable in the matter, the accused should have been found guilty but for the error in law, and pass a sentence warranted in law, or order a new trial.

Under s. 600 [now s 695], *Cr. Code*, this Court is given the authority to make any order that the Court of Appeal might have made. At the hearing before this Court, it was intimated that should the appeal of the Crown be maintained, this case should be finally disposed of, if possible, and that in such event, respondent could appropriately be given a suspended sentence.

Being of opinion that the accused should have been found guilty of common assault, had that offence been considered in the light of the law applicable to the facts of this case, I would maintain the appeal, set aside the verdict of acquittal with respect to common assault and enter a verdict of guilty of that offence. Prior to his acquittal in the Court below, respondent has been incarcerated during a number of weeks. It would appear more consonant with the representations made with respect to sentence, to sentence respondent to the time already spent by him in jail; and this is the sentence that I would pass.

[LOCKE J dissented on the basis that the Crown had no right to appeal from an acquittal under these circumstances: "Stated bluntly, the contention of the Crown is that where a trial Judge hearing a criminal charge fails not to deal with, but to consider independently, an offence included in the offence specifically charged, and this is done with the approval of counsel for the Crown, the provisions of s. 584 [now s 676] may be invoked to again place the accused in jeopardy. I do not think that it was ever contemplated when the legislation was enacted that it might be exercised in circumstances such as these."]

Appeal allowed; verdict of guilty of common assault entered.

R v Bernard
Supreme Court of Canada
[1988] 2 SCR 833

[At the accused's trial on a charge of sexual assault causing bodily harm contrary to s 246.2(c) (now s 272(c)) of the *Criminal Code*, the only issue left by the trial judge to the jury was the question of consent. The evidence indicated that the complainant was beaten about the face by the accused and that intercourse had taken place without her consent. The accused did not testify but in a statement to the police, which was admitted into evidence, the accused stated that he forced the complainant to have intercourse but he did it because he was drunk and when he realized what he was doing he got off the complainant. The trial judge directed the jury that the only evidence of drunkenness was in the accused's statement but that drunkenness was no defence to the charge alleged against the accused. An appeal by the accused from his conviction to the Ontario Court of Appeal was dismissed. On further appeal by the accused to the Supreme Court of Canada, the Court was asked to reconsider its decision in *Leary v The Queen* holding that the former offence of rape was an offence of general intent for which voluntary intoxication was no defence.]

McINTYRE J (with whom Beetz J concurred): ... A distinction has long been recognized in the criminal law between offences which require the proof of a specific intent and those which require only the proof of a general intent. This distinction forms the basis of the defence of drunkenness and it must be understood and kept in mind in approaching this case. ...

The general intent offence is one in which the only intent involved relates solely to the performance of the act in question with no further ulterior intent or purpose. The minimal intent to apply force in the offence of common assault affords an example. A specific intent offence is one which involves the performance of the *actus reus*, coupled with an intent or purpose going beyond the mere performance of the questioned act. Striking a blow or administering poison with the intent to kill, or assault with intent to maim or wound, are examples of such offences.

This distinction is not an artificial one nor does it rest upon any legal fiction. There is a world of difference between the man who in frustration or anger strikes out at his neighbour in a public house with no particular purpose or intent in mind, other than to perform the act of striking, and the man who strikes a similar blow with intent to cause death or injury. ...

It is not necessary for the purposes of this judgment to review in detail the authorities in this court on the question. It will be sufficient to summarize their effect in the following terms. Drunkenness in a general sense is not a true defence to a criminal act. Where, however, in a case which involves a crime of specific intent, the accused is so affected by intoxication that he lacks the capacity to form the specific intent required to commit the crime charged, it may apply. The defence, however, has no application in offences of general intent.

The criticism of the law with respect to the defence of drunkenness is based on two propositions. It is said, first, that the distinction between the general intent and specific intent offences is artificial and is little more than a legal fiction. Secondly, it is said that it is illogical, because it envisages a defence of drunkenness in certain situations and not in others; it is merely a policy decision made by judges and not based on principle or logic. It will be evident from what I have said that I reject the first ground of criticism. As to the second criticism, that it is based upon grounds of policy, I would say that there can be no doubt that considerations of policy are involved in this distinction. Indeed, in some cases, principally *Majewski* [[1977] AC 443 (HL)], the distinction has been defended on the basis that it is sound social policy. The fact, however, that considerations of policy have influenced the development of the law in the field cannot, in my view, be condemned. In the final analysis, all law should be based upon and consistent with sound social policy. No good law can be inconsistent with or depart from sound policy.

If the policy behind the present law is that society condemns those who, by the voluntary consumption of alcohol, render themselves incapable of self-control so that they will commit acts of violence causing injury to their neighbours, then in my view, no apology for such policy is needed, and the resulting law affords no affront to the well-established principles of the law or to the freedom of the individual ... .

In my view, the common law rules on the defence of drunkenness, though frequently the subject of criticism, have a rationality which not only accords with criminal law theory, but has also served society well. It is not questioned in this case that the defence of drunkenness, as it applies to specific intent offences, is supportable. It is submitted, however, that it should be extended to include all criminal charges. It is my view that this proposition is not sustainable ... .

The Chief Justice has expressed the view that evidence of self-induced intoxication should be a relevant consideration in determining whether the *mens rea* of any particular offence has been proved by the Crown. As I have indicated, I am unable to agree with this conclusion. The effect of such a conclusion would be that the more drunk a person becomes by his own voluntary consumption of alcohol or drugs, the more extended will be his opportunity for a successful defence against conviction for the offences caused by such drinking, regardless of the nature of the intent required for those offences ... .

This court in *Leary* approved the *Majewski* approach which has long been accepted in the law of Canada, and, for the reasons which I have set out, it is my opinion that this court's judgment in *Leary* ought not to be overruled. I must re-emphasize that the *Leary* rule does not relieve the Crown from its obligation to prove the *mens rea* in a general intent offence. The fact that an accused may not rely on voluntary intoxication in such offences does not have that effect because of the nature of the offence and the mental elements which must be shown. The requisite state of mind may be proved in two ways. First, there is the general proposition that triers of fact may infer *mens rea* from the *actus reus* itself: a person is presumed to have intended the natural and probable consequences of his actions. For example, in an offence involving the mere application of force, the minimal intent to apply that force will suffice to constitute the necessary *mens rea* and can be reasonably inferred from the act itself and the other evidence. Secondly, in cases where the accused was so intoxicated as to raise doubt as to the voluntary nature of his conduct, the Crown may meet its evidentiary obligation respecting the necessary blameworthy mental state of the accused by proving the fact of voluntary self-induced intoxication by drugs or alcohol. This was the approach suggested in *Majewski*. In most cases involving intoxication in general intent offences, the trier of fact will be able to apply the first proposition, namely, that the intent is inferable from the *actus reus* itself. As Fauteux J. observed in *George*, [[1960] SCR 871], at p. 879, it is almost metaphysically inconceivable for a person to be so drunk as to be incapable of forming the minimal intent to apply force. Hence, only in cases of the most extreme self-intoxication does the trier of fact need to use the second proposition, that is, that evidence of self-induced intoxication is evidence of the guilty mind, the blameworthy mental state.

The result ... is that, for these crimes, accused persons cannot hold up voluntary drunkenness as a defence. They cannot be heard to say: "I was so drunk that I did not know what I was doing." If they managed to get themselves so drunk that they did not know what they were doing, the reckless behaviour in attaining that level of intoxication affords the necessary evidence of culpable mental condition. Hence, it is logically impossible for an accused person to throw up his voluntary drunkenness as a defence to a charge of general intent. Proof of his voluntary drunkenness can be proof of his guilty mind ... .

It was argued by the appellant that the *Leary* rule converts the offence of sexual assault causing bodily harm into a crime of absolute liability in that the Crown need not prove the requisite intention for the completion of the offence. Therefore, it is said that *Leary* violates ss. 7 and 11(d) of the *Charter*. In *Re B.C. Motor Vehicle Act*, [1985] 2 S.C.R. 486, and in *R. v. Vaillancourt*, [1987] 2 S.C.R. 636, it was held that the requirement for a minimum mental state before the attachment of criminal liability is a principle of fundamental justice. Criminal offences, as a general rule, must have as one of their elements the requirement of a blameworthy mental state. The morally innocent ought not to be convicted. It is said that the *Leary* rule violates this fundamental premise. In my opinion, the *Leary* rule clearly does not offend this essential principle of criminal law but rather upholds it. The *Leary* rule recognizes that accused persons who have voluntarily consumed drugs or alcohol, thereby depriving themselves of self-control leading to the commission of a crime, are not morally innocent and are, indeed, criminally blameworthy. While the rule excludes consideration of voluntary intoxication in the approach to general intent offences, it none the less recognizes that it may be a relevant factor in those generally more serious offences where the *mens rea* must involve not only the intentional performance of the *actus reus* but, as well, the formation of further ulterior motives and purposes. It therefore intrudes upon the security of the person only in accordance with sound principle and within the established boundaries of the legal process. For these reasons, I would say that the *Charter* is not violated … .

I would not overrule the judgment of this court in *Leary* and I would confirm the law as it presently stands. Parliament at some time in the future may intervene in the matter with such statutory provisions as it may consider appropriate but failing that occurrence I would not enlarge the defence of drunkenness. …

In any event, should it be considered that I am wrong in my approach to the *Leary* case, this is none the less a case in which the provisions of s. 613(1)(b)(iii) [now s 686(1)(b)(iii)] of the *Criminal Code* should be applied.

WILSON J (with whom L'Heureux-Dubé J concurred): I have had the benefit of the reasons of the Chief Justice and of my colleagues McIntyre and La Forest JJ. I agree with McIntyre J. for the reasons given by him that sexual assault causing bodily harm is an offence of general intent requiring only the minimal intent to apply force. I agree with him also that in most cases involving general intent offences and intoxication the Crown will be able to establish the accused's blameworthy mental state by inference from his or her acts. I think that is the case here. The evidence of intoxication withheld from the trier of fact in this case could not possibly have raised a reasonable doubt as to the existence of the minimal intent to apply force. It is, accordingly, not necessary in this case to resort to self-induced intoxication as a substituted form of *mens rea*. And, indeed, I have some real concerns as to whether the imposition of criminal liability on that basis would survive a challenge under the *Canadian Charter of Rights and Freedoms*.

The facts are fully set out in the reasons of the Chief Justice and I refer to them only to underline why I agree with my colleague, McIntyre J., that the rule in *Leary v. The Queen*, [1978] 1 S.C.R. 29, should be preserved and applied in this case.

Sexual assault is a crime of violence. There is no requirement of an intent or purpose beyond the intentional application of force. It is first and foremost an assault. It is sexual in nature only because, objectively viewed, it is related to sex either on account of the area of the body to which the violence is applied or on account of words accompanying the violence. Indeed, the whole purpose, as I understand it, of the replacement of the offence of rape by the offence of sexual assault was to emphasize the aspect of violence and put paid to the benign concept that rape was simply the act of a man who was "carried away" by his emotions.

The appellant in his statement to the police admitted that he had forced the complainant to have sexual intercourse with him but claimed that because of his drunkenness he did not know *why* he had done this and that when he realized what he was doing he "got off" the complainant. There was evidence that the appellant had punched the complainant twice with his closed fist and had threatened to kill her. The doctor who examined the complainant testified that the complainant's right eye was swollen shut and that three stitches were required to close the wound. It is clear from this that there was intentional and voluntary, as opposed to accidental or involuntary, application of force.

The evidence of the appellant's intoxication consisted of his own statements to the police that he was drunk; the complainant's testimony that, while the appellant was acting out of character in making advances to her, he was able to walk, talk and put albums on the record-player; a friend's testimony that prior to the incident the appellant had been drinking at a bar and had become "very rowdy" although still capable of talking and walking straight. By his own admission, the appellant had sufficient wits about him after the violent assault to hide a bloodied towel and pillowcase from the police. There is no evidence that we are dealing here with extreme intoxication, verging on insanity or automatism, and as such capable of negating the inference that the minimal intent to apply force was present: see *R. v. Swietlinski* (1978), 44 C.C.C. (2d) 267 (Ont. C.A.), at p. 294, aff'd [1980] 2 S.C.R. 956. The evidence of intoxication in this case was simply not capable of raising a reasonable doubt as to the existence of the minimal intent required. In this I agree with McIntyre J.

I am less confident about the proposition accepted by my colleague that self-induced intoxication may substitute for the mental element required to be present at the time the offence was committed although I realize that there are statements in judgments of this court to that effect. I do not believe, however, that the court has clearly adopted that proposition. The decision of the House of Lords in *D.P.P. v. Majewski*, [1977] A.C. 443, may stand for the rather harsh proposition that even self-induced intoxication producing a state of automatism cannot constitute a defence to an offence of general intent such as assault but I doubt that our Canadian jurisprudence goes that far. ...

I believe that the *Leary* rule is perfectly consistent with an onus resting on the Crown to prove the minimal intent which should accompany the doing of the prohibited act in general intent offences. I view it as preferable to preserve the *Leary* rule in its more flexible form as Pigeon J. applied it, *i.e.*, so as to allow evidence of intoxication to go to the trier of fact in general intent offences only if it is evidence of extreme intoxication involving an absence of awareness akin to a state of insanity or automatism. Only in such a case is the evidence capable of raising a reasonable doubt as to the existence of the minimal intent required for the offence. I would not overrule *Leary*, as the Chief Justice would, and allow evidence of intoxication to go to the trier of fact in every case regardless of its possible relevance to the issue of the existence of the minimal intent required for the offence. ...

It is, in my view, not strictly necessary in this case to address the constitutionality of substituting self-induced intoxication as the *mens rea* for the minimal *mens rea* requirements of general intent offences. The issue would, in my view, only arise in those rare cases in which the intoxication is extreme enough to raise doubts as to the existence of the minimal intent which characterizes conscious and volitional conduct. However, as both the Chief Justice and McIntyre J. have addressed the issue, I will express my own somewhat tentative views upon it.

This court has affirmed as fundamental the proposition that a person should not be exposed to a deprivation of liberty unless the Crown proves the existence of a blameworthy or culpable state of mind: see *Re B.C. Motor Vehicle Act, supra*, at pp. 513-20. It does not follow from this, however, that those who, through the voluntary consumption of alcohol or drugs incapacitate themselves from knowing what they are doing, fall within the category of the "morally innocent" deserving of such protection. This is not to say that such persons do not have a right under s. 7 or s. 12 of the *Charter* to be protected against punishment that is disproportionate to their crime and degree of culpability: see *Re B.C. Motor Vehicle Act, supra*, at pp. 532-34; *R v. Smith (Edward Dewey)*, [1987] 1 S.C.R. 1045. They do, especially if the consequences of their becoming intoxicated were not intended or foreseen.

The real concern over the substituted form of *mens rea* arises, it seems to me, under s. 11(d) of the *Charter*. While this court has recognized that in some cases proof of an essential element of a criminal offence can be replaced by proof of a different element, it has placed stringent limitations on when this can happen. In *Vaillancourt, supra*, Lamer J. said at p. 656:

> Finally, the legislature, rather than simply eliminating any need to prove the essential element, may substitute proof of a different element. In my view, this will be constitutionally valid only if upon proof beyond reasonable doubt of the substituted element it would be unreasonable for the trier of fact not to be satisfied beyond reasonable doubt of the existence of the essential element. If the trier of fact may have a reasonable doubt as to the essential element notwithstanding proof beyond a reasonable doubt of the substituted element, then the substitution infringes ss. 7 and 11(d).

In *Whyte*, [[1988] 2 SCR 3], the Chief Justice approved the above statement at pp. 18-19, and added:

> In the passage from *Vaillancourt* quoted earlier, Lamer J. recognized that in some cases substituting proof of one element for proof of an essential element will not infringe the presumption of innocence if, upon proof of the substituted element, it would be unreasonable for the trier of fact not to be satisfied beyond a reasonable doubt of the existence of the essential element. This is another way of saying that a statutory presumption infringes the presumption of innocence if it requires the trier of fact to convict in spite of a reasonable doubt. Only if the existence of the substituted fact leads inexorably to the conclusion that the essential element exists, with no other reasonable possibilities, will the statutory presumption be constitutionally valid.

In my tentative view, it is unlikely that in those cases in which it is necessary to resort to self-induced intoxication as the substituted element for the minimal intent, proof of the substituted element will "inexorably" lead to the conclusion that the essential element of the minimal intent existed at the time the criminal act was committed. But I prefer to leave this question open as it is unnecessary to decide it in order to dispose of this appeal.

DICKSON CJ, dissenting (with whom Lamer J concurred and La Forest J expressed "general agreement"): … In my view, the only issue the court needs to address may be put as follows: should evidence of self-induced intoxication be considered by the trier of fact, along with all other relevant evidence, in determining whether the prosecution has proved beyond a reasonable doubt the *mens rea* required to constitute the offence? I am of the opinion that the court should answer that question in the affirmative.

I wish to make clear at the outset, however, that nothing in these reasons is intended to apply with respect to the quite distinct issues raised by offences, such as driving while impaired, where intoxication or the consumption of alcohol is itself an ingredient of the offence. The *mens rea* of such offences can be left for consideration another day. ...

In my dissent in *Leary*, I sought to advance the view that respect for basic criminal law principles required that the legal fiction, the artificial "specific" intent threshold requirement, be abandoned. I do not intend in these reasons to repeat what I said in *Leary*. With due regard for *stare decisis*, as to which I will have more to say in a moment, and with the greatest of respect for those of a contrary view, I would only add that nothing I have heard or read since the judgment in *Leary* has caused me to abandon or modify in the slightest degree the views of dissent which I there expressed. ...

The categories of "specific" intent on the one hand and "basic" or "general" intent on the other have evolved as an artificial device whereby evidence, otherwise relevant, is excluded from the jury's consideration. This court, in *Swietlinski*, has recognized that intoxication may as a matter of fact deprive an accused of "basic" or "general" intent. It is said, however, by those who support the classification that as a matter of policy, consideration of evidence of intoxication must be excluded. Indeed, a notable feature to be found in the analysis of many of those who support restricting the jury's use of evidence relating to drunkenness is the concession that while principle and logic lead in an opposite direction, the policy of protection of the public requires that principle and logic should yield: see, *e.g.*, *D.P.P. v. Majewski*, [1976] 2 All E.R. 142 at pp. 167-68, *per* Lord Edmund-Davies, quoted by Pigeon J. in *Leary, supra*, at pp. 52-53.

In my view, there are two fundamental problems with this approach. First, if the law is to be altered in the name of policy over principle, that is surely a task for Parliament rather than the courts. ...

Secondly, even if it were appropriate for the courts to bend principle in the name of policy, so far as I am aware, there is no evidence that the artificiality of the specific intent requirement is actually required for social protection.

An unrestrained application of basic *mens rea* doctrine would not, in my opinion, open a gaping hole in the criminal law inimical to social protection. There are several reasons for this. To the extent that intoxication merely lowers inhibitions, removes self-restraint or induces unusual self-confidence or aggressiveness, it would be of no avail to an accused, as such effects do not relate to the *mens rea* requirement for volitional and intentional or reckless conduct. Similarly, intoxication would be of no avail to an accused who got drunk in order to gain the courage to commit a crime or to aid in his defence. Thirdly, one can trust in the good sense of the jury and that of our trial judges to weigh all the evidence in a fair and responsible manner, and they are unlikely to acquit too readily those who have committed offences while intoxicated. ...

The real issue in this appeal, it seems to me, is whether the court should now overrule *Leary*. ...

Since *Leary* was decided, the *Canadian Charter of Rights and Freedoms* has come into force. This court has held that legislation which imposes the sanction of imprisonment without proof of a blameworthy state of mind violates the guarantee of fundamental justice contained in s. 7 of the *Charter* and must be struck down unless it can meet the exacting test of s. 1: see *Re B.C. Motor Vehicle Act*, [1985] 2 S.C.R. 486; *R. v. Vaillancourt*, [1987] 2 S.C.R. 636.

The appellant submits that *Leary* runs counter to s. 7 by providing that intoxication is no defence to a crime of general intent. In circumstances where the requisite mental intent is lacking due to an intoxicated condition, a general intent offence is converted into one of absolute liability in which proof of the commission of the *actus reus* by itself mandates conviction. It is also submitted that *Leary* runs counter to the presumption of innocence and the right to a fair hearing as guaranteed by s. 11(d) of the *Charter*, in so far as wrongful intent is irrebuttably presumed upon the showing of intoxication. ...

The effect of the majority holding in *Leary* is to impose a form of absolute liability on intoxicated offenders, which is entirely inconsistent with the basic requirement for a blameworthy state of mind as a prerequisite to the imposition of the penalty of imprisonment mandated by the above-cited authorities. I agree with the observation of Professor Stuart in *Canadian Criminal Law*, 2nd ed. (1987), that s. 7 of the *Charter* mandates the reversal of *Leary* and the assertion of "the fundamental principles of voluntariness and fault" in relation to intoxication and the criminal law: p. 378. ...

The majority holding in *Leary* also runs counter to the s. 11(d) right to be presumed innocent until proven guilty. With respect to crimes of general intent, guilty intent is in effect presumed upon proof of the fact of intoxication. Moreover, the presumption of guilt created by the *Leary* rule is irrebuttable. ...

In my view, the *Leary* rule cannot be upheld by reference to s. 1, as it cannot survive the "proportionality" inquiry. While the protection of the public, said to underlie the *Leary* rule, could serve as an important objective, in my view the *Leary* rule does not achieve that objective in a manner consistent with the proportionality test of *Oakes*, [[1986] 1 SCR 103]. *Oakes* requires that "the measures adopted must be carefully designed to achieve the objective in question." ...

The *Leary* rule in effect treats the deliberate act of becoming intoxicated as culpable in itself, but inflicts punishment measured by the unintended consequences of becoming intoxicated. Punishment acts as a deterrent where the conduct is intended or foreseen. There is no evidence to support the assertion that the *Leary* rule deters the commission of unintended crimes. Hence, there is no warrant for violating fundamental principles and convicting those who would otherwise escape criminal liability. ...

Finally, it is my view that there is a disproportionality between the effects of *Leary* on rights protected by the *Charter* and the objective of public safety. To paraphrase Lamer J. in *Re B.C. Motor Vehicle Act, supra*, at p. 521, it has not been demonstrated that risk of imprisonment of a few innocent persons is required to attain the goal of protecting the public from drunken offenders.

As stated in *R. v. Holmes*, [1988] 1 S.C.R. 914 at p. 940: "This effect, given the range of alternative legislative devices available to Parliament, is too deleterious to be justified as a reasonable limit under s. 1 of the *Charter*. Simply put, the provision exacts too high a price to be justified in a free and democratic society." ...

The *Leary* rule fits most awkwardly with that enunciated in *Pappajohn*. Lower courts have held that in the light of *Leary*, where intoxication is a factor in inducing a mistaken belief in consent, the jury must be instructed that while an honest but unreasonable belief will negate *mens rea* (*Pappajohn*) they are to disregard the effect that intoxication might have had in inducing that mistake (*Leary*). ...

In my view, the *Leary* qualification on the criminal law principle of general application with respect to mistake of fact unnecessarily and unduly complicates the jury's task.

Indeed, I find it difficult to imagine how it is humanly possible to follow the jury instruction apparently mandated by the combination of *Leary* and *Pappajohn*. This confusing and anomalous result is entirely the product of the deviation from basic criminal law principles which occurred in *Leary* and, accordingly, there is much to support the view that it should be overruled. ...

I have already indicated the confusion created by the combination of *Leary* and *Pappajohn*. I suggest that the distinction between "general" and "specific" intent which *Leary* mandates and the notorious difficulty in articulating a clear and workable definition of specific intent falls squarely within the principle enunciated in *Ranville* and *Vetrovec*. Because that category is based on policy rather than principle, classification of offences as falling within or without the specific intent category is necessarily an *ad hoc*, unpredictable exercise. ...

The trial judge made no reference in his charge to the jury to the requirement that the Crown prove that the accused acted with the requisite intent. In my view, this is fatal to the conviction. Although the Crown presented a strong case against the accused at trial, no request was made by the respondent that this court apply the provision of s. 613(1)(b)(iii) of the *Criminal Code*, and in any event, it is not for this court to speculate as to the likely result had the jury been properly instructed.

It follows that the appeal should be allowed, the conviction set aside, and a new trial ordered.

Appeal dismissed.

In *R v ADH*, 2013 SCC 28, [2013] 2 SCR 269, the Supreme Court of Canada was asked to define the fault element of s 218 of the *Criminal Code*. This provision prohibits abandoning a child under the age of 10 years in circumstances defined in that section. Justice Cromwell, for the majority, concluded that the Crown must prove a minimal level of subjective fault: "at least recklessness, that is, that the accused actually knew of the risk to the child's life or health." Justice Moldaver, in dissent, would have defined s 218 as a crime of penal negligence, or objective fault. Among his reasons for preferring this interpretation, he identified his concern that the majority's approach "would provide a defence to the errant parent or irresponsible caregiver who, by virtue of intoxication, could not or did not foresee the likely consequences of his or her dangerous conduct, whether it be locking a child in a car on a hot summer's day or exposing a child to the elements on a cold winter's night."

III. EXTREME INTOXICATION AND GENERAL INTENT

As you have seen, in *R v Bernard*, [1988] 2 SCR 833, the Court was split over whether the fault of voluntarily consuming intoxicants could substitute for the minimum fault requirement for an offence of general intent. However, in that case, the question was *obiter* because, on the facts before the Court, Bernard's intoxication had not reached the extreme level at which it becomes necessary to decide that question. In *R v Daviault*, presented with a case in which the trial judge found that the accused was extremely intoxicated, a majority of the Court adopted the approach first proposed by Wilson J in *Bernard*.

R v Daviault
Supreme Court of Canada
[1994] 3 SCR 63

[The accused was charged with sexual assault of an elderly woman who was an acquaintance of his wife. The accused was a chronic alcoholic. The accused testified that on the day of the offence he consumed seven or eight bottles of beer and at the request of the complainant brought a 40 oz bottle of brandy to her. The accused testified that he recalled having one glass of brandy. The complainant subsequently discovered that the bottle of brandy was empty. An expert witness testified that, assuming the accused had consumed the beers and the bottle of brandy, his blood alcohol content would have been between 400 mg and 600 mg per 100 ml of blood. That blood alcohol ratio would cause death or a coma in an ordinary person. The expert testified that an individual with this level of alcohol might suffer a blackout and lose contact with reality, and that his brain would temporarily dissociate from normal functioning. He would have no awareness of his actions and no memory of them the next day. The trial judge acquitted the accused on the basis that he had a reasonable doubt whether the accused by virtue of his extreme intoxication possessed the minimal intent necessary to commit the offence of sexual assault. An appeal by the Crown to the Quebec Court of Appeal was allowed on the basis that the trial judge erred in holding that intoxication is a defence to a general intent offence, such as sexual assault. The Court of Appeal substituted a conviction.]

CORY J (Lamer CJ and La Forest, L'Heureux-Dubé, McLachlin, and Iacobucci JJ concurring): Can a state of drunkenness which is so extreme that an accused is in a condition that closely resembles automatism or a disease of the mind as defined in s. 16 of the *Criminal Code*, R.S.C. 1985, c. C-46, constitute a basis for defending a crime which requires not a specific but only a general intent? That is the troubling question that is raised on this appeal.

The facts of this case and the judgments below are set out in the reasons of Justice Sopinka. Although I agree with my colleague on a number of issues, I cannot agree with his conclusion that it is consistent with the principles of fundamental justice and the presumption of innocence for the courts to eliminate the mental element in crimes of general intent. Nor do I agree that self-induced intoxication is a sufficiently blameworthy state of mind to justify culpability, and to substitute it for the mental element that is an essential requirement of those crimes. In my opinion, the principles embodied in our *Canadian Charter of Rights and Freedoms*, and more specifically in ss. 7 and 11(d), mandate a limited exception to, or some flexibility in, the application of the *Leary* rule. This would permit evidence of extreme intoxication akin to automatism or insanity to be considered in determining whether the accused possessed the minimal mental element required for crimes of general intent. ...

The distinction between crimes of specific and general intent has been acknowledged and approved by this Court on numerous occasions. (See *R. v. George*, [1960] S.C.R. 871, at p. 877 (Fauteux J.); and subsequent cases such as *Leary v. The Queen*, [1978] 1 S.C.R. 29; *Swietlinski v. The Queen*, [1980] 2 S.C.R. 956; *R. v. Chase*, [1987] 2 S.C.R. 293; *R. v. Bernard*, [1988] 2 S.C.R. 833; and *R. v. Quin*, [1988] 2 S.C.R. 825.) On this issue, I am in general agreement with Sopinka J.'s presentation. The categorization of crimes as being either specific or general intent offences and the consequences that flow from that categorization are now well established in this Court. However, as he observes, we are not dealing here with ordinary cases of intoxication but with the limited situation of very extreme intoxication and the need, under the *Charter*, to create an exception in situations where intoxication is such that the mental element is negated. Sopinka J. sees no need for such an exception. This is where I must disagree with my colleague. ...

What options are available with regard to the admissibility and significance of evidence of drunkenness as it may pertain to the mental element in general intent offences? One choice would be to continue to apply the *Leary* rule. Yet, as I will attempt to demonstrate in the next section, the rule violates the *Charter* and cannot be justified. Thus, this choice is unacceptable.

Another route would be to follow the *O'Connor* decision. Evidence relating to drunkenness would then go to the jury along with all other relevant evidence in determining whether the mental element requirement had been met. It is this path that is enthusiastically recommended by the majority of writers in the field. Yet it cannot be followed. It is now well established by this court that there are two categories of offences. Those requiring a specific intent and others which call for nothing more than a general intent. To follow *O'Connor* would mean that all evidence of intoxication of any degree would always go to the jury in general intent offences. This, in my view, is unnecessary. Further, in *Bernard, supra*, the majority of this court rejected this approach.

A third alternative, which I find compelling, is that proposed by Wilson J. in *Bernard*. I will examine the justifications for adopting this position in more detail shortly, but before doing that it may be helpful to review the nature of the *Charter* violations occasioned by a rigid application of the *Leary* rule. ...

In my view, the strict application of the *Leary* rule offends both ss. 7 and 11(d) of the *Charter* for a number of reasons. The mental aspect of an offence, or *mens rea*, has long been recognized as an integral part of crime. The concept is fundamental to our criminal law. That element may be minimal in general intent offences; none the less, it exists. In this case, the requisite mental element is simply an intention to commit the sexual assault or recklessness as to whether the actions will constitute an assault. The necessary mental element can ordinarily be inferred from the proof that the assault was committed by the accused. However, the substituted *mens rea* of an intention to become drunk cannot establish the *mens rea* to commit the assault. ...

It was argued by the respondent that the "blameworthy" nature of voluntary intoxication is such that it should be determined that there can be no violation of the *Charter* if the *Leary* approach is adopted. I cannot accept that contention. Voluntary intoxication is not yet a crime. Further, it is difficult to conclude that such behaviour should always constitute a fault to which criminal sanctions should apply. However, assuming that voluntary intoxication is reprehensible, it does not follow that its consequences in any given situation are either voluntary or predictable. Studies demonstrate that the consumption of alcohol is not the cause of the crime. A person intending to drink cannot be said to be intending to commit a sexual assault.

Further, self-induced intoxication cannot supply the necessary link between the minimal mental element or *mens rea* required for the offence and the *actus reus*. This must follow from reasoning in *R. v. DeSousa*, [1992] 2 S.C.R. 944, and *R. v. Théroux, supra*. Here, the question is not whether there is some symmetry between the physical act and the mental element but whether the necessary link exists between the minimal mental element and the prohibited act; that is to say that the mental element is one of intention with respect to the *actus reus* of the crime charged. As well, as Sopinka J. observes, the minimum *mens rea* for an offence should reflect the particular nature of the crime. See *R. v. Creighton*, [1993] 3 S.C.R. 3. I doubt that self-induced intoxication can, in all circumstances, meet this requirement for all crimes of general intent. …

In summary, I am of the view that to deny that even a very minimal mental element is required for sexual assault offends the *Charter* in a manner that is so drastic and so contrary to the principles of fundamental justice that it cannot be justified under s. 1 of the *Charter*. The experience of other jurisdictions which have completely abandoned the *Leary* rule, coupled with the fact that under the proposed approach, the defence would be available only in the rarest of cases, demonstrate that there is no urgent policy or pressing objective which needs to be addressed. Studies on the relationship between intoxication and crime do not establish any rational link. Finally, as the *Leary* rule applies to all crimes of general intent, it cannot be said to be well tailored to address a particular objective and it would not meet either the proportionality or the minimum impairment requirements. …

As I have said, the position adopted by Wilson J. in *Bernard* has much to commend it and should be adopted. …

There are some who argue that Wilson J.'s suggestion favours the extremely drunk while ignoring those who are less inebriated: see, for example, T. Quigley [& A Manson], in "Bernard on Intoxication: Principle, Policy and Points in Between—Two Comments" [(1989) 67 CR (3rd) 168], at pp. 171-3. I cannot agree with that contention. It must be remembered that those who are a "little" drunk can readily form the requisite mental element to commit the offence. The alcohol-induced relaxation of both inhibitions and socially acceptable behaviour has never been accepted as a factor or excuse in determining whether the accused possessed the requisite *mens rea*. Given the minimal nature of the mental element required for crimes of general intent, even those who are significantly drunk will usually be able to form the requisite *mens rea* and will be found to have acted voluntarily. In reality it is only those who can demonstrate that they were in such an extreme degree of intoxication that they were in a state akin to automatism or insanity that might expect to raise a reasonable doubt as to their ability to form the minimal mental element required for a general intent offence. Neither an insane person nor one in a state of automatism is capable of forming the minimum intent required for a general intent offence. Similarly, as the words themselves imply, "drunkenness akin to insanity or automatism" describes a person so severely intoxicated that he is incapable of forming even the minimal intent required of a general intent offence. The phrase refers to a person so drunk that he is an automaton. As such he may be capable of voluntary acts such as moving his arms and legs but is quite incapable of forming the most basic or simple intent required to perform the act prohibited by a general intent offence. I believe that Wilson J.'s modification of the *Leary* rule is a judge-fashioned remedy that can be adopted to remedy a judge-made law which, by eliminating the mental element of a crime, offends the *Charter*.

It is obvious that it will only be on rare occasions that evidence of such an extreme state of intoxication can be advanced and perhaps only on still rarer occasions is it likely to be successful. None the less, the adoption of this alternative would avoid infringement of the *Charter*.

I would add that it is always open to Parliament to fashion a remedy which would make it a crime to commit a prohibited act while drunk.

The appellant in this case is an elderly alcoholic. It is difficult if not impossible to present him in a sympathetic light. Yet any rule on intoxication must apply to all accused, including the young and inexperienced drinker. The strict rule in *Leary* is not a minor or technical infringement but a substantial breach of the *Charter* eliminating the mental elements of crimes of general intent in situations where the accused is in an extreme state of intoxication. I would think that this judge-made rule should be applied flexibly, as suggested by Wilson J., so as to comply with the *Charter*. Such an approach would mean that except in those rare situations where the degree of intoxication is so severe it is akin to automatism, drunkenness will not be a defence to crimes of general intent.

It should not be forgotten that if the flexible "Wilson" approach is taken, the defence will only be put forward in those rare circumstances of extreme intoxication. Since that state must be shown to be akin to automatism or insanity, I would suggest that the accused should be called upon to establish it on the balance of probabilities. This Court has recognized, in *R. v. Chaulk*, [1990] 3 S.C.R. 1303, that although it constituted a violation of the accused's rights under s. 11(d) of the *Charter*, such a burden could be justified under s. 1. In this case, I feel that the burden can be justified. Drunkenness of the extreme degree required in order for it to become relevant will only occur on rare occasions. It is only the accused who can give evidence as to the amount of alcohol consumed and its effect upon him. Expert evidence would be required to confirm that the accused was probably in a state akin to automatism or insanity as a result of his drinking. ...

Extreme intoxication akin to automatism or insanity should, like insanity, be established by the accused on a balance of probabilities. This I take to be the position put forward by Lamer C.J. in *R. v. Penno*, [*infra*]. At pages 877-78, the following appears:

> For these reasons, I am of the view that the offence of having care or control of a motor vehicle while one's ability to drive is impaired is a general intent offence. It follows, as was decided by a majority of this Court in *Bernard*, that no defence of intoxication can negate the *mens rea* of this offence, although the question is still open as to whether intoxication giving rise to a state of insanity or automatism could achieve such a result.
>
> The trial judge found that the appellant was very intoxicated. *However, the appellant did not prove, on a balance of probabilities, that his intoxication was so great as to constitute insanity or automatism*, nor was a state of insanity or automatism found by any of the judges in the courts below. On the facts of this case, I see no need to address the issue concerning the relevance of intoxication to negate the mens rea where such intoxication verges on insanity or automatism. [Emphasis added.]

Thus it is appropriate to place an evidentiary and legal burden on the accused to establish, on a balance of probabilities, that he was in a state of extreme intoxication that was akin to automatism.

SOPINKA J (Gonthier and Major JJ concurring) (dissenting): ... Sexual assault is a crime of general intent. In *Leary v. The Queen, supra*, a majority of this court held that drunkenness is not a defence to a crime of general intent. While some of the judges of this court have sought to overrule *Leary*, it has not happened. Accordingly, I agree with the Court of Appeal's decision that the trial judge was bound by the decision in *Leary*. Furthermore, I reject the appellant's submission that *Leary* ought to be overruled. ...

As a result, the decision in *Leary* still stands for the proposition that evidence of intoxication can only provide a defence for offences of specific intent but not for offences of general intent. Since sexual assault is a crime of general intent, intoxication is no defence to a charge of sexual assault. This rule is supported by sound policy considerations. One of the main purposes of the criminal law is to protect the public. This purpose would be frustrated if, as Lawton L.J. put it in the Court of Appeal in *Majewski*, [[1977] AC 443], at p. 456, "the more drunk a man became, provided he stopped short of making himself insane, the better chance he had of an acquittal." Society is entitled to punish those who of their own free will render themselves so intoxicated as to pose a threat to other members of the community. The fact that an accused has voluntarily consumed intoxicating amounts of drugs or alcohol cannot excuse the commission of a criminal offence unless it gives rise to a mental disorder within the terms of s. 16. Section 16 is not invoked in this case and, therefore, the circumstances in which alcohol or its effects may engage the provisions of that section are not in issue here. ...

Application of the *Leary* rule in circumstances such as those of the case at bar obviously permits the accused to be convicted despite the existence of a reasonable doubt as to whether he intended to perform the *actus reus* of the offence of sexual assault. In my view, this does not violate either ss. 7 or 11(d) of the *Charter*. None of the relevant principles of fundamental justice require that the intent to perform the *actus reus* of an offence of general intent be an element of the offence. In my opinion, the requirements of the principles of fundamental justice are satisfied by proof that the accused became voluntarily intoxicated.

The premise upon which the alleged breach of fundamental justice is based is that symmetry between the *actus reus*, or some aspect of it, and the *mens rea* is constitutionally required. This, it is said, is a principle of fundamental justice which is of universal application. This issue has been recently thrashed out in relation to whether consequences forming part of the *actus reus* must be foreseen on an objective or subjective basis or some variation thereof. In *R. v. Creighton*, [1993] 3 S.C.R. 3, this court divided on this issue with respect to the crime of unlawful act manslaughter. In the view of the Chief Justice, concurred in by three other members of the court, including myself, the mental element required was foreseeability of death on a modified objective standard. The majority opinion, however, adopted an objective standard of foreseeability but limited to bodily harm.

The second requirement of the principles of fundamental justice is that punishment must be proportionate to the moral blameworthiness of the offender. This was held to be a principle of fundamental justice in *R. v. Martineau*, [1990] 2 S.C.R. 633, and *R. v. Creighton, supra*. There are a few crimes in respect of which a special level of *mens rea* is constitutionally required by reason of the stigma attaching to a conviction and by reason of the severity of the penalty imposed by law. Accordingly, murder and attempted murder require a *mens rea* based on a subjective standard. No exception from the principle of fundamental justice should be made with respect to these offences and, as specific intent offences, drunkenness is a defence.

By contrast, sexual assault does not fall into the category of offences for which either the stigma or the available penalties demand as a constitutional requirement subjective intent to commit the *actus reus*. Sexual assault is a heinous crime of violence. Those found guilty of committing the offence are rightfully submitted to a significant degree of moral opprobrium. That opprobrium is not misplaced in the case of the intoxicated offender. Such individuals deserve to be stigmatized. Their moral blameworthiness is similar to that of anyone else who commits the offence of sexual assault and the effects of their conduct upon both their victims and society as a whole are the same as in any other case of sexual assault. Furthermore, the sentence for sexual assault is not fixed. To the extent that it bears upon his or her level of moral blameworthiness, an offender's degree of intoxication at the time of the offence may be considered during sentencing. Taking all of these factors into account, I cannot see how the stigma and punishment associated with the offence of sexual assault are disproportionate to the moral blameworthiness of a person like the appellant who commits the offence after voluntarily becoming so intoxicated as to be incapable of knowing what he was doing. The fact that the *Leary* rule permits an individual to be convicted despite the absence of symmetry between the *actus reus* and the mental element of blameworthiness does not violate a principle of fundamental justice. ...

For all of these reasons, in my opinion, the best course is for the court to reaffirm the traditional rule that voluntary intoxication does not constitute a defence to an offence of general intent, subject to the comments I have made with respect to improvements in the definition and application of the distinction between offences of specific and general intent. If a different approach is considered desirable because the *Leary* approach does not comport with social policy, Parliament is free to intervene. I note that this observation was made by McIntyre J. in *R. v. Bernard* but Parliament has not intervened. It has been suggested that Parliament should create a new offence of dangerous intoxication. Such a recommendation was made by the Butler Committee in England and by the Law Reform Commission in Canada: see "Butler Committee Report on Mentally Abnormal Offenders" (1975) (Cmnd. 6244, paras. 18.51-18.59), and Law Reform Commission of Canada, "Recodifying Criminal Law," Report 30, vol. 1 at pp. 27-8 (1986). Such legislation could be coupled with amendments to the *Criminal Code* to extend the defence of drunkenness to some or all offences to which it does not apply. Such changes, however, are for Parliament and not for this court to make.

There was some expectation in the majority judgment that Parliament would respond to the ruling by enacting a new offence that would contain intoxication as part of the offence: an offence of sexual assault while intoxicated or an offence of being drunk and dangerous. Leaving aside the wisdom of such a response, it is likely that such an intoxication-based offence would have been upheld under the Charter. In *R v Penno*, [1990] 2 SCR 865, the Supreme Court decided that intoxication could not be a defence to an offence in which it is an element. The offence in this case was care and control of a motor vehicle while impaired. McLachlin J (Sopinka and Gonthier JJ concurring) stated:

> Even if the accused is too drunk to know that he or she is assuming care and control of the motor vehicle, that does not matter, since the mental element of the offence lies in voluntarily becoming intoxicated. This interpretation recognizes that intoxication is excluded as a defence to impaired driving since it is the very gravamen of the offence.

As will be seen, however, Parliament did not respond with an intoxication-based offence, but rather with legislation that effectively deprives the accused of a *Daviault* defence of extreme intoxication for some offences.

Bill C-72 (later Bill C-32) was proposed as a response to *Daviault*. It was proclaimed into force as s 33.1 of the *Criminal Code* on September 15, 1995. In view of the importance of the preamble to any future litigation concerning the validity of s 33.1, the enacting legislation is reproduced below in its entirety:

BILL C-72

42-43-44 Elizabeth II, c 32, 1994-95

1st Session, 35th Parliament

The House of Commons of Canada

An Act to amend the *Criminal Code* (self-induced intoxication)

Preamble

WHEREAS the Parliament of Canada is gravely concerned about the incidence of violence in Canadian society;

WHEREAS the Parliament of Canada recognizes that violence has a particularly disadvantaging impact on the equal participation of women and children in society and on the rights of women and children to security of the person and to the equal protection and benefit of the law as guaranteed by sections 7, 15 and 28 of the *Canadian Charter of Rights and Freedoms*;

WHEREAS the Parliament of Canada recognizes that there is a close association between violence and intoxication and is concerned that self-induced intoxication may be used socially and legally to excuse violence, particularly violence against women and children;

WHEREAS the Parliament of Canada recognizes that the potential effects of alcohol and certain drugs on human behaviour are well known to Canadians and is aware of scientific evidence that most intoxicants, including alcohol, by themselves, will not cause a person to act involuntarily;

WHEREAS the Parliament of Canada shares with Canadians the moral view that people who, while in a state of self-induced intoxication, violate the physical integrity of others are blameworthy in relation to their harmful conduct and should be held criminally accountable for it;

WHEREAS the Parliament of Canada desires to promote and help to ensure the full protection of the rights guaranteed under sections 7, 11, 15 and 28 of the *Canadian Charter of Rights and Freedoms* for all Canadians, including those who are or may be victims of violence;

WHEREAS the Parliament of Canada considers it necessary to legislate a basis of criminal fault in relation to self-induced intoxication and general intent offences involving violence;

WHEREAS the Parliament of Canada recognizes the continuing existence of a common law principle that intoxication to an extent that is less than that which would cause a person to lack the ability to form the basic intent or to have the voluntariness required to commit a criminal offence of general intent is never a defence at law;

AND WHEREAS the Parliament of Canada considers it necessary and desirable to legislate a standard of care, in order to make it clear that a person who, while in a state of incapacity by reason of self-induced intoxication, commits an offence involving violence against another person, departs markedly from the standard of reasonable care that Canadians owe to each other and is thereby criminally at fault;

NOW, THEREFORE, Her Majesty, by and with the advice and consent of the Senate and House of Commons of Canada, enacts as follows:

1. The *Criminal Code* is amended by adding the following after section 33:

Self-induced intoxication
When defence not available

33.1(1) It is not a defence to an offence referred to in subsection (3) that the accused, by reason of self-induced intoxication, lacked the basic intent or the voluntariness required to commit the offence, where the accused departed markedly from the standard of care as described in subsection (2).

Criminal fault by reason of intoxication

(2) For the purposes of this section, a person departs markedly from the standard of reasonable care generally recognized in Canadian society and is thereby criminally at fault where the person, while in a state of self-induced intoxication that renders the person unaware of, or incapable of consciously controlling, their behaviour, voluntarily or involuntarily interferes or threatens to interfere with the bodily integrity of another person.

Application

(3) This section applies in respect of an offence under this Act or any other Act of Parliament that includes as an element an assault or any other interference or threat of interference by a person with the bodily integrity of another person.

Coming into force

2. This Act shall come into force on a day to be fixed by order of the Governor in Council.

Section 33.1 is drafted in awkward terms, not least because Parliament was faced with the difficult challenge of reversing the practical effect of *Daviault* without contradicting a pronouncement by the Supreme Court on a question of constitutional law.

In some respects, the state of the law is now more confusing than ever. There are three variations on the defence of intoxication. First, the common law rule in cases such as *Bernard* that restricts the defence to offences of specific intent continues to apply. Accordingly, the need to classify an offence as one of general or specific intent remains. Second, the expanded defence of extreme intoxication, as stated in *Daviault*, applies to offences of general intent. The application of this defence requires expert evidence concerning the nature and effect of the intoxicant and the defence cannot succeed unless it is proved on a balance of probabilities. Third, s 33.1 of the Code denies the defence of extreme intoxication to any offence of general intent that involves interference or threatened interference with the bodily integrity of another person, provided that, at the relevant time, the act was performed in a state of intoxication that shows a marked departure from the standard of reasonable care. Imagine the difficulty facing a judge who must deal with two or more of these variations in a single case. In the following extract, Gerry Ferguson considers the constitutionality of s 33.1.

G Ferguson, "The Intoxication Defence: Constitutionally Impaired and in Need of Rehabilitation"
(2012) 57 SCLR (2nd) 111 at 135-37 (footnotes omitted)

Parliament's main *Charter* defence to its abrogation of part of the *Daviault* defence in section 33.1 is a claim that even if section 33.1 involves an unconstitutional form of substituted fault, that violation of sections 7 and 11(d) is justified under section 1 of the *Charter*. Parliament tried to embolden its section 1 justification by emphasizing the government's pressing and substantial objective in enacting section 33.1, and by attempting to impair the section 7 and section 11(d) *Charter* infringement as little as reasonably possible by restricting section 33.1 to general intent offences involving assault or interference with bodily integrity. In regard to its pressing and substantial legislative objective, Bill C-72 contains a long Preamble which expressly sets out Parliament's concerns about permitting a defence of extreme intoxication to persons who commit assault-type offences. In particular, those concerns relate to the strong association between intoxication and violence, and the infringement of equality values that such a defence involves, since the victims of this form of drunken violence are disproportionately women and children. These claims are real and legitimate but may not be enough to overcome a section 1 *Charter* challenge. Certainly, the government was not entirely confident that section 33.1 would survive a constitutional challenge. In introducing Bill C-72 into the House of Commons and in defending it in the Senate, the Minister of Justice indicated that the government was seriously considering a reference of Bill C-72 to the Supreme Court before it was proclaimed. That reference did not occur. It is, however, very surprising that 17 years after its enactment, no appellate court in Canada has yet ruled on the constitutionality of section 33.1, although appellate courts have, from time to time, applied section 33.1 without commenting on its constitutional validity.

On the other hand, courts of first instance have considered the constitutionality of section 33.1 on several occasions and have reached different conclusions. There is virtual unanimity among those courts that section 33.1 does violate principles of fundamental justice in sections 7 and 11(d), as articulated in *Daviault*. These cases have generally ignored one strong feminist argument. That argument is that the removal of a defence of extreme intoxication in cases of general intent offences involving assault (by reliance on the device of substituted fault) should not be seen as a violation of principles of fundamental justice since it supports equality rights of women and children and is applied to a group of extremely intoxicated persons who are not morally blameless for the ultimate consequences of their conduct. This argument is, for example, well articulated by Professor Grant [I Grant, "Second Chances: Bill C-72 and the Charter" (1995) 33 Osgoode Hall LJ 379]. If the Supreme Court adopts this legitimate approach (and I cautiously predict that it will not), section 33.1 may survive a section 7 challenge. The Court will then be required to apply this same reasoning to conclude that the substituted fault in section 33.1 does not violate section 11(d) of the *Charter*. If that is the case, then the courts will not have to apply a section 1 *Charter* analysis to section 33.1 of the *Criminal Code*.

In regard to lower courts that have examined the constitutionality of section 33.1, the different conclusions reached by those courts arise from their difference of opinion as to whether section 33.1 is a reasonable limit on the violation of sections 7 and 11(d). In *R. v. Vickberg* [[1998] BCJ No 1034 (SC)], *R. v. Dow* [2010 QCCS 4276] and *R. v. N.(S.)* [[2012]

NUCJ No 3], the courts engaged in detailed analysis before concluding that section 33.1 did not violate section 1 of the *Charter*. On the other hand, in *R. v. Brenton* [[1999] NWTJ No 113 (SC)], *R. v. Dunn* [[1999] OJ No 5452 (Ct J (Gen Div))], *R. v. Jensen* [[2000] OJ No 4870 (Sup Ct)], *R. v. Cedeno* [2005 ONCJ 91] and *R. v. Fleming* [2010 ONSC 8022], the courts held that section 33.1 did violate section 1 of the *Charter*. ...

In my opinion, if the Supreme Court accepts the view that there is another reasonable alternative open to Parliament to achieve its objectives of denunciation of the offender's conduct and protection of society, especially women and children, from drunken violence, without any impairment of section 7 or section 11(d), then section 33.1 is bound to fail the minimal impairment test in section 1 of the *Charter*. Later in this paper, I argue that Parliament's objectives can indeed be achieved with no constitutional infringement by creating a set of penally negligent offences which apply when an accused's voluntary intoxication negates the requisite subjective fault for those offences.

As Ferguson says above, Parliament emphasized the desire to protect women and children from gendered violence when enacting s 33.1. In *R v SN*, Sharkey J offered a Nunavut perspective on the relevance of this concern:

R v SN
2012 NUCJ 2

SHARKEY J:

[48] I agree with the Crown position that the real object of s. 33.1 is the protection of women from alcohol-related or intoxicated violence and, in turn, the preservation of women's equality rights to full participation in Canadian society. The statistical data showing the extent to which women (and more particularly Aboriginal women) suffer from intoxicated violence is stunning.

[49] In Nunavut, where violent crime is several times the national average, it is anecdotal but true that the judges of this Court rarely see a case of violence against a woman— whether it be assault, spousal assault, sexual assault, or spousal manslaughter—where the offender is not intoxicated. So, it is within this context that I analyze the legislative objective of s. 33.1.

In *R v Brenton* (1999), 28 CR (5th) 308 (NWTSC), Vertes J held that the Crown had not demonstrated a pressing and substantial objective in respect of s 33.1 because of the rarity of successful claims to extreme intoxication. He held further:

It is only when the intoxication leads to a state of automatism or insanity that a defence would be available, according to *Daviault*, to a general intent offence.

Equal protection of the law comes from the fact that intentional violent behaviour is labelled as criminal conduct. Equal protection of the law comes from the principled enforcement of the law. Equal protection of the law does not entail, in my respectful opinion, imposing absolute liability for certain types of criminal offences. Excusing criminal conduct on the basis of intoxication is not the same thing as excusing conduct on the basis that it is involuntary and unintentional.

In many of the cases in which s 33.1 is raised, the trial judge has found that the accused's intoxication does not rise to the extreme level required to engage the potential defence. The fact that the constitutionality of s 33.1 has not yet been considered by appellate courts arguably speaks to the rarity of extreme intoxication—as Vertes J suggested in *Brenton*. However, the Supreme Court had occasion to apply s 33.1 in *Bouchard-Lebrun*, above. After that case was decided, Don Stuart criticized the Court for applying s 33.1 without first seeking submissions on the constitutionality of the section. *Bouchard-Lebrun* certainly seems like a missed opportunity for the Court to resolve the contradictory case law on this question and perhaps offers a hint that the Court is willing to apply s 33.1. If so, this raises questions about whether the Court will overrule *Daviault* or hold that while s 33.1 may violate s 7 (as interpreted by the majority in *Daviault* but not Justice Wilson in *Bernard*) and s 11(d), it can be justified under s 1 of the Charter as a reasonable response to intoxicated violence.

IV. INVOLUNTARY INTOXICATION

The limited defence of intoxication in s 33.1 of the Code applies only where the consumption of intoxicants is self-induced or voluntary. In most instances this issue poses little difficulty. In *Chaulk* this point was examined at length.

R v Chaulk
Nova Scotia Court of Appeal
2007 NSCA 84

BATEMAN JA:

[1] This is a Crown appeal from the acquittal of Shane Lee Chaulk on various charges. The events giving rise to the charges are not in dispute.

[2] In the early morning of May 29, 2005 there was a disturbance at an apartment building located at 39 Towerview Drive, Halifax. James MacDougall, who lived in apartment 91, was awakened by his teenage daughter and got up to investigate. He could hear loud yelling and screaming from the hallway, dominated by a male voice. In the hallway and terrified was Mr. MacDougall's female neighbour from apartment 90. He brought her into his apartment, locked and dead-bolted the door and dialled 911. As he was talking to the 911 operator, his door was broken in. Mr. Chaulk entered and threw the contents of Mr. MacDougall's desk, a computer and a large television onto the floor. An angry Mr. Chaulk, who is large in stature, yelling that he was going to kill Mr. MacDougall and his children, rushed Mr. MacDougall.

[3] Mr. MacDougall was able to contain Mr. Chaulk and calm him somewhat. Mr. Chaulk then removed all his clothes placing them in a pile at his feet. Spotting the female neighbour, he grabbed her by the blouse. She was able to break loose and run from the apartment. The police arrived at the apartment to find Mr. MacDougall pressing Mr. Chaulk against a wall to subdue him. He was naked, sweating profusely and babbling, vacillating between compliant and combative. They handcuffed him and took him to the hospital.

[4] He was charged with assaulting Mr. MacDougall (s. 266(a) *Criminal Code*); threatening to cause bodily harm to Mr. MacDougall (s. 264.1(1)(a) *Criminal Code*); break, enter and committing assault (s. 348(1)(b) *Criminal Code*) and mischief by wilfully damaging property (s. 430(4) *Criminal Code*).

[5] Mr. Chaulk was tried before Castor H.F. Williams J.P.C., who acquitted him of all charges, accepting Mr. Chaulk's defence of non-mental disorder automatism/extreme intoxication in relation to the first three charges. ... There is no appeal of the finding that Mr. Chaulk was operating in an automatic state when he committed the offences. The issue here is whether the judge erred in concluding that Mr. Chaulk's intoxicated state was not "self-induced." His conclusion turned on the evidence of Mr. Chaulk's drug and alcohol consumption that night.

· · ·

[7] It was Mr. Chaulk's defence that he committed the offences while extremely intoxicated and was therefore unable to form the necessary intent to commit the crimes. The Crown said that Mr. Chaulk's intoxication was "self induced," therefore s. 33.1 of the *Criminal Code* precludes his reliance on the defence of extreme intoxication for all but the property offence.

[8] In addressing the circumstances leading up to the events in question, Mr. Chaulk testified that after speaking briefly to an acquaintance "Mike," he attended a party at apartment 90, arriving sometime between 10:30 and 11 p.m. Mr. Chaulk did not know Mike's surname. Upon arrival he was met by Mike who introduced him to the two young women who lived in the apartment. He recognized some other acquaintances from school including someone named "Matt," whose surname he also did not know. Over the course of the next few hours Mr. Chaulk played video games and poker, consuming several beer (the number varied in his testimony from six to eight beer). He might have had some marijuana.

[9] It was Mr. Chaulk's evidence that he was getting bored and planned to leave the party. Matt offered him a "wake-up pill," which he took. He described the pill in direct examination:

A. It's kind of ... it's not real big. It's square, white. That's about it, I believe.
Q. Okay. And when it was provided to you, what format was it provided to you? How was it given to you?
A. He just handed it to me.
Q. Okay. What's it look like though?
A. It's just like a white paperish-type square thing. I don't know. It's like a capsule.
Q. A white paperish square?
A. It's kind of like a capsule size pill, flat thing. I don't know.

[10] Mr. Chaulk further testified that he was familiar with wake-up pills as over-the-counter caffeine pills. He thought the substance offered by Matt would help him stay awake.

[11] After taking the pill Mr. Chaulk continued to play cards. Within an hour or two his heart was pounding and things were looking weird. He attempted to call his mother but without success. He had no further recollection of specific events until he awoke in hospital around 10:30 a.m. the next morning. He did not recall his conversations with the doctors at the hospital.

[12] Dr. Margaret Dingle was working the QEII emergency room from 2 p.m. to 9 p.m. on the day of Mr. Chaulk's admission, he having been admitted around 8 a.m. that day in an agitated and confused state. He was first seen by a Dr. Petrie who opined that his state was consistent with exposure to chemicals or stimulant-type drugs. He administered Haldol and Ativan to control the agitation and sedate Mr. Chaulk.

[13] Dr. Dingle's notes of her interaction with Mr. Chaulk were admitted by consent. In addition she testified at the trial. She first consulted with him at 5 p.m. Having received the results of blood work and electrocardiogram tracings, she was concerned about the possibility of heart injury. She interviewed Mr. Chaulk to determine what, if any, drugs or medications he might have used leading up to his admission to hospital. Dr. Dingle acknowledged that she had no present recollection of her consultation with Mr. Chaulk. Her chart note indicated, however, that in response to asking him if he had taken drugs he told her he had consumed a mixture of acid, ecstasy and marijuana. She did not record the questions asked of Mr. Chaulk but testified that it is her practice to ask open-ended questions, rather than those that suggest an answer.

[14] Dr. Syed Akhtar, forensic psychiatrist, called by the defence opined that there was a reasonable probability that Mr. Chaulk's mental state fulfilled the criteria of non-insane automatism on the night in question. Dr. Akhtar had interviewed Mr. Chaulk in September 2005 at the request of the defence. Mr. Chaulk told Dr. Akhtar that he had been a heavy user of marijuana, starting in his teens and had tried ecstasy once but did not like its effects. He said he had not consumed alcohol or drugs that night, before arriving at the party. He further advised the doctor that he drank eight "Cold Shots" (bottles of high alcohol beer) at the party. When he was feeling pretty good he was offered and took a piece of paper with something on it. He was told it was caffeine. He reported to Dr. Akhtar that he had smoked a marijuana joint before consuming the beer.

[15] At trial Mr. Chaulk denied that he had tried ecstasy in the past, contrary to his report to Dr. Akhtar, and said his marijuana consumption that night had been limited to a puff. He testified that he does not consume illicit drugs other than, occasionally, some marijuana. He said he had never taken ecstasy or LSD and did not know that LSD was sometimes delivered on paper as "blotter acid."

. . .

(b) Self-Induced Intoxication and Criminal Code s. 33.1

[32] The recognition of the defence of extreme intoxication for general intent crimes in *Daviault, supra*, provoked a legislative response in the form of s. 33.1 of the *Criminal Code* which precludes that defence in the case of self-induced intoxication where the offence charged includes as an element, assaultive behaviour:

> 33.1(1) It is not a defence to an offence referred to in subsection (3) that the accused, *by reason of self-induced intoxication*, lacked the general intent or the voluntariness required to commit the offence, where the accused departed markedly from the standard of care as described in subsection (2).
>
> (2) For the purposes of this section, a person departs markedly from the standard of reasonable care generally recognized in Canadian society and is thereby criminally at fault where the person, while in a state of self-induced intoxication that renders the person

unaware of, or incapable of consciously controlling, their behaviour, voluntarily or involuntarily interferes or threatens to interfere with the bodily integrity of another person.

(3) This section applies in respect of an offence under this Act or any other Act of Parliament that includes as an element an assault or any other interference or threat of interference by a person with the bodily integrity of another person. (Emphasis added)

[33] Both parties approached this case as one of extreme intoxication. Once it was accepted by the trial judge that Mr. Chaulk was acting in a state akin to automatism, the remaining issue was whether s. 33.1 precluded him from arguing that he did not have the requisite mental element for the "assault" or that his conduct was not voluntary due to his automatic state. The constitutionality of s. 33.1 was and is not challenged. At issue is the meaning of "self-induced intoxication."

[34] It was common ground that the "wake-up pill" was, in fact, some form of intoxicating substance. The Crown said Mr. Chaulk's extreme intoxication was self-induced within the meaning of s. 33.1 because he should have known in accepting the "pill" he risked intoxication. Mr. Chaulk said he honestly thought he was taking a caffeine pill and, therefore, his state was not "self-induced."

. . .

[45] Thus, I conclude, since *R. v. King, supra*, the courts have consistently held that "voluntary intoxication" means the consuming of a substance where the person knew or had reasonable grounds for believing such might cause him to be impaired. (See also *R. v. McDowell*, [1980] O.J. No. 488 (Q.L.); 52 C.C.C. (2d) 298 (Ont. C.A.) *per* Martin J.A. at para. 14.) In *Regina v. Mack* (1975), 22 C.C.C. (2d) 257 (Alta. S.C.A.D.) Prowse J.A., commenting upon *R. v. King* [[1962] SCR 746], at p. 264 said:

> The effect of this decision is that if an accused knew or had any reasonable grounds for believing that the consumption of drugs or alcohol might cause him to be impaired, such evidence supports the conclusion that his condition was due to the voluntary consumption of drugs or alcohol and that intoxication voluntarily induced by itself does not rebut the rebuttable presumption that a man intends the natural consequences of his acts.

[46] Nor must the accused contemplate the extent of the intoxication or intend a certain level of intoxication. In *R. v. Honish* (1991), 68 C.C.C. (3d) 329; [1991] A.J. No. 1057 (Q.L.) (Alta. C.A.), aff'd *R. v. Honish*, [1993] 1 S.C.R. 458; [1993] S.C.J. No. 12 (Q.L.), the accused, after consuming alcohol had tried to kill himself by taking 45 tablets of an anti-depressant and 15 tablets of a sleeping pill. He had no memory thereafter of his involvement in a motor vehicle accident. The defence argued that the intoxication was involuntary because he did not know and had no reasonable grounds for believing that the drugs would cause him to be impaired. The trial judge found, as a fact, that Honish was warned by his doctor not to consume alcohol or other medication while taking the drugs and that there was a warning label on the bottle. Fraser J.A., as she then was, writing for the court, said at p. 339:

> ... The law concerning responsibility for one's acts following voluntary ingestion of intoxicating substances does not require that the consumer know to a nicety what the effect of the intoxicating substances will be. It is enough that he knows it might be dangerous and is recklessly indifferent with respect to ingestion or as to warnings relating to the effects of ingestion: *R. v. Rushton*, [1964] 1 C.C.C. 382, 48 M.P.R. 271 (N.S.C.A.); *R. v. Szymusik* (1972)

8 C.C.C. (2d) 407, [1972] 3 O.R. 602, 19 C.R.N.S. 373 (C.A.) (Ont. C.A.). In this case, the evidence supports the conclusion that Honish's consumption of the intoxicants falls within the category of reckless indifference.

[47] Synthesizing these authorities, the two judges dealing expressly with s. 33.1 would both apply an objective element to the issue of self-induced intoxication: *Vickberg, supra*, "… voluntarily ingesting a substance knowing or having reasonable grounds to know it might be dangerous …"; *Brenton, supra*—"… the risk of becoming intoxicated is within the contemplation or should be within the contemplation of the individual … ." This approach is consistent with the cases pre-dating the introduction of s. 33.1: *R. v. King, supra*, in giving meaning to "voluntary impairment,"—"… knew or had any reasonable grounds for believing might cause him to be impaired …"; *R. v. McDowell, supra*—"… knew or ought to have known that his ability might thereby be impaired." I would therefore express the test for self-induced intoxication as follows:

(i)   The accused voluntarily consumed a substance which;
(ii) S/he knew or ought to have known was an intoxicant and;
(iii) The risk of becoming intoxicated was or should have been within his/her contemplation.

[48] As I would allow the appeal on other grounds it is unnecessary to consider here how the judge's misstatement of the test would have affected the result.

Gerry Ferguson has criticized the prevailing approach to involuntary intoxication. He argues that when the accused does not know what intoxicant he or she is taking, or is unaware of its strength, the *Chaulk* approach deprives him or her of a defence by substituting objective fault for subjective *mens rea*. He also argues that persons whose inhibitions are reduced by the operation of involuntary intoxication should have access to a defence in circumstances in which they would not otherwise have committed the offence. See Gerry Ferguson, "The Intoxication Defence: Constitutionally Impaired and in Need of Rehabilitation" (2012) 57 SCLR (2nd) 111.

ADDITIONAL READING

Colvin, E & S Anand. *Principles of Criminal Law*, 3rd ed (Toronto: Carswell, 2007) at 467-501.

Ferguson, G. "The Intoxication Defence: Constitutionally Impaired and in Need of Rehabilitation" (2012) 57 SCLR (2nd) 111.

Grant, I. "Second Chances: Bill C-72 and the Charter" (1995) 33 Osgoode Hall LJ 379.

Healy, P. "Intoxication in the Codification of Canadian Criminal Law" (1994) 73 Can Bar Rev 515.

Healy, P. "Another Round on Intoxication" (1995) 33 CR (4th) 269.

Manning, M & P Sankoff. *Manning, Mewett & Sankoff: Criminal Law*, 4th ed (Toronto: Lexis-Nexis, 2009) ch 10.

Roach, K. *Criminal Law*, 6th ed (Toronto: Irwin Law, 2015) ch 7.

Smith, K. "Section 33.1: Denial of the Daviault Defence Should Be Held Constitutional" (2000) 28 CR (5th) 350.

Storey, T. "The Borderline Between Insanity and Intoxication" (2013) 77 J Crim L 194.

Stuart, D. *Canadian Criminal Law*, 6th ed (Toronto: Carswell, 2014) at 600.

Self-Defence

I. INTRODUCTION

All systems of criminal justice must address the question of when and whether an individual is permitted to use force to protect himself or herself against the aggression of another person. At the level of greatest generality, self-defence is a simple concept: the law should accommodate the right of a person to use reasonable force to defend himself or herself against apprehended harm. Yet as one descends from that level, a nest of difficult issues emerges. From what perspective should the risk of harm be assessed—the subjective view of the accused or the objective perspective of a reasonable person? What actions will the law permit an accused to take in response to a risk of harm? Under what conditions may one kill in self-defence? And if the law of self-defence will be based on some notion of "reasonableness"—if it will only protect reasonable apprehensions of harm and reasonable responses to that harm—what experiences, features, and perspectives should inform our understanding of the "reasonable person"?

In Canada, a statutory defence of self-defence was included in our first *Criminal Code* and remained relatively static until very recently. Through a set of interlocking provisions, the *Criminal Code* sought to address these questions by defining, with some precision, the circumstances in which an accused would be permitted to act in self-defence and the form of defensive action that would be allowed. Subsections 34(1) and 34(2) were at the heart of the old scheme:

> 34(1) Every one who is unlawfully assaulted without having provoked the assault is justified in repelling force by force if the force he uses is not intended to cause death or grievous bodily harm and is no more than is necessary to enable him to defend himself.
>
> (2) Every one who is unlawfully assaulted and who causes death or grievous bodily harm in repelling the assault is justified if

(a) he causes it under reasonable apprehension of death or grievous bodily harm from the violence with which the assault was originally made or with which the assailant pursues his purposes; and

(b) he believes, on reasonable grounds, that he cannot otherwise preserve himself from death or grievous bodily harm.

As interpreted by the courts, these subsections differentiated between circumstances in which an accused apprehended an assault that risked *death or grievous bodily harm* and situations in which the accused faced a risk of some lesser harm. Whether an accused who had *provoked* the initial assault could claim self-defence turned on this distinction. So too did the *degree* of self-defensive force permitted. A separate provision, s 37, imposing its own set of conditions, governed actions taken in defence of someone under a person's protection and served as a kind of "residual" self-defence provision, filling gaps left by ss 34(1) and 34(2). Yet another provision, s 35, seemed to have no meaningful role whatsoever. The result was a notoriously complex and, in some respects, incoherent statutory scheme. Appellate courts routinely ordered new trials on the basis of incorrect or inadequate jury charges on self-defence. The Supreme Court itself described these statutory provisions as "highly technical," "excessively detailed," and "internally inconsistent": *R v McIntosh*, [1995] 1 SCR 686 at para 16. The Court urged that "legislative action is required to clarify the *Criminal Code*'s self-defence regime."

That legislative action came in 2012, with amendments that created a single, simple provision governing all cases of self-defence and defence of others (as well as a new s 35, governing all forms of defence of property). Addressing the amendments before the Standing Senate Committee on Legal and Constitutional Affairs on May 12, 2012, the Honourable Rob Nicholson, Minister of Justice and Attorney General of Canada, explained the rationale and character of the proposed changes:

> In terms of defence of property and defence of the person, Bill C-26 would replace the current set of provisions with straightforward, easy-to-apply rules for each defence.
>
> The existing laws for both defences were included in the Criminal Code in 1892, but they are actually older than that. When I had a look at this for the first time, I found they actually mirror the legislation that was introduced into Upper Canada in 1840, and they have not been much changed since that time. Despite having relatively simple underlying principles, the laws are unnecessarily complex and confusing. For decades, these laws have been criticized by virtually every sort of criminal justice professional, from the courts to bar associations to academics to law enforcement agents.
>
> The complexity can have serious consequences. It complicates the charging decisions of police. It confuses juries and costs the justice system time, money and energy by giving rise to unnecessary grounds of appeal. The law can and must be clear and easily understood by the police, the public, prosecutors and the courts.
>
> Bill C-26 meets these objectives. It brings clarity and simplicity to the law without sacrificing any existing legal protection.
>
> The basic elements of both defences are the same. Whether a person is defending themselves or another person, or defending property in their possession, the general rule will be that they can undertake acts that may otherwise be criminal if they reasonably perceive a threat, they act for the purpose of defending against that threat, and their acts are judged to be reasonable in the circumstances.

Self-defence is a cornerstone of any criminal justice system. To complement the simpler self-defence rule, Bill C-26 proposes a non-exhaustive list of factors to help guide the determination of whether acts taken for a defensive purpose are reasonable. ...

The list is useful in many ways. It can improve charging and prosecution decisions and help guide judges in instructing juries. It also signals to the courts that they should continue to apply existing jurisprudence under the new defence.

Thus, although it incorporated aspects of the existing case law, the new s 34 represented a return to the conceptual foundations of self-defence: that one may act reasonably in response to a threat to oneself or another. Distinctions that previously took the form of hard rules are now reframed as factors to be considered in assessing the overall reasonableness of the accused's response in the circumstances. Consider the new self-defence provision:

34(1) A person is not guilty of an offence if

(a) they believe on reasonable grounds that force is being used against them or another person or that a threat of force is being made against them or another person;

(b) the act that constitutes the offence is committed for the purpose of defending or protecting themselves or the other person from that use or threat of force; and

(c) the act committed is reasonable in the circumstances.

(2) In determining whether the act committed is reasonable in the circumstances, the court shall consider the relevant circumstances of the person, the other parties and the act, including, but not limited to, the following factors:

(a) the nature of the force or threat;

(b) the extent to which the use of force was imminent and whether there were other means available to respond to the potential use of force;

(c) the person's role in the incident;

(d) whether any party to the incident used or threatened to use a weapon;

(e) the size, age, gender and physical capabilities of the parties to the incident;

(f) the nature, duration and history of any relationship between the parties to the incident, including any prior use or threat of force and the nature of that force or threat;

(f.1) any history of interaction or communication between the parties to the incident;

(g) the nature and proportionality of the person's response to the use or threat of force; and

(h) whether the act committed was in response to a use or threat of force that the person knew was lawful.

(3) Subsection (1) does not apply if the force is used or threatened by another person for the purpose of doing something that they are required or authorized by law to do in the administration or enforcement of the law, unless the person who commits the act that constitutes the offence believes on reasonable grounds that the other person is acting unlawfully.

The new s 34 is much simpler, with the heavy lifting to be done by a judge or jury's assessment of what was "reasonable in the circumstances."

And yet deciding what is "reasonable in the circumstances" raises certain difficult questions, ones that afflicted the law of self-defence under the old statutory regime and that remain relevant under the new provisions.

First is the fraught question of what perspective to assume when applying the criminal law. Ought one to assess the situation as it appears to the accused (a subjective analysis), from the perspective of the reasonable person (an objective analysis), or from the perspective of a reasonable person endowed with the same relevant characteristics and experiences as the accused (a modified objective standard)? For students of the criminal law, this issue comes up in many areas, including the law of *mens rea* and the approach to other defences, such as provocation.

As you read more about the law of self-defence, reflect on how a balance is struck between the objective and the subjective, and what social justice and policy implications follow on emphasizing one perspective over the other.

Whichever perspective is adopted, one wonders how much a jury is constrained by the niceties of legal doctrine applied to something as guided by instinct and assumptions about human behaviour as a situation involving a claim of self-defence. Consider the infamous case of the so-called subway vigilante, Bernhard Goetz, who shot four youths after one or two of them approached him, not displaying any weapons, and asked for $5. Goetz claimed that he was acting in self-defence when he stood up and fired five shots from the .38 calibre pistol that he was carrying in his waistband. In *People v Goetz*, 497 NE 3d 41 (1986), the New York Court of Appeals reversed the lower court, which had dismissed the charges on the basis that the grand jury had been misdirected that the relevant standard was whether the defendant's conduct was that of a *reasonable man* in the defendant's situation. The Court of Appeals confirmed that this objective perspective was, indeed, the legal approach required by New York state law. Chief Judge Wachtler explained that to ask merely whether the accused subjectively believed his or her conduct was reasonable and necessary "would allow citizens to set their own standards for the permissible use of force." Despite this legal ruling, the jury in the subsequent trial acquitted Goetz of attempted murder. The deliberations of the jury on this matter are revealed in Professor George Fletcher's book *A Crime of Self-Defense* (New York: Free Press, 1988) at 186-88:

> The District Attorney's office fought an appellate battle for nearly a year in order to establish the objective standard for assessing claims of self-defense. The fear and violent response of someone defending himself must be judged not solely by his own motives, but by the hypothetical fear and response of a reasonable person under the circumstances. But as the jury considered Goetz's motive to defend himself as a factor bearing on his intent to kill, they placed the entire burden of their analysis on his subjective perceptions and motives. It could only be these subjective motives—not the moral quality of his act as measured against the standard of reasonableness—that could influence the analysis whether he had a bad motive for shooting. Even an unreasonable belief in the necessity of self-defense was a good-faith belief, and if Goetz was acting in good faith, he did not have a criminal motive. …
>
> As a result of admitting a subjective theory of self-defense by the back door, the jury abandoned the task of judgment that the Court of Appeals had laid before it. They were supposed to consider not only whether Goetz had good motives, but whether he overreacted in formulating those motives. Their job was to get behind his intention and judge whether a reasonable person would have found shooting necessary under the circumstances. Yet they brought their common sense and their moral sensibilities to the instructions that [the trial judge] gave them, and as a result they fashioned a mode of analysis that no one expected.

The second question raised by a defence governed by what is "reasonable in the circumstances" concerns how the law imagines the reasonable person and her or his actions. Even if one assumes an objective perspective, what experiences, fears, and attributes should be considered when assessing the reasonableness of a response to force or threat of force? In

Canada the issue has arisen most forcefully in the context of claims of self-defence made by battered women charged with killing a domestic partner who, at the moment he was killed, did not seem to pose an immediate threat. How could that killing be reasonable in the circumstances? Beginning with the 1990 case of *R v Lavallee*, [1990] 1 SCR 852, the Supreme Court sought to address this question under the old provisions, seeking to understand the defence of self-defence in both its historical and contemporary social context. The resulting developments have left their mark on the new s 34, and it remains to be seen how well these new provisions will be able to respond to the lived realities of gender, racial, and social inequality.

Section II of this chapter will discuss the interpretation and applicability of the new self-defence provisions. Section III turns to a close examination of self-defence and domestic violence, focusing attention on the relationship between criminal law, inequality, and our understanding of the "reasonable person." Section IV concludes the chapter by briefly addressing defence of property.

II. INTERPRETING AND APPLYING THE SELF-DEFENCE PROVISIONS

The new s 34 has two central components. Subsection (1) sets out the elements of the new, simpler rule for self-defence. It provides that a person is not guilty of an offence if three conditions are met. First, the accused must "believe on reasonable grounds that force is being used against them or another person or that a threat of force is being made against them or another person." Second, an accused must have acted with the subjective purpose of protecting himself or herself (or others) from the use or threat of force. This condition serves to screen out acts motivated by vengeance, retribution, or some other non-defensive purpose. Finally, and at the heart of the defence, the act committed by the accused to defend against that force must be "reasonable in the circumstances." Thus, to establish an "air of reality" to self-defence, there must be some evidence upon which a properly instructed jury, acting reasonably, could find that (a) the accused had a reasonable belief that he or she, or another person, was subject to force or a threat of force; (b) the act was committed for the subjective purpose of protecting himself or herself or another from this force; and (c) the accused's act was reasonable in the circumstances.

Subsection (2) provides a list of factors that a judge or jury must consider when assessing the crucial issue of "reasonable in the circumstances." The list is not exhaustive, but it incorporates a number of the considerations that, whether explicit in the old statute or generated through judicial application of the old self-defence provisions, have proven relevant in cases of self-defence. For example, under the old legislation, if an accused had provoked the assault, it would categorically disentitle him or her from claiming self-defence; by contrast, the new provisions simply list, in paragraph (c), "the person's role in the incident" as one factor in assessing overall reasonableness. Whereas the old scheme required the accused to reasonably believe there was no reasonable alternative to acting as he or she did, the new s 34(2) merely cites "whether there were other means available to respond to the potential use of force" as one relevant circumstance. Section 34(2) rolls all such factors into a general assessment of whether the accused's act was "reasonable in the circumstances."

Addressing this aspect of the new legislation to the Standing Senate Committee on Legal and Constitutional Affairs, Justice Minister Rob Nicholson explained that "[w]hat is reasonable depends on the facts and circumstances of each individual case," but that "a number of factors commonly arise in self-defence cases and are familiar to the courts." He elaborated:

For instance, it will typically be relevant if either or both parties had a weapon, whether there was a pre-existing relationship between the parties, particularly one that included violence. Proportionality between the threat and the response is of course relevant. The greater the threat one faces, the greater the actions one can take to defend against that threat.

I should bring to this committee's attention the fact that there were a couple of changes made to this list of factors by the House of Commons. One change modified the opening words of proposed subsection 34(2) to clarify that all relevant circumstances pertaining to the accused, the other party and the incident must be taken into account.

Another change added the notion of "physical capabilities" to the factor that referred to the age, gender and sex of the parties. A new factor was added, namely "any history of interaction or communication between the parties to the incident." This could include a single exchange, and so is slightly different from the factor that deals with the "relationship" between the parties.

As you will see later in this chapter, these changes to the proposed legislation prior to its enactment reflected important developments in the case law on self-defence, most notably judicial recognition of the lived experience of women subject to persistent violence from their spouses and partners. Thus, despite the simplification of the self-defence provisions, understanding the legislation and predicting how these new provisions may be applied (and what relative weight may be given to the various factors) requires appreciation of the prior case law. Indeed, recall Justice Minister Nicholson's statement that Parliament intended that the courts "should continue to apply existing jurisprudence under the new defence."

These new provisions have other interesting features. First, unlike the prior legislation, which was limited to cases in which the accused committed some form of assault to repel an attack ("repelling force by force," in the language of the old s 34), the new provision speaks of a person not being guilty of "an offence" and refers generally to "the act committed." It appears that the defence can now be argued when an accused commits some other act—not solely an assault against an aggressor—to defend or protect himself or herself or another from an assault. Consider, for example, an accused who steals a car to escape an assault. Could he or she claim self-defence in answer to a charge of theft? This raises the issue of the relationship between self-defence and duress. Traditionally, self-defence was understood to be concerned with assaults committed to repel an attack, and duress was thought to apply to other offences committed when an accused is subject to a threat of force. With this expanded scope of offences to which self-defence can apply, how will the courts delineate the relative roles of self-defence and duress? Chapter 18, which discusses duress, touches on this issue, and examines the recent decision of *R v Ryan*, 2013 SCC 3, [2013] 1 SCR 14, which offers some suggestion of how the Court might distinguish the two defences.

At a more conceptual level, note also that, whereas the old legislation stated that an accused "is justified" if he or she acted in self-defence, the new provision states only that an accused is "not guilty of an offence" if it was committed in self-defence. Self-defence has traditionally been considered a quintessential justification—an instance in which the accused is thought to have acted *rightly*, rather than simply being excused as a so-called concession to human frailty. Does this change in language signal a different understanding of the defence? If so, will this shift have practical consequences?

Note also that s 34(3) separately treats the question of claims of self-defence when the offence is committed against a person seeking to administer or enforce the law, such as a police officer attempting to make an arrest. Section 34(3) prevents an accused from claiming self-defence in such circumstances unless the accused "believes on reasonable grounds that the other person is acting unlawfully." The real import of this section is that, if an accused seeks to rely on s 34(1) on a charge of resisting arrest or assaulting a police officer, his or her belief that a police officer is applying force unlawfully must also be reasonable. This modified objective standard limits access to self-defence; and yet, interestingly, it also suggests that, subject to satisfying the other conditions of s 34, an accused might plead self-defence if he or she reasonably—but wrongly—thought that a police officer lacked lawful authority.

Subjectivity and Objectivity in Self-Defence

An important aspect of s 34 is how it combines subjective and objective perspectives in the analysis of self-defence. Section 34(1)(a) refers to an accused committing an offence when "they believe on reasonable grounds" that he or she (or another person) is subject to a threat of force, thereby mixing subjective and objective components. Section 34(1)(b), by contrast, appears to be concerned solely with the subjective motivations of the accused. Finally, although s 34(1)(c) uses the objective language of "reasonableness," a number of the factors in s 34(2) used to determine if the accused's act was "reasonable in the circumstances" are aimed at placing the reasonable person in the shoes of the accused. For example, reference in paragraphs (e), (f), and (f.1) to the size, age, gender, and physical capabilities of those involved in the incident, and to the history of the relationships and communications between those involved, infuse the objective analysis with subjective considerations. The balancing of subjectivity and objectivity has long troubled this area of law and was the focal point of the Supreme Court of Canada's decision in the following case, decided under the old self-defence regime. As you read this case, focus on how the balance is struck and how the Court assesses the reasonableness of the accused's response.

R v Cinous

Supreme Court of Canada

2002 SCC 29, [2002] 2 SCR 3

[The accused, who supported himself through criminal acts, especially computer theft, was charged with murder. He was suspicious that the victim had stolen his revolver, and had tried to avoid him and a third party who had been with them when the revolver disappeared. The accused had heard rumours that the deceased and the third party intended to kill him. Several days after the revolver was stolen, the victim and the third party proposed that the accused join them in a theft. The accused said that the victim and the third party behaved suspiciously. When the victim put on latex surgical gloves, which in the accused's mind were worn to avoid getting blood on the wearer's hands, the accused, thinking he was soon to be killed, shot the deceased in the back of the head at a service station where they had stopped to purchase windshield wiper fluid. The accused was convicted at trial, but the Quebec Court of Appeal allowed his appeal, finding errors in the trial judge's instructions on self-defence. A majority of the Supreme Court of Canada allowed the appeal.]

McLACHLIN CJ and BASTARACHE J (L'Heureux-Dubé and LeBel JJ concurring):

[38] While we agree with the Court of Appeal that the trial judge made several errors in the charge to the jury, we do not agree that any of these, viewed individually or cumulatively, warrant overturning the conviction and ordering a new trial. It is our view that since the three conditions of self-defence were not all met on the facts of this case, the defence lacked the "air of reality" required in order to warrant leaving it with the jury. Since the defence should never have been put to the jury, any errors made in the charge to the jury relating to it are irrelevant. These errors of law can be safely set to one side, and s. 686(1)(b)(iii) should be applied in order to uphold the conviction.

[After a lengthy discussion of the "air of reality" test for putting defences to the jury, McLachlin CJ applied the law to the facts of the case. Recall that this case was decided under the old provisions and applied the elements of the defence found in those provisions; as you read this case, consider how these elements are dealt with in the new self-defence scheme.]

· · ·

[92] This brings us to the application of the air of reality test to the facts of this case. The question to be asked is whether there is evidence on the record upon which a properly instructed jury acting reasonably could acquit if it believed the evidence to be true.

[93] In *Pétel* ... , at p. 12, Lamer C.J. stated the three constitutive elements of self-defence under s. 34(2): "(1) the existence of an unlawful assault; (2) a reasonable apprehension of a risk of death or grievous bodily harm; and (3) a reasonable belief that it is not possible to preserve oneself from harm except by killing the adversary." All three of these elements must be established in order for the defence to succeed. The air of reality test must therefore be applied to each of the three elements. If any of these elements lacks an air of reality, the defence should not be put to the jury. ...

[94] Each of the three elements under s. 34(2) has both a subjective and an objective component. The accused's perception of the situation is the "subjective" part of the test. However, the accused's belief must also be reasonable on the basis of the situation he perceives. This is the objective part of the test. Section 34(2) makes the reasonableness requirement explicit in relation to the second and third conditions. *Pétel* held that the same standard applies to the first component of the defence, namely, the existence of an assault. With respect to each of the three elements, the approach is first to inquire about the subjective perceptions of the accused, and then to ask whether those perceptions were objectively reasonable in the circumstances.

[95] The air of reality analysis must be applied to each component of the defence, both subjective and objective. Evidence capable of supporting a particular finding of fact with respect to one component of the defence will not necessarily be capable of supporting other components of the defence. In the case of a defence of self-defence under s. 34(2), the testimony of the accused as to his perceptions does not necessarily constitute evidence reasonably capable of supporting the conclusion that the perception was reasonable.

[96] The difficult issue in this case is whether there is some evidence upon which a properly instructed jury acting reasonably could have concluded that the accused's purported perceptions were *reasonable* under the circumstances. Since reasonableness is inherently incapable of being established by direct evidence, the key question is whether there is evidence on the basis of which reasonableness could reasonably be inferred by a

jury. If a jury could not have reasonably come to the conclusion that the accused's perceptions were reasonable, even accepting that his testimonial evidence was true, then the defence should not have been put to the jury.

[97] There is no authority for the proposition that reasonableness is exempt from the air of reality test, or that evidence satisfying the air of reality test as to the subjective component of defence will automatically confer an air of reality upon the whole defence. Moreover, we consider that the introduction of such a requirement would constitute an unwarranted and illogical break with the rationale underlying air of reality analysis. The long-standing requirement is that the *whole defence* must have an air of reality, not just bits and pieces of the defence. See *Hebert* ... , at para. 16, per Cory J., holding that a defence of self-defence lacked an air of reality precisely in that the reasonableness of an accused's purported perception could not be supported by the evidence. See also *Thibert* ... , per Cory J., at paras. 6 and 7.

(1) The Putative Evidential Basis for the Defence

[98] The evidence relied upon in this case emanates from the accused's own testimony. While this Court has made it clear that a mere assertion by the accused of the elements of a defence will not be sufficient to clear the air of reality hurdle, that principle does not have any application to the present case. The accused's testimony goes beyond merely asserting the elements of the defence, and provides a comprehensive account of his perceptions and his explanation for them. As was stated above, credibility is not an issue in air of reality analysis. The issue is not whether the accused (or any other witness) should be believed. Rather, the question is whether, if the jury were to accept the construction of the evidence most favourable to the accused's position, the requisite inferences could reasonably be drawn.

[99] With these considerations in view, we now turn to a review of the relevant evidence.

[100] In his testimony, the accused pointed to many things that he perceived as indications that he was about to be attacked. The accused testified that he had heard rumors that the victim, Mike, and his companion, Ice, planned to kill him. He claimed to have received a specific warning to that effect by a friend of his.

[101] He testified that on the night in question, Mike and Ice did not take off their jackets when they came to his home. The accused testified that Ice put his hand under his coat, in what the accused took to be a suspicious gesture. The accused claimed that these facts led him to believe that Mike and Ice were armed, though they denied it when he asked them about it. They whispered to each other throughout the evening, which the accused also found suspicious.

[102] The accused testified that his suspicions were further aroused when he entered the van. He ascribed significance to the fact that Ice removed the gloves that he had initially been wearing and replaced them with a different pair, putting them on *before getting in the van*. He testified that this was unusual. He also testified that Mike sat behind the accused, on the passenger side, and was wearing latex surgical gloves. The accused testified that he associated wearing gloves of this type with a "burn" (i.e. an attack on a criminal by another criminal). He testified that this was based on limited personal experience of his own, and on movies that he had seen, in which hit men wore such gloves. The accused testified that Mike loudly snapped the gloves at some point during the ride, which he

interpreted as an overt threat. The accused testified that the gloves indicated that a plan to kill him existed and would be executed that very night.

[103] The accused further testified that the sudden change in the routine of the criminal group had meaning. He testified that Ice avoided eye contact with him, and that everyone in the van was uncharacteristically silent. He testified that Ice repeated the suspicious gesture that he had initially made in the apartment, placing his hand under his coat. He said that Ice did this both in the van and in the gas station. The accused testified that in the gang culture to which he belonged, this gesture is meant to communicate to rival gang members that one is armed. When pressed to say whether the purpose of Ice's gesture was to show he had a gun or to signal to the accused that he was going to kill him, the accused was reluctant to say it was a message that he would kill him. He nevertheless indicated that this gesture had added significance to him because there was a rumour that he was about to be killed.

[104] The accused testified that he felt trapped, and that he was convinced that Ice and the victim, Mike, were just waiting for the right moment to kill him. He testified that he felt that Ice and Mike had set a trap for him. He testified that he thought that Mike, who was sitting behind him, would be the one to kill him. He testified that he knew that Mike had used firearms before.

[105] When asked why he did not run away or call the police, the accused claimed not to have thought of these options. When pressed on cross-examination about not running away, he indicated that he felt he should not have to leave the van. With respect to calling the police, he also said: "I'm not used to calling the police, you know. I'm just not used to that. I never called the police in my life. People have been calling the police [on] me all my life. You know, I've been running away from the police all my life." He also stated that the police would have arrived too late to save him. He added that asking the police for help would have meant having to work for them as an informant. He said of being an informant: "that's the only way you can get protection, you know? And since I wasn't gonna do that, and I never will—you know what I'm saying?—so there was no way the police was going to protect me, no way!"

[106] It must now be determined whether a properly instructed jury acting reasonably could base an acquittal on the evidence reviewed above, assuming that evidence to be true. In order to make this determination, the evidence must be considered in relation to each of the three elements of self-defence under s. 34(2).

(2) The Existence of an Assault

[107] Lamer C.J. stated in *Pétel* ... that the existence of an actual assault is not a prerequisite for a defence under s. 34(2). Rather, the starting point is the perspective of the accused. Lamer C.J. stated at p. 13:

> The question that the jury must ask itself is therefore not "was the accused unlawfully assaulted?" but rather "did the accused reasonably believe, in the circumstances, that she was being unlawfully assaulted?"

Of course, in applying the air of reality test, the judge should not try to answer the question stated by Lamer C.J. The focus of the trial judge in air of reality analysis is narrower. The question is whether there is evidence upon which a jury acting reasonably *could* conclude that the accused reasonably believed he was about to be attacked, not whether the jury *should* so conclude. Assuming there is an air of reality to the whole defence, it will be up to the jury to decide whether or not the accused actually believed that he was about to be attacked, and whether or not that perception was reasonable.

[108] There is an air of reality to the subjective component of the defence. There is direct evidence on the accused's beliefs, in the form of the accused's testimony. It is open to the jury to believe this testimony. It is open to the jury to believe that the accused interpreted the various items pointed out in the evidence reviewed above as indicating that the victim and Ice were going to attack him.

[109] Whether a jury could reasonably infer on the basis of the evidence that the accused's perception of an attack was reasonable in the circumstances presents a more difficult issue. Nevertheless, here again it seems to us that the threshold test is met. A jury acting reasonably could draw an inference from the circumstances described by the accused, including particularly the many threatening indicators to which he testified, to the reasonableness of his perception that he was going to be attacked.

[110] We conclude that it would be possible for the jury reasonably to conclude that the accused believed that he was going to be attacked, and that this belief was reasonable in the circumstances. In coming to this conclusion, we do not express any opinion as to the substantive merits of the defence with respect to the first element of self-defence under s. 34(2). That question is reserved for the jury.

[111] The inquiry does not end here. In order for the defence to be put to the jury, there must also be an "air of reality" to the remaining two elements of self-defence under s. 34(2), namely the accused's reasonable perception of the risk of death or grievous bodily harm and his belief on reasonable grounds that there was no alternative to killing the victim.

(3) Reasonable Apprehension of Death or Grievous Bodily Harm

[112] The analysis as it relates to this second prong of self-defence under s. 34(2) follows substantially the same path as for the first prong. In order for this element of self-defence to clear the air of reality hurdle, it must be possible for the jury reasonably to infer from the evidence not only that the accused reasonably believed that he was facing an attack, but that he faced death or grievous bodily harm from that attack.

[113] The accused's testimony is unambiguously to the effect that he feared a deadly attack. It is open to the jury to accept this testimony, that is, to accept that he did in fact have this perception. There is therefore an air of reality to the subjective component of the defence.

[114] There is also an air of reality to the objective component of this element of the defence. On the particular facts of this case, this conclusion goes hand in hand with the determination that there is an air of reality to the first element of self-defence. That is, for the same reason that there is an air of reality to the reasonableness of the accused's perception he was going to be attacked, so too is there an air of reality to the accused's perception that the attack would be deadly. The accused's whole story is that he thought Ice and Mike were carrying out a plan to kill him, and that at least one of them was armed. The jury could not reasonably accept the accused's testimony that he believed that he was going to be attacked, but simultaneously disbelieve his claim that he thought the attack would be deadly. Similarly, the evidential basis for inferring the reasonableness of the

accused's perception that he was going to be attacked is also the evidential basis for inferring the reasonableness of his perception that the attack would be deadly.

[115] A jury acting reasonably could draw an inference from the circumstances described by the accused, including particularly the indications that Mike and Ice were armed, the rumors of a plan to assassinate him, the suspicious behaviour, and the wearing of the gloves, to the reasonableness of his perception that he was in mortal danger.

[116] Once again, we wish to stress that the conclusion that there is an air of reality to the second prong of this defence does not involve an appraisal of the substantive merits of the defence. This conclusion rests upon our assessment that a properly instructed jury acting reasonably *could* infer the reasonableness of the accused's perception that he faced a deadly attack. Whether a jury *should* come to such a conclusion is an entirely different question, which is entirely irrelevant to the air of reality analysis.

(4) Reasonable Belief in the Absence of Alternatives to Killing

[117] We now come to the third and final element of self-defence under s. 34(2). This requirement too has both a subjective and an objective component. The inquiry starts with the subjective perceptions of the accused at the relevant time, and then asks whether those perceptions were reasonable. It must be established both that the accused believed that he could not preserve himself except by shooting the victim, and that he held this belief on reasonable grounds.

[118] The inquiry into the inferences reasonably capable of being drawn by a jury must focus on the following sequence of events leading up to the accused's killing of Mike, the victim. The accused testified that he feared a deadly attack from Ice and, more particularly, from Mike, who was sitting behind him. The accused testified to the following sequence of events. Reasoning that Mike and Ice would be less likely to carry out their murderous plan in public view, the accused pulled into the well-lit parking lot of a service station. He then set about replenishing the van's supply of windshield washer fluid. He got out of the van, in which Ice and Mike continued to sit. He entered the service station. There, he had an exchange with the cashier, and realized that he did not have enough money to pay for the fluid. He exited the service station, and returned to the van, in which Mike and Ice still waited. He borrowed money from Ice. He then re-entered the service station, and bought the washer fluid. He exited the service station again. He regained the van, popped open the hood, and replenished the supply of fluid. When he was done, he put down the container, walked to the back door of the van, opened the door, and shot Mike in the head.

[119] The first question is whether there is an air of reality to the accused's claim that, at the time he shot the victim, he actually believed that he had no alternative. We believe that there is. The starting point in air of reality analysis is that the accused's evidence is assumed to be true. The accused's extensive direct testimony regarding his subjective perceptions at the relevant time amounts to more than a "mere assertion" of the element of the defence. Provided there is an air of reality to the whole defence, a jury is entitled to make a determination as to credibility, and to decide whether the accused really did believe that he could not preserve himself from death or grievous bodily harm except by killing the victim.

[120] A final issue remains. The question is whether there is anything in the testimony of the accused on the basis of which a properly instructed jury acting reasonably could infer the reasonableness of the accused's belief that he had no alternative but to kill the victim, at the end of the sequence of events described above. We conclude that there is no such evidence to be found in the accused's testimony, or in any other source.

[121] By specifying that an accused must believe *on reasonable grounds* that he had no alternative, Parliament injected an element of objectivity into the defence of self-defence. It is not enough for an accused to establish a subjective conviction that he had no choice but to shoot his way out of a dangerous situation. Nor is it enough for an accused to provide an explanation setting out just why he believed what he did was necessary. The accused must be able to point to a *reasonable ground* for that belief. The requirement is not just that the accused be able to articulate a reason for holding the belief, or point to some considerations that tended, in his mind, to support that belief. Rather, the requirement is that the belief that he had no other option but to kill must have been objectively *reasonable*.

[122] The accused testified that calling the police from within the service station would have been ineffective, as he believed that they would not have arrived in time to save him. This part of the accused's testimony may provide an evidential basis from which a jury acting reasonably could infer the reasonableness of the accused's belief that he could not have preserved himself from death by calling the police. There may even be an evidential basis from which a jury acting reasonably could infer a reasonable belief by the accused that it was unsafe to return to his apartment. But this is not an evidential foundation capable of supporting the defence of self-defence under s. 34(2).

[123] Section 34(2) does not require that an accused rule out *a few* courses of action other than killing. The requirement is that the accused have believed on reasonable grounds that there was *no alternative course of action* open to him at that time, so that he reasonably thought he was obliged to kill in order to preserve himself from death or grievous bodily harm. In this case, there is absolutely no evidence from which a jury could reasonably infer the reasonableness of a belief in the absence of alternatives. There is nothing in the evidence to explain why the accused did not wait in the service station rather than go back to the van. There is absolutely nothing to explain why he did not flee once he had left the van. Indeed, there is nothing to suggest the reasonableness of his conclusion that he needed to walk back to the van and shoot the victim.

[124] Self-defence under s. 34(2) provides a justification for killing. A person who intentionally takes another human life is entitled to an acquittal if he can make out the elements of the defence. This defence is intended to cover situations of last resort. In order for the defence of self-defence under s. 34(2) to succeed at the end of the day, a jury would have to accept that the accused believed *on reasonable grounds* that his own safety and survival depended on killing the victim at that moment. There is no evidence in the case on the basis of which a properly instructed jury acting reasonably could come to that conclusion. The inferences required for the defence to succeed are simply not capable of being supported by the accused's testimony.

[125] Since there is no evidential foundation for the third element of self-defence under s. 34(2), the defence as a whole lacks an air of reality.

[126] We conclude that the defence of self-defence under s. 34(2) should never have been put to the jury. The appeal should be allowed.

BINNIE J (Gonthier J concurring):

[127] I concur with the Chief Justice and Bastarache J., and with the reasons they have given, that the appeal should be allowed. I add these paragraphs on what I think is the decisive point.

[128] My colleagues have mobilized considerable scholarship for and against all aspects of the issues. When the smoke clears, this appeal comes down to a simple proposition. A criminal code that permitted preemptive killings within a criminal organization on the bare assertion by the killer that no course of action was reasonably available to him while standing *outside* a motor vehicle other than to put a shot in the back of the head of another member sitting *inside* the parked vehicle at a well-lit and populated gas station is a criminal code that would fail in its most basic purpose of promoting public order.

[129] The respondent says he did not consider going to the police, although he was outside the car and in a position to flee the scene. He said "I never called the police in my life." Even if the police unexpectedly got there before a shoot-out, they would ask for some information in return for protection. "That's how it works," he said. Accordingly, there was evidence that *subjectively*, as a self-styled criminal, he felt his only options were to kill or be killed. He wishes the jury to judge the reasonableness of his conduct by the rules of his criminal subculture, which is the antithesis of public order.

[130] A trial judge should be very slow to take a defence away from a jury. We all agree on that. Here, however, the only way the defence *could* succeed is if the jury climbed into the skin of the respondent and accepted as reasonable a sociopathic view of appropriate dispute resolution. There is otherwise no air of reality, however broadly or narrowly defined, to the assertion that on February 3, 1994, in Montréal, the respondent believed *on reasonable grounds* that he could not otherwise preserve himself from death or grievous bodily harm, as required by s. 34(2)(b) of the *Criminal Code*, R.S.C. 1985, c. C-46. The *objective* reality of his situation would necessarily be altogether ignored, contrary to the intention of Parliament as interpreted in our jurisprudence.

[131] If, in these circumstances, jurors gave effect to the plea of self-defence, the Crown could be expected to successfully attack the judge's erroneous instruction that left self-defence to their consideration. Even the most patient jurors are entitled to expect that if they are asked to consider a defence, and accept it, the verdict will not be reversed on appeal on the ground that as a matter of law there was no *objective* basis in the evidence for the judge to have put self-defence to them in the first place.

[Justice Arbour wrote a dissenting opinion, concurred in by Iacobucci and Major JJ.]

The question of how to assess the reasonableness of an accused's perceptions and responses—his or her apprehension of a threat, of the gravity and immediacy of that threat, and of the alternatives available to him or her—emerges again as the central issue in the next section of this chapter, which considers the courts' treatment of self-defence claims made in the context of domestic violence. Yet that issue has arisen in other situations as well. For example, should an accused's intoxication be relevant in assessing whether he or she acted in self-defence? In *Reilly v The Queen*, [1984] 2 SCR 396, Ritchie J, speaking for five members of the Court, rejected the accused's appeal that the trial judge erred in not instructing the jury to consider evidence of intoxication in deciding whether they had a reasonable doubt whether the accused acted in self-defence. He stated:

[Section 34(2)] places in issue the accused's state of mind at the time he caused death. The subsection can only afford protection to the accused if he apprehended death or grievous bodily harm from the assault he was repelling and if he believed he could not preserve himself from death or grievous bodily harm otherwise than by the force he used. Nonetheless, his apprehension must be a *reasonable* one and his belief must *be based upon reasonable and probable grounds*. The subsection requires that the jury consider, and be guided by, what they decide on the evidence was the accused's appreciation of the situation and his belief as to the reaction it required, so long as there exists an objectively verifiable basis for his perception.

Since s. 34(2) places in issue the accused's perception of the attack upon him and the response required to meet it, the accused may still be found to have acted in self-defence even if he was mistaken in his perception. Reasonable and probable grounds must still exist for this mistaken perception in the sense that the mistake must have been one which an ordinary man using ordinary care could have made in the same circumstances.

This statutory requirement of reasonableness is what distinguishes the defence provided by s. 34(2) from the general law upon mistake of fact expressed in *Pappajohn v. The Queen*, [1980] 2 S.C.R. 120. In the *Pappajohn* case it was held that an honest, but mistaken belief in facts which, if true, would render the accused's act innocent was sufficient to prevent him from forming the *mens rea* essential to all criminal liability; there was no legal necessity that the mistaken belief be based upon reasonable grounds. It was accepted that intoxication could potentially induce such a mistake of fact.

The fatal difficulty with the appellant's argument in this case is that although intoxication can be a factor in inducing an honest mistake, it cannot induce a mistake which must be based upon reasonable and probable grounds. The perspective of the reasonable man which the language of s. 34(2) places in issue here is the objective standard the law commonly adopts to measure a man's conduct. A reasonable man is a man in full possession of his faculties. In contrast, a drunken man is one whose ability to reason and to perceive is diminished by the alcohol he has consumed.

I should not be taken as saying that the defence under s. 34(2) can never be available to a person who is intoxicated. An intoxicated man may hold a reasonable belief, i.e. the same belief a sober man would form viewing the matter before him upon reasonable and probable grounds. Where he does so, however, it is in spite of his intoxication.

The requirement of an objective basis for the accused's perception of the facts, whether it be mistaken or accurate, eliminates any relevance that evidence of the accused's intoxication might have had to self-defence under s. 34(2). Naturally, if the accused is intoxicated, he is not deprived of the defence provided by the subsection so long as the objective test is met by the existence of reasonable and probable grounds for the accused's perception of the nature of the assault upon him and the response required to meet it.

Whereas the Supreme Court has thus held that the accused's intoxication should not normally factor into the modified objective standard, in *R v Nelson* (1992), 71 CCC (3d) 449, the Ontario Court of Appeal held that an accused's intellectual impairment was a feature that should be taken into consideration when assessing his or her reasonable beliefs and responses. The Court of Appeal reasoned that an accused's diminished intelligence that affects his or her perception of and reaction to an assault might mean that "his or her apprehension and belief could not be fairly measured against the perceptions of an 'ordinary man'" (at 467).

Similarly, in *R v Kagan*, 2004 NSCA 77, 185 CCC (3d) 417, a case in which an accused claiming self-defence suffered from Asperger's Syndrome, the Nova Scotia Court of Appeal indicated a jury should be told that it should consider evidence that, owing to his condition and in the circumstances of the case, the accused would have been highly anxious, paranoid, and distrustful, and that this might have affected his perception of the situation. Under the new self-defence provisions, factoring in such conditions and impairments would be part of considering "the relevant circumstances of the person," as mandated by s 34(2).

Proportionality and Other Aspects of "Reasonableness"

In addition to calling upon a judge or jury to contextualize the act by taking into account the characteristics and circumstances of the accused, and the character of the relationship between the parties and any past communications between them (paras (f) and (f.1)), many of the factors listed in s 34(2) direct the finder of fact's attention to considerations informing the proportionality between the threatened force and the act committed in self-defence. Section 34(2)(g) explicitly lists this central concern, stating that a judge or jury should consider "the nature and proportionality of the person's response to the use or threat of force," but a number of the other factors can also be grouped under this overarching concern for proportionality. Section 34(2) instructs the finder of fact to consider "the nature of the force or threat" (s 34(2)(a)); whether the force was "imminent and whether there were other means available to respond" to it (s 34(2)(b)); and whether weapons were involved in the incident (s 34(2)(d)).

In *R v Kong*, 2006 SCC 40, [2006] 2 SCR 347, the Supreme Court of Canada endorsed the decision reached by Wittman JA, writing in dissent at the Alberta Court of Appeal, 2005 ABCA 255. Taking guidance from the Supreme Court's decision in *Cinous*, which emphasized the modified objective approach that governs the assessment of self-defence, Justice Wittman helpfully explained how one should assess the proportionality of the force used by the accused:

> [208] ... a person is not expected to "weigh to a nicety" the exact measure of a defensive action or to stop and reflect upon the risk of deadly consequences from such action: *Kandola* at paras. 27 and 28 citing *Palmer v. The Queen* (1971), 55 Cr. App. R. 223 at 242. The principle has also been adopted and applied in *R. v. Ogal* (1928), 50 C.C.C. 71 (Alta. S.C.A.D.); *R. v. Preston* (1953), 106 C.C.C. 135 at 140 (B.C.C.A.); *R. v. Antley*, [1964] 2 C.C.C. 142 at 147 (Ont. C.A.), and *Baxter*.
>
> [209] The accused may be mistaken about the nature and extent of force necessary for self-defence provided the mistake was reasonable in the circumstances: *R. v. Nelson* (1992), 71 C.C.C. (3d) 449 at 468-9 (Ont. C.A.). In deciding whether the appellant's use of force was reasonable, the jury is to look to the circumstances to consider what a reasonable person in the accused's situation might do given the threatening attack and the force necessary to defend himself against that apprehended attack: *Baxter* at 110. The objective measurement of proportionate force in self-defence cases requires a tolerant approach .... .

An interesting and important issue related to this overall demand for a proportional response is whether an accused is under any obligation to "retreat" before using force in self-defence. Consider the following statement quoted with approval by the Supreme Court of the United States in 1895 (*Beard v US*, 158 US 550 at 561 (1895)): "a true man who is without fault is not obliged to fly from an assailant, who by violence or surprise maliciously seeks to take his life or do him enormous bodily harm." Note that in *R v Deegan*, 1979 ABCA 198, 49

CCC (2d) 417, the Alberta Court of Appeal adopted the following statement made by Holmes J in the US Supreme Court case of *Brown v United States of America*, 256 US 335 (1920):

> Many respectable writers agree that if a man reasonably believes that he is in immediate danger of death or grievous bodily harm from his assailant, he may stand his ground, and that if he kills him, he has not exceeded the bounds of lawful self-defence. That has been the decision of this court. *Beard v. United States*. Detached reflection cannot be demanded in the presence of an uplifted knife. Therefore, in this court, at least, it is not a condition of immunity that one in that situation should pause to consider whether a reasonable man might not think it possible to fly with safety, or to disable his assailant rather than to kill him.

The issue of whether an accused has a right to "stand his ground" or whether there is a so-called duty to retreat became central in the infamous killing of Trayvon Martin in Florida in 2012. George Zimmerman, a member of the local community watch, shot and killed the black teenager after an altercation between the two. Zimmerman took it upon himself to follow Martin because he felt that Martin was acting "suspiciously" and was concerned about robberies that had taken place in the community. Zimmerman was charged for the killing but claimed the protection of Florida's "Stand Your Ground" self-defence law. A jury acquitted him of second-degree murder and manslaughter. The national and international furor that ensued led the Florida governor to appoint a task force to review the state's self-defence laws.

Section 34 does not impose a requirement to retreat, but neither does it provide a right to "stand one's ground." Rather, the Canadian law of self-defence asks a judge or jury to consider the reasonable perceptions and the reasonable courses of action available to an accused in light of the totality of the situation, assessments to which the possibility of retreat might be relevant. As such, courts have held that whether an accused retreated in a given case may be a relevant factor in assessing a claim of self-defence: see *R v Druken*, 2002 NFCA 23, 164 CCC (3d) 115. Addressing the "duty to retreat" under the old self-defence provisions, the Ontario Court of Appeal concluded as follows in *R v Cain*, 2011 ONCA 298 at para 9, 278 CCC (3d) 228:

> ... s. 34(2) does not require defendants to retreat in the face of an assault, but rather permits defendants to stand their ground during the early stages of a confrontation. However, as the appellant properly concedes, the possibility of retreat is relevant to the second and third elements of the s. 34(2) defence, namely, the issues of whether the appellant did have a reasonable apprehension of death or grievous bodily harm, and whether the appellant had a reasonable belief that it was not otherwise possible to save himself from harm except by killing ... .

Note, however, that there are cases suggesting a more absolute rule that one is never required to flee *from one's own home* to escape an assault in order to claim self-defence. See *R v Forde*, 2011 ONCA 592, 277 CCC (3d) 1, in which the court concluded that "a jury is not entitled to consider whether an accused could have retreated from his or her own home in the face of an attack (or threatened attack) by an assailant in assessing the elements of self-defence under [the old] s. 34(2)" (para 55). See also *R v Docherty*, 2012 ONCA 784; *R v Jack* (1994), 91 CCC (3d) 446 (BCCA); and *R v Proulx* (1998), 127 CCC (3d) 511 (BCCA).

Another intriguing question related to the assessment of proportionality, as well as the accused's role in the event, is whether an accused who kills in the context of a consensual fistfight can claim self-defence. The Supreme Court of Canada considered this issue in *R v*

Paice, 2005 SCC 22, [2005] 1 SCR 339. In that case, decided under the old provisions, the accused was charged with manslaughter and, at trial, successfully claimed self-defence. After a dispute over a game of pool, the deceased had approached the accused in a bar and asked him, "do you want to go outside to fight?" Both went outside and, after exchanging threats, the deceased pushed the accused, causing him to stumble back several steps. The accused then swung his elbow at the deceased, knocking him to the ground, apparently unconscious. The accused then struck him two more times before he was pulled away. Writing for a majority of the Court, Justice Charron first addressed the legal principles arising from *R v Jobidon* (extracted in Chapter 1) regarding consent in the context of fistfights between adults. She clarified that, in order to vitiate consent, "*Jobidon* requires serious harm both intended and caused" (para 18). This being so, it was open to the trial judge in this case to find that, after the accused was pushed, he and the deceased were still involved in a consensual fistfight. On the issue of self-defence, Justice Charron reasoned that "[w]here a person willingly engages in mutual combat, he cannot later say that he did not provoke the assault" (para 20). Under the old provisions, unless the accused apprehended a threat of grievous bodily harm or death, if an accused provoked the assault he or she would be barred from claiming self-defence. Consequently, Justice Charron ordered a new trial in *Paice*. Under the new s 34, the fact that the accused and the deceased were involved in a consensual fistfight would presumably be one factor to take into account in assessing whether, given his or her "role in the incident," the accused's act was "reasonable in the circumstances."

For further discussion of this issue, see S Coughlan, "Annotation to Paice" (2005) 29 CR (6th) 3 and K Roach, "Jobidon Revisited in Paice" (2005) 50 Crim LQ 357.

Excessive Force and Self-Defence

Finally, it is important to recognize that this defence operates in an "all or nothing" fashion. That is, an accused who concedes that he or she committed the offence but claims to have acted in self-defence will simply be found guilty of the full offence if his or her act is judged not to have been reasonable in the circumstances. Consider, for example, a situation in which an accused is charged with murder but a judge or jury finds that "excessive force" was used in self-defence, contrary to the demand for proportionality between the apprehended threat and the accused's response. Should that person be found guilty of murder, or should the fact that he or she acted in the context of a reasonable apprehension of an unlawful assault reduce the offence to manslaughter, akin to the outcome of a successful provocation defence? In *Reilly v R* (1982), 66 CCC (2d) 146, Arnup JA, giving the judgment of the Ontario Court of Appeal, endorsed this approach:

> I have reached the conclusion that the doctrine of excessive force in self-defence rendering the accused guilty only of manslaughter instead of murder should be recognized in Ontario. Without deciding that there are no other requisites for its application in particular cases, I conclude also that the conditions stated by Martin J.A. in *Trecroce* (1980), 55 C.C.C. (2d) 202 should be applied. ...
>
> (a) The accused must have been justified in using some force to defend himself against an attack, real or *reasonably apprehended.*
> (b) The accused must have *honestly* believed that he was justified in using the force he did.
> (c) The force used was excessive only because it exceeded what the accused could *reasonably* have considered necessary. [Emphasis added.]

Yet the Supreme Court of Canada has rejected this approach to "excessive force" in self-defence. In *R v Faid*, [1983] 1 SCR 265, Dickson J (as he then was), giving the judgment for the seven-member Court, explained as follows:

> In *Brisson* I sought to explain why, in my opinion, a verdict of manslaughter, except in the circumstances to which I have earlier alluded, is not available where an accused acting in self-defence, as described in s. 34 of the *Code*, causes a death by the use of an excess of force. I am still of that opinion. The position of the Alberta Court of Appeal that there is a "half-way" house outside s. 34 of the *Code* is, in my view, inapplicable to the Canadian codified system of criminal law, it lacks any recognizable basis in principle, would require prolix and complicated jury charges and would encourage juries to reach compromise verdicts to the prejudice of either the accused or the Crown. Where a killing has resulted from the excessive use of force in self-defence the accused loses the justification provided under s. 34. There is no partial justification open under the section. Once the jury reaches the conclusion that excessive force has been used the defence of self-defence has failed. It does not follow automatically, however, that the verdict must be murder. The accused has become responsible for a killing. He has no justification on the basis of self-defence, but unless it is shown that the killing was accompanied by the intent required under s. 212(a) of the *Code*, it remains a killing without intent, in other words manslaughter. If the jury considers that excessive force has been used, and has resulted in a death, they must then ask themselves whether the accused, in causing the killing, possessed the intent described in s. 212(a) of the *Code*, that is, an intent to kill or cause bodily harm likely to cause death. If they are satisfied beyond a reasonable doubt that the intent was present, they should find the accused guilty of murder. However, in the event they found no such intent existed, or had a doubt as to its existence, they should convict of manslaughter. This conviction would rest upon the fact that an unlawful killing had been committed without the intent required to make it murder under s. 212(a).

This position is supported by the structure of s 34, and by s 26 of the *Criminal Code*, which provides that "[e]very one who is authorized by law to use force is criminally responsible for any excess thereof according to the nature and quality of the act that constitutes the excess." Consider, however, the polarizing effect of the absence of a "half-way house," as Justice Dickson called it, in the law of self-defence. For charges of murder met with claims of self-defence in which the principal issue is whether the accused used excessive force, the outcome will be either an outright acquittal or conviction for the highest offence known to law, with its mandatory penalty of life imprisonment. Recall the discussion, in Chapter 4, of plea bargaining and the challenge of wrongful convictions. This all-or-nothing structure of self-defence can put significant pressure on an accused to plead guilty to a lesser charge—such as manslaughter—rather than take the risk that a judge or jury will find that his or her act was excessive, or otherwise not reasonable in the circumstances. For reasons we will explore in the next section, this might be of particular concern in cases of gendered and domestic violence, a crucial issue in the development of the Canadian law of self-defence.

III. GENDERED VIOLENCE, "BATTERED WOMEN," AND SELF-DEFENCE

The experience of women subject to persistent violence from their domestic partners has been central to the recent development of the Canadian law of self-defence. Indeed, as you will see, the new s 34 bears the imprint of the judicial response to this issue. For many years, scholars and commentators drew attention to the criminal law's failure to respond to the particular circumstances of these women. A principal target of this criticism was the law of self-defence, which, as it had developed through judicial interpretation, would not accommodate battered women's claims that they had killed their abusers in justified self-defence. Justice Bertha Wilson would take an important jurisprudential step to address this gap in the law in the case of *R v Lavallee*. Before turning to that case, however, it is important to recognize that even the language of "battered women" is contentious and fails to clearly describe the character of the experiences at stake in the cases and issues examined in this section. The following extract from an in-depth study of Canadian cases involving women who killed a violent intimate partner provides helpful insight into this terminological issue and the experiences—and broader social and political dynamics—that such labels always incompletely capture.

> ### EA Sheehy, *Defending Battered Women on Trial: Lessons from the Transcripts*
> (Vancouver: University of British Columbia Press, 2014) at 12-13
> (footnotes omitted)
>
> For the purposes of this book, I use the term "battering" to describe the systemic use of threats and acts of violence, whether minor or serious, by male partners to get their way—to enforce their authority, to isolate, intimidate, and silence their female partners, and to control them. Also called "intimate terrorism" in the literature, battering is overwhelmingly committed by men against women, is motivated by the desire to dominate and achieve control over another, and tends to escalate over time. Battering draws on structural inequalities experienced by women—women's unequal access to social, political, and economic resources. Societies more rigidly stratified by gender have higher rates of battering.
>
> Battering is used to enforce women's traditional roles—to force women to serve their male partners by cooking and cleaning, bearing and raising children, and being sexually available; to restrict or supervise what women wear, whether they pursue educational or employment opportunities, and whom they associate with; and to reflect men "at twice their natural size." Melanie Randall sums up battering as "simultaneously express[ing] and reproduc[ing] sexual inequality on both individual and societal levels; it is both a cause and effect of sex inequality."
>
> Battering is distinguished from "situational couple violence," which denotes common couple violence in which women as well as men might on occasion use violence outside a larger pattern of control or coercion in order to get their way in a particular situation. Relationships are described as battering ones when there is evidence of threatening behaviour, sexual or physical abuse by the man, coupled with his effort to control and dominate the woman. In such cases, the implication is clear to both partners: if he needs to use more serious violence to achieve his goal, he will. Lisa A Goodman and Deborah

Epstein elaborate: "Even nonviolent control tactics take on a violent meaning through their implicit connection with potential physical harm."

The term "battered women" is used throughout this book, even though it implicitly suggests a category of women whose experiences are universal and who are somehow set apart from "other" women. In the context of criminal trials, in which nuance is abandoned by Crown and defence lawyers who present competing narratives about women on trial as either violent, manipulative frauds or wholly innocent, deserving wives and mothers, claiming the experience of battering carries particular risks. Women who fail in any way to meet the preconceptions of battered women can have their credibility destroyed and their chances of acquittal undercut. For example, in one case in my study of ninety-one women, the prosecutor argued at sentencing that the woman was "often drunk, profane, verbally abusive, physically aggressive, prone to lying and exaggeration, that she was not in fact the submissive, passive, vulnerable woman who lived in the state of learned helplessness." Some Canadian judges have attempted to disrupt this binary, insisting that, although a woman might use violence or coarse language or in other ways present as less than perfect, this does not mean that she has not experienced battering. Yet Crown attorneys and defence lawyers continue this battle for the hearts and minds of jurors by presenting contrasting and stark portraits of the woman's (and the deceased man's) goodness or evil.

To further complicate matters, many women, US author Martha R Mahoney explains, avoid calling themselves "battered." She identifies "the gap between my self-perceived competence and strength and my own image of battered women, the inevitable attendant loss of my own denial of painful experience, and the certainty that the listener cannot hear such a claim without filtering it through a variety of derogatory stereotypes." Even women convicted of killing their batterers might reject the label because they have grown up with male violence as a constant, internalized it as their fault, thought that the violence they experienced was not severe enough, or believed that if they fought back they could not be a battered woman. Thus, the practices of batterers and the consequences for women whose lives have been affected by them remain relatively invisible in our society and legal system and continue to be distorted by misconceptions.

As you will see, the following case, which was the Supreme Court of Canada's principal response to the issue of self-defence and battered women, brings us back to the question of how one imagines the "reasonable person" and the centrality of this question to the justice of the criminal law. Although decided under the old self-defence provisions, it is yet another case in which it is clear that existing jurisprudence will continue to inform interpretation and application of the law of self-defence in Canada.

R v Lavallee
Supreme Court of Canada
[1990] 1 SCR 852

[At trial, the accused was acquitted of murder by a judge and jury. The Manitoba Court of Appeal reversed and ordered a new trial, in part on the ground that expert testimony at trial relating to the reactions of the accused and other battered women should not be admitted in relation to her plea of self-defence.]

WILSON J: The appellant, who was 22 years old at the time, had been living with Kevin Rust for some three to four years. Their residence was the scene of a boisterous party on August 30, 1986. In the early hours of August 31 after most of the guests had departed the appellant and Rust had an argument in the upstairs bedroom which was used by the appellant. Rust was killed by a single shot in the back of the head from a .303 calibre rifle fired by the appellant as he was leaving the room.

The appellant did not testify but her statement made to police on the night of the shooting was put in evidence. Portions of it read as follows:

> Me and Wendy argued as usual and I ran in the house after Kevin pushed me. I was scared, I was really scared. I locked the door. Herb was downstairs with Joanne and I called for Herb but I was crying when I called him. I said, "Herb come up here please." Herb came up to the top of the stairs and I told him that Kevin was going to hit me actually beat on me again. Herb said he knew and that if I was his old lady things would be different, he gave me a hug. OK, we're friends, there's nothing between us. He said "Yeah, I know" and he went outside to talk to Kevin leaving the door unlocked. I went upstairs and hid in my closet from Kevin. I was so scared … . My window was open and I could hear Kevin asking questions about what I was doing and what I was saying. Next thing I know he was coming up the stairs for me. He came into my bedroom and said "Wench, where are you?" And he turned on my light and he said "Your purse is on the floor" and he kicked it. OK then he turned and he saw me in the closet. He wanted me to come out but I didn't want to come out because I was scared. I was so scared. [The officer who took the statement then testified that the appellant started to cry at this point and stopped after a minute or two.] He grabbed me by the arm right there. There's a bruise on my face also where he slapped me. He didn't slap me right then, first he yelled at me then he pushed me and I pushed him back and he hit me twice on the right hand side of my head. I was scared. All I thought about was all the other times he used to beat me, I was scared, I was shaking as usual. The rest is a blank, all I remember is he gave me the gun and a shot was fired through my screen. This is all so fast. And then the guns were in another room and he loaded it the second shot and gave it to me. And I was going to shoot myself. I pointed it to myself, I was so upset. OK and then he went and I was sitting on the bed and he started going like this with his finger [the appellant made a shaking motion with an index finger] and said something like "You're my old lady and you do as you're told" or something like that. He said "wait till everybody leaves, you'll get it then" and he said something to the effect of "either you kill me or I'll get you" that was what it was. He kind of smiled and then he turned around. I shot him but I aimed out. I thought I aimed above him and a piece of his head went that way.

The relationship between the appellant and Rust was volatile and punctuated by frequent arguments and violence. They would apparently fight for two or three days at a time or several times a week. Considerable evidence was led at trial indicating that the appellant was frequently a victim of physical abuse at the hands of Rust. Between 1983 and 1986 the appellant made several trips to hospital for injuries including severe bruises, a fractured nose, multiple contusions and a black eye. …

The need for expert evidence in … areas [of human behaviour] can, however, be obfuscated by the belief that judges and juries are thoroughly knowledgeable about "human nature" and that no more is needed. They are, so to speak, their own experts on human behaviour. This, in effect, was the primary submission of the Crown to this Court. …

Expert evidence on the psychological effect of battering on wives and common law partners must, it seems to me, be both relevant and necessary in the context of the present case. How can the mental state of the appellant be appreciated without it? The average member of the public (or of the jury) can be forgiven for asking: Why would a woman put up with this kind of treatment? Why should she continue to live with such a man? How could she love a partner who beat her to the point of requiring hospitalization? We would expect the woman to pack her bags and go. Where is her self-respect? Why does she not cut loose and make a new life for herself? Such is the reaction of the average person confronted with the so-called "battered wife syndrome." We need help to understand it and help is available from trained professionals. …

Laws do not spring out of a social vacuum. The notion that a man has a right to "discipline" his wife is deeply rooted in the history of our society. …

Fortunately, there has been a growing awareness in recent years that no man has a right to abuse any woman under any circumstances. Legislative initiatives designed to educate police, judicial officers and the public, as well as more aggressive investigation and charging policies all signal a concerted effort by the criminal justice system to take spousal abuse seriously. However, a woman who comes before a judge or jury with the claim that she has been battered and suggests that this may be a relevant factor in evaluating her subsequent actions still faces the prospect of being condemned by popular mythology about domestic violence. Either she was not as badly beaten as she claims or she would have left the man long ago. Or, if she was battered that severely, she must have stayed out of some masochistic enjoyment of it.

Expert testimony on the psychological effects of battering have been admitted in American courts in recent years. In *State v. Kelly*, 478 A.2d 364 at p. 378 (1984), the New Jersey Supreme Court commended the value of expert testimony in these terms:

> It is aimed at an area where the purported common knowledge of the jury may be very much mistaken, an area where jurors' logic, drawn from their own experience, may lead to a wholly incorrect conclusion, an area where expert knowledge would enable the jurors to disregard their prior conclusions as being common myths rather than common knowledge.

The court concludes at p. 379 that the battering relationship is "subject to a large group of myths and stereotypes." As such, it is "beyond the ken of the average juror and thus is suitable for explanation through expert testimony." I share that view. …

The bare facts of this case, which I think are amply supported by the evidence, are that the appellant was repeatedly abused by the deceased but did not leave him (although she twice pointed a gun at him), and ultimately shot him in the back of the head as he was leaving her room. The Crown submits that these facts disclose all the information a jury needs in order to decide whether or not the appellant acted in self-defence. I have no hesitation in rejecting the Crown's submission. …

In my view, there are two elements of the defence under s. 34(2) of the *Code* which merit scrutiny for present purposes. The first is the temporal connection in s. 34(2)(a) between the apprehension of death or grievous bodily harm and the act allegedly taken in self-defence. Was the appellant "under reasonable apprehension of death or grievous bodily harm" from Rust as he was walking out of the room? The second is the assessment in s. 34(2)(b) of the magnitude of the force used by the accused. Was the accused's belief that she could not "otherwise preserve herself from death or grievous bodily harm" except by shooting the deceased based "on reasonable grounds"?

The feature common to both 34(2)(a) and 34(2)(b) is the imposition of an objective standard of reasonableness on the apprehension of death and the need to repel the assault with deadly force. In *Reilly v. The Queen*, [1984] 2 S.C.R. 396, this Court considered the interaction of the objective and subjective components of s. 34(2) at p. 404:

> Subsection (2) of s. 34 places in issue the accused's state of mind at the time he caused death. The subsection can only afford protection to the accused if he apprehended death or grievous bodily harm from the assault he was repelling and if he believed he could not preserve himself from death or grievous bodily harm otherwise than by the force he used. Nonetheless, his apprehension must be a *reasonable* one and his belief must *be based upon reasonable and probable grounds*. The subsection requires that the jury consider, and be guided by, what they decide on the evidence was the accused's appreciation of the situation and his belief as to the reaction it required, so long as there exists an objectively verifiable basis for his perception.
>
> Since s. 34(2) places in issue the accused's perception of the attack upon him and the response required to meet it, the accused may still be found to have acted in self-defence even if he was mistaken in his perception. Reasonable and probable grounds must still exist for this mistaken perception in the sense that the mistake must have been one which an ordinary man using ordinary care could have made in the same circumstances. [Emphasis in original.]

If it strains credulity to imagine what the "ordinary man" would do in the position of a battered spouse, it is probably because men do not typically find themselves in that situation. Some women do, however. The definition of what is reasonable must be adapted to circumstances which are, by and large, foreign to the world inhabited by the hypothetical "reasonable man." ...

A. Reasonable Apprehension of Death

Section 34(2)(a) requires that an accused who intentionally causes death or grievous bodily harm in repelling an assault is justified if he or she does so "under reasonable apprehension of death or grievous bodily harm." In the present case, the assault precipitating the appellant's alleged defensive act was Rust's threat to kill her when everyone else had gone.

It will be observed that subsection 34(2)(a) does not actually stipulate that the accused apprehend *imminent* danger when he or she acts. Case law has, however, read that requirement into the defence: see *Reilly v. The Queen, supra; R. v. Baxter* (1975), 33 C.R.N.S. 22 (Ont. C.A.); *R. v. Bogue* (1976), 30 C.C.C. (2d) 403 (Ont. C.A.). The sense in which "imminent" is used conjures up the image of "an uplifted knife" or a pointed gun. The rationale for the imminence rule seems obvious. The law of self-defence is designed to ensure that the use of defensive force is really necessary. It justifies the act because the defender reasonably believed that he or she had no alternative but to take the attacker's life. If there is a significant time interval between the original unlawful assault and the accused's response, one tends to suspect that the accused was motivated by revenge rather than self-defence.

In the paradigmatic case of a one-time barroom brawl between two men of equal size and strength, this inference makes sense. How can one feel endangered to the point of firing a gun at an unarmed man who utters a death threat, then turns his back and walks out of the room? One cannot be certain of the gravity of the threat or his capacity to carry it out. Besides, one can always take the opportunity to flee or to call the police. If he comes back and raises his fist, one can respond in kind if need be. These are the tacit assumptions that underlie the imminence rule.

All of these assumptions were brought to bear on the respondent in *R. v. Whynot* (1983), 9 C.C.C. 449 (N.S. C.A.). The respondent, Jane Stafford, shot her sleeping common law husband as he lay passed out in his truck. The evidence at trial indicated that the deceased "dominated the household and exerted his authority by striking and slapping the various members and from time to time administering beatings to Jane Stafford and the others" (at p. 452). The respondent testified that the deceased threatened to kill all of the members of her family, one by one, if she tried to leave him. On the night in question he threatened to kill her son. After he passed out the respondent got one of the many shotguns kept by her husband and shot him. The Nova Scotia Court of Appeal held that the trial judge erred in leaving s. 37 (preventing assault against oneself or anyone under one's protection) with the jury. The Court stated at p. 464:

> I do not believe that the trial judge was justified in placing s. 37 of the *Code* before the jury any more than he would have been justified in giving them s. 34. Under s. 34 the assault must have been underway and unprovoked, and under s. 37 the assault must be such that it is necessary to defend the person assaulted by the use of force. No more force may be used than necessary to prevent the assault or the repetition of it. In my opinion, no person has the right in anticipation of an assault that may or may not happen, to apply force to prevent the imaginary assault.

The implication of the Court's reasoning is that it is inherently unreasonable to apprehend death or grievous bodily harm unless and until the physical assault is actually in progress, at which point the victim can presumably gauge the requisite amount of force needed to repel the attack and act accordingly. In my view, expert testimony can cast doubt on these assumptions as they are applied in the context of a battered wife's efforts to repel an assault. ...

[Wilson J then discussed the "Walker Cycle Theory of Violence," named after a pioneer researcher in the field of the battered woman syndrome, Dr. Lenore Walker.]

Dr. Walker first describes the cycle in the book, *The Battered Woman* (1979). In her 1984 book, *The Battered Woman Syndrome*, Dr. Walker reports the results of a study involving 400 battered women. Her research was designed to test empirically the theories expounded in her earlier book. At pp. 95-6 of *The Battered Woman Syndrome*, she summarizes the Cycle Theory as follows:

> A second major theory that was tested in this project is the Walker Cycle Theory of Violence (Walker, 1979). This tension reduction theory states that there are three distinct phases associated in a recurring battering cycle: (1) tension building, (2) the acute battering incident, and (3) loving contrition. During the first phase, there is a gradual escalation of tension

displayed by discrete acts causing increased friction such as name-calling, other mean intentional behaviors, and/or physical abuse. The batterer expresses dissatisfaction and hostility
but not in an extreme or maximally explosive form. The woman attempts to placate the
batterer, doing what she thinks might please him, calm him down, or at least, what will not
further aggravate him. She tries not to respond to his hostile actions and uses general anger
reduction techniques. Often she succeeds for a little while which reinforces her unrealistic
belief that she can control this man. ...

The tension continues to escalate and eventually she is unable to continue controlling his
angry response pattern. "Exhausted from the constant stress, she usually withdraws from
the batterer, fearing she will inadvertently set off an explosion. He begins to move more op-
pressively toward her as he observes her withdrawal. ... Tension between the two becomes
unbearable" (Walker, 1979, p. 59). The second phase, the acute battering incident, becomes
inevitable without intervention. Sometimes, she precipitates the inevitable explosion so as
to control where and when it occurs, allowing her to take better precautions to minimize
her injuries and pain.

"Phase two is characterized by the uncontrollable discharge of the tensions that have built
up during phase one" (p. 59). The batterer typically unleashes a barrage of verbal and physical
aggression that can leave the woman severely shaken and injured. In fact, when injuries do
occur it usually happens during this second phase. It is also the time police become involved,
if they are called at all. The acute battering phase is concluded when the batterer stops, usually bringing with its cessation a sharp physiological reduction in tension. This in itself is
naturally reinforcing. Violence often succeeds because it does work.

In phase three which follows, the batterer may apologize profusely, try to assist his victim,
show kindness and remorse, and shower her with gifts and/or promises. The batterer himself
may believe at this point that he will never allow himself to be violent again. The woman
wants to believe the batterer and, early in the relationship at least, may renew her hope in
his ability to change. This third phase provides the positive reinforcement for remaining in
the relationship, for the woman. In fact, our results showed that phase three could also be
characterized by an absence of tension or violence, and no observable loving-contrition
behaviour, and still be reinforcing for the woman.

Dr. Walker defines a battered woman as a woman who has gone through the battering
cycle at least twice. As she explains in her introduction to *The Battered Woman*, at p. xv:
"Any woman may find herself in an abusive relationship with a man once. If it occurs a
second time, and she remains in the situation, she is defined as a battered woman."

Given the relational context in which the violence occurs, the mental state of an accused at the critical moment she pulls the trigger cannot be understood except in terms
of the cumulative effect of months or years of brutality. As Dr. Shane explained in his
testimony, the deterioration of the relationship between the appellant and Rust in the
period immediately preceding the killing led to feelings of escalating terror on the part
of the appellant:

But their relationship some weeks to months before was definitely escalating in terms of
tension and in terms of the discordant quality about it. They were sleeping in separate bedrooms. Their intimate relationship was lacking and things were building and building and
to a point, I think, where it built to that particular point where she couldn't—she felt so
threatened and so overwhelmed that she had to—that she reacted in a violent way because

of her fear of survival and also because, I think because of her, I guess, final sense that she was—that she had to defend herself and her own sense of violence towards this man who had really desecrated her and damaged her for so long.

Another aspect of the cyclical nature of the abuse is that it begets a degree of predictability to the violence that is absent in an isolated violent encounter between two strangers. This also means that it may in fact be possible for a battered spouse to accurately predict the onset of violence before the first blow is struck, even if an outsider to the relationship cannot. Indeed, it has been suggested that a battered woman's knowledge of her partner's violence is so heightened that she is able to anticipate the nature and extent (though not the onset) of the violence by his conduct beforehand. ... In her article "Potential Uses for Expert Testimony: Ideas Toward the Representation of Battered Women Who Kill," 9 *Women's Rights Law Reporter* 227 (1986), psychologist Julie Blackman describes this characteristic at p. 229:

> Repeated instances of violence enable battered women to develop a continuum along which they can "rate" the tolerability or survivability of episodes of their partner's violence. Thus, signs of unusual violence are detected. For battered women, this response to the ongoing violence of their situations is a survival skill. Research shows that battered women who kill experience remarkably severe and frequent violence relative to battered women who do not kill. They know what sorts of danger are familiar and which are novel. They have had myriad opportunities to develop and hone their perceptions of their partner's violence. And, importantly, they can say what made the final episode of violence different from the others: they can name the features of the last battering that enabled them to know that this episode would result in life-threatening action by the abuser. ...

Of course, as Dr. Blackman points out, it is up to the jury to decide whether the distinction drawn between "typical" violence and the particular events the accused perceived as "life threatening" is compelling. According to the appellant's statement to police, Rust actually handed her a shotgun and warned her that if she did not kill him, he would kill her. I note in passing a remarkable observation made by Dr. Walker in her 1984 study, *The Battered Woman Syndrome*. Writing about the fifty battered women she interviewed who had killed their partners, she comments at p. 40:

> Most of the time the women killed the men with a gun; usually one of several that belonged to him. *Many of the men actually dared or demanded the woman use the gun on him first, or else he said he'd kill her with it.* (Emphasis added.)

Where evidence exists that an accused is in a battering relationship, expert testimony can assist the jury in determining whether the accused had a "reasonable" apprehension of death when she acted by explaining the heightened sensitivity of a battered woman to her partner's acts. Without such testimony I am skeptical that the average fact-finder would be capable of appreciating why her subjective fear may have been reasonable in the context of the relationship. After all, the hypothetical "reasonable man" observing only the final incident may have been unlikely to recognize the batterer's threat as potentially lethal. Using the case at bar as an example the "reasonable man" might have thought, as the majority of the Court of Appeal seemed to, that it was unlikely that Rust would make good on his threat to kill the appellant that night because they had guests staying overnight.

The issue is not, however, what an outsider would have reasonably perceived but what the accused reasonably perceived, given her situation and her experience.

Even accepting that a battered woman may be uniquely sensitized to danger from her batterer, it may yet be contended that the law ought to require her to wait until the knife is uplifted, the gun pointed or the fist clenched before her apprehension is deemed reasonable. This would allegedly reduce the risk that the woman is mistaken in her fear, although the law does not require her fear to be correct, only reasonable. In response to this contention, I need only point to the observation made by Huband J.A. that the evidence showed that when the appellant and Rust physically fought the appellant "invariably got the worst of it." I do not think it is an unwarranted generalization to say that due to their size, strength, socialization and lack of training, women are typically no match for men in hand-to-hand combat. The requirement imposed in *Whynot* that a battered woman wait until the physical assault is "underway" before her apprehensions can be validated in law would, in the words of an American court, be tantamount to sentencing her to "murder by installment": *State v. Gallegos*, 719 P.2d 1268 (N.M. 1986, at p. 1271). I share the view expressed by M.J. Willoughby in "Rendering Each Woman Her Due: Can a Battered Woman Claim Self-Defense When She Kills Her Sleeping Batterer" (1989), 38 *Kan. L. Rev.* 169, at p. 184, that "society gains nothing, except perhaps the additional risk that the battered woman will herself be killed, because she must wait until her abusive husband instigates another battering episode before she can justifiably act."

B. Lack of Alternatives to Self-Help

Subsection 34(2) requires an accused who pleads self-defence to believe "on reasonable grounds" that it is not possible to otherwise preserve him or herself from death or grievous bodily harm. The obvious question is if the violence was so intolerable, why did the appellant not leave her abuser long ago? This question does not really go to whether she had an alternative to killing the deceased at the critical moment. Rather, it plays on the popular myth already referred to that a woman who says she was battered yet stayed with her batterer was either not as badly beaten as she claimed or else she liked it. Nevertheless, to the extent that her failure to leave the abusive relationship earlier may be used in support of the proposition that she was free to leave at the final moment, expert testimony can provide useful insights. ...

The same psychological factors that account for a woman's inability to leave a battering relationship may also help to explain why she did not attempt to escape at the moment she perceived her life to be in danger. The following extract from Dr. Shane's testimony on direct examination elucidates this point:

> Q. Now, we understand from the evidence that on this night she went—I think you've already described it in your evidence—and hid in the closet?
>
> A. Yes.
>
> Q. Can you tell the jury why she, for instance, would stay in that house if she had this fear? Why wouldn't she [go] someplace else? Why would she have to hide in the closet in the same house?
>
> A. Well, I think this is a reflection of what I've been talking about, this ongoing psychological process, her own psychology and the relationship, that she felt trapped. There was no out for her, this learned helplessness, if you will, the fact that she felt paralyzed, she felt

tyrannized. She felt, although there were obviously no steel fences around, keeping her in, there were steel fences in her mind which created for her an incredible barrier psychologically that prevented her from moving out. Although she had attempted on occasion, she came back in a magnetic sort of a way. And she felt also that she couldn't expect anything more. Not only this learned helplessness about being beaten, beaten, where her motivation is taken away, but her whole sense of herself. She felt this victim mentality, this concentration camp mentality if you will, where she could not see herself be in any other situation except being tyrannized, punished and crucified physically and psychologically.

Of course, as Dr. Ewing adds, environmental factors may also impair the woman's ability to leave—lack of job skills, the presence of children to care for, fear of retaliation by the man, etc., may each have a role to play in some cases.

I emphasize at this juncture that it is not for the jury to pass judgment on the fact that an accused battered woman stayed in the relationship. Still less is it entitled to conclude that she forfeited her right to self-defence for having done so. I would also point out that traditional self-defence doctrine does not require a person to retreat from her home instead of defending herself: *R. v. Antley*, [1964] 2 C.C.C. 142, [1964] 1 O.R. 545, 42 C.R. 384 (C.A.). A man's home may be his castle but it is also the woman's home even if it seems to her more like a prison in the circumstances.

If, after hearing the evidence (including the expert testimony), the jury is satisfied that the accused had a reasonable apprehension of death or grievous bodily harm and felt incapable of escape, it must ask itself what the "reasonable person" would do in such a situation. The situation of the battered woman as described by Dr. Shane strikes me as somewhat analogous to that of a hostage. If the captor tells her that he will kill her in three days time, is it potentially reasonable for her to seize an opportunity presented on the first day to kill the captor or must she wait until he makes the attempt on the third day? I think the question the jury must ask itself is whether, given the history, circumstances and perceptions of the appellant, her belief that she could not preserve herself from being killed by Rust that night except by killing him first was reasonable. To the extent that expert evidence can assist the jury in making that determination, I would find such testimony to be both relevant and necessary. ...

Obviously the fact that the appellant was a battered woman does not entitle her to an acquittal. Battered women may well kill their partners other than in self-defence. The focus is not on who the woman is, but on what she did. In "The Meaning of Equality for Battered Women Who Kill Men in Self-Defence" (1985) 8 *Harv. Women's L.J.* 121, 149, Phyllis Crocker makes the point succinctly:

> The issue in a self-defence trial is not whether the defendant is a battered woman, but whether she justifiably killed her husband. The defendant introduces testimony to offer the jury an explanation of reasonableness that is an alternative to the prosecution's stereotypic explanations. It is not intended to earn her the status of a battered woman, as if that would make her not guilty. ...

Ultimately, it is up to the jury to decide whether, *in fact*, the accused's perceptions and actions were reasonable. Expert evidence does not and cannot usurp that function of the jury. The jury is not compelled to accept the opinions proffered by the expert about the effects of battering on the mental state of victims generally or on the mental state of the accused in particular. But fairness and the integrity of the trial process demand that the jury have the opportunity to hear them.

[The appeal was allowed and the verdict of acquittal restored. Dickson CJ and Lamer, L'Heureux-Dubé, Gonthier, and McLachlin JJ concurred with Wilson J. Sopinka J wrote a concurring opinion on a separate issue.]

The principles enunciated by Justice Wilson in *Lavallee* were discussed and applied in the following decision, which focuses on how previous threats made by the deceased may be relevant to the reasonableness of a battered woman's perceptions and response.

R v Pétel
Supreme Court of Canada
[1994] 1 SCR 3

[The accused, Colette Pétel, was charged with and convicted of second-degree murder in the killing of Alain Raymond on July 21, 1989. Raymond worked with Serge Edsell in the drug trade and since May 1989, Edsell had lived with the accused, her daughter, and her granddaughter. The accused testified that Edsell threatened her frequently and beat her daughter during this time.

On July 21, 1989 Edsell went to the accused's house, gave her his weapon to hide, forced her to weigh some cocaine, and threatened to kill her, her daughter, and her granddaughter. After consuming a small amount of drugs, the accused shot and wounded Edsell and, perceiving Raymond to be lunging at her, shot and killed him. During their deliberations, the jury asked whether threats or acts taking place in the months prior to July were relevant to determining whether the accused acted in self-defence under s 34(2). The judge replied:

> [T]hese earlier acts or threats help you to determine whether Alain Raymond or Serge Edsell attempted or threatened, because according to the evidence, if you believe it, this was a common plan, whether as I say Alain Raymond or Serge Edsell attempted or threatened on the evening of July 21, by an act or a gesture, to apply force to Mrs. Pétel, to her daughter or to her granddaughter, whether the assailant had or caused the alleged victim to believe on reasonable grounds that he had present ability to effect his purpose.
>
> So the previous facts help you to assess the situation, but the threat or the assault or the threat or the gesture that evening, in the context of ... the carrying out of an assault, that must be assessed on July 21.]

LAMER CJ (Sopinka, Cory, McLachlin, and Iacobucci JJ concurring): The accused appealed her conviction to the Court of Appeal. She argued that the charge to the jury on self-defence was erroneous. She submitted that the judge should have said that the previous threats were relevant in determining not only whether the victims threatened the accused and had present ability to effect their purpose, but also, which he failed to do, in determining the accused's state of mind regarding the imminence of the assault and the belief that she could not otherwise preserve herself from death. The accused based her arguments on *R. v. Lavallee*, [1990] 1 S.C.R. 852. ...

It can be seen from the wording of s. 34(2) of the *Code* that there are three constituent elements of self-defence, when as here the victim has died: (1) the existence of an unlawful assault; (2) a reasonable apprehension of a risk of death or grievous bodily harm; and (3) a reasonable belief that it is not possible to preserve oneself from harm except by killing the adversary.

In all three cases the jury must seek to determine how the accused perceived the relevant facts and whether that perception was reasonable. Accordingly, this is an objective determination. With respect to the last two elements, this approach results from the language used in the *Code* and was confirmed by this Court in *Reilly v. The Queen*, [1984] 2 S.C.R. 396, at p. 404:

> The subsection can only afford protection to the accused if he apprehended death or grievous bodily harm from the assault he was repelling and if he believed he could not preserve himself from death or grievous bodily harm otherwise than by the force he used. Nonetheless, his apprehension must be a *reasonable* one and his belief must *be based upon reasonable and probable grounds*. The subsection requires that the jury consider, and be guided by, what they decide on the evidence was the accused's appreciation of the situation and his belief as to the reaction it required, so long as there exists an objectively verifiable basis for his perception. [Emphasis in original.]

Some doubt may still exist as to whether this passage from *Reilly* also applies to the existence of an assault. For my part, I think that the word "situation" refers to the three elements of s. 34(2). An honest but reasonable mistake as to the existence of an assault is therefore permitted. ... The existence of an assault must not be made a kind of prerequisite for the exercise of self-defence to be assessed without regard to the perception of the accused. This would amount in a sense to trying the victim before the accused. In a case involving self-defence, it is the accused's state of mind that must be examined, and it is the accused (and not the victim) who must be given the benefit of a reasonable doubt. The question that the jury must ask itself is therefore not "was the accused unlawfully assaulted?" but rather "did the accused reasonably believe, in the circumstances, that she was being unlawfully assaulted?"

Moreover, *Lavallee, supra*, rejected the rule requiring that the apprehended danger be imminent. This alleged rule, which does not appear anywhere in the text of the *Criminal Code*, is in fact only a mere assumption based on common sense. As Wilson J. noted in *Lavallee*, this assumption undoubtedly derives from the paradigmatic case of self-defence, which is an altercation between two persons of equal strength. However, evidence may be presented (in particular expert evidence) to rebut this presumption of fact. There is thus no formal requirement that the danger be imminent. Imminence is only one of the factors which the jury should weigh in determining whether the accused had a reasonable apprehension of danger and a reasonable belief that she could not extricate herself otherwise than by killing the attacker.

[The chief justice found that the trial judge had made the following errors in his reply to the jury.]

First, the judge's answer suggested that the only relevance of the threats prior to July 21 was in enabling the jury to determine whether there had actually been an assault on the evening of July 21, that is, in the present case, death threats, and whether the assailant was in a position to carry out those threats. This in my view diverted the jury from the question it really should have been considering, namely the reasonable belief of the accused in the existence of an assault. Emphasizing the victims' acts rather than the accused's state of mind has the effect of depriving the latter of the benefit of any error, however reasonable. The jury's attention should not be diverted from its proper concern, the guilt of the accused, by an inquiry into the guilt of the victim.

Secondly, and this is the crucial point, the judge's answer might have led the jury to believe that the threats made before July 21 could serve no other purpose than to determine the existence of the assault and the assailant's ability, thus denying their relevance to reasonable apprehension of a danger of death or grievous bodily harm and to the belief that there was no solution but to kill the attacker.

The importance of failing to relate the earlier threats to the elements of self-defence cannot be underestimated. The threats made by Edsell throughout his cohabitation with the respondent are very relevant in determining whether the respondent had a reasonable apprehension of danger and a reasonable belief in the need to kill Edsell and Raymond. The threats prior to July 21 form an integral part of the circumstances on which the perception of the accused might have been based. The judge's answer to this question might thus have led the jury to disregard the entire atmosphere of terror which the respondent said pervaded her house. It is clear that the way in which a reasonable person would have acted cannot be assessed without taking into account these crucial circumstances. As Wilson J. noted in *Lavallee*, at p. 883:

> The issue is not, however, what an outsider would have reasonably perceived but what the accused reasonably perceived, given her situation and her experience.

By unduly limiting the relevance of the previous threats the judge in a sense invited the jury to determine what an outsider would have done in the same situation as the respondent.

The undisputed evidence that Edsell, her alleged attacker, handed over his weapon and asked his future victim to hide it, conduct that is odd to say the least for someone intending to kill, must have had a clear effect on the jury, indeed on any jury composed of reasonable individuals. In the Court of Appeal and in this Court, however, counsel for the Crown did not argue that, given the evidence in this case, no substantial wrong or miscarriage of justice occurred, and that s. 686(1)(b)(iii) of the *Criminal Code* should thus be applied. The Crown has the burden of showing that this provision is applicable: *Colpitts v. The Queen*, [1965] S.C.R. 739. This Court cannot apply it *proprio motu*. Having found an error of law in the judge's answer to the question by the jury, I must accordingly dismiss the appeal and affirm the order for a new trial.

[Gonthier J (La Forest, L'Heureux-Dubé, and Major JJ concurring) agreed with the chief justice's statement of the relevant law, but found no error in the judge's instructions to the jury and would have upheld the conviction.]

Appeal dismissed.

After years of lobbying by the Canadian Association of Elizabeth Fry Societies, the federal government appointed Justice Lynn Ratushny to conduct an inquiry of convicted women who might have benefited from the development in *Lavallee*. Justice Ratushny reviewed a total of 98 cases. She delivered her report in 1997, making recommendations about individual cases, and about the law in general: see Lynn Ratushny, *The Self-Defence Review—Final Report* (Ottawa: Department of Justice Canada, 1997). Justice Ratushny recommended relief in only seven of these cases. Ultimately, the federal government granted conditional pardons to two women (both of whom had already completed their sentences) and remission of the sentence of two others (both of whom had already been released on parole), referring a fifth case to the appropriate Court of Appeal. For a discussion of this report, see E Sheehy, "Review of the Self-Defence Review" (2000) 12 CJWL 197 and GT Trotter, "Justice, Politics and the Royal Prerogative of Mercy: Examining the Self-Defence Review" (2001) 26 Queen's LJ 339.

A rich literature has developed on the issue of battered woman syndrome: see e.g. EA Sheehy, *Defending Battered Women on Trial: Lessons from the Transcripts* (Vancouver: University of British Columbia Press, 2014); M Shaffer, "The Battered Woman Syndrome Revisited: Some Complicating Thoughts Five Years After R v Lavallee" (1997) 47 UTLJ 1; C Wells, "Battered Woman Syndrome and Defences to Homicide: Where Now?" (1994) 14 LS 266; I Leader-Elliott, "Battered but Not Beaten: Women Who Kill in Self-Defence" (1993) 15 Sydney L Rev 403; E Sheehy, J Stubbs & J Tolmie, "Defending Battered Women on Trial: The Battered Woman Syndrome and Its Limitations" (1992) 16 Crim LJ 369; C Boyle, "The Battered Wife Syndrome and Self-Defence: Lavallee v The Queen" (1990) 9 Can J of Fam L 171; and M Shaffer, "R v Lavallee: A Review Essay" (1990) 22 Ottawa L Rev 607.

An important concern raised post-*Lavallee* was that the case might be read as requiring battered women to exhibit traits that would fit them within a "syndrome," turning their perspectives and reactions in the circumstances into a kind of pathology, in order to have their experiences considered in the test for self-defence. Consider this extract from an article written by Professor Isabel Grant in the year after the *Lavallee* decision.

I Grant, "The Syndromization of Women's Experience"
(1991) 25 UBC L Rev 51 at 51-53 (footnotes omitted)

A fundamental problem with developing a category like the "battered woman syndrome" is that we risk transforming the reality of this form of gender oppression into a psychiatric disorder. The victim of spousal violence becomes the abnormal actor, the one whose conduct must be explained by an expert. When a woman uses force to defend herself, it is evaluated with reference to a male standard of reasonableness or to an exceptional standard for certain women, i.e. those who are "battered women." The focus is on the irrationality of a woman's response and on the need for medical terminology to transform that irrational response into a reasonable one for a "battered woman." She must either be reasonable "like a man" or reasonable "like a battered woman." Trapped in this dichotomy, the reasonable woman may disappear.

The element of the "battered woman syndrome" that is most likely to be associated with a form of mental abnormality is the concept of "learned helplessness." This term was originally coined to describe the behaviour of laboratory animals who have learned that their responses to negative stimuli had no impact on the environment around them. In the "battered woman" context, it refers to a woman's perceived inability to extricate herself from the battering environment. The woman is portrayed as helpless and choiceless.

> When a woman charged with murdering an abusive spouse is asserting a claim of self-defence, evidence is needed to show why the killing might have been a reasonable action. It is not clear why proof of prior helplessness is necessary. The focus on evidence of prior helplessness reflects our implicit acceptance of the stereotype that women must be abnormal if they do not leave an abusive relationship and that women who stay in such relationships should expect, tolerate (or perhaps even enjoy) violence.

It is not necessarily a "battered woman's" helplessness that renders her killing reasonable; it is the repetition and regularity of the abuse to which she has been subject and her perception of the threat to her life or safety. By relying on a syndrome explained by a psychiatrist to interpret the "perceived threat" we implicitly send the message that, without this evidence, the woman's perception of reality would not be trusted as reasonable.

There is a basic contradiction in using expert testimony on "battered woman syndrome" to justify a claim of self-defence for a woman who kills an abusive spouse. On the one hand, evidence of "battered woman syndrome" is used to portray the woman as weak and helpless; unable to escape the man who has dominated her. On the other hand, this evidence is being used to explain one instance where the woman did act to preserve her own safety. The act of killing is not the act of a "helpless" woman.

A woman who kills her batterer should not necessarily be seen as acting abnormally or pursuant to a psychiatric condition. In a situation where a woman is repeatedly beaten and threatened there may well be no other way out. It may have been quite rational for Ms. Lavallee to believe she had to kill her abuser to protect her own life. The fact that Ms. Lavallee remained in an abusive relationship does not mean she abandoned her right to defend herself.

These concerns were taken up in the concurring decision of Justice L'Heureux-Dubé in the following case, one that also provides a helpful review of the *Lavallee* decision.

R v Malott
Supreme Court of Canada
[1998] 1 SCR 123

MAJOR J (Lamer CJ and McLachlin, Cory, and Iacobucci JJ concurring):
[1] This appeal raises the adequacy of the trial judge's charge to the jury on the issue of battered woman syndrome as a defence to the charge of murder.

I. Facts

[2] The appellant, Margaret Ann Malott, and the deceased, Paul Malott, were common law spouses for about 19 years and had two children together. The appellant had previously been married for seven years to a man who violently abused her and their five children.

Mr. Malott abused Mrs. Malott physically, sexually, psychologically and emotionally. She had gone to the police, but Mr. Malott was a police informant on drug deals and the police told him of her complaints, resulting in an escalation of his violence towards her. A few months before the shooting, Mr. Malott separated from the appellant, took their son and went to live with his girlfriend, Carrie Sherwood. Mrs. Malott and their daughter continued to live at Mr. Malott's mother's house. Contact between Mr. and Mrs. Malott continued after the separation, as he dropped by his mother's home on a regular basis, often bringing Ms. Sherwood with him.

[3] On March 23, 1991, Mrs. Malott was scheduled to go to a medical centre with the deceased to get prescription drugs for use in the deceased's illegal drug trade. She took a .22 calibre pistol from Mr. Malott's gun cabinet, loaded it and carried it in her purse. After driving to the medical centre with Mr. Malott, she shot him to death. She then took a taxi to Ms. Sherwood's home, shot her and stabbed her with a knife. Ms. Sherwood survived and testified as a Crown witness.

[4] At trial, the appellant testified to the extensive abuse which she had suffered. The Crown conceded that the appellant had been subject to terrible physical and mental abuse at the hands of Mr. Malott. The appellant led expert evidence to show that she suffered from battered woman syndrome. The appellant raised three defences: self-defence, drug-induced intoxication and provocation, but relied primarily on self-defence. The jury found the appellant guilty of second degree murder in the death of Paul Malott and of attempted murder of Carrie Sherwood. The jury made a recommendation that because of the severity of the battered woman syndrome, the appellant should receive the minimum sentence.

[5] The appellant appealed both convictions. The appeal was heard by the Ontario Court of Appeal on May 28, 1996. [The Court of Appeal dismissed the appeal.] It is only the conviction for second degree murder of the deceased that is before this Court.

[Justice Major reviewed the majority decision in *Pétel*, which confirmed a subjective-objective approach to the three elements of self-defence under s 34(2). He continued, summarizing the relevance of expert evidence of battered woman syndrome to a claim of self-defence.]

[20] The admissibility of expert evidence respecting battered woman syndrome was not at issue in the present case. The admissibility of the expert evidence of Dr. Jaffe on battered woman syndrome was not challenged. However, once that defence is raised, the jury ought to be made aware of the principles of that defence as dictated by *Lavallee*. In particular, the jury should be informed of how that evidence may be of use in understanding the following:

1. Why an abused woman might remain in an abusive relationship. As discussed in *Lavallee*, expert evidence may help to explain some of the reasons and dispel some of the misconceptions about why women stay in abusive relationships.

2. The nature and extent of the violence that may exist in a battering relationship. In considering the defence of self-defence as it applies to an accused who has killed her violent partner, the jury should be instructed on the violence that existed in the relationship and its impact on the accused. The latter will usually but not necessarily be provided by an expert.

3. The accused's ability to perceive danger from her abuser. Section 34(2)(a) provides that an accused who intentionally causes death or grievous bodily harm in repelling an assault is justified if he or she does so "under reasonable apprehension of death or grievous bodily harm." In addressing this issue, Wilson J. for the majority in *Lavallee* rejected the requirement that the accused apprehend imminent danger. She also stated at pp. 882-83:

> Where evidence exists that an accused is in a battering relationship, expert testimony can assist the jury in determining whether the accused had a "reasonable" apprehension of death when she acted by explaining the heightened sensitivity of a battered woman to her partner's acts. Without such testimony I am skeptical that the average fact-finder would be capable of appreciating why her subjective fear may have been reasonable in the context of the relationship. After all, the hypothetical "reasonable man" observing only the final incident may have been unlikely to recognize the batterer's threat as potentially lethal. ...
>
> The issue is not, however, what an outsider would have reasonably perceived but what the accused reasonably perceived, given her situation and her experience.

4. Whether the accused believed on reasonable grounds that she could not otherwise preserve herself from death or grievous bodily harm. This principle was summarized in *Lavallee* as follows (at p. 890):

> By providing an explanation as to why an accused did not flee when she perceived her life to be in danger, expert testimony may also assist the jury in assessing the reasonableness of her belief that killing her batterer was the only way to save her own life.

[21] These principles must be communicated by the trial judge when instructing the jury in cases involving battered woman syndrome and the issue of self-defence.

C. Jury Charge in This Case

[22] In the present case, I am satisfied that the trial judge properly charged the jury with respect to the evidence on battered woman syndrome and how such evidence relates to the law of self-defence. ...

[31] My conclusion that the jury charge was adequate does not mean it was flawless. As with most jury charges, there is room for debate. In particular, it could be argued that it may have been desirable for the trial judge to have instructed the jury to a greater extent in making the connection between the evidence of battered woman syndrome and the legal issue of self-defence. However, in reviewing the trial judge's charge as a whole, I am satisfied that the jury were left with a sufficient understanding of the facts as they related to the relevant legal issues. ...

VI. Disposition

[34] The appeal is dismissed.

L'HEUREUX-DUBÉ J (McLachlin J concurring):

[35] I have read the reasons of my colleague Justice Major, and I concur with the result that he reaches. However, given that this Court has not had the opportunity to discuss the value of evidence of "battered woman syndrome" since *R. v. Lavallee*, [1990] 1 S.C.R. 852, and given the evolving discourse on "battered woman syndrome" in the legal community, I will make a few comments on the importance of this kind of evidence to the just adjudication of charges involving battered women.

[36] First, the significance of this Court's decision in *Lavallee*, which first accepted the need for expert evidence on the effects of abusive relationships in order to properly understand the context in which an accused woman had killed her abusive spouse in self-defence, reaches beyond its particular impact on the law of self-defence. A crucial implication of the admissibility of expert evidence in *Lavallee* is the legal recognition that historically both the law and society may have treated women in general, and battered women in particular, unfairly. *Lavallee* accepted that the myths and stereotypes which are the products and the tools of this unfair treatment interfere with the capacity of judges and juries to justly determine a battered woman's claim of self-defence, and can only be dispelled by expert evidence designed to overcome the stereotypical thinking. The expert evidence is admissible, and necessary, in order to understand the reasonableness of a battered woman's perceptions, which in *Lavallee* were the accused's perceptions that she had to act with deadly force in order to preserve herself from death or grievous bodily harm. Accordingly, the utility of such evidence in criminal cases is not limited to instances where a battered woman is pleading self-defence, but is potentially relevant to other situations where the reasonableness of a battered woman's actions or perceptions is at issue (e.g. provocation, duress or necessity). See *R. v. Hibbert*, [1995] 2 S.C.R. 973, at p. 1021.

[37] It is clear from the foregoing that "battered woman syndrome" is not a legal defence in itself such that an accused woman need only establish that she is suffering from the syndrome in order to gain an acquittal. As Wilson J. commented in *Lavallee*, at p. 890: "Obviously the fact that the appellant was a battered woman does not entitle her to an acquittal. Battered women may well kill their partners other than in self-defence." Rather, "battered woman syndrome" is a psychiatric explanation of the mental state of women who have been subjected to continuous battering by their male intimate partners, which can be relevant to the legal inquiry into a battered woman's state of mind.

[38] Second, the majority of the Court in *Lavallee* also implicitly accepted that women's experiences and perspectives may be different from the experiences and perspectives of men. It accepted that a woman's perception of what is reasonable is influenced by her gender, as well as by her individual experience, and both are relevant to the legal inquiry. This legal development was significant, because it demonstrated a willingness to look at the whole context of a woman's experience in order to inform the analysis of the particular events. But it is wrong to think of this development of the law as merely an example where an objective test—the requirement that an accused claiming self-defence must reasonably apprehend death or grievous bodily harm—has been modified to admit evidence of the subjective perceptions of a battered woman. More important, a majority of the Court accepted that the perspectives of women, which have historically been ignored, must now equally inform the "objective" standard of the reasonable person in relation to self-defence.

[39] When interpreting and applying *Lavallee*, these broader principles should be kept in mind. In particular, they should be kept in mind in order to avoid a too rigid and restrictive approach to the admissibility and legal value of evidence of a battered woman's experiences. Concerns have been expressed that the treatment of expert evidence on battered women syndrome, which is itself admissible in order to combat the myths and stereotypes which society has about battered women, has led to a new stereotype of the "battered woman": see, e.g., Martha Shaffer, "The battered woman syndrome revisited: Some complicating thoughts five years after *R. v. Lavallee*" (1997), 47 U.T.L.J. 1, at p. 9; Sheila Noonan, "Strategies of Survival: Moving Beyond the Battered Woman Syndrome," in Ellen Adelberg and Claudia Currie, eds., In Conflict with the Law: Women and the Canadian Justice System (1993), 247, at p. 254; Isabel Grant, "The 'syndromization' of women's experience," in Donna Martinson et al., "A Forum on Lavallee v. R.: Women and Self-Defence" (1991), 25 U.B.C. L. Rev. 23, 51, at pp. 53-54; and Martha R. Mahoney, "Legal Images of Battered Women: Redefining the Issue of Separation" (1991), 90 Mich. L. Rev. 1, at p. 42.

[40] It is possible that those women who are unable to fit themselves within the stereotype of a victimized, passive, helpless, dependent, battered woman will not have their claims to self-defence fairly decided. For instance, women who have demonstrated too much strength or initiative, women of colour, women who are professionals, or women who might have fought back against their abusers on previous occasions, should not be penalized for failing to accord with the stereotypical image of the archetypal battered woman. See, e.g., Julie Stubbs and Julia Tolmie, "Race, Gender, and the Battered Woman Syndrome: An Australia Case Study" (1995), 8 C.J.W.L. 122. Needless to say, women with these characteristics are still entitled to have their claims of self-defence fairly adjudicated, and they are also still entitled to have their experiences as battered women inform the analysis. Professor Grant, supra, at p. 52, warns against allowing the law to develop such that a woman accused of killing her abuser must either have been "reasonable 'like a man' or reasonable 'like a battered woman.'" I agree that this must be avoided. The "reasonable woman" must not be forgotten in the analysis, and deserves to be as much a part of the objective standard of the reasonable person as does the "reasonable man."

[41] How should the courts combat the "syndromization," as Professor Grant refers to it, of battered women who act in self-defence? The legal inquiry into the moral culpability of a woman who is, for instance, claiming self-defence must focus on the reasonableness of her actions in the context of her personal experiences, and her experiences as a woman, not on her status as a battered woman and her entitlement to claim that she is suffering from "battered woman syndrome." This point has been made convincingly by many academics reviewing the relevant cases: see, e.g., Wendy Chan, "A Feminist Critique of Self-Defense and Provocation in Battered Women's Cases in England and Wales" (1994), 6 Women & Crim. Just. 39, at pp. 56-57; Elizabeth M. Schneider, "Describing and Changing: Women's Self-Defense Work and the Problem of Expert Testimony on Battering" (1992), 14 Women's Rts. L. Rep. 213, at pp. 216-17; and Marilyn MacCrimmon, "The social construction of reality and the rules of evidence," in Donna Martinson et al., supra, 36, at pp. 48-49. By emphasizing a woman's "learned helplessness," her dependence, her victimization, and her low self-esteem, in order to establish that she suffers from "battered woman syndrome," the legal debate shifts from the objective rationality of her actions to preserve her own life to those personal inadequacies which apparently explain her failure

to flee from her abuser. Such an emphasis comports too well with society's stereotypes about women. Therefore, it should be scrupulously avoided because it only serves to undermine the important advancements achieved by the decision in *Lavallee*.

[42] There are other elements of a woman's social context which help to explain her inability to leave her abuser, and which do not focus on those characteristics most consistent with traditional stereotypes. As Wilson J. herself recognized in *Lavallee*, at p. 887, "environmental factors may also impair the woman's ability to leave—lack of job skills, the presence of children to care for, fear of retaliation by the man, etc. may each have a role to play in some cases." To this list of factors I would add a woman's need to protect her children from abuse, a fear of losing custody of her children, pressures to keep the family together, weaknesses of social and financial support for battered women, and no guarantee that the violence would cease simply because she left. These considerations necessarily inform the reasonableness of a woman's beliefs or perceptions of, for instance, her lack of an alternative to the use of deadly force to preserve herself from death or grievous bodily harm.

[43] How should these principles be given practical effect in the context of a jury trial of a woman accused of murdering her abuser? To fully accord with the spirit of *Lavallee*, where the reasonableness of a battered woman's belief is at issue in a criminal case, a judge and jury should be made to appreciate that a battered woman's experiences are both individualized, based on her own history and relationships, as well as shared with other women, within the context of a society and a legal system which has historically undervalued women's experiences. A judge and jury should be told that a battered woman's experiences are generally outside the common understanding of the average judge and juror, and that they should seek to understand the evidence being presented to them in order to overcome the myths and stereotypes which we all share. Finally, all of this should be presented in such a way as to focus on the reasonableness of the woman's actions, without relying on old or new stereotypes about battered women.

[44] My focus on women as the victims of battering and as the subjects of "battered woman syndrome" is not intended to exclude from consideration those men who find themselves in abusive relationships. However, the reality of our society is that typically, it is women who are the victims of domestic violence, at the hands of their male intimate partners. To assume that men who are victims of spousal abuse are affected by the abuse in the same way, without benefit of the research and expert opinion evidence which has informed the courts of the existence and details of "battered woman syndrome," would be imprudent.

[45] In the present appeal, it was uncontested that Margaret Ann Malott suffered years of horrible emotional, psychological, physical and sexual abuse at the hands of her husband, Paul Malott. Dr. Peter Jaffe, the psychologist who testified on Mrs. Malott's behalf, described her as having "one of the most severe cases" of battered woman syndrome that he had ever seen. I agree with Abella J.A. that in such circumstances, the trial judge could have more expansively explained and emphasized the relevance of the expert evidence on battered woman syndrome to Mrs. Malott's claim of self-defence. In this connection, the trial judge's charge to the jury was not perfect. But as my colleague Major J. correctly points out at para. 15, it is unrealistic for an appeal court to review a trial judge's charge to a jury based on a standard of perfection. In deference to this well-established principle,

I agree with Major J.'s conclusion that the charge was sufficient. For these reasons, I would dismiss the appeal.

Courts have taken the core idea from *Lavallee*—that "reasonableness" for the purposes of self-defence must be assessed in light of the experiences and position of the accused—and have applied that principle in settings beyond domestic violence.

- In *R v McConnell*, [1996] 1 SCR 1075, the Supreme Court of Canada endorsed the reasons of Conrad JA, dissenting at the Alberta Court of Appeal, in a case involving a federal inmate charged with first-degree murder. The accused testified that he thought that another group of inmates was going to kill him and he decided to take pre-emptive action. Justice Conrad accepted expert evidence of "prison environment syndrome" as establishing that "a person could believe he or she was being assaulted (a threat with present ability) without it being immediate": *R v McConnell*, 1995 ABCA 291 at para 77, 32 Alta LR (3d) 1.

- In *R v Kagan*, 2004 NSCA 77, 185 CCC (3d) 417, the accused was charged with the aggravated assault of his university roommate and claimed that he had acted in self-defence. The Nova Scotia Court of Appeal accepted forensic psychiatric evidence that the accused was suffering from Asperger's Syndrome, a form of high-functioning autism, and that this condition could have affected his perception of the situation. In particular, the jury ought to have been instructed that the effects of Asperger's should be considered when assessing whether the accused had a reasonable apprehension of grievous bodily harm or death and believed, on reasonable grounds, that there was no other means to protect himself.

- In *R v Nelson* (1992), 71 CCC (3d) 449, the Ontario Court of Appeal, relying heavily upon *Lavallee*, held that evidence of an accused's diminished intellectual capacity is a factor that is properly taken into account in applying s 34(2). A person with diminished intelligence, the court reasoned, "may be in a position similar to that of the accused in *Lavallee* in that his or her apprehension and belief could not be fairly measured against the perceptions of an 'ordinary man'" (at 467). Associate Chief Justice Morden explained that not every variation in the intellectual ability of an accused should be taken into account when assessing self-defence. Rather, his conclusion was that "where the accused has an intellectual impairment, not within his or her control, which relates to his or her ability to perceive and react to events—an impairment that clearly takes him or her out of the broad band of normal adult intellectual capacity—I think the deficit should be taken into account" (at 469).

One can readily discern the influence of *Lavallee* and subsequent cases—and, with this, the impact of the arguments and efforts made by feminist law reformers since the 1980s—on Parliament's amendments to the law of self-defence (see V MacDonnell, "The New Self-Defence Law: Progressive Development or Status Quo?" (2014) 92 Can Bar Rev 301). At a general level, the new s 34 mandates that the reasonableness of an accused's self-defensive act must be assessed in light of "the relevant circumstances of the person, the other parties and the act." This is a flexible and contextual test that avoids some of the bright-line rules (such as the judicially created imminence requirement) that troubled the law in the past.

More specifically, the listed factors to be considered include "the size, age, gender and physical capabilities of the parties to the incident" (s 34(2)(e)); "the nature, duration and history of any relationship between the parties to the incident, including any prior use or threat of force and the nature of that force or threat" (s 34(2)(f)); and "any history of interaction or communication between the parties to the incident" (s 34(2)(f.1)). These provisions go some distance toward absorbing the principles established in *Lavallee*, *Pétel*, and *Malott* into the self-defence scheme.

As this section has shown, a better crafted, interpreted, and applied law of self-defence is important. And yet the criminal law is ultimately limited in its ability to address the root causes of gendered violence. In *Defending Battered Women on Trial: Lessons from the Transcripts* (Vancouver: University of British Columbia Press, 2014), Elizabeth Sheehy offers a generally positive assessment of the new legislation in light of the lessons of her study, but also provides this crucial reminder (at 318, footnotes omitted):

> Most importantly, women's equality—economically, politically, legally, and socially—is a necessary condition for the elimination of male violence and women's need to resort to homicide to extricate themselves. In a speech given to the Canadian Bar Association a year after the *Lavallee* decision was released, Justice Wilson said that "[t]he economic, political and social inequality of women both fuels and justifies violence against women in society which values power over all else." As long as women are systematically subordinated to men, "they will suffer, at the minimum, ongoing physical domination and, at the maximum, physical and sexual abuse."
>
> Evan Stark and Anne Flitcraft argue that we must do more than protect women's safety, for what is safety without freedom? They state that "enormous hazards lie ahead if shelter is promoted as a concealed refuge from the violence of male-dominated family life, shelter occupants are defined as victims rather than as survivors, safety is emphasized over liberation, and a simulation of community is offered in lieu of direct challenges to existing community power structures." It is indisputable that societies in which women enjoy greater equality also record lower rates of male violence. We simply cannot expect to reduce or eliminate wife battering through criminal justice initiatives: we must support women's aspirations for freedom and equality and reshape our social, economic, legal, and political policies accordingly. There is no shortcut.

IV. DEFENCE OF PROPERTY

Among the amendments to the *Criminal Code* introduced in 2012 were relaxations to the law of citizen's arrest and a new provision governing defence of property. These amendments arose in the wake of highly publicized incidents involving small-business owners seeking to defend their stores from shoplifters.

The old provisions drew a distinction between defence of dwelling houses and defence of personal property. The new s 35 is not as structured and predictable as the old provisions, but provides a single, simple scheme for defence of property. It provides as follows:

> 35(1) A person is not guilty of an offence if
>
> (a) they either believe on reasonable grounds that they are in peaceable possession of property or are acting under the authority of, or lawfully assisting, a person whom they believe on reasonable grounds is in peaceable possession of property;
>
> (b) they believe on reasonable grounds that another person

(i) is about to enter, is entering or has entered the property without being entitled by law to do so,

(ii) is about to take the property, is doing so or has just done so, or

(iii) is about to damage or destroy the property, or make it inoperative, or is doing so;

(c) the act that constitutes the offence is committed for the purpose of

(i) preventing the other person from entering the property, or removing that person from the property, or

(ii) preventing the other person from taking, damaging or destroying the property or from making it inoperative, or retaking the property from that person; and

(d) the act committed is reasonable in the circumstances.

(2) Subsection (1) does not apply if the person who believes on reasonable grounds that they are, or who is believed on reasonable grounds to be, in peaceable possession of the property does not have a claim of right to it and the other person is entitled to its possession by law.

(3) Subsection (1) does not apply if the other person is doing something that they are required or authorized by law to do in the administration or enforcement of the law, unless the person who commits the act that constitutes the offence believes on reasonable grounds that the other person is acting unlawfully.

This section mimics many of the features of s 34, employing a mixed subjective-objective approach that focuses on whether "the act committed is reasonable in the circumstances." Like s 34, this defence is not limited to assaults; rather, it applies to any "offence" committed when an accused satisfies the four conditions outlined in s 35(1).

Although there is no list of contextual factors and considerations akin to s 34(2), on principle one would think a similar set of factors would have to inform the assessment of whether any act committed in defence of property is "reasonable in the circumstances." For example, it seems crucial that courts scrutinize the "nature and proportionality" of an accused's response to a threat to property. Consider *R v Szczerbaniwicz*, 2010 SCC 15, [2010] 1 SCR 455. In the course of an argument, the accused's wife threw his framed university diploma to the floor. He responded by pushing her "with such force that she landed on the staircase and sustained extensive bruises" (at para 23). The accused argued that his use of force was in defence of his property, but he was convicted at trial. On appeal, he argued that the court had failed to properly apply the "no more force than necessary" requirement, which was then a part of the law, by underemphasizing his subjective perceptions. Justice Abella, for the majority of the Supreme Court, rejected his appeal, characterizing the case as one "about a husband who lost his temper in an argument" and finding that the trial judge's finding that his use of force was disproportionate was "eminently justified" (at para 147). Justice Binnie, dissenting, described the accused's actions as "both morally objectionable and deeply unfortunate" (at para 34), but would have concluded that he was "acting in defence of property that was of considerable sentimental importance to him, as Mrs. Szczerbaniwicz fully appreciated at the time" (at para 35). He emphasized that "[t]he cases are clear that in these sort of 'quick response' situations an accused is not expected to 'weigh to a nicety' the exact measure of a defensive action or to stop and reflect upon the precise risk of consequences from such action" (at para 35).

For further discussion and interpretation of s 35, see K Roach, *Criminal Law*, 5th ed (Toronto: Irwin Law, 2012) at 342-51. He writes (at 343) that

[t]he omission of the concept of justification is more than a theoretical quibble with respect to the defence of property because the new section 35 omits the concept of using no more force than necessary that was found in the old defence of property provisions. … Section 35 does not specifically require the proportionality of the response be considered as one of the relevant factors in determining whether an act done to defend property is reasonable in their circumstances.

Should the law require proportionality between the harm inflicted and the harm avoided in claims of defence of property? Do you think that *Szczerbaniwicz* would be (or should be) decided differently under the new s 35?

ADDITIONAL READING

Brudner, A. "Constitutionalizing Self-Defence" (2011) 61 UTLJ 867.

Colvin, E & S Anand. *Principles of Criminal Law*, 3rd ed (Toronto: Carswell, 2007) at 306-23.

Ferguson, G. "Self-Defence: Selecting Applicable Defences" (2000) 5 Can Crim L Rev 179.

MacDonnell, V. "The New Self-Defence Law: Progressive Development or Status Quo?" (2014) 92 Can Bar Rev 301.

Manning, M & P Sankoff. *Manning, Mewett & Sankoff: Criminal Law*, 4th ed (Toronto: Lexis-Nexis, 2009) at 531-66.

Paciocco, DM. "The New Defense Against Force" (2014) 18 Can Crim L Rev 269.

Roach, K. *Criminal Law*, 6th ed (Toronto: Irwin Law, 2015) ch 9.

Sheehy, EA. *Defending Battered Women on Trial: Lessons from the Transcripts* (Vancouver: University of British Columbia Press, 2014).

Stewart, H. "The Role of Reasonableness in Self-Defence" (2003) 16 Can JL & Jur 317.

Stuart, D. *Canadian Criminal Law*, 7th ed (Toronto: Carswell, 2014) at 509-20.

Duress

The defence of duress is closely related to that of self-defence, discussed in the previous chapter, and necessity, the subject matter of the next. All address the criminal liability of people who find themselves in situations of extremity. In the case of self-defence (or defence of others), that extremity arises from someone apprehending the use of force against themselves or another person, and the response is to repel or resist that force. Necessity and duress concern situations in which individuals commit crimes under compulsion or coercion. The key distinction between the two is that necessity arises when *circumstances* have produced situations of imminent peril that compel the commission of an offence, whereas duress arises when criminal acts are committed by one who is subject to compulsion *from another person*. Indeed, necessity is sometimes simply referred to as "duress of circumstance."

The story of the defence of duress in Canada has unfolded with many twists and turns. There are really two types of duress defences in Canada. One is the *statutory defence*, preserved at common law and codified in highly restrictive form in s 17 of the *Criminal Code*. It reads as follows:

> 17. A person who commits an offence under compulsion by threats of immediate death or bodily harm from a person who is present when the offence is committed is excused for committing the offence if the person believes that the threats will be carried out and if the person is not a party to a conspiracy or association whereby the person is subject to compulsion, but this section does not apply where the offence that is committed is high treason or treason, murder, piracy, attempted murder, sexual assault, sexual assault with a weapon, threats to a third party or causing bodily harm, aggravated sexual assault, forcible abduction, hostage taking, robbery, assault with a weapon or causing bodily harm, aggravated assault, unlawfully causing bodily harm, arson or an offence under sections 280 to 283 (abduction and detention of young persons).

The other type of duress defence is the *common law defence*. This has somewhat different criteria, being essentially broader—lacking the strict requirements of immediacy and presence and not incorporating the long list of excluded offences found in s 17.

The contemporary development of the law of duress has been largely about sorting through the relationship between these two defences. As this chapter will show, the applicability of s 17 has been subject to progressive narrowing through common law interpretation and, more recently, constitutional analysis. The result is that despite the apparent codification of the defence, common law duress—a more permissive form of the defence than that codified in s 17—has taken on renewed and increased importance in Canadian criminal law. Recognizing that the defence of duress was in some disarray, the Supreme Court of Canada recently sought to bring clarity and coherence to it in *R v Ryan*, 2013 SCC 3, [2013] 1 SCR 14; this case raised the relationship between duress and self-defence, while showing the persistent shadow that spousal and gendered violence casts over this area of the law.

The bulk of this chapter charts the development of the law of duress in Canada from a starting point, with *R v Carker*, in which the statutory defence reigned supreme, to its contemporary state with *R v Ryan*, in which the common law requirements for the defence play the central role in the area, with s 17 now serving only to withdraw the defence from certain offenders charged with certain offences. The chapter concludes with short sections on the relationship between duress and excluded offences, duress and *mens rea*, and possibilities and considerations for reform of the defence of duress.

I. THE RELATIONSHIP BETWEEN THE COMMON LAW AND STATUTORY DEFENCES OF DURESS

In *R v Carker*, [1967] SCR 114, the accused was charged with mischief and argued duress. Unable to fit himself within the strict immediacy and presence requirements of s 17 of the *Criminal Code*, he argued that, given the Code's explicit preservation of common law excuses and justifications (s 7 at the time, now s 8(3)), he was also entitled to rely upon the common law defence of duress. Justice Ritchie, writing for the Court, held that "in respect of proceedings for an offence under the *Criminal Code* the common law rules and principles respecting 'duress' as an excuse or defence have been codified and exhaustively defined in s. 17" (at 117). *Carker* thus appeared to stand for the proposition that when the defence became part of our *Criminal Code* in 1892, the common law defence was effectively eclipsed by the statutory defence. The following case began the retreat from this position, narrowing the effect of s 17 and reinvigorating the common law defence.

Paquette v R
Supreme Court of Canada
[1977] 2 SCR 189

MARTLAND J (for the Court): The facts which give rise to this appeal are as follows: During the course of a robbery at the Pop Shoppe, in the City of Ottawa, on March 18, 1973, an innocent bystander was killed by a bullet from a rifle fired by one Simard. The robbery was committed by Simard and one Clermont, both of whom, together with the appellant, were jointly charged with non-capital murder. Simard and Clermont pleaded guilty to this charge.

The appellant was not present when the robbery was committed or when the shooting occurred. The charge against him was founded upon s. 21(2) of the *Criminal Code*.

The appellant made a statement to the police, which was admitted in evidence at the trial and which described his involvement in the matter as follows: On the day of the robbery Clermont telephoned the appellant for a ride as his own car was broken. Clermont asked the appellant where he used to work and was told at the Pop Shoppe. Clermont told him to drive to the Pop Shoppe because Clermont wanted to rob it, and, when the appellant refused, Clermont pulled his gun and threatened to kill him. Simard was picked up later and also a rifle. The appellant drove them to the Pop Shoppe. The appellant had been threatened with revenge if he did not wait for Clermont and Simard. The appellant, in his statement, stated he was afraid and drove around the block. After the robbery and homicide Clermont and Simard attempted twice, unsuccessfully, to get into the appellant's car. Three of the Crown's witnesses supported this later statement.

The trial judge charged the jury as follows:

> Now, the defence are asserting Paquette participated in this robbery because he was compelled to do so, and in that connection I charge you that if Paquette joined in the common plot to rob the Pop Shoppe under threats of death or grievous bodily harm, that would negative his having a common intention with Simard to rob the Pop Shoppe, and you must find Paquette not guilty.

The appellant was acquitted. The Crown appealed to the Court of Appeal for Ontario. The reasons delivered by that Court make it clear that the appeal would have been dismissed had it not been for the decision of this Court in *Dunbar v. The King* (1936), 67 C.C.C. 20; [1936] 4 D.L.R. 737 [which had held that duress was an issue of motive which does not negate intent under s 21(2) of the *Criminal Code*]. ...

Counsel for the Crown submits that the principles of law applicable to the excuse or defence of duress or compulsion are exhaustively codified in s. 17 of the *Criminal Code*, and that the appellant is precluded from relying upon this provision because of the exception contained at the end of it.

In my opinion the application of s. 17 is limited to cases in which the person seeking to rely upon it has himself committed an offence. If a person who actually commits the offence does so in the presence of another party who has compelled him to do the act by threats of immediate death or grievous bodily harm, then, if he believes the threats would be carried out, and is not a party to a conspiracy whereby he is subject to such compulsion, he is excused for committing the offence. The protection afforded by this section is not given in respect of the offences listed at the end of the section, which include murder and robbery.

The section uses the specific words "a person who commits an offence." It does not use the words "a person who is a party to an offence." This is significant in the light of the wording of s. 21(1) which, in paragraph (a), makes a person a party to an offence who "actually commits it." Paragraphs (b) and (c) deal with a person who aids or abets a person committing the offence. In my opinion s. 17 codifies the law as to duress as an excuse for the actual commission of a crime, but it does not, by its terms, go beyond that. *R. v. Carker*, [1967] S.C.R. 114, in which reference was made to s. 17 having codified the defence or excuse of duress, dealt with a situation in which the accused had actually committed the offence.

The appellant, in the present case, did not himself commit the offence of robbery or of murder. ...

[T]he appellant is entitled, by virtue of s. 7(3) of the *Code*, to rely upon any excuse or defence available to him at common law. The defence of duress to a charge of murder against a person who did not commit the murder, but who was alleged to have aided and abetted, was recently considered by the House of Lords in *Director of Public Prosecutions for Northern Ireland v. Lynch*, [1975] A.C. 653, in which the decided cases were fully reviewed. The facts in that case were as follows:

> The defendant drove a motor car containing a group of the I.R.A. in Northern Ireland on an expedition in which they shot and killed a police officer. On his trial for aiding and abetting the murder there was evidence that he was not a member of the I.R.A. and that he acted unwillingly under the orders of the leader of the group, being convinced that, if he disobeyed, he would himself be shot. The trial judge held that the defence of duress was not available to him and the jury found him guilty. The Court of Criminal Appeal in Northern Ireland upheld the conviction.

The House of Lords, by a 3 to 2 majority, held that on a charge of murder the defence of duress was open to a person accused as a principal in the second degree (aider and abettor) and ordered a new trial.

The conclusion of Lord Morris of Borth-y-Gest is stated at p. 677, as follows:

> Having regard to the authorities to which I have referred it seems to me to have been firmly held by our courts in this country that duress can afford a defence in criminal cases. A recent pronouncement was that in the Court of Appeal in 1971 in the case above referred to (*Reg. v. Hudson*, [1971] 2 Q.B. 202). The court stated that they had been referred to a large number of authorities and to the views of writers of textbooks. In the judgment of the court delivered by Lord Parker C.J. and prepared by Widgery L.J. the conclusion was expressed, at p. 206, that "... it is clearly established that duress provides a defence in all offences including perjury (except possibly treason or murder as a principal.")
>
> We are only concerned in this case to say whether duress could be a possible defence open to Lynch who was charged with being an aider and abettor. Relying on the help given in the authorities we must decide this as a matter of principle. I consider that duress in such a case can be open as a possible defence. Both general reasoning and the requirements of justice lead me to this conclusion.

Lord Wilberforce, at p. 682, cited with approval a passage from the dissenting reasons of Bray C.J., in *R. v. Brown and Morley*, [1968] S.A.S.R. 467 at 494:

> The reasoning generally used to support the proposition that duress is no defence to a charge of murder is, to use the words of Blackstone cited above, that "he ought rather to die himself, than escape by the murder of an innocent." Generally speaking I am prepared to accept this proposition. Its force is obviously considerably less where the act of the threatened man is not the direct act of killing but only the rendering of some minor form of assistance, particularly when it is by no means certain that if he refuses the death of the victim will be averted, or conversely when it is by no means certain that if he complies the death will be a necessary consequence. It would seem hard, for example, if an innocent passer-by seized in the street by a gang of criminals visibly engaged in robbery and murder in a shop and compelled at the point of a gun to issue misleading comments to the public, or *an innocent driver compelled at the point of a gun to convey the murderer to the victim*, were to have no defence. Are there any authorities which compel us to hold that he would not?

I am in agreement with the conclusion reached by the majority that it was open to Lynch, in the circumstances of that case, to rely on the defence of duress, which had not been put to the jury. If the defence of duress can be available to a person who has aided and abetted in the commission of murder, then clearly it should be available to a person who is sought to be made a party to the offence by virtue of s. 21(2). …

I would allow the appeal, set aside the judgment of the Court of Appeal, and restore the verdict of acquittal.

Appeal allowed.

Justice Martland's decision in *Paquette* narrowed the scope of s 17 of the *Criminal Code*. It was no longer an exhaustive definition of duress in Canadian criminal law. Rather, the restrictive s 17 defence, with its strict imminence and presence requirements and list of excluded offences for which an accused could not claim duress, would apply only to principal offenders—those charged with having actually committed the offence. Henceforth, secondary offenders (those who were parties rather than principals) would sidestep s 17 and have access to the generally more permissive common law version of the duress defence.

Accordingly, whether an accused would be characterized as a primary or a secondary offender became a crucial issue when duress was a live defence. Consider *R v Mena* (1987), 34 CCC (3d) 304 (Ont CA), in which the accused was charged with robbery, one of the offences excluded from duress under s 17 of the *Criminal Code*. The accused claimed duress, but on the facts of the case, it was uncertain whether the accused had actually committed the robbery or had merely aided the principal offender. If he was considered a primary offender, s 17 would deny him the defence of duress, whereas if he had only aided in the commission of the offence, a duress defence was possible. Justice Martin held (at 318) that, in such situations, the jury should be left to decide what role the accused had played and, as a consequence, whether he was entitled to a defence of duress:

> In the present case, the appellant had not inflicted any physical injury on the victim and claimed, as previously mentioned, that he had, in effect, made a pretence of securing him and had merely carried out part of the proceeds of the robbery at Yee's command. Assuming, as we are bound to do, that the jury took the most favourable view of the appellant's evidence, it was open to them to find that he had merely aided Yee and had not himself actually committed the offence of robbery and that, consequently, the common law defence of duress, if its requirements were met, was available to him as a secondary party to the robbery. In my view, it was an issue for the jury whether the appellant intended to act in concert with Yee or whether the acts performed by the appellant were the result of duress. If the jury, on a proper direction, found on the facts that the accused was a co-perpetrator of the offence of robbery, then s. 17 would render the defence of duress unavailable to the accused. The withdrawal of this issue from the jury constitutes a fundamental error: see *R. v. Kozak and Moore* (1975), 20 C.C.C. (2d) 175 at p. 180, 30 C.R.N.S. 7 (Ont. C.A.).

The reach and applicability of s 17 thus suffered its first blow through judicial interpretation in *Paquette*. And although the restrictive statutory defence still applied with full force for those charged as principal offenders, whenever strict limitations are put on a defence that operates as a response to human instinct in extreme situations, those limitations will eventually be subject to the pressure of difficult facts. So, in time, and in response to developments in the substantive review of criminal law under the Charter, the restrictions within s 17 were themselves brought into question, as in the following case.

R v Ruzic
Supreme Court of Canada
2001 SCC 24, [2001] 1 SCR 687

LeBEL J for the Court: ...

I. Facts

[2] The respondent Marijana Ruzic was born in Belgrade in the former Yugoslavia. She was 21 years old when she entered Canada. When heroin was discovered on her, she was charged with three offences, two of which proceeded to trial: possession and use of a false passport contrary to s. 368 of the *Criminal Code*, and unlawful importation of a narcotic contrary to s. 5(1) of the *Narcotic Control Act*, R.S.C. 1985, c. N-1.

[3] Ms. Ruzic admitted having committed both offences but claimed that she was then acting under duress and should thus be relieved from any criminal liability. She testified that, two months before her arrival in Canada, a man named Mirko Mirkovic approached her while she was walking her dog in the streets of Belgrade, where she lived in an apartment with her mother. She described him as a "warrior" and believed he was paid to kill people in the war. An expert witness testified at trial that, in 1994, large paramilitary groups roamed Belgrade and engaged in criminal and mafia-like activities. The same expert maintained that people living in Belgrade during that period did not feel safe. They believed the police could not be trusted. There was a real sense that the rule of law had broken down.

[4] From there began a series of encounters between Mirkovic and the respondent while she was walking her dog. Each time he approached her, he knew more about her, although she had shared no details of her life with him. He phoned her at home. He told her he knew her every move. Ms. Ruzic alleged that his behaviour became more and more intimidating, escalating to threats and acts of physical violence. On one occasion, he burned her arm with a lighter. On another, he stuck a syringe into her arm and injected her with a substance that smelled like heroin and made her nauseous. She indicated that these physical assaults were coupled with sexual harassment and finally threats against her mother.

[5] On April 25, 1994, Mirkovic phoned the respondent and instructed her to pack a bag and meet him at a hotel in central Belgrade. Once there, he allegedly strapped three packages of heroin to her body and indicated that she was to take them to a restaurant in Toronto. He gave her the false passport, a bus ticket from Belgrade to Budapest and some money. He told her to fly from Budapest to Athens, and then from Athens to Toronto. When she protested, he warned her that, if she failed to comply, he would harm her mother.

[6] Ms. Ruzic arrived in Budapest on April 26. Late that evening, she boarded a plane to Athens, where she arrived early the next day. She then purchased a ticket to Toronto. She missed that flight, exchanged her ticket for the next available flight, and left for Toronto two days later, on April 29.

[7] During the two months prior to her journey to Canada, Ms. Ruzic testified that she did not tell her mother or anyone else about Mirkovic. She was afraid he would harm whoever she told. She did not seek police protection because she believed the police in Belgrade were corrupt and would do nothing to assist her. She maintained that she followed

Mirkovic's instructions out of fear for her mother's safety. She made no attempt while in Budapest or Athens to seek the assistance of police or other government officials. Similarly, before her arrest, she did not ask any Canadian authorities for help. She asserted that she believed the only way she could protect her mother was to obey Mirkovic's orders.

$$\cdots$$

V. Analysis

A. Are Statutory Defences Owed Special Deference by Reviewing Courts?

$$\cdots$$

[22] Soon after the *Charter* came into force, Lamer J. (as he then was) pointed out in *Re B.C. Motor Vehicle Act, supra,* at pp. 496-97, that courts have not only the power but the duty to evaluate the substantive content of legislation for *Charter* compliance. In the realm of criminal law, the courts routinely review the definition of criminal offences to ensure conformity with *Charter* rights. This has included the *mens rea* element of an offence: e.g., *R. v. Vaillancourt,* [1987] 2 S.C.R. 636; *R. v. Wholesale Travel Group,* [1991] 3 S.C.R. 154. These powers and responsibilities extend equally to statutory defences. Courts would be abdicating their constitutional duty by abstaining from such a review. Defences and excuses belong to the legislative corpus that the *Charter* submits to constitutional review by the courts.

[23] Subject to constitutional review, Parliament retains the power to restrict access to a criminal defence or to remove it altogether. ...

[24] ... Thus, the issue is not whether the legislature may restrict or remove a criminal defence. It certainly can. The question for the courts is whether restricting the defence of duress accords with *Charter* rights.

$$\cdots$$

B. Is It a Principle of Fundamental Justice That Only Morally Voluntary Conduct Can Attract Criminal Liability?

[27] Whether it is a principle of fundamental justice under s. 7 of the *Charter* that morally involuntary conduct should not be punished is a novel question before this Court. We are thus called upon to canvass once more the contents of the "principles of fundamental justice," this time in the context of the defence of duress as framed by s. 17 of the *Criminal Code.*

$$\cdots$$

[29] The notion of moral voluntariness was first introduced in *Perka v. The Queen,* [1984] 2 S.C.R. 232, for the purpose of explaining the defence of necessity and classifying it as an excuse. It was borrowed from the American legal theorist George Fletcher's discussion of excuses in *Rethinking Criminal Law* (1978). A person acts in a morally involuntary fashion when, faced with perilous circumstances, she is deprived of a realistic choice whether to break the law. By way of illustration in *Perka,* Dickson J. evoked the situation of a lost alpinist who, on the point of freezing to death, breaks into a remote mountain cabin. The alpinist confronts a painful dilemma: freeze to death or commit a criminal offence. Yet as Dickson J. pointed out at p. 249, the alpinist's choice to break the law "is no true choice at all; it is remorselessly compelled by normal human instincts,"

here of self-preservation. The Court in *Perka* thus conceptualized the defence of necessity as an excuse. An excuse, Dickson J. maintained, concedes that the act was wrongful, but withholds criminal attribution to the actor because of the dire circumstances surrounding its commission. He summarized the rationale of necessity in this way, at p. 250:

> At the heart of this defence is the perceived injustice of punishing violations of the law in circumstances in which the person had no other viable or reasonable choice available; the act was wrong but it is excused because it was realistically unavoidable.

[30] Extending its reasoning in *Perka* to the defence of duress, the Court found in *R. v. Hibbert*, [1995] 2 S.C.R. 973, that it too rests on the notion of moral voluntariness. In the case of the defences of necessity and duress, the accused contends that he should avoid conviction because he acted in response to a threat of impending harm. The Court also confirmed in *Hibbert* that duress does not ordinarily negate the *mens rea* element of an offence. Like the defence of necessity, the Court classified the defence of duress as an excuse, like that of necessity. As such, duress operates to relieve a person of criminal liability only after he has been found to have committed the prohibited act with the relevant *mens rea*: see also *Bergstrom v. The Queen*, [1981] 1 S.C.R. 539, at p. 544 (per McIntyre J.).

[31] Thus duress, like necessity, involves the concern that morally involuntary conduct not be subject to criminal liability. Can this notion of "moral voluntariness" be recognized as a principle of fundamental justice under s. 7 of the *Charter*? Let us examine possible avenues which have been put forward by the respondent towards such recognition.

· · ·

[Justice LeBel first considered the possibility that "moral involuntariness" should be regarded as a principle of fundamental justice because it is an expression of the demand for "moral blameworthiness," recognized elsewhere in the Court's jurisprudence as an essential component of criminal liability. He rejected this approach, holding that to do so "would be contrary to the Court's conceptualization of duress as an excuse. Morally involuntary conduct is not always inherently blameless." He stated that "[o]nce the elements of the offence have been established, the accused can no longer be considered blameless. This Court has never taken the concept of blamelessness any further than this initial finding of guilt, nor should it in this case" (at para 41). Accordingly, he turned to the second argument for why "moral voluntariness" should be recognized as a principle of fundamental justice: the analogy with physical voluntariness.]

2. Moral Voluntariness and Voluntariness in the Physical Sense

[42] The respondent's second approach, which relates moral voluntariness back to voluntariness in the physical sense, rests on firmer ground. It draws upon the fundamental principle of criminal law that, in order to attract criminal liability, an act must be voluntary. Voluntariness in this sense has ordinarily referred to the *actus reus* element of an offence. It queries whether the actor had control over the movement of her body or whether the wrongful act was the product of a conscious will. Although duress does not negate ordinarily *actus reus* per se (just as it does not ordinarily negate *mens rea* as we have just seen), the principle of voluntariness, unlike that of "moral blamelessness," can remain relevant in the context of s. 7 even after the basic elements of the offence have been established. Unlike the concept of "moral blamelessness," duress in its "voluntariness"

perspective can more easily be constrained and can therefore more justifiably fall within the "principles of fundamental justice," even after the basic elements of the offence have been established.

. . .

[46] Punishing a person whose actions are involuntary in the physical sense is unjust because it conflicts with the assumption in criminal law that individuals are autonomous and freely choosing agents ... . It is similarly unjust to penalize an individual who acted in a morally involuntary fashion. This is so because his acts cannot realistically be attributed to him, as his will was constrained by some external force. As Dennis Klimchuk states in "Moral Innocence, Normative Involuntariness, and Fundamental Justice" (1998), 18 C.R. (5th) 96, at p. 102, the accused's agency is not implicated in her doing. In the case of morally involuntary conduct, criminal attribution points not to the accused but to the exigent circumstances facing him, or to the threats of someone else. ...

[47] Although moral involuntariness does not negate the *actus reus* or *mens rea* of an offence, it is a principle which, similarly to physical involuntariness, deserves protection under s. 7 of the *Charter*. It is a principle of fundamental justice that only voluntary conduct—behaviour that is the product of a free will and controlled body, unhindered by external constraints—should attract the penalty and stigma of criminal liability. Depriving a person of liberty and branding her with the stigma of criminal liability would infringe the principles of fundamental justice if the accused did not have any realistic choice. The ensuing deprivation of liberty and stigma would have been imposed in violation of the tenets of fundamental justice and would thus infringe s. 7 of the *Charter*.

C. Do the Immediacy and Presence Requirements in Section 17 Infringe the Principle of Involuntariness in the Attribution of Criminal Responsibility?

. . .

[50] The plain meaning of s. 17 is quite restrictive in scope. Indeed, the section seems tailor-made for the situation in which a person is compelled to commit an offence at gun point. The phrase "present when the offence is committed," coupled with the immediacy criterion, indicates that the person issuing the threat must be either at the scene of the crime or at whatever other location is necessary to make good on the threat without delay should the accused resist. Practically speaking, a threat of harm will seldom qualify as immediate if the threatener is not physically present at the scene of the crime.

. . .

[53] I agree with the respondent that a threat will seldom meet the immediacy criterion if the threatener is not physically present at or near the scene of the offence. The immediacy and presence requirements, taken together, clearly preclude threats of future harm.

[54] Neither the words of s. 17 nor the Court's reasons in *Carker* and *Paquette* dictate that the target of the threatened harm must be the accused. They simply require that the threat must be made to the accused. Section 17 may thus include threats against third parties. However, as discussed above, the language of s. 17 does not appear capable of supporting a more flexible interpretation of the immediacy and presence requirements. Even if the threatened person, for example, is a family member, and not the accused person, the threatener or his accomplice must be at or near the scene of the crime in order to effect the harm immediately if the accused resists. Thus, while s. 17 may capture threats

against third parties, the immediacy and presence criteria continue to impose consider-able obstacles to relying on the defence in hostage or other third party situations.

[55] Thus, by the strictness of its conditions, s. 17 breaches s. 7 of the *Charter* because it allows individuals who acted involuntarily to be declared criminally liable. Having said that, it will be interesting to see how the common law addresses the problem of duress, especially with respect to the immediacy component. In that regard, we will have the opportunity to see how the common law on duress in Canada, Great Britain, Australia, and even in some U.S. jurisdictions is often more liberal than what s. 17 provides and takes better account of the principle of voluntariness. This will confirm the view that s. 17 is overly restrictive and therefore breaches s. 7 of the *Charter*. We recall that the principles of fundamental justice may be distilled from the "legal principles which have historically been reflected in the law of this and other similar states" (*Seaboyer*, *supra*, at p. 603). Examining the common law of other states like Great Britain and Australia to confirm our interpretation of s. 7 will therefore be relevant. The analysis of duress in common law will also be useful as it will shed some light on the appropriate rules which had to be ap-plied to the defence of the accused in the case at bar and which will now be applied in all other cases, once s. 17 of the *Criminal Code* is partially struck down.

[Justice LeBel went on to canvass the common law of duress, noting that rather than strict immediacy and presence conditions, the common law imposed more flexible require-ments for a close temporal link between the threat of harm and the offence, no reasonable safe avenue of escape, and proportionality between the harm inflicted and the harm avoided. The Court would elaborate on these requirements in the *Ryan* decision, which follows in the next case.]

· · ·

E.   The Breach of Section 7 of the Charter: Conclusion in the Case at Bar

· · ·

[88] ... [Section] 17's reliance on proximity as opposed to reasonable options as the measure of moral choice is problematic. It would be contrary to the principles of funda-mental justice to punish an accused who is psychologically tortured to the point of seeing no reasonable alternative, or who cannot rely on the authorities for assistance. That indi-vidual is not behaving as an autonomous agent acting out of his own free will when he commits an offence under duress.

[89] The appellant's attempts at reading down s. 17, in order to save it, would amount to amending it to bring it in line with the common law rules. This interpretation badly strains the text of the provision and may become one more argument against upholding its validity.

[90] The underinclusiveness of s. 17 infringes s. 7 of the *Charter*, because the immedi-acy and presence requirements exclude threats of future harm to the accused or to third parties. It risks jeopardizing the liberty and security interests protected by the *Charter*, in violation of the basic principles of fundamental justice. It has the potential of convicting persons who have not acted voluntarily.

F. Can the Infringement Be Justified Under Section 1?

[91] Having found that the immediacy and presence requirements infringe s. 7 of the *Charter*, I turn now to consider whether the violation is a demonstrably justifiable limit under s. 1. The government, of course, bears the burden of justifying a *Charter* infringement. Consistent with its strategy in the courts below, the appellant made no attempt before this Court to justify the immediacy and presence criteria according to the s. 1 analysis. I therefore conclude at the outset that the appellant has failed to satisfy its onus under s. 1.

[92] Moreover, it is well established that violations of s. 7 are not easily saved by s. 1: *New Brunswick (Minister of Health and Community Services) v. G.(J.)*, [1999] 3 S.C.R. 46, at para. 99. Indeed, the Court has indicated that exceptional circumstances, such as the outbreak of war or a national emergency, are necessary before such an infringement may be justified: *R. v. Heywood*, [1994] 3 S.C.R. 761, at p. 802; *Re B.C. Motor Vehicle Act, supra*. No such extraordinary conditions exist in this case. Furthermore, I am inclined to agree with Laskin J.A. that the immediacy and presence criteria would not meet the proportionality branch of the s. 1 analysis. In particular, it seems to me these requirements do not minimally impair the respondent's s. 7 rights. Given the appellant's failure to make any submissions on the issue, the higher standard of justification for a violation of s. 7, and my doubts concerning proportionality, I conclude that the immediacy and presence conditions cannot be saved by s. 1.

. . .

VI. Disposition

[101] The appellant's submissions cannot be accepted. The immediacy and presence requirements of s. 17 of the *Criminal Code* infringe s. 7 of the *Charter*. As the infringement has not been justified under s. 1, the requirements of immediacy and presence must be struck down as unconstitutional. The Court of Appeal and the trial judge were right in allowing the common law defence of duress go to the jury, and the trial judge adequately instructed the jury on the defence.

[102] I would dismiss the appeal and confirm the acquittal of the respondent.

For critiques and assessments of the concept of moral involuntariness as developed in *Ruzic*, see S Yeo, "Challenging Moral Involuntariness as a Principle of Fundamental Justice" (2002) 28 Queen's LJ 335 and BL Berger, "Emotions and the Veil of Voluntarism: The Loss of Judgment in Canadian Criminal Defences" (2006) 51 McGill LJ 99.

With *Ruzic*, then, the statutory defence of duress suffered another blow. Now that the Supreme Court had struck down the immediacy and presence requirements, it seemed that the only remaining effect of s 17 was to make the duress defence unavailable to accused persons charged with having actually committed one of the listed offences. Without any legislative involvement whatsoever, we have travelled an enormous distance from the position set out in *Carker*, which in 1967 had held that s 17 exhaustively defined the law of duress in Canada.

There remained uncertainty, however, about whether the criteria for common law duress would now apply to principal offenders, who were still putatively governed by the statutory defence that had been chipped away at by *Paquette* and *Ruzic*. In the following case the

Supreme Court recognized the need for clarification of the defence of duress and brought the statutory and common law defences into harmony. The decision clearly articulated the law now governing duress in Canada, while exploring the relationship between duress and self-defence. It did so in the context of facts that raised, yet again, the abiding problem of spousal and gendered violence.

R v Ryan
Supreme Court of Canada
2013 SCC 3, [2013] 1 SCR 14

LeBEL and CROMWELL JJ (McLachlin CJ and Deschamps, Abella, Rothstein, Moldaver, and Karakatsanis JJ concurring):

I. Introduction

[1] This appeal raises a novel question: may a wife, whose life is threatened by her abusive husband, rely on the defence of duress when she tries to have him murdered? The Nova Scotia courts concluded that she may and acquitted the respondent, Nicole Ryan, of counselling the commission of her husband's murder. The Crown appeals.

[2] As we see it, the defence of duress is available when a person commits an offence while under compulsion of a threat made *for the purpose of compelling* him or her to commit it. That was not Ms. Ryan's situation. She wanted her husband dead because he was threatening to kill her and her daughter, not because she was being threatened for the purpose of compelling her to have him killed. That being the case, the defence of duress was not available to her, no matter how compelling her situation was viewed in a broader perspective. It is also our view, however, that the uncertainty surrounding the law of duress coupled with the Crown's change of position between trial and appeal created unfairness to Ms. Ryan's defence in this case. As a result, we would allow the appeal and enter a stay of proceedings.

[3] The appeal presents an opportunity to bring more clarity to the law of duress in Canadian criminal law. Some of the relevant law is statutory, but aspects of the provisions have been found to be unconstitutional. Other aspects of the relevant law are judge-made. The patchwork quilt nature of the present law has given rise to significant uncertainty about the parameters of both the statutory and common law elements of the defence and the relationship between them. In relation to this larger issue, our view is that the common law and statutory versions of the defence may be substantially harmonized in the manner we will set out in detail later in our reasons.

II. Overview of Facts and Proceedings

A. Facts

[4] The respondent, Nicole Ryan, has been the victim of a violent, abusive and controlling husband. She believed that he would cause her and their daughter serious bodily harm or death as he had threatened to do many times.

[5] In September of 2007, she began to think about having her husband murdered. Over the course of the next seven months, she spoke to at least three men whom she hoped would kill him. In December 2007 or January 2008, she paid one man $25,000 to carry out the killing, but he then refused, demanding more compensation. She approached another person and was contacted by a third, an undercover RCMP officer, posing as a "hit man." On March 27, 2008, she met with this individual and agreed to pay him to kill her husband. The agreed upon price was $25,000, with $2,000 paid in cash that day. The killing was to take place the coming weekend. Later that same night, she provided an address and a picture of her husband to the "hit man." Shortly after, she was arrested and charged with counselling the commission of an offence not committed contrary to s. 464(a) of the *Criminal Code*, R.S.C. 1985, c. C-46.

[6] ... The only issue at trial was whether the respondent's otherwise criminal acts were excused because of duress. ...

[7] The trial judge accepted the respondent's evidence that the relationship and the events she had described relating to that relationship were true. For example, Mr. Ryan's violent and threatening behaviour included outbursts at least once a week, where he would throw things at the respondent's head, physically assault her and threaten to kill her (trial judgment, at para. 17). The respondent testified that Mr. Ryan often told her that he would kill her and their daughter if she ever tried to leave him (para. 33), and that he would "burn the fucking house down" while she and her daughter were inside (para. 45).

[8] The trial judge had no difficulty in concluding that Mr. Ryan was a manipulative, controlling and abusive husband who sought to control the actions of the respondent, be they social, familial or marital. The judge found that the respondent's sole reason for her actions was her fear of her husband which arose from his threats of death and serious bodily harm to herself and their daughter (paras. 149-52). He also was satisfied that the respondent had led evidence to the requisite standard that she reasonably believed that Mr. Ryan would cause her and her daughter serious bodily injury and that there was no safe avenue of escape other than having him killed.

[9] The judge concluded that the respondent was in a very vulnerable state, had lost a considerable amount of weight, was dissociated and despondent. She had an intense and reasonable fear of Mr. Ryan, was feeling helpless, felt she had lost control and felt she was threatened with annihilation. While she had engaged the police and other agencies in an effort to assist her in the past, the evidence was that her problems were viewed as a "civil matter." She felt so vulnerable that the phone call of the undercover police officer appeared to her as the solution to all her problems (para. 73). On the basis of these findings, the trial judge found that the common law defence of duress applied, and acquitted the accused.

[The Crown appealed, arguing that duress applies only when an accused is forced by threats to commit an offence against a third party. The Nova Scotia Court of Appeal dismissed the appeal.]

B. Is Duress a Possible Defence?

. . .

[16] In this case ... we must resolve the question of whether the differences between duress and self-defence justify maintaining a meaningful juridical difference between

them. In our view, and with great respect to the contrary view of the Court of Appeal, they do. In other words, we conclude that the Court of Appeal erred in law when it found that there is "no principled basis" upon which the respondent should be excluded from relying on the defence of duress.

[17] With respect to the relationship between duress and necessity, Lamer C.J. in *Hibbert* concluded that the "the similarities between the two defences are so great that consistency and logic require that they be understood as based on the same juristic principles" and that to do otherwise "would be to promote incoherence and anomaly in the criminal law" (para. 54). Their common foundation is that both are excuses, "based on the idea of normative involuntariness" (para. 54), as Dickson J. (as he then was) had found in the case of the defence of necessity in *Perka v. The Queen*, [1984] 2 S.C.R. 232. The relationship among duress and necessity on one hand and self-defence on the other was less clear. All three apply in "essentially similar" situations: each is concerned with providing a defence to what would otherwise be criminal conduct because the accused acted in response to an external threat (para. 60). As the then Chief Justice explained in *Hibbert*,

> [t]he defences of self-defence, necessity and duress all arise under circumstances where a person is subjected to an external danger, and commits an act that would otherwise be criminal as a way of avoiding the harm the danger presents. [para. 50]

[18] However, there are also significant differences among the defences. ...

[20] First, self-defence is based on the principle that it is lawful, in defined circumstances, to meet force (or threats of force) with force: "an individual who is unlawfully threatened or attacked must be accorded the right to respond" (M. Manning and P. Sankoff, *Manning Mewett & Sankoff: Criminal Law* (4th ed. 2009), at p. 532). The attacker-victim is, as the Chief Justice put it, "the author of his or her own deserts" (para. 50). On the other hand, in duress and necessity, the victim is generally an innocent third party (see D. Stuart, *Canadian Criminal Law: A Treatise* (6th ed. 2011), at p. 511). Second, in self-defence, the victim simply attacks or threatens the accused; the motive for the attack or threats is irrelevant. In duress, on the other hand, *the purpose of the threat* is to compel the accused to commit an offence. To put it simply, self-defence is an attempt to stop the victim's threats or assaults by meeting force with force; duress is succumbing to the threats by committing an offence.

[21] However, these are not the only differences between duress and self-defence. It seems to us that there are two other significant differences which must be taken into account.

[22] One is that self-defence is completely codified by the provisions of the *Criminal Code*. Thus, Parliament has established the parameters of self-defence in their entirety. They are no longer found, even in part, in the common law. Duress, on the other hand, is partly codified and partly governed by judge-made law as preserved by s. 8(3) of the *Code*.

[23] Another is that the underlying rationales of the defences are profoundly distinct. The rationale underlying duress is that of moral involuntariness, which was entrenched as a principle of fundamental justice in *R. v. Ruzic* ... . [D]efences built on the principle of moral involuntariness are classified as excuses. The law excuses those who, although morally blameworthy, acted in a morally involuntary manner. The act remains wrong, but the author of the offence will not be punished because it was committed in circumstances in which there was realistically no choice ... [*Ruzic* at para 34; *Perka* at 248].

[24] Despite its close links to necessity and duress, self-defence, on the other hand, is a justification (*Perka*, at pp. 246 and 269). It "challenges the wrongfulness of an action which technically constitutes a crime" (*Perka*, at p. 246; see also H. Parent, *Traité de droit criminel* (2nd ed. 2005), vol. 1, *L'imputabilité*, at pp. 587-88) ... .

[25] We do not, for the present purpose, need to delve too deeply into the distinction between justifications and excuses and questions of exactly how and when the distinction is to be drawn in all cases. For the purposes of this appeal, the distinction simply expresses an underlying difference in principle between the two defences: while in a case of duress we excuse an act that we still consider to be wrong, the impugned act in a case of self-defence is considered right. The question then, is whether these differences support a principled distinction between duress and self-defence. In our view they do, for two main reasons.

[26] Given the different moral qualities of the acts involved, it is generally true that the justification of self-defence ought to be more readily available than the excuse of duress. And so it is. Unlike duress, self-defence does not require that any course of action other than inflicting the injury was "demonstrably impossible" or that there was "no other legal way out." ... Under the recently adopted provisions in Bill C-26, self-defence is available in circumstances in which a person believes on reasonable grounds that force is being used against him or her and responds reasonably for the purpose of self-defence: s. 34(1).

[27] Thus, if infliction of harm on a person who threatened or attacked the accused is not justified by the law of self-defence, it would be curious if the accused's response would nonetheless be excused by the more restrictive law of duress. For the sake of the coherence of the criminal law, the defence of self-defence ought to be more readily available, not less readily available, than the defence of duress in situations in which the accused responds directly against the source of the threat.

· · ·

[29] Duress cannot be extended so as to apply when the accused meets force with force, or the threat of force with force in situations where self-defence is unavailable. Duress is, and must remain, an applicable defence only in situations where the accused has been compelled to commit a specific offence under threats of death or bodily harm. This clearly limits the availability of the offence to particular factual circumstances. The common law elements of duress cannot be used to "fill" a supposed vacuum created by clearly defined statutory limitations on self-defence.

[30] This is even clearer when one considers—as explained above—the fundamental distinctions between both defences. Not only is one a justification and the other an excuse, but they also serve to avoid punishing the accused in completely different situations. If, for example, the accused was threatened with death or bodily harm without any element of compulsion, his or her only remedy is self-defence. If, on the other hand, the accused was compelled to commit a specific unlawful act under threat of death or bodily harm, the available defence is duress. ...

[31] Consider the result arrived at by the Court of Appeal in this case. The respondent responded to threats against her and her child of bodily harm and death in ways which, in the view of the Court of Appeal, would not entitle her to rely on the defence of self-defence. We add that the appeal to the Court was also presented on the assumption that self-defence was not potentially open to the respondent on these facts. For the purposes of these reasons, we do not need to decide this point. If this is the case, the extension of the law of duress to meet the respondent's situation has made the law incoherent at the level

of principle. Following the logic of the Court of Appeal's conclusions, duress, which deals with wrongful but excused conduct would be more readily available than self-defence, which addresses rightful conduct, in a situation in which the accused responded to threats by trying to eliminate them. And yet, according to the underlying rationale, excuses ought to be more restrictively defined than justifications (see, e.g., Stuart, at p. 511).

· · ·

[33] In our opinion, the Court of Appeal erred in law in finding that duress is a legally available defence on these facts. Duress is available only in situations in which the accused is threatened for the purpose of compelling the commission of an offence.

C. Remedy

[The Court then took the exceptional step of entering a stay of proceedings rather than ordering a new trial. Justices LeBel and Cromwell justified this remedy on the basis that the accused had made decisions about the conduct of her defence based on a law of duress that was unclear, that the protracted nature of the proceedings and "the abuse which she suffered at the hands of Mr. Ryan took an enormous toll on her," and that "on the record before us, it seems that the authorities were much quicker to intervene to protect Mr. Ryan than they had been to respond to her request for help in dealing with his reign of terror over her" (at para 35).]

D. Can the Law of Duress Be Clarified?

[36] This appeal underlines the need for further clarification of the law of duress. The statutory version of the defence applies to principals and the common law to parties. Important aspects of the statutory version were found to be unconstitutional in *Ruzic*, and the provision remains in place with two significant deletions as a result. The statutory version of the defence excludes a long list of offences from its operation, but various courts have found some of these exclusions to be unconstitutional. ... There is uncertainty about the similarities and differences between the common law and the statutory versions of the defence. Within the limits of the judicial role, in the development of the law, additional clarification is needed.

[37] In our view, after the decision of the Court in *Ruzic*, some reappraisal and some adjustment of both the interpretation of the statutory version of the defence and of the common law seems necessary. We begin with a recapitulation of what was decided in *Ruzic* and then address the various components of the statutory and common law versions of the defence.

· · ·

[Justices LeBel and Cromwell reviewed the decision in *Ruzic* and continued as follows:]

(2) The Statutory Defence of Duress Post-Ruzic

[43] What, therefore, remains of s. 17 after *Ruzic*? The Court did not strike down s. 17 in its entirety; it was found unconstitutional only "in part" (para. 1). As a result, the following four requirements of the statutory defence remain intact after the Court's ruling in *Ruzic*:

1. there must be a threat of death or bodily harm directed against the accused or a third party;
2. the accused must believe that the threat will be carried out;
3. the offence must not be on the list of excluded offences; and
4. the accused cannot be a party to a conspiracy or criminal association such that the person is subject to compulsion.

[44] However, the Court in *Ruzic* did not leave the statutory defence in place simply stripped of its unconstitutional portions. The Court supplemented the interpretation and application of s. 17 with elements from the common law defence of duress, which it found to be "more consonant with the values of the *Charter*" (para. 56). In other words, the Court in *Ruzic* used the common law standard to interpret the affirmative requirements of the statute (see D. M. Paciocco, "No-One Wants to Be Eaten: The Logic and Experience of the Law of Necessity and Duress" (2010), 56 *Crim. L.Q.* 240, at p. 273).

. . .

[46] In *Ruzic*, the Court articulated and analyzed the following three key elements of the common law defence of duress, which now operate in s. 17 cases alongside the four requirements remaining in the statutory defence: (1) no safe avenue of escape; (2) a close temporal connection; and (3) proportionality (see Parent, at pp. 549-50).

(a) No Safe Avenue of Escape

[47] The defence of duress "focuses on the search for a safe avenue of escape" (*Ruzic*, at para. 61). Following the decision in *Hibbert*, the Court in *Ruzic* concluded that the defence does not apply to persons who could have legally and safely extricated themselves from the situation of duress. In order to rely on the defence, the accused must have had no safe avenue of escape, as measured on the modified objective standard of the reasonable person similarly situated.

(b) A Close Temporal Connection

[48] There must be "a close temporal connection between the threat and the harm threatened" (*Ruzic*, at para. 96). The close connection between the threat and its execution must be such that the accused loses the ability to act voluntarily. The requirement of a close temporal connection between the threat and the harm threatened is linked with the requirement that the accused have no safe avenue of escape. As the Court in *Ruzic* indicated, a threat that is "too far removed in time ... would cast doubt on the seriousness of the threat and, more particularly, on claims of an absence of a safe avenue of escape" (para. 65).

. . .

[51] By reading in the requirements of safe avenue of escape and close temporal connection, the purely subjective standard becomes an evaluation based on a modified objective standard. These two elements, in conjunction with the belief that the threat will be carried out, must be analyzed as a whole: the accused cannot reasonably believe that the threat would be carried out if there was a safe avenue of escape and no close temporal connection between the threat and the harm threatened.

[52] The addition of the common law requirements to replace the now defunct immediacy and presence elements of s. 17 thus act to temper the once purely subjective belief as to the threat. Furthermore, they bring the statutory provision in line with the

principle of moral involuntariness. Considering that society's opinion of the accused's actions is an important aspect of the principle, it would be contrary to the very idea of moral involuntariness to simply accept the accused's subjective belief without requiring that certain external factors be present. ...

(c) Proportionality

[53] The defence of duress requires proportionality between the threat and the criminal act to be executed. In other words, the harm caused must not be greater than the harm avoided. Proportionality is measured on the modified objective standard of the reasonable person similarly situated, and it includes the requirement that the accused will adjust his or her conduct according to the nature of the threat: "The accused should be expected to demonstrate some fortitude and to put up a normal resistance to the threat" (*Ruzic*, at para. 62).

[54] Proportionality is a crucial component of the defence of duress because, like the previous two elements, it derives directly from the principle of moral involuntariness: only an action based on a proportionally grave threat, resisted with normal fortitude, can be considered morally involuntary. Furthermore, since the principle of moral involuntariness was judged to be a principle of fundamental justice in *Ruzic*, it must be read into s. 17 in order to comply with the statutory interpretation rule that courts must prefer the constitutional interpretation of a statute.

(3) *The Common Law Defence of Duress Post-Ruzic*

[55] Following this Court's analysis in *Ruzic*, we can conclude that the common law of duress comprises the following elements:

- an explicit or implicit threat of death or bodily harm proffered against the accused or a third person. The threat may be of future harm. Although, traditionally, the degree of bodily harm was characterized as "grievous," the issue of severity is better dealt with at the proportionality stage, which acts as the threshold for the appropriate degree of bodily harm;

- the accused reasonably believed that the threat would be carried out;

- the non-existence of a safe avenue of escape, evaluated on a modified objective standard;

- a close temporal connection between the threat and the harm threatened;

- proportionality between the harm threatened and the harm inflicted by the accused. This is also evaluated on a modified objective standard;

- the accused is not a party to a conspiracy or association whereby the accused is subject to compulsion and actually knew that threats and coercion to commit an offence were a possible result of this criminal activity, conspiracy or association.

[56] We will discuss these elements in turn.

.(a) Threat of Death or Bodily Harm

[57] For an accused to be able to rely on the common law defence of duress, there must have been a threat of death or bodily harm. This threat does not necessarily need to be directed at the accused (*Ruzic*, at para. 54). It can be either explicit or implied (*R. v. Mena* (1987), 34 C.C.C. (3d) 304 (Ont. C.A.), at p. 320; see also *R. v. McRae* (2005), 77 O.R. (3d) 1 (C.A.)).

• • •

[59] The harm threatened must be death or bodily harm. Traditionally, courts have qualified this bodily harm as needing to be "grievous" or "serious" (see, e.g., *Hibbert*, at paras. 21 and 23). However, this higher threshold is not necessary in light of the existence of the proportionality requirement—inherent in the principle of moral involuntariness—which acts as the ultimate barrier for those who seek to rely on the defence.

• • •

[63] Therefore, in order to fulfill this first requirement of the common law defence of duress, there must have been an explicit or implicit, present or future threat of death or bodily harm, directed at the accused or a third person.

(b) Reasonable Belief That Threat Will Be Carried Out

[64] In addition, the accused must have reasonably believed that the threat would be carried out. This element is analyzed on a modified objective basis, that is, according to the test of the reasonable person similarly situated.

(c) No Safe Avenue of Escape

[65] This element of the common law defence was specifically addressed in *Ruzic*, at para. 61. Once again, the test, evaluated on a modified objective basis, is that of a reasonable person similarly situated … . In other words, a reasonable person in the same situation as the accused and with the same personal characteristics and experience would conclude that there was no safe avenue of escape or legal alternative to committing the offence. If a reasonable person similarly situated would think that there *was* a safe avenue of escape, the requirement is not met and the acts of the accused cannot be excused using the defence of duress because they cannot be considered as morally involuntary.

(d) Close Temporal Connection

[66] The element of close temporal connection between the threat and the harm threatened … serves to restrict the availability of the common law defence to situations where there is a sufficient temporal link between the threat and the offence committed.

[67] This requirement in no way precludes the availability of the defence for cases where the threat is of future harm. For example, the accused in *Ruzic* was able to rely on the defence even though the threat was to harm her mother in the event that she did not smuggle the drugs from Belgrade to Toronto as ordered, a task that would take several days to accomplish.

[68] The first purpose of the close temporal connection element is to ensure that there truly was no safe avenue of escape for the accused. If the threat is too far removed from the accused's illegal acts, it will be difficult to conclude that a reasonable person similarly

situated had no option but to commit the offence. The temporal link between the threat and the harm threatened is necessary to demonstrate the degree of pressure placed on the accused.

[69] The second purpose of the close temporal connection requirement is to ensure that it is reasonable to believe that the threat put so much pressure on the accused that between this threat and the commission of the offence, "the accused los[t] the ability to act freely" (*Ruzic* at para. 65). It thus serves to determine if the accused truly acted in an involuntary manner.

(e) Proportionality

[70] Proportionality is inherent in the principle of moral involuntariness. "[T]his involuntariness is measured on the basis of society's expectation of appropriate and normal resistance to pressure" (*Perka*, at p. 259). Part of the analysis involves making a determination of whether the harm threatened is equal to or greater than the harm caused.

[71] The test for determining whether an act was proportional is therefore two-pronged, and was set out by Dickson J. in *Perka*, at p. 252:

> There must be some way of assuring proportionality. No rational criminal justice system, no matter how humane or liberal, *could excuse the infliction of a greater harm to allow the actor to avert a lesser evil.* ... According to Fletcher, this requirement is also related to the notion of voluntariness [(G.P. Fletcher, *Rethinking Criminal Law* (1978), at p. 804)]:
>
> ... [I]f the gap between the harm done and the benefit accrued becomes too great, the act is more likely to appear voluntary and therefore inexcusable. ... Determining this threshold is patently a matter of *moral judgment about what we expect people to be able to resist in trying situations.* A valuable aid in making that judgment is comparing the competing interests at stake and assessing the degree to which the actor inflicts harm beyond the benefit that accrues from his action. [Emphasis added.]

[72] In other words, the "moral voluntariness" of an act must depend on whether it is proportional to the threatened harm. To determine if the proportionality requirement is met, two elements must be considered: the difference between the nature and magnitude of the harm threatened and the offence committed, as well as a general moral judgment regarding the accused's behaviour in the circumstances. These elements are to be evaluated in conjunction on a modified objective basis.

[73] The first element of proportionality requires that the harm threatened was equal to or greater than the harm inflicted by the accused (*Ruzic*, at para. 62; also see *R. v. Latimer*, 2001 SCC 1, [2001] 1 S.C.R. 3, at para. 31). The second element of proportionality requires a more in-depth analysis of the acts of the accused and a determination as to whether they accord with what society expects from a reasonable person similarly situated in that particular circumstance. It is at this stage that we examine if the accused demonstrated "normal" resistance to the threat. Given that the defence of duress "evolved from attempts at striking a proper balance between those conflicting interests of the accused, of the victims and of society" (*Ruzic*, at para. 60), proportionality measured on a modified objective standard is key.

[74] The evaluation of the proportionality requirement on a modified objective standard differs from the standard used in the defence of necessity, which is purely objective.

While the defences of duress and necessity share the same juristic principles, according to Lamer C.J. in *Hibbert*, this does not entail that they must employ the same standard when evaluating proportionality. The Court in *Ruzic* noted that the two defences, although both categorized as excuses rooted in the notion of moral or normative involuntariness, target different types of situations. Furthermore, the temporality requirement for necessity is one of imminence, whereas the threat in a case of duress can be carried out in the future. It is therefore not so anomalous that the courts have attributed differing tests for proportionality, especially when we consider that the defences may apply under noticeably different factual circumstances.

(f) Participation in a Conspiracy or Criminal Association

[75] This statutory element has been recognized as also relevant to the common law. Recent jurisprudence has concluded that those who seek to rely on the common law defence of duress cannot do so if they knew that their participation in a conspiracy or criminal association came with a risk of coercion and/or threats to compel them to commit an offence: see *R. v. Li* (2002), 162 C.C.C. (3d) 360 (Ont. C.A.), at paras. 20-33; *R. v. Poon*, 2006 BCSC 1158 (CanLII), at para. 7; *R. v. M.P.D.*, 2003 BCPC 97, [2003] B.C.J. No. 771 (QL), at para. 61.

. . .

[77] … [C]ourts must take into account the accused's voluntary assumption of risk, a natural corollary of the unavailability of the defence of duress to those who wilfully engage in criminal conspiracies or organizations. This is consistent with the principle of moral involuntariness. An accused that, because of his or her criminal involvement, knew coercion or threats were a possibility cannot claim that there was no safe avenue of escape, nor can he or she truly be found to have committed the resulting offence in a morally involuntary manner.

[78] Therefore, to rely on the common law defence of duress, the accused must not be a party to a conspiracy or association whereby he or she is subject to compulsion and actually knew that threats and coercion to commit an offence were a possible result of this criminal activity, conspiracy or association. In *Ruzic*, at para. 70, LeBel J. states: "Like s. 17 of the *Criminal Code*, the English jurisprudence has precluded resort to the defence where the threats are made by a criminal organization which the accused voluntarily joined and *knew might pressure him to engage in criminal activity* (*R. v. Lewis* (1992), 96 Cr. App. R. 412; *R. v. Heath*, [1999] E.W.J. No. 5092 (QL))" (emphasis added).

[79] There is division of opinion as to whether the accused's knowledge of potential threats or coercion is evaluated on a subjective or objective standard. According to Yeo, the above-cited conclusion in *Ruzic* is consistent with Australian law, which only denies the defence of duress to those who were actually aware of the risk of being coerced by the criminal association (S. Yeo, "Defining Duress" (2002), 46 *Crim. L.Q.* 293, at p. 315). … Baker, however, seems to reject a purely subjective standard. According to him, the test should be whether the accused "[r]ecklessly or negligently placed himself in a situation in which it was probable that he would be forced to commit a criminal act" (para. 25-044).

[80] We think that the subjective standard is more in line with the principle of moral involuntariness. If the accused voluntarily puts him or herself in a position where he or she could be coerced, then we cannot conclude that there was no safe avenue of escape and that the ensuing actions were morally involuntary.

IV. Summary

[81] The defence of duress, in its statutory and common law forms, is largely the same. The two forms share the following common elements:

- There must be an explicit or implicit threat of present or future death or bodily harm. This threat can be directed at the accused or a third party.

- The accused must reasonably believe that the threat will be carried out.

- There is no safe avenue of escape. This element is evaluated on a modified object-ive standard.

- A close temporal connection between the threat and the harm threatened.

- Proportionality between the harm threatened and the harm inflicted by the ac-cused. The harm caused by the accused must be equal to or no greater than the harm threatened. This is also evaluated on a modified objective standard.

- The accused is not a party to a conspiracy or association whereby the accused is subject to compulsion and actually knew that threats and coercion to commit an offence were a possible result of this criminal activity, conspiracy or association.

[82] Certain differences remain.

[83] The first is that, as was established in *Paquette* and confirmed in *Ruzic*, the statu-tory defence applies to principals, while the common law defence is available to parties to an offence. The second is that the statutory version of the defence has a lengthy list of exclusions, whereas it is unclear in the Canadian common law of duress whether any offences are excluded. This results in the rather incoherent situation that principals who commit one of the enumerated offences cannot rely on the defence of duress while parties to those same offences, however, can.

[84] This is an unsatisfactory state of the law, but one which we think we are not able to confront in this case. Although we had the benefit of extensive argument about the parameters of the common law and statutory defences of duress, understandably no argu-ment was presented about the statutory exclusions. In addition, some courts have found some of these exclusions to be constitutionally infirm. We accordingly leave to another day the questions of the status of the statutory exclusions and what, if any, exclusions apply at common law.

V. Disposition

[85] We would allow the appeal and enter a stay of proceedings.

[Fish J agreed that the defence of duress was not available but also would have held that a stay of proceedings was not available. He would have ordered a new trial, "leaving it to the Crown to determine, in the exercise of its discretion, whether the public interest re-quires that a new trial be had."]

Consider the new self-defence provisions in s 34 of the *Criminal Code*, discussed in Chapter 17. If a case with facts similar to *Ryan* went to trial today, do you think that an accused could successfully rely on self-defence instead of duress? For an excellent discussion of the relationship between self-defence, necessity, and duress post-*Ryan* and in light of the new s 34, see S Coughlan, "The Rise and Fall of Duress: How Duress Changed Necessity Before Being Excluded by Self-Defence" (2013) 39:1 Queen's LJ 83.

The Supreme Court's decision in *Ryan* attempts to achieve substantial consistency between the statutory and common law defences of duress. Common law concepts of no safe escape, close temporal connection, and proportionality are grafted onto the s 17 defence as altered in *Ruzic*, while the Court imports into the common law the statutory bar on claims of duress made by someone who is "a party to a conspiracy or association whereby he or she is subject to compulsion." How does this interpretive effort in *Ryan* relate to the discussion in Chapter 1 of the sources of criminal law and nature of codification? In particular, why does the Court restrict the s 17 defence, as drafted by Parliament? Is this restriction justified, as the Court suggests, by its earlier decision in *Ruzic*? What about the Court reading the statutory restriction on those involved in criminal associations into the common law defence? Is that restriction consistent with the concept of excuse, especially as articulated by Chief Justice Dickson in *Perka v The Queen*, [1984] 2 SCR 232?

II. DURESS AND EXCLUDED OFFENCES

There are two issues with respect to excluded offences and the defence of duress. The first is the constitutionality of the statutory exclusion, in s 17 of the *Criminal Code*, of certain offences for which principal offenders cannot claim duress. This issue was not decided by the Supreme Court in *R v Ruzic*, because the offence charged was not one excluded under s 17 of the *Criminal Code* and the issue was alluded to but not taken up in the *Ryan* decision. Guided by the principles enunciated in *Ruzic*, the key question would be whether, by virtue of the exclusion of these offences, an accused could be convicted even though he or she acted in a morally involuntary manner. If so, the exclusion of these offences would seem to violate s 7 of the Charter. As the Supreme Court of Canada noted in *Ryan*, "some courts have found some of these exclusions to be constitutionally infirm" (para 84). For example, a Nova Scotia Provincial Court found that the exclusion of robbery violated s 7 of the Charter: *R v Fraser* (2002), 3 CR (6th) 309.

The second issue is whether some offences are excluded from the common law defence of duress, which still applies to parties to an offence. In *R v Ryan*, the Supreme Court of Canada commented that "it is unclear in the Canadian common law of duress whether any offences are excluded" (para 83). In *Paquette*, discussed earlier in this chapter, the Supreme Court previously held that the common law defence of duress could apply to a party to murder, and in *Hibbert* the Court contemplated that the common law defence could apply to attempted murder. In *Paquette*, the Supreme Court followed *Lynch v DPP*, [1975] 1 All ER 913 (HL), a decision that has subsequently been overruled by the House of Lords in *R v Howe*, [1987] 1 All ER 771 on the basis that duress should not excuse the commission of murder by either a principal offender or a party to the offence. Lord Hailsham concluded as follows in *Howe*:

> In general, I must say that I do not at all accept in relation to the defence of duress that it is either good morals, good policy or good law to suggest, as did the majority in *Lynch*'s case ... that the ordinary man of reasonable fortitude is not to be supposed to be capable of heroism if he is asked to take an innocent life rather than sacrifice his own. Doubtless in actual practice many will

succumb to temptation, as they did in *R. v. Dudley and Stephens*. But many will not, and I do not believe that as a "concession to human frailty" (see Smith and Hogan *Criminal Law* (5th ed., 1983) p. 215) the former should be exempt from liability to criminal sanctions if they do. I have known in my own lifetime of too many acts of heroism by ordinary human beings of no more than ordinary fortitude to regard a law as either "just or humane" which withdraws the protection of the criminal law from the innocent victim and casts the cloak of its protection on the coward and the poltroon in the name of a "concession to human frailty."

In *R v Gotts*, [1992] 1 All ER 832, the House of Lords further held that common law duress could not serve as a defence to attempted murder. There is also some suggestion in *Lynch* that duress was not considered a defence to certain forms of treason in English common law.

In *R v Aravena*, 2015 ONCA 250, the Court of Appeal for Ontario reassessed the Canadian position in light of the Supreme Court of Canada's ruling in *Ryan*. The case concerned a set of killings arising from internal strife within the Bandidos motorcycle gang. The central question in the appeal became whether three of the accused, who had aided and abetted in the murders, could claim the common law defence of duress. Consistent with the Supreme Court's earlier ruling in *Paquette*, the Court of Appeal held that common law duress is available to a secondary party to murder. In reasons that underscored the importance of the concept of moral involuntariness and the centrality of proportionality to the law of duress post-*Ryan*, Justices Doherty and Pardu wrote as follows:

> [52] As explained in *Ruzic*, at paras. 34-47, the concept of moral involuntariness as a principle of fundamental justice rests on an acceptance of individual autonomy and choice as essential preconditions to the imposition of criminal liability. If, on a reasonable assessment of the circumstances, it must be said that an accused had no realistic choice but to act as he did, fundamental justice requires that the accused not be branded a criminal for so acting. Society may regret or even deplore the accused's failure to "rise to the occasion," but it cannot, in a criminal justice system predicated on individual autonomy, justly criminalize and punish conduct absent a realistic choice: see *Perka*, at pp. 249-50. *Ryan*, at para. 40, confirmed the status of moral involuntariness as a principle of fundamental justice protected by s. 7 of the *Charter*.

> [53] Moral involuntariness does not depend exclusively on an individual's perception that she had no realistic choice but to act as she did. Moral involuntariness is measured, in part, "on the basis of society's expectation of appropriate and normal resistance to pressure": *Perka*, at p. 259. ...

> [54] The "social policy considerations" infused into the concept of moral voluntariness recognize that excuses which provide a defence for what is otherwise criminal behaviour cannot be entirely subjective. Excuses must take into account a variety of societal concerns, including the need to maintain social order and to protect persons who are the innocent victims of those who act under threats from others: *Ruzic*, at para. 58. ...

> [57] The proportionality requirement ultimately separates those society is prepared to excuse for yielding to threats from those society decides should not have succumbed to the pressure. Proportionality in the context of the duress defence is assessed on a "modified objective" standard: *Ryan*, at para. 72.

> [58] Proportionality is the product of two different but related evaluations. First, the harm threatened must be equal to or greater than the harm inflicted in response to the threat. Second, the accused's choice to inflict harm must "accord with what society expects from a reasonable person similarly situated in that particular circumstance": *Ryan*, at para. 73.

. . .

[61] Moral involuntariness as a principle of fundamental justice is a reflection of the central importance of individual autonomy and choice in the imposition of criminal liability. The statutory and common law defences of duress, as developed in *Hibbert*, *Ruzic* and *Ryan*, take moral voluntariness as both the rationale for the duress defence and as the justification for the strict limits on the availability of the defence. In doing so, the court has adhered to its oft repeated admonition that the common law must be developed and applied in accordance with the values and principles enshrined in the *Charter*. ...

[62] In the same way that the principle of moral involuntariness has played a central role in shaping the elements of the common law defence of duress, it must figure prominently in any assessment of whether any offences, and in particular murder, should be excluded from the reach of that defence. The Crown's claim that the common law defence of duress does not reach persons charged as parties to murder can be accepted only if the Crown can demonstrate either that the exclusion of murder is compatible with the principle of moral involuntariness or that the exclusion is a justifiable limitation on that principle.

[63] Whether excluding murder from the duress defence is consistent with the principle of moral involuntariness turns on the rationale underlying the defence and the interaction between that rationale and the proportionality requirement. Duress operates as an excuse and not a justification. While a person told to "kill or be killed" could perhaps never justify killing the innocent third party as the lesser of two evils, it is much more difficult to assert that the two harms are not of "comparable gravity": *R. v. Latimer*, 2001 SCC 1, [2001] 1 S.C.R. 3, at para. 31.

[64] Because duress operates as an excuse, harms of comparable gravity satisfy at least the first arm of the proportionality inquiry. The principle of moral involuntariness recognizes that the criminal law "is designed for the common man, not for a community of saints or heroes": *Ruzic*, at para. 40. The criminal law cannot demand acts of heroism, but must instead set standards of conduct "which ordinary men and women are expected to observe if they are to avoid criminal responsibility": *R. v. Howe*, [1987] A.C. 417 (H.L. Eng.), at p. 430; see also *Lynch*, at p. 670.

[65] Moral involuntariness by its very nature demands a fact-intensive inquiry. Neither prong of the proportionality requirement will always favour sacrificing one's own life over assisting in the murder of another. Choosing to aid in the murder of another will not always amount to choosing an evil greater than the evil threatened. For example, a person may be presented with a choice between taking the life of an innocent third party and the killing of her own child. The putative victims are equally innocent. Surely, the harms flowing from either choice are "of comparable gravity."

[66] Nor, on any realistic view, can a decision to assist in a murder to avoid a harm threatened always fall below the standard of what "society expects from a reasonable person similarly situated in [the] particular circumstance": *Ryan*, at para. 73. Consider, for example, a person who had no connection to the Bandidos or to the meeting at Kellestine's farm, but who happened to attend at the farm for some innocent purpose that night. Assume Kellestine's group took him captive and held him in the barn while Kellestine removed and murdered two of the victims. If that person was then ordered under threat of death by Kellestine to assist in the removal and murder of the next victim, would society expect the ordinary (not the heroic or exceptional) person to refuse Kellestine's order and give up his own life? Could it be said that the person had "a realistic choice"? We think not.

[67] In taking the view that the duress defence could excuse a choice to assist in a murder, we of course do not suggest that the defence would be readily made out. Indeed, the duress

defence is strictly limited and is not easily accessible in any situation. Moreover, the greater the harm caused by yielding to the threat, the more difficult it will be for an accused to make out the defence, particularly on the proportionality element. If an accused chooses to assist in a murder, it may well be that nothing short of a threat of immediate death to that person or some other person could ever satisfy the proportionality requirement.

· · ·

[73] In our view, while the victim's right to life is a crucial factor in assessing whether an accused's conduct is proportional and therefore morally involuntary, the victim's right to life cannot render conduct that is otherwise involuntary punishable under the criminal law. A proportionality requirement which looks to whether an accused had any realistic choice is an essential component of the moral involuntariness inquiry.

Justices Doherty and Pardu considered but rejected the English position that duress could not be a defence to murder. The argument for excluding murder from the defence of duress, they explained, is based on deterrence and the desire to vindicate innocent persons' right to life. They questioned the validity of the deterrence-based policy, expressing skepticism that excluding offences would have any deterrent effect on either those subject to serious threats, or those already involved in criminal activity who seek to coerce another. Justices Doherty and Pardu explained that, irrespectively, such a deterrence rationale "cannot withstand the head-on collision with the principle of moral involuntariness" and that, subject only to a justification pursuant to s 1 of the Charter, "criminal policy goals, no matter how legitimate, cannot be pursued at the expense of the constitutional protections afforded by s. 7" (at para 76). Justices Doherty and Pardu similarly rejected the English courts' argument that murder must be excluded from the duress defence in order to vindicate the innocent victim's right to life. They explained that this rationale is based on a justificatory understanding of duress—wherein the defence could only be available if the accused's act is the "lesser of two evils"—that is inconsistent with the Canadian understanding of the defence as excusatory in nature. Moreover, they noted that in some situations, an individual subject to threats will be unable to fully vindicate the right to life: "Whatever the threatened person decides, an innocent life may well be lost. A *per se* rule which excludes the defence of duress in all murder cases does not give the highest priority to the sanctity of life, but rather, arbitrarily, gives the highest priority to one of the lives placed in jeopardy" (at para 83).

Although *Aravena* was concerned with the applicability of the common law defence of duress to those charged as parties to murder, Justices Doherty and Pardu recognized that their heavy reliance on the principle of moral involuntariness—a principle of fundamental justice protected by s 7 of the Charter—would have implications for the constitutionality of the statutory exclusion of duress for principals charged with murder. They explained that, although the constitutionality of the exclusion of murder from the s 17 duress defence was not before the Court, "it follows from this analysis that, subject to any argument the Crown might advance justifying the exception as it applies to perpetrators under s. 1 of the Charter, the exception must be found unconstitutional" (at para 86). And having rejected both the deterrence and vindication of life justifications, it is difficult to imagine what a successful s 1 argument would look like. Might the Court of Appeal's decision in *Aravena* have sounded the death knell for the excluded offences in s 17?

Do you think that any offences ought to be excluded from the defence of duress? Recall that duress currently operates only as a full excuse: an accused claiming duress will either be fully liable for the offence charged or acquitted outright. Might it be that the creation of a partial defence of duress—whereby an accused would be still be criminally liable but punished less severely—would be a better means of balancing the various principles and policy considerations raised by claims of duress for the kinds of offences listed in s 17?

III. DURESS AND MENS REA

Before concluding this chapter by considering some reform options and considerations for the defence of duress, it is worthwhile to focus on the relationship between duress and *mens rea*. In *Ruzic*, the Court observed that "duress does not ordinarily negate the *mens rea* element of an offence" (at para 30), a proposition it derived from the following decision in *Hibbert*. You might recall this case from the section on subjective *mens rea* in Chapter 7. Consider the case afresh, having now studied the law of duress.

R v Hibbert
Supreme Court of Canada
[1995] 2 SCR 973

[The victim of the offence was the accused's friend. The accused testified that he was forced by the principal offender to accompany him to the victim's apartment building and to lure the victim down to the lobby. The accused stood by while the principal offender then shot the victim. In the charge to the jury, the trial judge instructed the jury that if the accused joined in the common plot to shoot the victim under threats of death or grievous bodily harm, that would negative his having a common intention with the principal offender to shoot the victim and he must be found not guilty. The trial judge also instructed the jury that the accused could not rely on the common law defence of duress if a safe avenue of escape existed. The accused was acquitted of attempted murder, but convicted of the included offence of aggravated assault. The accused's appeal to the Ontario Court of Appeal was dismissed.]

LAMER CJ: This appeal presents a number of important questions, each having to do with the role of duress as a defence to criminal charges. ... In particular, this Court must decide whether it is open to a person charged as a party to an offence to argue that, because his or her actions were coerced, he or she did not possess the *mens rea* necessary for party liability. This argument must be weighed against the alternative position—namely, that duress does not "negate" the *mens rea* for party liability, but that persons who commit certain criminal acts under duress may nonetheless be excused from criminal liability under the common law "defence of duress." It is also necessary for the Court to address certain questions having to do with limitations on this defence's availability. Specifically, we are asked to determine whether accused persons are foreclosed from recourse to the defence if they failed to avail themselves of a "safe avenue of escape" from the situation of coercion when such a safe avenue was available. If this is indeed the case, we must go on to consider whether the existence of such a "safe avenue" is to be determined on an objective basis, or from the subjective viewpoint of the accused.

[Having reviewed the factual background, the relevant statutory provisions, and the decisions below, Chief Justice Lamer turned to his analysis of the legal principles:]

B. The Relationship Between Mens Rea and the Defence of Duress

(1) The Common Law Defence of Duress in Canada

… *Paquette* stands for the proposition that duress can provide a "defence" in either of two distinct ways—as an excuse, or by "negating" *mens rea*. In the present case, the appellant argues that this is a correct view of the law, and submits that the trial judge erred by not placing both alternatives before the jury. What falls to be considered, therefore, is the validity of the proposition that the *mens rea* for party liability under the *Criminal Code* can be "negated" by threats of death or bodily harm. That is, the court is called upon to reconsider whether the second aspect of our judgment in *Paquette* reflects a correct understanding of the law of duress in Canada.

(2) Duress and Mens Rea

That threats of death or serious bodily harm can have an effect on a person's state of mind is indisputable. However, it is also readily apparent that a person who carries out the *actus reus* of a criminal offence in response to such threats will not necessarily lack the *mens rea* for that offence. Whether he or she does or not will depend both on what the mental element of the offence in question happens to be, and on the facts of the particular case. As a practical matter, though, situations where duress will operate to "negate" *mens rea* will be exceptional, for the simple reason that the types of mental states that are capable of being "negated" by duress are not often found in the definitions of criminal offences.

    In general, a person who performs an action in response to a threat will *know* what he or she is doing, and will be aware of the probable consequences of his or her actions. Whether or not he or she *desires* the occurrence of these consequences will depend on the particular circumstances. For example, a person who is forced at gunpoint to drive a group of armed ruffians to a bank will usually know that the likely result of his or her actions will be that an attempt will be made to rob the bank, but he or she may not desire this result—indeed, he or she may strongly wish that the robbers' plans are ultimately foiled, if this could occur without risk to his or her own safety. In contrast, a person who is told that his or her child is being held hostage at another location and will be killed unless the robbery is successful will almost certainly have an active subjective desire that the robbery succeed. While the existence of threats clearly has a bearing on the *motive* underlying each actor's respective decision to assist in the robbery, only the first actor can be said not to *desire* that the robbery take place, and neither actor can be said not to have knowledge of the consequences of their actions. …

[Lamer CJ first dealt with the meaning of the word "purpose" in s 21(1)(b) of the *Criminal Code*, which creates liability for a person who "does or omits to do anything for the purpose of aiding any person to commit" an offence. He then went on to discuss s 21(2) "in the interests of avoiding undue confusion in the law that applies to duress cases."]

(3) The Mens Rea Requirement for Party Liability Under Section 21

(a) Section 21(1)(b)

. . .

It is impossible to ascribe a single fixed meaning to the term "purpose." In ordinary usage, the word is employed in two distinct senses. One can speak of an actor doing something "on purpose" (as opposed to by accident), thereby equating purpose with "immediate intention." The term is also used, however, to indicate the ultimate ends an actor seeks to achieve, which imports the idea of "desire" into the definition. This dual sense is apparent in the word's dictionary definition.

... Our task in the present case is to consider the meaning of "purpose" as it is employed in s. 21(1)(b) of the *Code* in light of the parliamentary objective underlying the subsection. It must be emphasized, however, that the word "purpose" is employed in many different sections of the *Criminal Code*, in a number of distinct contexts. My conclusions in the present case on the proper interpretation of the word "purpose" as it is employed in s. 21(1)(b) of the *Code* are thus restricted to this particular subsection. It may well be that in the context of some other statutory provision a different interpretation of the term will prove to be the most appropriate.

The problems associated with the "purpose equals desire" interpretation are several. First, incorporating the accused's feelings about the desirability of the commission of an offence by the principal into the definition of the *mens rea* for "aiding" can result in distinctions being made which appear arbitrary and unreasonable in light of the policy underlying s. 21(1)(b). As Professor Colvin notes, under the "purpose equals desire" interpretation, a person would not be guilty of aiding in the commission of an offence if he or she were "genuinely opposed or indifferent to it" (p. 123). The reason for the aider's indifference or opposition would be immaterial. The perverse consequences that flow from this are clearly illustrated by the following hypothetical situation described by Mewett and Manning:

> If a man is approached by a friend who tells him that he is going to rob a bank and would like to use his car as a getaway vehicle for which he will pay him $100, when that person is ... charged under s. 21 for doing something for the purpose of aiding his friend to commit the offence, can he say "My purpose was not to aid the robbery but to make $100"? His argument would be that while he knew that he was helping the robbery, his desire was to obtain the $100 and he did not care one way or the other whether the robbery was successful or not. (*Criminal Law*, supra, at p. 112.)

I agree with the authors' conclusion that "[t]hat would seem an absurd result" (p. 112). ...

The leading English case on the issue of whether duress negates the *mens rea* of parties to offences (under the common law governing party liability) is the House of Lords' decision in *Lynch, supra*. As Professor G. Williams observes in his *Textbook of Criminal Law*, 2nd ed. (London: Stevens & Sons, 1983), at p. 624:

The view taken by the majority of the House of Lords in *Lynch* was that duress is a defence on its own, and does not negative either the doing of the act charged or the *mens rea*. This is plainly right.

The position at common law, of course, does not in and of itself determine the meaning to be ascribed to the word "purpose" in the context of s. 21(1)(b) of the *Code*. It can,

however, provide useful guidance when it comes to choosing between the two interpretations of the term that are available—one that accords with the common law position and
the other that contradicts it. In the absence of reason to believe that Parliament intended
its enactment of s. 21(1)(b) to radically alter the common law principles governing party
liability, the interpretation that accords with the common law would seem to also be the
most likely to accurately embody Parliament's intentions. This observation strengthens
my conclusion that Parliament's use of the term "purpose" in s. 21(1)(b) should not be seen
as incorporating the notion of "desire" into the mental state for party liability, and that
the word should instead be understood as being essentially synonymous with "intention." ...

For these reasons, I conclude that the expression "for the purpose of aiding" in
s. 21(1)(b), properly understood, does not require that the accused actively view the commission of the offence he or she is aiding as desirable in and of itself. As a result, the *mens
rea* for aiding under s. 21(1)(b) is not susceptible of being "negated" by duress. ...

(b) Section 21(2) and the Decision in Paquette

. . .

As was the case with the term "purpose" in s. 21(1)(b), the phrase "intention in common" [in s 21(2)] is capable of being understood in more than one sense. One possible
interpretation is that "intention in common" means no more than that the two persons
must have in mind the same unlawful purpose. Alternatively, however, it might be argued
that the requirement of "commonality" requires that the two persons' intentions match
in greater detail—in particular, that their motives or subjective views as to the desirability
of the commission of the "unlawful purpose" match up. If this latter interpretation were
adopted, it could be argued that although persons who assist others to commit criminal
acts as a result of threats made by the others would "intend" to provide such assistance,
their intention would not be "in common" with the intentions of the threatener, due to
the different motives and, possibly, views as to the immediate desirability of the criminal
activity at issue. In contrast, under the former interpretation a person would fall within
the ambit of s. 21(2) if they intended to assist in the commission of the same offence
envisioned by the principal, regardless of the fact that their intention might be due solely
to the principal's threats. Of course, it would be open to such a person to avoid criminal
liability through the common law defence of duress.

As noted earlier in *Paquette, supra*, Martland J. took the position that "intention in
common" meant something more than "intention to commit or aid in the same offence,"
arguing (at p. 423) that:

> A person whose actions have been dictated by fear of death or of grievous bodily injury
> cannot be said to have formed a genuine common intention to carry out an unlawful purpose
> with the person who has threatened him with those consequences if he fails to co-operate.

The phrase "intention in common" is certainly open to being interpreted in this manner.
However, notwithstanding the considerable weight I place on and the respect I have for
the opinion of Martland J., I have come to the conclusion that, in the context of s. 21(2),
the first interpretation discussed above is more consistent both with Parliament's intention
and with the interpretation of s. 21(1)(b) I have adopted in these reasons. Many of the
factors I considered earlier in the course of determining the meaning to be ascribed to

the term "purpose" in s. 21(1)(b) apply with similar force to the problem of interpreting s. 21(2) ... .

(4) Conclusions on Duress and Mens Rea

The conclusions that can be extracted from the discussion in the previous sections may be summarized as follows:

1. The fact that a person who commits a criminal act does so as a result of threats of death or bodily harm can in some instances be relevant to the question of whether he or she possessed the *mens rea* necessary to commit an offence. Whether or not this is so will depend, among other things, on the structure of the particular offence in question—that is, on whether or not the mental state specified by Parliament in its definition of the offence is such that the presence of coercion can, as a matter of logic, have a bearing on the existence of *mens rea*. If the offence is one where the presence of duress is of potential relevance to the existence of *mens rea*, the accused is entitled to point to the presence of threats when arguing that the Crown has not proven beyond a reasonable doubt that he or she possessed the mental state required for liability.

2. A person who commits a criminal act under threats of death or bodily harm may also be able to invoke an excuse-based defence (either the statutory defence set out in s. 17 or the common law defence of duress, depending on whether the accused is charged as a principal or as a party). This is so regardless of whether or not the offence at issue is one where the presence of coercion also has a bearing on the existence of *mens rea*.

3. The mental states specified in s. 21(1)(b) and (2) of the *Criminal Code* are not susceptible to being "negated" by duress. Consequently, it is not open to persons charged under these sections to argue that because their acts were coerced by threats they lacked the requisite *mens rea*. Such persons may, however, seek to have their conduct *excused* through the operation of the common law defence of duress.

It should be reiterated, however, that the holding in the present case is based on an interpretation of the particular terms of two specific offence-creating statutory provisions, s. 21(1)(b) and (2) of the *Criminal Code*. The question of whether other offences can be found, either in the *Code* or in some other statute, that are defined in such a way that the presence of coercion *is* relevant to the existence of *mens rea*, remains open.

[Lamer CJ then discussed the requirements for common law duress, including the "safe avenue of escape" requirement, addressed in the extract from *Ryan* in Section I of this chapter. He found errors in the trial judge's charge to the jury on the defence of duress, errors that he concluded might have had an effect on the verdict.]

Appeal allowed; new trial ordered.

As a result of *Hibbert*, duress will not raise a reasonable doubt about the subjective *mens rea* in ss 21(1)(b) and (c) and s 21(2). Given this, will duress ever be relevant to questions of fault? Should duress ever be relevant to fault?

IV. REFORM OF THE DEFENCE OF DURESS

This chapter has shown how the law of duress—governed both by s 17 of the *Criminal Code* and the common law—has shifted and changed through judicial interpretation. Although *Ryan* has brought greater clarity to the area, complexity remains, and new questions have arguably arisen given the new self-defence provisions found in s 34. Is there still a role for a separate law of duress? What meaning will the courts give to s 17 pursuant to the new s 34? Furthermore, as raised in the discussion of excluded offences above, are we satisfied with the "all or nothing" structure of duress, or might there be a role for duress as a partial excuse in some circumstances? Perhaps it is time for reform of the defence of duress in Canada.

Consider the following proposal and reasoning offered by the Law Reform Commission of Canada in 1987, in Report 31, *Recodifying Criminal Law* (1987) at 35:

> 3(8) Duress. No one is liable for committing a crime in reasonable response to threats of im-mediate serious harm to himself or another person unless he himself purposely causes the death of, or seriously harms, another person.

> **Comment**
>
> One's duty to obey the law may conflict with pressure stemming from the threats of others. Where the pressure is great and the breach of duty relatively small, the breach becomes unfit for punishment. This is the thrust of the criminal law defence of duress.
>
> The defence of duress is presently contained partly in section 17 of the *Criminal Code* and partly in the common law. According to the case-law, the section concerns the position of the actual committer; the common law that of other parties. Section 17 allows the defence only where there is a threat of immediate death or bodily harm from a person present, where the ac-cused is not a party to a conspiracy subjecting him to the duress and where the crime committed is not one of those listed in the section. The common law is less strict and detailed, does not re-quire the threatener to be present, has no rule on conspiracy and excludes duress only in the case of murder by an actual committer.
>
> Clause 3(8) simplifies and modifies the law in four ways. First, it specifies that the accused's response to the threat must be reasonable. Second, it provides the same rule for all parties. Third, it drops the need for the threatener's presence at the crime and the accused's absence from a conspiracy, on the ground that both are factors going ultimately to the reasonableness or other-wise of the accused's response. Finally, it abandons the *ad hoc* list of excluded crimes and re-places it with a general exclusion for an accused who himself purposely kills or seriously harms another person, the principle being that no one may put his own well-being before the life and bodily integrity of another innocent person.

Judicial reform is also possible. For example, as is discussed earlier in this chapter, the courts might eventually find that the list of excluded offences in s 17 should be struck down completely on the basis that barring access to duress for principals accused of these offences allows the conviction of those who acted in a morally involuntary manner. In such an even-tuality, the common law defence would effectively apply to all offenders.

The following is an extract from an article in which Professor Martha Shaffer persuasively argues for the need to consider the particular experiences of battered women in any reform to the law of duress.

M Shaffer, "Coerced into Crime: Battered Women and the Defence of Duress"
(1999) 4 Can Crim L Rev 272 at 307-8, 329-30 (footnotes omitted)

There is increasing evidence that battered women are frequently coerced into committing criminal offences by their abusers. Even as early as 1984, Lenore Walker, the American psychologist who coined the term "battered woman syndrome," speculated that up to 50 percent of the women serving time in U.S. prisons had been forced to commit offences by abusive partners. More recently battered women charged with criminal offences have begun with increasing frequency to raise duress claims as defences to their conduct. While this trend has been more pronounced in the United States than in Canada, Canadian courts have had to grapple with the impact of battering on duress claims in several cases.

Reported cases as well as social science evidence reveal that battered women have been involved in committing offences ranging from welfare fraud to drug trafficking to prostitution to child abuse to murder. Nonetheless, with few exceptions, battered women's duress claims have been rejected by the courts. Several possible explanations account for the resistance to battered women's claims. These include simple disbelief of the woman's claim that she was subject to abuse or that she acted under duress, evidentiary concerns regarding the admissibility of evidence of battering outside the self-defence context, and the doctrinal requirements of the defence of duress itself.

· · ·

An examination of the experiences of battered women who are forced by their abusers to commit offences reveals serious inadequacies in the existing law of duress from the standpoint of gender equality. ...

The experiences of battered women also demonstrate that gender should be a key consideration in assessing existing *Criminal Code* provisions and in reforming them. As feminists have frequently argued, all too often the law is drafted against the backdrop of a male norm. Thus, where women's experiences differ from those of men, the law may be incapable of responding to the realities of women's lives. The stories of battered women coerced into crime show how this has occurred in the context of the defence of duress. They also underscore the need for a new law of duress that is responsive to the legitimate claims of *both* men and women.

ADDITIONAL READING

Berger, BL. "Emotions and the Veil of Voluntarism: The Loss of Judgment in Canadian Criminal Defences" (2006) 51 McGill LJ 99.

Clarkson, CMV. "Necessary Action: A New Defence" [2004] Crim L Rev 81.

Colvin, E & S Anand. *Principles of Criminal Law*, 3rd ed (Toronto: Carswell, 2007) at 335-51.

Coughlan, S. "The Rise and Fall of Duress: How Duress Changed Necessity Before Being Excluded by Self-Defence" (2013) 39 Queen's LJ 83.

Horder, J. "Self-Defence, Necessity and Duress: Understanding the Relationship" (1998) 11 Can JL & Jur 143.

Manning, M & P Sankoff. *Manning, Mewett & Sankoff: Criminal Law*, 4th ed (Toronto: LexisNexis, 2009) at 475-89.

Paciocco, DM. "No-One Wants to Be Eaten: The Logic and Experience of the Law of Necessity and Duress" (2010) 56 Crim LQ 240.

Roach, K. *Criminal Law*, 6th ed (Toronto: Irwin Law, 2015) ch 9.

Shaffer, M. "Scrutinizing Duress: The Constitutional Validity of Section 17 of the Criminal Code" (1998) 40 Crim LQ 444.

Stuart, D. *Canadian Criminal Law*, 7th ed (Toronto: Carswell, 2014) at 521-37.

Yeo, S. "Defining Duress" (2002) 46 Crim LQ 293.

Necessity

Necessitas non habet legem; "Necessity knows no law." This well-known maxim reflects the theoretical basis of the defence of necessity: that in dire circumstances of looming peril, the claims of positive law seem to weaken. Do criminal prohibitions, usually crafted for a range of anticipated or "normal" situations continue to have legal and moral force in situations of extremity? What ought one to do when faced with a choice between breaking the law or obeying law but, in so doing, allowing a greater harm to take place? Furthermore, what should a just criminal law say about the moral blameworthiness of a person who, in such a situation, chooses to break the law? These questions are at the core of the defence of necessity.

Necessity is a controversial common law or judge-made defence that has been firmly recognized in Canadian law only since 1984. It is recognized in Canada as a defence for crimes committed in urgent situations of clear and imminent peril in which the accused has no safe avenue of escape or legal way out of the situation. As with self-defence and duress, considered in the previous two chapters, there is also an objective or reasonableness requirement to the necessity defence that requires the accused to reasonably resist the pressures that led to the commission of the crime. Controversially, the Supreme Court of Canada has insisted that necessity is only ever excusatory; it never *justifies* the commission of the crime.

The history of necessity as a defence in Canada is bound up with several very controversial cases. In Section I of this chapter we will examine a debate about the defence in Canada that revolved around the issue of whether necessity should have been a defence when a doctor was charged with violating Canada's old abortion law by performing an abortion outside of a hospital and without the approval of a hospital committee. Section II will consider the leading case of *Perka v The Queen*, in which the Supreme Court of Canada recognized necessity as a defence but divided on whether it is best conceived of as an excuse or a justification. It is in *Perka* that the Supreme Court set out the essential elements of the defence in Canada. A separate section will examine the rejection of the necessity defence in the famous *Latimer* case. The final section will examine the way that the defence of necessity has been codified in other jurisdictions, as well as proposals for its codification in Canada.

I. NECESSITY AND ABORTION

Morgentaler v The Queen
Supreme Court of Canada
[1976] 1 SCR 616

[The Supreme Court held (6:3) that the defence of necessity was not available to Dr. Henry Morgentaler, who had performed an abortion on a 26-year-old single woman in his clinic in contravention of the *Criminal Code*, which at the time allowed abortions to be performed only in a hospital if approved by a hospital committee. Dr. Morgentaler testified that he was afraid that the woman "might do something foolish" if he did not perform the abortion.]

DICKSON J (with whom five other members of the court concurred): ... In an attempt to escape the discipline of the statute, the appellant seeks to rely on an ill-defined and elusive concept sometimes referred to as the defence of necessity. The defence of necessity is as rare to Canadian jurisprudence as a s. 45 defence. [Section 45 protects from criminal liability those who perform a surgical operation with reasonable care.] Standard Canadian texts on criminal law either ignore or make scant reference to the subject. Save in the exceptional case of *R. v. Bourne*, [1939] 1 K.B. 687, to which I will later refer, the defence has never been raised successfully, so far as one can ascertain, in a criminal case in this country or in England. It was unavailing in *U.S. v. Holmes* (1842), 26 Fed. Cas. 36, where, following a shipwreck, the sailors threw 14 passengers overboard to lighten a lifeboat that was sinking and in *R. v. Dudley and Stephens* (1884), 14 Q.B.D. 273, where the accused, two seamen, after 18 days adrift in an open boat and starving, killed a youthful companion and fed on his flesh for four days, at the end of which time they were rescued. ... Necessity has been said to justify pulling down a house to prevent the spread of a fire, or the escape of prisoners from a burning prison and it has given rise to endless philosophizing on the right of a person in danger of drowning to push another from a floating plank in order to save himself. These are said to be examples of the defence of necessity, but no clear principle can be detected. It has been held that necessity cannot justify killing: *R. v. Dudley and Stephens*, *supra*, or the stealing of food by a starving man, Hale, *Pleas of Crown* i, 54 or the occupancy of empty housing by those in dire need of accommodation, *Southwark London Borough Council v. Williams*, [1971] 1 Ch. 734. The Courts have been reluctant to give recognition to the doctrine of necessity for, as Lord Denning, M.R., said in the *Williams* case, p. 744: "Necessity would open a door which no man could shut" and "The plea would be an excuse for all sorts of wrong-doing," and Lord Justice Edmund-Davies in the same case, p. 746 "... necessity can very easily become simply a mask for anarchy." The defence of necessity finds little support in the cases. Professor Glanville Williams, who has written frequently on abortion and the doctrine of necessity ((1952) 5 C.L.P. 128; (1953) 6 C.L.P. 216; *Sanctity of Life and the Criminal Law* (1957)) introduces the subject "Authorities on the defence of necessity" in his text on *Criminal Law* (2nd ed. 1961) with the qualified statement, p. 724: "Notwithstanding the doubts that have been expressed, it will here be submitted somewhat confidently that the defence is recognized in English Law." Compare, however, "The Necessity Plea in English Common Law" by P.R. Glazebrook,

1972A *Cambridge Law Journal*, 87, and see "The Defence of Necessity in Criminal Law: The Right to Choose the Lesser Evil" by Arnolds and Garland (1974), 65 *The Journal of Criminal Law and Criminology*, 289. On the authorities it is manifestly difficult to be categorical and state that there is a law of necessity, paramount over other laws, relieving obedience from the letter of the law. If it does exist it can go no further than to justify non-compliance in urgent situations of clear and imminent peril when compliance with the law is demonstrably impossible. No system of positive law can recognize any principle which would entitle a person to violate the law because on his view the law conflicted with some higher social value.

R. v. *Bourne, supra*, is sometimes quoted in support of the contention that there is a defence of necessity: for myself, I have some considerable reservations on the point. The *Bourne* decision may be regarded as exceptional and in a sense legislative. Although stated to exemplify the doctrine of necessity, the Judge did not specifically rely on necessity. At the time of *Bourne* the law was unclear as to the legal position of a medical practitioner who procured an abortion on a girl whose life or health was endangered by continued pregnancy. The English statute did not then contain, although it now does, any provision for therapeutic abortion akin to s. 251(4) of the *Code*. The trial Judge, through the word "unlawfully," imported such a concept and on the facts of that case it is of no surprise that the jury acquitted. The question of compliance with statutory law permitting therapeutic abortion did not arise. If the proponents of the existence of defence of necessity have to rely on the case of *Bourne*—and the only support in modern jurisprudence would seem to come from that case and one or two which followed it—to support their position, the very uniqueness of *Bourne* both on facts and law may lead one seriously to question whether a defence of necessity can really be said to exist. I do not think the *Bourne* case is of great assistance to the appellant. In *Bourne* the trial Judge imported into the charge the consideration of "preserving the life of the mother." That same concept finds statutory recognition in our abortion legislation but in the somewhat broader phraseology "likely to endanger her life or health." It is, therefore, clear that a medical practitioner who wishes to procure a miscarriage because continued pregnancy may endanger the life or health of his patient may legally do so if he secures the certificate mentioned in s. 251(4)(c). The defence of necessity, whatever that vague phrase may import, does not entitle a medical practitioner, in circumstances of time and place such as those under consideration, to procure an abortion on his own opinion of the danger to life and health.

Assuming the theoretical possibility of such a defence in the present case, it remains to be seen whether there is evidence to support it. ...

A defence of necessity at the very least must rest upon evidence from which a jury could find (i) that the accused in good faith considered the situation so emergent that failure to terminate the pregnancy immediately could endanger life or health and (ii) that upon any reasonable view of the facts compliance with the law was impossible. ...

Upon this evidence I think it perfectly clear the Court of Appeal did not err in concluding there was on the record little evidence of real and urgent medical need. More important, in answer to the question: "Was there any legal way out?" I think one must say that evidence from which a jury could conclude it was impossible for appellant to comply with the law is wholly wanting. The plain fact is that appellant made no attempt to bring himself within the bounds of legality in deciding to perform this abortion. ... I would hold, therefore, that the defence of necessity was not open to the appellant.

LASKIN CJ (with whom Judson and Spence JJ concurred) (dissenting): The appellant was charged with performing an illegal abortion on August 15, 1973, upon a 26-year-old unmarried female who had come to Canada from a foreign country in 1972 on a student visa. She was without family or close friends in Canada, ineligible to take employment and also ineligible for Medicare benefits. On becoming apprehensive of possible pregnancy in July, 1973, she consulted a physician in general practice who referred her to a gynecologist. He confirmed that she was pregnant, but refused assistance to procure an abortion. On her own initiative she canvassed five Montreal hospitals by telephone and learned that if an abortion was to be performed she would have to bear the fees of a surgeon and an anaesthetist, and could envisage two or three days' hospitalization at $140 per day. This was far beyond her means.

Throughout the period following her apprehension and the confirmation of her pregnancy and until the abortion performed by the appellant, she was anxious, unable to eat or sleep properly, prone to vomiting and quite depressed. Her condition had an adverse effect upon her studies and it was aggravated by her being told that the longer she delayed in having an abortion the more dangerous it would be. One hospital offered her an appointment (which would result in her case coming before the therapeutic abortion committee) at the end of August, 1973, when she would be eight to 10 weeks' pregnant. She got in touch with the appellant at the suggestion of a hospital or hospitals that she had contacted. There is some discrepancy between her evidence and that of the appellant as to the scope and nature of the conversation between them when she visited his clinic where the abortion was performed. In this appeal I think it proper to accept the evidence of the appellant who testified that his discussion with her went beyond asking whether she had previously had an abortion, when she realized she was pregnant and what his fee would be. He asserted that the conversation also encompassed reference to her country of origin, her vocation, her marital status and why an abortion was necessary. During the conversation the appellant said that he assessed the necessity of an abortion by reference to her state of anxiety, her inability to eat or sleep properly and the consequent adverse effect on her physical health. He also considered that her determination to have an abortion might lead her to do something foolish. The appellant was aware that his patient had approached a number of hospitals without success, but did not know that she had been offered an appointment at the end of August, 1973. ...

It appears quite clearly that what the Quebec Court of Appeal saw in the defence of necessity was urgency of such a nature as to make it impossible to obtain a lawful abortion under s. 251(4). The test it would apply parallels that which can rarely be met, if at all, where the charge against the accused is one arising out of homicide. I am not prepared to take the same stringent view of urgency and impossibility as did the Quebec Court of Appeal, and I would observe, moreover, that there is a danger here in usurping the function of the jury on that question according to the way in which it is defined. I do not doubt, of course, that the necessity must arise out of danger to life or health and not merely out of economic circumstances, although the latter may have an effect in producing the danger to life or health. ...

It was for the jury to say whether in such circumstances the harm sought to be avoided by performing the abortion was an immediate and physical one ... and whether there was enough of an emergency in this respect facing the accused as to make it certain that there could be no effective resort to the machinery of s. 251(4) to cope with the emergency.

I need hardly say that the sufficiency of evidence on any issue is a matter for the jury, which alone is charged to accept what it chooses and to weigh what it accepts in the light of the law given to it by the trial Judge.

R v Morgentaler, Smoling and Scott
Ontario Court of Appeal
(1985), 22 CCC (3d) 353

[The accused were charged with conspiracy to procure a miscarriage contrary to ss 251(1) and 423(1)(d) of the *Criminal Code*. The accused were acquitted and the Crown appealed to the Ontario Court of Appeal, arguing, *inter alia*, that the defence of necessity should not have been left to the jury. The court agreed and ordered a new trial.]

THE COURT: ... With respect, we think that the defence of necessity was misconceived. As has previously been noted, before a defence of necessity is available, the conduct of the accused must be truly involuntary in the sense ascribed in that term in the precedents cited. There was nothing involuntary in the agreement entered into in the case by the respondents. As stated by Fletcher, *Rethinking Criminal Law* (1978), pp. 811-2: "Planning, deliberating, relying on legal precedents—all of these are incompatible with the uncalculating response essential to 'involuntary' conduct."

Furthermore, there must be evidence that compliance with the law was demonstrably impossible, and that there was no legal way out.

Not only did the defendants fail to make every reasonable effort to comply with the law, but they consciously agreed to violate it. Their dissatisfaction with the state of the law, although perhaps relevant to the issue of motive, afforded no basis for the defence of necessity.

The constitutional validity of s. 251 having been upheld by the trial judge, it was not an issue for the jury to weigh the merits of the law enacted by Parliament and to be invited to resolve the public debate on abortion. Yet, it was on the basis of the dissatisfaction with the law that the defence sought to rely on the legal defence of necessity. ...

With respect, the defence of necessity is not premised on dissatisfaction with the law. The defence of necessity recognizes that the law must be followed, but there are certain factual situations which arise and which may excuse a person for failure to comply with the law. It is not the law which can create an emergency giving rise to a defence of necessity, but it is the facts of a given situation which may do so.

This was not a case where two or more doctors agreed to procure the miscarriage of a female person who was in immediate need of medical services in order to avoid danger to her life or health, and in which case the defence of necessity would be a live issue. The defence of necessity cannot be resorted to as an excuse for medical practitioners in Canada to agree in the circumstances of this case to procure abortions on their own opinion of the danger to life or health and at a place of their own choosing in complete disregard to the provisions of s. 251 of the *Criminal Code*.

Although it was for the jury to weigh the evidence, it is the function of an appellate court to examine the record with a view to ascertaining whether there is any evidence to support a defence. On the record before us including the evidence tendered by the Crown as well as for the defence, the defence of necessity was not open to the respondents, and the trial judge erred in leaving that defence to the jury.

[The Supreme Court did not decide whether the defence of necessity should have been left to the jury when on further appeal it held that the abortion law violated s 7 of the Charter. See *R v Morgentaler et al*, [1988] 1 SCR 30.]

II. THE CONCEPTUALIZATION OF NECESSITY AS AN EXCUSE OR JUSTIFICATION

Perka v The Queen
Supreme Court of Canada
[1984] 2 SCR 232

[The accused were charged with importing a narcotic and possession of a narcotic for the purpose of trafficking contrary to ss 5 and 4(2), respectively, of the *Narcotic Control Act*, RSC 1970, c N-1. The evidence led by the Crown indicated that 33.49 tons of marijuana worth $6 million or $7 million was seized from a ship found in Canadian waters on the west coast of Vancouver Island. The accused were members of the crew or officers of the ship or otherwise connected with the shipment of the marijuana. The accused adduced evidence as to the condition of the ship during poor weather conditions and the efforts that were made to remedy certain mechanical defects.

The defence presented evidence that the drugs were being shipped from Colombia to Alaska, and that there were engine breakdowns, overheating generators, and malfunctioning navigation devices, coupled with 8- to 10-foot swells and a rising wind. The accused therefore (according to the defence evidence) sought refuge on the west coast of Vancouver Island. In rebuttal, the Crown sought to adduce evidence as to the mechanical condition of the ship and, in particular, how easily the authorities were able to start the vessel, and as to how it performed subsequently. The Crown argued that the evidence of the ship's distress was a recent fabrication. The trial judge refused the Crown's application on the basis that the defence of necessity was one that could have been anticipated and that the evidence should have been led by the Crown in its case in chief. The accused were acquitted.

The British Columbia Court of Appeal ordered a new trial, holding that the Crown should have been allowed to call rebuttal evidence. The accused appealed to the Supreme Court of Canada. The five-member Court agreed with the Court of Appeal that a new trial should be awarded.]

DICKSON J (as he then was) stated for Ritchie, Chouinard, and Lamer JJ: ... Subsequent to *Morgentaler*, the courts appear to have assumed that a defence of necessity does exist in Canada ... .

In *Morgentaler, supra*, I characterized necessity as an "ill-defined and elusive concept." Despite the apparently growing consensus as to the existence of a defence of necessity that statement is equally true today. ...

Criminal theory recognizes a distinction between "justifications" and "excuses." A "justification" challenges the wrongfulness of an action which technically constitutes a crime. The police officer who shoots the hostage-taker, the innocent object of an assault who uses force to defend himself against his assailant, the good Samaritan who commandeers a car and breaks the speed laws to rush an accident victim to the hospital, these are all actors whose actions we consider *rightful*, not wrongful. For such actions people are often praised, as motivated by some great or noble object. The concept of punishment often seems incompatible with the social approval bestowed on the doer.

In contrast, an "excuse" concedes the wrongfulness of the action but asserts that the circumstances under which it was done are such that it ought not to be attributed to the actor. The perpetrator who is incapable, owing to a disease of the mind, of appreciating the nature and consequences of his acts, the person who labours under a mistake of fact, the drunkard, the sleepwalker: these are all actors of whose "criminal" actions we disapprove intensely, but whom, in appropriate circumstances, our law will not punish.

It will be seen that the two different approaches to the "defence" of necessity from Blackstone forward correspond, the one to a justification, the other to an excuse. ...

As a "justification" this residual defence ... would exculpate actors whose conduct could reasonably have been viewed as "necessary" in order to prevent a greater evil than that resulting from the violation of the law. As articulated, especially in some of the American cases, it involves a utilitarian balancing of the benefits of obeying the law as opposed to disobeying it, and when the balance is clearly in favour of disobeying, exculpates an actor who contravenes a criminal statute. This is the "greater good" formulation of the necessity defence: in some circumstances, it is alleged, the values of society, indeed of the criminal law itself, are better promoted by disobeying a given statute than by observing it.

With regard to this conceptualization of a residual defence of necessity, I retain the scepticism I expressed in *Morgentaler* [*v The Queen*, [1976] 1 SCR 616], at p. 678. It is still my opinion that, "[n]o system of positive law can recognize any principle which would entitle a person to violate the law because on his view the law conflicted with some higher social value." The *Criminal Code* has specified a number of identifiable situations in which an actor is justified in committing what would otherwise be a criminal offence. To go beyond that and hold that ostensibly illegal acts can be validated on the basis of their expediency, would import an undue subjectivity into the criminal law. It would invite the courts to second-guess the Legislature and to assess the relative merits of social policies underlying criminal prohibitions. Neither is a role which fits well with the judicial function. Such a doctrine could well become the last resort of scoundrels and, in the words of Edmund Davies L.J. in *Southwark London Borough Council v. Williams et al.*, [1971] Ch. 734 [at 746], it could "very easily become simply a mask for anarchy."

Conceptualized as an "excuse," however, the residual defence of necessity is, in my view, much less open to criticism. It rests on a realistic assessment of human weakness, recognizing that a liberal and humane criminal law cannot hold people to the strict obedience of laws in emergency situations where normal human instincts, whether of self-preservation or of altruism, overwhelmingly impel disobedience. The objectivity of the criminal law is preserved; such acts are still wrongful, but in the circumstances they are excusable. Praise is indeed not bestowed, but pardon is, when one does a wrongful act under pressure which, in the words of Aristotle in *The Nicomachean Ethics* (translator Rees, p. 49), "overstrains human nature and which no one could withstand."

· · ·

In *Morgentaler, supra* [at 678], I was of the view that any defence of necessity was restricted to instances of non-compliance "in urgent situations of clear and imminent peril when compliance with the law is demonstrably impossible." In my opinion, this restriction focuses directly on the "involuntariness" of the purportedly necessitous behaviour by providing a number of tests for determining whether the wrongful act was truly the only realistic reaction open to the actor or whether he was in fact making what in fairness could be called a choice. If he was making a choice, then the wrongful act cannot have been involuntary in the relevant sense.

The requirement that the situation be urgent and the peril be imminent, tests whether it was indeed unavoidable for the actor to act at all. ... At a minimum the situation must be so emergent and the peril must be so pressing that normal human instincts cry out for action and make a counsel of patience unreasonable.

The requirement that compliance with the law be "demonstrably impossible" takes this assessment one step further. Given that the accused had to act, could he nevertheless realistically have acted to avoid the peril or prevent the harm, without breaking the law? *Was there a legal way out?* I think this is what Bracton means when he lists "necessity" as a defence, providing the wrongful act was not "avoidable." The question to be asked is whether the agent had any real choice: could he have done otherwise? If there is a reasonable legal alternative to disobeying the law, then the decision to disobey becomes a voluntary one, impelled by some consideration beyond the dictates of "necessity" and human instincts.

The importance of this requirement that there be no reasonable legal alternative cannot be overstressed.

Even if the requirements for urgency and "no legal way out" are met, there is clearly a further consideration. There must be some way of assuring proportionality. No rational criminal justice system, no matter how humane or liberal, could excuse the infliction of a greater harm to allow the actor to avert a lesser evil. In such circumstances we expect the individual to bear the harm and refrain from acting illegally. If he cannot control himself we will not excuse him. ...

... If the conduct in which an accused was engaging at the time the peril arose was illegal, then it should clearly be punished, but I fail to see the relevance of its illegal character to the question of whether the accused's subsequent conduct in dealing with this emergent peril ought to be excused on the basis of necessity. At most the illegality—or if one adopts Jones J.A.'s approach, the immorality—of the preceding conduct will colour the subsequent conduct in response to the emergency as also wrongful. But that wrongfulness is never in any doubt. Necessity goes to *excuse* conduct, not to *justify* it. Where it is found to apply it carries with it no implicit vindication of the deed to which it attaches. That cannot be over-emphasized. Were the defence of necessity to succeed in the present case, it would not in any way amount to a vindication of importing controlled substances nor to a critique of the law prohibiting such importation. It would also have nothing to say about the comparative social utility of breaking the law against importing as compared to obeying the law. The question, as I have said, is never whether what the accused has done is wrongful. It is always and by definition, wrongful. The question is whether what he has done is voluntary. ...

It is now possible to summarize a number of conclusions as to the defence of necessity in terms of its nature, basis and limitations:

(1) the defence of necessity could be conceptualized as either a justification or an excuse;

(2) it should be recognized in Canada as an excuse, operating by virtue of s. 7(3) of the *Criminal Code*;

(3) necessity as an excuse implies no vindication of the deeds of the actor;

(4) the criterion is the moral involuntariness of the wrongful action;

(5) this involuntariness is measured on the basis of society's expectation of appropriate and normal resistance to pressure;

(6) negligence or involvement in criminal or immoral activity does not disentitle the actor to the excuse of necessity;

(7) actions or circumstances which indicate that the wrongful deed was not truly involuntary do disentitle;

(8) the existence of a reasonable legal alternative similarly disentitles; to be involuntary the act must be inevitable, unavoidable and afford no reasonable opportunity for an alternative course of action that does not involve a breach of the law;

(9) the defence only applies in circumstances of imminent risk where the action was taken to avoid a direct and immediate peril;

(10) where the accused places before the court sufficient evidence to raise the issue, the onus is on the Crown to meet it beyond a reasonable doubt.

In my view, the trial judge was correct in concluding that on the evidence before him he should instruct the jury with regard to necessity. There was evidence before him from which a jury might conclude that the accused's actions in coming ashore with their cargo of *cannabis* were aimed at self-preservation in response to an overwhelming emergency. I have already indicated that in my view they were not engaged in conduct that was illegal under Canadian criminal law at the time the emergency arose, and that even if they were, that fact alone would not disentitle them to raise the defence. ...

In the course of his charge on the issue of necessity the trial judge instructed the jury, using the specific words that appear in *Morgentaler*, to the effect that they must find facts which amount to "an urgent situation of clear and imminent peril when compliance with the law is demonstrably impossible" in order for the appellants' non-compliance with the law against importation and possession of *cannabis* to be excused. That is the correct test. It is, with respect, however, my view that in explaining the meaning and application of this test, the trial judge fell into error.

The trial judge was obliged, in my opinion, to direct the jury's attention to a number of issues pertinent to the test for necessity. Was the emergency a real one? Did it constitute an immediate threat of the harm purportedly feared? Was the response proportionate? In comparing this response to the danger that motivated it, was the danger one that society would reasonably expect the average person to withstand? Was there any reasonable legal alternative to the illegal response open to the accused? Although the trial judge did not explicitly pose each and every one of these questions in my view his charge was adequate to bring the consideration underlying them to the jury's attention on every issue except the last one, the question of a reasonable alternative.

WILSON J (concurring): ... Inasmuch as the Chief Justice's conclusion as to the defence of necessity seems clearly correct on the facts of this case and his disposition of the appeal manifestly just in the circumstances, I am dealing in these reasons only with the proposition very forcefully advanced by the Chief Justice in his reasons that the appropriate jurisprudential basis on which to premise the defence of necessity is exclusively that of excuse. My concern is that the learned Chief Justice appears to be closing the door on justification as an appropriate jurisprudential basis in some cases and I am firmly of the view that this is a door which should be left open by the court. ...

It may generally be said that an act is justified on grounds of necessity if the court can say that not only was the act a necessary one but it was rightful rather than wrongful. When grounded on the fundamental principle that a successful defence must characterize an act as one which the accused was within his rights to commit, it becomes immediately apparent that the defence does not depend on the immediacy or "normative involuntariness" of the accused's act unless, of course, the involuntariness is such as to be pertinent to the ordinary analysis of *mens rea*. The fact that one act is done out of a sense of immediacy or urgency and another after some contemplation cannot, in my view, serve to distinguish the quality of the act in terms of right or wrong. Rather, the justification must be premised on the need to fulfil a duty conflicting with the one which the accused is charged with having breached.

... [In] some circumstances defence counsel may be able to point to a conflicting duty which courts can and do recognize. For example, one may break the law in circumstances where it is necessary to rescue someone to whom one owes a positive duty of rescue (see *R. v. Walker* (1979), 48 C.C.C. (2d) 126, 5 M.V.R. 114 (Ont. Co. Ct.)), since failure to act in such a situation may itself constitute a culpable act or omission: see *R. v. Instan*, [1893] 1 Q.B. 450. Similarly, if one subscribes to the viewpoint articulated by Laskin C.J.C. in *Morgentaler, supra*, and perceives a doctor's defence to an abortion charge as his legal obligation to treat the mother rather than his alleged ethical duty to perform an unauthorized abortion, then the defence may be invoked without violating the prohibition enunciated by Dickson J. in *Morgentaler* against choosing a non-legal duty over a legal one ... .

Accordingly, where necessity is invoked as a justification for violation of the law, the justification must, in my view, be restricted to situations where the accused's act constitutes the discharge of a duty recognized by law. The justification is not, however, established simply by showing a conflict of legal duties. The rule of proportionality is central to the evaluation of a justification premised on two conflicting duties since the defence rests on the rightfulness of the accused's choice of one over the other.

As the facts before the court in the present case do not involve a conflict of legal duties it is unnecessary to discuss in detail how a court should go about assessing the relative extent of two evils. Suffice it to say that any such assessment must respect the notion of right upon which justification is based. The assessment cannot entail a mere utilitarian calculation of, for example, lives saved and deaths avoided in the aggregate but must somehow attempt to come to grips with the nature of the rights and duties being assessed. This would seem to be consistent with Lord Coleridge's conclusion that necessity can provide no justification for the taking of a life, such an act representing the most extreme form of rights violation. As discussed above, if any defence for such a homicidal act is to succeed, it would have to be framed as an excuse grounded on self-preservation. It could not possibly be declared by the court to be rightful. By contrast, the justification analysis would seem to support those cases in which fulfilment of the legal duty to save persons entrusted to one's care is preferred over the lesser offences of trespass or petty theft: see *Mouse's Case* (1608), 12 Co. Rep. 63, 77 E.R. 1341; *Amiens, Ch. corr., April 22, 1898, s. 1899.2.1* (*Ménard's Case*). The crucial question for the justification defence is whether the accused's act can be said to represent a furtherance of or a detraction from the principle of the universality of rights.

Appeals dismissed.

Although the view of Chief Justice Dickson undoubtedly establishes necessity as an excuse, as opposed to a justification, in Canadian law, the view of Justice Wilson that, in the case of conflicting legal duties, necessity might be conceptualized as a justification was adopted in the case of *Re A (Children) (Conjoined Twins: Surgical Separation)*, [2000] 4 All ER 961 (CA). In that case, the English Court of Appeal decided that an operation to separate conjoined infant twins, absent their parents' consent, would be justified and, therefore, lawful on the basis of the defence of necessity. Because there was no imminent peril, as contemplated in *Perka*, the Court found Justice Wilson's justification analysis, which does not necessarily require an emergency, to be more appealing.

As you read, Chief Justice Dickson makes clear that the mere fact that a person was engaged in illegal, immoral, or negligent activity when the necessitous situation emerged does not, on its own, disentitle the accused from relying on the defence of necessity. However, what if the creation of the perilous situation was foreseeable and the accused acted to bring it about anyway? In a part of *Perka* that you have not read, Chief Justice Dickson stated the following:

> If the necessitous situation was clearly foreseeable to a reasonable observer, if the actor contemplated or ought to have contemplated that his actions would likely give rise to an emergency requiring the breaking of the law, then I doubt whether what confronted the accused was in the relevant sense an emergency. His response was in that sense not "involuntary."

Canadian courts have wrestled with the question of whether and when the "fault" of the accused in bringing about a necessitous situation ought to disentitle the accused from claiming necessity. Consider the following scenarios that have arisen in recent cases:

- The accused went to a keg party to retrieve a stolen keg of beer. He knew that ownership of the keg was hotly contested, had exchanged threatening phone calls with the other group, and so anticipated that recovering the keg would be problematic and potentially volatile. When he arrived, a group of between 20 and 40 party-goers surrounded and attacked his car. Afraid, he backed the car out of the group, injuring two people in the process. He was charged with dangerous operation of a motor vehicle causing bodily harm and pleaded necessity. (*R v CWV*, 2004 ABCA 208.)

- The accused, who suffered from depression, lived in a tent in the forest about two hours out of town by foot. He was in the habit of fasting for long periods of time—up to 40 days in the past—and was now at the end of a 60-day fast. On the night in question, the accused (muscles atrophied from the fast) crawled and hobbled toward town for eight hours in cold winter weather to get food, which, if he had no money, he would scavenge from garbage cans. He testified that he thought he was in a desperate situation, facing starvation and hypothermia. He came upon an unoccupied townhouse, broke in, ate some food, and fell unconscious on the kitchen floor. He was charged with break and enter and mischief and pleaded necessity. (*R v Nelson*, 2007 BCCA 490, 228 CCC (3d) 302.)

III. NECESSITY AND THE LATIMER CASE

R v Latimer
Supreme Court of Canada
2001 SCC 1, [2001] 1 SCR 3

BY THE COURT:

[1] This appeal arises from the death of Tracy Latimer, a 12-year-old girl who had a severe form of cerebral palsy. Her father, Robert Latimer, took her life some seven years ago. He was found guilty of second degree murder. This appeal deals with three questions of law arising from his trial. First, did the trial judge mishandle the defence of necessity, resulting in an unfair trial? Second, was the trial unfair because the trial judge misled the jury into believing it would have some input into the appropriate sentence? Third, does the imposition of the mandatory minimum sentence for second degree murder constitute "cruel and unusual punishment" in this case, so that Mr. Latimer ("the appellant") should receive a constitutional exemption from the minimum sentence?

[2] We conclude that the answer to all three questions is no. The defence of necessity is narrow and of limited application in criminal law. In this case, there was no air of reality to that defence. The trial judge was correct to conclude that the jury should not consider necessity. While the timing of the removal of this defence from the jury's consideration was later in the trial than usual, it did not render the appellant's trial unfair or violate his constitutional rights. On the second issue, the trial judge did not prejudice the appellant's rights in replying to a question from the jury on whether it could offer input on sentencing. In answer to the third question, we conclude that the mandatory minimum sentence for second degree murder in this case does not amount to cruel and unusual punishment within the meaning of s. 12 of the *Canadian Charter of Rights and Freedoms*. The test for what amounts to "cruel and unusual punishment" is a demanding one, and the appellant has not succeeded in showing that the sentence in his case is "grossly disproportionate" to the punishment required for the most serious crime known to law, murder.

[3] We conclude that Mr. Latimer's conviction and sentence of life in prison with a mandatory minimum of 10 years' imprisonment for second degree murder should be upheld. This means that the appellant will not be eligible for parole consideration for 10 years, unless the executive elects to exercise the power to grant him clemency from this sentence, using the royal prerogative of mercy. The Court's role is to determine the questions of law that arise in this appeal; the matter of executive clemency remains in the realm of the executive, and it is discussed later in these reasons.

[4] The law has a long history of difficult cases. We recognize the questions that arise in Mr. Latimer's case are the sort that have divided Canadians and sparked a national discourse. This judgment will not end that discourse.

[5] Mr. Latimer perceived his daughter and family to be in a difficult and trying situation. It is apparent from the evidence in this case that he faced challenges of the sort most Canadians can only imagine. His care of his daughter for many years was admirable. His decision to end his daughter's life was an error in judgment. The taking of another life represents the most serious crime in our criminal law.

I. Facts

[6] The appellant, Robert Latimer, farmed in Wilkie, Saskatchewan. His 12-year-old daughter, Tracy, suffered a severe form of cerebral palsy. She was quadriplegic and her physical condition rendered her immobile. She was bedridden for much of the time. Her condition was a permanent one, caused by neurological damage at the time of her birth. Tracy was said to have the mental capacity of a four-month-old baby, and she could communicate only by means of facial expressions, laughter and crying. She was completely dependent on others for her care. Tracy suffered seizures despite the medication she took. It was thought she experienced a great deal of pain, and the pain could not be reduced by medication since the pain medication conflicted with her anti-epileptic medication and her difficulty in swallowing. Tracy experienced five to six seizures daily. She had to be spoon-fed, and her lack of nutrients caused weight loss.

[7] There was evidence that Tracy could have been fed with a feeding tube into her stomach, an option that would have improved her nutrition and health, and that might also have allowed for more effective pain medication to be administered. The Latimers rejected the feeding-tube option as being intrusive and as representing the first step on a path to preserving Tracy's life artificially.

[8] Tracy had a serious disability, but she was not terminally ill. Her doctors anticipated that she would have to undergo repeated surgeries, her breathing difficulties had increased, but her life was not in its final stages.

[9] Tracy enjoyed music, bonfires, being with her family and the circus. She liked to play music on a radio, which she could use with a special button. Tracy could apparently recognize family members and she would express joy at seeing them. Tracy also loved being rocked gently by her parents.

[10] Tracy underwent numerous surgeries in her short lifetime. In 1990, surgery tried to balance the muscles around her pelvis. In 1992, it was used to reduce the abnormal curvature in her back.

[11] Like the majority of totally involved, quadriparetic children with cerebral palsy, Tracy had developed scoliosis, an abnormal curvature and rotation in the back, necessitating surgery to implant metal rods to support her spine. While it was a successful procedure, further problems developed in Tracy's right hip: it became dislocated and caused her considerable pain.

[12] Tracy was scheduled to undergo further surgery on November 19, 1993. This was to deal with her dislocated hip and, it was hoped, to lessen her constant pain. The procedure involved removing her upper thigh bone, which would leave her lower leg loose without any connecting bone; it would be held in place only by muscle and tissue. The anticipated recovery period for this surgery was one year.

[13] The Latimers were told that this procedure would cause pain, and the doctors involved suggested that further surgery would be required in the future to relieve the pain emanating from various joints in Tracy's body. According to the appellant's wife, Laura Latimer, further surgery was perceived as mutilation. As a result, Robert Latimer formed the view that his daughter's life was not worth living.

[14] In the weeks leading up to Tracy's death, the Latimers looked into the option of placing Tracy in a group home in North Battleford. She had lived there between July and October of 1993, just prior to her death, while her mother was pregnant. The Latimers applied to place Tracy in the home in October, but later concluded they were not interested in permanently placing her in that home at that time.

[15] On October 12, 1993, after learning that the doctors wished to perform this additional surgery, the appellant decided to take his daughter's life. On Sunday, October 24, 1993, while his wife and Tracy's siblings were at church, Robert Latimer carried Tracy to his pickup truck, seated her in the cab, and inserted a hose from the truck's exhaust pipe into the cab. She died from the carbon monoxide.

[16] The police conducted an autopsy and discovered carbon monoxide in her blood. The appellant at first maintained that Tracy simply passed away in her sleep. He later confessed to having taken her life, and gave a statement to the investigating police and partially re-enacted his actions on videotape. Mr. Latimer also told police that he had considered giving Tracy an overdose of Valium, or "shooting her in the head."

[17] Mr. Latimer has been convicted of murder twice in this case. He was initially charged with first degree murder and convicted by a jury of second degree murder. The Court of Appeal for Saskatchewan upheld his conviction and life sentence with no eligibility for parole for 10 years, with Bayda C.J.S. dissenting on the sentence: *R. v. Latimer* (1995), 99 C.C.C. (3d) 481 ("*Latimer (No. 1)*"). The case was then appealed to this Court: [1997] 1 S.C.R. 217. It turned out that the prosecutor had interfered with the jury selection process. The Crown conceded that a new trial could not be avoided. In the second trial, Mr. Latimer was again convicted of second degree murder, and it is from that conviction that this appeal arises.

[18] During the second trial, two things occurred that, the appellant submits, resulted in an unfair trial. First, as counsel were about to make closing addresses to the jury, defence counsel asked the trial judge for a ruling on whether the jury could consider the defence of necessity. He wanted this ruling in advance of his closing submissions, since he planned to tailor his address to the judge's ruling. The trial judge, however, refused to make any ruling until *after* hearing counsel's closing addresses. Defence counsel made submissions, including some on the necessity defence. When counsel had concluded their addresses, the trial judge ruled that the jury was *not* entitled to consider necessity.

[19] Second, some time after beginning their deliberations, the jury sent a number of written questions to the trial judge, one of which was: "Is there any possible way we can have input to a recommendation for sentencing?" The trial judge told the jury it was not to concern itself with the penalty. He said:

> ... the penalty in any of these charges is not the concern of the jury. Your concern is, as I said, the guilt or innocence of the accused, and you must reach—that's your job, you reach that conclusion, and don't concern yourself what the penalty might be. We say that because we don't want you to be influenced one way or the other with what that penalty is. *So it may*

be that later on, once you have reached a verdict, you—we will have some discussions about that, but not at this stage of the game. You must just carry on and answer the question that was put to you, okay.

The appellant highlights the [italicized] passage as misleading the jury.

[20] After the jury returned with a guilty verdict, the trial judge explained the mandatory minimum sentence of life imprisonment, and asked the jury whether it had any recommendation as to whether Mr. Latimer's ineligibility for parole should exceed the minimum period of 10 years. Some jury members appeared upset, according to the trial judge, and later sent a note asking him if they could recommend less than the 10-year minimum. The trial judge explained that the *Criminal Code* provided only for a recommendation over the 10-year minimum, but suggested that the jury could make any recommendation it liked. The jury recommended one year before parole eligibility. The trial judge then granted a constitutional exemption from the mandatory minimum sentence, sentencing the appellant to one year of imprisonment and one year on probation, to be spent confined to his farm.

[21] The Court of Appeal for Saskatchewan affirmed Mr. Latimer's conviction but reversed the sentence. It imposed the mandatory minimum sentence for second degree murder of life imprisonment without eligibility for parole for 10 years. ...

III. Judicial History

[23] Mr. Latimer was tried by jury, during the course of which the trial judge made two rulings (besides his handling of the jury's inquiry as to sentence) that are at issue in this appeal. First, as previously outlined, he held that the jury was not entitled to consider the defence of necessity. Second, the trial judge granted a constitutional exemption from the mandatory minimum sentence for second degree murder: (1997), 121 C.C.C. (3d) 326 (Sask. Q.B.). The trial judge concluded that the mandatory sentence amounted to cruel and unusual punishment in this case. He reasoned that the exemption was a valid and appropriate remedy, given the particular circumstances of this offender, his motives, the public reaction to the mandatory sentence in Mr. Latimer's first trial, and his reduced level of criminal culpability.

[24] The Court of Appeal for Saskatchewan dismissed the appeal from conviction in a *per curiam* decision: (1998), 131 C.C.C. (3d) 191. The trial judge was correct to remove the defence of necessity from the jury, the Court of Appeal held, and the timing of the trial judge's ruling did not result in an unfair trial. The court reversed the trial judge's remedy of a constitutional exemption, commenting, at p. 216, that "the learned trial judge took too much upon himself in bypassing the judgment of this Court, the direction of Parliament, and the executive power of clemency." The Court of Appeal concluded that Mr. Latimer must serve the mandatory 10-year sentence before parole eligibility. ...

(1) The Availability of the Defence of Necessity

(a) The Three Requirements for the Defence of Necessity

[26] We propose to set out the requirements for the defence of necessity first, before applying them to the facts of this appeal. The leading case on the defence of necessity is

Perka v. The Queen, [1984] 2 S.C.R. 232. Dickson J., later C.J., outlined the rationale for the defence at p. 248:

> It rests on a realistic assessment of human weakness, recognizing that a liberal and humane criminal law cannot hold people to the strict obedience of laws in emergency situations where normal human instincts, whether of self-preservation or of altruism, overwhelmingly impel disobedience. The objectivity of the criminal law is preserved; such acts are still wrongful, but in the circumstances they are excusable. Praise is indeed not bestowed, but pardon is. ...

[27] Dickson J. insisted that the defence of necessity be restricted to those rare cases in which true "involuntariness" is present. The defence, he held, must be "strictly controlled and scrupulously limited" (p. 250). It is well-established that the defence of necessity must be of limited application. Were the criteria for the defence loosened or approached purely subjectively, some fear, as did Edmund Davies L.J., that necessity would "very easily become simply a mask for anarchy": *Southwark London Borough Council v. Williams*, [1971] Ch. 734 (C.A.), at p. 746.

[28] *Perka* outlined three elements that must be present for the defence of necessity. First, there is the requirement of imminent peril or danger. Second, the accused must have had no reasonable legal alternative to the course of action he or she undertook. Third, there must be proportionality between the harm inflicted and the harm avoided.

[29] To begin, there must be an urgent situation of "clear and imminent peril": *Morgentaler v. The Queen*, [1976] 1 S.C.R. 616, at p. 678. In short, disaster must be imminent, or harm unavoidable and near. It is not enough that the peril is foreseeable or likely; it must be on the verge of transpiring and virtually certain to occur. In *Perka*, Dickson J. expressed the requirement of imminent peril at p. 251: "At a minimum the situation must be so emergent and the peril must be so pressing that normal human instincts cry out for action and make a counsel of patience unreasonable." The *Perka* case, at p. 251, also offers the rationale for this requirement of immediate peril: "The requirement ... tests whether it was indeed unavoidable for the actor to act at all." Where the situation of peril clearly should have been foreseen and avoided, an accused person cannot reasonably claim any immediate peril.

[30] The second requirement for necessity is that there must be no reasonable legal alternative to disobeying the law. *Perka* proposed these questions, at pp. 251-52: "Given that the accused had to act, could he nevertheless realistically have acted to avoid the peril or prevent the harm, without breaking the law? *Was there a legal way out?*" (emphasis in original). If there was a reasonable legal alternative to breaking the law, there is no necessity. It may be noted that the requirement involves a realistic appreciation of the alternatives open to a person; the accused need not be placed in the last resort imaginable, but he must have no reasonable legal alternative. If an alternative to breaking the law exists, the defence of necessity on this aspect fails.

[31] The third requirement is that there be proportionality between the harm inflicted and the harm avoided. The harm inflicted must not be disproportionate to the harm the accused sought to avoid. See *Perka*, per Dickson J., at p. 252:

> No rational criminal justice system, no matter how humane or liberal, could excuse the infliction of a greater harm to allow the actor to avert a lesser evil. In such circumstances we

expect the individual to bear the harm and refrain from acting illegally. If he cannot control himself we will not excuse him.

Evaluating proportionality can be difficult. It may be easy to conclude that there is no proportionality in some cases, like the example given in *Perka* of the person who blows up a city to avoid breaking a finger. Where proportionality can quickly be dismissed, it makes sense for a trial judge to do so and rule out the defence of necessity before considering the other requirements for necessity. But most situations fall into a grey area that requires a difficult balancing of harms. In this regard, it should be noted that the requirement is not that one harm (the harm avoided) must always clearly outweigh the other (the harm inflicted). Rather, the two harms must, at a minimum, be of a comparable gravity. That is, the harm avoided must be either comparable to, or clearly greater than, the harm inflicted. As the Supreme Court of Victoria in Australia has put it, the harm inflicted "must not be out of proportion to the peril to be avoided": *R. v. Loughnan*, [1981] V.R. 443, at p. 448.

[32] Before applying the three requirements of the necessity defence to the facts of this case, we need to determine what test governs necessity. Is the standard objective or subjective? A subjective test would be met if the person believed he or she was in imminent peril with no reasonable legal alternative to committing the offence. Conversely, an objective test would not assess what the accused believed; it would consider whether in fact the person *was* in peril with no reasonable legal alternative. A modified objective test falls somewhere between the two. It involves an objective evaluation, but one that takes into account the situation and characteristics of the particular accused person. We conclude that, for two of the three requirements for the necessity defence, the test should be the modified objective test.

[33] The first and second requirements—imminent peril and no reasonable legal alternative—must be evaluated on the modified objective standard described above. As expressed in *Perka*, necessity is rooted in an objective standard: "involuntariness is measured on the basis of society's expectation of appropriate and normal resistance to pressure" (p. 259). We would add that it is appropriate, in evaluating the accused's conduct, to take into account personal characteristics that legitimately affect what may be expected of that person. The approach taken in *R. v. Hibbert*, [1995] 2 S.C.R. 973, is instructive. Speaking for the Court, Lamer C.J. held, at para. 59, that:

> it is appropriate to employ an objective standard that takes into account the particular circumstances of the accused, including his or her ability to perceive the existence of alternative courses of action.

While an accused's perceptions of the surrounding facts may be highly relevant in determining whether his conduct should be excused, those perceptions remain relevant only so long as they are reasonable. The accused person must, at the time of the act, honestly believe, on reasonable grounds, that he faces a situation of imminent peril that leaves no reasonable legal alternative open. There must be a reasonable basis for the accused's beliefs and actions, but it would be proper to take into account circumstances that legitimately affect the accused person's ability to evaluate his situation. The test cannot be a subjective one, and the accused who argues that *he* perceived imminent peril without an alternative would only succeed with the defence of necessity if his belief was reasonable given his circumstances and attributes. We leave aside for a case in which it arises the possibility that an honestly held but mistaken belief could ground a "mistake of fact" argument on the separate inquiry into *mens rea*.

[34] The third requirement for the defence of necessity, proportionality, must be measured on an objective standard, as it would violate fundamental principles of the criminal law to do otherwise. Evaluating the nature of an act is fundamentally a determination reflecting society's values as to what is appropriate and what represents a transgression. Some insight into this requirement is provided by George Fletcher, in a passage from *Rethinking Criminal Law* (1978), at p. 804. Fletcher spoke of the comparison between the harm inflicted and the harm avoided, and suggested that there was a threshold at which a person must be expected to suffer the harm rather than break the law. He continued:

> Determining this threshold is patently a matter of moral judgment about what we expect people to be able to resist in trying situations. A valuable aid in making that judgment is comparing the competing interests at stake and assessing the degree to which the actor inflicts harm beyond the benefit that accrues from his action.

The evaluation of the seriousness of the harms must be objective. A subjective evaluation of the competing harms would, by definition, look at the matter from the perspective of the accused person who seeks to avoid harm, usually to himself. The proper perspective, however, is an objective one, since evaluating the gravity of the act is a matter of community standards infused with constitutional considerations (such as, in this case, the s. 15(1) equality rights of the disabled). We conclude that the proportionality requirement must be determined on a purely objective standard.

(b) The Application of the Requirements for Necessity in This Case

[35] The inquiry here is not whether the defence of necessity should in fact *excuse* Mr. Latimer's actions, but whether the jury should have been left to consider this defence. The correct test on that point is whether there is an air of reality to the defence. In *R. v. Osolin*, [1993] 4 S.C.R. 595, at p. 676, Cory J. stated:

> ... a defence should not be put to the jury if a reasonable jury properly instructed would have been unable to acquit on the basis of the evidence tendered in support of that defence. On the other hand, if a reasonable jury properly instructed could acquit on the basis of the evidence tendered with regard to that defence, then it must be put to the jury. It is for the trial judge to decide whether the evidence is sufficient to warrant putting a defence to a jury as this is a question of law alone.

The question is whether there is sufficient evidence that, if believed, would allow a reasonable jury—properly charged and acting judicially—to conclude that the defence applied and acquit the accused.

[36] For the necessity defence, the trial judge must be satisfied that there is evidence sufficient to give an air of reality to each of the three requirements. If the trial judge concludes that there is no air of reality to any one of the three requirements, the defence of necessity should not be left to the jury.

[37] In this case, there was no air of reality to the three requirements of necessity.

[38] The first requirement is imminent peril. It is not met in this case. The appellant does not suggest he himself faced any peril; instead he identifies a peril to his daughter, stemming from her upcoming surgery which he perceived as a form of mutilation. Acute suffering can constitute imminent peril, but in this case there was nothing to her medical condition that placed Tracy in a dangerous situation where death was an alternative. Tracy was thought to be in pain before the surgery, and that pain was expected to continue, or increase, following the surgery. But that ongoing pain did not constitute an emergency in this case. To borrow the language of Edmund Davies L.J. in *Southwark London Borough Council, supra,* at p. 746, we are dealing not with an emergency but with "an obstinate and long-standing state of affairs." Tracy's proposed surgery did not pose an imminent threat to her life, nor did her medical condition. In fact, Tracy's health might have improved had the Latimers not rejected the option of relying on a feeding tube. Tracy's situation was not an emergency. The appellant can be reasonably expected to have understood that reality. There was no evidence of a legitimate psychological condition that rendered him unable to perceive that there was no imminent peril. The appellant argued that, for him, further surgery *did* amount to imminent peril. It was not reasonable for the appellant to form this belief, particularly when better pain management was available.

[39] The second requirement for the necessity defence is that the accused had no reasonable legal alternative to breaking the law. In this case, there is no air of reality to the proposition that the appellant had no reasonable legal alternative to killing his daughter. He had at least one reasonable legal alternative: he could have struggled on, with what was unquestionably a difficult situation, by helping Tracy to live and by minimizing her pain as much as possible. The appellant might have done so by using a feeding tube to improve her health and allow her to take more effective pain medication, or he might have relied on the group home that Tracy stayed at just before her death. The appellant may well have thought the prospect of struggling on unbearably sad and demanding. It was a human response that this alternative was unappealing. But it was a reasonable legal alternative that the law requires a person to pursue before he can claim the defence of necessity. The appellant was aware of this alternative but rejected it.

[40] The third requirement for the necessity defence is proportionality; it requires the trial judge to consider, as a question of law rather than fact, whether the harm avoided was proportionate to the harm inflicted. It is difficult, at the conceptual level, to imagine a circumstance in which the proportionality requirement could be met for a homicide. We leave open, if and until it arises, the question of whether the proportionality requirement could be met in a homicide situation. In England, the defence of necessity is probably not available for homicide: *R. v. Howe,* [1987] 1 A.C. 417 (H.L.), at pp. 453 and 429; Smith and Hogan, *Criminal Law* (9th ed. 1999), at pp. 249-51. The famous case of *R. v. Dudley and Stephens* (1884), 14 Q.B.D. 273, involving cannibalism on the high seas, is often cited as establishing the unavailability of the defence of necessity for homicide, although the case is not conclusive: see Card, Cross and Jones, *Criminal Law* (12th ed. 1992), at p. 352; Smith and Hogan, *supra,* at pp. 249 and 251. The Law Reform Commission of Canada has suggested the defence should not be available for a person who intentionally kills or seriously harms another person: *Report on Recodifying Criminal Law* (1987), at p. 36. American jurisdictions are divided on this question, with a number of them denying the necessity defence for murder: P.H. Robinson, *Criminal Law Defenses* (1984), vol. 2, at pp. 63-65; see also *United States v. Holmes,* 26 F. Cas. 360 (C.C.E.D. Pa.

1842) (No. 15,383). The American *Model Penal Code* proposes that the defence of necessity *would* be available for homicide: American Law Institute, *Model Penal Code and Commentaries* (1985), at §3.02, pp. 14-15; see also W.R. LaFave and A.W. Scott, *Substantive Criminal Law* (1986), vol. 1, at p. 634.

[41] Assuming for the sake of analysis only that necessity could provide a defence to homicide, there would have to be a harm that was seriously comparable in gravity to death (the harm inflicted). In this case, there was no risk of such harm. The "harm avoided" in the appellant's situation was, compared to death, completely disproportionate. The harm inflicted in this case was ending a life; that harm was immeasurably more serious than the pain resulting from Tracy's operation which Mr. Latimer sought to avoid. Killing a person—in order to relieve the suffering produced by a medically manageable physical or mental condition—is not a proportionate response to the harm represented by the non-life-threatening suffering resulting from that condition.

[42] We conclude that there was no air of reality to *any* of the three requirements for necessity. As noted earlier, if the trial judge concludes that even one of the requirements had no air of reality, the defence should not be left to the jury. Here, the trial judge was correct to remove the defence from the jury. In considering the defence of necessity, we must remain aware of the need to respect the life, dignity and equality of all the individuals affected by the act in question. The fact that the victim in this case was disabled rather than able-bodied does not affect our conclusion that the three requirements for the defence of necessity had no air of reality here. … Mr. Latimer's appeals against conviction and sentence are dismissed.

In Chapter 20, this book's chapter on sentencing, you will have an opportunity to consider Latimer's sentence appeal and the Court's holding that the mandatory minimum sentence of life imprisonment with no eligibility for parole for 10 years did not violate his s 12 Charter right against cruel and unusual punishment.

Latimer has attracted much popular and academic attention. For instance, see K Roach, "Crime and Punishment in the Latimer Case" (2001) 64 Sask L Rev 469; GT Trotter, "Necessity and Death: Lessons from Latimer and the Case of the Conjoined Twins" (2003) 40 Alta L Rev 817; A Manson, "Motivation, the Supreme Court and Mandatory Sentencing for Murder" (2001) 39 CR (5th) 65; B Sneiderman, "R v Latimer: Juries and Mandatory Penalties" (2001) 39 CR (5th) 29; and D Stuart, "A Hard Case Makes for Too Harsh Law" (2001) 39 CR (5th) 58.

Claims of necessity arise, by definition, in extraordinary and often unforeseeable circumstances. As you have learned, and as *Latimer* so vividly demonstrates, claims of necessity in such situations ultimately call upon courts to make judgments about what we are willing to demand from individuals faced with seemingly impossible situations. Such judgments are, ultimately, very much value-laden and express differing views of the moral limits of the criminal law (a theme introduced in Chapter 2).

Consider the case of *R v Kerr*, 2004 SCC 44, [2004] 2 SCR 371. The accused was an inmate in a maximum security institution who had received death threats from a man named Garon, a fellow inmate who was a member of a powerful prison gang that, on the evidence, was in effective control of the institution. Having received the threat, Kerr armed himself with two makeshift weapons. Garon approached Kerr the next morning, brandishing a weapon of his own. The two fought, stabbing each other multiple times with their homemade knives. Garon died of his wounds and Kerr was charged with second-degree murder and possession of a weapon for a dangerous purpose, contrary to s 88(1) of the *Criminal Code*. The trial judge acquitted Kerr on both counts, relying largely on self-defence. The Alberta Court of Appeal dismissed the appeal on the second-degree murder charge but allowed the appeal on the weapons charge and substituted a conviction. The Supreme Court restored the acquittal. Although the majority of the Court ultimately decided the case on other grounds, Arbour and LeBel JJ would have found that the defence of necessity applied on the basis that Kerr "had a reasonable belief that the circumstances afforded him no legal way out" and that "the harm he sought to avoid—in the words of the trial judge, 'a lethal attack'—outweighed the breach of s. 88(1)" (at para 96). Justice Binnie, dissenting in the case, took a different position on the necessity issue, reasoning (at para 68) that "[t]he argument that violent self-help in breach of the peace can be justified as 'necessity' has been rejected since medieval times as inimical to public order and should not be given new credence in 21st century Alberta."

Since the events of September 11, 2001, the defence of necessity has been at the centre of international debates as to whether the criminal law should excuse or justify extreme actions taken by government officials to prevent anticipated catastrophic harms. See e.g. K Ambos, "May a State Torture Suspects to Save the Life of Innocents?" (2008) 6 J Intl Criminal Justice 261; JD Ohlin, "The Bounds of Necessity" (2008) 6 J Intl Criminal Justice 289; KK Ferzan, "Torture, Necessity, and the Union of Law and Philosophy" (2004) 36 Rutgers LJ 183; and F Jessberger, "Bad Torture—Good Torture: What International Criminal Lawyers May Learn from the Recent Trial of Police Officers in Germany" (2005) 3 J Intl Criminal Justice 1059. In the last-mentioned article the author discusses a case in which a high-ranking Frankfurt Police official, Wolfgang Daschner, ordered that pain be inflicted on a kidnapping suspect (without causing injuries and with prior warning) in order to gather information in an attempt to save the missing boy. Having been threatened with physical pain that "he would never forget," the suspect disclosed the location of the boy, who, it turned out, he had already killed. Daschner and his subordinate were charged with criminal offences arising from these threats of torture. The Regional Court at Frankfurt found both guilty, concluding that the defence of necessity was not applicable, but held that, in the circumstances, no punishment should be imposed.

IV. NECESSITY AND CODIFICATION

Necessity remains a common law defence in Canada, preserved by s 8(3) of the *Criminal Code*. Other jurisdictions have codified versions of the defence that address some of the issues raised in this chapter. Consider, for example, the German *Criminal Code (Strafgesetzbuches)*, as amended in July 2009, which deals with necessity in the following way:

Section 34: Necessity as Justification

A person who, faced with an imminent danger to life, limb, freedom, honour, property or another legal interest which cannot otherwise be averted, commits an act to avert the danger from himself or another, does not act unlawfully, if, upon weighing the conflicting interests, in particular the affected legal interests and the degree of the danger facing them, the protected interest substantially outweighs the one interfered with. This shall apply only if and to the extent that the act committed is an adequate means to avert the danger.

Section 35: Necessity as Excuse

(1) A person who, faced with an imminent danger to life, limb or freedom which cannot otherwise be averted, commits an unlawful act to avert the danger from himself, a relative or person close to him, acts without guilt. This shall not apply if and to the extent that the offender could be expected under the circumstances to accept the danger, in particular, because he himself had caused the danger, or was under a special legal obligation to do so; the sentence may be mitigated pursuant to section 49(1) unless the offender was required to accept the danger because of a special legal obligation to do so.

(2) If at the time of the commission of the act a person mistakenly assumes that circumstances exist which would excuse him under subsection (1) above, he will only be liable if the mistake was avoidable. The sentence shall be mitigated pursuant to section 49(1).

The French *Code Penal* approaches the defence with a very simple provision that focuses on proportionality as the controlling concept:

Article 122-7

A person is not criminally liable if confronted with a present or imminent danger to himself, another person or property, he performs an act necessary to ensure the safety of the person or property, except where the means used are disproportionate to the seriousness of the threat.

The American Law Institute's *Model Penal Code* provides the following in s 3.02, which includes a subsection that deals with the issue, raised above, of an accused who had a role in bringing about the necessitous situation:

(1) Conduct which the actor believes to be necessary to avoid a harm or evil to himself or to another is justifiable, provided that:

(a) the harm or evil sought to be avoided by such conduct is greater than that sought to be prevented by the law defining the offense charged; and

(b) neither the Code nor other law defining the offense provides exceptions or defenses dealing with the specific situation involved; and

(c) a legislative purpose to exclude the justification claimed does not otherwise plainly appear.

(2) When the actor was reckless or negligent in bringing about the situation requiring a choice of harms or evils or in appraising the necessity for his conduct, the justification afforded by this Section is unavailable in a prosecution for any offense for which recklessness or negligence, as the case may be, suffices to establish culpability.

In 1987, the Law Reform Commission of Canada proposed the following codification of the defence of necessity and explained it in the commentary that follows:

Law Reform Commission of Canada, *Recodifying Criminal Law*
Report 31 (1987) at 36

3(9) Necessity.

(a) General Rule. No one is liable if:

(i) he acted to avoid immediate harm to the person or immediate serious damage to property;

(ii) such harm or damage substantially outweighed the harm or damage resulting from that crime; and

     (iii) such harm or damage could not effectively have been avoided by any lesser means.

     (b) Exception. This clause does not apply to anyone who himself purposely causes the death of, or seriously harms, another person.

Comment

The duty to obey the law may conflict with pressure stemming from natural forces or from some other source not covered by the more specific defences known to law. Such cases may be covered by the residual defence of necessity. Though not included in the present *Criminal Code*, it is well recognized by case-law and has been clarified by the Supreme Court of Canada. For the sake of comprehensiveness, clause 3(9) incorporates and codifies the rule laid down there.

     The application of the defence in any given case involves a judgment call. The trier of fact must consider whether the harm to be avoided was immediate; necessity relates only to emergencies. He must decide whether the harm avoided substantially outweighed the harm done, once again a matter for assessment.

     At common law it was clear that necessity was no defence to murder. This Code replaces that restriction with a more general one parallel to that used in duress and based on the same principle. The defence will not therefore avail one who himself purposely causes the death of, or seriously harms, another person.

The Sub-Committee of the Standing Committee on Justice and the Solicitor-General on the General Part of the Criminal Code stated in its Report of February 1993:

> The Law Reform Commission also proposed that the defence not be available to someone who caused bodily harm or death. The Commission reasoned that no one should harm or kill another person in order to save himself or herself. While it is sympathetic to this reasoning, the Sub-Committee would prefer not to put an express limitation on the actions that could be taken in necessitous circumstances. Such a limit may prove to be arbitrary and unjust.

In June 1993, the Department of Justice issued a white paper entitled *Proposals to Amend the Criminal Code (General Principles)*, which recommended that necessity should be codified, as "duress of circumstances," in the following way:

> 36(1) A person is not guilty of an offence, other than murder, to the extent that the person acts under
>
>   (a) duress of circumstances; or
>
>   (b) duress by threats.
>
> (2) A person acts under duress of circumstances if, otherwise than under duress by threats as described in subsection (3) or in defence of a person as described in section 37,
>
>   (a) the person acts to avoid what the person believes to be significant danger of imminent and otherwise unavoidable death or serious bodily harm to that person or another person,
>
>   (b) the person's acts are proportionate to the harm that the person seeks to avoid, and
>
>   (c) the person cannot reasonably be expected to act otherwise in response to the danger that the person believes to exist,
>
> but the defence of duress of circumstances is not available if the person, knowingly and without reasonable excuse, exposed themself to the danger.

As you know, no such proposal for codification or statutory reform has been implemented in Canada. Do you think that the necessity defence should be codified? If so, which of these approaches appeals to you and what features would you want to see in a codified necessity defence? Should (and could) a codified necesssity defence exclude certain offences, such as murder? Having studied the *Ruzic* case and the principle of moral voluntariness in Chapter 18, what constitutional limitations might there be on how the defence of necessity could be codified?

ADDITIONAL READING

Berger, BL. "A Choice Among Values: Theoretical and Historical Perspectives on the Defence of Necessity" (2002) 39 Alta L Rev 848.

Brudner, A. "A Theory of Necessity" (1987) 7 Oxford J Leg Stud 339.

Harel, A & A Sharon. "'Necessity Knows No Law': On Extreme Cases and Uncodifiable Necessities" (2011) 61 UTLJ 845.

Horder, J. "Self-Defence, Necessity and Duress: Understanding the Relationship" (1998) 11 Can JL & Jur 143.

Manning, M & P Sankoff. *Manning, Mewett & Sankoff: Criminal Law*, 4th ed (Toronto: Lexis-Nexis, 2009) at 489-500.

Paciocco, DM. "No-One Wants to Be Eaten: The Logic and Experience of the Law of Necessity and Duress" (2010) 56 Crim LQ 240.

Roach, K. *Criminal Law*, 6th ed (Toronto: Irwin Law, 2015) ch 9.

Stuart, D. *Canadian Criminal Law*, 7th ed (Toronto: Carswell, 2014) at 557-79.

Trotter, GT. "Necessity and Death: Lessons from Latimer and the Case of the Conjoined Twins" (2003) 40 Alta L Rev 817.

Yeo, S. "Revisiting Necessity" (2010) 56 Crim LQ 13.

Young, D. "Excuses and Intelligibility in Criminal Law" (2004) 53 UNBLJ 79.

Disposition

Sentencing

Legal philosophers have long debated both the justification for and purpose of punishment. Although Canadian criminal law reform has undoubtedly been touched by these debates, most participants in the justice system take as a given the imposition of a sentence as the natural endpoint of the criminal process for those found guilty of an offence, and focus instead on issues surrounding the measure and consequences of punishment. This chapter takes its lead from Canadian criminal law and attempts to sketch out a broad overview of the practice of sentencing. To be sure, this subject would require a work in its own right to comprehensively address. See e.g. A Manson et al, *Sentencing and Penal Policy in Canada: Cases, Materials, and Commentary*, 2nd ed (Toronto: Emond Montgomery, 2008). And yet, as you will see, these practices of sentencing are themselves deeply touched by the broader questions surrounding the nature and theory of punishment.

Contemporary sentencing law in Canada has essentially been marked by three principal developments. A consideration of each will provide the organizational structure of this chapter. Section I will introduce the current legislative framework for sentencing, with particular emphasis on the purposes and principles of sentencing. It will also briefly introduce the various sanctions available under Canadian law and the central role of judicial discretion in the sentencing process. Section II will address the sentencing of Aboriginal offenders and the (thus far) failed efforts of Parliament and the courts to reform the law of sentencing so as to ameliorate the overrepresentation of Aboriginal people in Canada's prisons. Finally, Section III will consider the impact of the *Charter of Rights and Freedoms* on sentencing, especially the application of s 12, which protects against cruel and unusual treatment or punishment. The focus will be on cases that present conflicts between Parliament's interests in deterring and denouncing crime through the use of mandatory minimum sentences and the importance of judicial discretion in tailoring sentences to both the offence and the offender's responsibility for the offence. As will be seen, s 12 of the Charter provides a constitutional limitation on the ability of Parliament to enact mandatory minimum sentences. This has proven important in recent years given the proliferation of mandatory minimum sentences under the current government's crime agenda.

I. THE LEGISLATIVE FRAMEWORK

There are provisions throughout the *Criminal Code* that bear upon the question of sentencing. Virtually every offence-creating provision also includes an accompanying subsection that specifies the minimum (if there is one) or the maximum punishment relating to that offence. Yet, general issues surrounding sentencing are dealt with rather comprehensively in part XXIII of the Code.

The Code did not always include an entire part dedicated to sentencing. The sentencing function was previously an exercise of judicial discretion tempered only by guidance provided in decisions of appellate courts. Typical of this approach is the following statement of the Supreme Court of Canada in *R v Lyons*, [1987] 2 SCR 309, per La Forest J:

> In a rational system of sentencing, the respective importance of prevention, deterrence, retribution and rehabilitation will vary according to the nature of the crime and the circumstances of the offender. No one would suggest that any of these functional considerations should be excluded from the legitimate purview of legislative or judicial decisions regarding sentencing.

In 1996, Parliament enacted Bill C-41. It came into force as the new part XXIII of the *Criminal Code*. This reform was the result of years of study and effort, the culmination of earlier work that included the Ouimet Committee, the Law Reform Commission, the Royal Commission on Sentencing, the Department of Justice, and the Daubney Committee in the House of Commons. Each had undertaken empirical work meant to test the implications of various sentencing options and correctional models. Finally, as Bill C-41 progressed through Parliament, its provisions were the subject of much evidence before the responsible committee and considerable debate.

The purpose behind these amendments and their implications are discussed in some detail in *R v Proulx*, below. Before reading that decision, however, it is worthwhile to gain a more detailed understanding of the provisions in the Code dealing with sentencing.

A. The Principles and Purposes of Sentencing

One of the key reforms introduced by Bill C-41 was the inclusion in the *Criminal Code* of a statement of principles and purposes concerning sentencing. As a result, and with some further additions over the intervening years, ss 718 to 718.2 now provide:

Purpose

718. The fundamental purpose of sentencing is to contribute, along with crime prevention initiatives, to respect for the law and the maintenance of a just, peaceful and safe society by imposing just sanctions that have one or more of the following objectives:

   (a) to denounce unlawful conduct;

   (b) to deter the offender and other persons from committing offences;

(c) to separate offenders from society, where necessary;

(d) to assist in rehabilitating offenders;

(e) to provide reparations for harm done to victims or to the community; and

(f) to promote a sense of responsibility in offenders, and acknowledgment of the harm done to victims and to the community.

Objectives—offences against children

718.01 When a court imposes a sentence for an offence that involved the abuse of a person under the age of eighteen years, it shall give primary consideration to the objectives of denunciation and deterrence of such conduct.

Objectives—offence against peace officer or other justice system participant

718.02 When a court imposes a sentence for an offence under subsection 270(1), section 270.01 or 270.02 or paragraph 423.1(1)(b), the court shall give primary consideration to the objectives of denunciation and deterrence of the conduct that forms the basis of the offence.

Fundamental principle

718.1 A sentence must be proportionate to the gravity of the offence and the degree of responsibility of the offender.

Other sentencing principles

718.2 A court that imposes a sentence shall also take into consideration the following principles:

(a) a sentence should be increased or reduced to account for any relevant aggravating or mitigating circumstances relating to the offence or the offender, and, without limiting the generality of the foregoing,

(i) evidence that the offence was motivated by bias, prejudice or hate based on race, national or ethnic origin, language, colour, religion, sex, age, mental or physical disability, sexual orientation, or any other similar factor, or

(ii) evidence that the offender, in committing the offence, abused the offender's spouse or common-law partner,

(ii.1) evidence that the offender, in committing the offence, abused a person under the age of eighteen years,

(iii) evidence that the offender, in committing the offence, abused a position of trust or authority in relation to the victim,

(iii.1) evidence that the offence had a significant impact on the victim, considering their age and other personal circumstances, including their health and financial situation,

(iv) evidence that the offence was committed for the benefit of, at the direction of or in association with a criminal organization, or

(v) evidence that the offence was a terrorism offence

shall be deemed to be aggravating circumstances;

(b) a sentence should be similar to sentences imposed on similar offenders for similar offences committed in similar circumstances;

(c) where consecutive sentences are imposed, the combined sentence should not be unduly long or harsh;

(d) an offender should not be deprived of liberty, if less restrictive sanctions may be appropriate in the circumstances; and

(e) all available sanctions other than imprisonment that are reasonable in the circumstances should be considered for all offenders, with particular attention to the circumstances of aboriginal offenders.

Without a doubt, one of the motivations for articulating the principles and objectives of sentencing was to provide greater certainty and even predictability to the sentencing process. As you review the cases below that post-date these amendments, consider whether these amendments have managed to achieve that purpose.

B. The Available Sentencing Tools

Subject to any statutorily prescribed minimum or maximum punishments and the very general guidance provided by the principles and purposes of sentencing, judges have considerable discretion in deciding upon the appropriate sentence. Further, the *Criminal Code* provides judges with a variety of options beyond simply sending an offender to jail. Indeed, as ss 718.2(d) and (e) make clear, imprisonment should be the last resort. As for other sentencing tools available, the following is a brief summary of the options available under the Code.

Absolute and Conditional Discharges

If an accused is found guilty of an offence for which no minimum punishment is prescribed by law and that is not punishable by 14 years' or life imprisonment, an absolute or conditional discharge can be given. This means that despite a finding of guilt, no conviction is registered. Under s 730 of the Code the discharge must be in "the best interests of the accused and not contrary to the public interest." A conditional discharge is accompanied by a probation order.

Probation

The making of probation orders is governed by s 731 of the Code. Probation orders may be imposed when an offender is conditionally discharged, fined, or imprisoned for less than two years. Further, one can be imposed when the passage of the sentence is suspended. The maximum duration of a probation order is three years.

The relevant provisions require certain conditions to be included. For example, every probation order must include a condition that the offender "keep the peace and be of good behaviour, [and] appear before the court when required to do so by the court."

In addition, judges have a fair amount of discretion to impose other conditions. For example, such orders often include conditions that an offender report to a probation officer, abide by a curfew, attend school or seek and maintain gainful employment, take counselling, and even perform up to 240 hours of community service. See *Criminal Code*, ss 731 to 733.1.

Restitution

Under s 738 of the *Criminal Code*, an offender who is convicted or subject to an absolute or conditional discharge can be required to make restitution for damage to property and pecuniary losses from bodily harm that result from the commission of the offence or the arrest of the offender. Reasonable moving and temporary housing costs may also be ordered in cases involving bodily harm or the threat of bodily harm to the offender's spouse or child.

Fines

Under s 734(2) of the *Criminal Code*, a court may fine an offender only if it is satisfied that the offender is able to pay the fine or work the fine off under a fine option program contemplated under s 736. There are also provisions in s 734.5 that allow licences to be denied for non-payment of fines and civil enforcement and imprisonment for defaulting on fines.

Conditional Sentences

One of the most important and controversial aspects of Bill C-41 was the creation of a new sanction—the conditional sentence. When first enacted, the relevant provision read:

> 742.1 Where a person is convicted of an offence, except an offence that is punishable by a minimum term of imprisonment, and the court
>> (a) imposes a sentence of imprisonment of less than two years, and
>> (b) is satisfied that serving the sentence in the community would not endanger the safety of the community and would be consistent with the fundamental purpose and principles of sentencing set out in sections 718 to 718.2,
> the court may, for the purpose of supervising the offender's behaviour in the community, order that the offender serve the sentence in the community, subject to the offender's complying with the conditions of a conditional sentence order made under section 742.3.

The next decision explains the purpose and significance of Bill C-41, while specifically addressing the considerations that should govern the imposition of conditional sentences. In the process, the decision also explains the use and purpose of probation orders.

R v Proulx
Supreme Court of Canada
2000 SCC 5, [2000] 1 SCR 61

[The 18-year-old accused, who had been driving for only seven weeks, was convicted of dangerous driving causing death and dangerous driving causing bodily harm. He had been drinking. The trial judge determined that a sentence of 18 months was appropriate, and despite the fact that the accused would not endanger the community, a conditional sentence of imprisonment would not be consistent with the other principles of sentencing in the *Criminal Code*. Accordingly, an 18-month sentence was imposed. The Court of Appeal allowed the appeal and substituted an 18-month conditional sentence. The Supreme Court of Canada restored the sentence of incarceration, but provided important guidance on the application of this sanction.]

LAMER CJ:

[1] By passing the *Act to amend the Criminal Code (sentencing) and other Acts in consequence thereof*, S.C. 1995, c. 22 ("Bill C-41"), Parliament has sent a clear message to

all Canadian judges that too many people are being sent to prison. In an attempt to remedy the problem of overincarceration, Parliament has introduced a new form of sentence, the conditional sentence of imprisonment.

. . .

[12] Since it came into force on September 3, 1996, the conditional sentence has generated considerable debate. With the advent of s. 742.1, Parliament has clearly mandated that certain offenders who used to go to prison should now serve their sentences in the community. Section 742.1 makes a conditional sentence available to a subclass of non-dangerous offenders who, prior to the introduction of this new regime, would have been sentenced to a term of incarceration of less than two years for offences with no minimum term of imprisonment.

[13] In my view, to address meaningfully the complex interpretive issues raised by this appeal, it is important to situate this new sentencing tool in the broader context of the comprehensive sentencing reforms enacted by Parliament in Bill C-41. I will also consider the nature of the conditional sentence, contrasting it with probationary measures and incarceration. Next, I will address particular interpretive issues posed by s. 742.1. I will first discuss the statutory prerequisites to the imposition of a conditional sentence. Thereafter, I will consider how courts should determine whether a conditional sentence is appropriate, assuming the prerequisites are satisfied. I conclude with some general comments on the deference to which trial judges are entitled in matters of sentencing and dispose of the case at hand in conformity with the principles outlined in these reasons.

V. Analysis

A. The 1996 Sentencing Reforms (Bill C-41)

[14] In September 1996, Bill C-41 came into effect. It substantially reformed Part XXIII of the *Code*, and introduced, *inter alia*, an express statement of the purposes and principles of sentencing, provisions for alternative measures for adult offenders and a new type of sanction, the conditional sentence of imprisonment.

[15] As my colleagues Cory and Iacobucci JJ. explained in *R. v. Gladue*, [1999] 1 S.C.R. 688, at para. 39, "[t]he enactment of the new Part XXIII was a watershed, marking the first codification and significant reform of sentencing principles in the history of Canadian criminal law." They noted two of Parliament's principal objectives in enacting this new legislation: (i) reducing the use of prison as a sanction, and (ii) expanding the use of restorative justice principles in sentencing (at para. 48).

(1) Reducing the Use of Prison as a Sanction

[16] Bill C-41 is in large part a response to the problem of overincarceration in Canada. It was noted in *Gladue*, at para. 52, that Canada's incarceration rate of approximately 130 inmates per 100,000 population places it second or third highest among industrialized democracies. In their reasons, Cory and Iacobucci JJ. reviewed numerous studies that uniformly concluded that incarceration is costly, frequently unduly harsh and "ineffective, not only in relation to its purported rehabilitative goals, but also in relation to its broader public goals" (para. 54). See also Report of the Canadian Committee on Corrections, *Toward Unity: Criminal Justice and Corrections* (1969); Canadian Sentencing Commission,

Sentencing Reform: A Canadian Approach (1987), at pp. xxiii-xxiv; Standing Committee on Justice and Solicitor General, *Taking Responsibility* (1988), at p. 75. Prison has been characterized by some as a finishing school for criminals and as ill-preparing them for reintegration into society: see generally Canadian Committee on Corrections, *supra*, at p. 314; Correctional Service of Canada, *A Summary of Analysis of Some Major Inquiries on Corrections—1938 to 1977* (1982), at p. iv. ...

[17] Parliament has sought to give increased prominence to the principle of restraint in the use of prison as a sanction through the enactment of s. 718.2(d) and (e). Section 718.2(d) provides that "an offender should not be deprived of liberty, if less restrictive sanctions may be appropriate in the circumstances," while s. 718.2(e) provides that "all available sanctions other than imprisonment that are reasonable in the circumstances should be considered for all offenders, with particular attention to the circumstances of aboriginal offenders." Further evidence of Parliament's desire to lower the rate of incarceration comes from other provisions of Bill C-41: s. 718(c) qualifies the sentencing objective of separating offenders from society with the words "where necessary," thereby indicating that caution be exercised in sentencing offenders to prison; s. 734(2) imposes a duty on judges to undertake a means inquiry before imposing a fine, so as to decrease the number of offenders who are incarcerated for defaulting on payment of their fines; and of course, s. 742.1, which introduces the conditional sentence. In *Gladue*, at para. 40, the Court held that "[t]he creation of the conditional sentence suggests, on its face, a desire to lessen the use of incarceration."

(2) Expanding the Use of Restorative Justice Principles in Sentencing

[18] Restorative justice is concerned with the restoration of the parties that are affected by the commission of an offence. Crime generally affects at least three parties: the victim, the community, and the offender. A restorative justice approach seeks to remedy the adverse effects of crime in a manner that addresses the needs of all parties involved. This is accomplished, in part, through the rehabilitation of the offender, reparations to the victim and to the community, and the promotion of a sense of responsibility in the offender and acknowledgment of the harm done to victims and to the community.

[19] Canadian sentencing jurisprudence has traditionally focussed on the aims of denunciation, deterrence, separation, and rehabilitation, with rehabilitation a relative late-comer to the sentencing analysis: see *Gladue*, at para. 42. With the introduction of Bill C-41, however, Parliament has placed new emphasis upon the goals of restorative justice. Section 718 sets out the fundamental purpose of sentencing, as well as the various sentencing objectives that should be vindicated when sanctions are imposed ... .

[20] Parliament has mandated that expanded use be made of restorative principles in sentencing as a result of the general failure of incarceration to rehabilitate offenders and reintegrate them into society. By placing a new emphasis on restorative principles, Parliament expects both to reduce the rate of incarceration and improve the effectiveness of sentencing. During the second reading of Bill C-41 on September 20, 1994 (*House of Commons Debates*, vol. IV, 1st Sess., 35th Parl., at p. 5873), Minister of Justice Allan Rock made the following statements:

A general principle that runs throughout Bill C-41 is that jails should be reserved for those who should be there. Alternatives should be put in place for those who commits offences but who do not need or merit incarceration. …

Jails and prisons will be there for those who need them, for those who should be punished in that way or separated from society … . [T]his bill creates an environment which encourages community sanctions and the rehabilitation of offenders together with reparation to victims and promoting in criminals a sense of accountability for what they have done.

It is not simply by being more harsh that we will achieve more effective criminal justice. We must use our scarce resources wisely.

B.   The Nature of the Conditional Sentence

[21] The conditional sentence was specifically enacted as a new sanction designed to achieve both of Parliament's objectives. The conditional sentence is a meaningful alternative to incarceration for less serious and non-dangerous offenders. The offenders who meet the criteria of s. 742.1 will serve a sentence under strict surveillance in the community instead of going to prison. These offenders' liberty will be constrained by conditions to be attached to the sentence, as set out in s. 742.3 of the *Code*. In case of breach of conditions, the offender will be brought back before a judge, pursuant to s. 742.6. If an offender cannot provide a reasonable excuse for breaching the conditions of his or her sentence, the judge may order him or her to serve the remainder of the sentence in jail, as it was intended by Parliament that there be a real threat of incarceration to increase compliance with the conditions of the sentence.

[22] The conditional sentence incorporates some elements of non-custodial measures and some others of incarceration. Because it is served in the community, it will generally be more effective than incarceration at achieving the restorative objectives of rehabilitation, reparations to the victim and community, and the promotion of a sense of responsibility in the offender. However, *it is also a punitive sanction capable of achieving the objectives of denunciation and deterrence*. It is this punitive aspect that distinguishes the conditional sentence from probation, and it is to this issue that I now turn.

(1) Comparing Conditional Sentences with Probation

[23] There has been some confusion among members of the judiciary and the public alike about the difference between a conditional sentence and a suspended sentence with probation. This confusion is understandable, as the statutory provisions regarding conditions to be attached to conditional sentences (s. 742.3) and probation orders (s. 732.1) are very similar. Notwithstanding these similarities, there is an important distinction between the two. While a suspended sentence with probation is primarily a rehabilitative sentencing tool, the evidence suggests that Parliament intended a conditional sentence to address both punitive and rehabilitative objectives.

· · ·

(b) Conditional Sentences Must Be More Punitive Than Probation

[28] Despite the similarities between the provisions and the fact that the penalty for breach of probation is potentially more severe than for breach of a conditional sentence, there are strong indications that Parliament intended the conditional sentence to be more

punitive than probation. It is a well accepted principle of statutory interpretation that no legislative provision should be interpreted so as to render it mere surplusage. It would be absurd if Parliament intended conditional sentences to amount merely to probation under a different name. While this argument is clearly not dispositive, it suggests that Parliament intended there to be a meaningful distinction between the two sanctions. I will now consider more specific arguments in support of this position.

[29] The conditional sentence is defined in the *Code* as a sentence of imprisonment. The heading of s. 742 reads "Conditional Sentence of Imprisonment." Furthermore, s. 742.1(a) requires the court to impose a sentence of imprisonment of less than two years before considering whether the sentence can be served in the community subject to the appropriate conditions. Parliament intended imprisonment, in the form of incarceration, to be more punitive than probation, as it is far more restrictive of the offender's liberty. Since a conditional sentence is, at least notionally, a sentence of imprisonment, it follows that it too should be interpreted as more punitive than probation.

· · ·

[32] Probation has traditionally been viewed as a rehabilitative sentencing tool. Recently, the rehabilitative nature of the probation order was explained by the Saskatchewan Court of Appeal in *R. v. Taylor* (1997), 122 C.C.C. (3d) 376. Bayda C.J.S. wrote, at p. 394:

> Apart from the wording of the provision, the innate character of a probation order is such that it seeks to influence the future behaviour of the offender. More specifically, it seeks to secure "the good conduct" of the offender and to deter him from committing other offences. *It does not particularly seek to reflect the seriousness of the offence or the offender's degree of culpability. Nor does it particularly seek to fill the need for denunciation of the offence or the general deterrence of others to commit the same or other offences. Depending upon the specific conditions of the order there may well be a punitive aspect to a probation order but punishment is not the dominant or an inherent purpose. It is perhaps not even a secondary purpose but is more in the nature of a consequence of an offender's compliance with one or more of the specific conditions with which he or she may find it hard to comply.* [Emphasis added.]

[33] Many appellate courts have struck out conditions of probation that were imposed to punish rather than rehabilitate the offender: see *R. v. Ziatas* (1973), 13 C.C.C. (2d) 287 (Ont. C.A.), at p. 288; *R. v. Caja* (1977), 36 C.C.C. (2d) 401 (Ont. C.A.), at pp. 402-3; *R. v. Lavender* (1981), 59 C.C.C. (2d) 551 (B.C.C.A.), at pp. 552-53; and *R. v. L.* (1986), 50 C.R. (3d) 398 (Alta. C.A.), at pp. 399-400. The impugned terms of probation in these cases were imposed pursuant to a residual clause in force at the time whose wording was virtually identical to that presently used in s. 742.3(2)(f).

[34] Despite the virtual identity in the wording of s. 742.3(2)(f) and the old residual clause applicable to probation orders, it would be a mistake to conclude that punitive conditions cannot now be imposed under s. 742.3(2)(f). Parliament amended the residual clause for probation, s. 732.1(3)(h), to read "for protecting society and for *facilitating the offender's successful reintegration into the community*" (emphasis added). It did so to make clear the rehabilitative purpose of probation and to distinguish s. 742.3(2)(f) from s. 732.1(3)(h). The wording used in s. 742.3(2)(f) does not focus principally on the rehabilitation and reintegration of the offender. If s. 742.3(2)(f) were interpreted as precluding punitive conditions, it would frustrate Parliament's intention in distinguishing

the two forms of sentence. Parliament would not have distinguished them if it intended both clauses to serve the same purpose.

[35] In light of the foregoing, it is clear that Parliament intended a conditional sentence to be more punitive than a suspended sentence with probation, notwithstanding the similarities between the two sanctions in respect of their rehabilitative purposes. I agree wholeheartedly with Vancise J.A., who, dissenting in *R. v. McDonald* (1997), 113 C.C.C. (3d) 418 (Sask. C.A.), stated, at p. 443, that conditional sentences were designed to "permit the accused to avoid imprisonment but not to avoid punishment."

[36] Accordingly, conditional sentences should generally include punitive conditions that are restrictive of the offender's liberty. Conditions such as house arrest or strict curfews should be the norm, not the exception. As the Minister of Justice said during the second reading of Bill C-41 (*House of Commons Debates, supra*, at p. 5873), "[t]his sanction is obviously aimed at offenders who would otherwise be in jail but who could be in the community under *tight* controls" (emphasis added).

[37] There must be a reason for failing to impose punitive conditions when a conditional sentence order is made. Sentencing judges should always be mindful of the fact that conditional sentences are only to be imposed on offenders who would otherwise have been sent to jail. If the judge is of the opinion that punitive conditions are unnecessary, then probation, rather than a conditional sentence, is most likely the appropriate disposition.

[38] The punitive nature of the conditional sentence should also inform the treatment of breaches of conditions. As I have already discussed, the maximum penalty for breach of probation is potentially more severe than that for breach of a conditional sentence. In practice, however, breaches of conditional sentences may be punished more severely than breaches of probation. Without commenting on the constitutionality of these provisions, I note that breaches of conditional sentence need only be proved on a balance of probabilities, pursuant to s. 742.6(9), whereas breaches of probation must be proved beyond a reasonable doubt.

[39] More importantly, where an offender breaches a condition without reasonable excuse, there should be a presumption that the offender serve the remainder of his or her sentence in jail. This constant threat of incarceration will help to ensure that the offender complies with the conditions imposed: see *R. v. Brady* (1998), 121 C.C.C. (3d) 504 (Alta. C.A.); J.V. Roberts, "Conditional Sentencing: Sword of Damocles or Pandora's Box?" (1997), 2 *Can. Crim. L. Rev.* 183. It also assists in distinguishing the conditional sentence from probation by making the consequences of a breach of condition more severe.

(2) Conditional Sentences and Incarceration

[40] Although a conditional sentence is by statutory definition a sentence of imprisonment, this Court, in *R. v. Shropshire*, [1995] 4 S.C.R. 227, at para. 21, recognized that there "is a very significant difference between being behind bars and functioning within society while on conditional release." See also *Cunningham v. Canada*, [1993] 2 S.C.R. 143, at p. 150, *per* McLachlin J. These comments are equally applicable to the conditional sentence. Indeed, offenders serving a conditional sentence in the community are only partially deprived of their freedom. Even if their liberty is restricted by the conditions attached to their sentence, they are not confined to an institution and they can continue to attend to their normal employment or educational endeavours. They are not deprived of their

private life to the same extent. Nor are they subject to a regimented schedule or an institutional diet.

. . .

[44] ... [A] conditional sentence, even with stringent conditions, will usually be a more lenient sentence than a jail term of equivalent duration: see also *Gagnon v. La Reine*, [1998] R.J.Q. 2636 (C.A.), at p. 2645; *Brady, supra*, at paras. 36 and 48 to 50. The fact that incarceration is a threatened punishment for those who breach their conditions provides further support for this conclusion. In order for incarceration to serve as a punishment for breach of a conditional sentence, logically it must be more onerous than a conditional sentence.

C. Application of Section 742.1 of the Criminal Code

. . .

(1) The Offender Must Be Convicted of an Offence That Is Not Punishable by a Minimum Term of Imprisonment

[48] This prerequisite is straightforward. The offence for which the offender was convicted must not be punishable by a minimum term of imprisonment. Offences with a minimum term of imprisonment are the only statutory exclusions from the conditional sentencing regime.

(2) The Court Must Impose a Term of Imprisonment of Less Than Two Years

[49] Parliament intended that a conditional sentence be considered only for those offenders who would have otherwise received a sentence of imprisonment of less than two years. There is some controversy as to whether this means that the judge must actually impose a term of imprisonment of a *fixed* duration before considering the possibility of a conditional sentence. Far from addressing purely methodological concerns, this question carries implications as to the role of ss. 718 to 718.2 in the determination of the appropriate sentence, the duration of the sentence, its venue and other modalities.

[50] A literal reading of s. 742.1(a) suggests that the decision to impose a conditional sentence should be made in two distinct stages. In the first stage, the judge would have to decide the appropriate sentence according to the general purposes and principles of sentencing (now set out in ss. 718 to 718.2). Having found that a term of imprisonment of less than two years is warranted, the judge would then, in a second stage, decide whether this same term should be served in the community pursuant to s. 742.1. At first sight, since Parliament said: "and the court (a) imposes a sentence of imprisonment of less than two years," it seems that the sentencing judge must first impose a term of imprisonment of a *fixed* duration before contemplating the possibility that this term be served in the community.

[51] This two-step approach was endorsed by the Manitoba Court of Appeal in the present appeal. However, this literal reading of s. 742.1 and the two-step approach it implies introduce a rigidity which is both unworkable and undesirable in practice.

. . .

(3)   The Safety of the Community Would Not Be Endangered by the Offender
*   Serving the Sentence in the Community*

[62] This criterion, set out in s. 742.1(b), has generated wide discussion in courts and among authors. I intend to discuss the following issues:

(a)   Is safety of the community a prerequisite to any conditional sentence?
(b)   Does "safety of the community" refer only to the threat posed by the specific offender?
(c)   How should courts evaluate danger to the community?
(d)   Is risk of economic prejudice to be considered in assessing danger to the community?

(a) A Prerequisite to Any Conditional Sentence

[63] As a prerequisite to any conditional sentence, the sentencing judge must be satisfied that having the offender serve the sentence in the community would not endanger its safety: see *Brady, supra,* at para. 58; *R. v. Maheu,* [1997] R.J.Q. 410, 116 C.C.C. (3d) 361 (C.A.), at p. 368 C.C.C.; *Gagnon, supra,* at p. 2641; [*R v Pierce* (1997), 114 CCC (3d) 23 (Ont CA)], at p. 39; [*R v Ursel* (1997), 96 BCAC 241] at pp. 284-86 (*per* Ryan J.A.). *If the sentencing judge is not satisfied that the safety of the community can be preserved, a conditional sentence must never be imposed.*

. . .

[65] … It is only once the judge is satisfied that the safety of the community would not be endangered, in the sense explained in paras. 66 to 76 below, that he or she can examine whether a conditional sentence "would be consistent with the fundamental purpose and principles of sentencing set out in sections 718 to 718.2." In other words, rather than being an overarching consideration in the process of determining whether a conditional sentence is appropriate, the criterion of safety of the community should be viewed as a condition precedent to the assessment of whether a conditional sentence would be a fit and proper sanction in the circumstances.

(b) "Safety of the Community" Refers to the Threat Posed by the Specific Offender

[66] The issue here is whether "safety of the community" refers only to the threat posed by the specific offender or whether it also extends to the broader risk of undermining respect for the law. The proponents of the broader interpretation argue that, in certain cases where a conditional sentence could be imposed, it would be perceived that wrongdoers are receiving lenient sentences, thereby insufficiently deterring those who may be inclined to engage in similar acts of wrongdoing, and, in turn, endangering the safety of the community.

[67] Leaving aside the fact that a properly crafted conditional sentence can also achieve the objectives of general deterrence and denunciation, I think the debate has been rendered largely academic in light of an amendment to s. 742.1(b) (S.C. 1997, c. 18, s. 107.1) which clarified that courts must take into consideration the fundamental purpose and principles of sentencing set out in ss. 718 to 718.2 in deciding whether to impose a conditional sentence. This ensures that objectives such as denunciation and deterrence will be dealt with in the decision to impose a conditional sentence. Since these factors will be

taken into account later in the analysis, there is no need to include them in the consideration of the safety of the community.

[68] In my view, the focus of the analysis at this point should clearly be on the risk posed by the individual offender while serving his sentence in the community. I would note that a majority of appellate courts have adopted an interpretation of the criterion referring only to the threat posed by the specific offender: see *Gagnon, supra*, at pp. 2640-41 (*per* Fish J.A.); *R. v. Parker* (1997), 116 C.C.C. (3d) 236 (N.S.C.A.), at pp. 247-48; *Ursel, supra*, at p. 260; *R. v. Horvath*, [1997] 8 W.W.R. 357 (Sask. C.A.), at p. 374; *Brady, supra*, at paras. 60-61; *Wismayer, supra*, at p. 44.

(c) How Should Courts Evaluate Danger to the Community?

[69] In my opinion, to assess the danger to the community posed by the offender while serving his or her sentence in the community, two factors must be taken into account: (1) the risk of the offender re-offending; and (2) the gravity of the damage that could ensue in the event of re-offence. If the judge finds that there is a real risk of re-offence, incarceration should be imposed. Of course, there is always some risk that an offender may re-offend. If the judge thinks this risk is minimal, the gravity of the damage that could follow were the offender to re-offend should also be taken into consideration. In certain cases, the minimal risk of re-offending will be offset by the possibility of a great prejudice, thereby precluding a conditional sentence. ...

(4) Consistent with the Fundamental Purpose and Principles of Sentencing Set Out in Sections 718 to 718.2

[77] Once the sentencing judge has found the offender guilty of an offence for which there is no minimum term of imprisonment, has rejected both a probationary sentence and a penitentiary term as inappropriate, and is satisfied that the offender would not endanger the community, the judge must then consider whether a conditional sentence would be consistent with the fundamental purpose and principles of sentencing set out in ss. 718 to 718.2.

[78] A consideration of the principles set out in ss. 718 to 718.2 will determine whether the offender should serve his or her sentence in the community or in jail. The sentencing principles also inform the determination of the duration of these sentences and, if a conditional sentence, the nature of the conditions to be imposed.

(a) Offences Presumptively Excluded from the Conditional Sentencing Regime?

[79] Section 742.1 does not exclude any offences from the conditional sentencing regime except those with a minimum term of imprisonment. Parliament could have easily excluded specific offences in addition to those with a mandatory minimum term of imprisonment but chose not to. As Rosenberg J.A. held in *Wismayer, supra*, at p. 31:

> Parliament clearly envisaged that a conditional sentence would be available even in cases of crimes of violence that are not punishable by a minimum term of imprisonment. Thus, s. 742.2 requires the court, before imposing a conditional sentence, to consider whether a firearms prohibition under s. 100 of the *Criminal Code* is applicable. Such orders may only be imposed for indictable offences having a maximum sentence of ten years or more "in the

commission of which violence against a person is used, threatened, or attempted" (s. 100(1)) and for certain weapons and drug offences (s. 100(2)).

Thus, a conditional sentence is available in principle for *all* offences in which the statutory prerequisites are satisfied.

. . .

[83] My difficulty with the suggestion that the proportionality principle presumptively excludes certain offences from the conditional sentencing regime is that such an approach focuses inordinately on the gravity of the offence and insufficiently on the moral blameworthiness of the offender. This fundamentally misconstrues the nature of the principle. Proportionality requires that *full consideration* be given to both factors. As s. 718.1 provides:

> A sentence must be proportionate to the gravity of the offence *and* the degree of responsibility of the offender. [Emphasis added.]

. . .

(v) SUMMARY

[113] In sum, in determining whether a conditional sentence would be consistent with the fundamental purpose and principles of sentencing, sentencing judges should consider which sentencing objectives figure most prominently in the factual circumstances of the particular case before them. Where a combination of both punitive and restorative objectives may be achieved, a conditional sentence will likely be more appropriate than incarceration. In determining whether restorative objectives can be satisfied in a particular case, the judge should consider the offender's prospects of rehabilitation, including whether the offender has proposed a particular plan of rehabilitation; the availability of appropriate community service and treatment programs; whether the offender has acknowledged his or her wrongdoing and expresses remorse; as well as the victim's wishes as revealed by the victim impact statement (consideration of which is now mandatory pursuant to s. 722 of the *Code*). This list is not exhaustive.

[114] Where punitive objectives such as denunciation and deterrence are particularly pressing, such as cases in which there are aggravating circumstances, incarceration will generally be the preferable sanction. This may be so notwithstanding the fact that restorative goals might be achieved by a conditional sentence. Conversely, a conditional sentence may provide sufficient denunciation and deterrence, even in cases in which restorative objectives are of diminished importance, depending on the nature of the conditions imposed, the duration of the conditional sentence, and the circumstances of the offender and the community in which the conditional sentence is to be served.

[115] Finally, it bears pointing out that a conditional sentence may be imposed even in circumstances where there are aggravating circumstances relating to the offence or the offender. Aggravating circumstances will obviously increase the need for denunciation and deterrence. However, it would be a mistake to rule out the possibility of a conditional sentence *ab initio* simply because aggravating factors are present. I repeat that each case must be considered individually.

[116] Sentencing judges will frequently be confronted with situations in which some objectives militate in favour of a conditional sentence, whereas others favour incarceration. In those cases, the trial judge will be called upon to weigh the various objectives in

fashioning a fit sentence. As La Forest J. stated in *R. v. Lyons*, [1987] 2 S.C.R. 309, at p. 329, "[i]n a rational system of sentencing, the respective importance of prevention, deterrence, retribution and rehabilitation will vary according to the nature of the crime and the circumstances of the offender." There is no easy test or formula that the judge can apply in weighing these factors. Much will depend on the good judgment and wisdom of sentencing judges, whom Parliament vested with considerable discretion in making these determinations pursuant to s. 718.3.

. . .

VIII. Disposition

[132] I would allow the appeal. Accordingly, the 18-month sentence of incarceration imposed by the trial judge should be restored. However, given that the respondent has already served the conditional sentence imposed by the Court of Appeal in its entirety, and that the Crown stated in oral argument that it was not seeking any further punishment, I would stay the service of the sentence of incarceration.

NOTE

As *Proulx* made clear, under s 742.1 of the *Criminal Code*, as it was originally enacted, there were relatively few restrictions on the availability of conditional sentences. Over the intervening years Parliament has added further restrictions. Prime Minister Harper's Conservative government was especially active in that regard. Today, s 742.1 provides as follows:

> 742.1 If a person is convicted of an offence and the court imposes a sentence of imprisonment of less than two years, the court may, for the purpose of supervising the offender's behaviour in the community, order that the offender serve the sentence in the community, subject to the conditions imposed under section 742.3, if
>
> (a) the court is satisfied that the service of the sentence in the community would not endanger the safety of the community and would be consistent with the fundamental purpose and principles of sentencing set out in sections 718 to 718.2;
>
> (b) the offence is not an offence punishable by a minimum term of imprisonment;
>
> (c) the offence is not an offence, prosecuted by way of indictment, for which the maximum term of imprisonment is 14 years or life;
>
> (d) the offence is not a terrorism offence, or a criminal organization offence, prosecuted by way of indictment, for which the maximum term of imprisonment is 10 years or more;
>
> (e) the offence is not an offence, prosecuted by way of indictment, for which the maximum term of imprisonment is 10 years, that
>
> > (i) resulted in bodily harm,
> >
> > (ii) involved the import, export, trafficking or production of drugs, or
> >
> > (iii) involved the use of a weapon; and
>
> (f) the offence is not an offence, prosecuted by way of indictment, under any of the following provisions:
>
> > (i) section 144 (prison breach),
> >
> > (ii) section 264 (criminal harassment),
> >
> > (iii) section 271 (sexual assault),
> >
> > (iv) section 279 (kidnapping),

(v)   section 279.02 (trafficking in persons—material benefit),

(vi)   section 281 (abduction of person under fourteen),

(vii)   section 333.1 (motor vehicle theft),

(viii)   paragraph 334(a) (theft over $5000),

(ix)   paragraph 348(1)(e) (breaking and entering a place other than a dwelling-house),

(x)   section 349 (being unlawfully in a dwelling-house), and

(xi)   section 435 (arson for fraudulent purpose).

Somewhat surprisingly, despite these additional restrictions, the rate at which conditional sentences are imposed has remained fairly constant. See M Dauvergne, "Adult Correctional Statistics in Canada, 2010/2011" (Ottawa: Statistics Canada, 2012) at 14-15, online: <http:// www.statcan.gc.ca/pub/85-002-x/2012001/article/11715-eng.pdf>. Can you think of a possible explanation for this?

C. Discretion in Sentencing and Its Limits

In those cases in which there is no mandatory minimum sentence, the very general guidance supplied by the principles and objectives of sentencing leaves judges with considerable discretion to fashion a sentence that is proportionate to the gravity of the offence and the degree of responsibility of the offender. This was true before Bill C-41 and remains true today, at least for those offences for which Parliament has not yet prescribed a mandatory minimum sentence. The next case discusses the wide discretion enjoyed by sentencing judges and also explains the limits on that discretion.

R v M(CA)
Supreme Court of Canada
[1996] 1 SCR 500

[The accused was sentenced by the trial judge to 25 years after pleading guilty to numerous counts of sexual assault and sexual offences against children. The BC Court of Appeal reduced the sentence to 18 years and 8 months. The Crown appealed.]

LAMER CJ (for the Court):

In my view, within the broad statutory maximum and minimum penalties defined for particular offences under the *Code*, trial judges enjoy a wide ambit of discretion under s. 717 in selecting a "just and appropriate" fixed-term sentence which adequately promotes the traditional goals of sentencing, subject only to the fundamental principle that the global sentence imposed reflect the overall culpability of the offender and the circumstances of the offence.

I conclude that the British Columbia Court of Appeal erred in applying as a principle of sentencing that fixed-term sentences under the *Criminal Code* ought to be capped at 20 years, absent special circumstances. ...

However, in the process of determining a just and appropriate fixed-term sentence of imprisonment, the sentencing judge should be mindful of the age of the offender in applying the relevant principles of sentencing. After a certain point, the utilitarian and normative goals of sentencing will eventually begin to exhaust themselves once a contemplated sentence starts to surpass any reasonable estimation of the offender's remaining natural life span. Accordingly, in exercising his or her specialized discretion under the *Code*, a sentencing judge should generally refrain from imposing a fixed-term sentence which so greatly exceeds an offender's expected remaining life span that the traditional goals of sentencing, even general deterrence and denunciation, have all but depleted their functional value. But with that consideration in mind, the governing principle remains the same: Canadian courts enjoy a broad discretion in imposing numerical sentences for single or multiple offences, subject only to the broad statutory parameters of the *Code* and the fundamental principle of our criminal law that global sentences be "just and appropriate." ...

In *Shropshire* (1995), 102 C.C.C. (3d) 193, this court recently articulated the appropriate standard of review that a court of appeal should adopt in reviewing the fitness of sentence under s. 687(1). In the context of reviewing the fitness of an order of parole ineligibility, Iacobucci J. described the standard of review as follows, at para. 46:

> An appellate court should not be given free rein to modify a sentencing order simply because it feels that a different order ought to have been made. The formulation of a sentencing order is a profoundly subjective process; the trial judge has the advantage of having seen and heard all of the witnesses whereas the appellate court can only base itself upon a written record. A variation in the sentence should only be made if the court of appeal is convinced it is not fit. *That is to say, that it has found the sentence to be clearly unreasonable.*

... The determination of a just and appropriate sentence is a delicate art which attempts to balance carefully the societal goals of sentencing against the moral blameworthiness of the offender and the circumstances of the offence, while at all times taking into account the needs and current conditions of and in the community. The discretion of a sentencing judge should thus not be interfered with lightly.

Sentencing is an inherently individualized process, and the search for a single appropriate sentence for a similar offender and a similar crime will frequently be a fruitless exercise of academic abstraction. As well, sentences for a particular offence should be expected to vary to some degree across various communities and regions in this country, as the "just and appropriate" mix of accepted sentencing goals will depend on the needs and current conditions of and in the particular community where the crime occurred. For these reasons, consistent with the general standard of review we articulated in *Shropshire*, I believe that a court of appeal should only intervene to minimize the disparity of sentences where the sentence imposed by the trial judge is in substantial and marked departure from the sentences customarily imposed for similar offenders committing similar crimes.

With the greatest respect, I believe the Court of Appeal erred in this instance by engaging in an overly interventionist mode of appellate review of the "fitness" of sentence which transcended the standard of deference we articulated in *Shropshire*.

As a second and independent ground of appeal, the Crown argues that the Court of Appeal erred in law by relying on the proposition that "retribution is not a legitimate goal of sentencing" (p. 116) in reducing the sentence imposed by Filmer Prov. Ct. J. to 18 years and eight months.

Retribution, as an objective of sentencing, represents nothing less than the hallowed principle that criminal punishment, in addition to advancing utilitarian considerations related to deterrence and rehabilitation, should also be imposed to sanction the moral culpability of the offender. In my view, retribution is integrally woven into the existing principles of sentencing in Canadian law through the fundamental requirement that a sentence imposed be "just and appropriate" under the circumstances. Indeed, it is my profound belief that retribution represents an important unifying principle of our penal law by offering an essential conceptual link between the attribution of *criminal liability* and the imposition of *criminal sanctions*. With regard to the attribution of criminal liability, I have repeatedly held that it is a principle of "fundamental justice" under s. 7 of the *Charter* that criminal liability may only be imposed if an accused possesses a minimum "culpable mental state" in respect of the ingredients of the alleged offence: see *R. v. Martineau* [(1990), 58 CCC (3d) 353, [1990] 2 SCR 633, 79 CR (3d) 129], at p. 360. See, similarly, *Reference re: Section 94(2) of the Motor Vehicle Act* [(1985), 23 CCC (3d) 289 (SCC) at 311]; *R. v. Vaillancourt* (1987), 39 C.C.C. (3d) 118, 47 D.L.R. (4th) 399, [1987] 2 S.C.R. 636. It is this mental state which gives rise to the "moral blameworthiness" which justifies the state in imposing the stigma and punishment associated with a criminal sentence: see *Martineau*, at p. 361. I submit that it is this same element of "moral blameworthiness" which animates the determination of the appropriate quantum of punishment for a convicted offender as a "just sanction." As I noted in *Martineau* in discussing the sentencing scheme for manslaughter under the *Code*, it is a recognized principle of our justice system that "punishment be meted out with regard to the level of moral blameworthiness of the offender" (p. 362): see the similar observations of W.E.B. Code in "Proportionate Blameworthiness and the Rule against Constructive Sentencing" (1992), 11 C.R. (4th) 40 at pp. 41-2.

However, the meaning of retribution is deserving of some clarification. The legitimacy of retribution as a principle of sentencing has often been questioned as a result of its unfortunate association with "vengeance" in common parlance: see, *e.g.*, *R. v. Hinch and Salanski*, [[1968] 3 CCC 39 (BCCA)], at pp. 43-4; *R. v. Calder* (1956), 114 C.C.C. 155 at p. 161, 23 C.R. 191, 17 W.W.R. 528 (Man. C.A.). But it should be clear from my foregoing discussion that retribution bears little relation to vengeance, and I attribute much of the criticism of retribution as a principle to this confusion. As both academic and judicial commentators have noted, vengeance has no role to play in a civilized system of sentencing: see [C Ruby, *Sentencing*, 4th ed (Toronto: Butterworths, 1994)], at p. 13. Vengeance, as I understand it, represents an uncalibrated act of harm upon another, frequently motivated by emotion and anger, as a reprisal for harm inflicted upon oneself by that person. Retribution in a criminal context, by contrast, represents an objective, reasoned and measured determination of an appropriate punishment which properly reflects the *moral culpability* of the offender, having regard to the intentional risk-taking of the offender, the consequential harm caused by the offender, and the normative character of the offender's conduct. Furthermore, unlike vengeance, retribution incorporates a principle of restraint; retribution requires the imposition of a just and appropriate punishment, and *nothing more*. As R. Cross has noted in *The English Sentencing System*, 2nd ed. (London: Butterworths, 1975), at p. 121: "The retributivist insists that the punishment must not be disproportionate to the offender's deserts."

Retribution, as well, should be conceptually distinguished from its legitimate sibling, denunciation. Retribution requires that a judicial sentence properly reflect the moral blameworthiness of that particular *offender*. The objective of denunciation mandates that a sentence should also communicate society's condemnation of that particular offender's *conduct*. In short, a sentence with a denunciatory element represents a symbolic, collective statement that the offender's conduct should be punished for encroaching on our society's basic code of values as enshrined within our substantive criminal law. As Lord Justice Lawton stated in *R. v. Sargeant* (1974), 60 Cr. App. R. 74 at p. 77: "society, through the courts, must show its abhorrence of particular types of crime, and the only way in which the courts can show this is by the sentences they pass." The relevance of both retribution and denunciation as goals of sentencing underscores that our criminal justice system is not simply a vast system of negative penalties designed to prevent objectively harmful conduct by increasing the cost the offender must bear in committing an enumerated offence. Our criminal law is also a system of values. A sentence which expresses denunciation is simply the means by which these values are communicated. In short, in addition to attaching negative consequences to undesirable behaviour, judicial sentences should also be imposed in a manner which positively instills the basic set of communal values shared by all Canadians as expressed by the *Criminal Code*.

As a closing note to this discussion, it is important to stress that neither retribution nor denunciation alone provides an exhaustive justification for the imposition of criminal sanctions. Rather, in our system of justice, normative and utilitarian considerations operate in conjunction with one another to provide a coherent justification for criminal punishment. As Gonthier J. emphasized in [*R v Goltz*, [1991] 3 SCR 485], at p. 495, the goals of the penal sanction are both "broad and varied." Accordingly, the meaning of retribution must be considered in conjunction with the other legitimate objectives of sentencing, which include (but are not limited to) deterrence, denunciation, rehabilitation and the protection of society. Indeed, it is difficult to perfectly separate these interrelated principles. And as La Forest J. emphasized in *Lyons*, the relative weight and importance of these multiple factors will frequently vary depending on the nature of the crime and the circumstances of the offender. In the final analysis, the overarching duty of a sentencing judge is to draw upon all the legitimate principles of sentencing to determine a "just and appropriate" sentence which reflects the gravity of the offence committed and the moral blameworthiness of the offender.

Appeal allowed; sentence of 25 years' imprisonment restored.

It is noteworthy that in codifying the objectives of sentencing in s 718, Parliament chose not to use the term "retribution"; however, it did expressly reference the need for a sentence to "denounce unlawful conduct" (see s 718(a)). Although retribution as a sentencing objective is not expressly mentioned in s 718, do you think it is implicit in the sentencing objectives identified by Parliament? Do you think it might be a motivating factor when Parliament enacts a mandatory minimum sentence?

Specific and general deterrence have also long been accepted sentencing objectives in Canada, so their express inclusion in s 718(b) is not surprising. However, among criminologists the notion that by imposing longer sentences of imprisonment on offenders crime will decrease because others who might be inclined to engage in similar behaviour will be deterred has been largely debunked. The research seems to suggest that certainty of apprehension is much more likely to deter prospective criminality than longer sentences. As Professors Anthony N. Doob and Cheryl M. Webster note:

> Although it is tempting to extend the search for consistent relationships between sentence severity and crime rates "just one last time" in the belief that general deterrent effects may still be lurking at the end of the next regression equation, one must recognize that sentencing policies currently in place in many jurisdictions are still based on the assumption that harsh sentences deter. There is no plausible body of evidence that supports policies based on this premise. On the contrary, standard social science norms governing the acceptance of the null hypothesis justify the present (always rebuttable) conclusion that sentence severity does not affect levels of crime.

See AN Doob & CM Webster, "Sentence Severity and Crime: Accepting the Null Hypothesis" (2003) 30 Crime & Justice 143 at 146. See also SN Durlauf & DS Nagin, "Imprisonment and Crime: Can Both Be Reduced?" (2011) 10 Criminology & Public Policy 13; PH Robinson & JM Darley, "Does Criminal Law Deter? A Behavioural Science Investigation" (2004) 24 Oxford J Leg Stud 173; M Tonry, "Learning from the Limitations of Deterrence Research" (2008) 37 Crime & Justice 279; TS Ulen, "Skepticism About Deterrence" (2014) 6 Loy U Chicago LJ 381; and CM Webster & AN Doob, "Searching for Sasquatch: Deterrence of Crime Through Sentence Severity" in J Petersilia & KR Reitz, eds, *Oxford Handbook on Sentencing and Corrections* (New York: Oxford University Press, 2012) 173.

Ordinarily, as *M(CA)* makes clear, appellate courts will afford sentencing judges substantial deference. Yet, as the next case illustrates, that deference has its limits, especially if sentencing judges allow their knowledge of the criminological research to trump the sentencing objectives legislated by Parliament.

R v Song
Ontario Court of Appeal
2009 ONCA 896, 100 OR (3d) 23

[The respondent pleaded guilty to a charge of producing marijuana. He was involved in a large-scale grow operation in a residential area. Police seized 1,400 marijuana plants. The operation involved a hydro bypass and theft of a substantial sum of electricity. The Crown had sought jail time, but the sentencing judge imposed a 12-month conditional sentence (essentially, a sentence of house arrest). The Crown appealed.]

BY THE COURT:

• • •

[4] The sentencing judge made ... errors in principle, in our view.

• • •

[7] ... [T]he sentencing judge refused to apply both the provisions of the Criminal Code, R.S.C. 1985, c. C-46 and binding jurisprudence mandating that general and specific deterrence be taken into account in arriving at an appropriate sentence in cases of this nature: Criminal Code, s. 718(b). See, also, R. v. Chen, [2007] O.J. No. 1153, 2007 ONCA 230, at para. 2; Nguyen, at para. 47; R. v. Dawson, 2004 CanLII 6662 (ON CA), [2004]

O.J. No. 3302, 189 O.A.C. 147 (C.A.); R. v. Koenders, 2007 BCCA 378, [2007] B.C.J. No. 1543, 221 C.C.C. (3d) 225 (C.A.), at paras. 20-21.

[8] Yet the sentencing judge discounted general deterrence, to the point of suggesting it would be "insane" to consider it. For example, in the course of an exchange with Crown counsel and in his reasons, he made the following comments:

During Submissions:

Crown: … I think there will be a general deterrence.

The Court: What's your basis for saying that? Because nobody has been deterred. People have been going to jail for drug offences for—for a couple of generations now and the drug—the drug plague is worse than it ever was.

Crown: Well, there's—yes. There's no statistical …

The Court: If—if something doesn't work, do I try doing it again and again to see if it does work?

Crown: I would …

The Court: I think there's …

Crown: There's no way of knowing …

The Court: Isn't that the definition of insanity?

Reasons:

And as I commented in submissions from counsel … I do not understand the idea of deterrence in this area. I do not know that there are, for example, fewer grow operations in Hamilton than there are in Brampton, even though you are likely to go to jail for real in Hamilton and less likely to do so here. I do know that in the United States, which makes us look like we are all living in Northwestern Europe by comparison, a country which has huge numbers of people serving life without parole for growing marijuana or trafficking in moderate amounts of it, that drugs are as available there, or perhaps more available than they are in jurisdictions where the laws are more lenient. I am given to understand the chances of a Dutch teenager smoking marijuana are substantially lower than they are of an American teenager smoking marijuana. And the Dutch teenager can walk down to the corner and get it at a coffee shop.

[9] There was no evidence to support any of these observations.

[10] Judges are entitled to hold personal and political opinions as much as anyone else. But they are not free to permit those views to colour or frame their trial and sentencing decisions. They are bound to apply the law as it stands. And this is the final error we wish to underline.

[11] The sentencing judge's reasons make it clear—albeit in breezy and colourful fashion—that he personally has little use for a sentencing regime that seeks to cope with marijuana offences by relying upon principles of deterrence and by the imposition of "real" jail sentences. This is reflected in the passage above, for example, and reinforced in the following excerpts:

The aggravating factors in a case like this are really the things that are incidental to the criminalization of the activity. Sources as conservative as The Economist Magazine and the Fraser Institute think-tank in this country, which are very, very conservative organizations maintain that drug prohibition is an absolute failure and that we would do less damage to ourselves if the whole undertaking were dismantled.

This is particularly appropriate in the case of marijuana, according to their arguments, because really what we're doing by prohibiting the production and consumption of marijuana is giving the Hell's Angels several billion dollars worth of income every year which is then turned into investments in what would otherwise be legitimate businesses.

So I quite frankly, simply, do not buy into the idea that by treating individuals like this harshly notwithstanding their lack of a record and the nature of the substance that they were producing that I am going to improve things at all. Likewise, the issue with home invasions, if this were not illegal then there would not be the home invasions. So, it is not an intrinsic aspect of growing marijuana that people are going to bust in on you with guns and try and take it away from you, it is rather a function of the fact that it is illegal.

[12] And, later in his reasons, he continued:

The really important factors in this case are that this is the least harmful drug covered by the Controlled Drugs and Substances Act. The Supreme Court of Canada had to basically ignore the harm principle, the John Stewart Mill fundamental principle of criminal law in order to uphold these laws and then promptly readopted it again in a subsequent case involving Montreal sex clubs.

[13] Whether these views have merit is a debate for another forum—one in which judges do not participate. Personal diatribes of the nature engaged in by the sentencing judge here are unhelpful, however, and demonstrate to us a lack of objectivity that undermines the deference generally afforded to judges. The principle of deference is not a license for the sentencing judge to defy settled jurisprudence, ignore the principles of the Criminal Code, or use his or her dais as a political podium.

Fitness of the Sentence

[14] These errors in principle reopen the fitness of the sentence for our consideration at large.

[15] Given the authorities referred to above, and applying conventional principles of sentencing, we find it very difficult to conclude that this is one of those rare cases where a conditional sentence is appropriate. Mr. Song was engaged in a large-scale commercial marijuana grow operation involving more than 1,400 plants worth a considerable amount of money, on any estimation, in the market. Even the trial judge acknowledged that the grow operation "might have yielded a fair amount of money eventually." The enterprise was carried on in a residential area and featured the theft of a considerable amount of electricity through a hydro bypass. While Mr. Song did plead guilty and had no prior criminal record, there was little else of a mitigating nature, and much of an aggravating nature, in the circumstances. Unlike in other cases, for example, there were no issues of ill-health, dire financial need or addiction to explain the operation. It was a purely commercial venture. Mr. Song was the person setting up and running the operation and held a significant degree of responsibility for it.

. . .

[18] The dilemma we face, however, is the practical reality that Mr. Song has completely served the sentence imposed on him. This court is reluctant to send people to, or back to, prison in such circumstances. Had we been dealing with this matter de novo at trial, a period of incarceration would clearly have been warranted. Indeed, had the matter come to us in a timely fashion before the conditional sentence had been served, we would have imposed a custodial term.

[19] In the end—without taking away from any of our observations above—we are not persuaded that it would serve the interests of justice to send Mr. Song to prison at this point. Accordingly, while leave to appeal sentence is granted, the appeal as to sentence must be dismissed.

Appeal dismissed.

Do you think the Court of Appeal would have been more deferential to the conclusions of the sentencing judge if the sources he relied upon had been properly before him as part of the record in the sentencing proceeding rather than matters of which he seemed to simply take judicial notice? If a judge has clear evidence before him or her that general deterrence simply does not work for a particular crime, should the judge be entitled to give that consideration diminished weight despite s 718(b) of the *Criminal Code*?

II. THE SENTENCING OF ABORIGINAL OFFENDERS

The overrepresentation of Aboriginal people within the criminal justice system is a long-standing and tragic reality in Canada; as you will read below, the Supreme Court of Canada has characterized it as "a crisis in the Canadian criminal justice system." Aboriginal adults and youth are disproportionately represented relative to their size in the overall population, both within our criminal courts and within our jails and prisons. The most recent statistics suggest that 28 percent of sentenced adult admissions are Aboriginal, whereas Aboriginal people make up about 4 percent of the adult population. For women, this overrepresentation is even more pronounced. Aboriginal women make up 43 percent of all women sentenced to provincial custody. (See "Admissions to Adult Correctional Services in Canada, 2011-2012" (2014) 34:1 Juristat.) Aboriginal youth constitute 39 percent of sentenced admissions, whereas Aboriginal people make up 7 percent of the youth population. (See "Admissions to Youth Correctional Services in Canada, 2011-2012" (2014) 34:2 Juristat.)

In an effort to at least begin the process of trying to redress this problem, Parliament included s 718.2(e) as part of the 1996 reforms. It provides that "all available sanctions other than imprisonment that are reasonable in the circumstances should be considered for all offenders, *with particular attention to the circumstances of aboriginal offenders*" (emphasis added). The Supreme Court first addressed the meaning of this legislative direction in the next case.

R v Gladue
Supreme Court of Canada
[1999] 1 SCR 688

CORY and IACOBUCCI JJ:

[1] On September 3, 1996, the new Part XXIII of the *Criminal Code*, R.S.C., 1985, c. C-46, pertaining to sentencing came into force. These provisions codify for the first time the fundamental purpose and principles of sentencing. This appeal is particularly concerned with the new s. 718.2(e). It provides that all available sanctions other than imprisonment that are reasonable in the circumstances should be considered for all offenders, with particular attention to the circumstances of aboriginal offenders. This appeal must consider how this provision should be interpreted and applied.

Factual Background

[2] The appellant, one of nine children, was born in McLennan, Alberta in 1976. Her mother, Marie Gladue, who was a Cree, left the family home in 1987 and died in a car accident in 1990. After 1987, the appellant and her siblings were raised by their father, Lloyd Chalifoux, a Metis. The appellant and the victim Reuben Beaver started to live together in 1993, when the appellant was 17 years old. Thereafter they had a daughter, Tanita. In August 1995, they moved to Nanaimo. Together with the appellant's father and two of her siblings, Tara and Bianca Chalifoux, they lived in a townhouse complex. By September 1995, the appellant and Beaver were engaged to be married, and the appellant was five months pregnant with their second child, a boy, whom the appellant subsequently named Reuben Ambrose Beaver in honour of his father.

[3] In the early evening of September 16, 1995, the appellant was celebrating her 19th birthday. She and Reuben Beaver, who was then 20, were drinking beer with some friends and family members in the townhouse complex. The appellant suspected that Beaver was having an affair with her older sister, Tara.

· · ·

[6] Mr. Gretchin saw the appellant run toward Beaver with a large knife in her hand and, as she approached him, she told him that he had better run. Mr. Gretchin heard Beaver shriek in pain and saw him collapse in a pool of blood. The appellant had stabbed Beaver once in the left chest, and the knife had penetrated his heart. As the appellant went by on her return to her apartment, Mr. Gretchin heard her say, "I got you, you fucking bastard." The appellant was described as jumping up and down as if she had tagged someone. Mr. Gretchin said she did not appear to realize what she had done. At the time of the stabbing, the appellant had a blood-alcohol content of between 155 and 165 milligrams of alcohol in 100 millilitres of blood.

[7] On June 3, 1996, the appellant was charged with second degree murder. On February 11, 1997, following a preliminary hearing and after a jury had been selected, the appellant entered a plea of guilty to manslaughter.

[8] There was evidence which indicated that the appellant had stabbed Beaver before he fled from the apartment. A paring knife found on the living room floor of their apartment had a small amount of Beaver's blood on it, and a small stab wound was located on Beaver's right upper arm.

[9] There was also evidence that Beaver had subjected the appellant to some physical abuse in June 1994, while the appellant was pregnant with their daughter Tanita. Beaver was convicted of assault, and was given a 15-day intermittent sentence with one year's probation. ...

[10] The appellant's sentencing took place 17 months after the stabbing. Pending her trial, she was released on bail and lived with her father. She took counselling for alcohol and drug abuse at Tillicum Haus Native Friendship Centre in Nanaimo, and completed Grade 10 and was about to start Grade 11. After the stabbing, the appellant was diagnosed as suffering from a hyperthyroid condition, which was said to produce an exaggerated reaction to any emotional situation. The appellant underwent radiation therapy to destroy some of her thyroid glands, and at the time of sentencing she was taking thyroid supplements which regulated her condition. During the time she was on bail, the appellant plead guilty to having breached her bail on one occasion by consuming alcohol.

[11] At the sentencing hearing, when asked if she had anything to say, the appellant stated that she was sorry about what happened, that she did not intend to do it, and that she was sorry to Beaver's family.

[12] In his submissions on sentence at trial, the appellant's counsel did not raise the fact that the appellant was an aboriginal offender but, when asked by the trial judge whether in fact the appellant was an aboriginal person, replied that she was Cree. When asked by the trial judge whether the town of McLennan, Alberta, where the appellant grew up, was an aboriginal community, defence counsel responded: "it's just a regular community." No other submissions were made at the sentencing hearing on the issue of the appellant's aboriginal heritage. Defence counsel requested a suspended sentence or a conditional sentence of imprisonment. Crown counsel argued in favour of a sentence of between three and five years' imprisonment.

[13] The appellant was sentenced to three years' imprisonment and to a ten-year weapons prohibition. Her appeal of the sentence to the British Columbia Court of Appeal was dismissed.

· · ·

[31] A core issue in this appeal is whether s. 718.2(e) should be understood as being remedial in nature, or whether s. 718.2(e), along with the other provisions of ss. 718 through 718.2, are simply a codification of *existing* sentencing principles. [Emphasis in original.] The respondent, although acknowledging that s. 718.2(e) was likely designed to encourage sentencing judges to experiment to some degree with alternatives to incarceration and to be sensitive to principles of restorative justice, at the same time favours the view that ss. 718-718.2 are largely a restatement of existing law. Alternatively, the appellant argues strongly that s. 718.2(e)'s specific reference to aboriginal offenders can have no purpose unless it effects a change in the law. The appellant advances the view that s. 718.2(e) is in fact an "affirmative action" provision justified under s. 15(2) of the *Canadian Charter of Rights and Freedoms*.

· · ·

[33] In our view, s. 718.2(e) is *more* than simply a re-affirmation of existing sentencing principles. [Emphasis in original.] The remedial component of the provision consists not only in the fact that it codifies a principle of sentencing, but, far more importantly, in its direction to sentencing judges to undertake the process of sentencing aboriginal offenders differently, in order to endeavour to achieve a truly fit and proper sentence in the particular

case. It should be said that the words of s. 718.2(e) do not alter the fundamental duty of the sentencing judge to impose a sentence that is fit for the offence and the offender. For example, as we will discuss below, it will generally be the case as a practical matter that particularly violent and serious offences will result in imprisonment for aboriginal offenders as often as for non-aboriginal offenders. What s. 718.2(e) does alter is the method of analysis which each sentencing judge must use in determining the nature of a fit sentence for an aboriginal offender. In our view, the scheme of Part XXIII of the *Criminal Code*, the context underlying the enactment of s. 718.2(e), and the legislative history of the provision all support an interpretation of s. 718.2(e) as having this important remedial purpose.

. . .

[38] The wording of s. 718.2(e) on its face, then, requires both consideration of alternatives to the use of imprisonment as a penal sanction generally, which amounts to a restraint in the resort to imprisonment as a sentence, and recognition by the sentencing judge of the unique circumstances of aboriginal offenders.

. . .

[40] It is true that there is ample jurisprudence supporting the principle that prison should be used as a sanction of last resort. It is equally true, though, that the sentencing amendments which came into force in 1996 as the new Part XXIII have changed the range of available penal sanctions in a significant way. The availability of the conditional sentence of imprisonment, in particular, alters the sentencing landscape in a manner which gives an entirely new meaning to the principle that imprisonment should be resorted to only where no other sentencing option is reasonable in the circumstances. The creation of the conditional sentence suggests, on its face, a desire to lessen the use of incarceration. The general principle expressed in s. 718.2(e) must be construed and applied in this light.

[41] Further support for the view that s. 718.2(e)'s expression of the principle of restraint in sentencing is remedial, rather than simply a codification, is provided by the articulation of the purpose of sentencing in s. 718.

. . .

[43] Section 718 now sets out the purpose of sentencing in the following terms:

> 718. The fundamental purpose of sentencing is to contribute, along with crime prevention initiatives, to respect for the law and the maintenance of a just, peaceful and safe society by imposing just sanctions that have one or more of the following objectives:
> (a) to denounce unlawful conduct;
> (b) to deter the offender and other persons from committing offences;
> (c) to separate offenders from society, where necessary;
> (d) to assist in rehabilitating offenders;
> (e) *to provide reparations for harm done to victims or to the community*; and
> (f) *to promote a sense of responsibility in offenders, and acknowledgment of the harm done to victims and to the community.* [Emphasis added.]

Clearly, s. 718 is, in part, a restatement of the basic sentencing aims, which are listed in paras. (a) through (d). What are new, though, are paras. (e) and (f), which along with para. (d) focus upon the restorative goals of repairing the harms suffered by individual victims and by the community as a whole, promoting a sense of responsibility and an acknowledgment of the harm caused on the part of the offender, and attempting to rehabilitate or heal the offender. The concept of restorative justice which underpins paras. (d), (e), and (f) is briefly discussed below, but as a general matter restorative justice involves some form of restitution and reintegration into the community. The need for offenders to take responsibility for their actions is central to the sentencing process: D. Kwochka, "Aboriginal Injustice: Making Room for a Restorative Paradigm" (1996), 60 *Sask. L. Rev.* 153, at p. 165. Restorative sentencing goals do not usually correlate with the use of prison as a sanction. In our view, Parliament's choice to include (e) and (f) alongside the traditional sentencing goals must be understood as evidencing an intention to expand the parameters of the sentencing analysis for all offenders. The principle of restraint expressed in s. 718.2(e) will necessarily be informed by this re-orientation.

[44] Just as the context of Part XXIII supports the view that s. 718.2(e) has a remedial purpose for all offenders, the scheme of Part XXIII also supports the view that s. 718.2(e) has a particular remedial role for aboriginal peoples. The respondent is correct to point out that there is jurisprudence which pre-dates the enactment of s. 718.2(e) in which aboriginal offenders have been sentenced differently in light of their unique circumstances. However, the existence of such jurisprudence is not, on its own, especially probative of the issue of whether s. 718.2(e) has a remedial role. There is also sentencing jurisprudence which holds, for example, that a court must consider the unique circumstances of offenders who are battered spouses, or who are mentally disabled. Although the validity of the principles expressed in this latter jurisprudence is unchallenged by the 1996 sentencing reforms, one does not find reference to these principles in Part XXIII. If Part XXIII were indeed a codification of principles regarding the appropriate method of sentencing different categories of offenders, one would expect to find such references. The wording of s. 718.2(e), viewed in light of the absence of similar stipulations in the remainder of Part XXIII, reveals that Parliament has chosen to single out aboriginal offenders for particular attention.

· · ·

D. The Context of the Enactment of Section 718.2(e)

[49] Further guidance as to the scope and content of Parliament's remedial purpose in enacting s. 718.2(e) may be derived from the social context surrounding the enactment of the provision. On this point, it is worth noting that, although there is quite a wide divergence between the positions of the appellant and the respondent as to how s. 718.2(e) should be applied in practice, there is general agreement between them, and indeed between the parties and all interveners, regarding the mischief in response to which s. 718.2(e) was enacted.

[50] The parties and interveners agree that the purpose of s. 718.2(e) is to respond to the problem of overincarceration in Canada, and to respond, in particular, to the more acute problem of the disproportionate incarceration of aboriginal peoples. They also agree that one of the roles of s. 718.2(e), and of various other provisions in Part XXIII, is to encourage sentencing judges to apply principles of restorative justice alongside or in the place of other, more traditional sentencing principles when making sentencing determinations. As the respondent states in its factum before this Court, s. 718.2(e) "provides the necessary flexibility and authority for sentencing judges to resort to the restorative model of justice in sentencing aboriginal offenders and to reduce the imposition of jail sentences where to do so would not sacrifice the traditional goals of sentencing."

[51] The fact that the parties and interveners are in general agreement among themselves regarding the purpose of s. 718.2(e) is not determinative of the issue as a matter of statutory construction. However, as we have suggested, on the above points of agreement the parties and interveners are correct. A review of the problem of overincarceration in Canada, and of its peculiarly devastating impact upon Canada's aboriginal peoples, provides additional insight into the purpose and proper application of this new provision.

(1) The Problem of Overincarceration in Canada

[52] Canada is a world leader in many fields, particularly in the areas of progressive social policy and human rights. Unfortunately, our country is also distinguished as being a world leader in putting people in prison. Although the United States has by far the highest rate of incarceration among industrialized democracies, at over 600 inmates per 100,000 population, Canada's rate of approximately 130 inmates per 100,000 population places it second or third highest: see Federal/Provincial/Territorial Ministers Responsible for Justice, *Corrections Population Growth: First Report on Progress* (1997), Annex B, at p. 1; Bulletin of U.S. Bureau of Justice Statistics, "Prison and Jail Inmates at Midyear 1998" (March 1999); The Sentencing Project, *Americans Behind Bars: U.S. and International Use of Incarceration, 1995* (June 1997), at p. 1. Moreover, the rate at which Canadian courts have been imprisoning offenders has risen sharply in recent years, although there has been a slight decline of late: see Statistics Canada, "Prison population and costs" in *Infomat: A Weekly Review* (February 27, 1998), at p. 5. This record of incarceration rates obviously cannot instil a sense of pride.

· · ·

[57] ... [A]lthough imprisonment is intended to serve the traditional sentencing goals of separation, deterrence, denunciation, and rehabilitation, there is widespread consensus that imprisonment has not been successful in achieving some of these goals. Overincarceration is a long-standing problem that has been many times publicly acknowledged but never addressed in a systematic manner by Parliament. In recent years, compared to other countries, sentences of imprisonment in Canada have increased at an alarming rate. The 1996 sentencing reforms embodied in Part XXIII, and s. 718.2(e) in particular, must be understood as a reaction to the overuse of prison as a sanction, and must accordingly be given appropriate force as remedial provisions.

(2) The Overrepresentation of Aboriginal Canadians in Penal Institutions

[58] If overreliance upon incarceration is a problem with the general population, it is of much greater concern in the sentencing of aboriginal Canadians. In the mid-1980s, aboriginal people were about 2 percent of the population of Canada, yet they made up 10 percent of the penitentiary population. In Manitoba and Saskatchewan, aboriginal people constituted something between 6 and 7 percent of the population, yet in Manitoba they represented 46 percent of the provincial admissions and in Saskatchewan 60 percent: see M. Jackson, "Locking Up Natives in Canada" (1988-89), 23 *U.B.C. L. Rev.* 215 (article originally prepared as a report of the Canadian Bar Association Committee on Imprisonment and Release in June 1988), at pp. 215-16. The situation has not improved in recent years. By 1997, aboriginal peoples constituted closer to 3 percent of the population of Canada and amounted to 12 percent of all federal inmates: Solicitor General of Canada,

Consolidated Report, *Towards a Just, Peaceful and Safe Society: The Corrections and Conditional Release Act—Five Years Later* (1998), at pp. 142-55. The situation continues to be particularly worrisome in Manitoba, where in 1995-96 they made up 55 percent of admissions to provincial correctional facilities, and in Saskatchewan, where they made up 72 percent of admissions. A similar, albeit less drastic situation prevails in Alberta and British Columbia: Canadian Centre for Justice Statistics, *Adult Correctional Services in Canada, 1995-96* (1997), at p. 30.

· · ·

[61] Not surprisingly, the excessive imprisonment of aboriginal people is only the tip of the iceberg insofar as the estrangement of the aboriginal peoples from the Canadian criminal justice system is concerned. Aboriginal people are overrepresented in virtually all aspects of the system. As this Court recently noted in *R. v. Williams*, [1998] 1 S.C.R. 1128, at para. 58, there is widespread bias against aboriginal people within Canada, and "[t]here is evidence that this widespread racism has translated into systemic discrimination in the criminal justice system."

[62] Statements regarding the extent and severity of this problem are disturbingly common. In *Bridging the Cultural Divide [A Report on Aboriginal People and Criminal Justice in Canada* (Ottawa: Royal Commission on Aboriginal Peoples, 1996)], at p. 309, the Royal Commission on Aboriginal Peoples listed as its first "Major Findings and Conclusions" the following striking yet representative statement:

> The Canadian criminal justice system has failed the Aboriginal peoples of Canada—First Nations, Inuit and Métis people, on-reserve and off-reserve, urban and rural—in all territorial and governmental jurisdictions. The principal reason for this crushing failure is the fundamentally different world views of Aboriginal and non-Aboriginal people with respect to such elemental issues as the substantive content of justice and the process of achieving justice.

[63] To the same effect, the Aboriginal Justice Inquiry of Manitoba described the justice system in Manitoba as having failed aboriginal people on a "massive scale," referring particularly to the substantially different cultural values and experiences of aboriginal people: *The Justice System and Aboriginal People, supra*, at pp. 1 and 86.

[64] These findings cry out for recognition of the magnitude and gravity of the problem, and for responses to alleviate it. The figures are stark and reflect what may fairly be termed a crisis in the Canadian criminal justice system. The drastic overrepresentation of aboriginal peoples within both the Canadian prison population and the criminal justice system reveals a sad and pressing social problem. It is reasonable to assume that Parliament, in singling out aboriginal offenders for distinct sentencing treatment in s. 718.2(e), intended to attempt to redress this social problem to some degree. The provision may properly be seen as Parliament's direction to members of the judiciary to inquire into the causes of the problem and to endeavour to remedy it, to the extent that a remedy is possible through the sentencing process.

· · ·

VI. Summary

[93] Let us see if a general summary can be made of what has been discussed in these reasons.

1. Part XXIII of the *Criminal Code* codifies the fundamental purpose and principles of sentencing and the factors that should be considered by a judge in striving to determine a sentence that is fit for the offender and the offence.

2. Section 718.2(e) mandatorily requires sentencing judges to consider all available sanctions other than imprisonment and to pay particular attention to the circumstances of aboriginal offenders.

3. Section 718.2(e) is not simply a codification of existing jurisprudence. It is remedial in nature. Its purpose is to ameliorate the serious problem of overrepresentation of aboriginal people in prisons, and to encourage sentencing judges to have recourse to a restorative approach to sentencing. There is a judicial duty to give the provision's remedial purpose real force.

4. Section 718.2(e) must be read and considered in the context of the rest of the factors referred to in that section and in light of all of Part XXIII. All principles and factors set out in Part XXIII must be taken into consideration in determining the fit sentence. Attention should be paid to the fact that Part XXIII, through ss. 718, 718.2(e), and 742.1, among other provisions, has placed a new emphasis upon decreasing the use of incarceration.

5. Sentencing is an individual process and in each case the consideration must continue to be what is a fit sentence for this accused for this offence in this community. However, the effect of s. 718.2(e) is to alter the method of analysis which sentencing judges must use in determining a fit sentence for aboriginal offenders.

6. Section 718.2(e) directs sentencing judges to undertake the sentencing of aboriginal offenders individually, but also differently, because the circumstances of aboriginal people are unique. In sentencing an aboriginal offender, the judge must consider:

    (A) The unique systemic or background factors which may have played a part in bringing the particular aboriginal offender before the courts; and

    (B) The types of sentencing procedures and sanctions which may be appropriate in the circumstances for the offender because of his or her particular aboriginal heritage or connection.

7. In order to undertake these considerations the trial judge will require information pertaining to the accused. Judges may take judicial notice of the broad systemic and background factors affecting aboriginal people, and of the priority given in aboriginal cultures to a restorative approach to sentencing. In the usual course of events, additional case-specific information will come from counsel and from a pre-sentence report which takes into account the factors set out in #6, which in turn may come from representations of the relevant aboriginal community which will usually be that of the offender. The offender may waive the gathering of that information.

8. If there is no alternative to incarceration the length of the term must be carefully considered.

9. Section 718.2(e) is not to be taken as a means of automatically reducing the prison sentence of aboriginal offenders; nor should it be assumed that an offender is receiving a more lenient sentence simply because incarceration is not imposed.

10. The absence of alternative sentencing programs specific to an aboriginal community does not eliminate the ability of a sentencing judge to impose a sanction that takes into account principles of restorative justice and the needs of the parties involved.

11. Section 718.2(e) applies to all aboriginal persons wherever they reside, whether on- or off-reserve, in a large city or a rural area. In defining the relevant aboriginal community for the purpose of achieving an effective sentence, the term "community" must be defined broadly so as to include any network of support and interaction that might be available, including in an urban centre. At the same time, the residence of the aboriginal offender in an urban centre that lacks any network of support does not relieve the sentencing judge of the obligation to try to find an alternative to imprisonment.

12. Based on the foregoing, the jail term for an aboriginal offender may in some circumstances be less than the term imposed on a non-aboriginal offender for the same offence.

13. It is unreasonable to assume that aboriginal peoples do not believe in the importance of traditional sentencing goals such as deterrence, denunciation, and separation, where warranted. In this context, generally, the more serious and violent the crime, the more likely it will be as a practical matter that the terms of imprisonment will be the same for similar offences and offenders, whether the offender is aboriginal or non-aboriginal.

VII. Was There an Error Made in This Case?

[94] From the foregoing analysis it can be seen that the sentencing judge, who did not have the benefit of these reasons, fell into error. He may have erred in limiting the application of s. 718.2(e) to the circumstances of aboriginal offenders living in rural areas or on-reserve. Moreover, and perhaps as a consequence of the first error, he does not appear to have considered the systemic or background factors which may have influenced the appellant to engage in criminal conduct, or the possibly distinct conception of sentencing held by the appellant, by the victim Beaver's family, and by their community. However it should be emphasized that the sentencing judge did take active steps to obtain at least some information regarding the appellant's aboriginal heritage. In this regard he received little if any assistance from counsel on this issue although they too were acting without the benefit of these reasons.

. . .

[96] In most cases, errors such as those in the courts below would be sufficient to justify sending the matter back for a new sentencing hearing. It is difficult for this Court to determine a fit sentence for the appellant according to the suggested guidelines set out herein on the basis of the very limited evidence before us regarding the appellant's

aboriginal background. However, as both the trial judge and all members of the Court of Appeal acknowledged, the offence in question is a most serious one, properly described by Esson J.A. as a "near murder." Moreover, the offence involved domestic violence and a breach of the trust inherent in a spousal relationship. That aggravating factor must be taken into account in the sentencing of the aboriginal appellant as it would be for any offender. For that offence by this offender a sentence of three years' imprisonment was not unreasonable.

[97] More importantly, the appellant was granted day parole on August 13, 1997, after she had served six months in the Burnaby Correctional Centre for Women. She was directed to reside with her father, to take alcohol and substance abuse counselling and to comply with the requirements of the Electronic Monitoring Program. On February 25, 1998, the appellant was granted full parole with the same conditions as the ones applicable to her original release on day parole.

[98] In this case, the results of the sentence with incarceration for six months and the subsequent controlled release were in the interests of both the appellant and society. In these circumstances, we do not consider that it would be in the interests of justice to order a new sentencing hearing in order to canvass the appellant's circumstances as an aboriginal offender.

[99] In the result, the appeal is dismissed.

Despite the Supreme Court's decision in *Gladue*, in the decade that followed that decision the overrepresentation of Aboriginal peoples within the criminal justice system in Canada only continued to worsen. The Supreme Court of Canada returned to the subject of sentencing Aboriginal offenders in *Ipeelee*. In its decision, the Court reaffirmed its decision in *Gladue*. It also seized the opportunity to correct errors it identified in the post-*Gladue* case law that, in its view, had significantly curtailed the scope and potential remedial impact of s 718.2(e).

R v Ipeelee
Supreme Court of Canada
2012 SCC 13, [2012] 1 SCR 433

[In this decision, the Court dealt with the cases of two Aboriginal offenders, Manasie Ipeelee and Frank Ladue. Both had long criminal records and each had been declared a "long-term offender" under part XXIV of the Code and made the subject of a long-term supervision order (LTSO, essentially a designation that facilitates the supervision of long-term offenders in the community for up to ten years after the completion of a sentence for a specific offence, due to concerns about the risk they pose to reoffend).

Ipeelee was an alcoholic with a history of committing violent offences when intoxicated. He was sentenced to six years' imprisonment followed by an LTSO after being designated a long-term offender. After his release from prison, Ipeelee committed an offence while intoxicated, thereby breaching a condition of his LTSO. He was sentenced to three years' imprisonment, less six months of pre-sentence custody at a 1:1 credit rate. The Court of Appeal dismissed the appeal he brought.

Ladue was a drug addict and alcoholic with a history of committing sexual assaults when intoxicated. He was sentenced to three years' imprisonment followed by an LTSO after being designated a long-term offender. After his release from prison, he failed a urinalysis test, thereby breaching a condition of his LTSO. Ladue was sentenced to three years' imprisonment for the breach, less five months of pre-sentence custody at a 1.5:1 rate. A majority of the Court of Appeal allowed Ladue's appeal and reduced the sentence to one year's imprisonment.]

LeBEL J (McLachlin CJ and Binnie, Deschamps, Fish, and Abella JJ concurring):

[58] The overrepresentation of Aboriginal people in the Canadian criminal justice system was the impetus for including the specific reference to Aboriginal people in s. 718.2(e). It was not at all clear, however, what exactly the provision required or how it would affect the sentencing of Aboriginal offenders. ...

[The Court then reviewed its earlier decision in *Gladue* before continuing.]

[62] ... Whereas Aboriginal persons made up 12 percent of all federal inmates in 1999 when *Gladue* was decided, they accounted for 17 percent of federal admissions in 2005 (J. Rudin, "Aboriginal Over-representation and *R. v. Gladue*: Where We Were, Where We Are and Where We Might Be Going," in J. Cameron and J. Stribopoulos, eds., *The Charter and Criminal Justice: Twenty-Five Years Later* (2008), 687, at p. 701). As Professor Rudin asks: "If Aboriginal overrepresentation was a crisis in 1999, what term can be applied to the situation today?" ("Addressing Aboriginal Overrepresentation Post-*Gladue*," at p. 452).

[63] Over a decade has passed since this Court issued its judgment in *Gladue*. As the statistics indicate, s. 718.2(e) of the *Criminal Code* has not had a discernible impact on the overrepresentation of Aboriginal people in the criminal justice system. Granted, the *Gladue* principles were never expected to provide a panacea. There is some indication, however, from both the academic commentary and the jurisprudence, that the failure can be attributed to some extent to a fundamental misunderstanding and misapplication of both s. 718.2(e) and this Court's decision in *Gladue*. The following is an attempt to resolve these misunderstandings, clarify certain ambiguities, and provide additional guidance so that courts can properly implement this sentencing provision.

· · ·

[80] An examination of the post-*Gladue* jurisprudence applying s. 718.2(e) reveals several issues with the implementation of the provision. These errors have significantly curtailed the scope and potential remedial impact of the provision, thwarting what was originally envisioned by *Gladue*.

[81] First, some cases erroneously suggest that an offender must establish a causal link between background factors and the commission of the current offence before being entitled to have those matters considered by the sentencing judge. The decision of the Alberta Court of Appeal in *R. v. Poucette*, 1999 ABCA 305, 250 A.R. 55, provides one example. In that case, the court concluded, at para. 14:

> It is not clear how Poucette, a 19 year old, may have been affected by the historical policies of assimilation, colonialism, residential schools and religious persecution that were mentioned by the sentencing judge. While it may be argued that all aboriginal persons have been

affected by systemic and background factors, *Gladue* requires that their influences be traced to the particular offender. Failure to link the two is an error in principle. ...

[82] This judgment displays an inadequate understanding of the devastating inter-generational effects of the collective experiences of Aboriginal peoples. It also imposes an evidentiary burden on offenders that was not intended by *Gladue*. As the Ontario Court of Appeal states in *R. v. Collins*, 2011 ONCA 182, 277 O.A.C. 88, at paras. 32-33:

> There is nothing in the governing authorities that places the burden of persuasion on an Aboriginal accused to establish a causal link between the systemic and background factors and commission of the offence. ...
>
> As expressed in *Gladue*, *Wells* and *Kakekagamick*, s. 718.2(e) requires the sentencing judge to "give attention to the unique background and systemic factors which may have played a part in bringing the particular offender before the courts": *Gladue* at para. 69. This is a much more modest requirement than the causal link suggested by the trial judge. ...

[83] As the Ontario Court of Appeal goes on to note in *Collins*, it would be extremely difficult for an Aboriginal offender to ever establish a direct causal link between his circumstances and his offending. The interconnections are simply too complex. The Aboriginal Justice Inquiry of Manitoba describes the issue, at p. 86:

> Cultural oppression, social inequality, the loss of self-government and systemic discrimination, which are the legacy of the Canadian government's treatment of Aboriginal people, are intertwined and interdependent factors, and in very few cases is it possible to draw a simple and direct correlation between any one of them and the events which lead an individual Aboriginal person to commit a crime or to become incarcerated.

Furthermore, the operation of s. 718.2(e) does not logically require such a connection. Systemic and background factors do not operate as an excuse or justification for the criminal conduct. Rather, they provide the necessary context to enable a judge to determine an appropriate sentence. This is not to say that those factors need not be tied in some way to the particular offender and offence. Unless the unique circumstances of the particular offender bear on his or her culpability for the offence or indicate which sentencing objectives can and should be actualized, they will not influence the ultimate sentence.

[84] The second and perhaps most significant issue in the post-*Gladue* jurisprudence is the irregular and uncertain application of the *Gladue* principles to sentencing decisions for serious or violent offences. As Professor Roach has indicated, "appellate courts have attended disproportionately to just a few paragraphs in these two Supreme Court judgments—paragraphs that discuss the relevance of *Gladue* in serious cases and compare the sentencing of Aboriginal and non-Aboriginal offenders" (K. Roach, "One Step Forward, Two Steps Back: *Gladue* at Ten and in the Courts of Appeal" ([2008-2009]), 54 *Crim. L.Q.* 470, at p. 472). The passage in *Gladue* that has received this unwarranted emphasis is the observation that "[g]enerally, the more violent and serious the offence the more likely it is as a practical reality that the terms of imprisonment for aboriginals and non-aboriginals will be close to each other or the same, even taking into account their different concepts of sentencing" (*Gladue*, at para. 79; see also *Wells*, at paras. 42-44). Numerous courts have erroneously interpreted this generalization as an indication that the *Gladue* principles do

not apply to serious offences (see, e.g., *R. v. Carrière*, 2002 CanLII 41803 (ON CA), (2002), 164 C.C.C. (3d) 569 (Ont. C.A.)).

[85] Whatever criticisms may be directed at the decision of this Court for any ambiguity in this respect, the judgment ultimately makes it clear [at para 82] that sentencing judges have a *duty* to apply s. 718.2(e): "There is no discretion as to whether to consider the unique situation of the Aboriginal offender; the only discretion concerns the determination of a just and appropriate sentence" .... . Similarly, in *Wells*, Iacobucci J. reiterated, at para. 50, that

> [t]he generalization drawn in *Gladue* to the effect that the more violent and serious the offence, the more likely as a practical matter for similar terms of imprisonment to be imposed on aboriginal and non-aboriginal offenders, was not meant to be a principle of universal application. In each case, the sentencing judge must look to the circumstances of the aboriginal offender.

. . .

[87] The sentencing judge has a statutory duty, imposed by s. 718.2(e) of the *Criminal Code*, to consider the unique circumstances of Aboriginal offenders. Failure to apply *Gladue* in any case involving an Aboriginal offender runs afoul of this statutory obligation. As these reasons have explained, such a failure would also result in a sentence that was not fit and was not consistent with the fundamental principle of proportionality. Therefore, application of the *Gladue* principles is required in every case involving an Aboriginal offender, including breach of an LTSO, and a failure to do so constitutes an error justifying appellate intervention.

VI. Application

A. Manasie Ipeelee

[88] Megginson J. sentenced Mr. Ipeelee to three years' imprisonment, less credit for pre-sentence custody. The Court of Appeal upheld that sentence. Both courts emphasized the serious nature of the breach, given the documented link between Mr. Ipeelee's use of alcohol and his propensity to engage in violence. As a result, both courts emphasized the objectives of denunciation, deterrence, and protection of the public.

[89] In my view, the courts below made several errors in principle warranting appellate intervention. First, the courts reached the erroneous conclusion that protection of the public is the paramount objective when sentencing for breach of an LTSO and that rehabilitation plays only a small role. As discussed, while protection of the public is important, the legislative purpose of an LTSO as a form of conditional release set out in s. 100 of the *CCRA* is to rehabilitate offenders and reintegrate them into society. The courts therefore erred in concluding that rehabilitation was not a relevant sentencing objective.

[90] As a result of this error, the courts below gave only attenuated consideration to Mr. Ipeelee's circumstances as an Aboriginal offender. Relying on *Carrière*, the Court of Appeal concluded that this was the kind of offence where the sentence will not differ as between Aboriginal and non-Aboriginal offenders, and relying on *W(HP)*, held that features of Aboriginal sentencing play little or no role when sentencing long-term offenders. Given certain trends in the jurisprudence discussed above, it is easy to see how the

court reached this conclusion. Nonetheless, they erred in doing so. These errors justify the Court's intervention.

[91] It is therefore necessary to consider what sentence is warranted in the circumstances. Mr. Ipeelee breached the alcohol abstention condition of his LTSO. His history indicates a strong correlation between alcohol use and violent offending. As a result, abstaining from alcohol is critical to managing his risk in the community. That being said, the conduct constituting the breach was becoming intoxicated, not becoming intoxicated and engaging in violence. The Court must focus on the actual incident giving rise to the breach. A fit sentence should seek to manage the risk of reoffence he continues to pose to the community in a manner that addresses his alcohol abuse, rather than punish him for what might have been. To engage in the latter would certainly run afoul of the principles of fundamental justice.

[92] At the time of the offence, Mr. Ipeelee was 18 months into his LTSO. He was living in Kingston, where there were few culturally-relevant support systems in place. There is no evidence, other than one isolated instance of refusing urinalysis, that he consumed alcohol on any occasion prior to this breach. Mr. Ipeelee's history indicates that he has been drinking heavily since the age of 11. Relapse is to be expected as he continues to address his addiction.

[93] Taking into account the relevant sentencing principles, the fact that this is Mr. Ipeelee's first breach of his LTSO and that he pleaded guilty to the offence, I would substitute a sentence of one year's imprisonment. Given the circumstances of his previous convictions, abstaining from alcohol is crucial to Mr. Ipeelee's rehabilitation under the long-term offender regime. Consequently, this sentence is designed to denounce Mr. Ipeelee's conduct and deter him from consuming alcohol in the future. In addition, it provides a sufficient period of time without access to alcohol so that Mr. Ipeelee can get back on track with his alcohol treatment. Finally, the sentence is not so harsh as to suggest to Mr. Ipeelee that success under the long-term offender regime is simply not possible.

B. Frank Ralph Ladue

[94] Bagnall Prov. Ct. J. sentenced Mr. Ladue to three years' imprisonment, less credit for pre-sentence custody. The majority of the Court of Appeal intervened and substituted a sentence of one year's imprisonment. Bennett J.A., writing for the majority, held that the sentencing judge made two errors warranting appellate intervention.

[95] First, the majority of the Court of Appeal held that the sentencing judge failed to give sufficient weight to Mr. Ladue's circumstances as an Aboriginal offender. Although she acknowledged Mr. Ladue's Aboriginal status in her reasons for sentence, she failed to give it any "tangible consideration" (para. 64). In my view, the Court of Appeal was right to intervene on this basis. The sentencing judge described Mr. Ladue's history in great detail, but she failed to consider whether and how that history ought to impact on her sentencing decision. As a result, she failed to give effect to Parliament's direction in s. 718.2(e) of the *Criminal Code*. As the Court of Appeal rightly concluded, this was a case in which the unique circumstances of the Aboriginal offender indicated that the objective of rehabilitation ought to have been given greater emphasis:

Mr. Ladue desires to succeed, as exhibited by his request not to be sent to Belkin House. However, he is addicted to drugs and alcohol, which can directly be related to how he was treated as an Aboriginal person. He has not reoffended in a manner which threatens the safety of the public. He will ultimately be released into the community without supervision. Unless he can manage his alcohol and drug addiction in the community he will very likely be a threat to the public. Repeated efforts at abstinence are not unusual for those dealing with addiction. Indeed, Mr. Ladue demonstrated that he is capable of abstinence as shown by his conduct a number of years ago. [para. 63]

[96] Second, the majority of the Court of Appeal held that a sentence of three years' imprisonment was not proportionate to the gravity of the offence and the degree of responsibility of the offender. The Court of Appeal placed particular emphasis on the manner in which Mr. Ladue came to arrive at Belkin House rather than Linkage House. In my view, this emphasis was entirely warranted. Mr. Ladue is addicted to opiates—incidentally, a form of the same drug he first began using while incarcerated in a federal penitentiary. He had arranged to be released to Linkage House where he would have access to culturally relevant programming and the resources of an Elder. Instead, as a result of errors made by correctional officials, he was released to Belkin House where he was immediately tempted by drugs. The Court of Appeal was therefore justified in reaching the following conclusion:

> I acknowledge that Mr. Ladue's repeated failure to abstain from substances while on release required some time back in prison. However, in my respectful opinion, a sentence of one year would properly reflect the principles and purpose of sentencing. I say this because it is enough time for Mr. Ladue to achieve sobriety, and enough time for the correctional staff to find an appropriate placement for him, preferably Linkage House or another halfway house which emphasizes Aboriginal culture and healing. In addition, a one-year sentence is more reflective of and more proportionate to the nature of his offence and his circumstances. … [T]he circumstances of Mr. Ladue's background played an instrumental part in his offending over his lifetime and his rehabilitation is critical to the protection of the public. [paras. 81-82]

[97] The judgment of the Court of Appeal is well founded. … As a result, I would dismiss the Crown's appeal and affirm the sentence of one year's imprisonment imposed by the majority of the Court of Appeal.

[Rothstein J wrote a separate concurring opinion upholding the three-year sentence for Mr. Ipeelee but also upholding the Court of Appeal's one-year sentence for Mr. Ladue.]

As mentioned above, the overrepresentation of Aboriginal adults and youth in prisons continues to rise despite s 718.2(e) of the Code and cases such as *Gladue* and *Ipeelee*. Why is this so? One factor may be the relative youth of Canada's Aboriginal population. Other factors may be socio-economic conditions including issues such as education, health, high child welfare apprehension rates, high criminal victimization rates especially among Aboriginal women and youth, and the ongoing legacy of residential schools. And, of course, as you have studied, institutional and systemic bias is always a matter of concern in the criminal justice system. As the Court recognized in *Gladue* (at para 65):

It is clear that sentencing innovation by itself cannot remove the causes of aboriginal offending and the greater problem of aboriginal alienation from the criminal justice system. The unbalanced ratio of imprisonment for aboriginal offenders flows from a number of sources, including poverty, substance abuse, lack of education, and the lack of employment opportunities for aboriginal people. It arises also from bias against aboriginal people and from an unfortunate institutional approach that is more inclined to refuse bail and to impose more and longer prison terms for aboriginal offenders. There are many aspects of this sad situation which cannot be addressed in these reasons. What can and must be addressed, though, is the limited role that sentencing judges will play in remedying injustice against aboriginal peoples in Canada. Sentencing judges are among those decision-makers who have the power to influence the treatment of aboriginal offenders in the justice system. They determine most directly whether an aboriginal offender will go to jail, or whether other sentencing options may be employed which will play perhaps a stronger role in restoring a sense of balance to the offender, victim, and community, and in preventing future crime.

In *Ipeelee* LeBel J similarly stated (at para 77):

The overwhelming message emanating from the various reports and commissions on Aboriginal peoples' involvement in the criminal justice system is that current levels of criminality are intimately tied to the legacy of colonialism (see, e.g., RCAP, at p. 309). As Professor Carter puts it, "poverty and other incidents of social marginalization may not be unique, but how people get there is. No one's history in this country compares to Aboriginal people's" (M. Carter, "Of Fairness and Faulkner" (2002), 65 *Sask. L. Rev.* 63, at p. 71). Furthermore, there is nothing in the *Gladue* decision which would indicate that background and systemic factors should not also be taken into account for other, non-Aboriginal offenders. Quite the opposite. Cory and Iacobucci JJ. specifically state, at para. 69, in *Gladue*, that "background and systemic factors will also be of importance for a judge in sentencing a non-aboriginal offender."

What is the relevance of *Gladue* and s 718.2(e) in the sentencing of disadvantaged offenders who are not Aboriginal? In *R v Hamilton* (2004), 186 CCC (3d) 129, the Ontario Court of Appeal stated:

[98] There can be no doubt that s. 718.2(e) applies to all offenders. Imprisonment is appropriate only when there is no other reasonable sanction. The closing words of the section recognize that restraint in the use of imprisonment is a particularly important principle with respect to the sentencing of aboriginal offenders. The restraint principle takes on added importance because the historical mistreatment of aboriginals by the criminal justice system as reflected in the highly disproportionate number of aboriginals sentenced to imprisonment, taken with aboriginal cultural views as to the purpose of punishment, can combine to make imprisonment ineffective in achieving the purpose or objectives of sentencing where the offender is an aboriginal: *R. v. Wells*, [[2000] 1 SCR 207, 141 CCC (3d) 368], at ... p. 385 C.C.C. The restraint principle is applied with particular force where the offender is an aboriginal not to somehow try to make up for historical mistreatment of aboriginals, but because imprisonment may be less effective than other dispositions in achieving the goals of sentencing where the offender is aboriginal.

[99] Parliament has chosen to identify aboriginals as a group with respect to whom the restraint principle applies with particular force. If it is shown that the historical mistreatment and cultural views of another group combine to make imprisonment ineffective in achieving the goals of sentencing, it has been suggested that a court may consider those factors in applying

the restraint principle in sentencing individuals from that group: see *R. v. Borde*, [(2003), 172 CCC (3d) 225 (Ont CA)], at ... p. 236 C.C.C. There was no evidence in the mass of material adduced in these proceedings to suggest that poor black women share a cultural perspective with respect to punishment that is akin to the aboriginal perspective. ...

[100] In any event, proportionality remains the fundamental principle of sentencing. Section 718.2(e) cannot justify a sentence which deprecates the seriousness of the offence. Where the offence is sufficiently serious, imprisonment will be the only reasonable response regardless of the ethnic or cultural background of the offender: *R. v. Wells*, *supra*, at p. 386 C.C.C.

• • •

[133] The fact that an offender is a member of a group that has historically been subject to systemic racial and gender bias does not in and of itself justify any mitigation of sentence. Lower sentences predicated on nothing more than membership in a disadvantaged group further neither the principles of sentencing, nor the goals of equality.

[134] A sentencing judge is, however, required to take into account all factors that are germane to the gravity of the offence and the personal culpability of the offender. That inquiry can encompass systemic racial and gender bias. As the court explained in *R. v. Borde*, *supra*, at ... p. 236 C.C.C.:

> However, the principles that are generally applicable to all offenders, including African-Canadians, are sufficiently broad and flexible to enable a sentencing court in appropriate cases to consider both the systemic and background factors that may have played a role in the commission of the offence. ...

[135] Reference to factors that may "have played a role in the commission of the offence" encompasses a broad range of potential considerations. Those factors include any explanation for the offender's commission of the crime. If racial and gender bias suffered by the offender helps explain why the offender committed the crime, then those factors can be said to have "played a role in the commission of the offence."

On the issue of Aboriginal offenders and sentencing, see generally M Jackson, "Locking Up Natives in Canada" (1989) 23 UBC L Rev 215; BP Archibald, "Sentencing and Visible Minorities: Equality and Affirmative Action in the Criminal Justice System" (1989) 12 Dal LJ 377; F Sugar & L Fox, "Nistum Peyako Séht'wawin Iskwewak: Breaking Chains" (1989-90) 3 CJWL 465; P Stenning & JV Roberts, "Empty Promises: Parliament, the Supreme Court and the Sentencing of Aboriginal Offenders" (2001) 64 Sask L Rev 137; J Rudin & K Roach, "Broken Promises: A Response to Stenning and Roberts, 'Empty Promises'" (2002) 65 Sask L Rev 3; R Pelletier, "The Nullification of Section 718.2(e): Aggravating Aboriginal Over-Representation in Canadian Prisons" (2001) 39 Osgoode Hall LJ 469; T Quigley, "Some Issues in Sentencing of Aboriginal Offenders" in R Gosse, JY Henderson & R Carter, eds, *Continuing Poundmaker and Riel's Quest: Presentations Made at a Conference on Aboriginal Peoples and Justice* (Saskatoon: Purich, 1994) 269; K Roach, "One Step Forward, Two Steps Back: Gladue at Ten and in the Courts of Appeal" (2009) 54 Crim LQ 470; JV Roberts & R Melchers, "The Incarceration of Aboriginal Offenders: Trends from 1978 to 2001" (2003) 45 Can J Corr 211; BR Pfefferle, "Gladue Sentencing: Uneasy Answers to the Hard Problem of Aboriginal Over-Incarceration" (2006) 32 Man LJ 113; J Rudin, "Aboriginal Over-Representation and R v Gladue: Where We Were, Where We Are and Where We Might Be Going" in J Cameron & J Stribopoulos, eds, *The Charter and Criminal Justice: Twenty-Five Years Later* (Markham, Ont: LexisNexis, 2008) 687; J Rudin, "Addressing Aboriginal

Overrepresentation Post-Gladue: A Realistic Assessment of How Social Change Occurs" (2009) 54 Crim LQ 447; D Milward & D Parkes, "Gladue: Beyond Myth and Towards Implementation in Manitoba" (2011) 35 Man LJ 84; and J Rudin, "Looking Backward, Looking Forward: The Supreme Court of Canada's Decision in R v Ipeelee" in BL Berger & J Stribopoulos, eds, *Unsettled Legacy: Thirty Years of Criminal Justice Under the Charter* (Markham, Ont: LexisNexis, 2012) 409.

III. CONSTITUTIONAL CONSIDERATIONS

The Charter added a new dimension to sentencing, creating constitutional limits on criminal punishment. The guarantee most relevant to sentencing is s 12, which provides that "[e]veryone has the right not to be subjected to any cruel and unusual treatment or punishment." In the following early Charter case, the Supreme Court of Canada used s 12 to rule a mandatory minimum sentence unconstitutional.

R v Smith (Edward Dewey)
Supreme Court of Canada
[1987] 1 SCR 1045

[The Supreme Court held 5:1 that s 5(2) of the *Narcotic Control Act*, RSC 1985, c N-1, a sentencing provision mandating a minimum sentence of seven years' imprisonment for importing narcotics, violated the prohibition of cruel and unusual punishment under s 12 of the Charter and was not justified under s 1 of the Charter.]

LAMER J (Dickson CJ concurring):
     Those who import and market hard drugs for lucre are responsible for the gradual but inexorable degeneration of many of their fellow human beings as a result of their becoming drug addicts. The direct cause of the hardship cast upon their victims and their families, these importers must also be made to bear their fair share of the guilt for the innumerable serious crimes of all sorts committed by addicts in order to feed their demand for drugs. Such persons, with few exceptions (as an example, the guilt of addicts who import not only to meet but also to finance their needs is not necessarily the same in degree as that of cold-blooded non-users), should, upon conviction, in my respectful view, be sentenced to and actually serve long periods of penal servitude. However, a judge who would sentence to seven years in a penitentiary a young person who, while driving back into Canada from a winter break in the U.S.A., is caught with only one, indeed, let's postulate, his or her first "joint of grass," would certainly be considered by most Canadians to be a cruel and, all would hope, a very unusual judge. ...
     In imposing a sentence of imprisonment, the judge will assess the circumstances of the case in order to arrive at an appropriate sentence. The test for review under s. 12 of the *Charter* is one of gross disproportionality, because it is aimed at punishments that are more than merely excessive. We should be careful not to stigmatize every disproportionate or excessive sentence as being a constitutional violation, and should leave to the usual sentencing appeal process the task of reviewing the fitness of a sentence. Section 12 will only be infringed where the sentence is so unfit having regard to the offence and the offender as to be grossly disproportionate.

In assessing whether a sentence is grossly disproportionate, the court must first consider the gravity of the offence, the personal characteristics of the offender and the particular circumstances of the case in order to determine what range of sentences would have been appropriate to punish, rehabilitate or deter this particular offender or to protect the public from this particular offender. The other purposes which may be pursued by the imposition of punishment, in particular the deterrence of other potential offenders, are thus not relevant at this stage of the inquiry. This does not mean that the judge or the legislator can no longer consider general deterrence or other penological purposes that go beyond the particular offender in determining a sentence, but only that the resulting sentence must not be grossly disproportionate to what the offender deserves. If a grossly disproportionate sentence is "prescribed by law," then the purpose which it seeks to attain will fall to be assessed under s. 1. Section 12 ensures that individual offenders receive punishments that are appropriate, or at least not grossly disproportionate, to their particular circumstances, while s. 1 permits this right to be overridden to achieve some important societal objective.

One must also measure the effect of the sentence actually imposed. If it is grossly disproportionate to what would have been appropriate, then it infringes s. 12. The effect of the sentence is often a composite of many factors and is not limited to the quantum or duration of the sentence but includes its nature and the conditions under which it is applied. Sometimes by its length alone or by its very nature will the sentence be grossly disproportionate to the purpose sought. Sometimes it will be the result of the combination of factors which, when considered in isolation, would not in and of themselves amount to gross disproportionality. For example, 20 years for a first offence against property would be grossly disproportionate, but so would three months of imprisonment if the prison authorities decide it should be served in solitary confinement. Finally, I should add that some punishments or treatments will always be grossly disproportionate and will always outrage our standards of decency: for example, the infliction of corporal punishment, such as the lash, irrespective of the number of lashes imposed, or, to give examples of treatment, the lobotomisation of certain dangerous offenders or the castration of sexual offenders. ...

The minimum seven-year imprisonment fails the proportionality test enunciated above and therefore *prima facie* infringes the guarantees established by s. 12 of the *Charter*. The simple fact that s. 5(2) provides for a mandatory term of imprisonment does not by itself lead to this conclusion. A minimum mandatory term of imprisonment is obviously not in and of itself cruel and unusual. ...

For example, a long term of penal servitude for he or she who has imported large amounts of heroin for the purpose of trafficking would certainly not contravene s. 12 of the *Charter*, quite the contrary. However, the seven-year minimum prison term of s. 5(2) is grossly disproportionate when examined in light of the wide net cast by s. 5(1).

... [T]he offence of importing enacted by s. 5(1) of the *Narcotic Control Act* covers numerous substances of varying degrees of dangerousness and totally disregards the quantity of the drug imported. The purpose of a given importation, such as whether it is for personal consumption or for trafficking, and the existence or non-existence of previous convictions for offences of a similar nature or gravity are disregarded as irrelevant. Thus, the law is such that it is inevitable that, in some cases, a verdict of guilt will lead to the imposition of a term of imprisonment which will be grossly disproportionate. ...

[In considering whether the infringement of s 12 was justified under s 1, Lamer J applied the test outlined in *R v Oakes*, [1986] 1 SCR 103, and stated:]

... In my view, the fight against the importing and trafficking of hard drugs is, without a doubt, an objective "of sufficient importance to warrant overriding a constitutionally protected right or freedom." ...

The certainty that all those who contravene the prohibition against importing will be sentenced to at least seven years in prison will surely deter people from importing narcotics. Therefore, rationality, the first prong of the proportionality test, has been met. But the Crown's justification fails the second prong, namely, minimum impairment of the rights protected by s. 12. Clearly there is no need to be indiscriminate. We do not need to sentence the small offenders to seven years in prison in order to deter the serious offender. ...

... The result sought could be achieved by limiting the imposition of a minimum sentence to the importing of certain quantities, to certain specific narcotics of the schedule, to repeat offenders, or even to a combination of these factors. ...

Having written these reasons some time ago, I have not referred to recent decisions of the courts or recent publications. However, I wish to refer to the Report of the Canadian Sentencing Commission entitled *Sentencing Reform: A Canadian Approach* (1987), which gives some support to my conclusion. The commission recommended the abolition of mandatory minimum penalties for all offences except murder and high treason because it was of the view that (p. 188): "... existing mandatory minimum penalties, with the exception of those prescribed for murder and high treason, serve no purpose that can compensate for the disadvantages resulting from their continued existence." ...

McINTYRE J (dissenting):

Punishment not *per se* cruel and unusual, may become cruel and unusual due to excess or lack of proportionality only where it is so excessive that it is an outrage to standards of decency. ...

... It is true, in general, that when a judge imposes a sentence, he considers the nature and gravity of the offence, the circumstances in which it was committed, and the character and criminal history of the offender, all with an eye to the primary purposes of punishment: rehabilitation, deterrence, incapacitation, and retribution. But ... sentencing is an imprecise procedure and there will always be a wide range of appropriate sentences. ...

... All that Parliament has done is to conclude that the gravity of the offence alone warrants a sentence of at least seven years' imprisonment. While, again, one may question the wisdom of this conclusion, I cannot agree that this makes the sentencing process arbitrary and, therefore, cruel and unusual in violation of s. 12 of the *Charter*. ...

Despite the result in this early s 12 case, *Smith* was not the harbinger of an era in which the courts would invalidate minimum sentences set by Parliament. Indeed, until the recent *Nur* decision discussed below, *Smith* was the only Supreme Court of Canada case in which an accused successfully argued that a sentence was cruel and unusual, contrary to s 12. Overall, courts displayed a reluctance to use s 12 to interfere with the punishments outlined in the *Criminal Code*. In the 1990s, Parliament enacted a series of mandatory minimum sentences of four years' imprisonment for various offences committed with a firearm. In *R v Morrisey*,

2000 SCC 39, [2000] 2 SCR 90, the Court held that the four-year minimum for causing death by criminal negligence with a firearm was not cruel and unusual punishment. It came to the same conclusion in *R v Ferguson*, 2008 SCC 6, [2008] 1 SCR 96 in relation to a case of man-slaughter with a firearm involving a police officer who shot and killed a prisoner during an altercation in a police holding cell. Consider the controversial *Latimer* case (discussed earlier in Chapter 19 on the defence of necessity, and presented below), in which the Supreme Court addressed the issue of cruel and unusual punishment and treatment.

R v Latimer
Supreme Court of Canada
2001 SCC 1, [2001] 1 SCR 3

[Latimer had been convicted of second-degree murder in the death of his severely disabled daughter. The *Criminal Code* provides for a mandatory sentence of life imprisonment for second-degree murder, with parole to be set between 10 and 25 years by the trial judge. In this case, not realizing the constraints imposed by the *Criminal Code*, the jury recommended that Latimer receive one year in prison. The trial judge purported to grant the accused a constitutional exemption from the mandatory sentence and imposed a sentence of one year's imprisonment and one year's probation. The Saskatchewan Court of Appeal affirmed Latimer's conviction, but set aside the sentence and imposed the mandatory sentence required by law. Latimer's appeal against both his conviction and sentence was dismissed by the Supreme Court of Canada. The following excerpt is restricted to the Court's reasons on the sentencing issue.]

BY THE COURT: …

(2) Application of Section 12 Principles

[80] The first factor to consider is the gravity of the offence. Recently, Gonthier J., in *Morrisey, supra*, provided important guidance for the proper assessment of the gravity of an offence for the purposes of a s. 12 analysis. Specifically, Gonthier J. noted, at para. 35, that an assessment of the gravity of the offence requires an understanding of (i) the character of the offender's actions, and (ii) the consequences of those actions.

[81] Certainly, in this case one cannot escape the conclusion that Mr. Latimer's actions resulted in the most serious of all possible consequences, namely, the death of the victim, Tracy Latimer.

[82] In considering the character of Mr. Latimer's actions, we are directed to an assessment of the criminal fault requirement or *mens rea* element of the offence rather than the offender's motive or general state of mind (*Morrisey* …). We attach a greater degree of criminal responsibility or moral blameworthiness to conduct where the accused knowingly broke the law (*Morrisey, supra*; *R. v. Martineau*, [1990] 2 S.C.R. 633, at p. 645). In this case, the *mens rea* requirement for second degree murder is subjective foresight of death: the most serious level of moral blameworthiness ([*R v Luxton*, [1990] 2 SCR 711] …).

[83] Parliament has classified murder offences into first and second degree based on its perception of relative levels of moral blameworthiness. Parliament has also provided

for differential treatment between them in sentencing, but only in respect of parole eligibility. As noted by Lamer C.J. in *Luxton* … :

> I must also reiterate that what we are speaking of here is a classification scheme for the purposes of sentencing. The distinction between first and second degree murder only comes into play when it has first been proven beyond a reasonable doubt that the offender is guilty of murder, that is, that he or she had subjective foresight of death: *R. v. Martineau*, handed down this day. There is no doubt that a sentencing scheme must exhibit a proportionality to the seriousness of the offence, or to put it another way, there must be a gradation of punishments according to the malignity of the offences. …

[84] However, even if the gravity of second degree murder is reduced in comparison to first degree murder, it cannot be denied that second degree murder is an offence accompanied by an extremely high degree of criminal culpability. In this case, therefore, the gravest possible consequences resulted from an act of the most serious and morally blameworthy intentionality. It is against this reality that we must weigh the other contextual factors, including and especially the particular circumstances of the offender and the offence.

[85] Turning to the characteristics of the offender and the particular circumstances of the offence we must consider the existence of any aggravating and mitigating circumstances. … Specifically, any aggravating circumstances must be weighed against any mitigating circumstances. In this regard, it is possible that prior to gauging the sentence's appropriateness in light of an appreciation of the particular circumstances weighed against the gravity of the offence, the mitigating and aggravating circumstances might well cancel out their ultimate impact. … Indeed, this is what occurs in this case. On the one hand, we must give due consideration to Mr. Latimer's initial attempts to conceal his actions, his lack of remorse, his position of trust, the significant degree of planning and premeditation, and Tracy's extreme vulnerability. On the other hand, we are mindful of Mr. Latimer's good character and standing in the community, his tortured anxiety about Tracy's well-being, and his laudable perseverance as a caring and involved parent. Considered together we cannot find that the personal characteristics and particular circumstances of this case displace the serious gravity of this offence.

[86] Finally, this sentence is consistent with a number of valid penological goals and sentencing principles. Although we would agree that in this case the sentencing principles of rehabilitation, specific deterrence and protection are not triggered for consideration, we are mindful of the important role that the mandatory minimum sentence plays in denouncing murder. Denunciation of unlawful conduct is one of the objectives of sentencing recognized in s. 718 of the *Criminal Code*. As noted by the Court in *R. v. M.(C.A.)*, [1996] 1 S.C.R. 500, at para. 81:

> The objective of denunciation mandates that a sentence should communicate society's condemnation of that particular offender's *conduct*. In short, a sentence with a denunciatory element represents a symbolic, collective statement that the offender's conduct should be punished for encroaching on our society's basic code of values as enshrined within our substantive criminal law. [Emphasis in original.]

Furthermore, denunciation becomes much more important in the consideration of sentencing in cases where there is a "high degree of planning and premeditation, and where the offence and its consequences are highly publicized, [so that] like-minded individuals may well be deterred by severe sentences": *R. v. Mulvahill and Snelgrove* (1993), 21 B.C.A.C. 296, at p. 300. This is particularly so where the victim is a vulnerable person with respect to age, disability, or other similar factors.

[87] In summary, the minimum mandatory sentence is not grossly disproportionate in this case. We cannot find that any aspect of the particular circumstances of the case or the offender diminishes the degree of criminal responsibility borne by Mr. Latimer. In addition, although not free of debate, the sentence is not out of step with valid penological goals or sentencing principles. The legislative classification and treatment of this offender meets the requisite standard of proportionality. ... Where there is no violation of Mr. Latimer's s. 12 right there is no basis for granting a constitutional exemption.

[88] Having said all this, we wish to point out that this appeal raises a number of issues that are worthy of emphasis. The sentencing provisions for second degree murder include both ss. 235 and 745(c). Applied in combination these provisions result in a sentence that is hybrid in that it provides for both a mandatory life sentence and a minimum term of incarceration. The choice is Parliament's on the use of minimum sentences, though considerable difference of opinion continues on the wisdom of employing minimum sentences from a criminal law policy or penological point of view.

[89] It is also worth referring again to the royal prerogative of mercy that is found in s. 749 of the *Criminal Code*, which provides "[n]othing in this Act in any manner limits or affects Her Majesty's royal prerogative of mercy." As was pointed out by Sopinka J. in *R. v. Sarson*, [1996] 2 S.C.R. 223, at para. 51, albeit in a different context:

> Where the courts are unable to provide an appropriate remedy in cases that the executive sees as unjust imprisonment, the executive is permitted to dispense "mercy," and order the release of the offender. The royal prerogative of mercy is the only potential remedy for persons who have exhausted their rights of appeal and are unable to show that their sentence fails to accord with the *Charter*.

[90] But the prerogative is a matter for the executive, not the courts. The executive will undoubtedly, if it chooses to consider the matter, examine all of the underlying circumstances surrounding the tragedy of Tracy Latimer that took place on October 24, 1993, some seven years ago. Since that time Mr. Latimer has undergone two trials and two appeals to the Court of Appeal for Saskatchewan and this Court, with attendant publicity and consequential agony for him and his family.

VI. *Disposition*

[91] Mr. Latimer's appeals against conviction and sentence are dismissed.

In *R v Ferguson*, 2008 SCC 6, [2008] 1 SCR 96, the Supreme Court affirmed that the only remedy for an unconstitutional mandatory sentence is to strike it down in its entirety, as opposed to fashioning exemptions from it for particular offenders. For a discussion of this decision, and the broader issues surrounding mandatory minimum sentences, see BL Berger, "A More Lasting Comfort? The Politics of Minimum Sentences, the Rule of Law and R v Ferguson" (2009) 47 SCLR (2nd) 101 and L Dufraimont, "R v Ferguson and the Search for a Coherent Approach to Mandatory Minimum Sentences Under Section 12" (2008) 42 SCLR (2nd) 459.

Beyond s 12, in recent years the Supreme Court has recognized that the organizing principle of sentencing law in Canada—proportionality—has achieved the status of a principle of fundamental justice under s 7 of the Charter. In *R v Ipeelee*, 2012 SCC 13, [2012] 1 SCR 433, LeBel J noted:

> [36] The *Criminal Code* goes on to list a number of principles to guide sentencing judges. The fundamental principle of sentencing is that the sentence must be proportionate to both the gravity of the offence and the degree of responsibility of the offender. As this Court has previously indicated, this principle was not borne out of the 1996 amendments to the *Code* but, instead, has long been a central tenet of the sentencing process (see, e.g., *R. v. Wilmott* (1966), 58 D.L.R. (2d) 33 (Ont. C.A.), and, more recently, *R. v. Solowan*, 2008 SCC 62, [2008] 3 S.C.R. 309, at para. 12, and *R. v. Nasogaluak*, 2010 SCC 6, [2010] 1 S.C.R. 206, at paras. 40-42). It also has a constitutional dimension, in that s. 12 of the *Canadian Charter of Rights and Freedoms* forbids the imposition of a grossly disproportionate sentence that would outrage society's standards of decency. In a similar vein, proportionality in sentencing could aptly be described as a principle of fundamental justice under s. 7 of the *Charter*.
>
> [37] The fundamental principle of sentencing (i.e., proportionality) is intimately tied to the fundamental purpose of sentencing—the maintenance of a just, peaceful and safe society through the imposition of just sanctions. Whatever weight a judge may wish to accord to the various objectives and other principles listed in the *Code*, the resulting sentence must respect the fundamental principle of proportionality. Proportionality is the *sine qua non* of a just sanction. First, the principle ensures that a sentence reflects the gravity of the offence. This is closely tied to the objective of denunciation. It promotes justice for victims and ensures public confidence in the justice system. As Wilson J. expressed in her concurring judgment in *Re B.C. Motor Vehicle Act*, [1985] 2 S.C.R. 486, at p. 533:
>
>> It is basic to any theory of punishment that the sentence imposed bear some relationship to the offence; it must be a "fit" sentence proportionate to the seriousness of the offence. Only if this is so can the public be satisfied that the offender "deserved" the punishment he received and feel a confidence in the fairness and rationality of the system.
>
> Second, the principle of proportionality ensures that a sentence does not exceed what is appropriate, given the moral blameworthiness of the offender. In this sense, the principle serves a limiting or restraining function and ensures justice for the offender. In the Canadian criminal justice system, a just sanction is one that reflects both perspectives on proportionality and does not elevate one at the expense of the other.

In *R v Anderson*, 2014 SCC 41 at para 21, [2014] 2 SCR 167, citing its decision in *Ipeelee*, the Court expressly recognized that proportionality is a principle of fundamental justice under s 7 of the Charter.

Over the past decade, Prime Minister Harper's Conservative government has added a number of mandatory minimum periods of imprisonment to a host of offences in the *Criminal Code* and the *Controlled Drugs and Substances Act*. See the *Tackling Violent Crime Act*, SC 2008, c 6 and the *Safe Streets and Communities Act*, SC 2012, c 1. As a result, the number of offences carrying mandatory minimum sentences has grown from less than 15 in the 1980s to over 75 today. As a result, courts in Canada met with new and growing numbers of claims under ss 7 and 12 of the Charter. A number of these courts began to rule that the mandatory minimum sentences were unconstitutional.

In *R v Nur*, 2015 SCC 15, the Supreme Court held (6:3) that two of these recently added mandatory minimums were inconsistent with s 12 of the Charter, and not reasonably justified under s 1. Section 95(2)(a) imposed mandatory minimum sentences for the offence of possessing prohibited or restricted firearms when the firearm is loaded or kept with readily accessible ammunition (s 95(1))—three years for a first offence and five years for a second or subsequent offence.

The decision in *Nur* dealt with the cases of two accused, Nur and Charles. Nur was sentenced to 40 months for his first contravention of s 95, whereas Charles received a seven-year sentence because he had prior related convictions. The Supreme Court was of the view that these sentences were appropriate in each of these cases and that the mandatory minimums would not occasion cruel and unusual punishment for either man. Nevertheless, reaffirming the continued relevance of reasonable hypotheticals for testing the validity of laws under s 12 of the Charter, the Court held that both mandatory minimums were unconstitutional and could not be saved under s 1. Characterizing sentencing as "inherently a judicial function" (at para 87), the majority concluded:

> [77] In summary, when a mandatory minimum sentencing provision is challenged, two questions arise. The first is whether the provision results in a grossly disproportionate sentence on the individual before the court. If the answer is no, the second question is whether the provision's reasonably foreseeable applications will impose grossly disproportionate sentences on others. This is consistent with the settled jurisprudence on constitutional review and rules of constitutional interpretation, which seek to determine the potential reach of a law; is workable; and provides sufficient certainty.
>
> . . .
>
> [82] Section 95(1) casts its net over a wide range of potential conduct. Most cases within the range may well merit a sentence of three years or more, but conduct at the far end of the range may not. At one end of the range, as Doherty J.A. observed, "stands the outlaw who carries a loaded prohibited or restricted firearm in public places as a tool of his or her criminal trade. ... [T]his person is engaged in truly criminal conduct and poses a real and immediate danger to the public" (para. 51). At this end of the range—indeed for the vast majority of offences—a three-year sentence may be appropriate. A little further along the spectrum stands the person whose conduct is less serious and poses less danger; for these offenders three years' imprisonment may be disproportionate, but not grossly so. At the far end of the range, stands the licensed and responsible gun owner who stores his unloaded firearm safely with ammunition nearby, but makes a mistake as to where it can be stored. For this offender, a three-year sentence is grossly disproportionate to the sentence the conduct would otherwise merit under the sentencing provisions of the *Criminal Code.*
>
> [83] Given the minimal blameworthiness of the offender in this situation and the absence of any harm or real risk of harm flowing from the conduct (i.e. having the gun in one residence as opposed to another), a three-year sentence would be grossly disproportionate. Similar examples can be envisaged. A person inherits a firearm and before she can apprise herself of the licence requirements commits an offence. A spouse finds herself in possession of her husband's firearm and breaches the regulation. We need not focus on a particular hypothetical. The bottom line is that s. 95(1) foreseeably catches licensing offences which involve little or no moral fault and little or no danger to the public. For these offences three years' imprisonment is grossly disproportionate to a fit and fair sentence. Firearms are inherently dangerous and the state is entitled to use

sanctions to signal its disapproval of careless practices and to discourage gun owners from making mistakes, to be sure. But a three-year term of imprisonment for a person who has essentially
committed a licensing infraction is totally out of sync with the norms of criminal sentencing set
out in the s. 718 of the *Criminal Code* and legitimate expectations in a free and democratic society. As the Court of Appeal concluded, there exists a "cavernous disconnect" between the severity
of the licensing-type offence and the mandatory minimum three-year term of imprisonment
(para. 176). Consequently, I conclude that s. 95(2)(a)(i) breaches s. 12 of the *Charter*.

· · ·

[103] I agree that the Court of Appeal erred in concluding that it was reasonably foreseeable
that a repeat offender could be a licensed owner of a prohibited or restricted firearm. This does
not end the analysis, however. The court must test the reasonably foreseeable applications of
s. 95(2)(a)(ii). Under the impugned mandatory minimum, a five-year term of imprisonment could
be imposed on an individual who breached a prohibition order imposed while on bail and who,
some years later, innocently came into possession of a restricted or prohibited firearm without
an authorization or a licence together with usable ammunition that he stored nearby and which
was readily accessible.

[104] A five-year minimum term of imprisonment for offenders such as these would be draconian. It goes far beyond what is necessary in order to protect the public, far beyond what is
necessary to express moral condemnation of the offender, and far beyond what is necessary to
discourage others from engaging in such conduct. In a phrase, such a sentence would be grossly
disproportionate. An offender in these circumstances has not caused any harm, nor is there a real
risk of harm to the public. Such an offender is not engaged in any criminal activity.

[105] There is little doubt that in many cases those who commit second or subsequent offences for the purpose of s. 95(2)(a)(ii) should be sentenced to terms of imprisonment, and some
for lengthy terms of imprisonment. The seven-year term of imprisonment imposed on Charles is
an example. But the five-year minimum term of imprisonment would be grossly disproportionate for less serious offenders captured by the provision.

[106] It follows that s. 95(2)(a)(ii) violates the guarantee against grossly disproportionate
punishment in s. 12 of the *Charter*.

The dissenting judges in *Nur* would have upheld the impugned laws, arguing that the
Crown would be unlikely to proceed by indictment in any of the hypotheticals constructed
by the majority, and if the Crown proceeded summarily rather than by indictment, the impugned mandatory minimums would not be triggered. If the Crown did proceed by indictment in such cases, the dissent argued that this would reflect an abuse of Crown discretion
and favoured the use of a case-specific s 7 abuse of process remedy rather than a wholesale
declaration of invalidity. In contrast, the majority concluded that prosecutorial discretion was
simply an inadequate safeguard of the constitutional interests of accused persons. In so
concluding, McLachlin CJ noted:

[96] ... [V]esting that much power in the hands of prosecutors endangers the fairness of the
criminal process. It gives prosecutors a trump card in plea negotiations, which leads to an unfair
power imbalance with the accused and creates an almost irresistible incentive for the accused to
plead to a lesser sentence in order to avoid the prospect of a lengthy mandatory minimum term of
imprisonment. As a result, the "determination of a fit and appropriate sentence, having regard to all
of the circumstances of the offence and offender, may be determined in plea discussions outside
of the courtroom by a party to the litigation" (R.M. Pomerance, "The New Approach to Sentencing

in Canada: Reflections of a Trial Judge" (2013), 17 *Can. Crim. L.R.* 305, at p. 313). We cannot ignore the increased possibility that wrongful convictions could occur under such conditions.

What is the future of mandatory minimum sentences in light of *Nur*? One commonly proposed remedy is to preserve judicial discretion by allowing judges to craft and justify exceptions from mandatory sentences. Yet the Court's decisions in *Ferguson* and *Nur* suggest that courts will not order such a result and that it will be up to Parliament to craft statutory exceptions as it has done with respect to firearm prohibitions in s 113.

Does your experience of studying criminal law, including material relating to the nature of offences and defences, make you more or less supportive of mandatory minimum sentences?

ADDITIONAL READING

Berger, BL. "A More Lasting Comfort? The Politics of Minimum Sentences, the Rule of Law and R v Ferguson" (2009) 47 SCLR (2nd) 101.

Crutcher, N. "The Legislative History of Mandatory Minimum Penalties of Imprisonment in Canada" (2001) 39 Osgoode Hall LJ 273.

Dufraimont, L. "R v Ferguson and the Search for a Coherent Approach to Mandatory Minimum Sentences Under Section 12" (2008) 42 SCLR (2nd) 459.

Healy, P. "Sentencing from There to Here and from Then to Now" (2013) 17 Can Crim L Rev 291.

Jobson, K & G Ferguson. "Towards a Revised Sentencing Structure for Canada" (1987) 66 Can Bar Rev 1.

Laxer, J. "The Constitutionality of Mandatory Minimum Sentences for Youth" (2013) 661 Crim LQ 71.

Manson, A. "Arbitrary Disproportionality: A New Charter Standard for Measuring the Constitutionality of Mandatory Minimum Sentences" (2012) 57 SCLR (2nd) 173.

Manson, A. *The Law of Sentencing* (Toronto: Irwin Law, 2001).

Manson, A et al. *Sentencing and Penal Policy in Canada: Cases, Materials, and Commentary*, 2nd ed (Toronto: Emond Montgomery, 2008).

Paciocco, DM. "The Law of Minimum Sentences: Judicial Responses and Responsibility" (2015) 19 Can Crim L Rev 173.

Paciocco, P. "Proportionality, Discretion, and the Roles of Judges and Prosecutors at Sentencing" (2014) 18 Can Crim L Rev 241.

Penney, S, V Rondinelli & J Stribopoulos. *Criminal Procedure in Canada* (Markham, Ont: Lexis-Nexis, 2011) ch 17.

Pomerance, RM. "The New Approach to Sentencing in Canada: Reflections of a Trial Judge" (2013) 17 Can Crim L Rev 305.

Roach, K. *Criminal Law*, 6th ed (Toronto: Irwin Law, 2015) ch 11.

Roach, K. "Searching for Smith: The Constitutionality of Mandatory Minimum Sentences" (2001) 39 Osgoode Hall LJ 367.

Roberts, JV & A von Hirsch. "Statute Sentencing Reform: The Purpose and Principles of Sentencing" (1995) 37 Crim LQ 220.

Roberts, JV & DP Cole, eds. *Making Sense of Sentencing* (Toronto: University of Toronto Press, 1999).

Roberts, JV & HH Bebbington. "Sentencing Reform in Canada: Promoting a Return to Principles and Evidenced-Based Policy" (2013) 17 Can Crim L Rev 327.

Ruby, CC, G Chan & NR Hasan. *Sentencing*, 8th ed (Markham, Ont: LexisNexis, 2012).

Sheehy, E. "The Discriminatory Effects of Bill C-15's Mandatory Minimum Sentences" (2010) 70 Criminal Reports (6th) 302.